The Routledge Drama Anthology and Sourcebook
From Modernism to Contemporary Performance

The *Routledge Drama Anthology and Sourcebook* is a groundbreaking compilation of the key movements in the history of modern theatre, from the late nineteenth century to contemporary performance practice. Each of the book's five sections comprises a selection of plays and performance texts that define the period, reproduced in full and accompanied by key theoretical writings of performers and critics that inform and contextualize their reading. Substantial introductions from experts in the field also provide these sections with an overview of the works and their significance.

The works span:
- Naturalism and symbolism
- The historical avant-garde
- Early political theatres
- The performance of ideology
- Contemporary performance

This textbook provides an unprecedented collection of comprehensive resource materials which will facilitate in-depth critical analysis. It enables a dialogue between Chekhov, Strindberg, Lorca, Marinetti and Artaud, Brecht, Churchill, Fornes, Ravenhill and Gómez-Peňa, among many other key practitioners.

Maggie B. Gale is Professor and Chair of Drama at the University of Manchester, England. Her publications include: *West End Women: Women on the London Stage 1918–1962* (1996); *British Theatre Between the Wars 1918–1939* (2000), with Clive Barker; *The Cambridge Companion to the Actress* (2007), with John Stokes, and *J. B. Priestley: Routledge Modern and Contemporary Dramatists* (2008).

John F. Deeney is Senior Lecturer in Drama at Manchester Metropolitan University, England. He is the author of many essays and articles on contemporary playwrights, editor of *Writing Live: An Investigation of the Relationship Between Writing and Live Art* (1998) and author of *Mark Ravenhill: Routledge Modern and Contemporary Dramatists* (2010).

Dan Rebellato is Professor of Contemporary Theatre at Royal Holloway, University of London. He is also an award-winning playwright and the author of *1956 and All That: The Making of Modern British Drama* (1999) and *Theatre and Globalization* (2009) as well as many essays and articles on post-war and contemporary British theatre and drama.

Routledge Drama Anthology and Sourcebook

From Modernism to Contemporary Performance

Edited by Maggie B. Gale and John F. Deeney
with Dan Rebellato

Routledge
Taylor & Francis Group

LONDON AND NEW YORK

First published 2010
by Routledge
2 Park Square, Milton Park, Abingdon, Oxon OX14 4RN

Simultaneously published in the USA and Canada
by Routledge
270 Madison Ave, New York, NY 10601

Routledge is an imprint of the Taylor & Francis Group, an informa business

Selection and editorial material © 2010 Maggie B. Gale and John F. Deeney
Individual chapters © the contributors

Typeset in Bembo MT Pro 11/14pt by Fakenham Photosetting Ltd, Fakenham, Norfolk

Printed and bound in Great Britain by MPG Books Group UK

British Library Cataloguing in Publication Data
A catalogue record for this book is available from the British Library

Library of Congress Cataloging in Publication Data
A catalog record for this book has been requested

ISBN 13: 978–0–415–46606–6 (hbk)
ISBN 13: 978–0–415–46662–2 (pbk)

Contents

Illustrations

owledgements

to thank the numerous people involved in the making of this anthology. Firstly,
artists and scholars who gave permission to reproduce their texts and photographs,
Tim Etchells and Forced Entertainment who let us use the latest 'version' of *Speak*
dly, to all the people at Routledge who were excited and engaged by the project
ncouraged us, especially when the task seemed too vast: Talia Rodgers, Moira
Piggott in particular. For those who have worked to clear permissions, thanks for
rk and patience. We would also like to thank all our students at the University
nd Manchester Metropolitan University, who have worked with many of the
d in this anthology over the past few years, and who have offered thoughtful
sponses to them. This project would not have been possible without the advice
ent of our friends and colleagues: John Stokes, Maria Delgado, Dan Rebellato,
es Thompson, Vicki Hutchison, Rose Whyman and Sue Cole. Many thanks to
ffered support such as Eamon McKay, Mel Kenyon, Andrew Quick and Robin
cially Aleksander Dundjerovic, for his initial work and advice in setting up the
advice and detailed responses to the anthology in its early stages and to the essays
hers and practitioners were vital, and for this we thank in particular Aikaterini
ison Jeffers, Linda Taylor and Shane Kinghorn. Special thanks to Hayley Bradley
rishly as an assistant on the project from early on, and to Oscar and Sol Partridge
colate and promises of cinema trips as a bribe when their mum needed to work
inally, enormous thanks to Jenny Hughes, who spent far more time and energy
le to expect, encouraging us, helping with shaping the ideas developed in this
iting and refining our writing for which we are both forever in her debt.

icated to the theatre and performance artists who have made our lives richer
k.

sh to thank the following for their permission to publish work in full or extracts.

se Raquin*, translated and © Pip Broughton, Oberon Books/Absolute Classics

, *Miss Julie, August Strindberg's Miss Julie*, new version translated by Frank
yright © 2000 Frank McGuinness. Kind permission of TGA, The Gersh
, and Casarotto Ramsay & Associates Limited, London.

he Three Sisters (Penguin) © 1954 Elisaveta Fen, pp. 247–330. Reproduced by
the Estate of Elisaveta Fen.

n We Dead Awaken, translation by William Archer, 1903. Public domain.

urice Maeterlinck, *Interior*, translation by Dan Rebellato. Reproduced by permission of SCP
Schmidt & Goldgrab on behalf of M. Louis Van Goitsenhoven Maeterlinck.

Emile Zola *Naturalism in the Theatre* (trans A. Bermel), in Eric Bentley, *The Theory of the Modern Stage*, pp. 351–72, 1968. Reprinted by permission of Helen Merrill, LLC. Copyright © Albert Bermel.

August Strindberg, *Preface to Miss Julie*, pp. 56–68. Copyright © 1998 Michael Robinson. Reprinted by permission of Oxford University Press.

Arthur Symons, 'A New Art of The Stage', in Eric Bentley, *The Theory of the Modern Stage*, pp. 138–47, 1968. Reproduced by kind permission of the Estate of Arthur Symons.

Maurice Maeterlinck, *The Modern Drama* (1904), in Bernard Dukore, *Dramatic Theory and Criticism*, pp. 731–6. Copyright © Dukore. Translated by Alfred Sutro, Reprinted from Maeterlinck, *The Double Garden*, NY Dodd Mead and Co. 1904. Reproduced by permission of SCP Schmidt & Goldgrab on behalf of M. Louis Van Goitsenhoven Maeterlinck.

Excerpt from 'Tragedy in Everyday Life', pp. 32–42 (translation by Dan Rebellato). Reproduced by permission of SCP Schmidt & Goldgrab on behalf of M. Louis Van Goitsenhoven Maeterlinck.

Pierre Quillard, *On the Complete Pointlessness of Accurate Staging*, pp. 180–3 (1891), newspaper article translated by Dan Rebellato. Copyright © Dan Rebellato 2009.

King Ubu: Copyright in this translation © The Estate of Kenneth McLeish 1997. Reprinted by permission of the publishers Nick Hern Books: www.nickernbooks.co.uk. Enquiries concerning any kind of performance of *King Ubu* should be directed to Nick Hern Books Ltd, 14 Larden Road, London W3 7ST, *fax* +44 (0) 20 8735 2500, *email* info@nickhernbooks.demon.co.uk. No performance may be given unless a licence has been obtained. The right of Kenneth McLeish to be identified as translator of this work has been asserted in accordance with the Copyright, Designs and Patents Act 1988.

Guillaume Apollinaire, *The Breasts of Tirésias*. English translation. Copyright © 1961 Louis Simpson. Originally published as *Les Mamelles de Tirésias* by Éditions Sic copyright © 1918. Reprinted by permission of Georges Borchardt, Inc., for Éditions Gallimard.

Antonin Artaud, *The Spurt of Blood*, from Antonin Artaud, *Collected Works*, vol. 1, pp. 62–5. Reproduced by kind permission of Calder Publications Ltd. Copyright © John Calder (Publishers) Ltd 1970.

Oskar Kokoschka, *Murderer the Women's Hope*, in *An Anthology of German Expressionist Drama*, ed. Walter Sokel, Cornell, 1984, pp. 17–22. Copyright © trans. Michael Hamburger. Translation reproduced by kind permission of the estate of Michael Hamburger.

Umberto Boccioni, *Bachelor Apartment*, *Genius and Culture* and *Feet* (Marinetti), from *Futurist Performance*. Copyright © 1971, 1986 Michael Kirby. English translation of manifestoes and playscripts. Copyright © 1971 Victoria Nes Kirby. Reprinted by permission of PAJ Publications.

Raoul Hausmann (1920), *Genius in a Jiffy or a Dadalogy*, in L. Senelick, ed. *Cabaret Performance: Europe 1890–1920*, New York: PAJ Publications, pp. 212–15, trans. Laurence Senelick 1989. Reproduced by kind permission of Laurence Senelick.

Federico García Lorca, *El Publico*. Copyright © Herederos de Federico García Lorca from *Obras Completas* (Galaxia/Gutenberg, 1966 edition). Translation © Caridad Svich and Herederos de Federico García Lorca. All rights reserved. For information regarding rights and permissions, please contact lorca@artslaw.co.uk or William Peter Kosmas, Esq, 8 Franklin Square, London W14 9UU.

Filippo Marinetti, 'The Meaning of the Music Hall', in *Theatre Quarterly* Vol 1: 3 (1971) (originally from the *Daily Express*). Reprinted by permission of the heirs of Filippo Marinetti. Courtesy of Fausto Piermaria Salvati, Vicedirettore Sezione OLAF –SIAE v. le della Letteratura 30, 00144 Roma, Italia.

Antonin Artaud, 'No More Masterpieces' and 'Theatre and the Plague' from Antonin Artaud, *The Theatre and Its Double*, pp. 7–22 and 55–63. Reproduced by kind permission of Calder Publications Ltd. Copyright © John Calder (Publishers) Ltd 1970.

André Breton, 'The First Surrealist Manifesto', pp. 66–71 and 'The Second Surrealist Manifesto', pp. 76–80 from *Surrealism* by Patrick Waldberg. Copyright © Dumont Schauberg, Cologne 1965. This edition © 1965 and 1997 Thames & Hudson Ltd, London. Reprinted by kind permission of Thames & Hudson and the estate of André Breton.

E. Prampolini, *Futurist Scenography (Manifesto)*, in E. T. Kirby, *Total Theatre: A Critical Anthology*, trans. Diana Clemmons from *Futurist Performance*. Copyright © Michael Kirby 1971, 1986. Reprinted by permission of PAJ Publications.

'Theater, Circus, Variety' by L. Moholy-Nagy from *The Theater of Bauhaus*, ed. Walter Gropius and Arthur Wensinger (Wesleyan University Press, 1971). Copyright © 1971 Walter Gropius and Arthur Wensinger. Reprinted by permission of Wesleyan University Press.

Cecily Hamilton and Christopher St John, *How the Vote was Won,* in *How the Vote Was Won*, ed. Carol Hayman and Dale Spender, Methuen Publishing Ltd, 1985, pp. 23–33. Copyright © 1985 Sir Leslie Bower.

Ernst Toller, *Hoppla, We're Alive!* Reprinted with the translator's corrections from *Ernst Toller Plays One: Transformation, Masses Man, Hoppla, We're Alive!: A Prologue and Five Acts.* Translated and edited by Alan Raphael Pearlman. London: Oberon Books Ltd, 2000. Original works © Katharine Weber. Sixteen photographs from the original production have not been included in this anthology but are available along with other important pictorial material in the Oberon edition.

Ronald Gow and Walter Greenwood, *Love on the Dole* in *Plays of the Thirties*, Pan Books Ltd, 1966, pp. 119–94. Copyright © 1938 Gow and Greenwood/Samuel French Acting Editions. Reprinted courtesy of Laurence Fitch Ltd.

Hallie Flanagan Davis, *E=MC²: A Living Newspaper about the Atomic Age*, London/NY: Samuel French, 1947/8. Copyright © 1947 Hallie Flanagan Davis. Copyright © 1948 Hallie Flanagan Davis. Reproduced with permission of Samuel French, Inc.

Ewan MacColl, *Johnny Noble* in *Agit-Prop to Theatre Workshop: Political Playscripts 1930–50*, ed.

Howard Goorney and Ewan MacColl, pp. 35–66, Manchester University Press, 1986. Copyright © Howard Goorney and Ewan MacColl. Reproduced by kind permission of Stella Goorney.

Susan Carlson, 'Suffrage Theatre: Community Activism and Political Commitment', in *A Companion to Modern British and Irish Drama*, ed. Mary Luckgurst, Oxford: Blackwell Publishing, 2006, pp. 99-109. Reproduced by permission of Blackwell Publishing Ltd.

'The Work of Art in the Age of its Technological Reproducibility, Second Version' reprinted by permission of the publisher from *The Work of Art in the Age of Its Technological Reproducibility, and Other Writings on Media*, by Walter Benjamin, ed. Michael W. Jennings, Brigid Doherty and Thomas Y. Levin, pp. 19–55, Cambridge, MA: The Belknap Press of Harvard University Press. Copyright © 2008 the President and Fellows of Harvard College. Reprinted by arrangement with the author and Writers House LLC, acting as agent for the author.

B. Brecht, 'Theatre for Pleasure or Theatre for Instruction' and 'The Street Scene', in *Brecht on Theatre*, ed. John Willett, London: Methuen, 1978, pp. 69–76 and pp. 120–9, translated by John Willett. Reproduced by kind permission of Suhrkamp Verlag. All rights reserved. And, Methuen Drama, an imprint of A & C Black Publishers.

Sheila Stowell, 'Rehabilitating Realism', in *Journal of Dramatic Theory and Criticism*, 6(2), 1992, pp. 81–8. Reprinted by kind permission of Sheila Stowell.

Marxism and Literary Criticism by Terry Eagleton. Copyright © 1976 University of California Press – Books. Reproduced by permission of University of California Press – Books in the format Textbook via Copyright Clearance Center.

Terry Eagleton, 'The Author as Producer', pp. 59–76, in *Marxism and Literary Criticism*. Copyright © 1975 Routledge. Reproduced by permission of Taylor & Francis Books UK and the author.

Blues for Mister Charlie. Copyright © 1964 James Baldwin. Copyright renewed. Reprinted by arrangement with the James Baldwin Estate.

The Cheviot, the Stag and the Black, Black Oil, in *Six-Pack: Plays for Scotland* by John McGrath is reproduced by permission of Polygon, an imprint of Birlinn Ltd: www.birlinn.co.uk.

Enter the Night?, in *What of the Night? Selected Plays by Maria Irene Fornes*. Copyright © 1993, 2008 Maria Irene Fornes. Reprinted by permission of PAJ Publications.

Far Away. Copyright © 2000 Caryl Churchill Ltd. Reprinted by permission of the publishers Nick Hern Books: www.nickhernbooks.co.uk. The right of Caryl Churchill to be identified as author of this work has been asserted in accordance with the Copyright, Designs and Patents Act 1988.

Mark Ravenhill, *Scenes from Family Life*, 2008, one of the Connections plays from the National Theatre 2008. Reprinted by kind permission of Casarotto Ramsay & Associates Limited, London.

Alan Sinfield, 'Theory of Cultural Production', in *Gay and After*, London: Serpent's Tail, 1998, pp. 146–59. Reproduced by kind permission of the author.

John McGrath, 'The Theory and Practice of Political Theatre', *Theatre Quarterly,* 9(35), 1979, pp. 43–54. Reproduced by kind permission of Elizabeth McGrath.

Howard Barker, 'Fortynine Asides for a Tragic Theatre', in H. Barker, *Arguments for a Theatre*, Manchester University Press, 1997, pp. 17–18. Reproduced by kind permission of the publisher.

Helen Gilbert and Joanne Tompkins, 'Introduction: Re-acting (to) Empire', in Gilbert and Tompkins, *Post-colonial Drama: Theory, Practice, Politics*, London: Routledge, 1996. Copyright © Gilbert and Tompkins, pp. 1–14. Reproduced by permission of Taylor & Francis Books UK.

Mark Ravenhill, 'Me, My iBook, and Writing in America', in *Contemporary Theatre Review*, 16(1), 2006, pp. 131–8, reprinted by permission of the publisher (Taylor & Francis Ltd, http://www.tandf.co.uk/journals).

Laurie Anderson, 'Excerpt from Anderson's Stage Directions for *Stories from the Nerve Bible*', pp. 161–7. Copyright © Laurie Anderson. Reproduced by kind permission of Laurie Anderson.

Robert Lepage and Marie Brassard, *The Polygraph*, trans. Gyllian Raby. Reproduced by kind permission of Robert Lepage, Marie Brassard and Gyllian Raby.

'Forced Entertainment', a new version of text from *Speak Bitterness,* in Tim Etchells, *Certain Fragments*, 2005 [1999] with an introduction by Tim Etchells in 2008. Printed here by courtesy of Tim Etchells and Forced Entertainment.

SuAndi, *The Story of M*, reproduced by kind permission of the author. Illustrations reproduced in this edition of the play are the copyright of the author.

Guillermo Gómez-Peña, 'Supernintendo Ranchero', from *BORDERScape 2000*, pp. 24–33, in Guillermo Gómez-Peña, *Dangerous Border Crossings*, London: Routledge, 2000. Reproduced by permission of Taylor & Francis Books UK.

Roland Barthes, extract from 'Myth Today', from *Mythologies*, translated by Annette Lavers. Translation copyright © 1972 Jonathan Cape Ltd. Reprinted by permission of Hill and Wang, a division of Farrar, Straus and Giroux, LLC. Also from *Mythologies* by Roland Barthes, published by Jonathan Cape. Reprinted by permission of The Random House Group Ltd.

Jean Baudrillard, 'The Divine Irreference of Images', pp. 3–7, and 'The Strategy of the Real', pp. 19–27, in *Simulacra and Simulation*, Ann Arbor: University of Michigan Press, 1994. Originally published in French by Éditions Galilée, 1981.

Hans-Thies Lehmann, 'Aspects: Text Space – Time – Body – Media', from *Postdramatic Theatre,* London: Routledge, pp. 145–74. German edition copyright © Verlag der Autoren, D-Frankfurt am Main, 1999; English edition copyright © Routledge 2006. Reproduced by permission of Taylor & Francis Books UK and Verlag der Autoren.

Eugenio Barba, 'Dramaturgy', pp. 66–71, and 'Montage', pp. 178–84, from *A Dictionary of Theatre Anthropology*. Copyright © 2006 (1991) Routledge. Reproduced by permission of Taylor & Francis Books UK and the author.

Nicholas Zurbrugg, ed., 'Laurie Anderson' (1991), in *Art, Performance, Media: 31 Interviews*, Minneapolis and London: University of Minnesota Press, 2004, pp. 25–34. Copyright © Laurie Anderson. Reproduced by kind permission of Laurie Anderson.

Guillermo Gómez-Peña, 'Away from the Surveillance Cameras of the Art World: Strategies for Collaboration and Community Activism', from Guillermo Gómez-Peña, *Dangerous Border Crossers*, pp. 167–87, London: Routledge, 2000. Reproduced by permission of Taylor & Francis Books UK.

Introduction

MAGGIE B. GALE

From modernism to contemporary practice: crisis and change

If I had to sum up the twentieth century, I would say it had raised the greatest hopes ever conceived by humanity, and destroyed all illusions and ideals. (Yehudi Menuhin qtd in Hobsbawm 2009: 2)

It works small the history thing. Small things make big changes. (Etchells 1999: 19)

THIS ANTHOLOGY AND SOURCEBOOK includes materials – plays, performance texts, critical essays, commentaries and interviews, theories and manifestos by practitioners and cultural critics – from the end of the nineteenth century to the early years of the twenty-first. As such it has an ambitious and challenging remit in terms of representation. The overarching agenda of the book necessitates the inclusion of a variety of texts that speak to significant innovations in the practice of theatre and performance, during a timeframe characterized by social and political crisis and change. The bulk of the materials come from the twentieth century, which historian Eric Hobsbawm has labelled an 'age of extremes' characterized by catastrophe, economic growth and decline, and culminating with the prediction of an 'apocalyptic future' (Hobsbawm 2009: 6). The texts in this volume encompass theatre and performance's reaction to, and interface with such a history, but as Etchells notes, it also reflects history as a series of 'small things' – individual plays and performances and even performers, that have transformed the ways in which we conceptualize and practise theatre as a social and cultural event and phenomenon.

The volume is divided into five parts: Naturalism and Symbolism: Early Modernist Practice; The Historical Avant-Garde: Performance and Innovation; Early Political Theatres; Ideology and Performance/The Performance of Ideology, and Contemporary Performance/The Contemporaneity of Practice. The parts cross over with each other chronologically; sometimes the materials are divided in terms of the artistic movements which they exemplify, at others they are divided according to the particular political or ideological agendas with which they are engaged. The introductory chapters to each of the five sections provide more detailed overviews of the historical and social contexts for the materials included, but in this introduction to the whole volume we want simply to draw out some of the themes repeated over the period which the volume covers.

Virtually all of the plays and texts in this volume reflect upon, are reflective of and sometimes collide with, a context of social, political and aesthetic transition with which Europe and America have been engaged from the late nineteenth century onwards. All areas of human experience have been radically changed by the impact of war, technological advances, economic crises and shifting relationships between the social classes and the individual and the state, during the period the volume covers. The terrible impact of two World Wars was felt by Europe and America across the classes, but the ripple effects were global with the redrawing of international boundaries in colonized territories and transformations in the power relations between colonizer and colonized, as well as an emergence of the United States as the dominant economic power. Some might suggest that the twentieth and twenty-first centuries thus far have been characterized by war itself, with very few countries ever existing in a state of peace. As performance theorist Richard Schechner writes in 2008, for all but very few of his own 70-plus years of lifetime, his country, the United States, has been at war. He points out that the economic cost of this has been significant, but more importantly he notes the high cost of war in terms of 'the cultural, the personal and the spiritual' (Schechner 2008: 7).

In the opening decade of the twenty-first century, the supposed divide between West and East and actual disparities between the rich and the poor appeared to be ever stronger. As an economic system, capitalism was challenged by the rise of communism in the earlier part of the twentieth century, only to re-emerge as an all-powerful globalized economic structure in the twenty-first century. Combined with this, the technological developments during the period covered in this volume, which transformed our production processes and transportation and communication systems, have completely altered the ways in which we live our lives – from increasing levels of geographical and social mobility to changing relationships between work and leisure time. They also threaten to potentially destroy the fine ecological balance of the physical world in which we live. The period covered in this volume has therefore been one of unprecedented change, much of which has created a consistent and vibrant revaluation of the ways in which art overall, and theatre and performance in particular, can be used to question and express experience and affect the world in which we live. In the final part of the volume we see artists embracing what Tim Etchells views as the 'small things [which] make big changes' (see above), whereby performance practice returns or perhaps re-embraces the complexities of individual experience and the expression of individuality, in a world where generality, uncertainty and the non-specificity of a 'global culture' appear to dominate.

The desire to use theatre as a means of thinking through the causal relationships between man/woman and their social environment embedded in the innovations brought about by the Naturalists in the late nineteenth century (see Part 1) is followed by the refusal of many in the historical avant-garde to see art as representational – art is not about meaning but should question and embrace the illogical, the anarchic, the subconscious and so on (see Part 2). The belief in theatre and performance as a form of social and political agency which drives much of the work of the practitioners whose work is placed in Parts 3 and 4 is complicated by the shift in beliefs brought about by the social upheavals and globalized contexts of the work in Part 5. Here a crisis of subjectivity prevails; artists question the terms by which we might define 'self', and what kinds of art we might usefully or meaningfully make in a culture in crisis. Running through each of the parts are questions about the potential of a theatre and performance practice which relies on text – this is as much to do with a predicament about and distrust of text (the written word and the power of language) as it is about the dominance of the play text as a form through which theatre and performance might be understood. Many of the practitioners we include in the volume, especially those in Parts 2 and 5, have been involved in undermining the dominance of text and the belief that text alone can represent experience or express meaning. Others have made formal textual innovations, breaking away from the traditional format of the well-made play prevalent in the late nineteenth century. All have been heavily influenced by innovations in art practices and theories of art generally, and some of the texts in this volume are hybrid forms which barely indicate what might be happening on stage or in front of our eyes (see 2.4 and 2.6) or which might more recognizably be viewed as performance poetry or prose (see 5.3 and 5.4).

The division of 'high' and 'low' culture dominant in the early years covered by this volume is problematized as early as 1896 in a play such as Alfred Jarry's *King Ubu* (2.1). Many of the practitioners whose work or ideas are included in the volume strongly argued against the idea of theatre as 'literary' and refuted its 'ownership' by the bourgeoisie or the ruling classes, instead celebrating popular cultural forms that they attempted to embrace in their work. The interrelationships between drama, text, performance, 'high' and 'low' art and theatricality are sometimes joyously and mischievously played with by, for example, the Surrealists at one end of the century (see 2.2) but also by artists like Tim Etchells and Forced Entertainment (5.3) at the closing end of the same century.

During the twentieth century, theatre has had to reposition itself alongside and in tandem with the development of other populist representational media such as film. The potential ways in which this repositioning might transform what we understand the role or function of art or theatre to be were critiqued early on by cultural philosophers such as Walter Benjamin (see 3.7), who questioned terms such as 'aura', 'replica' and 'authenticity' as part of a discussion about art practices in an age where 'art' objects could now be easily 'reproduced'. But the potential transformative effects of such media are fully embraced by later practitioners whose work is exemplified in Part 5 such as Laurie Anderson (see 5.1 and 5.10). Equally the spaces in which theatre and performance events take place have been transformed, from the large-scale proscenium-arch stages of the nineteenth century, to the intimate chamber theatres craved by practitioners such as Strindberg and Chekhov in the early part of the twentieth century, to the cabaret venues of the avant-garde and the non-theatre venues implied by the work of practitioners such as Ewan MacColl (3.5) and John McGrath (4.2), to the studio theatres and mass concert-hall performance spaces of the twenty-first century. There is a sense in which theorizing about how theatre and performance work as cultural products has removed the traditional boundaries we might use to define what is and what is not theatre: this in turn has influenced the kinds of spaces in which theatre might take place. If Antonin Artaud had lived to see the kinds of spaces and places in which theatre and performance took place in the opening decade of the twenty-first century, he would be very well placed to point out that his visionary ideas in the 1920s and 1930s were not simply the meanderings of a delusional dreamer.

One of the recurrent arguments about the unique quality of theatre and performance has focused on its reliance on interaction, on community and on its 'liveness' as an event, its non-reproducibility and inability to 'produce a tangible object which may enter into circulation as a marketable commodity' (Lehmann 2006: 16). This creates a problem in terms of what we use as a means of studying theatre and performance, especially historically. Ultimately 'you had to be there' to experience the event, but there are ephemera, an archive of possible materials which we might use to begin our studies and conversations about how that event might have functioned or what it might have signified. This anthology and sourcebook attempts therefore to provide a series of evidential 'objects' – texts – which it is hoped will provide a starting point for discussions about theatre and performance as a significant cultural product over a period of more than a hundred years. Some of the texts are more indicative than they are representational, but we have included photographic materials which can also be used as routes into discussing the 'texts' as theatre and performance rather than as literature. So, for example, the photographs of two productions of *Three Sisters* (see Figures 6 and 7) come from two different historical moments, but offer interesting scenographic commonalities in terms of the ways in which the text has been framed visually in performance. Each creates demarcated 'spaces' where action might happen simultaneously. Thus the early twentieth-century Russian staging might be part of a 'Naturalist' tradition, but is clearly linked or referred to by the recent German production, where the architectural lines imply a similar division of a domestic space, predicated on providing the possibility of simultaneous stage action.

Divisions of culture: modernism and postmodernism

Numerous 'texts' in this volume talk about how we might break away from 'traditional' theatre, with its passive audiences and silent auditoria. These might often discuss the ways in which popular performance forms influence theatre (for example, 2.9 and 2.13), as well as consistently reinvent what it is that theatre and performance might offer as cultural products created within a 'politics of culture'; for they are part of, and impact upon, a wider social and cultural milieu. Here, politics – in the broadest sense of the word – 'are the condition of which culture is the product' (Eagleton 2000: 122). For it is clear that political thinking and political change – who has access to power and how that access might affect our everyday lives – have impacted on theatre as much as any other cultural product during the period covered in this volume.

Whilst this introduction does not allow for extensive discussion of what we mean by politics or by culture, there are two things which it can offer. One is a framework within which the influence and nature of cultural transition, so integral to an understanding of many of the materials included in the volume, can be assessed. The second is a broad outline of some of the cultural movements from which the materials originate. Many of the materials in this volume, especially those in the earlier parts, respond to the cultural conditions from which they originate by means of manifestos for change and the transformation of theatre and, in turn, society. They represent 'emergent' cultures that challenged the 'residual' and 'dominant' cultures that surrounded them. Raymond Williams, the cultural and literary theorist whose ideas greatly influenced the development of cultural theory in the late decades of the twentieth century, uses the terms 'residual' (the extant sense of community, for example, or established social practices which may seem out of kilter with the contemporary moment), 'dominant' (those cultural practices which appear to be the 'norm', the predominant at any one time) and the 'emergent' (innovatory, 'alternative' or oppositional practices). He uses these to illustrate the ways in which no cultural product is isolated, but rather reacts against, is dispensed with or is appropriated by the present historical moment (see Williams 2005: 31–49).

Most of the texts in this volume, at the point of creation, fall into the category of emergent culture. However, as the introductions to each of the parts in the volume explore, the texts from the first half of the volume all came in fast succession. No sooner had Naturalism paved the way for a sociological perspective and a 'laboratory' of humanity through theatre (see Part 1), for example, than Symbolism interrupted by proposing that theatre was at its height of efficacy when working through the implied and the imagistic, through its poetic qualities as opposed to the constraints of realist text. Similarly, no sooner had Symbolism drawn us back into the poetic of language, than Dada and Futurism turned text on its head, deconstructing language and its relation to performance altogether (see Part 2). By the early 1920s, even though some Naturalist plays were still banned on the public English stage – viewed as socially risqué and unsuitable for a live performance by the British censor – Naturalism was part of the dominant culture and to some extent was fast becoming a residual culture from the late nineteenth century. For Williams, what came about during the twentieth century was in fact 'an increasingly close interweaving of all three categories', the residual, the dominant and the emergent (qtd in Eagleton 2000: 123). Certainly what we see in the many 'isms' of the Modernist and Postmodernist movements which dominate innovatory practice during the period covered in this volume is the deliberate interplay, manipulation, refusal and hybridizing of all of Williams' categories of cultural product, to different degrees depending on which texts we focus on.

Modernism, as the overarching artistic movement which frames the first three parts of this volume, is notoriously difficult to define. Before World War I, Modernist cultural practice was driven by experiment and was more positive in its outlook despite its desire to critique society and challenge cultural tradition. Thus a belief in progress underpinned the work of many of the early modernists such as the Naturalists. After World War I (1914–18), however, modernism was more characterized by fragmentation and a questioning of what might previously have been viewed as accepted knowledge – the chronology of time and the limitations of consciousness, for example. Immediately post-World War I, 'modernisms' traditionally grouped as the historical avant-garde, such as Futurism and Surrealism, often created a more violent and radical challenge to 'existing modes of representation' (Childs 2000: 4). Many of the practices they formulated have fed into developments typified in some postmodern theatre and performance practices at the opposite end of the century (see Parts 4 and 5). Here we see a move from an interrogation of the ways in which we look at and reflect reality, to postmodernism's questioning of any possibility of a consensual, united version or expression of reality as articulated in Baudrillard's 'The Strategy of the Real' (5.7).

Similarly, modernist practice beyond the avant-garde as explored in Part 3 questioned whose 'reality' we might represent. A belief in mankind's ability to control progress and to act upon the world rather than have it act upon them is integral to the work of Brecht in the mid-twentieth century (3.8 and 3.9) and John McGrath (4.2 and 4.7) in the latter half of the same century. With McGrath we see a playwright borrowing from the residue of past innovation to innovate through an appropriation of popular cultural forms in his present – an emergent cultural product influenced by its relation to past practices. Brechtian and Artaudian ideas continue to influence contemporary theatre and performance practices in a multitude of ways. Thus as practices which came under the umbrella of modernism melded and bled into each other, so too many of the theories produced in one historical moment find realization in another. We should also note that the postmodern – explored in more detail in Part 5 – cannot be totally distinguished from its antecedents. Although many argue that the postmodern marks a break from the modernist, as a post-World War II shift in cultural practices, general definitions allow for strong connections to be made between them. Thus the postmodern 'deliberately and playfully employs paradox to display its own artificiality and contradictions ... alludes to both high and popular culture' and is charac-terized by 'an incredulity to the grand narratives of progress ... [and] unsettles the stability of traditional notions of reason and rationality' (Macey 2000: 306-7). Such a description of a general movement influencing theatre and performance from the late 1950s onwards, however, could just as easily be applied to the historical avant-garde which flourished during the modernist period in the earlier part of the same century. The point here is not to confuse or to oversimplify, but to note the crossovers, cross-currents and meeting points between the cultural products included in this volume.

Whilst each of the introductory essays at the beginning of each part attempts to place the materials in the context of the politics of culture which Eagleton refers to, this introduction to the volume as a whole has been used to open up possible avenues of questioning. The *Routledge Drama Anthology and Sourcebook: From Modernism to Contemporary Performance* aims to provide a spectrum of materials, some of which connect, others which appear to stand on their own, but all of which represent some form of innovation driven by questions such as 'who is theatre for?', 'what can it represent and how might it represent it?', 'how does it function and how might we transform its functionality?' The editors have worked from the premise that the materials included are cultural products not literary works. They derive from a philosophical and pragmatic questioning of what theatre and performance are, and how they function within a politics of culture which runs from the alienating urban chaos of the late industrial revolution, through the social, political and domestic upheavals of the early and mid-twentieth century, to the globalized and seemingly anonymized culture of the first decade of the twenty-first century.

How to use this volume

The plays, performance texts and other critical texts included in this volume can and should be read both with and against each other. The contents to some extent are inevitably a compromise: pedagogically, we hope that there is a healthy and useful enough combination of the canonical and the marginal, the pan-European and American, the critical and the practical. Often copyright and financial constraints have been more influential over what has been excluded than any kind of intellectual or pedagogical rationale. For example, the omission of a play by Brecht is the result of a monopoly ownership of Brecht's works in English, although we were permitted to republish some of his theoretical work. In the last part, some contemporary practitioners were more conscious of whose work they would permit their own to be published alongside, and others simply had prohibitive fees. Other chosen documents came from a proactive desire to place certain materials against and alongside each other, however. Thus in Part 1, rather than have an early play by Ibsen we have included his last, in part to evidence the fluid nature of the infamous 'isms' of modernism: thus Ibsen is both a purveyor of Naturalism in the introduction to the part and a Symbolist in terms of the play we include, *When We Dead Awaken* (1.4). In Part 5, the texts cannot possibly represent the 'contemporary' *per se*, but it is hoped that they provide points of focus and a 'way in' to studying contemporary practices, the evidence for which is perhaps more readily accessible than the practice represented by the materials in the opening parts of the anthology. Many contemporary performance companies have sophisticated web page and archive holdings accessible to the public, with clips of their work accessible on YouTube – here you can even find film of Antonin Artaud and Bertolt Brecht in interview. Similarly there are perhaps many more publishers willing to publish contemporary plays than collections or new editions of older ones.

In light of this, we hope that the introductions to each of the parts give a clear and useful overview of the materials included and a steer as to the possible ways in which one might begin to engage with and discuss them. The short timelines on the opening page of each section give indicative information on events and innovations to provide a broad historical and cultural context, whilst the bibliography and further reading list at the end of each introduction offers a starting point for more in-depth investigation.

Theatre and Performance Studies have undergone a significant transformation over the past two decades, but the materials with which students still need to engage in order to understand the relationships between theatre and performance practices of the past and those of the present remain relatively constant as reference points. Whilst 'information' about historical theatre and performance practices has become more easily and speedily accessible through the internet, many of the texts and performance documents which one might wish to refer students to remain either inaccessible or too costly for the student purse. Many of the documents included in this anthology will be familiar and will often have been made available through photocopies or through limited library access only. Whilst there has always been a steady flow of new editions of say Chekhov or Ibsen's plays, a number of the texts included here have only been accessible in narrow or specialist focus anthologies or editions. Many of these came out during the 1970s and 1980s, when books were less expensive and curricula, perhaps, more specialist in focus, earlier in a programme of study. Many of these anthologies, often limited to just containing plays or just critical texts, are now out of print and do not provide the wider collection of materials included here.

Although the volume is divided into five parts, we refer the reader from one part to another wherever possible. So, for example, where Walter Benjamin's seminal essay, *The Work of Art in the Age of its Technological Reproducibility* (3.7), is placed in Part 3, it might also be used to analyse materials and ideas explored in both Part 2 and Part 5. Similarly, a play like Caryl Churchill's *Far Away* in Part 4 can be read alongside or against any of the plays in Part 4, but it could also be fruitfully placed against many of the plays/performance texts in Part 3 or even Part 5. The vision in operation when the volume was put together was that it could be multi-purpose in its potential usability, and that whilst the introduction and divisions of materials embrace an internal logic, the logic is not hermetically sealed to disallow any other grouping or connectivities being made between and amongst the texts included.

What we hope we have created in the *Routledge Drama Anthology and Sourcebook: From Modernism to Contemporary Performance* is a volume that students and teachers will buy and want to keep. It includes numerous plays and critical/performance texts seminal to an understanding of various developments in theatre and performance across Western Europe and America during the late nineteenth century and into the twenty-first. Such a volume, despite its obvious limitations in terms of global coverage, could be and has been used as the basis of a survey course for beginning and intermediary students, but it might just as easily be used as a general reference book for theatre and performance students, since it includes key plays and texts by a wide and various range of theorists and practitioners such as Zola, Maeterlinck, Brecht, Benjamin, Baudrillard, Barba, Churchill, Gómez-Peña and so on. We hope therefore that this volume allows for close, interconnected and fluid readings of the texts produced by some of the great European and American innovative theatre and performance artists and cultural theorists of the past 100-plus years.

Bibliography

Childs, Peter (2000) *Modernism*, London: Routledge.

Eagleton, Terry (2000) *The Idea of Culture*, Oxford: Blackwell.

Etchells, Tim (1999) *Certain Fragments,* London: Routledge.

Hobsbawm. Eric (2009 [1994]) *The Age of Extremes: 1914–1991*, London: Abacus.

Lehmann, Hans-Thies (2006) *Postdramatic Theatre*, London: Routledge.

Macey, David (2000) *The Penguin Dictionary of Critical Theory*, London: Penguin.

Schechner, Richard (2008) 'We Are, After All, At War', *The Drama Review*, 52(1) (T197), 7–10.

Williams, Raymond (2005 [1980]) *Culture and Materialism*, London: Verso.

Further reading

Bennett, Susan (1997) *Theatre Audiences: A Theory of Production and Reception*, London: Routledge.

Carey, John (1992) *The Intellectuals and the Masses: Pride and Prejudice among the Literary Intelligentsia 1880–1939*, London: Faber and Faber.

Eyre, Richard and Wright, Nicholas (2001) *Changing Stages: A View of British and American Theatre in the Twentieth Century*, London and New York: Random House.

Hughes, Robert (1991 [1980]) *The Shock of the New: Art and a Century of Change*, London: Thames and Hudson.

Kershaw, Baz (1992) *The Politics of Performance: Radical Theatre as Cultural Intervention*, London: Routledge.

McFarlane, James and Bradbury, Malcolm (eds) (1991 [1976]) *Modernism: A Guide to European Literature 1880–1930*, London: Penguin.

Wiles, David (2003) *A Short History of Western Performance Space*, Cambridge: Cambridge University Press.

Williams, Raymond (1973) *Drama from Ibsen to Brecht*, London: Pelican.

Part 1
Naturalism and Symbolism: Early Modernist Practice

Timeline

	Social, cultural and political context	Theatre
1848	*The Communist Manifesto*: Karl Marx and Friedrich Engels	
1859	*The Origin of Species*: Charles Darwin	
1861–2	Manifesto on the emancipation of serfs and social unrest in Russia	
1864		Imperial decree liberates Paris theatres and leads to an upsurge of new theatres being constructed
		Émile Zola's letter to Antony Valabrègue sets out his theory of the 'realist screen'
1866		In 'Books of Today and Tomorrow' (essay) Émile Zola coins the word 'Naturalism' to describe his scientific approach to literature (*L'Événement*)
1870	Education Act in Britain which provides equal access to elementary education for girls and boys	
1873		*Thérèse Raquin* (play): Émile Zola
		Saxe-Meiningen Theatre's first tour to Berlin
1874	First Impressionist Art Salon, Paris	
1876	Alexander Graham Bell invents the telephone	Wagner's *Ring* cycle premieres in Bayreuth
1877	Thomas Edison invents the phonograph	
1879		*A Doll's House*: Henrik Ibsen (Royal Theatre, Copenhagen)
1881		Electric lighting introduced into a number of British theatres
		Naturalist Novelists, Naturalism in the Theatre and *Our Dramatic Authors*: Émile Zola
1882		'On Realism: Some Viewpoints' (essay): August Strindberg
1883	The death of Karl Marx	
1885	Karl Benz patents the first gasoline-powered automobile (1885–6)	
1886		*Ghosts*: Henrik Ibsen (Meiningen Theatre)
		'Symbolist' (essay/manifesto): Jean Moréas (*Le Figaro*)
1887		Théâtre Libre founded by André Antoine in Paris
1888		Théâtre du Chat Noir opens its shadow puppet theatre
		Miss Julie: August Strindberg
1889		'On Modern Drama and Modern Theatre' (essay): August Strindberg
1890		Théâtre d'Art founded by Paul Fort

	Social, cultural and political context	Theatre
1891		*The Girl with the Severed Hands*: Pierre Quillard (Théâtre d'Art)
		'On the Complete Pointlessness of Accurate Staging' (essay): Pierre Quillard (*Revue d'Art Dramatique*)
		Intruder: Maurice Maeterlinck (Théâtre d'Art)
		The Blind: Maurice Maeterlinck (Théâtre d'Art)
1893		Théâtre de l'Oeuvre founded by Aurélien Lugné-Poë
		Miss Julie: August Strindberg (Théâtre Libre)
		The Weavers: Gerhart Hauptmann (Théâtre Libre)
1894	Thomas Edison opens his Kinetoscope Parlor in New York (early motion-picture device)	
1895	Auguste and Louis Lumière credited with the first public film screening in Paris	*Interior*: Maurice Maeterlinck (Théâtre de l'Oeuvre)
1896		Independent Theatre founded in Barcelona
		Ubu Roi: Alfred Jarry (Théâtre de l'Oeuvre)
		The Seagull: Anton Chekhov (Alexandrinsky Theatre, St Petersburg)
1897		Moscow Art Theatre founded by Konstantin Stanislavski and Vladimir Nemirovich-Danchenko
		Théâtre Antoine, successor to Théâtre Libre, founded, Paris
1898		*The Seagull*: Anton Chekhov (Moscow Art Theatre)
1899		*When We Dead Awaken*: Henrik Ibsen
1900	*The Interpretation of Dreams*: Sigmund Freud	
1901	Nobel Prize founded	*Three Sisters*: Anton Chekhov (Moscow Art Theatre)
1902		Death of Émile Zola
1903	The Wright brothers successfully fly an engine-powered aeroplane	
1904		*The Cherry Orchard*: Anton Chekhov (Moscow Art Theatre)
		Death of Chekhov
		Abbey Theatre, Dublin, founded
1905	Albert Einstein formulates his 'special theory of relativity'	Vsevolod Meyerhold opens the Moscow Art Studio Theatre
1906		Max Reinhardt founds the Kammerspielhaus in Berlin
		Death of Henrik Ibsen
1907	First Symbolist exhibition in Moscow (called *Blue Rose*)	Intimate Theatre, Stockholm, founded by August Strindberg and others
1908		*The Ghost Sonata*: August Strindberg (Intimate Theatre, Stockholm)
1911	Maurice Maeterlinck awarded the Nobel Prize for Literature	

Introduction

DAN REBELLATO

NATURALISM AND SYMBOLISM MARK the beginnings of modernist theatre and in many ways provided the template for much that followed. André Antoine's Théâtre Libre (1887–94) was perhaps the first independent experimental theatre company in the modern world and the Symbolist theatres that followed, while fiercely opposed to the Naturalism with which the Théâtre Libre was associated, followed Antoine's lead in choosing intimate small theatre spaces, producing short plays performed by amateur casts, and publishing journals to explain their work and ideas. Most modernist theatres which followed were a response to, and rejection of, Naturalism. For that reason, it is sometimes supposed that Naturalism was not a modernist theatre and that modernism emerged precisely in reaction to a perceived conservatism on the Naturalist stage.

In fact, Naturalism was foundational to modernist theatre practice and caused as much scandal, controversy and outrage as any of the radical, experimental theatres that came after it. The term 'naturalism', in particular, has become flattened out to refer to any theatrical production where the set and the acting attempt vaguely to resemble real life. Similarly, the term 'symbolism' can refer to any attempt to represent things and ideas through symbols. Naturalist and Symbolist theatre in their particular historical moments had a much more specific character and remit. The naturalism of Robert De Niro's acting or the symbolism in a play like Samuel Beckett's *Waiting for Godot* are very different from the Naturalism of *Thérèse Raquin* or the Symbolism of Maurice Maeterlinck's work.

The nineteenth century

Modernism was so called because it sought to capture the distinctive spirit of the modern age. The nineteenth century had wrought enormous changes across European society and culture. Industrialization, which had begun in Britain in the eighteenth century, had spread across Europe through the nineteenth century. This altered the economic organization of society which meant the emergence of unprecedentedly large industrial processes, including the building of huge factories, large-scale industrial machinery, whole towns of housing for the workers who operated it and, as a result, a transformation in the geography of Europe. Revolutionary developments in technology saw the invention, for example, of the typewriter, the battery, the light bulb, photography and cinema, the steam train and the bicycle, the elevator and escalator, phonograph, gramophone, telephone, and numerous industrial processes that would feed the development and spread of industrial capitalism across Europe.

By the beginning of the twentieth century, Europe's capital cities had expanded: thus London had gone from a population of under one million in 1800 to around six and a half million by 1900, and Paris from just over half a million to nearly three million. The emergence of cities as the centres of industry and the relative decline of agriculture meant a great migration from the countryside to the city. Cities were transformed to accommodate their new residents. This rapid expansion, with new classes being thrown together in the new city spaces, created new forms of cultural and social anxiety. There were new opportunities for vice and criminality and, not unconnected, new relationships between those with wealth and those with power.

The Eiffel Tower, and the 'Universal Exposition' of 1888 which it was built to mark, were examples of Paris's heightened awareness of itself as a powerful global city, a centre for international industry, culture and finance. Modernist theatre was also marked by these cosmopolitan flows of people and ideas. The repertoires of the Théâtre Libre and the Théâtre de l'Oeuvre – the two main Naturalist and Symbolist theatres in Paris – were pan-European, showing work from, among others, Sweden (Strindberg), Norway (Ibsen), Germany (Hauptmann), Belgium (Maeterlinck), Britain (Shelley) and Italy (Verga). Otherwise, Naturalism and Symbolism had very different relations to these dramatic changes. Symbolism, as the cultural theorist Walter Benjamin remarked (1999: 41), was an attempt to shield art from the onslaught of the modern world to appeal beyond it to something timeless, mysterious, profoundly unscientific. Naturalism, on the other hand, was to embrace the modern world with campaigning enthusiasm, bringing the scientific age's distinctive forms of analysis to bear on itself.

It was the emergence of a substantial middle class in Paris that gave Naturalism its main audience, while the city provided Naturalism with its subject matter. Thus much of Émile Zola's work focused on the particular conditions of Parisian life, showing particular delight in addressing the social problems and contradictions arising from rapid urban change – alcoholism, prostitution, consumerism, class conflict, decline of religion and so on. The critics who so vehemently railed against Naturalism did so in urban-industrial metaphors; when Strindberg's *Miss Julie* (1.2) was published in 1888, they called it 'water from … [a] dirty sewer' (Meyer 1985: 198). Ibsen distances himself from Zola in the same terms: 'Zola descends into the sewer to bathe in it; I to cleanse it' (qtd in Meyer 1974, 514–15).

As the income of the rising industrial class outstripped that of the declining aristocracy (whose income derived from land, which was suffering from economic competition with the Americas), the middle class bought up the gentry's town houses. These houses, with their steps up to the front door, literally elevated its residents above the mess and chaos of the city. Curtains and shutters prevented the public from seeing in. Naturalism, with its preference for making invisible the fourth wall, was a way of seeing into these homes, of showing the middle class to itself, stripped of its carefully presented respectability, laid bare in its greed, lust and hypocrisy. Pastor Manders, hearing of Mr Alving's affair with a maid, voices this architectural clash between outward respectability and domestic vice: 'all that in this very house! In this house!' (Ibsen 1994: 118).

Naturalism and the nineteenth-century stage

An immediate literary precedent for Naturalism lay in the rise of the 'realist' novel of the 1830s in the work of Balzac, Flaubert and Stendhal. A little later, in the 1850s, 'realism' emerged as a force in the visual arts, gaining particular notoriety when Gustave Courbet's paintings were rejected by the Paris International Exposition of 1855. It was in this atmosphere of controversy that Émile Zola began writing, first as a critic, then as a novelist. He was a great supporter of Courbet and his approach to the novel was entirely in the spirit of Flaubert's famous remark that 'great art is scientific and impersonal' (qtd in Cruickshank 1969: 3). However, Zola thought the term 'realism' too narrow and exclusive and instead, in an article for *L' Événement* published on

15 July 1866, coined the term 'Naturalism' to describe his new approach and for the next fifteen years campaigned for it indefatigably in the novel and, from the mid-1870s, on the stage. Zola collected many of his essays and articles in a series of books, including *The Experimental Novel* (1880) and *Naturalist Novelists, Naturalism in the Theatre* and *Our Dramatic Authors* in (1881). Zola had considerable success as a novelist and adapted some of his own novels for the stage, including *L'Assommoir* (1879), *Nana* (1881), *Pot-Bouille* (1883), *Le Ventre de Paris* (1887), and *Germinal* (1888). Only *Thérèse Raquin* (1873), however, adapted from his novel of 1867, has had any substantial theatrical afterlife.

If Zola thought that by using the word 'Naturalism' rather than 'Realism' he would avoid controversy, he was mistaken. The French stage in the 1870s was dominated by three playwrights – that 'illustrious trinity' wrote Antoine half in mockery, half in awe (1964: 2) – Émile Augier, Victorien Sardou and Alexandre Dumas *fils*, the masters of the 'well-made play'. This form, developed and perfected through the century, was loosely based on Aristotle's rules for dramatic construction and took its hero through an increasingly complicated plot, characterized by secrets and misunderstandings, before being completely resolved in the 'scène à faire' (or 'obligatory scene') in which all secrets are revealed, all misunderstandings resolved. The moral world-view of the well-made play – usually articulated by a 'raisonneur', a character who voices the author's own moral judgment – was generally conservative. Further, the neatness of the narrative prevented it from connecting with the messy realities of nineteenth-century Europe, which had seen the unification of Germany and Italy, the spread of colonial empires, and multiple wars and revolutions. Yet, as the Naturalist playwright Henry Becque noted in 1888, 'from all these events we have not taken the action of a single drama, not one' (Schumacher 1996: 53).

Shortly after the publication of *Thérèse Raquin*, Zola's novel was condemned in the French newspaper *Le Figaro*. The article was entitled 'La Littérature Putride' (Putrid Literature) and its author, 'Ferragus', denounced *Thérèse Raquin* as 'a puddle of dirt and blood' and Naturalism as 'a monstrous school of novelists that tries to replace the eloquence of the body with the eloquence of the charnel house, that specializes in clinical abnormalities, that gathers the diseased together and invites us to admire their blemishes, that takes its inspiration from that great teacher, cholera, and make spurt forth the pus of conscience'. 'Ferragus' was a pseudonym for Louis Ulbach, a satirical writer and friend of Zola, so it is quite possible that Zola put him up to writing the article to gain publicity for his book. Nonetheless, his arguments shed light on the curious place of the theatre within French culture in his belief that *Thérèse Raquin*'s (1.1) characters could not possibly be put on stage: they are 'impossible phantoms, who reek of death, who have never breathed life, who are but nightmares of reality' (Ferragus 1868: 1).[1] Zola invites us to treat his characters with contempt and disgust and, suggests Ferragus, this is not acceptable in the theatre.

What Ferragus means by this is that actors should be met with admiration, complicit laughter or tragic empathy, and nothing else. It would be unseemly to play a role that repelled the audience's sympathy. Indeed, Naturalist plays, if they weren't banned outright, were sometimes modified to conform to prevailing theatrical taste: when Ibsen's *A Doll's House* was first produced in Germany, for example, Hedwig Niemann-Raabe, the actress playing Nora, refused to play the ending in which Nora leaves her husband and children, declaring '*I* would never leave *my* children' (Meyer 1974: 480). To prevent the production from falling through, Ibsen had to write a new closing sequence in which Nora sees her children, imagines them motherless, and declares 'Oh, this is a sin against myself, but I cannot leave them' (Ibsen 1994: 87–8).

Thus Naturalism was a long time coming to the French stage. Zola's campaign was conducted as much in hope as conviction. In 'Naturalism in the Theatre' (1.6), perhaps as tacit acknowledgement of his own shortcomings as a dramatist, he confesses to not knowing what form Naturalist theatre will take, only the ideas it must embody, and he fervently bids a 'genius to come … with the expected word, the solution to the problem, the formula for real life on stage, combining it with the illusions necessary in the theatre' (106: 134). Zola presumed this genius would be a writer; though, as we will see, it was a director who would first make Naturalism a theatrical reality.

But what is 'Naturalism'? Even in its era, the term meant different things to different people. For Zola, it is very much the application of scientific method to the production of literature and theatre. For Strindberg, it was 'the poetic portrayal of nature' (Strindberg 1992: 512–13). Ibsen was uninterested in aligning himself with any movement.[2] However, one can see in Naturalism two main strands, which I will call 'the sociological imagination' and a 'visual culture'. Broadly, the first conveys something of Naturalism's attitude to the world, the second conveys its style of representing the world. Neither entails the other and much Naturalist theatre leans in one of the two directions.

The sociological imagination

'We are an age of method, of experimental science,' wrote Zola (1.6: 131), aligning the Naturalist movement with the nineteenth century's revolution in scientific ideas, in particular its impact on the study of society. Particularly important were Ernest Renan, Auguste Comte and Hippolyte Taine with their shared belief in bringing the principles of scientific investigation to bear on literature, religion and history, respectively. Comte, in particular, is one of the founders of modern sociology, which has its origins in the application of scientific method to the study of society (Comte's preferred term for such study was 'social physics' [1983: 77]). While their names have somewhat receded in importance, they were part of the climate of thought in the 1900s that produced the twentieth century, for good and bad. They certainly had a defining influence on Zola's conception of Naturalism.

For Renan, science had shown religion to be redundant; as he wrote in his posthumously published *The Future of Science*, 'It is not one single argument, but all the modern sciences together that produce this great conclusion: there is no such thing as the supernatural' (Renan 1890: 47). Such sceptical attitudes towards religion that he represents can be found in the generally unsympathetic representation of religious beliefs in Naturalist plays, including Kristin in *Miss Julie*, whose banal pieties are pointedly inadequate to the more complex dilemmas unfolding before us.

In his *Course in Positive Philosophy* (1830–42), Comte suggests that the history of humanity has fallen into three intellectual stages: 'the theological, or fictitious; the metaphysical, or abstract; and the scientific, or positive' (Comte 1983: 71). In the first, the world is explained through false religious ideas; in the second, the religious ideas have been abandoned in favour of abstract concepts; in the third, the positive stage, 'the mind has given over the vain search after absolute notions, the origin and destination of the universe, and the causes of phenomena, and applies itself to the study of their laws' (ibid: 72). These kinds of 'teleological' arguments were more popular in the nineteenth century than in ours and can be found in the work of thinkers as diverse as G.W.F. Hegel and Karl Marx (whose youngest daughter, Eleanor, was an early translator of Ibsen's work into English).

Comte's view of history confirmed Zola's view that Naturalism was progressive and modern, *the* literary and theatrical form of the positivist age. Indeed, Comte's three-stage history of human ideas finds its way, somewhat reinterpreted, into Zola's 'Naturalism in the Theatre'. Thus in his declaration that 'an irresistible current carries our society towards the study of reality ... the great naturalistic school, which has spread secretly, irrevocably, often making its way in darkness but always advancing, can finally come out triumphantly into the light of day' (1.6: 129), one can see traces of Comte's teleology. In describing previous forms of theatre as a 'necessary link' (ibid: 130) or a 'necessary revolution', the article shows a Comtean confidence in Naturalism as the inevitable outcome of theatre history.

For Zola, Comte's three phases of thought – theological, metaphysical and scientific – map onto three phases of French theatre: Classical, Romantic and Naturalist. The Classical theatre that dominated the seventeenth and eighteenth centuries arose from the rediscovery of ancient Greek theatre and, in particular, Aristotle's *Poetics* which attempts to codify its rules. Associated with dramatists like Jean Racine and Pierre Corneille, neoclassicism was characterized by a certain grand austerity, heightened poetic language, stories drawn from classical mythology, great psychological complexity and with reason favoured over passion. Romanticism emerged in the theatre in the 1830s and now Shakespeare, rather than ancient Greece, provided the model. All the formal purity of neoclassicism was abandoned; action was vivid and intense, emotions ran high, the stories mixed comedy and tragedy, and often had medieval and Renaissance settings. Zola suggests that classicism, with its ancient cosmology, corresponds to the theological phase, while Romanticism, with its grand passions, its evocation of higher causes for which to fight, its speculation about the nature of the universe, corresponds to the metaphysical. With the advent of Naturalism, says Zola in clearly Comtean terms, we are seeing 'the gradual substitution of physiological man for metaphysical man' (ibid: 135).

A still greater influence on Zola's thinking comes from critic and historian Hippolyte Taine for whom the best way to understand a society is to read its literature. 'If the work is rich and one knows how to interpret it', Taine wrote, 'one can find in there the psychology of a soul, often of a century, and sometimes of an entire race. In this respect a great poem, a beautiful novel, the memoirs of a great man are more instructive than a mountain of historians and their history books' (Taine 1863: xlv). Taine believed that a work of literature bore the traces of three forces acting on it from the society in which it emerged: *race, milieu* and *moment*. Taine did not merely believe these were influences amongst others: these were the only possible causes of all events (xxxiii). Together, '*race, environment, moment*, in other words the internal dynamic, the external pressure and the momentum already acquired ... will impose a shape and direction on anything new' (xxxiii, xxx). Taine's *moment, milieu* and *race* find themselves paraphrased loosely in Strindberg's preface to *Miss Julie* (1.7), in which he describes his main character as a victim of 'the errors of an age, of circumstances, and of her own deficient constitution' (1.7: 141). If Comte left Zola with the belief that Naturalism was the modern theatre form *par excellence*, Taine persuaded him that literature and drama were unparalleled means of capturing the spirit of the age.

The word 'naturalism', before Zola picked it up, was a philosophical term denoting a belief that all things are part of the natural world, that nothing – not free will, ethics, passions, religion or art – escaped the laws of cause and effect and the natural forces at work in the physical universe. The publication of Charles Darwin's *The Origin of Species* (1859) was a naturalistic landmark in this sense: it erased much of the distinction between human beings and animals. It encouraged many thinkers – sociologists, economists and artists – to see animal behaviour in the patterns of human society. Although Darwin's evolutionary processes are only visible over hundreds of years, at the end of the century 'Social Darwinism' had appeared: this was a – probably illegitimate – application of Darwin's principle of 'natural selection' to human cultures, suggesting that ordinary human interactions were 'really' competitions for status and power. Naturalism in the theatre was, to some extent, part of this overexuberant adoption of Darwinian themes. Zola carries some of this meaning over into his view of the world and of art; of the novel *Thérèse Raquin* he writes:

> In *Thérèse Raquin* I set out to study, not characters, but temperaments. Therein lies the whole essence of the book. I chose to portray individuals existing under the sovereign dominion of their nerves and their blood, devoid of free will and drawn into every act of their lives by the inescapable promptings of their flesh. (Zola 1992: 1–2)

Taine's philosophically naturalist remark that 'vice and virtue are products just like vitriol and sugar' (1863: xv) was Zola's epigraph to the first edition of *Thérèse Raquin*.

Influenced by French physiologist Claude Bernard, who sought to apply the principles of scientific enquiry to the practice of medicine and surgery, Zola compared the Naturalist author to a surgeon: 'I like to think of him as an anatomist of the soul and the flesh,' he wrote in 1866. 'He dissects man, studies the play of the passions, explores each fibre, analyses the whole organism. Like a surgeon, he has neither shame nor revulsion when he explores human wounds. He cares only for truth and lays before us the corpse of our heart. Modern science has provided him with the tools of analysis and the experimental method' (qtd in Becker 2002: 256). Defending his characterization of Thérèse and Laurent in his preface to *Thérèse Raquin* he insists: 'I simply carried out on two living bodies the same analytical examination that surgeons perform on corpses' (Zola 1992: 2).

Many Naturalist playwrights had connections with the world of medical science: Chekhov was a practising doctor; Ibsen was a pharmacist's apprentice for six years; Strindberg studied medicine for two years and in 1887 published a collection of stories and essays entitled *Vivisections: A Retired Doctor's Observations*. This is not to say that they were all reliable supporters of the latest scientific ideas: Zola's *Thérèse Raquin* uncomfortably marries a contemporary scientific viewpoint with the ancient theory of the 'humours' (1992: xvi–xxii). Ibsen's *Ghosts* (1881) relies on the belief that syphilis is hereditary. Strindberg's openness to the new science was, to put it mildly, undiscriminating, and *Miss Julie* makes reference to telepathy in the battle between its antagonists (60). Chekhov, despite or perhaps because of his medical training, depicts most of his doctors as depressed, weary, cynical, even accidentally murderous.

Nonetheless, there is, widespread in Naturalist theatre, a determination to observe the world with all its flaws and disorders with the unsentimental clarity of a scientist, refusing any mystical, spiritual or otherwise non-physical explanations, crowned by a belief that the theatre has the vital social purpose of recording the observable truth of the world that is too important to be restrained by theatrical convention or moral squeamishness.

Visual culture

A determination to depict the truth of the world, understood in materialist terms, does not necessarily entail visual realism. It is therefore important to understand that Naturalism's visual style, its preference for a relation of resemblance between the stage and the world, is a particular – and contestable – decision. 'Realism' has never been a theatre movement as such; in the arts, realism doesn't mean much more than a determination to represent reality, however that reality is understood. The Naturalist version of realism understands reality in the sociological terms that I have described and chooses to represent that world through copying its surfaces – the details of human behaviour and its environment.

Changes in theatre technology made new kinds of realism possible through the nineteenth century. The move from oil to gas lighting at the beginning of the century, then to limelight in the mid-century, and finally to electric lighting towards the century's end, meant that the stage could be lit more brightly, with a whiter light, the intensity, level and direction of which could increasingly be controlled. This demanded increasingly sophisticated scene painting, as the backcloths were more exposed by the light; it also made obsolete some conventions of the early nineteenth century, including footlights, heavy stylized make-up and the necessity for the actor to stand downstage facing the audience if they were to be seen.

Particularly influential in making use of these innovations to create new realistic stage effects was the Meiningen Court Theatre, established in 1866 by George II, Duke of Saxe-Meiningen, a small independent state in the heart of what is now Germany. The Meiningen company became famous for the detailed, historically accurate composition of their stage pictures, in particular their crowd scenes, which were arranged with particular eye to realistic effect. André Antoine saw them in Brussels in 1888 and admired the 'extraordinarily convincing crowd scenes' and the sight of an actor with his back to the audience who thereby 'gives the impression that he is oblivious to the presence of the public and thus creates the perfect illusion' (Schumacher 1996: 80). Stanislavski saw them when they toured to Russia and the meticulously realized sound effects at the Moscow Art Theatre owed much to the similarly innovative sound design at the Meiningen.

If human beings are the products of their environment, then the environment must be represented with particular care. Zola's remark that 'the environment must determine the character' (1.6: 136) is directly echoed by Antoine's insistence that 'it is the environment that determines the movements of the character, not the movements of the characters that determine the environment' (qtd in Whitton 1987: 21). In both instances the French word for environment, 'milieu', both stands for 'set design' and reminds us of the second of Taine's forces. As such, Naturalism demanded a new detail and precision in stage design, the better to demonstrate the social and environmental forces acting on the characters. The actors, meanwhile, were required to subsume themselves within the ensemble and the stage picture so as to represent the place of the human within the natural world. The dramatist's medium being language, he or she has limited power to determine through words the stage environment. Naturalism gave new independent responsibility to the stage designer.

Jean Jullien's book *Le Théâtre Vivant* (1892) provides us with two widely used phrases to describe Naturalist theatre. One is that a Naturalist play is 'a slice of life'; the other is that the play is seen through 'a *fourth wall*, transparent for the audience, opaque for the actor' (1892: 11; my emphasis). The 'fourth wall' requires not only the actor to not acknowledge the audience, but the audience to join in the make-believe. To encourage this, the auditorium lights were dimmed; this is now so common in European and North American theatre as to seem unremarkable but at the Théâtre Libre, where they started dimming the house lights a year into their operation, it occasioned giggles and facetious kissing sounds (Chothia 1991: 64).

All of these techniques came together in perhaps the most important European theatre company of the nineteenth century, the Théâtre Libre, founded by André Antoine in March 1887. The Théâtre Libre was quickly associated with Naturalism, though in fact its repertoire was an eclectic mixture of Naturalist plays, farces, tragedies, poetic dramas, Symbolist plays, historical epics and documentary performances. Antoine was a member of the new middle class, initially supporting his company from his job as clerk at the Gas Company and the Palais de Justice; it was an amateur operation, a beneficiary of an Imperial decree deregulating the theatre industry in 1864, and it struggled on for barely seven years under Antoine's leadership. Yet it directly inspired the foundation of a dozen other experimental theatres across Europe, including Berlin's Freie Bühne (1889), London's Independent Theatre (1891), the Moscow Art Theatre (1897), as well as many theatres in Paris (see Henderson 1971).

August Strindberg: *Miss Julie* (1.2)

One theatre artist directly inspired by the example of the Théâtre Libre was August Strindberg, who formed the Scandinavian Experimental Theatre in 1888 to perform two one-act plays he had written that summer: *Miss Julie* and *Creditors*. *Miss Julie* and its preface reflect both Strindberg's brief but fervent advocacy of Zolaesque Naturalism and his own equally fervent misogyny. His philosophical naturalism was greatly influenced by his recent reading of the German philosopher Friedrich Nietzsche, from whom he appears to have taken the idea that the world is divided into the naturally weak and naturally strong, both groups engaged in perpetual, but unequal, battle for supremacy. For Strindberg, the weak included the lower classes, socialists and women. In the preface, he declares that a woman is a 'stunted form of human being' compared to 'man, the lord of creation, the creator of culture' (1.7: 141). Any talk of equality between men and women is absurd, he decides, because men and women are entirely different species; it would be as meaningless as demanding equality between ants and elephants. Feminism, an emergent political movement across Europe in the late nineteenth century, was therefore an attempt to deny nature or – and this is Strindberg at his most Nietzschean – for the weak to defeat the strong by stealth. In this he undoubtedly has his eye on Ibsen, whose *A Doll's House* (1879) was considered a form of feminist challenge to patriarchal convention.[3]

The play exploits some of this spurious logic. Julie is a woman whose upbringing and aristocratic privilege has encouraged her to try to dominate the men around her; challenging the traditional passive female position, she leads when dancing and was seen training her fiancé like a dog. She invades the scullery and flirts with the servants. However, when circumstances conspire to place her and Jean together in the latter's bedroom, her 'true' weakness as a woman is revealed, and she submits sexually to her servant. The possibility of equality between them is articulated in the play by Jean – 'Maybe deep down there is not such a difference between us all as people think' (1.2: 56) – but later it becomes clear that this was simply part of his seduction. Jean's male 'superiority' is revealed and, Strindberg suggests, there is no possible outcome for her than her own death. It is the tragedy of a woman trying to defy her nature.

Although it is unlikely that many modern theatregoers would be convinced by Strindberg's views about men and women, it is worth considering the view of feminist critic and thinker Germaine Greer, who has argued that Strindberg's genius lay in his unflinching honesty: in his torrid misogyny he 'glimpsed the archetypal conflict in all its terrible grandeur' and laid it bare (Greer 1986: 207). Perhaps one might defend this play as more honest about patriarchal attitudes and the 'battle of the sexes' than the more reasoned and liberal debates of Ibsen or Shaw. Let's also not overlook that Strindberg gives Julie a speech of violent female sexual revenge that has rarely been equalled for force and power:

JULIE: ... I'm weak – am I – I'd like to see your blood, your brains smashed on the chopping block. I want to see every one of your sex swimming in a lake of blood like this one. I think I could drink out of your skull – I could wash my feet in your ripped stomach – I could roast your heart and eat. So you think I am weak ... (1.2: 64).

On the other hand, one can consider the play as being complicated by Strindberg's own adherence to the principles of Naturalism. The preface shows just how closely Strindberg has followed the debates around Zola's work and the emergence of the Théâtre Libre. He calls for the lowering of the house lights and the actors to turn their backs on the audience, and describes the scenography in terms of a fourth wall, all of which recalls the Théâtre Libre's principles of staging (1.7: 145), while his description of his characters as animals and his insistence that characters 'merge with their milieu' (ibid: 144) recall Zola. Some of his ideas go further; for example, in his suggestion that actors might improvise some of their dialogue (ibid), there is a moment where this is suggested in the play (1.2: 62), and in his desire to create spaces for 'monologue, mime and ballet' (1.7: 143 and 1.2: 53 and 57 for wordless and dance sequences).

But where the play is most modern is in its conception of character; unlike Zola's simplistic notion of individuals being ruled by a single temperament which Strindberg criticizes (1.7: 140), or Taine's neat tripartite account of the forces acting on human action, Strindberg's characters are multiple: 'conglomerates of past and present stages of culture, bits out of books and newspapers, scraps of humanity, torn shreds of once fine clothing now turned to rags, exactly as the human soul is patched together' (ibid: 140). Strindberg lists at least thirteen different reasons to explain Julie's action, from the 'festive atmosphere of Midsummer Night' to the fact that she is menstruating during the action of the play (ibid: 139). This has an effect on the tumbling dialogue that frequently darts from thought to thought, giving a potent sense of a mind's wandering journey through a subject (e.g. 1.2: 56, 64, 65). The multiplicity of motives creates rich ambiguities in the play that perhaps undermine Strindberg's misogynistic intentions. Similarly, the psychological density of the play raises questions it cannot fully answer: what did happen in Jean's bedroom? Is Julie's fate truly inevitable? So many different thoughts crowd together in the play to explain the action that it becomes difficult to limit it to a woman's battle against her femininity.

In addition, the battle of the sexes threads through the play's battles between Naturalism and theatricality. Strindberg seems to conceive Naturalism as a 'masculine' form of theatre: in his preface, he explicitly addresses his thoughts on Naturalism only to men, since he believes women 'would rather be beautiful than truthful' (1.7: 145). Jean's talent for deception and seduction is repeatedly described in terms of theatre (1.2: 54, 56, 67), and the preface to the play sees non-Naturalistic conventions as false. But the play is itself not always rigorously Naturalistic: several images – Julie and Jean's dreams of falling and climbing (ibid: 55), the peasants' dance (ibid: 57) and the rather Ibsenite image of the greenfinch (or 'siskin') being beheaded (ibid: 64) – all take on meanings in the play beyond the strictly material and logical. The sexual politics of the play are worked out at the level of theatrical form as well as content.

Thérèse Raquin (1.1) and the contradictions of Naturalism

'Zola's *Thérèse Raquin*', wrote August Strindberg, 'will be accounted the first milestone of naturalist drama, thus ascribing the origin of the latter to 1873' (Strindberg 1996: 76). That was the year Zola's adaptation of his own novel opened at the Théâtre de la Renaissance. The play closed after seventeen performances which, for the time, was moderately successful, and was performed by a number of the Naturalist theatres across Europe. It is Zola's only play to be regularly revived and adapted.

The play, in some respects, programmatically represents Zola's naturalistic ideas. In the first few minutes we are given various aspects of *race*, *milieu* and *moment*, from Camille's sickly physiology to the Raquin family background, from the geography of their youth to the urban environment of Paris. Unlike the book, which is able to roam freely between different locations, the entire play is set in one room. This has the benefit of creating an even more cramped setting to suggest the pressing in of the bourgeois *milieu* on the lives of the characters. Animal imagery supports the Naturalistic representation of these characters as natural beings. The first act establishes, like an equation, a series of conditions – (a) Camille is weak, (b) Laurent is strong, (c) Thérèse is strong also, (d) They are having an affair, (e) Laurent may soon not be able to take time off work to see Thérèse, (f) Camille has agreed to go boating – such as to make the outcome seem like an inevitable consequence.

Within the play, Zola places a few images to steer the audience to an appreciation of his Naturalist intentions. Laurent is an artist and his work is admired as being lifelike – even to the point where it does not flatter its subject. Meanwhile much fun is had with the character of Michaud, who enjoys gruesome stories of what we would now call 'true crime': he horrifies Thérèse with his tales of the murderers who walk the streets unidentified, their victims undiscovered. His salacious voyeurism is presumably to be distinguished from the clinical objectivity of the Naturalist.

Later in the play, however, Laurent fails to recognize the portrait he's painted, believing it is actually Camille come back to accuse him, a moment that might stand as a metaphor for the way works of art can elude the grasp of their makers. Indeed, *Thérèse Raquin* does not consistently fulfil Zola's dream of a Naturalist theatre: the play is heavily indebted to the conventions of the well-made play and of the melodramatic stage. Zola artfully misdirects the audience, inviting us to think Thérèse dislikes Laurent before pulling off a major reversal in the fifth scene of Act 1. While this is ingenious, it works more as a technical plot twist than a Naturalist exposition of a human case study. The same is true of some of the play's elegant literary touches, such as the symmetry of Thérèse adding extra sugar to the syllabub in Act 1, and adding too much salt to the soup in Act 4. These seem out of place in a 'slice of life'. The play tips into melodrama from the end of Act 3 when Mme Raquin overhears Laurent's confession: 'She suddenly has an attack of spasms, staggers as far as the bed, tries to balance, but seizing onto one of the white bed curtains, leans against the wall a moment, panting and fearful' (1.1: 44). Such moments seem uncritically copied from the conventions of the mid-century Paris Boulevard theatre. When Thérèse asks, 'What is the good of acting out this comedy of the past?' (1.1: 43), she might have been referring to the play itself.

In a very early attempt to explain Naturalism in a letter to his friend, the poet and critic Antony Valabrègue, Zola suggested that art was like a window onto the world, and the type of art was the type of glass, or 'screen', in that window. Unlike the 'classical' or 'romantic' screen, what characterizes the 'realist'[4] screen is that it is

> a simple pane of glass, very thin and clear, which aims to be so perfectly transparent that images pass straight through it and are therefore reproduced in all their reality. Thus a precise, accurate, and simple reproduction that does not alter line or colour. The realist screen denies its own existence … However clear, thin, and transparent it may be, it has its own tint and a certain thickness; it colours objects, it refracts everything as something else. Nonetheless, I gladly consider the images it offers the most real; it achieves a high degree of exact reproduction.
>
> (Becker 2002: 238)

Zola claims that the realist screen is entirely transparent; then he accepts that such a transparency is impossible; and then he seems to put that consideration to one side. The image of the transparent screen suggests that the stage need only represent the *appearance* of the world. However, Naturalist theatre represents more of an experimental project than this suggests. It broke theatrical form, it introduced new subject matter, it expressed new attitudes towards the world and expressed those attitudes in new ways. As such, it cannot but have drawn attention to itself as theatre, in the choices it made, and in the artistic and political decisions underlying the performances. In such circumstances, it will have been difficult, perhaps impossible, to look transparently through the theatrical screen to the world it is depicting. All of these contradictions are part of what continues to fascinate theatre makers and audiences about Naturalism. It perhaps explains why, well over a century later, it is not uncommon to find writers, actors, directors and theatre companies wishing to challenge Naturalism, to seek out alternative forms. It is also why those same people return to those early Naturalist plays to subvert them and explore and exploit their contradictions.

The Symbolist movement

Barely three years after the Théâtre Libre had opened its doors, Naturalism was challenged by a rival avant-garde theatre movement. Symbolist theatre – declared Paul Fort, director of Théâtre d'Art – would not concern itself, like Naturalism, with the 'trivial and accidental details of actuality' (qtd in Whitton 1987: 28). In the manifesto that announced the Symbolist movement, Jean Moréas neatly belittled Naturalism as 'a legitimate but ill-advised protest against the blandishments of a few then-fashionable novelists' (1886: 2). Symbolism had a much grander aim: nothing less than to represent the mystical harmony of the universe.

Just as Naturalist theatre was rehearsed in the novel, Symbolist theatre was prefigured in poetry. Charles Baudelaire's *Les Fleurs du Mal* (The Flowers of Evil) (1857) and Arthur Rimbaud's 'Le Bateau Ivre' (The Drunken Boat) (1871), and *Une Saison en Enfer* (A Season in Hell) (1873) were particular inspirations in their elusive attempts to capture mysterious patterns beyond what was known. Baudelaire's poem 'Correspondances' (1857) is an important example as it presents an experience of the world thick with mysterious symbols between which there are curious harmonies, where a perfume can resemble a child's body, the sound of an oboe or a verdant meadow.

The Symbolists were interested in everything the Naturalists usually tried to repress in their work: ambiguity, metaphor, mysticism. The 'symbols' of Symbolism were those images that seemed to have more significance than is explained by their mere existence. As the critic John Cruickshank put it, writing of the great poet and theorist of Symbolism Stéphane Mallarmé, his poems 'aspire towards mystical presences hinted at by such things as blue sky, open windows, the sound of bells, a woman's hair, ships leaving port' (Cruickshank 1969: 142). In the specifically literary figures of symbol, metaphor, allegory, echo, parallel, repetition and rhyme, usually non-literal connections are drawn between two quite different experiences or objects. This affinity is a third quality that gives us a glimpse, so the Symbolists felt, of a broader cosmic harmony far deeper and more fundamental than the banal and accidental happenstance of material life.

Where the Naturalists pronounced the end of the supernatural and the ubiquity of material reality, the Symbolists denounced material reality as an illusion and sought experiences of the supernatural. Put another way, Naturalism was materialist and Symbolism was idealist. Where the Naturalists saw clarity and transparency as virtues, the Symbolists preferred to be ambiguous, cryptic, difficult. Where the Naturalists sought a wide public for their work, the Symbolists were avowedly elitist, preferring to speak to a small coterie of close initiates. Where the Naturalists embraced the modern world and believed themselves to be its direct expression, the Symbolists turned away from it and sought the ancient and the timeless. Where the preferred environment of the Naturalists was a scientific laboratory, the Symbolists would probably have been more at home in a cathedral.

Like the Naturalists, the Symbolists faced enormous difficulties in realizing their ideas on the stage but if anything their problem was more fundamental. One of their most devoted admirers, Camille Mauclair, admitted that 'if ever a literary movement has been incapable by its very essence of adapting itself to the stage, it was Symbolism' (qtd in Whitton 1987: 32). The problem was the materiality of the stage itself; how was it possible to attain a glimpse of the 'Eternal' on a solid stage made of wood, with painted backdrops, fleshly actors? Many Symbolists considered great plays to be better read than performed; Maurice Maeterlinck, perhaps Symbolism's most accomplished playwright, believed that 'most of the great poems of humanity are not fit for the stage. Lear, Hamlet, Othello, Macbeth, Anthony and Cleopatra cannot be represented, and it is dangerous to see them on the stage. Something of Hamlet died for us the day we saw him die onstage' (qtd in Dorra 1995: 145). Mallarmé bemoaned 'the solid set and the real actor' of the conventional theatre (1885: 195). In 1902, the Russian Symbolist writer Bryusov wrote in reference to the avalanche at the end of Ibsen's *When We Dead Awaken* (1.4) performed by the Moscow Art Theatre, 'When an avalanche of cotton batting comes crashing down on stage, the spectators ask each other: how did they do that? If Rubek and Irene simply went backstage, the spectator would more readily believe in their destruction' (Schumacher 1996: 220). The Symbolists were entranced by the mystical power of words and saw the clumsy materialism of the stage as a barrier to the 'Infinite'.

An early clue to a possible Symbolist staging practice came from the work of the composer Richard Wagner, in particular his vision of the *Gesamtkunstwerk* (total work of art). There was a view, associated with Walter Pater but very widespread, that all art aspired towards the condition of music. Music's communicative form being abstract and (usually) non-literal suggested itself as a direct example of art that was not mimetic of anything in the world and which might, therefore, represent some higher reality than mere appearance. The example of music encouraged writers to think more abstractly about words not just as bearers of meaning but also as bearers of rhythms, textures, their own kind of music. And if music and poetry could represent complementary arts that led towards the higher Idea, perhaps other art forms could too. Ultimately, the most perfect expression of the Idea might be a 'total work of art' that combined all others in a single experience. And what art form seems to combine all others? 'There is only one medium,' wrote Richard Wagner, 'in which all these united artforms can transform their intentions into glorious reality, and that is the drama' (qtd in Schumacher 1996: 162).

Symbolist staging

Paul Fort was only 18 years old and still a student when he formed the Théâtre d'Art as an avowedly Symbolist theatre. It was a short-lived enterprise, existing for less than sixteen months and producing only eight productions. Their second performance in January 1891 was given over to a raw but potent staging of Shelley's *The Cenci*, uncut and lasting until 2.00 a.m. However, it was unusual for Théâtre d'Art to give an evening over to one play; more often, bills would contain several items – plays, staged poems and readings. Also, it was not uncommon for evenings to be interrupted by arguments and fights in the auditorium, ending late in the night.

The Théâtre d'Art produced some of the most radically experimental theatre of the nineteenth century, setting a template for later experiments in Expressionism, Dada and Surrealism (see Part 2). In particular, there was a consistent attempt to find a way of bypassing the materiality of the theatre and restore the poetic in language to the stage. In March 1891 the Théâtre d'Art staged Pierre Quillard's *The Girl with the Severed Hands*. The play is a medieval verse fantasy about a girl mutilated by her abusive father, who escapes to a mystical land where her hands are restored and a choir of angels bid her to accept the love of a Poet-King. At the Théâtre d'Art, a thin gauze separated the audience from the stage; upstage was a gold backcloth adorned with paintings of angels kneeling in prayer. In front of the gauze to the left stood a narrator, Susan Gay, wearing a long blue robe and standing at a lectern. She intoned the stage directions while the poetic dialogue was recited without expression by the actors behind the gauze.

Several features of this staging are worth pointing out. The lack of movement and of any distracting 'realistic' detail allows the audience to concentrate on the words. As Pierre Quillard wrote, in a newspaper article responding to criticisms of that evening, '*The word creates the set and everything else as well*' (1.11: 163). The gold backcloth was a '*pure ornamental fiction which completes the illusion with colour and lines analogous to the drama*' (ibid: 164); in other words, rather than creating a realistic setting for the action, the backcloth is a symbolic analogy for the play, corresponding to an aspect of its atmosphere or ideas. The gauze served two purposes: first, it distanced the actors, made them harder to see, simplified their physical outline, making them seem less individual. Second, it served as a kind of analogy for the relation of the Symbolist to everyday life: by looking through the gauze's surface to discern its mystical depths, the audience was rehearsing their penetration of the surface of ordinary life to the deeper realities beyond. The narrator at the front of the gauze is like the Symbolist, a guide leading us through to the Ideal. The theatre, as Quillard puts it, is '*a chance to dream*' (ibid).

The lack of intonation in the verse-speaking was one attempt to solve the problem of the actor's presence. Camille Mauclair insisted that actors 'have no value except as incarnations of the Idea they symbolise' (qtd in Carlson 1993: 290). Aurélien Lugné-Poë, introducing his own Symbolist company, the Théâtre de l'Oeuvre, declared: 'the greatest virtue of the actor will be to efface himself' (qtd in Braun 1982: 46). There was considerable interest in finding alternatives to human performers; many theatre makers associated with Symbolism, including Alfred Jarry, Edward Gordon Craig, Paul Margueritte and Fyodor Sologub, were interested in using puppets, Margueritte admiring the way they seem to 'possess a quaint and mysterious life' (qtd in Henderson 1971: 134). Maeterlinck wrote some of his plays for puppets, and mused, 'one should perhaps eliminate the living being from the stage', considering a bewildering range of alternatives, from masks, sculptures, wax figures, shadows, reflections to even 'a projection of symbolic forms, or a being who would appear to be alive without being alive? I do not know; but the absence of man seems essential to me' (qtd in Dorra 1995: 145–6). In 1888, the Petit Théâtre de la Galerie Vivienne and Théâtre du Chat Noir opened puppet and shadow-puppet theatres, respectively.

If puppets were not feasible the next best thing was to turn human beings into puppets. This was initially achieved by minimizing the distinctive and individual human qualities of the actor but stripping the voice of any kind of conversational intonation, and the body of its ordinary movements and gestures. This was not always very effective; as one contemporary reviewer noted, the actors 'assume a perpetually ecstatic and visionary air. As if hallucinating, they stare before them, gazing afar, very far, vaguely, very vaguely. Their voices are cavernous, their diction chopped. They endeavour to give the impression that they are deranged. This is in order to awaken us to a sense of the Beyond' (qtd in Whitton 1987: 34). Correspondingly, Strindberg, in his Symbolist phase, described ideal acting as being somewhat like sleepwalking (1967: 23).

Maurice Maeterlinck and Symbolist playwriting

Where the Naturalists favoured precise, contemporary locations, the Symbolists preferred mystical, other-worldly locations, not anchored in time or space. Maeterlinck's *The Blind* (1891), for example, is set in 'an ancient forest in the North, with an aura of timelessness, beneath a sky deep in stars'. Maeterlinck, who moved to Paris in 1886, was quickly welcomed by the Symbolists. Strindberg initially dismissed his work – but after a stormy period in his life when he began to abandon Naturalism in favour of new, more fragmented and personal theatre forms, he revised his opinion: 'The theatre I seek is Maeterlinck's and not that of the past' (qtd in Mayer 1985), later recalling that on this rereading 'he struck me like a new country and a new age' (521).

Maeterlinck's plays are distinguished by stillness and inactivity, though this is not to say that they are not dramatic. In his famous essay 'Tragedy in Everyday Life' (1.10), Maeterlinck suggests that 'an old man sitting in his armchair, just waiting beneath his lamp … lives, in reality, a profound, more human and more universal life than the lover who strangles his mistress, the captain who carries off the battle, or "the husband who avenges his honour"' (1.10: 160). Both poles of Symbolism saw the complex twisting narratives of Naturalism to be burdened with the bustle of everyday life and favoured stillness, contemplation and image. Maeterlinck's particular achievement was to recognize that this stillness and silence – and what might be going on within it – were worth dramatic attention, and in his best plays he strips away the grand rhetoric, the knights and castles, keeping the language very simple and the characters ordinary. The result is a series of one-act plays that find mystery and horror within everyday experience. In *Intruder* (1891), a family sit waiting for a nurse to attend their mother who has just given birth. The daughters somehow sense a figure, unseen by anyone else, enter the garden, then the house, climb the stairs and pass into the mother's antechamber, at which point the Nurse appears, announcing her death. In *The Blind* (1891), six blind men and six blind women are lost in a forest, because, unbeknown to them, their guide has died and his body sits lifeless among them.

In *Interior* (1894, 1.5), we are looking at the rear of a house. Through the windows, a family is sitting quietly together of an evening, unaware that one of the daughters has drowned. There is a telling homology between the stage picture in this play and the staging innovations of the Théâtre d'Art. The two men function like the narrator in Pierre Quillard's play, standing before the house, which has affinities with the gauze screen of that production. But the relations of the image are reversed; what we look at through the gauze is precisely a Naturalist setting, a domestic interior. Outside the house, we know the horrible truth about the death, news of which is imminently going to strike them and destroy their calm. Visually it is reframing a Naturalist play within a set of Symbolist concerns, reminding us that there is more to life than our particular existence. In the theatre there is a further visual rhyme: the windows of the house form a kind of proscenium arch; because it is dark outside and light indoors, the family cannot see the strangers in their garden. This reproduces the relationship we have, as a theatre audience, with the two strangers; we sit in the dark, watching them while they are unaware of our presence. In turn, this prompts the question, is someone watching *us*, aware of some cosmic injustice about to befall us? Symbolism gloried in drawing attention to the processes of theatre itself, creating theatre about theatre – or 'metatheatre' – which used the artifice and artistry of the theatre to talk about the world, contrasting with the Naturalists who wanted as far as possible for that artistry to be transparent.

Ibsen and Chekhov: between Symbolism and Naturalism

As we have seen, the Symbolists and Naturalists were opposed in many things. However, they also had much in common and their aggressively contrary viewpoints should not hide their shared roots in late nineteenth-century philosophy, science and ideas. Both Naturalism and Symbolism began as writers' theatres but their respective theatrical visions demanded the creation of the director to organize the visual field. They each demanded the effacement of the actor and endeavoured to contain some aspect of theatricality, whether that be its fictionalizing, metaphorical productivity or its dully material, physical existence. Symbolism's gauze is, in some ways, a version of the Naturalist 'fourth wall', both of them allowing access to some secret truth of the world; both conceived human beings as determined by forces outside of their control and of which they are usually unaware, whether they be natural laws or cosmic correspondences. Mallarmé, for example, declared that the poet's 'role is to understand and apply the universal laws of Analogy', which sounds Naturalistic, until the final word (qtd in Cruickshank 1969: 138). Naturalism being deterministic and Symbolism being fatalistic, they shared a belief that the future was fixed, even if we cannot know how.

Naturalism and Symbolism were, in many ways, contemporaries, in dialogue with each other, sharing theatre spaces, audiences and writers. Many of the major playwrights of the era were championed by both the Symbolists and the Naturalists. Some, like Strindberg and Hauptmann, moved very decisively from one to the other. Others, like Ibsen and Chekhov, maintained an ambiguous relationship with both. Henrik Ibsen is now so frequently considered to be a stern Naturalist that it can be surprising to read in a Symbolist journal of the time someone declaring, 'don't let [the Naturalists] get their hands on Ibsen' (qtd in Henderson 1971: 113). Ibsen had two successful productions at the Théâtre Libre but a commercial production of *Hedda Gabler* in 1891 was a failure. It fell to the Symbolists, and especially Lugné-Poë at the Théâtre de l'Oeuvre, to premiere most of his plays in Paris, including *Rosmersholm, An Enemy of the People* (1893), *The Master Builder* (1894), *Little Eyolf, Brand* (1895), *The Pillars of Society, Peer Gynt* (1896), *Love's Comedy* and *John Gabriel Borkman* (1897).

Why were the Symbolists so enamoured of Ibsen? Despite Ibsen's reputation as a Naturalist, his work shows signs of the sociological imagination only in four plays: *The Pillars of Society, A Doll's House, Ghosts* and *An Enemy of the People*. In each of these plays, a vision of society is plainly set out and truth is held out as an absolute virtue that must be defended regardless of the consequences. Over time, Ibsen's work increasingly exploited metaphor and symbolism. Although his characters and settings remained contemporary, the psychological worlds they inhabited became abstracted and elevated – literally so; *The Master Builder, John Gabriel Borkman* and *When We Dead Awaken* (1.4) all feature various kinds of journeys upwards.

By the time we reach his last play, *When We Dead Awaken*, Ibsen's stagecraft has begun to closely resemble some aspects of Symbolist theatre. The play is structured around two encounters in the first act that lead to two journeys up a mountain. Despite the grand sweep of the play's movement, it is a play of stillness and memory. Maia begins the play by expressing the idea that beneath the bustle of activity she seems to detect silence and death (1.4: 99), which, as with the images of dead women walking through the gardens at night (1.4: 102), sounds like something that might be expressed in a Maeterlinck play. The movement of the play lifts the action away from the sociality of the town to the sublime isolation of the mountain, an environment – like the medieval forests of the Symbolists – good for growing metaphors.

Rubek is an artist and in what we hear of his history we see a battle between Naturalism and Symbolism. The busts he sculpts of people secretly show them, he suggests, as animals underneath (ibid: 101), which, taken together with the play's frequent animal images, points towards a certain Naturalistic view of the world. But Rubek's greatest work, *The Resurrection Day*, embodied quite different ideas. He wanted to 'embody the pure woman as I saw her awakening on the Resurrection Day ... filled with a sacred joy at finding herself unchanged' (ibid: 106). (Some Symbolists, too, demanded that the stage treat woman as 'the eternal Object' [Henderson 1971: 113].) Rubek is confronted with Irene, the model who sat for him, and protests – like Zola – that as an artist he had to shut off any erotic feelings towards his subject. However, like Laurent in *Thérèse Raquin*, the artwork seemed to change beyond his control. He began to add other images and moved the Woman away from the centre, Meiningen-like, to create an overall image; in doing so he lost the sense of transcendence and the image fell back down to earth. The working title of *When We Dead Awaken* was *The Resurrection Day* and it is not hard to see the play as working through Ibsen's own disengagement from realism. *When We Dead Awaken* was first published in mid-December 1899 and first performed in Stuttgart on 26 January 1900, and as such marks a transition between the nineteenth- and twentieth-century theatre.

A year later, Chekhov's *Three Sisters* (1.3) premiered at the Moscow Art Theatre. By all accounts, the final curtain came down in silence, the audience too moved even to applaud.

Chekhov is an exquisite realist: his characters have the complexity Strindberg was aiming for in *Miss Julie* and his plotting escapes the conventions of the well-made play in a way that even Ibsen never managed. Chekhov once claimed that 'a writer must be as objective as a chemist; he must renounce subjectivity in life and know that dunghills play an important part in the landscape and evil passions are as much part of life as good ones' (qtd in Rayfield 1997: 149). This highly Zolaesque sentiment is reflected in his plays' unheroic characters. Key to understanding Chekhov is that we may be moved by the characters' plight, but we are not obliged to *like* any of them. The Prozorov sisters are self-obsessed, spoiled and consumed with their social superiority; and Colonel Vershinin is a philosophizing bore who embarks on an affair with Masha, leaving his suicidal wife at home. Chebutykin is a drunken surgeon who self-pityingly treats a botched operation as his own tragedy rather than the patient's.

Chekhov was a meticulous observer of human behaviour but, like Maeterlinck, found drama in silence and stillness and points a way towards the later twentieth-century dramaturgy of Samuel Beckett and Harold Pinter. Where Chekhov seems to be moving in a Symbolist direction in *Three Sisters* is in his deployment of stillness and subtext. The play has a vigorous plot that keeps one's interest and moves the action and characters forward, but this is disguised in various ways – first, several important actions take place offstage (like the departure of the soldiers) or only half visibly (like Irina's birthday party); second, when decisive actions do take place the audience's attention is elsewhere (when Soliony and Toozenbach fight their duel, it is offstage and Masha is now crying about being parted from Vershinin); third, each act begins with the promise of great activity and ends in stasis. Act 3, for example, begins with a bustle of activity, the sisters joining the relief effort to support those made homeless by the fire; by the end of the play they have forgotten about the fire and are left 'huddled together' on the stage (1.3: 96). As a result, the play, without being lethargic or boring, stages lethargy and boredom. It is a play in which silence speaks.

Conclusion

Modern theatre begins on the Théâtre Libre's tiny stage in Montmartre, Paris in March 1887. From there comes an almost inexhaustible procession of experimental companies, most of them both promoting and challenging Naturalism, adopting and rejecting many of its characteristics. Integrally linked to Naturalism, Symbolism pushed the stage to unprecedented levels of formal innovation, challenging the theatre's relation with its audience and the world. As John Henderson suggests, both Naturalism and Symbolism were present at the birth of the avant-garde: Naturalism worked to strip the theatre of its decorative self-indulgence; Symbolism restored poetry to the stage and made the theatre into what Maurice Maeterlinck called 'the temple of dreams' (qtd in Dorra 1995: 144). The plays in this part show the journey from one genre to another and, read alongside and against each other, give an insight into the interrelation between two movements situated at the start of the modernist period in theatre.

Notes

1. All translations from original sources, unless otherwise indicated, are by the author.
2. In fact, most of the Naturalist writers seemed rather to dislike each other. Strindberg, while sometimes admitting to admiration of his Scandinavian colleague, more often thought of Ibsen as 'my enemy' (Strindberg 1992: 522), while Ibsen agreed, famously hanging a portrait of Strindberg ('my mortal enemy') above his desk claiming that

he liked to see those 'demonic eyes' staring down at him while he worked (Meyer 1974: 770). Ibsen also thought Tolstoy mad (823), while Tolstoy, in *What is Art?* (1897), mocked Ibsen and Zola, and pronounced Chekhov's *The Seagull* 'utterly worthless' (624). Chekhov in his turn partly wrote *The Seagull* in mockery of Ibsen's *The Wild Duck* and smirked his way through a performance of *When We Dead Awaken* (Rayfield 1997: 519). This should be borne in mind as a corrective to the impression that theatrical Naturalism was any kind of disciplined international dramatic movement.

3. Strindberg's disdain for Ibsen makes its way into the preface to *Miss Julie*; in its reference to 'pretentious talk of the joy of life', he is making a dig at Ibsen's *Ghosts* (Ibsen 1994: 145).
4. This is two years before he adopted the word 'Naturalism' to describe the new movement.

Bibliography

Antoine, A. (1964) *Memories of the Théâtre Libre*, Miami: University of Miami Press.

Becker, C. (2002) *Zola: Le Saut dans les Étoiles*, Paris: Presses de la Sorbonne Nouvelle.

Benjamin, W. (1999) *The Arcades Project*, Cambridge, MA: Harvard University Press.

Braun, E. (1982) *The Director and the Stage: From Naturalism to Grotowski*, London: Methuen.

Carlson, M. (1993) *Theories of the Theatre: A Historical and Critical Survey from the Greeks to the Present*, Ithaca and London: Cornell University Press.

Chothia, J. (1991) *André Antoine*, Cambridge: Cambridge University Press.

Comte, A. (1983) *Auguste Comte and Positivism: The Essential Writings*, Chicago and London: University of Chicago Press.

Cruickshank, J. (1969) *French Literature and its Background 5: The Late Nineteenth Century*, Oxford: Oxford University Press.

Deak, F. (1993) *Symbolist Theater: The Formation of an Avant-Garde*, Baltimore and London: Johns Hopkins University Press.

Dorra, H. (1995) *Symbolist Art Theories: A Critical Anthology*, Berkeley and Los Angeles: University of California Press.

Ferragus (1868) 'Lettres de Ferragus III: La Littérature Putride', *Le Figaro*, 23 January: 1.

Greer, G. (1986) *The Madwoman's Underclothes: Essays and Occasional Writings 1968-85*, London: Picador.

Henderson, J. A. (1971) *The First Avant-Garde 1887-1894: Sources of the Modern French Theatre*, London: Harrap.

Ibsen, H. (1980) *Plays: Two*, London: Methuen.

Ibsen, H. (1994) *Four Major Plays*, Oxford: Oxford University Press.

Jullien, J. (1892) *Le Théâtre Vivant*, Paris: Charpentier & Fasquelle.

Maeterlinck, M. (1979) *Théâtre*, Geneva: Slatkine Reprints.

Mallarmé, S. (1885) 'Richard Wagner: Rêverie d'un Poëte Français', *La Revue Wagnérienne*, 8 August: 195.

Meyer, M. (1974) *Ibsen*, Harmondsworth: Penguin.

Meyer, M. (1985) *Strindberg: A Biography*, London: Secker and Warburg.

Moréas, J. (1886) 'Le Symbolisme', *Le Figaro*, Supplément Littéraire, 18 September: 2–3.

Quillard, P. (1976) *The Girl with Cut-Off Hands*, *The Drama Review*, 20(3), 123–8.

Rayfield, D. (1997) *Anton Chekhov: A Life*, London: HarperCollins.

Renan, E. (1890) *L'Avenir de la Science: Pensées de 1848*, Paris: Calmann Lévy.

Schumacher, C. (ed.) (1996) *Naturalism and Symbolism in European Theatre*, Theatre in Europe: A Documentary History, Cambridge: Cambridge University Press.

Strindberg, A. (1967) *Open Letters to the Intimate Theater*, Seattle and London: University of Washington Press.

Strindberg, A. (1992) *Letters*, vol. II: 1892–1912, Chicago: University of Chicago Press.

Strindberg, A. (1996) *Selected Essays*, Oxford: Oxford University Press.

Taine, H. (1863) *Histoire de la Littérature Anglaise*: vol. 1, Paris: Hachette.

Whitton, D. (1987) *Stage Directors in Modern France*, Manchester: Manchester University Press.

Zola, É. (1992) *Thérèse Raquin*, Oxford: Oxford University Press.

Further reading

Bentley, E. (ed.) (1976) *The Theory of the Modern Stage: An Introduction to Modern Theatre and Drama*, Harmondsworth: Penguin.

Bradbury, M. and J. McFarlane (eds) (1976) *Modernism 1890–1930*, Pelican Guides to European Literature, Harmondsworth: Penguin.

Cardullo, B. and R. Knopf (eds) (2001) *Theater of the Avant-Garde: A Critical Anthology*, New Haven and London: Yale University Press.

Chadwick, C. (1971) *Symbolism*, London: Methuen.

Deak, F. (1976) 'Symbolist Staging at the Théâtre d'Art', *The Drama Review* (20(3) (T71), 117–22.

Emeljanow, V. (ed.) (1981) *Chekhov: The Critical Heritage*, London: Routledge.

Garner Jr, S. B. (2000) 'Physiologies of the Modern: Zola, Experimental Medicine, and the Naturalist Stage', *Modern Drama*, 43(4), 67–79.

Gerould, D. (1985) *Doubles, Demons, and Dreamers: An International Collection of Symbolist Drama*, New York: PAJ.

Gottlieb, V. (ed.) (2005) *Anton Chekhov at the Moscow Art Theatre: Archive Illustrations of the Original Productions*, Abingdon: Routledge.

Harrison, C., P. Wood and with J. Gaiger (eds) (1998) *Art in Theory 1815–1900: An Anthology of Changing Ideas*, Oxford: Blackwell.

McFarlane, J. (ed.) (1994) *The Cambridge Companion to Ibsen*, Cambridge Companions to Literature, Cambridge: Cambridge University Press.

Moi, T. (2006) *Henrik Ibsen and the Birth of Modernism*, Oxford: Oxford University Press.

Shattuck, R. (1969) *The Banquet Years: The Origins of the Avant-Garde in France from 1885 to World War I*, London: Jonathan Cape.

Stanislavski, K. (2008) *An Actor's Work: A Student's Diary*, Abingdon: Routledge.

Stanislavski, K. (2008) *My Life in Art*, Abingdon: Routledge.

Szondi, P. (1987) *Theory of the Modern Drama*, Cambridge and Oxford: Polity and Blackwell.

West, T. G. (1980) *Symbolism: An Anthology*, London: Methuen.

Worth, K. (1985) *Maeterlinck's Plays in Performance*, Cambridge: Chadwyck-Healey.

Zola, É. (1964) *The Experimental Novel and Other Essays*, New York: Haskell House.

1.1 THÉRÈSE RAQUIN (1873)

ÉMILE ZOLA

Translated by Pip Broughton

Émile Zola (1840–1902) was a French novelist and public intellectual who coined the term Naturalism in 1866 to refer to his new scientific model of fiction writing. Over the next fifteen years, he mounted a ceaseless press campaign for Naturalism in the novel and the theatre and gathered these articles in a series of books: The Experimental Novel *(1880),* Naturalist Novelists *(1881),* Naturalism in the Theatre *(1881) and* Our Dramatic Authors *(1881). Critical of the worn-out conventions of Romanticism and the artificiality of the well-made play, his ideas were widely admired by Antoine, Strindberg and Chekhov, and prepared the way for the emergence of stage Naturalism in the 1880s.* Thérèse Raquin *was originally published in serial form for the journal* L'Artiste*, then published as a novel in 1867. Zola adapted the novel for the stage in 1873. The play has often been revived – sometimes readapted from the original novel and often in radically non-Naturalist styles – and has also been made into three films, seven TV series, two operas and a Broadway musical. This translation was written by Pip Broughton for the Warehouse Theatre, Croydon, London in 1984.*

Characters
LAURENT
CAMILLE
THÉRÈSE RAQUIN
MADAME RAQUIN
GRIVET
MICHAUD
SUZANNE

The set

A large bedroom which also serves as dining room and parlour. The room is in the Pont-Neuf Passage. It is high, dark, in a state of decay, hung with faded grey wallpaper, furnished with threadbare poor furniture, littered with haberdashery cardboard boxes.

At the back: a door; to the right of the door, a wardrobe; to the left, a writing-desk. On the left: upstage, on a slant, a bed in an alcove with a window looking out onto a bare wall; midstage, a little door; downstage, a work-table. On the right: upstage, the top of the spiral staircase leading down to the shop; downstage, a fireplace; on the mantelpiece a columned clock and two bunches of artificial flowers under glass; photographs hang either side of the mirror. In the middle of the room: a round table with waxed tablecloth; two armchairs, one blue, the other green; other various chairs.

The set remains the same throughout the four acts.

Act 1

Eight o'clock one Thursday summer evening, after dinner. The table has not yet been cleared; the window is half open. There is a feeling of peace, of a sense of middle-class calm.

Scene 1

LAURENT, THÉRÈSE, MME RAQUIN, CAMILLE

CAMILLE is sitting in an armchair stage right, stiffly posing for his portrait, wearing his Sunday best. LAURENT is painting, standing at his easel in front of the window. Next to LAURENT sits THÉRÈSE, in a daydream, her chin in her hand. MME RAQUIN is finishing clearing the table.

CAMILLE: (*After a long pause.*) All right if I talk? Won't disturb you, will it?

LAURENT: Not in the least, so long as you don't move.

CAMILLE: I fall asleep after dinner if I don't talk ... You're lucky, you're healthy. You can eat anything ... I shouldn't have had that second helping of syllabub, it always makes me ill. My stomach is so delicate ... You like syllabub, don't you?

LAURENT: Oh yes. It's delicious – so sweet.

CAMILLE: We know what you like here. Mother spoils you – she makes syllabub specially for you, even though she knows what it does to me ... That's true, isn't it, Thérèse, that Mother spoils Laurent?

THÉRÈSE: (*Without raising her head.*) Yes.

MME RAQUIN: (*Carrying a pile of plates.*) Don't listen to them, Laurent. It was Camille who told me how much you love it, and Thérèse who wanted to put the extra sugar in it.

CAMILLE: Mother, you're such an egoist.

MME RAQUIN: *Me*, an egoist?!

CAMILLE: Yes, you ... (*To LAURENT.*) Mother likes you because you're from Vernon, like her. Remember, when we were little, she used to give us money ...

LAURENT: And you bought loads of apples.

CAMILLE: And you, you bought little penknives ... What a stroke of luck it was bumping into each other here in Paris, I still can't believe it – after all that time! Oh, I was getting so bored, I was dying of boredom! Every evening, when I got home from the office, it was so miserable here ... Can you still see properly?

LAURENT: Not really, but I want to get this finished.

CAMILLE: It's nearly eight o'clock. These Summer evenings are so long ... I wanted to be painted in sunlight – that would have been more attractive. Instead of this dingy background, you could have done a landscape. But in the mornings I barely even have time to swallow my coffee before I have to set off for the office ... I say, this can't be particularly good for the old digestive system, sitting still like this after a meal.

LAURENT: Don't worry, this is the last session.

MME RAQUIN comes back in and finishes clearing the table, then wipes it with a cloth.

CAMILLE: You would have got a better light in the mornings, though. We don't get the sun in here, but it shines onto the wall opposite; that lights the room ... I really don't know why Mother got it into her head to rent this place. It's so damp. When it rains, it's like being in a cellar.

LAURENT: Bah! One place is as good as another for work purposes.

CAMILLE: I daresay you're right. They've got the haberdashery shop downstairs. It keeps them busy. I never go down there.

LAURENT: But the flat itself is comfortable though, isn't it?

CAMILLE: Not really! Apart from this room where we eat and sleep, we've only got the one room for Mother. You can't count the kitchen, which is a black hole no bigger than a cupboard. Nothing closes properly, so it's freezing cold. At night-time we get an abominable draught under that little door to the staircase. (*He indicates the little door, stage left.*)

MME RAQUIN: (*Who has finished her clearing up.*) My poor Camille, you're never satisfied. I did it all for the best. You're the one who wanted to come and work in Paris. I'd have been happy to open up another haberdashery shop in Vernon. But when you married your cousin Thérèse, I had to work again, in case you had children.

CAMILLE: Yes, well, I thought we'd be living in a busy street with lots of people passing. I could've sat at the window and watched the cars – that would've been fun ... But here all I can see when I open the shutter is that big wall opposite and the glass roof of the passage below. The wall is black, the glass roof is all dirty from dust and cobwebs ... I still prefer the windows at Vernon. You could watch the Seine from there, though that wasn't much fun either.

MME RAQUIN: I offered you the chance of going back there.

CAMILLE: Good God, no! Not now that I've found Laurent at the office ... After all I'm out all day, I don't care if the street is damp, just so long as you're happy.

MME RAQUIN: Then don't tease me any more about the flat.

Bell from shop.

Thérèse, the shop.

THÉRÈSE seems not to have heard and stays still.

All right, I'll go. (*She goes down the spiral staircase.*)

Scene 2

LAURENT, THÉRÈSE, CAMILLE

CAMILLE: I don't like to contradict her, but the street is very unhealthy. I'm afraid of another collapsed lung. I'm not strong like you two ... (*Silence.*) I say, can I have a rest? I can't feel my left arm any more.

LAURENT: Just a few more brush strokes and I'm finished.

CAMILLE: No good. I can't hold it any longer. I've got to walk about a bit. (*He gets up, paces, then goes over to THÉRÈSE.*) I've never been able to understand how my wife manages to stay perfectly still for hours at a time, without even moving a finger. It gets on my nerves, she's always miles away. Doesn't it bother you, Laurent, to feel her like that next to you? Come on, Thérèse, bustle up. Having fun are you?

THÉRÈSE: (*Without moving.*) Yes.

CAMILLE: I hope you're having a good time. Only animals amuse themselves like that … When her father, Captain Degans, left her with Mother, those huge black eyes of hers used to frighten me … And the Captain! – now *he* was a terrifying man. He died in Africa; never set foot in Vernon again … That's right, isn't it, Thérèse? (*No reply.*) She'll talk herself to death! (*He kisses her.*) You're a good girl, though. We haven't quarrelled once since Mother married us … You're not cross with me, are you?

THÉRÈSE: No.

LAURENT: (*Slapping* CAMILLE *on the shoulder.*) Come on, Camille, only ten minutes more.

CAMILLE sits.

Turn your head to the left … That's it, now don't move!

CAMILLE: (*After a silence.*) Any news of your father?

LAURENT: No, the old man's forgotten me. Anyway I never write to him.

CAMILLE: Strange, though – between father and son. I couldn't do it.

LAURENT: Nah! My father always had his own ideas. He wanted me to be a lawyer, so I could handle his endless lawsuits with his neighbours. When he found out that I was blowing his money on visiting painters' workshops instead of law lessons, he stopped my allowance … Who wants to be a lawyer!

CAMILLE: It's a good job. You've got to be brainy and the money's not bad.

LAURENT: I bumped into an old college friend of mine who paints. So I started to study painting, too.

CAMILLE: You should have kept it up. You might have won awards by now.

LAURENT: I couldn't. I was dying of hunger. So I chucked in the painting, and looked for a proper job.

CAMILLE: But you still know how to draw.

LAURENT: I'm not very good … What I liked about painting was that it was fun and not too tiring … God, how I missed that bloody studio when I started working at the office! I had this couch, where I slept in the afternoons. That couch could tell a story or two – what a life!

CAMILLE: You mean, you had affairs with the models?

LAURENT: Of course. There was one superb blonde …

THÉRÈSE rises slowly and goes down to the shop.

Oh look! We've chased away your wife.

CAMILLE: You don't imagine she was listening, do you! She's not very clever. But she's a perfect nurse when I'm ill. Mother has taught her how to make the infusions.

LAURENT: I don't think she likes me very much.

CAMILLE: Oh you know, women! Haven't you finished yet?

LAURENT: Yes, you can get up now.

CAMILLE: (*Getting up and coming to look at the portrait.*) Finished? Have you really finished?

LAURENT: Just the frame to go on now.

CAMILLE: It's a huge success, isn't it. (*He leans over the spiral staircase.*) Mother! Thérèse! Come and look, Laurent's finished!

Scene 3

LAURENT, CAMILLE, MME RAQUIN, THÉRÈSE

MME RAQUIN: What? Finished already?

CAMILLE: (*Holding the portrait in front of himself.*) Yes … Come and look.

MME RAQUIN: (*Looking at the portrait.*) Oh! … Look at that! Particularly the mouth, the mouth is very striking … Don't you think so, Thérèse?

THÉRÈSE: (*Without approaching.*) Yes.

She goes to the window where she day-dreams, her forehead against the glass.

CAMILLE: And the dress-suit, my wedding suit. I've only ever worn it four times! … And the collar looks like real material!

MME RAQUIN: And the arm of the chair!

CAMILLE: Amazing! Real wood! … My armchair, we bought it at Vernon; no-one but me may sit in it. Mother's is blue. (*Indicating other chair.*)

MME RAQUIN: (*To* LAURENT *who has put away the easel and paints.*) Why have you put a dark patch under the left eye?

LAURENT: That's the shadow.

CAMILLE: (*Putting the portrait on the easel, between the alcove and the window.*) It might have been more attractive without the shadow … but never mind, I think I look very distinguished, as if I were out visiting.

MME RAQUIN: My dear Laurent, how can we thank you? Are you sure you won't let Camille pay for the materials?

LAURENT: He's the one to thank for having sat for me!

CAMILLE: No, no, that won't do. I'll go and buy a bottle of something. Damn it, we'll drink to your work of art!

LAURENT: Oh, well, if you insist, I'll just go and get the frame. Remember it's Thursday. Monsieur Grivet and the Michauds must find the portrait in its place.

He goes out. CAMILLE *takes off his jacket, changes tie, puts on an overcoat which his mother gives him and goes to follow* LAURENT.

Scene 4

THÉRÈSE, MME RAQUIN, CAMILLE

CAMILLE: (*Hesitating and coming back.*) What shall I buy?

MME RAQUIN: It must be something that Laurent likes. He's such a good, dear child! He's practically one of the family.

CAMILLE: Yes, he's a real brother … What about a bottle of anisette?

MME RAQUIN: Are you sure he'd like that? A light wine would be better, perhaps, with some cakes?

CAMILLE: (*To THÉRÈSE.*) You're not saying much. Do you remember if he likes Malaga?

THÉRÈSE: (*Leaving the window and moving downstage.*) I'm sure he does. He likes everything. He eats and drinks like a pig.

MME RAQUIN: My child ...!

CAMILLE: Do tell her off. She can't stand him. He's already noticed, he told me so. It's not very nice ... (*To THÉRÈSE.*) I can't allow you to be against my friends. What have you got against him?

THÉRÈSE: Nothing ... He's always here. Lunch, dinner, he eats here all the time. You always put the best food on his plate. Laurent this, Laurent that. It gets on my nerves, that's all ... He's not particularly amusing, either. He's a greedy, lazy pig.

MME RAQUIN: Be charitable, Thérèse. Laurent is not happy. He lives in an attic and eats very badly at that place of his. It gives me pleasure to see him eat a good meal and feel warm and cosy here with us. He makes himself at home, has a smoke, that's nice to see ... He's all alone in the world, the poor boy.

THÉRÈSE: Do what you like. Pamper him, coddle him, it's all the same to me.

CAMILLE: I know! I'll get a bottle of champagne, that'll be perfect.

MME RAQUIN: Yes, that'll pay him back for the portrait nicely ... Don't forget the cakes.

CAMILLE: It's only half-past eight. Our friends won't arrive until nine. They'll get such a surprise! Champagne! (*He goes.*)

MME RAQUIN: (*To THÉRÈSE.*) You'll light the lamp, won't you, Thérèse. I'm going down to the shop.

Scene 5

THÉRÈSE, later joined by LAURENT

THÉRÈSE, left alone, stays still a moment, looking around, then at last she lets out a sigh. Silently she moves downstage and stretches with lassitude and boredom. Then she hears LAURENT enter by the small side door and she smiles, shaking with joy. During this scene it gets darker and darker as night falls.

LAURENT: Thérèse ...

THÉRÈSE: Laurent, my darling ... I felt you would come back, my love. (*She takes his hands and leads him downstage.*) I haven't seen you for a whole week. Every afternoon I waited for you, hoping you'd be able to escape from the office ... If you hadn't come, I'd have done something stupid ... *Why* have you stayed away for a whole week? I can't stand it any longer. Shaking hands every evening in front of the others you seem so cold.

LAURENT: I'll explain.

THÉRÈSE: You're afraid, aren't you? You big baby! Where could we be safer? (*She raises her voice and moves a few paces.*) Who could guess we loved each other? Who would ever come and look for us in this room?

LAURENT: (*Pulling her back and taking her in his arms.*) Be sensible ... No, I'm not afraid to come here.

THÉRÈSE: Then you're afraid of me, admit it ... You're afraid that I love you too much, that I'll upset your life.

LAURENT: Why do you doubt me? Don't you know I can't sleep because of you. I'm going mad. ME! Who never took women seriously ... Thérèse, I'm afraid because you have awoken something in the depths of my being – a man I never knew existed. Sometimes, it's true, I am not calm. It can't be natural to love anyone as I love you; and I'm afraid it will get out of control.

THÉRÈSE: (*Her head resting on his shoulder.*) That would be a pleasure without end, a long walk in the sun. (*They kiss.*)

LAURENT: (*Extricating himself rapidly.*) Did you hear someone on the stairs? (*They both listen.*)

THÉRÈSE: It's only the damp making the stairs creak. (*They come together again.*) Come here, let's love each other without fear, without regret. If only you knew ... Oh, what a childhood I had! I have been brought up in the damp atmosphere of a sick man's room.

LAURENT: My poor Thérèse.

THÉRÈSE: Oh yes! I was so miserable. For hours on end I would squat in front of the fire stupidly watching over his infusions. If I moved, my aunt scolded me – mustn't wake Camille up, must we? I used to stammer; my hands shook like an old woman's. I was so clumsy that even Camille made fun of me. And yet I felt strong. I could feel my child's fists clench, I wanted to smash everything ... They told me my mother was the daughter of a nomadic African chief. It must be true; so often I dreamt of escaping; roaming the roads and running barefoot in the dust, begging like a gypsy ... you see, I preferred starving in the wild to their hospitality.

She has raised her voice: LAURENT, distressed, crosses the room and listens at the staircase.

LAURENT: Keep your voice down, your aunt will come up.

THÉRÈSE: Let her come up! It's their fault if I'm a liar. (*She leans on the table, arms crossed.*) I don't know why I ever agreed to marry Camille. It was a prearranged marriage. My aunt simply waited until we were of age. I was only twelve years old when she said, 'You will love your cousin, you will look after him.' She wanted him to have a nurse, an infusion-maker. She adored this puny child that she had wrestled from death twenty times, and she trained me to be his servant ... And I never protested. They had made me cowardly. I felt pity for the child. When I played with him I could feel my fingers sink into his limbs like putty. On the evening of the wedding, instead of going to my room at the left on the top of the stairs, I went in Camille's, which was on the right. That was all ... But you ... you, my Laurent ...

LAURENT: You love me? (*He takes her in his arms and slowly sits her down in the chair to the right of the table.*)

THÉRÈSE: I love you. I loved you the day Camille pushed you into the shop, remember? – when you'd bumped into each other at the office ... I really don't know how I loved you. It was more like hate. The very sight of you drove me mad, I couldn't bear it. The moment you were there, my nerves were strained to breaking point, yet I waited achingly for you to come, for the pain. When you were painting just now, I was nailed to the stool, at your feet, no matter how hard I secretly tried to fight it.

LAURENT: (*Kneeling at her feet.*) I adore you.

THÉRÈSE: And our only time of pleasure, Thursday evenings, when Grivet and old Michaud would arrive regular as clockwork, those Thursday evenings used to drive me mad – the eternal games of dominoes, eternal Thursdays, the same imbecilic boredom ... But now I feel proud and revenged. When we sit round the table exchanging polite remarks I can bask in such wicked pleasure; I sit there sewing and put on my half-baked expression while you all play dominoes; and in the midst of this bourgeois peace I'm reliving our moments of ecstasy.

LAURENT: (*Thinking he has heard a noise, getting up, terrified.*) I'm sure you're talking too loud. We'll be caught. I tell you your aunt will come up. (*He listens at the door to the spiral staircase.*) Where is my hat?

THÉRÈSE: (*Quietly getting up.*) Do you really think she will come up? (*She goes to the staircase and returns with lowered voice.*) Yes, you're right, you'd better go. You will come tomorrow, at two o'clock?

LAURENT: No, it's not possible.

THÉRÈSE: Why not?

LAURENT: The head-clerk has threatened to sack me if I'm absent again.

THÉRÈSE: You mean we won't see each other any more? You're leaving me? This is where all this caution has been leading? Oh, you coward!

LAURENT: No, we can have a peaceful existence, the two of us. It's only a matter of looking, of waiting for circumstances to change. How often I've dreamt of having you all to myself for a whole day; then my desire would grow and I wanted you for a month of happiness, then a year, then all my life ... All our lives to be together ... all our life to love each other. I would leave my job and would start painting again. You would do whatever you wished. We would adore each other for ever, for ever ... You'd be happy, wouldn't you?

THÉRÈSE: (*Smiling, swooning on his chest.*) Oh yes, very, very happy.

LAURENT: (*Breaking away from her, in a low voice.*) If only you were free ...

THÉRÈSE: (*Dreamily.*) We would marry, we would no longer be afraid of anything. Oh, Laurent, what a sweet life it would be.

LAURENT: All I can see are your eyes shining in the dim light, those eyes that would drive me mad. We must now say farewell, Thérèse.

THÉRÈSE: You're not coming tomorrow?

LAURENT: No. Trust me. If we have to spend some time apart without seeing each other, you must tell yourself that we are working towards our future happiness. (*He kisses her and then exits hastily through the secret door.*)

THÉRÈSE: (*Alone. A moment's silence as she dreams.*) If only I were free.

Scene 6

THÉRÈSE, MME RAQUIN, CAMILLE

MME RAQUIN: What, you still haven't lit the lamp! Oh, you daydreamer. Never mind, it's ready. I'll get it. (*She goes out to her bedroom.*)

CAMILLE: (*Arrives with a bottle of champagne and a box of cakes.*) Where is everyone? Why is it so dark in here?

THÉRÈSE: My aunt has gone for the lamp.

CAMILLE: Ah. (*Shaking.*) Oh it's you! You gave me a fright ... You could at least talk in a more natural tone of voice ... You know I hate it when people play jokes in the dark.

THÉRÈSE: I'm not playing jokes.

CAMILLE: I caught sight of you just then, all white like a ghost ... It's ridiculous, pranks like that ... Now if I wake up during the night, I'm going to think that a woman in white is pacing round my bed waiting to strangle me ... It's all very well for you to laugh.

THÉRÈSE: I'm not laughing.

MME RAQUIN: (*Enters with lamp.*) What's wrong?

The scene brightens.

CAMILLE: It's Thérèse, she's scaring me, she thinks it's funny. I nearly dropped the bottle of champagne ... That would have been three francs wasted.

MME RAQUIN: What? You only paid three francs? (*She takes bottle.*)

CAMILLE: Yes, I went as far as the boulevard St Michel, where I'd seen some advertised for three francs in a grocer's. It's just as good as the eight franc bottle. Everyone knows that the shopkeepers are a load of frauds. Here are the cakes.

MME RAQUIN: Give them to me. I'll put everything on the table so as to surprise Grivet and Michaud when they arrive. Could you get me two plates, Thérèse?

They set everything on the table, the champagne between two plates of cakes. Then THÉRÈSE *goes and sits at her work table and begins to sew.*

CAMILLE: Ah, quarter to nine. On the stroke of nine Monsieur Grivet will arrive. He's exactitude itself ... You will be nice to him, won't you? I know he's only the deputy chief clerk but he could be useful as regards my promotion. He's a very powerful man, so don't underestimate him. The old boys at the office swear that in twenty years he's never once been a minute late ... Laurent is wrong to say he won't make his mark.

MME RAQUIN: Our friend Michaud is just as precise. When he was Police Superintendent at Vernon he arrived home precisely at eight o'clock exactly, do you remember? We always complimented him on it.

CAMILLE: Yes, but since he's retired and moved to Paris with his niece, he's become somewhat more erratic. That little Suzanne is always leading him up the garden path ... But all the same I find it most agreeable to have good friends and to entertain them once a week. Anything more regular would cost too much ... Oh, I've just remembered, before they arrive, I wanted to tell you, I hatched a plan when I was walking back.

MME RAQUIN: What plan?

CAMILLE: Mother, you know I promised to take Thérèse to Saint-Ouen one Sunday before the weather turns. She hates walking out round town with me, even though it is much more fun than the countryside. She says I wear her out, that I don't walk properly ... So, I thought it'd be an idea to go for a walk in Saint-Ouen this coming Sunday, and to take Laurent with us.

MME RAQUIN: Yes, my children, you do that. My legs aren't good enough to come with you, but I think that's an excellent idea ... That will make you square with Laurent for the portrait.

CAMILLE: Laurent is so funny in the countryside ... Remember, Thérèse, the time we took him to Suresnes? He's so strong, like a horse! He can jump over streams of water and can throw stones to amazing heights. What a joker! On the wooden horse at Suresnes he did this impersonation of a hunt, cracking the whip, kicking the spurs. You know, he did it so well that a wedding party nearby almost wept with laughter. The bride almost had a seizure! Really! ... Remember, Thérèse?

THÉRÈSE: He'd certainly had enough to drink at dinner to stimulate his wit.

CAMILLE: Oh you! You don't understand people having fun. If I had to rely on you for entertainment I would have a truly tedious time at Saint-Ouen ... All she does – she just sits on the ground staring into the water ... Now, if I bring Laurent, it's to keep me amused ... Where the devil has he gone to get that frame? (*Bell rings in shop.*) Ah, that'll be him. Monsieur Grivet still has seven minutes left.

Scene 7

Same and LAURENT

LAURENT: (*Holding the frame.*) They always take so long in that shop. (*Looking at MME RAQUIN and CAMILLE who are talking in hushed voices.*) I bet you're plotting some treat.

CAMILLE: Guess.

LAURENT: You're going to invite me to dinner tomorrow night and there'll be chicken and rice.

MME RAQUIN: You greedy pig!

CAMILLE: Better than that ... On Sunday I'm taking Thérèse to Saint-Ouen and you're coming with us ... Would you like that?

LAURENT: Would I like to! (*He takes the portrait and a small hammer from MME RAQUIN.*)

MME RAQUIN: You will be careful, won't you, Laurent. I leave Camille in your hands. You are strong. I am happier when I know he is with you.

CAMILLE: Mother, you're such a worrier, it's boring. Just think, I can't even go to the end of the road without her imagining some catastrophe has happened ... It's awful always being treated like a little boy ... What we'll do, we'll take a cab as far as the ramparts, that way we'll only have to pay for the one journey. Then we'll walk back along the tow-path, spend the afternoon on the island, and in the evening we'll have a fish stew by the riverside. Is that settled, then?

LAURENT: (*Fixing the painting into the frame.*) Yes ... but we could add the finishing touch to the programme.

CAMILLE: How?

LAURENT: (*Glancing at THÉRÈSE.*) With a trip on a rowing boat.

MME RAQUIN: No, no, no boating. I wouldn't feel happy.

THÉRÈSE: You don't think Camille would risk going on the water, do you? He's much too scared.

CAMILLE: Me scared?!

LAURENT: That's true, I forgot you were frightened of the water. When we used to go paddling in the Seine at Vernon, you'd just stay on the bank, shivering ... All right, we'll give the boat a miss.

CAMILLE: But that's not true! *I'm* not scared! ... We *shall* take a boat. What the devil are you doing, making me out to be an idiot? We'll see which of the three of us is the least brave. It's Thérèse who's frightened.

THÉRÈSE: My poor child, you look pale with fear already.

CAMILLE: Tease me if you like ... We'll see! We'll see!

MME RAQUIN: Camille, my good Camille, give up this idea; do it for me.

CAMILLE: Please, Mother, don't torment me. You know it only makes me ill.

LAURENT: Very well, your wife will decide.

THÉRÈSE: Accidents can happen anywhere.

LAURENT: That's very true ... in the street – your foot could slip, a tile could fall on your head.

THÉRÈSE: Besides, you know how much I adore the Seine.

LAURENT: (*To CAMILLE.*) All right then, that's settled. You win! We will take a boat.

MME RAQUIN: (*Aside to LAURENT, who's hanging up portrait.*) I can't tell you how worried this outing makes me. Camille is so insistent. You see how carried away he gets.

LAURENT: Don't be afraid. I'll be there ... I must just quickly hang up the portrait. (*He hangs portrait over mantelpiece.*)

CAMILLE: It will catch the light there, won't it? (*Shop bell rings and the clock strikes nine.*) Nine o'clock. Here's Monsieur Grivet.

Scene 8

The same plus GRIVET

GRIVET: I'm first to arrive ... Good evening Ladies and Gentlemen.

MME RAQUIN: Good evening, Monsieur Grivet ... shall I take your umbrella? (*She takes it.*) Is it raining?

GRIVET: It's threatening to. (*She goes to put it to the left of fireplace.*) Not in that corner, not in that corner; you know my little habits ... In the other corner. There, thank you.

MME RAQUIN: Give me your galoshes.

GRIVET: No, no, I'll put them away myself. (*He sits on the chair she offers him.*) I have my own little system. Yes, yes, I like everything to be in its place, you understand. (*He places galoshes next to umbrella.*) That way I don't worry.

CAMILLE: Do you not bring any news, Monsieur Grivet?

GRIVET: (*Getting up and coming centre stage.*) I left the office at half-past four, dined at six at the Little Orléans restaurant, read my paper at seven at the Café Saturnin; and it being Thursday today, instead of going to bed at nine as is my habit, I came here. (*Reflecting.*) Yes, that's all, I think.

LAURENT: You didn't see anything on your way here?

GRIVET: Oh yes, of course, forgive me ... There was a crowd of people in the rue Saint-André-des-Arts. I had to cross to the other pavement ... That did put me out ... You understand, in the mornings I walk to the office along the left-hand pavement, and, in the evenings, I return along the other ...

MME RAQUIN: The right-hand pavement.

GRIVET: No, no, no, no. Allow me. (*Miming the action.*) In the mornings, I go like this, and in the evenings, I come back ...

LAURENT: Oh, very good. (*Clapping.*)

GRIVET: Always by way of the left-hand pavement, you see. I always keep to the left, like the railways. It's the best way of not getting lost *en route*.

LAURENT: But what was the crowd doing on the pavement?

GRIVET: I don't know. How should I know?

MME RAQUIN: No doubt, some accident.

GRIVET: Why, of course, that's true, it must have been an accident ... I hadn't thought of that ... My word, you put my mind at rest by saying it was an accident. (*He sits down at the table, on the left.*)

MME RAQUIN: Ah! Here's Monsieur Michaud.

Scene 9

The same plus MICHAUD *and* SUZANNE

SUZANNE *takes off her shawl and hat and goes to chat quietly to* THÉRÈSE, *who is still sitting at her work desk.* MICHAUD *shakes hands with everyone.*

MICHAUD: I believe I am late.

GRIVET, *who has taken out his watch and shows it with an air of triumph.*

I know, six minutes past nine. It was this little one's fault. (*Indicating* SUZANNE.) We had to stop at every shop. (*He goes to place his cane next to* GRIVET's *umbrella.*)

GRIVET: No, forgive me, but that's my umbrella's place ... You know full well that I don't like that. I have left you the other corner of the fireplace for your cane.

MICHAUD: Very well, very well, don't let's get angry.

CAMILLE: (*Aside to* LAURENT.) I say, I do believe Monsieur Grivet is annoyed because there's champagne. He's looked at the bottle three times without saying a thing. It's amazing that he's not more surprised than that!

MICHAUD: (*Turning and catching sight of the champagne.*) Well, blow me! You're going to send us home in a proper state. Cakes and champagne!

GRIVET: Gosh, champagne. I've drunk champagne only four times in my whole life.

MICHAUD: Whose saint's day are you celebrating?

MME RAQUIN: We are celebrating the portrait of Camille that Laurent finished this evening. (*She takes the lamp and goes over to the portrait to illuminate it.*) Look! (*They all follow her, except* THÉRÈSE, *who stays at her work table, and* LAURENT, *who leans on the fireplace.*)

CAMILLE: It's very striking, isn't it? I look as though I'm out visiting.

MICHAUD: Yes, yes.

MME RAQUIN: It's still quite fresh. You can still smell the paint.

GRIVET: That's what it is. I thought I could smell something ... That's the advantage of photographs – they don't smell.

CAMILLE: Yes, but when the paint dries ...

GRIVET: Oh, certainly, when the paint dries ... And it dries quite quickly ... But they painted a shop in the Rue de la Harpe and that took five days to dry!

MME RAQUIN: Well, Monsieur Michaud, do you think it's good?

MICHAUD: It's very good; very, very good. (*They all return and* MME RAQUIN *puts the lamp on the table.*)

CAMILLE: If you could serve tea now, Mother. We shall drink the champagne after the game of dominoes.

GRIVET: (*Sitting down again.*) Quarter past nine. We'll hardly have time to get a good game in.

MME RAQUIN: It'll only take five minutes ... You stay there, Thérèse, since you are not feeling well.

SUZANNE: (*Cheerfully.*) I am feeling very well. I will help you, Madame Raquin. I like playing the housewife. (*They go out to the kitchen.*)

Scene 10

THÉRÈSE, GRIVET, CAMILLE, MICHAUD, LAURENT

CAMILLE: Nothing new to report, Monsieur Michaud?

MICHAUD: No, nothing ... I took my niece to the Luxembourg to do her sewing. Oh, yes, of course, yes, there *is* news! There's the tragedy at the rue St-André-des-Arts.

CAMILLE: What tragedy? Monsieur Grivet saw a big crowd there on his way here.

MICHAUD: The crowd hasn't dispersed since this morning. (*To GRIVET.*) They were all looking up into the air, weren't they?

GRIVET: I couldn't say. I changed pavements ... So it *was* an accident? (*He puts on his skull-cap and cuffs, which were in his pocket.*)

MICHAUD: Yes, at the Hotel de Bourgogne they found a woman's body cut into four pieces, in the trunk belonging to a traveller who has since disappeared.

GRIVET: Is it possible?! Cut into four pieces! How can you cut a woman into four pieces?

CAMILLE: It's disgusting!

GRIVET: And I walked right past the place! ... I remember now, everyone was looking up into the air ... Did they see anything up there? – Was there anything to see?

MICHAUD: You could see the window of the bedroom where the crowd claim the trunk was found ... but they were, in fact, wrong. The window of the bedroom in question looked out onto the courtyard.

LAURENT: Has the murderer been arrested?

MICHAUD: No, one of my ex-colleagues who is conducting the inquiry told me this morning he is working in the dark and the murderer is still at large.

GRIVET chuckles, nodding his head.

The law is going to have some difficulty finding him!

LAURENT: But has the identity of the victim been established?

MICHAUD: No. The body was naked, and the head was not in the trunk.

GRIVET: It must have got mislaid.

CAMILLE: Please, dear sir! Your woman cut into four pieces is making my flesh creep.

GRIVET: Why, no! It's fun to be frightened, when one is absolutely sure that one is in no danger oneself. Monsieur Michaud's stories of his time as Police Superintendent are so amusing ... Remember the one about the policeman's body that had been buried in a carrot-patch and his fingers were pulled up with the carrots? He told us that story last autumn ... I found that one very interesting. What the devil, we know there aren't any murderers lurking behind our backs here. This is a house of God ... Now in a wood, that's different. If I were crossing a dark wood with Monsieur Michaud, I would ask him to keep quiet.

LAURENT: (*To MICHAUD.*) Do you think many crimes go unpunished?

MICHAUD: Yes, unfortunately. Disappearances, slow deaths, suffocations, sinister crushings, without a trace of blood, without a single cry. The law arrives and can't find any clues. There's more than one murderer freely walking the streets in broad daylight right now, you know.

GRIVET: (*Chuckling louder.*) Don't make me laugh. And no-one arrests them?

MICHAUD: If they are not arrested, my dear Monsieur Grivet, it is because nobody suspects they are murderers.

CAMILLE: So what's wrong with the police?

MICHAUD: Nothing's wrong with the force. But they can't do the impossible. I say again, there are criminals who right now are living, loved and respected ... You are wrong to scoff, Monsieur Grivet.

GRIVET: Let me scoff, let me scoff, leave me in peace.

MICHAUD: Maybe one of these men is an acquaintance of yours, and you shake hands with him every day.

GRIVET: Oh no, don't say things like that. That's not true, you know full well that's not true. I could tell you a story or two.

MICHAUD: Tell us your story, then.

GRIVET: Certainly ... It's the story of the thieving magpie. (*MICHAUD shrugs his shoulders.*) You may know it. You know everything. Once there was a servant-girl who was imprisoned for having stolen some table silver. Two months later some men were cutting down a poplar tree and they found the silver in a magpie's nest. The thief was the magpie! The girl was released ... so you see, the guilty are always punished.

MICHAUD: (*Sneering.*) So, did they put the magpie into prison?

GRIVET: (*Annoyed.*) A magpie in prison! A magpie in prison? Michaud is so stupid!

CAMILLE: Come, that's not what Monsieur Grivet meant. You are confusing things.

GRIVET: The police are inefficient, that's all ... It's immoral.

CAMILLE: Laurent, do you think that people can kill like that without anyone knowing about it?

LAURENT: What *I* think? (*He crosses the room, slowly getting nearer to THÉRÈSE.*) I think that Monsieur Michaud is making fun of you. He's trying to frighten you with his stories. How can he know what he claims nobody knows ... And if there are people out there who are that clever, good luck to them, that's what I say! (*Close to THÉRÈSE.*) Look, your wife is less gullible than you.

THÉRÈSE: Of course, what you don't know, doesn't exist.

CAMILLE: All the same, I'd prefer it if we talked about something else. Would you mind, let's talk about something else ...

GRIVET: With pleasure, let's talk about something else.

CAMILLE: Why, we haven't brought up the chairs from the shop ... Come and give me a hand, would you. (*He goes down.*)

GRIVET: (*Getting up, moaning.*) Is that what he calls talking about something else, going to fetch chairs?

MICHAUD: Are you coming, Monsieur Grivet?

GRIVET: After you ... The magpie in prison! Magpie in prison! Has anyone seen such a thing? ... For an ex-Police Superintendent, you have just told us a load of poppycock, Monsieur Michaud.

They go down the stairs.

LAURENT: (*Seizing THÉRÈSE's hands, lowering voice.*) Do you swear to obey me?

THÉRÈSE: (*Same.*) Yes, I belong to you. Do what you want with me.

CAMILLE: (*From below.*) Laurent, you lazy-bones … You could at least have come and helped with the chairs, instead of leaving it to your elders and betters.

LAURENT: (*Raising voice.*) I stayed to flirt with your wife. (*To* THÉRÈSE, *gently.*) Have hope. We shall live together happily for ever.

CAMILLE: (*From below, laughing.*) Oh, that! I give my consent. Try to please her.

LAURENT: (*To* THÉRÈSE.) And remember what you said: what you don't know, doesn't exist. (*They hear steps on the stairs.*) Careful.

They separate hastily. THÉRÈSE *resumes her bored attitude by her work desk.* LAURENT *breaks stage right. The others come back up, each with a chair, laughing heartily.*

CAMILLE: (*To* LAURENT.) Oh, Laurent, you're such a card. Your jokes will be the death of me. All that palaver just to get out of carrying up a chair.

MME RAQUIN *and* SUZANNE *enter with tea.*

GRIVET: Ah! At last, here's the tea.

Scene 11

The same plus MME RAQUIN *and* SUZANNE

MME RAQUIN: (*To* GRIVET, *who's taken out his watch.*) Yes, it took me a quarter of an hour. Now, sit down and we will catch up on lost time.

GRIVET *sits downstage left, behind him* LAURENT. MME RAQUIN'S *armchair to the right:* MICHAUD *sits behind her. Finally, at the back in the centre,* CAMILLE *in his armchair.* THÉRÈSE *stays at her work table.* SUZANNE *joins her when she has finished serving the tea.*

CAMILLE: (*Sitting.*) There, I'm in my chair. Pass the box of dominoes, Mother.

GRIVET: (*Beatifically.*) This is such a pleasure. Every Thursday, I wake up and say to myself, 'Why, this evening I shall go to the Raquins and play dominoes.' You won't believe how much …

SUZANNE: (*Interrupting.*) Shall I sweeten yours, Monsieur Grivet?

GRIVET: With pleasure, Miss, how charming you are. Two lumps, remember? (*Resuming.*) Indeed, you won't believe how much …

CAMILLE: (*Interrupting.*) Aren't you coming, Thérèse?

MME RAQUIN: (*Passing him the box of dominoes.*) Leave her. You know she is not feeling well. She doesn't like playing dominoes … If we get a customer, why she can go down to the shop.

CAMILLE: It's upsetting, when everyone else is enjoying themselves, to have someone there who isn't. (*To* MME RAQUIN.) Come along, Mother, will you not sit down?

MME RAQUIN: (*Sitting.*) Yes, yes, here I am.

CAMILLE: Is everyone sitting comfortably?

MICHAUD: Certainly, and this evening I am going to thrash you, Monsieur Grivet … Mme Raquin, your tea is a touch stronger than last Thursday … But Monsieur Grivet was saying something.

GRIVET: Me? I was saying something?

MICHAUD: Yes, you had started a sentence.

GRIVET: A sentence? You think so? That surprises me.

MICHAUD: No, I assure you. Isn't that right, Mme Raquin? Monsieur Grivet said, 'Indeed, you won't believe how much … '

GRIVET: 'Indeed, you won't believe how much.' No, I don't remember, nothing of the sort … If you are making fun of me, Monsieur Michaud, you know full well that I find that mediocre.

CAMILLE: Is everyone sitting comfortably? Then I shall begin.

He noisily empties the box. Silence, while the players shuffle the dominoes and deal.

GRIVET: Monsieur Laurent is not playing and is forbidden to give advice. There, everyone take seven. No cheating, do you hear Monsieur Michaud? No cheating. (*Silence.*) Ah, me to start. I've got the double six!

End of Act 1.

Act 2

Ten p.m. The lamp is on. One year has passed without change to the room. Same peace. Same intimacy. MME RAQUIN *and* THÉRÈSE *are in mourning.*

Scene 1

THÉRÈSE, GRIVET, LAURENT, MICHAUD, MME RAQUIN, SUZANNE

All are seated exactly as at the end of Act 1. THÉRÈSE *at her work table looking dreamy and unwell, her embroidery work on her knee.* GRIVET, MICHAUD *and* MME RAQUIN *at the round table. But* CAMILLE'S *chair is empty. A silence during which* MME RAQUIN *and* SUZANNE *serve tea, exactly repeating their motions of Act 1.*

LAURENT: You should relax, Mme Raquin. Give me the box of dominoes.

SUZANNE: Shall I sweeten yours, Monsieur Grivet?

GRIVET: With pleasure, Mademoiselle. You're so charming. Two lumps, remember? You're the only one to sweeten me.

LAURENT: (*Holding the domino box.*) Here are the dominoes. Do sit down, Mme Raquin. (*She sits.*) Is everyone sitting comfortably?

MICHAUD: Certainly, and tonight I am going to thrash you, Monsieur Grivet. Just let me put a little rum in my tea. (*He pours the rum.*)

LAURENT: Is everyone sitting comfortably? … Then I shall begin. (*He noisily empties the box. The players shuffle and share out dominoes.*)

GRIVET: This is such a pleasure ... There, everybody take seven. No cheating. Do you hear, Monsieur Michaud, no cheating ...? (*Silence.*) No, it's not me to start today.

MME RAQUIN: (*Bursting suddenly into tears.*) I can't. I can't.

LAURENT and MICHAUD get up and SUZANNE comes over to stand behind MME RAQUIN's armchair.

When I see you all sitting round the table like in the old days, I remember, it breaks my heart ... My poor Camille used to be here.

MICHAUD: For heaven's sake, Mme Raquin, do try to be sensible.

MME RAQUIN: Forgive me, my old friend. I can't go on ... You remember how he loved playing dominoes. He was the one who always emptied the box, exactly as Laurent did just now. And if I didn't sit down straight away, he would scold me. I was always afraid of contradicting him – it always made me ill. Oh, those were such happy evenings. And now his chair is empty, you see!

MICHAUD: Come on, old girl, you mustn't upset yourself. You'll make yourself ill.

SUZANNE: (*Hugging MME RAQUIN.*) Don't cry, please. It hurts us all so much.

MME RAQUIN: You are right. I must be brave. (*She cries.*)

GRIVET: (*Pushing away his dominoes.*) I suppose it'd be better if we didn't play. It's a shame that it affects you in this way. Your tears won't bring him back.

MICHAUD: We are all mortal.

MME RAQUIN: Alas.

GRIVET: Our only intention in coming round here is to offer you some diversion.

MICHAUD: You must forget, my poor friend.

GRIVET: Certainly. Hang it all ... Let us not get downcast. We'll play for two sous a game, all right? Yes?

LAURENT: In a minute. Give Mme Raquin time to compose herself ... We all weep for our dear Camille.

SUZANNE: Listen to them, dear lady. We all weep for him, we weep for him with you. (*She sits at her feet.*)

MME RAQUIN: Yes, you are all so good ... Don't be angry with me for upsetting the game.

MICHAUD: We're not angry with you. It's just that it's a year now since the terrible incident happened and you should learn to think about it more calmly.

MME RAQUIN: I hadn't counted the days. I am crying because the tears come to my eyes. Forgive me. I can still see my dear boy beaten by the murky Seine water, and then I see him as a tiny boy falling asleep between two blankets as I sing to him. What a terrible way to die! How he must have suffered! I knew something terrible would happen. I begged him to abandon the idea of that boat trip. He wanted to be so brave ... If only you knew how I tended him in his cradle. Once when he had typhoid I held him for three weeks on end without a wink of sleep.

MICHAUD: (*Getting up.*) You've still got your niece. You mustn't distress her. You mustn't distress the kind friend who saved her, and whose eternal regret it will be that he was unable to rescue Camille as well. Your sorrow is selfish. You're bringing tears to Laurent's eyes.

LAURENT: These memories are so painful.

MICHAUD: Come now, you did all you could. When the boat capsized, by colliding with a stake, I believe – one of those stakes used to support the eel-nets, if I remember correctly ...

LAURENT: I believe so. The jolt sent all three of us flying into the water.

MICHAUD: Then, when you had fallen in, you were able to grab hold of Thérèse?

LAURENT: I was rowing, she was sitting next to me. All I had to do was to grab her clothes. When I dived back in, Camille had disappeared ... He had been sitting at the front of the boat, dipping his hands in the water ... he even made jokes, he said, 'Golly, it isn't half cold. It wouldn't be very nice to take a header in that brew.'

MICHAUD: You mustn't reawaken these painful memories. You acted like a hero – you dived in again three times.

GRIVET: (*Getting up.*) So I believe ... There was a superb article about it in my paper the next day. It said that Monsieur Laurent deserved a medal. I got goose pimples just reading how three people had fallen into the river while their dinner stood waiting for them at the bankside restaurant. And then a week later when they found poor Monsieur Camille, there was another article. (*To MICHAUD.*) Do you remember, it was Monsieur Laurent who came to fetch you to identify the body with him.

MME RAQUIN is seized by another weeping fit.

MICHAUD: (*Angrily, in lowered voice.*) Really, Monsieur Grivet, couldn't you have kept quiet? Mme Raquin was just beginning to calm down. Did you *have* to refer to such details?

GRIVET: (*Piqued, in lowered voice.*) A thousand pardons, it was you who started the story of the accident ... Seeing as we can't play, we have to say something.

MICHAUD: (*Raising his voice gradually.*) What! If you haven't quoted that article in your paper a hundred times! It's most disagreeable, understand? Now, Mme Raquin won't stop crying for *another* quarter of an hour.

GRIVET: (*Shouting.*) Well you started it.

MICHAUD: What! No. Damn it! You did.

GRIVET: You'll be calling me a fool in a minute.

MME RAQUIN: My dear friends, please don't argue.

They move upstage, muttering their discontent.

I will be good. I won't cry any more. These conversations are a great comfort. It helps to talk of my loss, it reminds me how much I owe you all ... My dear Laurent, give me your hand. Are you angry?

LAURENT: Yes, with myself, for not being able to give *both* of them back to you.

MME RAQUIN: (*Holding his hand.*) You are my child, and I love you. Every night I pray for you. You tried to save my son. Every night I beseech the Heavens to watch over your precious life … You see, my son is up there and he will hear my prayers. You will owe your happiness to him. Each time you find joy, say to yourself that it was I who prayed and Camille who granted it.

LAURENT: Dear Madame Raquin!

MICHAUD: That's good, very good.

MME RAQUIN: (*To SUZANNE.*) And now my little one, back to your place. Look, I'm smiling – for you.

SUZANNE: Thank you. (*She gets up and kisses her.*)

MME RAQUIN: (*Slowly taking up the dominoes game.*) Who's to start?

GRIVET: Oh! Are you sure? … Oh, how kind!

GRIVET, MICHAUD and LAURENT sit in their places.

Who's to start?

MICHAUD: Me. There! (*He starts the game.*)

SUZANNE: (*Who has moved over to THÉRÈSE.*) My dear friend, shall I tell you about the blue prince?

THÉRÈSE: The blue prince?

SUZANNE: (*Takes a stool and sits next to THÉRÈSE.*) There's so much to tell. I'll whisper it to you, I don't want my uncle to know. Imagine, this young man … It's a young man, he's got a blue suit and a very fine chestnut moustache that really suits him.

THÉRÈSE: Be careful, your uncle is listening.

SUZANNE half rises and watches the players.

MICHAUD: (*Furiously to GRIVET.*) But you passed on five a minute ago, and now you're playing fives all over the place.

GRIVET: I passed on five? You are mistaken. Apologise!

MICHAUD protests, the game continues.

SUZANNE: (*Sitting again, in lowered voice.*) No need to worry about uncle when he plays dominoes …! This young man used to come to the Luxembourg Gardens every day. You know my uncle usually sits on the terrace, by the third tree from the left, just by the newspaper kiosk? Well, the blue prince would sit by the fourth tree. He would put a book on his knee. Every time he turned the page he would look across at me. (*She stops from time to time to glance furtively at the players.*)

THÉRÈSE: Is that all?

SUZANNE: Yes, that's all that happened in the Luxembourg Gardens … oh no, I forget … one day he saved me from a hoop that a little girl threw at me at top speed. He gave the hoop a hard hit and it span off in the other direction – that made me smile. It made me think of lovers who throw themselves at wild horses. The blue prince must have had the same idea: he started smiling too as he bowed to me.

THÉRÈSE: Is that the end of the story?

SUZANNE: No! That's just the beginning. The day before yesterday, my uncle had gone out. I was feeling very bored, because our maid is very stupid. So, to keep myself amused, I got out the big telescope – you know, the one that my uncle had in Vernon? Do you know that from our terrace you can see right to the edge of Paris? I was looking in the direction of Saint Sulpice …

MICHAUD: (*Angrily, to GRIVET.*) What! No! A six! Go on, play it!

GRIVET: It's a six, it's a six, I can see very well. Heavens, I'll have to do my sums. (*The game continues.*)

SUZANNE: Wait! … I saw chimneys, oh! so many chimneys, fields of them, oceans of them! When I moved the telescope slightly the chimneys started to march, faster and faster until they fell onto each other, marching at the double. The whole telescope was full of them … Suddenly, who do I see between two chimneys …? Guess! … The blue prince.

THÉRÈSE: So he's a chimney sweep, your blue prince?

SUZANNE: No, silly. He was on a terrace like me, and what's even funnier, he was looking through a telescope, like me. I recognised him, of course, with his blue suit and moustache.

THÉRÈSE: So where does he live?

SUZANNE: But I don't know. You see I only saw him in the telescope. It was without doubt a long way away in the direction of Saint Sulpice. When I looked with my bare eyes, all I could see was grey, with blue patches of the slate roofs. Then I almost lost the spot. The telescope moved and I had to retrace an enormous journey across the sea of chimneys. Now I've got a landmark, the weathercock of the house next door.

THÉRÈSE: Have you seen him again?

SUZANNE: Yes, yesterday, today, every day … Am I doing anything wrong? If only you knew how little and sweet he looks in the telescope. He's hardly any bigger than that; just like a little figure; I'm not frightened of him at all … But I don't know where he is; I don't even know if what you see in the telescope is real. It's all so far away … When he goes like this (*She blows a kiss.*) I draw back and all I can see is the grey again. I can believe that the blue prince didn't do that (*She repeats gesture of blowing a kiss.*) can't I, since he's not there any more, no matter how hard I stare out …

THÉRÈSE: (*Smiling.*) You do me good … love your blue prince forever – in your dreams.

SUZANNE: Oh no! Sh, the game's over.

MICHAUD: So, it's us two, the final set, Monsieur Grivet.

GRIVET: Are you ready, Monsieur Michaud? (*They mix up the pieces.*)

MME RAQUIN: (*Pushing her armchair stage right.*) Laurent, as you're on your feet, would you do me the favour of fetching my wool basket. I must have left it on the chest of drawers in my bedroom. Take the lamp.

LAURENT: There's no need. (*He goes out of the upstage door.*)

MICHAUD: You've got a true son, there. He's so obliging.

MME RAQUIN: Yes, he's very good to us. I entrust him with our little errands; and in the evenings, he helps us to shut up shop.

GRIVET: The other day I saw him selling some needles like a real shop girl. Ha! Ha! A shop girl with a beard!

He laughs. LAURENT *comes back suddenly, with a wild look in his eyes, as if he were being followed. For a moment he leans against the wardrobe.*

MME RAQUIN: Whatever's the matter?

MICHAUD: (*Rising.*) Are you not well?

GRIVET: Did you bump into something?

LAURENT: No, it's nothing, thank you. A fit of dizziness. (*He moves unsurely downstage.*)

MME RAQUIN: And the wool basket?

LAURENT: The basket ... I don't know ... I haven't got it.

SUZANNE: What! You were frightened. A man frightened!

LAURENT: (*Attempting to laugh.*) Frightened? Frightened of what? ... I didn't find the basket.

SUZANNE: Wait, I'll find it. And if I find your ghost, I'll bring him back with me. (*She goes.*)

LAURENT: (*Recovering gradually.*) You see, it's soon gone.

GRIVET: You are living too well. It's bad blood, that's your trouble.

LAURENT: (*Shaking.*) Yes, bad blood.

MICHAUD: (*Resitting.*) You need a refreshing infusion.

MME RAQUIN: As a matter of fact I've noticed you've been distracted for quite some time now. I'll prepare you some red vine-leaf. (*To* SUZANNE *returning with basket.*) Ah, you've found it!

SUZANNE: It was on the chest of drawers. (*To* LAURENT.) Monsieur Laurent, I didn't see your ghost. I must have scared him.

GRIVET: What a lot of spirit that girl has.

Bell from shop.

SUZANNE: Don't disturb yourselves. I'll go. (*She goes down.*)

GRIVET: A treasure, a real treasure. (*To* MICHAUD.) Let's say I've got thirty-two points to your twenty-eight.

MME RAQUIN: (*Having searched in the basket that she's placed on the fireplace.*) No, I can't find the wool I need. I'll have to go down for it (*She goes down.*)

Scene 2
THÉRÈSE, LAURENT, GRIVET, MICHAUD

GRIVET: (*In a lowered voice.*) It's not as jolly here as it used to be. The game was almost jeopardised just now.

MICHAUD: (*Ditto.*) What do you expect? When there's been a death in the house? ... But rest assured, I've found a way of bringing back our good old Thursdays. (*They play.*)

THÉRÈSE: (*Quietly to* LAURENT.) You're frightened, aren't you?

LAURENT: (*Quietly.*) Yes. Shall I come to you tonight?

THÉRÈSE: No, we must wait. Let's wait a bit longer. We must be careful.

LAURENT: We've been careful for a year. It's been a year since I last touched you. It would be so easy. I could come back through the little door. We are free now. Alone together in your room we wouldn't be afraid.

THÉRÈSE: No, let's not spoil the future. We need so much happiness, Laurent. Will we ever find enough?

LAURENT: Have confidence. We will find peace and happiness in each other's arms. We will fight the fear together. When shall I come?

THÉRÈSE: On our wedding night. It won't be long now ... Careful, my aunt.

MME RAQUIN: (*From off.*) Thérèse, will you come down. You're needed in the shop.

THÉRÈSE *goes out, wearily. They all watch her go.*

Scene 3
LAURENT, GRIVET, MICHAUD, MME RAQUIN

MICHAUD: Did you notice Thérèse just then? She can't hold her head up and is looking extremely pale.

MME RAQUIN: I watch her every day, the rings under her eyes, her hands that suddenly start shaking feverishly.

LAURENT: Yes, and her cheeks have the pink flame of consumption.

MME RAQUIN: Yes, you were the first to point it out to me, my darling Laurent, and now I see things getting worse. Will no pain be spared me!

MICHAUD: Rubbish, you're worrying about nothing. It's only her nerves. She'll recover.

LAURENT: No, she is heart-broken. There seems to be a feeling of farewell in her long silence, in her pale smiles ... It will be a long, slow death.

GRIVET: My dear man, you are being of small consolation. You ought to be cheering her up, not filling her head with macabre thoughts.

MME RAQUIN: Alas, my friend, Laurent is right. The sickness is in her heart. She has no wish to be consoled. Each time I try to make her see reason, she gets impatient, even angry. She is hiding in her pain like a wounded animal.

LAURENT: We must resign ourselves to it.

MME RAQUIN: That would be the final blow ... She's all I have. I was hoping she would be there to close my eyes. If she goes, I'll be all alone here in this shop ... left to die in a corner ... Oh, see how unhappy I am. What ill wind is shaking our house? (*She weeps.*)

GRIVET: (*Timidly.*) Well, are we playing or not?

MICHAUD: Wait, can't you. Damn you. (*He gets up.*) Look, I'm determined to find a cure. What the devil, at her age she can't be inconsolable ... Did she weep a lot after the terrible catastrophe at Saint-Ouen?

MME RAQUIN: No, she was never one for crying. She simply suffered a silent grief. She seemed overwhelmed by a weariness of mind and body; she seemed dazed, like after a long walk, but recently she's become extremely fearful.

LAURENT: (*Shaking.*) Extremely fearful?

MME RAQUIN: Yes ... One night I heard her shouting out in her sleep. I ran to her ... She didn't recognise me, she was babbling deliriously.

LAURENT: A nightmare ... And she was talking? What did she say?

MME RAQUIN: I couldn't make out the words. She was crying out for Camille ... Now in the evenings she doesn't dare go up to bed without the lamp. In the mornings she is exhausted, she drags herself around listlessly and looks at me blankly, it upsets me so ... I know only too well that she will leave us, that she wishes to join my other poor child.

MICHAUD: Very well, old girl, my enquiry is complete. I shall tell you exactly what I think. But first may we be left alone?

LAURENT: You wish to be left alone with Mme Raquin?

MICHAUD: Yes.

GRIVET: (*Getting up.*) Very well, we're going. You know you owe me two games, Monsieur Michaud. Remind me. I'll be waiting for you.

GRIVET and LAURENT go out.

Scene 4

MICHAUD and MME RAQUIN

MICHAUD: Now then, my old girl, I'll be blunt ...

MME RAQUIN: What is your advice? If only we could save her!

MICHAUD: (*Lowering his voice.*) You must marry her off.

MME RAQUIN: Marry her off! Oh, how cruel! It would be like losing my dear Camille all over again.

MICHAUD: Come, come, let's face the facts. I'm acting as your doctor and as your doctor I prescribe marriage.

MME RAQUIN: No, it's not possible ... You've seen her fears. She'd never accept. She hasn't forgotten my son. I begin to doubt your sense of delicacy, Michaud. Thérèse can't possibly remarry with Camille still in her heart. That would be a profanation.

MICHAUD: Don't start using big words with me! A woman who is afraid to go to her room alone at night is in need of a husband, damn it!

MME RAQUIN: What? And introduce a stranger to our midst! It would cloud the rest of my old age. We might make the wrong choice, disturb the little peace we have left ... No, no. Let me die in my mourning clothes. (*She sits.*)

MICHAUD: Obviously we have to find a good soul who would be both a good husband for Thérèse and a good son for you, who would replace Camille perfectly. In a word ... well, how about ... Laurent!

MME RAQUIN: Laurent!

MICHAUD: Why yes! They'd make such a lovely couple. That is my advice, old friend, they must be married.

MME RAQUIN: Those two, Michaud!

MICHAUD: I was sure you would be amused. I've been toying with the idea for some time now. Think it over and have faith in my professional experience. If, in order to add a final joy to your old age, you decide to marry Thérèse off and save her from this slow, consuming grief, then where would you find a better husband than Laurent?

MME RAQUIN: But they've always been like brother and sister.

MICHAUD: Come now, just think of yourself! I only want to see you all happy. It will be like the good old days again. You will have two children to comfort you in your old age.

MME RAQUIN: Do not tempt me ... You're right, I am in such need of consolation. But I fear we might be doing wrong ... My poor Camille would punish us for forgetting him so quickly.

MICHAUD: Who's talking about forgetting him? Laurent is forever mentioning his name. He'll still be part of the family, damn it.

MME RAQUIN: I am old. My legs are bad. All I ask is to die happy.

MICHAUD: You see, I've managed to convince you. It's the only way of avoiding a stranger in your midst. You would be simply strengthening your bond of friendship. And I want to see you a grandmother with little ones climbing on your knee ... You are smiling, you see, I knew I'd make you smile.

MME RAQUIN: Oh, it's wrong, it's wrong to smile. I feel so confused, my friend. They will never consent. They never think of such things.

MICHAUD: Bah, we will hustle things on. They are far too reasonable not to realise that their marriage is necessary to the happiness of this household. That's the logic we must use to them. I'll speak to Laurent. I'll talk him into it while I help him close up the shop. Meanwhile, you speak to Thérèse. And we'll have them engaged this very evening.

MME RAQUIN: (*Rising.*) I'm all of a tremble. (THÉRÈSE *enters.*)

MICHAUD: Look, here she is. I'll leave you. (*He goes.*)

Scene 5

MME RAQUIN and THÉRÈSE

MME RAQUIN: (*To* THÉRÈSE, *who enters, dejected.*) What's wrong with you, my child? You haven't said a word all evening. I beg you, try to be less sad. For the gentlemen's sake. (THÉRÈSE *makes a vague gesture.*) I know, I know you can't control sadness ... Are you in pain?

THÉRÈSE: No, I'm just very tired.

MME RAQUIN: If you are in pain, you must say so. It's not right to suffer without allowing us to look after you. Perhaps you're getting palpitations? Pains in your chest?

THÉRÈSE: No ... I don't know ... It's nothing ... It's as if everything in me has gone to sleep.

MME RAQUIN: Dear child ... you cause me so much anxiety, with your long silences. You are all I have.

THÉRÈSE: Are you asking me to forget?

MME RAQUIN: I didn't say that. I can't say that ... But it is my duty to see if there can be any consolation for you. I mustn't impose my mourning on you ... Tell me, frankly.

THÉRÈSE: I am so tired.

MME RAQUIN: You must tell me. You spend too much time alone and you are bored, is that it? At your age to be constantly weeping!

THÉRÈSE: I don't understand what you're trying to say.

MME RAQUIN: Nothing. I was just asking. I want to know what's wrong. I know it can't be much fun living alone with a sad old woman. I do understand. And your room is so big, so dark and perhaps you want ...

THÉRÈSE: I don't *want* anything.

MME RAQUIN: Listen. Don't be angry. I know it's a wicked idea we've had but ... We've thought you should remarry.

THÉRÈSE: Me! Never! Never! Why do you doubt me?

MME RAQUIN: (*Very emotional.*) I said to them, she can't have forgotten him, he's still in her heart ... It was they who forced me ... And they are right, you see, my child. This house is too sad. Soon everyone will desert us. Oh, you must listen to them.

THÉRÈSE: Never!

MME RAQUIN: Yes. Remarry. I can't remember how they put it ... they were so convincing ... I did agree with them. I took it upon myself to persuade you ... If you like, I'll call Michaud. He'll explain much better than I can.

THÉRÈSE: My heart is closed, it won't listen. Please can't you all leave me in peace? Remarry, good God, to whom!

Figure 1 The Italian actress Giacinta Pezzana as the mother in *Thérèse Raquin* at the Teatro dei Fiorentini in 1879.

Figure 2 Charlotte Emmerson as Thérèse and Ben Daniels as Laurent in *Thérèse Raquin* from a new version by Nicholas Wright, directed by Marianne Elliot at the Royal National Theatre, London in 2006. (Photographer: Simon Annand and by permission of the Royal National Theatre archive.)

MME RAQUIN: They have had a good idea. They have found you someone. Michaud is below right now talking to Laurent.

THÉRÈSE: Laurent! The person you've chosen is Laurent! But I don't love him, don't want to love him.

MME RAQUIN: They are right, I promise you. Laurent is practically one of the family. You know how kind he is, how helpful he is to us. At first, like you, I felt hurt; it seemed wrong. Then, when I thought more about it, I realised that it would be more faithful to Camille's memory for you to marry his friend, your rescuer.

THÉRÈSE: But I still weep, still want to weep!

MME RAQUIN: And I am pleading against these tears of yours and against my own ... You see, they only want us to be happy. They said I'd have two children, they said it'd surround me with something sweet and joyful to ease the wait for death ... I am selfish, I need to see you smile ... Do it for me.

THÉRÈSE: My sweet suffering. You know I have always resigned myself, that my only wish was to please you.

MME RAQUIN: Yes, you are a good girl. (*Trying to smile.*) Next spring will be my last. We will work out a cosy life together, we three. Laurent will love us both ... You

Figure 3 Charlotte Emmerson as Thérèse and Ben Daniels as Laurent in *Thérèse Raquin* from a new version by Nicholas Wright, directed by Marianne Elliot at the Royal National Theatre, London in 2006. (Photographer: Simon Annand and by permission of the Royal National Theatre archive.)

know, I'm marrying him too, a little ... You will lend him to me for my little errands, for my old woman's whims.

THÉRÈSE: Dear aunt ... I was so sure you would let me weep in peace.

MME RAQUIN: You give your consent, yes?

THÉRÈSE: Yes.

MME RAQUIN: (*Very moved.*) Thank you, my daughter. You make me so happy. (*Falls into armchair.*) Oh, my dear son, my poor dead child, I was the first to betray you.

Scene 6

THÉRÈSE, MME RAQUIN, MICHAUD, then: SUZANNE, GRIVET and LAURENT

MICHAUD: (*Quietly to MME RAQUIN.*) I've persuaded him. But my God, it wasn't without the greatest difficulty. He will do it for your sake, you understand; I pleaded your case ... He'll be up in a minute, he's just locking up the front ... and Thérèse?

MME RAQUIN: She consents.

MICHAUD crosses to THÉRÈSE, upstage left, and whispers to her.

SUZANNE: (*Arrives, followed by GRIVET, in mid-conversation.*) No, Monsieur Grivet, no! You are such an egoist, I *won't* dance with you at the wedding. So you never got married so as not to disturb your little habits?

GRIVET: Certainly, Miss.

SUZANNE: Huh, the objectionable man! ... Not a single step of the quadrille, do you hear? (*She goes over to join THÉRÈSE and MICHAUD.*)

GRIVET: All little girls think it's fun to get married. I've tried it five times. (*To MME RAQUIN.*) You remember the last time, that large unfeeling lady teacher. The banns were published, everything was going perfectly, until she confessed to drinking milky coffee in the mornings. I loathe milky coffee, *I* drink hot chocolate and have done for thirty years now. That would have upset my entire existence, so I broke it off. I did the right thing, didn't I?

MME RAQUIN: (*Smiling.*) Without doubt.

GRIVET: Ah! It's such a pleasure when people get on with each other. That's how Michaud saw straight away that Thérèse and Laurent were made for each other.

MME RAQUIN: (*Gravely.*) You are right, my friend. (*She gets up.*)

GRIVET: That's what the song says. (*He sings.*) Oh dear mother, shall I say, what torments me, night and day. (*Looks at watch.*) Gracious! Five to eleven! (*He sits down and puts on his galoshes, picks up his umbrella.*)

LAURENT: (*Who has come up, goes over to MME RAQUIN.*) I have just been discussing your happiness with Monsieur Michaud. Your children wish to make you happy ... dear Mother.

MME RAQUIN: (*Very moved.*) Yes, call me your mother, my good Laurent.

LAURENT: Thérèse. Do you wish to give our mother a sweet and peaceful life?

THÉRÈSE: I do. We have a duty to fulfil.

MME RAQUIN: Oh, my children! (*Taking the hands of* THÉRÈSE *and* LAURENT *and holding them in her own hands.*) Marry her, Laurent: make her happy and my son will thank you. You make me so happy. I pray to the Heavens that we shall not be punished.

End of Act 2.

Act 3

Three a.m. The room is decorated, all white. Big open fire. One lamp burning. White curtains round the bed: bedspread edged with lace, squares of lace on the chairs. Large bouquets of roses everywhere, on the sideboard, mantelpiece, table.

Scene 1

THÉRÈSE, MME RAQUIN, SUZANNE, MICHAUD, GRIVET

THÉRÈSE, MME RAQUIN and SUZANNE in wedding outfits enter. MME RAQUIN and SUZANNE have already taken off their hats and shawls. THÉRÈSE is in grey silk: she goes to sit: she seems tired. SUZANNE stands at the door and argues a moment with GRIVET and MICHAUD (wearing black), who want to follow the women.

SUZANNE: No, uncle. No, Monsieur Grivet. You can't come into the bride's bedroom. What you're doing is very improper.

GRIVET and MICHAUD enter all the same.

MICHAUD: (*Quietly to* SUZANNE.) Sh, sh, it's a joke. (*To* GRIVET.) Have you got the packet of nettles, Monsieur Grivet?

GRIVET: Certainly, they've been in my pocket since this morning. They caused me a lot of bother both at the church and at the restaurant. (*He approaches the bed slyly.*)

MME RAQUIN: (*With a smile.*) Come on now, gentlemen, you can't be present for the undressing of the bride.

MICHAUD: The undressing of the bride! Oh, my dear lady, what a charming thought! If you need any help with the pins, here we are at your service. (*He joins* GRIVET.)

SUZANNE: (*To* MME RAQUIN.) I've never seen my uncle look so jolly. He was so red, very red during the dessert.

MME RAQUIN: Let them laugh. You're allowed to have fun on a wedding night. At Vernon we used to get up to all sorts of tricks. The wedding couple weren't allowed to get a wink of sleep all night.

GRIVET: (*In front of the bed.*) My word, this bed is so soft. Have a feel, Monsieur Michaud.

MICHAUD: By jove, three mattresses at least. (*Whispers.*) Have you hidden the stinging nettles in the bed?

GRIVET: (*Whispers.*) Right in the middle.

MICHAUD: (*Bursting out laughing.*) Ha! Ha! You are such a joker, honestly!

GRIVET: (*Also giggling.*) Ha, ha! This one will work all right.

MME RAQUIN: (*Smiling.*) Gentlemen, the bride is waiting.

SUZANNE: Look, will you leave? You're getting annoying now.

MICHAUD: Right, very well, we're going.

GRIVET: (*To* THÉRÈSE.) Our compliments, Madame, and good night.

THÉRÈSE: (*Getting up and sitting down again.*) Thank you, gentlemen.

GRIVET: You're not angry are you, my dear lady?

MME RAQUIN: What, my old friend, on a wedding night?! Goodnight.

MICHAUD and GRIVET leave slowly, spluttering with laughter.

SUZANNE: (*Shutting the door behind them.*) And don't come back. Uncle, wait for me downstairs. Only the groom will be allowed in and then only when we allow it.

Scene 2

THÉRÈSE, MME RAQUIN, SUZANNE

MME RAQUIN: You should get undressed, Thérèse. It's nearly three o'clock.

THÉRÈSE: I am exhausted. What with the ceremony, the coach-ride, that interminable meal ... Leave that for a moment, please.

SUZANNE: (*To* MME RAQUIN.) Yes, it was so hot in that restaurant. It gave me a headache, but it went away in the cab. You are the one who must be tired, with your bad legs! Remember what the doctor said.

MME RAQUIN: He said a severe shock might be fatal, but today I just felt so happy. Everything went very smoothly, didn't you think? It was all very proper.

SUZANNE: The Mayor looked perfect, didn't he? When he began to read from his little red book, the groom bowed his head ... Monsieur Grivet's signature in the register looked superb.

MME RAQUIN: At the church, the priest was very touching.

SUZANNE: Ooh, and everyone was crying. I was watching Thérèse; she looked so serious ... And then this afternoon, there were so many people on the streets. We must have travelled twice round Paris. People gave us funny looks ... Half of the wedding party was asleep by the time we got to the restaurant. (*She laughs.*)

MME RAQUIN: Thérèse, you ought to get undressed, my child.

THÉRÈSE: Just a bit longer please. Keep talking, just a bit longer.

SUZANNE: Can I be your chamber-maid? Wait. Now, let me do it all. In that way, you won't get more tired.

MME RAQUIN: Give me her hat.

SUZANNE: (*Gives the hat to* MME RAQUIN.) There, you see, you don't even have to move. Oh, but I'm afraid you'll have to stand up if you want me to take off your dress.

THÉRÈSE: (*Standing up.*) How you torment me!

MME RAQUIN: It's late, my daughter.

SUZANNE: (*Unhooking the dress.*) A husband, that must be awful. One of my friends who got married cried and cried. Your waist is so small and you aren't holding yourself in. You're right to wear long bodices. Ah, this hook is really sticking. I've got a good mind to go and fetch Monsieur Grivet. (*She laughs.*)

THÉRÈSE: Hurry up, I've got the shivers.

SUZANNE: We'll go in front of the fire.

They both cross to the fire.

Oh! You've got a rip in your flounce. Oh, this silk is magnificent, so strong … Why you are so nervous, my darling friend. I can feel you shaking when I touch you, just like Thisbe. She's the cat my uncle gave me. I'm trying so hard not to tickle you.

THÉRÈSE: I'm a bit feverish.

SUZANNE: Nearly finished. There! (*She makes THÉRÈSE step out of the dress and hands it to MME RAQUIN.*) Finished! And now I will brush your hair for the night, would you like that?

MME RAQUIN: That's it. (She takes the dress out of the upstage door.)

SUZANNE: (*Having sat THÉRÈSE down in front of the fire.*) Now you're all nice and pink. You looked as pale as death just now.

THÉRÈSE: It's the fire.

SUZANNE: (*Standing behind her, brushing her hair.*) Lower your head a touch. You have such superb hair. Tell me, my dear friend, I'd like to ask a few questions. I'm so curious, you know … Your heart is beating so very fast, and that's why you are shaking, is that right?

THÉRÈSE: My heart isn't seventeen years old like yours, my dear.

SUZANNE: I hope I'm not annoying you! It's just I've been thinking all day long that if I were in your place I'd be so foolish; so I promised myself to watch how you prepared yourself for the night so that I wouldn't seem too awkward when it was my turn … You seem a bit sad, but you have courage; I'd be afraid of sobbing like an idiot.

THÉRÈSE: Is the blue prince such an awful prince, then?

SUZANNE: Don't tease me. You look good with your hair down. You look like a queen in those pictures … No plaits, just a simple bun, yes?

THÉRÈSE: Yes, just a simple knot, please. (*MME RAQUIN returns and takes a white nightdress from the wardrobe.*)

SUZANNE: (*Brushing THÉRÈSE's hair.*) If you promise not to laugh, I'll tell you what I would be feeling in your place. I would be happy, oh, but happy like I'd never been before. And then, I'd be terribly scared. I'd think I was floating on a cloud, approaching something unknown, sweet and terrifying, with very gentle music, and very delicate perfumes. And I'd step into a white light, pushed forward in spite of myself by a joy that was so thrilling I would think I was dying … That's how you feel, isn't it?

THÉRÈSE: Yes … (*Softly.*) Music, perfumes, a great light, all the springtime of youth and love.

SUZANNE: You're still trembling.

THÉRÈSE: I can't get warm.

MME RAQUIN: (*Coming to sit by the fireplace.*) I'll warm your nightdress for you. (*She holds it against the fire.*)

SUZANNE: And when the blue prince was waiting, like Monsieur Laurent is doing, I would maliciously make him wait. Then, when he'd come to the door, oh! Then I would come over all silly, I'd make myself very small, very, very small, so that he couldn't find me. I don't know after that. I can't think about it, without feeling funny.

MME RAQUIN: (*Turning the nightdress, smiling.*) You ought not to think about it, little one. Children think of nothing but dolls, flowers and husbands.

SUZANNE: (*To THÉRÈSE.*) Is that not what you're feeling?

THÉRÈSE: Yes, it is. I'd have preferred not to have been married in winter, or in this room. At Vernon, in May, the acacia are in flower, the nights are warm.

SUZANNE: There! That's your hair done. Now you can put on your nice warm nightdress.

MME RAQUIN: (*Helping THÉRÈSE on with her nightdress.*) It's burning my hands.

SUZANNE: I hope you're not cold now.

THÉRÈSE: Thank you.

SUZANNE: (*Looking at THÉRÈSE.*) Ah, you are lovely. You look like a true bride in the lace.

MME RAQUIN: Now we will leave you alone, my child.

THÉRÈSE: Alone, no! Wait, I'm sure I've still something to tell you.

MME RAQUIN: No, don't talk; I'm avoiding talking, you note. I don't want to start us crying. If you knew what an effort it's been ever since this morning. My heart is breaking, and yet I must be, I *am* happy … It's all over. You saw how jolly our old friend Michaud was, you must be jolly, too.

THÉRÈSE: Yes, you are right. I've got a headache. Goodbye.

MME RAQUIN: Goodbye … Tell me, my daughter, you're not feeling sorrowful, you're not hiding anything from me …? What makes me strong is the thought of having made you happy … You will love your husband; he deserves both of our affection. You will love him like you loved … No, I've got nothing to say to you, I don't want to say anything. We have done the best we can and I wish you much happiness, my daughter, for all the comfort you are giving me.

SUZANNE: Anyone would think you were leaving Thérèse to a pack of wolves in a dark den. The den smells good. There are roses everywhere. Like a cosy nest.

THÉRÈSE: These flowers must have been expensive. You are mad.

MME RAQUIN: I know you love the springtime; I wanted to give you a corner of spring in your room for your wedding night. You could live out Suzanne's dream, and believe that you are visiting the garden of paradise. You see, you are smiling. Be happy amidst your roses. Good night my daughter (*She kisses her.*) Good night, little one.

SUZANNE: And me, aren't you going to give me a kiss, dear friend?

THÉRÈSE kisses her.

Now you've gone all pale again. The blue prince is here. Oh! It's wonderful, a room like this full of roses.

Scene 3

LAURENT and THÉRÈSE

THÉRÈSE, now alone. She slowly moves back to sit by the fire. Silence. LAURENT enters slowly, still in his wedding outfit. He closes the door and advances with embarrassment. Takes off his jacket and waistcoat.

LAURENT: Thérèse, my dear love …

THÉRÈSE: (*Pushing him away.*) No, wait, I'm cold.

LAURENT: (*After a silence.*) At last, we are alone, my Thérèse, far from the others, free to love each other … Life ahead is ours, this room is ours, you are mine, dear wife, because I won you, and you gave yourself willingly. (*He goes to kiss her.*)

THÉRÈSE: (*Pushing him away.*) No, in a minute, I am freezing.

LAURENT: My poor angel! Give me your feet so I can warm them with my hands. (*He kneels in front of her and tries to take her foot, which she withdraws.*) The time has come, you see. Remember, we've been waiting for a year, been working for a year towards this night of love. We need it, don't we, as payment for all our caution, our suffering, our pain?

THÉRÈSE: I remember … Don't stay there. Sit down a minute. Let's talk.

LAURENT: (*Getting up.*) Why are you shaking? I've closed the door, and I am your husband … Before, when I came to you, you never trembled, you laughed, you spoke out loud despite the risk of being found out. Now, you are talking in a whisper as if someone were listening through the walls … Come, we can raise our voices, and laugh, and love each other. It is our wedding night. No one will come.

THÉRÈSE: (*Terrified.*) Don't say that. Don't say that …! You are even paler than I am, Laurent, and you are stammering to get your words out. Don't pretend to be brave. Let's wait until we dare before we kiss. You are afraid of looking ridiculous by not taking me and kissing me. You are a child. We are not a normal newly wedded couple. Sit down. Let's talk.

He sits. She changes her tone of voice to a familiar and casual one.

It was very windy today.

LAURENT: Yes, it was a very cold wind. But it died down a little this afternoon.

THÉRÈSE: Yes. The apricot trees will do well not to flower too early.

LAURENT: In March, bouts of frost are very bad for fruit trees. You must remember, at Vernon …

He stops. Both dream an instant.

THÉRÈSE: (*Quietly.*) At Vernon, that was our childhood. (*Assuming her familiar and indifferent tone of voice.*) Put a log on the fire, will you? It's beginning to be quite pleasant in here. Is it four o'clock yet?

LAURENT: (*Looking at the clock.*) No, not yet. (*He moves left and sits at the other end of the room.*)

THÉRÈSE: It's surprising, how long the night is … Do you dislike cab rides as I do? There is nothing more stupid than riding for hours. It puts me to sleep … And I detest eating in restaurants.

LAURENT: One is always more comfortable at home.

THÉRÈSE: That's not so in the country.

LAURENT: One can eat some excellent things in the country. Do you remember, the pleasure gardens by the water … (*He gets up.*)

THÉRÈSE: Shut up! (*Suddenly getting up, rough voice.*) Why do you bring back those memories! I can hear them, pounding in your head and in mine, and the whole cruel story unfolds in front of my eyes … No, let's not say anything, let us not think any more. Underneath your words, I hear others; I hear what you are thinking but don't say. Am I right? Just then you were thinking of the accident? Shut up! (*A silence.*)

LAURENT: Thérèse, say something, I implore you. This silence is too heavy to bear. Speak to me.

THÉRÈSE: (*Going to sit stage right, her hands clutching her forehead.*) Close your eyes. Try to disappear.

LAURENT: No. I need to hear your voice. Say something, anything you like, like you did just now, that the weather is bad, that the night is long …

THÉRÈSE: All the same I think, I can't not think. You are right, silence is bad, it is better to talk … (*Trying to smile, in a jolly tone.*) The town hall was so cold this morning. My feet were frozen. But I managed to warm them on a little stove in the church. Did you notice the little stove? It was just by the place where we knelt down.

LAURENT: Of course. Grivet stood over it throughout the whole ceremony. That devil Grivet had a triumphant smile on his face. He was so funny, wasn't he? (*They both force themselves to laugh.*)

THÉRÈSE: The church was a bit dark, due to the weather. Did you notice the lace of the altar cloth? That lace costs ten francs a metre at least, better than any we've got in the shop. The smell of the incense hung around; it smelt so sweet, it made me feel sick … At first I thought we were alone inside that huge church; that pleased me. (*Her voice getting muffled.*) Then, I heard singing. You must have noticed it in a chapel on the other side of the nave.

LAURENT: (*Hesitating.*) I think I saw some people with candles.

THÉRÈSE: (*Suddenly seized by terror.*) It was a funeral. When I looked up I was confronted by the black cloth and the white cross … The coffin passed close to us. I watched it. A poor, short, narrow, shabby coffin. Some poor creature, sordid and destitute.

She has gradually moved towards LAURENT and brushes his shoulder. They both shake. Pause. Then she resumes in a low voice.

Laurent, did you see him at the morgue?

LAURENT: Yes.

THÉRÈSE: Did he look as though he had suffered a lot?

LAURENT: Horribly.

THÉRÈSE: His eyes were wide open, and he looked straight at you?

LAURENT: Yes. He looked revolting, blue and swollen with the water. And he was smiling; the corner of his mouth was twisted.

THÉRÈSE: You say you think he was smiling … Tell me, tell me everything, tell me how he looked. In my long sleepless nights, I've never seen him clearly, and I have a passion, a passion to see him.

LAURENT: (*In a terrible voice, shaking THÉRÈSE.*) Shut up! Wake up! We are both half asleep. What are you talking about? If I answered you, I was lying. I saw nothing. Nothing. Nothing. What is this ridiculous game we are playing?

THÉRÈSE: Ah! Feel how the words rise to our lips in spite of ourselves. Everything leads us back to him … the apricot trees in flower, the pleasure gardens by the river, the coffin … There can no longer be any indifferent conversation between us. He is at the bottom of all our thoughts.

LAURENT: Kiss me.

THÉRÈSE: I understand full well that you were talking about nothing but him, and that I replied about nothing but him. The awful story has formed inside us and we must complete it aloud.

LAURENT: (*Trying to take her in his arms.*) Kiss me Thérèse. Our kisses will cure us. We married so that we could find peace in each other's arms. Kiss me, and let us forget, dear wife.

THÉRÈSE: (*Pushing him away.*) No! I beg you, do not torment me. Just one more minute … Reassure me, be good and light-hearted like before. (*A silence. LAURENT walks away, then he suddenly goes out of the main door, as if he's had a sudden idea.*)

Scene 4

THÉRÈSE alone

THÉRÈSE: He's left me alone … Don't leave me, Laurent, I am yours. He's gone, and I am alone, now … I think the lamp is going out. If it goes out … If I am left in the dark … I don't want to be alone. I don't want it to be night … Oh, why did I not let him kiss me? I don't know what was wrong with me, my lips were icy cold; I thought his kiss would have killed me … Where can he have gone? (*A*

knock at the little side door.*) Oh my God, now the other one has come back! He's come back for my wedding night. Can you hear him? He's knocking on the wood of the bed, he's calling me to my pillow … Go away. I'm frightened … (*She stays still, trembling, hands over her eyes. Another knock, she gradually calms herself and smiles.*) No, it's not the other one, it's my dear lover, it's my dear … Thank you for that good thought, Laurent. I recognise your signal.

She goes and opens. LAURENT enters.

Scene 5

LAURENT and THÉRÈSE

They repeat exactly the same gestures as in Act 1 Scene Five.

THÉRÈSE: It's you, my Laurent! (*She flings her arms round his neck.*) I knew you would come, my dear love. I was thinking about you. It is so long since I've been able to hold you like this, all to myself.

LAURENT: Remember how you held me till I fell asleep. And I would dream of a way to stop us having to separate for ever … Tonight, that beautiful dream is fulfilled. Thérèse … you are there leaning against my chest for ever.

THÉRÈSE: An endless pleasure, a long walk in the sun.

LAURENT: Kiss me, then, dear wife.

THÉRÈSE: (*Suddenly breaking away, with a shout.*) No, then no! What is the good of acting out this comedy of the past? We don't love each other any more. We have murdered our love. Do you think I can't feel how cold you are in my arms? Let us stay calm and not move.

LAURENT: You are mine. I will have you. I will cure you of this nervous fear. What would be cruel, would be not to love each other any more, to find only a nightmare instead of the happiness we dreamt of. Come, put your arms round my neck again.

THÉRÈSE: No, we must not tempt suffering.

LAURENT: You must understand how ridiculous it is to spend the night like this; when we have loved each other so fearlessly. No one will come.

THÉRÈSE: (*Terrified.*) You've just said that. Don't repeat yourself, I implore you … He might come.

LAURENT: Do you want to drive me mad? (*He goes towards her.*) I have given up too much, for you to refuse me now.

THÉRÈSE: (*Breaking away from him.*) Mercy! The sound of our kisses will call him I'm afraid, look, I'm afraid.

LAURENT goes to seize her in his arms, when he catches sight of CAMILLE's portrait, hanging above the sideboard.

LAURENT: (*Terrified, staggering backwards, pointing with his finger.*) There! There! Camille.

THÉRÈSE: I told you so. I felt a cold breeze behind my back. Where is he?

LAURENT: There, in the shadow.

THÉRÈSE: Behind the bed?

LAURENT: No, on the right. He's quite still, staring. He's watching us, staring ... He looks just as I saw him, pale and smudgy, with that twisted smile at the corner of his mouth.

THÉRÈSE: (*Looking.*) But, it's his portrait that you can see!

LAURENT: His portrait?

THÉRÈSE: Yes, the painting you did, you know?

LAURENT: No, I don't know. You think it's his portrait? I saw his eyes move ... Look. They're moving now. His portrait. Then go and take it down.

THÉRÈSE: No, I don't dare.

LAURENT: I beg you, do it.

THÉRÈSE: No.

LAURENT: Then let us turn it to face the wall, then we won't be afraid any more; perhaps we'll be able to kiss.

THÉRÈSE: No, why don't you do it yourself?

LAURENT: His eyes are still looking at me. I tell you his eyes are moving! They are following me, they are crushing me ... (*He slowly approaches.*) I will look down, and then I won't see him any more. (*He takes down the portrait in a single furious movement.*)

Scene 6

LAURENT, MME RAQUIN, THÉRÈSE

MME RAQUIN: (*In the doorway.*) What's wrong? I heard someone shouting.

LAURENT: (*Still holding the portrait and looking at it in spite of himself.*) He looks terrible. He looks just like he did when we threw him into the water.

MME RAQUIN: (*Advancing, staggering.*) Oh, just God! They killed my child!

THÉRÈSE, desperate, cries out in terror; LAURENT, bewildered, throws the portrait onto the bed, and falls back in front of MME RAQUIN, who stammers.

Murderers, murderers!

She suddenly has an attack of spasms, staggers as far as the bed, tries to balance, but seizing onto one of the white bed curtains, leans against the wall a moment, panting and fearful. LAURENT, hounded by her looks, hides behind THÉRÈSE.

LAURENT: It's the attack they warned her of. The paralysis is rising to her throat.

MME RAQUIN: (*Making a final supreme effort.*) My poor child. The wretches, the ...

THÉRÈSE: It's horrible. She's all twisted, like in a vice. I don't dare help her. (*MME RAQUIN, thrown backwards, overwhelmed, collapses onto a chair.*)

MME RAQUIN: Misery! ... I can't ... I can't ... (*She freezes stiff in her chair, her eyes fixed on THÉRÈSE and LAURENT.*)

THÉRÈSE: She's dying.

LAURENT: No, her eyes are living, her eyes are threatening us. Oh, that those lips and limbs were of stone!

End of Act 3.

Act 4

Five p.m. Five months later. The room is dark and humid once more. Dirty curtains. Neglected housework; dust, rags and clothes lying around on the furniture, dirty crockery left on the chairs. A rolled-up mattress thrown behind the bed curtain.

Scene 1

THÉRÈSE, SUZANNE

They are sitting at the work table, sewing.

THÉRÈSE: (*Gaily.*) So, at long last you found out where the blue prince lives? Love can't make you as stupid as they say, then.

SUZANNE: I wouldn't know. Myself, I'm pretty smart. In the end, you understand, it wasn't the least bit amusing to see my prince half a league away, always well-behaved like a picture. Between you and me, he was *too* well-behaved, much too much so.

THÉRÈSE: (*Laughing.*) So you like your lovers to be wicked, do you?

SUZANNE: Well, a lover you're not afraid of can't be a serious lover, can he? When I caught sight of my prince far away against the sky surrounded by chimney-pots, I thought I was looking at one of those angels in my Mass book who stand with their feet in the clouds. Very nice, but in the end extremely boring, you see! So, when it was my birthday, I told Uncle to give me a map of Paris.

THÉRÈSE: A map of Paris?

SUZANNE: Yes ... Uncle was rather surprised, too ... When I got the map ... I set to work. I worked so hard! I drew lines with a ruler, measured distances with a pair of compasses, added, multiplied. And, when I thought I'd found the prince's terrace, I stuck a pin in the map on the spot. Then, the next day, I forced Uncle to take a walk along the road where the house was.

THÉRÈSE: (*Cheerfully.*) My dear, it's such an amusing story. (*Looking at the clock and suddenly becoming very withdrawn.*) Five o'clock already. Laurent will be home.

SUZANNE: What's wrong? Just now you were so cheerful.

THÉRÈSE: (*Recovering.*) So the map helped you to discover the blue prince's address?

SUZANNE: Mm? No, my map was no help at all. Oh, if you only knew where it led me! One day it led me to a huge ugly house, where they make shoe polish; another day to a photographer's shop; another time to a seminary, then a prison, I don't know where else ... You're not laughing. Come on, it *is* funny. ... Are you feeling unwell?

THÉRÈSE: No, I thought my husband would be home. When you get married, you must frame that lucky map of yours!

SUZANNE: (*Getting up and moving stage right, passing behind THÉRÈSE.*) I've just told you it was useless. Haven't you been listening? Anyway, one afternoon, I went to the flower market at Saint Sulpice; I wanted to get some nasturtiums for our terrace. Who do I see in the middle of the market …? The blue prince, loaded down with flowers, pots in his pockets, pots under his arms, pots in his hands. He looked quite embarrassed with all his pots when he caught sight of me … Then he followed me; he didn't know how to get rid of the pots, poor dear! He said they were all for his terrace! Then, he made friends with Uncle, asked for my hand, and now I am marrying him – so there you are! I made a paper bird with the map and all I ever look at through the telescope is the moon … My dear friend, have you been listening?

THÉRÈSE: Yes, and your story is beautiful. And you still have your blue sky, and your flowers and your laughter. Oh, my dear, with your blue bird, if only you knew. (*Looks at the clock.*) Five o'clock. It is five o'clock isn't it? I must lay the table.

SUZANNE: I'll help you.

THÉRÈSE gets up. SUZANNE helps her to lay the table, three places.

Oh, how heartless of me to be so cheerful here, when I know that your happiness has been saddened by the cruel affliction of poor Mme Raquin … How is she today?

THÉRÈSE: She still can't move or talk but she doesn't seem to be in pain.

SUZANNE: The doctor did warn it could happen; she was always overdoing it … The paralysis has been merciless. As if she'd been struck by lightning and turned to stone, the poor, dear lady … When she's here with us, all stiff in her chair, her face all taut and white, her pale hands on her lap, she reminds me of one of those awful statues of mourning you see in churches, sitting at the feet of the tombs. I don't know why, but she makes me feel terrified. Can she still not move her hands?

THÉRÈSE: Her hands are dead like her legs.

SUZANNE: Oh Lord, it's such a shame! Uncle says she can't even hear or understand any more. He says it would be a Godsend for her mind to go completely.

THÉRÈSE: He's wrong. She can hear and understand everything. Her intelligence is still lucid and her eyes are alive.

SUZANNE: Yes, they seem to have got bigger; they are quite enormous now. They look so black and terrible in her dead face. I'm not easily scared as a rule, but during the night when I think of the poor lady I start to shake all over. You know those stories of people being buried alive? I imagine that she has been buried alive and that she is lying there at the bottom of a ditch with a ton of soil weighing on her chest preventing her from shouting out … What can she think about all day long? It's awful to be like that and yet to think all the time, *all* the time … But you are both so good to her!

THÉRÈSE: We are only doing our duty.

SUZANNE: And you are the only one who can understand what she's saying with her eyes, aren't you? I can't under-

stand her at all. Monsieur Grivet prides himself on being able to interpret her slightest wish, yet he always replies at cross-purposes. She's so lucky that she's got you by her; she doesn't want for anything. Uncle's forever saying, 'The Raquins, that's a house of God.' Your happiness will come back, you'll see. Has the doctor given her any hope?

THÉRÈSE: Very little.

SUZANNE: I was here last time he came and he said the poor lady might possibly recover her voice and the use of her limbs.

THÉRÈSE: We mustn't count on it. We daren't count on it.

SUZANNE: Oh, but you must, you must have hope. (*They have finished laying the table and move downstage.*) And where's Monsieur Laurent? We hardly see him nowadays.

THÉRÈSE: Since he stopped working at the office and took up painting again, he leaves first thing in the morning and doesn't get home until the evening. He's working very hard – on a large painting that he wants to send to the next Salon.

SUZANNE: Monsieur Laurent has changed into a real gentleman. He no longer laughs too loud, he looks so distinguished. I never used to think I would like him as a husband, whereas now he would be just right … If you promise not to tell anyone, I'll tell you a secret …

THÉRÈSE: I'm hardly a gossip, you know.

SUZANNE: That's true, you keep everything to yourself. Then let me tell you that yesterday we were passing your husband's studio in the rue Mazarin, when Uncle suddenly had the idea of paying him a visit. Monsieur Laurent hates being disturbed, as you know, but he made us quite welcome … you'll never guess what he's working on.

THÉRÈSE: He's working on a big painting.

SUZANNE: No, the canvas for the big painting is still all white. We found him surrounded by lots of little canvases on which he had done rough sketches, children's heads, women's faces, old men … Uncle was most impressed; he claims that all of a sudden your husband has become a great painter; and he can't just be flattering him, because he always used to be so critical of his work. What I noticed was that all the faces seemed to resemble each other. They looked like …

THÉRÈSE: Who did they look like?

SUZANNE: I don't want to upset you … They all looked like poor Monsieur Camille.

THÉRÈSE: (*Shaking.*) Oh no … You must have imagined it.

SUZANNE: No, I assure you. All the children, women, old men, they have all got something that reminded me of the person I've just mentioned. My uncle thought they needed more colour, they are so pale. And they've all got a smile in the corner of their mouth.

We hear LAURENT at the door.

Ah! Here's your husband. Don't say anything. I think he wants to give you a surprise with all those faces.

Scene 2

LAURENT, SUZANNE, THÉRÈSE

LAURENT: Good evening, Suzanne. Have you both been working hard?

THÉRÈSE: Yes.

LAURENT: I am exhausted. (*He sinks wearily into a chair.*)

SUZANNE: It must be tiring having to stand up to paint, all day long.

LAURENT: I didn't do any work today. I walked as far as Saint-Cloud and then back again. Walking does me so much good ... Thérèse, is the supper ready?

THÉRÈSE: Yes.

SUZANNE: I must go.

THÉRÈSE: Your uncle promised to fetch you; you must wait. You are not disturbing us.

SUZANNE: Well, then, I'll go down to the shop; I want to steal some tapestry needles.

As she is about to go down, the bell rings.

Why, a customer! Well, then, she will be served. (*She goes down.*)

Scene 3

LAURENT, THÉRÈSE

LAURENT: (*Pointing to the mattress left at the foot of the bed.*) Why didn't you hide the mattress? The idiots don't need to know that we sleep in separate beds. (*He gets up.*)

THÉRÈSE: You hide it. I do what I like.

LAURENT: (*Roughly.*) Woman, let's not start quarrelling. It's not night-time yet.

THÉRÈSE: Huh! So much the better for you if you can amuse yourself out of doors, if you can wear yourself out walking all day long. I'm fine when you are not there. As soon as you come back, all hell opens up ... At least let me rest during the daytime since we don't sleep at night.

LAURENT: (*In a more gentle tone.*) Your voice is even more harsh than mine, Thérèse.

THÉRÈSE: (*After a silence.*) Are you going to bring in my aunt for supper? No, you'd better wait until the Michauds have gone; I'm always afraid when she is here when they are. For a while now I've seen an unrelenting thought in her eyes. She will find some way of talking, you'll see.

LAURENT: Bah! I get more afraid when he goes to her room. Michaud is bound to want to see his old friend. What on earth could she tell him? She can't even lift a finger. (*He goes out of door to MME RAQUIN's bedroom.*)

Scene 4

THÉRÈSE, MICHAUD, SUZANNE, then LAURENT and MME RAQUIN in a chair, rigid and silent, white hair, dressed in black

MICHAUD: Oh! The table is laid.

THÉRÈSE: Why, of course, Monsieur Michaud.

MICHAUD: So you are still living well, I see. These lovers have got a devilish appetite ... On with your hat, Suzanne ... (*Looking sad.*) And where is our good Mme Raquin?

LAURENT comes in, pushing MME RAQUIN. He sits her at the table to her laid place.

Ah, here she is, the old girl. Her eyes are shining – she is happy to see us. (*To MME RAQUIN.*) We two are old friends, aren't we ...? Do you remember when I was Police Superintendent? I believe we first met at the time of the Wolf's Throat murder. You must remember, this woman and this man who had murdered a haulier, and I myself had to go and arrest them in their hovel. Damn it, they were guillotined at Rouen.

Scene 5

THÉRÈSE, LAURENT, MICHAUD, SUZANNE, MME RAQUIN, GRIVET

GRIVET: (*Who has heard MICHAUD's last few words.*) Ah! You're telling the story of the haulier; yes, I know that one. You told me that one, and I found it greatly interesting ... Monsieur Michaud has a nose for sniffing out criminals. Good evening to you, one and all.

MICHAUD: And what are you doing here at this time, Monsieur Grivet?

GRIVET: Well, I was passing, and I thought I'd treat myself to a little debauchery; I've come for a chat with dear Mme Raquin. Oh! Were you about to sit down to eat, I hope I'm not disturbing you?

LAURENT: Not in the least.

GRIVET: It's just that we understand each other so well. A single glance and I know exactly what she means.

MICHAUD: Then, you'd better tell me what she means by staring at me all the time.

GRIVET: Wait, I can read her eyes like a book. (*He sits in front of MME RAQUIN.*) Now, let's chat like old friends ... Have you got something you want to ask Monsieur Michaud? No? Nothing at all, just as I thought. (*To MICHAUD.*) You are making yourself out to be so important. She doesn't need you, you understand, it's me she wants to talk to. (*Turning back to MME RAQUIN.*) Now, what did you say? Yes, yes, I understand; you are hungry.

SUZANNE: (*Leaning against the back of the chair.*) Would you prefer if we left, dear Madame?

GRIVET: Gracious me! She *is* hungry ... And she is inviting me to stay for a game this evening ... A thousand pardons, Mme Raquin, but I can't accept, you know my little habits. But on Thursday, yes, I promise.

MICHAUD: Tut. She didn't say anything at all, Monsieur Grivet. Where do you get that idea from? Let me question her.

LAURENT: (*To THÉRÈSE, who has got up.*) Keep an eye on your aunt. You were right, she's got a terrible glint in her eye.

MICHAUD: Let's see, old girl, you know I am at your command. Why are you looking at me in this way? If only you could find a way of telling me what you want.

SUZANNE: You see what Uncle is saying, your every wish is sacred to us.

GRIVET: Hah. I've already explained what she wants – it's obvious.

MICHAUD: (*Insisting.*) You can't make yourself understood, can you, old girl. (*To* LAURENT, *who has come to the table.*) Laurent, look, how strangely she is continually staring at me.

LAURENT: No, I can't see anything special in her eyes.

SUZANNE: What about you, Thérèse, you can understand her slightest whim?

MICHAUD: Yes, please help us. Ask her for us.

THÉRÈSE: You are mistaken. She doesn't want anything, she always looks like that. (*She comes over and leans on the table opposite* MME RAQUIN, *but cannot stand to look her in the eyes.*) That's right, isn't it? You don't want anything …? No, nothing, I assure you. (*She moves away.*)

MICHAUD: Well, then, perhaps Monsieur Grivet was right.

GRIVET: Please yourselves, damn you. But I know what she says; she is hungry and she invites me to stay for a game.

LAURENT: Why don't you accept, Monsieur Michaud, you are more than welcome.

MICHAUD: Thank you, but I am busy this evening.

THÉRÈSE: (*Quietly, to* LAURENT.) For pity's sake, don't keep them here a moment longer.

MICHAUD: Goodbye, my friends. (*He is about to go.*)

GRIVET: Oh yes, goodnight, goodnight. (*He gets up and follows* MICHAUD.)

SUZANNE: (*Goes to kiss* MME RAQUIN.) Ah! Look! Her fingers are moving!

MICHAUD *and* GRIVET *let out a shout of surprise and cross over to* MME RAQUIN.

THÉRÈSE: (*Quietly to* LAURENT.) Oh God! She has made a superhuman effort. This is the punishment! (*They huddle together.*)

MICHAUD: (*To* MME RAQUIN.) Why, you are like a little girl again. Look at your fingers dancing the gavotte now.

A silence, during which MME RAQUIN *continues to move her fingers, with her eyes rooted on* THÉRÈSE *and* LAURENT.

GRIVET: Oho! We've become a proper little wanderer, haven't we, with our hands roving all over the place!

THÉRÈSE: (*Quietly.*) Great God, she is reviving – the stone statue is coming back to life.

LAURENT: (*Quietly.*) Be strong. Hands can't talk.

SUZANNE: It's as if she's making shapes on the tablecloth.

GRIVET: Yes, what is she doing?

MICHAUD: Can't you see? She is writing. That's a capital T.

THÉRÈSE: (*Quietly.*) Hands do talk, Laurent!

GRIVET: By God, it's true, she is writing. (*To* MME RAQUIN.) Take it gently and I will try to follow you. (*After a silence.*) No, start again, I lost you there. (*After another silence.*) It's incredible, I read: T.H.R.E.E.S. Threes! She undoubtedly wants me to stay for a game!

SUZANNE: No, Monsieur Grivet she has written the name of my dear friend, Thérèse.

MICHAUD: Really, Monsieur Grivet, can't you even read? (*Reading.*) 'Thérèse and.' Continue, Mme Raquin.

LAURENT: (*To* THÉRÈSE.) Revenging hand, hand once dead coming out of the coffin, each finger becoming a mouth. She shall not finish! (*He goes to take a knife from his pocket.*)

THÉRÈSE: (*Holding him back.*) For pity's sake, you will betray us!

MICHAUD: It's perfect, I understand, 'Thérèse and Laurent.' She is writing your names, my friends.

GRIVET: Both your names, upon my honour. It's incredible.

MICHAUD: (*Reading.*) 'Thérèse and Laurent have.' Have what? What do they have, these two dear children?

GRIVET: Oh! She's stopped … keep going, keep going.

MICHAUD: Finish the sentence, just a little effort …

MME RAQUIN *looks at* THÉRÈSE *and* LAURENT *for a long-held stare.*

Yes, we all want to know the end of the sentence.

She remains a moment motionless, enjoying the terror of the two murderers, then her hand falls.

Oh! She's let her hand drop, damn it.

SUZANNE: (*Touching the hand.*) It is stuck to her knee again like a hand of stone.

THÉRÈSE: I thought I saw our punishment. The hand is silent now. We are saved.

LAURENT: Don't fall. Lean on me. I thought I was choking.

The three gather round MME RAQUIN's *chair.*

GRIVET: It's too annoying that she didn't finish the sentence.

MICHAUD: Yes, I was following perfectly. What can she have wanted to say?

SUZANNE: That she is grateful for the care that Thérèse and Laurent heap upon her.

MICHAUD: This little one is brighter than we are. 'Thérèse and Laurent have all my blessings.' Of course, damn it, there's the finished sentence. That's right, isn't it, Mme Raquin, you are doing them justice. (*To* THÉRÈSE *and* LAURENT.) You are two courageous souls, you deserve a good reward, in this world or the next.

LAURENT: You would do as we do.

GRIVET: They are already rewarded. Do you know that in this district they are known as the turtle doves?

MICHAUD: Ah, and it was *we* who married them … Are you coming Monsieur Grivet? We must let them get on with their supper, after all. (*Coming back to* MME RAQUIN.) Have patience, old girl. Your little hands will come back to life, and your legs too. It's a good sign to have been able to move your fingers just a little; your recovery is near at hand. Goodbye. (*He leaves.*)

SUZANNE: (*To* THÉRÈSE.) Till tomorrow, good friend. (*She leaves.*)

GRIVET: (*To* MME RAQUIN.) There, I said we understood

each other perfectly. Take courage, we will start up our Thursday dominoes again, and we will beat Monsieur Michaud between the two of us; yes, we will thrash him. (*On his way out, to* THÉRÈSE *and* LAURENT.) Goodbye, turtle doves, you are two turtle doves.

As MICHAUD, SUZANNE *and* GRIVET *leave by the spiral staircase,* THÉRÈSE *goes out of the upstage door and returns with the soup.*

Scene 6

THÉRÈSE, LAURENT, MME RAQUIN

During this scene, MME RAQUIN's *face reflects the emotions that she is feeling: anger, horror, and joy, total revenge. Her burning eyes hound the murderers, sharing their outbursts and sobs.*

LAURENT: She would have given us up.

THÉRÈSE: Shut up, leave her alone. (*She serves the soup.*)

LAURENT: (*Sitting at the table upstage.*) Do you think she would spare us if she could speak? Michaud and Grivet had a peculiar smile on their faces when they were talking about our happiness. They'll end up knowing everything, you'll see. Grivet put his hat on to one side, didn't he?

THÉRÈSE: (*Putting down the soup tureen.*) Yes, I believe so.

LAURENT: He buttoned his frock-coat and he put a hand into his pocket on his way out. At the office he always used to button his frock-coat like that when he wanted to look important. And the way he said, 'Goodbye, turtle doves.' The imbecile.

THÉRÈSE: (*Coming back.*) Be quiet; don't make it worse than it already is.

LAURENT: When he twists his mouth in that stupid manner, you know, it must be to laugh at us. I don't trust these people who play the fool ... They know everything, I assure you.

THÉRÈSE: They are too innocent ... It would be one end, if they gave us up; but they see nothing, they will continue to traipse through our pitiful lives with their oblivious bourgeois tread. (*She sits at the table.*) Let us talk about something else. You must be mad to raise the subject when she is still here.

LAURENT: I haven't got a spoon.

THÉRÈSE goes and fetches a spoon from the sideboard, gives it to LAURENT *and sits.*

Are you not going to feed her?

THÉRÈSE: Yes, when I've finished my soup.

LAURENT: (*Tasting the soup.*) Your soup is dreadful, it's too salty. (*He pushes it away.*) It's one of your wicked tricks. You know I hate salt.

THÉRÈSE: Laurent, please don't pick an argument with me. I am very tired. The tension just now has left me shattered.

LAURENT: Yes, make yourself listless ... you torture me with your petty annoyances.

THÉRÈSE: You want us to have a quarrel, don't you?

LAURENT: I 'want' you to stop talking to me in that tone of voice.

THÉRÈSE: Oh really! (*In a rough voice, pushing away her plate.*) Very well, just as you please, we will not eat any more this evening, we will tear each other apart, and my aunt can listen. It's a treat we give her every day now.

LAURENT: Do you calculate the blows you give me? Why, you spy on me, you try to touch my open wounds and then you are happy when the pain drives me mad.

THÉRÈSE: It wasn't me who found the soup too salty! Here we go! The most ridiculous pretext is enough, isn't it! You just want to argue all evening, to dull your nerves so that you can sleep a little during the night.

LAURENT: You don't sleep any more than I do.

THÉRÈSE: Oh, you have made my whole existence appalling. As soon as night falls, we begin to shake. You know who is there, between us. Oh, what torture it is in this room!

LAURENT: It's your fault.

THÉRÈSE: My fault! Is it my fault if, instead of the rich life you dreamt of, all you have created is fear and disgust?

LAURENT: Yes, it's your fault.

THÉRÈSE: Stop it! I am not an idiot! Don't think I don't know you. You've always been a calculating thing. When you took me as your mistress, it was because I didn't cost anything ... You don't even dare deny it ... Oh, don't you see, I hate you!

LAURENT: Who's looking for a quarrel now, me or you?

THÉRÈSE: I hate you. You killed Camille!

LAURENT: (*Gets up and sits down again.*) Be quiet! (*Pointing to* MME RAQUIN.) A moment ago, you told me to be silent in front of her. Do not force me to recall the facts, to tell the truth all over again in her presence.

THÉRÈSE: Oh, let her hear, let her suffer! Haven't I suffered? The *truth* is that you killed Camille.

LAURENT: You're lying, admit that you are lying ... If I threw him into the river, it was because you pushed me into the murder.

THÉRÈSE: Me? Me?

LAURENT: Yes, you. Don't play the innocent, don't make me drag it from you by force ... I need you to confess to your crime, I need you to accept your share of the guilt. That gives me relief and calms me.

THÉRÈSE: But it wasn't I who killed Camille.

LAURENT: Yes it was, a thousand times yes! You were on the bank, and I said to you quietly, 'I am going to throw him into the river.' You consented, you got into the boat ... You see very well that you killed him with me.

THÉRÈSE: That's not true ... I was mad, I don't know what I did any more. I never wanted to kill him.

LAURENT: And, in the middle of the Seine, when I capsized the boat, didn't I warn you? You grabbed onto my neck. You left him to drown *like a dog.*

THÉRÈSE: It is not true, you killed him!

LAURENT: And, in the cab on the way back, didn't you put your hand into mine? Your hand fired my heart.

THÉRÈSE: *You* killed him.

LAURENT: (*To* MME RAQUIN.) She doesn't remember. She's deliberately not remembering. (*To* THÉRÈSE.) You intoxicated me with your caresses, here, in this room. You pushed me against your husband, you wanted to get rid of him. He didn't please you, he used to shiver with fever, you said. Three years ago was I like this? Was I a wretch then? I used to be an upright gentleman, I didn't do any harm to anyone ... I wouldn't have even crushed a fly.

THÉRÈSE: *You* killed him!

LAURENT: Twice you turned me into a cruel brute ... I used to be prudent and peaceful. And look at me now, I tremble at the least shadow like an easily frightened child. My nerves are just as wretched as yours. You have led me to adultery, to murder, without my even noticing. Now when I look back, I remain stupefied by what I have done. In my dreams I see policemen, the court, the guillotine, pass before my eyes. (*He rises.*) You play the innocent in vain – at night your teeth chatter with terror. You know very well that if the ghost were to come, he would strangle you first.

THÉRÈSE: (*Getting up.*) Don't say that. You killed him. (*Both standing at the table.*)

LAURENT: Listen, it is cowardly to refuse your share of the crime. You want to make my guilt the heavier, don't you? Since you push me to the edge, I prefer to make an end of it. You see, I am quite calm. (*He takes his hat.*) I am going to tell the whole story to the Police Superintendent for the area.

THÉRÈSE: (*Jeering.*) What a good idea!

LAURENT: We will *both* be arrested, we will soon see what the judge thinks of your innocence.

THÉRÈSE: Do you think you can scare me? I am more weary than you. I am the one who will go to the magistrate, if you don't.

LAURENT: I don't need you to accompany me – I will be able to tell them everything myself.

THÉRÈSE: Oh no, every time we quarrel, when you run out of reasons, you always bring up this threat. Well, today I want it to be serious. I am not a coward, like you. I am ready to follow you to the scaffold. Come on, let's go, I'll come with you. (*She goes with him as far as the spiral staircase.*)

LAURENT: (*Stammering.*) As you wish, we'll go together to the police.

He goes down – THÉRÈSE *remains immobile, listening; she is gradually seized by a fit of shaking and terror –* MME RAQUIN *turns her head, her face lit up by a fierce smile.*

THÉRÈSE: He's gone down. He's still down there. Will he have the courage to give us up? ... I don't want that, I will run after him, grab his arm and bring him back ... And what if he shouts out the whole story in the street. Oh, my God, I was wrong to push him to the limit. I should

have been more reasonable ... (*Listening.*) He's stopped in the shop, the bell hasn't rung. What can he be doing? He's coming back up, oh I can hear him coming back up the stairs. I knew he was too much of a coward. (*Suddenly.*) The coward! Coward!

LAURENT: (*Coming in, sits down. He is broken, head in his hands.*) I can't, I can't.

THÉRÈSE: (*In a mocking tone.*) Oh! Back already, are you? What did they say? Oh, how I pity you, you have no blood in your veins.

LAURENT: (*In a lower voice.*) I can't.

THÉRÈSE: You ought to be helping me to carry the terrible memory, but you are feebler than I am ... How can you ask us to forget?

LAURENT: So you accept your part of the crime now, do you?

THÉRÈSE: Yes. I am guilty. If you like, I am more guilty than you. I should have saved my husband from your clutches. Camille was so good.

LAURENT: Let's not start again, I beg you. How you revel when you have driven me frantic. Don't look at me. Stop smiling. I will escape from you when I wish to. (*He takes out a little bottle from his pocket.*) Here is the remission, here is the peaceful sleep. Two drops of prussic acid will be enough.

THÉRÈSE: Poison! Oh no, you are too cowardly. I dare you to drink it. Drink, go on, Laurent, drink just a little, to see ...

LAURENT: Be quiet. Don't push me any further.

THÉRÈSE: I am calm, you won't drink it ... Camille was good, do you hear, and I wish you were in his place in the ground.

LAURENT: Be quiet!

THÉRÈSE: Why, you don't know a woman's heart. How can you expect me not to hate you, drenched as you are in Camille's blood?

LAURENT: (*Pacing back and forth, as if hallucinating.*) Will you be quiet! I can hear something hammering in my head. It will shatter my skull ... What is this infernal game of yours, to have regrets now, to weep louder and louder? I am living with him all the time now. He did this, he did that, he was good, he was generous. Oh, misery! I am going mad ... He is living with us. He sits on my chair, he sits at the table next to me, uses our furniture. He used to eat off my plate, he's still eating off it. I don't know any more, I am him, I am Camille ... I've got his wife, I've got his place at table, I've got his sheets. I am Camille, Camille, Camille!

THÉRÈSE: It's a cruel game *you're* playing putting his face in all your paintings.

LAURENT: Oh, so you know that, do you? (*Lowering his voice.*) Talk softer, it's terrible, my hands are no longer my own. I can't even paint any more, it's always his face that takes shape under my hand. No, these hands are no longer mine. They will kill me in the end, if I don't cut them off. They are his hands, he has taken them from me.

THÉRÈSE: It's the punishment.

LAURENT: Tell me I haven't got Camille's mouth. (*He kisses her.*) Look, did you hear that? I pronounced that phrase just as Camille would have done. Listen, 'I've got his mouth. I've got his mouth.' That's it, isn't it? I talk like him, I laugh like him. He is always there, in my head, punching with his clenched fists.

THÉRÈSE: It is the punishment.

LAURENT: (*Violently.*) Go away woman, you are driving me mad. Go away, or I'll ... (*He throws her to the ground in front of the table and raises his foot.*)

THÉRÈSE: (*On the ground.*) Kill me, like the other, make an end of it all ... Camille never laid a hand on me. You, you are a monster ... But kill me, like the other!

LAURENT, demented, backs away and breaks upstage. He sits down, his head in his hands. Meanwhile, MME RAQUIN manages to push a knife off the table, which lands in front of THÉRÈSE. THÉRÈSE slowly turns her head at this noise: she looks in turn at MME RAQUIN and at the knife.

You pushed it and made it fall. Your eyes are burning like two hell-holes. I know what you are saying. You are right, this man is making my existence intolerable. If he wasn't always there, reminding me of what I long to forget, I would be peaceful, I would work out a gentle life for myself. (*To MME RAQUIN, as she picks up the knife.*) You're looking at the knife, aren't you? Yes. I am holding the knife and I don't want this man to torture me any longer ... He killed Camille, who was in his way ... He is in my way! (*She gets up, with the knife in her fist.*)

LAURENT: (*Who gets up, hiding the bottle of poison in his hand.*) Let us make peace, let us finish our meal, shall we?

THÉRÈSE: If you like. (*To herself.*) I will never be patient enough to wait till night. The knife is burning my hand.

LAURENT: What are you thinking about? Sit down at the table ... Wait, I will serve you with something to drink. (*He pours some water into a glass.*)

THÉRÈSE: Better to end it all now. (*She approaches with the knife raised. But she sees LAURENT pour the poison into the glass.*) What are you pouring into it, Laurent?

LAURENT: (*Likewise sees the knife.*) Why are you raising your arm?

A silence.

Drop the knife!

THÉRÈSE: Drop the poison.

They look at each other with a terrible stare: then they let the bottle and knife drop.

LAURENT: At the same moment, in each mind, the same thought, the horrible thought.

THÉRÈSE: Remember how we adored each other with such passionate kisses, Laurent? And here we are, face to face, with poison and a knife. (*She glances towards MME RAQUIN and shrieks with shock.*) Laurent, look!

LAURENT: (*Getting up and turning towards MME RAQUIN with terror.*) She was there, waiting to watch us die!

THÉRÈSE: But can't you see her lips are moving? She is smiling ... Oh, what a terrible smile!

LAURENT: She's coming back to life.

THÉRÈSE: She's going to speak, I tell you, she's going to speak!

LAURENT: I know how to stop her. (*He goes to leap on MME RAQUIN when she slowly rises to her feet. He staggers back, reeling.*)

MME RAQUIN: (*Standing up, in a low, deep voice.*) Murderer of the child, dare to strike the mother!

THÉRÈSE: Oh mercy! Don't hand us over to the police.

MME RAQUIN: Hand you over! No, no ... I thought of it, just now when I regained my strength. I began to write your act of indictment on the table. But I stopped myself; I thought that human justice would be too quick. And I want to watch your slow death, here in this room, where you stole from me all my happiness.

THÉRÈSE: (*Sobbing, throwing herself at MME RAQUIN's feet.*) Forgive me ... My fears are suffocating me ... I am a miserable wretch ... If you wish to raise your foot, I will deliver up my head, on the floor – here, so that you can crush it ... Pity ... have pity!

MME RAQUIN: (*Leaning on the table.*) Pity? Did you have any for the poor child I adored? Don't ask for pity. I have no more pity. You have torn out my heart.

LAURENT falls to his knees.

I will not save you from each other. May your remorse make you lash out at each other like enraged beasts. I shall not give you up to justice. You are mine, only mine, and I am watching over you.

THÉRÈSE: It is too much not to be punished ... We will judge each other, and we will condemn each other.

She picks up the bottle of prussic acid, drinks greedily and falls to the ground at MME RAQUIN's feet. LAURENT, who has seized the bottle, also drinks and falls.

MME RAQUIN stands over them, watching.

MME RAQUIN: Dead. They're dead.

1.2 MISS JULIE (1888)

AUGUST STRINDBERG

In a new version by Frank McGuinness (from a literal translation by Charlotte Barslund)

August Strindberg (1849–1912) wrote Miss Julie in 1888. It was quickly identified as one of the first plays which embraced the principles of Naturalism and showed how they could be manifested in theatre. Miss Julie has since become part of the canon of modernist plays, though it was originally banned or refused performances in a number of countries, including Strindberg's homeland of Sweden, where it had to wait eighteen years for its first professional production. André Antoine mounted a celebrated production of the play at the Théâtre Libre in 1893 and it was often performed and adapted for the stage in Europe and America during the twentieth century. The play raises issues of gender, sexual politics and class relevant to the emancipatory era for which it was originally written, but which have a resonance still. The version printed here is by Frank McGuinness and was commissioned for a production at Theatre Royal, Haymarket in London in 2000, directed by Michael Boyd.

Characters

MISS JULIE
JEAN
KRISTIN

The stage

A large kitchen whose ceilings and side walls are hidden by drapes and borders. The back wall stretches in up from stage left. On the same wall there are shelves with copper, cast-iron and pewter pots. The shelves are decorated with embossed paper. Stage right three-quarters of a large arched exit is visible with two glass doors. Through them there is a fountain with a cupid, and flowering lilac bushes and tall upright poplars can be seen. The corner and some of the hood of a large tiled stove can be seen stage left. At stage right one end of the servants' white-painted pine dinner table stands surrounded by some chairs. The stove is decorated with leafy birch twigs. The floor is strewn with juniper twigs. On the end of the table there is a large Japanese spice jar with lilacs in bloom. There is an ice-box, a draining board and a sink. Above the door there is a large, old-fashioned bell, and on its left side there is a fixed speaking tube. Frying something in a pan, Kristin stands by the stove. She wears a light-coloured cotton dress and an apron. Jean enters, dressed in livery. He carries a large pair of riding boots with spurs. He places them somewhere visible on the floor.

JEAN: Off her head. The mistress. Julie. She's off her head, tonight.

KRISTIN: So – he's here now?

JEAN: The Count – I took his Lordship to the station. I come back, I'm going past the barn, I walk into the dance. What do I see? Miss Julie, dancing with the gamekeeper. She's leading. Then she catches sight of me. She runs full into my arms. She asks me to dance. She starts to waltz – never seen the like of it. She's off her head.

KRISTIN: She always was, but she's been worse the past two weeks since her engagement's been called off.

JEAN: What was the story there? Tell me that. He might not have had money but he had standing. People like that – if it's not one thing, it's something else. (*He sits down at the end of the table.*) I for one find it strange that a lady would rather stay at home with their servants than go off with her father to see her relatives. It's Midsummer Eve.

Figure 4 The first production in Stockholm of *Miss Julie* in November 1906, at The People's Theatre.

KRISTIN: Maybe she can't face people after the bother with her fiancé.

JEAN: Maybe. But at least he was his own man. Do you know what happened, Kristin? Do you know that I saw it all – though I pretended I saw nothing.

KRISTIN: You saw it?

JEAN: I did – I certainly did. The stable yard one evening, the two of them, Miss Julie putting him through his paces, that's what she called it. Do you know what happened? She had her riding whip and she made him leap over it. Like a dog. He leapt twice, and he felt the touch of the whip from her hand. Then he let her have it across the left cheek, he smashed the whip into a thousand pieces, and departed from the scene.

KRISTIN: That's what happened, is it? No. Just as you say?

JEAN: That's it exactly. Now come on, Kristin, have you anything nice for me?

She takes something from the frying pan and sets the table for JEAN.

KRISTIN: A bit of kidney, that's all. I cut it off the roast veal.

JEAN smells the food.

JEAN: Excellent. Delicious – a great *délice*. (*He touches the plate.*) You could have warmed the plate.

KRISTIN: Listen to him – more fussy than the Count himself when he sits down to eat.

She runs her hands affectionately through his hair. He responds crossly.

JEAN: Don't touch me. I'm a sensitive man, you know that.

KRISTIN: It's only because I'm mad about you and you know that.

JEAN eats and KRISTIN opens a bottle of beer.

JEAN: Beer? On Midsummer Eve? I think not, thank you. I can do something better for myself. (*He opens a drawer and takes out a bottle of red wine with yellow sealing wax on the cork.*) Look – yellow sealing wax. A glass if you please. One with a stem – this you drink *pur*.

KRISTIN returns to the stove and puts a small pot on it.

KRISTIN: God help the one who gets him for a husband. Such a fuss he makes.

JEAN: Is that so? I'd put money on you being delighted to land a strapping man like myself. I imagine you don't lose much face when people call me your intended. (*He tastes the wine.*) Good. Very good. Temperature not quite perfect though. (*He heats the glass in his hand.*) Dijon – that's where we bought this. Without the bottle it set us back four francs a litre. There's duty on top of that. What are you cooking now? It stinks like hell.

KRISTIN: Some dirty feed Miss Julie wants for her bitch, Diana.

JEAN: Kristin, would you please express yourself in a more ladylike manner? And why are you standing here sweating for that dog on Midsummer Eve? Is she not well?

KRISTIN: She's not well. She smelt out the gamekeeper's dog. Now she has a pack of pups inside her. Miss Julie wants rid of them.

JEAN: Miss Julie gets on her high horse about one thing and doesn't give a tinker's curse about another. Just like her dead mother, the Countess. She was in her element in the kitchen and the barn, but she'd go nowhere with just the one horse. Her cuffs might need washing, but every button had to bear the coat of arms. As for Miss Julie, she does not give a damn about herself and her reputation. She was leaping about the barn at the dance and she tore the gamekeeper from Anna's arms, she wanted to dance with him. We'd never do a thing like that. That's what happens when the gentry demean themselves. That's when they fall. Still, she is a grand looking woman. Magnificent. The shoulder on her! And everything else.

KRISTIN: Take it easy, will you? I know what Klara says, and she dresses her.

JEAN: Klara be damned. You women would eat each other out of jealousy. I've been out riding with her – and the way she dances.

KRISTIN: Jean – will you dance with me when I'm finished?

JEAN: I will, of course, yes.

KRISTIN: Is that a promise?

JEAN: Promise? When I say I will, then I will. The dinner was lovely, thank you.

He puts the cork in the bottle. MISS JULIE, *in the doorway, speaks offstage.*

JULIE: I will soon return. Carry on – carry on.

JEAN hides the bottle in the drawer. He gets up respectfully. MISS JULIE *enters and goes to* KRISTIN *at the stove.*

JULIE: Have you finished it?

KRISTIN indicates JEAN's *presence.* JEAN *asks gallantly:*

JEAN: Are the ladies conversing in secrets?

MISS JULIE hits him in the face with her handkerchief.

JULIE: Nosy-nosy.

JEAN: The beautiful smell of violets.

MISS JULIE flirts back.

JULIE: Impudent. He knows all about perfumes too. He certainly knows how to dance. Do not peep – just go away.

JEAN replies with a mixture of cheek and respect:

JEAN: Are the ladies brewing some witch's spell especially for Midsummer Eve? Will someone be telling fortunes? Will the stars show the man you'll marry?

MISS JULIE concludes sharply:

JULIE: If you can see that, then you must have extraordinary eyesight. (*She turns to Kristin.*) Throw that in a bottle, cork it tightly. Now, Jean, come and dance with me.

JEAN is reluctant.

JEAN: I don't wish to be disrespectful, but I promised this dance to Kristin.

JULIE: She can have another, can't she? What do you say, Kristin? May I borrow Jean? Will you let me?

KRISTIN: Not for me to say. If Miss Julie lowers herself to him, he could hardly say no. Let him go. He should thank her for the honour.

JEAN: I honestly want to cause no offence, but I doubt if it's wise that Miss Julie should have the same partner twice in a row. People soon get the wrong notion in these cases –

MISS JULIE flares up:

JULIE: Cases – what is he talking about? What are these notions – explain.

JEAN is evasive.

JEAN: If Miss Julie doesn't care to follow me, then I will have to explain. It does not look well if you favour one servant above others – they might come to expect the same –

JULIE: Favour! The idea of it! I am shocked! I am mistress of this house. I honour the servants' dance with my presence. When I actually want to dance, I wish to do so with a partner who can lead. That way I do not look ridiculous.

JEAN: Miss Julie's word is my command.

MISS JULIE grows gentler.

JULIE: Not command – don't say that. We're happy tonight – celebrating – we've stripped away all the titles. Give me your arm, go on. Kristin, don't worry. I won't run away with your fiancé.

JEAN offers her his arm and escorts MISS JULIE off the stage.

PANTOMIME

This is acted as if the actress really is alone in the room. She turns her back to the audience. She doesn't look into the auditorium. There is the faint violin music of a Scottish reel. KRISTIN hums to the music as she clears up after JEAN. She washes the plate, dries it and puts it away in a cupboard. She takes off her cook's apron. She takes out a small mirror from a drawer in the table. She tilts it against the jar of lilacs. She lights a candle, heats a hairpin and curls her fringe. She goes to the door and listens. She returns again to the table. She finds MISS JULIE's handkerchief. She picks it up and smells it, spreads it out pensively, smoothes it, stretches it and folds it into four parts.

Jean enters on his own.

JEAN: Off her head – she really is. Dancing in that manner. People standing mocking her behind the doors. Well, Kristin, what do you say to that?

KRISTIN: She's not herself, it's her time of the month and then she's always strange. But what about yourself – will you dance with me now?

JEAN: I hope you're not cross because I left.

KRISTIN: I'm not. Very little to make me cross there. I do know my place.

JEAN puts his arms around her waist.

JEAN: Kristin, you're a sound girl and you'll make a sound wife.

MISS JULIE enters, is unpleasantly surprised and remarks with forced jollity:

JULIE: So you have abandoned your partner – how charming.

JEAN: Not so, Miss Julie. I've run back to the one I left behind.

MISS JULIE paces the floor.

JULIE: No one dances as well as you do, do you know that? Why are you wearing your uniform on Midsummer Eve? Take if off immediately.

JEAN: Then I must ask you, Mam, to excuse yourself – my black coat is hanging over there.

JULIE: Is he shy in front of me? Too shy to change a jacket? Run into your room and then toddle back. No, maybe you should stay and I won't peep.

JEAN: Whatever you wish, my lady.

He exits the stage right.

His arm is visible as he changes his jacket.

JULIE: Jean is so casual with you – is he really your fiancé?

KRISTIN: Fiancé? He is my intended, if you like. That's what we call it.

JULIE: Call it?

KRISTIN: Well, Miss Julie, yourself, had a fiancé and –

JULIE: That's true, but we were properly engaged –

KRISTIN: So properly the engagement ended.

JEAN enters wearing a black coat and black hat.

JULIE: *Très gentil, monsieur Jean, très gentil – très gentil.*

JEAN: *Vous voulez plaisanter, Madame.*

JULIE: *Et vous voulez parler français.* Where did you learn it?

JEAN: Switzerland. I was *sommelier* in one of the biggest hotels at Lucerne.

JULIE: In those clothes you look so like a gentleman. *Charmant.* (*She sits down at the table.*)

JEAN: You're flattering me.

MISS JULIE is hurt.

JULIE: I'm flattering you?

JEAN: I'm modest by nature. That modesty prevents me from imagining that you would utter truthful compliments to one in my position, so I must take the liberty of assuming that you have exaggerated – you have indulged in flattery.

JULIE: Where did you learn such phraseology? You must have gone to the theatre often.

JEAN: I have indeed. I have been in many theatres – I have.

JULIE: Weren't you born here on the estate?

JEAN: My father worked as a labourer on the next-door estate – the Attorney's. I used to see Miss Julie when she was a child, but Miss Julie did not notice me.

JULIE: No – is that so?

JEAN: Yes, that's so, I remember very clearly once – no, I can't speak about that.

JULIE: You can, you can, just for me. Make one exception.

JEAN: I can't really. Perhaps another time.

JULIE: Another time may never arrive. What's the danger in telling me now?

JEAN: No danger – I just don't want to. Look at that one.

He points to KRISTIN who has fallen asleep in a chair by the stove.

JULIE: That one will make the most divine wife – she will. Does she snore as well, perhaps?

JEAN: She doesn't – she does talk in her sleep though.

MISS JULIE asks cynically:

JULIE: She talks in her sleep – how do you know?

He replies cheekily:

JEAN: I've heard her.

There is a pause and they watch each other.

JULIE: Sit down – won't you?

JEAN: In your presence I am now allowed to sit?

JULIE: If I command you?

JEAN: I'll obey.

JULIE: Sit down – no, wait. Fetch me something to drink first.

JEAN: I don't know if we have anything cold. Beer – that's all – I think.

JULIE: That's all right. I have simple tastes. Beer suits me more than wine.

He takes a bottle of beer from the ice-box. He looks in the cupboard for a glass and plate. He serves her.

Thank you. Have one yourself – go on.

JEAN: I'm not a beer man. But if Miss Julie commands –

JULIE: Commands? My good sir, I believe it is manners to keep your lady company.

JEAN: That is absolutely true. (*He opens another bottle and takes a glass.*)

JULIE: Now – drink a toast to me.

He hesitates.

I do believe the poor boy is shy.

On his knees, parodying, he raises his glass.

JEAN: Oh mistress mine!

JULIE: Bravo! Kiss my shoe – now – you have to – then it is finished.

He hesitates, but then grasps her foot gamely and kisses it lightly.

Excellent. You should have been an actor.

He gets up.

JEAN: This is not right, Miss Julie. What if someone came in and saw us –

JULIE: What if?

JEAN: People gossip. That's what if. If Miss Julie knew how their tongues were wagging up there just now –

JULIE: What were they saying? Talking about me? Sit down.

He sits down.

JEAN: I don't want to insult you – there were statements made that cast aspersions of the kind that – you know yourself. You're not a child. They see a lady on her own drinking at night with a man, even a servant, then –

JULIE: What then? Anyway, we're not on our own. Kristin, she's here.

JEAN: She's dead to the world.

She rises.

JULIE: Kristin? Are you sleeping?

KRISTIN mumbles in her sleep.

Kristin? She has a gift for this. Sleeping.

KRISTIN mutters in her sleep.

KRISTIN: Boots – polish the Count's – coffee – hurry – make coffee – hurry.

MISS JULIE grabs KRISTIN's nose.

JULIE: Wake up.

JEAN answers her sternly:

JEAN: Don't disturb her sleep.

MISS JULIE reacts sharply:

JULIE: What?

JEAN: A woman slaving over a stove all day has the right to be tired at night-time. You should respect the sleep –

MISS JULIE is pacing the floor.

JULIE: A beautiful thought – it does him great credit. Thank you. (*She offers him her hand.*) Now gather some lilacs with me.

JEAN: With Miss Julie?

JULIE: Me!

JEAN: That is not right. Absolutely not.

JULIE: I don't follow your way of thinking. Have you imagined something and you believe it?

JEAN: I don't, but the servants will –

JULIE: Believe I'm in love with a servant?

JEAN: I'm not an arrogant man, but there have been cases, and the servants will say anything. Nothing is sacred.

JULIE: I do believe the man's an aristocrat.

JEAN: I am. Yes.

JULIE: I demean myself –

JEAN: Miss Julie, don't demean yourself. Listen to me. Not a living soul will believe you did it by choice. People will swear that you fell.

JULIE: I think more of people than you do. Go on – come on. (*She looks at him pleadingly.*)

JEAN: You're a strange being – do you know that?

JULIE: Am I? Are you? Yes. Everything is strange. Life itself. All of us. Everything. A mess, tossing and turning across the water and then it sinks – it sinks. I'm suddenly thinking of a dream I always have. I'm on top of a pillar. I've climbed up here, and I see no way of getting down, but I do not have the courage to throw myself. I want so much to fall, but I don't fall, and I'll have no peace until I come down, no rest until down I come, down to the field. And when I reach the field, I want to walk into the earth. Have you ever felt anything like that?

JEAN: No. When I dream, I'm lying beneath a big tree in a deep forest. I want to get up, right up to the top, I want to be able to see where the sun shines bright over the whole countryside. I want to rob the bird's nest and steal the golden eggs. I climb and I climb, but the tree trunk is thick, it's slippery, and the first branch is so far away. I do know that if I could only reach that first branch, then I could climb to the top – like stepping up a ladder. I've not reached it yet, I can't, but I will, even if I'm only dreaming.

JULIE: I'm standing talking to you about dreams – come on. To the fields.

She offers him her arm and they move to go.

JEAN: If we step on top of nine flowers tonight, Miss Julie, then our dreams will come true this Midsummer Night.

They go to the doorway. JEAN puts one hand up to his eye.

JULIE: What have you got in your eye? Let me see.

JEAN: Nothing. Just dirt. It'll pass.

JULIE: My dress – the sleeve has scratched you. Sit down, I'll help you.

She takes his arm and sits him down. She clasps his head and pulls it backwards. With the corner of her handkerchief she tries to clean his eye.

Sit still. Absolutely still. (*She slaps his hand.*) Do as I tell you. Now – now – a big strong boy – (*She feels his upper arm.*) Such strength.

JEAN warns her:

JEAN: Miss Julie –

KRISTIN wakes up and walks sleepily offstage right to lie down.

JULIE: Yes, monsieur Jean.

JEAN: *Attention. Je ne suis qu'un homme.*

JULIE: Sit still. Listen to me. Say thank you, kiss my hand.

JEAN: Miss Julie, listen to me. Kristin has gone to lie down. Listen to me – will you?

JULIE: First kiss my hand.

JEAN: Listen to me.

JULIE: First kiss my hand.

JEAN: Yes, but on your own head be it.

JULIE: Be what?

JEAN: You're twenty-five – are you still a child? Do you not know you can be burnt playing with fire?

JULIE: Not me – I'm insured.

JEAN: You are not – no. Even if you are, there is still dangerous fire around here.

JULIE: Are you referring to yourself?

JEAN: I am. I am a young man –

JULIE: Of beautiful appearance. What arrogance. Beyond belief. You are Don Juan, perhaps. Or Joseph. My God, I believe he is a Joseph.

JEAN: You believe that.

JULIE: I'm half frightened.

JEAN tries to put his arms around her and kiss her. She slaps him across the face.

JULIE: No.

JEAN: Are you playing or are you serious?

JULIE: Serious.

JEAN: You always are – even when you're playing. That's what's dangerous. Now I'm tired of playing. Give me permission to return to my work. The Count will need his boots on time, and it's well after midnight.

JULIE: Put the boots away.

JEAN: No. That's my job – I do it well, that's my duty. I've never imagined myself as your playmate, I never will be, I think too much of myself to be that.

JULIE: Proud, aren't you?

JEAN: Sometimes I am, other times I'm not.

JULIE: Have you ever known love?

JEAN: We don't say that word. There's been girls I like. One time I couldn't get the girl I wanted, and I was sick. I couldn't eat, I couldn't drink for love, just like the princes in the Arabian Nights.

JULIE: Who was she?

JEAN is silent.

Who was she?

JEAN: You can't make me tell you that.

JULIE: If I ask you as a friend – an equal – who was she?

JEAN: You.

MISS JULIE sits down.

JULIE: How entertaining.

JEAN: If you like, yes. Ridiculous. That was the story I couldn't tell you before. I will now. Do you know what the world looks like from down here – no, you don't. You're like the hawk and the falcon. They fly so high above you rarely see their backs. I lived in a hovel on the estate. Seven brothers and sisters – a pig as well – in a dirty field where there wasn't a tree growing. From the window though, I could see the wall around the Count's park, and the orchard of apples rising above it. It was the Garden of Eden. And standing guard there were multitudes of evil angels with their swords on fire. But still I was like the other lads – I discovered the way to the tree of life – you despise me now –

JULIE: Do I? All boys thieve apples.

JEAN: You say that now, but you still despise me. It doesn't matter. I went with my mother one day into the vegetable garden to weed the onion beds. There was a Turkish pavilion beside the garden. Jasmine trees shaded it, the honeysuckle drowned it. I didn't know what it was for but I'd never set eyes before on such a beautiful building. People went in and out again, and one day the door was left open. I sneaked in, I saw the wall covered with pictures, kings and emperors. Red curtains with tassels covered the windows. Do you know where I was now – you do – I – (*He picks a lilac flower and holds it under MISS JULIE's nose.*) I'd never been inside a big house – never seen anything but the church, but this was more lovely. No matter where my thoughts wandered, they always came back to – that. Bit by bit the desire was eating me that one day I would enjoy the pleasure of –. *Enfin*, I did sneak in, I saw and wondered. Then somebody came in, into the beautiful pavilion. There was one exit for the gentry out of there. For my kind there was another. I had to climb through that stinking pit – no choice in it.

MISS JULIE has taken the lilac and let it drop on to the table.

I leapt out and I ran through the raspberries, all across the strawberries and I finished up on the rose terrace. I could see a pink dress there – a pair of white stockings.

It was you. I crawled under a pile of weeds. Imagine me hiding under thistles prickling me, all damp and soiled and stinking. I watched you walk among the roses. I thought that if it's true a thief can get into Heaven and live among the angels, then it's strange that the child of a man who labours on God's earth can't enter the park and play with the Count's daughter.

MISS JULIE asks painfully:

JULIE: Wouldn't all poor children think the same thing as you did if they were where you were?

JEAN hesitates at first, then is convinced.

JEAN: All poor – they would – yes – of course.

JULIE: Poverty must be awful.

In deep pain, JEAN is very moved.

JEAN: Miss Julie – Miss Julie. A dog might lie on the Countess's sofa, a lady's hand might caress a horse's nose, but a poor child – (*He walks.*) A man might pull himself up by his own boot laces, if he has it in him. So they say, but how often does that happen? So, do you know what I did? I waded into the stream with my clothes on. Hauled out and beaten blue. The next Sunday, my father and the rest of the house had gone off to my grandmother's, I arranged that I could stay at home. I washed myself with warm water and soap. I donned my Sunday best and went to church where I would see you. I did see you and I went home wanting to die – going to die. I wanted to do it beautifully – in complete comfort, with no pain. I remembered then it was dangerous to sleep under an elder bush. We had one which was just bursting into bloom. I ripped all its flowers from it and I made a bed in the oat bin. Oats are so smooth – have you noticed? They touch like skin, human soft – anyway, I slammed the lid shut and nodded off. I fell asleep and woke up a very sick boy. But as you can see, I did not die. What was I doing? Don't ask me. I had no hope of winning. You were a sign that I should abandon hope of ever rising from the class I was born into.

JULIE: You know, you have a charming way with words. Did you go to school?

JEAN: A short while. I have read a lot of novels and I've gone to the theatre. I've heard the gentry talking as well – that's where I learned the most.

JULIE: You stand there listening to us speak, do you?

JEAN: I do. And I've heard plenty, let me tell you, when I'm sitting on the coachman's seat or rowing the boat. I once heard Miss Julie and a lady friend –

JULIE: Did you – what did you hear?

JEAN: That would be telling, wouldn't it? I did raise my eyebrows a little – where did you learn those words? That I couldn't understand. Maybe deep down there is not such a difference between us all as people think.

JULIE: How dare you. We don't behave the way you do when we're engaged.

JEAN fixes her with his eyes.

JEAN: You're sure? Miss Julie, please don't act the innocent –

JULIE: I gave my love to a good-for-nothing.

JEAN: Women always say that – afterwards.

JULIE: Always?

JEAN: I'd say always. I've heard it said so many times in so many different cases.

JULIE: What cases?

JEAN: This one for instance. The last time –

JULIE: Stop. I don't want to hear any more.

JEAN: She didn't either. Very strange. So I ask your permission to go to bed.

She answers softly:

JULIE: Go to bed? On Midsummer Eve?

JEAN: Yes. I'm not in the mood for leaping about with the herd up there.

JULIE: Get the key to the boat and row me out on the lake. I want to see the sun rise.

JEAN: Is that wise?

JULIE: Are you worried about my reputation?

JEAN: Why shouldn't I be? I'd prefer not to be taken for a fool. I'd prefer not to be sacked without a reference now that I'm starting to stand on my own two feet. And I think I have a certain obligation to Kristin.

JULIE: I understand – it's Kristin now –

JEAN: It's you as well. Take my advice, go upstairs and go to bed.

JULIE: Am I to do as you command?

JEAN: Yes, for once – for your own sake. I'm begging you. Night's falling. Tiredness is like drink, it makes your head light. Go to bed. If I'm not mistaken, I can hear people coming to look for me. If they find the two of us, you have had it.

The crowd's voices are heard singing.

VOICES:
A lady she walked by the shore
She was wanting to wash her feet
She was looking for sailors and more
And a handsome young man she did meet

Will you lie down with me on the sand
And I'll take you from here to Peru
I'll kiss more than your lily white hand
I'll leave your dainty cheek black and blue

The lady she laid on her back
Her petticoats sheets in the wind
The bucko he emptied his sack
And they called it original sin

Will you lie down with me on the sand

And I'll take you from here to Peru
I'll kiss more than your lily white hand
I'll leave your dainty cheek black and blue

A lady she walked by the shore
She was wanting to wash her feet
She was looking for sailors and more
And a handsome young man she did meet

JULIE: I know my servants. I love them the way they love me. You'll see. Let them come.

JEAN: They do not love you, Miss Julie. They eat your food, and afterwards they spit at you. Believe me. Listen to them. Listen to the words they are singing. No, don't listen.

She listens.

JULIE: What are they singing?

JEAN: A dirty song. About you and me.

JULIE: Damn them – they're filth –

JEAN: A pack of cowards. When you're in that kind of fight, you can only run –

JULIE: Run where? We can't get out. We can't go in to Kristin.

JEAN: We can't. My room? We have to. And you can trust me. I am your friend – a genuine friend.

JULIE: What if – what if they look in there?

JEAN: I'll bolt the door. If they break it down, I'll shoot. Come on. (*He gets on his knees.*) Come on.

MISS JULIE asks urgently:

JULIE: Promise me –

JEAN: I swear.

DANCE

Peasants enter in their best clothes, with flowers in their hats, led by a fiddler. A keg of beer and a bottle of schnapps, decorated with leaves, are placed on the table. Glasses are found. They drink. They form a circle and dance, singing 'A Lady She Walked by the Shore'. When this is over, they exit, singing. MISS JULIE enters on her own. She sees the mess in the kitchen and clasps her hands. She takes a powder puff and powders her face. JEAN enters, excited.

JEAN: You saw that – you heard it. Do you think we can stay here?

JULIE: We can't, no. What are we going to do?

JEAN: Leave, go abroad, far away.

JULIE: Go abroad? All right – where?

JEAN: Switzerland, or the Italian Lakes – you've never been there?

JULIE: No. Is it beautiful there?

JEAN: The summer lasts for ever. Orange trees and laurels.

JULIE: How will we live there?

JEAN: I'll open a hotel – first-class service, first-class guests.

JULIE: A hotel?

JEAN: Believe me, that's the way to live. New people all the time, new language. There's no such thing as an idle minute to complain or to worry. Always something to do – endless work. The bell rings night and day. The train whistles. The carriage coming and going. And the gold piles in. That's the life.

JULIE: Yes, that's living. And me –

JEAN: The mistress of the house. The hotel's pride and joy. You have looks, you have style – it has to be a success, it's bound to. Mighty. You'll rule like a queen behind the counter – you'll press an electric bell and the slaves will come running. The guests file past your throne and lay their gifts upon your table – you'll terrify them. You won't believe how it puts the wind up people to be presented with a bill. I'll salt the bills and you'll sugar them with your sweetest smile. We'll get away from this place. (*He takes a timetable from his pocket.*) The next train, now. We'll hit Malmö by six-thirty, Hamburg tomorrow morning, eight-forty. Frankfurt – Basle – a day later through the St Gothard Pass into Como, let me see, in three days. Three days.

JULIE: This is all grand, but Jean, give me courage – you must. Tell me you love me. Put your arms about me.

He hesitates.

JEAN: I want to – but I daren't. Not in this house again. I have no doubt – I love you – can you doubt that, Miss Julie?

She answers shyly, very womanly:

JULIE: Julie. Call me Julie. We're equals now. Julie.

He is tormented.

JEAN: I can't. We are not equals as long as we're standing in this house. The past is between us, there's the Count. I respect him more than any other I've ever met. If I see his gloves lying on a chair it's enough to make me a small child. If I hear the bell ringing I leap like a frightened horse. I can see him, boots standing there, so straight and proud, and I can feel my back bending. (*He kicks the boots.*) Old woman's talk – bigotry – we drank it in our mother's milk and it's as easy to spew out. We'll go to another country – a republic – they will grovel before me in my servant's uniform. They can grovel, I won't. I wasn't born to do that. I have something in me. I have a man's nature. If I can only grab that first branch, then watch me climb. I might be a servant today, but next year I'll own a hotel. In ten years' time I'll be living off my money. I'll travel then to Romania and get myself a decoration. I may – note that I say may – just end up a Count.

JULIE: Good, excellent.

JEAN: In Romania you can buy a Count's title and then I'll make you a Countess after all. My Countess.

JULIE: I'm leaving all that behind me. I care nothing about that. Say you love me. If you don't – yes, if you don't – what am I?

JEAN: I'll say it till it's coming out your ears – just wait – but not here, not here. Above all else show no feelings in this place, or we'll be lost. We have to look at things with a cold eye. Behave like logical people.

He takes out a cigar, cuts it and lights it.

You sit there – I'll sit here – we'll talk as if nothing happened.

JULIE: God almighty, have you no feelings?

JEAN: Feelings? I am the most passionate man, but I can control myself.

JULIE: You kissed my shoe a minute ago – and now –

JEAN: That was then – now we've other things to talk about.

JULIE: Don't speak so roughly to me.

JEAN: I'm speaking wisely. We've made one foolish mistake, we're not making another. The Count could walk in at any minute and before that happens we have to decide what's to be our destiny. What do you make of my plans for our future – do you approve?

JULIE: They seem sensible enough, but I do have one question. Such a big undertaking is going to need a lot of capital. Do you have any?

He chews on his cigar.

JEAN: Me? I certainly do. I'm an expert in my field, I have enormous experience. I'm fluent in many languages. That's what I call capital.

JULIE: But it won't buy you a railway ticket.

JEAN: Very true – that's why I'm looking for a partner who can provide the funds.

JULIE: Where are you going to find one at such short notice?

JEAN: That's your job if you want to come with me.

JULIE: I can't do that, I own nothing myself.

There is a pause.

JEAN: Then that's that –

JULIE: So.

JEAN: Things stay as they are.

JULIE: Do you think I'll live in this house as your whore? Do you think I'll let people point the finger at me? Do you think I can look my father in the face after this? No. Get me away from this place. I am humiliated – I am disgraced. Christ, what have I done – Christ – (*She sobs.*)

JEAN: Please don't start on that same old song. What have you done? The same as many have done before you.

She screams convulsively.

JULIE: You take me now. I've fallen – I'm falling –

JEAN: Fall down to my level and I'll lift you up again.

JULIE: What power drove me to you? The terror of the weak before the strong? As I fall, you rise – is that it? Or was it love? Is this love? Do you know what love is?

JEAN: I'd say I do, yes. Do you think I've not done it before?

JULIE: The way you speak and the way you think –

JEAN: It's what I learned, it's what I'm like. Don't act the lady – we're two peas in the pod now. That's right, girl, come on and I'll feed you a drink. (*He opens the drawer in the table and takes out the wine bottle. He fills up two used wine glasses.*)

JULIE: That wine – where did you get it?

JEAN: The cellar.

JULIE: My father's burgundy.

JEAN: Isn't it good enough for his son-in-law?

JULIE: And I was drinking beer – me –

JEAN: Just goes to show you have poorer taste than myself.

JULIE: Thief.

JEAN: Are you going to tell Daddy?

JULIE: Jesus, have I been aiding and abetting a thief? Have I been drunk or dreaming this Midsummer Night? A night of innocent games –

JEAN: Innocent my arse.

She paces up and down the room.

JULIE: Am I the most unfortunate alive on this earth?

JEAN: Why are you unfortunate? Look what you've won. Think of Kristin in there. Maybe you don't believe she has feelings as well.

JULIE: I did think so once. Not now. A servant is a servant –

JEAN: And a whore is a whore.

She is on her knees with her hands clasped.

JULIE: God above, end my life. Save me from the filth I've fallen into. Save me – please.

JEAN: I must admit I am sorry for you. When I was hiding in the onion beds watching you in the rose garden you must know I was entertaining the same dirty thoughts every other boy thinks.

JULIE: You said you would die for me.

JEAN: In the oat bin? Talking rubbish.

JULIE: You were lying?

Jean begins to grow sleepy.

JEAN: I suppose I was. I think I read the story in some newspaper – a chimney sweep lay down in a box of lilacs – he'd been ordered to pay child maintenance –

JULIE: And that's your like, is it?

JEAN: I had to think of something. Women fall for fancy stories.

JULIE: Pig.

JEAN: *Merde.*

JULIE: Now you've seen the hawk on its back –

JEAN: Not quite on its back –

JULIE: And I was to be the first branch –

JEAN: But the branch was rotten –

JULIE: I was to be the sign above the hotel –

JEAN: And I was to be the hotel –

JULIE: Trapped behind your counter, tempting the guests, cheating on the bills –

JEAN: I would do that myself –

JULIE: Could a human being sink so low in the dirt?

JEAN: Then clean it.

JULIE: Servant – lackey – get to your feet when I speak.

JEAN: Servant's whore – lackey's lick – shut up and get out. You stand here telling me that I'm filth? None of my kind has acted the filthy way you did tonight. Do you think any serving girl would throw herself at a man the way you did? Have you ever seen a girl from my class hand herself over like that? I've seen it with animals, I've seen it with whores. Oh, I know your class lets it happen. What do they call it? Being liberated. Emancipated – something fancy like that. Yes, I've seen great ladies wag their arses at soldiers and waiters.

She is crushed.

JULIE: That's right. Hit me. Walk on me. I deserve no better. I'm an unfortunate woman – so help me. Show me how to get out of this if you know a way.

He speaks more gently.

JEAN: I won't deny my share in the honour of seducing you – that would be shaming myself. But do you really believe a man in my position would have dared to look at you unless you offered the invitation yourself? I am still amazed –

JULIE: And are you proud of it –

JEAN: Why should I not be? I do admit though that I won too easily to give me complete pleasure.

JULIE: Go on – hit me again.

He gets up.

JEAN: No – forgive what I have just said. I wouldn't hit a defenceless man, let alone a woman. Yes, it's good to learn that you blinded us beneath you with fool's gold – the hawk's back was not too fine, the porcelain cheeks were powdered and the elegant nails had black beneath them. The handkerchief may smell of perfume but it's soiled. Still, it hurts me to know that what I wanted amounted to so little, so very, very little. It hurts me to see you fall so low that you're far beneath your cook. It hurts me the way flowers in the harvest are washed away by the rain and churned into dirt.

JULIE: You're talking as if you're already looking down on me.

JEAN: I do – I do. You see, I could make you a Countess, but you can never turn me into a Count.

JULIE: But I'm still the child of a Count, and you can never be that.

JEAN: True, but I could father Counts if –

JULIE: You thieve – I don't.

JEAN: Thieving's not that bad. There's worse you could learn to do. By the way, as a servant of this establishment I count myself to some extent a part of the family. A child of the house, you might say. It's not really thieving when the child grabs a berry from the branches that are full.

(*His passion is aroused once more.*) Miss Julie, you are an extraordinary woman. Far too good for my like. You were drunk, you made a mistake, and you want to cover that up by believing that you're in love with me. You are not – maybe you fancy my fine features – and so your love's no better than mine. Me though, I'd hate to be your animal, and I can never win your heart.

JULIE: Are you sure about that?

JEAN: You're going to say that I can. I should be able to love you absolutely. You are beautiful, and wealthy – (*He moves closer to her and takes her hand.*) Clever, kind when you choose to be, and when you have a man on fire, those flames will never die.

He puts his arms around her waist.

You're a strong wine – warm – the smell is powerful – and to kiss you –

He attempts to lead her offstage, but she quickly frees herself.

JULIE: Get your hands off me. You won't win me like that – no.

JEAN: How then? No sweet nothings – not like that – no caresses? Not by planning the future, saving you from disgrace – how do I win you?

JULIE: How? I don't know how. I do not know. I hate you the way I hate a rat, but I can't get away from you.

JEAN: Escape with me.

She straightens up.

JULIE: Escape – we'll escape, yes. I am tired out. Get me a glass of wine.

JEAN pours the wine.
MISS JULIE looks at her watch.

JULIE: We have to talk first – we have a bit of time – (*She empties her glass and holds it out for more.*)

JEAN: Stop drinking so much – you'll get drunk.

JULIE: Who cares?

JEAN: Who cares? It's bad manners to get drunk. What were you going to say to me?

JULIE: We must escape. But first of all we need to talk – I mean I need to talk. So far you've done all the talking. You've told me about your life. I want to tell you now about mine. Before we begin our journey, we have to know each other completely.

JEAN: Hold on. Make sure you won't regret spilling out your life's secrets.

JULIE: Are you not my friend?

JEAN: Sometimes I am, but don't count on me.

JULIE: You don't mean that. Anyway, my secrets are every-body's business. My mother had no noble blood. She came from very ordinary stock. She was reared in the ideas of her time – woman's emancipation, equality, all that sort of thing. And she loathed marriage. When my

father proposed, she said she could never be his wife, but he could be her lover. He told her he didn't wish the woman he loved to receive less respect than he himself would. She told him that such things meant nothing to her, and being madly in love he agreed to her terms. From that day on his own kind didn't recognise him. This imprisoned him in family life, and that did not satisfy him. I was born and, as far as I can understand it, my mother did not want that. My mother wanted to rear me as a child of nature. I also had to learn everything a boy is taught. I was to become an example of how a woman could be just as good as a man. I wore boy's clothes. I was taught to tame horses, but never to milk in the barn. I had to groom and harness. I had to learn about farming – hunting – even slaughtering. It was frightening. Throughout the estate men were ordered to do women's work, and the women to do men's. So, the estate fell to ruin. We were the laughing stock of the whole neigh-bourhood. My father must have finally come out from under his spell. He turned against it all and everything was changed to the way he wanted it. My parents were soon married quietly. My mother took ill – I don't know from what – she hid in the garden – some nights she stayed outside. You've heard about the big fire – that came next. The house, the stable, the barn – all burned down in mysterious circumstances. It was probably an act of arson, because the catastrophe happened the day after the quarterly insurance had run out. My father had sent the renewal premium, but it was delayed – the servant carrying it was careless – and it didn't arrive on time. (*She fills the glass and drinks wine.*)

JEAN: Don't drink any more.

JULIE: Who cares? We were left with the clothes we stood in. We had to sleep in the carriages. My father had neglected most of his old friends. They had forgotten him completely. He didn't know where to get money to build the house up again. My mother remembered a friend from her youth. A brickmaker – he lived near here. My mother urged my father to borrow from this man. He did borrow and he was not allowed to pay a penny interest. That astonished him. So the house rose again from the ashes. (*She drinks again.*) Do you know who burned down the house?

JEAN: Your most exalted mother?

JULIE: Do you know who the brickmaker was?

JEAN: Your mother's lover.

JULIE: Do you know whose money it was?

JEAN: Hold on – I don't know – whose?

JULIE: My mother's.

JEAN: Then it was the Count's as well, unless they made a marriage settlement.

JULIE: There was no settlement. My mother had a small fortune. She didn't want my father to manage it. She gave it into the safe keeping of her – friend.

JEAN: And he did keep it.

JULIE: He did. My father finds this all out, but he can't take him to court, he can't pay his wife's lover back, and he can't prove that it is his wife's money. He wanted to shoot himself – they say he tried and failed. He recovered. He made my mother pay for what she had done. I loved my father, but I sided with my mother. I didn't know the ins and outs of it all. I've learned from her to hate men – she hated all men, you've heard that – I swore to her I would not be a slave to any man.

JEAN: Then you got yourself engaged to the County Attorney.

JULIE: So that he would become my slave.

JEAN: Did he not want to?

JULIE: He wanted to, but I wouldn't let him. I grew bored of him.

JEAN: I saw it – in the stableyard.

JULIE: What did you see?

JEAN: What I saw. He broke off the engagement.

JULIE: Lie. I did that. Has he claimed he did, the good-for-nothing?

JEAN: He's not that, I think. Miss Julie, you hate men.

JULIE: Yes. Always – almost. I get weak – then – Christ –

JEAN: You hate me as well?

JULIE: I hate you. I would like to put you down like an animal –

JEAN: Have the animal put down, and those who abused it get two years' hard labour, isn't that the law?

JULIE: It is.

JEAN: That law doesn't apply. No animals here. What are we going to do?

JULIE: Get away from here.

JEAN: And torment each other to death?

JULIE: No. Two days to love – eight days – as long as you can love – and then – die.

JEAN: Die? Ridiculous. It's better to open a hotel.

She is not listening to him.

JULIE: By Lake Como. The sun shines there all the time. The laurels are green at Christmas, and the oranges burn red –

JEAN: It pisses rain on Lake Como. The only oranges I saw were on fruit stalls. But it's a nice trap for tourists. There's loads of villas there for happy couples to rent. There's big profit in that. Do you know why? They lease for six months – and they leave after three weeks.

She asks naively:

JULIE: Three weeks? Why?

JEAN: They fight. But the rent still has to be paid. Then they lease it out again. That's the way it happens. There's plenty of love – even if it doesn't last too long.

JULIE: You don't want to die with me?

JEAN: I don't want to die at all. I enjoy my life, and I think suicide is sinful, it's against God who gave us life.

JULIE: You believe in God?

JEAN: Naturally I do, yes. I go to church every second Sunday. Look, I'm really tired of this – I'm off to bed.

JULIE: I see – you believe I can be tossed aside like that? Do you know when a man shames a woman he owes her a debt?

JEAN takes out his wallet and throws a silver coin on the table.

JEAN: There you go. I wouldn't be in debt to anyone.

MISS JULIE pretends not to have noticed the insult.

JULIE: Do you know what the law says –

JEAN: It's sad the law doesn't say when a woman's seduced a man, how she should be punished.

JULIE: Do you see any other escape – we go away, get married and then separate.

JEAN: And if I do not want to be part of this damaging marriage?

JULIE: Damaging?

JEAN: Most definitely. You see I come from a much better background than you do. None of my ancestors indulged in arson.

JULIE: You're sure of that?

JEAN: You can't contradict it – nobody recorded my family's history, apart from the parish. I've looked up your breeding in a book on the drawing-room table. Do you know who started your noble line? He was a miller. During the war with Denmark he let the king screw his wife. I can't boast such ancestors. I don't have a single ancestor, but I can become one myself.

JULIE: This is what I get for giving my heart to a dog – for dishonouring my family –

JEAN: Dishonour – yes, well, I told you so. You shouldn't drink because then you start talking. And really one should not talk.

JULIE: I do regret it – I really do. If you loved me at least –

JEAN: For the last time – what are you talking about? Do you want me to weep? Will I leap over your riding whip? Will I kiss you? Trick you into running away to Lake Como, stay with you for three weeks and then – what will I do then? What will you do? This is beginning to pain me. That's what happens when a man interferes in women's business. Miss Julie, I see the misery you're in. I know you're suffering, but I do not understand you. We're not like you. We don't have your sort of hatred. Love's like a game to us. When we've time off work, we play, but we don't have all night and day like you do! I think you're a sick woman, and your mother was seriously mad. Whole parishes about here have been affected by her kind of madness.

JULIE: Be gentle with me – you're talking to me now like a human being.

JEAN: You act like a human being as well. You spit on me, yet you won't let me wipe the spit dry – on you.

JULIE: Just help me, will you? What way should I go?

JEAN: In Christ's name, I wish I knew myself.

JULIE: Crazy – I've been insane – but there must surely be some way of saving myself.

JEAN: Calm – just be calm. Nobody knows a thing.

JULIE: That's not possible. Those people know – Kristin knows.

JEAN: They don't imagine anything like this happening – they couldn't.

She hesitates.

JULIE: But it could happen again.

JEAN: True.

JULIE: And what will they do?

JEAN: What will they do – I didn't think of that, have I taken leave of my senses? There's only one thing to do – get away. Now. You have to go on your own – everything's lost if I'm seen to follow you. Just get away – anywhere –

JULIE: Anywhere – on my own – I can't –

JEAN: You must. Before the Count comes back. We know what's going to happen if you stay. The harm's done. If you fall once, you fall again – you get to care less and less. That way you're found out. Just leave. Write to the Count later on. Tell him everything. But don't mention my name. He'll never ever guess that. And I don't imagine he would be too keen to know.

JULIE: Come with me and I'll go.

JEAN: Woman, are you a lunatic? Miss Julie runs off with her servant. It would be read in every newspaper the day after tomorrow. The Count could not survive that.

JULIE: How do I leave? How do I stay? Help me. I am worn out – my very bones are aching. Order me what to do. Force me to do something – I can't think anything, I can't do anything.

JEAN: Do you see now what you're cut from? Why do you give yourself such airs and walk the earth as if you owned it? All right, I'll order you. Get upstairs – get dressed. Get money together for the journey – then get downstairs.

She asks half-audibly:

JULIE: Come upstairs with me.

JEAN: To your bedroom? You're off your head again – (*He hesitates a moment.*) No – get out – now.

He takes her hand and leads her offstage. She asks as she exits:

JULIE: Jean, speak kindly to me.

JEAN: You don't give orders of kindness, you bark them. Now you know what it feels like.

On his own, JEAN heaves a sigh of relief. He sits down by the table and takes out a notebook and pencil. He calculates something out loud. This continues in dumb mime until KRISTIN enters dressed for church. She holds a shirtfront and a white tie in her hand.

KRISTIN: I've slept like a log.

JEAN: Dressed for church already, are you?

KRISTIN: I am. What about yourself? You promised to come to communion with me today.

JEAN: I did, true enough. I see you've got my Sunday best. Come on then.

He sits down. KRISTIN starts to dress him in the shirtfront and white tie. There is a pause. He asks sleepily:

JEAN: What's the reading for today?

KRISTIN: John the Baptist getting his head chopped off.

JEAN: That one goes on and on. Watch, you're hanging me. I could sleep for a month, I really could.

KRISTIN: Well, what has the big man been doing up all night? Look at the green face on him.

JEAN: I've been stuck here talking to Miss Julie.

KRISTIN: That lady does not know the meaning of modesty.

There is a pause.

JEAN: Kristin?

KRISTIN: What?

JEAN: Isn't it peculiar when you think of it – her –

KRISTIN: What's peculiar?

JEAN: Everything.

There is a pause. KRISTIN looks at the half-empty glasses standing on the table.

KRISTIN: Have you been boozing together as well?

JEAN: We have.

KRISTIN: To hell with you – it's not possible – is it?

He considers this briefly.

JEAN: Yes – it is.

KRISTIN: I don't believe it – I can't, no – oh God –

JEAN: You're not jealous of her, are you?

KRISTIN: Not of her – no. Klara or Sofi – either of them – I would have had your eyes. That's the way it is. Why – I don't know. But it's a dirty act.

JEAN: Are you in a rage against her?

KRISTIN: A rage against you. That was a rotten thing to do – really rotten. Foolish girl. I'll tell you one thing. I won't stay any longer in this house when I can no longer look up to my betters.

JEAN: Why do you have to look up to them?

KRISTIN: The smart boy here can explain that to me. Do you want to dance attendance on people who have no decency? Do you? We'll all be tarred with the same brush, I say.

JEAN: Yes, but it's comforting for us to know they're not a bit better.

KRISTIN: I take no comfort from it. If they are the dregs, there's not much point in us trying to improve ourselves. Think of the Count. Think of the suffering that man's endured in his day. Good Jesus. I will stay no longer in this house. And she did it with the likes of this boy. If it had been the County Attorney – if it had been someone from her own class –

JEAN: What then?

KRISTIN: Well, you're no better nor worse than you should be, but there are distinctions between people. No, I cannot get over this. Miss Julie so haughty, so hard on all men – who would believe she'd throw herself at any man – especially a man like this. She's the one who insisted the bitch should be put down because she ran after the gamekeeper's dog. I'm saying it out straight. I'll stay here no longer. Come the twenty-fourth of October, I'll be gone.

JEAN: What then?

KRISTIN: Then you might start looking for work seeing that we're supposed to get married. That's what then.

JEAN: So what should I look for? When I'm a married man I can't get a position like this.

KRISTIN: No, you can't. You'll have to look for a job as a caretaker or a porter in a government office. The money at the Civil Service is bad, but it's a safe job with a pension for the wife and children –

He grimaces.

JEAN: Is that so? I don't intend to die just yet for my wife and children. I must admit my ambitions were slightly higher.

KRISTIN: Oh, you have ambitions, do you? You have obligations as well. You might think of them.

JEAN: Don't preach to me about obligations. I know what I've got to do. (*He listens to what's happening offstage.*) We'll have time enough to think about that. Get yourself ready, we'll head off to church.

KRISTIN: Who's that wandering about upstairs?

JEAN: Maybe it's Klara.

KRISTIN: It wouldn't be the Count – he wouldn't have come home and no one's heard him?

JEAN is frightened.

Figure 5 Sandra Prinsoo and John Kani as Miss Julie and Jean in The Baxter Theatre Centre's 1985 production of *Miss Julie*. (Photographer: Bee Berman. Reprinted by permission of The Baxter Theatre Centre, Cape Town, South Africa.)

JEAN: The Count? No – that's not true – he would have rang for me – I know that.

KRISTIN exits.

KRISTIN: God, look down on us. I've never found myself in the likes of this before.

The sun rises. It lights the tops of the trees in the park. The light moves slowly until it falls in a slant through the windows. JEAN goes over to the door and gives MISS JULIE a sign. MISS JULIE enters dressed in travelling clothes. She carries a small bird-cage, covered with a towel. She places it on a chair.

JULIE: I'm ready now.

JEAN: Hold your tongue. Kristin is awake.

MISS JULIE is growing increasingly nervous.

JULIE: Does she suspect anything?

JEAN: Nothing – she knows nothing. Christ, the look of you.

JULIE: What? How do I look?

JEAN: You're as pale as a ghost. I'm sorry to say this – your face is filthy.

JULIE: Let me clean it then. (*She goes to the washing bowl and cleans her face and hands.*) Give me a towel. Look – the sun's rising.

JEAN: Then the demons' work is done.

JULIE: They were busy last night. Jean, listen to me. Come with me. I have the money now.

He hesitates.

JEAN: Enough money?

JULIE: Enough to make a start. Come with me – I can't travel alone today. It's Midsummer. Imagine being stuck on that train, surrounded by people. Every eye would be fixed on me. I wouldn't be able to breathe. We would have to stop at every train station when what we want to do is fly, fly. No. I can't, I can't. The memories would start. I'd remember when I was a child – the church on Midsummer Day was thick with leaves and branches. Birch twigs and lilacs. We'd feast at the happy table, friends, relations – and the afternoon in the garden, dancing, music, flowers, playing games. You can run away for the rest of your life, but the memories, they weigh you down like your luggage. They bring you remorse, they hurt your conscience.

JEAN: I will go with you. It has to be now before it's too late. I mean now, this minute.

JULIE: Get dressed then. (*She takes the bird-cage.*)

JEAN: Take no luggage. That will give the game away.

JULIE: Nothing, no. Only what we can carry and ourselves.

JEAN has taken his hat.

JEAN: What's that – what have you there?

JULIE: My greenfinch – that's all. I can't leave it behind.

JEAN: Is that so – we're bringing a bird-cage, are we? You are off your head. Let it go.

JULIE: This is all I'm taking from my own home. The one living creature that cares for me since Diana betrayed me. Don't be cruel. Let me keep it.

JEAN: I'm saying, let it go. Keep your voice down. Kristin will hear us.

JULIE: I'm not handing it to strangers – I'd rather kill it.

JEAN: Give me the bastard and I'll wring its neck.

JULIE: All right, but don't let it suffer, don't – I can't, no –

JEAN: Give me it – I can do it.

She takes the bird from the cage and kisses it.

JULIE: My tiny Serine, are you going to die and leave Mama?

JEAN: Please, no scenes. We're talking about your life, your survival. Come on, quickly.

He takes the bird from her, goes to the chopping board and takes the kitchen axe. MISS JULIE turns away.

JEAN: You wasted your time learning to shoot with a gun. Better for you to behead a few chickens. (*He chops.*) You might not faint then at the sight of a drop of blood.

She screams.

JULIE: Take my life as well – take it. That creature is innocent. You can kill it and your hands don't shake. I despise – I hate you. There is blood between us. I curse the day I set eyes on you, I curse the day I was conceived in my mother's womb.

JEAN: Your curses won't help you. Get a move on.

She approaches the chopping board as if drawn against her will.

JULIE: No – not yet – I don't want to – I can't – I need to see – ssh, there's a carriage coming up the road – (*She listens, her eyes firmly fixed all the while on the chopping board and axe.*) I can't stomach the sight of blood – that's what you think – I'm weak – am I – I'd like to see your blood, your brains smashed on the chopping block. I want to see every one of your sex swimming in a lake of blood like this one. I think I could drink out of your skull – I could wash my feet in your ripped stomach – I could roast your heart and eat. So you think I am weak. You think I love you – and blessed be your seed in my womb. You think I'll carry your child beneath my heart and my blood will nourish it – I'll give you a child and I'll take your name. Tell me, what is your name? I've never heard your surname. Have you got one? I don't suppose you do. So I'll become Mrs Doorman – or maybe Mrs Shitspreader – you are a dog who wears my collar – you are the son of a labourer – you wear my coat of arms on your buttons. I have to share you with my cook. I am my servant's rival. Dear sweet God! You think I'm a coward who wants to run away. No, I'll stay now. What will be, will be. My father will return home. He'll find his desk broke open. His money vanished. He'll ring then – on that bell there. Ring twice for his lackey. He'll send for the police. And I will tell him everything. Everything. It will be wonderful to put an end to this – if only that could be the end. His heart will break. He will die. That will be the end for each and every one of us. Quiet – we will all be at peace – eternal rest – they break the coat of arms over the coffin – the Count's line has ended. The lackey's child survives in an orphanage – he will win the praise of the gutter and end up behind bars.

JEAN: Listen to the spouting of the royal blood. Well done, Miss Julie. Bury the miller in his sack.

KRISTIN enters, dressed for church, with a hymn-book in her hand. MISS JULIE rushes towards her. She falls into her arms, as if seeking protection.

JULIE: Kristin, help me. Save me from this man.

KRISTIN is unmoved and cold.

KRISTIN: What sort of racket are you making on a Sunday morning? (*She notices the chopping board.*) Look at the state of that. What are you doing? Why are you roaring and screaming like this?

JULIE: You're a woman, Kristin, and you're my friend. Take care against that good-for-nothing.

JEAN is disconcerted.

JEAN: The ladies are engaged in conversation, so I'll go and shave.

He slips out stage right.

JULIE: You have to understand me – you have to listen –

KRISTIN: I do not understand this carry on. Where is my lady going dressed in travelling clothes? Why is Jean wearing a hat? Why is that?

JULIE: Kristin, listen to me, I'll tell you everything, listen –

KRISTIN: I want to know nothing –

JULIE: Listen – you have to listen –

KRISTIN: About what? This silly nonsense with Jean, is that it? I do not care in the slightest. But if you think you'll trick him into eloping with you, I can put a sure stop to your gallop.

MISS JULIE is even more nervous.

JULIE: Please be calm, Kristin, and listen to me. I can't stay here – Jean can't stay here – we have to get away.

KRISTIN eyes her and MISS JULIE brightens up.

JULIE: So I've had this idea, you see. The three of us go together – go abroad – Switzerland. We start a hotel together – I've money, you see – Jean and I, we'd take care of everything. And I thought that you would take charge of the kitchen. Wouldn't that be lovely? Say yes, please. Come away with us – then everything will be settled. Say yes, do, please.

She embraces KRISTIN and pats her back. KRISTIN eyes her coldly and thoughtfully. MISS JULIE speaks at great speed.

JULIE: Kristin, you've never travelled. Get out and see the world – do. Such fun to travel by train. New people constantly – new places – we'll visit the zoo in Hamburg – you'll like that – the theatre and the opera – in Munich we'll get to the museum – Rubens, Raphael, great painters you know – you have heard about Munich – where King Ludwig lived – the king who went mad, you know – we'll see his castle – exactly like in fairy tales and it's not far from there to Switzerland – the Alps, you know – the Alps – imagine – snow on top in the middle of the summer – oranges grow there and laurels green all year round.

JEAN can be seen in the wings sharpening his razor on a strap which he holds with his teeth and left hand. He listens to the conversation with a pleased expression, nodding approval in places. MISS JULIE speaks with even greater speed than before.

JULIE: We'll open a hotel – I'll keep guard behind the counter and Jean will greet the guests – does the shopping – writes a letter – believe me, it's a fine life – the train whistles, the carriage arrives, the bell rings upstairs, it rings in the restaurant – I'll write the bills – I'll salt them, I will – you would not believe how paying bills scares the wits out of the guests – you – you will be in charge of the kitchen. You won't be standing over a stove – no – no – you'll be well-dressed because you'll be introduced to people – and I'm not flattering you – you'll land yourself a husband one fine day with your looks. You'll see – a grand English gentleman – these people are very easy to – (*She slows down.*) Land. We'll grow rich. Build ourselves a villa at Lake Como. It does rain there – sometimes it does rain – but – (*Her voice falters.*) The sun has to shine there once in a while – just when it's at its darkest – and – then – if it doesn't – we can go back home, can't we – and just go back – (*She pauses.*) Here – or some place else –

KRISTIN: Stop this. Do you yourself believe any of it, Miss Julie?

MISS JULIE is crushed.

JULIE: Do I believe it?

KRISTIN: Yes.

MISS JULIE is exhausted.

JULIE: I don't know. I don't believe in anything any more. (*She collapses on the bench and drops her head between her arms on the table.*) Nothing at all. Nothing.

KRISTIN turns to where JEAN is standing.

KRISTIN: So he was thinking of doing a runner.

Disconcerted, JEAN puts the razor down on the table.

JEAN: A runner? That's putting it too harshly. You've heard

what Miss Julie is proposing. She may be exhausted without her night's sleep but we can still carry out her proposal.

KRISTIN: Listen to that. Was the intention that I would cook for that –

JEAN *interrupts sharply:*

JEAN: Keep a decent tongue in your head when you're addressing your mistress. Do you hear?

KRISTIN: Mistress?

JEAN: Yes.

KRISTIN: Listen to that. Listen to him.

JEAN: Listen to you – listen more and talk less. Miss Julie is your mistress. You spit on her now but you might spit on yourself for the same reason.

KRISTIN: I've always had enough respect for myself –

JEAN: Enough to spit on others –

KRISTIN: Enough to never lower myself beneath my station. No man can say that the Count's cook threw herself at the stableboy or the pig-keeper. No man can say that.

JEAN: Yes, you've been enjoying yourself with the right gentleman – that's been your good luck.

KRISTIN: A right gentleman, yes – he steals oats from the Count's stables –

JEAN: You're a fine one to talk. You take your cut from the grocery money – you take bribes from the butcher.

KRISTIN: What are you saying?

JEAN: And you, yes you, you can no longer respect your betters.

KRISTIN: Are you coming to church? After your big talk you could do with a good sermon.

JEAN: I'm not going to church today, no. Go by yourself, fall on your knees and confess your sins.

KRISTIN: I'll do that, yes. And I'll come home and forgive you as well. The Saviour suffered on the cross. He died for all our sins. If we come to him with faith, if we repent, he will take all our guilt on himself.

JEAN: Will he forgive those who stole food?

JULIE: Do you believe that, Kristin?

KRISTIN: As sure as I'm alive, as I'm standing here, that is my faith. The faith of my childhood. I've stayed firm in it, Miss Julie. Where there is a multitude of sin, there is a multitude of grace.

JULIE: If I had your faith – if I –

KRISTIN: You can't have it. It comes only through the grace of God and he does not grant it to everyone –

JULIE: So who does he grant it to?

KRISTIN: The last shall be the first – that's the great mystery of grace, Miss Julie. God doesn't have favourites. The last –

JULIE: So he favours the last –

KRISTIN *continues:*

KRISTIN: Shall be first, and it is easier for a camel to pass through the eye of a needle than for a rich man to enter

the Kingdom of God. That's the way God planned it, Miss Julie. Well I'm going now – going on my own. I'll tell the stableboy when I'm leaving not to lend anybody any horses – someone might want to do a runner before the Count gets home. Farewell. (*She exits.*)

JEAN: There goes the devil. And all this because of a greenfinch.

MISS JULIE *is numb.*

JULIE: Leave the greenfinch out of it. Do you see any ending – any way out of this?

JEAN: No.

JULIE: If you were in my place, what would you do?

JEAN: Me – in your place – wait a minute. If I were of noble blood – If I were a woman who – fell – I don't know. I do – I do know.

She has taken the razor and makes a gesture.

JULIE: This?

JEAN: Yes. But I wouldn't do it. Make a note of that. That's the difference between us.

JULIE: You're a man, and I am a woman – what difference is that?

JEAN: The same difference between a man and a woman.

MISS JULIE *has the razor in her hand.*

JULIE: I want to. I can't. My father couldn't either, the time he should have.

JEAN: No, he shouldn't have. He needed his revenge first.

JULIE: And now through me, my mother gets her revenge.

JEAN: Have you never loved your father, Miss Julie?

JULIE: I love him with all my heart and soul, but I loathe him too. I did that without knowing it. He brought me up to hate my own sex. I am woman, and I am man. Who's to blame for what happened? My father? My mother? Myself? Is it myself? Have I nothing that is mine? Every thought I've had, I took from my father. Every passion I've felt came from my mother. And the last hope – everybody is equal – that I got from the man I was to marry, and for that reason I call him good-for-nothing. How can it be my own fault? Should I blame Jesus, like Kristin did – no, I won't do that. I think too much of myself, I know myself too well – thank you, Father, for teaching me that. A rich man can't enter the Kingdom of God – what a lie. Kristin has money saved in the bank – so she's barred for sure. Who's to blame? Who gives a curse who's to blame? In the end I will take the blame on my own two shoulders, and I will face the music.

JEAN: Yes, but –

The bell rings sharply twice. MISS JULIE *leaps to her feet.* JEAN *changes his coat.*

JEAN: The Count – he's home. What if Kristin – (*He goes to the speaking tube, taps it and listens.*)

JULIE: Has he been to his desk yet?

JEAN listens. The audience does not hear what the Count says.

JEAN: Yes, my Lord. (*He listens.*) At once, my Lord. (*He listens.*) In half an hour – yes.

She is even more distressed.

JULIE: What did he say? In the name of Jesus, what did he say?

JEAN: His boots – his coffee – he wants them in half an hour.

JULIE: Half an hour, I am worn out. I can do nothing. I can't say I'm sorry, can't run away, can't stay, I cannot live, I cannot die. Help me. Bark me an order and I'll obey like a dog. Save my honour, save my name – do me that one last favour. You know what I want to do. I can't. Force me to do it. Command me to do it.

JEAN: I can't – I don't know why either – I don't understand – I put on this coat and it makes me – I can't order you about – now since the Count spoke to me – I can't say what I mean – but – I will live and die a servant – if that man the master were to walk in and order me to cut my throat, I believe I would do it here and now.

JULIE: Pretend you're him, and I'm you. You acted so well when you were on your knees – then you had blue blood – or have you ever been to the theatre and seen a hypnotist –

JEAN indicates he has.

JULIE: He says, take the broom, and you take it. He says, sweep, and you sweep.

JEAN: You have to be asleep first though –

MISS JULIE is in ecstasy.

JULIE: I think I'm sleeping already. I think the whole room is filled with smoke. You look like an iron stove, and it looks like a man dressed in black, wearing a top hat, and your eyes, they're like coal glowing when the fire's dying, and your face is the colour of ashes.

The sun's rays stretch across the floor and lighten JEAN.

JULIE: It's so warm – so very warm – (*She rubs her hands as if warming them before a fire.*) Full of light – peace –

JEAN takes the razor and puts it in her hand.

JEAN: Here – go into the daylight – into the barn – and –

He whispers in her ear. She is awake now.

JULIE: Thank you. I can go to my rest now. Tell me this – the first and the last – can the first receive the gift of grace? Tell me, even if you don't believe it.

JEAN: The first? I can't, no. Miss Julie – wait. You're no longer among the first. You're standing among the last.

JULIE: I am among the last. I am the last. Still – I can't go now. Tell me again to go.

JEAN: I can't – I can't.

JULIE: And the last shall be the first.

JEAN: Stop thinking about it – stop. You're draining my strength, you're turning me into a coward. Look, I think I heard the bell – no. Will we put some paper round it? Frightened of a bell, so frightened. It's not just a bell – there is someone behind it – a hand makes it move – and something else makes the hand move – put your hands over your ears – put your hands over your ears – just do that. I will, and he'll ring louder. He'll keep ringing until you answer. It will be too late then. The police will be here – then –

The bell rings twice, forcefully. JEAN startles, then straightens up.

Savage – there is no other way out – go.

MISS JULIE exits through the door with complete determination.

1.3 THREE SISTERS (1900)

ANTON CHEKHOV

Translated by Elisaveta Fen

Anton Chekhov (1860–1904) wrote Three Sisters *fitfully through the spring, summer and winter of 1900, suffering greatly from tuberculosis. In October, he read a first draft of the play to the Moscow Art Theatre, who were to produce the play, and received a muted reaction from the company, some of whom were expecting a comedy, but the play became one of the Art Theatre's greatest successes. Along with* The Seagull, Uncle Vanya *and* The Cherry Orchard, Three Sisters *has become one of the most widely performed plays of the twentieth century. The puzzles of the play – why don't the sisters just go to Moscow? What happened to Vershinin's wife? – have fostered their own minor industry of radical reworkings, sequels and homages, including The Wooster Group's* Brace Up!, *Brian Friel's* Afterplay, *Dijana Milošević's* The Story of Tea, *Janusz Glowacki's* The Fourth Sister, *Beth Henley's* Crimes of the Heart *and Diane Samuels'* Three Sisters on Hope Street, *several movies, a ballet,* Winter Dreams, *choreographed by Kenneth MacMillan, and a rock musical,* Three Sistahs. *The translation from Russian republished here is by Elisaveta Fen and was originally published in 1959 by Penguin Classics.*

Characters

PROZOROV ANDREY SERGHYEEVICH
NATASHA (Natalia Ivanovna), his fiancée, afterwards his wife
OLGA (Olga Serghyeevna, Olia) ⎫
MASHA (Maria Serghyeevna) ⎬ his sisters
IRENA (Irena Serghyeevna) ⎭
KOOLYGHIN, Fiodor Ilyich, master at the High School for boys, husband of Masha
VERSHININ, Alexandr Ignatyevich, Lieutenant-Colonel, Battery Commander
TOOZENBACH, Nikolai Lvovich, Baron, Lieutenant in the Army
SOLIONY, Vassily Vassilich, Captain
CHEBUTYKIN, Ivan Romanych, Army Doctor
FEDOTIK, Aleksey Petrovich, Second Lieutenant
RODÉ, Vladimir Karlovich, Second Lieutenant
FERAPONT (Ferapont Spiridonych), an old porter from the County Office
ANFISA, the Prozorovs' former nurse, an old woman of 80

The action takes place in a county town.

Act 1

A drawing-room in the Prozorovs' house; it is separated from a large ballroom[1] at the back by a row of columns. It is midday; there is cheerful sunshine outside. In the ballroom the table is being laid for lunch. OLGA, *wearing the regulation dark-blue dress of a secondary school mistress, is correcting her pupils' work, standing or walking about as she does so.* MASHA, *in a black dress, is sitting reading a book, her hat on her lap.* IRENA, *in white, stands lost in thought.*

OLGA: It's exactly a year ago that Father died, isn't it? This very day, the fifth of May – your Saint's day, Irena. I remember it was very cold and it was snowing. I felt then as if I should never survive his death; and you had fainted and were lying quite still, as if you were dead. And now – a year's gone by, and we talk about it so easily. You're wearing white, and your face is positively radiant ...

A clock strikes twelve.

The clock struck twelve then, too. (*A pause.*) I remember when Father was being taken to the cemetery there was a military band, and a salute with rifle fire. That was because he was a general, in command of a brigade. And yet there weren't many people at the funeral. Of course, it was raining hard, raining and snowing.

IRENA: Need we bring up all these memories?

Baron TOOZENBACH, CHEBUTYKIN *and* SOLIONY *appear behind the columns by the table in the ballroom.*

OLGA: It's so warm today that we can keep the windows wide open, and yet there aren't any leaves showing on the birch trees. Father was made a brigadier eleven years ago, and then he left Moscow and took us with him. I remember so well how everything in Moscow was in blossom by now, everything was soaked in sunlight and warmth. Eleven years have gone by, yet I remember everything about it, as if we'd only left yesterday. Oh, Heavens! When I woke up this morning and saw this flood of sunshine, all this spring sunshine, I felt so moved and so happy! I felt such a longing to get back home to Moscow!

CHEBUTYKIN: (*to* TOOZENBACH.) The devil you have!

TOOZENBACH: It's nonsense, I agree.

MASHA: (*absorbed in her book, whistles a tune under her breath*)

OLGA: Masha, do stop whistling! How can you? (*A pause.*) I suppose I must get this continual headache because I have to go to school every day and go on teaching right into the evening. I seem to have the thoughts of someone quite old. Honestly, I've been feeling as if my strength and youth were running out of me drop by drop, day after day. Day after day, all these four years that I've been working at the school.... I just have one longing and it seems to grow stronger and stronger....

IRENA: If only we could go back to Moscow! Sell the house, finish with our life here, and go back to Moscow.

OLGA: Yes, Moscow! As soon as we possibly can.

(CHEBUTYKIN *and* TOOZENBACH *laugh.*)

IRENA: I suppose Andrey will soon get a professorship. He isn't likely to go on living here. The only problem is our poor Masha.

OLGA: Masha can come and stay the whole summer with us every year in Moscow.

MASHA: (*Whistles a tune under her breath.*)

IRENA: Everything will settle itself, with God's help. (*Looks through the window.*) What lovely weather it is today! Really, I don't know why there's such joy in my heart. I remembered this morning that it was my Saint's day, and suddenly I felt so happy, and I thought of the time when we were children, and Mother was still alive. And then such wonderful thoughts came to me, such wonderful stirring thoughts!

OLGA: You're so lovely today, you really do look most attractive. Masha looks pretty today, too. Andrey could be good-looking, but he's grown so stout. It doesn't suit him. As for me, I've just aged and grown a lot thinner. I suppose it's through getting so irritated with the girls at school. But today I'm at home, I'm free, and my headache's gone, and I feel much younger than I did yesterday. I'm only twenty-eight, after all.... I suppose everything that God wills must be right and good, but I can't help thinking sometimes that if I'd got married and stayed at home, it would have been a better thing for me: (*A pause.*) I would have been very fond of my husband.

TOOZENBACH: (*To* SOLIONY.) Really, you talk such a lot of nonsense, I'm tired of listening to you. (*Comes into the drawing-room.*) I forgot to tell you: Vershinin, our new battery commander, is going to call on you today. (*Sits down by the piano.*)

OLGA: I'm very glad to hear it.

IRENA: Is he old?

TOOZENBACH: No, not particularly. Forty, forty-five at the most. (*Plays quietly.*) He seems a nice fellow. Certainly not a fool. His only weakness is that he talks too much.

IRENA: Is he interesting?

TOOZENBACH: He's all right, only he's got a wife, a mother-in-law and two little girls. What's more, she's his second wife. He calls on everybody and tells them that he's got a wife and two little girls. He'll tell you about it, too, I'm sure of that. His wife seems to be a bit soft in the head. She wears a long plait like a girl, she is always philosophizing and talking in high-flown language, and then she often tries to commit suicide, apparently just to annoy her husband. I would have run away from a wife like that years ago, but he puts up with it, and just grumbles about it.

SOLIONY: (*Enters the drawing-room with* CHEBUTYKIN.) Now I can only lift sixty pounds with one hand, but with two I can lift two hundred pounds, or even two hundred and forty. So I conclude from that that two men are not just twice as strong as one, but three times as strong, if not more.

CHEBUTYKIN: (*Reads the paper as he comes in.*) Here's a recipe for falling hair ... two ounces of naphthaline, half-a-bottle of methylated spirit ... dissolve and apply once a day.... (*Writes it down in a notebook.*) Must make a note of it. (*To* SOLIONY.) Well, as I was trying to explain to you, you cork the bottle and pass a glass tube through the cork. Then you take a pinch of ordinary powdered alum, and ....

IRENA: Ivan Romanych, dear Ivan Romanych!

CHEBUTYKIN: What is it, my child, what is it?

IRENA: Tell me, why is it I'm so happy today? Just as if I were sailing along in a boat with big white sails, and above me the wide, blue sky, and in the sky great white birds floating around?

CHEBUTYKIN: (*Kisses both her hands, tenderly.*) My little white bird!

IRENA: You know, when I woke up this morning, and after I'd got up and washed, I suddenly felt as if everything in the world had become clear to me, and I knew the way I ought to live. I know it all now, my dear Ivan Romanych. Man must work by the sweat of his brow whatever his class, and that should make up the whole meaning and purpose of his life and happiness and contentment. Oh, how good it must be to be a workman, getting up with the sun and breaking stones by the roadside – or a shepherd – or a schoolmaster teaching the children – or an engine-driver on the railway. Good Heavens! it's better to be a mere ox or horse, and work, than the sort of young woman who wakes up at twelve, and drinks her coffee in bed, and then takes two hours dressing.... How dreadful! You know how you long for a cool drink in hot weather? Well, that's the way I long for work. And if I don't get up early from now on and really work, you can refuse to be friends with me any more, Ivan Romanych.

CHEBUTYKIN: (*Tenderly.*) So I will, so I will....

OLGA: Father taught us to get up at seven o'clock and so Irena always wakes up at seven – but then she stays in bed till at least nine, thinking about something or other. And with such a serious expression on her face, too! (*Laughs.*)

IRENA: You think it's strange when I look serious because you always think of me as a little girl. I'm twenty, you know!

TOOZENBACH: All this longing for work.... Heavens! how well I can understand it! I've never done a stroke of work in my life. I was born in Petersburg, an unfriendly, idle city – born into a family where work and worries were simply unknown. I remember a valet pulling off my boots for me when I came home from the cadet school.... I grumbled at the way he did it, and my mother looked on in admiration. She was quite surprised when other people looked at me in any other way. I was so carefully protected from work! But I doubt whether they succeeded in protecting me for good and all – yes, I doubt it very much! The time's come: there's a terrific thunder-cloud advancing upon us, a mighty storm is coming to freshen us up! Yes, it's coming all right, it's quite near already, and it's going to blow away all this idleness and indifference, and prejudice against work, this rot of boredom that our society is suffering from. I'm going to work, and in twenty-five or thirty years' time every man and woman will be working. Every one of us!

CHEBUTYKIN: I'm not going to work.

TOOZENBACH: You don't count.

SOLIONY: In twenty-five years' time you won't be alive, thank goodness. In a couple of years you'll die from a stroke – or I'll lose my temper with you and put a bullet in your head, my good fellow. (*Takes a scent bottle from his pocket and sprinkles the scent over his chest and hands.*)

CHEBUTYKIN: (*Laughs.*) It's quite true that I never have done any work. Not a stroke since I left the university. I haven't even read a book, only newspapers. (*Takes another newspaper out of his pocket.*) For instance, here.... I know from the paper that there was a person called Dobroliubov, but what he wrote about I've not the faintest idea.... God alone knows....

Someone knocks on the floor from downstairs.

There! They're calling me to come down: there's someone come to see me. I'll be back in a moment.... (*Goes out hurriedly, stroking his beard.*)

IRENA: He's up to one of his little games.

TOOZENBACH: Yes. He looked very solemn as he left. He's obviously going to give you a present.

IRENA: I do dislike that sort of thing ....

OLGA: Yes, isn't it dreadful? He's always doing something silly.

MASHA: 'A green oak grows by a curving shore, And round that oak hangs a golden chain' .... (*Gets up as she sings under her breath.*)

OLGA: You're sad today, Masha.

MASHA: (*Puts on her hat, singing.*)

OLGA: Where are you going?

MASHA: Home.

IRENA: What a strange thing to do.

TOOZENBACH: What! Going away from your sister's party?

MASHA: What does it matter? I'll be back this evening. Goodbye, my darling. (*Kisses* IRENA.) And once again – I wish you all the happiness in the world. In the old days when Father was alive we used to have thirty or forty officers at our parties. What gay parties we had! And today – what have we got today? A man and a half, and the place is as quiet as a tomb. I'm going home. I'm depressed today, I'm sad, so don't listen to me. (*Laughs through her tears.*) We'll have a talk later, but goodbye for now, my dear. I'll go somewhere or other....

IRENA: (*Displeased.*) Really, you are a....

OLGA: (*Tearfully.*) I understand you, Masha.

SOLIONY: If a man starts philosophizing, you call that philosophy, or possibly just sophistry, but if a woman or a couple of women start philosophizing you call that ... what would you call it, now? Ask me another!

MASHA: What are you talking about? You are a disconcerting person!

SOLIONY: Nothing.
'He had no time to say "Oh, oh!"
Before that bear had struck him low'....

A pause.

MASHA: (*To* OLGA, *crossly.*) Do stop snivelling!

Enter ANFISA *and* FERAPONT, *the latter carrying a large cake.*

ANFISA: Come along, my dear, this way. Come in, your boots are quite clean. (*To* IRENA.) A cake from Protopopov, at the Council Office.

IRENA: Thank you. Tell him I'm very grateful to him. (*Takes the cake.*)

FERAPONT: What's that?

IRENA: (*Louder.*) Tell him I sent my thanks.

OLGA: Nanny, will you give him a piece of cake? Go along, Ferapont, they'll give you some cake.

FERAPONT: What's that?

ANFISA: Come along with me, Ferapont Spiridonych, my dear. Come along. (*Goes out with* FERAPONT.)

MASHA: I don't like that Protopopov fellow, Mihail Potapych, or Ivanych, or whatever it is. It's best not to invite him here.

IRENA: I haven't invited him.

MASHA: Thank goodness.

Enter CHEBUTYKIN, *followed by a soldier carrying a silver samovar. Murmurs of astonishment and displeasure.*

OLGA: (*Covering her face with her hands.*) A samovar! But this is dreadful! (*Goes through to the ballroom and stands by the table.*)

IRENA: My dear Ivan Romanych, what are you thinking about?

TOOZENBACH: (*Laughs.*) Didn't I tell you?

MASHA: Ivan Romanych, you really ought to be ashamed of yourself!

CHEBUTYKIN: My dear, sweet girls, I've no one in the world but you. You're dearer to me than anything in the world! I'm nearly sixty, I'm an old man, a lonely, utterly unimportant old man. The only thing that's worth anything in me is my love for you, and if it weren't for you, really I would have been dead long ago. (*To* IRENA.) My dear, my sweet little girl, haven't I known you since the very day you were born? Didn't I carry you about in my arms?... didn't I love your dear mother?

IRENA: But why do you get such expensive presents?

CHEBUTYKIN: (*Tearfully and crossly.*) Expensive presents!... Get along with you! (*To the orderly.*) Put the samovar over there. (*Mimics* IRENA.) Expensive presents!

The orderly takes the samovar to the ballroom.

ANFISA: (*Crosses the drawing-room.*) My dears, there's a strange colonel just arrived. He's taken off his coat and he's coming up now. Irenushka, do be nice and polite to him, won't you? (*In the doorway.*) And it's high time we had lunch, too.... Oh, dear! (*Goes out.*)

TOOZENBACH: It's Vershinin, I suppose.

Enter VERSHININ.

TOOZENBACH: Lieutenant-Colonel Vershinin!

VERSHININ: (*To* MASHA *and* IRENA.) Allow me to introduce myself – Lieutenant-Colonel Vershinin. I'm so glad, so very glad to be here at last. How you've changed! Dear, dear, how you've changed!

IRENA: Please, do sit down. We're very pleased to see you, I'm sure.

VERSHININ: (*Gayly.*) I'm so glad to see you, so glad! But there were three of you, weren't there? – three sisters. I remember there were three little girls. I don't remember their faces, but I knew your father, Colonel Prozorov, and I remember he had three little girls. Oh, yes, I saw them myself. I remember them quite well. How time flies! Dear, dear, how it flies!

TOOZENBACH: Alexandr Ignatyevich comes from Moscow.

IRENA: From Moscow? You come from Moscow?

VERSHININ: Yes, from Moscow. Your father was a battery commander there, and I was an officer in the same brigade. (*To* MASHA.) I seem to remember your face a little.

MASHA: I don't remember you at all.

IRENA: Olia, Olia! (*Calls towards the ballroom.*) Olia, do come!

OLGA *enters from the ballroom.*

IRENA: It seems that Lieutenant-Colonel Vershinin comes from Moscow.

VERSHININ: You must be Olga Serghyeevna, the eldest. And you are Maria.... And you are Irena, the youngest ....

OLGA: You come from Moscow?

VERSHININ: Yes. I studied in Moscow and entered the service there. I stayed there quite a long time, but then I was put in charge of a battery here – so I moved out here, you see. I don't really remember you, you know, I only remember that there were three sisters. I remember your father, though, I remember him very well. All I need to do is to close my eyes and I can see him standing there as if he were alive. I used to visit you in Moscow.

OLGA: I thought I remembered everybody, and yet ....

VERSHININ: My Christian names are Alexandr Ignatyevich.

IRENA: Alexandr Ignatyevich, and you come from Moscow! Well, what a surprise!

OLGA: We're going to live there, you know.

IRENA: We hope to be there by the autumn. It's our home town, we were born there.... In Staraya Basmannaya Street.

Both laugh happily.

MASHA: Fancy meeting a fellow townsman so unexpectedly! (*Eagerly.*) I remember now. Do you remember, Olga, there was someone they used to call 'the lovesick Major'? You were a Lieutenant then, weren't you, and you were in love with someone or other, and everyone used to tease you about it. They called you 'Major' for some reason or other.

VERSHININ: (*Laughs.*) That's it, that's it.... 'The lovesick Major', that's what they called me.

MASHA: In those days you only had a moustache.... Oh, dear, how much older you look! (*Tearfully.*) How much older!

VERSHININ: Yes, I was still a young man in the days when they called me 'the lovesick Major'. I was in love then. It's different now.

OLGA: But you haven't got a single grey hair! You've aged, yes, but you're certainly not an old man.

VERSHININ: Nevertheless, I'm turned forty-two. Is it long since you left Moscow?

IRENA: Eleven years. Now what are you crying for, Masha, you funny girl? ... (*Tearfully.*) You'll make me cry, too.

MASHA: I'm not crying. What was the street you lived in?

VERSHININ: In the Staraya Basmannaya.

OLGA: We did, too.

VERSHININ: At one time I lived in the Niemietzkaya Street. I used to walk from there to the Krasny Barracks, and I remember there was such a gloomy bridge I had to cross. I used to hear the noise of the water rushing under it. I remember how lonely and sad I felt there. (*A pause.*) But what a magnificently wide river you have here! It's a marvellous river!

OLGA: Yes, but this is a cold place. It's cold here, and there are too many mosquitoes.

VERSHININ: Really? I should have said you had a really good healthy climate here, a real Russian climate. Forest, river ... birch trees, too. The dear, unpretentious birch trees — I love them more than any of the other trees. It's nice living here. But there's one rather strange thing, the station is fifteen miles from the town. And no one knows why.

SOLIONY: I know why it is. (*Everyone looks at him.*) Because if the station were nearer, it wouldn't be so far away, and as it is so far away, it can't be nearer.

An awkward silence.

TOOZENBACH: You like your little joke, Vassily Vassilich.

OLGA: I'm sure I remember you now. I know I do.

VERSHININ: I knew your mother.

CHEBUTYKIN: She was a good woman, God bless her memory!

IRENA: Mamma was buried in Moscow.

OLGA: At the convent of Novo-Dievichye.

MASHA: You know, I'm even beginning to forget what she looked like. I suppose people will lose all memory of us in just the same way. We'll be forgotten.

VERSHININ: Yes, we shall all be forgotten. Such is our fate, and we can't do anything about it. And all the things that seem serious, important and full of meaning to us now will be forgotten one day — or anyway they won't seem important any more. (*A pause.*) It's strange to think that we're utterly unable to tell what will be regarded as great and important in the future and what will be thought of as just paltry and ridiculous. Didn't the great discoveries of Copernicus — or of Columbus, if you like — appear useless and unimportant to begin with? — whereas some rubbish, written up by an eccentric fool, was regarded as a revelation of great truth?

It may well be that in time to come the life we live today will seem strange and uncomfortable and stupid and not too clean, either, and perhaps even wicked ...

TOOZENBACH: Who can tell? It's just as possible that future generations will think that we lived our lives on a very high plane and remember us with respect. After all, we no longer have tortures and public executions and invasions, though there's still a great deal of suffering!

SOLIONY: (*In a high-pitched voice as if calling to chickens.*) Cluck, cluck, cluck! There's nothing our good Baron loves as much as a nice bit of philosophizing.

TOOZENBACH: Vassily Vassilich, will you kindly leave me alone? (*Moves to another chair.*) It's becoming tiresome.

SOLIONY: (*As before.*) Cluck, cluck, cluck!...

TOOZENBACH: (*To* VERSHININ.) The suffering that we see around us — and there's so much of it — itself proves that our society has at least achieved a level of morality which is higher....

VERSHININ: Yes, yes, of course.

CHEBUTYKIN: You said just now, Baron, that our age will be called great; but people are small all the same.... (*Gets up.*) Look how small I am.

A violin is played offstage.

MASHA: That's Andrey playing the violin; he's our brother, you know.

IRENA: We've got quite a clever brother.... We're expecting him to be a professor. Papa was a military man, but Andrey chose an academic career.

OLGA: We've been teasing him today. We think he's in love, just a little.

IRENA: With a girl who lives down here. She'll be calling in today most likely.

MASHA: The way she dresses herself is awful! It's not that her clothes are just ugly and old-fashioned, they're simply pathetic. She'll put on some weird-looking, bright yellow skirt with a crude sort of fringe affair, and then a red blouse to go with it. And her cheeks look as though they've been scrubbed, they're so shiny! Andrey's not in love with her — I can't believe it; after all, he has got some taste. I think he's just playing the fool, just to annoy us. I heard yesterday that she's going to get married to Protopopov, the chairman of the local council. I thought it was an excellent idea. (*Calls through the side door.*) Andrey, come here, will you? Just for a moment, dear.

Enter ANDREY.

OLGA: This is my brother, Andrey Serghyeevich.

VERSHININ: Vershinin.

ANDREY: Prozorov. (*Wipes the perspiration from his face.*) I believe you've been appointed battery commander here?

OLGA: What do you think, dear? Alexandr Ignatyevich comes from Moscow.

ANDREY: Do you, really? Congratulations! You'll get no peace from my sisters now.

VERSHININ: I'm afraid your sisters must be getting tired of me already.

IRENA: Just look, Andrey gave me this little picture frame today. (*Shows him the frame.*) He made it himself.

VERSHININ: (*Looks at the frame, not knowing what to say.*) Yes, it's ... it's very nice indeed.... .

IRENA: Do you see that little frame over the piano? He made that one, too.

ANDREY waves his hand impatiently and walks off.

OLGA: He's awfully clever, and he plays the violin, and he makes all sorts of things, too. In fact, he's very gifted all round. Andrey, please, don't go. He's got such a bad habit – always going off like this. Come here!

MASHA and IRENA take him by the arms and lead him back, laughing.

MASHA: Now just you come here!

ANDREY: Do leave me alone, please do!

MASHA: You are a silly! They used to call Alexandr Ignatyevich 'the lovesick Major', and he didn't get annoyed.

VERSHININ: Not in the least.

MASHA: I feel like calling you a 'lovesick fiddler'.

IRENA: Or a 'lovesick professor'.

OLGA: He's fallen in love! Our Andriusha's in love!

IRENA: (*Clapping her hands.*) Three cheers for Andriusha! Andriusha's in love!

CHEBUTYKIN: (*Comes up behind ANDREY and puts his arms round his waist.*) 'Nature created us for love alone.' ... (*Laughs loudly, still holding his paper in his hand.*)

ANDREY: That's enough of it, that's enough.... (*Wipes his face.*) I couldn't get to sleep all night, and I'm not feeling too grand just now. I read till four o'clock, and then I went to bed, but nothing happened. I kept thinking about one thing and another ... and it gets light so early; the sun just pours into my room. I'd like to translate a book from the English while I'm here during the summer.

VERSHININ: You read English, then?

ANDREY: Yes. My father – God bless his memory – used to simply wear us out with learning. It sounds silly, I know, but I must confess that since he died I've begun to grow stout, as if I'd been physically relieved of the strain. I've grown quite stout in a year. Yes, thanks to Father, my sisters and I know French and German and English, and Irena here knows Italian, too. But what an effort it all cost us!

MASHA: Knowing three languages in a town like this is an unnecessary luxury. In fact, not even a luxury, but just a sort of useless encumbrance ... it's rather like having a sixth finger on your hand. We know a lot of stuff that's just useless.

VERSHININ: Really! (*Laughs.*) You know a lot of stuff that's useless! It seems to me that there's no place on earth, however dull and depressing it may be, where intelligence and education can be useless. Let us suppose that among the hundred thousand people in this town, all of them, no doubt, very backward and uncultured, there are just three people like yourselves. Obviously, you can't hope to triumph over all the mass of ignorance around you; as your life goes by, you'll have to keep giving in little by little until you get lost in the crowd, in the hundred thousand. Life will swallow you up, but you'll not quite disappear, you'll make some impression on it. After you've gone, perhaps six more people like you will turn up, then twelve, and so on, until in the end most people will have become like you. So in two or three hundred years life on this old earth of ours will have become marvellously beautiful. Man longs for a life like that, and if it isn't here yet, he must imagine it, wait for it, dream about it, prepare for it, he must know and see more than his father and his grandfather did. (*Laughs.*) And you're complaining because you know a lot of stuff that's useless.

MASHA: (*Takes off her hat.*) I'll be staying to lunch.

IRENA: (*With a sigh.*) Really, someone should have written all that down.

ANDREY has left the room, unnoticed.

TOOZENBACH: You say that in time to come life will be marvellously beautiful. That's probably true. But in order to share in it now, at a distance so to speak, we must prepare for it and work for it.

VERSHININ: (*Gets up.*) Yes.... What a lot of flowers you've got here! (*Looks round.*) And what a marvellous house! I do envy you! All my life I seem to have been pigging it in small flats, with two chairs and a sofa and a stove which always smokes. It's the flowers that I've missed in my life, flowers like these!... (*Rubs his hands.*) Oh, well, never mind!

TOOZENBACH: Yes, we must work. I suppose you're thinking I'm a sentimental German. But I assure you I'm not – I'm Russian. I don't speak a word of German. My father was brought up in the Greek Orthodox faith. (*A pause.*)

VERSHININ: (*Walks up and down the room.*) You know, I often wonder what it would be like if you could start your life over again – deliberately, I mean, consciously.... Suppose you could put aside the life you'd lived already, as though it was just a sort of rough draft, and then start another one like a fair copy. If that happened, I think the thing you'd want most of all would be not to repeat yourself. You'd try at least to create a new environment for yourself, a flat like this one, for instance, with some flowers and plenty of light.... I have a wife, you know, and two little girls; and my wife's not very well, and all that.... Well, if I had to start my life all over again, I wouldn't marry.... No, no!

Enter KOOLYGHIN, in the uniform of a teacher.

KOOLYGHIN: (*Approaches* IRENA.) Congratulations, dear sister – from the bottom of my heart, congratulations on your Saint's day. I wish you good health and everything a girl of your age ought to have! And allow me to present you with this little book.... (*Hands her a book.*) It's the history of our school covering the whole fifty years of its existence. I wrote it myself. Quite a trifle, of course – I wrote it in my spare time when I had nothing better to do – but I hope you'll read it nevertheless. Good morning to you all! (*To* VERSHININ.) Allow me to introduce myself. Koolyghin's the name; I'm a master at the secondary school here. And a town councillor. (*To* IRENA.) You'll find a list in the book of all the pupils who have completed their studies at our school during the last fifty years. *Feci quod potui, faciant melior a potentes.* (*Kisses* MASHA.)

IRENA: But you gave me this book last Easter!

KOOLYGHIN: (*Laughs.*) Did I really? In that case, give it me back – or no, better give it to the Colonel. Please do take it, Colonel. Maybe you'll read it some time when you've nothing better to do.

VERSHININ: Thank you very much. (*Prepares to leave.*) I'm so very glad to have made your acquaintance....

OLGA: You aren't going, are you?... Really, you mustn't.

IRENA: But you'll stay and have lunch with us! Please do.

OLGA: Please do.

VERSHININ: (*Bows.*) I see I've intruded on your Saint's day party. I didn't know. Forgive me for not offering you my congratulations. (*Goes into the ballroom with* OLGA.)

KOOLYGHIN: Today is Sunday, my friends, a day of rest; let us rest and enjoy it, each according to his age and position in life! We shall have to roll up the carpets and put them away till the winter.... We must remember to put some naphthaline on them, or Persian powder.... The Romans enjoyed good health because they knew how to work *and* how to rest. They had *mens sana in corpore sano.* Their life had a definite shape, a form.... The director of the school says that the most important thing about life is form.... A thing that loses its form is finished – that's just as true of our ordinary, everyday lives. (*Takes* MASHA *by the waist and laughs.*) Masha loves me. My wife loves me. Yes, and the curtains will have to be put away with the carpets, too.... I'm cheerful today, I'm in quite excellent spirits.... Masha, we're invited to the director's at four o'clock today. A country walk has been arranged for the teachers and their families.

MASHA: I'm not going.

KOOLYGHIN: (*Distressed.*) Masha, darling, why not?

MASHA: I'll tell you later.... (*Crossly.*) All right, I'll come, only leave me alone now.... (*Walks off.*)

KOOLYGHIN: And after the walk we shall all spend the evening at the director's house. In spite of weak health, that man is certainly sparing no pains to be sociable. A first-rate, thoroughly enlightened man! A most excellent person! After the conference yesterday he said to me: 'I'm tired,

Fiodor Ilyich. I'm tired!' (*Looks at the clock, then at his watch.*) Your clock is seven minutes fast. Yes, 'I'm tired,' he said.

The sound of the violin is heard offstage.

OLGA: Will you all come and sit down, please! Lunch is ready. There's a pie.

KOOLYGHIN: Ah, Olga, my dear girl! Last night I worked up to eleven o'clock, and I felt tired, but today I'm quite happy. (*Goes to the table in the ballroom.*) My dear Olga!

CHEBUTYKIN: (*Puts the newspaper in his pocket and combs his beard.*) A pie? Excellent!

MASHA: (*Sternly to* CHEBUTYKIN.) Remember, you mustn't take anything to drink today. Do you hear? It's bad for you.

CHEBUTYKIN: Never mind. I've got over that weakness long ago! I haven't done any heavy drinking for two years. (*Impatiently.*) Anyway, my dear, what does it matter?

MASHA: All the same, don't you dare to drink anything. Mind you don't now! (*Crossly, but taking care that her husband does not hear.*) So now I've got to spend another of these damnably boring evenings at the director's!

TOOZENBACH: I wouldn't go if I were you, and that's that.

CHEBUTYKIN: Don't you go, my dear.

MASHA: Don't go, indeed! Oh, what a damnable life! It's intolerable.... (*Goes into the ballroom.*)

CHEBUTYKIN: (*Follows her.*) Well, well!...

SOLIONY: (*As he passes* TOOZENBACH *on the way to the ballroom.*) Cluck, cluck, cluck!

TOOZENBACH: Do stop it, Vassily Vassilich. I've really had enough of it....

SOLIONY: Cluck, cluck, cluck!...

KOOLYGHIN: (*Gaily.*) Your health, Colonel! I'm a schoolmaster ... and I'm quite one of the family here, as it were. I'm Masha's husband. She's got a sweet nature, such a very sweet nature!

VERSHININ: I think I'll have a little of this dark vodka. (*Drinks.*) Your health! (*To* OLGA.) I do feel so happy with you people!

Only IRENA *and* TOOZENBACH *remain in the drawing-room.*

IRENA: Masha's a bit out of humour today. You know, she got married when she was eighteen, and then her husband seemed the cleverest man in the world to her. It's different now. He's the kindest of men, but not the cleverest.

OLGA: (*Impatiently.*) Andrey, will you please come?

ANDREY: (*Offstage.*) Just coming. (*Enters and goes to the table.*)

TOOZENBACH: What are you thinking about?

IRENA: Oh, nothing special. You know, I don't like this man Soliony, I'm quite afraid of him. Whenever he opens his mouth he says something silly.

TOOZENBACH: He's a strange fellow. I'm sorry for him, even though he irritates me. In fact, I feel more sorry for him than irritated. I think he's shy. When he's alone with me, he can be quite sensible and friendly, but in company he's offensive and bullying. Don't go over there just yet, let them get settled down at the table. Let me stay beside you for a bit. Tell me what you're thinking about. (*A pause.*) You're twenty ... and I'm not thirty yet myself. What years and years we still have ahead of us, a whole long succession of years, all full of my love for you!...

IRENA: Don't talk to me about love, Nikolai Lvovich.

TOOZENBACH: (*Not listening.*) Oh, I long so passionately for life, I long to work and strive so much, and all this longing is somehow mingled with my love for you, Irena. And just because you happen to be beautiful, life appears beautiful to me! What are you thinking about?

IRENA: You say that life is beautiful. Maybe it is – but what if it only seems to be beautiful? Our lives, I mean the lives of us three sisters, haven't been beautiful up to now. The truth is that life has been stifling us, like weeds in a garden. I'm afraid I'm crying.... So unnecessary.... (*Quickly dries her eyes and smiles.*) We must work, work! The reason we feel depressed and take such a gloomy view of life is that we've never known what it is to make a real effort. We're the children of parents who despised work....

Enter NATALIA IVANOVNA. She is wearing a pink dress with a green belt.

NATASHA: They've gone in to lunch already.... I'm late.... (*Glances at herself in a mirror, adjusts her dress.*) My hair seems to be all right.... (*Catches sight of IRENA.*) My dear Irena Serghyeevna, congratulations! (*Gives her a vigorous and prolonged kiss.*) You've got such a lot of visitors.... I feel quite shy.... How do you do, Baron?

OLGA: (*Enters the drawing-room.*) Oh, there you are, Natalia Ivanovna! How are you, my dear?

They kiss each other.

NATASHA: Congratulations! You've such a lot of people here, I feel dreadfully shy....

OLGA: It's all right, they're all old friends. (*Alarmed, dropping her voice.*) You've got a green belt on! My dear, that's surely a mistake!

NATASHA: Why, is it a bad omen, or what?

OLGA: No, but it just doesn't go with your dress ... it looks so strange....

NATASHA: (*Tearfully.*) Really? But it isn't really green, you know, it's a sort of dull colour.... (*Follows OLGA to the ballroom.*)

All are now seated at the table; the drawing-room is empty.

KOOLYGHIN: Irena, you know, I do wish you'd find yourself a good husband. In my view it's high time you got married.

CHEBUTYKIN: You ought to get yourself a nice little husband, too, Natalia Ivanovna.

KOOLYGHIN: Natalia Ivanovna already has a husband in view.

MASHA: (*Strikes her plate with her fork.*) A glass of wine for me, please! Three cheers for our jolly old life! We keep our end up, we do!

KOOLYGHIN: Masha, you won't get more than five out of ten for good conduct!

VERSHININ: I say, this liqueur's very nice. What is it made of?

SOLIONY: Black beetles!

IRENA: Ugh! ugh! How disgusting!

OLGA: We're having roast turkey for dinner tonight, and then apple tart. Thank goodness, I'll be here all day today ... this evening, too. You must all come this evening.

VERSHININ: May I come in the evening, too?

IRENA: Yes, please do.

NATASHA: They don't stand on ceremony here.

CHEBUTYKIN: 'Nature created us for love alone.' ... (*Laughs.*)

ANDREY: (*Crossly.*) Will you stop it, please? Aren't you tired of it yet?

FEDOTIK and RODÉ come in with a large basket of flowers.

FEDOTIK: Just look here, they're having lunch already!

RODÉ: (*In a loud voice.*) Having their lunch? So they are, they're having lunch already.

FEDOTIK: Wait half a minute. (*Takes a snapshot.*) One! Just one minute more!... (*Takes another snapshot.*) Two! All over now.

They pick up the basket and go into the ballroom where they are greeted uproariously.

RODÉ: (*Loudly.*) Congratulations, Irena Serghyeevna! I wish you all the best, everything you'd wish for yourself! Gorgeous weather today, absolutely marvellous. I've been out walking the whole morning with the boys. You do know that I teach gym at the high school, don't you?...

FEDOTIK: You may move now, Irena Serghyeevna, that is, if you want to. (*Takes a snapshot.*) You do look attractive today. (*Takes a top out of his pocket.*) By the way, look at this top. It's got a wonderful hum.

IRENA: What a sweet little thing!

MASHA: 'A green oak grows by a curving shore, And round that oak hangs a golden chain.' ... A green chain around that oak.... (*Peevishly.*) Why do I keep on saying that? Those lines have been worrying me all day long!

KOOLYGHIN: Do you know, we're thirteen at table?

RODÉ: (*Loudly.*) You don't really believe in these old superstitions, do you? (*Laughter.*)

KOOLYGHIN: When thirteen people sit down to table, it means that some of them are in love. Is it you, by any chance, Ivan Romanych?

CHEBUTYKIN: Oh, I'm just an old sinner.... But what I can't make out is why Natalia Ivanovna looks so embarrassed.

Loud laughter. NATASHA runs out into the drawing-room, ANDREY follows her.

ANDREY: Please, Natasha, don't take any notice of them! Stop ... wait a moment.... Please!

Figure 6 From the Moscow Art Theatre 1901 production of *Three Sisters*.

NATASHA: I feel so ashamed.... I don't know what's the matter with me, and they're all laughing at me. It's awful of me to leave the table like that, but I couldn't help it.... I just couldn't.... (*Covers her face with her hands.*)

ANDREY: My dear girl, please, please don't get upset. Honestly, they don't mean any harm, they're just teasing. My dear, sweet girl, they're really good-natured folks, they all are, and they're fond of us both. Come over to the window, they can't see us there.... (*Looks round.*)

NATASHA: You see, I'm not used to being with a lot of people.

ANDREY: Oh, how young you are, Natasha, how wonderfully, beautifully young! My dear, sweet girl, don't get so upset! Do believe me, believe me.... I'm so happy, so full of love, of joy.... No, they can't see us here! They can't see us! How did I come to love you, when was it? ... I don't understand anything. My precious, my sweet, my innocent girl, please – I want you to marry me! I love you, I love you as I've never loved anybody.... (*Kisses her.*)

Enter two officers and, seeing NATASHA and ANDREY kissing, stand and stare in amazement.

Act 2

The scene is the same as in Act 1.

It is eight o'clock in the evening. The faint sound of an accordion is heard coming from the street.

The stage is unlit. Enter NATALIA IVANOVNA in a dressing-gown, carrying a candle. She crosses the stage and stops by the door leading to ANDREY's room.

NATASHA: What are you doing, Andriusha? Reading? It's all right, I only wanted to know.... (*Goes to another door, opens it, looks inside and shuts it again.*) No one's left a light anywhere....

ANDREY: (*Enters with a book in his hand.*) What is it, Natasha?

NATASHA: I was just going round to see if anyone had left a light anywhere. It's carnival week, and the servants are so excited about it ... anything might happen! You've got to watch them. Last night about twelve o'clock I happened to go into the dining-room, and – would you believe it? – there was a candle alight on the table. I've not found out who lit it. (*Puts the candle down.*) What time is it?

ANDREY: (*Glances at his watch.*) Quarter past eight.

NATASHA: And Olga and Irena still out. They aren't back from work yet, poor things! Olga's still at some teachers' conference, and Irena's at the post office. (*Sighs.*) This morning I said to Irena: 'Do take care of yourself, my dear.' But she won't listen. Did you say it was a quarter past eight? I'm afraid Bobik is not at all well. Why does he get so cold? Yesterday he had a temperature, but today he feels quite cold when you touch him.... I'm so afraid!

ANDREY: It's all right, Natasha. The boy's well enough.

NATASHA: Still, I think he ought to have a special diet. I'm so anxious about him. By the way, they tell me that some carnival party's supposed to be coming here soon after nine. I'd rather they didn't come, Andriusha.

ANDREY: Well, I really don't know what I can do. They've been asked to come.

NATASHA: This morning the dear little fellow woke up and looked at me, and then suddenly he smiled. He recognized me, you see. 'Good morning, Bobik,' I said, 'good morning, darling precious!' And then he laughed. Babies understand everything, you know, they understand us perfectly well. Anyway, Andriusha, I'll tell the servants not to let that carnival party in.

ANDREY: (*Irresolutely.*) Well … it's really for my sisters to decide, isn't it? It's their house, after all.

NATASHA: Yes, it's their house as well. I'll tell them, too…. They're so kind…. (*Walks off.*) I've ordered sour milk for supper. The doctor says you ought to eat nothing but sour milk, or you'll never get any thinner. (*Stops.*) Bobik feels so cold. I'm afraid his room is too cold for him. He ought to move into a warmer room, at least until the warm weather comes. Irena's room, for instance – that's just a perfect room for a baby: it's dry, and it gets the sun all day long. We must tell her: perhaps she'd share Olga's room for a bit…. In any case, she's never at home during the day, she only sleeps there…. (*A pause.*) Andriusha, why don't you say anything?

ANDREY: I was just day-dreaming. … There's nothing to say, anyway….

NATASHA: Well…. What was it I was going to tell you? Oh, yes! Ferapont from the Council Office wants to see you about something.

ANDREY: (*yawns*). Tell him to come up.

NATASHA goes out. ANDREY, bending over the candle which she has left behind, begins to read his book. Enter FERAPONT in an old shabby overcoat, his collar turned up, his ears muffled in a scarf.

ANDREY: Hullo, old chap! What did you want to see me about?

FERAPONT: The chairman's sent you the register and a letter or something. Here they are. (*Hands him the book and the letter.*)

ANDREY: Thanks. That's all right. Incidentally, why have you come so late? It's gone eight already.

FERAPONT: What's that?

ANDREY: (*Raising his voice.*) I said, why have you come so late? It's gone eight already.

FERAPONT: That's right. It was still daylight when I came first, but they wouldn't let me see you. The master's engaged, they said. Well, if you're engaged, you're engaged. I'm not in a hurry. (*Thinking that ANDREY has said something.*) What's that?

ANDREY: Nothing. (*Turns over the pages of the register.*) Tomorrow's Friday, there's no meeting, but I'll go to the office just the same … do some work. I'm so bored at home! … (*A pause.*) Yes, my dear old fellow, how things do change, what a fraud life is! So strange! Today I picked up this book, just out of boredom, because I hadn't anything to do. It's a copy of some lectures I attended at the University…. Good Heavens! Just think – I'm secretary of the local council now, and Protopopov's chairman, and the most I can ever hope for is to become a member of the council myself! I – a member of the local council! I, who dream every night that I'm a professor in Moscow University, a famous academician, the pride of all Russia!

FERAPONT: I'm sorry, I can't tell you. I don't hear very well.

ANDREY: If you could hear properly I don't think I'd be talking to you like this. I must talk to someone, but my wife doesn't seem to understand me, and as for my sisters … I'm afraid of them for some reason or other, I'm afraid of them laughing at me and pulling my leg…. I don't drink and I don't like going to pubs, but my word! how I'd enjoy an hour or so at Tyestov's, or the Great Moscow Restaurant! Yes, my dear fellow, I would indeed!

FERAPONT: The other day at the office a contractor was telling me about some business men who were eating pancakes in Moscow. One of them ate forty pancakes and died. It was either forty or fifty, I can't remember exactly.

ANDREY: You can sit in some huge restaurant in Moscow without knowing anyone, and no one knowing you; yet somehow you don't feel that you don't belong there…. Whereas here you know everybody, and everybody knows you, and yet you don't feel you belong here, you feel you don't belong at all…. You're lonely and you feel a stranger.

FERAPONT: What's that? (*A pause.*) It was the same man that told me – of course, he may have been lying – he said that there's an enormous rope stretched right across Moscow.

ANDREY: Whatever for?

FERAPONT: I'm sorry, I can't tell you. That's what he said.

ANDREY: What nonsense! (*Reads the book.*) Have you ever been to Moscow?

FERAPONT: (*After a pause.*) No. It wasn't God's wish. (*A pause.*) Shall I go now?

ANDREY: Yes, you may go. Goodbye.

FERAPONT goes out.

Goodbye. (*Reading.*) Come in the morning to take some letters…. You can go now. (*A pause.*) He's gone.(*A bell rings.*) Yes, that's how it is…. (*Stretches and slowly goes to his room.*)

Singing is heard offstage; a nurse is putting a baby to sleep. Enter MASHA and VERSHININ. While they talk together, a maid lights a lamp and candles in the ballroom.

MASHA: I don't know. (*A pause.*) I don't know. Habit's very important, of course. For instance, after Father died, for a long time we couldn't get accustomed to the idea that we hadn't any orderlies to wait on us. But, habit apart, I think it's quite right what I was saying. Perhaps it's different in other places, but in this town the military certainly do seem to be the nicest and most generous and best-mannered people.

VERSHININ: I'm thirsty. I could do with a nice glass of tea.

MASHA: (*Glances at her watch.*) They'll bring it in presently. You see, they married me off when I was eighteen. I was afraid of my husband because he was a school-master, and I had only just left school myself. He seemed terribly learned

Figure 7 *Drei Schwestern* (Three Sisters) at the Schaubühne am Lehniner Platz in Berlin, 2009. (Photograph Arno Declair.)

then, very clever and important. Now it's quite different, unfortunately.

VERSHININ: Yes.... I see....

MASHA: I don't say anything against my husband – I'm used to him now – but there are such a lot of vulgar and unpleasant and offensive people among the other civilians. Vulgarity upsets me, it makes me feel insulted, I actually suffer when I meet someone who lacks refinement and gentle manners, and courtesy. When I'm with the other teachers, my husband's friends, I just suffer.

VERSHININ: Yes, of course. But I should have thought that in a town like this the civilians and the army people were equally uninteresting. There's nothing to choose between them. If you talk to any educated person here, civilian or military, he'll generally tell you that he's just worn out. It's either his wife, or his house, or his estate, or his horse, or something.... We Russians are capable of such elevated thoughts – then why do we have such low ideals in practical life? Why is it, why?

MASHA: Why?

VERSHININ: Yes, why does his wife wear him out, why do his children wear him out? And what about *him* wearing out his wife and children?

MASHA: You're a bit low-spirited today, aren't you?

VERSHININ: Perhaps. I haven't had any dinner today. I've had nothing to eat since morning. One of my daughters is a bit off colour, and when the children are ill, I get so worried. I feel utterly conscience-stricken at having given them a mother like theirs. Oh, if only you could have seen her this morning! What a despicable woman! We started quarrelling at seven o'clock, and at nine I just walked out and slammed the door. (*A pause.*) I never talk about these things in the ordinary way. It's a strange thing, but you're the only person I feel I dare complain to. (*Kisses her hand.*) Don't be angry with me. I've nobody, nobody but you.... (*A pause.*)

MASHA: What a noise the wind's making in the stove! Just before Father died the wind howled in the chimney just like that.

VERSHININ: Are you superstitious?

MASHA: Yes.

VERSHININ: How strange. (*Kisses her hand.*) You really are a wonderful creature, a marvellous creature! Wonderful, marvellous! It's quite dark here, but I can see your eyes shining.

MASHA: (*Moves to another chair.*) There's more light over here.

VERSHININ: I love you, I love you, I love you. ... I love your eyes, I love your movements.... I dream about them. A wonderful, marvellous being!

MASHA: (*Laughing softly.*) When you talk to me like that, somehow I can't help laughing, although I'm afraid at the same time. Don't say it again, please. (*Half-audibly.*) Well, no ... go on. I don't mind.... (*Covers her face with her hands.*) I don't mind.... Someone's coming.... Let's talk about something else....

Enter IRENA and TOOZENBACH through the ballroom.

TOOZENBACH: I have a triple-barrelled name – Baron Toozenbach-Krone-Alschauer – but actually I'm a Russian. I was baptized in the Greek-Orthodox faith, just like yourself. I haven't really got any German characteristics, except maybe the obstinate patient way I keep on pestering you. Look how I bring you home every evening.

IRENA: How tired I am!

TOOZENBACH: And I'll go on fetching you from the post office and bringing you home every evening for the next twenty years – unless you send me away.... (*Noticing* MASHA *and* VERSHININ, *with pleasure.*) Oh, it's you! How are you?

IRENA: Well, here I am, home at last! (*To* MASHA.) A woman came into the post office just before I left. She wanted to send a wire to her brother in Saratov to tell him her son had just died, but she couldn't remember the address. So we had to send the wire without an address, just to Saratov. She was crying and I was rude to her, for no reason at all. 'I've no time to waste,' I told her. So stupid of me. We're having the carnival crowd today, aren't we?

MASHA: Yes.

IRENA: (*Sits down.*) How nice it is to rest! I am tired!

TOOZENBACH: (*Smiling.*) When you come back from work, you look so young, so pathetic, somehow.... (*A pause.*)

IRENA: I'm tired. No, I don't like working at the post office, I don't like it at all.

MASHA: You've got thinner.... (*Whistles.*) You look younger, too, and your face looks quite boyish.

TOOZENBACH: It's the way she does her hair.

IRENA: I must look for another job. This one doesn't suit me. It hasn't got what I always longed for and dreamed about. It's the sort of work you do without inspiration, without even thinking.

Someone knocks at the floor from below.

That's the Doctor knocking. (*To* TOOZENBACH.) Will you answer him, dear? ... I can't.... I'm so tired.

TOOZENBACH: (*knocks on the floor.*)

IRENA: He'll be up in a moment. We must do something about all this. Andrey and the Doctor went to the club last night and lost at cards again. They say Andrey lost two hundred roubles.

MASHA: (*With indifference.*) Well, what are we to do about it?

IRENA: He lost a fortnight ago, and he lost in December, too. I wish to goodness he'd lose everything we've got, and soon, too, and then perhaps we'd move out of this place. Good Heavens, I dream of Moscow every night. Sometimes I feel as if I were going mad. (*Laughs.*) We're going to Moscow in June. How many months are there till June? ... February, March, April, May ... nearly half-a-year!

MASHA: We must take care that Natasha doesn't get to know about him losing at cards.

IRENA: I don't think she cares.

Enter CHEBUTYKIN. *He has been resting on his bed since dinner and has only just got up. He combs his beard, then sits down at the table and takes out a newspaper.*

MASHA: There he is. Has he paid his rent yet?

IRENA: (*Laughs.*) No. Not a penny for the last eight months. I suppose he's forgotten.

MASHA: (*Laughs.*) How solemn he looks sitting there!

They all laugh. A pause.

IRENA: Why don't you say something, Alexandr Ignatyevich?

VERSHININ: I don't know. I'm just longing for some tea. I'd give my life for a glass of tea! I've had nothing to eat since morning....

CHEBUTYKIN: Irena Serghyeevna!

IRENA: What is it?

CHEBUTYKIN: Please come here. *Venez ici!*

IRENA goes over to him and sits down at the table.

I can't do without you.

IRENA lays out the cards for a game of patience.

VERSHININ: Well, if we can't have any tea, let's do a bit of philosophizing, anyway.

TOOZENBACH: Yes, let's. What about?

VERSHININ: What about? Well ... let's try to imagine what life will be like after we're dead, say in two or three hundred years.

TOOZENBACH: All right, then.... After we're dead, people will fly about in balloons, the cut of their coats will be different, the sixth sense will be discovered, and possibly even developed and used, for all I know.... But I believe life itself will remain the same; it will still be difficult and full of mystery and full of happiness. And in a thousand years' time people will still be sighing and complaining: 'How hard this business of living is!' – and yet they'll still be scared of death and unwilling to die, just as they are now.

VERSHININ: (*After a moment's thought.*) Well, you know ... how shall I put it? I think everything in the world is bound to change gradually – in fact, it's changing before our very eyes. In two or three hundred years, or maybe in a thousand years – it doesn't matter how long exactly – life will be different. It will be happy. Of course, we shan't be able to enjoy that future life, but all the same, what we're living for now is to create it, we work and ... yes, we suffer in order to create it. That's the goal of our life, and you might say that's the only happiness we shall ever achieve.

MASHA: (*Laughs quietly.*)

TOOZENBACH: Why are you laughing?

MASHA: I don't know. I've been laughing all day today.

VERSHININ (*To* TOOZENBACH.) I went to the same cadet school as you did but I never went on to the Military Academy. I read a great deal, of course, but I never know what books I ought to choose, and probably I read a lot of stuff that's not worth anything. But the longer I live the more I seem to long for knowledge. My hair's going grey and I'm getting on in years, and yet how little I know, how little! All the same, I think I do know one thing which is not only true but also most important. I'm sure of it. Oh, if only I could convince you that there's not going to be any happiness for our own generation, that there mustn't be and won't be.... We've just got to work and work. All the happiness is reserved for our descendants, our remote descendants. (*A pause.*) Anyway, if I'm not to be happy, then at least my children's children will be.

FEDOTIK and RODÉ enter the ballroom; they sit down and sing quietly, one of them playing on a guitar.

TOOZENBACH: So you won't even allow us to dream of happiness! But what if I *am* happy?

VERSHININ: You're not.

TOOZENBACH: (*Flinging up his hands and laughing.*) We don't understand one another, that's obvious. How can I convince you?

MASHA: (*Laughs quietly.*)

TOOZENBACH: (*Holds up a finger to her.*) Show a finger to her and she'll laugh! (*To* VERSHININ.) And life will be just the same as ever not merely in a couple of hundred years' time, but in a million years. Life doesn't change, it always goes on the same; it follows its own laws, which don't concern us, which we can't discover anyway. Think of the birds that migrate in the autumn, the cranes, for instance: they just fly on and on. It doesn't matter what sort of thoughts they've got in their heads, great thoughts or little thoughts, they just fly on and on, not knowing where or why. And they'll go on flying no matter how many philosophers they happen to have flying with them. Let them philosophize as much as they like, as long as they go on flying.

MASHA: Isn't there some meaning?

TOOZENBACH: Meaning? ... Look out there, it's snowing. What's the meaning of that? (*A pause.*)

MASHA: I think a human being has got to have some faith, or at least he's got to seek faith. Otherwise his life will be empty, empty.... How can you live and not know why the cranes fly, why children are born, why the stars shine in the sky! ... You must either know why you live, or else ... nothing matters ... everything's just wild grass.... (*A pause.*)

VERSHININ: All the same, I'm sorry my youth's over.

MASHA: 'It's a bore to be alive in this world, friends,' that's what Gogol says.

TOOZENBACH: And I feel like saying: it's hopeless arguing with you, friends! I give you up.

CHEBUTYKIN: (*Reads out of the paper.*) Balsac's marriage took place at Berdichev.[2]

IRENA: (*Sings softly to herself.*)

CHEBUTYKIN: Must write this down in my notebook. (*Writes.*) Balsac's marriage took place at Berdichev. (*Reads on.*)

IRENA: (*Playing patience, pensively.*) Balsac's marriage took place at Berdichev.

TOOZENBACH: Well, I've thrown in my hand. Did you know that I'd sent in my resignation, Maria Serghyeevna?

MASHA: Yes, I heard about it. I don't see anything good in it, either. I don't like civilians.

TOOZENBACH: Never mind. (*Gets up.*) What sort of a soldier do I make, anyway? I'm not even good-looking. Well, what does it matter? I'll work. I'd like to do such a hard day's work that when I came home in the evening I'd fall on my bed exhausted and go to sleep at once. (*Goes to the ballroom.*) I should think working men sleep well at nights!

FEDOTIK: (*To* IRENA.) I've got you some coloured crayons at Pyzhikov's, in Moscow Street. And this little penknife, too....

IRENA: You still treat me as if I were a little girl. I wish you'd remember I'm grown up now. (*Takes the crayons and the penknife, joyfully.*) They're awfully nice!

FEDOTIK: Look, I bought a knife for myself, too. You see, it's got another blade here, and then another ... this thing's for cleaning your ears, and these are nail-scissors, and this is for cleaning your nails....

RODÉ: (*In a loud voice.*) Doctor, how old are you?

CHEBUTYKIN: I? Thirty-two.

Laughter.

FEDOTIK: I'll show you another kind of patience. (*Sets out the cards.*)

The samovar is brought in, and ANFISA *attends to it. Shortly afterwards* NATASHA *comes in and begins to fuss around the table.*

SOLIONY: (*Enters, bows to the company and sits down at the table.*)

VERSHININ: What a wind, though!

MASHA: Yes. I'm tired of winter. I've almost forgotten what summer is like.

IRENA: (*Playing patience.*) I'm going to go out. We'll get to Moscow!

FEDOTIK: No, it's not going out. You see, the eight has to go on the two of spades. (*Laughs.*) That means you won't go to Moscow.

CHEBUTYKIN: (*Reads the paper.*) Tzitzikar. Smallpox is raging....

ANFISA: (*Goes up to* MASHA.) Masha, the tea's ready, dear. (*To* VERSHININ.) Will you please come to the table, your Excellency? Forgive me, your name's slipped my memory....

MASHA: Bring it here, Nanny. I'm not coming over there.

IRENA: Nanny!

ANFISA: Comi-ing!

NATASHA: (*To* SOLIONY.) You know, even tiny babies understand what we say perfectly well! 'Good morning, Bobik,' I said to him only today, 'Good morning, my precious!' – and then he looked at me in such a special sort of way. You may say it's only a mother's imagination, but it isn't, I do assure you. No, no! He really is an extraordinary child!

SOLIONY: If that child were mine, I'd cook him up in a frying pan and eat him. (*Picks up his glass, goes into the drawing-room and sits down in a corner.*)

NATASHA: (*Covers her face with her hands.*) What a rude, ill-mannered person!

MASHA: People who don't even notice whether it's summer or winter are lucky! I think I'd be indifferent to the weather if I were living in Moscow.

VERSHININ: I've just been reading the diary of some French cabinet minister – he wrote it in prison. He got sent to prison in connection with the Panama affair. He writes with such a passionate delight about the birds he can see through the prison window – the birds he never even noticed when he was a cabinet minister. Of course, now he's released he won't notice them any more.... And in the same way, you won't notice Moscow once you live there again. We're not happy and we can't be happy: we only want happiness.

TOOZENBACH: (*Picks up a box from the table.*) I say, where are all the chocolates?

IRENA: Soliony's eaten them.

TOOZENBACH: All of them?

ANFISA: (*Serving VERSHININ with tea.*) Here's a letter for you, Sir.

VERSHININ: For me? (*Takes the letter.*) From my daughter. (*Reads it.*) Yes, of course.... Forgive me, Maria Serghyeevna, I'll just leave quietly. I won't have any tea. (*Gets up, agitated.*) Always the same thing....

MASHA: What is it? Secret?

VERSHININ: (*In a low voice.*) My wife's taken poison again. I must go. I'll get away without them seeing me. All this is so dreadfully unpleasant. (*Kisses MASHA's hand.*) My dear, good, sweet girl.... I'll go out this way, quietly.... (*Goes out.*)

ANFISA: Where's he off to? And I've just brought him some tea! What a queer fellow!

MASHA: (*Flaring up.*) Leave me alone! Why do you keep worrying me? Why don't you leave me in peace? (*Goes to the table, cup in hand.*) I'm sick and tired of you, silly old woman!

ANFISA: Why.... I didn't mean to offend you, dear.

ANDREY's voice: (*Offstage*). Anfisa!

ANFISA: (*Mimics him.*) Anfisa! Sitting there in his den! ... (*Goes out.*)

MASHA: (*By the table in the ballroom, crossly*.) Do let me sit down somewhere! (*Fumbles up the cards laid out on the table.*) You take up the whole table with your cards! Why don't you get on with your tea?

IRENA: How bad-tempered you are, Mashka!

MASHA: Well, if I'm bad-tempered, don't talk to me, then. Don't touch me!

CHEBUTYKIN: (*Laughs.*) Don't touch her! ... Take care you don't touch her!

MASHA: You may be sixty, but you're always gabbling some damn nonsense or other, just like a child....

NATASHA: (*Sighs.*) My dear Masha, need you use such expressions? You know, with your good looks you'd be thought so charming, even by the best people – yes, I honestly mean it – if only you wouldn't use these expressions of yours! *Je vous prie, pardonnez moi, Marie, mais vous avez des manières un peu grossières.*

TOOZENBACH: (*With suppressed laughter.*) Pass me.... I say, will you please pass me.... Is that cognac over there, or what? ...

NATASHA: *Il parait que mon Bobik déjà ne dort pas....* I think he's awake. He's not been too well today. I must go and see him ... excuse me. (*Goes out.*)

IRENA: I say, where has Alexandr Ignatyevich gone to?

MASHA: He's gone home. His wife's done something queer again.

TOOZENBACH: (*Goes over to SOLIONY with a decanter of cognac.*) You always sit alone brooding over something or other – though what it's all about nobody knows. Well, let's make it up. Let's have a cognac together. (*They drink.*) I suppose I'll have to play the piano all night tonight – a lot of rubbishy tunes, of course.... Never mind!

SOLIONY: Why did you say 'let's make it up'? We haven't quarrelled.

TOOZENBACH: You always give me the feeling that there's something wrong between us. You're a strange character, no doubt about it.

SOLIONY: (*Recites.*) 'I am strange, but who's not so? Don't be angry, Aleko!'

TOOZENBACH: What's Aleko got to do with it? ... (*A pause.*)

SOLIONY: When I'm alone with somebody I'm all right, I'm just like other people. But in company, I get depressed and shy, and ... I talk all sorts of nonsense. All the same, I'm a good deal more honest and well-intentioned than plenty of others. I can prove I am.

TOOZENBACH: You often make me angry because you keep on pestering me when we're in company – but all the same, I do like you for some reason.... I'm going to get drunk tonight, whatever happens! Let's have another drink!

SOLIONY: Yes, let's. (*A pause.*) I've never had anything against you personally, Baron. But my temperament's rather like Lermontov's. (*In a low voice.*) I even look a little like Lermontov, I've been told.... (*Takes a scent bottle from his pocket and sprinkles some scent on his hands.*)

TOOZENBACH: I have sent in my resignation! Finished! I've been considering it for five years, and now I've made up my mind at last. I'm going to work.

SOLIONY: (*Recites.*) 'Don't be angry, Aleko.... Away, away with all your dreams!'

During the conversation ANDREY enters quietly with a book in his hand and sits down by the candle.

TOOZENBACH: I'm going to work!

CHEBUTYKIN: (*Comes into the drawing-room with IRENA.*) And the food they treated me to was the genuine Caucasian stuff: onion soup, followed by chehartma – that's a meat dish, you know.

SOLIONY: Chereshma isn't meat at all; it's a plant, something like an onion.

CHEBUTYKIN: No-o, my dear friend. Chehartma isn't an onion, it's roast mutton.

SOLIONY: I tell you chereshma is a kind of onion.

CHEBUTYKIN: Well, why should I argue about it with you? You've never been to the Caucasus and you've never tasted chehartma.

SOLIONY: I haven't tasted it because I can't stand the smell of it. Chereshma stinks just like garlic.

ANDREY: (*Imploringly.*) Do stop it, friends! Please stop it!

TOOZENBACH: When's the carnival crowd coming along?

IRENA: They promised to be here by nine – that means any moment now.

TOOZENBACH: (*Embraces* ANDREY *and sings.*) 'Ah, my beautiful porch, my lovely new porch, my ...'³

ANDREY: (*Dances and sings.*) 'My new porch all made of maple-wood....'

CHEBUTYKIN: (*Dances.*) 'With fancy carving over the door....'

Laughter.

TOOZENBACH: (*Kisses* ANDREY.) Let's have a drink, the devil take it! Andriusha, let's drink to eternal friendship. I'll come with you when you go back to Moscow University.

SOLIONY: Which university? There are two universities in Moscow.

ANDREY: There's only one.

SOLIONY: I tell you there are two.

ANDREY: Never mind, make it three. The more the merrier.

SOLIONY: There are two universities in Moscow.

Murmurs of protest and cries of 'Hush!'

There are two universities in Moscow, an old one and a new one. But if you don't want to listen to what I'm saying, if my conversation irritates you, I can keep silent. In fact I can go to another room.... (*Goes out through one of the doors.*)

TOOZENBACH: Bravo, bravo! (*Laughs.*) Let's get started, my friends, I'll play for you. What a funny creature that Soliony is! ... (*Sits down at the piano and plays a waltz.*)

MASHA: (*Dances alone.*) The Baron is drunk, the Baron is drunk, the Baron is drunk....

Enter NATASHA.

NATASHA: (*To* CHEBUTYKIN.) Ivan Romanych! (*Speaks to him, then goes out quietly.* CHEBUTYKIN *touches* TOOZENBACH *on the shoulder and whispers to him.*)

IRENA: What is it?

CHEBUTYKIN: It's time we were going. Goodnight.

IRENA: But really.... What about the carnival party?

ANDREY: (*Embarrassed.*) The carnival party's not coming. You see, my dear, Natasha says that Bobik isn't very well, and so. ... Anyway, I don't know ... and I certainly don't care....

IRENA: (*Shrugs her shoulders.*) Bobik's not very well! ...

MASHA: Never mind, we'll keep our end up! If they turn us out, out we must go! (*To* IRENA.) It isn't Bobik who's not well, it's her.... There! ... (*Taps her forehead with her finger.*) Petty little bourgeois housewife!

ANDREY goes to his room on the right. CHEBUTYKIN *follows him. The guests say goodbye in the ballroom.*

FEDOTIK: What a pity! I'd been hoping to spend the evening here, but of course, if the baby's ill.... I'll bring him some toys tomorrow.

RODÉ: (*In a loud voice.*) I had a good long sleep after lunch today on purpose, I thought I'd be dancing all night. I mean to say, it's only just nine o'clock.

MASHA: Let's go outside and talk it over. We can decide what to do then.

Voices are heard saying 'Goodbye! God bless you!' and TOOZENBACH *is heard laughing gaily. Everyone goes out.* ANFISA *and a maid clear the table and put out the lights. The nurse sings to the baby offstage. Enter* ANDREY, *wearing an overcoat and hat, followed by* CHEBUTYKIN. *They move quietly.*

CHEBUTYKIN: I've never found time to get married, somehow ... partly because my life's just flashed past me like lightning, and partly because I was always madly in love with your mother and she was married....

ANDREY: One shouldn't marry. One shouldn't marry because it's so boring.

CHEBUTYKIN: That may be so, but what about loneliness? You can philosophize as much as you like, dear boy, but loneliness is a dreadful thing. Although, really ... well, it doesn't matter a damn, of course! ...

ANDREY: Let's get along quickly.

CHEBUTYKIN: What's the hurry? There's plenty of time.

ANDREY: I'm afraid my wife may try to stop me.

CHEBUTYKIN: Ah!

ANDREY: I won't play cards tonight, I'll just sit and watch. I'm not feeling too well.... What ought I to do for this breathlessness, Ivan Romanych?

CHEBUTYKIN: Why ask me, dear boy? I can't remember – I simply don't know.

ANDREY: Let's go through the kitchen.

They go out. A bell rings. The ring is repeated, then voices and laughter are heard.

IRENA: (*Coming in.*) What's that?

ANFISA: (*In a whisper.*) The carnival party.

The bell rings again.

IRENA: Tell them there's no one at home, Nanny. Apologize to them.

ANFISA goes out. IRENA *walks up and down the room, lost in thought. She seems agitated. Enter* SOLIONY.

SOLIONY: (*Puzzled.*) There's no one here.... Where is everybody?

IRENA: They've gone home.

SOLIONY: How strange! Then you're alone here?

IRENA: Yes, alone. (*A pause.*) Well ... Goodnight.

SOLIONY: I know I behaved tactlessly just now, I lost control of myself. But you're different from the others, you stand out high above them – you're pure, you can see where the truth lies.... You're the only person in the world who can possibly understand me. I love you.... I love you with a deep, infinite ...

IRENA: Do please go away. Goodnight!

SOLIONY: I can't live without you. (*Follows her.*) Oh, it's such a delight just to look at you! (*With tears.*) Oh, my happiness! Your glorious, marvellous, entrancing eyes – eyes like no other woman's I've ever seen....

IRENA: (*Coldly.*) Please stop it, Vassily Vassilich!

SOLIONY: I've never spoken to you of my love before ... it makes me feel as if I were living on a different planet.... (*Rubs his forehead.*) Never mind! I can't force you to love me, obviously. But I don't intend to have any rivals – successful rivals, I mean.... No, no! I swear to you by everything I hold sacred that if there's anyone else, I'll kill him. Oh, how wonderful you are!

Enter NATASHA carrying a candle.

NATASHA: (*Pokes her head into one room, then into another, but passes the door leading to her husband's room.*) Andrey's reading in there. Better let him read. Forgive me, Vassily Vassilich, I didn't know you were here. I'm afraid I'm not properly dressed.

SOLIONY: I don't care. Goodbye. (*Goes out.*)

NATASHA: You must be tired, my poor dear girl. (*Kisses IRENA.*) You ought to go to bed earlier.

IRENA: Is Bobik asleep?

NATASHA: Yes, he's asleep. But he's not sleeping peacefully. By the way, my dear, I've been meaning to speak to you for some time but there's always been something ... either you're not here, or I'm too busy.... You see, I think that Bobik's nursery is so cold and damp.... And your room is just ideal for a baby. Darling, do you think you could move into Olga's room?

IRENA: (*Not understanding her.*) Where to?

The sound of bells is heard outside, as a 'troika' is driven up to the house.

NATASHA: You can share a room with Olia for the time being, and Bobik can have your room. He is such a darling! This morning I said to him: 'Bobik, you're my very own! My very own!' And he just gazed at me with his dear little eyes.

The door bell rings.

That must be Olga. How late she is!

A maid comes up to NATASHA and whispers in her ear.

NATASHA: Protopopov! What a funny fellow! Protopopov's come to ask me to go for a drive with him. In a troika! (*Laughs.*) Aren't these men strange creatures! ...

The door bell rings again.

Someone's ringing. Shall I go for a short drive? Just for a quarter of an hour? (*To the maid.*) Tell him I'll be down in a minute.

The door bell rings.

That's the bell again. I suppose it's Olga. (*Goes out.*)

The maid runs out; IRENA sits lost in thought. Enter KOOLYGHIN and OLGA, followed by VERSHININ.

KOOLYGHIN: Well! What's the meaning of this? You said you were going to have a party.

VERSHININ: It's a strange thing. I left here about half an hour ago, and they were expecting a carnival party then.

IRENA: They've all gone.

KOOLYGHIN: Masha's gone, too? Where has she gone to? And why is Protopopov waiting outside in a troika? Who's he waiting for?

IRENA: Please don't ask me questions. I'm tired.

KOOLYGHIN: You ... spoilt child!

OLGA: The conference has only just ended. I'm quite worn out. The headmistress is ill and I'm deputizing for her. My head's aching, oh, my head, my head.... (*Sits down.*) Andrey lost two hundred roubles at cards last night. The whole town's talking about it....

KOOLYGHIN: Yes, the conference exhausted me, too. (*Sits down.*)

VERSHININ: So now my wife's taken it into her head to try to frighten me. She tried to poison herself. However, everything's all right now, so I can relax, thank goodness. ... So we've got to go away? Well, Goodnight to you, all the best. Fiodor Illych, would you care to come along with me somewhere or other? I can't stay at home tonight, I really can't.... Do come!

KOOLYGHIN: I'm tired. I don't think I'll come. (*Gets up.*) I'm tired. Has my wife gone home?

IRENA: I think so.

KOOLYGHIN: (*Kisses IRENA's hand.*) Goodnight. We can rest tomorrow and the day after tomorrow, two whole days! Well, I wish you all the best. (*Going out.*) How I long for some tea! I reckoned on spending the evening in congenial company, but – *o, fallacem hominum spem!* Always use the accusative case in exclamations.

VERSHININ: Well, it looks as if I'll have to go somewhere by myself. (*Goes out with KOOLYGHIN, whistling.*)

OLGA: My head aches, oh, my head.... Andrey lost at cards ... the whole town's talking.... I'll go and lie down. (*Going out.*) Tomorrow I'm free. Heavens, what a joy! Tomorrow

I'm free, and the day after tomorrow I'm free.... My head's aching, oh, my poor head....

IRENA: (*Alone.*) They've all gone. No one's left.

Someone is playing an accordion in the street. The nurse sings in the next room.

NATASHA: (*Crosses the ballroom, wearing a fur coat and cap. She is followed by the maid.*) I'll be back in half an hour. I'm just going for a little drive. (*Goes out.*)

IRENA: (*Alone, with intense longing.*) Moscow! Moscow! Moscow!

Act 3

A bedroom now shared by OLGA *and* IRENA. *There are two beds, one on the right, the other on the left, each screened off from the centre of the room. It is past two o'clock in the morning. Offstage the alarm is being sounded on account of a fire which has been raging for some time. The inmates of the house have not yet been to bed.* MASHA *is lying on a couch, dressed, as usual, in black.* OLGA *and* ANFISA *come in.*

ANFISA: Now they're sitting down there, under the stairs.... I keep telling them to come upstairs, that they shouldn't sit down there, but they just cry. 'We don't know where our Papa is,' they say, 'perhaps he's got burned in the fire.' What an idea! And there are people in the yard, too ... half-dressed....

OLGA: (*Takes a dress out of a wardrobe.*) Take this grey frock, Nanny.... And this one.... This blouse, too.... And this skirt. Oh, Heavens! what is happening! Apparently the whole of the Kirsanovsky Street's been burnt down.... Take this ... and this, too.... (*Throws the clothes into* ANFISA's *arms.*) The poor Vershinins had a fright. Their house only just escaped being burnt down. They'll have to spend the night here ... we mustn't let them go home. Poor Fedotik's lost everything, he's got nothing left....

ANFISA: I'd better call Ferapont, Oliushka, I can't carry all this.

OLGA: (*Rings.*) No one takes any notice when I ring. (*Calls through the door.*) Is anyone there? Will someone come up, please!

A window, red with the glow of the fire, can be seen through the open door. The sound of a passing fire engine is heard.

How dreadful it all is! And how tired of it I am!

Enter FERAPONT.

Take this downstairs please.... The Kolotilin girls are sitting under the stairs ... give it to them. And this, too....

FERAPONT: Very good, Madam. Moscow was burned down in 1812 just the same. Mercy on us! ... Yes, the French were surprised all right.

OLGA: Go along now, take this down.

FERAPONT: Very good. (*Goes out.*)

OLGA: Give it all away, Nanny dear. We won't keep anything, give it all away.... I'm so tired, I can hardly keep on

my feet. We mustn't let the Vershinins go home. The little girls can sleep in the drawing-room, and Alexandr Ignatyevich can share the downstairs room with the Baron. Fedotik can go in with the Baron, too, or maybe he'd better sleep in the ballroom. The doctor's gone and got drunk – you'd think he'd done it on purpose; he's so hopelessly drunk that we can't let anyone go into his room. Vershinin's wife will have to go into the drawing-room, too.

ANFISA: (*Wearily.*) Don't send me away, Oliushka, darling! Don't send me away!

OLGA: What nonsense you're talking, Nanny! No one's sending you away.

ANFISA: (*Leans her head against* OLGA's *breast.*) My dearest girl! I do work, you know, I work as hard as I can.... I suppose now I'm getting weaker, I'll be told to go. But where can I go? Where? I'm eighty years old. I'm over eighty-one!

OLGA: You sit down for a while, Nanny.... You're tired, you poor dear.... (*Makes her sit down.*) Just rest a bit. You've turned quite pale.

Enter NATASHA.

NATASHA: They're saying we ought to start a subscription in aid of the victims of the fire. You know – form a society or something for the purpose. Well, why not? It's an excellent idea! In any case it's up to us to help the poor as best we can. Bobik and Sofochka are fast asleep as if nothing had happened. We've got such a crowd of people in the house; the place seems full of people whichever way you turn. There's flu about in the town.... I'm so afraid the children might catch it.

OLGA: (*Without listening to her.*) You can't see the fire from this room; it's quiet in here.

NATASHA: Yes.... I suppose my hair is all over the place. (*Stands in front of the mirror.*) They say I've got stouter, but it's not true! I'm not a bit stouter. Masha's asleep ... she's tired, poor girl.... (*To* ANFISA, *coldly.*) How dare you sit down in my presence? Get up! Get out of here!

ANFISA goes out. A pause.

I can't understand why you keep that old woman in the house.

OLGA: (*Taken aback.*) Forgive me for saying it, but I can't understand how you. ...

NATASHA: She's quite useless here. She's just a peasant woman, her right place is in the country. You're spoiling her. I do like order in the home, I don't like having useless people about. (*Strokes* OLGA's *cheek.*) You're tired, my poor dear! Our headmistress is tired! You know, when my Sofochka grows up and goes to school, I'll be frightened of you.

OLGA: I'm not going to be a headmistress.

NATASHA: You'll be asked to, Olechka. It's settled.

OLGA: I'll refuse. I couldn't do it.... I wouldn't be strong enough. (*Drinks water.*) You spoke so harshly to Nanny just now.... You must forgive me for saying so, but I just can't stand that sort of thing ... it made me feel quite faint....

NATASHA: (*Agitated.*) Forgive me, Olia, forgive me. I didn't mean to upset you.

MASHA gets up, picks up a pillow and goes out in a huff.

OLGA: Please try to understand me, dear.... It may be that we've been brought up in a peculiar way, but anyway I just can't bear it. When people are treated like that, it gets me down, I feel quite ill.... I simply get unnerved....

NATASHA: Forgive me, dear, forgive me! ... (*Kisses her.*)

OLGA: Any cruel or tactless remark, even the slightest discourtesy, upsets me....

NATASHA: It's quite true, I know I often say things which would be better left unsaid – but you must agree with me, dear, that she'd be better in the country somewhere.

OLGA: She's been with us for thirty years.

NATASHA: But she can't do any work now, can she? Either I don't understand you, or you don't want to understand me. She can't work, she just sleeps or sits about.

OLGA: Well, let her sit about.

NATASHA: (*In surprise.*) What do you mean, let her sit about? Surely she is a servant! (*Tearfully.*) No, I don't understand you, Olia! I have a nurse for the children and a wet nurse and we share a maid and a cook. Whatever do we want this old woman for? What for?

The alarm is sounded again.

OLGA: I've aged ten years tonight.

NATASHA: We must sort things out, Olia. You're working at your school, and I'm working at home. You're teaching and I'm running the house. And when I say anything about the servants, I know what I'm talking about.... That old thief, that old witch must get out of this house tomorrow! ... (*Stamps her feet.*) How dare you vex me so? How dare you? (*Recovering her self-control.*) Really, if you don't move downstairs, we'll always be quarrelling. This is quite dreadful!

Enter KOOLYGHIN.

KOOLYGHIN: Where's Masha? It's time we went home. They say the fire's getting less fierce. (*Stretches.*) Only one block got burnt down, but to begin with it looked as if the whole town was going to be set on fire by that wind. (*Sits down.*) I'm so tired, Olechka, my dear. You know, I've often thought that if I hadn't married Masha, I'd have married you, Olechka. You're so kind. I'm worn out. (*Listens.*)

OLGA: What is it?

KOOLYGHIN: The doctor's got drunk just as if he'd done it on purpose. Hopelessly drunk.... As if he'd done it on purpose. (*Gets up.*) I think he's coming up here.... Can you hear him? Yes, he's coming up. (*Laughs.*) What a fellow, really! ... I'm going to hide myself. (*Goes to the wardrobe and stands between it and the wall.*) What a scoundrel!

OLGA: He's been off drinking for two years, and now suddenly he goes and gets drunk.... (*Walks with NATASHA towards the back of the room.*)

CHEBUTYKIN enters; walking firmly and soberly he crosses the room, stops, looks round, then goes to the wash-stand and begins to wash his hands.

CHEBUTYKIN: (*Glumly.*) The devil take them all ... all the lot of them! They think I can treat anything just because I'm a doctor, but I know positively nothing at all. I've forgotten everything I used to know. I remember nothing, positively nothing....

OLGA and NATASHA leave the room without his noticing.

The devil take them! Last Wednesday I attended a woman at Zasyp. She died, and it's all my fault that she did die. Yes.... I used to know a thing or two twenty-five years ago, but now I don't remember anything. Not a thing! Perhaps I'm not a man at all, but I just imagine that I've got hands and feet and a head. Perhaps I don't exist at all, and I only imagine that I'm walking about and eating and sleeping. (*Weeps.*) Oh, if only I could simply stop existing! (*Stops crying, glumly.*) God knows.... The other day they were talking about Shakespeare and Voltaire at the club.... I haven't read either, never read a single line of either, but I tried to make out by my expression that I had. The others did the same. How petty it all is! How despicable! And then suddenly I thought of the woman I killed on Wednesday. It all came back to me, and I felt such a swine, so sick of myself that I went and got drunk....

Enter IRENA, VERSHININ and TOOZENBACH. TOOZENBACH is wearing a fashionable new civilian suit.

IRENA: Let's sit down here for a while. No one will come in here.

VERSHININ: The whole town would have been burnt down but for the soldiers. They're a fine lot of fellows! (*Rubs his hands with pleasure.*) Excellent fellows! Yes, they're a fine lot!

KOOLYGHIN: (*Approaches them.*) What's the time?

TOOZENBACH: It's gone three. It's beginning to get light.

IRENA: Everyone's sitting in the ballroom and nobody thinks of leaving. That man Soliony there, too.... (*To CHEBUTYKIN.*) You ought to go to bed, Doctor.

CHEBUTYKIN: I'm all right.... Thanks.... (*Combs his beard.*)

KOOLYGHIN: (*Laughs.*) Half seas over, Ivan Romanych! (*Slaps him on the shoulder.*) You're a fine one! *In vino veritas*, as they used to say in Rome.

TOOZENBACH: Everyone keeps asking me to arrange a concert in aid of the victims of the fire.

IRENA: Well, who'd you get to perform in it?

TOOZENBACH: It could be done if we wanted to. Maria

Serghyeevna plays the piano wonderfully well, in my opinion.

KOOLYGHIN: Yes, wonderfully well!

IRENA: She's forgotten how to. She hasn't played for three years ... or maybe it's four.

TOOZENBACH: Nobody understands music in this town, not a single person. But I do – I really do – and I assure you quite definitely that Maria Serghyeevna plays magnificently. She's almost a genius for it.

KOOLYGHIN: You're right, Baron. I'm very fond of Masha. She's such a nice girl.

TOOZENBACH: Fancy being able to play so exquisitely, and yet having nobody, nobody at all, to appreciate it!

KOOLYGHIN: (Sighs.) Yes.... But would it be quite proper for her to play in a concert? (A pause.) I don't know anything about these matters, my friends. Perhaps it'll be perfectly all right. But you know, although our director is a good man, a very good man indeed, and most intelligent, I know that he does hold certain views.... Of course, this doesn't really concern him, but I'll have a word with him about it, all the same, if you like.

CHEBUTYKIN: (Picks up a china clock and examines it.)

VERSHININ: I've got my clothes in such a mess helping to put out the fire, I must look like nothing on earth. (A pause.) I believe they were saying yesterday that our brigade might be transferred to somewhere a long way away. Some said it was to be Poland, and some said it was Cheeta, in Siberia.

TOOZENBACH: I heard that, too. Well, the town will seem quite deserted.

IRENA: We'll go away, too!

CHEBUTYKIN: (Drops the clock and breaks it.) Smashed to smithereens!

A pause. Everyone looks upset and embarrassed.

KOOLYGHIN: (Picks up the pieces.) Fancy breaking such a valuable thing! Ah, Ivan Romanych, Ivan Romanych! You'll get a bad mark for that!

IRENA: It was my mother's clock.

CHEBUTYKIN: Well, supposing it was. If it was your mother's, then it was your mother's. Perhaps I didn't smash it. Perhaps it only appears that I did. Perhaps it only appears to us that we exist, whereas in reality we don't exist at all. I don't know anything, no one knows anything. (Stops at the door.) Why are you staring at me? Natasha's having a nice little affair with Protopopov, and you don't see it. You sit here seeing nothing, and meanwhile Natasha's having a nice little affair with Protopopov.... (Sings.) Would you like a date?... (Goes out.)

VERSHININ: So.... (Laughs.) How odd it all is, really! (A pause.) When the fire started, I ran home as fast as I could. When I got near, I could see that our house was all right and out of danger, but the two little girls were standing there, in the doorway in their night clothes. Their mother wasn't there. People were rushing about, horses, dogs

... and in the kiddies' faces I saw a frightened, anxious, appealing look, I don't know what!... My heart sank when I saw their faces. My God, I thought, what will these children have to go through in the course of their poor lives? And they may live a long time, too! I picked them up and ran back here with them, and all the time I was running, I was thinking the same thing: what will they have to go through?

The alarm is sounded. A pause.

When I got here, my wife was here already ... angry, shouting!

Enter MASHA carrying a pillow; she sits down on the couch.

VERSHININ: And when my little girls were standing in the doorway with nothing on but their night clothes, and the street was red with the glow of the fire and full of terrifying noises, it struck me that the same sort of thing used to happen years ago, when armies used to make sudden raids on towns, and plunder them and set them on fire.... Anyway, is there any essential difference between things as they were and as they are now? And before very long, say, in another two or three hundred years, people may be looking at our present life just as we look at the past now, with horror and scorn. Our own times may seem uncouth to them, boring and frightfully uncomfortable and strange.... Oh, what a great life it'll be then, what a life! (Laughs.) Forgive me, I'm philosophizing my head off again ... but may I go on, please? I'm bursting to philosophize just at the moment. I'm in the mood for it. (A pause.) You seem as if you've all gone to sleep. As I was saying: what a great life it will be in the future! Just try to imagine it.... At the present time there are only three people of your intellectual calibre in the whole of this town, but future generations will be more productive of people like you. They'll go on producing more and more of the same sort until at last the time will come when everything will be just as you'd wish it yourselves. People will live their lives in your way, and then even you may be outmoded, and a new lot will come along who will be even better than you are.... (Laughs.) I'm in quite a special mood today. I feel full of a tremendous urge to live.... (Sings.)

'To Love all ages are in fee,
The passion's good for you and me.' ... (Laughs.)

MASHA: (Sings.) Tara-tara-tara....

VERSHININ: Tum-tum....

MASHA: Tara-tara. ...

VERSHININ: Tum-tum, tum-tum.... (Laughs.)

Enter FEDOTIK.

FEDOTIK: (Dancing about.) Burnt, burnt! Everything I've got burnt!

All laugh.

IRENA: It's hardly a joking matter. Has everything really been burnt?

FEDOTIK: (*Laughs.*) Everything, completely. I've got nothing left. My guitar's burnt, my photographs are burnt, all my letters are burnt. Even the little note-book I was going to give you has been burnt.

Enter SOLIONY.

IRENA: No, please go away, Vassily Vassilich. You can't come in here.

SOLIONY: Can't I? Why can the Baron come in here if I can't?

VERSHININ: We really must go, all of us. What's the fire doing?

SOLIONY: It's dying down, they say. Well, I must say it's a peculiar thing that the Baron can come in here, and I can't. (*Takes a scent bottle from his pocket and sprinkles himself with scent.*)

VERSHININ: Tara-tara.

MASHA: Tum-tum, tum-tum.

VERSHININ: (*Laughs, to SOLIONY.*) Let's go to the ballroom.

SOLIONY: Very well, we'll make a note of this. 'I hardly need to make my moral yet more clear: That might be teasing geese, I fear!' (*Looks at TOOZENBACH.*) Cluck, cluck, cluck! (*Goes out with VERSHININ and FEDOTIK.*)

IRENA: That Soliony has smoked the room out.... (*Puzzled.*) The Baron's asleep. Baron! Baron!

TOOZENBACH: (*Waking out of his dose.*) I must be tired. The brick-works.... No, I'm not talking in my sleep. I really do intend to go to the brick-works and start working there quite soon. I've had a talk with the manager. (*To IRENA, tenderly.*) You are so pale, so beautiful, so fascinating.... Your pallor seems to light up the darkness around you, as if it were luminous, somehow.... You're sad, you're dissatisfied with the life, you have to live.... Oh, come away with me, let's go away and work together!

MASHA: Nikolai Lvovich, I wish you'd go away.

TOOZENBACH: (*Laughs.*) Oh, you're here, are you? I didn't see you. (*Kisses IRENA's hand.*) Goodbye, I'm going. You know, as I look at you now, I keep thinking of the day – it was a long time ago, your Saint's day – when you talked to us about the joy of work.... You were so gay and high-spirited then.... And what a happy life I saw ahead of me! Where is it all now? (*Kisses her hand.*) There are tears in your eyes. You should go to bed, it's beginning to get light ... it's almost morning.... Oh, if only I could give my life for you!

MASHA: Nikolai Lvovich, please go away! Really now....

TOOZENBACH: I'm going. (*Goes out.*)

MASHA: (*Lies down.*) Are you asleep, Fiodor?

KOOLYGHIN: Eh?

MASHA: Why don't you go home?

KOOLYGHIN: My darling Masha, my sweet, my precious Masha....

IRENA: She's tired. Let her rest a while, Fyedia.

KOOLYGHIN: I'll go in a moment. My wife, my dear, good wife! ... How I love you! ... only you!

MASHA: (*Crossly.*) *Amo, amas, amat, amamus, amatis, amant!*

KOOLYGHIN: (*Laughs.*) Really, she's an amazing woman! – I've been married to you for seven years, but I feel as if we were only married yesterday. Yes, on my word of honour, I do! You really are amazing! Oh, I'm so happy, happy, happy!

MASHA: And I'm so bored, bored, bored! (*Sits up.*) I can't get it out of my head.... It's simply disgusting. It's like having a nail driven into my head. No, I can't keep silent about it any more. It's about Andrey.... He's actually mortgaged this house to a bank, and his wife's got hold of all the money – and yet the house doesn't belong to him, it belongs to all four of us! Surely, he must realize that, if he's got any honesty.

KOOLYGHIN: Why bring all this up, Masha? Why bother about it now? Andriusha owes money all round.... Leave him alone.

MASHA: Anyway, it's disgusting. (*Lies down.*)

KOOLYGHIN: Well, we aren't poor, Masha. I've got work, I teach at the county school, I give private lessons in my spare time.... I'm just a plain, honest man.... *Omnia mea mecum porto*, as they say.

MASHA: I don't ask for anything, but I'm just disgusted by injustice. (*A pause.*) Why don't you go home, Fiodor?

KOOLYGHIN: (*Kisses her.*) You're tired. Just rest here for a while.... I'll go home and wait for you.... Go to sleep. (*Goes to the door.*) I'm happy, happy, happy! (*Goes out.*)

IRENA: The truth is that Andrey is getting to be shallow-minded. He's ageing and since he's been living with that woman he's lost all the inspiration he used to have! Not long ago he was working for a professorship, and yet yesterday he boasted of having at last been elected a member of the County Council. Fancy him a member, with Protopopov as chairman! They say the whole town's laughing at him, he's the only one who doesn't know anything or see anything. And now, you see, everyone's at the fire, while he's just sitting in his room, not taking the slightest notice of it. Just playing his violin. (*Agitated.*) Oh, how dreadful it is, how dreadful, how dreadful! I can't bear it any longer, I can't, I really can't! ...

Enter OLGA. She starts arranging things on her bedside table.

IRENA: (*Sobs loudly.*) You must turn me out of here! Turn me out; I can't stand it any more!

OLGA: (*Alarmed.*) What is it? What is it, darling?

IRENA: (*Sobbing.*) Where.... Where has it all gone to? Where is it? Oh, God! I've forgotten.... I've forgotten everything ... there's nothing but a muddle in my head.... I don't remember what the Italian for 'window' is, or for 'ceiling'.... Every day I'm forgetting more and more, and life's slipping by, and it will never, never come back.... We shall never go to Moscow.... I can see that we shall never go....

Figure 8 From the Moscow Art Theatre 1901 production of *Three Sisters*.

OLGA: Don't, my dear, don't....

IRENA: (*Trying to control herself.*) Oh, I'm so miserable! ... I can't work, I won't work! I've had enough of it, enough! ... First I worked on the telegraph, now I'm in the County Council office, and I hate and despise everything they give me to do there.... I'm twenty-three years old, I've been working all this time, and I feel as if my brain's dried up. I know I've got thinner and uglier and older, and I find no kind of satisfaction in anything, none at all. And the time's passing ... and I feel as if I'm moving away from any hope of a genuine, fine life, I'm moving further and further away and sinking into a kind of abyss. I feel in despair, and I don't know why I'm still alive, why I haven't killed myself....

OLGA: Don't cry, my dear child, don't cry.... It hurts me.

IRENA: I'm not crying any more. That's enough of it. Look, I'm not crying now. Enough of it, enough! ...

OLGA: Darling, let me tell you something.... I just want to speak as your sister, as your friend.... That is, if you want my advice.... Why don't you marry the Baron?

IRENA: (*Weeps quietly.*)

OLGA: After all, you do respect him, you think a lot of him.... It's true, he's not good-looking, but he's such a decent, clean-minded sort of man.... After all, one doesn't marry for love, but to fulfil a duty. At least, I think so, and I'd marry even if I weren't in love. I'd marry anyone that proposed to me, as long as he was a decent man. I'd even marry an old man.

IRENA: I've been waiting all this time, imagining that we'd be moving to Moscow, and I'd meet the man I'm meant for there. I've dreamt about him and I've loved him in my dreams.... But it's all turned out to be nonsense ... nonsense....

OLGA: (*Embracing her.*) My darling sweetheart, I understand everything perfectly. When the Baron resigned his commission and came to see us in his civilian clothes, I thought he looked so plain that I actually started to cry.... He asked me why I was crying.... How could I tell him? But, of course, if it were God's will that he should marry you, I'd feel perfectly happy about it. That's quite a different matter, quite different!

NATASHA, carrying a candle, comes out of the door on the right, crosses the stage and goes out through the door on the left without saying anything.

MASHA: (*Sits up.*) She goes about looking as if she'd started the fire.

OLGA: You're silly, Masha. You're the stupidest person in our family. Forgive me for saying so.

A pause.

MASHA: My dear sisters, I've got something to confess to you. I must get some relief, I feel the need of it in my heart. I'll confess it to you two alone, and then never again, never to anybody! I'll tell you in a minute. (*In a low voice.*) It's a secret, but you'll have to know everything. I can't keep silent any more. (*A pause.*) I'm in love, in love.... I love that man.... You saw him here just now.... Well, what's the good? ... I love Vershinin....

OLGA: (*Goes behind her screen.*) Don't say it. I don't want to hear it.

MASHA: Well, what's to be done? (*Holding her head.*) I thought he was queer at first, then I started to pity him ... then I began to love him ... love everything about him – his voice, his talk, his misfortunes, his two little girls....

OLGA: Nevertheless, I don't want to hear it. You can say any nonsense you like, I'm not listening.

MASHA: Oh, you're stupid, Olia! If I love him, well – that's my fate! That's my destiny.... He loves me, too. It's all rather frightening, isn't it? Not a good thing, is it? (*Takes IRENA by the hand and draws her to her.*) Oh, my dear! ... How are we going to live through the rest of our lives? What's going to become of us? When you read a novel, everything in it seems so old and obvious, but when you fall in love yourself, you suddenly discover that you don't really know anything, and you've got to make your own decisions.... My dear sisters, my dear sisters! ... I've confessed it all to you, and now I'll keep quiet.... I'll be like that madman in the story by Gogol – silence ... silence! ...

Enter ANDREY followed by FERAPONT.

ANDREY: (*Crossly.*) What do you want? I don't understand you.

FERAPONT: (*Stopping in the doorway, impatiently.*) I've asked you about ten times already, Andrey Serghyeevich.

ANDREY: In the first place, you're not to call me Andrey Serghyeevich – call me 'Your Honour'.

FERAPONT: The firemen are asking Your Honour if they may drive through your garden to get to the river. They've been going a long way round all this time – it's a terrible business!

ANDREY: All right. Tell them it's all right.

FERAPONT goes out.

They keep on plaguing me. Where's Olga?

OLGA comes from behind the screen.

I wanted to see you. Will you give me the key to the cupboard? I've lost mine. You know the key I mean, the small one you've got ...

OLGA silently hands him the key. IRENA goes behind the screen on her side of the room.

ANDREY: What a terrific fire! It's going down though. That Ferapont annoyed me, the devil take him! Silly thing he made me say.... Telling him to call me 'Your Honour'! ... (*A pause.*) Why don't you say anything, Olia? (*A pause.*) It's about time you stopped this nonsense ... sulking like this for no reason whatever.... You here, Masha? And Irena's here, too. That's excellent! We can talk it over then, frankly and once for all. What have you got against me? What is it?

OLGA: Drop it now, Andriusha. Let's talk it over tomorrow. (*Agitated.*) What a dreadful night!

ANDREY: (*In great embarrassment.*) Don't get upset. I'm asking you quite calmly, what have you got against me? Tell me frankly.

VERSHININ'S VOICE: (*Offstage.*) Tum-tum-tum!

MASHA: (*In a loud voice, getting up.*) Tara-tara-tara! (*To* OLGA.) Goodbye, Olia, God bless you! (*Goes behind the screen and kisses* IRENA.) Sleep well.... Goodbye, Andrey. I should leave them now, they're tired ... talk it over tomorrow.... (*Goes out.*)

OLGA: Really, Andriusha, let's leave it till tomorrow.... (*Goes behind the screen on her side of the room.*) It's time to go to bed.

ANDREY: I only want to say one thing, then I'll go. In a moment.... First of all, you've got something against my wife, against Natasha. I've always been conscious of it from the day we got married. Natasha is a fine woman, she's honest and straightforward and high-principled.... That's my opinion. I love and respect my wife. You understand that I respect her, and I expect others to respect her, too. I repeat: she's an honest, high-principled woman, and all your grievances against her – if you don't mind my saying so – are just imagination, and nothing more.... (*A pause.*) Secondly, you seem to be annoyed with me for not making myself a professor, and not doing any academic work. But I'm working in the Council Office, I'm a member of the County Council, and I feel my service

there is just as fine and valuable as any academic work I might do. I'm a member of the County Council, and if you want to know, I'm proud of it! (*A pause.*) Thirdly ... there's something else I must tell you.... I know I mortgaged the house without asking your permission.... That was wrong, I admit it, and I ask you to forgive me.... I was driven to it by my debts.... I'm in debt for about thirty-five thousand roubles. I don't play cards any more, I've given it up long ago. ... The only thing I can say to justify myself is that you girls get an annuity, while I don't get anything ... no income, I mean.... (*A pause.*)

KOOLYGHIN: (*Calling through the door.*) Is Masha there? She's not there? (*Alarmed.*) Where can she be then? It's very strange.... (*Goes away.*)

ANDREY: So you won't listen? Natasha is a good, honest woman, I tell you. (*Walks up and down the stage, then stops.*) When I married her, I thought we were going to be happy, I thought we should all be happy.... But ... oh, my God! ... (*Weeps.*) My dear sisters, my dear, good sisters, don't believe what I've been saying, don't believe it.... (*Goes out.*)

KOOLYGHIN: (*Through the door, agitated.*) Where's Masha? Isn't Masha here? Extraordinary! (*Goes away.*)

The alarm is heard again. The stage is empty.

IRENA: (*Speaking from behind the screen.*) Olia! Who's that knocking on the floor?

OLGA: It's the doctor, Ivan Romanych. He's drunk.

IRENA: It's been one thing after another all night. (*A pause.*) Olia! (*Peeps out from behind the screen.*) Have you heard? The troops are being moved from the district ... they're being sent somewhere a long way off.

OLGA: That's only a rumour.

IRENA: We'll be left quite alone then.... Olia!

OLGA: Well?

IRENA: Olia, darling, I do respect the Baron.... I think a lot of him, he's a very good man.... I'll marry him, Olia, I'll agree to marry him, if only we can go to Moscow! Let's go, please do let's go! There's nowhere in all the world like Moscow. Let's go, Olia! Let's go!

Act 4

The old garden belonging to the Prozorovs' house. A river is seen at the end of a long avenue of fir-trees, and on the far bank of the river a forest. On the right of the stage there is a verandah with a table on which champagne bottles and glasses have been left. It is midday. From time to time people from the street pass through the garden to get to the river. Five or six soldiers march through quickly.

CHEBUTYKIN, radiating a mood of benevolence which does not leave him throughout the act, is sitting in a chair in the garden. He is wearing his army cap and is holding a walking stick, as if ready to be called away at any moment. KOOLYGHIN, with a decoration round his neck and with his moustache shaved off, TOOZENBACH and IRENA are standing on the verandah saying Goodbye to FEDOTIK and

RODÉ, *who are coming down the steps. Both officers are in marching uniform.*)

TOOZENBACH: (*Embracing* FEDOTIK.) You're a good fellow, Fedotik; we've been good friends! (*Embraces* RODÉ.) Once more, then.... Goodbye, my dear friends!

IRENA: Au revoir!

FEDOTIK: It's not 'au revoir'. It's Goodbye. We shall never meet again!

KOOLYGHIN: Who knows? (*Wipes his eyes, smiling.*) There! you've made me cry.

IRENA: We'll meet some time.

FEDOTIK: Perhaps in ten or fifteen years' time. But then we'll hardly know one another.... We shall just meet and say: 'How are you?' coldly.... (*Takes a snapshot.*) Wait a moment.... Just one more, for the last time.

RODÉ: (*Embraces* TOOZENBACH.) We're not likely to meet again.... (*Kisses* IRENA'S *hand.*) Thank you for everything ... everything!

FEDOTIK: (*Annoyed.*) Do just wait a second!

TOOZENBACH: We'll meet again if we're fated to meet. Do write to us. Be sure to write.

RODÉ: (*Glancing round the garden,*) Goodbye, trees! (*Shouts.*) Heigh-ho! (*A pause.*) Goodbye, echo!

KOOLYGHIN: I wouldn't be surprised if you got married out there, in Poland.... You'll get a Polish wife, and she'll put her arms round you and say: Kohane![4] (*Laughs.*)

FEDOTIK: (*Glances at his watch.*) There's less than an hour to go. Soliony is the only one from our battery who's going down the river on the barge. All the others are marching with the division. Three batteries are leaving today by road and three more tomorrow – then the town will be quite peaceful.

TOOZENBACH: Yes, and dreadfully dull, too.

RODÉ: By the way, where's Maria Serghyeevna?

KOOLYGHIN: She's somewhere in the garden.

FEDOTIK: We must say Goodbye to her.

RODÉ: Goodbye. I really must go, or I'll burst into tears. (*Quickly embraces* TOOZENBACH *and* KOOLYGHIN, *kisses* IRENA'S *hand.*) Life's been very pleasant here....

FEDOTIK: (*To* KOOLYGHIN.) Here's something for a souvenir for you – a note-book with a pencil.... We'll go down to the river through here. (*They go off, glancing back.*)

RODÉ: (*Shouts.*) Heigh-ho!

KOOLYGHIN: (*Shouts.*) Goodbye!

At the back of the stage FEDOTIK *and* RODÉ *meet* MASHA, *and say Goodbye to her; she goes off with them.*

IRENA: They've gone.... (*Sits down on the bottom step of the verandah.*)

CHEBUTYKIN: They forgot to say Goodbye to me.

IRENA: Well, what about you?

CHEBUTYKIN: That's true, I forgot, too. Never mind, I'll be seeing them again quite soon. I'll be leaving tomorrow. Yes ... only one more day. And then, in a year's time I'll

be retiring. I'll come back here and finish the rest of my life near you. There's just one more year to go and then I get my pension.... (*Puts a newspaper in his pocket and takes out another.*) I'll come back here and lead a reformed life. I'll be a nice, quiet, well-behaved little man.

IRENA: Yes, it's really time you reformed, my dear friend. You ought to live a different sort of life, somehow.

CHEBUTYKIN: Yes. ... I think so, too. (*Sings quietly.*) Tarara-boom-di-ay.... I'm sitting on a tomb-di-ay....

KOOLYGHIN: Ivan Romanych is incorrigible! Incorrigible!

CHEBUTYKIN: Yes, you ought to have taken me in hand. You'd have reformed me!

IRENA: Fiodor's shaved his moustache off. I can't bear to look at him.

KOOLYGHIN: Why not?

CHEBUTYKIN: If I could just tell you what your face looks like now – but I daren't.

KOOLYGHIN: Well! Such are the conventions of life! *Modus vivendi*, you know. The director shaved his moustache off, so I shaved mine off when they gave me an inspectorship. No one likes it, but personally I'm quite indifferent. I'm content. Whether I've got a moustache or not, it's all the same to me. (*Sits down.*)

ANDREY *passes across the back of the stage pushing a pram with a child asleep in it.*

IRENA: Ivan Romanych, my dear friend, I'm awfully worried about something. You were out in the town garden last night – tell me what happened there?

CHEBUTYKIN: What happened? Nothing. Just a trifling thing. (*Reads his paper.*) It doesn't matter anyway.

KOOLYGHIN: They say that Soliony and the Baron met in the town garden outside the theatre last night and ....

TOOZENBACH: Don't, please! What's the good? ... (*Waves his hand at him deprecatingly and goes into the house.*)

KOOLYGHIN: It was outside the theatre.... Soliony started badgering the Baron, and he lost patience and said something that offended him.

CHEBUTYKIN: I don't know anything about it. It's all nonsense.

KOOLYGHIN: A school-master once wrote 'nonsense' in Russian over a pupil's essay, and the pupil puzzled over it, thinking it was a Latin word. (*Laughs.*) Frightfully funny, you know! They say that Soliony's in love with Irena and that he got to hate the Baron more and more.... Well, that's understandable. Irena's a very nice girl. She's a bit like Masha, she tends to get wrapped up in her own thoughts. (*To* IRENA.) But your disposition is more easy-going than Masha's. And yet Masha has a very nice disposition, too. I love her, I love my Masha.

From the back of the stage comes a shout: 'Heigh-ho!'

IRENA: (*Starts.*) Anything seems to startle me today. (*A pause.*) I've got everything ready, too. I'm sending my luggage off after lunch. The Baron and I are going to get married tomorrow, and directly afterwards we're moving to the brick-works, and the day after tomorrow I'm starting work at the school. So our new life will begin, God willing! When I was sitting for my teacher's diploma, I suddenly started crying for sheer joy, with a sort of feeling of blessedness.... (*A pause.*) The carrier will be coming for my luggage in a minute....

KOOLYGHIN: That's all very well, but somehow I can't feel that it's meant to be serious. All ideas and theories, but nothing really serious. Anyway, I wish you luck from the bottom of my heart.

CHEBUTYKIN: (*Moved.*) My dearest girl, my precious child! You've gone on so far ahead of me, I'll never catch you up now. I've got left behind like a bird which has grown too old and can't keep up with the rest of the flock. Fly away, my dears, fly away, and God be with you! (*A pause.*) It's a pity you've shaved your moustache off, Fiodor Illyich.

KOOLYGHIN: Don't keep on about it, please! (*Sighs.*) Well, the soldiers will be leaving today, and everything will go

Figure 9 Lynn Redgrave, Vanessa Redgrave and Gemma Redgrave in Robert Strura's 1991 production of *Three Sisters*. (Photograph: John Haynes.)

back to what it was before. Anyway, whatever they say, Masha is a good, loyal wife. Yes, I love her dearly and I'm thankful for what God has given me. Fate treats people so differently. For instance, there's an excise clerk here called Kozyrev. He was at school with me and he was expelled in his fifth year because he just couldn't grasp the *ut consecutivum*. He's dreadfully hard up now, and in bad health, too, and whenever I meet him, I just say to him: 'Hullo, *ut consecutivum!*' 'Yes', he replies, 'that's just the trouble – *consecutivum*' ... and he starts coughing. Whereas I – I've been lucky all my life. I'm happy, I've actually been awarded the order of Saint Stanislav, second class – and now I'm teaching the children the same old *ut consecutivum*. Of course, I'm clever, cleverer than plenty of other people, but happiness does not consist of merely being clever....

In the house someone plays 'The Maiden's Prayer'.

IRENA: Tomorrow night I shan't have to listen to the 'Maiden's Prayer'. I shan't have to meet Protopopov.... (*A pause.*) By the way, he's in the sitting-room. He's come again.

KOOLYGHIN: Hasn't our headmistress arrived yet?

IRENA: No, we've sent for her. If you only knew how difficult it is for me to live here by myself, without Olia! She lives at the school now; she's the headmistress and she's busy the whole day. And I'm here alone, bored, with nothing to do, and I hate the very room I live in. So I've just made up my mind – if I'm really not going to be able to live in Moscow, that's that. It's my fate, that's all. Nothing can be done about it. It's God's will, everything that happens, and that's the truth. Nikolai Lvovich proposed to me.... Well, I thought it over, and I made up my mind. He's such a nice man, it's really extraordinary how nice he is.... And then suddenly I felt as though my soul had grown wings, I felt more cheerful and so relieved somehow that I wanted to work again. Just to start work! ... Only something happened yesterday, and now I feel as though something mysterious is hanging over me....

CHEBUTYKIN: Nonsense!

NATASHA: (*Speaking through the window.*) Our headmistress!

KOOLYGHIN: Our headmistress has arrived! Let's go indoors.

Goes indoors with IRENA.

CHEBUTYKIN: (*Reads his paper and sings quietly to himself.*) Tarara-boom-di-ay.... I'm sitting on a tomb-di-ay....

MASHA walks up to him; ANDREY *passes across the back of the stage pushing the pram.*

MASHA: You look very comfortable sitting here....

CHEBUTYKIN: Well, why not? Anything happening?

MASHA: (*Sits down.*) No, nothing. (*A pause.*) Tell me something. Were you in love with my mother?

CHEBUTYKIN: Yes, very much in love.

MASHA: Did she love you?

CHEBUTYKIN: (*After a pause.*) I can't remember now.

MASHA: Is my man here? Our cook Marfa always used to call her policeman 'my man'. Is he here?

CHEBUTYKIN: Not yet.

MASHA: When you have to take your happiness in snatches, in little bits, as I do, and then lose it, as I've lost it, you gradually get hardened and bad-tempered. (*Points at her breast.*) Something's boiling over inside me, here. (*Looking at* ANDREY, *who again crosses the stage with the pram.*) There's Andrey, our dear brother.... All our hopes are gone. It's the same as when thousands of people haul a huge bell up into a tower. Untold labour and money is spent on it, and then suddenly it falls and gets smashed. Suddenly, without rhyme or reason. It was the same with Andrey....

ANDREY: When are they going to settle down in the house? They're making such a row.

CHEBUTYKIN: They will soon. (*Looks at his watch.*) This is an old-fashioned watch: it strikes.... (*Winds his watch which then strikes.*) The first, second and fifth batteries will be leaving punctually at one o'clock. (*A pause.*) And I shall leave tomorrow.

ANDREY: For good?

CHEBUTYKIN: I don't know. I may return in about a year. Although, God knows ... it's all the same....

The sounds of a harp and a violin are heard.

ANDREY: The town will seem quite empty. Life will be snuffed out like a candle. (*A pause.*) Something happened yesterday outside the theatre; everybody's talking about it. I'm the only one that doesn't seem to know about it.

CHEBUTYKIN: It was nothing. A lot of nonsense. Soliony started badgering the Baron, or something. The Baron lost his temper and insulted him, and in the end Soliony had to challenge him to a duel. (*Looks at his watch.*) I think it's time to go. ... At half-past twelve, in the forest over there, on the other side of the river.... Bang-bang! (*Laughs.*) Soliony imagines he's like Lermontov. He actually writes poems. But, joking apart, this is his third duel.

MASHA: Whose third duel?

CHEBUTYKIN: Soliony's.

MASHA: What about the Baron?

CHEBUTYKIN: Well, what about him? (*A pause.*)

MASHA: My thoughts are all in a muddle.... But what I mean to say is that they shouldn't be allowed to fight. He might wound the Baron or even kill him.

CHEBUTYKIN: The Baron's a good enough fellow, but what does it really matter if there's one Baron more or less in the world? Well, let it be! It's all the same.

The shouts of 'Ah-oo!' and 'Heigh-ho!' are heard from beyond the garden.

That's Skvortsov, the second, shouting from the boat. He can wait.

ANDREY: I think it's simply immoral to fight a duel, or even to be present at one as a doctor.

CHEBUTYKIN: That's only how it seems.... We don't exist, nothing exists, it only seems to us that we do.... And what difference does it make?

MASHA: Talk, talk, nothing but talk all day long! ... (*Starts to go.*) Having to live in this awful climate with the snow threatening to fall at any moment, and then on the top of it having to listen to all this sort of talk.... (*Stops.*) I won't go into the house, I can't bear going in there.... Will you let me know when Vershinin comes? ... (*Walks off along the avenue.*) Look, the birds are beginning to fly away already! (*Looks up.*) Swans or geese.... Dear birds, happy birds.... (*Goes off.*)

ANDREY: Our house will seem quite deserted. The officers will go, you'll go, my sister will get married, and I'll be left alone in the house.

CHEBUTYKIN: What about your wife?

Enter FERAPONT *with some papers.*

ANDREY: My wife is my wife. She's a good, decent sort of woman ... she's really very kind, too, but there's something about her which pulls her down to the level of an animal ... a sort of mean, blind, thick-skinned animal – anyway, not a human being. I'm telling you this as a friend, the only person I can talk openly to. I love Natasha, it's true. But at times she appears to me so utterly vulgar, that I feel quite bewildered by it, and then I can't understand why, for what reasons I love her – or, anyway, did love her....

CHEBUTYKIN: (*Gets up.*) Well, dear boy, I'm going away tomorrow and it may be we shall never see each other again. So I'll give you a bit of advice. Put on your hat, take a walking stick, and go away.... Go away, and don't ever look back. And the further you go, the better.

SOLIONY passes across the back of the stage accompanied by two officers. Seeing CHEBUTYKIN, *he turns towards him, while the officers walk on.*

SOLIONY: It's time, Doctor. Half past twelve already. (*Shakes hands with* ANDREY.)

CHEBUTYKIN: In a moment. Oh, I'm tired of you all. (*To* ANDREY.) Andriusha, if anyone asks for me, tell them I'll be back presently. (*Sighs.*) Oh-ho-ho!

SOLIONY: 'He had no time to say "Oh, oh!"'
Before that bear had struck him low.' ...
(*Walks off with him.*) What are you groaning about, old man?

CHEBUTYKIN: Oh, well!

SOLIONY: How do you feel?

CHEBUTYKIN: (*Crossly.*) Like a last year's bird's-nest.

SOLIONY: You needn't be so agitated about it, old boy. I shan't indulge in anything much, I'll just scorch his wings a little, like a woodcock's. (*Takes out a scent bottle and sprinkles scent over his hands.*) I've used up a whole bottle today, but my hands still smell. They smell like a corpse. (*A pause*.) Yes.... Do you remember that poem of Lermontov's?

'And he, rebellious, seeks a storm,
  As if in storms there were tranquillity.' ...

CHEBUTYKIN: Yes.

'He had no time to say "Oh, oh!"
  Before that bear had struck him low.'

Goes out with SOLIONY.

Shouts of 'Heigh-ho!' 'Ah-oo!' are heard. Enter ANDREY *and* FERAPONT.

FERAPONT: Will you sign these papers, please?

ANDREY: (*With irritation*.) Leave me alone! Leave me alone, for Heaven's sake. (*Goes off with the pram*.)

FERAPONT: Well, what am I supposed to do with the papers then? They are meant to be signed, aren't they? (*Goes to back of stage*.)

Enter IRENA *and* TOOZENBACH, *the latter wearing a straw hat.* KOOLYGHIN *crosses the stage, calling: 'Ah-oo! Masha! Ah-oo!'*

TOOZENBACH: I think he's the only person in the whole town who's glad that the army is leaving.

IRENA: That's quite understandable, really. (*A pause*.) The town will look quite empty.

TOOZENBACH: My dear, I'll be back in a moment.

IRENA: Where are you going?

TOOZENBACH: I must slip back to the town, and then ... I want to see some of my colleagues off.

IRENA: It's not true.... Nikolai, why are you so absent-minded today? (*A pause*.) What happened outside the theatre last night?

TOOZENBACH: (*With a movement of impatience*). I'll be back in an hour.... I'll be back with you again. (*Kisses her hands*.) My treasure! ... (*Gazes into her eyes*.) It's five years since I first began to love you, and still I can't get used to it, and you seem more beautiful every day. What wonderful, lovely hair! What marvellous eyes! I'll take you away tomorrow. We'll work, we'll be rich, my dreams will come to life again. And you'll be happy! But – there's only one 'but', only one – you don't love me!

IRENA: I can't help that! I'll be your wife, I'll be loyal and obedient to you, but I can't love you.... What's to be done? (*Weeps*.) I've never loved anyone in my life. Oh, I've had such dreams about being in love! I've been dreaming about it for ever so long, day and night ... but somehow my soul seems like an expensive piano which someone has locked up and the key's got lost. (*A pause*.) Your eyes are so restless.

TOOZENBACH: I was awake all night. Not that there's anything to be afraid of in my life, nothing threatening.... Only the thought of that lost key torments me and keeps me awake. Say something to me.... (*A pause*.) Say something!

IRENA: What? What am I to say? What?

TOOZENBACH: Anything.

IRENA: Don't, my dear, don't.... (*A pause*.)

TOOZENBACH: Such trifles, such silly little things sometimes become so important suddenly, for no apparent reason! You laugh at them, just as you always have done, you still regard them as trifles, and yet you suddenly find they're in control, and you haven't the power to stop them. But don't let us talk about all that! Really, I feel quite elated. I feel as if I was seeing those fir-trees and maples and birches for the first time in my life. They all seem to be looking at me with a sort of inquisitive look and waiting for something. What beautiful trees – and how beautiful, when you think of it, life ought to be with trees like these!

Shouts of 'Ah-oo! Heigh-ho!' are heard.

I must go, it's time.... Look at that dead tree, it's all dried-up, but it's still swaying in the wind along with the others. And in the same way, it seems to me that, if I die, I shall still have a share in life somehow or other. Goodbye, my dear.... (*Kisses her hands*.) Your papers, the ones you gave me, are on my desk, under the calendar.

IRENA: I'm coming with you.

TOOZENBACH: (*Alarmed*.) No, no! (*Goes off quickly, then stops in the avenue*.) Irena!

IRENA: What?

TOOZENBACH: (*Not knowing what to say*.) I didn't have any coffee this morning. Will you tell them to get some ready for me? (*Goes off quickly*.)

IRENA *stands, lost in thought, then goes to the back of the stage and sits down on a swing. Enter* ANDREY *with the pram;* FERAPONT *appears.*

FERAPONT: Andrey Serghyeech, the papers aren't mine, you know, they're the office papers. I didn't make them up.

ANDREY: Oh, where has all my past life gone to? – the time when I was young and gay and clever, when I used to have fine dreams and great thoughts, and the present and the future were bright with hope? Why do we become so dull and commonplace and uninteresting almost before we've begun to live? Why do we get lazy, indifferent, useless, unhappy? ... This town's been in existence for two hundred years; a hundred thousand people live in it, but there's not one who's any different from all the others! There's never been a scholar or an artist or a saint in this place, never a single man sufficiently outstanding to make you feel passionately that you wanted to emulate him. People here do nothing but eat, drink and sleep.... Then they die and some more take their places, and they eat, drink and sleep, too, – and just to introduce a bit of variety into their lives, so as to avoid getting completely stupid with boredom, they indulge in their disgusting gossip and vodka and gambling and law-suits. The wives deceive their husbands, and the husbands lie to their wives, and pretend they don't see anything and don't hear anything.... And all this overwhelming vulgarity and pettiness crushes the children and puts out any spark they might have in them, so that they, too, become miserable, half-dead creatures, just like one another and just like their parents! ... (*To* FERAPONT, *crossly.*) What do you want?

FERAPONT: What? Here are the papers to sign.

ANDREY: What a nuisance you are!

FERAPONT: (*Hands him the papers.*) The porter at the finance department told me just now ... he said last winter they had two hundred degrees of frost in Petersburg.

ANDREY: I hate the life I live at present, but oh! the sense of elation when I think of the future! Then I feel so light-hearted, such a sense of release! I seem to see light ahead, light and freedom. I see myself free, and my children, too, – free from idleness, free from *kvass*, free from eternal meals of goose and cabbage, free from after-dinner naps, free from all this degrading parasitism! ...

FERAPONT: They say two thousand people were frozen to death. They say everyone was scared stiff. It was either in Petersburg or in Moscow, I can't remember exactly.

ANDREY: (*With sudden emotion, tenderly.*) My dear sisters, my dear good sisters! (*Tearfully.*) Masha, my dear sister! ...

NATASHA: (*Through the window.*) Who's that talking so loudly there? Is that you, Andriusha? You'll wake Sofochka. Il ne faut pas faire du bruit, la Sophie est dormie déjà. Vous êtes un ours. (*Getting angry.*) If you want to talk, give the pram to someone else. Ferapont, take the pram from the master.

FERAPONT: Yes, Madam. (*Takes the pram.*)

ANDREY: (*Shamefacedly.*) I was talking quietly.

NATASHA: (*In the window, caressing her small son.*) Bobik! Naughty Bobik! Aren't you a naughty boy!

ANDREY: (*Glancing through the papers.*) All right, I'll go through them and sign them if they need it. You can take them back to the office later. (*Goes into the house, reading the papers.*)

FERAPONT wheels the pram into the garden.

NATASHA: (*In the window.*) What's Mummy's name, Bobik? You darling! And who's that lady? Auntie Olia. Say: 'Hullo, Auntie Olia.'

Two street musicians, a man and a girl, enter and begin to play on a violin and a harp; VERSHININ, OLGA and ANFISA come out of the house and listen in silence for a few moments; then IRENA approaches them.

OLGA: Our garden's like a public road; everybody goes through it. Nanny, give something to the musicians.

ANFISA: (*Giving them money.*) Go along now, God bless you, good people!

The musicians bow and go away.

Poor, homeless folk! Whoever would go dragging round the streets playing tunes if he had enough to eat? (*To* IRENA.) How are you, Irenushka? (*Kisses her.*) Ah, my child, what life I'm having! Such comfort! In a large flat at the school with Oliushka – and no rent to pay, either! The Lord's been kind to me in my old age. I've never had such a comfortable time in my life, old sinner that I am! A big flat, and no rent to pay, and a whole room to myself, with my own bed. All free. Sometimes when I wake up in the night I begin to think, and then – Oh, Lord! Oh, Holy Mother of God! – there's no one happier in the world than me!

VERSHININ: (*Glances at his watch.*) We shall be starting in a moment, Olga Serghyeevna. It's time I went. (*A pause.*) I wish you all the happiness in the world ... everything.... Where's Maria Serghyeevna?

IRENA: She's somewhere in the garden. I'll go and look for her.

VERSHININ: That's kind of you. I really must hurry.

ANFISA: I'll come and help to look for her. (*Calls out.*) Mashenka, ah-oo!

Goes with IRENA *towards the far end of the garden.*

Ah-oo! Ah-oo!

VERSHININ: Everything comes to an end. Well, here we are – and now it's going to be 'Goodbye'. (*Looks at his watch.*) The city gave us a sort of farewell lunch. There was champagne, and the mayor made a speech, and I ate and listened, but in spirit I was with you here.... (*Glances round the garden.*) I've grown so ... so accustomed to you.

OLGA: Shall we meet again some day, I wonder?

VERSHININ: Most likely not! (*A pause.*) My wife and the two little girls will be staying on here for a month or two. Please, if anything happens, if they need anything....

OLGA: Yes, yes, of course. You needn't worry about that. (*A pause.*) Tomorrow there won't be a single officer or soldier in the town.... All that will be just a memory, and, of course, a new life will begin for us here.... (*A pause.*) Nothing ever happens as we'd like it to. I didn't want to be a headmistress, and yet now I am one. It means we shan't be going to live in Moscow....

VERSHININ: Well.... Thank you for everything. Forgive me if ever I've done anything.... I've talked a lot too much, far too much.... Forgive me for that, don't think too unkindly of me.

OLGA (*Wipes her eyes.*) Now ... why is Masha so long coming?

VERSHININ: What else can I tell you now it's time to say 'Goodbye'? What shall I philosophize about now? ... (*Laughs.*) Yes, life is difficult. It seems quite hopeless for a lot of us, just a kind of impasse.... And yet you must admit that it is gradually getting easier and brighter, and it's clear that the time isn't far off when the light will spread everywhere. (*Looks at his watch.*) Time, it's time for me to go.... In the old days the human race was always making war, its entire existence was taken up with campaigns, advances, retreats, victories.... But now all that's out of date, and in its place there's a huge vacuum, clamouring to be filled. Humanity is passionately seeking something to fill it with and, of course, it will find something some day. Oh! If only it would happen soon! (*A pause.*) If only we could educate the industrious people and make the educated people industrious.... (*Looks at his watch.*) I really must go....

OLGA: Here she comes!

Enter MASHA.

VERSHININ: I've come to say Goodbye....

OLGA walks off and stands a little to one side so as not to interfere with their leave-taking.

MASHA: (*Looking into his face.*) Goodbye! ... (*A long kiss.*)

OLGA: That'll do, that'll do.

MASHA: (*Sobs loudly.*)

VERSHININ: Write to me.... Don't forget me! Let me go ... it's time. Olga Serghyeevna, please take her away ... I must go ... I'm late already.... (*Deeply moved, kisses* OLGA's *hands, then embraces* MASHA *once again and goes out quickly.*)

OLGA: That'll do, Masha! Don't, my dear, don't....

Enter KOOLYGHIN.

KOOLYGHIN: (*Embarrassed.*) Never mind, let her cry, let her. ... My dear Masha, my dear, sweet Masha.... You're my wife, and I'm happy in spite of everything.... I'm not complaining, I've no reproach to make – not a single one.... Olga here is my witness.... We'll start our life over again in the same old way, and you won't hear a word from me ... not a hint....

MASHA: (*Suppressing her sobs.*) 'A green oak grows by a curving shore, And round that oak hangs a golden chain.' ... 'A golden chain round that oak.' ... Oh, I'm going mad.... By a curving shore ... a green oak....

OLGA: Calm yourself, Masha, calm yourself. ... Give her some water.

MASHA: I'm not crying any more....

KOOLYGHIN: She's not crying any more ... she's a good girl.

The hollow sound of a gun-shot is heard in the distance.

MASHA: 'A green oak grows by a curving shore, And round that oak hangs a golden chain.' ... A green cat ... a green oak ... I've got it all mixed up.... (*Drinks water.*) My life's messed up.... I don't want anything now.... I'll calm down in a moment.... It doesn't matter.... What *is* 'the curving shore'? Why does it keep coming into my head all the time? My thoughts are all mixed up.

Figure 10 Steffi Kühnert (Olga), Jule Böwe (Irina) and Bibiana Beglau (Masha) in *Drei Schwestern* (Three Sisters) at the Schaubühne am Lehniner Platz in Berlin, 2009. (Photographer: Arno Declair.)

Enter IRENA.

OLGA: Calm down, Masha. That's right ... good girl! ... Let's go indoors.

MASHA: (*Irritably.*) I'm not going in there! (*Sobs, but immediately checks herself.*) I don't go into that house now, and I'm not going to....

IRENA: Let's sit down together for a moment, and not talk about anything. I'm going away tomorrow, you know.... (*A pause.*)

KOOLYGHIN: Yesterday I took away a false beard and a moustache from a boy in the third form. I've got them here. (*Puts them on.*) Do I look like our German teacher? ... (*Laughs.*) I do, don't I? The boys are funny.

MASHA: It's true, you do look like that German of yours.

OLGA: (*Laughs*). Yes, he does.

MASHA cries.

IRENA: That's enough, Masha!

KOOLYGHIN: Very much like him, I think!

Enter NATASHA.

NATASHA: (*To the maid.*) What? Oh, yes. Mr Protopopov is going to keep an eye on Sofochka, and Andrey Serghyeevich is going to take Bobik out in the pram. What a lot of work these children make! ... (*To IRENA.*) Irena, you're really leaving tomorrow? What a pity! Do stay just another week, won't you? (*Catching sight of KOOLYGHIN, shrieks; he laughs and takes off the false beard and moustache.*) Get away with you! How you scared me! (*To IRENA.*) I've grown so accustomed to you being here.... You mustn't think it's going to be easy for me to be without you. I'll get Andrey and his old violin to move into your room: he can saw away at it as much as he likes there. And then we'll move Sofochka into his room. She's such wonderful child, really! Such a lovely little girl! This morning she looked at me with such a sweet expression, and then she said: 'Ma-mma!'

KOOLYGHIN: It's quite true, she is a beautiful child.

NATASHA: So tomorrow I'll be alone here. (*Sighs.*) I'll have this fir-tree avenue cut down first, then that maple tree over there. It looks so awful in the evenings.... (*To IRENA.*) My dear, that belt you're wearing doesn't suit you at all. Not at all good taste. You want something brighter to go with that dress.... I'll tell them to put flowers all round here, lots of flowers, so that we get plenty of scent from them.... (*Sternly.*) Why is there a fork lying on this seat? (*Going into the house, to the maid.*) Why is that fork left on the seat there? (*Shouts.*) Don't answer me back!

KOOLYGHIN: There she goes again!

A band plays a military march offstage; all listen.

OLGA: They're going.

Enter CHEBUTYKIN.

MASHA: The soldiers are going. Well. ... Happy journey to them! (*To her husband.*) We must go home.... Where's my hat and cape? ...

KOOLYGHIN: I took them indoors. I'll bring them at once.

OLGA: Yes, we can go home now. It's time.

CHEBUTYKIN: Olga Serghyeevna!

OLGA: What is it? (*A pause.*) What?

CHEBUTYKIN. Nothing.... I don't know quite how to tell you.... (*Whispers into her ear.*)

OLGA: (*Frightened.*) It can't be true!

CHEBUTYKIN: Yes ... a bad business.... I'm so tired ... quite worn out.... I don't want to say another word.... (*With annoyance.*) Anyway, nothing matters! ...

MASHA: What's happened?

OLGA: (*Puts her arms round IRENA.*) What a dreadful day! ... I don't know how to tell you, dear....

IRENA: What is it? Tell me quickly, what is it? For Heaven's sake! ... (*Cries.*)

CHEBUTYKIN: The Baron's just been killed in a duel.

IRENA: (*Cries quietly.*) I knew it, I knew it....

CHEBUTYKIN: (*Goes to the back of the stage and sits down.*) I'm tired.... (*Takes a newspaper out of his pocket.*) Let them cry for a bit.... (*Sings quietly to himself.*) Tarara-boom-di-ay, I'm sitting on a tomb-di-ay.... What difference does it make? ...

The three sisters stand huddled together.

MASHA: Oh, listen to that band! They're leaving us ... one of them's gone for good ... for ever! We're left alone ... to start our lives all over again. We must go on living ... we must go on living....

IRENA: (*Puts her head on OLGA's breast*). Some day people will know why such things happen, and what the purpose of all this suffering is.... Then there won't be any more riddles.... Meanwhile we must go on living ... and working. Yes, we must just go on working! Tomorrow I'll go away alone and teach in a school somewhere; I'll give my life to people who need it.... It's autumn now, winter will soon be here, and the snow will cover everything ... but I'll go on working and working! ...

OLGA: (*Puts her arms round both her sisters.*) How cheerfully and jauntily that band's playing – really I feel as if I wanted to live! Merciful God! The years will pass, and we shall all be gone for good and quite forgotten.... Our faces and our voices will be forgotten and people won't even know that there were once three of us here.... But our sufferings may mean happiness for the people who come after us.... There'll be a time when peace and happiness reign in the world, and then we shall be remembered kindly and blessed. No, my dear sisters, life isn't finished for us yet! We're going to live! The band is playing so cheerfully and joyfully – maybe, if we wait a little longer, we shall find out why we live, why we suffer. ... Oh, if we only knew, if only we knew!

The music grows fainter and fainter. KOOLYGHIN, *smiling happily, brings out the hat and the cape.* ANDREY *enters; he is pushing the pram with* BOBIK *sitting in it.*

CHEBUTYKIN: (*Sings quietly to himself.*) Tarara-boom-diay.... I'm sitting on a tomb-di-ay.... (*Reads the paper.*) What does it matter? Nothing matters!

OLGA: If only we knew, if only we knew! ...

Notes

1 A large room, sparsely furnished, used for receptions and dances in Russian houses.
2 A town in western Russia well known for its almost exclusively Jewish population.
3 A traditional Russian dance-song.
4 A Polish word meaning 'beloved'.

1.4 WHEN WE DEAD AWAKEN (1899)

HENRIK IBSEN

Translated by William Archer

Henrik Ibsen (1828–1906). When We Dead Awaken *was the last play written by Ibsen. He was concerned that his health would fail him, believing that the play would be 'the best and the biggest I have ever written'. It is subtitled 'A Dramatic Epilogue' because he intended it to bring to an end the great sequence of twelve prose plays he had been writing since 1877 and which included all of his Naturalist plays. He had been drifting away from strict Naturalism since* The Wild Duck *but this play treads on Symbolist territory more decisively than ever: it is a play of stillness, memory, atmosphere, of persuasion and obsession, metaphor and symbol. The play was poorly received at the time, though a young James Joyce thought it one of Ibsen's finest achievements. The play is less often performed than the other prose plays, not least because of the technical challenge of producing the closing avalanche. The translation from Norwegian printed here was written by William Archer in 1903.*

Characters

PROFESSOR ARNOLD RUBEK, a sculptor
MRS MAIA RUBEK, his wife
THE INSPECTOR at the Baths
ULFHEIM, a landed proprietor
A STRANGER LADY
A SISTER OF MERCY
Servants, Visitors to the Baths and Children

The First Act passes at a bathing establishment on the coast; the Second and Third Acts in the neighbourhood of a health resort, high in the mountains.

Act 1

Outside the Bath Hotel. A portion of the main building can be seen to the right. An open, park-like place with a fountain, groups of fine old trees, and shrubbery. To the left, a little pavilion almost covered with ivy and Virginia creeper. A table and chair outside it. At the back a view over the fjord, right out to sea, with headlands and small islands in the distance. It is a calm, warm and sunny summer morning.

PROFESSOR RUBEK *and* MRS MAIA RUBEK *are sitting in basket chairs beside a covered table on the lawn outside the hotel, having just breakfasted. They have champagne and seltzer water on the table, and each has a newspaper.* PROFESSOR RUBEK *is an elderly man of distinguished appearance, wearing a black velvet jacket, and otherwise in light summer attire.* MAIA *is quite young, with a vivacious expression and lively, mocking eyes, yet with a suggestion of fatigue. She wears an elegant travelling dress.*

Figure 11 *When We Dead Awaken*, Theater Ibsen, Skien, Norway, 2006, directed by Morten Traavik. (Photographer: Dag Jenssen.)

MAIA: (*Sits for some time as though waiting for the* PROFESSOR *to say something, then lets her paper drop with a deep sigh.*) Oh dear, dear, dear – !

RUBEK: (*Looks up from his paper.*) Well, Maia? What is the matter with you?

MAIA: Just listen how silent it is here.

RUBEK: (*Smiles indulgently.*) And you can hear that?

MAIA: What?

RUBEK: The silence?

MAIA: Yes, indeed I can.

RUBEK: Well, perhaps you are right, *mein Kind*. One can really hear the silence.

MAIA: Heaven knows you can – when it's so absolutely overpowering as it is here –

RUBEK: Here at the Baths, you mean?

MAIA: Wherever you go at home here, it seems to me. Of course there was noise and bustle enough in the town. But I don't know how it is – even the noise and bustle seemed to have something dead about it.

RUBEK: (*With a searching glance.*) You don't seem particularly glad to be at home again, Maia?

MAIA: (*Looks at him.*) Are you glad?

RUBEK: (*Evasively.*) I – ?

MAIA: Yes, you, who have been so much, much further away than I. Are you entirely happy, now that you are at home again?

Figure 12 *When We Dead Awaken*, Theater Ibsen, Skien, Norway, 2006, directed by Morten Traavik. (Photographer: Dag Jenssen.)

RUBEK: No – to be quite candid – perhaps not entirely happy –

MAIA: (*With animation.*) There, you see! Didn't I know it!

RUBEK: I have been too long abroad. I have drifted quite away from all this – this home life.

MAIA: (*Eagerly, drawing her chair nearer him.*) There, you see, Rubek! We had much better get away again! As quickly as ever we can.

RUBEK: (*Somewhat impatiently.*) Well, well, that is what we intend to do, my dear Maia. You know that.

MAIA: But why not now – at once? Only think how cosy and comfortable we could be down there, in our lovely new house –

RUBEK: (*Smiles indulgently.*) We ought by rights to say: our lovely new home.

MAIA: (*Shortly.*) I prefer to say house – let us keep to that.

RUBEK: (*His eyes dwelling on her.*) You are really a strange little person.

MAIA: Am I so strange?

RUBEK: Yes, I think so.

MAIA: But why, pray? Perhaps because I'm not desperately in love with mooning about up here – ?

RUBEK: Which of us was it that was absolutely bent on our coming north this summer?

MAIA: I admit, it was I.

RUBEK: It was certainly not I, at any rate.

MAIA: But good heavens, who could have dreamt that everything would have altered so terribly at home here? And in so short a time, too! Why, it is only just four years since I went away –

RUBEK: Since you were married, yes –

MAIA: Married? What has that to do with the matter?

RUBEK: (*Continuing.*) – since you became the Frau Professor, and found yourself mistress of a charming home – I beg your pardon – a very handsome house, I ought to say. And a villa on the Lake of Taunitz, just at the point that has become most fashionable, too –. In fact it is all very handsome and distinguished, Maia, there's no denying that. And spacious too. We need not always be getting in each other's way –

MAIA: (*Lightly.*) No, no, no – there's certainly no lack of house-room, and that sort of thing –

RUBEK: Remember, too, that you have been living in altogether more spacious and distinguished surroundings – in more polished society than you were accustomed to at home.

MAIA: (*Looking at him.*) Ah, so you think it is *I* that have changed?

RUBEK: Indeed I do, Maia.

MAIA: I alone? Not the people here?

RUBEK: Oh yes, they too – a little, perhaps. And not at all in the direction of amiability. That I readily admit.

MAIA: I should think you must admit it, indeed.

RUBEK: (*Changing the subject.*) Do you know how it affects me when I look at the life of the people around us here?

MAIA: No. Tell me.

RUBEK: It makes me think of that night we spent in the train, when we were coming up here –

MAIA: Why, you were sound asleep all the time.

RUBEK: Not quite. I noticed how silent it became at all the little roadside stations. I heard the silence – like you, Maia –

MAIA: H'm, – like me, yes.

RUBEK: – and that assured me that we had crossed the frontier – that we were really at home. For the train stopped at all the little stations – although there was nothing doing at all.

MAIA: Then why did it stop – though there was nothing to be done?

RUBEK: Can't say. No one got out or in; but all the same the train stopped a long, endless time. And at every station I could make out that there were two railway men walking up and down the platform – one with a lantern in his hand – and they said things to each other in the night, low, and toneless, and meaningless.

MAIA: Yes, that is quite true. There are always two men walking up and down and talking –

RUBEK: – of nothing. (*Changing to a livelier tone.*) But just wait till tomorrow. Then we shall have the great luxurious steamer lying in the harbour. We'll go on board her, and sail all round the coast – northward ho! – right to the polar sea.

MAIA: Yes, but then you will see nothing of the country – and of the people. And that was what you particularly wanted.

RUBEK: (*Shortly and snappishly.*) I have seen more than enough.

MAIA: Do you think a sea voyage will be better for you?

RUBEK: It is always a change.

MAIA: Well, well, if only it is the right thing for you –

RUBEK: For me? The right thing? There is nothing in the world the matter with me.

MAIA: (*Rises and goes to him.*) Yes, there is, Rubek. I am sure you must feel it yourself.

RUBEK: Why my dearest Maia – what should be amiss with me?

MAIA: (*Behind him, bending over the back of his chair.*) That you must tell me. You have begun to wander about without a moment's peace. You cannot rest anywhere – neither at home nor abroad. You have become quite misanthropic of late.

RUBEK: (*With a touch of sarcasm.*) Dear me – have you noticed that?

MAIA: No one that knows you can help noticing it. And then it seems to me so sad that you have lost all pleasure in your work.

RUBEK: That too, eh?

MAIA: You that used to be so indefatigable – working from morning to night!

RUBEK: (*Gloomily.*) Used to be, yes –

MAIA: But ever since you got your great masterpiece out of hand –

RUBEK: (*Nods thoughtfully.*) 'The Resurrection Day' –

MAIA: – The masterpiece that has gone round the whole world, and made you so famous –

RUBEK: Perhaps that is just the misfortune, Maia.

MAIA: How so?

RUBEK: When I had finished this masterpiece of mine – (*Makes a passionate movement with his hand*) – for 'The Resurrection Day' is a masterpiece! Or was one in the beginning. No, it is one still. It must, must, must be a masterpiece!

MAIA: (*Looks at him in astonishment.*) Why, Rubek – all the world knows that.

RUBEK: (*Short, repellently.*) All the world knows nothing! Understands nothing!

MAIA: Well, at any rate it can divine something –

RUBEK: Something that isn't there at all, yes. Something that never was in my mind. Ah yes, that they can all go into ecstasies over! (*Growling to himself.*) What is the good of working oneself to death for the mob and the masses – for 'all the world'!

MAIA: Do you think it is better, then – do you think it is worthy of you, to do nothing at all but portrait-bust now and then?

RUBEK: (*With a sly smile.*) They are not exactly portrait-busts that I turn out, Maia.

MAIA: Yes, indeed they are – for the last two or three years – ever since you finished your great group and got it out of the house –

RUBEK: All the same, they are no mere portrait-busts, I assure you.

MAIA: What are they, then?

RUBEK: There is something equivocal, something cryptic, lurking in and behind these busts – a secret something, that the people themselves cannot see –

MAIA: Indeed?

RUBEK: (*Decisively.*) I alone can see it. And it amuses me unspeakably. – On the surface I give them the 'striking likeness', as they call it, that they all stand and gape at in astonishment – (*Lowers his voice.*) – but at bottom they are all respectable, pompous horse-faces, and self-opinionated donkey-muzzles, and lop-eared, low-browed dog-skulls, and fatted swine-snouts – and sometimes dull, brutal bull-fronts as well –

MAIA: (*Indifferently.*) All the dear domestic animals, in fact.

RUBEK: Simply the dear domestic animals, Maia. All the animals which men have bedevilled in their own image – and which have bedevilled men in return. (*Empties his champagne-glass and laughs.*) And it is these double-faced works of art that our excellent plutocrats come and order of me. And pay for in all good faith – and in good round figures too – almost their weight in gold, as the saying goes.

MAIA: (*Fills his glass.*) Come, Rubek! Drink and be happy.

RUBEK: (*Passes his hand several times across his forehead and leans back in his chair.*) I am happy, Maia. Really happy – in a way. (*Short silence.*) For after all there is a certain happiness in feeling oneself free and independent on every hand – in having at one's command everything one can possibly wish for – all outward things, that is to say. Do you not agree with me, Maia?

MAIA: Oh yes, I agree. All that is well enough in its way. (*Looking at him.*) But do you remember what you promised me the day we came to an understanding on – on that troublesome point –

RUBEK: (*Nods.*) – on the subject of our marriage, yes. It was no easy matter for you, Maia.

MAIA: (*Continuing unruffled.*) – and agreed that I was to go abroad with you, and live there for good and all – and enjoy myself. – Do you remember what you promised me that day?

RUBEK: (*Shaking his head.*) No, I can't say that I do. Well, what did I promise?

MAIA: You said you would take me up to a high mountain and show me all the glory of the world.

RUBEK: (*With a slight start.*) Did I promise you that, too?

MAIA: Me too? Who else, pray?

RUBEK: (*Indifferently.*) No, no, I only meant did I promise to show you – ?

MAIA: – all the glory of the world? Yes, you did. And all that glory should be mine, you said.

RUBEK: That is a sort of figure of speech that I was in the habit of using once upon a time.

MAIA: Only a figure of speech?

RUBEK: Yes, a schoolboy phrase – the sort of thing I used to say when I wanted to lure the neighbours' children out to play with me, in the woods and on the mountains.

MAIA: (*Looking hard at him.*) Perhaps you only wanted to lure me out to play, as well?

RUBEK: (*Passing it off as a jest.*) Well, has it not been a tolerable amusing game, Maia?

MAIA: (*Coldly.*) I did not go with you only to play.

RUBEK: No, no, I daresay not.

MAIA: And you never took me up with you to any high mountain, or showed me –

RUBEK: (*With irritation.*) – all the glory of the world? No, I did not. For, let me tell you something: you are not really born to be a mountain-climber, little Maia.

MAIA: (*Trying to control herself.*) Yet at one time you seemed to think I was.

RUBEK: Four or five years ago, yes. (*Stretching himself in his chair.*) Four or five years – it's a long, long time, Maia.

MAIA: (*Looking at him with a bitter expression.*) Has the time seemed so very long to you, Rubek?

RUBEK: I am beginning now to find it a trifle long. (*Yawning.*) Now and then, you know.

MAIA: (*Returning to her place.*) I shall not bore you any longer.

She resumes her seat, takes up the newspaper and begins turning over the leaves. Silence on both sides.

RUBEK: (*Leaning on his elbows across the table, and looking at her teasingly.*) Is the Frau Professor offended?

MAIA: (*Coldly, without looking up.*) No, not at all.

Visitors to the baths, most of them ladies, begin to pass, singly and in groups, through the park from the right, and out to the left.

Waiters bring refreshments from the hotel, and go off behind the pavilion.

THE INSPECTOR, *wearing gloves and carrying a stick, comes from his rounds in the park, meets visitors, bows politely and exchanges a few words with some of them.*

THE INSPECTOR: (*Advancing to* PROFESSOR RUBEK'S *table and politely taking off his hat.*) I have the honour to wish you good morning, Mrs Rubek. – Good morning, Professor Rubek.

RUBEK: Good morning, good morning Inspector.

THE INSPECTOR: (*Addressing himself to* MRS RUBEK.) May I venture to ask if you have slept well?

MAIA: Yes, thank you; excellently – for my part. I always sleep like a stone.

THE INSPECTOR: I am delighted to hear it. The first night in a strange place is often rather trying. – And the Professor – ?

RUBEK: Oh, my night's rest is never much to boast of – especially of late.

THE INSPECTOR: (*With a show of sympathy.*) Oh – that is a pity. But after a few weeks' stay at the Baths – you will quite get over that.

RUBEK: (*Looking up at him.*) Tell me, Inspector – are any of your patients in the habit of taking baths during the night?

THE INSPECTOR: (*Astonished.*) During the night? No, I have never heard of such a thing.

RUBEK: Have you not?

THE INSPECTOR: No, I don't know of anyone so ill as to require such treatment.

RUBEK: Well, at any rate there is someone who is in the habit of walking about the park by night?

THE INSPECTOR: (*Smiling and shaking his head.*) No, Professor – that would be against the rules.

MAIA: (*Impatiently.*) Good Heavens, Rubek, I told you so this morning – you must have dreamt it.

RUBEK: (*Drily.*) Indeed? Must I? Thank you! (*Turning to* THE INSPECTOR.) The fact is, I got up last night – I couldn't sleep – and I wanted to see what sort of night it was –

THE INSPECTOR: (*Attentively.*) To be sure – and then – ?

RUBEK: I looked out at the window – and caught sight of a white figure in there among the trees.

MAIA: (*Smiling to* THE INSPECTOR.) And the Professor declares that the figure was dressed in a bathing costume –

RUBEK: – or something like it, I said. Couldn't distinguish very clearly. But I am sure it was something white.

THE INSPECTOR: Most remarkable. Was it a gentleman or a lady?

RUBEK: I could almost have sworn it was a lady. But then after it came another figure. And that one was quite dark – like a shadow – .

THE INSPECTOR: (*Starting.*) A dark one? Quite black, perhaps?

RUBEK: Yes, I should almost have said so.

THE INSPECTOR: (*A light breaking in upon him.*) And behind the white figure? Following close upon her – ?

RUBEK: Yes – at a little distance –

THE INSPECTOR: Aha! Then I think I can explain the mystery, Professor.

RUBEK: Well, what was it then?

MAIA: (*Simultaneously.*) Was the Professor really not dreaming?

THE INSPECTOR: (*Suddenly whispering, as he directs their attention towards the background on the right.*) Hush, if you please! Look there – don't speak loud for a moment.

A slender lady, dressed in fine, cream-white cashmere and followed by a SISTER OF MERCY *in black, with a silver cross hanging by a chain on her breast, comes forward from behind the hotel and crosses the park towards the pavilion in front on the left. Her face is pale, and its lines seem to have stiffened; the eyelids are drooped and the eyes appear as though they saw nothing. Her dress comes down to her feet and clings to the body in perpendicular folds. Over her head, neck, breast, shoulders and arms she wears a large shawl of white crêpe. She keeps her arms crossed upon her breast. She carries her body immovably, and her steps are stiff and measured. The* SISTER'S *bearing is also measured, and she has the air of a servant. She keeps her brown piercing eyes incessantly fixed upon the lady. Waiters, with napkins on their arms, come forward in the hotel doorway, and cast curious glances at the strangers, who take no notice of anything, and, without looking round, enter the pavilion.*

RUBEK: (*Has risen slowly and involuntarily, and stands staring at the closed door of the pavilion.*) Who was that lady?

THE INSPECTOR: She is a stranger who has rented the little pavilion there.

RUBEK: A foreigner?

THE INSPECTOR: Presumably. At any rate they both came from abroad – about a week ago. They have never been here before.

RUBEK: (*Decidedly; looking at him.*) It was she I saw in the park last night.

THE INSPECTOR: No doubt it must have been. I thought so from the first.

RUBEK: What is this lady's name, Inspector?

THE INSPECTOR: She has registered herself as 'Madame de Satow, with companion'. We know nothing more.

RUBEK: (*Reflecting.*) Satow? Satow – ?

MAIA: (*Laughing mockingly.*) Do you know anyone of that name, Rubek? Eh?

RUBEK: (*Shaking his head.*) No, no one. – Satow? It sounds Russian – or in all events Slavonic. (*To* THE INSPECTOR.) What language does she speak?

THE INSPECTOR: When the two ladies talk to each other, it is in a language I cannot make out at all. But at other times she speaks Norwegian like a native.

RUBEK: (*Exclaims with a start.*) Norwegian? You are sure you are not mistaken?

THE INSPECTOR: No, how could I be mistaken in that?

RUBEK: (*Looks at him with eager interest.*) You have heard her yourself?

THE INSPECTOR: Yes. I myself have spoken to her – several times. – Only a few words, however, she is far from communicative. But –

RUBEK: But Norwegian it was?

THE INSPECTOR: Thoroughly good Norwegian – perhaps with a little north-country accent.

RUBEK: (*Gazing straight before him in amazement, whispers.*) That too?

MAIA: (*A little hurt and jarred.*) Perhaps this lady has been one of your models, Rubek? Search your memory.

RUBEK: (*Looks cuttingly at her.*) My models?

MAIA: (*With a provoking smile.*) In your younger days, I mean. You are said to have had innumerable models – long ago, of course.

RUBEK: (*In the same tone.*) Oh no, little Frau Maia. I have in reality had only one single model. One and only one – for everything I have done.

THE INSPECTOR: (*Who has turned away and stands looking out to the left.*) If you'll excuse me, I think I will take my leave. I see someone coming whom it is not particularly agreeable to meet. Especially in the presence of ladies.

RUBEK: (*Looking in the same direction.*) That sportsman there? Who is it?

THE INSPECTOR: It is a certain Mr Ulfheim, from –

RUBEK: Oh, Mr Ulfheim –

THE INSPECTOR: – the bear-killer, as they call him –

RUBEK: I know him.

THE INSPECTOR: Who does not know him?

RUBEK: Very slightly, however. Is he on your list of patients – at last?

THE INSPECTOR: No, strangely enough – not as yet. He comes here only once a year – on his way up to his hunting-grounds. – Excuse me for the moment –

Makes a movement to go into the hotel.

ULFHEIM'S VOICE: (*Heard outside.*) Stop a moment, man! Devil take it all, can't you stop? Why do you always scuttle away from me?

THE INSPECTOR: (*Stops.*) I am not scuttling at all, Mr Ulfheim.

ULFHEIM enters from the left followed by a servant with a couple of sporting dogs in leash. ULFHEIM *is in shooting costume, with high boots and a felt hat with a feather in it. He is a long, lank, sinewy personage, with matted hair and beard and a loud*

voice. His appearance gives no precise clue to his age, but he is no longer young.

ULFHEIM: (*Pounces upon* THE INSPECTOR.) Is this a way to receive strangers, hey? You scamper away with your tail between your legs – as if you had the devil at your heels.

THE INSPECTOR: (*Calmly, without answering him.*) Has Mr Ulfheim arrived by the steamer?

ULFHEIM: (*Growls.*) Haven't had the honour of seeing any steamer. (*With his arms akimbo.*) Don't you know that I sail my own cutter? (*To the servant.*) Look well after your fellow-creatures, Lars. But take care you keep them ravenous, all the same. Fresh meat-bones – but not too much meat on them, do you hear? And be sure it's reeking raw and bloody. And get something in your own belly while you're about it. (*Aiming a kick at him.*) Now then, go to hell with you.

The servant goes out with the dogs, behind the corner of the hotel.

THE INSPECTOR: Would not Mr Ulfheim like to go into the dining-room in the meantime?

ULFHEIM: In among all the half-dead flies and people? No, thank you a thousand times, Mr Inspector.

THE INSPECTOR: Well, well, as you please.

ULFHEIM: But get the housekeeper to prepare a hamper for me as usual. There must be plenty of provender in it – and lots of brandy –! You can tell her that I or Lars will come and play Old Harry with her if she doesn't –

THE INSPECTOR: (*Interrupting.*) We know your ways of old. (*Turning.*) Can I give the waiter any orders, Professor? Can I send Mrs Rubek anything?

RUBEK: No thank you; nothing for me.

MAIA: Nor for me.

THE INSPECTOR *goes into the hotel.*

ULFHEIM: (*Stares at them for a moment; then lifts his hat.*) Why, blast me if here isn't a country tyke that has strayed into regular tip-top society.

RUBEK: (*Looking up.*) What do you mean by that, Mr Ulfheim?

ULFHEIM: (*More quietly and politely.*) I believe I have the honour of addressing no less a person than the great Sculptor Rubek.

RUBEK: (*Nods.*) I remember meeting you once or twice – the autumn when I was last at home.

ULFHEIM: That's many years ago, now. And then you weren't so illustrious as I hear you've since become. At that time even a dirty bear-hunter might venture to come near you.

RUBEK: (*Smiling.*) I don't bite even now.

MAIA: (*Looks with interest at* ULFHEIM.) Are you really and truly a bear-hunter?

ULFHEIM: (*Seating himself at the next table, nearer the hotel.*) A bear-hunter when I have the chance, madam. But I make the best of any sort of game that comes in my way – eagles, and wolves, and women, and elks and reindeer – if only it's fresh and juicy and has plenty of blood in it.

Drinks from his pocket-flask.

MAIA: (*Regarding him fixedly.*) But you like bear-hunting best?

ULFHEIM: I like it best, yes. For then one can have the knife handy at a pinch. (*With a slight smile.*) We both work in a hard material, madam – both your husband and I. He struggles with his marble blocks, I daresay; and I struggle with tense and quivering bear-sinews. And we both of us win the fight in the end – subdue and master our material. We never rest till we've got the upper hand of it, though it fight never so hard.

RUBEK: (*Deep in thought.*) There's a great deal of truth in what you say.

ULFHEIM: Yes, for I take it the stone has something to fight for too. It is dead, and determined by no manner of means to let itself be hammered into life. Just like the bear when you come and prod him up in his lair.

MAIA: Are you going up into the forests now to hunt?

ULFHEIM: I am going right up into the high mountain. – I suppose you have never been in the high mountain, madam?

MAIA: No, never.

ULFHEIM: Confound it all then, you must be sure and come up there this very summer! I'll take you with me – both you and the Professor, with pleasure.

MAIA: Thanks. But Rubek is thinking of taking a sea trip this summer.

RUBEK: Round the coast – through the island channels.

ULFHEIM: Ugh – what the devil would you do in those damnable sickly gutters – floundering about in the brackish ditchwater? Dishwater I should rather call it.

MAIA: There, you hear, Rubek!

ULFHEIM: No, much better come up with me to the mountain – away, clean away, from the trail and taint of men. You can't think what that means for me. But such a little lady –

He stops.

The SISTER OF MERCY *comes out of the pavilion and goes into the hotel.*

ULFHEIM: (*Following her with his eyes.*) Just look at her, do! That night-crow there! – Who is it that's to be buried?

RUBEK: I have not heard of anyone –

ULFHEIM: Well, there's someone on the point of giving up the ghost, then – in one corner. or another. – People that are sickly and rickety should have the goodness to see about getting themselves buried – the sooner the better.

MAIA: Have you ever been ill yourself, Mr Ulfheim?

ULFHEIM: Never. If I had, I shouldn't be here. – But my nearest friends – they have been ill, poor things.

MAIA: And what did you do for your nearest friends?

ULFHEIM: Shot them, of course.

RUBEK: (*Looking at him.*) Shot them?

MAIA: (*Moving her chair back.*) Shot them dead?

ULFHEIM: (*Nods.*) I never miss, madam.

MAIA: But how can you possibly shoot people!

ULFHEIM: I am not speaking of people –

MAIA: You said your nearest friends –

ULFHEIM: Well, who should they be but my dogs?

MAIA: Are your dogs your nearest friends?

ULFHEIM: I have none nearer. My honest, trusty, absolutely loyal comrades – When one of them turns sick and miserable – bang! – and there's my friend sent packing – to the other world.

The SISTER OF MERCY *comes out of the hotel with a tray on which is bread and milk. She places it on the table outside the pavilion, which she enters.*

ULFHEIM: (*Laughs scornfully.*) That stuff there – is that what you call food for human beings! Milk and water and soft, clammy bread. Ah, you should see my comrades feeding. Should you like to see it?

MAIA: (*Smiling across to the PROFESSOR and rising.*) Yes, very much.

ULFHEIM: (*Also rising.*) Spoken like a woman of spirit, madam! Come with me, then! They swallow whole great thumping meat-bones – gulp them up and then gulp them down again. Oh, it's a regular treat to see them. Come along and I'll show you – and while we're about it, we can talk over this trip to the mountains –

He goes out by the corner of the hotel, MAIA *following him.*

Almost at the same moment the STRANGE LADY *comes out of the pavilion and seats herself at the table.*

THE LADY *raises her glass of milk and is about to drink, but stops and looks across at* RUBEK *with vacant, expressionless eyes.*

RUBEK: (*Remains sitting at his table and gazes fixedly and earnestly at her. At last he rises, goes some steps towards her, stops, and says in a low voice.*) I know you quite well, Irene.

THE LADY: (*In a toneless voice, setting down her glass.*) You can guess who I am, Arnold?

RUBEK: (*Without answering.*) And you recognise me, too, I see.

THE LADY: With you it is quite another matter.

RUBEK: With me? – How so?

THE LADY: Oh, you are still alive.

RUBEK: (*Not understanding.*) Alive – ?

THE LADY: (*After a short pause.*) Who was the other? The woman you had with you – there at the table?

RUBEK: (*A little reluctantly.*) She? That was my – my wife.

THE LADY: (*Nods slowly.*) Indeed. That is well, Arnold. Someone, then, who does not concern me –

RUBEK: (*Nods.*) No, of course not –

THE LADY: – one whom you have taken to you after my lifetime.

RUBEK: (*Suddenly looking hard at her.*) After your – ? What do you mean by that, Irene?

IRENE: (*Without answering.*) And the child? I hear the child is prospering too. Our child survives me – and has come to honour and glory.

RUBEK: (*Smiles as at a far-off recollection.*) Our child? Yes, we called it so – then.

IRENE: In my lifetime, yes.

RUBEK: (*Trying to take a lighter tone.*) Yes, Irene. – I can assure you 'our child' has become famous all the wide world over. I suppose you have read about it.

IRENE: (*Nods.*) And has made its father famous too. – That was your dream.

RUBEK: (*More softly, with emotion.*) It is to you I owe everything, everything, Irene – and I thank you.

IRENE: (*Lost in thought for a moment.*) If I had then done what I had a right to do, Arnold –

RUBEK: Well? What then?

IRENE: I should have killed that child.

RUBEK: Killed it, you say?

IRENE: (*Whispering.*) Killed it – before I went away from you. Crushed it – crushed it to dust.

RUBEK: (*Shakes his head reproachfully.*) You would never have been able to, Irene. You had not the heart to do it.

IRENE: No, in those days I had not that sort of heart.

RUBEK: But since then? Afterwards?

IRENE: Since then I have killed it innumerable times. By daylight and in the dark. Killed it in hatred – and in revenge – and in anguish.

RUBEK: (*Goes close up to the table and asks softly.*) Irene – tell me now at last – after all these years – why did you go away from me? You disappeared so utterly – left not a trace behind –

IRENE: (*Shaking her head slowly.*) Oh Arnold – why should I tell you that now – from the world beyond the grave.

RUBEK: Was there someone else whom you had come to love?

IRENE: There was one who had no longer any use for my love – any use for my life.

RUBEK: (*Changing the subject.*) H'm – don't let us talk any more of the past –

IRENE: No, no – by all means let us not talk of what is beyond the grave – what is now beyond the grave for me.

RUBEK: Where have you been, Irene? All my inquiries were fruitless – you seemed to have vanished away.

IRENE: I went into the darkness – when the child stood transfigured in the light.

RUBEK: Have you travelled much about the world?

IRENE: Yes. Travelled in many lands.

RUBEK: (*Looks compassionately at her.*) And what have you found to do, Irene?

IRENE: (*Turning her eyes upon him.*) Wait a moment; let me see – Yes, now I have it. I have posed on the turntable in variety-shows. Posed as a naked statue in living pictures. Raked in heaps of money. That was more than I could do with you; for you had none. – And then I turned the heads of all sorts of men. That, too, was more than I could do with you, Arnold. You kept yourself better in hand.

RUBEK: (*Hastening to pass the subject by.*) And then you have married, too?

IRENE: Yes; I married one of them.

RUBEK: Who is your husband?

IRENE: He was a South American. A distinguished diplomatist. (*Looks straight in front of her with a stony smile.*) Him I managed to drive quite out of his mind; mad – incurably mad; inexorably mad. – It was great sport, I can tell you – while it was in the doing. I could have laughed within me all the time – if I had anything within me.

RUBEK: And where is he now?

IRENE: Oh, in a churchyard somewhere or other. With a fine handsome monument over him. And with a bullet rattling in his skull.

RUBEK: Did he kill himself?

IRENE: Yes, he was good enough to take that off my hands.

RUBEK: Do you not lament his loss, Irene?

IRENE: (*Not understanding.*) Lament? What loss?

RUBEK: Why the loss of Herr von Satow, of course.

IRENE: His name was not Satow.

RUBEK: Was it not?

IRENE: My second husband is called Satow. He is a Russian –

RUBEK: And where is he?

IRENE: Far away in the Ural Mountains. Among all his gold-mines.

RUBEK: So he lives there?

IRENE: (*Shrugs her shoulders.*) Lives? Lives? In reality I have killed him –

RUBEK: (*Start.*) Killed – !

IRENE: Killed him with a fine sharp dagger which I always have with me in bed –

RUBEK: (*Vehemently.*) I don't believe you, Irene!

IRENE: (*With a gentle smile.*) Indeed you may believe it, Arnold.

RUBEK: (*Looks compassionately at her.*) Have you never had a child?

IRENE: Yes, I have had many children.

RUBEK: And where are your children now?

IRENE: I killed them.

RUBEK: (*Severely.*) Now you are telling me lies again!

IRENE: I have killed them, I tell you – murdered them pitilessly. As soon as ever they came into the world. Oh, long, long before. One after the other.

RUBEK: (*Sadly and earnestly.*) There is something hidden behind everything you say.

IRENE: How can I help that? Every word I say is whispered into my ear.

RUBEK: I believe I am the only one that can divine your meaning.

IRENE: Surely you ought to be the only one.

RUBEK: (*Rests his hands on the table and looks intently at her.*) Some of the strings of your nature have broken.

IRENE: (*Gently.*) Does not that always happen when a young warm-blooded woman dies?

RUBEK: Oh Irene, have done with these wild imaginings –! You are living! Living – living!

IRENE: (*Rises slowly from her chair and says, quivering.*) I was dead for many years. They came and bound me – laced my arms together behind my back –. Then they lowered me into a grave-vault, with iron bars before the loop-hole. And with padded walls – so that no one on the earth above could hear the grave-shrieks –. But now I am beginning, in a way, to rise from the dead. (*She seats herself again.*)

RUBEK: (*After a pause.*) In all this, do you hold me guilty?

IRENE: Yes.

RUBEK: Guilty of that – your death, as you call it.

IRENE: Guilty of the fact that I had to die. (*Changing her tone to one of indifference.*) Why don't you sit down, Arnold?

RUBEK: May I?

IRENE: Yes. – You need not be afraid of being frozen. I don't think I am quite turned to ice yet.

RUBEK: (*Moves a chair and seats himself at her table.*) There, Irene. Now we two are sitting together as in the old days.

IRENE: A little way apart from each other – also as in the old days.

RUBEK: (*Moving nearer.*) It had to be so, then.

IRENE: Had it?

RUBEK: (*Decisively.*) There had to be a distance between us –

IRENE: Was it absolutely necessary, Arnold?

RUBEK: (*Continuing.*) Do you remember what you answered when I asked if you would go with me out into the wide world?

IRENE: I held up three fingers in the air and swore that I would go with you to the world's end and to the end of life. And that I would serve you in all things –

RUBEK: As the model for my art –

IRENE: – in frank, utter nakedness –

RUBEK: (*With emotion.*) And you did serve me, Irene – so bravely – so gladly and ungrudgingly.

IRENE: Yes with all the pulsing blood of my youth, I served you!

RUBEK: (*Nodding, with a look of gratitude.*) That you have every right to say.

IRENE: I fell down at your feet and served you, Arnold! (*Holding her clenched hand towards him.*) But you, you, – you – !

RUBEK: (*Defensively.*) I never did you any wrong! Never, Irene!

IRENE: Yes, you did! You did wrong to my innermost, inborn nature –

RUBEK: (*Starting back.*) I –!

IRENE: Yes, you! I exposed myself wholly and unreservedly to your gaze – (*More softly.*) And never once did you touch me.

RUBEK: Irene, did you not understand that many a time I was almost beside myself under the spell of all your loveliness?

IRENE: (*Continuing undisturbed.*) And yet – if you had touched me, I think I should have killed you on the spot. For I

had a sharp needle always upon me – hidden in my hair – (*Strokes her forehead meditatively.*) But after all – after all – that you could –

RUBEK: (*Looks impressively at her.*) I was an artist, Irene.

IRENE: (*Darkly.*) That is just it. That is just it.

RUBEK: An artist first of all. And I was sick with the desire to achieve the great work of my life. (*Losing himself in recollection.*) It was to be called 'The Resurrection Day' – figured in the likeness of a young woman, awakening from the sleep of death –

IRENE: Our child, yes –

RUBEK: (*Continuing.*) It was to be the awakening of the noblest, purest, most ideal woman the world ever saw. Then I found you. You were what I required in every respect. And you consented so willingly – so gladly. You renounced home and kindred – and went with me.

IRENE: To go with you meant for me the resurrection of my childhood.

RUBEK: That was just why I found in you all that I required – in you and in no one else. I came to look on you as a thing hallowed, not to be touched save in adoring thoughts. In those days I was still young, Irene. And the superstition took hold of me that if I touched you, if I desired you with my senses, my soul would be profaned, so that I should be unable to accomplish what I was striving for. – And I still think there was some truth in that.

IRENE: (*Nods with a touch of scorn.*) The work of art first – then the human being.

RUBEK: You must judge me as you will; but at that time I was utterly dominated by my great task – and exultantly happy in it.

IRENE: And you achieved your great task, Arnold.

RUBEK: Thanks and praise be to you, I achieved my great task. I wanted to embody the pure woman as I saw her awakening on the Resurrection Day. Not marvelling at anything new and unknown and undivined; but filled with a sacred joy at finding herself unchanged – she, the woman of earth – in the higher, freer, happier region – after the long, dreamless sleep of death. (*More softly.*) Thus did I fashion her. – I fashioned her in your image, Irene.

IRENE: (*Laying her hands flat upon the table and leaning against the back of her chair.*) And then you were done with me –

RUBEK: (*Reproachfully.*) Irene!

IRENE: You had no longer any use for me –

RUBEK: How can you say that!

IRENE: – and began to look about you for other ideals –

RUBEK: I found none, none after you.

IRENE: And no other models, Arnold?

RUBEK: You were no model to me. You were the fountainhead of my achievement.

IRENE: (*Is silent for a short time.*) What poems have you made since? In marble I mean. Since the day I left you.

RUBEK: I have made no poems since that day – only frittered away my life in modelling.

IRENE: And that woman, whom you are now living with – ?

RUBEK: (*Interrupting vehemently.*) Do not speak of her now! It makes me tingle with shame.

IRENE: Where are you thinking of going with her?

RUBEK: (*Slack and weary.*) Oh, on a tedious coasting-voyage to the North, I suppose.

IRENE: (*Looks at him, smiles almost imperceptibly, and whispers.*) You should rather go high up into the mountains. As high as ever you can. Higher, higher, – always higher, Arnold.

RUBEK: (*With eager expectation.*) Are you going up there?

IRENE: Have you the courage to meet me once again?

RUBEK: (*Struggling with himself, uncertainly.*) If we could – oh, if only we could – !

IRENE: Why can we not do what we will? (*Looks at him and whispers beseechingly with folded hands.*) Come, come, Arnold! Oh, come up to me – !

MAIA enters, glowing with pleasure, from behind the hotel, and goes quickly up to the table where they were previously sitting.

MAIA: (*Still at the corner of the hotel, without looking around.*) Oh, you may say what you please, Rubek, but – (*Stops, as she catches sight of IRENE.*) – Oh, I beg your pardon – I see you have made an acquaintance.

RUBEK: (*Curtly.*) Renewed an acquaintance. (*Rises.*) What was it you wanted with me?

MAIA: I only wanted to say this: you may do whatever you please, but *I* am not going with you on that disgusting steamboat.

RUBEK: Why not?

MAIA: Because I want to go up on the mountains and into the forests – that's what I want. (*Coaxingly.*) Oh, you must let me do it, Rubek. – I shall be so good, so good afterwards!

RUBEK: Who is it that has put these ideas into your head?

MAIA: Why he – that horrid bear-killer. Oh you cannot conceive all the marvellous things he has to tell about the mountains. And about life up there! They're ugly, horrid, repulsive, most of the yarns he spins – for I almost believe he's lying – but wonderfully alluring all the same. Oh, won't you let me go with him? Only to see if what he says is true, you understand. May I, Rubek?

RUBEK: Yes, I have not the slightest objection. Off you go to the mountains – as far and as long as you please. I shall perhaps be going the same way myself.

MAIA: (*Quickly.*) No, no, no, you needn't do that! Not on my account!

RUBEK: I want to go to the mountains. I have made up my mind to go.

MAIA: Oh thanks, thanks! May I tell the bear-killer at once?

RUBEK: Tell the bear-killer whatever you please.

MAIA: Oh thanks, thanks, thanks! (*Is about to take his hand; he repels the movement.*) Oh, how dear and good you are today, Rubek!

She runs into the hotel.

At the same time the door of the pavilion is softly and noiselessly set ajar. The SISTER OF MERCY *stands in the opening, intently on the watch. No one sees her.*

RUBEK: (*Decidedly, turning to* IRENE.) Shall we meet up there then?

IRENE: (*Rising slowly.*) Yes, we shall certainly meet. – I have sought for you so long.

RUBEK: When did you begin to seek for me, Irene?

IRENE: (*With a touch of jesting bitterness.*) From the moment I realised that I had given away to you something rather indispensable, Arnold. Something one ought never to part with.

RUBEK: (*Bowing his head.*) Yes, that is bitterly true. You gave me three or four years of your youth.

IRENE: More, more than that I gave you – spend-thrift as I then was.

RUBEK: Yes, you were prodigal, Irene. You gave me all your naked loveliness –

IRENE: – to gaze upon –

RUBEK: – and to glorify –

IRENE: Yes, for your own glorification. – And the child's.

RUBEK: And yours too, Irene.

IRENE: But you have forgotten the most precious gift.

RUBEK: The most precious –? What gift was that?

IRENE: I gave you my young, living soul. And that gift left me empty within – soulless. (*Looking at him with a fixed stare.*) It was that I died of, Arnold.

The SISTER OF MERCY *opens the door wide and makes room for her. She goes into the pavilion.*

RUBEK: (*Stands and looks after her; then whispers.*) Irene!

Act 2

Near a mountain resort. The landscape stretches, in the form of an immense treeless upland, towards a long mountain lake. Beyond the lake rises a range of peaks with blue-white snow in the clefts. In the foreground on the left a purling brook falls in severed streamlets down a steep wall of rock, and thence flows smoothly over the upland until it disappears to the right. Dwarf trees, plants and stones along the course of the brook. In the foreground on the right a hillock, with a stone bench on the top of it. It is a summer afternoon, towards sunset.

At some distance over the upland, on the other side of the brook, a troop of children is singing, dancing and playing. Some are dressed in peasant costume, others in town-made clothes. Their happy laughter is heard, softened by distance, during the following.

PROFESSOR RUBEK *is sitting on the bench, with a plaid over his shoulders, and looking down at the children's play.*

Presently, MAIA *comes forward from among some bushes on the upland to the left, well back, and scans the prospect with her hand shading her eyes. She wears a flat tourist cap, a short skirt, kilted up, reaching only midway between ankle and knee, and high, stout lace-boots. She has in her hand a long alpenstock.*

MAIA: (*At last catches sight of* RUBEK *and calls.*) Hallo!

She advances over the upland, jumps over the brook, with the aid of her alpenstock, and climbs up the hillock.

MAIA: (*Panting.*) Oh, how I have been rushing around looking for you, Rubek.

RUBEK: (*Nods indifferently and asks.*) Have you just come from the hotel?

MAIA: Yes, that was the last place I tried – that fly-trap.

RUBEK: (*Looking at her for moment.*) I noticed that you were not at the dinner-table.

MAIA: No we had our dinner in the open air, we two.

RUBEK: 'We two'? What two?

MAIA: Why, I and that horrid bear-killer, of course.

RUBEK: Oh he.

MAIA: Yes. And first thing tomorrow morning we are going off again.

RUBEK: After bears?

MAIA: Yes. Off to kill a brown-boy.

RUBEK: Have you found the tracks of any?

MAIA: (*With superiority.*) You don't suppose that bears are to be found in the naked mountains, do you?

RUBEK: Where, then?

MAIA: Far beneath. On the lower slopes; in the thickest parts of the forest. Places your ordinary town-folk could never get through –

RUBEK: And you two are going down there tomorrow?

MAIA: (*Throwing herself down among the heather.*) Yes, so we have arranged. – Or perhaps we may start this evening. – If you have no objection, that's to say?

RUBEK: I? Far be it from me to –

MAIA: (*Quickly.*) Of course Lars goes with us – with the dogs.

RUBEK: I feel no curiosity as to the movements of Mr Lars and his dogs. (*Changing the subject.*) Would you not rather sit properly on the seat?

MAIA: (*Drowsily.*) No, thank you. I'm lying so delightfully in the soft heather.

RUBEK: I can see that you are tired.

MAIA: (*Yawning.*) I almost think I'm beginning to feel tired.

RUBEK: You don't notice it till afterwards – when the excitement is over –

MAIA: (*In a drowsy tone.*) Just so. I will lie and close my eyes. (*A short pause. With sudden impatience.*) Ugh, Rubek – how can you endure to sit there listening to these children's screams! And to watch all the capers they are cutting, too!

RUBEK: There is something harmonious – almost like music – in their movements, now and then; amid all the clumsiness. And it amuses me to sit and watch for these isolated moments – when they come.

MAIA: (*With a somewhat scornful laugh.*) Yes, you are always, always an artist.

RUBEK: And I propose to remain one.

MAIA: (*Lying on her side, so that her back is turned to him.*) There's not a bit of the artist about him.

RUBEK: (*With attention.*) Who is it that's not an artist?

MAIA: (*Again in a sleepy tone.*) Why, he – the other one, of course.

RUBEK: The bear-hunter, you mean?

MAIA: Yes. There's not a bit of the artist about him – not the least little bit.

RUBEK: (*Smiling.*) No, I believe there's no doubt about that.

MAIA: (*Vehemently, without moving.*) And so ugly as he is! (*Plucks up a tuft of heather and throws it away.*) So ugly, so ugly! Isch!

RUBEK: Is that why you are so ready to set off with him – out into the wilds?

MAIA: (*Curtly.*) I don't know. (*Turning towards him.*) You are ugly, too, Rubek.

RUBEK: Have you only just discovered it?

MAIA: No, I have seen it for long.

RUBEK: (*Shrugging his shoulders.*) One doesn't grow younger. One doesn't grow younger, Frau Maia.

MAIA: It's not that sort of ugliness that I mean at all. But there has come to be such an expression of fatigue, of utter weariness, in your eyes – when you deign, once in a while, to cast a glance at me.

RUBEK: Have you noticed that?

MAIA: (*Nods.*) Little by little this evil look has come into your eyes. It seems almost as though you were nursing some dark plot against me.

RUBEK: Indeed? (*In a friendly but earnest tone.*) Come here and sit beside me, Maia; and let us talk a little.

MAIA: (*Half rising.*) Then will you let me sit upon your knee? As I used to in the early days?

RUBEK: No, you mustn't – people can see us from the hotel. (*Moves a little.*) But you can sit here on the bench – at my side.

MAIA: No, thank you; in that case I'd rather lie here, where I am. I can hear you quite well here. (*Looks inquiringly at him.*) Well, what is it you want to say to me?

RUBEK: (*Begins slowly.*) What do you think was my real reason for agreeing to make this tour?

MAIA: Well – I remember you declared, among other things, that it was going to do me such a tremendous lot of good. But – but –

RUBEK: But – ?

MAIA: But now I don't believe the least little bit that that was the reason –

RUBEK: Then what is your theory about it now?

MAIA: I think now that it was on account of that pale lady.

RUBEK: Madame von Satow – !

MAIA: Yes, she who is always hanging at our heels. Yesterday evening she made her appearance up here too.

RUBEK: But what in all the world – !

MAIA: Oh, I know you knew her very well indeed – long before you knew me.

RUBEK: And had forgotten her, too – long before I knew you.

MAIA: (*Sitting upright.*) Can you forget so easily, Rubek?

RUBEK: (*Curtly.*) Yes, very easily indeed. (*Adds harshly.*) When I want to forget.

MAIA: Even a woman who has been a model to you?

RUBEK: When I have no more use for her –

MAIA: One who has stood to you undressed?

RUBEK: That means nothing – nothing for us artists. (*With a change of tone.*) And then – may I venture to ask – how was I to guess that she was in this country?

MAIA: Oh, you might have seen her name in a Visitor's List – in one of the newspapers.

RUBEK: But I had no idea of the name she now goes by. I had never heard of any Herr von Satow.

MAIA: (*Affecting weariness.*) Oh well then, I suppose it must have been for some other reason that you were so set upon this journey.

RUBEK: (*Seriously.*) Yes, Maia – it was for another reason. A quite different reason. And that is what we must sooner or later have a clear explanation about.

MAIA: (*In a fit of suppressed laughter.*) Heavens, how solemn you look!

RUBEK: (*Suspiciously scrutinising her.*) Yes, perhaps a little more solemn than necessary.

MAIA: How so – ?

RUBEK: And that is a very good thing for us both.

MAIA: You begin to make me feel curious, Rubek.

RUBEK: Only curious? Not a little bit uneasy.

MAIA: (*Shaking her head.*) Not in the least.

RUBEK: Good. Then listen. – You said that day down at the Baths that it seemed to you I had become very nervous of late –

MAIA: Yes, and you really have.

RUBEK: And what do you think can be the reason of that?

MAIA: How can I tell – ? (*Quickly.*) Perhaps you have grown weary of this constant companionship with me.

RUBEK: Constant – ? Why not say 'everlasting'?

MAIA: Daily companionship, then. Here have we two solitary people lived down there for four or five mortal years, and scarcely have an hour away from each other. – We two all by ourselves.

RUBEK: (*With interest.*) Well? And then – ?

MAIA: (*A little oppressed.*) You are not a particularly sociable man, Rubek. You like to keep to yourself and think your own thoughts. And of course I can't talk properly to you about your affairs. I know nothing about art and that sort of thing – (*With an impatient gesture.*) And care very little either, for that matter!

RUBEK: Well, well; and that's why we generally sit by the fireside, and chat about your affairs.

MAIA: Oh, good gracious – I have no affairs to chat about.

RUBEK: Well, they are trifles, perhaps; but at any rate the time passes for us in that way as well as another, Maia.

MAIA: Yes, you are right. Time passes. It is passing away from you, Rubek. – And I suppose it is really that that makes you so uneasy –

RUBEK: (*Nods vehemently.*) And so restless! (*Writhing in his seat.*) No, I shall soon not be able to endure this pitiful life any longer.

MAIA: (*Rises and stands for a moment looking at him.*) If you want to get rid of me, you have only to say so.

RUBEK: Why will you use such phrases? Get rid of you?

MAIA: Yes, if you want to have done with me, please say so right out. And I will go that instant.

RUBEK: (*With an almost imperceptible smile.*) Do you intend that as a threat, Maia?

MAIA: There can be no threat for you in what I said.

RUBEK: (*Rising.*) No, I confess you are right there. (*Adds after a pause.*) You and I cannot possibly go on living together like this –

MAIA: Well? And then – ?

RUBEK: There is no 'then' about it. (*With emphasis on his words.*) Because we two cannot go on living together alone – it does not necessarily follow that we must part.

MAIA: (*Smiles scornfully.*) Only draw away from each other a little, you mean?

RUBEK: (*Shakes his head.*) Even that is not necessary.

MAIA: Well then? Come out with what you want to do with me.

RUBEK: (*With some hesitation.*) What I now feel so keenly – and so painfully – that I require, is to have someone about me who really and truly stands close to me –

MAIA: (*Interrupts him anxiously.*) Don't I do that, Rubek?

RUBEK: (*Waving her aside.*) Not in that sense. What I need is the companionship of another person who can, as it were, complete me – supply what is wanting in me – be one with me in all my striving.

MAIA: (*Slowly.*) It's true that things like that are a great deal too hard for me.

RUBEK: Oh no, they are not at all in your line, Maia.

MAIA: (*With an outburst.*) And heaven knows I don't want them to be, either!

RUBEK: I know that very well. – And it was with no idea of finding any such help in my life-work that I married you.

MAIA: (*Observing him closely.*) I can see in your face that you are thinking of someone else.

RUBEK: Indeed? I have never noticed before that you were a thought-reader. But you can see that, can you?

MAIA: Yes, I can. Oh, I know you so well, so well, Rubek.

RUBEK: Then perhaps you can also see who it is I am thinking of?

MAIA: Yes, indeed I can.

RUBEK: Well? Have the goodness to – ?

MAIA: You are thinking of that – that model you once used for – (*Suddenly letting slip the train of thought.*) Do you know, the people down at the hotel think she's mad.

RUBEK: Indeed? And pray what do the people down at the hotel think of you and the bear-killer?

MAIA: That has nothing to do with the matter. (*Continuing the former train of thought.*) But it was this pale lady you were thinking of.

RUBEK: (*Calmly.*) Precisely, of her. – When I had no more use for her – and when, besides, she went away from me – vanished without a word –

MAIA: Then you accepted me as a sort of makeshift, I suppose?

RUBEK: (*More unfeelingly.*) Something of the sort, to tell the truth, little Maia. For a year or a year and a half I had lived there lonely and brooding, and had put the last touch – the very last touch, to my work. 'The Resurrection Day' went out over the world and brought me fame – and everything else that heart could desire. (*With greater warmth.*) But I no longer loved my own work. Men's laurels and incense nauseated me, till I could have rushed away in despair and hidden myself in the depths of the woods. (*Looking at her.*) You, who are a thought-reader – can you guess what then occurred to me?

MAIA: (*Lightly.*) Yes, it occurred to you to make portrait-busts of gentlemen and ladies.

RUBEK: (*Nods.*) To order, yes. With animals' faces behind the masks. Those I threw in gratis – into the bargain, you understand. (*Smiling.*) But that was not precisely what I had in my mind.

MAIA: What, then?

RUBEK: (*Again serious.*) It was this, that all the talk about the artist's vocation and the artist's mission, and so forth, began to strike me as being very empty, and hollow, and meaningless at bottom.

MAIA: Then what would you put in its place?

RUBEK: Life, Maia.

MAIA: Life?

RUBEK: Yes, is not life in sunshine and in beauty a hundred times better worth while than to hang about to the end of your days in a raw, damp hole, and wear yourself out in a perpetual struggle with lumps of clay and blocks of stone?

MAIA: (*With a little sigh.*) Yes, I have always thought so, certainly.

RUBEK: And then I had become rich enough to live in luxury and in indolent, quivering sunshine. I was able to build myself the villa on the Lake of Taunitz, and the palazzo in the capital, – and all the rest of it.

MAIA: (*Taking up his tone.*) And last but not least, you could afford to treat yourself to me, too. And you gave me leave to share in all your treasures.

RUBEK: (*Jesting, so as to turn the conversation.*) Did I not promise to take you up to a high enough mountain and show you all the glory of the world?

MAIA: (*With a gentle expression.*) You have perhaps taken me up with you to a high enough mountain, Rubek – but you have not shown me all the glory of the world.

RUBEK: (*With a laugh of irritation.*) How insatiable you are, Maia.! Absolutely insatiable! (*With a vehement outburst.*) But do you know what is the most hopeless thing of all, Maia? Can you guess that?

MAIA: (*With quiet defiance.*) Yes, I suppose it is that you have gone and tied yourself to me – for life.

RUBEK: I would not have expressed myself so heartlessly.

MAIA: But you would have meant it just as heartlessly.

RUBEK: You have no clear idea of the inner workings of an artist's nature.

MAIA: (*Smiling and shaking her head.*) Good heavens, I haven't even a clear idea of the inner workings of my own nature.

RUBEK: (*Continuing undisturbed.*) I live at such high speed, Maia. We live so, we artists. I, for my part, have lived through a whole lifetime in the few years we two have known each other. I have come to realise that I am not at all adapted for seeking happiness in indolent enjoyment. Life does not shape itself that way for me and those like me. I must go on working – producing one work after another – right up to my dying day. (*Forcing himself to continue.*) That is why I cannot get on with you any longer, Maia – not with you alone.

MAIA: (*Quietly.*) Does that mean, in plain language, that you have grown tired of me?

RUBEK: (*Bursts forth.*) Yes, that is what it means! I have grown tired – intolerably tired and fretted and unstrung – in this life with you! Now you know it. (*Controlling himself.*) These are hard, ugly words I am using. I know that very well. And you are not at all to blame in this matter; – that I willingly admit. It is simply and solely I myself, who have once more undergone a revolution – (*Half to himself.*) – and awakening to my real life.

MAIA: (*Involuntarily folding her hands.*) Why in all the world should we not part then?

RUBEK: (*Looks at her in astonishment.*) Should you be willing to?

MAIA: (*Shrugging her shoulders.*) Oh yes – if there's nothing else for it, then –

RUBEK: (*Eagerly.*) But there is something else for it. There is an alternative –

MAIA: (*Holding up her forefinger.*) Now you are thinking of the pale lady again!

RUBEK: Yes, to tell the truth, I cannot help constantly thinking of her. Ever since I met her again. (*A step nearer her.*) For now I will tell you a secret, Maia.

MAIA: Well?

RUBEK: (*Touching his own breast.*) In here, you see – in here I have a little bramah-locked casket. And in that casket all my sculptor's visions are stored up. But when she disappeared and left no trace, the lock of the casket snapped to. And she had the key – and she took it away with her. – You, little Maia, you had no key; so all that the casket contains must lie unused. And the years pass! And I have no means of getting at the treasure.

MAIA: (*Trying to repress a subtle smile.*) Then get her to open the casket for you again –

RUBEK: (*Not understanding.*) Maia – ?

MAIA: – for here she is, you see. And no doubt it's on account of this casket that she has come.

RUBEK: I have not said a single word to her on this subject!

MAIA: (*Looks innocently at him.*) My dear Rubek – is it worth while to make all this fuss and commotion about so simple a matter?

RUBEK: Do YOU think this matter is so absolutely simple?

MAIA: Yes, certainly I think so. Do you attach yourself to whoever you most require. (*Nods to him.*) I shall always manage to find a place for myself.

RUBEK: Where do you mean?

MAIA: (*Unconcerned, evasively.*) Well – I need only take myself off to the villa, if it should be necessary. But it won't be; for in town – in all that great house of ours – there must surely, with a little good will, be room enough for three.

RUBEK: (*Uncertainly.*) And do you think that would work in the long run?

MAIA: (*In a light tone.*) Very well, then – if it won't work, it won't. It is no good talking about it.

RUBEK: And what shall we do then, Maia – if it does not work?

MAIA: (*Untroubled.*) Then we two will simply get out of each other's way – part entirely. I shall always find something new for myself, somewhere in the world. Something free! Free! Free! – No need to be anxious about that, Professor Rubek! (*Suddenly points off to the right.*) Look there! There we have her.

RUBEK: (*Turning.*) Where?

MAIA: Out on the plain. Striding – like a marble statue. She is coming this way.

RUBEK: (*Stands gazing with his hand over his eyes.*) Does not she look like the Resurrection incarnate? (*To himself.*) And her I could displace – and move into the shade! Remodel her –. Fool that I was!

MAIA: What do you mean by that?

RUBEK: (*Putting the question aside.*) Nothing. Nothing that you would understand.

IRENE advances from the right over the upland. The children at their play have already caught sight of her and run to meet her. She is now surrounded by them; some appear confident and at ease, others uneasy and timid. She talks low to them and indicates that they are to go down to the hotel; she herself will rest a little beside the brook. The children run down over the slope to the left, half way to the back. IRENE goes up to the wall of rock, and lets the rillets of the cascade flow over her hands, cooling them.

MAIA: (*In a low voice.*) Go down and speak to her alone, Rubek.

RUBEK: And where will you go in the meantime?

MAIA: (*Looking significantly at him.*) Henceforth I shall go my own ways.

She descends from the hillock and leaps over the brook, by aid of her alpenstock. She stops beside IRENE.

MAIA: Professor Rubek is up there, waiting for you, madam.

IRENE: What does he want?

MAIA: He wants you to help him to open a casket that has snapped to.

IRENE: Can I help him in that?

MAIA: He says you are the only person that can.

IRENE: Then I must try.

MAIA: Yes, you really must, madam.

She goes down by the path to the hotel. In a little while PROFESSOR RUBEK comes down to IRENE, but stops with the brook between them.

IRENE: (*After a short pause.*) She – the other one – said that you had been waiting for me.

RUBEK: I have waited for you year after year – without myself knowing it.

IRENE: I could not come to you, Arnold. I was lying down there, sleeping the long, deep, dreamful sleep.

RUBEK: But now you have awakened, Irene!

IRENE: (*Shakes her head.*) I have the heavy, deep sleep still in my eyes.

RUBEK: You shall see that day will dawn and lighten for us both.

IRENE: Do not believe that.

RUBEK: (*Urgently.*) I do believe it! And I know it! Now that I have found you again –

IRENE: Risen from the grave.

RUBEK: Transfigured!

IRENE: Only risen, Arnold. Not transfigured.

He crosses over to her by means of stepping-stones below the cascade.

RUBEK: Where have you been all day, Irene?

IRENE: (*Pointing.*) Far, far over there, on the great dead waste –

RUBEK: (*Turning the conversation.*) You have not your – your friend with you today, I see.

IRENE: (*Smiling.*) My friend is keeping a close watch on me, none the less.

RUBEK: Can she?

IRENE: (*Glancing furtively around.*) You may be sure she can – wherever I may go. She never loses sight of me – (*Whispering.*) Until, one fine sunny morning, I shall kill her.

RUBEK: Would you do that?

IRENE: With the utmost delight – if only I could manage it.

RUBEK: Why do you want to?

IRENE: Because she deals in witchcraft. (*Mysteriously.*) Only think, Arnold – she has changed herself into my shadow.

RUBEK: (*Trying to calm her.*) Well, well, well – a shadow we must all have.

IRENE: I am my own shadow. (*With an outburst.*) Do you not understand that!

RUBEK: (*Sadly.*) Yes, yes, Irene, I understand.

He seats himself on a stone beside the brook. She stands behind him, leaning against the wall of rock.

IRENE: (*After a pause.*) Why do you sit there turning your eyes away from me?

RUBEK: (*Softly, shaking his head.*) I dare not – I dare not look at you.

IRENE: Why dare you not look at me any more?

RUBEK: You have a shadow that tortures me. And I have the crushing weight of my conscience.

IRENE: (*With a glad cry of deliverance.*) At last!

RUBEK: (*Springs up.*) Irene – what is it!

IRENE: (*Motioning him off.*) Keep still, still, still! (*Draws a deep breath and says, as though relieved of a burden.*) There! Now they let me go. For this time. – Now we can sit down and talk as we used to – when I was alive.

RUBEK: Oh, if only we could talk as we used to.

IRENE: Sit there where you were sitting. I will sit here beside you.

He sits down again. She seats herself on another stone, close to him.

IRENE: (*After a short interval of silence.*) Now I have come back to you from the uttermost regions, Arnold.

RUBEK: Aye, truly, from an endless journey.

IRENE: Come home to my lord and master –

RUBEK: To our home; – to our own home, Irene.

IRENE: Have you looked for my coming every single day?

RUBEK: How dared I look for you?

IRENE: (*With a sidelong glance.*) No, I suppose you dared not. For you understood nothing.

RUBEK: Was it really not for the sake of someone else that you all of a sudden disappeared from me in that way?

IRENE: Might it not quite well be for your sake, Arnold?

RUBEK: (*Looks doubtfully at her.*) I don't understand you – ?

IRENE: When I had served you with my soul and with my body – when the statue stood there finished – our child as you called it – then I laid at your feet the most precious sacrifice of all – by effacing myself for all time.

RUBEK: (*Bows his head.*) And laying my life waste.

IRENE: (*Suddenly firing up.*) It was just that I wanted! Never, never should you create anything again – after you had created that only child of ours.

RUBEK: Was it jealousy that moved you, then?

IRENE: (*Coldly.*) I think it was rather hatred.

RUBEK: Hatred? Hatred for me?

IRENE: (*Again vehemently.*) Yes, for you – for the artist who had so lightly and carelessly taken a warm-blooded body, a young human life, and worn the soul out of it – because you needed it for a work of art.

RUBEK: And you can say that – you who threw yourself into my work with such saint-like passion and such ardent joy? – that work for which we two met together every morning, as for an act of worship.

IRENE: (*Coldly, as before.*) I will tell you one thing, Arnold.

RUBEK: Well?

IRENE: I never loved your art, before I met you. – Nor after either.

RUBEK: But the artist, Irene?

IRENE: The artist I hate.

RUBEK: The artist in me too?

IRENE: In you most of all. When I unclothed myself and stood for you, then I hated you, Arnold –

RUBEK: (*Warmly.*) That you did not, Irene! That is not true!

IRENE: I hated you, because you could stand there so unmoved –

RUBEK: (*Laughs.*) Unmoved? Do you think so?

IRENE: – at any rate so intolerably self-controlled. And because you were an artist and an artist only – not a man! (*Changing to a tone full of warmth and feeling.*) But that statue in the wet, living clay, that I loved – as it rose up, a vital human creature, out of those raw, shapeless masses – for that was our creation, our child. Mine and yours.

RUBEK: (*Sadly.*) It was so in spirit and in truth.

IRENE: Let me tell you, Arnold – it is for the sake of this child of ours that I have undertaken this long pilgrimage.

RUBEK: (*Suddenly alert.*) For the statue's – ?

IRENE: Call it what you will. I call it our child.

RUBEK: And now you want to see it? Finished? In marble, which you always thought so cold? (*Eagerly.*) You do not know, perhaps, that it is installed in a great museum somewhere – far out in the world?

IRENE: I have heard a sort of legend about it.

RUBEK: And museums were always a horror to you. You called them grave-vaults –

IRENE: I will make a pilgrimage to the place where my soul and my child's soul lie buried.

RUBEK: (*Uneasy and alarmed.*) You must never see that statue again! Do you hear, Irene! I implore you –! Never, never see it again!

IRENE: Perhaps you think it would mean death to me a second time?

RUBEK: (*Clenching his hands together.*) Oh, I don't know what I think. – But how could I ever imagine that you would fix your mind so immovably on that statue? You, who went away from me – before it was completed.

IRENE: It was completed. That was why I could go away from you – and leave you alone.

RUBEK: (*Sits with his elbows upon his knees, rocking his head from side to side, with his hands before his eyes.*) It was not what it afterwards became.

IRENE: (*Quietly but quick as lightning, half-unsheathes a narrow-bladed sharp knife which she carried in her breast, and asks in a hoarse whisper.*) Arnold – have you done any evil to our child?

RUBEK: (*Evasively.*) Any evil? – How can I be sure what you would call it?

IRENE: (*Breathless.*) Tell me at once: what have you done to the child?

RUBEK: I will tell you, if you will sit and listen quietly to what I say.

IRENE: (*Hides the knife.*) I will listen as quietly as a mother can when she –

RUBEK: (*Interrupting.*) And you must not look at me while I am telling you.

IRENE: (*Moves to a stone behind his back.*) I will sit here, behind you. – Now tell me.

RUBEK: (*Takes his hands from before his eyes and gazes straight in front of him.*) When I had found you, I knew at once how I should make use of you for my life-work.

IRENE: 'The Resurrection Day' you called your life-work. – I call it 'our child'.

RUBEK: I was young then – with no knowledge of life. The Resurrection, I thought, would be most beautifully and exquisitely figured as a young unsullied woman – with none of our earth-life's experiences – awakening to light and glory without having to put away from her anything ugly and impure.

IRENE: (*Quickly.*) Yes – and so I stand there now, in our work?

RUBEK: (*Hesitating.*) Not absolutely and entirely so, Irene.

IRENE: (*In rising excitement.*) Not absolutely –? Do I not stand as I always stood for you?

RUBEK: (*Without answering.*) I learned worldly wisdom in the years that followed, Irene. 'The Resurrection Day' became in my mind's eye something more and something – something more complex. The little round plinth on which your figure stood erect and solitary – it no longer afforded room for all the imagery I now wanted to add –

IRENE: (*Gropes for her knife, but desists.*) What imagery did you add then? Tell me!

RUBEK: I imagined that which I saw with my eyes around me in the world. I had to include it – I could not help it, Irene. I expanded the plinth – made it wide and spacious. And on it I placed a segment of the curving, bursting earth. And up from the fissures of the soil there now swarm men and women with dimly suggested animal-faces. Women and men – as I knew them in real life.

IRENE: (*In breathless suspense.*) But in the middle of the rout there stands the young woman radiant with the joy of light? – Do I not stand so, Arnold?

RUBEK: (*Evasively.*) Not quite in the middle. I had unfortunately to move that figure a little back. For the sake of the general effect, you understand. Otherwise it would have dominated the whole too much.

IRENE: But the joy in the light still transfigures my face?

RUBEK: Yes, it does, Irene – in a way. A little subdued perhaps – as my altered idea required.

IRENE: (*Rising noiselessly.*) That design expresses the life you now see, Arnold.

RUBEK: Yes, I suppose it does.

IRENE: And in that design you have shifted me back, a little toned down – to serve as a background-figure – in a group.

She draws the knife.

RUBEK: Not a background-figure. Let us say, at most, a figure not quite in the foreground – or something of that sort.

IRENE: (*Whispers hoarsely.*) There you uttered your own doom.

On the point of striking.

RUBEK: (*Turns and looks up at her.*) Doom?

IRENE: (*Hastily hides the knife, and says as though choked with agony.*) My whole soul – you and I – we, we, we and our child were in that solitary figure.

RUBEK: (*Eagerly, taking off his hat and drying the drops of sweat upon his brow.*) Yes, but let me tell you, too, how I have placed myself in the group. In front, beside a fountain – as it were here – sits a man weighed down with guilt, who cannot quite free himself from the earth-crust. I call him remorse for a forfeited life. He sits there and dips his fingers in the purling stream – to wash them clean – and he is gnawed and tortured by the thought that never, never will he succeed. Never in all eternity will he attain to freedom and the new life. He will remain for ever prisoned in his hell.

IRENE: (*Hardly and coldly.*) Poet!

RUBEK: Why poet?

IRENE: Because you are nerveless and sluggish and full of forgiveness for all the sins of your life, in thought and in act. You have killed my soul – so you model yourself in remorse, and self-accusation, and penance – (*Smiling.*) – and with that you think your account is cleared.

RUBEK: (*Defiantly.*) I am an artist, Irene. And I take no shame to myself for the frailties that perhaps cling to me. For I was born to be an artist, you see. And, do what I may, I shall never be anything else.

IRENE: (*Looks at him with a lurking evil smile, and says gently and softly.*) You are a poet, Arnold. (*Softly strokes his hair.*) You dear, great, middle-aged child, – is it possible that you cannot see that!

RUBEK: (*Annoyed.*) Why do you keep on calling me a poet?

IRENE: (*With malign eyes.*) Because there is something apologetic in the word, my friend. Something that suggests forgiveness of sins – and spreads a cloak over all frailty. (*With a sudden change of tone.*) But I was a human being – then! And I, too, had a life to live, – and a human destiny to fulfil. And all that, look you, I let slip – gave it all up in order to make myself your bondwoman. – Oh, it was self-murder – a deadly sin against myself! (*Half whispering.*) And that sin I can never expiate!

She seats herself near him beside the brook, keeps close, though unnoticed, watch upon him, and, as though in absence of mind, plucks some flowers from the shrubs around them.

IRENE: (*With apparent self-control.*) I should have borne children in the world – many children – real children – not such children as are hidden away in grave-vaults. That was my vocation. I ought never to have served you – poet.

RUBEK: (*Lost in recollection.*) Yet those were beautiful days, Irene. Marvellously beautiful days – as I now look back upon them –

IRENE: (*Looking at him with a soft expression.*) Can you remember a little word that you said – when you had finished – finished with me and with our child? (*Nods to him.*) Can you remember that little word, Arnold?

RUBEK: (*Looks inquiringly at her.*) Did I say a little word then, which you still remember?

IRENE: Yes, you did. Can you not recall it?

RUBEK: (*Shaking his head.*) No, I can't say that I do. Not at the present moment, at any rate.

IRENE: You took both my hands and pressed them warmly. And I stood there in breathless expectation. And then you said: 'So now, Irene, I thank you from my heart. This,' you said, 'has been a priceless episode for me.'

RUBEK: (*Looks doubtfully at her.*) Did I say 'episode'? It is not a word I am in the habit of using.

IRENE: You said 'episode'.

RUBEK: (*With assumed cheerfulness.*) Well, well – after all, it was in reality an episode.

IRENE: (*Curtly.*) At that word I left you.

RUBEK: You take everything so painfully to heart, Irene.

IRENE: (*Drawing her hand over her forehead.*) Perhaps you are right. Let us shake off all the hard things that go to the heart. (*Plucks off the leaves of a mountain rose and strews them on the brook.*) Look there, Arnold. There are our birds swimming.

RUBEK: What birds are they?

IRENE: Can you not see? Of course they are flamingoes. Are they not rose-red?

RUBEK: Flamingoes do not swim. They only wade.

IRENE: Then they are not flamingoes. They are sea-gulls.

RUBEK: They may be sea-gulls with red bills, yes. (*Plucks broad green leaves and throws them into the brook.*) Now I send out my ships after them.

IRENE: But there must be no harpoon-men on board.

RUBEK: No, there shall be no harpoon-men. (*Smiles to her.*) Can you remember the summer when we used to sit like this outside the little peasant hut on the Lake of Taunitz?

IRENE: (*Nods.*) On Saturday evenings, yes, – when we had finished our week's work –

RUBEK: – And taken the train out to the lake – to stay there over Sunday –

IRENE: (*With an evil gleam of hatred in her eyes.*) It was an episode, Arnold.

RUBEK: (*As if not hearing.*) Then, too, you used to set birds swimming in the brook. They were water-lilies which you –

IRENE: They were white swans.

RUBEK: I meant swans, yes. And I remember that I fastened a great furry leaf to one of the swans. It looked like a burdock-leaf –

IRENE: And then it turned into Lohengrin's boat – with the swan yoked to it.

RUBEK: How fond you were of that game, Irene.

IRENE: We played it over and over again.

RUBEK: Every single Saturday, I believe, – all the summer through.

IRENE: You said I was the swan that drew your boat.

RUBEK: Did I say so? Yes, I daresay I did. (*Absorbed in the game.*) Just see how the sea-gulls are swimming down the stream!

IRENE: (*Laughing.*) And all your ships have run ashore.

RUBEK: (*Throwing more leaves into the brook.*) I have ships enough in reserve. (*Follows the leaves with his eyes, throws more into the brook, and says after a pause.*) Irene, – I have bought the little peasant hut beside the Lake of Taunitz.

IRENE: Have you bought it? You often said you would, if you could afford it.

RUBEK: The day came when I could afford it easily enough; and so I bought it.

IRENE: (*With a sidelong look at him.*) Then do you live out there now – in our old house?

RUBEK: No, I have had it pulled down long ago. And I have built myself a great, handsome, comfortable villa on the site – with a park around it. It is there that we – (*Stops and corrects himself.*) – there that I usually live during the summer.

IRENE: (*Mastering herself.*) So you and – and the other one live out there now?

RUBEK: (*With a touch of defiance.*) Yes. When my wife and I are not travelling – as we are this year.

IRENE: (*Looking far before her.*) Life was beautiful, beautiful by the Lake of Taunitz.

RUBEK: (*As though looking back into himself.*) And yet, Irene –

IRENE: (*Completing his thought.*) – yet we two let slip all that life and its beauty.

RUBEK: (*Softly, urgently.*) Does repentance come too late, now?

IRENE: (*Does not answer, but sits silent for a moment; then she points over the upland.*) Look there, Arnold, – now the sun is going down behind the peaks. See what a red glow the level rays cast over all the heathery knolls out yonder.

RUBEK: (*Looks where she is pointing.*) It is long since I have seen a sunset in the mountains.

IRENE: Or a sunrise?

RUBEK: A sunrise I don't think I have ever seen.

IRENE: (*Smiles as though lost in recollection.*) I once saw a marvellously lovely sunrise.

RUBEK: Did you? Where was that?

IRENE: High, high up on a dizzy mountain-top. – You beguiled me up there by promising that I should see all the glory of the world if only I –

She stops suddenly.

RUBEK: If only you – ? Well?

IRENE: I did as you told me – went with you up to the heights. And there I fell upon my knees and worshipped you, and served you. (*Is silent for a moment; then says softly.*) Then I saw the sunrise. (*Turning at him with a scornful smile.*) With you – and the other woman?

RUBEK: (*Urgently.*) With me – as in our days of creation. You could open all that is locked up in me. Can you not find it in your heart, Irene?

IRENE: (*Shaking her head.*) I have no longer the key to you, Arnold.

RUBEK: You have the key! You and you alone possess it! (*Beseechingly.*) Help me – that I may be able to live my life over again!

IRENE: (*Immovable as before.*) Empty dreams! Idle – dead dreams. For the life you and I led there is no resurrection.

RUBEK: (*Curtly, breaking off.*) Then let us go on playing.

IRENE: Yes, playing, playing – only playing!

They sit and strew leaves and petals over the brook, where they float and sail away.

Up the slope to the left at the back come ULFHEIM *and* MAIA *in hunting costume. After them comes the servant with the leash of dogs, with which he goes out to the right.*

RUBEK: (*Catching sight of them.*) Ah! There is little Maia, going out with the bear-hunter.

IRENE: Your lady, yes.

RUBEK: Or the other's.

MAIA: (*Looks around as she is crossing the upland, sees the two sitting by the brook, and calls out.*) Goodnight, Professor! Dream of me. Now I am going off on my adventures!

RUBEK: (*Calls back to her.*) What sort of an adventure is this to be?

MAIA: (*Approaching.*) I am going to let life take the place of all the rest.

RUBEK: (*Mockingly.*) Aha! So you too are going to do that, little Maia?

MAIA: Yes. And I've made a verse about it, and this is how it goes: (*Sings triumphantly.*) I am free! I am free! I am free! No more life in the prison for me! I am free as a bird! I am free! For I believe I have awakened now – at last.

RUBEK: It almost seems so.

MAIA: (*Drawing a deep breath.*) Oh – how divinely light one feels on waking.

RUBEK: Goodnight, Frau Maia – and good luck to –

ULFHEIM: (*Calls out, interposing.*) Hush, hush! – for the devil's sake let's have none of your wizard wishes. Don't you see that we are going out to shoot –

RUBEK: What will you bring me home from the hunting, Maia?

MAIA: You shall have a bird of prey to model. I shall wing one for you.

RUBEK: (*Laughs mockingly and bitterly.*) Yes, to wing things – without knowing what you are doing – that has long been quite in your way.

MAIA: (*Tossing her head.*) Oh, just let me take care of myself for the future, and I wish you then –! (*Nods and laughs roguishly.*) Goodbye – and a good, peaceful summer night on the upland!

RUBEK: (*Jestingly.*) Thanks! And all the ill-luck in the world over you and your hunting!

ULFHEIM: (*Roaring with laughter.*) There now, that is a wish worth having!

MAIA: (*Laughing.*) Thanks, thanks, thanks, Professor!

They have both crossed the visible portion of the upland, and go out through the bushes to the right.

RUBEK: (*After a short pause.*) A summer night on the upland! Yes, that would have been life!

IRENE: (*Suddenly, with a wild expression in her eyes.*) Will you spend a summer night on the upland – with me?

RUBEK: (*Stretching his arms wide.*) Yes, yes, – come!

IRENE: My adored lord and master!

RUBEK: Oh Irene!

IRENE: (*Hoarsely, smiling and groping in her breast.*) It will be only an episode – (*Quickly, whispering.*) Hush! – do not look round, Arnold!

RUBEK: (*Also in a low voice.*) What is it?

IRENE: A face that is staring at me.

RUBEK: (*Turns involuntarily.*) Where! (*With a start.*) Ah –!

The SISTER OF MERCY's *head is partly visible among the bushes beside the descent to the left. Her eyes are immovably fixed on* IRENE.

IRENE: (*Rises and says softly.*) We must part then. No, you must remain sitting. Do you hear? You must not go with me. (*Bends over him and whispers.*) Till we meet again – tonight – on the upland.

RUBEK: And you will come, Irene?

IRENE: Yes, surely I will come. Wait for me here.

RUBEK: (*Repeats dreamily.*) Summer night on the upland. With you. With you. (*His eyes meet hers.*) Oh, Irene – that might have been our life. – And that we have forfeited – we two.

IRENE: We see the irretrievable only when –

Breaks off.

RUBEK: (*Looks inquiringly at her.*) When – ?

IRENE: When we dead awaken.

RUBEK: (*Shakes his head mournfully.*) What do we really see then?

IRENE: We see that we have never lived. (*She goes towards the slope and descends.*)

The SISTER OF MERCY *makes way for her and follows her.* PROFESSOR RUBEK *remains sitting motionless beside the brook.*

MAIA: (*Is heard singing triumphantly among the hills.*) I am free! I am free! I am free! No more life in the prison for me! I am free as a bird! I am free!

Act 3

A wild riven mountain-side, with sheer precipices at the back. Snow-clad peaks rise to the right, and lose themselves in drifting mists. To the left, on a stone-scree, stands an old, half-ruined hut. It is early morning. Dawn is breaking. The sun has not yet risen.

MAIA comes, flushed and irritated, down over the stone-scree on the left. ULFHEIM follows, half angry, half laughing, holding her fast by the sleeve.

MAIA: (*Trying to tear herself loose.*) Let me go! Let me go, I say!

ULFHEIM: Come, come! Are you going to bite now? You're as snappish as a wolf.

MAIA: (*Striking him over the hand.*) Let me, I tell you? And be quiet!

ULFHEIM: No, confound me if I will!

MAIA: Then I will not go another step with you. Do you hear? – not a single step!

ULFHEIM: Ho, ho! How can you get away from me, here, on the wild mountain-side?

MAIA: I will jump over the precipice yonder, if need be –

ULFHEIM: And mangle and mash yourself up into dogs'-meat! A juicy morsel! (*Lets go his hold.*) As you please. Jump over the precipice if you want to. It's a dizzy drop. There's only one narrow footpath down it, and that's almost impassable.

MAIA: (*Dusts her skirt with her hand, and looks at him with angry eyes.*) Well, you are a nice one to go hunting with!

ULFHEIM: Say rather, sporting.

MAIA: Oh! So you call this sport, do you?

ULFHEIM: Yes, I venture to take that liberty. It is the sort of sport I like best of all.

MAIA: (*Tossing her head.*) Well – I must say! (*After a pause; looks searchingly at him.*) Why did you let the dogs loose up there?

ULFHEIM: (*Blinking his eyes and smiling.*) So that they too might do a little hunting on their own account, don't you see?

MAIA: There's not a word of truth in that! It wasn't for the dogs' sake that you let them go.

ULFHEIM: (*Still smiling.*) Well, why did I let them go then? Let us hear.

MAIA: You let them go because you wanted to get rid of Lars. He was to run after them and bring them in again, you said. And in the meantime –. Oh, it was a pretty way to behave!

ULFHEIM: In the meantime?

MAIA: (*Curtly breaking off.*) No matter!

ULFHEIM: (*In a confidential tone.*) Lars won't find them. You may safely swear to that. He won't come with them before the time's up.

MAIA: (*Looking angrily at him.*) No, I daresay not.

ULFHEIM: (*Catching at her arm.*) For Lars – he knows my – my methods of sport, you see.

MAIA: (*Eludes him, and measures him with a glance.*) Do you know what you look like, Mr Ulfheim?

ULFHEIM: I should think I'm probably most like myself.

MAIA: Yes, there you're exactly right. For you're the living image of a faun.

ULFHEIM: A faun?

MAIA: Yes, precisely; a faun.

ULFHEIM: A faun! Isn't that a sort of monster? Or a kind of a wood demon, as you might call it?

MAIA: Yes, just the sort of creature you are. A thing with a goat's beard and goat-legs. Yes, and the faun has horns too!

ULFHEIM: So, so! – Has he horns too?

MAIA: A pair of ugly horns, just like yours, yes.

ULFHEIM: Can you see the poor little horns *I* have?

MAIA: Yes. I seem to see them quite plainly.

ULFHEIM: (*Taking the dogs' leash out of his pocket.*) Then I had better see about tying you.

MAIA: Have you gone quite mad? Would you tie me?

ULFHEIM: If I am a demon, let me be a demon! So that's the way of it! You can see the horns, can you?

MAIA: (*Soothingly.*) There, there, there! Now try to behave nicely, Mr Ulfheim. (*Breaking off.*) But what has become of that hunting-castle of yours, that you boasted so much of? You said it lay somewhere hereabouts.

ULFHEIM: (*Points with a flourish to the hut.*) There you have it, before your very eyes.

MAIA: (*Looks at him.*) That old pigsty!

ULFHEIM: (*Laughing in his beard.*) It has harboured more than one king's daughter, I can tell you.

MAIA: Was it there that that horrid man you told me about came to the king's daughter in the form of a bear?

ULFHEIM: Yes, my fair companion of the chase – this is the scene. (*With a gesture of invitation.*) If you would deign to enter.

MAIA: Isch! If ever I set foot in it –! Isch!

ULFHEIM: Oh, two people can doze away a summer night in there comfortably enough. Or a whole summer, if it comes to that!

MAIA: Thanks! One would need to have a pretty strong taste for that kind of thing. (*Impatiently.*) But now I am tired both of you and the hunting expedition. Now I am going down to the hotel – before people awaken down there.

ULFHEIM: How do you propose to get down from here?

MAIA: That's your affair. There must be a way down somewhere or other, I suppose.

ULFHEIM: (*Pointing towards the back.*) Oh, certainly! There is a sort of way – right down the face of the precipice yonder –

MAIA: There, you see. With a little goodwill –

ULFHEIM: – but just you try if you dare go that way.

MAIA: (*Doubtfully.*) Do you think I can't?

ULFHEIM: Never in this world – if you don't let me help you.

MAIA: (*Uneasily.*) Why, then come and help me! What else are you here for?

ULFHEIM: Would you rather I should take you on my back –?

MAIA: Nonsense!

ULFHEIM: – or carry you in my arms?

MAIA: Now do stop talking that rubbish!

ULFHEIM: (*With suppressed exasperation.*) I once took a young girl – lifted her up from the mire of the streets and carried her in my arms. Next my heart I carried her. So I would have borne her all through life – lest haply she should dash her foot against a stone. For her shoes were worn very thin when I found her –

MAIA: And yet you took her up and carried her next your heart?

ULFHEIM: Took her up out of the gutter and carried her as high and as carefully as I could. (*With a growling laugh.*) And do you know what I got for my reward?

MAIA: No. What did you get?

ULFHEIM: (*Looks at her, smiles and nods.*) I got the horns! The horns that you can see so plainly. Is not that a comical story, madam bear-murderess?

MAIA: Oh yes, comical enough! But I know another story that is still more comical.

ULFHEIM: How does that story go?

MAIA: This is how it goes. There was once a stupid girl, who had both a father and a mother – but a rather poverty-stricken home. Then there came a high and mighty seigneur into the midst of all this poverty. And he took the girl in his arms – as you did – and travelled far, far away with her –

ULFHEIM: Was she so anxious to be with him?

MAIA: Yes, for she was stupid, you see.

ULFHEIM: And he, no doubt, was a brilliant and beautiful personage?

MAIA: Oh, no, he wasn't so superlatively beautiful either. But he pretended that he would take her with him to the top of the highest of mountains, where there were light and sunshine without end.

ULFHEIM: So he was a mountaineer, was he, that man?

MAIA: Yes, he was – in his way.

ULFHEIM: And then he took the girl up with him – ?

MAIA: (*With a toss of the head.*) Took her up with him finely, you may be sure! Oh no! he beguiled her into a cold, clammy cage, where – as it seemed to her – there was neither sunlight nor fresh air, but only gilding and great petrified ghosts of people all around the walls.

ULFHEIM: Devil take me, but it served her right!

MAIA: Yes, but don't you think it's quite a comical story, all the same?

ULFHEIM: (*Looks at her moment.*) Now listen to me, my good companion of the chase –

MAIA: Well, what is it now?

ULFHEIM: Should not we two tack our poor shreds of life together?

MAIA: Is his worship inclined to set up as a patching-tailor?

ULFHEIM: Yes, indeed he is. Might not we two try to draw the rags together here and there – so as to make some sort of a human life out of them?

MAIA: And when the poor tatters were quite worn out – what then?

ULFHEIM: (*With a large gesture.*) Then there we shall stand, free and serene – as the man and woman we really are!

MAIA: (*Laughing.*) You with your goat-legs yes!

ULFHEIM: And you with your –. Well, let that pass.

MAIA: Yes, come – let us pass – on.

ULFHEIM: Stop! Whither away, comrade?

MAIA: Down to the hotel, of course.

ULFHEIM: And afterward?

MAIA: Then we'll take a polite leave of each other, with thanks for pleasant company.

ULFHEIM: Can we part, we two? Do you think we can?

MAIA: Yes, you didn't manage to tie me up, you know.

ULFHEIM: I have a castle to offer you –

MAIA: (*Pointing to the hut.*) A fellow to that one?

ULFHEIM: It has not fallen to ruin yet.

MAIA: And all the glory of the world, perhaps?

ULFHEIM: A castle, I tell you –

MAIA: Thanks! I have had enough of castles.

ULFHEIM: – with splendid hunting-grounds stretching for miles around it.

MAIA: Are there works of art too in this castle?

ULFHEIM: (*Slowly.*) Well, no – it's true there are no works of art; but –

MAIA: (*Relieved.*) Ah! that's one good thing, at any rate!

ULFHEIM: Will you go with me, then – as far and as long as I want you?

MAIA: There is a tame bird of prey keeping watch upon me.

ULFHEIM: (*Wildly.*) We'll put a bullet in his wing, Maia!

MAIA: (*Looks at him a moment, and says resolutely.*) Come then, and carry me down into the depths.

ULFHEIM: (*Puts his arm round her waist.*) It is high time! The mist is upon us!

MAIA: Is the way down terribly dangerous?

ULFHEIM: The mountain is more dangerous still.

She shakes him off, goes to the edge of the precipice and looks over, but starts quickly back.

ULFHEIM: (*Goes towards her, laughing.*) What? Does it make you a little giddy?

MAIA: (*Faintly.*) Yes, that too. But go and look over. Those two, coming up –

ULFHEIM: (*Goes and bends over the edge of the precipice.*) It's only your bird of prey – and his strange lady.

MAIA: Can't we get past them – without their seeing us?

ULFHEIM: Impossible! The path is far too narrow. And there's no other way down.

MAIA: (*Nerving herself.*) Well, well – let us face them here, then!

ULFHEIM: Spoken like a true bear-killer, comrade!

PROFESSOR RUBEK and IRENE appear over the edge of the precipice at the back. He has his plaid over his shoulders; she has a fur cloak thrown loosely over her white dress, and a swansdown hood over her head.

RUBEK: (*Still only half visible above the edge.*) What, Maia! So we two meet once again?

MAIA: (*With assumed coolness.*) At your service. Won't you come up?

PROFESSOR RUBEK *climbs right up and holds out his hand to* IRENE, *who also comes right to the top.*

RUBEK: (*Coldly to* MAIA.) So you, too, have been all night on the mountain, – as we have?

MAIA: I have been hunting – yes. You gave me permission, you know.

ULFHEIM: (*Pointing downward.*) Have you come up that path there?

RUBEK: As you saw.

ULFHEIM: And the strange lady too?

RUBEK: Yes, of course. (*With a glance at* MAIA.) Henceforth the strange lady and I do not intend our ways to part.

ULFHEIM: Don't you know, then, that it is a deadly dangerous way you have come?

RUBEK: We thought we would try it, nevertheless. For it did not seem particularly hard at first.

ULFHEIM: No, at first nothing seems hard. But presently you may come to a tight place where you can neither get forward nor back. And then you stick fast, Professor! Mountain-fast, as we hunters call it.

RUBEK: (*Smiles and looks at him.*) Am I to take these as oracular utterances, Mr Ulfheim?

ULFHEIM: Lord preserve me from playing the oracle! (*Urgently, pointing up towards the heights.*) But don't you see that the storm is upon us? Don't you hear the blasts of wind?

RUBEK: (*Listening.*) They sound like the prelude to the Resurrection Day.

ULFHEIM: They are storm-blasts from the peaks, man! Just look how the clouds are rolling and sinking – soon they'll be all around us like a winding-sheet!

IRENE: (*With a start and shiver.*) I know that sheet!

MAIA: (*Drawing* ULFHEIM *away.*) Let us make haste and get down.

ULFHEIM: (*To* PROFESSOR RUBEK.) I cannot help more than one. Take refuge in the hut in the meantime – while the storm lasts. Then I shall send people up to fetch the two of you away.

IRENE: (*In terror.*) To fetch us away! No, no!

ULFHEIM: (*Harshly.*) To take you by force if necessary – for it's a matter of life and death here. Now, you know it. (*To* MAIA.) Come, then – and don't fear to trust yourself in your comrade's hands.

MAIA: (*Clinging to him.*) Oh, how I shall rejoice and sing, if I get down with a whole skin!

ULFHEIM: (*Begins the descent and calls to the others.*) You'll wait, then, in the hut, till the men come with ropes, and fetch you away.

ULFHEIM, *with* MAIA *in his arms, clambers rapidly but warily down the precipice.*

IRENE: (*Looks for some time at* PROFESSOR RUBEK *with terror-stricken eyes.*) Did you hear that, Arnold? – Men are coming up to fetch me away! Many men will come up here –

RUBEK: Do not be alarmed, Irene!

IRENE: (*In growing terror.*) And she, the woman in black – she will come too. For she must have missed me long ago. And then she will seize me, Arnold! And put me in the strait-waistcoat. Oh, she has it with her, in her box. I have seen it with my own eyes –

RUBEK: Not a soul shall be suffered to touch you.

IRENE: (*With a wild smile.*) Oh no – I myself have a resource against that.

RUBEK: What resource do you mean?

IRENE: (*Drawing out the knife.*) This!

RUBEK: (*Tries to seize it.*) Have you a knife?

IRENE: Always, always – both day and night – in bed as well!

RUBEK: Give me that knife, Irene!

IRENE: (*Concealing it.*) You shall not have it. I may very likely find a use for it myself.

RUBEK: What use can you have for it, here?

IRENE: (*Looks fixedly at him.*) It was intended for you, Arnold.

RUBEK: For me!

IRENE: As we were sitting by the Lake of Taunitz last evening –

RUBEK: By the Lake of –

IRENE: – outside the peasant's hut – and playing with swans and water-lilies –

RUBEK: What then – what then?

IRENE: – and when I heard you say with such deathly, icy coldness – that I was nothing but an episode in your life –

RUBEK: It was you that said that, Irene, not I.

IRENE: (*Continuing.*) – then I had my knife out. I wanted to stab you in the back with it.

RUBEK: (*Darkly.*) And why did you hold your hand?

IRENE: Because it flashed upon me with a sudden horror that you were dead already – long ago.

RUBEK: Dead?

IRENE: Dead. Dead, you as well as I. We sat there by the Lake of Taunitz, we two clay-cold bodies – and played with each other.

RUBEK: I do not call that being dead. But you do not understand me.

IRENE: Then where is the burning desire for me that you fought and battled against when I stood freely forth before you as the woman arisen from the dead?

RUBEK: Our love is assuredly not dead, Irene.

IRENE: The love that belongs to the life of earth – the beautiful, miraculous earth-life – the inscrutable earth-life – that is dead in both of us.

RUBEK: (*Passionately.*) And do you know that just that love – it is burning and seething in me as hotly as ever before?

IRENE: And I? Have you forgotten who I now am?

RUBEK: Be who or what you please, for aught I care! For me, you are the woman I see in my dreams of you.

IRENE: I have stood on the turn-table naked – and made a show of myself to many hundreds of men – after you.

RUBEK: It was I that drove you to the turn-table – blind as I then was − I, who placed the dead clay-image above the happiness of life − of love.

IRENE: (*Looking down.*) Too late − too late!

RUBEK: Not by a hairsbreadth has all that has passed in the interval lowered you in my eyes.

IRENE: (*With head erect.*) Nor in my own!

RUBEK: Well, what then! Then we are free − and there is still time for us to live our life, Irene.

IRENE: (*Looks sadly at him.*) The desire for life is dead in me, Arnold. Now I have arisen. And I look for you. And I find you. − And then I see that you and life lie dead − as I have lain.

RUBEK: Oh, how utterly you are astray! Both in us and around us life is fermenting and throbbing as fiercely as ever!

IRENE: (*Smiling and shaking her head.*) The young woman of your Resurrection Day can see all life lying on its bier.

RUBEK: (*Throwing his arms violently around her.*) Then let two of the dead − us two − for once live life to its uttermost − before we go down to our graves again!

IRENE: (*With a shriek.*) Arnold!

RUBEK: But not here in the half darkness! Not here with this hideous dank shroud flapping around us −

IRENE: (*Carried away by passion.*) No, no − up in the light, and in all the glittering glory! Up to the Peak of Promise!

RUBEK: There we will hold our marriage-feast, Irene − oh, my beloved!

IRENE: (*Proudly.*) The sun may freely look on us, Arnold.

RUBEK: All the powers of light may freely look on us − and all the powers of darkness too. (*Seizes her hand.*) Will you then follow me, oh my grace-given bride?

IRENE: (*As though transfigured.*) I follow you, freely and gladly, my lord and master!

RUBEK: (*Drawing her along with him.*) We must first pass through the mists, Irene, and then −

IRENE: Yes, through all the mists, and then right up to the summit of the tower that shines in the sunrise.

The mist-clouds close in over the scene − PROFESSOR RUBEK and IRENE, hand in hand, climb up over the snow-field to the right and soon disappear among the lower clouds. Keen storm-gusts hurtle and whistle through the air. The SISTER OF MERCY appears upon the stone-scree to the left. She stops and looks around silently and searchingly.

MAIA: I am free! I am free! I am free! No more life in the prison for me! I am free as a bird! I am free!

Suddenly a sound like thunder is heard from high up on the snow-field, which glides and whirls downwards with headlong speed. PROFESSOR RUBEK and IRENE can be dimly discerned as they are whirled along with the masses of snow and buried in them.

SISTER OF MERCY: (*Gives a shriek, stretches out her arms towards them and cries.*) Irene!

Stands silent a moment, then makes the sign of the cross before her in the air, and says.

Pax vobiscum!

MAIA's triumphant song sounds from still farther down below.

1.5 **INTERIOR** (1894)

MAURICE MAETERLINCK

Translated by Dan Rebellato

Maurice Maeterlinck (1862–1949) *was a well-known and controversial* fin-de-siècle *Belgian playwright and essayist. His most popular collection,* The Treasure of the Humble *(1896), included the essay* Tragedy in Everyday Life *(see 1.10), which offers a new approach to the writing of Symbolist drama. He shared the Symbolist aversion to the theatre, claiming, 'I always enjoy reading a play far more than I do seeing it acted', finding the fleshly presence of the actor damaging to the delicate ideas embodied in fine poetic language. For this reason he may have conceived* Interior *and some other plays (*The Blind *and* Intruder*) as puppet plays, although when it was first performed at the Théâtre de l'Oeuvre in March 1895* Interior *was performed by actors. In* Interior, *he uses the device of two men watching a family at peace, unaware of the terrible news that they are about to receive, to reflect on our – and, by implication, Naturalism's – tendency to ignore the ubiquity of death and the cruel ironies of fate. In its use of silence, hesitation and rich haunting atmosphere it looks forward to some aspects of 'absurd drama' in the 1950s and 1960s. It is translated from French for the present volume by Dan Rebellato.*

Characters

In the garden
THE OLD MAN
THE STRANGER
MARY
MARTHA
A FARMHAND
THE CROWD

In the house
THE FATHER
THE MOTHER
THE TWO GIRLS
THE CHILD

An old garden planted with willows. A house at the back, with three of its ground-floor windows lit up. We can clearly make out a family spending an evening together by the light of the lamp. THE FATHER *is sitting next to the fire.* THE MOTHER, *one elbow on the table, stares into space. Two young girls, dressed in white, are embroidering, dreaming and smiling in the calm of the room. A child sleeps, its head on the mother's left shoulder. When one of them gets up, walks or makes a movement, their movements appear serious, slow, sparse and as if hypnotized by the distance, the light and the slight veil of the windows.*

THE OLD MAN *and* THE STRANGER *cautiously make their way into the garden.*

OLD MAN: We're in the part of the garden that goes up round the back of the house. They never come here. The doors are on the other side. – They're locked and the shutters are closed. But there are no shutters this side and I saw the light … Yes; they're spending an evening by the light of the lamp. It's good that they didn't hear us; the mother or the young girls might have come out and then what would we have done? …

STRANGER: What are we going to do?

OLD MAN: First, I want to check they're all in the room. Yes, I can see the father sitting by the fire. He's waiting, his hands on his knees … the mother's leaning on the table.

STRANGER: She's looking at us …

OLD MAN: No; she is looking at nothing in particular. Her eyes aren't blinking. She can't see us; we're in the shade of the great trees. But don't get any nearer … the dead girl's two sisters are also in the room. They are working slowly at their embroidery; and the little child's asleep. The clock in the corner says nine … they suspect nothing and they say nothing.

STRANGER: Could we attract the father's attention, signal to him in some way? He's turned his head towards us. Would you like me to tap on one of the windows? One of them will have to find out before the others …

OLD MAN: I don't know what to do … we must be very careful … the father is old and frail … the mother too; and the sisters are too young … they never will love anyone the way they loved her … I've never seen a happier household … No, no, don't go near the window; that's the worst thing we could do … better to say it as simply as possible, like it's something ordinary, and not to seem too sad; otherwise, their grief has to compete with yours and they won't know what to do … let's go round to the other part of the garden. We'll knock on the door and go in like nothing's happened. I'll go in first; they won't be surprised to see me; I sometimes drop in of an evening, to bring them flowers or fruit, spend a couple of hours with them.

STRANGER: Why do I need to go with you? You go on your own; I'll wait till I'm called … they've never seen me … I'm just a passer-by; I'm a stranger …

OLD MAN: Better if I'm not alone. Bad news brought by two people is less blunt, less heavy … I was thinking about this on the way here … if I go in alone, I'll have to speak immediately; they'd know everything in a few words and I'd have nothing more to say; and the silence after bad news is terrifying … that's when the heart breaks. If we go in together, I can, for example, work my way round to telling them: she was found like this … floating on the river, her hands clasped together …

STRANGER: Her hands were not clasped; her arms were limp by her sides …

OLD MAN: You see how you let your tongue run away with itself … and the misfortune gets lost in the details … but if I go in alone, I know them: from the first words it'll all be so dreadful, God knows what will happen … but if we take turns to speak, they'll be listening to us and not to the terrible news … don't forget that the mother will be there and her life is so fragile … it's as well that the first wave founders on a handful of silly words … you have to be a bit roundabout with wretched people like this and make sure they are cushioned. Even the most careless visitors, without knowing it, take some of the sadness away with them … it just disperses soundlessly or effortlessly, like the air or the light …

STRANGER: Your clothes are wet and dripping on the flagstones.

OLD MAN: Just the bottom of my coat, I got it wet in the water. You look cold. You've got mud all down your front … I didn't notice it on the way, it was so dark …

STRANGER: I went into the water up to my waist.

OLD MAN: Did you find her long before I arrived?

STRANGER: Barely minutes before. I was on my way to the village; it was already late and getting dark on the river bank. I was walking, following the river because it was lighter than the path, and I see something strange by a clump of reeds … I get closer and see her hair rising almost in a circle round her head, swirling with the current …

In the room, the two young girls turn their heads towards the window.

OLD MAN: Did you see the two sisters' hair flutter on their shoulders?

STRANGER: They turned their heads this way … turned their heads that's all. Was I talking too loudly? (*The two young girls resume their original position.*) They've turned back now … I went into the water up to my waist and managed to grab her hand and drag her onto the bank easily enough … She was as beautiful as her sisters …

OLD MAN: Maybe more beautiful … I don't know why, I've lost my nerve …

STRANGER: What are you talking about, nerve? We did all anyone could … She'd been dead over an hour.

OLD MAN: She was alive this morning! … I met her coming out of church … She said she was going away, going to see her grandmother on the other side of that river where you found her … She'd didn't know when she'd be back … she seemed to be about to ask me something; but her courage failed her and she hurried off. I saw nothing but now I start to wonder … She smiled like one of those who smile instead of speaking for fear of being misunderstood … It always seemed like her hope was tinged with sorrow … her eyes were dim and she barely looked at me …

STRANGER: Some of the farmhands told me that they saw her wandering on the bank until the evening … They thought she was looking for flowers … it might be that her death …

OLD MAN: Who can say … what can we ever know? …

Maybe she was the type of person who doesn't like to talk but inside is carrying any number of reasons to end their life ... you can't see into the soul like you can into that room. Everyone's like this ... They come out with trivialities; and no one suspects anything's wrong ... you can spend months with someone who is no longer of this world, whose soul can't hold itself down any more; you talk to them without a second thought: and you see what happens ... they look like lifeless dolls but so many things are going on in their souls ... They don't know what they are themselves ... She would have lived like the others do ... She would have said up to her death: 'Sir, Madam, it looks like rain this morning' or even: 'Let's have dinner, we'll be thirteen at table': or even: 'The fruit hasn't ripened yet.' They smile, talking of falling blossom, and they cry in the dark ... Not even an angel could see what has to be seen; and we humans can only understand with hindsight ... Yesterday evening, there she was, by the lamp like her sisters, and if this hadn't happened you wouldn't be looking at them like this, but now we can't help look at them this way ... I feel like I'm looking at them for the first time ... Something new must enter our ordinary lives before we can understand them ... They're by your side, you look at them and look at them, but only really see them at the moment when they go for good ... And meanwhile, the strange little soul that she must have had; the poor, simple, unfathomable little soul that she must have had, dear child, to say what she must have said, to do what she must have done! ...

STRANGER: At this moment, they are smiling silently in their room ...

OLD MAN: They're relaxed ... they're not expecting her this evening ...

STRANGER: They smile without moving ... but now the father is placing a finger to his lips ...

OLD MAN: He's indicating the child asleep at its mother's breast ...

STRANGER: She doesn't dare lift her eyes, for fear of disturbing its sleep ...

OLD MAN: They are not working any more ... there is a heavy silence.

STRANGER: They have let the ball of white wool fall to the floor ...

OLD MAN: They are looking at the child ...

STRANGER: They don't know that they are being looked at ...

OLD MAN: We, too, are being looked at ...

STRANGER: They've raised their eyes ...

OLD MAN: But they can't see anything ...

STRANGER: They seem happy, but, I don't know, there's still something ...

OLD MAN: They think they're safe in there ... they have locked the doors; and the windows have iron bars on them ... they have reinforced the walls of their old

house; they have bolted the three oak doors ... they have foreseen everything they could foresee ...

STRANGER: We're going to have to tell them eventually ... someone might turn up and tell them straight out ... there was a crowd of farmhands in the meadow where the dead girl was found ... if one of them knocks on the door ...

OLD MAN: Martha and Mary are with the little dead girl. The farmhands were going to make a stretcher out of leaves and branches; and I told the oldest to come and warn us immediately, as soon as they set off. Let's wait till she arrives; she'll go in with me ... we shouldn't have seen them like this ... I thought all we had to do was knock on the door, just go in, find the words to say and say them ... But I have spent too long watching them under their lamp.

MARY enters.

MARY: They're coming, grandfather.

OLD MAN: Is that you? – Where are they?

MARY: They are at the foot of the last hills.

OLD MAN: Are they coming in silence?

MARY: I told them to pray quietly. Martha is with them ...

OLD MAN: Are there many of them?

MARY: The whole village is walking alongside the pallbearers. They brought lanterns but I told them to put them out ...

OLD MAN: Which way are they coming?

MARY: They are coming along the footpaths. They are walking slowly ...

OLD MAN: It's time ...

MARY: Have you told them, grandfather?

OLD MAN: You can see perfectly well that we haven't ... they are still waiting by the lamp ... Look, my child, look: you'll see something of life ...

MARY: Oh! How calm they seem! ... it's almost like a dream ...

STRANGER: Be careful, I saw the two sisters give a start ...

OLD MAN: They are getting up ...

STRANGER: I think they're coming towards the windows ...

At this point, one of the two sisters comes up to the first window, the other, to the third; and, pressing their hands on the panes stare for a long time into the darkness.

OLD MAN: No one comes to the window in the middle ...

MARY: They are looking ... listening ...

OLD MAN: The older one smiles but doesn't see ...

MARY: And the second has eyes full of fear ...

OLD MAN: Be careful; we don't know how far beyond the body the soul can reach ...

A long silence. MARY *nestles up to* THE OLD MAN'*s chest and hugs him.*

MARY: Grandfather! ...

OLD MAN: Don't cry, my child ... our turn will come ...

Silence.

STRANGER: They've been looking for a long time ...

OLD MAN: They could look for a hundred thousand years and not see anything, the poor girls ... the night is too dark ... they're looking over here but the bad news is coming from over there ...

STRANGER: Lucky they are looking this way ... I don't know what that is coming from the direction of the meadows.

MARY: I think it's the crowd ... they are so far away you can barely make them out ...

STRANGER: They are following the path as it rises and falls ... see, they appear again on that slope lit by the moon ...

MARY: Oh! Looks like there's a lot of them ... they were already coming in from the outskirts of the town when I arrived ... They are taking the long route ...

OLD MAN: They'll get here nonetheless, yes I can see them too. They're crossing the meadows ... they look so small you can scarcely pick them out from the grasses ... you might think they were children playing in the moonlight; and if the girls see them they wouldn't understand ... they may well have their backs to it, but each step brings misery closer and it's been getting nearer for over two hours. They can't stop it, any more than the ones bringing it ... it's their master too and they must serve it ... it has its aim and follows its path ... it's unstoppable and has only one thought ... they have to submit to its power. They are sad but they come ... they have pity but they must draw nearer.

MARY: The older one's not smiling any more, grandfather.

STRANGER: They're moving away from the windows.

MARY: They're kissing their mother.

STRANGER: The older one is stroking the sleeping child's curls ...

MARY: Oh, look! The father wants a kiss too ...

STRANGER: Now silence ...

MARY: They're returning to their mother's side ...

STRANGER: And the father's eyes are fixed on the great pendulum on the clock.

MARY: It's like they're praying without knowing it ...

STRANGER: It's like they're listening to their souls ...

Silence.

MARY: Grandfather, don't tell them, not this evening.

OLD MAN: You see how you also lose your nerve. I knew we shouldn't watch them. I'm nearly eighty-three and it's the first time I've seen life like this. Why does everything they do seem so strange and so serious to me? ... they're waiting for night to fall, that's all, by the lamp, just like we would by ours. But I feel like I'm looking at them from high up, from another world, because I know a little truth that they don't ... is that it, my children? But tell me why you're so pale too? Is there something else, perhaps, which cannot be said, but makes us weep? I didn't know life had anything this sad in it, anything which could terrify those who saw it ... even if nothing had happened it would have terrified me to see them so still ... they have too much faith in this world ... there they are separated from the enemy by thin window panes ... they think they're safe because they've locked the door and they don't realize that what happens happens in the soul and that the world doesn't stop at their front door ... they are so certain of their little life, they have no idea how much more others know about it; and I, just a poor old man, I hold here, a couple of steps from their door, all their little happiness between my two old hands, and dare not open them ...

MARY: Have pity, grandfather ...

OLD MAN: We can pity them, my child, but no one pities us ...

MARY: Tell them tomorrow, grandfather, tell them when it gets light ... they won't be so sad ...

OLD MAN: You may be right ... it would be better to leave all this tonight. And light is gentle on sadness ... But what would they say to us tomorrow? Misfortune makes us resentful; and those it hits want to be told before everyone else knows. They don't like it handled by strangers ... it would be like we'd stolen something from them.

STRANGER: Besides, there's no more time; I can already hear the murmur of prayers ...

MARY: They're here ... they're passing behind the hedges ...

MARTHA enters.

MARTHA: Here I am. I led them here. I told them to wait on the road.

The cries of children can be heard.

Ah, the children are still crying ... I told them not to come ... but they also wanted to see and their mother wouldn't listen to me ... I'm going to tell them ... No, they've gone quiet – Is everything ready? – I've brought the little ring we found on her. I laid her out on the stretcher myself. She looked like she was asleep. It was very difficult; her hair wouldn't do what I wanted ... I got them to pick daisies ... it's sad, there were no other flowers ... what are you doing here? Why aren't you with them?

She looks through the windows.

They're not crying? ... They ... haven't you told them?

OLD MAN: Martha, Martha, there is too much life in your soul, you wouldn't understand.

MARTHA: Why wouldn't I?

After a silence, and in a very serious, reproachful tone –

You should have told them, grandfather.

OLD MAN: Martha, you don't understand ...

MARTHA: I'll have to tell them.

OLD MAN: Stay here, my child, and watch for a moment.

MARTHA: Oh, they are so sad! ... They mustn't be kept waiting any longer.

OLD MAN: Why not?

MARTHA: I don't know ... but it's not possible, not any more!

OLD MAN: Come here, my child.

MARTHA: They're so patient!

OLD MAN: Come here, my child.

MARTHA: (*Turning around.*) Where are you, grandfather? I'm so sad I can't make you out ... I, I don't know what to do now.

OLD MAN: Don't look at them any more; not until they know the full story.

MARTHA: I want to go in with you.

OLD MAN: No Martha, wait here ... sit with your sister on the old stone bench by the wall of the house, and turn away ... you are too young, the memory would stay with you forever ... you shouldn't see what a face looks like when its eyes are filled with death ... there may be tears ... Don't turn round ... There may be nothing ... Above all, don't turn round if you hear nothing ... you never know in advance what path despair will take ... a few tiny sobs from the very depths and that's usually all ... I don't know what I'll do when I hear them ... it's not part of this life ... kiss me, my child, before I go.

The murmur of prayers gets gradually nearer. A part of the crowd enters the garden. We can hear the patter of soft footsteps and the murmur of low voices.

STRANGER: (*To the crowd.*) Stay here ... don't go near the window ... where is she?

FARMHAND: Who?

STRANGER: The others ... the pallbearers? ...

FARMHAND: They're taking the path that leads to the door.

THE OLD MAN leaves. MARTHA and MARY are seated on the bench, backs to the windows. Low muttering in the crowd.

STRANGER: Be quiet! ... Not a sound.

The older sister gets up and goes to the bolts on the door.

MARTHA: Is she opening it?

STRANGER: Far from it, she's locking it.

Silence.

MARTHA: Hasn't grandfather gone in?

STRANGER: No ... she's going back to sit next to her mother ... the others aren't stirring and the child's slept through the whole thing.

Silence.

MARTHA: My little sister, give me your hands.

MARY: Martha.

They hug and embrace.

STRANGER: He must have knocked ... they all raised their heads at the same time ... they're looking at each other ...

MARTHA: Oh! Oh! My poor sister ... I'm going to start crying too ...

She stifles her sobs on her sister's shoulder.

STRANGER: He must be knocking again ... the father's looking up this time. He's getting up.

MARTHA: My sister, my sister, I want to go in too ... they mustn't be alone any longer.

MARY: Martha, Martha.

She holds her back.

STRANGER: The father is at the door ... he's drawing back the bolts ... cautiously, he opens it ...

MARTHA: Oh! ... you can't see ...

STRANGER: What?

MARTHA: The pallbearers ...

STRANGER: He's not opened it very much ... I can only see the edge of the front garden and the fountain ... he's not letting go of the door ... he draws back ... He's saying something like 'Ah, it's you! ... ' He raises his arms ... He's closing the door carefully ... Your grandfather's inside ...

The crowd has got up close to the windows. MARTHA and MARY rise hesitantly, before approaching as well, arms tight around each other. The dead girl's sisters get up; THE MOTHER gets up too, after having carefully sat the child in her armchair, in such a way that from outside the child can be seen sleeping, the head a little to one side, in the centre of the room. THE MOTHER goes up to meet THE OLD MAN and holds out her hand, but withdraws it before he has time to take it. One of the young girls goes to take the visitor's coat and the other offers him an armchair. But THE OLD MAN declines with a small gesture. THE FATHER smiles, bemused. THE OLD MAN looks towards the windows.

STRANGER: He can't bring himself to tell them ... He's looking at us.

Muttering in the crowd.

STRANGER: Be quiet! ...

THE OLD MAN, seeing the faces at the windows, quickly averts his gaze. One of the young girls is still offering the same armchair, and he finally sits down and rubs his forehead repeatedly.

STRANGER: He's sitting down ...

The other people in the room sit down as well, while THE FATHER speaks at length. Eventually THE OLD MAN opens his mouth and the sound of his voice appears to draw their attention. THE FATHER interrupts. THE OLD MAN carries on and, little by little, the others become still. Suddenly THE MOTHER gives a start, and stands up.

MARTHA: Oh! The mother begins to understand! ...

She turns around and buries her face in her hands. Further murmuring from the crowd. Some jockey for position. Children cry to be lifted up so that they can see too. Most of the mothers comply.

STRANGER: Silence! ... He hasn't told them yet ...

THE MOTHER can be seen, anxiously questioning THE OLD MAN. He says a few words more, then abruptly all the others get up too and seem to be asking him questions. He gives a slow nod of affirmation.

STRANGER: He's said it ... He's come right out with it! ...

VOICES IN THE CROWD: He's said it! ... He's said it! ...

STRANGER: There's not a sound to be heard.

THE OLD MAN gets up as well; and without turning round be indicates the door behind him. THE MOTHER, THE FATHER and the two young girls hurry to the door, which THE FATHER can't immediately get open. THE OLD MAN makes to stop THE MOTHER going out.

VOICES IN THE CROWD: They're coming out! They're coming out!

Pandemonium in the garden. Everyone hurls themselves towards the other side of the house and disappears, apart from THE STRANGER who stays at the windows. In the room, the double doors finally open; they all run out at once. The starry sky can be seen, the lawn and the fountain in the moonlight, while in the middle of the abandoned room, the child continues to sleep peacefully in the armchair. Silence.

STRANGER: The child has not awoken ...

He leaves.

Notes

This is a new translation of Maeterlinck's play. The play was originally published in French in 1894 and collected in *Théâtre* (3 vols), ed. Martine de Rougemont, Paris and Brussels, 1901–2.

1.6 Naturalism in the Theatre (1881)

ÉMILE ZOLA

Translated by Albert Bermel

Naturalism

I

EACH WINTER AT THE beginning of the theatre season I fall prey to the same thoughts. A hope springs up in me, and I tell myself that before the first warmth of summer empties the playhouses, a dramatist of genius will be discovered. Our theatre desperately needs a new man who will scour the debased boards and bring about a rebirth in an art degraded by its practitioners to the simple-minded requirements of the crowd. Yes, it would take a powerful personality, an innovator's mind, to overthrow the accepted conventions and finally install the real human drama in place of the ridiculous untruths that are on display today. I picture this creator scorning the tricks of the clever hack, smashing the imposed patterns, remaking the stage until it is continuous with the auditorium, giving a shiver of life to the painted trees, letting in through the backcloth the great, free air of reality.

Unfortunately, this dream I have every October has not yet been fulfilled, and is not likely to be for some time. I wait in vain, I go from failure to failure. Is this, then, merely the naive wish of a poet? Are we trapped in today's dramatic art, which is so confining, like a cave that lacks air and light? Certainly, if dramatic art by its nature forbids this escape into less restricted forms, it would indeed be vain to delude ourselves and to expect a renaissance at any moment. But despite the stubborn assertions of certain critics who do not like to have their standards threatened, it is obvious that dramatic art, like all the arts, has before it an unlimited domain, without barriers of any kind to left or right. Inability, human incapacity, is the only boundary to an art.

To understand the need for a revolution in the theatre, we must establish clearly where we stand today. During our entire classical period tragedy ruled as an absolute monarch. It was rigid and intolerant, never granting its subjects a touch of freedom, bending the greatest minds to its inexorable laws. If a playwright tried to break away from them he was condemned as witless, incoherent and bizarre; he was almost considered a dangerous man. Yet even within the narrow formula genius did build its monument of marble and bronze. The formula was born during the Greek and Latin revival; the artists who took it over found in it a pattern that would serve for great works. Only later, when the imitators – that line of increasingly weaker and punier disciples – came along, did the faults in the formula show up: outlandish situations, improbabilities, dishonest uniformity, and uninterrupted, unbearable declaiming. Tragedy maintained such a sway that two hundred years had to pass before it went out of date. It tried slowly to become more flexible, but without success, for the authoritarian principles in which it was grounded formally forbade any concession to new ideas, under pain of death. Just when it was trying to broaden its scope, it was overturned, after a long and glorious reign.

In the eighteenth century romantic drama was already stirring inside tragedy. On occasion the three unities were violated, more importance was given to scenery and extras, violent climaxes were now staged, where formerly they had been described in speeches so that the majestic tranquillity of psychological analysis might not be disturbed by physical action. In addition, the passion of the *grande époque* was replaced by commonplace acting; a grey rain of mediocrity and staleness soaked the stage. One can visualize tragedy, by the beginning of this century, as a long, pale, emaciated figure without a drop of blood under its white skin, trailing its tattered robes across a gloomy stage on which the footlights had gone dark of their own accord. A rebirth of dramatic art out of a new formula was inevitable. It was then that romantic drama noisily planted its standard in front of the prompter's box. The hour had come; a slow ferment had been at work; the insurrection advanced on to terrain already softened-up for the victory. And never has the word insurrection seemed more apt, for romantic drama bodily seized the monarch tragedy and, out of hatred for its impotence, sought to destroy every memory of its reign. Tragedy did not react; it sat still on its throne, guarding its cold majesty, persisting with its speeches and descriptions. Whereas romantic drama made action its rule, excesses of action that leapt to the four corners of the stage, hitting out to right and left, no longer reasoning or analysing, giving the public a full view of the blood-drenched horror of its climaxes. Tragedy had chosen antiquity for its setting, the eternal Greeks and Romans, immobilizing the action in a room or in front of the columns of a temple; romantic drama chose the Middle Ages, paraded knights and ladies, manufactured strange sets with castles pinnacled over sheer gorges, armories crowded with weapons, dungeons dripping with moisture, ancient forests pocked with moonlight. The war was joined on all fronts; romantic drama ruthlessly made itself the armed adversary of tragedy and assaulted it with every method that defied the old formula.

This raging hostility, which characterized the romantic drama at its high tide, needs to be stressed, for it offers a precious insight. The poets who led the movement undoubtedly talked about putting real passion on stage and laying claim to a vast new realm that would encompass the whole of human life with its contradictions and inconsistencies; it is worth remembering, for example, that romantic drama fought above all for a mixture of laughter and tears in the same play, arguing that joy and pain walk side by side on earth. Yet truth, reality, in fact counted for little – even displeased the innovators. They had only one passion, to overthrow the tragic formula that inhibited them, to crush it once and for all under a stampede of every kind of audacity. They did not want their heroes of the Middle Ages to be more real than the heroes of tragic antiquity; they wanted them to appear as passionate and splendid as their predecessors had appeared cold and correct. A mere skirmish over dress and modes of speech, nothing more: one set of puppets at odds with another. Togas were torn up in favour of doublets; a lady, instead of addressing her lover as 'My lord', called him 'My lion'. After the transition fiction still prevailed; only the setting was different.

I do not want to be unfair to the romantic movement. Its effect has been outstanding and unquestionable; it has made us what we are: free artists. It was, I repeat, a necessary revolution, a violent struggle that arose just in time to sweep away a tragic convention that had become childish. Still, it would be ridiculous to arrest the evolution of dramatic art at romanticism. These days, especially, it is astounding to read certain prefaces in which the 1830 movement is announced as the triumphal entry into human truth. Our forty-year distance is enough to let us see clearly that the alleged truth of the romanticists is a persistent and monstrous exaggeration of reality, a fantasy that has declined into excesses. Tragedy, to be sure, is another type of falseness, but it is not *more* false. Between the characters who pace about in togas, endlessly discussing their passions with confidants, and the characters in doublets who perform great feats and flit about like insects drunk with the sun, there is nothing to choose; both are equally and totally unacceptable. Such people have never existed. Romantic heroes are only tragic heroes bitten by the *mardi gras* bug, hiding behind false noses, and dancing the dramatic cancan after drinking. For the old sluggish rhetoric the 1830 movement substituted an excited, full-blooded rhetoric, and that is all.

Without believing that art progresses, we can still say that it is continuously in motion, among all civilizations, and that this motion reflects different phases of the human mind. Genius is made manifest in every formula, even in the most primitive and innocent ones, though the formulas become transmuted according to the intellectual breadth of each civilization; that is incontestable. If Aeschylus was great, Shakespeare and Molière showed themselves to be equally great, each within his differing civilization and formula. By this I mean that I set apart the creative genius who knows how to make the most of the formula of his time. There is no progress in human creation but there is a logical succession to the formulas, to methods of thought and expression. Thus, art takes the same strides as humanity, is its very language, goes where it goes, moves with it towards light and truth; but for that, we could never judge whether a creator's efforts were more or less great, depending on whether he comes at the beginning or end of a literature.

In these terms, it is certain that when we left tragedy behind, the romantic drama was a first step in the direction of the naturalistic drama, towards which we are now advancing. The romantic drama cleared the ground, proclaimed the freedom of art. Its love of action, its mixture of laughter and tears, its research into accuracy of costume and setting show the movement's impulse towards real life. Is this not how things happen during every revolution against a secular regime? One begins by breaking windows, chanting and shouting, wrecking relics of the last regime with hammer blows. There is a first exuberance, an intoxication with the new horizons faintly glimpsed, excesses of all kinds that go beyond the original aims and degenerate into the despotism of the old, hated system, those very abuses the revolution has just fought against. In the heat of the battle tomorrow's truths evaporate. And not until all is calm and the fever has abated is there any regret for the broken windows, any understanding of how the effort has gone awry, how the new laws have been prematurely thrown together so that they are hardly any improvement over the laws that were destroyed. Well, the whole history of romantic drama is there. It may have been the formula necessary for its time, it may have had truthful intuitions, it may have been the form that will always be celebrated because a great poet used it to compose his masterpieces. At the present time it is, none the less, a ridiculous, outdated formula, with a rhetoric that offends us. We now wonder why it was necessary to push in windows, wave swords, bellow without a break, to go a scale too shrill in sentiment and language. All that leaves us cold, it bores and annoys us. Our condemnation of the romantic formula is summed up in one severe remark: To destroy one rhetoric it was not necessary to invent another.

Today, then, tragedy and romantic drama are equally old and worn out. And that is hardly to the credit of the latter, it should be said, for in less than half a century it has fallen into the same state of decay as tragedy, which took two centuries to die. There it lies, flattened in its turn, overwhelmed by the same passion it showed in its own battle. Nothing is left. We can only guess at what is to come. Logically all that can grow up on that free ground conquered in 1830 is the formula of naturalism.

II

It seems impossible that the movement of inquiry and analysis, which is precisely the movement of the nineteenth century, can have revolutionized all the sciences and arts and left dramatic art to one side, as if isolated. The natural sciences date from the end of the last century; chemistry and physics are less than a hundred years old; history and criticism have been renovated, virtually re-created since the Revolution; an entire world has arisen; it has sent us back to the study of documents, to experience, made us realize that to start afresh we must first take things back to the beginning, become familiar with man and nature, verify what is. Thenceforward, the great naturalistic school, which has spread secretly, irrevocably, often making its way in darkness but always advancing, can finally come out triumphantly into the light of day. To trace the history of this movement, with the misunderstandings that might have impeded it and the multiple causes that have thrust it forward or slowed it down, would be to trace the history of the century itself. An irresistible current carries our society towards the study of reality. In the novel Balzac has been the bold and mighty innovator who has replaced the observation of the scholar with the imagination of the poet. But in the theatre the evolution seems slower. No eminent writer has yet formulated the new idea with any clarity.

I certainly do not say that some excellent works have not been produced, with characters in them who are ingeniously examined and bold truths taken right on to the stage. Let me, for instance, cite certain plays by M. Dumas *fils*, whose talent I scarcely admire, and M. Émile Augier, the most humane and powerful of all. Still, they are midgets beside Balzac; they lack the genius to lay down the formula. It must be said that one can never tell quite when a movement is getting under way; generally its source is remote and lost in the earlier movement from which it emerged. In a manner of speaking, the naturalistic current has always existed. It brings with it nothing absolutely novel. But it has finally flowed into a period favourable to it; it is succeeding and expanding because the human mind has attained the necessary maturity. I do not, therefore, deny the past; I affirm the present. The strength of naturalism is precisely that it has deep roots in our national literature which contains plenty of wisdom. It comes from the very entrails of humanity; it is that much the stronger because it has taken longer to grow and is found in a greater number of our masterpieces.

Certain things have come to pass and I point them out. Can we believe that *L'Ami Fritz* would have been applauded at the Comédie-Française twenty years ago? Definitely not! This play, in which people eat all the time and the lover talks in such homely language, would have disgusted both the classicists and the romantics. To explain its success we must concede that as the years have gone by a secret fermentation has been at work. Lifelike paintings, which used to repel the public, today attract them. The majority has been won over and the stage is open to every experiment. This is the only conclusion to draw.

So that is where we stand. To explain my point better – I am not afraid of repeating myself – I will sum up what I have said. Looking closely at the history of our dramatic literature, one can detect several clearly separated periods. First, there was the infancy of the art, farces and the mystery plays of the Middle Ages, the reciting of simple dialogues which developed as part of a naïve convention, with primitive staging and sets. Gradually, the plays became more complex but in a crude fashion. When Corneille appeared he was acclaimed most of all for his status as an innovator, for refining the dramatic formula of the time, and for hallowing it by means of his genius. It would be very interesting to study the pertinent documents and discover how our classical formula came to be created. It corresponded to the social spirit of the period. Nothing is solid that is not built on necessity. Tragedy reigned for two centuries because it satisfied the exact requirements of those centuries. Geniuses of differing temperaments had buttressed it with their masterpieces. And it continued to impose itself long afterwards, even when second-rate talents were producing inferior work. It acquired a momentum. It persisted also as the literary expression of that society, and nothing would have overthrown it if the society had not itself disappeared. After the Revolution, after that profound disturbance that was meant to transform everything and give birth to a new world, tragedy struggled to stay alive for a few more years. Then the formula cracked and romanticism broke through. A new formula asserted itself. We must look back at the first half of the century to understand the meaning of this cry for liberty. The young society was in the tremor of its infancy. The excited, bewildered, violently unleashed people were still racked by a dangerous fever; and in the first flush of their new liberty they yearned for prodigious adventures and superhuman love affairs. They gaped at the stars; some committed suicide, a very curious reaction to the social enfranchisement which had just been declared at the cost of so much blood. Turning specifically to dramatic literature, I maintain that romanticism in the theatre was an uncomplicated revolt, the invasion by a victorious group who took over the stage violently with drums beating and flags flying. In these early moments the combatants dreamed of making their imprint with a new form; to one rhetoric they opposed another: the Middle Ages to Antiquity, the exalting of passion to the exalting of duty. And that was all, for only the scenic conventions were altered. The characters remained marionettes in new clothing. Only the exterior aspect and the language were modified. But for the period that was enough. Romanticism had taken possession of the theatre in the name of literary freedom and it carried out its revolutionary task with incomparable bravura. But who does not see today that its role could extend no farther than that? Does romanticism have anything whatever to say about our present society? Does it meet one of our requirements? Obviously not. It is as outmoded as a jargon we no longer follow. It confidently expected to replace classical literature which had lasted for two centuries because it was based on social conditions. But romanticism was based on nothing but the fantasy of a few poets or, if you will, on the passing malady of minds overwhelmed by historical events; it was bound to disappear with the malady. It provided the occasion for a magnificent flowering of lyricism; that will be its eternal glory. Today, however, with the evolution accomplished, it is plain that romanticism was no more than the necessary link between classicism and naturalism. The struggle is over; now we must found a secure state. Naturalism flows out of classical art, just as our present society has arisen from the wreckage of the old society. Naturalism alone corresponds to our social needs; it alone has deep roots in the spirit of our times; and it alone can provide a living, durable formula for our art, because this formula will express the nature of our contemporary intelligence. There may be fashions and passing fantasies that exist outside naturalism but they will not survive for long. I say again, naturalism is the expression of our century and it will not die until a new upheaval transforms our democratic world.

Only one thing is needed now: men of genius who can fix the naturalistic formula. Balzac has done it for the novel and the novel is established. When will our Corneilles, Molières and Racines appear to establish our new theatre? We must hope and wait.

III

The period when romantic drama ruled now seems distant. In Paris five or six of its playhouses prospered. The demolition of the old theatres along the Boulevard du Temple was a catastrophe of the first order. The theatres became separated from one another, the public changed, different fashions arose. But the discredit into which the drama has fallen proceeds mostly from the exhaustion of the genre – ridiculous, boring plays have gradually taken over from the potent works of 1830.

To this enfeeblement we must add the absolute lack of new actors who understand and can interpret these kinds of plays, for every dramatic formula that vanishes carries away its interpreters with it. Today the drama, hunted from stage to stage, has only two houses that really belong to it, the Ambigu and the Théâtre-Historique. Even at the Saint-Martin the drama is lucky to win a brief showing for itself, between one great spectacle and the next.

An occasional success may renew its courage. But its decline is inevitable; romantic drama is sliding into oblivion, and if it seems sometimes to check its descent, it does so only to roll even lower afterwards. Naturally, there are loud complaints. The tail-end romanticists are desperately unhappy. They swear that except in the drama – meaning their kind of drama – there is no salvation for dramatic literature. I believe, on the contrary, that we must find a new formula that will transform the drama, just as the writers in the first half of the century transformed tragedy. That is the essence of the matter. Today the battle is between romantic drama and naturalistic drama. By romantic drama I mean every play that mocks truthfulness in its incidents and characterization, that struts about in its puppet-box, stuffed to the belly with noises that flounder, for some idealistic reason or other, in pastiches of Shakespeare and Hugo. Every period has its formula; ours is certainly not that of 1830. We are an age of method, of experimental science; our primary need is for precise analysis. We hardly understand the liberty we have won if we use it only to imprison ourselves in a new tradition. The way is open: we can now return to man and nature.

Finally, there have been great efforts to revive the historical drama. Nothing could be better. A critic cannot roundly condemn the choice of historical subjects, even if his own preferences are entirely for subjects that are modern. It is simply that I am full of distrust. The manager one gives this sort of play to frightens me in advance. It is a question of how history is treated, what unusual characters are presented bearing the names of kings, great captains or great artists, and what awful sauce they are served up in to make the history palatable. As soon as the authors of these concoctions move into the past they think everything is permitted: improbabilities, cardboard dolls, monumental idiocies, the hysterical scribblings that falsely represent local colour. And what strange dialogue – François I talking like a haberdasher straight out of the Rue Saint-Denis, Richelieu using the words of a criminal from the Boulevard du Crime, Charlotte Corday with the weeping sentimentalities of a factory girl.

What astounds me is that our playwrights do not seem to suspect for a moment that the historical genre is unavoidably the least rewarding, the one that calls most strongly for research, integrity, a consummate gift of intuition, a talent for reconstruction. I am all for historical drama when it is in the hands of poets of genius or men of exceptional knowledge who are capable of making the public see an epoch come alive with its special quality, its manners, its civilization. In that case we have a work of prophecy or of profoundly interesting criticism.

But unfortunately I know what it is these partisans of historical drama want to revive: the swaggering and sword-play, the big spectacle with big words, the play of lies that shows off in front of the crowd, the gross exhibition that saddens honest minds. Hence my distrust. I think that all this antiquated business is better left in our museum of dramatic history under a pious layer of dust.

There are, undeniably, great obstacles to original experiments: we run up against the hypocrisies of criticism and the long education in idiocies that has been foisted on the public. This public, which titters at every childishness in melodramas, nevertheless lets itself be carried away by outbursts of fine sentiment. But the public is changing. Shakespeare's public and Molière's are no longer ours. We must reckon with shifts in outlook, with the need for reality which is everywhere getting more insistent. The last few romantics vainly repeat that the public wants this and the public wants that; the day is coming when the public will want the truth.

IV

The old formulas, classical and romantic, were based on the rearrangement and systematic amputation of the truth. They determined on principle that the truth is not good enough; they tried to draw out of it an essence, a 'poetry', on the pretext that nature must be expurgated and magnified. Up to the present the different literary schools disputed only over the question of the best way to disguise the truth so that it might not look too brazen to the public. The classicists adopted the toga; the romantics fought a revolution to impose the coat of mail and the doublet. Essentially the change of dress made little difference; the counterfeiting of nature went on. But today the naturalistic thinkers are telling us that the truth does not need clothing; it can walk naked. That, I repeat, is the quarrel.

Writers with any sense understand perfectly that tragedy and romantic drama are dead. The majority, though, are badly troubled when they turn their minds to the as-yet-unclear formula of tomorrow. Does the truth seriously ask them to give up the grandeur, the poetry, the traditional epic effects that their ambition tells them to put into their plays? Does naturalism demand that they shrink their horizons and risk not one flight into fantasy?

I will try to reply. But first we must determine the methods used by the idealists to lift their works into poetry. They begin by placing their chosen subject in a distant time. That provides them with costumes and makes the framework of the story vague enough to give them full scope for lying. Next, they generalize instead of particularizing; their characters are no longer living people but sentiments, arguments, passions that have been induced by reasoning. This false framework calls for heroes of marble or cardboard. A man of flesh and bone with his own originality would jar in such a legendary setting. Moreover, when we see the characters in romantic drama or tragedy walking about they are stiffened into an attitude, one representing duty, another patriotism, a third superstition, a fourth maternal love; thus, all the abstract ideas file by. Never the thorough analysis of an organism, never a character whose muscles and brain function as in nature.

These, then, are the mannerisms that writers with epic inclinations do not want to give up. For them poetry resides in the past and in abstraction, in the idealizing of facts and characters. As soon as one confronts them with daily life, with the people who fill our streets, they blink, they stammer, they are afraid; they no longer see clearly; they find everything ugly and not good enough for art. According to them, a subject must enter the lies of legend, men must harden and turn to stone like statues before the artist can accept them and make them fit the disguises he has prepared.

Now, it is at this point that the naturalistic movement comes along and says squarely that poetry is everywhere, in everything, even more in the present and the real than in the past and the abstract. Each event at each moment has its poetic, superb aspect. We brush up against heroes who are great and powerful in different respects from the puppets of the epic-makers. Not one playwright in this century has brought to life figures as lofty as Baron Hulot, Old Grandet, César Birotteau, and all the other characters of Balzac, who are so individual and so alive. Beside these real, giant creations Greek and Roman heroes quake; the heroes of the Middle Ages fall flat on their faces like lead soldiers.

With the superior works being produced in these times by the naturalistic school – works of high endeavour, pulsing with life – it is ridiculous and false to park our poetry in some antiquated temple and bury it in cobwebs. Poetry flows at its full force through everything that exists; the truer to life, the greater it becomes. And I mean to give the word poetry its widest definition, not to pin it down exclusively to the cadence of two rhymes, nor to bury it in a narrow coterie of dreamers, but to restore its real human significance which concerns the expansion and encouragement of every kind of truth.

Take our present environment, then, and try to make men live in it: you will write great works. It will undoubtedly call for some effort; it means sifting out of the confusion of life the simple formula of naturalism. Therein lies the difficulty: to do great things with the subjects and characters that our eyes, accustomed to the spectacle of the daily round, have come to see as small. I am aware that it is more convenient to present a marionette to the public and name it Charlemagne and puff it up with such tirades that the public believes it is watching a colossus; it is more convenient than taking a bourgeois of our time, a grotesque, unsightly man, and drawing sublime poetry out of him, making him, for example, Père Goriot, the father who gives his guts for his daughters, a figure so gigantic with truth and love that no other literature can offer his equal.

Nothing is as easy as persuading the managers with known formulas; and heroes in the classical or romantic taste cost so little labour that they are manufactured by the dozen, and have become standardized articles that clutter up our literature. But it takes hard work to create a real hero, intelligently analysed, alive and performing. That is probably why naturalism terrifies those authors who are used to fishing up great men from the troubled waters of history. They would have to burrow too deeply into humanity, learn about life, go straight for the greatness of reality and make it function with all their power. And let nobody gainsay this true poetry of humanity; it has been sifted out in the novel and can be in the theatre; only the method of adaptation remains to be found.

I am troubled by a comparison; it has been haunting me and I will now free myself of it. For two long months a play called *Les Danicheff* has been running at the Odéon. It takes place in Russia. It has been very successful here, but is apparently so dishonest, so packed with gross improbabilities, that the author, a Russian, has not even dared to show it in his country. What can you think of this work which is applauded in Paris and would be booed in St Petersburg? Well, imagine for a moment that the Romans could come back to life and see a performance of *Rome vaincue*. Can you hear their roars of laughter? Do you think the play would complete one performance? It would strike them as a parody; it would sink under the weight of mockery. And is there one historical play that could be performed before the society it claims to portray? A strange theatre, this, which is plausible only among foreigners, is based on the disappearance of the generations it deals with, and is made up of so much misinformation that it is good only for the ignorant!

The future is with naturalism. The formula will be found; it will be proved that there is more poetry in the little apartment of a bourgeois than in all the empty, worm-eaten palaces of history; in the end we will see that everything meets in the real: lovely fantasies that are free of capriciousness and whimsy, and idylls, and comedies, and dramas. Once the soil has been turned over, the task that seems alarming and unfeasible today will become easy.

I am not qualified to pronounce on the form that tomorrow's drama will take; that must be left to the voice of some genius to come. But I will allow myself to indicate the path I consider our theatre will follow.

First, the romantic drama must be abandoned. It would be disastrous for us to take over its outrageous acting, its rhetoric, its inherent thesis of action at the expense of character analysis. The finest models of the genre are, as has been said, mere operas with big effects. I believe, then, that we must go back to tragedy – not, heaven forbid, to borrow more of its rhetoric, its system of confidants, its declaiming, its endless speeches, but to return to its simplicity of action and its unique psychological and physiological study of the characters. Thus understood, the tragic framework is excellent; one deed unwinds in all its reality, and moves the characters to passions and feelings, the exact analysis of which constitutes the sole interest of the play – and in a contemporary environment, with the people who surround us.

My constant concern, my anxious vigil, has made me wonder which of us will have the strength to raise himself to the pitch of genius. If the naturalistic drama must come into being, only a genius can give birth to it. Corneille and Racine made tragedy. Victor Hugo made romantic drama. Where is the as-yet-unknown author who must make the naturalistic drama? In recent years experiments have not been wanting. But either because the public was not ready or because none of the beginners had the necessary staying-power, not one of these attempts has had decisive results.

In battles of this kind, small victories mean nothing; we need triumphs that overwhelm the adversary and win the public to the cause. Audiences would give way before the onslaught of a really strong man. This man would come with the expected word, the solution to the problem, the formula for a real life on stage, combining it with the illusions necessary in the theatre. He would have what the newcomers have as yet lacked: the cleverness or the might to impose himself and to remain so close to truth that his cleverness could not lead him into lies.

And what an immense place this innovator would occupy in our dramatic literature! He would be at the peak. He would build his monument in the middle of the desert of mediocrity that we are crossing, among the jerry-built houses strewn about our most illustrious stages. He would put everything in question and remake everything, scour the boards, create a world whose elements he would lift from life, from outside our traditions. Surely there is no more ambitious dream that a writer of our time could fulfil. The domain of the novel is crowded; the domain of the theatre is free. At this time in France an imperishable glory awaits the man of genius who takes up the work of Molière and finds in the reality of living comedy the full, true drama of modern society ...

Physiological man

... In effect, the great naturalistic evolution which comes down directly from the fifteenth century to ours has everything to do with the gradual substitution of physiological man for metaphysical man. In tragedy metaphysical man, man according to dogma and logic, reigned absolutely. The body did not count; the soul was regarded as the only interesting piece of human machinery; drama took place in the air, in pure mind. Consequently, what use was the tangible world? Why worry about the place where the action was located? Why be surprised at a baroque costume or false declaiming? Why notice that Queen Dido was a boy whose budding beard forced him to wear a mask? None of that mattered; these trifles were not worth stooping to; the play was heard out as if it were a school essay or a law case; it was on a higher plane than man, in the world of ideas, so far away from real man that any intrusion of reality would have spoiled the show.

Such is the point of departure – in Mystery plays, the religious point; the philosophical point in tragedy. And from that beginning natural man, stifling under the rhetoric and dogma, struggled secretly, tried to break free, made lengthy, futile efforts, and in the end asserted himself, limb by limb. The whole history of our theatre is in this conquest by the physiological man, who emerged more clearly in each period from behind the dummy of religious and philosophical idealism. Corneille, Molière, Racine, Voltaire, Beaumarchais and, in our day, Victor Hugo, Émile Augier, Alexandre Dumas *fils*, even Sardou, have had only one task, even when they were not completely aware of it: to increase the reality of our corpus of drama, to progress towards truth, to sift out more and more of the natural man and impose him on the public. And inevitably, the evolution will not end with them. It continues; it will continue forever. Mankind is very young ...

Costume, stage design, speech

Modern clothes make a poor spectacle. If we depart from bourgeois tragedy, shut in between its four walls, and wish to use the breadth of larger stages for crowd scenes we are embarrassed and constrained by the monotony and the uniformly funereal look of the extras. In this case, I think, we should take advantage of the variety of garb offered by the different classes and occupations. To elaborate: I can imagine an author setting one act in the main marketplace of Les Halles in Paris. The setting would be superb, with its bustling life and bold possibilities. In this immense setting we could have a very picturesque ensemble by displaying the porters wearing their large hats, the saleswomen with their white aprons and vividly coloured scarves, the customers dressed in silk or wool or cotton prints, from the ladies accompanied by their maids to the female beggars on the prowl for anything they can pick up off the street. For inspiration it would be enough to go to Les Halles and look about. Nothing is gaudier or more interesting. All of Paris would enjoy seeing this set if it were realized with the necessary accuracy and amplitude.

And how many other settings for popular drama there are for the taking! Inside a factory, the interior of a mine, the gingerbread market, a railway station, flower stalls, a racetrack, and so on. All the activities of modern life can take place in them. It will be said that such sets have already been tried. Unquestionably we have seen factories and railway stations in fantasy plays; but these were fantasy stations and factories. I mean, these sets were thrown together to create an illusion that was at best incomplete. What we need is detailed reproduction: costumes supplied by trades-people, not sumptuous but adequate for the purposes of truth and for the interest of the scenes. Since everybody mourns the death of the drama our playwrights certainly ought to make a try at this type of popular, contemporary drama. At one stroke they could satisfy the public hunger for spectacle and the need for exact studies which grows more pressing every day. Let us hope, though, that the playwrights will show us real people and not those whining members of the working class who play such strange roles in boulevard melodrama.

As M. Adolphe Jullien has said – and I will never be tired of repeating it – everything is interdependent in the theatre. Lifelike costumes look wrong if the sets, the diction, the plays themselves are not lifelike. They must all march in step along the naturalistic road. When costume becomes more accurate, so do sets; actors free themselves from bombastic declaiming; plays study reality more closely and their characters are more true to life. I could make the same observations about sets I have just made about costume. With them, too, we may seem to have reached the highest possible degree of truth, but we still have long strides to take. Most of all we would need to intensify the illusion in reconstructing the environments, less for their picturesque quality than for dramatic utility. The environment must determine the character. When a set is planned so as to give the lively impression of a description by Balzac; when, as the curtain rises, one catches the first glimpse of the characters, their personalities and behaviour, if only to see the actual locale in which they move, the importance of exact reproduction in the decor will be appre-ciated. Obviously, that is the way we are going. Environment, the study of which has transformed science and literature, will have to take a large role in the theatre. And here I may mention again the question of metaphysical man, the abstraction who had to be satisfied with his three walls in tragedy – whereas the physiological man in our modern works is asking more and more compel-lingly to be determined by his setting, by the environment that produced him. We see then that the road to progress is still long, for sets as well as costume. We are coming upon the truth but we can hardly stammer it out.

Another very serious matter is diction. True, we have got away from the chanting, the plainsong, of the seventeenth century. But we now have a 'theatre voice', a false recitation that is very obtrusive and very annoying. Everything that is wrong with it comes from the fixed tradi-tional code set up by the majority of critics. They found the theatre in a certain state and, instead of looking to the future, and judging the progress we are making and the progress we shall make by the progress we have already made, they stubbornly defend the relics of the old conventions, swearing that these relics must be preserved. Ask them why, make them see how far we have travelled; they will give you no logical reason. They will reply with assertions based on a set of conditions that are disappearing.

In diction the errors come from what the critics call 'theatre language'. Their theory is that on stage you must not speak as you do in everyday life. To support this viewpoint they pick examples from traditional practices, from what was happening yesterday – and is happening still – without taking account of the naturalistic movement, the phases of which have been established for us by M. Jullien's book [*Histoire du Costume au Théâtre,* 1880]. Let us realize that there is no such thing as 'theatre language'. There has been a rhetoric which grew more and more feeble and is now dying out. Those are the facts. If you compare the declaiming of actors under Louis XIV with that of Lekain, and if you compare Lekain's with that of our own artists today, you will clearly distinguish the phases, from tragic chanting down to our search for the natural, precise tone, the cry of truth. It follows that 'theatre language', that language of booming sonority, is vanishing. We are moving towards simplicity, the exact word spoken without emphasis, quite naturally. How many examples I could give if I had unlimited space! Consider the powerful effect that Geoffroy has on the public; all his talent comes from his natural personality. He holds the public because he speaks on stage as he does at home. When a sentence sounds outlandish he cannot pronounce it; the author has to find another one. That is the fundamental criticism of so-called 'theatre language'. Again, follow the diction of a talented actor and at the same time watch the public; the cheers go up, the house is in raptures when a truthful accent gives the words the exact value they must have. All the great successes of the stage are triumphs over convention.

Alas, yes, there is a 'theatre language'. It is the clichés, the resounding platitudes, the hollow words that roll about like empty barrels, all that intolerable rhetoric of our vaudevilles and dramas, which is beginning to make us smile. It would be very interesting to study the style of such talented authors as MM. Augier, Dumas and Sardou. I could find much to criticize, especially in the last two with their conventional language, a language of their own that they put into the mouths of all their characters, men, women, children, old folk; both sexes and all ages. This irritates me, for each character has his own language, and to create living people you must give them to the public not merely in accurate dress and in the environments that have made them what they are, but with their individual ways of thinking and expressing themselves. I repeat that that is the obvious aim of our theatre. There is no theatre language regulated by such a code as 'cadenced sentences' or sonority. There is simply a kind of dialogue that is growing more precise and is following – or rather, leading – sets and costumes towards naturalistic progress. When plays are more truthful, the actors' diction will gain enormously in simplicity and naturalness.

To conclude, I will repeat that the battle of the conventions is far from being finished, and that it will no doubt last forever. Today we are beginning to see clearly where we are going, but steps are still impeded by the melting slush of rhetoric and metaphysics.

Note

Translated by Albert Bermel, 1968. Selected extracts from *Naturalism in the Theatre,* from Eric Bentley, *The Theory of the Modern Stage,* London: Penguin, 1968, pp. 351–72.

1.7 **Preface to Miss Julie** (1888)

AUGUST STRINDBERG

Translated by Michael Robinson

LIKE ART IN GENERAL, the theatre has long seemed to me a *Biblia pauperum*,[1] a Bible in pictures for those who cannot read what is written or printed, and the dramatist a lay preacher who peddles the ideas of the day in a popular form, so popular that the middle classes which form the bulk of the audience can, without too much mental effort, understand what is going on. That is why the theatre has always been an elementary school for the young, the semi-educated, and women, who still retain the primitive capacity for deceiving themselves or for letting themselves be deceived, that is, for succumbing to illusions and to the hypnotic suggestions of the author. Nowadays, therefore, when the rudimentary and undeveloped kind of thinking that takes the form of fantasy appears to be evolving into reflection, investigation, and analysis, it seems to me that the theatre, like religion, is about to be discarded as a dying form of art, which we lack the necessary preconditions to enjoy. This supposition is supported by the serious theatrical crisis now prevailing throughout Europe, and especially by the fact that in England and Germany, those cultural heartlands which have nurtured the greatest thinkers of our age, the drama is dead, along with most of the other fine arts.

Again, in other countries people have believed in the possibility of creating a new drama by filling the old forms with new contents; but this approach has failed, partly because there has not yet been time to popularize the new ideas, so the public has not been able to understand what was involved; partly because party differences have so inflamed emotions that pure, dispassionate enjoyment has become impossible in a situation where people's innermost thoughts have been challenged and an applauding or whistling majority has brought pressure to bear on them as openly as it can do in a theatre; and partly because we have not yet found the new form for the new content, and the new wine has burst the old bottles.

In the following play I have not tried to accomplish anything new, for that is impossible, but merely to modernize the form according to what I believe are the demands a contemporary audience would make of this art. To that end I have chosen, or let myself be moved by, a theme that may be said to lie outside current party strife, for the problem of rising or falling on the social ladder, of higher or lower, better or worse, man or woman is, has been, and always will be of lasting interest. When I took this theme from a real incident that I heard about some years ago, it seemed to me a suitable subject for a tragedy, not least because of the deep impression it made on me; for it still strikes us as tragic to see someone favoured by fortune go under, and even more to see a whole family die out. But the time may come when we shall have become so highly developed, so enlightened, that we shall be able to look with indifference at the brutal, cynical, heartless drama that life presents, when we shall have laid aside those inferior, unreliable instruments of thought called feelings, which will become superfluous and harmful once our organs of judgement have matured. The fact that the heroine arouses our pity merely depends on our weakness in not being able to resist the fear that the same fate might overtake us. A highly sensitive spectator may still not feel that such pity is enough, while the man with faith in the future will probably insist on some positive proposals to remedy the evil, some kind of programme, in other words. But in the first place there is no such thing as absolute evil, for after all, if one family falls another now has the good fortune to rise, and this alternate rising and falling is one of life's greatest pleasures, since happiness is only relative. And of the man with a programme who wants to remedy the unpleasant fact that the bird of prey eats the dove and lice eat the bird of prey, I would ask: why should it be remedied? Life is not so idiotically mathematical that only the big eat the small; it is just as common for a bee to kill a lion or at least to drive it mad.

If my tragedy makes a tragic impression on many people, that is their fault. When we become as strong as the first French revolutionaries, we shall feel as much unqualified pleasure and relief at seeing the thinning out in our royal parks of rotten, superannuated trees, which have stood too long in the way of others with just as much right to their time in the sun, as it does to see an incurably ill man finally die. Recently, my tragedy *The Father* was criticized for being so tragic, as though tragedies were supposed to be merry. One also hears pretentious talk about the joy of life, and theatre managers commission farces as though this joy of life lay in behaving stupidly and depicting people as if they were all afflicted with St Vitus' dance or congenital idiocy. I find the joy of life in its cruel and powerful struggles, and my enjoyment comes from getting to know something, from learning something. That is why I have chosen an unusual case, but an instructive one, an exception, in other words, but an important exception that proves the rule, even though it may offend those who love the commonplace. What will also bother simple minds is that my motivation of the action is not simple, and that there is not a single point of view. Every event in life – and this is a fairly new discovery! – is usually the result of a whole series of more or less deep-seated motives, but the spectator usually selects the one that he most easily understands or that best flatters his powers of judgement. Someone commits suicide. 'Business worries', says the business man. 'Unrequited love', say the ladies. 'Physical illness', says the sick man, 'Shattered hopes', says the failure. But it may well be that the motive lay in all of these things, or in none of them, and that the dead man concealed his real motive by emphasizing quite a different one that shed the best possible light on his memory.

I have motivated Miss Julie's tragic fate with an abundance of circumstances: her mother's 'bad' basic instincts; her father's improper bringing-up of the girl; her own nature and the influence her fiancé's suggestions had on her weak, degenerate brain; also, and more immediately: the festive atmosphere of Midsummer Night; her father's absence; her period; her preoccupation with animals; the intoxicating effect of the dance; the light summer night; the powerful aphrodisiac influence of the flowers; and finally chance that drives these two people together in a room apart, plus the boldness of the aroused man.

So my treatment has not been one-sidedly physiological nor obsessively psychological. I have not attributed everything to what she inherited from her mother nor put the whole blame on her period, nor just settled for 'immorality', nor merely preached morality – lacking a priest, I've left that to the cook!

I flatter myself that this multiplicity of motives is in tune with the times. And if others have anticipated me in this, then I flatter myself that I am not alone in my paradoxes, as all discoveries are called.

As regards characterization, I have made my figures fairly 'characterless' for the following reasons:

Over the years the word 'character' has taken on many meanings. Originally it no doubt meant the dominant trait in a person's soul-complex, and was confused with temperament. Later it became the middle-class expression for an automaton, so that an individual whose nature had once and for all set firm or adapted to a certain role in life, who had stopped growing, in short, was called a character, whereas someone who goes on developing, the skilful navigator on the river of life who does not sail with cleated sheets but tacks with every change in the wind in order to luff again, was called characterless. In a derogatory sense, of course, because he was so hard to catch, classify, and keep track of. This bourgeois concept of the immobility of the soul was transferred to the stage, which has always been dominated by the bourgeoisie. There a character became a man who was fixed and set, who invariably appeared drunk or comical or sad; and all that was needed to characterize him was to give him a physical defect, a club-foot, a wooden leg, a red nose, or some continually repeated phrase such as 'That's capital' or 'Barkis is willin', etc.[2] This elementary way of viewing people is still to be found in the great Molière. Harpagon is merely a miser, although he could have been both a miser and an excellent financier, a splendid father, and a good citizen; and even worse, his 'defect' is extremely advantageous to his daughter and his son-in-law, who are his heirs and therefore ought not to criticize him even if they do have to wait a while before jumping into bed together. So I do not believe in simple stage characters, and the summary judgements that authors pass on people – this one is stupid, that one brutal, this one jealous, that one mean – ought to be challenged by naturalists, who know how richly complicated the soul is, and who are aware that 'vice' has a reverse side, which is very much like virtue.

As modern characters, living in an age of transition more urgently hysterical at any rate than the one that preceded it, I have depicted the figures in my play as more split and vacillating, a mixture of the old and the new, and it seems to me not improbable that modern ideas may also have permeated down by way of newspapers and kitchen talk to the level of the servants. That is why the valet belches forth certain modern ideas from within his inherited slave's soul. And I would remind those who take exception to the characters in our modern plays talking Darwinism,[3] while holding up Shakespeare to our attention as a model, that the gravedigger in *Hamlet* talks the then-fashionable philosophy of Giordano Bruno (Bacon),[4] which is even more improbable since the means of disseminating ideas were fewer then than now. Besides, the fact of the matter is, 'Darwinism' has existed in every age, ever since Moses' successive history of creation from the lower animals up to man; it is just that we have discovered and formulated it now!

My souls (characters) are conglomerates of past and present stages of culture, bits out of books and newspapers, scraps of humanity, torn shreds of once fine clothing now turned to rags, exactly as the human soul is patched together, and I have also provided a little evolutionary history by letting the weaker repeat words stolen from the stronger, and allowed these souls to get 'ideas', or suggestions as they are called, from one another, from the milieu (the death of the siskin),[5] and from objects (the razor). I have also facilitated *Gedankenübertragung* via an inanimate medium (the Count's boots, the bell). Finally, I have made use of 'waking suggestion', a variation of hypnotic suggestion, which is now so well known and popularized that it cannot arouse the ridicule or scepticism it would have done in Mesmer's time.[6]

Miss Julie is a modern character, which does not mean that the man-hating half-woman has not existed in every age, just that she has now been discovered, has come out into the open and made herself heard. Victim of a superstition (one that has seized even stronger minds) that woman, this stunted form of human being who stands between man, the lord of creation, the creator of culture, [and the child],[7] is meant to be the equal of man or could ever be, she involves herself in an absurd struggle in which she falls. Absurd because a stunted form, governed by the laws of propagation, will always be born stunted and can never catch up with the one in the lead, according to the formula: A (the man) and B (the woman) start from the same point C; A (the man) with a speed of, let us say, 100 and B (the woman) with a speed of 60. Now, the question is, when will B catch up with A? – Answer: *Never!* Neither with the help of equal education, equal voting rights, disarmament, or temperance – no more than two parallel lines can ever meet and cross.

The half-woman is a type who thrusts herself forward and sells herself nowadays for power, decorations, honours, or diplomas as formerly she used to do for money. She is synonymous with degeneration. It is not a sound species for it does not last, but unfortunately it can propagate itself and its misery in the following generation; and degenerate men seem unconsciously to select their mates among them so that they increase in number and produce creatures of uncertain sex for whom life is a torment. Fortunately, however, they succumb, either because they are out of harmony with reality or because their repressed instincts erupt uncontrollably or because their hopes of attaining equality with men are crushed. The type is tragic, offering the spectacle of a desperate struggle against nature, a tragic legacy of Romanticism which is now being dissipated by Naturalism, the only aim of which is happiness. And happiness means strong and sound species. But Miss Julie is also a relic of the old warrior nobility that is now giving way to the new aristocracy of nerve and brain; a victim of the discord which a mother's 'crime' has implanted in a family; a victim of the errors of an age, of circumstances, and of her own deficient constitution, which together form the equivalent of the old-fashioned concept of Fate or Universal Law. The naturalist has erased guilt along with God, but he cannot erase the consequences of an action – punishment, prison, or the fear of it – for the simple reason that these consequences remain, whether or not he acquits the individual. For an injured party is less forbearing than those who have not been harmed may be, and even if her father found compelling reasons not to seek his revenge, his daughter would wreak vengeance on herself, as she does here, because of her innate or acquired sense of honour which the upper classes inherit – from where? From barbarism, from their original Aryan home, from the chivalry of the Middle Ages, all of which is very beautiful, but a real disadvantage nowadays where the preservation of the species is concerned. It is the nobleman's *harakiri*, the inner law of conscience which makes a Japanese slit open his own stomach when someone insults him, and which survives in modified form in that privilege of the nobility, the duel. That is why Jean, the servant, lives, but Miss Julie, who cannot live without honour, does not. The slave has this advantage over the earl, he lacks this fatal preoccupation with honour, and there is in all of us Aryans a little of the nobleman or Don Quixote, which means that we sympathize with the suicide who has committed a dishonourable act and thereby lost his honour, and we are noblemen enough to suffer when we see the mighty fallen and reduced to a useless corpse, yes, even if the fallen should rise again and make amends through an honourable act. The servant Jean is the type who founds a species, someone in whom the process of differentiation may be observed. He was a poor tied-worker's son and has now brought himself up to be a future nobleman. He has been quick to learn, has finely developed senses (smell, taste, sight) and an eye for beauty. He has already come up in the world, and is strong enough not to be concerned about exploiting other people. He is already a stranger in his environment, which he despises as stages in a past he has put behind him, and which he fears and flees, because people there know his secrets, spy out his intentions, regard his rise with envy, and look forward to his fall with pleasure. Hence his divided, indecisive character, wavering between sympathy for those in high positions and hatred for those who occupy them. He calls himself an aristocrat and has learnt the secrets of good society, is polished on the surface but coarse underneath, and already wears a frock-coat with style, although there is no guarantee that the body beneath it is clean.

He respects Miss Julie but is afraid of Kristin because she knows his dangerous secrets, and he is sufficiently callous not to allow the events of the night to interfere with his future plans. With the brutality of a slave and the indifference of a master he can look at blood without fainting, and shake off misfortune without further ado. That is why he escapes from the struggle unscathed and will probably end up the proprietor of a hotel; and even if *he* does not become a Romanian count, his son will probably go to university and possibly become a government official.

Moreover, the information he gives about life as the lower classes see it from below is quite important – when he speaks the truth, that is, which he does not often do, for he tends to say what is to his own advantage rather than what is true. When Miss Julie supposes that everyone in the lower classes finds the pressure from above oppressive, Jean naturally agrees since his intention is to gain sympathy, but he immediately corrects himself when he sees the advantage of distinguishing himself from the common herd.

Apart from the fact that Jean is rising in the world, he is also superior to Miss Julie in that he is a man. Sexually he is the aristocrat because of his masculine strength, his more finely developed senses, and his ability to take the initiative. His inferiority arises mainly from the social milieu in which he temporarily finds himself and which he will probably discard along with his livery.

His slave mentality expresses itself in his respect for the Count (the boots) and his religious superstition; but he respects the Count mainly as the occupant of the high position that he covets; and this respect remains even when he has conquered the daughter of the house and seen how empty that pretty shell is.

I do not believe there can be any love in a 'higher' sense between two such different natures, so I let Miss Julie imagine she loves him as a means of protecting or excusing herself; and I let Jean suppose he could fall in love with her if his social circumstances were different. I suspect that love is rather like the hyacinth, which has to put its roots down into the darkness *before* it can produce a strong flower. Here it shoots up, blooms, and goes to seed all in a moment, and that is why it dies so quickly.

Kristin, finally, is a female slave. Standing over the stove all day has made her subservient and dull; like an animal her hypocrisy is unconscious and she overflows with morality and religion, which serve as cloaks and scapegoats for her sins whereas a stronger character would have no need of them because he could bear his guilt himself or explain it away. She goes to church to unload her household thefts onto Jesus casually and deftly, and to recharge herself with a new dose of innocence.

Moreover, she is a minor character, and therefore my intention was only to sketch her in as

I did the Pastor and the Doctor in *The Father*, where I just wanted to depict ordinary people as country parsons and provincial doctors usually are. And if some people have found my minor characters abstract, that is because ordinary people are to some extent abstract when working; which is to say, they lack individuality and show only one side of themselves while performing their tasks, and as long as the spectator feels no need to see them from several sides, my abstract depiction will probably suffice.

Finally, where the dialogue is concerned I have somewhat broken with tradition by not making my characters catechists who sit around asking stupid questions in order to elicit a witty reply. I have avoided the symmetrical, mathematical artificiality of French dialogue and allowed my characters' brains to work irregularly as they do in real life, where no subject is ever entirely exhausted before one mind discovers by chance in another mind a cog in which to engage. For that reason the dialogue also wanders, providing itself in the opening scenes with material that is later reworked, taken up, repeated, expanded, and developed, like the theme in a musical composition.

The action is sufficiently fecund, and since it really concerns only two people I have restricted myself to them, introducing only one minor character, the cook, and letting the father's unhappy spirit hover above and behind it all. I have done this because it seems to me that what most interests people today is the psychological process; our inquiring minds are no longer satisfied with simply seeing something happen, we want to know how it happened. We want to see the strings, look at the machinery, examine the double-bottomed box, try the magic ring to find the seam, and examine the cards to discover how they are marked.

In this regard I have had in mind the monographic novels of the Goncourt brothers,[8] which have attracted me more than anything else in contemporary literature.

As for the technical aspects of the composition, I have, by way of experiment, eliminated all act divisions. I have done this because it seems to me that our declining susceptibility to illusion would possibly be disturbed by intervals, during which the spectator has time to reflect and thereby escape from the suggestive influence of the dramatist-hypnotist. My play probably runs for about an hour and a half, and since people can listen to a lecture, a sermon, or a conference session for that length of time or even longer, I imagine that a ninety-minute play should not exhaust them. I attempted this concentrated form as long ago as 1872, in one of my first attempts at drama, *The Outlaw*, but with scant success. I had written the piece in five acts, but when it was finished I noticed what a disjointed and disturbing effect it had. I burned it and from the ashes arose a single, long, carefully worked-out act of fifty printed pages, which played for a full hour. Consequently the form is not new, though it seems to be my speciality, and current changes in taste may well have made it timely. In due course I would hope to have an audience so educated that it could sit through a single act lasting an entire evening, but this will require some preliminary experimentation. Meanwhile, in order to provide resting places for the audience and the actors without breaking the illusion for the audience I have used three art forms that belong to the drama, namely the monologue, mime, and ballet, all of which were part of classical tragedy, monody having become monologue and the chorus, ballet.

Nowadays our realists have banished the monologue as implausible, but given appropriate motivation it becomes plausible, and I can therefore use it to advantage. It is perfectly plausible for a speaker to walk up and down alone in his room reading his speech aloud, that an actor should run through his role aloud, a servant girl talk to her cat, a mother prattle to her child, an old maid chatter to her parrot, or a sleeper talk in his sleep. And in order to give the actor a chance, for once, to work on his own and to escape for a moment from the hectoring of an author, I have not written out the monologues in detail but simply suggested them. For, in so far as it does not influence the action, it is quite immaterial what is said while asleep or to the cat, and a talented actor who is absorbed in the situation and mood of the play can probably improvise better than the author, who cannot calculate in advance just how much needs to be said, or for how long, before the theatrical illusion is broken.

As we know, some Italian theatres have returned to improvisation, producing actors who are creative in their own right, although in accordance with the author's intentions. This could really be a step forward or a fertile, new form of art that may well deserve the name *creative*.

Where a monologue would be implausible, I have resorted to mime, and here I leave the actor even greater freedom to create – and so win independent acclaim. But in order not to try the audience beyond its limits, I have let the music – well-motivated by the Midsummer dance, of course – exert its beguiling power during the silent action, and I would ask the musical director to select this music with great care so that the wrong associations are not aroused by recollections of the latest operettas or dance tunes or by the use of ultra-ethnographic folk music.

I could not have substituted a so-called crowd scene for the ballet I have introduced because crowd scenes are always badly acted, with a pack of simpering idiots seeking to use the occasion to show off and so destroy the illusion. Since ordinary people do not improvise their malicious remarks but use ready-made material that can be given a double meaning, I have not composed a malicious song but taken a little-known singing game which I noted down myself in the neighbourhood of Stockholm. The words do not hit home precisely, but that is the intention, for the cunning (weakness) of the slave does not permit him to attack directly. So: no speaking buffoons in a serious play, no coarse smirking over a situation that puts the lid on a family's coffin.

As for the scenery, I have borrowed the asymmetry and cropped framing of impressionist painting, and believe I have thereby succeeded in strengthening the illusion; for not being able to see the whole room or all the furniture leaves us free to conjecture, that is, our imagination is set in motion and we complete the picture ourselves. This also means that I have avoided those tiresome exits through doors, particularly stage doors that are made of canvas and sway at the slightest touch; they do not even permit an angry father to express his anger after a bad dinner by going out and slamming the door behind him 'so the whole house shakes'. (In the theatre it sways!) I have likewise restricted myself to a single set, both to allow the characters time to merge with their milieu and to break with the custom of expensive scenery. But when there is only a single set, one is entitled to demand that it be realistic. Yet nothing is more difficult than to get a room on stage to resemble a real room, no matter how easy the scene-painter finds erupting volcanoes and waterfalls. Even if the walls do have to be of canvas, it is surely time to stop painting shelves and kitchen utensils on them. There are so many other stage conventions in which we are asked to believe that we might be spared the effort of believing in painted saucepans.[9]

I have placed the rear wall and the table at an angle so that the actors have to play face on or in half profile when they are seated opposite each other at the table. In a production of *Aida* I have seen an angled backdrop which led the eye out into an unknown perspective, nor did it give the impression of having been put there simply to protest the boredom of straight lines.

Another perhaps desirable innovation would be the removal of the footlights. I understand that the purpose of lighting from below is to make the actors' faces fatter, but I would like to ask: why all actors have to have fat faces? Does not this underlighting obliterate a great many features in the lower parts of the face, especially around the jaws, distort the shape of the nose, and cast shadows over the eyes? Even if this is not the case, one thing is certain: it hurts the actors' eyes, so that their full expressiveness is lost, for footlights strike the retina in places that are normally protected (except in sailors, who cannot avoid seeing the sun reflected in water), and therefore we seldom see any other play of the eyes except crude glances either to the side or up to the balcony, when the white of the eye is visible. This probably also accounts for the tiresome way that actresses in particular have of fluttering their eyelashes. And when anyone on stage wants to speak with the eyes, the actor has sadly no alternative but to look straight at the audience, with which he or she then enters into direct contact outside the frame of the set – a bad habit rightly or wrongly called 'counting the house'.

Would not sufficiently strong side lighting (using parabolic reflectors or something similar) give the actor this new resource, of strengthening his facial expression by means of the face's greatest asset: the play of the eyes?

I have hardly any illusions about getting the actor to play for the audience and not with it, although this would be desirable. Nor do I dream of seeing the full back of an actor[10] throughout an important scene, but I do fervently wish that vital scenes should not be performed next to the prompter's box, as duets designed to elicit applause, but rather located to that part of the stage the action dictates. So, no revolutions, simply some small modifications, for to turn the stage into a room with the fourth wall removed and some of the furniture consequently facing away from the audience, would probably have a distracting effect, at least for the present.

When it comes to a word about make-up I dare not hope to be heard by the ladies, who would rather be beautiful than truthful. But the actor really might consider whether it is to his advantage to paint his face with an abstract character that will sit there like a mask. Picture an actor who gives himself a pronounced choleric expression by drawing a line with soot between his eyes, and suppose that, in spite of being in so permanently enraged a state, he needs to smile on a certain line. What a horrible grimace that would be! And how can the old man get the false forehead of his wig to wrinkle with anger when it is as smooth as a billiard ball?

In a modern psychological drama, where the subtlest movements of the soul should be mirrored more in the face than in gestures and sounds, it would probably be best to experiment with strong side lighting on a small stage and with actors wearing no make-up, or at least a bare minimum.

If we could then dispense with the visible orchestra with its distracting lights and faces turned towards the audience; if we could have the stalls raised so that the spectator's eyes were on a line higher than the actor's knees; if we could get rid of the private proscenium boxes with their giggling drinkers and diners; if we could have complete darkness in the auditorium; and finally, and most importantly, if we had a *small* stage and a *small* auditorium, then perhaps a new drama might arise, and the theatre would at least be a place where educated people might once again enjoy themselves. While waiting for such a theatre, we shall just have to go on writing for our desk drawers, preparing the repertoire whose time will come.

I have made an attempt! If it fails, there will surely be time to try again!

Notes

1. A 'poor man's Bible', a medieval work of edification richly illustrated with pictures from the Bible, aimed at those with little or no education.
2. The Yarmouth carrier Barkis' recurring phrase in *David Copperfield* (1850) by Charles Dickens (1812–70). Strindberg was otherwise an enthusiastic admirer of Dickens' novels.
3. Darwin's *Origin of Species* appeared in 1859 and had been translated into Swedish in 1871.
4. Italian philosopher Giordano Bruno (1548–1600) was burnt at the stake by the Inquisition. Bacon is the English statesman and philosopher Francis Bacon (1561–1626). The theory that Bacon wrote Shakespeare's plays was one to which Strindberg sometimes subscribed.
5. Siskin is translated as greenfinch by McGuinness.
6. The German doctor and practitioner of hypnotism Anton Mesmer (1734–1815) was mainly active in Vienna and Paris.
7. 'and the child' was inserted by the translator to make sense of a passage that closely echoes similar arguments in Strindberg's essays and letters on women. This paragraph has not been included in previous translations of the *Preface*.
8. Edmond (1822–96) and Jules (1830–70) de Goncourt together wrote several novels of psychological realism focusing closely on a central female character (e.g. *Soeur Philomène* (1861) and *Germaine Lacerteux* (1864)).
9. The use of real props was already standard practice at the court theatre of the Duke of Saxe-Meiningen (1826–1914), as was the kind of asymmetrical set design which Strindberg is advocating here.
10 The acting style associated with the newly opened Théâtre Libre in Paris; Strindberg was hoping this *Preface* would help sell the play to its director, André Antoine (1858–1943).

From *Miss Julie and Other Plays*, translated with an introduction and notes (edited) by Michael Robinson, Oxford and New York: Oxford University Press, 1998, pp. 56–68. Notes: pp. 291–3.

1.8 A New Art of the Stage (1907)

ARTHUR SYMONS

1

IN THE REMARKABLE EXPERIMENTS of Mr Gordon Craig, I seem to see the suggestion of a new art of the stage, an art no longer realistic, but conventional, no longer imitative, but symbolical. In Mr Craig's staging there is the incalculable element; the element that comes of itself, and cannot be coaxed into coming. But in what is incalculable there may be equal parts of inspiration and of accident. How much, in Mr Craig's staging, is inspiration, how much is accident? That is, after all, the important question.

Mr Craig, it is certain, has a genius for line, for novel effects of line. His line is entirely his own; he works in squares and straight lines, hardly ever in curves. He drapes the stage into a square with cloths; he divides these cloths by vertical lines, carrying the eye straight up to an immense height, fixing it into a rigid attention. He sets squares of pattern and structure on the stage; he forms his groups into irregular squares, and sets them moving in straight lines, which double on themselves like the two arms of a compass; he puts square patterns on the dresses, and drapes the arms with ribbons that hang to the ground, and make almost a square of the body when the arms are held out at right angles. He prefers gestures that have no curves in them; the arms held straight up, or straight forward, or straight out sideways. He likes the act of kneeling, in which the body is bent into a sharp angle; he likes a sudden spring to the feet, with the arms held straight up. He links his groups by an arrangement of poles and ribbons, something in the manner of a maypole; each figure is held to the centre by a tightly stretched line like the spoke of a wheel. Even when, as in this case, the pattern forms into a circle, the circle is segmented by straight lines.

This severe treatment of line gives breadth and dignity to what might otherwise be merely fantastic. Mr Craig is happiest when he can play at children's games with his figures, as in almost the whole of *The Masque of Love*.[1] When he is entirely his own master, not dependent on any kind of reality, he invents really like a child, and his fairy-tale comes right, because it is not tied by any grown-up logic. Then his living design is like an arabesque within strict limits, held in from wandering and losing itself by those square lines which rim it implacably round.

Then, again, his effects are produced simply. Most of the costumes in *The Masque of Love* were made of sacking, stitched roughly together. Under the cunning handling of the light, they gave you any illusion you pleased, and the beggars of the masque were not more appropriately clothed than the kings and queens. All had dignity, all reposed the eye.

The aim of modern staging is to intensify the reality of things, to give you the illusion of an actual room, or meadow, or mountain. We have arrived at a great skill in giving this crude illusion of reality. Our stage painters can imitate anything, but what they cannot give us is the emotion which the playwright, if he is an artist, wishes to indicate by means of his scene. It is the very closeness of the imitation which makes our minds unable to accept it. The eye rebounds, so to speak, from this canvas as real as wood, this wood as real as water, this water which is actual water. Mr Craig aims at taking us beyond reality; he replaces the pattern of the thing itself by the pattern which that thing evokes in his mind, the symbol of the thing. As, in conventional art, the artist unpicks the structure of the rose to build up a mental image of the rose, in some formal pattern which his brain makes over again, like a new creation from the beginning, a new organism, so, in this new convention of the stage, a plain cloth, modulated by light, can stand for space or for limit, may be the tight walls of a tent or the sky and the clouds. The eye loses itself among these severe, precise, and yet mysterious lines and surfaces; the mind is easily at home in them; it accepts them as readily as it accepts the convention by which, in a poetical play, men speak in verse rather than in prose.

Success, of course, in this form of art lies in the perfecting of its emotional expressiveness. Even yet Mr Craig has not done much more, perhaps, than indicate what may be done with the material which he finds in his hands. For instance, the obvious criticism upon his mounting of *Acis and Galatea*[2] is, that he has mounted a pastoral, and put nothing pastoral into his mounting. And this criticism is partly just. Yet there are parts, especially the end of Act I, where he has perfectly achieved the rendering of pastoral feeling according to his own convention. The tent is there with its square walls, not a glimpse of meadow or sky comes into the severe design, and yet, as the nymphs in their straight dresses and straight ribbons lie back laughing on the ground, and the children, with their little modern brown straw hats, toss paper roses among them, and the coloured balloons (which you may buy in the street for a penny) are tossed into the air, carrying the eye upward, as if it saw the wind chasing the clouds, you feel the actual sensation of a pastoral scene, of country joy, of the spring and the open air, as no trickle of real water in a trough, no sheaves of real corn among painted trees, no imitation of a flushed sky on canvas, could trick you into feeling it. The imagination has been caught; a suggestion has been given which strikes straight to the 'nerves of delight'; and be sure those nerves, that imagination, will do the rest, better, more effectually, than the deliberate assent of the eyes to an imitation of natural appearances.

Take again some of those drawings of stage scenery which we have not yet been able to see realized, the decoration for Hofmannsthal's *Elektra* and *Venice Preserved*, and for *Hamlet* and for *The Masque of London*. Everywhere a wild and exquisite scenic imagination builds up shadowy structures which seem to have arisen by some strange hazard, and to the sound of an unfamiliar music, and which are often literally like music in the cadences of their design. All have dignity, remoteness, vastness; a sense of mystery, an actual emotion in their lines and faint colours. There is poetry in this bare prose framework of stage properties, a quality of grace which is almost evasive, and seems to point out new possibilities of drama, as it provides new, scarcely hoped for, possibilities to the dramatist.

Take, for instance, *The Masque of London*. It is Piranesi, and it is London of today, seen in lineal vision, and it is a design, not merely on paper, but built up definitely between the wings of the stage. It is a vast scaffolding, rising out of ruins, and ascending to toppling heights; all its crazy shapes seem to lean over in the air, and at intervals a little weary being climbs with obscure patience. In one of the *Hamlet* drawings we see the room in the castle at Elsinore into which Ophelia is to come with her bewildered singing; and the room waits, tall, vague, exquisitely still and strange, a ghostly room, prepared for beauty and madness. There is another room, with tall doors and windows and abrupt pools of light on the floor; and another, with its significant shadows, its two enigmatic figures, in which a drama of Maeterlinck might find its own atmosphere awaiting it. And in yet another all is gesture; walls, half-opened doors, half-seen windows, the huddled people at a doorway, and a tall figure of a woman raised up in the foreground, who seems to motion to them vehemently. Colour cooperates with line in effects of rich and yet delicate vagueness; there are always the long, straight lines, the sense of height and space, the bare surfaces, the subtle, significant shadows, out of which Mr Craig has long since learned to evoke stage pictures more beautiful and more suggestive than any that have been seen on the stage in our time.

The whole stage art of Mr Craig is a protest against realism, and it is to realism that we owe whatever is most conspicuously bad in the mounting of plays at the present day. Wagner did some of the harm; for he refused to realize some of the necessary limitations of stage illusion, and persisted in believing that the stage artist could compete successfully with nature in the production of landscape, light, and shadow. Yet Wagner himself protested against the heaps of unrealizing detail under which Shakespeare was buried, in his own time, on the German stage, as he is buried on the English stage in our own. No scene-painter, no scene-shifter, no limelight man, will ever delude us by his moon or meadow or moving clouds or water. His business is to aid the poet's illusion, that illusion of beauty which is the chief excuse for stage plays at all, when once we have passed beyond the 'rose-pink and dirty drab', in Meredith's sufficing phrase, of stage romance and stage reality. The distinction, the incomparable merit, of Mr Craig is that he conceives his setting as the poet conceives his drama. The verse in most Shakespearean revivals rebounds from a backcloth of metallic solidity; the scenery shuts in the players, not upon Shakespeare's dream, but upon as nearly as possible 'real' historical *bric-à-brac*. What Mr Craig does, or would do if he were allowed to do it, is to open all sorts of 'magic casements', and to thrust back all kinds of real and probable limits, and to give at last a little scope for the imagination of the playwright who is also a poet.

I do not yet know of what Mr Craig is capable, how far he can carry his happy natural gifts towards mastery. But he has done so much already that I want to see him doing more; I want to see him accepting all the difficulties of his new art frankly, and grappling with them. For the staging of Maeterlinck, especially for such a play as *La Mort de Tintagiles* [Maeterlinck's *The Death of Tintagiles*, 1894], his art, just as it is, would suffice. Here are plays which exist anywhere in space, which evade reality, which do all they can to become disembodied in the very moment in which they become visible. They have atmosphere without locality, and that is what Mr Craig can give us so easily. But I would like to see him stage an opera of Wagner, *Tristan*, or the *Meistersinger* even. Wagner has perfected at Bayreuth his own conception of what scenery should be; he has done better than any one else what most other stage-craftsmen have been trying to do. He allows more than they do to convention, but even his convention aims at convincing the eye; the dragon of the *Ring* is as real a beast as Wagner could invent in his competition with nature's invention of the snake and the crocodile. But there are those who prefer Wagner's music in the concert-room to Wagner's music even at Bayreuth. Unless the whole aim and theory of Wagner was wrong, this preference is wrong. I should like, at least as an experiment, to see what Mr Craig would make of one of the operas. I am not sure that he would not reconcile those who prefer Wagner in the concert-room to this new kind of performance on the stage. He would give us the mind's attractive symbols of all these crude German pictures; he would strike away the footlights from before these vast German singers, and bring a ghostly light to creep down about their hoods and untightened drapings; he would bring, I think, the atmosphere of the music for the first time upon the stage.

Then I would like to see Mr Craig go further still; I would like to see him deal with a purely modern play, a play which takes place indoors, in the house of middle-class people. He should mount the typical modern play, Ibsen's *Ghosts*. Think of that room 'in Mrs Alving's country-house, beside one of the large fjords in Western Norway'. Do you remember the stage directions? In the first act the glimpse, through the glass windows of the conservatory, of 'a gloomy fjord landscape, veiled by steady rain'; in the second 'the mist still lies heavy over the landscape'; in the third the lamp burning on the table, the darkness outside, the 'faint glow from the conflagration'. And always 'the room as before'. What might not Mr Craig do with that room! What, precisely, I do not know; but I am sure that his method is capable of an extension which will take in that room, and, if it can take in that room, it can take in all of modern life which is of importance to the playwright.

2

Most people begin with theory, and go on, if they go on, to carry their theory into practice. Mr Gordon Craig has done a better thing, and, having begun by creating a new art of the stage on the actual boards of the theatre, has followed up his practical demonstration by a book of theory, in which he explains what he has done, telling us also what he hopes to do. *The Art of the Theatre* is a little book, hardly more than a pamphlet, but every page is full of original thought. Until I read it, I was not sure how much in Mr Craig's work was intention and how much happy accident. Whether or not we agree with every part of his theory, he has left no part unthought out. His theory, then, in brief, is this: he defines the theatre as 'a place in which the entire beauty of life can be unfolded, and not only the external beauty of the world, but the inner beauty and meaning of life'. He would make the theatre a temple in which a continual ceremony unfolds and proclaims the beauty of life, and, like the churches of other religions, it is to be, not for the few, but for the people. The art of the theatre is to be 'neither acting nor the play, it is not scene nor dance, but it consists of all the elements of which these things are composed: action, which is the very spirit of acting; words, which are the body of the play; line and colour, which are the very heart of the scene; rhythm, which is the very essence of dance'. The art of the theatre is addressed in the first place to the eyes, and the first dramatist spoke through 'poetic action, which is dance, or prose action, which is gesture'. In the modern theatre a play is no longer 'a balance of actions, words, dance and scene, but it is either all words or all scene'. The business of the stage director, who is to be the artist of the theatre, is to bring back the theatre to its true purpose. He begins by taking the dramatist's play, and sets himself to interpret it visibly on the boards. He reads it and gets his general impression:

> he first of all chooses certain colours, which seem to him to be in harmony with the spirit of the play, rejecting other colours as out of tune. He then weaves into a pattern certain objects – an arch, a fountain, a balcony, a bed – using the chosen object as the centre of his design. Then he adds to this all the objects which are mentioned in the play, and which are

necessary to be seen. To these he adds, one by one, each character which appears in the play, and gradually each movement of each character, and each costume.... While this pattern for the eye is being devised, the designer is being guided as much by the sound of the verse or prose as by the sense or spirit.

At the first rehearsal the actors are all in their stage dresses, and have all learned their words. The picture is there; the stage director then lights his picture. He then sets it in motion, teaching each actor to 'move across our sight in a certain way, passing to a certain point, in a certain light, his head at a certain angle, his eyes, his feet, his whole body in tune with the play'. The play is then ready to begin, we may suppose? By no means. 'There will not be any play,' says the stage director to the sheep-like playgoer who has been meekly drifting with the current of dialogue, 'there will not be any play in the sense in which you use the word. When,' he is told, 'the theatre has become a masterpiece of mechanism, when it has invented a technique, it will without any effort develop a *creative art* of its own.' And that art is to be created out of three things, the three bare necessities of the stage: action, 'scene and voice. By action is meant 'both gestures and dancing, the prose and poetry of action'; by scene, 'all which comes before the eye, such as the lighting, costume, as well as the scenery'; by voice,

the spoken word or the word which is sung, in contradiction to the word which is read; for the word written to be spoken and the word written to be read are two entirely different things.

Up to this last surprising point, which, however, has been stealthily led up to by a very persuasive semblance of logic, how admirable is every definition and every suggestion! Everything that is said is as self-evidently true as it is commonly and consistently neglected. Who will deny that the theatre is a visible creation of life, and that life is, first of all, action; to the spectator, in the stalls or in the street, a thing first of all seen, and afterwards, to the measure of one's care or capability, heard and understood? That life should be created over again in the theatre, not in a crude material copy, but in the spirit of all art, 'by means of things that do not possess life until the artist has touched them': this also will hardly be denied. This visible creation of life is (until the words come into it) like a picture, and it is made in the spirit of the painter, who fails equally if in his picture he departs from life, or if he but imitates without interpreting it. But is it not, after all, through its power of adding the life of speech to the life of motion that the theatre attains its full perfection? Can that perfection be attained by limiting its scope to what must remain its only materials to work with: action, scene and voice?

The question is this: whether the theatre is the invention of the dramatist, and of use only in so far as it interprets his creative work; or whether the dramatist is the invention of the theatre, which has made him for its own ends, and will be able, when it has wholly achieved its mechanism, to dispense with him altogether, except perhaps as a kind of prompter. And the crux of the question is this: that to the supreme critic of literature, to Charles Lamb, a play of Shakespeare, *Lear* or *Hamlet*, seems too great for the stage, so that when acted it loses the rarest part of its magic; while to the ideal stage director, to Mr Gordon Craig, *Hamlet* should not be acted because it is not so calculated for the theatre that it depends for its ultimate achievement on gesture, scene, costume, and all that the theatre has to offer; not, that is, that it is greater or less in its art, but that it is different. If we are content to believe both, each from his own point of view, is it not Craig who will seem the more logical? For why, it will be asked, should the greatest dramatist of the world have produced his greatest work under an illusion, that is for acting? Why should all the vital drama of the world, the only drama that is vital as literature, have been thus produced? If all this has indeed been produced under an illusion, and in the face of nature, how invaluable must such an illusion be, and how careful should we be to refrain from destroying any of its power over the mind!

An illusion is one thing, a compromise is another, and every art is made up in part of more and more ingenious compromises. The sculptor, who works in the round, and in visible competition with the forms of life, has to allow for the tricks of the eye. He tricks the eye that he may suggest, beyond the literal contour, the movement of muscle and the actual passage of blood under the skin, the momentary creasing of flesh; and he balances his hollows and bosses that he may suggest the play of air about living flesh: all his compromises are with fact, to attain life. May not the art of the dramatist be in like manner a compromise with the logic of his mechanism, a deliberate and praiseworthy twisting of ends into means? The end of technique is not in itself, but in its service to the artist; and the technique, which Mr Craig would end with, might, if it were carried out, be utilized by the dramatist to his own incalculable advantage.

Notes

1. A reference to the production of the masque from Purcell's *Dioclesian* in 1901.
2. A reference to the production of Handel's *Acis and Galatea* in 1902.

Originally published in *Studies in Seven Arts*, New York: Dutton, 1907.

1.9 **The Modern Drama** (1904)

MAURICE MAETERLINCK

Translated by Alfred Sutro

• • • T HE FIRST THING THAT strikes us in the drama of the day is the decay, one might almost say the creeping paralysis, of external action. Next we note a very pronounced desire to penetrate deeper and deeper into human consciousness, and place moral problems upon a high pedestal; and finally the search, still very timid and halting, for a kind of new beauty, that shall be less abstract than was the old.

It is certain that, on the actual stage, we have far fewer extraordinary and violent adventures. Bloodshed has grown less frequent, passions less turbulent; heroism has become less unbending, courage less material and less ferocious. People still die on the stage, it is true, as in reality they still must die, but death has ceased — or will cease, let us hope, very soon — to be regarded as the indispensable setting, the *ultima ratio*, the inevitable end, of every dramatic poem. In the most formidable crises of our life — which, cruel though it may be, is cruel in silent and hidden ways — we rarely look to death for a solution; and for all that the theatre is slower than the other arts to follow the evolution of human consciousness, it will still be at last compelled, in some measure, to take this into account.

When we consider the ancient and tragical anecdotes that constitute the entire basis of the classical drama; the Italian, Scandinavian, Spanish or mythical stories that provided the plots, not only for all the plays of the Shakespearian period, but also — not altogether to pass over an art that was infinitely less spontaneous — for those of French and German romanticism, we discover at once that these anecdotes are no longer able to offer us the direct interest they presented at a time when they appeared highly natural and possible, at a time, when at any rate, the circumstances, manners, and sentiments they recalled were not yet extinct in the minds of those who witnessed their reproduction.

To us, however, these adventures no longer correspond with a living and actual reality. Should a youth of our time love, and meet obstacles not unlike those which, in another order of ideas and events, beset Romeo's passion, we need no telling that his adventure will be embellished by none of the features that gave poetry and grandeur to the episode of Verona. Gone beyond recall is the entrancing atmosphere of a lordly, passionate life; gone the brawls in picturesque streets, the interludes of bloodshed and splendor, the mysterious poisons, the majestic, complaisant tombs! And where shall we look for that exquisite summer's night, which owes its vastness, its savor, the very appeal that it makes to us, to the shadow of an heroic, inevitable death that already lay heavy upon it? Divest the story of Romeo and Juliet of these beautiful trappings, and we have only the very simple and ordinary desire of a noble-hearted, unfortunate youth for a maiden whose obdurate parents deny him her hand. All the poetry, the splendor, the passionate life of this desire, result from the glamour, the nobility, tragedy, that are proper to the environment wherein it has come to flower; nor is there a kiss, a murmur of love, a cry of anger, grief or despair, but borrows its majesty, grace, its heroism, tenderness – in a word, every image that has helped it to visible form – from the beings and objects around it; for it is not in the kiss itself that the sweetness and beauty are found, but in the circumstance, hour, and place wherein it was given. Again, the same objections would hold if we chose to imagine a man of our time who should be jealous as Othello was jealous, possessed of Macbeth's ambition, unhappy as Lear; or, like Hamlet, restless and wavering, bowed down beneath the weight of a frightful and unrealisable duty.

These conditions no longer exist. The adventure of the modern Romeo – to consider only the external events which it might provoke – would not provide material for a couple of acts. Against this it may be urged that a modern poet, who desires to put on the stage an analogous poem of youthful love, is perfectly justified in borrowing from days gone by a more decorative setting, one that shall be more fertile in heroic and tragical incident. Granted; but what can the result be of such an expedient? Would not the feelings and passions that demand for their fullest, most perfect expression and development the atmosphere of today (for the passions and feelings of a modern poet must, in despite of himself, be entirely and exclusively modern) would not these suddenly find themselves transplanted to a soil where all things prevented their living? ...

But we need dwell no further on the necessarily artificial poems that arise from the impossible marriage of past and present. Let us rather consider the drama that actually stands for the reality of our time, as Greek drama stood for Greek reality, and the drama of the Renaissance for the reality of the Renaissance. Its scene is a modern house, it passes between men and women of today. The names of the invisible protagonists – the passions and ideas – are the same, more or less, as of old. We see love, hatred, ambition, jealousy, envy, greed; the sense of justice and idea of duty; pity, goodness, devotion, piety, selfishness, vanity, pride, etc. But although the names have remained more or less the same, how great is the difference we find in the aspect and quality, the extent and influence, of these ideal actors! Of all their ancient weapons not one is left them, not one of the marvelous moments of olden days. It is seldom that cries are heard now; bloodshed is rare, and tears not often seen. It is in a small room, round a table, close to the fire, that the joys and sorrows of mankind are decided. We suffer, or make others suffer, we love, we die, there in our corner; and it were the strangest chance should a door or a window suddenly, for an instant, fly open, beneath the pressure of extraordinary despair or rejoicing. Accidental, adventitious beauty exists no longer; there remains only an external poetry that has not yet become poetic. And what poetry, if we probe to the root of things – what poetry is there that does not borrow nearly all of its charm, nearly all of its ecstasy, from elements that are wholly external? Last of all, there is no longer a God to widen, or master, the action; nor is there an inexorable fate to form a mysterious, solemn, and tragical background for the slightest gesture of man; nor the somber and abundant atmosphere that was able to ennoble even his most contemptible weaknesses, his least pardonable crimes.

There still abides with us, it is true, a terrible unknown; but it is so diverse and elusive, it becomes so arbitrary, so vague and contradictory, the moment we try to locate it, that we cannot evoke it without great danger; cannot even, without the mightiest difficulty avail ourselves of it, though in all loyalty, to raise to the point of mystery the gestures, actions, and words of the men we pass every day. The endeavor has been made; the formidable, problematic enigma of heredity, the grandiose but improbable enigma of inherent justice, and many others beside, have each in their turn been put forward as a substitute for the vast enigma of the Providence or Fatality of old.

And it is curious to note how these youthful enigmas, born but of yesterday, already seem older, more arbitrary, more unlikely, than those whose places they took in an access of pride …

… Incapable of outside movement, deprived of external ornament, daring no longer to make serious appeal to a determined divinity or fatality, [the modern drama] has fallen back on itself, and seeks to discover, in the regions of psychology and of moral problems, the equivalent of what once was offered by exterior life. It has penetrated deeper into human consciousness; but has encountered difficulties there no less strange than unexpected.

To penetrate deeply into human consciousness is the privilege, even the duty, of the thinker, the moralist, the historian, novelist, and, to a degree, of the lyrical poet; but not of the dramatist. Whatever the temptation, he dare not sink into inactivity, become mere philosopher or observer. Do what one will, discover what marvels one may, the sovereign law of the stage, its essential demand, will always be *action*. With the rise of the curtain, the high intellectual desire within us undergoes transformation; and in place of the thinker, psychologists, mystic or moralist there stands the mere instinctive spectator, the man electrified negatively by the crowd, the man whose one desire it is to see something happen … And there are no words so profound, so noble and admirable, but they will soon weary us if they leave the situation unchanged, if they lead to no action, bring about no decisive conflict, or hasten no definite solution.

But whence is it that action arises in the consciousness of man? In its first stage it springs from the struggle between diverse conflicting passions. But no sooner has it raised itself somewhat – and this is true, if we examine it closely, of the first stage also – than it would seem to be solely due to the conflict between a passion and a moral law, between a duty and a desire. Hence the eagerness with which modern dramatists have plunged into all the problems of contemporary morality; and it may safely be said that at this moment they confine themselves almost exclusively to the discussion of these different problems.

This movement was initiated by the dramas of Alexandre Dumas *fils*, dramas which brought the most elementary of moral conflicts on to the stage; dramas, indeed, whose entire existence was based on problems such as the spectator, who must always be regarded as the ideal moralist, would never put to himself in the course of his whole spiritual existence, so evident is their solution. Should the faithless husband or wife be forgiven? Is it well to avenge infidelity by infidelity? Has the illegitimate child any rights? Is the marriage of inclination – such is the name it bears in those regions – preferable to the marriage for money? Have parents the right to oppose a marriage for love? Is divorce to be deprecated when a child has been born of the union? Is the sin of the adulterous wife greater than that of the adulterous husband? etc., etc.

Indeed, it may be said here that the entire French theatre of today, and a considerable proportion of the foreign theatre, which is only its echo, exist solely on questions of this kind, and on the entirely superfluous answers to which they give rise.

On the other hand, however, the highest point of human consciousness is attained by the dramas of Björnson, of Hauptmann, and, above all, of Ibsen. Here we touch the limit of the resources of modern dramaturgy. For, in truth, the further we penetrate into the consciousness of man, the less struggle do we discover. It is impossible to penetrate far into any consciousness unless that consciousness be very enlightened; for, whether we advance ten steps, or a thousand, in the depths of a soul that is plunged in darkness, we shall find nothing there that can be unexpected, or new; for darkness everywhere will only resemble itself. But a consciousness that is truly enlightened will possess passions and desires infinitely less exacting, infinitely more peaceful and patient, more salutary, abstract, and general, than are those that reside in the ordinary consciousness. Thence, far less struggle – or at least a struggle of far less violence – between these nobler and wiser passions; and this for the very reason that they have become vaster and loftier; for if there be nothing more restless, destructive and savage than a dammed-up stream, there is nothing more tranquil, beneficent and silent than the beautiful river whose banks ever widen.

Again, this enlightened consciousness will yield to infinitely fewer laws, admit infinitely fewer doubtful or harmful duties. There is, one may say, scarcely a falsehood or error, a prejudice, half-truth or convention, that is not capable of assuming, that does not actually assume, when the occasion presents itself, the form of a duty in an uncertain consciousness. It is thus that honor, in the chivalrous, conjugal sense of the word (I refer to the honor of the husband, which is supposed to suffer by the infidelity of the wife), that revenge, a kind of morbid prudishness, pride, vanity, piety to certain gods, and a thousand other illusions, have been, and still remain, the unquenchable source of a multitude of duties that are still regarded as absolutely sacred, absolutely incontrovertible, by a vast number of inferior consciousnesses. And these so-called duties are the pivot of almost all the dramas of the Romantic period, as of most of those of today. But not one of these somber, pitiless duties, that so fatally impel mankind to death and disaster, can readily take root in the consciousness that a healthy, living light has adequately penetrated; in such there will be no room for honor or vengeance, for conventions that clamor for blood. It will hold no prejudices that exact tears, no injustice eager for sorrow. It will have cast from their throne the gods who insist on sacrifice, and the love that craves for death. For when the sun has entered into the consciousness of him who is wise, as we may hope that it will some day enter into that of all men, it will reveal one duty, and one alone, which is that we should do the least possible harm and love others as we love ourselves; and from this duty no drama can spring.

Let us consider what happens in Ibsen's plays. He often leads us far down into human consciousness, but the drama remains possible only because there goes with us a singular flame, a sort of red light, which, somber, capricious – unhallowed, one almost might say – falls only on singular phantoms. And indeed nearly all the duties which from the active principle of Ibsen's tragedies are duties situated no longer within, but without, the healthy, illumined consciousness; and the duties we believe we discover outside this consciousness often come perilously near an unjust pride, or a kind of soured and morbid madness.

Let it not be imagined, however – for indeed this would be wholly to misunderstand me – that these remarks of mine in any way detract from my admiration for the great Scandinavian poet. For, if it be true that Ibsen has contributed few salutary elements to the morality of our time, he is perhaps the only writer for the stage who has caught sight of, and set in motion, a new, though still disagreeable poetry, which he has succeeded in investing with a kind of savage, gloomy beauty and grandeur (surely too savage and gloomy for it to become general or definitive); as he is the only one who owes nothing to the poetry of the violently illumined dramas of antiquity or of the Renaissance.

But, while we wait for the time when human consciousness shall recognize more useful passions and less nefarious duties, for the time when the world's stage shall consequently present more happiness and fewer tragedies, there still remains in the depths of every heart of loyal intention a great duty of charity and justice that eclipses all others. And it is perhaps from the struggle of this duty against our egoism and ignorance that the veritable drama of our century shall spring. When this goal has been attained – in real life as on the stage – it will be permissible perhaps to speak of a new theatre, a theatre of peace, and of beauty without tears.

Note

This excerpt from Maurice Maeterlinck's, *The Double Garden* (New York: Dodd, Mead & Co., 1904) was translated by Alfred Sutro.

1.10 Tragedy in Everyday Life (1896)

MAURICE MAETERLINCK

Translated by Dan Rebellato

THERE IS A TRAGIC aspect to everyday life which is much more real, much more profound and much more akin to our real self than the tragedy of grand adventures. We can all sense it but it's not easy to demonstrate, because the essence of this tragedy is neither merely psychological nor material. It's not in a determined struggle of one person against another, one desire against another, or the eternal battle between passion and duty. Rather it means making visible what is overwhelming in the simple fact of being alive. Rather it means making visible the existence of a soul in itself, in the midst of an unsleeping vastness. Instead, it would mean making heard, beneath the commonplace exchanges of reason and sentiment, the more sombre, uninterrupted dialogue between the individual and his destiny. Instead, it would mean making us follow the hesitant and painful footsteps of someone approaching or retreating from truth, from beauty, or from God. Again, it means showing us and making us listen to a thousand things that the tragic poets let us glimpse only in passing. But this is the essential point: should we not try to show those things first of all? What we hear within King Lear, within Macbeth, within Hamlet, for example, the mysterious song of the infinite, the portentous silence of souls or the gods, the eternity which rumbles towards the horizon, the destiny or fate that one perceives inwardly without being able to say how — is there any way of bringing those to the fore and, by some unprecedented reversal of roles, distancing us from the actors? And is it rash to claim that the real tragedy of life, the ordinary, deep and universal tragedy, only begins at the moment when what we call adventures, misfortunes and perils have passed? Does joy not have a longer reach than woe, and do some of its powers not touch the human soul? Is it absolutely necessary to wail like the Atrides for an eternal God to manifest himself in our life and does he never come to us when we are seated motionless beneath a lamp? When you think about it, isn't stillness, watched over by the stars, a terrible thing; and does a sense of life unfold in tumult or in silence? Shouldn't a great unease come over us when we are told at the end of those stories, 'They lived happily ever after'? What happens while they live happily? Isn't there more that is serious and substantial to be found in happiness, in a simple moment of peace, than in the excitation of the passions? Isn't it then that the march of time and many other hidden currents become finally visible as the hours rush headlong into nothing? Doesn't this all cut deeper than the dagger blows of conventional drama? Isn't it when a man believes himself to be protected against the approach of death that the strange and silent tragedy of being and infinity opens the doors to its own theatre? Is it when I flee from a drawn sword that my existence touches on its most interesting feature? Is it always in a kiss that it is most sublime? Are there not other moments in which one hears more constant and purer voices? Does your soul only flourish at night in the heart of a thunderstorm? You might well think that's what we've always believed. Most of our tragic authors find dramatic life only in violence and history; and one might well say that all of our theatre is anachronistic and that the dramatic art is as behind the times as sculpture. It's not the same for the fine arts or serious music, for example, which recognized the need to bring out those hidden qualities, grave and astonishing of life today. They realized that a life that discards surface decoration only grows in depth, meaning and spiritual weight. A good painter won't paint Marius, conqueror of the Cimbri, or the assassination of the Duke of Guise any more because the psychology of victory or murder is primitive and abnormal, and the empty clamour of a violent act drowns out more profound but hesitant and discreet voices. He or she will depict a house lost in the countryside, an open door at the end of a corridor, a face or hands at rest; these simple images could add something to our awareness of life; and once we have it, we can never lose it.

But like those mediocre painters who waste their time in painting historical scenes, our tragic authors devote their works to the violence of their stories. And they claim it's entertainment to show us the same kinds of thing that used to delight barbarians accustomed to the conspiracies, murders and treacheries they show us. But most of our lives are spent far away from blood, cries and swords, and the tears of men have become silent, invisible and almost spiritual ...

When I go to the theatre, I feel like I am spending a few hours among my ancestors, who had a simple, harsh and brutal understanding of life, which I no longer recognize and in which I can no longer take part. I watch a deceived husband kill his wife, a woman poisoning her lover, a son avenge his father, a father who slays his children, children who bring about their father's death, assassinated kings, virgins deflowered, merchants imprisoned, and that whole sublime tradition – alas! So superficial, and so materialistic: blood, fake tears and death. Who can show me someone who doesn't just have one *idée fixe* and can take the time to live without having to put a rival or a mistress to death?

I had come in hope of seeing something of how life is tied to its source and its mystery by links which I have neither the opportunity nor strength to perceive every day. I had come in hope of glimpsing a moment of the beauty, grandeur and gravity of my humble everyday existence. I had hoped I might be shown some kind of presence, some power or some god who lived alongside me in my own room. I longed for unfamiliar heightened moments among my most mundane hours; and mostly I just got a man telling me at great length of his jealousy, or why he is going to poison someone or why he has to kill himself.

I admire Othello, but he seems to me not to live the noble daily life of a Hamlet, who, because he does not act, has time to live. Othello is admirably jealous. But isn't it perhaps an old error to think that it is at the moments where we are possessed by this kind of passion (or others of similar intensity) that we truly live? I have come to believe that an old man sitting in his armchair, just waiting beneath his lamp, hearing without knowing it all the eternal laws which range around his house, interpreting without understanding the silence of doors and windows and, in the frail voice of the light, giving himself up to the presence of his soul and his destiny, his head slightly inclined to one side, not realizing that the powers of the world all throng around him, watching over him in the room like attentive servants, unaware that the sun itself is keeping the little table on which he leans from tipping into the void, and that there is no star in the heavens nor an impulse in the soul which is indifferent to the movement of a closing eyelid or a rising thought – I have come to believe that this motionless old man lives, in reality, a profound, more human and more universal life than the lover who strangles his mistress, the captain who carries off the battle, or 'the husband who avenges his honour'.

It will perhaps be said that a motionless life would be barely visible, that one really needs to animate it with varied movement and that these varied movements must necessarily resolve themselves only into the small number of passions employed hitherto. I'm not so sure a static theatre is impossible. As far as I can see, it already exists. The majority of Aeschylus' tragedies are static tragedies. I'm not talking about *Prometheus* and *The Suppliants* where nothing happens; but the great tragedy of *The Libation Bearers*, certainly the most terrible drama of antiquity, which lurks like a bad dream around the tomb of Agamemnon, until murder erupts, like a bolt of lightning, from of the accumulated layering of prayers. From this point of view, look at several other of the best ancient tragedies: *Eumenides, Antigone, Electra, Oedipus at Colonnus*. 'They admired,' says Racine in his preface to *Berenice*, 'they admired Sophocles' *Ajax*, which consists only in Ajax killing himself from sorrow after his rage at being refused the armour of Achilles. They admired *Philoctetes*, the whole of which concerns Ulysses coming to seize Hercules' arrows. *Oedipus* itself, although full of recognition scenes, is less substantial than the simplest contemporary tragedy.'

What is this but motionless life? Usually, there isn't even psychological action, which is a thousand times better than material action and which it seems impossible to do without, but which it manages nonetheless to do away with or to reduce remarkably, so as not to let anything get in the way of the place of man in the universe. In these plays, we are no longer among barbarians, and man no longer acts in the heat of primitive passions which are not the only things of interest about him. We have time to watch him in repose. It's no longer a matter of a singular violent moment in existence, but of existence itself. There are thousands of laws, more powerful and revered than the laws of passion; but these gentle laws, discreet and silent, like everything endowed with irresistible force, are only sensed in the twilight and contemplation in the still hours of one's life.

When Ulysses and Neoptolemus come to demand Hercules' armour from Philoctetes, their action is in itself as simple and unremarkable as that of a man today going into a house to visit a sick person, a traveller who knocks on the door of an inn, or a mother who waits by the fire for her child to return. Sophocles cursorily stamps the character of his heroes. But perhaps the main interest of tragedy is found not in the struggle between cunning and loyalty, between patriotism, resentment and stubborn pride? There is something else; and that is the higher existence of man which must be made visible. The poet adds to ordinary life that unknown element which is the secret of poets, and all at once it appears in its extraordinary grandeur, in its submission to mysterious powers, in its infinite connections and its solemn woe. A chemist releases some mysterious droplets into a test tube which only seems to contain clear water: and at once a world of crystals springs up at its rim and reveals to us everything that has been in suspension, where our partial vision saw nothing. Thus in *Philoctetes*, the slender psychology of its three principal characters is just the glass of the test tube containing the clear water of ordinary life into which the poet releases the revelatory droplets of his genius ...

Also, is it not in the words, rather than the actions, that we find the beauty and grandeur of the most beautiful and grandest tragedies? Do we find these qualities only in words that accompany and explain action? No; there must be something more than the superficially necessary dialogue.

It is almost only those words which at first appear unnecessary which give the work its value. It is in them that the soul may recognize itself. Alongside the necessary dialogue, there is almost always another dialogue which seems superfluous. Look carefully and you will see that it's the only thing that the soul hears deeply, because this is the only place where the soul is addressed. You will also recognize that it's the quality and expanse of this empty dialogue which determines the quality and the inexpressible reach of the work. For certain in ordinary dramas the necessary dialogue in no way responds to reality; and what makes for the mysterious beauty of the most beautiful tragedies is found precisely in the words which are spoken alongside the apparently rigid truth. What sustains the poem are those words that are true to the deeper and incomparably more immediate truth of the invisible soul. One might even say that the poem gets closer to beauty and to a higher truth to the extent that it eliminates words which explain action and replaces them with words which explain not what is sometimes called 'the state of the soul' but those unknown elusive and ceaseless struggles of the soul towards its beauty and its truth. This is also the measure of how far it approaches true life. It happens to everyone in their everyday life that they have to negotiate very serious situations through words. Imagine it for a second. At such moments, is it always (or ever?) what you say or how you respond that matters the most? Are other forces, other words which we do not hear, at work determining what happens? What I say often counts for little; but my presence, the attitude of my soul, my future and past, what will be born in me, what has died in me, a secret thought, the stars supporting me, my destiny, thousands of mysteries encircling me, surrounding you − that is what speaks to you at that moment of tragedy and that is what answers. Beneath each of my words and beneath each of yours, all of that exists, and it is principally this that we see and principally this that we hear, despite ourselves. If you appeared, you 'the scorned husband', 'the deceived lover', 'the abandoned wife', with the intention of killing me, it is not my most eloquent pleas that would stay your hand. But it may be that you will come up against one of these unforeseen forces and that my soul, which knows that they throng around me, utters a secret word which disarms you. Those are the realms in which these episodes are decided, this is the dialogue for whose echo one should listen. And it's that echo − extremely weak and intermittent, it's true − which one really hears in a few of those works which I have spoken a little about. But couldn't one try to get a little nearer to those realms in which everything takes place 'really'?

I think the effort is being made. Recently, working on *The Master Builder*, the play of Ibsen's in which this 'second level' dialogue resonates most tragically, I tried once again to clumsily penetrate its secrets. And yet, these are the analogous traces of the hand of the same blind man on the same wall and which direct themselves also towards the same glimmers. In *The Master Builder*, I would asked what has the poet added to life to make it appear so strange, so profound and so disturbing beneath its apparent simplicity? It's not easy to discern and the old master keeps more than one secret. It is even as though what he wanted to say is nothing against what he was *compelled* to say. He has released certain powers of the soul which had never been given their freedom, and perhaps he was taken over by them. 'See, Hilde,' exclaims Solness, 'See! There is sorcery in you just as there is in me. It is that sorcery which stirs up the powers out there. And we *have* to accept them. Whether you want to or not, you *have to*.'[1]

There is sorcery in them just as in all of us. Hilde and Solness are, I think, the first heroes who felt themselves to be living in the environment of their soul and the essential life that they have discovered in themselves, beyond everyday life, terrifies them. Hilde and Solness are two souls that have glimpsed their position in the true life. There is more than one way to know someone. There are, for example, two or three people that I see more or less every day. It is probable for a long time that I will only identify them by their gestures, their outward and inward habits, their ways of feeling, acting and thinking. But, in a really long friendship, there comes a curious moment when we perceive, as it were, the exact place of our friend in relation to the unknown which surrounds us, and the attitude of destiny towards him. It's from that moment on that he really belongs to us. We have seen once and for all the way things are through his eyes. We know that however much he withdraws to the privacy of his home, and stays as still as he can for fear of disturbing something in the great chasms of the future, his caution will do no good, and those numberless things destined for him will knock at each of his doors in turn, and find him wherever he hides himself. And yet, we also know that he will go out, seeking pointlessly for any adventure. He will always come back empty-handed. The day our eyes are opened like this, it is as though a perfect science beyond the scope of mere reason were born in our soul, and we know that events which may seem to be within his grasp, within such a man's reach, will never come to pass.

From that moment, a special part of the soul presides over the friendship even of the dullest and the most humble. There is a kind of transposition of life. And when we bump into one of those who knows us like this, while all the time talking to us about the snow falling or the women passing by, there is in each of us a little something that acknowledges, examines, questions without knowing it; takes an interest in circumstances and speaks of events impossible for us to understand ...

I believe that Hilde and Solness find themselves in that state and understand each other like this. Their conversations do not resemble anything that we have heard before now, because the poet has tried to contain that internal and external dialogue in the same language. Who knows what new forces govern this sleepwalking drama? Everything said in it both conceals and reveals the sources of an unknown life. And if at times we are overwhelmed, we must not lose sight of the fact that, to our dim eyes, our soul often seems a wholly deranged force, and that there are many aspects to mankind more fertile, more profound and more interesting than those of reason and intelligence ...

Notes

1. The quotation comes from near the end of Act 2. See Henrik Ibsen, *Four Major Plays*, trans. James MacFarlane and Jens Arup, ed. James MacFarlane. World's Classics. 2nd edn. Oxford: Oxford University Press, 1994, p. 323.

The extract is from *Le Trésor des Humbles* (The Treasure of the Humble), Préface de Marc Rombaut, Lecture d'Albert Spinette. Espace Nord. Bruxelles: Éditions Labor, 1986, pp. 101–10. Translated by Dan Rebellato. This is a chapter from Maeterlinck's book of poetic-philosophical meditations, *The Treasure of the Humble*. Here he defends the stillness, silence and mystery of his plays, which stand in sharp contrast to the clamorous action of Romantic drama, the intricate plotting of the well-made play and the mundane detail of naturalism. Instead he argues for a kind of anti-dramatic drama of stillness and contemplation, the better to reveal our place in the mysterious universe.

1.11 On the Complete Pointlessness of Accurate Staging (1891)

PIERRE QUILLARD

Translated by Dan Rebellato

Sir,

IN THE 15TH APRIL issue of *Revue d'Art Dramatique*, your contributor M. Pierre Véber reported, with politely ironic neutrality, on the performance at the Théâtre d'Art, on Friday 27 March.[1] He briefly refers to one of the aspects of what we attempted that evening, in *The Girl with the Severed Hands*: a complete simplification of the dramatic means. Please permit me a little space to set out in a little more detail and without obscurity the innovation in staging I attempted. Also, the *mise en scène* necessarily depends on the dramatic system adopted, and since there are symbols, the *mise en scène* is a sign and a symbol in itself.

Nowhere is the inanity of Naturalism more clearly apparent than in the theatre. Think of the splendours of the Théâtre Libre. Time and time again, we've watched Monsieur Antoine die there with accomplished art (for want of a better word); men and women, whores and pimps have had the most banal conversations there and made the crudest remarks, *just like in real life*; each statement, on its own, was truthful and the author might have heard them from his caretaker, his lawyer, or from people passing on the street or any dull ordinary person you like. But this dialogue showed nothing whatever of how one character differed from his neighbour or what constitutes in him the *quid proprium* that distinguishes one monad from another. To create the complete illusion of life, it was thought clever to build scrupulously accurate sets, real fountains murmuring centre stage and meat dripping blood on the butcher's stall.[2] And yet, despite the meticulous care with which the whole exterior of things is represented, the drama was misplaced and unfathomable and the illusion entirely lacking. The truth is that Naturalism, by which I mean making use of specific facts, of trifling and arbitrary documents, is the very opposite of theatre.

The whole of drama is above all a synthesis: Prometheus, Orestes, Oedipus, Hamlet, Don Juan are creatures of a general humanity, in whom a single-minded and commanding passion is embodied with extraordinary intensity. The poet has breathed supernatural life into them; he created them by force of language, and set them off across the world, pilgrims in eternity. Dress them in tattered smocks and if Aeschylus or Shakespeare has crowned them, they will be kings, and their absent ermine robes will shine forth joyously, if they gleam in the verse. A universe unfolds around them, sadder or more magnificent than our own, and the grotesque backcloths of the travelling circus are the dream architecture that the poet places in the mind of the willing spectator. *The word creates the set and everything else as well.*

So what's left of the stagehand's job? All that's required is that the staging does not disturb the illusion in any way and to do that it should be as simple as possible. I write 'a marvellous palace'; even if a scene-painter were somehow to represent it using the most ingenious artistry they can devise, the effect produced by all that trickery will never equal 'a marvellous palace' for anyone; in each person's soul these words evoke a particular, personal image, which will be in conflict with any crude scenic representation; far from aiding the free play of the imagination, painted canvas impairs it. *The set must be a pure ornamental fiction which completes the illusion with colour and lines analogous to the drama.* Generally, a backdrop and some moveable drapes are all you need to suggest the infinite multiplicity of time and place. The spectator will not be distracted from the action any more by noises in the wings, or an incongruous prop; he will give himself up completely to the will of the poet and see, depending on his soul, terrible and enchanting figures and imaginary worlds that none but he will enter; the theatre will be what it has to be: *a chance to dream.*

This aesthetic is by no means new, indeed it is as old as history. In the first act of *The Recognition of Śakuntalā*, on a motionless chariot, the driver mimes the passion of a race; the horses, he says, 'thrust the air apart, their wake / Is thunder; in our tracks they leave for dust / The very dust they raised ...';[3] for those willing souls who were present at the traditional recital of this ancient masterpiece, this is undoubtedly a more perfect illusion of a wild-horse ride than that given to those sophisticated Parisians, sitting in the *Variétés* watching the horses of *Paris Pont de Mer*;[4] the latter know perfectly well that it's nothing more than ingenious stage machinery, but the former wouldn't even have contemplated such childish artifice. We need only recall Greek theatre and its masks, or the featureless stages of classical tragedy. These are similar means by which an informed spectator would collaborate in the drama: why would he not give himself, now as then, to this sacred art when he happily puts up with vaudeville's most wretched contrivances?

At least for one evening the audience didn't have to ignore the inadequacy of the set: listening to and deservedly applauding Mme Rachilde's *Lady Death*;[5] however, the characters were *contemporary* and perhaps one might have expected some confusion or surprise; but they existed, *in themselves*, over and above their time and its happenstance, with such independence that no one noticed how unusual the middle-class dining room was in which they moved; for everyone, the stage perfectly represented the sombre, black-draped smoking room where Paul Dartigny dies, since the dialogue hung funeral veils over your face and deepened the mysterious and sacred shadow around you.

It would be childish arrogance to say that all drama should be like this in the future. But we might say that an art form of this kind in which the poet, putting aside all other means and using only the word and the human voice, has no room for trickery – the work stands quite naked, stripped of make-up, reveals right away its native beauty or its original stain. Perhaps this kind of honesty is arrogant, but nothing is without risk.

Notes

1. Pierre Véber, 'Au Théâtre d'Art', *Revue d'Art Dramatique*, 22 (1891): 115–17. The passage to which Quillard seems particularly to be responding is: 'finally, Mr Quillard's experiment may be summarized as follows: a complete simplification of the dramatic means; a narrator, placed at the corner of the proscenium describes the stage, the setting and the action. The main focus is on poetic language. Theatre as such disappears entirely, to make way for a series of declamations in dialogue form, a kind of decorative poetry. Maeterlinck never went so far' (p. 117). – *Translator.*

2. On 20 October 1888, Antoine staged Giovanni Verga's *Cavelleria Rusticana* and Fernand Icres' *The Butchers* and his decisions to create a working fountain for the Verga and to hang real meat in the butcher's shop set attracted both admiration and ridicule. – *Translator*.

3. I have quoted these lines from a modern translation of this first-millennium Sanskrit play: Kālidāsa, *The Recognition of Śakuntalā*, trans. W. J. Johnson, World's Classics, Oxford: Oxford University Press, 2001, pp. 7–8. The play was eventually performed at the Théâtre de l'Oeuvre in December 1895. – *Translator*.

4. *Paris Port de Mer* was a spectacular theatrical revue by Henri Blondeau and Hector Monréal which opened at the Théâtre des Variétés in March 1891 and included a celebrated staging of a horse race. – *Translator*.

5. Mme Rachilde's *Lady Death* (*Madame La Mort*) was performed on the same evening as Quillard's *The Girl with the Severed Hands*. Its central character is Paul Dartigny. – *Translator*.

Pierre Quillard (1864–1912) was a poet, playwright and journalist who published his first play, *The Girl with the Severed Hands,* in *La Pléiade* (1886), a journal he had co-founded two years earlier. This mystical work was performed at the Théâtre d'Art in March 1891, in a visionary and experimental production. When a reviewer in *Revue d'Art Dramatique* lightly mocked the evening, Quillard wrote a celebrated defence of Symbolist theatre practices (and attacked Naturalism as he did so), which we publish here. His 'On the Complete Pointlessness of Accurate Staging' is translated for the present volume by Dan Rebellato from Pierre Quillard, 'De l'inutilité absolue de la mise on sciène exacte', *Revue d'Art Dramatique,* 22 (1 May 1891): 180–3.

Part 2
The Historical Avant-Garde: Performance and Innovation

Timeline

	Social, cultural and political context	Theatre
1893	*On the Psychical Mechanism of Hysterical Phenomena*: Sigmund Freud and Josef Breuer	
1895	First films made	
1896		*King Ubu* (*Ubu Roi*): Alfred Jarry, Paris
1900	*The Interpretation of Dreams*: Sigmund Freud	
1901	*A Dream Play*: August Strindberg	
1902	First transatlantic radiotelegraph message (Guglielmo Marconi)	
1907		Alfred Jarry dies
1909		*Foundation and Manifesto of Futurism* published on the front page of Parisian newspaper *Le Figaro*
		Murderer the Women's Hope: Oskar Kokoschka
1910		First Futurist *serate*, Italy
1911		*On the Art of the Theatre*: Edward Gordon Craig
		Manifesto of Futurist Playwrights (*The Pleasure of Being Booed*)
1912	The sinking of the *Titanic*	
1913	Post-Impressionism and Cubism introduced in New York	Marinetti's *Variety Theatre Manifesto*
1914	Start of the First World War (1914–1918)	
1916		Dada exhibitions and Cabaret Voltaire, Zurich
1917	America enters the First World War	*The Breasts of Tiresias*: Guillaume Apollinaire
	Russian Revolution	First Dada Exhibition, Paris
	Carl Jung's *The Psychology of the Unconscious* translated into English	Tristan Tzara launches the movement Dada and publishes *Dada 1*
	Marcel Duchamp, famous for his Dada 'ready-mades', submits his sculpture *Fountain* (a porcelain urinal, signed by R. Mutt) to an exhibition of the Society for Independent Artists in New York	Pablo Picasso creates the designs for Jean Cocteau's *Parade*, Paris
1918	End of the First World War	*Baal*: Bertolt Brecht (first produced in 1923)
		Gas: Georg Kaiser, Berlin
1919	*The Cabinet of Dr Caligari* (Expressionist film)	
1920	The League of Nations formed	First Paris Dada event

	Social, cultural and political context	Theatre
1921		*The Wedding on the Eiffel Tower*: Jean Cocteau
		Dada Festival at the Salle Gaveau, with performance of work by Tristan Tzara and André Breton
1922	Mussolini elected to power in Italy	
1924		*First Surrealist Manifesto*: André Breton
1925		*The Spurt of Blood*: Antonin Artaud (unperformed until the late 1960s)
1926		Théâtre Alfred Jarry founded in Paris by Antonin Artaud and Roger Vitrac
1927	*Metropolis* (Expressionist film by Fritz Lang, Germany)	
1929	Surrealist artist Salvador Dalí collaborates with the Surrealist film director Luis Buñuel on the film *Un Chien Andalou* (*An Andalusian Dog*)	*The Second Surrealist Manifesto*: André Breton
1930		*The Public*: Federico García Lorca (unfinished play)
1932		*First Manifesto of the Theatre of Cruelty*: Antonin Artaud
1933		*Second Manifesto of The Theatre of Cruelty*: Antonin Artaud
1936	Start of the Spanish Civil War (1936–9) First public television broadcast	Federico García Lorca dies

Introduction

MAGGIE B. GALE

What has our culture lost in 1980 that the *avant-garde* had in 1890? Ebullience, idealism, confidence, the belief that there was plenty of territory to explore, and above all the sense that art, in the most disinterested and noble way, could find the necessary metaphors by which a radically changing culture could be explained to its inhabitants. (Hughes 1991: 9)

The Modernists struggled against entrenched rules and conventions, yet never challenged the guardians of established cultural institutions ... avant-garde art was not only characterized by opposition, protest, negativity; it also experimented with new forms of expression and antici-pated in its creations a liberated arts practice. (Berghaus 2005: 39)

THE HISTORICAL AVANT-GARDE, WHICH provides the overarching framework for the materials included in Part 2, is named as such here and elsewhere in order to distin-guish between it and 'new' avant-garde art and performance which emerged towards the end of the twentieth century, some materials from which can be found in Part 5. It is historical in that it is firmly located within the turbulence of Europe at the end of the nineteenth century and the years immediately preceding and following the First World War (1914–18). The historical avant-garde includes a wide range of art practices. Here we focus on four prominent and inter-connecting movements within the historical avant-garde – Dada, Surrealism, Expressionism and Futurism – often characterized by their anti-establishment, anti-traditionalist, politically and socially inflammatory and intertextual or hybrid nature.

The historical avant-garde: a context

The performance and critical texts included here provide a series of pointers that help navigate a map of experimental practice which burst the seams of conventional theatre at the time, and have continued to influence the development of performance as a social practice, aesthetic proposition and cultural product in the twenty-first century. Many of these movements proposed a radical transformation in the meaning and function of theatre as well as challenged existing forms and practices. They also linked theatre to developments in innovative art practices as opposed to those in literature and mark a definite turning point in the move away from performance being dominated by literary text.

A number of historians and critics have noted the elitism inherent in a great deal of modernist thinking and arts practice thus: 'the avant-garde typically expresses itself through obscure and innovative techniques deliberately resisting easy assimilation into popular or mass culture' (Edgar and Sedgwick 2008: 33). The paradox, which will become apparent as this introduction develops, is that much avant-garde theorizing about the role and function of theatre and performance sought to respond to and engage the 'masses' and counter the lack of representation or connection they found in the bourgeois theatres of the day. However, John Carey suggests that the modernists stigmatized what they saw as 'the masses', the crowd, the common man, playing into cultural anxieties about the new levels of relatively increased social agency which the proletariat had access to during the early twentieth century (see Carey 1992). Numerous theoretical and performance texts produced by the historical avant-garde made reference to the validity of popular cultural and performance forms which they perceived as the art of the masses. For example, they embraced popular non-literary performance – circus, variety or, as in the case of Antonin Artaud, traditional non-Western performance styles (Balinese dance) – as a means of extricating theatre and performance from the stranglehold of the bourgeois and the literary, the text, the word. In practice this was achieved on different levels and to varying degrees, but it is clear that an antagonism towards the domination of literary text, which we also find in some of the postmodern contemporary practice explored in Part 5 of this volume, finds its roots in the ideas and performance practices of the historical avant-garde, at the opposite end of the century.

The end of the nineteenth and beginning of the twentieth century were times of great social and cultural upheaval, and the devastation caused by the First World War had a profound impact globally and locally. The historical avant-garde both developed before and cut across the war and operated, albeit in a constant state of flux, until well into the middle of the twentieth century. Whilst it often removed itself from a direct engagement with the 'class' war (see Part 3), many practitioners whose work is aligned with the historical avant-garde were driven by political concerns from one end of the political spectrum to another – from the political left to fascism. However, these artists of the historical avant-garde shared a subversive and countercultural agenda. The desire to create social and cultural disturbance through art was paramount. As had the Naturalists and the Symbolists before them, these artists asked questions about the function, purpose and cultural value of the artwork. They innovated and embraced a wide variety of artistic forms – poetry, film, photography, painting and performance – often creating hybrid performance events.

The historical avant-garde: definitions

If we examine the origins of the term 'avant-garde' we can see its close connection with a utopian vision of society in which artists and their artworks are at the vanguard of visionary social developments. Thus Aronson notes:

> The historical roots of the term 'avant-garde' lie in French military terminology. The term was apparently first tied to art by Henri de Saint Simon (1760–1825) ... In his last major work *Opinions littéraires, philosophiques et industrielles* (1925) [he] ... proposed a utopian society to be led by a triumvirate of scientists, industrialist-artisans, and artists, with the last constituting an elite force within this group of leaders. (Aronson, 2000: 6)

The historical avant-garde set out to restructure 'the way in which an audience views and experiences the very act of theatre, which in turn must transform the way in which the spectators view themselves and their world' (ibid: 7). Whilst this idea is also central to many of the ideas and practices explored in each part of this anthology, as is the challenge to the historical avant-garde to 'transform society while standing apart from it' (ibid: 6), there is no other movement which so radically transformed what we understand as performance. Günter Berghaus notes that the historical avant-garde 'modified the categories of representation and enriched them with new techniques that went beyond the traditional "art holding a mirror to nature" concepts connected with Realism and to some extent Naturalism' (Berghaus 2005: 33; see also Part 1). It is certainly the case that a performance text such as Alfred Jarry's *King Ubu*, for example (see 2.1), or Lorca's *The Public* (2.8) could not be further removed in terms of an artistic agenda from a play such as Strindberg's *Miss Julie* (1.2). But go further forward in the career of a playwright such as Strindberg and a play like *Ghost Sonata* (1907) might have much more in common. Similarly, despite its lack of logic or sense of cause and effect, Apollinaire's Surrealist *The Breasts of Tiresias* (2.2) has very little immediately in common with Kokoschka's Expressionist *Murderer the Women's Hope* (2.4). At times there are only broad similarities and common discourses between the work and theory of those who we would consider to belong to the movement we call the historical avant-garde. Certainly many critiqued what they saw as the 'destructive forces of industrialisation' and the ways in which the rapid development of the 'urban wastelands' of the mid- to late nineteenth century had created a society in which man experienced alienation and estrangement (Berghaus 2005: 32). But others, such as the Futurists, famously celebrated the possibilities of destruction brought about by war, the alienating characteristics of urban and industrial modernization and so on. It is necessary therefore to utilize a number of frameworks for the reading and comparing of materials from such a diversity of artists as represent some of the 'isms' of the historical avant-garde. Here Christopher Innes's framework of the philosophical, the populist and the primitive is useful.

The historical avant-garde: the philosophical, the populist and the primitive

Innes has suggested that although the 'signature' of the historical avant-garde was an 'unremitting hostility to contemporary civilisation', there was always an underlying agenda to find a 'utopian alternative to the *status quo*' (Innes 1993: 6). He identifies three strands to this project: the philosophical, the populist and the primitive. In line with the ideas promoted by the Russian anarchist philosopher Mikhail Bakunin (1814–76), the politics of the historical avant-garde in general terms leaned towards the anarchistic, founded as they were upon a belief in individualism and a 'fluid sense of individual fulfillment' (ibid). Certainly some of the propositions put forward by the historical avant-garde adhere to this, but there are still inherent contradictions: for example, many of their political ideas implied collective action, as in fact did Bakunin's and his followers'. What many of the historical avant-garde did share in common, however, was a determined anti-establishment position manifest in their continual barrage against the cultural dominance of the bourgeoisie. They saw the bourgeoisie as watering down or flattening out the revolutionary potential of the arts, promoting and consuming a level of mediocrity, which in turn reflected upon nothing but the staid quality of their own lives.

Innes also sees the historical avant-garde as connecting to 'populist' culture in its alignment with Mikhail Bakhtin's (1895–1975) identification of the 'counter-cultural' potential of the carnivalesque (ibid: 7). Writing in the 1930s, philosopher and cultural theorist Bakhtin described the performance of carnival – with its reversals of hierarchy, sensual materiality, and displays of both the grotesque and the beautiful, its mixture of the bodily and the communal – as revolutionary. He saw folk traditions as 'multi-tonal or dialogic' – a model that allows for fluid interchange of ideas and experience rather than the solidification of culture as represented by the bourgeois hegemony. Reflecting on what he viewed to be the contemporary crisis in Russian culture, Bakhtin saw carnival as belonging to 'the borderline between art and life' (Bakhtin 1984: 7). This deconstruction and reformulation of the relationship between art and life are also central to a great deal of practice within the historical avant-garde. Similarly for Bakhtin, physical, embodied, communal and festive cultures should be valued against the literary, hierarchical, non-collective world of bourgeois art. Others have pointed to the way in which Bakhtin's 'carnivalesque' validates the collective experience and the democratic and utopian vision of the 'texture of public life' which carnival offers (Hirschkop and Shepherd 1989: 35). We can see echoes of these ideas in Jarry's *King Ubu* (2.1) and Apollinaire's *The Breasts of Tiresias* (2.2), but for now it is important to note the carnivalesque as framing Innes's identification of the populist strand of the historical avant-garde.

The last aspect of Innes's framework for analysis here is the primitive. Whilst some of the historical avant-garde, such as the Futurists, celebrated the excitement and promise of catastrophe provided by the speed and impact of technological development on our experience of the world, others showed a generic 'hostility to modern society and all the artistic forms that reflect its assumptions' (Innes 1993: 9). There was a significant element of the historical avant-garde that turned to the non-European – to African art or Balinese dance, for example. Here the attraction was related to a desire to move away from what was seen as the rational, the intellectual, the logical – towards art which reflected the primal, the ritualistic, the shamanistic, the earthy, the spiritual and the subliminal. Numerous critics and artists have pointed to the ways in which this turn to the primitive might be viewed in retrospect as a form of colonialism – an imbuing of non-Western art with an essentialist character of the exotic 'other'. As contemporary performance artist Coco Fusco notes, from the perspective of the end of the twentieth century, there appears to have been a belief amongst the historical avant-garde that 'Western art traditions could be subverted through the appropriation of the perceived performative nature of the "non-Western"' (Fusco 2002: 270). Fusco points to the ways in which the historical avant-garde fetishized the 'primitive' – aligning it with a binary of civilized versus savage (see *The Breasts of Tiresias* – 2.2). It is certainly the case that the historical avant-garde adopted particular aspects of non-Western cultures and often decontextualized them as a means of finding an alternative to the staid bourgeois culture with which they saw themselves as being surrounded. Here Elin Diamond's observation is pertinent, 'primitivism sits on a pile of simple ahistorical essentialisms . . . To the "civilized" eye, the primitive signifies an enticing and inferior otherness, a projection of white culture's repressed libidinal forces' (Diamond 2006: 113). Whilst she notes that primitivism was a 'pervasive aesthetic' adopted by numerous and differing modernist playwrights, she sees it as one of modernism's many 'trans-atlantic curiosities' (ibid: 114). Looking back on modernist practice from the standpoint of the twenty-first century, it is easy to see the colonial context of what was thought at the time to be a radical and revolutionary cultural positioning. For Innes, however, the exploration of the framework of 'primitivism' is useful as a way into an analysis of the nature and influence of the performance practice of the historical avant-garde. Whilst noting its colonial roots, he states that 'the attempt to reproduce the effects of the "primitive" . . . helps to explain avant-garde elements that might otherwise seem puzzling, such as the apparent incompatibility of stressing emotional authenticity and using stylized movement or unnatural gesture to express it' (Innes 1993: 18). This is particularly apparent in works such as Artaud's *Spurt of Blood* (2.3) and Kokoschka's *Murderer the Women's Hope* (2.4), to which we will return later.

Taking into account Innes's three tropes which might be used as frameworks for exploring the historical avant-garde – the philosophical, the populist and the primitive – it is useful to turn to an exploration of the play that signalled the beginnings of the historical avant-garde, Jarry's seminal *King Ubu* (2.1), which although written and first performed at the end of the nineteenth century, heavily influenced and is integral to an understanding of the development of the historical avant-garde in Europe.

Alfred Jarry (1873–1907) and *King Ubu* (2.1)

Alfred Jarry's *King Ubu* opens with a play on the French word for shit, 'Merde' or as it is translated in the version included in this anthology, 'Shikt'. The uproar and outrage after this utterance in the original production notoriously halted the stage action (Meltzer 1994: 110–11). First produced in the respected and largely middle-class Parisian theatre of 1896, the play caused a public outcry. Jarry himself was no stranger to controversy and even courted it; 'eccentric to the point of mania and lucid to the point of hallucination', Jarry's public persona reflected his alcoholism and his disrespect for the social habits of the bourgeoisie (Shattuck and Taylor 1980: 9). Known for his social pranks, such as painting himself entirely green with the intention of eliciting shock from his friends when he entered a café, Jarry became obsessed with the character he created in King Ubu. He wrote many plays and sketches centred on Ubu, as well as numerous articles on philosophy, art, politics and theatre (see Schumacher 1985). Jarry's collection of articles which he titled *The Green Candle* was not published until over sixty years after his death in 1969 (ibid: 33) but his novel, *Exploits and Opinions of Dr Faustroll, Pataphysician*, published in 1898, was later recognized by the Surrealists as 'one of the most influential books written in the nineteenth century' (ibid: 34). The novel juxtaposes medical, scientific and legal language in a mixture of storytelling, scenario description and lists. This is not a novel which in any way relates to the standard narrative prose of the late nineteenth century – the opening of the seventh chapter gives some indication as to its estrangement from the familiar aspects of the traditional novel: 'Across the foliated space of the twenty-seven equivalents, Faustroll conjured up into the third dimension' (Jarry 1980: 190). Similarly, although the play *King Ubu* bears little relation to any dramatic text which came before it in terms of character, action or plot, it adapts the deceptively conventional structuring device of a well-made play, in five acts divided into short scenes.

The play opens with Ma Ubu persuading Ubu to take up arms:

MA UBU: ... Thane of Four-door, you used to be. Now who follows you? Fifty sausage-knotters in procession. Forget Four-door. Get your loaf measured for the crown of Baloney. (2.1: 192)

Her ambitious suggestions for Ubu's career development and the reference to the Thane of Four-door (an indirect reference to the place Cawdor in *Macbeth*) immediately reminds us of Lady Macbeth. Indeed, Jarry deliberately plays with the classic, subverting and borrowing at will from Shakespeare's play. With his army officer Dogpile and the Barmpots, Ubu sets out to conquer through violence, dishonesty and sheer dogged determination. Jarry speeds the audience through the five short acts which move from private rooms to palace courtyards, to the parade ground, to a cave in the mountains, to a dungeon, to a camp outside the city, to 'the middle of nowhere' and finally ends 'on board a ship skimming the ocean'. An unspeakable monster who is content to destroy everyone in his path, Ubu is pompous and violent but also witty. He is 'amoral, anti-social ... self serving' and greedy, and, as Innes notes, 'a figure symbolizing all that bourgeois morality condemns is claimed to be representative of the real basis of bourgeois society' (Innes 1993: 23). Claude Schumacher suggests that the 'basic material' of the play is 'that of all revenge tragedies – or Shakespeare's histories', pointing out however that just as Jarry had no intention of writing a 'history play so too none of the characters in the play relate to any "real" people', just as the country in which the play is set – 'Poland' – is 'devoid of any geographical reality' (Schumacher 1985: 45). Jarry subverted an existing cultural referent to create something new and this he had in common with many of the historical avant-garde whom he later inspired.

For Jarry, 'a play ought to be a kind of public holiday' (Shattuck and Watson Taylor 1965: 87) – an idea which links directly to the carnivalesque – and this is borne out in the playfulness of *King Ubu*. Just as the text is removed from the traditional dramatic literature of its day – it has more in common with the Surrealist and later Absurdist texts (see Esslin 2001) – so too the staging requirements of the play went beyond anything available in the theatre of the time – such quick location changes were not possible in a box set or proscenium-arch theatre with minimally flexible stage machinery. Jarry disliked the staging conventions of the '1890s as an unacceptable compromise between artefact and nature', and wanted for his play 'an abstract set, an artificial environment' (Schumacher 1985: 48). He made the set with innovative artists of the day including Pierre Bonnard and Henri Toulouse-Lautrec, and in his famous letter to director Lugné-Poë (see Part 1: Introduction) Jarry insisted on the use of masks, cardboard horses' heads – referring to the fact that he had originally wanted to write *King Ubu* as a puppet play – plain backdrop, crowds being played by single performers, special vocal intonation and non-referential costumes, 'divorced as far as possible from local colour or chronology' (Melzer 1994: 110–11). The testimony from W. B. Yeats is perhaps most useful in its ability to give a sense of the way in which the play created the potential for a seismic cultural shift:

> I go to the first performance of Jarry's *Ubu Roi* … with Rhymer … [who] explains to me what is happening on the stage. The players are supposed to be dolls, toys, marionettes, and now they are all hopping like wooden frogs, and I can see for myself that the chief personage, who is some kind of king, carries for a sceptre a brush of the kind we use to clean a closet [toilet]. Feeling bound to support the most spirited party, we have shouted for the play … I am very sad … after our own verse … what more is possible? After us the Savage God. (qtd in ibid: 118)

Yeats astutely observed, in retrospect, that for all the innovation and advance made by the new wave of artists at the end of the nineteenth century – and this would include those whose work was discussed in Part 1 of this anthology – what Jarry's play indicated, anarchic, fast-paced and irreverent as it is, was a completely new direction, the response to which combined 'disgust and wonder, fear and awe, distance and familiarity', a form of what would later be termed as 'estrangement' (Taxidou 2007: 1; and see Part 3).

Jarry died in abject poverty at a young age, but not before he had befriended the influential art critic – amongst his many other occupations – Guillaume Apollinaire (1880–1918). Apollinaire, who also died very young, was one of a coterie of artists which included Pablo Picasso (1881–1973) and Max Jacob (1876–1944), and was central to the artistic and philosophical developments brought about by the historical avant-garde, especially those of the Surrealists. Before moving on to explore Surrealism and its impact on theatre and performance practice, however, it is useful to briefly explore Dada, the movement which preceded it and which, in part, Surrealism was a reaction to.

Dada

The sense of the improvisational, the rough and ready, was a common feature of a great deal of historical avant-garde performance. Much of Dada performance happened in a cabaret setting and had an improvisational feel. During the First World War, many artists fled to Zurich which was not operating under the same censorious atmosphere created in many European cities by the war. Here there were no ration stamps and 'newspapers printed what they pleased' (Melzer 1994: 11). It was in this atmosphere of relative freedom that Dada and Dadaism developed at the Cabaret Voltaire where, from 1916, cabaret evenings with an audience capacity of around fifty and organized by a group of artists including Hugo Ball (1886–1927), Emmy Hennings (1885–1948), Hans Arp (1886–1966) and Tristan Tzara (1896–1963) – who heavily influenced the Surrealists – took place. The evenings consisted of performances centred on poetry, music and language play, where the semantic meaning of words give way to their tonal and rhythmic qualities, just as the word Dada has no meaning but is, rather, a play on sounds. As the cabaret developed so the performances became more experimental in nature with consistent use of masks and sound poems. For Hugo Ball, 'The Dadaist loves the extraordinary and the absurd ... He therefore welcomes any kind of mask. Any game of hide and seek, with its inherent power to deceive' (Melzer 1994: 33), and his reading of what happens to the performer when they wear a mask takes us back to Innes's recognition of the historical avant-garde's obsession with the primitive to some extent. 'Man suddenly finds himself placed before an image of himself which he didn't suspect existed and which plunges him into terror ... at the limits of his reason' (ibid: 33). Melzer notes that the conceptualization and practice of Dada happened incrementally with theory and practice developing alongside one another. She identifies key characteristics of this development, with simultaneity and montage as central: so one poem might be read/performed by any number of performers in different rhythms at the same time as each other, for example. There was within Dada, which is perhaps why Tristan Tzara formed an early association with the Surrealists, a refusal to adhere to logic or to pander to the desire to 'make meaning' in art. Heavily influenced by painters such as Wassily Kandinsky (1886–1944), there are relatively few extant performance texts compared to the artworks and poetry produced from within Dada. As a movement, Dada's boundaries are blurred and its definitions flexible, as Melzer notes: 'Dada's raging manifestos do not help to clarify the movement; rather, they reinforce its many ambiguities' (ibid: 57). This was deliberate for a movement which critiqued the commodification of art objects and focused more on experimenting with art as *process* and as *action*. Such a critique of the commodification of art is no more evident than in the famous *Fountain* by Marcel Duchamp, a porcelain urinal signed by the imaginary artist R. Mutt and submitted to an exhibition of contemporary art in New York (Part 2: Timeline). *Fountain* is a ready-made, everyday object transformed into 'art' through its cultural/commodity framing – it has a title, is signed by an 'artist' and is submitted to a gallery as an exhibit.

In the Dada performance text included in this volume, *Genius in a Jiffy or a Dadalogy* by Raoul Hausmann (2.7), there is a critical exploration of the relationship between the artist and the artwork. The text was written in 1920 by Hausmann (1886–1971), who had been part of the Expressionist movement in Germany, working on the art/philosophy magazine *Der Sturm*. A painter and photographer by trade, he developed a photomontage technique the use of which became common practice amongst the avant-garde. Hausmann's play opens on a darkened stage where 'breakfast rolls rain down in the moonlight' (2.7: 177). The Engineer Dada enters the stage, 'Out of the past', and states that he is expecting something to happen in the 'present revolutionary atmosphere' (ibid). He curses those who know nothing about art, one of whom, the Dadasophist, enters the stage and complains that he has sprained his hand and can't produce, calling the Engineer a 'wage-slave'. The Engineer tells him to get on with his work and that he should be paid for his own ideas. They then discuss the meaning of Dada, get '*eaten up by two Berlin Daily editors*' and someone in the audience shouts that 'Dada's a hoax'. The text is playful but almost entirely self-referential, reflecting the infighting and disagreement which was characteristic of many of the movements within the historical avant-garde, but in particular amongst the conflictual Dadaists, whose desire to constantly reinvent themselves and the philosophy of Dada is one reason why the movement in its purest form was short-lived. Although only a brief text, Hausmann's play typifies the Dadaist 'adversarial position towards accepted moral attitudes and assailed them by means of satire' (Senelick 1989: 9). Such hostility to traditional art forms and the deliberate embracing of the illogical and the satirical characterize a great deal of Surrealist practice, and is epitomized in the earliest 'surrealist' drama, *The Breasts of Tiresias*.

Guillaume Apollinaire and *The Breasts of Tiresias* (2.2)

Named by Apollinaire as a 'surrealist drama', his 1917 play *The Breasts of Tiresias* caused as much outrage as Jarry's had done more than twenty years earlier. The play has all the aesthetic and philosophical earmarks of the Surrealist movement, which, led by André Breton (1896–1966), was to follow in Paris in the mid-1920s. Apollinaire had a coterie of followers, and it was they who flocked to see the production of the play along with the critics of many of the leading Parisian newspapers and journals. As with Jarry's earlier play, the structure of *The Breasts of Tiresias* adheres to a traditional act and scene format; even so the production caused great scandal because of its subject matter, modes and registers of performance, and the synthetic décor such as masks, a patchwork of houses on the backdrop, unconventional musical instruments and the giant child's wooden horse ridden by the Policeman. Set largely in the public space of 'The market place at Zanzibar', the play exposes an anxiety about the 'battle of the sexes' as much as it suggests a bizarre world in which one of the Husband's young children is an entrepreneurial businessman making his father a great deal of money in 'the curdled milk trade', and another is a best-selling novelist. Thérèse (Tiresias) opens the play by declaring that:

> I am a feminist and I do not recognize the authority of men … Men have been doing what they like long enough … I want to make war and not make children. No Mister Husband you won't give me orders. (2.2: 209)

After this her breasts, 'one red, the other blue', fly off 'like toy balloons', but 'remain attached by strings' and she sprouts a beard and moustache. Whilst the theme of the play is clearly underpinned by cultural anxiety around women's increased levels of social agency, it is neither a feminist nor an anti-feminist text. Athough Apollinaire states his disquiet, in the preface to the play, about the falling French birth rate, 'we don't make children in France anymore because we don't make love enough. That is all there is to it!' (Apollinaire 1964: 59), this is not a polemical play despite its astute social and cultural critique. The text vacillates between declaration and dialogue, between fast-paced banter and ranting provocation. Music and dialogue intersect and interplay with one another as the action is punctuated by a cacophony of sounds. This is a play which makes unashamed reference to the 'primitive' in its setting and its appropriation of a 'savage' protocol of human relations. More than anything, however, the comic and grotesque are embedded within the anti-logic of the text: the play 'tells a story' but not in any strictly chronological sense nor in any way which allows us to identify with any of the characters, some of whom represent social types – Policeman, Reporter – or simply an embodied object – Kiosk.

Apollinaire, as is the case for many of the historical avant-garde artists who followed him, theorized about the need to transform the theatre, to make it more reflective of the disorientating chaos of a world – that is, Europe – in flux. He also wanted it to embrace more popular performance forms, and move away from concrete representation towards abstraction. As he states in the preface to the play:

> After all, the stage is no more the life it represents than the wheel is a leg. Consequently it is legitimate … to bring to the theatre new and striking aesthetic principles which accentuate the roles of the actors and increase the effect of the production … to protest against that 'realistic' theatre which is predominating theatrical art today. This 'realism', which is no doubt suited to the cinema, is, I believe, as far removed as possible from the art of drama. (Apollinaire 1964: 59–60)

For Apollinaire, theatre has the potential to raise 'humanity above the mere appearance of things' (ibid) and he saw the refusal to pander to tradition as a means of achieving this. Similar to the Symbolists who came before him (see Part 1), Apollinaire believed theatre and performance could thrive on the exploration of what lies under the surface of the 'real' with which the Naturalists were concerned; that theatre could explore the repressed, the unstated and so on. We can see this belief reflected in the *Surrealist Manifestos* which are examined later (2.11), but a further investigation of both Apollinaire's suggestions for the production and the original critical reception of the play gives us a better sense of how his ideas were borne out in practice.

In the prologue he suggests that 'We're trying to bring a new spirit into the theatre' and that a new theatre would be a 'circular theatre with two stages':

> One in the middle and the other like a ring
> Around the spectators permitting
> The full unfolding of our modern art
> Often connecting in unseen ways as in life
> Sounds gestures colors cries tumults
> Music dancing acrobatics poetry painting
> Choruses actions and multiple sets
>
> …
>
> For the theatre must not be 'realistic'
> (Apollinaire 1964: 66)

This call for a new spirit for theatre, with the integration and hybridization of different art forms on a stage which has more in common with a circus ring, resonates with many of the ideas developed by others who were part of the historical avant-garde such as Artaud and Meyerhold (see Part 3: Introduction).

The production was full of noise and action, with the stage wings covered in long strips of coloured paper, and the actors dressed in extraordinary costumes which made them appear as puppets or dolls – note the similarity with the original production of *King Ubu*. One actor played the newspaper kiosk and was covered in newspapers, another played 'the people of Zanzibar' and used 'all manner of musical sound effects' – a toy flute, cymbals, 'wood blocks and broken dishes', the noise of which was interspersed with the action on the rest of the stage (Melzer 1994: 129–30). The reaction to the production was equally full of commotion, and some reports suggest the crowd went crazy. One critic likened the play to Jarry's but like 'Jarry to the twentieth power' (ibid). Melzer notes that in the days following the event, critics were at a loss as to how to define the performance. We have to remember that France was still at war during 1917 and such a play as *The Breasts of Tiresias* did not fit into any ready-made framework; although similar in impact to Jarry's play some twenty years earlier, nothing like it had been witnessed in the theatres of Paris. Whilst other experiments had been taking place in the arts in Europe, many of which – including those of the Dada artists in Zurich in 1916 – Apollinaire would have been aware of, his play signalled a new direction in performance, as André Breton later testified:

> Never again, as at that evening, did I plumb the depths of the gap which would separate the new generation from that preceding it. (Qtd in Melzer 1994: 133)

André Breton and the *First* and *Second Surrealist Manifesto* (2.11)

Influenced by the Dadaist Tristan Tzara (1896-1963), with whom he later argued, André Breton wrote the *First Surrealist Manifesto* in 1924. Whilst the word 'surreal' carries the connotations of 'bizarre', 'outlandish' or simply 'weird' in contemporary parlance, surrealism as defined by Breton was rooted in a connection with the irrational, the subconscious and the world of the dream. As Breton states:

> SURREALISM, noun, masc., Pure psychic automatism by which it is intended to express, either verbally or in writing, the true function of thought. Thought dictated in the absence of all control exerted by reason, and outside all aesthetic or moral preoccupations.
>
> ENCYCL. *Philos.* Surrealism is based on the belief in the superior reality of certain forms of association heretofore neglected, in the omnipotence of the dream, and in the disinterested play of thought. It leads to the permanent destruction of all other psychic mechanisms and to its substitution for them in the solution of the principal problems of life. (2.11: 270)

Breton's project involved a validation of the irrational and an attack on the fragmentation of consciousness – the 'dream' should be integrated into our view of 'reality' – it was also a call for man to 'escape from the control of reason as well as from the imperatives of a moral order' (Waldberg 1978: 17). The automatic writing practised by some of the Surrealists was not some form of message received from a 'spiritual' world, rather it was a technique which aimed at releasing thoughts and images from the unconscious, through disengaging the rational and intellectual conventionally considered to be at the root of the creative process of writing. Similarly, Surrealist art explores the workings of the mind beyond its ability to rationally formulate 'reality'. As Breton states in the *First Surrealist Manifesto* (2.11), 'Could not the dreams as well be applied to the solution of life's fundamental problems?' (ibid: 267). For Breton, because the rational mind functioned in a prohibitive environment and in the dream world, 'The agonizing question of possibility does not arise' (ibid: 268), creativity is stilted without recourse to the irrational world of dreams. Breton was familiar with Freud's ideas and psychoanalytic technique (see Freud 2006 and 1937) in part through his work as a medic helping the shell-shocked soldiers of the First World War. Here he observed that when the 'critical faculty of the subject' is removed from the process of the production of text, something new, vital, 'unencumbered by any reticence', emerges (ibid: 269). The Surrealists philosophized about areas related to performance but did not engage with performance at the same level as they did with art and writing. Their influence is more discernible from a historical perspective. By the time of the *Second Surrealist Manifesto* in 1929 (2.11) Breton was more assertively linking a re-evaluation of the dream state with the call to political and ideological arms, seeing the 'raising of problems of love, dream, madness, art and religion' as paramount to any revolutionary impulse.

What Surrealism offers is a conceptualization of the possibilities of art, and in turn, theatre and performance, which implicate the individual, the unconscious and the irrational. This connects to Jarry and Apollinaire's ideas and practice of theatre, and further, links to the innovative theatre theories of Artaud. The Surrealists were largely located in Paris during the 1920s but their ideas reverberated well into the 1930s and 1940s and well beyond Paris. Similarly, Antonin Artaud, originally affiliated with the Surrealist movement for a short time, created theories of theatre and performance which have been seminal to the development of innovative practice throughout the mid- and late twentieth-century European theatre. That his ideas and his practice had less impact in his own lifetime is a reflection of the 'conservative' state of much theatre during that historical moment. It is also a reflection of the fact that, for numerous reasons – economic, technical and practical – many of his ideas were simply unrealizable. This volume includes two of Artaud's writings on theatre, *No More Masterpieces* and *Theatre and the Plague* (2.10) – which later became part of the seminal collection of his theatre theories, *The Theatre and Its Double* (Artaud 1981) as well as the extraordinary, filmic performance text *The Spurt of Blood* (2.3). An examination of these pieces helps to map out Artaud's ideas and their connection to the historical avant-garde and beyond.

Antonin Artaud (1896–1948)

Artaud worked as an actor (noted in particular for his role as Massieu the monk in Dreyer's film *Le Passion de Jeanne d'Arc*), director and writer during the 1920s and 1930s, but he is less remembered for his actual professional theatre work than for his ideas about theatre. Little is written, for example, about his running of the Alfred Jarry Theatre in Paris during the mid-1920s, where, along with Roger Vitrac, he introduced Paris to numerous experimental European plays: although one critic of the time noted his 'strikingly sensitive, intelligent, careful illustration of the subtlest meanings in the text' in relation to his production of Strindberg's *A Dream Play* in the mid-1920s (qtd in Leach 2004: 159). Plagued by mental illness and poverty, he was one of the most prolific theatre theorists of the early part of the twentieth century and he also wrote extensively about the occult, philosophy and culture. His ideas have influenced numerous theatre groups and directors throughout the twentieth century – notably Jean-Louis Barrault and Peter Brook in Europe and The Living Theatre in America, and after his death his ideas have achieved an almost cult status (see Hayman 1977 and Esslin 1976).

For Artaud, as for many of the artists of the historical avant-garde, life and art were almost indistinguishable. He wanted to make theatre significant outside the framework of dominant bourgeois culture. As with the Surrealists, his was a project of disruption to create theatre which moved its audiences physically, emotionally and intellectually. Artaud used a host of metaphors and analogies to present his ideas about theatre, one of the most infamous being his comparison of theatre with the plague (see 2.10). Here he proposed that theatre must create societal upheaval, a psycho-physical reaction similar to that created by the plague: he wanted audiences to be shifted from a position of passive consumption to one of active involvement, bringing about physiological as much as social upheaval:

> For if theatre is like the plague, this is not just because it acts on large groups and disturbs them in one and the same way. There is both something victorious and vengeful in theatre just as in the plague ... The plague takes dormant images, latent disorder and suddenly carries them to the point of the most extreme gestures ... Like the plague, theatre is a powerful appeal through illustration to those powers which return the mind to the origins of its inner struggles ... If fundamental theatre is like the plague, this is not because it is contagious, but because like the plague it is a revelation, urging forward the exteriorisation of a latent undercurrent of cruelty through which all the perversity of which the mind is capable, whether in a person or a nation, becomes localised. (2.10: 260)

Just as the Surrealists wanted art to 'infect' us, to reach into our subconscious, to stay with us after the event, so too Artaud believed that theatre had the potential to alter not only the way we perceive our world but the world itself in which we live. Although Artaud's was not an ideological or political mission, he often refers to the 'masses' in a way which enlists them as part of a revolutionary project. In *No More Masterpieces* he critiques the way in which the classics have been appropriated by the social elite and have lost their power to move us: 'Past masterpieces are fit for the past, they are no good to us.' He proposes that it is 'senseless to criticise the masses for having no sense of the sublime, when we ourselves confuse the sublime with one of those formal, moreover always dead, exhibits' (2.10: 261). We should note here that Artaud was writing at a time when the 'popular' performance forms embraced by the early Surrealists and the Futurists (see Marinetti's *The Meaning of the Music Hall*: 2.9) were considered to be somehow a lower form of art on a hierarchy which placed opera and the theatrical production of classical texts high on the ladder of artistic forms. Artaud also turned to the gestural and hieroglyphic nature of non-Western art forms in traditions such as Balinese dance which he witnessed for the first time at the Paris Colonial Exposition of 1931. Here, he perceived a performance form which was predicated on a non-textual language as more capable, he thought, of expressing the human experience, and 'answering the needs of the times' (ibid), without pandering to 'middle-class conformity' (2.10: **57**). Artaud believed that theatre has the 'power to affect the appearance and structure of things' (ibid: 263) as did, for example, Brecht (see Part 3), but he used psycho-logical models and proposed that actors should make use of ecstatic and shamanistic states such as trance. Like Apollinaire, he suggested that the audience should literally be at the centre of the performance with the action happening around them; this way theatre might affect them in the same way vibration affects the movement of a snake as a 'very long massage': he wanted to bring the audience like 'charmed snakes ... back to the subtlest ideas through their anatomies' (ibid: 264). For Artaud the theatre could be a place where 'violent physical images pulverise, mesmerise the audience's sensibilities, caught in the drama as if in a vortex of higher forces'. As Esslin notes, Artaud's theories express a desire to create a theatre capable of communicating the 'fullness of human experience and emotion through bypassing the discursive use of language and by establishing contact between the artist and his audience at a level above – or perhaps below – the merely cerebral appeal of the verbal plane' (Esslin 1976: 70). To some extent we are limited in our ability to map Artaud's ideas against his actual practice as very few of his performance texts have survived. Where they have, it is sometimes difficult to imagine them working in practice, certainly on the stages of his day.

The Spurt of Blood (1925: 2.3)

Unproduced professionally until 1964, by Peter Brook and Charles Marowitz in London (see Hayman 1977), *The Spurt of Blood* is a short text that reads as a blueprint for performance, a *performance score* rather than a play. For Christopher Innes the text is rife with the 'hallucinatory shock effects of surrealistic film' (Innes 1984: 92). Peopled by characters with names which reflect their social or public roles – KNIGHT, WETNURSE, PRIEST, WHORE and so on – the performance text has production requirements which would have been impossible in the context of the available technologies of the era in which it was written. It has a filmic quality, as Innes has noted, evidenced in the extensive stage directions, '*At that moment two stars collide, and a succession of limbs of flesh fall. Then feet, hands, scalps, masks ... falling slower and slower as if through space ... and a scarab which lands with heart-breaking, nauseating slowness*' (2.3: 219). Similarly the performance 'score' ends with an extraordinary and grotesque image: '*A host of scorpions crawl out from under the WETNURSE's dress and start swarming in her vagina which swells and splits, becomes transparent and shimmers like the sun*.' The text, which could last half an hour or two hours depending on the production choices made, begins with romantic clichés – 'I love you and everything is fine', 'I love you, I am great' – but disintegrates into the ridiculous:

> ... the KNIGHT *enters and throws himself on the* WETNURSE, *shaking her violently*.
> KNIGHT: (*In a terrible voice*.) Where did you put it? Give me my Gruyère.

The Spurt of Blood is full of violent and sexual imagery, and unlike Eve who bit the apple in the Garden of Eden, the WHORE bites God's wrist, eliciting a 'spurt of blood' which flies across the stage, at which point the stage is strewn with dead bodies. This is not a performance text aimed at exploring or expressing some kind of 'meaning' in a social sense; rather we are bombarded with the chaotic imagery of culture in a state of disintegration and a world in disarray. Far more potent and virulent than anything by Apollinaire, the text expresses a strange apocalyptic vision. The imagery is, however, almost ritualistic and this it shares with an earlier performance text by the

Expressionist painter Oskar Kokoschka (1886–1980), although Innes suggests that Artaud knew nothing of Kokoschka's *Murderer the Women's Hope* (1909, 2.4).

Expressionism and *Murderer the Women's Hope* (1909: 2.4)

Expressionism begins to emerge in art at the end of the nineteenth century. It signified the move away from literal representation towards a style which embraced the externalizing of internal psychology and social angst and as a means of exploring feeling, thought and spirit: as such it had some common features with other 'isms' of the historical avant-garde. In art, Expressionism was often characterized by intense colour, by the manipulation of spatial construction, by canvases filled with the irregular rhythms of frenetic brushstrokes – a famous early example of this being Edvard Munch's (1863–1944) 1893 painting, *The Scream*. What is manifest here is a representation of an internal state of mind rather than an attempt to replicate an external 'reality'. Thus the artist's subjective vision of the world is imposed onto the representation of it. Just as the Surrealists and the Symbolists before them (see Part 1) had no interest in representing surface reality, so, too, the Expressionists made use of emblematic modes. Later forms of Expressionist playwriting in America, typified by works such as Elmer Rice's *The Adding Machine* (1923) or Sophie Treadwell's *Machinal* (1928) – retitled *The Life Machine* in the first English production – made use of the abstraction present in earlier Expressionism. Here stark sets and telegraph-type speech – short, rhythmic, repetitive language – convey the internal states of characters who embodied social angst, or the alienation created by technological development whereby man/woman was often pitted against machine, as is the case with Mr Zero, the accountant soon to be replaced by the adding machine of the title of the Elmer Rice play. Here the Expressionist style links more to early German film, such as *The Cabinet of Dr Caligari* (1919) or Fritz Lang's *Metropolis* (1927), than a text like Kokoschka's, but the sense of alienation, of ritualized existence, of extremes of human emotion resonate (see Styan 1981: 3). Styan notes that early Expressionist drama in Germany was a reaction against the 'pre-war authority of the family and community ... and ... the mechanization of life' (ibid). He sees it as a 'violent drama of youth', and Kokoschka is not untypical in spirit. Styan gives a useful breakdown of the key characteristics of early Expressionist drama which it is worth noting in shorthand here. First, the atmosphere was often 'vividly dreamlike and nightmarish'; plot and structure were 'disjointed, broken into episodes' without the conflict or sense of cause and effect of a well-made play; characters were often social types rather than individuals; dialogue switched between the 'poetical' and 'telegraphese' – short words or speeches delivered in a rhythmical or repetitive manner; and lastly the acting or performance style was puppet-like and gestural (ibid: 4–5). Many of these characteristics can be found in Kokoschka's performance text.

Murderer the Women's Hope (2.4) opens under a night sky with torches offering the only light. Figures appear in relief before a tower with a large red grille as its door. The characters have clothes covered in symbols and are 'savage in appearance'. The text has the feeling of a medieval procession as a CHORUS walks around the stage. The ritualistic quality of the language builds as the piece progresses – WOMAN is spellbound by the mystical qualities of THE MAN who strode 'through the fire, his feet unharmed' (2.4: 223). The girls warn WOMAN that they must escape and the movement and fearful expressions of the crowd climax in a moment of threat in which the MEN are sadistically ordered to brand WOMAN with a hot iron, to mark her: 'THE MAN: (*Enraged.*) My men, now brand her with my sign, hot iron into her red flesh' (ibid). In her struggle WOMAN manages to wound THE MAN. Her need for revenge is heightened to the point where she states that she will not let him live: 'you feed on me, weaken me, woe to you … Your love imprisons me …', at which point she writhes on the steps to the tower in convulsions. THE MAN then kills the frenzied crowd as they attempt to escape, their torches showering them with sparks, and the stage is left piled with dead bodies as, '*From very far away*' we hear the crowing of cocks.

A man who courted public controversy, Kokoschka wrote the play, 'as an antedote to the torpor that, for the most part, one experiences in the theatre today' (Berghaus 2005: 65). The text has a prehistoric feel – located as it is in some ancient place – and focuses on a primal version of the battle of the sexes. The females are constructed in animalistic terms: WOMAN '*creeps round the cage like a panther*' and the violence in the play is almost sadomasochistic in tone. Again, parallels might be drawn with Artaud's *The Spurt of Blood*, similarly violent in terms of the imagery and the relationship between male and female that it depicts. There is also a strong reference in both to the 'primitive' framed by a Western notion of the uncivilized rather than, as in Apollinaire's 'Zanzibar', as a reference to a particular non-Western geography. With its reference to resurrection the play might suggest that 'murder becomes an act of spiritual liberation and the murderer "the only hope of womankind"' (ibid 67). What is clear is that any number of readings of the text are possible. For Styan it is 'unique in its violent eroticism' with scenes which 'correspond to the seven stations of the cross' (Styan 1981: 45). He also notes that the actors in the first production were not given the script, and the improvisational and free expressive form of the text alongside its musical and gestural properties present the possibility that in fact the extant text came out of its performance as much as the other way round (ibid).

Expressionist theatre, perhaps more than any other of the 'isms' of the historical avant-garde, developed a number of styles which altered the formal qualities of the text in a sustained manner. For example, although a later play such as *Hoppla, We're Alive!* (3.2), explored in Part 3, could not be more different from Kokoschka's text, we can identify a resonance with earlier Expressionist plays. The Expressionists were less concerned with the politics of the aesthetics of performance than were the Dadaists, and did not engage in the same level of self-reflection and critique of the artwork as other modernists. Such conscious critique was however absolutely embedded within Futurist performance practice, evidenced here in Umberto Boccioni's *Genius and Culture* and *Bachelor Apartment* (2.5), and in Marinetti's *Feet* (2.6).

Futurism – Filippo Tommaso Marinetti (1876–1944) and Umberto Boccioni (1882–1916)

The Futurists shared much with the other historical avant-garde movements that developed during the first three decades of the twentieth century – an abhorrence of tradition, a desire to disrupt, a belief in art as action and process, and so on. Marinetti is viewed as the founding father of Futurism, which declared itself – through the publication on the front page of Parisian daily newspaper *Le Figaro* of the *Foundation and Manifesto of Futurism* in 1909 – by launching a 'violently upsetting incendiary manifesto'. The manifesto lays out the tenets of Italian Futurism and is worth quoting at some length here. Marinetti states that the Futurists intended to:

sing of the love of danger … courage, audacity, and revolt will be the essential elements of our poetry … the world's magnificence has been enriched by … the beauty of speed … no work without an aggressive character can be a masterpiece … we will glorify war – the world's only hygiene – militarism, patriotism, the destructive gesture of freedom-bringers, beautiful ideas worth dying for and scorn for woman ... we will sing of the polyphonic tides of revolution.

Whilst historians have noted Marinetti's leanings towards fascism – he became a great friend of the Fascist Italian dictator Benito Mussolini – others point to his earlier associations with the 'amorphous pool of radicals and subversives of the extreme Left in Italy' (Berghaus 2005: 95). Futurism's intention to 'effect a total overhaul of society' was not, however, based on socialist ideological affiliations, and politically, Marinetti had far more in common with anarchist beliefs and those which later developed into the foundations of fascism. Fascism works through autocratic systems of representation rather than dialectical ones, and gained power as a political movement in Europe – specifically Germany, Spain and Italy – during the 1920s and 1930s. Walter Benjamin (see Part 3: Introduction and 3.7) argued vociferously against both Marinetti's glorification of war, and Futurism's aestheticization of politics, and from a contemporary standpoint it is difficult to disassociate an appreciation of Futurism from its ultimate foundations in an exclusionary politics. Keeping this in mind, the task here is to look at the ways in which the Futurists influenced developments in theatre and performance, and Marinetti's *The Meaning of the Music Hall* (2.9) along with Enrico Prampolini's *Futurist Scenography* (2.12) go some way towards opening this discussion. Originally published in an English newspaper, the *Daily Mail*, in 1913, Marinetti's analysis of the British popular music hall, which flourished as a mode of performance practice from the last decades of the nineteenth century into the first few of the twentieth, is an interesting one. For Marinetti the music hall thrived on having 'no masters, no dogmas' and on subsisting 'on the moment', it set out to entertain the audience with the comic or the 'startling to the imagination'. Here the audience 'does not remain static and stupidly passive, but participates noisily in the action'. Based on the expression and display of physical skill, risk and daring, many music hall acts appealed to the Futurists for whom text-based theatres were the epitomy of bourgeois indulgence. Marinetti makes direct reference to the primitive in relation to this performance form and states that Futurism could perfect 'variety theatre by transforming it into the theatre of wonders' (2.9: 251). Enrico Prampolini's (1894–1956) suggestions for theatre are more concerned with the specifics of production, and reveal a desire to develop a 'dynamic synthesis' in production, to move away from classicism towards intuitive staging that makes use of the poetic and vibrant qualities of colour; the non-representational where the scenography, and specifically the lighting, will come across as a character in and of itself (see 2.12). Between the two we can see an embracing of both so-called 'low' and 'high art'. Whilst Marinetti perhaps misunderstood and underestimated the 'traditions' which operated within the music hall, he focused on its populist appeal. Prampolini, on the other hand, wanted to create 'luminous dynamic architectures' in staging, which, like many of Artaud's ideas, would have been technically unrealizable in his historical moment.

The Futurist performances of which, Marinetti's *Feet* (2.6) and the Boccioni texts would have been a component were called *serate*, evenings of performances, readings of manifestos and exhibitions of Futurist artworks, in large theatres. Most *serate* turned into a battleground where the audience noisily and sometimes violently disrupted the performances, which, much to the joy of the Futurists, brought their ideas more noticeably into the public realm. By around 1914 the disruptive potential of these evenings had reached its limit, as the element of surprise was harder to manufacture and Marinetti turned to other performance escapades to develop Futurism's performance practices (see Berghaus 2005).

The scripts or *sintesi* which we have reprinted here do not really give a full sense of the vibrant, violent and disruptive essence of Futurism; what they do give us, however, is a sense – especially in the case of *Feet* (2.6) – of what the Futurists might have been aiming to achieve in performance. *Genius and Culture* and *Bachelor Apartment* (2.5) subvert bourgeois domestic settings, and link with Dada's critique of the commodification of both artist and artwork as the CRITIC in the former states:

> I am not a man, I am a critic. I am a man of culture. The artist is a man, a slave, a baby ... In him nature is chaos. The critic and history are between nature and the artist. History is history, in other words subjective fact. (2.5: 226)

Thus, whilst the artist is human, the critic can remove himself from humanity and be 'a man of culture', which he can critique subjectively, and present his critique as fact or truth. Similarly the relationship between the sexes in both texts is presented in what might now be seen as rather traditionalist terms, with the woman in *Genius and Culture* (2.5) as the supportive nurturer of the artist and as the manipulative seductress in *Bachelor Apartment* (2.5). Marinetti's *Feet* (2.6), however, does more in terms of performative innovation. Broken into seven sections, scenes or simply moments, the audience sit in front of a stage curtain which is only a third raised above the stage and therefore see only 'legs in action'. The actors are required to give 'greatest expression to the attitudes and movements of their lower extremities' (2.6: 228). Attention is drawn to the seven 'episodes', none of which lasts longer than a few lines of text, via our hearing of snippets of conversation, just as a camera might focus on small elements of a larger scene. So, we see the bottom of two armchairs whilst we witness a failed seduction scene as A BACHELOR says, 'All, all for one of your kisses' and A MARRIED WOMAN replies, 'No! ... Don't talk to me like that! ...'. Later our attention is drawn to three women sitting on a couch having a conversation about which of three men sitting on another couch they prefer. The last episode is simply a man running away – presumably offstage – whilst another kicks at him shouting 'Imbecile!' What the performance text achieves is a retuning of our attention: we are asked, as it were, to fill in the missing pieces, there is no exposition – we don't know where we are, who is there or why – there is minimal reference to the usual signifiers which operate in theatre and they are manipulated so as to remove the possibility of presenting a picture or a scene. Just as a camera pans in on specific aspects of a filmic composition, so Marinetti plays with our desire to know where we are and what the characters on stage are doing there; we cannot see their faces, their expressions, nor can we identify or empathize with them in any real way. Something else apart from our intellect comes into play. Marinetti's text genuinely opens up questions about how performance works as practice, linking him with others from the avant-garde such as Artaud and Moholy-Nagy (1895–1946), who, like Marinetti, turned to an analysis of variety and circus performance as a way of breaking theatre and performance away from the dominance of text.

László Moholy-Nagy's *Theater, Circus, Variety* (2.13) is self-explanatory and has been included in this volume because of the way it discusses the relationship between popular performance forms and innovative theories of staging. Like others from the historical avant-garde, Moholy-Nagy believed that the actor has to work in synchronicity with the other elements of staging (sound, motion, space, form) in a 'theatre of totality' which he saw as an 'organism' – something removed from the traditional storytelling qualities of bourgeois theatre which did not facilitate the 'creative relationships and reciprocal tensions' which he believed a theatre of totality could achieve.

As we have seen, much of the historical avant-garde can be identified with a desire to genuinely investigate the potential of theatre and performance beyond its subservience to text, to literature and the written word. Some played with language and sound, removing meaning through the repetition or deconstruction of the tonal and rhythmic qualities of language, and through creating a different hierarchy between language and the other elements of theatre, the visual, the physical and so on. This introduction draws to its close with an exploration of one of the most original and poetic attempts to investigate the nature of theatre as an expressive art form, Federico García Lorca's (1898–1936) unfinished and rarely performed *The Public* (2.8). Moholy-Nagy's definition of stagecraft is a useful way into this text:

> The result is nothing more than literature if a reality or a potential reality, no matter how imaginative, is formulated or visually expressed without the creative forms peculiar only to the stage. It is not until the tensions concealed in the utmost economy of means are brought into universal and dynamic interaction that we have creative stagecraft. (2.13: 277)

Federico García Lorca's *The Public* (2.8)

Lorca's unfinished play removes us from the sanctuary of logic or recognizable reality into a metatheatrical drama of a bizarre combination of characters, from the DIRECTOR and his SERVANT to a ROMAN EMPEROR, a PAJAMA COSTUME, a FIGURE WITH VINE LEAVES and four very articulate and troublesome WHITE HORSES. Lorca – friend of the Surrealist Salvador Dalí and a hero of the Spanish avant-garde who met a tragic death at the beginning of the Spanish Civil War (1936–39) – created a play which makes constant references to the relationship between the theatre work and its audience. The play is full of disguise and deception, of poetic language which conjures imagery rather than delineates action. Divided into 'Frames', the staging was once again extraordinarily challenging for the European theatre of the day, which is one reason, perhaps, why *The Public* was not produced professionally until the late 1980s. 'Frame Three', for example, requires a 'wall of sand', and 'Frame Six' a 'giant eye and a cluster of trees with clouds'. Just as Artaud envisioned a stage composition which removed itself entirely from the representational, so, too, Lorca juxtaposes magical, poetic and imagistic metaphors. Lorca's is a play which proposes, as Delgado suggests, an engagement 'with the politics and function of theatre' in the play's 'metatheatricality' (Delgado 2008: 135). Delgado also notes the play's lack of a 'cumulative structural pattern' present in other of Lorca's works and points to the fact of his 'characters mutating without warning . . . functioning under different names', and entering and leaving the stage for 'no palpable reason' (ibid 155–6). Like many of the other plays and performance texts in this section, there is still, many years after it was written, a sense of the impossible reach of *The Public* in terms of its potential realization in production: unlike the majority of Lorca's work, it is still only rarely performed.

Conclusion

The historical avant-garde was a movement made up of different and interconnected elements; it had no formal beginning or end. Its inventions and practices, however, reverberate through to the early twenty-first century, as Harding notes:

> whether one defines the avant-garde solely as an ephemeral movement inseparably intertwined with a modernist past, or whether one recognises in the radical aesthetic movements from the early part of the century the emergence of ... an 'avant-garde urge' that has continued to thrive in contemporary theater, our understanding of that urge ... is largely contingent upon a sense of the dynamics that characterized the historical avant-garde. (Harding 2000: 6)

These dynamic theories about art, and more specifically theatre and performance, which the varying movements within the historical avant-garde developed, created public outrage and disturbance, even though some of them could not be realized in practice within the technological limitations of their time. Many of these ideas have become embedded in the approach to theatre of practitioners working at the other end of the century (see Part 5). Evaluation of work produced by the historical avant-garde has to take this into account. Whilst the reverberations of the Naturalists fairly quickly influenced dominant bourgeois theatre cultures, those created by the historical avant-garde took a longer time to impact on dominant performance practices. At the same time, their self-conscious and self-reflective writings help us to locate them culturally at the absolute cutting edge of art practices in the early decades of the twentieth century. As stated at the beginning of this volume and this particular section however, it is important to recognize the crossovers between one art/performance movement and another. As the timeline at the beginning of this part illustrates, Dada, Surrealism, Expressionism and Futurism were all practices which interrelated and circulated during the same decades. The reach of Part 2 has been largely France, Germany, Italy and Spain, but the avant-garde in Russia and Germany equally influenced far less esoteric and far more politically directed performance, as is evident in the theatre practices in England, Germany and the United States discussed in Part 3. Where the historical avant-garde refused to adhere specifically or permanently to a particular ideological position, some of their ideas were often adopted by those who wanted to transform theatre as part of a 'class' war and a battle with a political system subservient to the economic inequities of capitalism.

Bibliography

Apollinaire, Guillaume (1964) *The Breasts of Tiresias*, trans. Louis Simpson, in Michael Benedikt and George Welwarth (eds), *Modern French Theatre: An Anthology of Plays from Jarry to Ioneso*, London: Faber and Faber, pp. 55–92.

Aronson, Arnold (2000) *American Avant-Garde Theatre: A History*, London: Routledge.

Artaud, Antonin (1981 [1964]) *The Theatre and Its Double*, London: John Calder.

Bakhtin, Mikhail (1984 [1965]) *Rabelais and His World*, Bloomington: Indiana University Press.

Berghaus, Günter (2005) *Theatre, Performance and the Historical Avant-Garde*, Basingstoke: Palgrave Macmillan.

Carey, John (1992) *The Intellectuals and the Masses*, London: Faber and Faber.

Delgado, Maria (2008) *Lorca: Routledge Modern and Contemporary Dramatists*, London: Routledge.

Diamond, Elin (2006) 'Deploying/Destroying the Primitivist Body in Hurston and Brecht', in Alan Ackerman and Martin Puchner (eds), *Against Theatre: Creative Destructions on the Modernist Stage*, Basingstoke: Palgrave Macmillan, pp. 112–32.

Edgar, Andrew and Peter Sedgwick (2008) *Cultural Theory: The Key Concepts*, London: Routledge.

Esslin, Martin (1976) *Antonin Artaud: The Man and His Work*, London: John Calder.

Esslin, Martin (2001 [1961]) *The Theatre of the Absurd*, London: Methuen.

Freud, Sigmund (2006 [1899]) *The Interpretation of Dreams*, Raleigh, NC: Hayes Barton Press.

Freud, Sigmund (1937 [1933]) *New Introductory Lectures on Psychoanalysis*, London: Hogarth.

Fusco, Coco (2002) 'The Other History of Intercultural Performance', in Rebecca Schneider and Gabrielle Cody (eds), *Re-Direction*, London: Routledge, pp. 266–90.

Harding James M. (2000) *Contours of the Theatrical Avant-Garde*, Ann Arbor: University of Michigan Press.

Hayman, Ronald (1977) *Artaud and After*, Oxford: Oxford University Press.

Hirschkop, Ken and David Shepherd (1989) *Bakhtin and Cultural Theory*, Manchester: Manchester University Press.

Hughes, Robert (1991 [1980]) *The Shock of the New: Art and the Century of Change*, London: Thames and Hudson.

Innes, Christopher (1984) *Holy Theatre: Ritual and the Avant-Garde*, London: Routledge.

Innes, Christopher (1993) *Avant-Garde Theatre 1892–1992*, London: Routledge.

Jarry, Alfred (1980 [1898]) *Exploits and Opinions of Dr Faustroll, Pataphysician*, in Roger Shattuck and Simon Watson Taylor (eds), *Selected Works of Alfred Jarry*, London: Eyre Methuen, pp. 173–256.

Leach, Robert (2004) *Makers of Modern Theatre*, London: Routledge.

Melzer, Annabelle (1994 [1980]) *Dada and Surrealist Performance*, Baltimore and London: Johns Hopkins University Press.

Rice, Elmer (1956 [1923]) *The Adding Machine,* New York: Samuel French.

Schumacher, Claude (1985) *Alfred Jarry and Guillaume Apollinaire*, London: Methuen.

Senelick, Laurence (ed.) (1989) *Cabaret Performance: Europe 1890–1920,* New York: PAJ.

Shattuck, Roger and Simon Watson Taylor (eds) (1980 [1965]) *Selected Works of Alfred Jarry*, London: Eyre Methuen.

Styan, J. L. (1981) *Modern Drama in Theory and Practice 3: Expressionism and Epic Theatre*, Cambridge: Cambridge University Press.

Olga, Taxidou (2007) *Modernism and Performance: Jarry to Brecht*, Basingstoke: Palgrave Macmillan.

Treadwell, Sophie (2011 [1928]) 'Machinal', in Maggie B. Gale and Gillie Bush Bailey (eds), *Performance Texts by Women 1880–1930: An Anthology of Texts by British and American Women of the Modernist Period*, Manchester: Manchester University Press.

Waldberg, Patrick (1978 [1965]) *Surrealism*, London: Thames and Hudson.

Further reading

Benson, Timothy (1987) *Berlin Dada*, Ann Arbor: University of Michigan Press.

Bürger, Peter (1984) *Theory of the Avant-Garde*, Minneapolis: University of Minnesota Press.

Dukore, Bernard F. and Daniel Gerould (1976) *Avant-Garde Drama: A Casebook, 1918–1939*, New York: Crowell.

Goldberg, RoseLee (1979) *Performance: Live Art, 1900 to the Present*, New York: Harry N. Abrams.

Jarry, Alfred (1980 [1898]) 'Twelve Theatrical Topics', in Roger Shattuck and Simon Watson Taylor (eds), *Selected Works of Alfred Jarry*, London: Eyre Methuen, pp. 86–90.

Kolocotroni, Vassiliki, Jane Goldman and Olga Taxidou (eds) (1998) *Modernism: An Anthology of Sources and Documents*, Edinburgh: Edinburgh University Press.

Kirby, E. T. (1969) *Total Theatre: A Critical Anthology*, New York: Dutton.

Murphy, Richard (1999) *Theorising the Avant-Garde: Modernism, Expressionism, and the Problems of Postmodernity*, Cambridge: Cambridge University Press.

Puchner, Martin (2002) *Stagefright: Modernism, Anti-theatricality and Drama*, Baltimore and London: Johns Hopkins University Press.

Singleton, Brian (1998) *Artaud: Le Théâtre et son Double* (Critical Guides to French Texts No. 118), London: Grant and Cutler.

Sokel, W. H. (ed.) (1963) *Anthology of German Expressionist Drama*, New York: Anchor Books.

2.1 **KING UBU** (1896)

ALFRED JARRY

Translated by Kenneth McLeish

Alfred Jarry (1873–1907). Born in France, the son of a merchant, Jarry went on to become an iconic hero of the Surrealist movement founded over a decade after his death. Echoes of his ideas and visions for theatre can also be found in the European 'absurdist' theatre which found currency after World War II. Best known for his Ubu *plays, which focus on the adventures of the treacherous and deeply unpleasant Père Ubu and his entourage, Jarry also wrote poetry, prose and journalism. He was both involved with, and critical of, the Symbolist movement in Paris. Originally produced in Paris in 1896, Jarry's* King Ubu *was a sensation which bought him notoriety. Known as an eccentric figure and an alcoholic, he died young and impoverished. This translation was produced at the Gate Theatre, London, in 1997, directed by John Wright.*

Characters

PA UBU
MA UBU
DOGPILE
GOOD KING WENCESLAS
QUEEN ROSAMOND
PRINCE WILLY
PRINCE SILLY
PRINCE BILLIKINS
BIG BAD BERNIE
WALLOP
MCCLUB
FAST FREDDIE
NORBERT NURDLE
TSAR ALEXIS OF ALL THE RUSSKIES
NICK NACKERLEY
GENERAL CUSTARD
MAJOR F. FORT
BEAR
BARMPOTS, BANKERS, CASHHOUNDS, CHAPS, CITIZENS, CLERKS, COUNCILLORS, FLUNKEYS, GHOSTS, GUARDS, JUDGES, MESSENGERS, NOBS, PARTISANS, SEAFARERS, SOLDIERS, TURNKEYS.

Act 1

1

PA UBU, MA UBU

PA UBU: Shikt.

MA UBU: Pa Ubu, language.

PA UBU: Watch it, Ma Ubu. I'll bash your head in.

MA UBU: Not my head, Pa Ubu. Someone else's.

PA UBU: Stagger me sideways, what d'you mean?

MA UBU: Come on, Pa Ubu. You *like* what you are?

PA UBU: Stagger me sideways, girl, of course I like it. Shikt, who wouldn't? Captain of the Guard, Eye and Ear of Good King Wenceslas, Past President of the Battalions of Baloney, Thane of Four-door. What more d'you want?

MA UBU: You're joking. Thane of Four-door, you used to be. Now who follows you? Fifty sausage-knotters in procession. Forget Four-door. Get your loaf measured for the crown of Baloney.

PA UBU: Ma Ubu, what are you on about?

MA UBU: As if you didn't know.

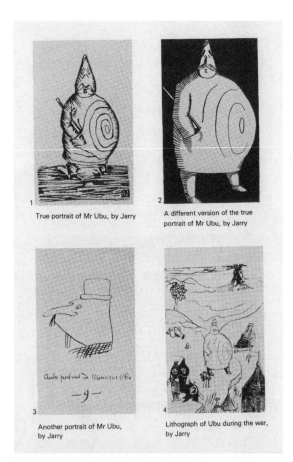

1 True portrait of Mr Ubu, by Jarry

2 A different version of the true portrait of Mr Ubu, by Jarry

3 Another portrait of Mr Ubu, by Jarry

4 Lithograph of Ubu during the war, by Jarry

Figure 13 Four Portraits of Mr Ubu by Alfred Jarry

PA UBU: Stagger me sideways. Good King Wenceslas is still alive, for starters. And even if he wasn't, he's got a million kids.

MA UBU: So, do in the lot of them. Take over.

PA UBU: Watch it, Ma Ubu, or it's jug for you.

MA UBU: Idiot! If I'm in jug, who'll patch your pants?

PA UBU: So let 'em *see* my bum.

MA UBU: No: plant it on a throne. Just think of it. A pile of cash, big as you like. Bangers for breakfast. A golden coach.

PA UBU: If I was king, I'd have a big hat. Like that one I had in Four-door, till those bastards nicked it.

MA UBU: *And* a brolly. *And* a cloak so long that it brushed the floor.

PA UBU: I can't resist. Shickastick, if I catch him on his own, he's for it.

MA UBU: At last, Pa Ubu. A proper man at last.

PA UBU: Just a minute. I'm Captain of the Guard. Murder Good King Wenceslas? His Maj of Baloney? I'd rather die.

MA UBU: (*Aside.*) Shikt. (*Aloud.*) You want to be Daddy Mouse forever? *Poor* Daddy Mouse?

PA UBU: Blubberit, stagger me sideways, I'd rather be poor, honest Daddy Mouse than Big Fat Cat that Nicked the Cream.

MA UBU: What about the brolly? The cloak? The great big hat?

PA UBU: What about them, Ma Ubu?

He goes, slamming the door.

MA UBU: Snikt, what a tight-arse. Never mind. Slipalipt, I'm loosening him. With God's good help, not to mention mine, I'll be Queen of Baloney by Saturday.

2

Room in PA UBU's house, with a table set for a feast. PA UBU, MA UBU.

MA UBU: Well, they're late. Our guests.

PA UBU: Yes. Stagger me sideways, I'm starving. Ma Ubu, you look really ugly today. Because we've got company?

MA UBU: (*Shrugging.*) Shikt.

PA UBU: (*Grabbing a roast chicken.*) Dagit, I'm hungry. I'll get stuck into this. Chicken, right? Snot bad.

MA UBU: Put that down. Leave something for the guests.

PA UBU: There's plenty. I won't touch another thing. Look out the window, Ma Ubu. See if our guests are here.

MA UBU: (*Going to the window.*) No sign of them.

PA UBU snatches his chance and snitches a slice of meat.

Here they are. Captain Dogpile and his Barmpots. Pa Ubu, what are you eating?

PA UBU: Nothing. Collops.

MA UBU: Collops. Collops. Dagnagit, put them down!

PA UBU: Stagger me sideways, I'll dot you one.

The door opens.

3

PA UBU, MA UBU, DOGPILE, BARMPOTS

MA UBU: Good evening, gents. So naice to see you. Do sit down.

DOGPILE: Ma Ubu, good evening. Where's Pa Ubu?

PA UBU: Here! Godnagit, stagger me sideways, I'm not that small.

DOGPILE: Good evening, Pa Ubu. Lads, siddown.

All sit.

PA UBU: Pff! Any bigger, I'd have smashed the chair.

DOGPILE: Oi, Ma Ubu, what's for dinner?

MA UBU: I'll tell you.

PA UBU: I like this part.

MA UBU: Baloney soup. Calfcollops. Chicken. Pâté de dog. Turkey bum. Charlotte Russe.

PA UBU: That's enough. Snurk! More?

MA UBU: (*Continuing.*) Ice cream, lettuce, apples, hotpot, tartyfarts, cauliflower shikt.

PA UBU: Dagnagit, I'm paying for this. What d'you take me for, a bank?

MA UBU: Ignore him. He's barmy.

PA UBU: I'll barm your bum.

MA UBU: Shut up, Pa Ubu. Eat your burger.

PA UBU: Burger me, it's bad.

DOGPILE: Bleah, it's horrible.

MA UBU: Nagnancies, what d'you *want*?

PA UBU: (*Striking his forehead.*) Got it! Hang on. I won't be long.

Exit.

MA UBU: Nah, gents, collops.

DOGPILE: Very nice. All gone.

MA UBU: Some turkeybum?

DOGPILE: Fantastic. Great! Up Ma Ubu.

ALL: Up Ma Ubu.

PA UBU returns, carrying a disgusting brush.

PA UBU: What about three cheers for Pa Ubu?

He pokes the brush at the guests.

MA UBU: Idiot, what are you doing?

PA UBU: It's lovely. Taste it, taste it.

Several of them taste and die, poisoned.

PA UBU: Ma Ubu, pass the tartyfarts. I'll hand them round.

MA UBU: Here.

PA UBU: Out, out, the lot of you. Captain Dogpile, I want a word.

THE OTHERS: Hey! We haven't finished.

PA UBU: Oh yes you have. Out, out! Dogpile, sit.

No one moves.

Still here? Stagger me sideways, where are those tartyfarts? I'll see to you.

He starts hurling tartyfarts.

ALL: Erg! Foo! Aagh!

PA UBU: Shikt, shikt, shikt. D'you get it? Out!

ALL: Bastard! Swine!

PA UBU: They've gone. What a lousy dinner. Dogpile, walkies.

Exeunt.

4

PA UBU, MA UBU, DOGPILE

PA UBU: Here, Dogpile. Diddums like oo dindins?

DOGPILE: Lovely. All but the shikt.

PA UBU: The shikt was great.

MA UBU: Shickun son goo. That's French.

PA UBU: Captain Dogpile, I'm going to make you Lord de Lawdy.

DOGPILE: Pardon, Pa Ubu? I thought you were skint.

PA UBU: In a day or two, with your help, I'll be King of Baloney.

DOGPILE: You're going to kill Good King Wenceslas?

PA UBU: Aren't you the clever one?

DOGPILE: If you're doing for Good King Wenceslas, count me in. I'm his mortal enemy. Me and my Barmpots.

PA UBU: (*Falling on his neck.*) Dogpile! Darling!

DOGPILE: Puah, you stink, Pa Ubu. Don't you ever wash?

PA UBU: What if I don't?

MA UBU: He doesn't know how to.

PA UBU: I'll stample you.

MA UBU: Shiktface.

PA UBU: Out, Dogpile. That's all for now. I'll make you Lord de Lawdy. That's a promise. Stagger me sideways, I swear, on Ma Ubu's head.

MA UBU: Hey …

PA UBU: Shut it, girl.

Exeunt.

5

PA UBU, MA UBU, MESSENGER

PA UBU: Hey you. What is it? Piss off. Who needs you?

MESSENGER: Sirrah, you're summoned. By his Majesty.

Exit.

PA UBU: Oh shikt. Dogalmighty, stagger me sideways, they know. I'm done for. Chopped. Oh dear.

MA UBU: You great jelly. Get on with it.

PA UBU: I know, I'll say it was her ... and that Dogpile.

MA UBU: Lardbelly, just you try.

PA UBU: Just watch me.

He goes. MA UBU *runs after him.*

MA UBU: Pa Ubu! No! Pa Ubu! I'll let you have sausage.

PA UBU: (*Off.*) Sausage, ha! Haha! HaHA!

6

The royal palace. GOOD KING WENCESLAS, *surrounded by his officers;* DOGPILE; *princes* SILLY, WILLY *and* BILLIKINS. *Enter* PA UBU.

PA UBU: It was them, not me. Ma Ubu, Dogpile. They did it.

KING: Did what, Pa Ubu?

DOGPILE: He's pissed.

KING: One knows how it feels.

PA UBU: Of course I'm pissed. From drinking toasts.

KING: Pa Ubu, it is our purpose to reward your loyal service as Captain of the Guard. From this day on, be known as Baron Stretcholand.

PA UBU: Good ole Majesty, how kind, how kind.

KING: Never mind all that, Pa Ubu. Just turn up at the Posh Parade tomorrow.

PA UBU: I will, I will. But first, your Maj ... a little gift.

He gives him a kazoo.

KING: A kazoo? What shall we do with it? We'll give it to Billikins.

BILLIKINS: Pa Ubu's orf his chump.

PA UBU: Right, 'scuse me, time to piss off.

He turns and falls.

Gor! Nyai! Stagger me sideways, I've knackered my kneecap and gurdled my gob.

KING: (*Getting up.*) I say, Pa Ubu, are you all right?

PA UBU: All right? I'm done for. What'll become of poor old Ma?

KING: One shall look after her.

PA UBU: How kind. But don't think that'll save you.

Exit.

7

PA UBU's *house.* PA UBU, MA UBU, BIG BAD BERNIE, WALLOP, MCCLUB, DOGPILE, BARMPOTS, SOLDIERS.

PA UBU: OK, lads. Time to get this plot moving. Who's got an idea? Me first. Me first.

DOGPILE: Pa Ubu, go on.

PA UBU: This is it, lads. It's simple. I stuff his lunch with arsenic. He shoves it down his gob, drops dead, and I nab his throne.

ALL: Ooh! Cheeky monkey! Aren't you the naughty one?

PA UBU: Good, innit? Dogpile, got anything better?

DOGPILE: I suggest: one slash of the sabre, to slice him in snippets from snitch to shoe.

ALL: Yay! Our hero! Whee! Yeehah!

PA UBU: And suppose he kicks you up the bum? Have you forgotten those stout iron shoes he wears for Posh Parades? In any case, now I know, I'll tell him. There'll be a big reward.

MA UBU: Coward, traitor, lardbag.

ALL: Boo! Hiss!

PA UBU: Watch it, or I'll drop you lot in as well. Oh, all right. For your sakes, lads, I'll do it. Dogpile, stand by to slice.

DOGPILE: Hang on. Why don't we all pile in on him, yelling and shouting? We've got to scare off his guards.

PA UBU: Got it! I stamp on his toe. He kicks me. I shout 'SHIKT' – and that's the signal. You all pile in.

MA UBU: Then as soon as he's dead, you grab the crown.

DOGPILE: And I and the lads see to the rest of them.

PA UBU: Right. Especially that bastard Billikins.

They start to go. He drags them back.

Hang on. Haven't we forgotten something? The solemn oath?

DOGPILE: How do we do that, without a bible?

PA UBU: We'll use Ma Ubu. Swear on her.

ALL: Yay. Good. Right.

PA UBU: OK. You all swear to kill Good King Wenceslas ... properly?

ALL: We swear. We'll kill him. Up Pa Ubu. Yay.

End of Act 1.

Act 2
1

The royal palace. GOOD KING WENCESLAS, QUEEN ROSAMOND, SILLY, WILLY, BILLIKINS.

KING: Prince Billikins, this morning you were very cheeky to Pa Ubu, one's Captain of the Guard, one's Baron Stretcholand. One therefore grounds you. Stay away from one's Posh Parade.

QUEEN: Hang on, Wence. You need the whole family there. Security.

KING: One means what one says. Don't bibblebabble, madam. You tire one's ears.

BILLIKINS: Mighty majesty, pater: one submits.

QUEEN: You're really going through with it, your Maj? This Posh Parade?

KING: Madam, why not?

QUEEN: I told you before. I had a dream. He smote you with his smiters, chucked you in the river and nabbed the crown. That lion and unicorn put it on his head.

KING: Whose head?

QUEEN: Pa Ubu's head.

KING: Absurd. His Lord High Ubuness is the soul of loyalty. He'd let wild horses mangle him to mincemeat before he harmed a hair of one's head.

QUEEN, BILLIKINS: You're just so *wrong*.

KING: Enough. We'll show you how much one trusts Count Ubu. One will attend the Posh Parade dressed just as one is. No sword, no armour.

QUEEN: Alack! O woe! I'll not clap eyes on you no moe.

KING: Come, Willy. Come Silly.

They go. The QUEEN *and* BILLIKINS *go to the window.*

QUEEN, BILLIKINS: God and St Nick protect you.

QUEEN: Billikins, come with me to church. We'll pray for them.

2

The parade ground. The BALONIAN ARMY, GOOD KING WENCESLAS, WILLY, SILLY, PA UBU, DOGPILE *and his* BARMPOTS, BIG BAD BERNIE, WALLOP, McCLUB.

KING: Baron Ubu, stand beside one, you and your chaps. It's time to inspect the troops.

PA UBU: (*Aside to his men.*) Any minute now. (*To the king.*) Right behind you, sire.

UBU's *men gather round the* KING.

KING: Ah! The Forty-seventh Mounted Foot and Mouth. Aren't they something?

PA UBU: They're rubbish. Look at that one, there. Oi, monkey's armpit, have you forgotten how to shave?

KING: He looks smooth enough to one. Pa Ubu, what's up?

PA UBU: This.

He stamps on his foot.

KING: Bastard.

PA UBU: SHIKT! It's time!

DOGPILE: Pile on, lads.

They all attack the KING. *One* BARMPOT *explodes.*

KING: One's done for! Help! One's dead.

WILLY: (*To* SILLY.) I say. Up and at 'em, what?

PA UBU: I've got the crown. See to the rest of them.

DOGPILE: Get the bastards. Now!

The PRINCES *run for it. All chase them.*

3

QUEEN ROSAMOND, BILLIKINS

QUEEN: Oh that's better. I love a good pray.

BILLIKINS: There's nothing to be afraid of.

Huge shouting, off.

What's that? I say, my brothers. Pa Ubu and his badlads, after them.

QUEEN: God save us. Saints and martyrs! They're gaining on them.

BILLIKINS: The whole bally army, following Pa Ubu. Where's his Majesty? Oh! I say!

QUEEN: Willy's down. Poor Willy's shot.

BILLIKINS: Silly!

SILLY *turns.*

Look out!

QUEEN: He's surrounded.

BILLIKINS: He's done for. Dogpile's sliced him like salami.

QUEEN: Saints and martyrs! They've broken into the palace. They're climbing the stairs. They're foaming at the mouth.

QUEEN, BILLIKINS: (*On their knees.*) God save us. Please.

BILLIKINS: If I get my hands on that bounder Ubu . . .

4

The same. The door is broken down. PA UBU *and the* BARMPOTS *burst in.*

PA UBU: Yeah, Billikins? What will you do?

BILLIKINS: Good god, man, I'll defend my mater. To the last drop of blood. Take one step further, make one's day.

PA UBU: Dogpile, I'm scared. I'm off.

SOLDIER: (*Advancing.*) Billikins, on guard!

BILLIKINS: On guard yourself.

He bops his bonce.

QUEEN: Bully for Billy! One for you!

OTHERS: (*Advancing.*) We'll see to you, Billikins. We'll take good care of you.

BILLIKINS: Bounders! Ruffians! Take that! And that!

He whirls his sabre and massacres them.

PA UBU: He's a slinky little slicer. But that won't save his bacon.

BILLIKINS: Mater, escape by the secret passage.

QUEEN: What about you, son? What about you?

BILLIKINS: I'll follow.

PA UBU: Grab the queen. Oh, she's gone. Right, you bastard . . .

He advances on BILLIKINS.

BILLIKINS: Cry God for Billikins and Sangorge!

He nicks UBU's *napper with a savage swordslice.*

Mater, wait for me!

He escapes by the secret passage.

5

A cave in the mountains. BILLIKINS, QUEEN ROSAMOND.

BILLIKINS: We'll be quite safe here.

QUEEN: Oh, Billikins. Ah.

She falls on the snow.

BILLIKINS: What's the matter, mater?

QUEEN: I'm ill, Bill. I've only two hours to live.

BILLIKINS: Good lord. Hypothermia?

QUEEN: So many blows. How could I endure? His majesty murdered, our family finished – and you, last remnant of the royal race, forced to flee, here in the hills, like a common catnapper.

BILLIKINS: And forced by *him*, what's more. That bounder Ubu. That oik. That swine. When I think how the pater larded him with honours, lorded him – for this! The very next morning, a knife in the guts. That's hardly cricket. Not fair at all.

QUEEN: Oh Billikins, remember how happy we were before Pa Ubu came! Ah me, what a change is here.

BILLIKINS: Chin up, mater. We'll bide our time. We'll watch for the sunrise. We'll remember who we are.

QUEEN: The sunrise! Ah child, for you perhaps, glad dawn. But these poor eyes won't live to see it.

BILLIKINS: What's up? She's white. She's limp. Anyone there? I say . . . ? Oh lord, her heart's not beating. She's dead. Good grief, yet another of Pa Ubu's victims.

He hides his face in his hands and sobs.

It isn't fair. Alone at fourteen years old, with such violent vengeance to bally bear.

He surrenders himself to the most violent despair. Meanwhile, the ghosts of GOOD KING WENCESLAS, SILLY, WILLY *and* QUEEN ROSAMOND, *plus their* ANCESTORS, *fill the cave.*

The senior GHOST *goes to* BILLIKINS *and prods him tenderly.*

GHOST: Bear with me, Billikins. In life, I was Vaslav the Versatile, first king and founder of our royal line. To you, now, I hand this holy task: our vengeance.

He gives him a big sword.

And this great big sword. Let it not rest nor sleep till that traitor dieth, till it encompasseth his death.

All the GHOSTS *disappear, leaving* BILLIKINS *in a state of exaltation.*

6

The royal palace. PA UBU, MA UBU, DOGPILE.

PA UBU: I bloody will not. Bumbrains! Why should I bankrupt myself for them?

DOGPILE: It's traditional, Pa Ubu. Coronation . . . goodies for everyone. People expect it.

MA UBU: Loads to eat, a mint of money, or you'll be out by Tuesday.

PA UBU: Mintomoney, no. Loadsteat, fine. Knacker three old nags. That's good enough for lardipuffs like them.

MA UBU: Look who's talking. Lardipuffs!

PA UBU: I keep telling you, I'm here to make my pile. Mine, every penny, mine.

MA UBU: You've got the Balonian Big Bank. What more d'you want?

DOGPILE: I know. In the cathedral. There's hidden treasure. I know where it is. We'll give them that.

PA UBU: Just you try. One finger . . .

DOGPILE: Pa Ubu, unless you give them something, they'll never pay their taxes.

PA UBU: You're kidding.

MA UBU: No he's not.

PA UBU: Oh, all right. Do what you like. Three million cash, a billion chopsansteaks. Just leave some for me!

Exeunt.

7

Palace courtyard, full of people. PA UBU, *crowned.* MA UBU, DOGPILE, FLUNKEYS *staggering with meat.*

PEOPLE: Up Ubu. Hurray! Up Ubu. Yay!

PA UBU: (*Throwing gold.*) There. There. I'm not doing this because I like it. It was Ma's idea. Be sure and pay your taxes.

ALL: We will. We will.

DOGPILE: Ma Ubu, look. They're fighting for the cash. It's hell down there.

MA UBU: Fooagh, look: he's had his brains bashed in.

PA UBU: Lovely! Bring more gold.

DOGPILE: Suppose we had a race?

PA UBU: Brilliant. (*To the* PEOPLE.) Friends, you see this golden treasure chest? Stuffed with money. Thirty zillion nicker. Balonian bazoomas, every pee of it: no rubbish. Anyone who wants to be in the race, go over there. Start when I wave my hanky. First here gets the lot. If you don't win, the consolation prize is this other chest. You share it: everyone gets something.

ALL: Yeehah! God save the king. Up Ubu. It was never like this when Good King Wenceslas was king.

PA UBU: (*Joyfully to* MA UBU.) Listen to them!

The PEOPLE *line up at one side of the courtyard.*

One, two, three. Are you ready?

ALL: Yes! Yes!

PA UBU: Go!

They surge forward. Jostling, tumult.

DOGPILE: They're coming! They're coming!

PA UBU: Him in front, he's flagging.

MA UBU: No, he's not. Come on!

DOGPILE: Ah, he came too soon. Come on, the other one! Come on!

The runner who had been second wins.

ALL: Fast Freddie! Hurray! Hurray!

FAST FREDDIE: Sire, what can I say? Your majesty, your majesty …

PA UBU: Tsk, it's nothing. Freddie, lovey, take your money. Enjoy. Mwah, mwah. And the rest of you, here's yours. One coin each, until they're done.

ALL: Yay! Fast Freddie, Pa Ubu! Hurray! Hurray!

PA UBU: All right, it's dinner time. You're all invited. In you go!

PEOPLE: In! Up Ubu! Hurray!

They go into the palace. We hear the noise of revelry, and it lasts all night. Curtain.

End of Act 2.

Act 3

1

The palace. PA UBU, MA UBU.

PA UBU: Stagger me sideways, I've dunnit: king. I've had the party … got the angover … Next, the great big cloak.

MA UBU: Very naice, Pa Ubu. It's naice being royal.

PA UBU: You said it, girl.

MA UBU: We've such a lot to thank him for.

PA UBU: Who?

MA UBU: Captain Dogpile. Lord de Lawdy.

PA UBU: Lord de Lawdy? You're joking. Now I don't need him any more, he can stuff his lordship.

Figure 14 *Ubu* directed by Jean Vilar at the Théàtre National Populaire, in 1958. (Photographer: Bernand.)

MA UBU: Bad idea, Pa Ubu. He may turn nasty.

PA UBU: I'm so frightened! Him and that Billikins.

MA UBU: You've not frightened of Billikins?

PA UBU: Tickle me taxes, he's fourteen years old! A spottibot!

MA UBU: Pa Ubu, be careful. Be naice to him. Bribe him.

PA UBU: More money down the tubes! I've spent sixty squillion already.

MA UBU: I'm telling you, Billikins'll win. He's got justice fighting on his side.

PA UBU: So bloody what? We've got injustice, haven't we? You piss me off, Ma Ubu. I'll settle you.

He chases her out.

2

Great hall of the palace. PA UBU, MA UBU, OFFICERS, SOLDIERS, BIG BAD BERNIE, WALLOP, MCCLUB, NOBS IN CHAINS, BANKERS, LAWYERS, CLERKS.

PA UBU: Bring the nob-box, the nob-hook, the nob-knife, the nob-ledger – and the nobs.

The NOBS are pushed forward, roughly.

MA UBU: Pa Ubu, please. Go easy.

PA UBU: Listen up. Royal decree. To enrich the state, I'm going to do in all the nobs and snitch their loot.

NOBS: Ooh! Aah! Help!

PA UBU: Bring me Nob Number One. And the nob-hook. All those condemned to death, I shove down this hole. Down to the Slushpile to be debrained. (*To the* NOB.) What's your name, dogbum?

NOB: Viscount of Vitebsk.

PA UBU: How much is that worth?

NOB: Three million a year.

PA UBU: Guilty!

He hooks him down the chute.

MA UBU: You're so strict.

PA UBU: Next nob. What's your name?

Silence.

Answer, bogbrain.

SECOND NOB: Protector of Pinsk. Not to mention Minsk.

PA UBU: Ducky. Down you go. Next! What an ugly bastard. Who are you?

THIRD NOB: Holder of Hanover, Halle and Harrogate.

PA UBU: Three in one? Down the tube. Next nob. Name?

FOURTH NOB: Proud Palatine of Polock.

PA UBU: Pollocks to that, mate. Down the tube. What's biting you, Ma Ubu?

MA UBU: You're being so fierce.

PA UBU: I'm working. Making my fortune. I'll hear the list now. Clerk of the Court, MY list. MY titles. Read MY list to ME.

CLERK: Viscount of Vitebsk. Protector of Pinsk. Holder of Hanover, Halle, Harrogate. Palatine of Polock.

PA UBU: Yes. *Well ...?*

CLERK: That's all.

PA UBU: What d'you mean, that's all? Come here, nobs. The lot of you. I'm not rich enough yet, so you're all for the chop. You've got it, I need it. Stuff the nobs down the tube.

The NOBS are stuffed down the hatch.

Get a nurdle on. I've laws to pass.

SEVERAL: Big deal.

PA UBU: Lawyers first, then bankers.

SEVERAL LAWYERS: Objection! Nolle prosequi. Status quo.

PA UBU: Shikt. Law Number One: judges' salaries. Abolished.

JUDGES: What'll we live on? We're skint. All skint.

PA UBU: Live on the fines.

FIRST JUDGE: Impossible.

SECOND JUDGE: Outrageous.

THIRD JUDGE: Unheard-of.

FOURTH JUDGE: Beyond the pale.

JUDGES: Under these conditions, we refuse to judge.

PA UBU: All judges down the tube!

They struggle, in vain.

MA UBU: What're you doing, Pa Ubu? Who'll do the judging, now?

PA UBU: Watch and see. Who's next, now? Bankers.

BANKERS: No change!

PA UBU: First off, I want half of all charges.

BANKERS: You're joking.

PA UBU: And here *are* some charges: property, ten percent, commerce and industry, twenty-five percent, marriage and death fifty nicker each.

FIRST BANKER: Pa Ubu, it just isn't viable.

SECOND BANKER: It doesn't add up.

THIRD BANKER: Neither ult nor inst.

PA UBU: Take the piss, would you? Down the tube!

The BANKERS are downchuted.

MA UBU: Fine king you are, killing the whole world.

PA UBU: Don't worry, girl. I'll go from town to town myself, collect the cash.

3

Rude hut in the Balonian countryside. PEASANTS.

PEASANT: (*Entering.*) I come with news. His majesty's no more. His sons no more. Save Billikins. He got away. His mummy too. They're in the hills. Pa Ubu's nabbed the throne.

ANOTHER PEASANT: And that's not all. I've just been to town and they were carting corpses and the corpses belonged to three hundred executed nobles and five hundred executed

judges and they're doubling the taxes and Pa Ubu's coming to collect them in person.

ALL: Alack! What now? Pa Ubu's a rotten swine and his family's no better. Or so they say.

PEASANT: Hark! What's that? There's someone at the door.

PA UBU: (*Outside.*) Rumblestuffsticks! Open up! By shikt, by Dikt, by good saint Nickt, cashknackers, slashpacks, I want your tax!

The door is broken down. UBU bursts in, with a pack of CASHHOUNDS.

4

PA UBU: Who's the oldest?

A PEASANT steps forward.

PEASANT: Norbert Nurdle.

PA UBU: Right. Listen. Rumblestuffsticks, I said listen. D'you want these frensomine to clip your clackers?

PEASANT: But your Majesty hasn't said anything.

PA UBU: Wrong, pal. I've been flapping my gob for the whole last hour. Fetch out your tax-pot, now, or die. Cashandlers, the cashcart.

The cashcart is brought in.

PEASANT: The point is, sire, we're covered by limited liability. The documents were based on an assessment of wundruntunty poundipees. And we paid in full, the Feast of St Multiple Ult.

PA UBU: So what? I've changed the rules. It was in the paper: all taxes to be paid twice over, except those I may dream up later, to be paid three times. Simple, innit? I make my fortune, snickersnack, then kill the whole world and buggeroff.

PEASANTS: Lord Ubu, have pity. We're honest, simple folk. We're poor.

PA UBU: Tough titty. Pay. Unless you want the rest of it. Neck-knotting, noodle-nackering. Rumblestuffsticks, I am the bloody king.

PEASANTS: You aren't. Revolution! Up Billikins. His majesty. The king.

PA UBU: Cashcarters, kill.

A battle begins. The house is wrecked. None escape except old NORBERT, who legs it across the plain. UBU is left alone, scooping cash.

5

Dungeon. UBU, with DOGPILE in chains.

PA UBU: It's just what happens, mate. You ask for what I owe you, I say no, you turn nasty, you end up here. Goldalmighty! It's perfect. Couldn't be better. You've got to agree.

DOGPILE: Pa Ubu, beware. Five days you've held this throne. You've killed. You just don't care. Dead corpses scream and groan for vengeance. Pa Ubu, beware.

PA UBU: Very good: a poet, and don't you know it. If you once got out of here ...! Oh yes, oh yes. How lucky for me that this dank deep dungeon, enclosed by craggy castle, has never popped a prisoner yet. Night night, sleep tight, keep hold of your nicker-nack, the rats here bite.

Exit. TURNKEYS *bolt all the doors.*

6

Palace of TSAR ALEXIS OF ALL THE RUSSKIES. TSAR ALEXIS, *his* COURTIERS, DOGPILE.

ALEXIS: Base mercenary wretch! Wast even thou who conspired to do in our good king cousin, Wenceslas?

DOGPILE: I'm sorry, sire. Pa Ubu made me. I didn't want to.

ALEXIS: Big liar. Never mind. What d'you want now?

DOGPILE: Pa Ubu dungeoned me for treason. I managed to escape. I've been on the road five days, five nights. Galloping. On a horse. To beg your royal pardon.

ALEXIS: What practical proof presentest thou?

DOGPILE: My soldier's sword. And this detailed plan of the castle.

ALEXIS: We accept the sword. But burn the plan, by Genghis. We'll not come top by cheating.

DOGPILE: One of good king Wenceslas' sons, young Billikins, still lives. To see him on the throne, I'd give my all.

ALEXIS: In the Brave Balonian Battalions, what place hadst thou?

DOGPILE: Commander of the fifth phalanx of fusiliers. Pa Ubu's personal protectors.

ALEXIS: OK. Thou'rt now lieutenant of lancers. Sub. If thou dost well, thou gets rewarded. If thou betray'st us, watch out.

DOGPILE: I lack not courage, sire.

ALEXIS: Good. Vanish from our presence. Scat.

Exit.

7

UBU'S *council chamber.* PA UBU, MA UBU, COUNCILLORS.

PA UBU: Order. I declare this meeting open. Stretch your ears and flab your gobs. Agenda: one, cashcount. Two, my new idea: how to keep it sunny and do away with rain.

COUNCILLOR: Lord Ubu, brilliant.

MA UBU: Licker.

PA UBU: Queen of my shikt, button it. We're not doing badly, lords. Our brass-knuckle boys bring in the bacon. Our mother-muggers work miracles. Everywhere you look, you see nothing but houses crumbling and citizens grumbling under the burden of our bills.

COUNCILLOR: The new taxes, Lord Ubu. What about them?

MA UBU: They're rubbish. Tax on marriages: three pee. Pa Ubu's chasing people in the street and forcing them into church.

PA UBU: Stuffsticks! Chancelloress of the Exchequeress, I'm talking.

Enter MESSENGER.

What's he want? Blugger off, cat-basket, or I'll trundle your trollops and snaggle your snipes.

MA UBU: Too late. He's gone. He left this postcard.

PA UBU: You read it. I'm depressed. I've forgotten how to read. Get a grundle on. It'll be from Dogpile.

MA UBU: So it is. 'Having a lovely taime. Tsar Alexis of all the Russkies really naice. Invading tomorrow to put Billikins back on throne and stuff your guts. Regards ...'

PA UBU: I'm done for. The naughty man's coming to hurt me. St Nickerless, oelpme, I'll give you all my taxes. God, tell me what to do. I'll even pray. Oh what am I to do?

He sobs and sobs.

MA UBU: Pa Ubu, there's only one thing for it. War.

ALL: Hurrah! Fight! Yay!

PA UBU: Oh brilliant. Thrashed again.

FIRST COUNCILLOR: Call up the army.

SECOND COUNCILLOR: Lines of supply.

THIRD COUNCILLOR: Forts, cannons, balls.

FOURTH COUNCILLOR: Cash for our boys.

PA UBU: Ah! No. What d'you take me for? Me, pay? No chance. Stagger me sideways, we'll fight if you're all so eager. But pay? Not me.

ALL: War! War! Yay!

8

In camp outside UBU'S *capital city.* PA UBU, MA UBU, SOLDIERS, BARMPOTS.

SOLDIERS AND BARMPOTS: Up Baloney! Up Ubu!

PA UBU: Ma Ubu, give me my breastplate. My poky-stick. I'll be so loaded, I won't be able to run if they're after me.

MA UBU: Coward.

PA UBU: Godnag this shikastick. This nobhook. They won't stay put. I'll never be ready. The Russkies'll come and kill me.

SOLDIER: Lord Ubu, your snackersnicks are falling down.

PA UBU: I dead you, hookynobbyshikastick. Slicymug. Piff, paff, pah.

MA UBU: What does he look like? His breastplate, his iron hat. Like an armour-plated pumpkin.

PA UBU: Time to mount. Bring forth Cashnag.

MA UBU: Whadyoo say?

PA UBU: Cashnag. My ... charger.

MA UBU: He can't carry you. He's not been fed since Tuesday. He's a bag of bones.

PA UBU: You're joking. Twelve pee a day and still can't carry me? You're pulling my leg, cornswobbit, you're pocketing the cash.

MA UBU blushes and lowers her eyes.

Bring Cashnag Two. Rumblestuffsticks, I refuse to walk.

An enormous horse is brought in.

I'll mount. There's no air up here. I'm dizzy. I'll fall.

The horse moves off.

Help! Make it stand still. I'll fall.

MA UBU: What an idiot. He's on. He's off again.

PA UBU: Godnagit, I thought I'd had it that time. Never mind. I'm off. To war. I'll kill the whole world. Especially those who don't march in step. Ubu be angry, Ubu pullout oo teef, oo tongue.

MA UBU: Pa Ubu, farewell.

PA UBU: I forgot to tell you. Take over while I'm gone. I've got the cashledger with me, so keep your sticky hands to yourself, all right? I'm leaving Big Bad Bernie to look after you. Ma Ubu, farewell.

MA UBU: Pa Ubu, tata. Give that Tsar whatfor.

PA UBU: Watch me. Nose-knotting, teeth-twisting, tongue-tearing, noodlenackering.

Fanfares as the army marches off.

MA UBU: (*Alone.*) Hangdock he's gone. Lardifard! Right. Get organised, kill Billikins and grab the loot.

Act 4
1

Royal crypt in the cathedral

MA UBU: Where is it, the treasure? None of these stones sound hollow. I've done it right: thirteen steps along the wall from the tomb of Vaslav the Versatile. Just a minute: this one sounds hollow. Ma Ubu, to work! Prise it open. Mff! Won't budge. I'll use the cashook. It's never failed before. Haho! Kings' bones, and gold. Into the sack, all of it. Aeeh, what's that noise? Is ... anybody ... there? Nothing. Get a nurdle on. All of it. You need to see daylight, don't you, cash? Had it up to here with tombs? Put back the stone ... Ah! That noise again. I'm scared. I've had enough. I'll come back for the rest some other time. Tomorrow.

VOICE: (*From the tomb of STANLEY THE USUALLY SILENT.*) Never, Ma Ubu.

MA UBU shrieks and flees through the secret door, lugging the cashsack.

2

Square in the capital. BILLIKINS, CHAPS, SOLDIERS, PEOPLE.

BILLIKINS: I say, chaps, three cheers for Baloney and Good King Wenceslas. That bounder Ubu's legged it. There's no one left but Mater Ubu and Big Bad Bernie. I've an idea. Suppose I lead you chaps, chuck 'em out and restore my royal race?

ALL: Yay! Billikins! I say!

BILLIKINS: And when we've done that, we'll abolish all the taxes imposed by that great oik Ub.

ALL: Hurray! I say! On to the palace. Exterminate!

BILLIKINS: Oh look. Ma Ubu and her guards. There, on the palace steps.

MA UBU: What is it, gents? Oh, Billikins.

The CROWD throws stones.

FIRST GUARD: There's not a window left.

SECOND GUARD: They got me. Ah.

THIRD GUARD: I'm done for. Oh.

BILLIKINS: Keep chucking, chaps.

BIG BAD BERNIE: Hoho! Heehee! Haha!

He draws his sword and rushes among them, creating horrible havoc.

BILLIKINS. You swine. On guard.

They fight a duel.

BIG BAD BERNIE: Aah. Eeh. Ooh.

BILLIKINS: I win. Ma Ubu now.

Trumpets sound.

Jolly good. Here come the upper crust. Don't let her get away.

MA UBU runs away, with all the BALONIANS after her. Shots; stones.

3

With UBU's army, marching in Russkiland

PA UBU: Hobblit, daggit, naggit, we're passing out. Curdled. Oi, squaddie, hump this cash-helmet. Sarge, take the clacker-snips, the poky-stick. That's better. I tell you again: our cashness is curdled.

The SOLDIERS obey.

WALLOP: Seeyou, pal. Whirthell they Russkies?

PA UBU: It's bloody marvellous. Not enough cash for a chariot that fits. I ask you. To stop the nag knackering under us, our cashness has had to walk. Leading the bleeder. Just wait till we get back to Baloney. Five minutes with our physics set, our poofiprofs, we'll invent a wind-cart to waft us wherever we want. Us and our army. Well?

MCCLUB: Sorsor, Nick Nackerley. Sure tis a rush he's in.

PA UBU: All right, all right. What's up?

NICK NACKERLEY: Lord, all is lost. The Balonians have broken out. Big Bad Bernie's dead. Ma Ubu's hiding in the hills.

PA UBU: Polecat! Vulture! Fruitbat! Where did that lot come from? Puddle me. Who's responsible? Billikins, betya. Where have you come from?

NICK NACKERLEY: Baloney, sire.

PA UBU: Shikt, son, if I thought this was true we'd all be on our way home right now. But see here, sonny, you've got cloud for brains. You're dreaming, sonnikins. Go to the front line. Take a look: Russkies. We'll make a sortie, sunshine. Give it all we've got: shikthooks, cashpikes, everything.

GENERAL CUSTARD: Pa Ubu, look. Wusskies.

PA UBU: You're right. Russkies. Brilliant. If we'd some way out of here. But we haven't. We're on a hill; we're sitting ducks.

SOLDIERS: Russkies! Woe! The foe!

PA UBU: Time to get organised. For battle. We'll stay up here. No point in going down there. I'll stand in the middle. Like a living citadel. You can all protect me. Stuff your guns with bullets. Eight bullets means eight dead Russkies, eight more bastards off my back. Light armed Foot, down there. Wait till they charge, then killem. Heavy Horse, hang back, then charge. Artillery here, all round this windmill. If anything moves, shoot it. Me? Us? We'll wait inside the windmill. We'll stick our cashcannon through the window, bar the door with our poky-stick, and if anyone breaks in, they'll be really in the shikt.

OFFICERS: Sah! Sah! Sah!

PA UBU: We'll win, no problem. What time is it?

A cuckoo crows three times.

GENERAL CUSTARD: Eleven a.m.

PA UBU: Dinner time. They'll not attack till twelve. General Laski, tell the men: fall out and pee, then fall back in and start the Cashnal Anthem.

GENERAL CUSTARD: Sah. Weady, chaps? By the wight in thwees. Left wight, left wight.

Exit CUSTARD *and* ARMY. *Impressive orchestral introduction.* PA UBU *sings. The* ARMY *comes back in time to join in the chorus.*

PA UBU: God save our gracious me,
Long live our noble me,
Pour me some –

SOLDIERS: Beer, beer, beer, beer, beer, beer, beer, beer.

PA UBU: Fill up your tanks and then
Unzip your pants and then
All start to –

SOLDIERS: Pee, pee, pee, pee, pee, pee, pee, pee.

PA UBU: Soon as you've room for more
Flap gob and start to pour,
Fill up with –

SOLDIERS: Beer, beer, beer, beer, beer, beer, beer, beer.

PA UBU: I love it. I love you all.

SOLDIERS AND BARMPOTS: Till, till, till, till,
Tax, tax, tax, tax,
Up Ubu, up Ubu,
Ting, ting-a-ting.

PA UBU: I love it. I love you all.

A Russkie cannonball flies in and smashes the windmill's sail.

Ahoo! Help! They got me. No, I lied. They didn't.

4

PA UBU, GENERAL CUSTARD, MAJOR F. FORT, TSAR ALEXIS, DOGPILE, SOLDIERS, BARMPOTS, UBU'S ARMY, RUSSKIE ARMY

MAJOR F. FORT: (*Arriving.*) Lord Ubu, the Russkies are attacking.

PA UBU: Don't look at me. Snot my fault. Cashofficers, prepare for battle.

GENERAL CUSTARD: Another cannon ball.

PA UBU: I'm off. It's raining lead and iron. My cashness could get seriously croaked. Down the hill.

They all rush down the hill. Battle has begun. They vanish in the clouds of smoke at the foot of the hill.

RUSSKIE: (*Slashing.*) Yah! Take that.

GENERAL CUSTARD: Ouch. That weally hurt.

PA UBU: Say your prayers, pigbreath. Put that down. You don't scare me.

RUSSKIE: Oh, don't I? Right.

He fires.

PA UBU: Oh! I'm hit, I'm leaking, I'm buried. Only kidding. Here!

He tears strips off him.

You, Custard. Start again.

GENERAL CUSTARD: Forward. Push. Mark the man, not the ball. We're winning.

PA UBU: You think so? What are these, then? Black eyes, not medals, mate.

RUSSKIE CAVALRYMEN: Make way! His Totality the Tsar.

TSAR ALEXIS arrives, with DOGPILE in disguise.

BALONIAN SOLDIER: Help! The Tsar.

ANOTHER: He's crossed the ditch.

ANOTHER: Who's that bastard with him? The one with the big sword. Yike! That's four he's sliced.

DOGPILE: Had enough? Want more? Who the hell are you? Ha! Hey! Any more of you?

He massacres Balonians.

PA UBU: Don't just stand there. Grab him. Slab the whole lot of them. We're winning. Up ours!

ALL: Up ours! Godnagit. Grab them. Get that big bastard. Now.

DOGPILE: Sangorge. Ow.

PA UBU: (*Recognising him.*) It's Dogpile. Well, well, well. Have we something nice for you? You like things hot. Cashkindlers, light the fire. Yarg! Ooh! I'm dead. A cannonball. Our favverwichartinevven, forgivmasins. No doubt, a cannonball.

DOGPILE: It was a water pistol.

PA UBU: Bastard. Now you're for it.

He runs at him and tears strips off him.

GENERAL CUSTARD: Lord Ubu, we're winning.

PA UBU: Of course we are. I'm exhausted. I'm black and blue. I've gottosiddown. I'm globbed.

GENERAL CUSTARD: Pa Ubu, it's the Tsar you want to glob.

PA UBU: You're right. Shiktsword, hup! Cashook, ha-hey! There's work to do. How's my dear little poky-stick? All ready to tsap that Tsar? Ha-ho! Bring Cashnag, my charger, here.

He hurls himself at TSAR ALEXIS.

RUSSKIE OFFICER: Look out, sire!

PA UBU: Go stuff yourself. Ow! What are you doing? Can't we discuss this? I'm sorry, master. Don't be cross. I didn't do it on purpose.

He legs it. TSAR ALEXIS runs after him.

Oh shikt, he's after me. He's furious. Oh brilliant, here's the ditch. The ditch in front, and him behind. Nothing for it. Eyes shut and –

He jumps the ditch. TSAR ALEXIS falls in.

TSAR ALEXIS: I've fallen in.

POLSKIES: He's ditched! Hurrah!

PA UBU: Hm. Dare I look? He's fallen in. They're bashing his bonce. That's good. Keep at it, lads. Kick him, strangle him, smash the swine. I daren't watch. It's all come out exactly as we predicted. One's poky-stick did sterling work. One would have completely done him in if dire, sudden dread hadn't drained one's deadliness. One was unexpectedly compelled to do a runner. We owe our present safety, in part, to our own imperial skill as horseman and in part to the hocks and withers of our charger Cashnag, whose speed is equalled only by his strength and whose swiftness is sung in song and story – oh and the deepness of the ditch which loomed at the feet of the foe of yourumble serfint chancellstecker. Bloody good speech. Why thangyew. Pity no one else was listening. Back to work!

The Russkie Light Horse make a sortie and rescue TSAR ALEXIS.

GENERAL CUSTARD: We've weally had it now.

PA UBU: I'm off, then. Balonians, quick march. This way. No, that way.

BALONIANS: Run for it!

PA UBU: You said it. Stop pushing. Don't jostle. Make room for me.

He is jostled.

Watch it. Wanna coppa cashclub? He's gone. Right, leg it, and fast before that Laski sees us.

He goes. Soon afterwards, we see TSAR ALEXIS and the RUSSKIE ARMY routing the Balonians.

5

Cave in the hills. It is snowing. PA UBU, WALLOP, MCCLUB.

PA UBU: Fweeorg. It's cold. Brass monkeys. My cashness is not enjoying this.

WALLOP: Seeyou, pal. How's the terror? How's the running?

PA UBU: The terror's gone. I've still got the runs.

MCCLUB: (*Aside.*) Osor, osor.

PA UBU: Hey McClub. Your snickersnack. Howizzit?

MCCLUB: Fine sor, tanksforaskin. Except it's not well at all, atall. I can't get the bullet out. Seesor, it's dragging on the ground.

PA UBU: That'll teach you. Button it up, next time. You want to be like me. Lion-hearted, but cautious. I massacred four of them, in person, not counting the ones that were dead already when I did 'em.

WALLOP: Seeyou, McClub. What happened to wee Nick Nackerley?

MCCLUB: Brained by a bullet.

PA UBU: Behold, as the flowers of the field are felled, hoed by the heedless, heartless hoe of the heedless, heartless hoer who heartlessly hacks their heads, so now Nick Nackerley. Proud as a poppy, dead as a dandelion. Fiercely he fought, but there were just too-too many Russkies.

WALLOP: Seeyou.

MCCLUB: Sorsor.

ECHO: Ee-oo-aw.

WALLOP: Wossaht? Whairsma-weenife?

PA UBU: Not more Russkies. I'm sick of them. Where are you? I'll blugger the lotayoo.

6

Enter a BEAR.

MCCLUB: Osor, osor.

PA UBU: Oh look. Nice doggie. Here boy. Miaow, miaow.

WALLOP: Jings, it's a fooky bear, anabigyin.

PA UBU: A bear! A fookybear! It'll eat me. Dog protect me. It's coming for me. No, it's biting McClub. What a relief.

The BEAR attacks MCCLUB. WALLOP goes for it with his knife. UBU climbs a rock.

MCCLUB: Help. Wallop. Sorsorelp.

PA UBU: Get stuffed. We're saying our prayers. It's you it's eating: not our turn.

WALLOP: Ahavit, Ahavit.

MCCLUB: Pull. It's weakening, sohtis.

PA UBU: For wotweerabowtoreseev.

MCCLUB: Sorosor.

WALLOP: It's got me in its fangs. Ah hate this.

PA UBU: Thelordsmasheperd.

MCCLUB: There. Got it.

WALLOP: It's bleeding. Yay!

In the midst of the BARMPOTS' *cheers, the* BEAR *roars in agony and* PA UBU *continues to mutter prayers.*

MCCLUB: Hold it tight. I'll get my nuclear knuckleduster.

PA UBU: Makethmetoliedown.

WALLOP: Hurry up. Ahcannycope.

PA UBU: Greenpasturesleadeathme.

MCCLUB: There. Here.

Huge explosion. The BEAR *falls dead.*

WALLOP AND MCCLUB: Ta-RA!

PA UBU: Stillwatersby amen. Well? Is it dead yet? Can I come down off this rock?

WALLOP: (*Scornfully.*) Please yersel.

PA UBU: (*Climbing down.*) Well, aren't you lucky? Still alive, still slushing the snow – and all thanks to my imperial cashness. Who was it who nabbled his nidgets and gabbled his gob saying prayers for you? Who acked it with oliness as bravely as Barmpot McClubere banged it withis brass-nuckle bomlet? Who urried up this illere to itch is words igher in eaven's earole?

WALLOP: Yerbum.

PA UBU: What a monster. Thanks to me: dinner. Look at its belly. The Greeks could have used it for a woodenorse. Room for plenty more inside – as we very nearly saw for ourselves, dear friends.

WALLOP: Ma gut thinks ma throat's been cut. What's teat?

MCCLUB: Bear.

PA UBU: No, no, no, no, no. Are you going to eat it raw? We've nothing to light a fire.

WALLOP: We've pustols, flunts.

PA UBU: So we have. And now I remember, there's a bunchatrees just up the road, crammed with dry wood. McClub, go fetch.

MCCLUB *trudges off across the snow.*

WALLOP: Right. Lord Ubu, you carve.

PA UBU: Ah no. It may not be really dead. In any case, you're half eaten already. Bitten to bits. You do it. I'll light the fire, ready for when he brings the wood.

WALLOP *starts carving up the* BEAR.

Ah! He moved.

WALLOP: Lord Ubu, he's cold.

PA UBU: Tut. So much nicer hot. He'll give my cashness indigestion.

WALLOP: (*Aside.*) He's terrible. (*Aloud.*) Lord Ubu, give us a hand. Ahcannycope.

PA UBU: I can't. I won't. I'm tired.

MCCLUB: (*Returning.*) Snojoke. Snoin. Slike the North Pole, sohtis, or the West Pole. Safter teatime. Lbedark in anhour. Lessgeta move on while we can still see. At all.

PA UBU: Hear that, Wallop? Get on. Both of you, gerron. Carvim, cookim, I'm starvinere.

WALLOP: Seeyou, fatso. Ifye willniwork, yecannyeat.

PA UBU: See if I care. I like it raw. It's you two who'll suffer. I'm going to sleep.

MCCLUB: Sleep, is it? Sure and we'll do the job ourselves. He'll not see none of it, willewallop? Praps a bit of a bone or two.

WALLOP: The fire's beginnintaeburn.

PA UBU: That's better. Warmer. Russkies, everywhere. What a victory. Ah.

He falls asleep.

MCCLUB: Now, master Wallop, what say you? Nick Nackerley brought news: what truth was in't? The common talk is this: Ma Ubu deposéd stands. In my nostrils, it hath the smell of truth.

WALLOP: Purrameatonablurryfire.

MCCLUB: Nay, matters more urgent crave attention. And ere we act, we must have certain news.

WALLOP: Thou hast the right of it. Pa Ubu sleepeth. Shall we leave him where he lieth, or thtay with him?

MCCLUB: Night bringeth counsel. Knit up the ravelled sleeve of sleep, and when Dawn's candles prick we'll know just what to do.

WALLOP: Nay. While yet tis dark, snatch our chance and scarper.

MCCLUB: After you.

They go.

7

PA UBU: (*Talking in his sleep.*) Russkies, don't shoot. There's someone here. Whosat? Dogpile. Can't bearim. Bear. As bad as Billikins. He's after me as well. Gerroff. Shoo. Buggeroff. Nick Nackerley, now. The Tsar. Can't touch ME-hee. Missussubu. What you got there, girl? Wheredyoo get that gold? Thassmine, you old bag, you been diggin in the cathedral. Digginup my tomb. I've been dead for years. Billikins done me in. Laid to rest in the Cathedral. Next to Vaslav the Versatile. And in the cemetery, next to Roger the Ratbag. And in that prison cell, next to Dogpile. Not him again. Bear, buggeroff. Satanspawn, begawn. What d'you mean, can't hear me? Oh, the Barmpots lopped your lugoils. Debrainin, snackersnikin, taxnabbin, boozinanboozin, thassalife. For Barmpots, Cashlads, his right royal cashness, me.

He snores and sleeps.

Act 5

1

Night. PA UBU *asleep.* MA UBU *comes in. She doesn't see him. It's pitch dark.*

MA UBU: At last, somewhere to hide. No one about. Suits me. What a journey! Four days; one end of Baloney to the other. Whatever *could* have happened, *happened*, all at once. Fatso nags out of it on his charger. I creep into the crypt to nabisloot. Next thing, Billikins and his berserkers are almost stoning me to death. I lose my protector, Big Bad Bernie, who was so besotted with my charms that he fell in a heap every time he saw me, and every time he didn't, which is a sign of real true love. Said he'd be sliced into snippets for my sake, poor lamb. And so he was. By Billikins. Slish, slash, slosh. Aah. I nearly died. Anyway, I escape. They're all after me. Foaming with fury. I leave the palace. Down to the river. Guards on every bridge. I swim across: that'll foolem. Nobs pile after me. I'm surrounded, on every side. They're foaming at the mouth. At last I make it. One end of Baloney to the other. Four days, tramping through the snow in my own queendom, as used to be, till I end up here. Safe. Four days, I haven't et or drunk. Billikins was too close for that. Nehmind, I made it. Bleah, I'm famished. I'm freezing. What happened to old lardibags, I mean to my lord and master? Not to mention Cashnag. Died of hunger, poor old devil. Nehmind, eh? *And* I forgot the treasure. Left it in the palace. Finders keepers. Who cares?

PA UBU: (*Stirring in his sleep.*) Arrest Ma Ubu. Snackersnicker.

MA UBU: Aee. Where is this? I don't believe it. Dog, no! Pa Ubu sleepineer? That's queer. Wake him gently. Oi, gutbag, shake a leg.

PA UBU: Bloodyell, didyeseet? That bear? It was brain against bruin. Brian won, completely gobbled and globbed that brown. Wait till it's light, lads: you'll see, you'll see.

MA UBU: He's babbling. Dafter than when he started. Who's he on about?

PA UBU: McClub! Wallop! Sakashikt, where are you? I'm scared. Someone said something. Who? Not ... the bear? Shikt. Matches, matches ... Lostem in the fight.

MA UBU: (*Aside.*) Exploit the state he's in, the dark. Pretend to be a spook. Make him promise to forgiveusour cashpassin.

PA UBU: Dogalmighty. There is someone there. O-elp. I wish I was dead.

MA UBU: (*Making her voice huge.*) True, Ubu, too troo. There's someone here. The voice of doom looms from the tomb. Your fairy godmother: speciality, good advice.

PA UBU: Get stuffed.

MA UBU: Interrupt me not, or I shut my gob and you get stuffed.

PA UBU: Cornswobbit. Not another word. Do go on, your spookiness.

MA UBU: We were just going to say, Master Ubu, what a naughty little boy you are.

PA UBU: Naughty. What? Yes. Yes.

MA UBU: Godnagit, shuttit!

PA UBU: A swearing fairy.

MA UBU: (*Aside.*) Shikt. (*Aloud.*) Master Ub, you're married?

PA UBU: To vinegar-features, of course I am.

MA UBU: You mean, to the most charming waife in all the world.

PA UBU: I mean, a porcupine. Prickles everywhere. You don't know where to grab.

MA UBU: Try grabbing naicely. She could be ever so naice.

PA UBU: So full of lice?

MA UBU: Listen! Willy little boy! Sit up straight, fold your arms, pay attention! (*Aside.*) Get a nurdle on. It's nearly dawn. (*Aloud.*) Master Ub, your waife is soft and sweet, without a fault.

PA UBU: Ah, rubbish. It's *all* her fault.

MA UBU: Dognagit. She's true to you, too troo.

PA UBU: Of course she is. Who else'd have her?

MA UBU: Bastard! (*Recovering.*) Your waife steals not your gold.

PA UBU: Rubbish.

MA UBU: Not a penny peeeece.

PA UBU: So wottabat dear ole Cashnag? Three months, nothing teat, dragged by the bridle halfway round the world, dead in harness, poor old devil.

MA UBU: Not troo! Your waife is sweeeet and you're a beeeest.

PA UBU: Stuff yoo! My wife's a tart and you're a fart.

MA UBU: Master Ub, beware. You murdered Good King Wenceslas.

PA UBU: Not my fault. Ma Ubu made me.

MA UBU: You had Willy and Silly done to death.

PA UBU: Tough titty. They were after me.

MA UBU: You broke your word to Dogpile. Then you killed him.

PA UBU: He wanted to be Lord de Lawdy. So did I. Now no one is. That proves it. It wasn't me.

MA UBU: There's only one way to redeeeem your siiiiiins.

PA UBU: What is it? I'll do anything, be good, be nice, be famous.

MA UBU: You must forgive Ma Ubu for snafflin a bit of snitch.

PA UBU: Forgive her, yes. When she pays it back, when I blatterer blackanbloo, when she gives ole Cashnag the kissolife.

MA UBU: He's hooked on that horse. Yike, I'm done for: dawn.

PA UBU: So now I've proof, my own missus was robbinme. You told me. She's additnow. Guilty as charged, verdict of you all, hanged by the neck, signed, sealed delivered, no appeal. Hey up: dawn. Cashnagit, it's her. Ma Ubu.

MA UBU: (*Offendedly.*) Coursitsnot. I'll dooooo for yoooo.

PA UBU: Come off it, nagbag.

MA UBU: Cheeky devil.

PA UBU: I can see it's you. What the L U doinere?

MA UBU: Big Bad Bernie's dead and the Balonians are after me.

PA UBU: Thassalaff. The Russkies a rafterME. And when they catch me –

MA UBU: They can keep you.

PA UBU: They can keep this fookybear. Here, catch.

He throws the BEAR at her.

MA UBU: (*Collapsing under it.*) Ai. Yarg. Bleah. I can't breathe. It's biting me. It's eating me. It's digesting me.

PA UBU: It's dead, you fool. Just a minute, spose-it snot? Salive? O-eck.

He climbs his rock again.

Our fetherwich artineven.

MA UBU: (*Throwing off the BEAR.*) Where's he gone?

PA UBU: Yike. She'sere! Protectusfromevil. Is it dead?

MA UBU: It's all right, ploppipants, it's cold. How did it get here?

PA UBU: (*Mumbling.*) I dunno. Yes I do. It was going to eat Wallop and McClub, but I killed it with a pilaprayer.

MA UBU: Wallop, McClub, a pilaprayer? Cashnagit, he's off his nut.

PA UBU: *You're* off *your* nut, naggybag.

MA UBU: So tell me about your fighting.

PA UBU: Won't. Too long. I was very, very brave, and they all kept hitting me.

MA UBU: Even the Balonians?

PA UBU: 'Up Wence!' they shouted. 'Up Billikins!' They were really after me. And they crushed poorole Custard.

MA UBU: See if I care. Billikins bashed up Big Bad Bernie.

PA UBU: See if I care. They knackered Nick Nackerley.

MA UBU: See if I care.

PA UBU: Right, naggybag, that does it. Cumere. Down on thy knees, avaunt.

He forces her to her knees.

Base wretch, thou'rt for it now.

MA UBU: You and whose army?

PA UBU: Denosing, deluggering, debumming, debraining, demarrowing, deswimbladdering, deneckeration. Whadd-yoo thinko THIS?

He tears strips off her.

MA UBU: Ow. Pa Ubu. No.

Huge noise outside the cave.

2

PA UBU, MA UBU, BILLIKINS, CHAPS

BILLIKINS and his CHAPS rush into the cave.

BILLIKINS: This way, chaps. Yay! Up Baloney!

PA UBU: Hang on, I'm busy. My better half.

BILLIKINS: (*Bashing him.*) Take that, you pig, you dog, you louse, you chicken, you unmitigated swine.

PA UBU: (*Giving as good as he gets.*) Take that, pintpot, poultice, salad-bowl, squirt, stuffed shirt.

MA UBU: (*Having a bash as well.*) Take that, babyface, pisspant, noserag, bumwipe, bib.

The CHAPS pile on. The UBS defend themselves as best they can.

PA UBU: There's millions of em.

MA UBU: So kick their heads in.

PA UBU: Stagger me sideways, yes. Haha, haHA. Another one! I wish I'd Cashnag ere.

BILLIKINS: Bashem. On! On! On!

VOICE: (*Off.*) Up Ubu. His Cashness. Yaaah!

PA UBU: At last. The Ubbibums. This way, cashhounds, eel, inere.

The BARMPOTS pile in and pile on.

McCLUB: Start runnin, Balonians, sotis, yaah.

WALLOP: Seeyooboo, pushyerweewayoot. Taethedoor. Then run.

BILLIKINS: I say. That hurt.

BARMPOT: No it didn't.

BILLIKINS: Oh, right. Willy me.

ANOTHER BARMPOT: They're nearly out. On, on, on, on.

WALLOP: Thisway. Ahcanseeablurrysky. CumOHN.

McCLUB: Osor, don't panic. Run.

PA UBU: Now I've flapped in my pants. Cornswobbit, NOW! Bangem, blobem, gashem, globem. HaHAH.

WALLOP: Two left. Behind you. There.

PA UBU: (*Bashing them with the BEAR.*) One, two. Feeoo! There! I'm out. Run for it. This way. After meeeeeeee!

3

The Middle of Nowhere. It's snowy. THE UBS and the BARMPOTS, legging it.

PA UBU: We've made it. They've given up.

MA UBU: He's gone to be crowned, that Billikins.

PA UBU: He can keep his crown.

MA UBU: Pa Ubu, you're right.

They disappear into the distance.

4

On board a ship skimming the ocean. On deck, PA UBU *and all the rest.*

CAPTAIN: What a balmy breeze.

PA UBU: Observe with what prodigious speed we skim the waves. At a rough estimate, one million knots per hour. Reef knots, every one of them. It's what we sailors call a breeze behind.

WALLOP: Blowtoot yerbum.

Sudden squall. The ship yaws.

PA UBU: Yike. Eee. We're done for. We're sinking. We're drowning. It's your fault. It's your boat.

CAPTAIN: All hands to the forestopspritsal. Chocks away.

PA UBU: Idiot. Stackinussall thisside. What if the wind changes? We'll fall in. Fishll finishuss.

CAPTAIN: Luff the portcullis. Steady Eddy.

PA UBU: Stuff steady. Get a nurdle on. I want to get there. If we never get there, it'll be all your fault. We've got to get there. Oh here, let me. Splice the mainbrace. Any more for the skylark? Keelhaul the binnacle. Mr Christian, avast behind. What? What?

All scream with laughter. The wind rises.

CAPTAIN: Break out the pipsal and pass to port.

PA UBU: You eardim, pass the port.

They're kicking their legs in the air with laughing. A wave hits the ship.

Hey, that was a biggun. We know what we're doing.

MA UBU, WALLOP: Lovely day for a cruise.

A second wave hits the ship.

WALLOP: (*Soaked.*) Seeyou, repent or die.

PA UBU: Waiter! Oi, waiter! A drop to drink.

They all settle down to drink.

MA UBU: How naice to visit Engelland once more. One's favourite little country. One's hice in the highlands. One's dear old friends.

PA UBU: Not far now. Just passing Germany.

WALLOP: Jings, ahcannywait taeseemawee Wales.

MCCLUB: Sure and aren't they are tales we'll have to tell?

PA UBU: Firstoff, I'm off to London. His Cashness Prince of the Piggybank.

MA UBU: How naice. Ow what ai waive.

MCCLUB: Twas the Dogger Bank, suretwas.

WALLOP: Seejimmy thileaskye.

PA UBU: They call it the Isle of Sky because it's blue.

MA UBU: Pa Ubu, you know everything.

PA UBU: Course I do. Swot got me ere ina firstplace.

2.2 THE BREASTS OF TIRESIAS (1917)

GUILLAUME APOLLINAIRE

Translated by Louis Simpson

Guillaume Apollinaire (1880–1918). Born of a Polish noblewoman and, it is thought, a Swiss-Italian aristocrat, Apollinaire adopted his French name after emigrating to France. A poet, critic and writer, Apollinaire is often credited with inventing the word 'surrealism'. The Breasts of Tiresias *is frequently viewed as the first 'surrealist' play and was made into an opera with music by François Poulenc in 1947. Apollinaire was certainly one of the heroes of the Surrealist movement but also had a working relationship with the Cubists, Picasso and Braque. Apollinaire, although from noble stock, worked for a living and at one point wrote erotic prose as a means of earning an income. Having fought and been wounded during World War I, he died during the post-World War I Spanish flu epidemic in 1918 aged 38. This translation was made in 1961.*

Don't hope for rest risk everything you own
Learn what is new for everything must be known
When a prophet speaks you must be looking on
And make children that's the point of my tale
The child is wealth and the only wealth that's real

Characters
DIRECTOR
THÉRÈSE–TIRESIAS and the FORTUNETELLER
HUSBAND
POLICEMAN
REPORTER FROM PARIS
SON
KIOSK
LACOUF
PRESTO
PEOPLE OF ZANZIBAR
LADY
CHORUS

Prologue

In front of the lowered curtain the DIRECTOR, *in evening dress and carrying a swagger stick, emerges from the prompt box*

DIRECTOR: So here I am once more among you
I've found my ardent company again
I have also found a stage
But to my dismay found as before
The theatre with no greatness and no virtue
That killed the tedious nights before the war
A slanderous and pernicious art
That showed the sin but did not show the savior
Then the hour struck the hour of men
I have been at war like all other men

In the days when I was in the artillery
On the northern front commanding my battery
One night when the gazing of the stars in heaven
Pulsated like the eyes of the newborn
A thousand rockets that rose from the opposite trench
Suddenly woke the guns of the enemy

I remember as though it were yesterday
I heard the shells depart but no explosions
Then from the observation post there came
The trumpeter on horseback to announce
That the sergeant there who calculated
From the flashes of the enemy guns
Their angle of fire had stated
That the range of those guns was so great
That the bursts no longer could be heard
And all my gunners watching at their posts
Announced the stars were darkening one by one
Then loud shouts arose from the whole army
    THEY'RE PUTTING OUT THE STARS WITH SHELLFIRE
The stars were dying in that fine autumn sky
As memory fades in the brain
Of the poor old men who try to remember
We were dying there of the death of stars
And on the somber front with its livid lights
We could only say in despair
    THEY'VE EVEN MURDERED
    THE CONSTELLATIONS
But in a great voice out of a megaphone
The mouth of which emerged
From some sort of supreme headquarters
The voice of the unknown captain who always saves
    us cried
    THE TIME HAS COME TO LIGHT THE STARS AGAIN
And the whole French front shouted together
    FIRE AT WILL
The gunners hastened
The layers calculated
The marksmen fired
And the sublime stars lit up again one by one
Our shells rekindled their eternal ardor
The enemy guns were silent dazzled
By the scintillating of all the stars

There is the history of all the stars

And since that night I too light one by one
All the stars within that were extinguished

So here I am once more among you
My troupe don't be impatient
Public wait without impatience

I bring you a play that aims to reform society
It deals with children in the family
The subject is domestic
And that is the reason it's handled in a familiar way

The actors will not adopt a sinister tone
They will simply appeal to your common sense
And above all will try to entertain you
So that you will be inclined to profit

From all the lessons that the play contains
And so that the earth will be starred with the glances
of infants
Even more numerous than the twinkling stars
Hear O Frenchmen the lesson of war
And make children you that made few before

We're trying to bring a new spirit into the theatre
A joyfulness voluptuousness virtue
Instead of that pessimism more than a hundred years
old
And that's pretty old for such a boring thing
The play was created for an antique stage
For they wouldn't have built us a new theatre
A circular theatre with two stages
One in the middle the other like a ring
Around the spectators permitting
The full unfolding of our modern art
Often connecting in unseen ways as in life
Sounds gestures colors cries tumults
Music dancing acrobatics poetry painting
Choruses actions and multiple sets

Here you will find actions
Which add to the central drama and augment it
Changes of tone from pathos to burlesque
And the reasonable use of the improbable
And actors who may be collective or not
Not necessarily taken from mankind
But from the universe

For the theatre must not be 'realistic'

It is right for the dramatist to use
All the illusions he has at his disposal

As Morgana did on Mount Gibel
It is right for him to make crowds speak and
inanimate things
If he wishes
And for him to pay no more heed to time
Than to space

His universe is his stage
Within it he is the creating god
Directing at his will
Sounds gestures movements masses colors
Not merely with the aim
Of photographing the so-called slice of life
But to bring forth life itself in all its truth

For the play must be an entire universe
With its creator
That is to say nature itself
And not only
Representation of a little part
Of what surrounds us or has already passed

Pardon me my friends my company

Pardon me ladies and gentlemen
For having spoken a little too long
It's been so long since I have been among you

But out there there's still a fire
Where they're putting out the smoking stars
And those who light them again demand that you
Lift yourselves to the height of those great flames
And also burn

O public
Be the unquenchable torch of the new fire

Act 1

The market place at Zanzibar, morning. The scene consists of houses, an area opening on the harbor and whatever else can evoke in Frenchmen the idea of the game of zanzibar.[1] A megaphone shaped like a dice box and decorated with dice is in the foreground. On the courtyard side, the entrance to a house; on the garden side, a newspaper kiosk with a large display and a picture of the newspaper woman which is able to move its arm; it is also decorated with a mirror on the side facing the stage. In the background, the collective speechless person who represents the people of Zanzibar is present from the rise of the curtain. He is sitting on a bench. A table is at his right, and he has ready to hand the instruments he will use to make the right noise at the right moment: revolver, musette, bass drum, accordion, snare drum, thunder, sleigh bells, castanets, toy trumpet, broken dishes. All the sounds marked to be produced by an instrument are made by the people of Zanzibar, and everything marked to be spoken through the megaphone is to be shouted at the audience.

Scene 1

THE PEOPLE OF ZANZIBAR, THÉRÈSE

THÉRÈSE: (*Blue face, long blue dress decorated with monkeys and painted fruit. She enters when the curtain has risen, but from the moment that the curtain begins to rise she attempts to dominate the sound of the orchestra.*)
No Mister husband
You won't make me do what you want

(*In a hushing voice.*)

I am a feminist and I do not recognize the authority of men

(*In a hushing voice.*)

Besides I want to do as I please
Men have been doing what they like long enough
After all I too want to go and fight the enemy
I want to be a soldier hup two hup two
I want to make war (*Thunder.*) and not make children
No Mister husband you won't give me orders

(*She bows three times, backside to the audience.*)

(*In the megaphone.*)

Because you made love to me in Connecticut
Doesn't mean I have to cook for you in Zanzibar
VOICE OF HUSBAND: (*Belgian accent.*)
Give me lard I tell you give me lard

Broken dishes.

THÉRÈSE: Listen to him he only thinks of love

(*She has a fit of hysterics.*)

But you don't understand you fool

(*Sneeze.*)

That after being a soldier I want to be an artist

(*Sneeze.*)

Exactly exactly

(*Sneeze.*)

I also want to be a deputy a lawyer a senator

(*Two sneezes.*)

Minister president of the state

(*Sneeze.*)

And I want to be a doctor or psychiatrist
Give Europe and America the trots
Making children cooking no it's too much

(*She cackles.*)

I want to be a mathematician philosopher chemist
A page in a restaurant a little telegraphist
And if it pleases me I want
To keep that old chorus girl with so much talent

(*Sneeze cackle, after which she imitates the sound of a train.*)

VOICE OF HUSBAND: (*Belgian accent.*)
   Give me lard I tell you give me lard
THÉRÈSE: Listen to him he only thinks of love
   Little tune on the musette.
   Why don't you eat your old sausage feet

Bass drum.

But I think I'm growing a beard
My bosom is falling off

(*She utters a loud cry and opens her blouse from which her breasts emerge, one red, the other blue, and as she lets go of them they fly off, like toy balloons, but remain attached by strings.*)

Fly away birds of my frailty
   Et cetera
How pretty are feminine charms
They're awfully sweet
You could eat them

(*She pulls on the balloon strings and makes them dance.*)

But enough of this nonsense
Let's not go in for aeronautics
There is always some advantage in being virtuous
Vice is a dangerous business after all
That is why it is better to sacrifice beauty
That may be a cause of sin
Let us get rid of our breasts

(*She strikes a lighter and makes them explode; then she makes a face, thumbing her nose with both hands at the audience and throws them the balls she has in her bodice.*)

That is to say
It's not just my beard my mustache is growing too

(*She caresses her beard and strokes her mustache, which have suddenly sprouted.*)

What the devil
I look like a wheatfield that's waiting for the harvester

(*In the megaphone.*)

I feel as virile as the devil
I'm a stallion
From my head on down
I'm a bull

(*Without the megaphone.*)

I'll be a torero
But let's not reveal

My future to everyone hero
Conceal your arms
And you my husband less virile than I
You can sound the alarms
As much as you want

(*Cackling, she goes and admires herself in the mirror attached to the newspaper kiosk.*)

Scene 2

THE PEOPLE OF ZANZIBAR, THÉRÈSE, the HUSBAND

HUSBAND: (*Enters with a big bouquet of flowers, sees that she is not looking at him, and throws the flowers into the auditorium. From this point on, the HUSBAND loses his Belgian accent.*)
   I want lard I tell you
THÉRÈSE: Eat your old sausage feet
HUSBAND: (*While he speaks Thérèse cackles louder and louder. He approaches as though to hit her, then laughing.*)
   Ah but it isn't my wife Thérèse

(*A pause then in a severe manner. In the megaphone.*)

Who is this rascal who's wearing her clothes

(*He goes over to examine her and comes back. In the megaphone.*)

No doubt he's a murderer and he has killed her

(*Without the megaphone.*)

Thérèse my little Thérèse where are you

(*He reflects with his head in his hands, then plants himself squarely, fists on hips.*)

But you, you base rascal who have disguised yourself like Thérèse
I will kill you

(*They fight, she overpowers him.*)

THÉRÈSE: You're right I'm no longer your wife
HUSBAND: Goodness
THÉRÈSE: And yet I am Thérèse
HUSBAND: Goodness
THÉRÈSE: But Thérèse who is no longer a woman
HUSBAND: This is too much
THÉRÈSE: And as I have become a fine fellow
HUSBAND: It must have escaped my attention
THÉRÈSE: From now on I'll have a man's name Tiresias
HUSBAND: (*Hands clasped.*) Sweetiest

She goes off.

Scene 3

THE PEOPLE OF ZANZIBAR, the HUSBAND

VOICE OF TIRESIAS: I'm moving house
HUSBAND: Sweetiest

(*She throws out of the window a chamberpot, a basin, and a urinal. the husband picks up the chamberpot.*)

The piano

(*He picks up the urinal.*)

The violin

(*He picks up the basin.*)

The butter dish the situation is becoming grave

Scene 4

The same. TIRESIAS, LACOUF, PRESTO.

TIRESIAS *returns with clothes, a cord, various odd objects. She throws down everything, hurls herself on the* HUSBAND. *Upon the last reply by* THE HUSBAND, PRESTO *and* LACOUF, *armed with cardboard revolvers, having emerged with a solemn bearing from below the stage, advance into the auditorium, while* TIRESIAS, *over-powering her husband, takes off his trousers, undresses herself, hands him her skirt, ties him up, puts on the trousers, cuts her hair, and puts on a top hat. This stage business goes on until the first revolver shot.*

PRESTO: Old Lacouf I've lost at zanzi with you
   All that I hope to lose
LACOUF: Mister Presto I've won nothing
   And then what has Zanzibar got to do with it you are in Paris
PRESTO: In Zanzibar
LACOUF: In Paris
PRESTO: This is too much
   After ten years of friendship
   And all the bad things I've always said about you
LACOUF: Too bad did I ever ask you for a favor you are in Paris
PRESTO: In Zanzibar the proof is I've lost everything
LACOUF: Mister Presto we'll have to fight
PRESTO: We'll have to

They go up solemnly on to the stage and take positions at the rear facing each other.

Figure 15 Presto, The People of Zanzibar and Lacouf in *Les Mamelles de Tirésias*, 24 June 1917. (*La Rampe*, 12 July 1917.)

LACOUF: On equal terms
PRESTO: Fire at will
   All shots are natural

They aim at each other. THE PEOPLE OF ZANZIBAR *fire two shots and they fall.*

TIRESIAS: (*Who is ready, starts at the sound and exclaims.*)
   Ah dear Freedom so you've been conquered at last
   But first let's buy a newspaper
   And see what has just happened

She buys a newspaper and reads it; meanwhile THE PEOPLE OF ZANZIBAR *set up a placard on each side of the stage.*

> PLACARD FOR PRESTO:
> As he lost at Zanzibar
> Mister Presto has lost his pari
> Mutuel bet for we're in Paris
>
> PLACARD FOR LACOUF
> Mister Lacouf has won nothing
> Since the scene's at Zanzibar
> Just as the Seine's at Paris

As soon as THE PEOPLE OF ZANZIBAR *return to their place,* PRESTO *and* LACOUF *get up,* THE PEOPLE OF ZANZIBAR *fire a revolver shot, and the duelists fall down again.* TIRESIAS *throws down the newspaper in astonishment.*

(*In the megaphone.*)

Now the universe is mine
The women are mine mine is the government
I'm going to make myself town councilor
But I hear a noise
Maybe I'd better go away

She goes off cackling while the HUSBAND *imitates the sound of a locomotive.*

Scene 5

THE PEOPLE OF ZANZIBAR, *the* HUSBAND, *the* POLICEMAN

POLICEMAN: (*While* THE PEOPLE OF ZANZIBAR *play the accordion the mounted policeman makes his horse caper, drags one dead man into the wings so that his feet alone remain visible, makes a circuit of the stage, does the same with the other body, makes another circuit of the stage and, seeing the* HUSBAND *tied up in the foreground*):
   I smell a crime here
HUSBAND: Ah! since at last there's an agent of the government
   Of Zanzibar
   I'm going to challenge him
   Hey Mister if you've got any business with me
   Be kind enough to take
   My army papers out of my left pocket
POLICEMAN: (*In the megaphone.*) What a pretty girl

(*Without the megaphone.*)

Tell me pretty maiden
Who has been treating you so shamefully
HUSBAND: (*Aside.*) He takes me for a young lady

(*To the policeman.*)

If it's a marriage that you have in mind
THE POLICEMAN *puts his hand on his heart.*

Then begin by getting me out of this

The POLICEMAN *unties him, tickling him; they laugh and the* POLICEMAN *continues to say What a pretty girl.*

Scene 6

The same. PRESTO, LACOUF.
As soon as the POLICEMAN *begins to untie the* HUSBAND, PRESTO *and* LACOUF *return to the spot where they fell.*

PRESTO: I'm beginning to be tired of being dead
Imagine there are people
Who think it's more honorable to be dead than alive
LACOUF: Now you can see you were not in Zanzibar
PRESTO: Yet that's the place to live
But it disgusts me to think that we fought a duel
Certainly death is regarded
Much too favorably
LACOUF: What do you expect people think too well
Of mankind and its remains
In the stool of jewelers
Do you think there are pearls and diamonds
PRESTO: Greater marvels have been seen
LACOUF: So Mister Presto
We don't have luck with pari-mutuels
But now you can see that you were in Paris

PRESTO: In Zanzibar
LACOUF: Aim
PRESTO: Fire

THE PEOPLE OF ZANZIBAR *fire a revolver shot, and they fall. The* POLICEMAN *has finished untying the* HUSBAND.

POLICEMAN: You're under arrest

PRESTO *and* LACOUF *run off in the direction opposite where they entered. Accordion.*

Scene 7

THE PEOPLE OF ZANZIBAR, the POLICEMAN, the HUSBAND (*dressed as a woman*)

POLICEMAN: The local duelists
Won't prevent me saying that I think it's
Like a lovely ball of rubber when I touch you
HUSBAND: Kerchoo

Broken dishes.

POLICEMAN: A cold bewitching
HUSBAND: Kitchi

Snare drum. The HUSBAND *removes the skirt, which is impeding his movements.*

POLICEMAN: Loose woman

(*He winks.*)

So what if she's pretty
HUSBAND: (*Aside.*) Really he's right
Since my wife is a man
It's right for me to be a woman

(*To the* POLICEMAN *bashfully.*)

Figure 16 Guillaume Apollinaire and members of the cast of *Les Mamelles de Tirésias*, 24 June 1917.

I am a decent woman-mister
My wife is a man-lady
She's taken the piano the violin the butter dish
She's a soldier minister mover of shit

POLICEMAN: Mother of tits

HUSBAND: They've burst she's a lady psychiatrist

POLICEMAN: She's the mother of swans
   Ah, how they sing when they're dying
   Listen

Musette, a sad tune.

HUSBAND: After all it's a matter of curing people
   Music will do it
   As well as any other panacea

POLICEMAN: That's fine no resisting

HUSBAND: I refuse to continue this conversation

(In the megaphone.)

Where is my wife

VOICES OF WOMEN: *(In the wings.)* Long live Tiresias
   No more children no more children

Thunder and bass drum. The HUSBAND *makes a face at the audience and puts a hand to his ear like an ear trumpet, while the* POLICEMAN, *taking a pipe out of his pocket, offers it to him. Bells.*

POLICEMAN: Hey, Sweetheart, smoke a cigar
   And I'll play my violin

HUSBAND: The baker of Zanzibar
   Has a wife who changes her skin

POLICEMAN: She carries a joke too far

THE PEOPLE OF ZANZIBAR *hang up a placard with this ritornelle and it stays there.*

Hey, Sweetheart, smoke a cigar
And I'll play my violin
The baker of Zanzibar
Has a wife who changes her skin
She carries a joke too far

POLICEMAN: Miss or Mrs. I'm crazy with love
   For you
   And I want to marry you I do

HUSBAND: Kerchoo
   But don't you see that I am only a man

POLICEMAN: No matter what I could marry you
   By proxy

HUSBAND: Nonsense
   You'd do better making children

POLICEMAN: Hah! the idea

VOICES OF MEN: *(In the wings.)* Long live Tiresias
   Long live General Tiresias
   Long live Deputy Tiresias

The accordion plays a military march.

VOICES OF WOMEN *(In the wings.)* No more children No more children

Scene 8

The same. The KIOSK.
The KIOSK *with the moving arm of the newspaper woman proceeds slowly towards the other end of the stage.*

HUSBAND: Famous representative of authority
   You hear I believe it's been said with clarity
   Women at Zanzibar want political rights
   And suddenly renounce their reproductive nights
   No more children No more children you hear them shout
   To fill Zanzibar there are elephants about
   Monkeys and serpents mosquitoes and ostriches
   And just as in beehives enough sterile bitches
   But bees at least make wax and bring in the honey
   Woman is only a neuter under the sky
   And you can take my word for it Mister gendarme

(In the megaphone.)

Zanzibar needs children

(Without the megaphone.)

Go and sound the alarm
Shout it at the crossroads and on the avenue
In Zanzibar we'll have to make children anew
Women won't make them Worse luck Let men populate
But yes exactly I'm letting you have it straight
And I'll make them myself

POLICEMAN AND KIOSK: You

KIOSK: *(In the megaphone which the husband holds out to her.)*
   A story like this should go far
   It's much too good to restrict it to Zanzibar
   You that shed tears at the play
   Wish for children that conquer
   Observe the measureless ardor
   Born of the changing of sex

HUSBAND: Return this very night and see how nature can
   Provide you with progeny without a woman

POLICEMAN: I shall return this night to see how nature can
   Provide you with progeny without a woman
   Don't keep me cooling my heels with no reward
   I'm coming back tonight and take you at your word

KIOSK: What a jerk is the gendarme
   Who's in charge of Zanzibar
   The burlesque theatre and the bar
   For this fellow hold more charm
   Than repeopling Zanzibar

Scene 9

THE SAME. PRESTO.

PRESTO: *(Tickling the* HUSBAND.*)* What do you think their name should be

They are just the same as we
Yet they're not men as you can see
POLICEMAN: I shall return this night to see how nature can
Provide you with progeny without a woman
HUSBAND: Well then return this night and see how nature can
Provide me with progeny without a woman
ALL: (*In chorus. They dance, the* HUSBAND *and* POLICEMAN *together,* PRESTO *and the* KIOSK *paired off and sometimes changing partners.* THE PEOPLE OF ZANZIBAR *dance alone playing the accordion.*)
Hey, Sweetheart, smoke a cigar
And I'll play my violin
The baker of Zanzibar
Has a wife who changes her skin
She carries a joke too far

Act 2
Scene 1

The same place, the same day, just as the sun goes down. The same scenery to which have been added several cradles containing the newborn. An empty cradle stands next to an enormous bottle of ink, a gigantic pot of glue, a huge fountain pen, and a tall pair of scissors.

HUSBAND: (*He has a child on each arm. Continuous crying of children on the stage, in the wings and in the auditorium throughout the scene ad lib. The stage directions only indicate when and where the crying is redoubled.*)
Ah! what a thrill being a father
40,049 children in one day alone
My happiness is complete
Quiet quiet

Crying of children in the background.

Domestic happiness
No woman on my hands

(*He lets the children fall.*)

Quiet

Crying of children from the left side of the auditorium.

Modern music is amazing
Nearly as amazing as the stage sets of the new painters
Who flourish far from the Barbarians
At Zanzibar
You don't have to go to the Ballet Russe or the Vieux-Colombier
Quiet quiet

Crying of children from the right side of the auditorium. Bells.

The time's come to swat 'em with belts on the bottom
But let's not rush matters I think that I'll go
And buy them bicycles and when they have got 'em
Then every virtuoso
May exercise
And vocalize
To the open skies

Gradually the children quiet down, he applauds.

Bravo bravo

A knock.

Come in

Scene 2

The same. The REPORTER FROM PARIS.

REPORTER: (*His face is blank; he has only a mouth. He enters dancing. Accordion.*)
Hands up
Hullo Mister Husband
I'm a Reporter from a Paris paper
HUSBAND: From Paris
Make yourself at home
REPORTER: (*Makes a circuit of the stage dancing.*)
The papers of Paris

(*In the megaphone.*)

a town in America

(*Without the megaphone.*)

Hurrah

A revolver shot, THE REPORTER *unfolds the American flag.*

Have announced that you've discovered
The way for men
To make children
HUSBAND: (*The* REPORTER *folds the flag and wraps it around himself like a belt.*)
That's right
REPORTER: And how's it done
HUSBAND: Willpower sir that's the whole secret
REPORTER: Are they Negroes or like other people
HUSBAND: It all depends on how you look at it

Castanets.

REPORTER: You're wealthy I suppose

(*He does a dance step.*)

HUSBAND: Not at all
REPORTER: How will you bring them up?
HUSBAND: After they've been bottle fed
I hope that they'll feed me instead
REPORTER: In short you are something of a daughter-father
A maternalized paternal instinct I guess
HUSBAND: To the contrary Sir it's all pure selfishness
The child is the wealth of the family
It's worth more than cash and a legacy

THE REPORTER *takes notes.*

See that little fellow asleep in his cradle

The child cries. THE REPORTER *tiptoes across to look at him.*

His first name is Arthur and already he's made

A million for me in the curdled milk trade

Toy trumpet.

REPORTER: He's advanced for his age
HUSBAND: Joseph over there
    The child cries.
    he's a novelist

The REPORTER goes over to look at Joseph.

His last novel sold 600,000 copies
Permit me to offer you one

A big book placard is lowered; it has several pages on the first of which is printed:
What Luck!
A Novel.
Read it at your leisure

The REPORTER lies down; the HUSBAND turns the pages on which may be read one word to the page:
A lady whose name was Cambron.
REPORTER: *(Stands up and speaks into the megaphone.)*
    A lady whose name was Cambron

(He laughs into the megaphone uttering the four vowels: a, e, i, o.)
HUSBAND: Nevertheless it has a certain urbanity of expression
REPORTER: *(Without the megaphone.)* Ah! ah! ah! ah!
HUSBAND: A certain precociousness
REPORTER: Eh! eh!
HUSBAND: That you don't find in the streets
REPORTER: Hands up
HUSBAND: Finally just as it stands
    The novel has put in my hands
    Almost two hundred thousand francs
    Plus a literary prize
    Consisting of twenty cases of dynamite

(Backs away.)

REPORTER: Good-bye
HUSBAND: Don't be afraid they're in my safety deposit vault
REPORTER: All right
    Don't you have a daughter
HUSBAND: Sure I do this one divorced

She cries. The REPORTER goes over to look at her.

From the potato king
Gets a hundred thousand dollars alimony
And this *(She cries.)* no one in Zanzibar is as artistic as she

The REPORTER shadow boxes.

She recites lovely poems on gloomy evenings
Her fire and genius earn in a year
What a poet earns in fifty thousand years
REPORTER: Congratulations my dear
    But you've got some dust

On your dust coat

The HUSBAND smiles gratefully at the REPORTER as he picks up the speck of dust.

Since you're so rich lend me a hundred sous
HUSBAND: Put the dust back

All the children cry. The HUSBAND chases the REPORTER, kicking him. He goes off dancing.

Scene 3
THE PEOPLE OF ZANZIBAR, *the* HUSBAND

HUSBAND: Ah yes it's as simple as a periscope
    The more children I have
    The richer I'll be and the better able to live
    It's said that the cod produces enough eggs in a day
    To supply the whole world for a whole year
    With cod paste and garlic
    Isn't it wonderful to have a numerous family
    Then who are those idiotic economists
    Who've made us believe that the child
    Means poverty
    Whereas it's just the opposite
    Did you ever hear of a cod that died in poverty
    So I'm going to keep on making children
    First we'll make a reporter
    So I'll know everything
    I'll predict the rest
    And invent the remainder

(He starts tearing up newspapers with his teeth and hands; he tramples. His movements must be very quick.)

He must be adaptable to every job
And able to write for every party

(He puts the torn newspapers in the empty cradle.)

What a fine reporter he'll be
Reporting lead articles
Et cetera
He'll have to have blood from an ink bottle

(He takes the bottle of ink and pours it into the cradle.)

He'll need a backbone

(He puts a huge fountain pen into the cradle.)

A brain for not thinking with

(He empties the glue pot into the cradle.)

A tongue to drivel with

(He puts the scissors into the cradle.)

Also he'll have to be able to sing
Come on sing

Thunder.

Scene 4

The same. The SON.

HUSBAND repeats: "One, two!" till the end of the son's monologue. This scene goes very quickly.

SON: Dear daddy if you want a closer look
At the activities of every crook
You've got to let me have some pocket money
The tree of print is leafy every bough
Flaps like a banner the fruit hangs in bunches
Papers have grown you ought to pick them now
And make the little kiddies salad lunches
If you let me have five hundred francs
I won't tell what I know about you
If you don't I'll tell all for I'm frank
And I fix fathers brothers sisters too
When you marry I'll tell them that your bride's
Pregnant three times over
I'll compromise you and I'll write besides
That you've stolen killed given rung bored
HUSBAND: Bravo there's a vocalist

THE SON gets out of the cradle.

SON: Dear parents in one man
If you want to know what happened yesterday evening
Here it is
A great conflagration destroyed Niagara Falls
HUSBAND: So what
SON: Alcindor the engineer
Put a gas mask on and played
The horn till twelve o'clock or near
For a murderous brigade
Listen and you still may hear
HUSBAND: So long as he doesn't do it here
SON: The Princess of Bergame they say
Is marrying a girl today
Just a meeting on the subway

Castanets.

HUSBAND: What's it to me do I know all those people
I want reliable news about my friends
SON: (*He rocks a cradle.*) We hear from Montrouge
That Mister Picasso's
New picture can move
As this cradle does
HUSBAND: Bravo bravo
For the brush of Picasso
O my son
Some other time I know right now
All that I need to know
About yesterday
SON: I'm going away to make tomorrow's news
HUSBAND: Good luck

Exit the SON.

Scene 5

THE PEOPLE OF ZANZIBAR, the HUSBAND

HUSBAND: That one didn't work out
I think I'll disinherit him

At this moment radio placards enter: Ottawa – fire j.c.b. industries STOP 20,000 prose poems destroyed STOP president expresses sympathy. Rome – h.nr.m.t.ss. director villa medicis finishes portrait SS. Avignon – great artist g.rg.s braque has just invented process intensive cultivation of paintbrushes. Vancouver delayed bulletin – Dogs mister Paul Léaut.d on strike.

Stop stop
That was a lousy idea trusting the Press
They'll drive me crazy
The whole damn day
It's got to stop

(*In the megaphone.*)

Hullo hullo Miss
I don't want your telephone service
I'm de-subscribing

(*Without the megaphone.*)

I'm changing my program no more useless mouths
Economize economize
First off all I'll make a little tailor
When I'm dressed up I can take a walk
And as I'm not so bad to look at
Attract a lot of pretty girls

Scene 6

The same. The POLICEMAN.

POLICEMAN: Fine things you've been up to
You've kept your word
40,050 children in a day
You're rocking the boat
HUSBAND: I'm getting rich
POLICEMAN: But the population of Zanzibar
Famished by this excess of mouths to feed
Will soon be dying of hunger
HUSBAND: Give them cards that makes up for everything
POLICEMAN: Where do we get them?
HUSBAND: From The Fortuneteller
POLICEMAN: That's clear enough
HUSBAND: Of course for we're thinking of the future

Scene 7

The same. The FORTUNETELLER.

FORTUNETELLER: (*She enters at the rear of the auditorium. Her skull is lighted with electricity.*)
Chaste citizens of Zanzibar here I am
HUSBAND: Still another
I just don't count

FORTUNETELLER: I thought that you wouldn't have any
  objections
  To having your fortune told

POLICEMAN: You are well aware Madame
  You're practicing an illegal occupation
  It's amazing the things people do
  To avoid working

HUSBAND: (*To the* POLICEMAN.) No scandal in my house

FORTUNETELLER: (*To a spectator.*) You Sir will shortly
  Give birth to triplets

HUSBAND: Competition already

A LADY: (*In the audience.*) Madame Fortuneteller
  I think he's deceiving me

Broken dishes.

FORTUNETELLER: Keep him in the hay box

She climbs onto the stage; crying of children, accordion.

  Look an incubator

HUSBAND: If you're the barber give me a haircut

FORTUNETELLER: The girls of New York
  Only pick mirabelles
  Only eat ham from York
  That's why they're such belles

HUSBAND: The ladies of Paris
  Beat all competitors
  Cats like little mice
  And ladies we like yours

FORTUNETELLER: That is your smiles

ALL: (*In chorus.*) And then sing night and day
  Scratch if you itch and choose
  The white or the black either way
  Luck is a game win or lose
  Just keep your eye on the play
  Just keep your eye on the play

FORTUNETELLER: Chaste citizens of Zanzibar
  Who have given up childbearing
  Listen to me wealth and honor
  Pineapple groves and herds of elephants
  By right will belong
  Before very long
  To those who will claim them with armies of infants

All the children start crying on the stage and in the auditorium. The FORTUNETELLER *deals the cards and they come tumbling down from the ceiling. Then the children are quiet.*

  You who are so fertile

HUSBAND and POLICEMAN: Fertile fertile

FORTUNETELLER: (*To the* HUSBAND.) You'll be a millionaire ten
  times over

The HUSBAND *falls down in a sitting position.*

FORTUNETELLER: (*To the* POLICEMAN.) You who don't make
  children

You'll die in the most abject poverty

POLICEMAN: You've insulted me
  I arrest you in the name of Zanzibar

FORTUNETELLER: Laying hands on a woman shame on you

She claws and strangles him. The HUSBAND *offers her a pipe.*

HUSBAND: Hey, Sweetheart, smoke a cigar
  And I'll play my violin
  The baker of Zanzibar
  Has a wife who changes her skin

FORTUNETELLER: She carries a joke too far

HUSBAND: I'm going to turn you into the chief of police
  Murderer

THÉRÈSE: (*Taking off her fortuneteller's costume.*)
  Dear husband don't you recognize me

HUSBAND: Thérèse or should I say Tiresias

The POLICEMAN *revives.*

THÉRÈSE: Tiresias is officially
  Head of the Army in Room A at City Hall
  But don't worry
  I'm bringing back in a moving van
  The piano the violin the butter dish
  And three influential ladies whose lover I have become

POLICEMAN: Thanks for thinking of me

HUSBAND: My general my deputy
  Thérèse I meant to say
  You're as flat-chested as a bedbug

THÉRÈSE: So what! Let's go where the berries
  And banana blossoms are
  Let's hunt elephants on safaris
  As they do in Zanzibar
  Come and rule the heart of Thérèse

HUSBAND: Thérèse

THÉRÈSE: Throne or tomb no matter what
  But this I'm sure of that we've got
  To love or I'll die on the spot

HUSBAND: Dear Thérèse you must no longer be
  As flat-chested as a bedbug

(*He takes out of the house a bouquet of balloons and a basket of balls.*)

  Here's a whole supply

THÉRÈSE: We've both of us done without them
  Let's continue

HUSBAND: That's true let's not make matters complicated
  Let's go and dunk our bread

THÉRÈSE: (*She releases the toy balloons and throws the balls at the audience.*) Fly away birds of my frailty
  Go and feed all the children
  Of the new population

ALL: (*In chorus.* THE PEOPLE OF ZANZIBAR *dance jingling bells.*)
  And then sing night and day
  Scratch if you itch and choose

The white or the black either way
Luck is a game win or lose
Just keep your eye on the play

Note

1. Zanzibar – commonly known as *zanzi* – a game of chance played with three dice and a dice box. Each player in turn throws the dice. An ace counts 100 points, a six 60, and the other numbers their face value. The player with the highest total wins. The game can be decided in one throw, in three throws, by leaving out one or two dice at each throw, or in several extra throws. In case of a tie, the players each throw once. There are many kinds of *zanzi*; the notorious *chemin de fer* is one of them – played with three throws of the dice; at each throw one of the dice is left out. – *Translator.*

2.3 THE SPURT OF BLOOD (1925)

ANTONIN ARTAUD

Translated by Victor Corti

Antonin Artaud (1896–1948). Artaud spent a great deal of his life in sanatoriums and asylums in France. Suffering from depression, addiction to opiates and cancer, he died before the theatre had developed either technologically or aesthetically to a level whereby the majority of his innovative visions for theatre could be put into working practice. An actor, poet, playwright and theorist, Artaud is best known for his theories on the function, purpose and practice of theatre gathered together in The Theatre and Its Double *(see document 2.10). He ran the Alfred Jarry Theatre in Paris in the mid 1920s where* The Spurt of Blood *was reportedly to be produced, but it was not premiered until some forty years later. His vision for theatre involved a reconceptualization of the role of the audience in the making and experience of the artwork, and his ideas have been adopted and debated by most innovative practitioners of the twentieth and twenty-first centuries. This translation was made in 1970.*

YOUNG MAN: I love you and everything is fine.

GIRL: (*In a quickened, throbbing voice.*) You love me and everything is fine.

YOUNG MAN: (*Lower.*) I love you and everything is fine.

GIRL: (*Lower still.*) You love me and everything is fine.

YOUNG MAN: (*Suddenly turns aside.*) I love you.

Silence.

YOUNG MAN: Face me.

GIRL: (*Same business, faces him.*) There.

YOUNG MAN: (*On an exalted, high-pitched tone.*) I love you, I am great, I am lucid, I am full, I am dense.

GIRL: (*Same high-pitched tone.*) We love each other.

YOUNG MAN: We are intense. Ah, what a well-made world.

Silence: Noise like a huge wheel spinning, blowing out wind. A hurricane comes between them. At that moment two stars collide, and a succession of limbs of flesh fall. Then feet, hands, scalps, masks, colonnades, porticoes, temples and alembics, falling slower and slower as if through space, then three scorpions one after the other and finally a frog, and a scarab which lands with heart-breaking, nauseating slowness.

YOUNG MAN: (*Shouting at the top of his voice.*) Heaven's gone crazy. (*Looks up at the sky.*) Let's run off. (*Pushes the GIRL off ahead of him.*)

A Mediaeval KNIGHT in enormous armour enters, followed by a WETNURSE holding her bosom up with her hands and panting because of her swollen breasts.

KNIGHT: Leave your teats alone. Hand me my papers.

WETNURSE: (*Giving a shrill cry.*) Oh! Oh! Oh!

KNIGHT: Now what's the matter with you, dammit?

WETNURSE: Our girl there, with him.

KNIGHT: Shush, there's no girl there!

WETNURSE: I tell you they are fucking.

KNIGHT: And what do I care if they are fucking.

WETNURSE: Lecher.

KNIGHT: Balloon.

WETNURSE: (*Thrusting her hands in pockets as big as her breasts.*) Pimp.

(*She tosses his papers over hastily.*)

KNIGHT: Philte, Let me eat.

WETNURSE runs off. He then gets up and pulls a huge slice of Gruyère cheese out of each paper. He suddenly coughs and chokes.

KNIGHT: (*Mouth full.*) Ehp. Ehp. Bring your breasts over here, bring your breasts over here. Where's she gone?

He runs off. YOUNG MAN returns.

Figure 17 A sequence from Artaud's *The Spurt of Blood*, directed by Peter Brook and Charles Marowitz for the *Theatre of Cruelty* season at the LAMDA Theatre, London in 1964.

YOUNG MAN: I saw, I knew, I understood. Here is the main square, the priest, the cobbler, the vegetable stalls, the church portals, the red light, the scales of justice. I can't go on!

A PRIEST, *a* COBBLER, *a* BEADLE, *a* WHORE, *a* JUDGE, *and a* BARROW-WOMAN *advance onto the stage like shadows.*

YOUNG MAN: I have lost her, bring her back.
ALL: (*On a different tone.*) Who, who, who, who.
YOUNG MAN: My wife.
BEADLE: (*Very blustering.*) Your wife, huh, joker!
YOUNG MAN: Joker! She might be yours!
BEADLE: (*Striking his forehead.*) He could be right!

He runs off.

The PRIEST *steps forward next and puts his arm around the* YOUNG MAN'*s shoulders.*

PRIEST: (*As if confessing someone.*) What part of her body did you refer to most often?

YOUNG MAN: To God.

The PRIEST, *disconcerted at this reply, immediately assumes a Swiss accent.*

PRIEST: (*With a Swiss accent.*) But that's out of date. We don't look at it in that way. You'll have to ask the volcanoes and earthquakes about that. We gratify ourselves with man's minor indecencies in the confessional. There it is, that's all, that's life.
YOUNG MAN: (*Very impressed.*) Ah, that's it, that's life! Well, it's a mess.
PRIEST: (*Still with a Swiss accent.*) Of course.

It suddenly becomes night. The earth quakes. Thunder rages, lightning zig-zagging everywhere and its flashes light up the characters who run about, bump into one another, fall down, get up again and run like mad.
At a given moment a huge hand seizes the WHORE'*s hair which catches fire and swells up visibly.*

A GIGANTIC VOICE: Bitch! Look at your body!

The WHORE'*s body appears completely naked and hideous under her blouse and skirt which turn transparent.*

WHORE: God, let go of me.

She bites GOD'*s wrist. A great spurt of blood slashes across the stage, while in the midst of the brightest lightning flash we see the* PRIEST *making the sign of the cross.*

When the lights come up again, the characters are all dead and their corpses lie all over the ground. Only the WHORE *and* YOUNG MAN *are left, devouring each other with their eyes. The* WHORE *falls into the* YOUNG MAN'*s arms.*

WHORE: (*With a sigh, as if in an orgiastic climax.*) Tell me how it happened.

The YOUNG MAN *hides his head in his hands.*

The WETNURSE *returns carrying the* GIRL *under her arms like a parcel.*

The GIRL *is dead. She drops her on the ground where she sprawls out and becomes as flat as a pancake.*

The WETNURSE'*s breasts are gone. Her chest is completely flat.*

At that moment, the KNIGHT *enters and throws himself on the* WETNURSE, *shaking her violently.*

KNIGHT: (*In a terrible voice.*) Where did you put it? Give me my Gruyère.
WETNURSE: (*Brazenly.*) Here!

She lifts up her dress.

The YOUNG MAN wants to run off but he freezes like a paralysed puppet.

YOUNG MAN: (*In a ventriloquist's voice and as if hovering in mid-air.*) Don't hurt Mummy.
KNIGHT: Damn her.

He hides his face in horror.

A host of scorpions crawl out from under the WETNURSE'S dress and start swarming in her vagina which swells and splits, becomes transparent and shimmers like the sun.

The YOUNG MAN and WHORE fly off like mad.

GIRL: (*Gets up, dazzled.*) The Virgin! Ah, that's what he was looking for.

Notes

From Antonin Artaud, *Collected Works Volume 1*, London: John Calder, 1978, pp. 62–5.

2.4 MURDERER THE WOMEN'S HOPE (1907)

OSKAR KOKOSCHKA

Translated by Michael Hamburger

Oskar Kokoschka (1886–1980) was an Austrian artist and poet as well as playwright. His play Murderer the Women's Hope *exemplifies Kokoschka's disdain for realism as a mode of expression – it is rather a text predicated on the dream state, and is often called the first Expressionist drama. The play contains echoes of elements of Strindberg's* Dance of Death, *was not produced professionally until 1916 and was adapted into an opera (by Paul Hindemith) in 1920. Better known for his painting than for his theatre, Kokoschka became an exile during the rise of Nazism.*

Persons

MAN
WOMAN
CHORUS: MEN *and* WOMEN

Night sky. Tower with large red iron grille as door; torches the only light; black ground, rising to the tower in such a way that all the figures appear in relief.

The MAN *in blue armor, white face, kerchief covering a wound, with a crowd of men – savage in appearance, gray-and-red kerchiefs, white-black-and-brown clothes, signs on their clothes, bare legs, long-handled torches, bells, din – creeping up with handles of torches extended and lights; wearily, reluctantly try to hold back the adventurer, pull his horse to the ground; he walks on, they open up the circle around him, crying out in a slow crescendo.*

MEN: We were the flaming wheel around him,
    We were the flaming wheel around you, assailant of locked fortresses!

Hesitantly follow him again in chain formation; he, with the torch bearer in front of him, heads the procession.

MEN: Lead us, pale one!

While they are about to pull his horse to the ground, WOMEN *with their leader ascend steps on the left.*

WOMAN, *red clothes, loose yellow hair, tall.*

WOMAN: (*Loud.*) With my breath I fan the yellow disc of the sun, my eye collects the jubilation of the men, their stammering lust prowls around me like a beast.

FEMALE ATTENDANTS separate themselves from her, only now catch sight of the stranger.

FIRST FEMALE ATTENDANT: His breath attaches itself to the virgin!
FIRST MAN: (*To the others.*) Our master is like the moon that that rises in the East.
SECOND GIRL: (*Quiet, her face averted.*) When will she be enfolded joyfully?

Listening, alert, the CHORUS *walks round the whole stage, dispersed in groups; The* MAN *and the* WOMAN *meet in front of the gate.*

Pause.

WOMAN: (*Observes him spellbound, then to herself.*) Who is the stranger that has looked on me?

GIRLS press to the fore.

FIRST GIRL: (*Recognizes him, cries out.*) His sister died of love.

SECOND GIRL: O the singing of Time, flowers never seen.

MAN: (*Astonished; his procession halts.*) Am I real? What did the shadows say?

Raising his face to her.

Did you look at me, did I look at you?

WOMAN: (*Filled with fear and longing.*) Who *is* the pallid man? Hold him back.

FIRST GIRL: (*With a piercing scream, runs back.*) Do you let him in? It is he who strangles my little sister praying in the temple.

FIRST MAN: (*To the GIRL.*) We saw him stride through the fire, his feet unharmed.

SECOND MAN: He tortured animals to death, killed neighing mares by the pressure of his thighs.

THIRD MAN: Birds that ran before us he made blind, stifled red fishes in the sand.

MAN: (*Angry, heated.*) Who is she that like an animal proudly grazes amidst her kin?

FIRST MAN: She divines what none has understood.

SECOND MAN: She perceives what none has seen or heard.

THIRD MAN: They say shy birds approach her and let themselves be seized.

GIRLS in time with the MEN.

FIRST GIRL: Lady, let us flee. Extinguish the flares of the leader.

SECOND GIRL: Mistress, escape!

THIRD GIRL: He shall not be our guest or breathe our air. Let him not lodge with us, he frightens me.

MEN, hesitant, walk on, WOMEN crowd together anxiously.

The WOMAN goes up to the MAN, prowling, cautious.

FIRST GIRL: He has no luck.

FIRST MAN: She has no shame.

WOMAN: Why do you bind me, man, with your gaze? Ravening light, you confound my flame! Devouring life overpowers me. O take away my terrible hope – and may torment overpower you.

MAN: (*Enraged.*) My men, now brand her with my sign, hot iron into her red flesh.

MEN carry out his order. First the CHORUS, with their lights, struggle with her, then the OLD MAN with the iron; he rips open her dress and brands her.

WOMAN: (*Crying out in terrible pain.*) Beat back those men, the devouring corpses.

She leaps at him with a knife and strikes a wound in his side. the MAN falls.

MEN: Free this man possessed, strike down the devil. Alas for us innocents, bury the conqueror. We do not know him.

MAN: (*In convulsions, singing with a bleeding, visible wound.*) Senseless craving from horror to horror, unappeasable rotation in the void. Birth pangs without birth, hurtling down of the sun, quaking of space. The end of those who praised me. Oh, your unmerciful word.

MEN: We do not know him; spare us. Come, you singing girls, let us celebrate our nuptials on his bed of affliction.

GIRLS: He frightens us; you we loved even before you came.

Three masked men on the wall lower a coffin on ropes; the wounded man, hardly stirring now, is placed inside the tower. WOMEN retire with the MEN. The OLD MAN rises and locks the door, all is dark, a torch, quiet, blue light above in the cage.

WOMAN: (*Moaning and revengeful.*) He cannot live, nor die; how white he is!

She creeps round the cage like a panther. She crawls up to the cage inquisitively, grips the bars lasciviously, inscribes a large white cross on the tower, cries out.

Open the gate; I must be with him.

Shakes the bars in despair.

MEN AND WOMEN: (*Enjoying themselves in the shadows, confused.*) We have lost the key – we shall find it – have you got it? – haven't you seen it? – we are not guilty of your plight, we do not know you –

They go back again. A cock crows, a pale light rises in the background.

WOMAN: (*Slides her arm through the bars and prods his wound, hissing maliciously, like an adder.*) Pale one, do you recoil? Do you know fear? Are you only asleep? Are you awake? Can you hear me?

MAN: (*Inside, breathing heavily, raises his head with difficulty; later, moves one hand; then slowly rises, singing higher and higher, soaring.*) Wind that wanders, time repeating time, solitude, repose and hunger confuse me.

Worlds that circle past, no air, it grows long as evening.

WOMAN: (*Incipient fear.*) So much light is flowing from the gap, so much strength from the pale as a corpse he's turned.

Once more creeps up the steps, her body trembling, triumphant once more and crying out with a high voice.

THE MAN *has slowly risen, leans against the grille, slowly grows.*

WOMAN: (*Weakening, furious.*) A wild beast I tame in this cage; is it with hunger your song barks?

MAN: Am I the real one, you the dead ensnared? Why are you turning pale?

Crowing of cocks.

WOMAN: (*Trembling.*) Do you insult me, corpse?

MAN: (*Powerfully.*) Stars and moon! Woman! In dream or awake, I saw a singing creature brightly shine. Breathing, dark things become clear to me. Who nourishes me?

WOMAN covers him entirely with her body; separated by the grille, to which she clings high up in the air like a monkey.

MAN: Who suckles me with blood? I devour your melting flesh.

WOMAN: I will not let you live, you vampire, piecemeal you feed on me, weaken me, woe to you, I shall kill you – you fetter me – you I caught and caged – and you are holding me – let go of me. Your love imprisons me – grips me as with iron chains – throttles me – let go – help! I lost the key that kept you prisoner.

Lets go the grille, writhes on the steps like a dying animal, her thighs and muscles convulsed.

The MAN *stands upright now, pulls open the gate, touches the* WOMAN – *who rears up stiffly, dead white – with his fingers. She feels that her end is near, highest tension, released in a slowly diminishing scream; she collapses and, as she falls, tears away the torch from the hands of the rising leader. The torch goes out and covers everything in a shower of sparks. He stands on the highest step;* MEN *and* WOMEN *who attempt to flee from him run into his way, screaming.*

CHORUS: The devil! Tame him, save yourselves, save yourselves if you can – all is lost!

He walks straight towards them. Kills them like mosquitoes and leaves red behind. From very far away, crowing of cocks.

Note

This version of the play was originally published in Walter H. Sokel, ed., *An Anthology of German Expressionist Drama*, Ithaca, NY: Cornell Paperbacks, 1984, pp. 17–22.

2.5 GENIUS AND CULTURE *and* BACHELOR APARTMENT (*C.* 1909–16)

UMBERTO BOCCIONI

Translated by Victoria Nes Kirby

Umberto Boccioni (1882–1916), more famous as an Italian painter than a playwright, became one of the main protagonists in the development of the theory and practice of Futurism, being one of the authors of the 'Manifesto of Futurist Painters' in 1910. Later in his career he turned from painting and writing to sculpture, but was a proactive participant in Futurist performance events and exhibitions. He died after a riding accident during World War I. The translations were made in 1971.

Genius and Culture

In the centre, a costly dressing table with a mirror in front of which a very elegant WOMAN, *already dressed to leave, finishes putting on rouge. At the right, a* CRITIC, *an ambiguous being, neither dirty nor clean, neither old nor young, neutral, is sitting at a table over-burdened with books and papers, on which shines a large paper knife, neither modern nor antique. He turns his shoulder to the dressing table. At left,* THE ARTIST, *an elegant youth, searches in a large file, sitting on thick cushions on the floor.*

THE ARTIST: (*Leaving the file, and with his head between his hands.*) It's terrible! (*Pause.*) I must get out of here! To be renewed! (*He gets up, tearing the abstract designs from the file with convulsive hands.*) Liberation!! These empty forms, worn out. Everything is fragmentary, weak! Oh! Art! ... who, who will help me!? (*He looks around; continues to tear up the designs with sorrowful and convulsive motions.*)

THE WOMAN is very near him, but doesn't hear him. THE CRITIC *becomes annoyed, but not very, and going near her, takes a book with a yellow jacket.*

THE CRITIC: (*Half-asking* THE WOMAN, *and half-talking to himself.*) But what's the matter with that clown that he acts and shouts that way?

THE WOMAN: (*Without looking.*) Oh well, he is an artist ... he wants to renew himself, and he hasn't a cent!

THE CRITIC: (*Bewildered.*) Strange! An artist! Impossible! For twenty years I have profoundly studied this marvelous phenomenon, but I can't recognize it. (*Obviously with archeological curiosity.*) That one is crazy! Or a protester! He wants to change! But creation is a serene thing. A work of art is done naturally, in silence, and in recollection, like a night-ingale sings ... Spirit, in the sense that Hegel means spirit ...

THE WOMAN: (*Intrigued.*) And if you know how it is done, why don't you tell him? Poor thing! He is distressed ...

THE CRITIC: (*Strutting.*) For centuries, the critic has told the artist how to make a work of art.... Since ethics and aesthetics are functions of the spirit ...

THE WOMAN: But you, you've never made any?

THE CRITIC: (*Nonplussed.*) Me? ... Not me!

THE WOMAN: (*Laughing with malice.*) Well, then, you know how to do it, but you don't do it. You are neutral. How boring you must be in bed! (*She continues putting on her rouge.*)

THE ARTIST: (*Always walking back and forth sorrowfully, wringing his hands.*) Glory! Ah! Glory! (*Tightening his fists.*) I am strong! I am young! I can face anything! Oh! Divine electric lights ... sun ... To electrify the crowds ... Burn them! Dominate them!

THE WOMAN: (*Looking at him with sympathy and compassion.*) Poor thing! Without any money ...

THE ARTIST: (*Struck.*) Ah! I am wounded! I can't resist any longer! (*Toward* THE WOMAN, *who doesn't hear him.*) Oh! A woman! (*Toward* THE CRITIC, *who has already taken and returned a good many books, and who leafs through them and cuts them.*) You! You, sir, who are a man, listen ... Help me!

THE CRITIC: Calm down ... let's realize the differences. I am not a man, I am a critic. I am a man of culture. The artist is a man, a slave, a baby, therefore, he makes mistakes. I don't see myself as being like him. In him nature is chaos. The critic and history are between nature and the artist. History is history, in other words subjective fact, that is to say fact, in other words history. Anyway it is itself objective.

At these words, THE ARTIST, *who has listened in a stupor, falls on the cushions as if struck by lightning.* THE CRITIC, *unaware of this, turns, and goes slowly to the table to consult his books.*

THE WOMAN: (*Getting up dumbfounded.*) My God! That poor youth is dying! (*She kneels in front of* THE ARTIST *and caresses him kindly.*)

THE ARTIST: (*Reviving.*) Oh! Signora! Thank you! Oh! Love ... maybe love ... (*Revives more and more.*) How beautiful you are! Listen ... Listen to me ... If you know what a terrible thing the struggle is without love! I want to love, understand?

THE WOMAN: (*Pulling away from him.*) My friend, I understand you ... but now I haven't time. I must go out ... I am expected by my friend. It is dangerous.... He is a man ... that is to say, he has a secure position ...

THE CRITIC: (*Very embarrassed.*) What's going on? I don't understand anything ...

THE WOMAN: (*Irritated.*) Shut up, idiot! You don't understand anything.... Come! Help me to lift him! We must cut this knot that is choking his throat!

THE CRITIC: (*Very embarrassed.*) Just a minute ... (*He carefully lays down the books and puts the others aside on the chair.*) Hegel ... Kant ... Hartmann ... Spinoza.

THE WOMAN: (*Goes near the youth, crying irritably.*) Run! ... come here, help me to unfasten it.

THE CRITIC: (*Nonplussed.*) What are you saying?

THE WOMAN: Come over here! Are you afraid! Hurry ... back here there is an artist who is dying because of an ideal.

THE CRITIC: (*Coming closer with extreme prudence.*) But one never knows! An impulse ... a passion ... without control ... without culture ... in short, I prefer him dead. The artist must be ... (*He stumbles, and falls clumsily on the artist, stabbing his neck with the paper knife.*)

THE WOMAN: (*Screaming and getting up.*) Idiot! Assassin! You have killed him. You are red with blood!

THE CRITIC: (*Getting up, still more clumsily.*) I, Signora? How?! I don't understand.... Red? Red? Yours is a case of color blindness.

THE WOMAN: Enough! Enough! (*Returns to her dressing table.*) It is late. I must go! (*Leaving.*) Poor youth! He was different and likable! (*Exits.*)

THE CRITIC: I can't find my bearings! (*Looks attentively and long at the dead* ARTIST.) Oh my God! He is dead! (*Going over to look at him.*) The artist is really dead! Ah ... he is breathing. I will make a monograph. (*He goes slowly to his table. From a case, he takes a beard a meter long and applies it to his chin. He puts on his glasses, takes paper and pencil, then looks among his books without finding anything. He is irritated for the first time and pounds his fists, shouting.*) Aesthetics! Aesthetics! Where is Aesthetics? (*Finding it, he passionately holds a large volume to his chest.*) Ah! Here it is! (*Skipping, he goes to crouch like a raven near the dead artist. He looks at the body, and writes, talking in a loud voice.*) Toward 1915, a marvelous artist blossomed ... (*He takes a tape measure from his pocket and measures the body.*) Like all the great ones, he was 1.68 [meters] tall, and his width ... (*While he talks, the curtain falls.*)

Bachelor Apartment (Theatrical Synthesis)

Idiotic interior of an elegant youth's bachelor apartment — prints on the walls, a very low divan, several vases of flowers, as in all bachelor apartments. A newly acquired painting is in front of the divan on an easel.

THE YOUTH: (*Listening eagerly near the door.*) Here we are! (*Opens it.*) Good morning! ... How are you?

THE WOMAN: (*Advancing, with a certain reserve.*) Good morning (*Looking around her.*) It's nice in here ...

THE YOUTH: (*With fervor.*) How beautiful you are! Very elegant! Thank you for coming ... I doubted ...

THE WOMAN: Why? Where is the painting? I came to see it.

THE YOUTH: It's this one. (*He takes her by the hand and conducts her in front of the painting. While* THE WOMAN *looks at it squinting,* THE YOUTH *takes her in his arms and kisses the nape of her neck.*)

THE WOMAN: (*Struggling energetically.*) Sir! What are you thinking of? ... These are really cowardly ...

THE YOUTH: Excuse me. (*He grasps her again forcefully and speaks close to her mouth.*) You are very beautiful! You are mine! You must be mine! ...

THE WOMAN: (*Struggling in a way that makes her seem serious.*) Sir! Leave me alone! ... I'll call for someone! I am a respectable woman! ... Leave me alone!

THE YOUTH: (*Mortified, letting her go.*) You are right. I ask your pardon ... I don't know what I am doing ... I will leave you.

THE WOMAN: Open the door for me! I want to get out of here!

THE YOUTH: (*Going to open the door.*) Go!

With this word, THE WOMAN lets her fur coat fall, and appears in black silk panties, with her bosom, shoulders, and arms nude. With coquetry and modesty, she runs to crouch on the divan.

THE WOMAN: You are timid, after all.... Turn that painting, and come here! ...

Note

From Michael Kirby, *Futurist Performance,* New York: Dutton, 1971, pp. 234–5.

2.6 **FEET** (1919)

FILIPPO TOMMASO MARINETTI

Translated by Victoria Nes Kirby

Filippo Tommaso Marinetti (1876–1944) trained as a lawyer in Italy but did not practise professionally. He was the founder of Futurist movement, largely through the publication of the Futurist Manifesto *in 1909. His aesthetic ideas were predicated on a celebration of speed, violence and the machine. Marinetti wrote many treatises on performance (see 2.9) and organized numerous theatrical evenings, most of which ended in riots. He was a follower of Mussolini's political party and without doubt the radical anarchic elements of Futurism are somewhat outweighed by its fascist tendencies. The text of* Feet, *however, offers a firm departure from the Surrealist performance texts and engages us with the possibilities of the mechanics and processes of theatre and performance. This translation was made in 1971.*

A curtain edged in black should be raised to about the height of a man's stomach. The public sees only legs in action. The actors must try to give the greatest expression to the attitudes and movements of their lower extremities.

1
Two armchairs
(one facing the other)

A BACHELOR
A MARRIED WOMAN

HIM: All, all for one of your kisses! …
HER: No! … Don't talk to me like that! …

2

A MAN WHO IS WALKING BACK AND FORTH

MAN: Let's meditate …

3
A desk

A SEATED MAN WHO IS NERVOUSLY MOVING HIS RIGHT FOOT

SEATED MAN: I must find … To cheat, without letting myself cheat!

3a

A MAN WHO IS WALKING SLOWLY WITH GOUTY FEET
A MAN WHO IS WALKING RAPIDLY

THE RAPID ONE: Hurry! Vile passéist!
THE SLOW ONE: Ah! What fury! There is no need to run! He who goes slowly is healthy …

4
A couch

THREE WOMEN

ONE: Which one do you prefer?
ANOTHER: All three of them.

A couch

THREE OFFICIALS

ONE: Which one do you prefer?
ANOTHER: The second one.

> *(The second one must be the woman who shows the most legs of the three.)*

5
A table

A FATHER
A BACHELOR
A YOUNG GIRL

THE FATHER: When you have the degree you will marry your cousin.

6
A pedal-operated sewing machine

A GIRL WHO IS WORKING

THE GIRL: I will see him on Sunday!

7

A MAN WHO IS RUNNING AWAY
A FOOT THAT IS KICKING AT HIM

THE MAN WHO IS GIVING THE KICK: Imbecile!

Note

From Michael Kirby, *Futurist Performance,* New York: Dutton, 1971, pp. 290–1.

2.7 GENIUS IN A JIFFY *OR* A DADALOGY (1920)

RAOUL HAUSMANN

Translated by Laurence Senelick

Raoul Hausmann (1886–1971). A painter and writer, born in Vienna, Hausmann was a committed member of the Expressionist movement but moved into Dada practice in Berlin, as an organizer of events and contributor to Dadaist journals in the late 1910s. He invented a particular method of photomontage and moved more into the field of photography as his career developed. During the war he had 'banned artist' status until 1944. This translation was made in 1989.

The stage is horribly dark, breakfast rolls rain down in the moonlight. A house once stood left. Out of the past enters ENGINEER DADA *followed by the* DADASOPHIST.

ENGINEER DADA: I feel so abandoned. – My eyes indeed were the first to see the light, but in the present revolutionary atmosphere … I believe something is bound to happen. The same thing goes for Byronic collars and penny-dreadful poetry. Otherwise things'll get very bad. I'd like to sing a song. A little bit of art. (*He sings.*)

> Herr Hölz he plays the gramophone,
> It drives Herr Ebert mad,
> Herr Seeckt's behind the fence alone,
> And wants to bash him bad.

A good song, a beautiful song. And yet people say I have bad teeth. Those nitwits, the Dadaists; when I think of the meatheads there are who understand nothing about taking photographs. For example there's the Dadasophist, imagines he could be something. Nothing but a … hush, here he comes now.

DADASOPHIST: Ah, good morning, Engineer, I'm glad I ran into you. Button up my left ear for me, I have until this evening to write a poem for *Schall und Rauch*, but I've sprained my hand and can't reach my head.

ENGINEER DADA: You are a nasty fellow. You ask me to do things you wouldn't do yourself. I'll have Grosz make a sketch of you, so you can see just how ugly you are. But strain your brain for 5.75 marks, no soldier in the Baltic provinces makes that much, it's overpaying – and

concoct a political poem. You can't do it by yourself, I must first engineer it properly. You Prague stevedore!

DADASOPHIST: I – I need just a piece of paper – and then my chamberpot brain whizzes away like a spinning top. – Give me a kick, you capitalist wage-slave, it'll do my stomach good and then you'll see.

ENGINEER DADA: (*Boxes his ears.*)

DADASOPHIST: (*Blubbers.*)

> The fat bourgeois guzzles a bottle of wine,
> At night screws his dear wife in bed,
> Hopes his hero Herr Kapp will manage just fine, -
> And then the dumb ARPshole drops dead!!

– there! didn't I say so? good, right?

ENGINEER DADA: Why, man – You're bigger than Mehring and Huelsenbeck put together. Kerr will have to deliver a revised verdict on you and I myself will raise your honorarium to six marks. You must see to it that Kurt Wolff publishes you, perhaps under the title: My name is Rolf or I am a Beast; man, you ought to give me ten marks for that! That's an invaluable idea! Straight from me!

DADASOPHIST: Man, I may have a trust-fund, but I have to pay so much luxury tax I cannot give you any money. I would rather recite another poem. Listen:

> Let malicious people rap,
> Profiteering's there for all.

Goods? nah, just hand out pure crap,
Profiteering leads the ball.
Sure, laws against it have been framed,
But if your granddad's clever,
If Sklarz or Scheidemann he's named,
No laws can hurt you ever!
So, man, it's clear for all to see
You're totally secure!
Go profiteering stalwartly,
In good company, be sure:
Ebert, Fritze, the Kaiser, it appears,
Are all enrolled among the profiteers.

ENGINEER DADA: Oh, that won't do – nope, nope, NOPE – it won't work if you dare list our illustrious sovereign as a profiteer! Suppress that! When I was back in New York at the Nocker Bocker, a fellow dared make indecent remarks about President Wilson – well, I can tell you, it made me feel very bad – believe you me. I had to leave America right away and that affected the exchange rate so adversely for me that I wished there had been another big Kapp or rather Ludendorff uprising, because if I were to film it, the rate of exchange would go up again. But now – well, bore a hole in the asphalt, take a telescope and then you can keep an eye on the exchange rate! Otherwise, if nothing special happens, they'll say I've engineered the world atlas of the Dadaists, the Dadaco, so well that Hänisch will order a million copies for school textbooks! By the way, my man, Dadaism – well, what exactly is it?

Both break into a lament, the sky turns light blue, blood and walking-sticks rain down, – both Dadaists are eaten up by two Berlin Daily editors, and a voice from the audience says:

Dada's a hoax!
Is there an anti-Semite organizer in the house?

Note

The name-dropping refers to the turbulent political and artistic scene in post-war Germany. Max Hölz, a Spartacist, in 1920 had led a Communist revolt in Vogtland which he proclaimed a Soviet Republic; he was a promoter of the General Strike of 1921. Wolfgang Kapp had led a monarchist revolt against the republican government, seized Berlin and had himself proclaimed imperial chancellor; he was abetted by half-mad General Erich Ludendorff, who was later a participant in the Hitler beer-hall Putsch. The revolt failed after the general strike, and Friedrich Ebert resumed power as first president of the German Reich. Hans von Seekt, a military hero, was commander-in-chief of the Reichswehr; Phillip Scheidemann, who had urged a compromise peace during the war, was proclaimed first Prime Minister of the republic but resigned when the Reichstag accepted the terms of the Treaty of Versailles. Konrad Hänisch, a Social Democrat and Minister for Public Worship and Education, had convened a Schoolbook Conference in 1920. Alfred Kerr was Berlin's most influential drama critic. Kurt Wolff founded a new publishing house devoted to avant-garde and experimental works. – *Translator.*

From Laurence Senelick, ed., *Cabaret Performance: Europe 1890–1920*, New York: PAJ Publications, 1989, pp. 212–15.

2.8 THE PUBLIC (1930)

FEDERICO GARCÍA LORCA

Adapted/translated by Caridad Svich

Federico García Lorca (1898–1936) is Spain's foremost playwright, whose plays are produced in theatres all over the world and are frequently adapted into choreographed works, films, operas and so on. A fascination with his personal life has somewhat overshadowed the analysis and appreciation of his oeuvre which embraces folk culture and the poetic as major components of the theatrical art. The author of a number of works and treatises on theatre, Lorca was a friend of Salvador Dalí. The original play was left unfinished, unpublished and unproduced. This version was written in 1930 and there is documentation that a second draft was completed in 1936. The first professional production of The Public, *a co-production of Piccolo Teatro di Milano and the Centro Dramatico Nacional of Madrid, took place in Milan and Madrid in the 1986–7 theatre season under the direction of esteemed Catalan director (and García Lorca expert) Lluis Pasqual. This English-language version is based on Antonio Monegal's Spanish edition of the play published by Alianza Editorial/Biblioteca García Lorca in 2000. The version of Lorca's* The Public *printed here was translated by playwright Caridad Svich.*

Figures
DIRECTOR
SERVANT
FIRST MAN (Gonzalo)
SECOND MAN
THIRD MAN
BOY, played by an actress
HELEN
And HORSES

And: FIGURE WITH VINE LEAVES, FIGURE WITH BELLS, ROMAN EMPEROR, CENTURION, JULIET, FIRST WHITE HORSE, THREE WHITE HORSES, HARLEQUIN COSTUME, BALLERINA COSTUME, PAJAMA COSTUME, THE IDIOT SHEPHERD, MALE NUDE, MALE NURSE, THIRD MAN, FOUR LADIES (theatre patrons), FIRST STUDENT, SECOND STUDENT, THIRD STUDENT, FOURTH STUDENT, FIFTH STUDENT, MAGICIAN, LADY IN BLACK, and TWO THIEVES

Suggested doubling (Translator):
FIRST MAN (Gonzalo) may also play Figure with Vine Leaves, Male Nude and Magician;
SECOND MAN may also play Figure with Bells and Fifth Student;
THIRD MAN may also play Roman Emperor and Male Nurse;
SERVANT may also play Centurion, First White Horse, the Idiot Shepherd and Lady (theatre patron);
HELEN may also play Juliet and Lady (theatre patron);
BOY (played by an actress) may also play Harlequin Costume;
FOUR HORSES from Frame One may also play Three White Horses and Black Horse from Frame Three, and Four Students in Frame Five;
And the Ballerina Costume, Pajama Costume, Two Ladies and Thieves may be played by puppets.

As this is a play that revels in actor (and scenic transformation), other multiple doubling ideas are encouraged. Historically, the play has been performed with as little as eight actors, and as many as thirty. This version suggests a cast of ten.

Frame One

The DIRECTOR's Room. The DIRECTOR of the open air theatre is seated. He wears a bolero-cut jacket. Blue decor. A huge handprint is on the wall. The windows are X-ray negatives.

SERVANT: Sir.

DIRECTOR: What?

SERVANT: The public

DIRECTOR: Show them in.

FOUR WHITE HORSES enter.

DIRECTOR: What can I do for you?

The HORSES blow their trumpets.

If I were a man capable of sighing, such sounds would do indeed. My theatre will always be the open air theatre. (*Furiously.*) But I have lost my fortune. If I hadn't, I would poison the air. A little syringe to pick the scab off the wound would be enough for me. Get out of here! Out of my house, horses! Someone's just invented a bed for sleeping with horses. (*Sobbing.*) My dear little horses.

HORSES: (*Sobbing.*) For three hundred coins.[1] Two hundred coins, for a bowl of soup, for an empty bottle of perfume. For a drop of your spit, for one of your nail-clippings …

DIRECTOR: Out! Out! Out! (*He rings a bell.*)

HORSES: For nothing. Before your feet used to smell. We were three years old. We waited for you in the toilet, behind doors … We would fill your bed with tears.

The SERVANT enters.

DIRECTOR: Get my whip!

HORSES: Your shoes were stewed in sweat, but we knew, we understood that our relationship is the same as the one the moon has with the apples rotting on the grass.

DIRECTOR: (*To SERVANT.*) Open the doors.

HORSES: No, no, no. It's abominable. You're covered now with down, and you eat the whitewash of the walls that are not yours.

SERVANT: I won't open the door. I don't want to go out onto the stage.

DIRECTOR: (*Striking him.*) Open it!

FIRST AND SECOND HORSE: (*Furiously.*) Abominable!

THIRD AND FOURTH HORSE: Ble-nam-I-boa!

FIRST AND SECOND HORSE: (*Challenging.*) Abominable.

THIRD AND FOURTH HORSE: Ble-nam-I-boa.

The HORSES raise their golden trumpets and dance slowly to the rhythm of their chant.

The SERVANT opens the door.

DIRECTOR: Open air theatre! Go on, go now. Open air theatre. Get out of here.

The HORSES leave.

(*To SERVANT.*) Carry on. (*He sits at the table.*)

SERVANT: Sir.

DIRECTOR: What?

SERVANT: The public!

DIRECTOR: Show them in.

The DIRECTOR changes his blond wig for a dark one. THREE MEN enter. They wear frock coats, and have dark beards. They are identical.

FIRST MAN: Are you the Director of the Open Air Theatre?

DIRECTOR: At your service.

FIRST MAN: We wanted to congratulate you on your latest show.

DIRECTOR: Thank you.

THIRD MAN: Most original.

FIRST MAN: And such a lovely title too. *Romeo and Juliet.*

DIRECTOR: A man and a woman who fall in love.

FIRST MAN: Romeo can be a bird, and Juliet a stone. Romeo can be a grain of salt, and Juliet a map.

DIRECTOR: But they'll never stop being Romeo and Juliet.

FIRST MAN: And in love. Do you think they were really in love?

DIRECTOR: Good sir … I'm not inside …

FIRST MAN: Enough! Enough! You've incriminated yourself.

SECOND MAN: (*To FIRST MAN.*) Take care now for you're to blame. Why knock on a theatre's door? Call on a forest and it would easily offer up the sound of its sap for your ears. But a theatre?

FIRST MAN: It is precisely on theatres that we must call, because …

THIRD MAN: So that the truth of tombs be known.

SECOND MAN: Tombs with playbills, spotlights, and long rows of seats.

DIRECTOR: Gentlemen …

FIRST MAN: Yes, yes, Director of the Open Air Theatre, author of *Romeo and Juliet.*

SECOND MAN: How did Romeo piss, Mister Director? Or is it not pleasant to watch Romeo piss? How many times did he pretend to fling himself from the tower only to be catapulted into the drama of his own pain? What went on, Mister Director … when there was nothing going on? And the tomb scene: why didn't you walk down the steps of the tomb at the end? You could have seen an angel there, making off with Romeo's sex, while leaving another, your sex, which suited him better. And what if I tell you that the main character in the drama was a poisonous flower? What would you say? Answer me.

DIRECTOR: Gentlemen, that's not what it's about.

FIRST MAN: (*Interrupting.*) That is precisely what it's about. We have to bury the theatre – that's clear – because everyone's a coward. And I will have to shoot myself.

SECOND MAN: Gonzalo!

FIRST MAN: (*Slowly.*) I will have to shoot myself so that a new theatre can rise: the theatre beneath the sand.

DIRECTOR: Gonzalo ...

FIRST MAN: What ...? (*Pause.*)

DIRECTOR: (*Demonstratively.*) I can't. It would ruin everything. It'd be as if I was blinding my own children. And what do I do with the public? What happens to the audience if I take away the handrails from the bridge? The mask would come to devour me. I saw a man devoured by a mask once. The strongest young men of the city rammed wads of old newspaper up his ass with blood-stained sticks. And once in America, the mask strung a young man up by his own intestines.

FIRST MAN: Sublime!

SECOND MAN: Why don't you say this in your theatre?

THIRD MAN: Isn't it the beginning of a plot?

DIRECTOR: More like an ending.

THIRD MAN: An end brought about by fear.

DIRECTOR: That is clear. You don't suppose, sir, that I will put the mask on the stage.

FIRST MAN: Why not?

DIRECTOR: What about morality? And the spectators' stomachs?

FIRST MAN: There are those who throw up at the sight of someone turning a squid inside out. There are others who pale if the word 'cancer' is spoken in a deliberate manner. But you know full well tin-plate, plaster, glitter, and, as a last resort, cardboard can work wonders. After all, anyone can afford cardboard. (*He stands.*) But what you want to do is to deceive us. You want to deceive us so things go on the same way they always have, and we won't be able to do anything for our dead. It's your fault that nasty flies fell into four thousand glasses of orange juice I set out, and now I have to tear up roots again.

DIRECTOR: (*Stands up.*) I do not argue, sir. What is it you want from me? Have you a new play to show me?

FIRST MAN: Could there be a play newer than we with our beards ... and you?

DIRECTOR: And I?

FIRST MAN: Yes ... you.

SECOND MAN: Gonzalo!

FIRST MAN: (*Looking at the DIRECTOR.*) I recognize him still, it's as if I see him again the morning he caught that hare, which was a vision of speed, and tucked it into a little briefcase full of books. And I remember too the day he discovered how to part his hair down the middle, and how he placed a rose behind each ear. Do you recognize me now?

DIRECTOR: This is not the plot. For heaven's sake. (*Shouts.*) Helen. Helen. (*Runs to the door.*)

FIRST MAN: I'm going to put you on the stage, whether you like it or not. You've put me through too much. Quick! The screen! The screen!

The THIRD MAN brings on a folding screen and sets it up stage center.

DIRECTOR: (*Sobbing.*) The public will see me then. My theatre will be ruined. I've put on the best shows of the season, but now ...!

The HORSES' trumpets sound. FIRST MAN goes to the back wall and opens the door.

FIRST MAN: Come inside with us. You have a place in this drama. Everyone has. (*To the DIRECTOR.*) And you! Get behind the screen.

SECOND and THIRD man push the DIRECTOR behind the screen.

He immediately appears on the other side of the screen as a BOY dressed in white satin with a white ruff round his neck, carrying a small black guitar. The BOY should be played by an actress.

FIRST MAN: Enrique! Enrique! (*Covers his face with his hands.*)

SECOND MAN: Don't make me go behind the screen. Leave me alone. Gonzalo!

DIRECTOR: (*Coldly, strumming his guitar.*) Gonzalo, I will spit on you. I want to spit on you a great deal; and I want to take some little scissors and rip up your jacket. Give me some silk and thread. I want to sew; I want to embroider. I don't like tattoos, but I shall embroider you, with silk thread.

THIRD MAN (BOY): Wherever you like.

FIRST MAN: (*Weeps.*) Enrique! Enrique!

DIRECTOR: I shall embroider your flesh. I'd like to watch you sleep on the roof. How much money do you have in your pockets? Burn it!

FIRST MAN strikes a match, and burns his money.

I can never see precisely how it is that images vanish in the flame. Have you no more money? You're poor, Gonzalo! What about my lipstick? Rouge? How tiresome you are.

SECOND MAN: (*Timidly.*) I have lipstick. (*Gets lipstick from under his beard, and holds it out.*)

DIRECTOR: Thanks ... but ... you're here as well? Get behind the screen! You too! I don't know how you put up with him, Gonzalo.

DIRECTOR shoves the second man behind the screen.

SECOND MAN reappears as a WOMAN in black pajama pants with a crown of poppies on her head. She carries a lorgnette in her hand with blond mustachios attached to it, which she will use for effect as needed, putting it over her mouth.

SECOND MAN: (*Dryly.*) Give me the lipstick.

DIRECTOR: Ha, ha ha. Oh Maximiliana, Empress of Bavaria. You are a bad bad girl.

SECOND MAN: (*Puts lorgnette to her mouth.*) I'd advise a bit of silence.

DIRECTOR: Bad bad woman. Helen! Helen!

FIRST MAN: (*Loudly.*) Don't call Helen.

DIRECTOR: And why not? She loved me very much when I had my open air theatre. Helen!

HELEN appears stage left, dressed in ancient Greek manner. Her eyebrows are blue, her hair is white and her feet are chalk-white. Her dress is open down the front, and we see she wears rose-colored tights. SECOND MAN *raises his lorgnette to his mouth.*

HELEN: The same again?

DIRECTOR: Once more.

THIRD MAN (BOY): What, have you made an appearance, Helen? Why have you appeared if you won't love me?

HELEN: Who told you that? Why do you love me so much? I would kiss your feet if you punished me, or if you went out with other women. But all you do is worship me, and me alone. We must put an end to this once and for all.

DIRECTOR: (*To* THIRD MAN.) And me? Don't you remember me? Have you forgotten how I tore out my nails for you? Don't you remember? How could I have gone with other women, and not with you? Why have I called you, Helen? Why did I call you, my torturer?

HELEN: (*To* THIRD MAN.) Go with him! And admit the truth you've been hiding from me. It makes no difference to me that you were drunk, as if that were an excuse: you kissed his face, you lay in the same bed.

THIRD MAN (BOY): Helen!

THIRD MAN goes behind screen quickly and reappears as himself without a beard, pale-faced, and with a whip in his hand. He wears leather cuffs with inlaid gold studs. He whips the DIRECTOR.

THIRD MAN: You always talk, you always lie, and I am going to finish you off: no mercy.

HORSES: (*Off.*) Mercy. Mercy.

HELEN: You could go on whipping him for a whole century and I still wouldn't believe you.

THIRD MAN goes to HELEN *and grips her wrists.*

You can mutilate my fingers for a hundred years; you won't extract a single moan from me.

THIRD MAN: We'll see who's stronger.

HELEN: I am, I always will be.

SERVANT enters.

(*To* SERVANT.) Take me away from here. Quickly. Take me away.

The SERVANT *goes behind the screen and reappears unchanged.*

Take me away. Far away from here.

The SERVANT *embraces her.*

DIRECTOR: Let us begin.

FIRST MAN: Whenever you wish.

HORSES: (*Off.*) Mercy. Mercy.

The HORSES *sound their trumpets. Freeze. Slow curtain.*

Frame Two
Roman Ruin

A FIGURE, *covered entirely with red vine leaves, is playing a flute while seated on a fallen capital. Another* FIGURE, *covered completely with little golden bells, dances center stage.*

FIGURE WITH BELLS: If I turned into a cloud?

FIGURE WITH VINE LEAVES: I would turn myself into an eye.

FIGURE WITH BELLS: If I turned myself into a turd?

FIGURE WITH VINE LEAVES: I would turn into a fly.

FIGURE WITH BELLS: If I turned into an apple?

FIGURE WITH VINE LEAVES: I would turn into a kiss.

FIGURE WITH BELLS: If I turned myself into a breast?

FIGURE WITH VINE LEAVES: I would turn myself into a white bedsheet.

VOICE: (*Off.*) (*Sarcastically.*) Bravo!

FIGURE WITH BELLS: And if I were to turn into a moonfish?

FIGURE WITH VINE LEAVES: I would turn into a knife.

FIGURE WITH BELLS: (*Stops dancing.*) But … why? Why do you torment me? If you love me, why won't you follow where I want to lead you? If I turned into a moonfish, you could turn into a wave or seaweed; or if you wanted something a little more distant, because you don't want to kiss me, you could turn into a full moon; but a knife? You take pleasure in interrupting my dance. And dancing is the only way I have of loving you.

FIGURE WITH VINE LEAVES: When you wander midst the objects of the house, and circle the bed, I follow you. But I don't follow you where you, in your wisdom, choose to take me. If you turned into a moonfish, I'd slit your belly with a knife, because I'm a man. That is all I am: a man, more of a man than Adam. And I want you to be more of a man than I. Such a man that as you were to pass by, the leaves and the branches would fall silent. But you're not a man. If I didn't have this flute, you'd be in the moon, a moon covered in little lace hankies and drops of woman's blood.

FIGURE WITH BELLS: (*Shyly.*) And if I were to turn myself into an ant?

FIGURE WITH VINE LEAVES: (*Vigorously.*) I would turn myself into earth.

FIGURE WITH BELLS: (*Forcefully.*) And if I turn into earth?

FIGURE WITH VINE LEAVES: (*Weakly.*) I would turn into water.

FIGURE WITH BELLS: (*Roused.*) And if I turned into water?

FIGURE WITH VINE LEAVES: (*Weaker.*) I would turn into a moonfish.

FIGURE WITH BELLS: (*Trembling.*) And if I turned myself into a moonfish?

FIGURE WITH VINE LEAVES: (*Rising.*) I would turn into a knife, into a knife sharpened during four long springs.

FIGURE WITH BELLS: Take me to the bath. Drown me. That's the only way you'll see me naked. Do you think I'm afraid of blood? I know how to master you. You think I don't know you? I could so master you that if I were to say … 'And if I were to turn into a moonfish?,' you would say 'I would turn into a little sack of spawn.'

FIGURE WITH VINE LEAVES: Get an axe, and cut off my legs. Let the insects crawl out of the ruins, and leave me. I detest you. I'd like to see how base you really are. I spit on you.

FIGURE WITH BELLS: You want me to go? Goodbye. I'm easy. If I walk down amongst the ruins, I'll find love and love to spare.

FIGURE WITH VINE LEAVES: (*Despairing.*) Where are you going? Where are you going?

FIGURE WITH BELLS: Don't you want me to go?

FIGURE WITH VINE LEAVES: (*Softly.*) No, don't go. If I turned into a grain of sand?

FIGURE WITH BELLS: I would turn into a whip.

FIGURE WITH VINE LEAVES: And if I turned myself into a little sack of spawn?

FIGURE WITH BELLS: I would turn into another whip: a whip made of guitar strings.

FIGURE WITH VINE LEAVES: Don't beat me!

FIGURE WITH BELLS: A whip made from ship's ropes.

FIGURE WITH VINE LEAVES: Don't strike my stomach!

FIGURE WITH BELLS: A whip made from the stamens of an orchid.

FIGURE WITH VINE LEAVES: You will end by blinding me.

FIGURE WITH BELLS: Blind, yes, because you're not a man. I'm the man around here. I'm so much a man that I faint when the hunters awaken. I'm so much a man that a sharp pain shoots through my teeth when someone snaps a flower's stalk, no matter how small it is. I'm a giant. I'm such a giant that I can embroider a rose on the fingernail of a newborn baby.

FIGURE WITH VINE LEAVES: These white ruins are torture. I'm waiting for night to fall, so I can grovel at your feet.

FIGURE WITH BELLS: No, no. Why say that to me? You should be making me do that. Aren't you a man? A man who's more of a man than Adam?

FIGURE WITH VINE LEAVES: (*Falls down.*) Ah …

FIGURE WITH BELLS: (*Approaches quietly.*) And if I should turn myself into a capital?

FIGURE WITH VINE LEAVES: Poor me.

FIGURE WITH BELLS: You would turn into the shadow of a capital, and nothing more. And then Helen would come to my bed. My dear Helen. While you would be lying underneath the cushions, drenched in sweat; not your own sweat, but the sweat of coachmen, stokers, and cancer surgeons. And then I would turn myself into a moonfish, and you would be nothing more than a little powder compact passed from hand to hand.

FIGURE WITH VINE LEAVES: Ah.

FIGURE WITH BELLS: More tears? I shall have to throw a faint so that the field workers come here. I shall have to call out to the workmen, the tall workmen filled with machete scars who work night and day dredging up mud from the river. Get up, coward. Yesterday I was at a blacksmith's, and I ordered a chain. Don't crawl away from me. A chain. Yes. And I wept all night long because my ankles and wrists hurt, even though I didn't have it on.

FIGURE WITH VINE LEAVES blows a silver whistle.

What are you doing?

FIGURE WITH VINE LEAVES blows the whistle again.

I know what you want, but I've still time to run away.

FIGURE WITH VINE LEAVES: Run away, then.

FIGURE WITH BELLS: I'll defend myself with blades of grass.

FIGURE WITH VINE LEAVES: Try to defend yourself.

FIGURE WITH VINE LEAVES blows the whistle. A BOY in red tights drops in from above.

BOY: The Emperor! The Emperor! The Emperor!

FIGURE WITH VINE LEAVES: The Emperor.

FIGURE WITH BELLS: I'll pretend I'm you. Don't show yourself. It could cost me my life.

BOY: The Emperor! The Emperor! The Emperor!

FIGURE WITH BELLS: It was all a game between us. Just a game we played. And now I'll serve the Emperor using your voice. You can stretch out over there behind the big capital. I never told you before, but over there there's a cow that cooks for the soldiers.

FIGURE WITH VINE LEAVES: The Emperor! We haven't got a chance. You've torn the spider's web, and I can feel my big feet become small and disgusting.

FIGURE WITH BELLS: Would you like some tea? Where can I find a hot drink amongst these ruins?

BOY: (*On the ground.*) The Emperor! The Emperor! The Emperor!

A trumpet sounds. The ROMAN EMPEROR appears. He is accompanied by a CENTURION who wears a yellow tunic and whose skin is gray, and also by the FOUR WHITE HORSES with their trumpets from the first frame.[2] The boy approaches the EMPEROR. The EMPEROR takes the BOY into his arms, and they disappear into the ruins.

CENTURION: The Emperor seeks the one.

FIGURE WITH VINE LEAVES: I'm the one.

FIGURE WITH BELLS: I'm the one.

CENTURION: Which one of the two is …?

FIGURE WITH VINE LEAVES: I am.

FIGURE WITH BELLS: I am.

CENTURION: The Emperor will divine which one of you two is the one. With a knife, or with a gob of spit. Cursed are you and all your sort. Because of you, I have to roam about and sleep on sand. My wife is as majestic as a mountain. Gives birth from four or five different places at the same time, and snores at noon beneath the trees. I have two hundred children, and I'll have more yet. Cursed be all of you.

The CENTURION spits, and sings to himself. A long, sustained cry from behind the ruins.

The EMPEROR reappears, mopping his forehead. He takes off his black gloves, revealing red ones, which he then takes off to reveal alabaster hands.

EMPEROR: (*Casually*.) Which of the two is the one?

FIGURE WITH VINE LEAVES: I am, my lord.

EMPEROR: One is one, and always one. I've cut the heads off more than forty young men who wouldn't admit it.

CENTURION: (*Spits*.) One is one and nothing more than one.

EMPEROR: And not two.

CENTURION: Because if there was two of them, the Emperor wouldn't be out searching the streets.

EMPEROR: (*To* CENTURION.) Strip them.

FIGURE WITH BELLS: I'm one, my lord. He's just a beggar who lives in the ruins, and nourishes himself with weeds.

EMPEROR: Step aside.

FIGURE WITH VINE LEAVES: You know me. You know who I am.

He strips off the vine leaves, and stands nude before the EMPEROR. *His skin is alabaster white.*

EMPEROR: (*Embraces him*.) One is one.

FIGURE WITH VINE LEAVES: And always one. If you will kiss me, I will open my mouth and let your sword pierce my throat.

EMPEROR: And I will.

FIGURE WITH VINE LEAVES: And leave my lover's head amongst the ruins: the head of one who was always one.

EMPEROR: (*Sighs*.) One.

CENTURION: (*To* EMPEROR.) It's not easy, but there you have him.

FIGURE WITH VINE LEAVES: He has what he can never have.

FIGURE WITH BELLS: It's treason! Treason!

CENTURION: Shut your mouth, you old rat! Broomstick's son!

FIGURE WITH BELLS: Gonzalo! Help! Gonzalo!

FIGURE WITH BELLS pulls one of the columns, and it unfolds into the white folding screen from the First Frame. From behind it the THREE BEARDED MEN, and the DIRECTOR are seen.[3]

FIRST MAN: Treason!

FIGURE WITH BELLS: He has betrayed us.

DIRECTOR: Treason!

The EMPEROR embraces the FIGURE WITH VINE LEAVES. Curtain.

Frame Three

A wall of sand. A transparent, gelatinous moon is painted on the wall above left. Stage center there is an immense green leaf.

FIRST MAN: (*Entering*.) That's not what's needed. After all that has happened it would be unfair of me to once again speak to children and contemplate the joys of heaven.

SECOND MAN: Evil place this.

DIRECTOR: Did you see the wrestling?

THIRD MAN: (*Entering*.) They should both have died. I've never seen a bloodier feast.

FIRST MAN: Two lions; two demigods.

SECOND MAN: Two demigods, except they've got an anus.

FIRST MAN: The anus is man's punishment. It's man's failure, shame and death. Both of them had an anus. Neither of them could match the pure beauty of marble that gleams, protecting intimate desires beneath an immaculate surface.

THIRD MAN: When the moon comes out, the children in the fields gather together to shit.

FIRST MAN: Behind the rushes, by fresh still water, we have found the traces of men who sully the nudity's freedom.

THIRD MAN: They should have both died.

FIRST MAN: (*Vigorous*.) They should have both won!

THIRD MAN: How?

FIRST MAN: By being men, and not letting themselves be dragged down by false desires; by being men: whole and complete. Can a man ever stop being a man?

SECOND MAN: Gonzalo!

FIRST MAN: They both lost, and now their exploits will just be a source of ridicule and mockery for people.

THIRD MAN: Neither of them were men, as are neither of you; I am repulsed by you both.

FIRST MAN: Back there, behind the revelers, is the Emperor. Why don't you go and strangle him? I admit your courage, just as I justify your beauty. Why don't you throw yourself on him and tear into his neck with your teeth?

DIRECTOR: Why don't you?

FIRST MAN: Because I can't, because I don't want to, and because I'm weak.

DIRECTOR: (*Indicating the* THIRD MAN.) But he can. He wants to. He's strong. (*Loudly*.) The Emperor is in the ruins.

THIRD MAN: Let him who wants to breathe in his breath go.

FIRST MAN: You!

THIRD MAN: I could only convince you if I had my whip.

FIRST MAN: You know I won't resist you, but I'd still despise you for being a coward.

SECOND MAN: A coward!

DIRECTOR: (*Looking at the* THIRD MAN. *Loudly*.) The Emperor, who drinks our blood, is in the ruins!

THIRD MAN hides his face in his hands.

FIRST MAN: (*To* DIRECTOR.) That's the one; do you recognize him now? He's the brave lad, who in the café and in books rolls up our veins in long fish bones. That's the man who makes love with the Emperor under cover, and seeks him out in dockside bars. Enrique, look closely at him. Look what tiny bunches of grapes fall over his shoulders. He doesn't fool me. Now I will kill the Emperor. And not with a knife, but only these two frail hands, which are women's envy.

DIRECTOR: No, he must go. Wait a minute.

THIRD MAN sits in a chair and weeps.

THIRD MAN: I won't be able to debut my new cloud pajamas! Ah! I haven't told you yet, but I've found a marvelous new drink that only a few blacks in Honduras know about.

DIRECTOR: We should be in some dank reservoir. Not here. We should be under the ooze where the dead frogs rot.

SECOND MAN: (*Embracing* FIRST MAN.) Gonzalo, why do you love him so much?

FIRST MAN: (*To the* DIRECTOR.) I'll bring you the Emperor's head.

DIRECTOR: I can't think of a better gift for Helen.

SECOND MAN: Gonzalo, stay here and let me wash your feet.

FIRST MAN: The Emperor's head burns the bodies of all women.

DIRECTOR: (*To* FIRST MAN.) What you don't know is that Helen can soften her hands in phosphorus and quicklime. Go on, take the knife. Helen. My dear Helen!

THIRD MAN: My eternal love. Let no one here speak of Helen.

DIRECTOR: (*Trembling.*) No one must mention her name. It's best if we calm ourselves. If we just forget about the theatre, we'll be able to (do so). No one must mention her name.

FIRST MAN: Helen.

DIRECTOR: (*To* FIRST MAN.) Shut up! I'll see you later behind the big warehouse, so shut up.

FIRST MAN: I'd rather get it over with, once and for all. Helen! (*Starts to exit.*)

DIRECTOR: (*To* FIRST MAN.) Wait. And if I were to turn into a little jasmine dwarf?

SECOND MAN: (*To* FIRST MAN.) Let's go. Don't let him fool you. I'll accompany you to the ruins.

DIRECTOR: (*Embracing* FIRST MAN.) I will turn myself into a little pill of aniseed containing the essence of the rushes growing near all the rivers and you will be a Chinese mountain covered with tiny living harps.

FIRST MAN: (*Eyes half closed.*) No, no, not a Chinese mountain. I'll be a skin of ancient wine that will fill your throat with leeches.

FIRST MAN and DIRECTOR fight.

THIRD MAN: We should pull them apart.

SECOND MAN: Before they devour each other.

THIRD MAN: Although I'd get my freedom.

The DIRECTOR and FIRST MAN continue to fight in silence.

SECOND MAN: I'd get my death.

THIRD MAN: If I have a slave...

SECOND MAN: It's because I am a slave.

THIRD MAN: We're both slaves, but we can break our chains each in his own way.

FIRST MAN: I'll call Helen!

DIRECTOR: I'll call Helen!

FIRST MAN: No. Please!

DIRECTOR: No, don't call her! I'll turn into whatever you want.

They disappear right, fighting.

THIRD MAN: We could give them a shove and they'd fall down the well. Then you and I would be free.

SECOND MAN: You'd be free. I'd be more enslaved than ever.

THIRD MAN: It doesn't matter. I'll push them in. I'm longing to live in my verdant country again, and be a shepherd, and drink the water from the rock streams.

SECOND MAN: You seem to forget that I can be strong when I put my mind to it. I was still a child when I used to yoke up my father's ox-team. My bones may be covered with tiny orchids, but there's a mantle of muscle there to be used when I want to.

THIRD MAN: (*Gently.*) It'll be better for them, and for us too. Come on! It's a deep well.

SECOND MAN: I won't let you!

They fight. SECOND MAN *pushes* THIRD MAN *and they disappear stage left.*

The wall opens and we see the sepulchre of Juliet in Verona. Realistic décor. Rose bushes and ivy. Moon. JULIET *is stretched out on the tomb. She wears a white opera gown, which has a train. Her pink celluloid breasts are exposed.*

JULIET: (*Jumping out of the tomb.*) Please. I haven't run into a single friend in all this time despite the fact that I've gone through more than three thousand empty arches. A little help, please. A little help, and a sea of dreams.

She sings:

A sea of dreams
A sea of white earth
And of empty arches across the sky.
My train trails the seaweed and the tide
My train trails through time.
A sea of time,
A beach of woodcutter worms
And a glass dolphin through the cherry trees.
Oh, pure asbestos at day's end. Oh ruin!
Solitude without arches. A sea of dreams!

A tumult of swords and voices are heard from the back of the stage.

People, and even more people. They'll end up in my tomb next, and sleeping on my little cot. I'm not interested in discussions about love or theatre; what I want is ... to Love.

The FIRST WHITE HORSE appears; he carries a sword.

FIRST WHITE HORSE: To Love.

JULIET: Yes. A love that lasts only for a moment.

FIRST WHITE HORSE: I waited for you in the garden.

JULIET: You mean in the tomb.

FIRST WHITE HORSE: You're as crazy as ever. Juliet, when are you going to notice the perfection of one day? One day: a morning, and an afternoon.

JULIET: And a night.

FIRST WHITE HORSE: Night is not day. In one day you could shed your anguish, and stave off the power of the impenetrable marble walls.

JULIET: How?

FIRST WHITE HORSE: Mount my rump.

JULIET: What for?

FIRST WHITE HORSE: (*Drawing close to her.*) I'll carry you away from here.

JULIET: Where?

FIRST WHITE HORSE: To dark places; in dark places there are soft branches. The cemetery of wings has a thousand dense surfaces.

JULIET: (*Trembling.*) And what will you give me there?

FIRST WHITE HORSE: I will give you the silent core of darkness.

JULIET: Day?

FIRST WHITE HORSE: Lightless moss: a touch that can devour tiny worlds with the tips of your fingers.

JULIET: I thought you were the one who was going to teach me the perfection of one day.

FIRST WHITE HORSE: So as to take you into the night.

JULIET: (*Furiously.*) And what's the night to me? Stupid horse. What can I learn from night's stars, its clouds, or its drunks? I must get some rat poison to rid myself of such bothersome people. But I don't want to kill rats. Rats play for me on small pianos, and little lacquered brushes.

FIRST WHITE HORSE: Juliet, the night isn't just one moment, but one moment can last an entire night.

JULIET: (*Sobs.*) That's enough; I don't want to hear any more from you. Why do you want to take me away? Words of love are lies, broken mirrors, and footsteps on water. Afterwards you will leave me again in the tomb, like everyone else does; trying to convince anyone who'll listen that real love is impossible. I'm tired of it. And I rise up to ask for help, so that all those people who prattle on and theorize about my heart and who pry open my mouth with tiny marble forceps, may be thrown out of my tomb once and for all.

FIRST WHITE HORSE: Day is a seated ghost.

JULIET: Yet I've known of women killed by the sun's light.

FIRST WHITE HORSE: Understand a single day fully, and you will come to love every night.

JULIET: The same from all of them! The same from all of them! From all the men, trees, horses, all the same. Everything you want to teach me, I already know. The moon pushes gently at empty houses, brings down stone pillars, and gives worms little torches to light their way into cherries. The moon carries masks of meningitis into bedrooms, fills the wombs of pregnant women with cold water, and, when I least expect it, flings handfuls of grass on my shoulders. Don't look at me, dear horse, with such longing, for I know it well. When I was very small, in Verona, I used to see beautiful cows grazing in the meadows; Later I saw them in my picture-books, but I always remembered them best when I passed by the butcher's shop.

FIRST WHITE HORSE: Love that lasts only for a moment.

JULIET: Yes, one minute, and Juliet will be alive, happy, and free from the swarm of magnifying stares. Juliet at her beginning, Juliet on the verge of the big city.

The tumult of voices and swords is again heard rise from the back of the stage,

FIRST WHITE HORSE: Love. To love. Love
Love of the snail – nail, nail.
Who points his horns to the sun.
Love. To love. Love.
Of the horse who licks
its block of salt.

He dances.

JULIET: There were forty of them yesterday, and I was asleep. Spiders came, and little girls too, and the young woman raped by a dog, who covered herself with geraniums, and yet I remained calm. When nymphs speak of cheese, they may mean mermaid's milk, or clover juice. But now there are four of them, four boys, who wanted to fix a little clay phallus on me, and paint a moustache on me.

FIRST WHITE HORSE: Love. To love. Love.
Love of Aphrodite's priest for a he-goat
And of the mule for the snail – nail, nail.
Who points his horns to the sun.
Love. To love. Love.
Of Jupiter in the stable
With the peacock
And the horse who whinnies inside the cathedral.

JULIET: Four young men, horse. I heard them playing about for a long time, but I didn't wake until the knives were drawn.

The BLACK HORSE appears, with black plume, and a wheel in hand.

BLACK HORSE: Four young men? Everyone. Asphodel in one field, the other side newly seeded. The dead carry on their discussions, and the living go to it with the scalpel. Everyone.

FIRST WHITE HORSE: On the shores of the Dead Sea beautiful apples are born out of the ashes, the very best ashes.

BLACK HORSE: So fresh. What flesh. Like dew. I eat ashes.

JULIET: No, no, ashes aren't good to eat. Who's talking about ashes?

FIRST WHITE HORSE: I'm not talking about ashes; I'm talking about ashes formed like apples.

BLACK HORSE: Form. Form. It's a blood craving.

JULIET: Chaos.

BLACK HORSE: A blood craving, and the monotony of the wheel.

The THREE WHITE HORSES appear, carrying long black-lacquered walking canes.

THREE WHITE HORSES: Form and ashes. Ashes and form. Mirror. And a golden loaf for the man who can end it.

JULIET: (*Wrings her hands.*) Form and ashes.

BLACK HORSE: Yes. You know full well how I decapitate doves.

When someone says rock, I hear air; when someone says air, I hear emptiness; when someone says emptiness, I hear headless dove.

FIRST WHITE HORSE: Love. Love. Love.
Of the moon for the eggshell
Of the egg yolk for the moon
And the cloud for the eggshell.

THREE WHITE HORSES: (*Striking the ground with their sticks.*)
Love. Love. Love.
Of cowdung for the sun
Of the sun for a dead cow
And the blackbeetle for the sun.

BLACK HORSE: You can waggle your sticks however much you want, but things will go on as they will and as they must. Damn you! Louts! Because of you, I have to scour the woods for resin several times a week, and plug up my ears to restore the silence I need. (*Persuasively.*) Come on Juliet, I've laid linen sheets out for you. Any minute now there will be a fine rain, crowned by ivy, soaking the skies and walls.

THREE WHITE HORSES: We have three black canes.

FIRST WHITE HORSE: And a sword.

THREE WHITE HORSES: (*To JULIET.*) We must pass through your womb to find the resurrection of horses.

BLACK HORSE: Juliet, it's three in the morning; if you're not careful, they'll lock the gate; and you won't be able to get back in.

THREE WHITE HORSES: She'll still have the fields, and the mountains on the horizon.

BLACK HORSE: Pay them no mind Juliet. Out in the fields there's a snot-eating farm hand, an enormous foot that squashes little mice, and an army of worms that slime their way through the overgrown grass.

FIRST WHITE HORSE: She'll still have her hard little breasts. They've just invented a bed for sleeping with horses.

THREE WHITE HORSES: (*Brandishing their sticks.*) And we want to go to bed.

FIRST WHITE HORSE: With Juliet. I was in the tomb last night, and I know everything that went on.

THREE WHITE HORSES: We want to go to bed.

FIRST WHITE HORSE: Because we are real horses, coach horses; we smash the woodwork of our stalls, and the shutters of the stable with our shafts.

THREE WHITE HORSES: Take off your clothes Juliet; show your rump, and we'll whip it with our tails; we want to be reborn.

JULIET seeks refuge with the BLACK HORSE.

BLACK HORSE: She's crazy, crazier than crazy.

JULIET: (*Pulling herself together.*) I'm not frightened of you. You want to sleep with me, right? Very well, it is I who wants to sleep with you, understand? I'm in charge. I give the orders. I mount you. And I trim your manes with my scissors.

BLACK HORSE: Who goes through whom? Oh, love, love that needs to pass its light through dark heat! Oh sea resting on twilight and on the flower of a corpse's ass.

JULIET: (*Vigorously.*) I'm not a slave. You can't prick my breasts with amber daggers. Nor am I an oracle for those who tremble with lust by the city's gates. I dream of the fragrance of fig trees, and of the slim waist of a man scything wheat. Nobody goes through me. I go through you!

BLACK HORSE: Sleep, sleep, and sleep.

The THREE WHITE HORSES hold up their canes, and from the ferrules shoot three jets of water.

THREE WHITE HORSES: We piss on you, we piss on you. As we piss on a mare, as a she-goat pisses on the muzzle of her billy, as the heavens piss on magnolia blossoms and turn them to leather.

BLACK HORSE: (*To JULIET.*) Go to your place. Let no one go through you.

JULIET: Must I be silent then? A newborn baby is beautiful.

THREE WHITE HORSES: Beautiful indeed. And he'd draw his tail across all of heaven.

FIRST MAN enters right, with the DIRECTOR, who is transformed now as a white Harlequin.

FIRST MAN: That's enough, gentlemen!

DIRECTOR: Open air theatre!

FIRST WHITE HORSE: No, now we've opened up the real theatre, the theatre beneath the sand; under the sand of the arena.

BLACK HORSE: So that the truth about tombs can be told.

THREE WHITE HORSES: Tombs with advertisements, gaslights, and long rows of seats.

FIRST MAN: Yes! Now we've taken the first step. But I know for sure that three of you are in hiding, the three of you still float on the surface.

The THREE WHITE HORSES gather together, nervous.

You're used to the coachman's whip, and the blacksmith's pincers, and you're frightened of the truth.

BLACK HORSE: When the last suit of blood has been taken off, truth will be a nuisance, a wasted crabshell, or a scrap of leather tossed behind a window.

WHITE HORSE: They must make their exits immediately. They're afraid of the public. I know the truth.
I know they're not here to seek Juliet out; they hide their true desires in their wounding eyes.

BLACK HORSE: Not a desire, all desires, as do you.

FIRST MAN: I only have one desire.

FIRST WHITE HORSE: Nobody can forget his mask.

FIRST MAN: I don't wear a mask.

DIRECTOR: There's nothing but masks; I was right, Gonzalo. If we mock the mask, it'll hang us from a tree, as it did with that young man in America.

JULIET: (*Sobs.*) The mask.

FIRST WHITE HORSE: Form.

DIRECTOR: In the middle of the street it's the mask that steals us and guards us against the indiscreet blush that rises to our cheeks. In the bedroom, when we pick our noses, or delicately explore our rumps, the plaster of the mask presses so hard on our flesh that we can barely stretch out on the bed.

FIRST MAN: (*To DIRECTOR.*) My struggle with the mask was over when I managed to see you naked. (*Embraces him.*)

FIRST WHITE HORSE: (*Mocking.*) A lake is only a surface.

DIRECTOR: (*Annoyed.*) Or an expanse.

FIRST WHITE HORSE: (*Laughing.*) An expanse is but a thousand surfaces.

DIRECTOR: (*To FIRST MAN.*) Don't embrace me, Gonzalo. Your love is only alive before witnesses. Haven't you given me enough kisses already in the ruins? I abhor your elegance and theatricality.

They fight.

FIRST MAN: I display my love for you in front of others because I hate the mask, and because I have been able to tear if off your face.

DIRECTOR: Why am I so weak?

FIRST MAN: (*Struggling.*) I love you.

DIRECTOR: (*Struggling.*) I spit on you.

JULIET: They're fighting!

BLACK HORSE: They're making love.

THREE WHITE HORSES: Love. Love. Love.
Love of one with two.
The love of three which suffocates
for being one between two.

FIRST MAN: I'll strip your skeleton

DIRECTOR: My skeleton has seven lights.

FIRST MAN: That's easy enough; I've seven hands.

DIRECTOR: My skeleton has seven shadows.

THREE WHITE HORSES: Leave him be, leave him be.

FIRST WHITE HORSE: (*To FIRST MAN.*) I order you to leave him.

The HORSES separate the FIRST MAN and the DIRECTOR.

DIRECTOR: I'm a slave to the lion, but I can be a friend of the horse.

FIRST WHITE HORSE: (*Embracing him.*) Love.

DIRECTOR: I'll place my hands in the biggest pots of money so I can throw coins in the mud, and cover bill-notes with breadcrumbs.

JULIET: (*To BLACK HORSE.*) Please!

BLACK HORSE: (*Wary.*) Wait.

FIRST MAN: The time hasn't come yet for the horses to carry off the naked body, a body paled by my very own tears.

The THREE WHITE HORSES hold the FIRST MAN back.

(*Urgently.*) Enrique!

DIRECTOR: Enrique? Here's your Enrique.

The DIRECTOR swiftly strips off his costume, and throws it behind a column. Underneath he wears a thin ballerina costume. From behind the column appears the white HARLEQUIN COSTUME wearing a pale yellow mask.

HARLEQUIN COSTUME: I'm cold. Electric light. Bread. They were burning rubber. (*Stops, very still.*)

DIRECTOR: (*To FIRST MAN.*) You won't come with me now. I'm Wilhemina, and I belong with the horses.

FIRST WHITE HORSE: Moon, vixen and a pitcher in a dive bar.

DIRECTOR: Horses and ships and regiments and even the storks will go through me. I am open wide.

THREE WHITE HORSES: Wilhemina!

DIRECTOR: Not Wilhemina, I'm not Wilhemina: I'm La Dominga of the Islands.

DIRECTOR takes off the ballet costume and he's dressed in body tights covered with little bells. Throws the tulle behind the column and goes, followed by the HORSES. The BALLERINA COSTUME appears.

BALLERINA COSTUME: Wi-wilhe-wilhemi- wilhemina; namile-namelile … Let me in or let me out. (*Falls to the ground asleep.*)

FIRST MAN: Enrique! Careful on the steps.

DIRECTOR: (*From off.*) Moon and vixen of the drunken sailors.

JULIET: (*To the BLACK HORSE.*) Give me my sleeping draught.

BLACK HORSE: Sand.

FIRST MAN: (*Shouts.*) To a moonfish. I just wish you were a moonfish. Turn into a moonfish.

(*Flings himself off, upstage.*)

HARLEQUIN COSTUME: Enrique. Electric light. Bread. They were burning rubber.

Enter left THIRD MAN and SECOND MAN. SECOND MAN is the woman in the black pajamas and poppies of Frame One. The THIRD MAN is unchanged.

SECOND MAN: He loves me so much he'll kill for us if he sees us together; let's go. I'll serve you from now on. And forever.

THIRD MAN: Your beauty shone through the columns.

JULIET: (*To couple.*) We'll close the door.

SECOND MAN: A theatre's door never closes.

JULIET: My dear friend, it's raining hard.

It begins to rain. THIRD MAN takes out a mask that has an expression of burning passion, and puts it on.

THIRD MAN: (*Gallantly.*) Couldn't you let me sleep here?

JULIET: What for?

THIRD MAN: To enjoy you.

He whispers to her.

SECOND MAN: (*To the* BLACK HORSE.) Did you see a man with dark hair and black beard leave? He wore patent leather shoes that squeaked a little.

BLACK HORSE: I didn't see him.

THIRD MAN: (*To* JULIET.) Who better than I to protect you?

JULIET: And who more deserving of your love than your girl friend?

THIRD MAN: My girl friend? (*Furiously.*) I lose out every time and it's always your fault. She's not my girl friend; she's a mask, a mop, a sickly lapdog.

He strips the SECOND MAN *violently of his pajamas and wig. The* SECOND MAN *is revealed as in Frame One, except for the beard.*

SECOND MAN: Have mercy!

THIRD MAN: (*To* JULIET.) I brought him here, disguised, so the scoundrels wouldn't get to him. (*To* SECOND MAN.) Kiss my hand; kiss your bodyguard's hand.

The PAJAMA COSTUME *with poppies appears; the face of this apparition is as white and smooth as an ostrich's egg.* THIRD MAN *pushes* SECOND MAN *off right.*

SECOND MAN: Have mercy!

The PAJAMA COSTUME *sits on the steps and slowly beats his featureless face with his hands, until the end of the scene. The* THIRD MAN *takes a large red cape from his pocket, places it over his shoulders, and wraps his arms around* JULIET.

THIRD MAN: My love.
    'arise, fair sun, and kill the envious moon …'
    The wind shall break the cypress boughs …

JULIET: It doesn't go like that.

THIRD MAN: 'It is the East and Juliet …'
    In India the wind visits every woman
    whose hands are made of water.

BLACK HORSE: (*Shaking the wheel.*) It will close now!

JULIET: Rain is beating down!

THIRD MAN: Wait, wait, the nightingale sings now.

JULIET: (*Trembling.*) The nightingale. Dear God, the nightingale.

BLACK HORSE: Don't let it catch you out here.

Grabs her quickly and lays her out in the tomb.

JULIET: (*Falling asleep.*) The nightingale …

BLACK HORSE: (*Leaving.*) Tomorrow I'll be here with sand.

JULIET: Tomorrow.

THIRD MAN: (*By the tomb.*) My love, come back to me. The wind breaks the leaves on the maple trees. What have you done? (*Embraces her.*)

VOICE: (*Off.*) Enrique!

HARLEQUIN COSTUME: Enrique.

BALLERINA COSTUME: Wilhemina, finish it, end all. (*Weeps.*)

THIRD MAN: Wait, wait. Now the nightingale sings.

A ship's horn is heard. The THIRD MAN *takes off his mask and places it on* JULIET's *face, then covers her with his red cape.*

It's raining too much.

He opens an umbrella and tiptoes silently off.

FIRST MAN: (*Entering.*) Enrique, how did you get back?

HARLEQUIN COSTUME: (*Echoing.*) Enrique, how did you get back?

FIRST MAN: Why do you mock me?

HARLEQUIN COSTUME: Why do you mock me?

FIRST MAN: (*Embraces the* HARLEQUIN.) After you'd crushed the grass and the horses, you had to come back for my tireless love.

HARLEQUIN COSTUME: The horses!

FIRST MAN: Tell me. Tell me you came back for me.

HARLEQUIN COSTUME: (*Weakly*) I'm cold. Electric light. Bread. They were burning rubber.

FIRST MAN: (*Embraces him violently.*) Enrique!

HARLEQUIN COSTUME: (*Weaker still.*) Enrique.

BALLERINA COSTUME: (*Softly.*) Wilhemina.

FIRST MAN: (*Throws* HARLEQUIN COSTUME *down, and climbs up the stairs.*) Enrique!

HARLEQUIN COSTUME: (*On the ground.*) Enrique …

The figure with the egg-shaped face continues to strike himself incessantly with his hands. Over the noise of the rain, a nightingale sings. Curtain.

Song of the Idiot Shepherd[4]

Blue curtain. Center stage is a large wardrobe full of white masks of diverse expression. In front of each mask there is a little light. The IDIOT SHEPHERD *enters stage right. He's dressed in rough animal skins. On his head he wears a funnel of feathers and little wheels. He plays a hurdy-gurdy and dances slowly.*

SHEPHERD: The idiot shepherd keeps the masks.
    The masks
    Of the beggars and the poets
    who murder the fish-hawks
    when they fly over still water.
    The mask
    Of the children who use their fists
    And rot under toadstools.
    The masks
    Of eagles who bear crutches.
    The mask of the mask
    That was once made of Cretan plaster
    turned into violet powder
    At Juliet's assassination:
    Divine, diviner, divine the riddle
    Of a theatre without orchestra stalls
    And a sky filled with chairs:
    The empty husk of the mask.
    Bleat, bleat, bleat, my masks.

The masks bleat like sheep and one of them coughs.

The horses eat the toadstool

And rot underneath the corks.
The eagles use their fists
And bathe themselves in mud
Behind the comet,
And the comet devours the fish-hawk
That drew blood on the poet's breast.
Bleat, bleat, bleat, my masks!
Europe tears her tits,
Asia is left without orchestra stalls,
And America is a crocodile
That doesn't even need a mask.
A little music, a little noise
Of wounded pricks and (poisoned) bottles.

*He pushes the wardrobe, which is on wheels, forward and exits.
The masks bleat.*

Frame Five

*Stage center is a bed, facing the public and perpendicular as if painted
by a primitive. A red nude figure crowned with blue thorns is on the
bed. Upstage, archways and stairs leading to the boxes of the theatre.
To the right is the façade of a university building. As the curtain rises,
we hear the sharp burst of applause.*

MALE NUDE: When will it all be done?

MALE NURSE: (*Enters quickly.*) When the disturbances are over.

MALE NUDE: What is it they want?

MALE NURSE: They demand the death of the Theatre Director.

MALE NUDE: And what are they saying about me?

MALE NURSE: Nothing.

MALE NUDE: And what about Gonzalo? Any word?

MALE NURSE: They're searching for him in the ruins.

MALE NUDE: I want to die. How many glasses of blood have
they extracted from me?

MALE NURSE: Fifty. I'll give you your gall now; and then I'll be
back at eight. I'll be back to deepen the wound on your
right side with a scalpel.

MALE NUDE: It's the one richer in vitamins.

MALE NURSE: Yes.

MALE NUDE: Did they let the people out from under the
arena?

MALE NURSE: On the contrary; the military have set up barricades at all the exits.

MALE NUDE: How far to Jerusalem?

MALE NURSE: Three stations, if there's enough coal.

MALE NUDE: Oh Father, take away this cup of sorrows.

MALE NURSE: Shut up. This is the third thermometer you've
broken.

*The STUDENTS enter. They wear black university gowns, with
red academic sashes.*

FIRST STUDENT: Why don't we file through the bars?

SECOND STUDENT: The alley's packed with armed men. It's too
difficult to get away through there.

THIRD STUDENT: And the horses?

FIRST STUDENT: The horses managed to get out by dashing
through the roof over the stage.

FOURTH STUDENT: I saw them when I was locked in the tower.
They were going up the hill altogether. The Theatre
Director was with them.

FIRST STUDENT: Isn't there an orchestra pit in this theatre?

SECOND STUDENT: Even the orchestra pit is packed with
people, we're better off here.

*We hear the sharp burst of applause. The MALE NURSE raises the
MALE NUDE to a sitting position and arranges his pillows.*

MALE NUDE: I'm thirsty.

MALE NURSE: They've sent into the theatre for some water.

FOURTH STUDENT: The first grenade thrown in the revolution
blasted the Professor of Rhetoric's head off.

SECOND STUDENT: To the great delight of his wife; she'll be so
busy now she'll need two taps on her tits.

THIRD STUDENT: They say that a horse used to go up to the
terrace with her at night.

FIRST STUDENT: Precisely. She saw everything that was going
on onstage through the skylight and she's the one who
gave the alarm.

FOURTH STUDENT: And even though the poets got a ladder to
climb up and kill her, she kept on yelling, and won the
crowd to her side.

SECOND STUDENT: What's her name?

THIRD STUDENT: Helen.

FIRST STUDENT: (*Aside.*) Selene, the moon goddess.

SECOND STUDENT: (*To FIRST STUDENT.*) What's the matter with
you?

FIRST STUDENT: I'm scared to go out into the open.

*The TWO THIEVES come down the stairs. FOUR LADIES in
evening dress rush out of the boxes (there's also a boy with them).
The STUDENTS continue their discussion.*

FIRST LADY; Will the coaches still be at the door?

SECOND LADY: How awful!

THIRD LADY: They found the Director in the tomb.

FIRST LADY: And Romeo?

FOURTH LADY: They were stripping him naked as we came
out.

BOY: The public wants the poet to be dragged through the
street by horses.

FIRST LADY: But why? It was a charming play; what's more,
the revolution had no right to desecrate a tomb.

SECOND LADY: The diction was spirited, and the actors looked
lovely; why must we lick the skeletons?

BOY: You're right. The tomb scene was prodigiously executed.
However, I found out it was false when I saw Juliet's
feet: they were tiny.

SECOND LADY: Scrumptious! Would you have them be any
different?

BOY: No, but they were too small to be a woman's feet.
They were too perfect, too feminine. They were a man's
feet: feet invented by a man.

SECOND LADY: How awful!

The murmur of voices and the clash of swords is heard in the theatre.

THIRD LADY: Can't we get out?

BOY: The revolution has reached the Cathedral by now. Let's take the stairs.

They exit.

FOURTH STUDENT: The rioting broke out when they realized Romeo and Juliet were really in love.

SECOND STUDENT: Quite the opposite: the riot broke out when they realized that they didn't love one another and that they could never love one another.

FOURTH STUDENT: The audience had the intelligence to figure it out, and that's why they protested.

SECOND STUDENT: Precisely. The skeletons were in love. They were yellow with ardor. But the costumes were not in love, and every so often, the audience noticed that Juliet's dress had tiny dirty toads all over its train.

FOURTH STUDENT: People forget the costumes during a performance. The revolution broke out when they found the real Juliet gagged and trussed under the seats, packed in with wads of cotton wool so she couldn't cry out.

FIRST STUDENT: That's the mistake everyone makes, and that's why theatre is in its death throes. The audience should try to penetrate the silk and cardboard erected by the poet in his bedroom. Romeo can be a bird, and Juliet a stone; Romeo can be a grain of salt, and Juliet a map. What does it matter to an audience?

FOURTH STUDENT: It doesn't, but a bird cannot be a cat, and a stone can't be the crest of a wave.

SECOND STUDENT: It's a question of form, of masks. A cat can be a frog, and the winter moon can very well be a bundle of firewood covered in maggots hardened by the frost. The public must trust their sleep to words; they mustn't see through the plaster column to the bleating sheep and the clouds passing in the heavens.

FOURTH STUDENT: That's why the revolution broke out. The director opened up the trapdoors, and people could see how poison from fake veins had brought real death to many children. It's not the disguised forms that bring life, but rather the slightest barometer of difference behind such things.

SECOND STUDENT: When all's said and done, must Romeo necessarily be a man, and Juliet a woman, for the tomb scene to be genuine and profound in production?

FIRST STUDENT: It isn't necessary at all. That's what the director was trying to show us with his brilliance.

FOURTH STUDENT: (*Annoyed.*) It's not necessary? Then by all means stop the machines, (stop progress), throw seeds of wheat on your fields of steel.

SECOND STUDENT: And what would happen? Mushrooms would o'ertake us or maybe hearts would beat more

intensely with more passion. The way it is now, people know how much nourishment there is in a wheat grain, but pay no mind at all to how nourishing fungus can be.

FIFTH STUDENT: (*Rising out of one of the boxes.*) The Judge has arrived and before the couple is assassinated they are going to be forced to repeat the tomb scene.

FOURTH STUDENT: Let's go, you'll see how right I am.

SECOND STUDENT: Yes, let's go, we'll see the last truly feminine Juliet that'll ever be seen on the stage.

They exit rapidly.

MALE NUDE: Oh Father, forgive them, for they know not what they do.

MALE NURSE: (*To the THIEVES.*) Why do you arrive at this hour?

THIEVES: The prompter made a mistake.

MALE NURSE: Have you had your injections already?

THIEVES: Yes.

The THIEVES sit at the foot of the bed with lighted church candles. The stage is in shadow. The PROMPTER arrives.

MALE NURSE: Is it the proper time to give the warning?

PROMPTER: Please forgive me. But Joseph of Arimathea's beard is missing.

MALE NURSE: Is the operating theatre ready?

PROMPTER: It just needs the candlesticks, the chalice and the flasks of camphorated oil.

MALE NURSE: Hurry up.

PROMPTER exits.

MALE NUDE: How much longer?

MALE NURSE: Not very long. The third bell has already rung. When the Emperor puts on his Pontius Pilate disguise.

BOY: (*Appears with the LADIES.*) Please! Don't let fear dictate your actions.

FIRST LADY: It's just horrible to get lost in a theatre, and not be able to find the exit.

SECOND LADY: So far what has frightened me the most has been the cardboard wolf and those four snakes in the tin tank.

THIRD LADY: When we were climbing the mountain over by the ruin, we thought we could see the light of dawn; but we just bumped into the curtains. My gold lamé slippers are stained with oil.

FOURTH LADY: (*Peering out from behind the arches.*) They're doing the tomb scene again. The fire will break through the doors now. I saw the attendants a moment ago and their hands are already too burned for them to contain it.

BOY: We could get onto one of the balconies by the branches of that tree, and call for help from there.

MALE NURSE: (*Shouts.*) When are you going to start the death knell?

One bell is heard.

THIEVES: (*Raising their candlesticks.*) Holy, Holy, Holy.

MALE NUDE: Father, into thy hands I commend my spirit.

MALE NURSE: You are two minutes early.

MALE NUDE: But the nightingale has already sung.

MALE NURSE: True. And the chemists await the agony.

MALE NUDE: For the agony of man: lonely men on platforms and in trains.

MALE NURSE: (*Looks at his watch. Calls.*) Bring the shroud. Carefully now, or the coming wind will blow off your wigs. Quick.

THIEVES: Holy, Holy, Holy

MALE NUDE: All has been consummated.

The bed turns on its axis. The MALE NUDE *disappears. On the other side of the bed, dying* FIRST MAN *is stretched out, still in white tie and tails and with a black beard.*

FIRST MAN: (*Closing his eyes.*) Agony!

The stage is lit with the silvery flicker of a black-and-white movie; the arches and the upstage area are tinted with fine blue light.

The THIEVES *and the* MALE NURSE *exit dancing, facing the audience.*

The STUDENTS *enter from under the arches carrying small flashlights.*

FOURTH STUDENT: The reaction of the audience was abominable.

FIRST STUDENT: Abominable. A spectator must never be part of the play. When people visit an aquarium they don't kill the sea snakes or the water rats or the leprous fish; no, they cast their eyes over the fish tanks and they learn something.

FOURTH STUDENT: Romeo is a man of thirty and Juliet is a fifteen-year-old boy. The audience's condemnation is absolute.

SECOND STUDENT: The Director concealed it brilliantly from the majority of the audience, but the horses and the rioting wrecked his plans.

FOURTH STUDENT: What is truly inexcusable is that they have assassinated them.

FIRST STUDENT: And that they have also assassinated the real Juliet, who was moaning under the seats.

FOURTH STUDENT: Out of sheer curiosity and nothing else. They wanted to see what they were made of.

THIRD STUDENT: And what did they get out of it? Blood, and utter disorientation.

FOURTH STUDENT: The re-staging of the scene was splendid, though, because there was no doubt that they loved one another completely, even if personally I don't think it's right. When the nightingale sang, I couldn't hold back my tears.

THIRD STUDENT: Nor could anyone else, but then they started brandishing sticks and knives. You see, words are stronger than they are, and when ideology goes on the rampage, it tramples fearlessly over the most innocent truths.

FIFTH STUDENT: (*Happily.*) Look, I got hold of one of Juliet's shoes. The nuns were laying her out for burial and I nicked it.

FOURTH STUDENT: (*Somber.*) Which Juliet?

FIFTH STUDENT: Which Juliet do you think? The one on stage, the one with the most beautiful feet in the world.

FOURTH STUDENT: But didn't you realize the Juliet in the tomb was a boy in disguise? A director's trick? And the real Juliet was tied up and gagged under the seats?

FIFTH STUDENT: (*Laughing.*) Well I want her. She looked so lovely. If she was a boy in disguise I don't care. On the other hand I wouldn't have nicked a shoe off that young woman under the seats; she was all covered with dust, groaning and mewing like a poor cat.

THIRD STUDENT: And they killed her.

FIFTH STUDENT: Because they're out of their minds. I go up to the mountains twice a day, and when I finish studying, I guard a huge herd of bulls that I have to fight every minute to win. I don't have time to think whether she is a man or a woman or a boy but only that she gives me pleasure. She fills me with joy.

FIRST STUDENT: Splendid! And if I decide to fall in love with a crocodile?

FIFTH STUDENT: You fall in love.

FIRST STUDENT: And if I want to fall in love with you?

FIFTH STUDENT: You fall in love. And I'll carry you on my shoulders among the crags.

FIRST STUDENT: And we will destroy everything.

FIFTH STUDENT: Households, families.

FIRST STUDENT: We'll go in with our football boots anywhere anyone speaks of love and we'll splatter their mirrors with mud.

FIFTH STUDENT: And we'll burn the prayer books that the priests use to say Mass.

FIRST STUDENT: Come. Let's go now!

FIFTH STUDENT: I've got four hundred bulls; we'll get my father's heavy ropes, the ones he made himself, and we'll hitch up to the mountain, and let loose a volcano.

FIRST STUDENT: Joy. The joy little boys and girls and frogs and wooden barrel taps feel.

PROMPTER: (*Enters.*) Gentlemen, it's time for the practical geometry class!

FIRST MAN: Agony.

The stage is in half light. The STUDENTS *switch on their flashlights and go into the university.*

PROMPTER: Don't take it out on the windowpanes.

FIFTH STUDENT: (*Fleeing through the arches with* FIRST STUDENT.) Joy! Joy! Joy!

FIRST MAN: Agony. The loneliness of a young man in dreams full of elevators and trains that take him at astronomical speeds. The loneliness of buildings, of street corners, of beaches where you will never appear …

FIRST LADY: (*On the stairs.*) Are we back at the same piece of scenery? How awful!

BOY: There has to be a real door here somewhere!

SECOND LADY: Please! Don't let go of my hand!

BOY: When dawn comes, we'll make our way by the skylight.

THIRD LADY: I'm starting to feel cold in this dress.

FIRST MAN: (*Weakly.*) Enrique, Enrique!

FIRST LADY: What was that?

BOY: Calm down.

The stage is dark. The BOY's torch illuminates the face of the FIRST MAN, who is now dead. Curtain.

Frame Six

The DIRECTOR's room. Same decor as Frame One. To the left on the floor is a large horse's head. To the right a giant eye and a cluster of trees with clouds leaning on the walls. The DIRECTOR enters with the MAGICIAN. The MAGICIAN wears tails, white tie, ankle-length white satin cape, and top hat. The DIRECTOR is dressed as in the first frame.

DIRECTOR: A magician cannot solve this problem, neither can a doctor, an astronomer, or anybody. It's very easy to turn the lions loose, and then rain sulfur on them. Please don't talk anymore.

MAGICIAN: It seems to me that you, a man of masks, forget that we magicians use a black velvet curtain.

DIRECTOR: When people are in heaven. But tell me, what kind of curtain do we use in a place where's so much violence in the wind that it tears the clothes off people's backs, where even little children carry knives to slash the curtains?

MAGICIAN: The magician's black velvet curtain assumes there is an order in the mystery of a trick. Why did you choose to stage such a hackneyed tragedy, rather than an original play?

DIRECTOR: In order to show what happens every day in all the great cities and in the countryside. I chose a story that happened once, that in spite of its originality, is accepted by everybody. I could have chosen *Oedipus*, or *Othello*. On the other hand, had I raised the curtain on an original truth the stalls would have been blood-stained from the very first scene.

MAGICIAN: If you'd made use of Diana's flower, which Shakespeare uses, in his darker mood, ironically in *A Midsummer Night's Dream*, the show would in all probability have succeeded. If love is pure chance, and Titania Queen of the Fairies falls in love with an ass, then there's nothing special if Gonzalo, by the same process, sits in a club with a boy dressed in white sitting on his knee.

DIRECTOR: I beg you, please don't talk any more.

MAGICIAN: Put up a wire arch, a curtain, and a tree with real leaves; run the curtain back and forth and if the timing is executed properly, nobody will be surprised if the tree turns into a snake's egg. But what you wanted to do was to murder the dove, and replace it with a lump of marble full of tiny, prattling gobs of spit.

DIRECTOR: There was no other way to do it. My friends and

I opened the tunnel under the sand without the citizens noticing. We were helped by workmen, and by students, who now deny they were there, despite the fact that their hands are cut and sore. When we reached the tomb, we raised the curtain.

MAGICIAN: And what theatre can come from out of a tomb?

DIRECTOR: All theatre comes from a raw confined place. All true theatre has the foul stench of a rotting moon. When the costumes do the talking, the living become little bone buttons lining Calvary's walls. I made the tunnel to show the shape, the form, of a power that has been hidden. The audience had no choice but to pay attention to the story once it had possessed and enthralled them.

MAGICIAN: Without the slightest effort, I can turn a bottle of ink into a severed hand with antique rings.

DIRECTOR: (*Annoyed.*) But that's a lie. That's theatre. The reason I spent three days, battling with roots and sudden springs of water, was to destroy theatre.

MAGICIAN: I knew that.

DIRECTOR: And to demonstrate that if Romeo and Juliet die their agonizingly long deaths only to awaken with a smile on their face when the curtain falls, then my characters set fire to the curtain, and die for real before an audience's eyes. The horses, the sea, the army of grass stopped me. But one day, when they burn down all the theatres, they'll find, in the couches, behind the mirrors, in golden papier-mâché goblets, the gathering of our dead imprisoned by our public. We have to destroy theatre, or live in the theatre! There's no point in booing from the windows. And if dogs howl tenderly, we must raise the curtain without a care. I knew a man who used to sweep the roof, and clean the skylights and railings, simply out of politeness to the heavens.

MAGICIAN: If you go up one more step, a man will be nothing more than a blade of grass to you.

DIRECTOR: Not a blade of grass, but rather a navigator.

MAGICIAN: I can turn a navigator into a sewing needle.

DIRECTOR: That's exactly what happens in theatre. And that's why I risked pulling off a very difficult poetic trick: in the hope that love would burst forth and transform us, and give new form to our costumes.

MAGICIAN: It astonishes me when I hear you say love.

DIRECTOR: Astonishes you? Why?

MAGICIAN: I see a landscape of sand in a troubled mirror.

DIRECTOR: And what else?

MAGICIAN: And a dawn that will never come to an end.

DIRECTOR: It's possible.

MAGICIAN: (*Taps the horse's head with the tips of his fingers indifferently.*) Love.

DIRECTOR: (*Sits at the table.*) It astonishes me when you say love.

MAGICIAN: Astonishes you? Why?

DIRECTOR: I see that each grain of sand is turning into a busy little ant.

MAGICIAN: And what else?

DIRECTOR: That night falls every five minutes.

MAGICIAN: (*Looks at him steady.*) It's possible. (*Pause.*) But what can we expect of people who open up the theatre beneath the sand? If you were to open that door, this theatre would fill with madmen, rainstorms, monstrous leaves and sewer rats. Whoever thought one could break down all the doors of drama with one play?

DIRECTOR: It's only by breaking down all the doors that a play can be truly itself, using its own eyes to see that the law is a wall that dissolves in the tiniest drop of blood. It disgusts me to see a dying man tracing a door on the wall with his finger before quietly going to sleep. A real play is a circle of arches where the wind, the moon and living creatures enter and exit without finding a place to rest. You walk here on the boards of a theatre where a real drama has been presented, where a real fight occurred, a fight that cost the lives of all the actors. (*He breaks down.*)

SERVANT: (*Rushes in.*) Sir ...

DIRECTOR: What is it?

Enter the WHITE HARLEQUIN COSTUME, *and a* LADY *dressed in black. A thick black veil conceals her face.*

Figure 18 The magician (Walter Vidarte) making his final entry in the closing scene of *The Public* directed by Lluís Pasqual, in Madrid, 1987. (Photographer: Ros Ribas.)

LADY IN BLACK: Where is my son?

DIRECTOR: What son?

LADY IN BLACK: Gonzalo, my son.

DIRECTOR: (*Annoyed.*) When the show was over he rushed down under the stage with that boy there – the one that's with you. Later the prompter saw him stretched out on the imperial bed they have in the prop room. Don't ask me anything. Today everything's buried.

HARLEQUIN COSTUME: (*Weeping.*) Enrique.

LADY IN BLACK: Where is my son? This morning the fishermen brought me a huge, pale rotting moonfish and they said to me 'Here's your son.' A steady trickle of blood ran from its mouth and little children laughed and daubed the soles of their boots red. When I had shut the door, I could tell the market people were dragging it to sea.

HARLEQUIN COSTUME: To the sea.

DIRECTOR: The show finished hours ago. What happened afterwards is not my responsibility.

LADY IN BLACK: I'll press charges. I'll demand justice in front of everyone. (*Starts to exit.*)

MAGICIAN: Madam, there is no exit that way.

LADY IN BLACK: You're right; the foyer is in complete darkness. (*Goes towards the stage right door.*)

DIRECTOR: Nor that way either. You will fall through the skylight.

MAGICIAN: Madam. Allow me. I will show you the way.

He takes off his cape and covers her with it. He makes two or three passes with his hands, pulls away the cape and the LADY *has disappeared. The* SERVANT *pushes* HARLEQUIN *off left. The* MAGICIAN *takes out a large white fan and begins to fan himself, while singing softly.*

DIRECTOR: I'm cold

MAGICIAN: What?

DIRECTOR: I said I'm cold.

MAGICIAN: (*Fans himself.*) That's a pretty word 'cold.'

DIRECTOR: Thanks for everything.

MAGICIAN: Not at all. Getting things offstage is easy, the difficult bit is getting them on.

DIRECTOR: It's much more difficult to replace them with something else.

SERVANT: (*Enters.*) It's getting a bite cold. Do you want the heat on?

DIRECTOR: No, we'll have to put up with it all because we've broken down the doors, we've taken the roof off; we're left with the four bare walls of drama.

The servant goes out through the center door.

No matter, there's still soft grass to sleep on.

MAGICIAN: To sleep!

DIRECTOR: In the end, to sleep is to sow a seed.

SERVANT: (*Reenters.*) Sir, I can't stand the cold.

DIRECTOR: I told you, we have to put up with it, no matter what kind of vulgar conjuring trick it is, we mustn't let ourselves be beaten down by it. Do your duty.

The DIRECTOR puts on gloves, turns up his coat collar, shaking violently.

MAGICIAN: (*Fanning himself.*) But is coldness a bad thing?

DIRECTOR: (*Weakly.*) Cold is a dramatic element like any other.

SERVANT: (*At the door, shaking, hands against his chest.*) Sir!

DIRECTOR: What?

SERVANT: (*Falling to his knees.*) The public is here.

DIRECTOR: (*Falls face down on the table.*) Show them in.

The MAGICIAN seated near the horse's head, whistles and fans himself gleefully. The entire left-hand corner of the set breaks open, and a sky is revealed. It has long, brightly lit clouds. A slow rain of white gloves falls rigidly and evenly.

VOICE: (*Off.*) Sir.

VOICE: (*Off.*) What?

VOICE: (*Off.*) The public.

VOICE: (*Off.*) Show them in.

The MAGICIAN waves the fan in the air vigorously. Snowflakes begin to fall onstage.

Slow curtain.

Notes

1. The word translated in this text as 'coins' is *pesetas* in the original. – *Translator.*

2. The appearance of the Four Horses here may also be executed in purely visual terms, either as puppets or a singular image. – *Translator.*

3. If there is doubling as suggested, then the three men and Director in this brief sequence may be heard from Off. – *Translator.*

4. The Song of the Idiot Shepherd is placed before Frame Five in the Monegal edition of the text, but in other previous editions it is placed after Frame Five. – *Translator.*

2.9 The Meaning of the Music Hall (1913)

FILIPPO TOMMASO MARINETTI

WE FUTURISTS ARE PROFOUNDLY disgusted with the contemporary stage because it stupidly fluctuates between historic reconstruction (*pastiche* or plagiarism) and a minute, wearying, photographic reproduction of actuality. We delight in frequenting the music-hall or variety theatre, smoking concert, circus, cabaret and night club, which offer today the only theatrical entertainment worthy of the true Futurist spirit.

Futurism exalts the variety theatre because, born as it were with us, it fortunately has no tradition, no masters, no dogmas, and subsists on the moment. The variety theatre is absolutely practical because it aims at entertaining and amusing the public by performances either comic or startling to the imagination. The authors, actors, and mechanics of the variety theatre exist and conquer their difficulties only for one purpose, that of everlastingly startling by new inventions. Hence the absolute impossibility of stagnation or repetition, the desperate emulation of brain and muscle to beat all previous records in agility, speed, strength, complexity and grace.

Futuristic wonder

The variety theatre offering the most lucrative medium for endless inventive effort most naturally produces what I call the *Futuristic Wonder*, a product of modern mechanism. It presents caricature in its fullest form, foolery of the deepest kind, impalpable and delicious irony, absorbing and decisive symbols, torrents of irrepressible hilarity, profound analogies between human beings and the animal, the vegetable, and the mechanical world; swift revelations of cynicism, a network of spritely wit, puns, and cock-and-bull stories which pleasantly fan the intellect: all the scales of laughter to relax the nerves; all the scales of such fun, foolery, doltishness, absurdity as insensibly urge the soul to the very edge of madness; all the new meanings of light, sound, noise, and speech and their mysterious, inexplicable correspondence with the most unexplored centres of our sensibility.

The modern variety theatre is the overflowing melting-pot of all those elements which are combining to prepare our new sensibility. It lends itself to the ironical decomposition of all our worn-out prototypes – the beautiful, the great, the solemn, the religious, the fierce, the seductive, the terrible; and also to the abstract forecasting of those new prototypes which shall succeed them.

The variety theatre is the only kind of theatre where the public does not remain static and stupidly passive, but participates noisily in the action, singing, beating time with the orchestra, giving force to the actor's words by unexpected tags and queer improvised dialogue.

Ideal school of sincerity

The variety theatre is the ideal school for sincerity for man, in that it brutally strips woman of all her veils of the romantic phrases, sighs, and sobs which mask and deform her. On the other hand, it shows up all the most admirable animal qualities of woman, her powers of attack and of seduction, of treachery and of resistance. The variety theatre is a school for heroism by reason of its various record difficulties to be beaten and record efforts to be surpassed, which produce on its stage a strong and healthy atmosphere of danger (looping the loop on a bicycle, in a motor car, or on horseback). The variety theatre is the only school to be recommended to adolescents and young people of promise, because it explains in the swiftest and most striking manner the most mysterious sentimental problems of life and the most complicated political events. In fact, the variety theatre explains and most luminously illustrates the dominating laws of life:

> The interpenetration of separate rhythms.
> The inevitable nature of lying and contradiction.
> The synthetic combination of speed with transformation (*Fregoli*).

The variety theatre is, of course, anti-academical, primitive, and ingenuous, and therefore all the more significant by reason of the unforeseen nature of all its fumbling efforts and the coarse simplicity of its resources (singers who walk methodically round the stage after every verse, like caged beasts). The variety theatre destroys all that is solemn, sacred, earnest, and pure in Art – with a big A. It collaborates with Futurism in the destruction of the immortal masterpieces by plagiarizing them, parodying them, and by retailing them without style, apparatus, or pity, just like any ordinary turn. And that is why we loudly applaud the execution of *Parsifal* in forty minutes.

To provoke immense rows

Futurism wants to perfect the variety theatre by transforming it into the theatre of wonders and of records. It is absolutely necessary to abolish every vestige of logic in the performances of the variety theatre; to exaggerate luxury; multiply contrasts and give the supreme place on the stage to the improbable and the absurd. (Example: to oblige singers to dye their necks, their arms, and especially their hair all colours, hitherto unused for purposes of seduction: green hair, violet arms, blue neck, orange chignons, etc.) Futurism wants to abolish those Parisian revues whose *compere* and *commere* merely replace the chorus of the Greek tragedy. Out upon logic and consecutive ideas!

To introduce surprise and some necessity for action in the audience, I hazard a few random suggestions. To smear gum on a stall so that its occupant may be stuck to his seat and excite general hilarity. Naturally the evening coats or dress would be paid for by the management. To sell the same place to ten different persons; obstructions, discussions and quarrels will necessarily follow. To offer free seats to ladies and gentlemen who are notoriously cracked, irritable, or eccentric – calculated to provoke immense rows by bizarre or objectionable behaviour.

To debauch systematically all classical art, producing, for instance, in one single evening all the Greek, French and Italian tragedies in abridged form. To enliven the works of Beethoven, Wagner, Bach, Bellini, Chopin by cutting into them with Neapolitan songs. To soap carefully the planks of the stage so that the actors may slip up at the most tragic moments.

To encourage in every way the genus of the American Eccentric, all his mechanical grotesque effects, his coarse imagination, his immense brutality, his surprise waistcoat and his baggy trousers, deep as a ship's hold, from which will be brought out, with a thousand other cargoes, the great Futurist hilarity which shall rejuvenate the face of the earth.

Note

From the original publication (in the British newspaper the *Daily Mail*):

In those literary and artistic circles where Life and Decadence meet on equal terms at midnight, Signor Marinetti has created something like a furore by his unexampled power of explaining and illustrating the philosophy of Futurism in terms which are capable of being comprehended, after supper, by the merely human brain. In the article which we print below he attempts to show what the modern music-hall is – as seen through his own remarkable temperament. We accept no responsibility for this effusion, which is sure to interest both those who understand it and those who do not: except to the extent that in the interest of the latter class, who are possibly less numerous than we suppose, it has been slightly – very slightly – edited.

Daily Mail, 21 November 1913

2.10 Theatre and the Plague *and* No More Masterpieces (1938)

ANTONIN ARTAUD

Translated by Victor Corti

Theatre and the Plague

IN THE ARCHIVES OF the small town of Caligari, Sardinia, lies an account of an astonishing historic occurrence.

One night about the end of April or the beginning of May, 1720, some twenty days before the ship *Grand-Saint-Antoine* reached Marseilles, where its landing coincided with the most wondrous outbreak of plague that erupted throughout the city's archives, Saint-Rémys, the Sardinian Viceroy, perhaps rendered more sensitive to that most baleful virus by his restricted monarchical duties, had a particularly agonising dream. He saw himself plague-ridden and saw the disease ravage his tiny state.

Society's barriers became fluid with the effects of the scourge. Order disappeared. He witnessed the subversion of all morality, the breakdown of all psychology, heard his lacerated, utterly routed bodily fluids murmur within him in a giddy wasting away of matter, they grew heavy and were then gradually transformed into carbon. Was it too late to ward off the scourge? Although organically destroyed, crushed, extirpated, his very bones consumed, he knew one does not die in dreams, that our will-power even operates *ad absurdum*, even denying what is possible, in a kind of metamorphosis of lies reborn as truth.

He awoke. He would show himself able to drive away these plague rumours and the miasmas of the Oriental virus.

The *Grand-Saint-Antoine*, a month out of Beyreut, requested permission to enter the harbour and dock there. At this point the Viceroy gave an insane order, an order thought raving mad, absurd, stupid and despotic both by his subjects and his suite. He hastily dispatched a pilot's boat and men to the supposedly infected vessel with orders for the *Grand-Saint-Antoine* to tack about that instant and make full sail away from the town or be sunk by cannon shot. War on the plague. The autocrat did not do things by halves.

In passing, we ought to note the unusually influential power the dream exerted on him, since it allowed him to insist on the savage fierceness of his orders despite the gibes of the populace and the scepticism of his suite, when to do so meant riding roughshod not only over human rights, but even over the most ordinary respect for life, over all kinds of national and international conventions, which in the face of death, no longer apply.

Be that as it may, the ship held her course, made land at Leghorn and sailed into Marseilles' roads where she was allowed to dock.

The Marseilles authorities have kept no record of what happened to her plague-infected cargo. We roughly know what happened to the members of her crew; they did not all die of the plague but were scattered over various countries.

The *Grand-Saint-Antoine* did not bring the plague to Marseilles, it was already there, at a particular stage of renewed activity, but its centres had been successfully localised.

The plague brought by the *Grand-Saint-Antoine* was the original, Oriental virus, hence the unusually horrible aspect, the widespread flaring up of the epidemic, and dates from its arrival and dispersion throughout the town.

This prompts a few thoughts.

This plague, which apparently revived a virus, was able to wreak as great havoc on its own, since the Captain was the only member of the ship's crew who did not catch the plague. Then again it did not seem that the newly arrived infected men had ever been in direct contact with those others confined to their quarantine districts. The *Grand-Saint-Antoine* passed within hailing distance of Caligari, Sardinia, but did not leave the plague there, yet the Viceroy picked up certain of its emanations in his dreams. For one cannot deny that a substantial though subtle communication was established between the plague and himself. It is too easy to lay the blame for communication of such a disease on infection by contact alone.

But this communication between Saint-Rémys and the plague, though of sufficient intensity to release imagery in his dreams, was after all not powerful enough to infect him with the disease.

Nevertheless, the town of Caligari, learning some time later that the ship driven from its shores by the miraculously enlightened though despotic Prince's will was the cause of the great Marseilles epidemic, recorded the fact in its archives where anyone may find it.

The 1720 Marseilles plague has given us what may pass as the only clinical description we have of the scourge.

But one wonders whether the plague described by Marseilles doctors was exactly the same as the 1347 Florence epidemic which produced the *Decameron*. Histories and holy books, the Bible among them, certain old medical treatises, describe the outward symptoms of all kinds of plagues whose malignant features seem to have impressed them far less than the demoralising and prodigious effect they produced in their minds. No doubt they were right, for medicine would be hard put to establish any basic difference between the virus Pericles died of before Syracuse (if the word virus is anything more than a verbal convenience) and that appearing in the plague described by Hippocrates, which, as recent medical treatises inform us, are a kind of fictitious plague. These same treatises hold the only genuine plague comes from Egypt, arising from the cemeteries uncovered by the subsiding Nile. The Bible and Herodotus both call attention to the lightning appearance of a plague that decimated 180,000 men of the Assyrian army in one night, thereby saving the Egyptian Empire. If this fact is true, we ought to consider the scourge as the immediate medium or materialisation of a thinking power in close contact with what we call fate.

This, with or without the army of rats that hurled itself on the Assyrian troops that night, and gnawed away their accoutrements in a few hours. The above event ought to be compared with the epidemic that broke out in 660 B.C. in the Holy City of Mekao, Japan, on the occasion of a mere change of government.

The 1502 Provence plague, which gave Nostradamus his first opportunity to practise his powers of healing, also coincided with the most profound political upheavals, the downfall or death of kings, the disappearance and destruction of whole provinces, earthquakes, all kinds of magnetic phenomena, exodus of the Jews, proceeding or following on disasters or havoc of a political or cosmic order, those causing them being too idiotic to foresee them, or not really depraved enough to desire their after effects.

However mistaken historians or doctors may have been about the plague I think one might agree on the idea of the disease as a kind of psychic entity, not carried by a virus. If we were to analyse closely all the facts on contagious plagues given in history or contained in archives, we would have difficulty in singling out one properly established occurrence of contagious contact, and the example Boccaccio cites of swine that died because they sniffed at sheets in which the plague-ridden had been wrapped scarcely suggests more than a kind of strange affinity between swine-flesh and the nature of the plague, something which would have to be gone into very thoroughly.

Since the concept of a truly morbid entity does not exist, there are forms the mind can provisionally agree on to designate certain phenomena, and it seems our minds might agree on a plague described in the following manner.

Before any pronounced physical or psychological sickness appears, red spots appear all over the body, the sick person only suddenly noticing them when they turn black. He has no time to be alarmed by them before his head feels on fire, grows overwhelmingly heavy and he collapses. Then he is seized with terrible fatigue, a focal, magnetic, exhausting tiredness, his molecules are split in two and drawn towards their annihilation. His fluids wildly jumbled in disorder, seem to race though his body. His stomach heaves, his insides seem to want to burst out between his teeth. His pulse sometimes slows down until it becomes a shadow, a latent pulse, at other times it races in accordance with his seething inner fever, the streaming wanderings of his mind. His pulse beating as fast as his heart, growing intense, heavy, deafening; those eyes, first inflamed, then glazed. That hugely swollen panting tongue, first white, then red, then black, as if charred and cracked, all heralding unprecedented organic disturbances. Soon the fluids, furrowed like the earth by lightning, like a volcano tormented by subterranean upheavals, seek an outlet. Fiery cones are formed at the centre of each spot and around them the skin rises up in blisters like air bubbles under a skin of lava. These blisters are surrounded by rings, the outer one, just like Saturn's ring at maximum radiance, indicating the outer edge of the bubo.

The body is streaked with them. Just as volcanoes have their own chosen locations on earth, the bubos have their own chosen spots over the expanse of the human body. Bubos appear around the anus, under the armpits, at those precious places where the active glands steadily carry out their functions, and through these bubos the anatomy discharges either its inner putrefaction, or in other cases, life itself. A violent burning sensation localised in one spot, more often than not indicates that the life force has lost none of its strength and that abatement of the sickness or even a cure may be possible. Like silent rage, the most terrible plague is one that does not disclose its symptoms.

Once open, a plague victim's body exhibits no lesions. The gall bladder, which filters heavier, solid organic waste, is full, swollen to bursting point with a sticky black liquid, so dense it suggests new matter. Arterial and veinal blood is also black and sticky. The body is as hard as stone. On the walls of the stomach membrane countless blood sources have arisen and everything points to a basic disorder in secretion. But there is neither loss nor destruction as in leprosy or syphilis. The intestines themselves, the site of the bloodiest disorders, where matter reaches an unbelievable degree of decomposition and calcification, are not organically affected. The gall bladder, from which the hardest matter must be virtually torn as in some human sacrifices, with a sharp knife, an obsidian instrument, hard and glazed – the gall bladder is hypertrophied and fragile in places, yet intact, without an iota missing, any visible lesions or loss of matter.

However, in some cases, the lesioned brain and lungs blacken and become gangrenous. The softened, chopped up lungs fall in chips of an unknown black substance, the brain fissured, crushed and disintegrated, is reduced to powder, to a kind of coal black dust.

Two notable observations can be made about the above facts. The first is that the plague syndrome is complete without any gangrene in the lungs or brain and the plague victim dies without any putrefaction in his limbs. Without underestimating the disease, the anatomy does not need localised physical gangrene to make up its mind to die.

The second remark is that the only two organs really affected and injured by the plague, the brain and lungs, are both dependant on consciousness or the will. We can stop breathing or thinking, speed up our breath, induce any rhythm we choose, make it conscious or unconscious at will, bring about a balance between both kinds of breathing; automatic, under direct control of the sympathetic nerve, and the other, which obeys each new conscious mental reflex.

We can also speed up, slow down or accent our thoughts. We can regulate the subconscious interplay of the mind. We cannot control the filtering of the fluids by the liver, the redistribution of the blood within the anatomy, by the heart and arteries, control digestion, stop or speed up the elimination of substances in the intestines. Hence the plague seems to make its presence known in those places, to have a liking for all those physical localities where human will-power, consciousness and thought are at hand or in a position to occur.

During the 1880s, a French doctor called Yersin, working on the corpses of Indo-Chinese who had died of the plague, isolated one of these round-headed, short-tailed bacilli only visible under a microscope, and called it the plague microbe. In my eyes, this is only a much smaller, infinitely smaller material factor, which appears at any moment during the development of the virus, but does not help to explain the plague at all. And I would rather this doctor had told me why all great plagues last five months, with or without a virus, after which the virulence dies down, and how the Turkish Ambassador passing through Languedoc towards the end of 1720 could draw an imaginary line from Nice to Bordeaux passing through Avignon and Toulouse, as the outer geographic limit of the scourge's spread, events having proved him correct.

From the above it is apparent that the disease has a mental physiognomy whose laws cannot be scientifically specified and it would be useless to try and fix its geographic source, since Egyptian plague is not Oriental plague, nor is it Hippocrates', nor that of Syracuse, nor that in Florence, nor the Black Death which accounted for fifty million lives in medieval Europe. No one can say why the plague strikes a fleeing coward and spares a rake satisfying himself on the corpses of the dead. Why isolation, chastity or solitude are ineffectual against the scourge's attacks or why a group of debauchees who have retired to the countryside, such as Boccaccio, his two well-equipped companions and their seven lustful devotees, could calmly await the hot weather when the plague subsides. Or why in a nearby castle, turned into a warlike fortress ringed with troops barring anyone from entering, the plague turned the garrison and all the occupants into corpses yet spared the guards, alone exposed to infection. Equally, who could explain why the sanitary cordons set up with great numbers of troops by Mahmet Ali about the end of the last century at the time of a fresh outbreak of Egyptian plague, effectively protected convents, schools, prisons and palaces. And that many plague epidemics with all the characteristics of Oriental plague, could suddenly have broken out in medieval Europe in those parts without any contact with the East.

Out of these peculiarities, mysteries, contradictions and traits, we ought to be able to construct the mental features of a disease which saps the anatomy and life, until it is torn apart and causes spasms, like pain which, as it intensifies, strikes deeper, increases its resources and means of access in every ramification of our sensibility.

But out of the mental freedom with which the plague evolves, without any rats, germs or contact, we can deduce the dark, ultimate action of a spectacle I am going to try and analyse.

Once the plague is established in a city, normal social order collapses. There is no more refuse collection, no more army, police or municipality. Pyres are lit to burn the dead whenever men are available. Each family wants its own. Then wood, space and fire grow scarce, families fight around the pyres, soon to be followed by general flight since there are too many corpses. The streets are already choked with crumbling pyramids of the dead, the vermin gnawing at the edges. The stench rises in the air like tongues of flame. Whole streets are blocked by mounds of dead. Then the houses are thrown open and raving plague victims disperse through the streets howling, their minds full of horrible visions. The disease gnawing at their vitals, running through their whole anatomy, is discharged in mental outbursts. Other plague victims who, without bubos or delirium, pain or rashes, examine themselves proudly in the mirror, feeling in splendid health, only to fall dead with their shaving dishes in their hands, full of scorn for other victims.

Over the thick, bloody, noxious streaming gutters, the colour of anguish and opium, spurting from the corpses, strange men clothed in wax, with noses a mile long and glass eyes, mounted on kinds of Japanese sandals made up of a double arrangement of wooden slabs, a horizontal one in the form of a sole, with the uprights isolating them from the infected liquids, pass by chanting absurd litanies, though their sanctity does not prevent them falling into the holocaust in turn. These ignorant doctors only show their fear and childishness.

The scum of the populace, immunised so it seems by their frantic greed, enter the open houses and help themselves to riches they know will serve no purpose or profit. At this point, theatre establishes itself. Theatre, that is to say that momentary pointlessness which drives them to useless acts without immediate profit.

The remaining survivors go berserk; the virtuous and obedient son kills his father, the continent sodomise their kin. The lewd become chaste. The miser chucks handfuls of his gold out of the windows, the Soldier Hero sets fire to the town he had formerly risked his life to save. Dandies deck themselves out and stroll among the charnel-houses. Neither a concept of lack of sanctions nor one of imminent death are enough to motivate such pointlessly absurd acts among people who did not believe death could end anything. How else can we explain that upsurge of erotic fever among the recovered victims who, instead of escaping, stay behind, seeking out and snatching sinful pleasure from the dying or even the dead, half crushed under the pile of corpses where chance had lodged them.

But if a major scourge is needed to make this frenzied pointlessness appear and if that scourge is called the plague, we might perhaps attempt to determine the value of this pointlessness in relation to our whole personality. The condition of a plague victim who dies without any material destruction, yet with all the stigmata of an absolute, almost abstract disease upon him, is in the same condition as an actor totally penetrated by feelings without any benefit or relation to reality. Everything in the actor's physical aspect, just as in the plague victim, shows life has reacted to a paroxysm, yet nothing has happened.

Between the shrieking plague-ridden who run in pursuit of their imaginings, and actors in pursuit of their sensibility, between a living man who invents characters he would never have thought of dreaming up without the plague, bringing them to life amidst an audience of corpses and raving lunatics, and the poet who inopportunely invents characters entrusting them to an equally inert or delirious audience, there are other analogies which account for the only important truths, placing theatre action like that of the plague, on a par with a true epidemic.

Whereas plague imagery related to an advanced state of physical disorganisation is like the last outbursts of waning mental strength, the imagery of poetry in the theatre is a mental power which begins its trajectory in the tangible and gets along without reality. Once launched in fury, an actor needs infinitely more virtue to stop himself committing a crime, than a murderer needs to perpetrate his crime, and this is where, in their pointlessness, these acts of stage feeling appear as something infinitely more valid than those feelings worked out in life.

Compared with a murderer's fury that exhausts itself, a tragic actor's remains enclosed with a circle. The murderer's anger has accomplished an act, and is released, losing contact with the power that inspired, but will no longer sustain it. The actor's has assumed a form that denies itself progressively as it is released, merging with universality.

If we are now prepared to accept this mental picture of the plague, we can consider the plague victim's disturbed fluids as a solidified, substantial aspect of a disorder which on other levels is equivalent to the clashes, struggles, disasters and devastation brought about by events. Just as it is not impossible that the unconsumed despair of a lunatic screaming in an asylum can cause the plague, so by a kind of reversibility of feelings and imagery, in the same way we can admit that outward events, political conflicts, natural disasters, revolutionary order and wartime chaos, when they occur on a theatre level are released into the audience's sensitivity with the strength of an epidemic.

In *The City of God*, St Augustine points to the similarity of the plague which kills without destroying any organs and theatre which, without killing, induces the most mysterious changes not only in the minds of individuals but in a whole nation.

'Know then,' he writes, 'you who are ignorant of this, that these plays, exhibitions of shameless folly and licence, were established at Rome not by the vicious craving of men but by the appointment of your gods. Much more pardonably might you have rendered divine honours to Scipio[1] than to gods such as these; indeed, the gods were not so moral as their pontiff! ...

'They enjoined that plays be exhibited in their honour to stay a physical pestilence, while their pontiff prohibited the theatre to prevent a moral pestilence. If then there remains in you sufficient mental enlightenment to prefer the soul to the body, choose whom you will worship. But these astute and wicked spirits, foreseeing that in due course the pestilence would shortly cease, took occasion to infect not the bodies, but the morals of their worshippers, with a far more serious disease. And in this plague these gods found great enjoyment because it benighted the minds of men with so gross a darkness and dishonoured them with so foul a deformity, that even quite recently some of those who fled from the sack of Rome and found refuge in Carthage were so infected with the disease that day after day they seemed to contend with one another who should most madly run after the actors in the theatre.'

There is no point in trying to give exact reasons for this infectious madness. It would be as much use trying to find reasons why the nervous system after a certain time is in tune with the vibrations of the subtlest music and is eventually somehow lastingly modified by it. Above all we must agree stage acting is a delirium like the plague, and is communicable.

The mind believes what it sees and does what it believes; that is the secret of fascination. And in his book, St Augustine does not doubt the reality of this fascination for one moment.

Yet conditions must be found to give birth to a spectacle that can fascinate the mind. It is not just a matter of art.

For if theatre is like the plague, this is not just because it acts on large groups and disturbs them in one and the same way. There is both something victorious and vengeful in theatre just as in the plague, for we clearly feel that spontaneous fire the plague lights as it passes by is nothing but a gigantic liquidation.

Such a complete social disaster, such organic disorder overflowing with vice, this kind of wholesale exorcism constricting the soul, driving it to the limit, indicates the presence of a condition which is an extreme force and where all the powers of nature are newly rediscovered the instant something fundamental is about to be accomplished.

The plague takes dormant images, latent disorder and suddenly carries them to the point of the most extreme gestures. Theatre also takes gestures and develops them to the limit. Just like the plague, it reforges the links between what does and does not exist in material nature. It rediscovers the idea of figures and archetypal symbols which act like sudden silences, fermata, heart stops, adrenalin calls, incendiary images surging into our abruptly woken minds. It restores all our dormant conflicts and their powers, giving these powers names we acknowledge as signs. Here a bitter clash of symbols takes place before us, hurled one against the other in an inconceivable riot. For theatre can only happen the moment the inconceivable really begins, where poetry taking place on stage, nourishes and superheats created symbols.

These symbols are symbols of full-blown powers held in bondage until that moment and unusable in real life, exploding in the guise of incredible images giving existence and the freedom of the city to acts naturally opposed to social life.

A real stage play upsets our sensual tranquillity, releases our repressed subconscious, drives us to a kind of potential rebellion (since it retains its full value only if it remains potential), calling for a difficult heroic attitude on the part of the assembled groups.

As soon as the curtain goes up on Ford's *'Tis Pity She's a Whore* to our great surprise we see before us a man launched on a most arrogant defence of incest, exerting all his youthful, conscious strength both in proclaiming and justifying it.

He does not hesitate or waver for one instant, thereby demonstrating just how little all the barriers mean that might be set up against him. He is heroically guilty, boldly, openly heroic. Everything drives him in this direction, inflames him, there is no heaven and no earth for him, only the strength of his tumultuous passion, and Annabella's unsubmissive love does not fall short of his.

'I weep', she says, 'not with remorse, but for fear I shall not be able to satisfy my passion.' They are both falsifiers, hypocrites and liars for the sake of their superhuman passion obstructed, persecuted by the law, but which they place above the law.

Revenge for revenge, crime for crime. While we believed them threatened, hunted, lost and we were ready to feel pity for them as victims, they show themselves ready to trade blow for blow with fate and threat for threat.

We follow them from one demand to the other, from one excess to the next. Annabella is caught, convicted of adultery and incest, she is trampled upon, insulted, dragged along by the hair but to our great astonishment instead of trying to make excuses she provokes her executioner even more and sings out in a kind of stubborn heroism. This is final rebellion, exemplary love without respite, making the audience gasp with anxiety in case anything should ever end it.

If one is looking for an example of total freedom in rebellion, Ford's *'Tis Pity* offers us this poetic example coupled with a picture of ultimate danger.

And just when we think we have reached a climax of horror and bloodshed, of flaunted laws, in short, poetry consecrating rebellion, we are obliged to continue in a vortex nothing can stop.

At the end we tell ourselves there must be retribution and death for such boldness and for such an irresistible crime.

Yet it is not so. Giovanni, the lover, inspired by a great impassioned poet, places himself above retribution and crime by a kind of indescribably passionate crime, places himself above threats, above horror by an even greater horror that baffles both law and morals and those who dare to set themselves up as judges.

A clever trap is laid; orders are given for a great banquet where henchmen and hired assassins hide among the guests, ready to pounce on him at the first sign. But this lost, hunted hero inspired by love, will not allow anyone to judge that love.

He seems to say, you want my love's flesh and blood but I mean to hurl it in your face, I intend to splatter you with the blood of a love whose level you could never attain.

And he kills his beloved and rips out her heart as if to eat his fill of it in the midst of that feast where the guests had hoped to devour him themselves.

He kills his rival before his execution, his sister's husband who had dared to come between himself and his mistress, slaying him in a final duel which then appears as his own death throes.

Like the plague, theatre is a powerful appeal through illustration to those powers which return the mind to the origins of its inner struggles. And we clearly sense Ford's passionate example is only a symbol for a much greater and absolutely fundamental task.

The terrifying apparition of Evil produced in unalloyed form at the Eleusinian Mysteries being truly revealed, corresponded to the darker moments in certain ancient tragedies which all theatre must rediscover.

If fundamental theatre is like the plague, this is not because it is contagious, but because like the plague it is a revelation, urging forward the exteriorisation of a latent undercurrent of cruelty through which all the perversity of which the mind is capable, whether in a person or a nation, becomes localised.

Just like the plague there is an evil time, the victory of dark powers, a higher power nourishing them until they have died out.

In theatre, as in the plague, there is a kind of strange sun, an unusually bright light by which the difficult, even the impossible suddenly appears to be our natural medium. And Ford's *'Tis Pity She's a Whore* is lit by the brilliance of that strange sun just as is all worthwhile theatre. It resembles the plague's freedom where, step by step, stage by stage, the victim's character swells out, where the survivors gradually become imposing, superhuman beings.

Now one may say all true freedom is dark, infallibly identified with sexual freedom, also dark, without knowing exactly why. For the Platonic Eros, the genetic meaning of a free life, disappeared long ago beneath the turbid surface of the *Libido* we associate with everything sullied, despicable and ignominious in being alive, to rush headlong with our customary, impure vitality, with constantly renewed strength, in the direction of life.

Thus all great Myths are dark and one cannot imagine all the great Fables, aside from a mood of slaughter, torture and bloodshed, telling the masses about the original division of the sexes and the slaughter of essences that came with creation.

Theatre, like the plague, is made in the image of this slaughter, this essential division. It unravels conflicts, liberates powers, releases potential and if these and the powers are dark, this is not the fault of the plague or theatre, but life.

We do not see that life as it stands and as it has been made offers us much cause for exaltation. It seems as though a colossal abcess, ethical as much as social, is drained by the plague. And like the plague, theatre is collectively made to drain abcesses.

It may be true that the poison of theatre, when injected in the body of society, destroys it as St Augustine asserted, but it does so as a plague, a revenging scourge, a redeeming epidemic when credulous ages were convinced they saw God's hand in it, while it was nothing more than a natural law applied, where all gestures were offset by another gesture, every action by a reaction.

Like the plague, theatre is a crisis resolved either by death or cure. The plague is a superior disease because it is an absolute crisis after which there is nothing left except death or drastic purification. In the same way, theatre is a disease because it is a final balance that cannot be obtained without destruction. It urges the mind on to delirium which intensifies its energy. And finally from a human viewpoint we can see that theatre action is as beneficial as the plague, impelling us to see ourselves as we are, making the masks fall and divulging our world's lies, aimlessness, meanness, and even two-facedness. It shakes off stifling material dullness which even overcomes the senses' clearest testimony, and collectively reveals their dark powers and hidden strength to men, urging them to take a nobler, more heroic stand in the face of destiny than they would have assumed without it.

And the question we must now ask ourselves is to know whether in this world that is slipping away, committing suicide without realising it, a nucleus of men can be found to impress this higher idea of theatre on the world, to bring back to all of us a natural, occult equivalent of the dogma we no longer believe.

No More Masterpieces

ONE OF THE REASONS for the stifling atmosphere we live in, without any possible escape or remedy, which is shared by even the most revolutionary among us – is our respect for what has been written, expressed or painted, for whatever has taken shape, as if all expression were not finally exhausted, has not arrived at the point where things must break up to begin again, to make a fresh start.

We must finally do away with the idea of masterpieces reserved for a so-called elite but incomprehensible to the masses, since the mind has no red-light districts like those used for illicit sexual relations.

Past masterpieces are fit for the past, they are no good to us. We have the right to say what has been said and even what has not been said in a way that belongs to us, responding in a direct and straightforward manner to present-day feelings everybody can understand.

It is senseless to criticise the masses for having no sense of the sublime, when we ourselves confuse the sublime with one of those formal, moreover always dead, exhibits. And if, for example, the masses today no longer understand *Oedipus Rex*, I would venture to say *Oedipus Rex* is at fault as a play and not the masses.

In *Oedipus Rex* there is the incest theme and the idea that nature does not give a rap for morality. And there are wayward powers at large we would do well to be aware of, call them *fate* or what you will.

In addition, there is the presence of a plague epidemic which is the physical incarnation of these powers. But all this is clothed in language which has lost any contact with today's crude, epileptic rhythm. Sophocles may speak nobly, but in a manner that no longer suits the times. His speeches are too refined for today, as if he were speaking beside the point.

Yet the masses tremble at railway disasters, are familiar with earthquakes, plagues, revolutions and wars as well as being sensitive to the disturbing anguish of love and are capable of becoming conscious of all those grand ideas. They ask only to become conscious of them, but on condition we know how to speak their language and that notions of these things are not brought to them invested in a sophistication belonging to dead periods we will never relive.

Just as in former times, the masses today are thirsting for mystery. They only ask to become conscious of the laws by which fate reveals itself and perhaps to guess at the secret of its apparitions.

Let us leave textual criticism to teachers and formal criticism to aesthetes, and acknowledge that what has already been said no longer needs saying; that an expression twice used is of no value since it does not have two lives. Once spoken, all speech is dead and is only active as it is spoken. Once a form is used it has no more use, bidding man find another form, and theatre is the only place in the world where a gesture, once made, is never repeated in the same way.

If the masses do not frequent literary masterpieces, this is because the masterpieces are literary, that is to say set in forms no longer answering the needs of the times.

Far from accusing the masses, the public, we must accuse the formal screen we place between ourselves and the masses and that form of a new idolatry, the idolising of set masterpieces, an aspect of middle-class conformity.

The conformity that makes us confuse the sublime, the concepts, and the objects with the forms they have acquired in our minds through the ages – our affected, snobbish, aesthetic mentality the public no longer understands.

It is useless in all this to accuse the public's bad taste while it slakes its thirst with inanities, as long as we have not given the public a worth-while show. And I defy anyone to point out a worth-while show *here*, worth-while in the highest sense of theatre, since the last great Romantic melodramas, that is a hundred years ago.

The public, which mistakes the bogus for truth, has the sense of what is true and always reacts to it when it appears. Today, however, we must look for it in the street, not on stage. And if the crowds in the street were given a chance to show their dignity as human beings, they would always do so.

If the masses have grown unused to going to the theatre, if we have all finally come to regard theatre as an inferior art, a means of coarse distraction, using it as an outlet for our worst instincts, this is because we have for too long been told theatre is all lies and illusion. Because for four hundred years, that is since the Renaissance, we have become accustomed to purely descriptive, narrative theatre, narrating psychology.

People exerted their ingenuity to bring to life on stage credible but detached beings, with the show on one side and the masses on the other – and the masses were shown only a mirror of themselves.

Shakespeare himself is responsible for this abberation and decline, this isolationist concept of theatre, holding that a stage performance ought not to affect the public, or that a projected image should not cause a shock to the anatomy, leaving an indelible impression on it.

If man in Shakespeare's plays is sometimes concerned with what is above him, it is always finally to determine the result of that concern within man, that is, psychology.

Psychology persists in bringing the unknown down to a level with the known, that is to say with the everyday and pedestrian. And psychology has caused this abasement and fearful loss of energy which appears to me to have really reached its limit. And it seems both theatre and ourselves want nothing more to do with psychology.

Besides, I think we are all agreed on this point of view and in order to censure psychological drama there is no need to stoop as low as disgusting modern French theatre.

Plots dealing with money, money troubles, social climbing, the pangs of love unspoilt by altruism, sexuality sugar-coated with eroticism yet shorn of mystery, are not theatre even if they are psychology. This anxiety, debauchery and lust, before which we are only Peeping Toms gratifying our instincts, tends to go sour and turn into revolution. This is something we must realise.

But that is not our most serious concern.

In the long run, Shakespeare and his followers have instilled a concept of art for art's sake in us, art on the one hand and life on the other, and we might rely on this lazy, ineffective idea as long as life outside held good, but there are too many signs that everything which used to sustain our lives no longer does so and we are all mad, desperate and sick. And I urge *us* to react.

This concept of unworldly art, charm-poetry existing solely to charm away the hours, is a decadent notion, an unmistakable symptom of the emasculatory force within us.

Our literary admiration for Rimbaud, Jarry, Lautréamont and a few others, which drove two men to suicide, but turned into nothing more than café chit-chat for the rest, belongs to the idea of literary poetry, detached art, emasculated mental activity which has no effect and produces nothing. And I note that just when personal poetry, involving only its creator as he creates, became rife in a most excessive way, theatre was held in great contempt by poets who never had either a feeling for immediate group action, effectiveness or danger.

Let us do away with this foolish adherence to texts, to *written* poetry. Written poetry is valid once and then ought to be torn up. Let dead poets make way for the living. And we ought after all to be able to see it is our adulation for what has already been done, however fine and worthy it may be, that fossilises us, makes us stagnate and prevents us contacting that underlying power called thinking energy, vital power, determination of exchange, lunar periods or what have you.

Poetry plain and simple, unformed and unwritten, underlies textual poetry. And just as masks, once used in magic rituals, are no longer fit for anything but to be put in museums – in the same way, the poetic effectiveness of a text is exhausted – theatre's effectiveness and poetry is exhausted least quickly of all, since it permits the action of movement and spoken things, never reproduced twice.

We must know what we want. If we are all prepared for war, the plague, famine and slaughter, we have no need to say so, we have only to go on as we are. To go on behaving as snobs, to flock to hear such and such a singer, to see such and such a wonderful show which never transcends the world of art (even the *Ballets Russes* at the height of their splendour never transcended the world of art), such and such an exhibition of painting where impressive forms dazzle us here and there, only by chance, and without being truly conscious of the powers they could arouse.

This empiricism, chance, personalism and anarchy must come to an end.

No more personal poems benefiting those who write them more than those who read them.

Once and for all, enough of these displays of closed, conceited, personal art.

Our anarchy and mental confusion are a function of the anarchy of everything else – or rather everything else is a function of that anarchy.

I am not of the opinion that civilisation must change so theatre can change, but I do believe theatre used in the highest and most difficult sense has the power to affect the appearance and structure of things. And bringing two impassioned revelations together on stage, two living fires, two nervous magnetisms, is just as complete, as true, even as decisive as bringing together two bodies in short-lived debauchery is in life.

For this reason I suggest a Theatre of Cruelty.

With this mania we all have today for belittling everything, as soon as I said 'cruelty' everyone took it to mean 'blood'. But a '*theatre of cruelty*' means theatre that is difficult and cruel for myself first of all. And on a performing level, it has nothing to do with the cruelty we practise on one another, hacking at each other's bodies, carving up our individual anatomies, or, like ancient Assyrian Emperors, posting sackfuls of human ears, noses or neatly dissected nostrils, but the far more terrible, essential cruelty objects can practise on us. We are not free and the sky can still fall on our heads. And above all else, theatre is made to teach us this.

Either we will be able to revert through theatre by present-day means to the higher idea of poetry underlying the Myths told by the great tragedians of ancient times, with theatre able once more to sustain a religious concept, that is to say without any meditation or useless contemplation, without diffuse dreams, to become conscious and also be in command of certain predominant powers, certain ideas governing everything; and since ideas when they are effective generate their own energy, rediscover within us that energy which in the last analysis creates order and increases the value of life, or else we might as well abdicate now without protest, and acknowledge we are fit only for chaos, famine, bloodshed, war and epidemics.

Either we restore one focal attitude and necessity in all the arts, finding correspondences between a gesture in painting or on stage, and a gesture made by lava in a volcanic eruption, or we must stop painting, gossiping, writing or doing anything at all.

I suggest theatre today ought to return to the fundamental magic notion reintroduced by psychoanalysis, which consists in curing a patient by making him assume the external attitude of the desired condition.

I suggest we ought to reject the empiricism of random images produced by the subconscious, calling them poetic and therefore hermetic images, as if that kind of trance brought about by poetry does not reverberate throughout our whole sensibility, in every nerve, as if poetry were a shadowy power with invariable motions.

I suggest we ought to return through theatre to the idea of a physical knowledge of images, a means of inducing trances, just as Chinese medicine knows the points of acupuncture over the whole extent of the human anatomy, down to our most sensitive functions.

Theatre can reinstruct those who have forgotten the communicative power or magic mimicry of gesture, because a gesture contains its own energy, and there are still human beings in theatre to reveal the power of these gestures.

To practice art is to deprive a gesture of its reverberations throughout the anatomy, whereas these reverberations, if the gesture is made in the conditions and with the force required, impels the anatomy and, through it, the whole personality to adopt attitudes that correspond to that gesture.

Theatre is the only place in the world, the last group means we still possess of directly affecting the anatomy, and in neurotic, basely sensual periods like the one in which we are immersed, of attacking that base sensuality through physical means it cannot withstand.

Snakes do not react to music because of the mental ideas it produces in them, but because they are long, they lie coiled on the ground and their bodies are in contact with the ground along almost their entire length. And the musical vibrations communicated to the ground affect them as a very subtle, very long massage. Well I propose to treat the audience just like those charmed snakes and to bring them back to the subtlest ideas through their anatomies.

First of all by crude means, these gradually becoming more refined. But these crude, direct means hold its attention from the start.

For this reason the audience is in the centre in the 'Theatre of Cruelty', while the show takes place around them.

In such a show there is continual amplification; the sounds, noises and cries are first sought for their vibratory qualities, secondly for what they represent.

Lighting occurs in its turn in these progressively refined means. Lighting made not only to give colour or to shed light, but containing its own force, influence and suggestiveness. For light in a green cave does not predispose the organism sensually in the same way as light on a very windy day.

Following on sound and lighting there is action and action's dynamism. This is where theatre, far from imitating life, communicates wherever it can with pure forces! And whether we accept or deny them, there is none the less a manner of speaking which gives the name forces to whatever gives birth to forceful images in our subconscious, to outwardly motiveless crime.

Violent, concentrated action is like lyricism; it calls forth supernatural imagery, a bloodshed of images, a bloody spurt of images inside the poet's head as well as in the audience's.

Whatever conflicts may obsess the mentality of the times, I defy any spectator infused with the blood of violent scenes, who has felt higher action pass through him, who has seen the rare, fundamental motions of his thought illuminated in extraordinary events – violence and bloodshed having been placed at the service of violence in thought – once outside the theatre, I defy him to indulge in thoughts of war, riot or motiveless murder.

The idea may seem puerile and advanced when stated in this way. And some will claim one example encourages another, that an attitude to cure encourages a cure, or murder to murder. Everything depends on the manner and purity with which things are done. There are risks. But we must not forget that while theatre action is violent it is not biased and theatre teaches us just how useless action is since once it is done it is over, as well as the superior use of that state of mind unused by action but which, if *turned about*, sublimates.

Therefore I propose a theatre where violent physical images pulverise, mesmerise the audience's sensibilities, caught in the drama as if in a vortex of higher forces.

Theatre, abandoning psychology, must narrate the unusual, stage nature's conflicts, nature's subtle powers arising first and foremost as extraordinary derivative powers. Theatre bringing on trances just as the whirling Dervishes or the Assouas induce trances. It must be aimed at the system by exact means, the same means as the sympathetic music used by some tribes which we admire on records but are incapable of originating among ourselves.

One runs risks, but I consider that in present-day conditions they are worth running. I do not believe we have succeeded in reanimating the world we live in and I also do not believe it worth hanging onto. But I propose something to get us out of the slump, instead of continuing to moan about it, about the boredom, dullness and stupidity of everything.

Note

1. Scipio Nasica, High Pontiff, who ordered that the theatres in Rome be razed to the ground and their cellars filled.

From Antonin Artaud, *The Theatre and Its Double,* London: John Calder, 1977, pp. 7–22 and 55–63. Translated by Victor Corti, 1970.

2.11 First Surrealist Manifesto (1924) *and* Second Surrealist Manifesto (1929)

ANDRÉ BRETON

Translated by Patrick Waldberg

First Surrealist Manifesto (extract)

WE ARE STILL LIVING under the reign of logic, but the logical processes of our time apply only to the solution of problems of secondary interest. The absolute rationalism which remains in fashion allows for the consideration of only those facts narrowly relevant to our experience. Logical conclusions, on the other hand, escape us. Needless to say, boundaries have been assigned even to experience. It revolves in a cage from which release is becoming increasingly difficult. It too depends upon immediate utility and is guarded by common sense. In the guise of civilization, under the pretext of progress, we have succeeded in dismissing from our minds anything that, rightly or wrongly, could be regarded as superstition or myth; and we have proscribed every way of seeking the truth which does not conform to convention. It would appear that it is by sheer chance that an aspect of intellectual life – and by far the most important in my opinion – about which no one was supposed to be concerned any longer has, recently, been brought back to light. Credit for this must go to Freud. On the evidence of his discoveries a current of opinion is at last developing which will enable the explorer of the human mind to extend his investigations, since he will be empowered to deal with more than merely summary realities. Perhaps the imagination is on the verge of recovering its rights. If the depths of our minds conceal strange forces capable of augmenting or conquering those on the surface, it is in our greatest interest to capture them; first to capture them and later to submit them, should the occasion arise, to the control of reason. The analysts themselves can only gain by this. But it is important to note that there is no method fixed *a priori* for the execution of this enterprise, that until the new order it can be considered the province of poets as well as scholars, and that its success does not depend upon the more or less capricious routes which will be followed.

It was only fitting that Freud should appear with his critique on the dream. In fact, it is incredible that this important part of psychic activity has still attracted so little attention. (For, at least from man's birth to his death, thought presents no solution of continuity; the sum of dreaming moments – even taking into consideration pure dream alone, that of sleep – is from the point of view of time no less than the sum of moments of reality, which we shall confine to waking moments.) I have always been astounded by the extreme disproportion in the importance and seriousness assigned to events of the waking moments and to those of sleep by the ordinary observer. Man, when he ceases to sleep, is above all at the mercy of his memory, and the memory normally delights in feebly retracing the circumstance of the dream for him, depriving it of all actual consequence and obliterating the only *determinant* from the point at which he thinks he abandoned this constant hope, this anxiety, a few hours earlier. He has the illusion of continuing something worthwhile. The dream finds itself relegated to a parenthesis, like the night. And in general it gives no more counsel than the night. This singular state of affairs seems to invite a few reflections:

1 Within the limits to which its performance is restricted (or what passes for performance), the dream, according to all outward appearances, is continuous and bears traces of organization. Only memory claims the right to edit it, to suppress transitions and present us with a series of dreams rather than *the dream*. Similarly, at no given instant do we have more than a distinct representation of realities whose co-ordination is a matter of will.[1] It is important to note that nothing leads to a greater dissipation of the constituent elements of the dream. I regret discussing this according to a formula which in principle excludes the dream. For how long, sleeping logicians, philosophers? I would like to sleep in order to enable myself to surrender to sleepers, as I surrender to those who read me with their eyes open, in order to stop the conscious rhythm of my thought from prevailing over this material. Perhaps my dream of last night was a continuation of the preceding night's, and will be continued tonight with an admirable precision. *It could be*, as they say. And as it is in no way proven that, in such a case, the 'reality' with which I am concerned even exists in the dream state, or that it does not sink into the immemorial, then why should I not concede to the dream what I sometimes refuse to reality – that weight of self-assurance which by its own terms is not exposed to my denial? Why should I not expect more of the dream sign than I do of a daily increasing degree of consciousness? Could not the dreams as well be applied to the solution of life's fundamental problems? Are these problems the same in one case as in the other, and do they already exist in the dream? Is the dream less oppressed by sanctions than the rest? I am growing old and, perhaps more than this reality to which I believe myself confined, it is the dream, and the detachment that I owe to it, which is ageing me.

2 I return to the waking state. I am obliged to retain it as a phenomenon of interference. Not only does the mind show a strange tendency to disorientation under these conditions (this is the clue to slips of the tongue and lapses of all kinds whose secret is just beginning to be surrendered to us), but when functioning normally the mind still seems to obey none other than those suggestions which rise from that deep night I am commending. Sound as it may be, its equilibrium is relative. The mind hardly dares express itself and, when it does, is limited to stating that this idea or that woman *has an effect on it*. What effect it cannot say; thus it gives the measure of its subjectivism and nothing more. The idea, the woman, *disturbs* it, disposes it to less severity. Their role is to isolate one second of its disappearance and remove it to the sky in that glorious acceleration that it can be, that it is. Then, as a last resort, the mind invokes chance – a more obscure divinity than the others – to whom it attributes all its aberrations. Who says that the angle from which that idea is presented which affects the mind, as well as what the mind loves in that woman's eye, is not *precisely* the same thing that attracts the mind to its dream and reunites it with data lost through its own error? And if things were otherwise, of what might the mind not be capable? I should like to present it with the key to that passage.

3 The mind of the dreaming man is fully satisfied with whatever happens to it. The agonizing question of possibility does not arise. Kill, plunder more quickly, love as much as you wish. And if you die, are you not sure of being roused from the dead? Let yourself be led. Events will not tolerate deferment. You have no name. Everything is inestimably easy.

What power, I wonder, what power so much more generous than others confers this natural aspect upon the dream and makes me welcome unreservedly a throng of episodes whose strangeness would overwhelm me if they were happening as I write this? And yet I can believe it with my own eyes, my own ears. That great day has come, that beast has spoken.

If man's awakening is harsher, if he breaks the spell too well, it is because he has been led to form a poor idea of expiation.

4 When the time comes when we can submit the dream to a methodical examination, when by methods yet to be determined we succeed in realizing the dream in its entirety (and that implies a memory discipline measurable in generations, but we can still begin by recording salient facts), when the dream's curve is developed with an unequalled breadth and regularity, then we can hope that mysteries which are not really mysteries will give way to the great Mystery. I believe in the future resolution of these two states – outwardly so contradictory – which are dream and reality, into a sort of absolute reality, a *surreality*, so to speak. I am aiming for its conquest, certain that I myself shall not attain it, but too indifferent to my death not to calculate the joys of such possession.

They say that not long ago, just before he went to sleep, Saint-Pol-Roux placed a placard on the door of his manor at Camaret which read: THE POET WORKS.

There is still a great deal to say, but I did want to touch lightly, in passing, upon a subject which in itself would require a very long exposition with a different precision. I shall return to it. For the time being my intention has been to see that justice was done to that *hatred of the marvellous* which rages in certain men, that ridicule under which they would like to crush it. Let us resolve, therefore: the Marvellous is always beautiful, everything marvellous is beautiful. Nothing but the Marvellous is beautiful.

... One night, before falling asleep, I became aware of a most bizarre sentence, clearly articulated to the point where it was impossible to change a word of it, but still separate from the sound of any voice. It came to me bearing no trace of the events with which I was involved at that time, at least to my conscious knowledge. It seemed to me a highly insistent sentence – a sentence, I might say, *which knocked at the window*. I quickly took note of it and was prepared to disregard it when something about its whole character held me back. The sentence truly astounded me. Unfortunately I still cannot remember the exact words to this day, but it was something like: 'A man is cut in half by the window'; but it can only suffer from ambiguity, accompanied as it was by the feeble visual representation of a walking man cut in half by a window perpendicular to the axis of his body.[2] It was probably a simple matter of a man leaning on the window and then straightening up. But the window followed the movements of the man, and I realized that I was dealing with a very rare type of image. Immediately I had the idea of incorporating it into my poetic material, but no sooner had I invested it with poetic form than it went on to give way to a scarcely intermittent succession of sentences which surprised me no less than the first and gave me the impression of such a free gift that the control which I had had over myself up to that point seemed illusory and I no longer thought of anything but how to put an end to the interminable quarrel which was taking place within me.[3]

Totally involved as I was at the time with Freud, and familiar with his methods of examination which I had had some occasion to practise on the sick during the war, I resolved to obtain from myself what one seeks to obtain from a patient – a spoken monologue uttered as rapidly as possible, over which the critical faculty of the subject has no control, unencumbered by any reticence, which is *spoken thought* as far as such a thing is possible. It seemed to me, and still does – the manner in which the sentence about the man cut in two came to me proves it – that the speed of thought is no greater than that of words, and that it does not necessarily defy language or the moving pen. It was with this in mind that Philippe Soupault (with whom I had shared these first conclusions) and I undertook to cover some paper with writing, with a laudable contempt for what might result in terms of literature. The ease of realization did the rest. At the end of the first day we were able to read to each other around fifty pages obtained by this method, and began to compare our results. Altogether, those of Soupault and my own presented a remarkable similarity, even including the same faults in construction: in both cases there was the illusion of an extraordinary verve, a great deal of emotion, a considerable assortment of images of a quality such as we would never have been capable of achieving in ordinary writing, a very vivid graphic quality, and here and there an acutely comic passage. The only difference between our texts seemed to me essentially due to our respective natures (Soupault's is less static than mine) and, if I may hazard a slight criticism, due to the fact that he had made the mistake of distributing a few words in the way of titles at the head of certain pages – no doubt in the spirit of mystification. On the other hand, I must give him credit for maintaining his steadfast opposition to the slightest alteration in the course of any passage which seemed to me rather badly put. He was completely right on this point, of course.[4] In fact it is very difficult to appreciate the full value of the various elements when confronted by them. It can even be said to be impossible to appreciate them at the first reading. These elements are outwardly *as strange to you who have written them as to anyone else*, and you are naturally distrustful of them. Poetically speaking, they are especially endowed with a very high degree of *immediate absurdity*. The peculiarity of this absurdity, on closer examination, comes from their capitulation to everything – both inadmissible and legitimate – in the world, to produce a revelation of a certain number of premises and facts generally no less objective than any others.

In homage to Guillaume Apollinaire – who died recently, and who appears to have consistently obeyed a similar impulse to ours without ever really sacrificing mediocre literary means – Soupault and I used the name SURREALISM to designate the new mode of pure expression which we had at our disposal and with which we were anxious to benefit our friends. Today I do not believe anything more need be said about this word. The meaning which we have given it has generally prevailed over Apollinaire's meaning. With even more justification we could have used SUPERNATURALISM, employed by Gerard de Nerval in the dedication of *Filles de Feu*.[5] In fact, Nerval appears to have possessed to an admirable extent the *spirit* to which we refer. Apollinaire, on the other hand, possessed only the *letter* of surrealism (which was still imperfect) and showed himself powerless to give it the theoretical insight that engages us. Here are two passages by Nerval which appear most significant in this regard:

'I will explain to you, my dear Dumas, the phenomenon of which you spoke above. As you know, there are certain story-tellers who cannot invent without identifying themselves with the characters from their imagination. You know with what conviction our old friend Nodier told how he had had the misfortune to be guillotined at the time of the Revolution; one became so convinced that one wondered how he had managed to stick his head back on.'

'... And since you have had the imprudence to cite one of the sonnets composed in this state of SUPERNATURALIST reverie, as the Germans would say, you must hear all of them. You will find them at the end of the volume. They are hardly more obscure than Hegel's metaphysics or Swedenborg's MEMORABLES, and would lose their charm in explication, if such a thing were possible, so concede me at least the merit of their expression ...'[6]

It would be dishonest to dispute our right to employ the word SURREALISM in the very particular sense in which we intend it, for it is clear that before we came along this word amounted to nothing. Thus I shall define it once and for all:

SURREALISM, noun, masc., Pure psychic automatism by which it is intended to express, either verbally or in writing, the true function of thought. Thought dictated in the absence of all control exerted by reason, and outside all aesthetic or moral preoccupations.

ENCYCL. *Philos.* Surrealism is based on the belief in the superior reality of certain forms of association heretofore neglected, in the omnipotence of the dream, and in the disinterested play of thought. It leads to the permanent destruction of all other psychic mechanisms and to its substitution for them in the solution of the principal problems of life.

Notes (edited)

1. We must take into consideration the *thickness* of the dream. I usually retain only that which comes from the superficial layers. What I prefer to visualize in it is everything that sinks at the awakening, everything that is not left to me of the function of that preceding day, dark foliage, absurd branches. In 'reality', too, I prefer to *fall*.
2. Had I been a painter, this visual representation would undoubtedly have dominated the other. It is certainly my previous disposition which decided it. Since that day I have had occasion to concentrate my attention voluntarily on similar apparitions, and I know that they are not inferior in clarity to auditory phenomena. Armed with a pencil and a blank sheet of paper, it would be easy for me to follow its contours. This is because here again it is not a matter of drawing, *it is only a matter of tracing*. I would be able to draw quite well a tree, a wave, a musical instrument – all things of which I am incapable of furnishing the briefest sketch at this time. Sure of finding my way, I would plunge into a labyrinth of lines which at first would not seem to contribute to anything. And upon opening my eyes I would experience a very strong impression of '*jamais vu*' ...
3. Knut Hamsun attributes the kind of revelation by which I have just been possessed to *hunger*, and he may well be right. (The fact is I was not eating everyday at that period) ... Apollinaire affirmed that Chirico's paintings had been executed under the influence of cenesthesiac pains (migraines, colic).
4. I believe increasingly in the infallibility of my thought in regard to myself, and it is too accurate. Nevertheless, in this *writing down of thoughts*, where one is at the mercy of the first exterior distraction, 'transports' can be produced. It would be inexcusable to seek to ignore them. By definition, thought is strong and incapable of being at fault. We must attribute those obvious weaknesses to suggestions which come from outside.
5. And also by Thomas Carlyle in *Sartor Resartus* Chapter VIII: 'Natural Supernaturalism', 1833–4.
6. See also L'Idéoréalisme by Saint-Pol-Roux.

Second Surrealist Manifesto (1929)

IN SPITE OF THE individual courses peculiar to each of its past and present participants, in the end surrealism's overall tendency will be readily admitted to have been nothing so much as the provocation, from an intellectual and moral point of view, of the most universal and serious kind of *crisis of conscience*, and it will be agreed that the attainment or non-attainment of this result can decide its historical success or defeat.

From an intellectual point of view, it was and still is necessary to expose by every available means the factitious character of the old contradictions hypocritically calculated to hinder every unusual agitation on the part of man, and to force its recognition at all costs, if only to give mankind some faint idea of its abilities and to challenge it to escape its universal shackles to some meaningful extent. The bugbear of death, the music-halls of the beyond, the shipwreck of the loftiest intellect in sleep, the crushing curtain of the future, the towers of Babel, the mirrors of inconsistency, the insurmountable silver-splashed wall of the brain – all of these striking images of human catastrophe are perhaps nothing but images. There is every reason to believe that there exists a certain point in the mind at which life and death, real and imaginary, past and future, communicable and incommunicable, high and low, cease to be perceived in terms of contradiction. Surrealist activity would be searched in vain for a motive other than the hope to determine this point. Thus it is sufficiently obvious that it would be absurd to attribute to that activity a uniquely destructive, or constructive, direction: the point in question is, *a fortiori*, that construction and destruction can no longer be brandished against each other. It is also clear that surrealism is not interested in taking much account of what is produced peripherally under the pretext of art – which is really anti-art – philosophy or anti-philosophy, in short, everything that does not conclude in the annihilation of being into a blind, inner splendour which would be no more the essence of ice than of fire. What indeed could be expected from the surrealist experience by those who retain some anxiety about the place they will occupy *in the world*? On that mental plane from which one can undertake for oneself alone the perilous – but, we believe, supreme – recognition, there can be no question of attaching the least importance to the footsteps of those who come or go, since these footsteps occur in a region where, by definition, surrealism has no ear. Surrealism should not be at the mercy of this or that man's whim; if it declares that it can, by its own means, deliver thought from an ever harsher bondage, put it back on the path of total understanding, restore its original purity, then that is enough to justify its being judged only by what it had done and by what remains to be done in order to keep its promise.

Surrealism, particularly in regard to its means of undertaking the investigation of the elements of reality and unreality, reason and unreason, reflection and impulse, knowledge and 'fatal' ignorance, utility and inutility, etc., presents at least one analogy with historical materialism in that it departs from the 'colossal abortion' of the Hegelian system. It seems impossible to me that limits can be assigned – those of the economic plan, for example – to the practice of a philosophy definitely adaptable to negation and the negation of negation. How can they acknowledge that the dialectic method can only be validly applied to the solution of social problems? Surrealism's whole ambition is to furnish that method with possibilities of application not at all concurrent in the most immediate realms of consciousness. With all due respect to certain narrow-minded revolutionaries, I really do not see why we should abstain from raising problems of love, dream, madness, art and religion,[1] provided that we consider them in the same light in which they, and we too, consider Revolution. And I do not hesitate to say that before surrealism nothing systematic had been done in this direction, and that when we found it, *the dialectic method was* – for us too – *inapplicable in its Hegelian form*. For us too it was a question of the need to have done with idealism as such (the creation of the word surrealism alone should prove that) and to return to Engel's example of the need to stop clinging to the juvenile development: 'The rose is a rose. The rose is not a rose. But the rose is still a rose.' Nevertheless – forgive me this digression – it was necessary to set 'the rose' into action conducive to less favourable contradictions, where it might be in succession something from the garden, something with a particular role in a dream, something impossible to separate from the 'optical bouquet', something which can totally change its nature by passing into automatic writing, something which has none of the rose's properties except those the painter has decided to retain in a surrealist painting, and finally, something entirely different from itself, which returns to the garden. This is a far cry from any idealistic conception, and we would not even mention it if we might stop being continuously exposed to attacks of elementary materialism, attacks which emanate both from those who, out of decadent conservatism, have no desire to clarify the relation of thought to matter, and from those who, out of a misunderstood revolutionary sectarianism and in defiance of what is needed, confuse this materialism with that which Engels essentially distinguished from it and which he defined as above all an *intuition of the world* called upon to prove and fulfill itself: *In the course of the development of philosophy, idealism became untenable and was denied by modern materialism. The latter, which is the negation of negation, is not simply a restoration of the old materialism: to those solid foundations it adds the entire conception of philosophy and the natural sciences in the course of a two-thousand-year evolution as well as the product of this long history itself.* We also intend to make it understood as a point of departure that for us philosophy is *outclassed*. This is the fate, I think, of all those for whom reality has not only a theoretical importance but for whom it is also a question of life and death to appeal passionately to that reality, as Feuerbach insisted: ours to give as we *totally*, unreservedly give our support to the principle of historical materialism, his to throw in the face of the astounded intellectual world the idea that 'man is what he eats' and that a future revolution would have a better chance of success if the people received better food, such as peas instead of potatoes.

Our support of the principle of historical materialism – there is no way of playing on these words. Let that depend only on us – I mean provided communism does not treat us merely as strange animals determined to practise star-gazing and defiance in its ranks – and we shall show ourselves capable of doing our full duty from a revolutionary point of view. This, unfortunately, is a pledge which interests only us: for example, two years ago I myself could not enter, freely and unobserved, the headquarters of the French Party, where nevertheless so many disreputable individuals – police and others – are allowed to carry on as though they were in a boiler factory. In the course of three interrogations of several hours' length, I had to defend surrealism against the childish accusation of being in essence a political movement with a clearly anti-communist and counter-revolutionary bent. Needless to say, I expected nothing from the thorough investigation of my ideas on the part of those who were judging me. 'If you are a Marxist', Michel Marty shouted at one of us around that time, 'you do not need to be a surrealist.' Surrealists that we were, it was of course not we who boasted of it in those circumstances: this label had preceded us in spite of ourselves just as that of 'relativists' might have preceded the followers of Einstein, or 'psychoanalysts' those of Freud. How can one not be terribly worried about such a weakening of the ideological level of a party which not long before had emerged so brilliantly armed with two of the best minds of the nineteenth century! One hardly knows: the little that I can conclude from my own personal experience in this regard can be measured by the following. They asked me to give a report on the Italian situation in the 'Gas' cell, specifying that I was to rely upon statistical facts alone (steel production, etc.) and *especially no ideology*. I could not.

Note (edited)

1. For some time now false quotation has been one of the methods most frequently employed against me ... a contributor to the *Exquisite Corpse* sharply reprimands me under the pretext that I wrote : 'I vow never to wear the French uniform again.' *I'm, sorry, but that was not me.*

From Patrick Waldberg, *Surrealism*, London: Thames and Hudson, 1978, pp. 66–72 and 76–80.

2.12 Futurist Scenography (Manifesto) (1915)

ENRICO PRAMPOLINI

Translated by Diana Clemmons

April–May 1915

*L*ET'S REFORM THE STAGE. To admit, to believe that a stage has existed up until today is to affirm that artistically man is absolutely blind. The stage is not equivalent to a photographic enlargement of a rectangle of reality or to a relative synthesis, but to the adoption of a theoretical system and subjective scenographic material completely opposed to the so-called objective scenography of today.

It is not only a question of reforming the conception of the structure of the *mise-en-scène*; one must create an abstract entity which identifies itself with the scenic action of the play.

It is wrong to view the stage separately, as a pictorial fact: (a) because we are no longer dealing with scenography but with simple painting; (b) we are returning to the past (that is to say to the past ... present) where the stage expresses one subject, the play develops another.

These two forces which have been diverging (playwright and scenographer) must converge to form a multiple synthesis of the play.

The stage must live the theatrical action in its dynamic synthesis; it must express the essence of the character conceived by the author just as an actor at once expresses and lives it within himself. Therefore, in order to reform the stage one must:

1   Deny exact reconstruction of that which the playwright has conceived, thus abandoning resolutely every factual relationship, every comparison between object and subject and vice versa; all these relationships weaken direct emotion with indirect sensations.
2   Substitute for scenic action an emotional order which awakens all sensations necessary to the development of the play; the resulting atmosphere will provide the interior milieu.
3   *Absolute synthesis* in material expression of the stage, which means not the pictorial synthesis of all the elements, but synthesis excluding those elements of scenic architecture which are incapable of producing new sensations.
4   The scenic architecture will have to be a connection for the audience's intuition rather than a picturesque and elaborate collaboration.
5   The colors and the stage will have to arouse in the spectator those emotional values which neither the poet's words nor the actor's gestures can evoke.

There are no theatre reformers today: Dresa and Rouché experimented in France with ingenuous and infantile expressions; Meyerhold and Stanislavsky in Russia with revivals of sickening classicism (we leave out the Assyrian-Persian-Egyptian-Nordic plagiarist Bakst); Adolphe Appia, Fritz Erler, Littman Fuchs and Max Reinhardt (organizer) in Germany have attempted reforms directed more toward tedious elaboration, rich in glacial exteriors, than toward the essential idea of interpretive reform; Granville-Barker and Gordon Craig in England have made some limited innovations, some objective syntheses.

Displays and material simplifications, not rebellion against the past. It is this necessary revolution which we intend to provoke, because no one has had the artistic austerity to renovate the interpretive conception of the element to be expressed.

Our scenography is a monstrous thing. Today's scenographers, sterile whitewashers, still prowl around the dusty and stinking corners of classical architecture.

We must rebel and assert ourselves and say to our poet and musician friends: this action demands this stage rather than that one.

Let us be artists too, and no longer merely executors. Let us create the theatre, give life to the play with all the evocative power of our art.

It goes without saying that we need plays suited to our sensibility, which implies a more intense and synthetic conception in the scenic development of subjects.

Let's renovate the stage. The absolutely new feature that our innovation will give the theatre is *the abolition of the painted stage.* The stage will no longer be a colored backdrop, but an *uncolored electro-mechanical architecture, powerfully vitalized by chromatic emanations from a luminous source,* produced by electric reflectors, with multicolored panes of glass, arranged, coordinated analogically with the swing-mirror of each scenic action.

With the luminous irradiation of these sheaves, of these planes of colored lights, the dynamic combinations will give marvelous results of mutual permeation, of intersection of lights and shadows. From these will be born blank surrenders, corporalities luminous with exultation. These assemblages, these unreal shocks, this exuberance of sensations combined with dynamic stage architectures which will move, unleashing metallic arms, knocking over plastic frameworks, amidst an essentially new, modern noise, will augment the vital intensity of the scenic action.

On a stage illuminated in such a way the actors will gain unforeseen dynamic effects which are neglected or very seldom employed in today's theatres, mostly because of the ancient prejudice that one must imitate, represent reality.

What's the use?

Is it that the scenographers believe it absolutely necessary to represent this reality? Idiots! Don't you understand that your efforts, your useless realistic preoccupations have no effect other than that of diminishing the intensity and emotional content, which can be attained precisely through the interpretive equivalents of these realities, i.e., abstractions?

Let's create the theatre. In the above lines we have upheld the idea of a dynamic theatre as opposed to the static theatre of old; with the fundamental principles which we shall set forth, we intend not only to carry the theatre to its most advanced expression, but also to attribute the essential values which belong to it and which no one has thought of presenting till now.

Let's exchange the roles. Instead of the illuminated stage, let's create the *illuminant stage: luminous expression which will irradiate the colors demanded by the theatrical action with all its emotional power.*

The material means of expressing this illuminant stage consist in employing electrochemical colors, fluorescent tubes which have the chemical property of being susceptible to electric current and diffusing luminous colorations of all tonalities according to the combinations of fluorine with other such gases. The desired effects of luminosity will be obtained by stimulating these gases (systematically arranged according to the proper design on this immense sceno–dramatic architecture) with electric neon (ultraviolet) tubes. But the Futurist scenographic and choreographic evolution must not stop there. In the final synthesis human actors will no longer be tolerated, like children's jumping jacks, or today's super-marionettes recommended by recent reformers; neither one nor the other can sufficiently express the multiple aspects conceived by the playwright.

In the totally realizable époque of Futurism we shall see the luminous dynamic architectures of the stage emanate from chromatic incandescences which, mounting tragically or showing themselves voluptuously, will inevitably arouse new sensations and emotional values in the spectator.

Vibrations, luminous forms (produced by electric currents and colored gases) will wriggle and writhe dynamically, and these veritable actor-gases of an unknown theatre will have to replace living actors. By shrill whistles and strange noises these actor-gases will be able to give the unusual significations of theatrical interpretations quite well; they will be able to express these multiform emotive qualities with much more effectiveness than some celebrated actor or other can with his displays. These exhilarant, explosive gases will fill the audience with cheerfulness or terror and it will perhaps become an actor itself, too. But these words are not our last. We still have much to say. Let us first carry out what we have set forth above.

Note

From E. T. Kirby, *Total Theatre: A Critical Anthology*, New York: Dutton, 1969, pp. 89–95. Reprinted from *Archivi del Futurismo*, vol. I, Rome: De Luca Editore, translated by Diana Clemmons.

2.13 Theater, Circus, Variety (1924)

LÁSZLÓ MOHOLY-NAGY

Translated by Arthur S. Wensinger

1. The historical theater

THE HISTORICAL THEATER WAS essentially a disseminator of information or propaganda, or it was an articulated concentration of action (*Aktionskonzentration*) derived from events and doctrines in their broadest meaning – that is to say, as 'dramatized' legend, as religious (cultist) or political (proselytizing) propaganda, or as compressed action with a more or less transparent purpose behind it.

The theater differed from the eyewitness report, simple storytelling, didactic moralizing, or advertising copy through its own particular synthesis of the elements of presentation: SOUND, COLOR (LIGHT), MOTION, SPACE, FORM (OBJECTS AND PERSONS).

With these elements, in their accentuated but often uncontrolled interrelationships, the theater attempted to transmit an articulated experience.

In early epic drama (*Erzählungsdrama*) these elements were generally employed as illustration, subordinated to narration or propaganda. The next step in this evolution led to the drama of action (*Aktionsdrama*), where the elements of dynamic-dramatic movement began to crystallize: the theater of improvisation, the *commedia dell'arte*. These dramatic forms were progressively liberated from a central theme of logical, intellectual-emotional action which was no longer dominant. Gradually their moralizing and their tendentiousness disappeared in favor of an unhampered concentration on action: Shakespeare, the opera.

With August Stramm,[1] drama developed away from verbal context, from propaganda, and from character delineation, and toward explosive activism. Creative experiments with MOTION AND SOUND (speech) were made, based on the impetus of human sources of energy, that is, the 'passions.' Stramm's theater did not offer narrative material, but action and tempo, which, unpremeditated, sprang almost AUTOMATICALLY and in headlong succession from the human impulse for motion. But even in Stramm's case action was not altogether free from literary encumbrance.

'Literary encumbrance' is the result of the unjustifiable transfer of intellectualized material from the proper realm of literary effectiveness (novel, short story, etc.) to the stage, where it incorrectly remains a dramatic end in itself. The result is nothing more than literature if a reality or a potential reality, no matter how imaginative, is formulated or visually expressed without the creative forms peculiar only to the stage. It is not until the tensions concealed in the utmost economy of means are brought into universal and dynamic interaction that we have creative stagecraft (*Bühnengestaltung*). Even in recent times we have been deluded about the true value of

L. MOHOLY-NAGY   Human Mechanics (Variety)

Figure 19 Moholy-Nagy, *Human Mechanics (Variety)*. (Photographer: uncredited.)

creative stagecraft when revolutionary, social, ethical, or similar problems were unrolled with a great display of literary pomp and paraphernalia.

2. Attempts at a theater form for today
a) Theater of Surprises: Futurists, Dadaists, Merz[2]

In the investigation of any morphology, we proceed today from the all-inclusive functionalism of goal, purpose, and materials.

From this premise the FUTURISTS, EXPRESSIONISTS, and DADAISTS (MERZ) came to the conclusion that phonetic word relationships were more significant than other creative literary means, and that the logical–intellectual content (*das Logisch-Gedankliche*) of a work of literature was far from its primary aim. It was maintained that, just as in representational painting it was not the content as such, not the objects represented which were essential, but the interaction of colors, so in literature it was not the logical–intellectual content which belonged in the foreground, but the effects which arose from the word-sound relationships. In the case of some writers this idea has been extended (or possibly contracted) to the point where word relationships are transformed into

L. MOHOLY-NAGY   The Benevolent Gentlemen (Circus Scene)

Figure 20 Moholy-Nagy, *The Benevolent Gentleman (Circus Scene)*. (Photographer: uncredited.)

exclusively phonetic sound relationships, thereby totally fragmenting the word into conceptually disjointed vowels and consonants.

This was the origin of the Dadaist and Futurist 'Theater of Surprises,' a theater which aimed at the elimination of logical-intellectual (literary) aspects. Yet in spite of this, man, who until then had been the sole representative of logical, causal action and of vital mental activities, still dominated.

b) The Mechanized Eccentric (*Die mechanische Exzentrik*)

As a logical consequence of this there arose the need for a MECHANIZED ECCENTRIC, a concentration of stage action in its purest form (*eine Aktionskonzentration der Bühne in Reinkultur*). Man, who no longer should be permitted to represent himself as a phenomenon of spirit and mind through his intellectual and spiritual capacities, no longer has any place in this concentration of action. For, no matter how cultured he may be, his organism permits him at best only a certain range of action, dependent entirely on his natural body mechanism.

The effect of this body mechanism (*Körpermechanik*) (in circus performance and athletic events, for example) arises essentially from the spectator's astonishment or shock at the potentialities of his *own* organism as demonstrated to him by others. This is a subjective effect. Here the human body is the sole medium of configuration (*Gestaltung*). For the purposes of an objective *Gestaltung* of movement this medium is limited, the more so since it has constant reference to sensible and perceptive (i.e., again literary) elements. The inadequacy of 'human' *Exzentrik* led to the demand for a precise and fully controlled organization of form and motion, intended to be a synthesis of dynamically contrasting phenomena (space, form, motion, sound, and light). This is the Mechanized Eccentric.

3. The coming theater: Theater of Totality

Every form process or *Gestaltung* has its general as well as its particular premises, from which it must proceed in making use of its specific media. We might, therefore, clarify theater production (*Theatergestaltung*) if we investigated the nature of its highly controversial media: the human *word* and the human action, and, at the same time, considered the endless possibilities open to their creator – man.

The origins of MUSIC as conscious composition can be traced back to the melodic recitations of the heroic saga. When music was systematized, permitting only the use of HARMONIES (KLÄNGE) and excluding so-called SOUNDS (GERÄUSCHE), the only place left for a special sound form (*Geräuschgestaltung*) was in literature, particularly in poetry. This was the underlying idea from which the Expressionists, Futurists, and Dadaists proceeded in composing their sound-poems (*Lautgedichte*). But today, when music has been broadened to admit sounds of all kinds, the sensory-mechanistic effect of sound interrelationships is no longer a monopoly of poetry. It belongs, as much as do harmonies (*Töne*), to the realm of music, much in the same way that the task of painting, seen as color creation, is to organize clearly primary (apperceptive)[3] color effect. Thus the error of the Futurists, the Expressionists, the Dadaists, and all those who built on such foundations becomes clear. As an example: the idea of an *Exzentrik* which is ONLY mechanical.

It must be said, however, that those ideas, in contradistinction to a literary-illustrative viewpoint, have unquestionably advanced creative theater precisely because they were diametrically opposed. They canceled out the predominance of the exclusively logical-intellectual values. But once the predominance has been broken, the associative processes and the language of man, and consequently man himself in his totality as a formative medium for the stage, may not be barred from it. To be sure, he is no longer to be pivotal – as he is in traditional theater – but is to be employed ON AN EQUAL FOOTING WITH THE OTHER FORMATIVE MEDIA.

Man as the most active phenomenon of life is indisputably one of the most effective elements of a dynamic stage production (*Bühnengestaltung*), and therefore he justifies on functional grounds the utilization of his totality of action, speech, and thought. With his intellect, his dialectic, his adaptability to any situation by virtue of his control over his physical and mental powers, he is – when used in any concentration of action (*Aktionskonzentration*) – destined to be primarily a configuration of these powers.

And if the stage didn't provide him full play for these potentialities, it would be imperative to create an adequate vehicle.

But this utilization of man must be clearly differentiated from his appearance heretofore in traditional theater. While there he was only the interpreter of a literarily conceived individual or type, in the new THEATER OF TOTALITY he will use the spiritual and physical means at his disposal PRODUCTIVELY and from his own INITIATIVE submit to the overall action process.

While during the Middle Ages (and even today) the center of gravity in theater production lay in the representation of the various *types* (hero, harlequin, peasant, etc.), it is the task of the FUTURE ACTOR to discover and activate that which is COMMON to all men.

In the plan of such a theater the traditionally 'meaningful' and causal interconnections can NOT play the major role. In the consideration of stage setting as an *art form*, we must learn from the creative artist that, just as it is impossible to ask what a man (as organism) is or stands for, it is inadmissible to ask the same question of a contemporary nonobjective picture which likewise is a *Gestaltung*, that is, an organism.

The contemporary painting exhibits a multiplicity of color and surface interrelationships, which gain their effect, on the one hand, from their conscious and logical statement of problems, and on the other, from the unanalyzable intangibles of creative intuition.

In the same way, the Theater of Totality with its multifarious complexities of light, space, plane, form, motion, sound, man – and with all the possibilities for varying and combining these elements – must be an ORGANISM.

Thus the process of integrating man into creative stage production must be unhampered by moralistic tendentiousness or by problems of science or the INDIVIDUAL. Man may be active only as the bearer of those functional elements which are organically in accordance with his specific nature.

It is self-evident, however, that all *other* means of stage production must be given positions of effectiveness equal to man's, who as a living psychophysical organism, as the producer of incomparable climaxes and infinite variations, demands of the coformative factors a high standard of quality.

4. How shall the Theater of Totality be realized?

One of two points of view still important today holds that theater is the concentrated activation (*Aktionskonzentration*) of sound, light (color), space, form, and motion. Here man as co-actor is not necessary, since in our day equipment can be constructed which is far more capable of executing the *purely mechanical* role of man than man himself.

The other, more popular view will not relinquish the magnificent instrument which is man, even though no one has yet solved the problem of how to employ him as a creative medium on the stage.

Is it possible to include his human, logical functions in a present-day concentration of action on the stage, without running the risk of producing a copy from nature and without falling prey to Dadaist or Merz characterization, composed of an eclectic patchwork whose seeming order is purely arbitrary?

The creative arts have discovered pure media for their constructions: the primary relationships of color, mass, material, etc. But how can we integrate a sequence of human movements and thoughts on an equal footing with the controlled, 'absolute' elements of sound, light (color), form, and motion? In this regard only summary suggestions can be made to the creator of the new theater (*Theatergestalter*). For example, the REPETITION of a thought by many actors, with identical words and with identical or varying intonation and cadence, could be employed as a means of creating synthetic (i.e., unifying) creative theater. (This would be the CHORUS – but not the attendant and passive chorus of antiquity!) Or mirrors and optical equipment could be used to project the gigantically enlarged faces and gestures of the actors, while their voices could be amplified to correspond with the visual MAGNIFICATION. Similar effects can be obtained from the SIMULTANEOUS, SYNOPTICAL, and SYNACOUSTICAL reproduction of thought (with motion pictures, phonographs, loud-speakers), or from the reproduction of thoughts suggested by a construction of variously MESHING GEARS (*eine* ZAHNRADARTIG INEINANDERGREIFENDE *Gedankengestaltung*).

Independent of work in music and acoustics, the literature of the future will create its own 'harmonies,' at first primarily adapted to its own media, but with far-reaching implications for others. These will surely exercise an influence on the word and thought constructions of the stage.

This means, among other things, that the phenomena of the subconscious and dreams of fantasy and reality, which up to now were central to the so called 'INTIMATE ART THEATER' ('KAMMER-SPIELE'), may no longer be predominant. And even if the conflicts arising from today's complicated social patterns, from the world-wide organization of technology, from pacifist-utopian and other kinds of revolutionary movements, can have a place in the art of the stage, they will be significant only in a transitional period, since their treatment belongs properly to the realms of literature, politics, and philosophy.

We envision TOTAL STAGE ACTION (GESAMTBÜHNENAKTION) as a great dynamic-rhythmic process, which can compress the greatest clashing masses or accumulations of media – as qualitative and quantitative tensions – into elemental form. Part of this would be the use of simultaneously inter-penetrating sets of contrasting relationships, which are of minor importance in themselves, such as: the tragicomic, the grotesque-serious, the trivial-monumental; hydraulic spectacles; acoustical and other 'pranks'; and so on. Today's CIRCUS, OPERETTA, VAUDEVILLE, the CLOWNS in America and elsewhere (Chaplin, Fratellini) have accomplished great things, both in this respect and in eliminating the subjective – even if the process has been naïve and often more superficial than incisive. Yet it would be just as superficial if we were to dismiss great performances and 'shows' in this genre with the word *Kitsch*. It is high time to state once and for all that the much disdained masses, despite their 'academic backwardness,' often exhibit the soundest instincts and preferences. Our task will always remain the creative understanding of the true, and not the imagined, needs.

5. The means

Every *Gestaltung* or creative work should be an unexpected and new organism, and it is natural and incumbent on us to draw the material for surprise effects from our daily living. Nothing is more effective than the exciting new possibilities offered by the familiar and yet not properly evaluated elements of modern life – that is, its idiosyncrasies: individuation, classification, mechanization. With this in mind, it is possible to arrive at a proper understanding of stagecraft through an investigation of creative media other than man-as-actor himself.

In the future, SOUND EFFECTS will make use of various acoustical equipment driven electrically or by some other mechanical means. Sound waves issuing from unexpected sources – for example, a speaking or singing arc lamp, loud-speakers under the seats or beneath the floor of the auditorium, the use of new amplifying systems – will raise the audience's acoustic surprise-threshold so much that unequal effects in other areas will be disappointing.

Color (LIGHT) must undergo even greater transformation in this respect than sound.

Developments in painting during the past decades have created the organization of absolute color values and, as a consequence, the supremacy of pure and luminous chromatic tones. Naturally the monumentality and the lucid balance of their harmonies will not tolerate the actor with indistinct or splotchy make-up and tattered costuming, a product of misunderstood Cubism, Futurism, etc. The use of precision-made metallic masks and costumes and those of various other composition materials will thus become a matter of course. The pallid face, the subjectivity of expression, and the gestures of the actor in a colored stage environment are therefore eliminated without impairing the effective contrast between the human body and any mechanical construction. Films can also be projected onto various surfaces and further experiments in space illumination will be devised. This will constitute the new ACTION OF LIGHT, which by means of modern technology will use the most intensified contrasts to guarantee itself a position of importance equal to that of all other theater media. We have not yet begun to realize the potential of light for sudden or blinding illumination, for flare effects, for phosphorescent effects, for bathing the auditorium in light synchronized with climaxes or with the total extinguishing of lights on the stage. All this, of course, is thought of in a sense totally different from anything in current traditional theater.

From the time that stage objects became mechanically movable, the generally traditional, horizontally structured organization of movement in space has been enriched by the possibility of vertical motion. Nothing stands in the way of making use of complex APPARATUS such as film, automobile, elevator, airplane, and other machinery, as well as optical instruments, reflecting-equipment, and so on. The current demand for dynamic construction will be satisfied in this way, even though it is still only in its first stages.

There would be a further enrichment if the present isolation of the stage could be eliminated. In today's theater, STAGE AND SPECTATOR are too much separated, too obviously divided into active and passive, to be able to produce creative relationships and reciprocal tensions.

It is time to produce a kind of stage activity which will no longer permit the masses to be silent spectators, which will not only excite them inwardly but will let them *take hold and participate* – actually allow them to fuse with the action on the stage at the peak of cathartic ecstasy.

To see that such a process is not chaotic, but that it develops with control and organization, will be one of the tasks of the thousand-eyed NEW DIRECTOR, equipped with all the modern means of understanding and communication.

It is clear that the present peep-show stage is not suitable for such organized motion.

The next form of the advancing theater – in cooperation with future authors – will probably answer the above demands with SUSPENDED BRIDGES AND DRAWBRIDGES running horizontally, diagonally, and vertically within the space of the theater; with platform stages built far into the auditorium; and so on. Apart from rotating sections, the stage will have movable space constructions and DISKLIKE AREAS, in order to bring certain action moments on the stage into prominence, as in film 'close-ups.' In place of today's periphery of orchestra loges, a runway joined to the stage could be built to establish – by means of a more or less caliper-like embrace – a closer connection with the audience.

The possibilities for a VARIATION OF LEVELS OF MOVABLE PLANES on the stage of the future would contribute to a genuine organization of space. Space will then no longer consist of the interconnections of planes in the old meaning, which was able to conceive of architectonic delineation of space only as an enclosure formed by opaque surfaces. The new space originates from free-standing surfaces or from linear definition of planes (WIRE FRAMES, ANTENNAS), so that the surfaces stand at times in a very free relationship to one another, without the need of any direct contact.

As soon as an intense and penetrating concentration of action can be functionally realized, there will develop simultaneously the corresponding auditorium ARCHITECTURE. There will also appear COSTUMES designed to emphasize function and costumes which are conceived only for single moments of action and capable of sudden transformations.

There will arise an enhanced *control* over all formative media, unified in a harmonious effect and built into an organism of perfect equilibrium.

Notes

1. August Stramm (1874–1915) was a Westphalian poet and dramatist and the strongest of the members of the circle known as the *Sturmdichter*. His works belong to the early phase of Expressionism and are in a radically elliptical, powerful, and antisyntactical style. – *Translator*.
2. The phenomenon known as *Merz* is closely connected with the Dadaist movement of the post-World War I period in Germany and Switzerland. The term was coined in 1919 by the artist Kurt Schwitters and came from one of his collages in which was incorporated a scrap of newspaper with only the center part of the word 'kom*merz*iell' on it. A whole series of his collages was called *Merzbilder*. From 1923 to 1932, with Arp, Lissitzsky, Mondrian, and many others, Schwitters published the magazine *Merz*; and at about the same period the Merz Poets caused a great furor. The movement was characterized by playfulness, earnest experimentalism, and what seems to have been a great need for self-expression and for shocking the bourgeoisie. – *Translator*.
3. 'Apperceptive' signifies here, in contrast to 'associative,' an elementary step in observation and conceptualization (psychophysical assimilation), e.g., to assimilate a color = apperceptive process. The human eye reacts without previous experience to red with green, blue with yellow, etc. An object = assimilation of color + matter + form = connection with previous experience = associative process. – *Translator*.

From *The Theatre of the Bauhaus*, ed. Walter Gropius and A. Wensinger, Baltimore: Johns Hopkins University Press, 1961, reprinted by Wesleyan University Press, 1996, pp. 17–48.

Part 3
Early Political Theatres

Timeline

	Social, cultural and political context	Theatre
1848	*The Communist Manifesto*: Karl Marx and Friedrich Engels	
1859	*The Origin of Species*: Charles Darwin	
1861–2	Manifesto on the emancipation of serfs and social unrest in Russia	
1869	John Stuart Mill: *The Subjection of Women*	
1892	Strikes by and massacres of workers in Russia	
1893	Independent Labour Party founded in Britain	
1903	Emmeline Pankhurst founds the Women's Social and Political Union	
1904		*John Bull's Other Island*: George Bernard Shaw
1905	Polish Revolution First Russian Revolution	
1908		Actresses' Franchise League founded in London
1909	*Marriage as a Trade*: Cicely Hamilton Violence starts in the women's suffrage movement in Britain, including arson attacks and damage to buildings	*How the Vote Was Won*: Cicely Hamilton and Christopher St John Campaign against state censorship by British playwrights and theatre workers
1910	Mexican Revolution	
1914	Start of the First World War (1914–18)	
1916	Easter Rising in Dublin suppressed by the British Army	
1917	Russian Revolution; Tsar of Russia abdicates America enters the First World War	
1918	End of the First World War German Revolution	*Baal*: Bertolt Brecht (unproduced until 1923)
1919	Treaty of Versailles	
1920	The League of Nations formed	
1921	Irish Free State established	
1923		The Blue Blouse theatre collective (1923–8)
1924	Lenin dies, Joseph Stalin becomes leader of the Soviet Union (Russia)	
1926	British General Strike	Workers' Theatre Movement (1926–35)

	Social, cultural and political context	Theatre
1927	Hunger marches by the unemployed (until 1936) (UK) First 'talking' movie	*Hoppla, We're Alive!*: Ernst Toller Brecht collaborates with Piscator
1929	Wall Street Crash (USA) leading to world economic crisis	
1930		*The Modern Theatre is the Epic Theatre* (essay): Bertolt Brecht
1933	Hitler becomes Chancellor of Germany Roosevelt elected President of the United States (1933–1945)	Brecht leaves Germany (until 1949), under fear of Nazi persecution, eventually finding exile in the USA. His best-known plays, including *Mother Courage and Her Children*, *Life of Galileo* and *The Good Person of Szechwan*, written during this period
1934		Ronald Gow and Walter Greenwood: *Love on the Dole*
1935		Federal Theatre Project (USA, 1935–9), formed out of Roosevelt's 'New Deal' programme
1936	Start of the Spanish Civil War (1936–9) First public television broadcast	Unity Theatre (London) established
1938	House Committee on Un-American Activities established (USA, 1938–75)	*Our Town*: Thornton Wilder Bertolt Brecht writes *The Street Scene* and *The Popular and the Realistic* (essays): published respectively in 1950 and 1958
1939	Start of the Second World War (1939–45)	
1945	End of the Second World War Atomic bomb dropped on Hiroshima and Nagasaki Labour Party wins landslide general election victory	Theatre Workshop (UK) established, their first production Ewan MacColl's *Johnny Noble*
1947		*E=mc²*: Hallie Flanagan Davis

Introduction

MAGGIE B. GALE AND JOHN F. DEENEY

As soon as the public and the theatre have worked together to achieve a common desire for a revolutionary culture, almost any bourgeois play, no matter whether it demonstrates the decay of bourgeois society or whether it brings out the capitalist principle with special clarity, will serve to strengthen the notion of the class struggle and to add to our revolutionary understanding of its historical necessity. (Erwin Piscator 1920 [Piscator 1980: 45])

PARTS 1 AND 2 of this anthology have covered periods of theatrical activity inspired by some kind of radical or revolutionary agenda for theatre. The Naturalists, no matter how 'conservative' their work appears to be today, were breaking away from the dominant Romantic traditions of the middle-class theatres of the mid- to late nineteenth century. Similarly, the Symbolists believed that the Naturalist aesthetic limited the expressive possibilities of the stage. The historical avant-garde, in all of its manifestations, believed that the function of theatre went beyond questions of entertainment or education. For them the artwork's revolutionary potential lay in the investigation of both the function of theatre and performance and the deliberate and vibrant challenge to existing aesthetic conventions. Whilst the movements examined in the previous two parts cross over with the period covered here – roughly from the early 1910s to the late 1940s – the materials examined in this part directly engage with *materialist* politics and ideology. This imperative created a reconceptualization of theatre's relationship with its audience, by primarily presenting the world as a place upon which *we can act*, that we can change, that we have the agency to affect, rather than simply as something which *acts upon us*.

Ibsen, Strindberg, Chekhov and others, such as George Bernard Shaw with the 'play of ideas', in the later nineteenth and early twentieth centuries engaged with the possibility of a theatre which could present and discuss the social problems of their day. However, the political theatres we examine here are directly concerned with social and political revolution, equality, citizenship, class difference and social agency. If Naturalism was enclosed by the domestic setting (see Part 1), the political theatres of the early twentieth century sought a revolution in dramatic form and theatrical presentation which capitalized on the theatre's status, disruptive potential and aesthetic power within the public space. Similar to the historical avant-garde (see Part 2), the political theatres we examine here demanded a fundamental questioning of the audience's relationship to theatre and, in turn, to the world.

Not all of the plays in this part come out of the shared desire for a revolutionary culture as expressed by Piscator (quoted above). However, they do all share a radical revisioning of the relationship between the individual and the society in which they live. Just as the Naturalists were concerned with the consequences of industrialization for the individual, so, too, the political theatres of the 1920s to 1940s reflected the social unrest which many saw as linked to the exploitative and alienating society created by industrialization.

From the turn of the twentieth century, there were 'revolutions' and political uprisings, the like of which we have not seen since – all over Europe and in South America. Revolutions in

Poland (1905), Mexico (1910), Russia (1905 and 1917) and after the end of the First World War in Germany in 1918 – were both direct responses to and motivated by a newly organized form of class struggle. This struggle was shaped by the writings of Karl Marx (1818–83), who, along with other key nineteenth-century thinkers, such as Friedrich Engels (1820–95), offered a materialist analysis of history that denaturalized a social hierarchy which placed power in the hands of a small social elite: the ruling classes. A materialist historical analysis does not see history simply in terms of the official chronology of events: the 'progression' of the monarchy and ruling elite, or of a series of wars. Rather it places the ruling elite and the proletariat – the working classes – in relation to one another, within an antagonistic and potentially revolutionary framework of cause and effect. Again, although the earlier plays in this part do not present as strong a critique of the existing class system as the subsequent plays, they link injustice to a capitalist system and see the latter as a political system predicated on economic inequality.

The introduction to Part 2 of this anthology implies the fluid movement of culture between European cities in the 1910s and 1920s, as well as the impact of the regrouping of European states during the late nineteenth century. The First World War (1914–18) in some ways reduced the levels of fluidity in terms of cultural exchange; nevertheless, the later plays in this part are influenced by German and Russian ideas about the relationship of the political to the production of art and culture. As Piscator implies above, the development of political theatre cannot happen without the development of a new audience. The political theatres of the 1910s to 1940s were not, by and large, written for a commercialized theatre industry, although some such as *Love on the Dole* (3.3) found huge success there. The political theatres we engage with here were largely more makeshift, did not aspire to literary sophistication, and were inspired not by economic imperatives but by primarily political and educative ones. In addition, as with the theatre and performance in other parts of this anthology, the *practice* of political theatre was as important as the product.

Writing in the mid-1970s, Michael Kirby made the distinction between political theatre which engages in issues of government or party politics, and that which aims simply to 'change the beliefs and opinions of the spectator' (Kirby 1975: 132). He also notes however that some political theatres do 'not proselytise', are 'not didactic' and 'do not support particular alternatives' (ibid: 135). This broad framework for the definition of political theatre is one we adopt here. But we also note the move to critique, in the 1980s and 1990s, the relationship between form and content in the art and political equation, whereby realism is seen as a coercive form *per se*.

The term 'political theatre' is a contentious one which is in part why this section names political theatres in the plural. During the 1980s and 1990s, scholarship differentiated between political theatres influenced by Brecht – theatres of the political left – and other theatres which were political in content and perhaps explored political issues, but did not challenge or develop traditional or dominant theatrical forms. For some the lack of an engagement in a rethinking of form meant that there was an inherent acceptance of the status quo – thus theatre produced without this engagement might fail somehow to qualify for the term 'political'. In addition, Holderness draws attention to intention in the definition of political theatre:

Theatre may be 'political' without becoming 'political theatre', in the sense that a play may represent political matters or address political issues, in exactly the same way as a play can represent love … or poverty or madness … the politics of a truly political theatre must be a matter of conscious choice and deliberate intention. (Holderness 1992: 2–3)

What Holderness does here is to make a distinction between what may or may not be 'truly' political theatre. What we wish to do in this part, however, is to suggest, like Kirby, that it is possible to see the history of theatre in the twentieth century as providing a spectrum of political theatres – some of which make use of, in Raymond Williams's terms, a dominant cultural form, and some of which utilize an emergent one (Williams 2005: 40). This part therefore includes plays and performance texts which are political in each of the senses implied above by Holderness – the part moves from texts which explore social worlds through a directly politically oriented lens, to those which manipulate the theatrical form to create what Walter Benjamin (cultural critic and friend of Brecht) calls theatre as a *politicized art* (see below).

Political realisms in England – *How the Vote Was Won* (3.1)

Originally created in the form of a pamphlet (Spender and Hayman 1985: 19), Hamilton and St John's play *How the Vote Was Won* (1909, 3.1) was embedded in a theatrical/political movement specifically dedicated, in a society where women's citizenship did not extend to their having political power through the right to vote, to the promotion of 'votes for women'. Following in the footsteps of Shaw (see Innes 1998), and in line with other playwrights experimenting with the 'play of ideas', Hamilton and St John's play theatricalized a complex and high-profile political debate. Hamilton, the author of *Marriage as a Trade* (1909), which provided a radical investigation of the inequities of the economic foundations of marriage, was a key member of the Women Writers' Suffrage League. Both Hamilton and St John were involved to varying degrees in the Actresses' Franchise League, a politically inspired theatre organization set up in 1908 to enable and promote the involvement of women from the theatre profession in the struggle for the vote (see Holledge 1981 and Stowell 1992). The play has minimal production requirements and therefore has the potential to tour at low cost and with considerable flexibility – one of the common features of later 'political' plays. *How the Vote Was Won* was originally produced in the English Edwardian commercial theatre. Strangely for a play which contains such overt propaganda, it was a great critical success. Thus, the *Pall Mall Gazette* noted that, 'The fact that it is so acutely controversial is not at all against it – is, in fact, a virtue rather than a defect, for the Theatre of Ideas is upon us' (Spender and Hayman 1985: 20). Other critics praised the play for its fast-paced humour and for the ways in which Horace, the clerk from Brixton, is outwitted by the very same women he considers to be his social and intellectual inferiors. What this reception does not evidence, however, is the extraordinary levels of cultural anxiety which the suffragettes created in their campaign for votes for women: some genuinely thought that giving women the vote would unleash a completely unmanageable political force – a 'petticoat' government (see Ramelson 1976). Of course this political campaign was part of a general movement to increase the levels of participation in the formal political arena – working-class men in Britain did not receive the full vote until 1918 and women, not universally, until 1928. The message of the play is no less radical for the positive reception which it originally garnered. *How the Vote Was Won*, as with much suffrage drama, made a strategic intervention into a dominant theatrical form: comedy and farce, to some extent the staple of the commercial theatre of the day, are made subversive through the politically propagandistic message the play explores.

The premise of the play is that there is to be a General Strike by women. In a political environment where women are being told that they do not or cannot support themselves economically, but are, rather, under the financial care of their men, they decide to go on strike and return to the homes of their male relatives or to the state-funded poor houses and workhouses. The opening of the play sees Horace's wife Ethel being informed of the ensuing strike and left to fend for herself by her female servants. Disbelieving the situation, as the play progresses, she slowly realizes, as does Horace, that the women – his sister, his aunt, his niece, his cousin and even a very distant female relation – mean business. They all descend upon his household and present the argument that if men *really* support women economically, then why on earth should women work at all. As the country grinds to a halt – England cannot survive without the input of female labour – so Horace's politics reverse and he ends up, albeit in order to return his life to his own control, presenting himself as the hero of the hour:

HORACE: You may depend on me – all of you – to see justice done. When you want a thing done, get a man to do it! Votes for Women! (3.1: 318)

The play performs a dialectic. The thesis – that women work for a living contributing to the state and therefore should have equal citizenship – is placed directly against the antithesis – that women are the weaker sex reliant upon male custodianship and therefore in receipt of political agency *through* men. The synthesis, that men and women's labour is interconnected and interdependent, is played out theatrically through the use of comedy and farce.

Realism as a 'prison house' form?

Some late-twentieth-century literary theory suggests that realism, here the reproduction of observable reality in theatrical performance, is a 'prison house' form: that realism cannot be used to present a radical agenda because it presents the world 'as it is' rather than presenting it as being alterable (see Belsey 1985; Case 1989; Dolan 1988 and 1990). Stowell, in her article 'Rehabilitating Realism' (3.10), argues for a more subtle and layered analysis of the power of realism to address the issue of social change in theatre. She suggests that presenting the world 'as it is' does not negate the possibility of a sophisticated reading of theatre and performance, whereby the audience can understand the distinction 'between reproduction and reinforcement' (3.10: 485). Here, what Stowell is foregrounding is the capacity of an audience to acknowledge 'the possibility of cumulative experience … the significance of a play's process' (ibid). Audiences don't necessarily accept drama as 'truth', but rather as a perspective upon it. Stowell counteracts, what became in the 1980s, the dominant perception of realism as being a form characterized by 'closure', by its inability to offer resistant readings of the world and through prescribed meaning in the mind of the spectator. Here, closure refers to the ways in which a text appears to offer no alternative to the status quo. For example, in *Three Sisters* (1.3) we are exposed to their world and gain a greater understanding of it, but one might argue that the sisters are trapped within a fatalistic universe in which they lack agency. When we make use of Stowell's position it is easy to see *How the Vote Was Won*, despite its conventional form, as political theatre which offers a resistant reading of a dominant ideology. At the end of the play, Horace is still convinced that he is from a superior sex, but has in fact joined the struggle for votes for women, a struggle which at the beginning of the play he found abhorrent.

Carlson (3.6) writes of the suffrage theatre, which proliferated during the first decade of the twentieth century in England in particular, as an 'example of a politically inspired theatre', which 'made new assumptions about theatrical space, domestic space and public space simultaneously' (3.6: 442). Thus, in *How the Vote Was Won*, the authors simplify the staging requirements of a 'domestic' play and explore the possibility of social change through the investigation of the damaging effects of an ideology based on gender inequality.

Love on the Dole (3.3)

Whilst *How the Vote Was Won* explores the gendered dynamics of inequality, Gow and Greenwood's *Love on the Dole* (1934) focuses on issues of class inequality in a post-First World War, post-General Strike (1926), post-Wall Street Crash (1929) northern English town. The economic crises of the late 1920s had bought both England and America almost to the point of industrial standstill. During the 1920s and 1930s England and Scotland saw the beginnings of a politicized theatre movement influenced by the Blue Blouse agitprop theatre from Russia and the ideas of Piscator and Meyerhold (which we discuss later in this introduction). Gow and Greenwood's play, as with Hamilton and St John's, does not borrow directly from the theatre theory of figures such as Piscator or Brecht. It is no less political, however, because the narrative takes us through a process of understanding the injustices of a particular economic system, through the downfall and destruction of Larry Meath. The form the play takes is one of a realist, well-made play, with the classical fall of the hero through the progression of the three acts. If Zolaesque and Ibsenite Naturalism dramatized the hold of the family unit over the individual (see Part 1: Introduction), then Greenwood and Gow show the traditional patriarchal order in disarray. Greenwood, who wrote the original novel from which the play was adapted, came from Salford in north-west England (Hanky Park in the play), and was from a family which had been impoverished during the economic crisis of the 1920s – he had first-hand experience of the world about which he was writing.

Love on the Dole opens with a speaker, offstage in a public space, decrying the pitfalls of capitalism:

unemployment and pauperdom, that is the legacy of the Industrial Revolution. That is the price we pay for the system. And that is the price you'll go on paying till you waken up to the fact that the remedy's in your own hands. You've got votes – why don't you use them? Why don't you think? (3.3: 367).

Gow and Greenwood frame their story of a northern family destroyed by economic recession with an analysis of the class system and a call to action. The fate of the Hardcastle family might be seen as a microcosm of the conditions of the English working classes in the interwar period. By the end of the play, both the family patriarch and the son are offered work, and an escape from poverty, through Sally's acceptance of a job from the local business magnate. The implication is that her job involves more than labour, and that she has had to 'sell' not only her soul, but her body, in order to escape from the cycle of poverty in which the residents of Hanky Park live. Her romantic attachment to Larry Meath, a revolutionary thinker, is brought to a sudden halt by his death during a demonstration which goes horribly wrong. Interestingly, as in *How the Vote Was Won*, the play explores the value of female labour within the context of a traditionally patriarchal culture. Hugely successful on tour and in London's West End, the play was adapted into a very successful film starring Deborah Kerr in 1941. The significance of *Love on the Dole* is the way in which it synthesizes an analysis of class, gender and social deprivation. It achieved this at a time when the majority of plays in the British commercial theatre not only centred around the lives of the middle and upper classes, but rarely contained working-class characters in more than stereotyped or derisory roles – servants, shop workers and so on. The play made use of the 'prison house' *form* of realism, but, like the earlier suffrage play, it subverts conventional content, paving the way for a theatre which engages far more with the lives of the majority as opposed to the elite. Thus, although the form is not innovative in the way that the theatre we will go on to explore appears to be, it is a play which, as Piscator states above, rehearses the potential of a 'common desire for a revolutionary culture'. The play anticipates the move to a more socially engaged theatre in the late 1950s and 1960s – with writers such as Shelagh Delaney (*A Taste of Honey*, 1958) in England and Lorraine Hansberry (*A Raisin in the Sun*, 1959) in the United States.

Brecht and realism in revolt

The work we explore in the next section of this introduction connects more strongly with what current theatre history classes as 'political theatre' – where the dramaturgical and theatrical form is heavily influenced by Piscator and Brecht and also by Russian theatrical innovations such as those developed by Meyerhold. Generically, here the means of production and the function of the illusory qualities of the theatrical event – particularly those associated with Naturalism – are deconstructed and dismantled in favour of a practice that, through acknowledging its own theatrical and fictive qualities, develops new ways in which to represent and engage with the contemporary world.

Vsevolod Meyerhold (1874–1940) was a key practitioner and theorist in the development of twentieth-century theatre. Beginning his theatrical career as an actor in Stanislavski's and Nemirovich-Danchenko's newly formed Moscow Art Theatre in 1898, Meyerhold eventually came to see the Art Theatre's 'fourth wall' aesthetic as limiting the creative possibilities of the stage. From 1902, and now as a director, Meyerhold began developing a practice that foregrounded the theatre's very theatricality. Not only hugely influenced by the classics and the contemporary Symbolist dramatists such as Maeterlinck (see Part 1), Meyerhold also turned to theatrical and performance forms such as *commedia dell'arte* and the circus (see 2.13) that counteracted an emphasis on individual psychology. He experimented with anti-illusionistic staging methods, established the use of a 'forestage' (built over the orchestra pit and extending into the auditorium) and was responsible for importing Soviet-inspired 'constructivism' – the movement that emphasized an artwork's functionality and social objective – into stage design. 'Biomechanics' was the highly physicalized system of actor-training that Meyerhold began to formally develop in the 1920s. It emphasized not only the 'social dimension' to the actor's work, but how the expressive possibilities of acting were rooted in a scientific understanding of the interrelationship between 'intention', 'realization' and 'reaction' (see Leach 2004). If the 1917 Russian Revolution garnered Meyerhold's full support, then the emancipatory promise that this event held was reflected by Meyerhold in a theatre that uniquely sought to fuse the poetic, the popular and the political. With productions such as *The Government Inspector* (staged 1926), Meyerhold – not untypically – treated Gogol's original text as a blueprint open to adaptation. His aim 'was to combine in unexpected ways grotesque contradictions, a broken rhythm, the forestage, stock characters in stock situations, improvising actors, and a noisy, engaged audience' (ibid: 74). Despite his early support for the revolution, Meyerhold was an outspoken opponent of Socialist Realism (see below) and was eventually murdered by the state in the Stalinist purges of the 1940s.

Unlike much of the work discussed in this introduction, it is perhaps the more 'formal' aspects of Meyerhold's experimental and modernist interventions that are most relevant to a discussion of 'political theatre'. His use of constructivist design and the 'forestage', for example, clearly anticipates aspects of both Piscator and Brecht's practice. However, Meyerhold's rejection of theatrical realism was, like those who followed him, not concerned with formal innovation *per se*, but founded on the critical issue of *how* the theatre might effectively mediate contemporary realities.

Brecht shared many of Meyerhold's concerns and for him the realist project was limited in terms of its potential political efficacy by the formalistic boundaries of the well-made play. Brecht is often seen as being directly anti-realist, but in fact his evolving theatre practice demonstrates a deeper and more complex engagement with realism and the modern drama. Brecht's 'realism', which transformed the German theatre, developed in part alongside a Stalinist-Russian appropriation of realism – Socialist Realism – which narrowly redrew the form in terms of the singular and premeditated social messages it could convey in stark state-approved terms: Socialist Realism required the presentation of the 'real' as the state both perceived it and wanted it to be projected through theatre. It is important, therefore, not to confuse Brecht's political agenda around realism with state-approved Stalinist artworks.

In his essay *The Street Scene* (3.8), Brecht points to developments in German theatre after the First World War, whereby practitioners made use of banners, choruses, film and projection to create what became known as 'Epic' theatre. He draws a distinction between 'Epic' and 'Dramatic' theatre by means of pointing to the opposing ways in which narrative functions. In Epic theatre 'narrative' is opposed to 'plot', 'argument' to 'suggestion' and 'reason' to 'feeling'. Whereas in 'Dramatic' theatre, 'thought determines being' and 'man is unalterable', in Epic theatre, 'social being determines thought' and 'man is able to alter' (Brecht 2001: 37). Epic theatre borrows from the classical canon in the way in which it expands narrative to deal with not only the specifics of everyday and domestic life – the microcosmic – but gives the broader macrocosmic picture of social relations as they are conditioned by economic factors. Thus characters are presented in an evolving social and political context. Epic theatre pivots on the relationship between cause and effect, narrative is often episodic and the flow is broken by interruption, focusing our direct attention away from the dramatic events. We might be drawn out of the action in order to critically reflect rather than empathize. This Brecht calls the *Verfremdungseffekt* – variously translated as the A-Effect, the alienation effect and distancation – 'a technique of taking the human social incidents to be portrayed and labelling them as something striking, something that calls for explanation, is not to be taken for granted, not just natural' (3.8: 472). Thus all events on stage within Epic theatre have an intentional 'socially practical significance' (ibid: 470).

Discussions of Brecht's practice have often focused on the material aesthetics and self-conscious display of theatrical elements, such as direct address, the use of placards, the use of narrative-breaking song and so on. However, it is important to distinguish between aesthetics – the choices made in terms of presentation – and what might be called here, for our purposes, 'method' – the choices made in terms of what is to be represented and the cumulative effects of these choices (see Jameson 1998). Brecht was as interested in the social and political function of theatre as he was in unpicking the ways in which the presentation of theatre might be revisioned. He was not anti-realist, therefore, but wanted to make use of realist modes in a more creative, sophisticated and revolutionary way:

> Realist writing, of which history offers many widely varying examples, is likewise conditioned by the question of how, when and for what class it is made use of ... Our conception of *realism* needs to be broad and political, free from aesthetic restrictions and independent of convention. *Realist* means: laying bare society's causal network/ showing up the dominant viewpoint as the viewpoint of the dominators/writing from the standpoint of the class which has prepared the broadest solutions for the most pressing problems afflicting human society/emphasises the dynamics of development/concrete and so as to encourage abstraction. (Brecht 2001: 109)

Terry Eagleton argues in *The Author as Producer* (3.11) that Brecht wanted to 'extend' realism's 'scope', as he notes that for Brecht realism is 'less a specific literary style or *genre* ... than a kind of art which discovers social laws and developments'. Thus, realism 'is quite compatible with the widest uses of fantasy and invention' (3.11: 492). Theatre can offer social and political critique at the same time as tapping into the 'non-real', the imaginary and the entertaining. Brecht constantly emphasized the necessity for *Spaß* – fun – in efficacious theatre practice, and a kind of 'realism in revolt' was one way in which he saw this could be achieved.

Brecht and Benjamin's reconfiguration of the function and practice of theatre

Although Brecht focused on the possibilities of theatre's consciousness-raising potential, he was also concerned to capitalize upon its power to entertain; he did not separate the two functions. In *Theatre for Pleasure or Theatre for Instruction* (3.9), Brecht proposes that the educative and instructive qualities of theatre are part of both its pleasure and its knowledge-making apparatus. He states that 'we have to defend the epic theatre against the suspicion that it is a highly disagreeable, humourless, indeed strenuous affair' (3.9: 477). In this, and following in the footsteps of Meyerhold and Piscator, Brecht was seeking to fundamentally redefine the relationship between the stage and the audience. Like many of the movements within the historical avant-garde explored in Part 2, Brecht saw the stage/audience relationship as integral to the function of the contemporary artwork and fundamental to modern theatre. Removing the primacy of emotional identification with characters and their situations, Brecht's 'theatre for the scientific age', unlike the Surrealists who focused more on interior psychological landscapes (see Part 2), focused on the exterior, on the sociological, the empirical and the observable. His audience were to critique and judge rather than empathize or become engulfed by the aesthetic.

This redirecting and reshaping of the audience's engagement in the theatre event – which played out in staging and design as well as text and acting style – although present to different degrees in the work explored in the previous two parts of this volume, are fundamental to Brecht's perception of the function of theatre. Similarly in *The Work of Art in the Age of its Technological Reproducibility* (3.7), Walter Benjamin notes that the technological advances of the modern age have given a new meaning to participation – the relationship between the artist, the artwork and spectatorship. Like Brecht, he believed that art has a social function, and like Brecht he believed that art could and should be interventionist. Benjamin proposed that the artist should not '*aestheticize*' politics as did the Futurists (see Part 2), but rather engage in a practice of '*politicizing art*' (3.7: 461). In other words, whilst the Futurists in Benjamin's view made an aesthetic of a political position, Brecht wanted to politicize art, in particular theatre.

Focusing on the theme of replication, Walter Benjamin reconceptualizes the function of art during the modernist period: he called for 'theses defining the tendencies of the development of art under the present conditions of production' (ibid: 445). In simple terms, technology intervenes in the space between the artist and the artwork, and a 'reproduction' of the real becomes mechanized – thus the photograph can reproduce reality not only more efficiently in terms of its representation of a surface reality, but with a more conscious and manipulated agenda of critique as well as having the possibility of being circulated to a mass audience. Benjamin acknowledges the artistry involved in mechanized art – film, photography and so on – arguing that the artist and the machine can work together and develop the aesthetic potential of technology. He suggests that while art in the past was largely made for, reflective of and consumed by an elite, art in the modern world was being consumed by a larger and more diverse audience: 'The masses are a matrix from which all customary behaviour toward works of art is today emerging newborn' (ibid: 459). Thus, 'the greatly increased mass of participants' is integral to a change in the functional dynamics of spectatorship, unleashing the political potential of representational practices in a more overt fashion, and to a greater degree, than in previous centuries. Benjamin's essay discusses at great length elements of the artwork such as originality, authenticity and aura as defining art's potential uniqueness. Technical reproducibility militates against such qualities, removing a sense of immediacy from the artwork, but permitting an enhanced form of critical engagement on the part of both artist and spectator.

Cultural critic Terry Eagleton notes in *The Author as Producer* (3.11), that Benjamin, using Brecht as his exemplar, defines a politicized and Marxist-based art form as one in which the artist must not only demonstrate a 'commitment' to a revolutionary politics, he or she must also seek to transform the material forces of artistic production. As Eagleton explains, '[d]ismantling the traditional naturalistic theatre, with its illusion of reality, Brecht produced a new kind of drama based on a critique of the ideological assumptions of bourgeois theatre' (3.11: 489). This was arguably a far more organized and systematic critique than that with which the Surrealists engaged. Many of the political theatres in Europe and the United States of the mid- to late twentieth century have been heavily influenced by the filtering through and transformation of a Marxist-informed philosophy of theatre which Brecht provided. The translation of these ideas for theatre practice has made acceptable – and in some cases normative – the idea of collaborative working practices, the removal of the proscenium arch and the idea of the 'fourth wall', the embracing of and re-engagement with popular performance techniques and their combination with the literary or poetic text, the integration of song and choreographed movement and a breaking down, to some extent, of the hierarchies inherent to a more traditional, commercially oriented theatre. Indeed many of the practices related to the texts discussed in Parts 4 and 5 of this volume, despite their seemingly vast differences, owe a debt to the ways in which Brecht revolutionized theatre.

Hoppla, We're Alive! (3.2)

Equally seminal to the history of European political theatre is the work of Ernst Toller (1893-1939) and specifically his play *Hoppla, We're Alive!* (3.2). The text as reproduced in this volume offers a unique insight into a play that in its authorship demonstrates the idiosyncrasies of a creative and frequently tense working partnership. Toller's collaborator Erwin Piscator, theatre theorist and the director of *Hoppla*, influenced Brecht in the 1920s. Employing the newly available technological developments in theatre – film projection, an abstract set design, other new scenic innovations and choreography – Piscator's work anticipated the subsequent refinements of Brecht's Epic theatre model, particularly in terms of breaking down scenic illusion.

The play opens with a prologue set in 1919 which sees the incarceration of the revolutionary political agitator Karl Thomas in a mental asylum. Jumping to 1927, the play then follows Thomas's life in Weimar Germany and his inability, after being released from the asylum, to reconcile his political convictions with those of his former comrades. The revolution he was fighting for appears to have been forgotten. The Weimar Republic was formed after the First World War as a liberal democracy which replaced the governance of the former imperial order; it is viewed as ending during the early 1930s when Hitler came to power. Thomas's former comrades have accommodated to the new status quo – what was imagined as revolutionary led to a reality far less powerfully radical. Thomas is falsely accused of the murder of Kilman, one-time revolutionary comrade but now a government minister. But immediately prior to being exonerated for the crime, Thomas commits suicide in his prison cell, an act preceded by the following speech:

KARL THOMAS: ... Where to? Where to? ... The stone walls press nearer and nearer ... I am freezing ... and it is dark ... and the glacier of darkness clutches me mercilessly ... Where to? Where to? ... To the highest mountain ... To the highest tree ... The Deluge. (3.2: 356)

Whilst, on the one hand, Toller seems to be arguing for the necessity of revolutionary political action, the character of Karl Thomas also functions as a kind of Everyman figure in an Expressionist *Stationendrama*; the protagonist's journey to spiritual awakening in this particular dramatic form, modelled on the journey Christ took to his death in the 'Stations of the Cross' (see also Styan 1981: 45 on Kokoschka's *Murderer the Women's Hope*, 2.4). Nevertheless, *Hoppla, We're Alive!*, and particularly in Piscator's production, sought to reflect the material conditions of life in 1920s Germany – Thomas may be an Expressionist hero/anti-hero but his angst is not vague or unnamable, it is driven by his disillusionment at what he perceives as the failure of the revolution. The play also exemplifies the 'New Objectivity', an artistic movement in 1920s Germany that was opposed to Expressionism. For Alan Pearlman, *Hoppla, We're Alive!* is in part 'a "state of the nation" play in its severe critique of the hypocrisy of Weimar society' (Pearlman 2000: 44). Like Brecht's *Baal* (1918), the play dramatizes idealism as being at odds with political and social reality.

Piscator's production made use of multiple layers of scaffolding, allowing for the simultaneous playing of scenes, the use of montage and an emblematic form of staging that created a form of realism without the suffocating detailed 'reproduction' of the 'real'. Piscator's aim was to produce and communicate the multiple strands of modern life and he did this by integrating and juxta-posing live action with technology and other media – film, sound, projection, music, song and dance. These features distinguished the original production of the play as key to the development of a mature political theatre aesthetic by connecting events onstage to wider political realities.

Between the Prologue and Act 1 – Karl Thomas's period of incarceration and a passage of eight years in the timeline of the play – Piscator created a seven-minute 'film interlude' in order to 'establish a dramatic connection between Thomas's fate and war and revolution' (Piscator 1980: 211). Based on factual information and key historical events, such as the Treaty of Versailles (1919) and Lenin's death (1924), an astonishing 3,000 feet of film was shot for this. The original footage was then edited and spliced with genuine documentary film. In the interlude between Acts 4 and 5, the famous 1920s Charleston dance was performed by innovative Expressionist choreographer and dancer Mary Wigman's (1886–1973) female dance troupe. Dressed in skeleton costumes and using ultraviolet light to generate luminosity, the dance functioned like a Brechtian A-Effect; the Charleston – a signifier of 1920s middle-class sexual liberation and decadence – when 'performed by skeletons was a powerful comment … on the precarious nature of German prosperity in 1927', thus forging a comedic and provocative defamiliarization of the familiar (Patterson 1981: 145).

The influence of Sergei Eisenstein's (1898-1948) essay *The Montage of Attractions* (1923) can clearly be detected in Piscator's work. Eisenstein, a Soviet film maker and theorist, proposed, through the use of montage, juxtaposition of chosen images placed in non-chronological order. An 'attraction' therefore, was 'any aggressive moment of theatre', anything which 'subjects the audience to … specific emotional shocks' (Eisenstein qtd in Leach 2004: 89). Similarly, the performance practice developed by the Blue Blouse movement in Russia can clearly be seen in Toller and Piscator's work and in the work of many of the 'political' theatre groups which emerged during the late 1920s and early 1930s in Europe and North America.

The Blue Blouse and 'agitprop'

The Blue Blouse, a Soviet Union-based theatre collective that operated from 1923 to 1928, remains a phenomenon of unparalleled scale and significance in the history of political theatre. The movement was integral to the development of a particular mode of performance 'using whatever materials were available' (Deák 1973: 35). This style of performance came to be known as 'agitprop' – agitation combined with propaganda. Here, the agitation is the vibrant theatricality and the propaganda is the conscious desire to represent a specific ideological position with a focus on a particular theme such as workers' rights. By the late 1920s some 500 groups formed the professional wing of the movement, bolstered by an additional 8,000 amateur companies – and these performed all over the Soviet Union (see Deák 1973 and McGrath 1981: 27). Named after the workers' blue uniforms – in which its members also performed – the Blue Blouse operated in post-revolutionary Russia 'to explain current events and government policy in popular, clear, entertaining ways to a predominantly peasant and largely illiterate population' (Jackson 2007: 69). The form this theatre took was necessarily makeshift and mobile. It was often performed on platforms mounted on mobile vehicles and playing in non-conventional theatre spaces such as public meeting halls, bars and outside factory gates, and utilizing a huge range of performance and dramatic forms. Actual social and political subject matter was mediated through monologue and dialogue, dance and gymnastics, popular and folk song, jazz, the employment of techniques derived from carnival, circus, cartoon, *commedia dell'arte* and so forth (McGrath 1981: 26–7). The drawing together of such elements was by no means haphazard – the Blue Blouse was a tightly organized and disciplined operation, requiring well-trained and highly skilled performers: '[i]t was seen as imperative to harness the entertaining features of each piece to the ultimate goal, that of winning over ordinary people to the immediate and urgent task of transforming society and of equipping them with the knowledge to enable them … to play their part' (Jackson 2007: 70).

The immediacy, directness and simplicity of Blue Blouse's performance work, particularly through the use of popular cultural forms, strategically sought to work in dialogue with working-class audiences. Similarly, rather than reaching out to a more generalized middle-class theatregoing audience as *Love on the Dole* did, much political theatre – of which the ballad opera *Johnny Noble* (3.5) is a pertinent example – was made specifically for, about and often by a working-class demographic. Often vital to this theatre was a conscious critique of class difference and the dominant Naturalist theatre. Agitprop advanced the possibility, in terms of Benjamin's later ideas, of theatre as a *politicized art*: it takes a didactic position, and so exploits the educational potential of theatre. This does not mean, however, that it was a dry or simplistic theatrical form. Just as documentary theatre operates on a basis of layering and juxtaposing fact, image and movement, as pioneered in Piscator's work of the 1920s, so too agitprop theatre uses a sophisticated bricolage of performance styles and conventions to forge new forms of mediation between education and entertainment, as Brecht's theory and practice of theatre later expanded upon.

If we turn to Brecht's most deliberately 'educational' plays, for example, it is possible to see how he intended a political theatre in which the educative and the entertaining could be combined and placed in productive relationship with each other. Thus, in Brecht's *Lehrstücke* (Learning Plays – such as *The Measures Taken* [1930]) it is tempting to read the self-conscious promotion of Marxist ideology as a crude form of dramaturgy. However, in these plays Brecht was forging an experimental form in which the individual subject's role and function within the dominant ideology was opened up in a kind of 'laboratory': the *Lehrstücke* facilitated dialogic exploration. It is not surprising that Brecht intended the *Lehrstück* to be performed in non-conventional theatre spaces – such as schools – and by non-professional actors. The techniques Brecht advocated for this included the sharing of roles by performers in order to forge an aesthetic that was based on a scientific objectivity, rather than Aristotelian empathy. The *Lehrstücke* and the agitprop of the Blue Blouse movement suggest a form of simplicity, which when mediated theatrically is intended to produce a complex 'reading' by the audience.

Political theatre / politicized art – *Johnny Noble* (3.5)

In Britain, political theatre developed rapidly in the 1920s and 1930s. It worked directly against both the privately run independent subscription theatres and the commercialized theatre system which dominated the theatre industry – theatres owned or run by a small management elite in London, and touring circuits owned by businessmen and theatre impresarios (see Barker and Gale 2000). The political theatres explored by Raphael Samuel *et al.* in *Theatres of the Left* (Samuel *et al.* 1985; see also Davies 1987) were run on a largely amateur basis and were independent from the idiosyncrasies of an industry swamped by costs, its profit-making imperatives and a perception that theatre was largely for entertainment. The commercial theatres did not see themselves as part and parcel of a revolutionary cultural project. With the growing popularity of film as a mass art form, and numerous theatres converted to cinemas by the 1930s, the economic instability of the commercial theatre sector became increasingly prohibitive in terms of investment in experimentation and new forms. Whereas many European theatres received state funding, the British theatre did not benefit from a system of state funding and subsidy for the arts until the mid-1940s.

During the decades which followed the First World War, as indicated above, the social unrest created by war, economic decline and the gradual dismantling of the British Empire intensified. *Love on the Dole* (see 3.3) shows an England divided by a failing economy and an increasingly politicized working class. Modernists in the arts tended to configure 'the masses' as threatening the balance of society, as a threat to the social order, as lacking intellectual insight and as watering down the purity of art (see Carey 1992). The mobilization of the masses, evidenced by the General Strike of 1926, a series of high-profile hunger marches across Britain between 1927 and 1936 and the increasing viability of the Labour Party – seen by many as representing the working classes – as fit for government, all signified a tectonic shift in the political landscape. A number of theatre artists believed theatre to have a huge potential as a revolutionary tool for the workers' struggle. Theatrical forms were adopted to articulate political ideas and to intervene in debates around social struggle. The Workers' Theatre Movement in the UK (1926–35) emphasized class struggle and 'saw itself as a theatre of action, dealing with immediate issues … it turned from naturalistic drama and the discussion play to agit-prop, in the form of sketches, cabaret and review' (Samuel *et al.* 1985: 33). Radical in its outlook, the movement contained groups with names like the Red Players and the Rebel Players. Theatre groups within the movement had direct contact with similar companies in Europe and borrowed from the techniques developed by Piscator in Germany and the Blue Blouse movement in Russia, but affiliations were also both locally and nationally networked. Here theatre was being utilized directly as part of a political interventionist project to politicize, educate and entertain.

Produced in the mid-1940s, Ewan MacColl's *Johnny Noble* (3.5) directly reflects the work which was developed within the Workers' Theatre Movement in terms of both its politicizing content and its formal properties. An 'episodic play with singing', MacColl exploits a range of what we might now understand to be Brechtian devices – direct address to the audience, an epic form where the play has a sequence of interconnected but self-contained scenes without the traditional structure of the 'Act' and the demand for an acting style which provides commentary as well as exposition. Not dissimilar to *Hoppla, We're Alive!*, the play follows a hero's journey from disenfranchisement to political awakening. Whereas in *Hoppla* self-realization leads to the hero's downfall, in *Johnny Noble* it leads to a sense of belonging and purpose. The narrative framework of the play takes the form of a 'romance' between Johnny, an out-of-work sailor, and Mary, whose family members have been killed in shipping accidents whilst working in the disintegrating fishing industry in the north-east of England. First performed in the mid-1940s after the Second World War, the play is set during the economic depression of the early 1930s and opens with two narrators declaring the stage as a 'microcosm of the world' and that, 'On this dead stage we'll make society appear'. Having removed the illusionistic conceit of Naturalist theatre, the narrators move on to set the scene of a 'derelict' town where life choices are limited by the lack of employment and the oppression of the working man by a failing economic system dependent on supply and demand. The 'characters' have depersonalized emblematic names – 1ST YOUTH, SEAMAN and MOTHER – which indicate their functional roles in the play. Johnny and Mary are separated at first by her refusal to live under the strain of being married to someone who works at sea – a precarious and dangerous occupation, through which her father was lost – and then by Johnny's need to find alternative employment.

The 'story' of the play is unravelled through music and song, dance and announcement (through the 'microphone voice') and the reporting of contemporary significant events – the march of the unemployed to London in 1931, the Spanish Civil War, the rise of fascism in Europe and so on. Johnny's journey across Britain reveals a land blighted by unemployment. He eventually joins a ship bound for Spain, which has to dodge Franco's sea blockade in order to deliver vital supplies to the besieged Spanish people. MacColl shows the link between personal experience and political consciousness when one of the characters questions why Johnny would risk his life for a 'foreigner': to which the 1ST NARRATOR replies, 'If a man in Spain dies because he opens his mouth to speak his mind, that's everybody's business' (3.5: 429). Thus what appears at first to be a simple story of love obstructed by circumstance, becomes an examination of the interrelationship between the political and the personal. MacColl simplifies the cause and effect dynamic of history to some extent, and this has been a criticism of the political theatres that focus on the transformation of the individual. Some might argue that his 'working class' are stereotyped in ways which are ultimately no different from those adopted by more conservative playwrights (see e.g. Jean in *Miss Julie* 1.2). But for the political theatres of the period, representation of a class unrepresented on the mainstream stages was in and of itself a significant statement. Depicting Johnny Noble's story through the media of popular music, folk song and dance emphasizes the 'romantic' dimension to the hero's awakening but also breaks up the primacy of the text and performs a Brechtian A-Effect in distancing the audience from the simply psychological/biographical narrative. Throughout the text MacColl makes the connection between the experience of the individual and the lives of countless other nameless workers.

At the end of the play, Johnny returns from the Second World War to a country which has arguably not been socially reconstructed through war: economic conditions remained exploitative. The working classes remained oppressed – their lives were as little valued when they were fighting for their country as they were when the industries they helped to build and maintain through their labour collapsed:

The members of the CHORUS *straighten up like men coming out of a dream.*

JOHNNY: The war wasn't fought for this. They said it would be different. They said ... We fought for something better ...

2ND R. BOY: Time you forgot the fighting, Johnny. You can't fight tradition. You can't fight history. (3.5: 433–4)

After a mock fight between Johnny Noble and an imaginary 'Johnny Privilege', and a further demand that Johnny forget about the war and enjoy the momentary 'trade boom', Johnny is reminded by MAN of what happened to his comrades, those who died meaningless deaths as part of the machinery of war. This is the final call to arms of the play where Johnny is inspired to take action by the statement:

MAN: You've two hands and a brain and there's plenty of you. Take the world in your hands, Johnny, and wipe it clean. It's up to you, Johnny.

Johnny's reply signifies the transformation of the masses from passive acceptance to political agency:

JOHNNY: ... It's our world. It's up to us. We can do it, can't we? (ibid: 434)

One of the inaugural productions of the ground-breaking Theatre Workshop which MacColl had founded with his then partner Joan Littlewood (see Goorney 2008 [1981]; Holdsworth 2006), *Johnny Noble* typifies a great deal of political theatre of its day as well as having a resonance for later plays from the repoliticized theatres of the late 1960s and 1970s such as *The Cheviot, the Stag and the Black, Black Oil* (see 4.2). One cannot underestimate the potency of a play like *Johnny Noble* in the immediate post-Second World War world – a world turned upside down by the spread of fascism throughout Europe, the terrors of the Holocaust, the realities of which were only just emerging, the loss of countless millions of young in the fighting and the birth of the nuclear age precipitated by the dropping of the atomic bomb on Hiroshima and Nagasaki in Japan. Today, the play appears to suffer from an overt romanticism and oversimplification. Indeed, it has been criticized for dramatizing 'the politicisation of the individual but fail[ing] to say very much about the social and political change that is its background' (Chambers and Prior 1987: 32). However, it must be remembered that the post-war world, characterized in Britain by the birth of the welfare state, the landslide Labour government of 1945–51 and the extension of education provision, also appeared to promise a removal of class inequalities. Although the play does not provide a sophisticated materialist analysis of history, present, for example, in a play like Brecht's *Mother Courage* (1939), it nevertheless presents a historically justified, if idealistic, call to arms: it is a play which expresses hope for the possibility of a new and fairer world. Similarly, Hallie Flanagan Davis's (1889–1969) $E=mc^2$ (3.4) calls upon its audience to wake up to, and act upon, the factual realities of nuclear armament and to take responsibility for their capacity to stop the catastrophic proliferation of the weapons of mass destruction which a nuclear arms race would create.

$E=mc^2$: A Living Newspaper about the Atomic Age (3.4)

In $E=mc^2$, first produced in 1947, the naïve statement by a US Marine at the opening of the play: ' we've got the bomb and it's going to end the war damn quick' (3.4: 396), is completely counteracted through the progression of the play, where the factual information about nuclear weaponry is critically unravelled to argue a case against ever using such atomic warfare again:

> STAGE MANAGER: …The only way to obliterate that shadow is to throw across the sky a tremendous affirmation of man's will to save himself from destruction – Whether we can do it and do it in time, rests not alone with the scientists, but with the psychologist – the economist – the philosopher – the artist – with you and with me. For it is still – in this moment of time – December 13, 1947 – by some desperate miracle – *our world*. (ibid: 417)

Flanagan Davis's play was generated through her collaborative work as leader of the Federal Theatre Project (FTP) in the United States during the 1930s. It was also influenced by her sponsored research of European and Soviet theatres, including a visit to Meyerhold and the Blue Blouse groups in 1926 (Taxidou 2007: 201). The Federal Theatre Project (1935–9) was embedded in a United States' government initiative by the then Works Progress Administration to create employment for out-of-work artists (see Fraden 1994). Although the arts received less than 1 per cent of the total funding available, this project represents the intervention of state funding in United States' theatre which hitherto, unlike some of the European examples we have given, was unprecedented. For President Roosevelt the arts had a significant role to play in his famous New Deal programme for democracy in a time of economic depression. For Flanagan Davis, 'theatre was more than a private enterprise … it was also a public interest which, if properly fostered, might come to be a social and educative force' (Flanagan 1940 qtd in Jackson 2007). The FTP commissioned plays by established playwrights such as Elmer Rice (see Part 2: Introduction) but also created their own plays and performances through collaborative methods of script composition. Relatively short lived for economic as well as political reasons – some critics saw the work of the FTP as leaning too far towards leftist politics – the FTP reached out to and served a wide and varied constituency. Although $E=mc^2$ was written after the end of the Second World War and almost ten years after the demise of the FTP as a functioning, funded organization, the play bears a strong resemblance in form and use of dialectic to both earlier FTP pieces such as the 'Living Newspaper'-styled *One Third of a Nation* (1938, see Jackson 2007) and the style of *Johnny Noble*, as well as paying tribute to the influence of the Blue Blouse agitprop technique.

The Living Newspaper was a form developed by political theatre practitioners in Europe, the Soviet Union and the United States. As a form the Living Newspaper was just that: it dramatized, in what we might now call a magazine format, issues of contemporary import using 'documentary reportage techniques' (Jackson 2007: 88). It was not dissimilar to techniques used in the political German theatre of the 1920s, whereby there were narrators/news reporters, and actors played functional roles such as, in the case of $E=mc^2$, Newsboy, Policeman, Atom and so on. The Living Newspaper format 'dealt with significant issues and events of the time, making full use of the theatre's resources in order to show ordinary people how their own lives were being affected by those events and what they themselves could do to try to change things for the better. A mix of the campaigning, the didactic and the interventionist' (ibid). The staging of the piece reflects a stripped-down Brechtian aesthetic employing film and projection. Flanagan Davis notes that the play was originally produced with 'no front curtain, a small stage with several movable units and two small side stages with gauze front curtains which made possible instantaneous revelation' (3.4: 419).

$E=mc^2$ is a play for the 'scientific age' in a way in which Brecht might never have imagined. Written immediately after the Second World War, it is historically located at the beginning of both the Cold War and the growth of anti-socialist and anti-communist sentiment, which were exemplified in House Committee on Un-American Activities (see Part 3: Timeline). The premise of the play is that the atomic bomb was viewed by an uneducated public as a positive invention which brought with it an unprecedented political power and potential global superiority. The play engages directly with social and ethical questions arising from scientific developments, characterized by an objective analysis of the material consequences of nuclear science and weapons proliferation. It begins with a poetic declaration of fact by the character of the STAGE MANAGER, who notes that people's reactions to the bombings were largely expressed in personal terms – how it affected their own localized lives. $E=mc^2$ gradually discourses the globalized impact of the deathly atom bomb and argues for both an individual and a universal response. Discussions within the play are held between and amongst representatives of the state – the army, politicians, representatives of the 'new' atomic science and ordinary people. The dialogue moves us away from the idea, expressed by Francis Lightfoot, a physicist, that the atom bomb has created a world where 'Yesterday, man was a slave; today, he's free! – Matter – obeys him' (ibid: 399).

$E=mc^2$ is without question an anti-war play, but it does not derive from a specific Marxist-inspired agenda as say Toller or MacColl's play. It makes reference to class hierarchies, but is less interested in an analysis of class structure and its link to an economic system than it is in placing all the classes together in search of a common goal. From this point of view, the politics of $E=mc^2$ links us back to *How the Vote Was Won* in the ways in which it takes a particular political and social issue, in its historical and material context, and expresses its relevance to all classes. Flanagan Davis employs the radical forms of the Living Newspaper and agitprop combined to relatively liberal ends – the message of the play is not underpinned by the same kind of ideological radicalism that motivated other figures we have discussed in this introduction, such as Toller and Brecht. With its 'dancing atoms', direct address and epic scope, the play can be linked to later *politicized art* but also represents one of the first examples of what might be viewed as a play which appropriates a radical form for a relatively liberal analysis. It does not fundamentally seek to question the economic and social inequities of the superstructure of mid-twentieth-century American society, but rather the ways in which the populace might potentially influence, as opposed to revolutionize, society's development.

Conclusion: the Legacies of early political theatres

It is tempting to view many of the plays and theatre practices discussed here as no longer directly pertinent to an early twenty-first-century world. Certainly, the principal belief systems that underpin their authorship were put to the test throughout the twentieth century. Only seventy years after the 1917 Bolshevik Revolution, 'Really Existing Socialism' – the various forms of human, social and economic oppression that the Marxist dream had turned into – began its rapid disintegration across Eastern Europe. China, the largest nation state on the planet, remains politically communist but has economically embraced capitalism. The communist outpost of Cuba, which in 1962 forced a showdown between the United States and the Soviet Union and brought the world to the brink of nuclear Armageddon, functions now – to outsiders at least – as a kind of nostalgic twilight-zone-cum-vacation destination.

Interestingly, of all the plays considered in this part, it is arguably *How the Vote Was Won* that achieved most in terms of envisioning a closing of the gap between political idealism and reality; full equality of citizenship between women and men has not yet been achieved, but the crusade and eventual victory of 'votes for women' remains a milestone in this particular long march. As a 'campaigning play', *How the Vote Was Won* represents something truly exceptional: an efficacious form of cooperation between political agitation and theatre practice. Of course, it may be argued that the play's very specific focus (and the campaign which surrounded it) made this possible, compared to say the more expansive – even fairy-tale – belief in working-class emancipation that informs *Johnny Noble*. Also, we should not forget here that a dramatist's political and ideological beliefs, however deeply held, do not preclude a desire for dialogue, debate and the posing of difficult questions. Ernst Toller was a committed Marxist, but *Hoppla, We're Alive!*, as we have seen, candidly dramatizes both the human and social consequences of a failed revolution.

In terms of the relevance of all of this to our current world, Terry Eagleton reminds us that 'Marxist ideas have stubbornly outlived Marxist political practice', and as a form of 'critique' Marxism 'has to be assessed by how much it illuminates [contemporary] works of art' (Eagleton 2002: viii). We will consider the implications of this view more fully in the next part. However, it is startling to consider the extent to which the original theatrical proprietors of a supposedly discredited ideology have exerted their influence in late twentieth- and early twenty-first-century dramaturgical and theatre practices. The Brazilian theatre director Augusto Boal's (1931–2009) 'interventionist' theatre practices, from 'Theatre of the Oppressed' to 'Legislative Theatre', have had an international impact in developing forms of participatory theatre that seek to effect positive change and activate agency in people's private, public and collective lives. Boal's starting point was Brecht. Boal's work is, today, considered an exemplar of 'applied theatre' or 'social theatre', which would also include 'theatre-in-education' in the UK, a particularly unique and extensive movement during the 1970s and 1980s that brought socially relevant theatre into schools, and 'theatre for development', theatre that is made in collaboration with communities in the developing world, oppressed by war, political corruption and/or the forces of nature. In the United States the Epic form finds a potent resonance and contemporary relevance even in the mainstream, with Tony Kushner's two-part *Angels in America* (1991–2). In the UK, the political dramatists who emerged in the 1960s and 1970s, such as Edward Bond, Howard Brenton, Caryl Churchill (see 4.4), David Edgar and David Hare, developed dramatic forms that are indebted to the ideas of Brecht particularly, but also Toller and Piscator. Mark Ravenhill, for example (see 4.5), one of the playwrights seen to have reinvigorated the British theatre for a new and younger audience in the 1990s, used Toller's *Hoppla, We're Alive!* as the prototype for his play *Some Explicit Polaroids* (1999), about the failure of the socialist project in modern-day England. Such playwrights and practitioners can be seen to have built their political and aesthetic project on the works of their predecessors, but adapted the original theories and practices to a theatre much changed by the film and media industries and, in the UK especially, by new funding structures and the dominance of the subsidized 'super theatres' – the Royal National Theatre, the Royal Court, the Royal Shakespeare Theatre and so on. The next part turns to practitioners whose politics are informed by evolving understandings of what we mean by the 'political' – by identity politics, but also by the wider and more pressing contemporary politics of globalization and its effect on the individual subject and the world in which s/he operates.

Bibliography

Barker, Clive and Maggie B. Gale (eds) (2000), *British Theatre Between the Wars, 1918–1939*, Cambridge: Cambridge University Press.

Belsey, Catherine (1985) 'Constructing the Subject: Deconstructing the Text', in J. Newton and D. Rosenfelt (eds), *Feminist Criticism and Social Change: Sex, Class and Race in Literature and Culture*, New York: Methuen, pp. 45–64.

Brecht, Bertolt (2001 [1964]) *Brecht on Theatre*, ed. and trans. J. Willett, London: Methuen.

Carey, John (1992) *The Intellectuals and the Masses: Pride and Prejudice Among the Literary Intelligentsia, 1800-1939*, London: Faber and Faber.

Case, Sue-Ellen (1989) 'Towards a Butch/Femme Aesthetic', in L. Hart (ed.), *Making a Spectacle: Feminist Essays on Contemporary Women's Theatre*, Ann Arbor: University of Michigan Press, pp. 282–99.

Chambers, Colin and M. Prior (1987) *Playwrights' Progress: Patterns of Post-War British Drama*, Oxford: Amber Lane Press.

Davies, Andrew (1987) *Other Theatres: The Development of Alternative and Experimental Theatre in Britain*, Basingstoke: Macmillan.

Deák, Frantisek (1973) 'Blue Blouse', *The Drama Review: TDR*, 17 (1) (March), 35–46.

Dolan, Jill (1988) *The Feminist Spectator as Critic*, Ann Arbor: University of Michigan Press.

Dolan, Jill (1990) ' "Lesbian" Subjectivity in Realism: Dragging at the Margins of Structure and Ideology', in Sue-Ellen Case (ed.), *Performing Feminisms: Feminist Critical Theory and Theatre*, Baltimore: Johns Hopkins University Press, pp. 40–53.

Eagleton, Terry (2002 [1976]) *Marxism and Literary Criticism*, London: Routledge.

Flanagan, Hallie (1940) *Arena: The Story of the Federal Theatre*, New York: Duell, Sloane and Pearce.

Fraden, R. (1994) *Blueprints for a Black Federal Theatre, 1935–1939*, Cambridge: Cambridge University Press.

Goorney, Howard (2008 [1981]) *The Theatre Workshop Story*, London: Methuen.

Holderness, Graham (1992) 'Introduction', in G. Holderness, (ed.), *The Politics of Theatre and Drama*, Basingstoke: Macmillan, pp. 1–17.

Holdsworth, Nadine (2006) *Joan Littlewood* (Routledge Performance Practitioners), London: Routledge.

Holledge, Julie (1981) *Innocent Flowers*, London: Virago.

Innes, Christopher (ed.) (1998) *The Cambridge Companion to George Bernard Shaw*, Cambridge: Cambridge University Press.

Jackson, Anthony (2007) *Theatre, Education and the Making of Meanings: Art or Instrument?*, Manchester: Manchester University Press.

Jameson, Fredric (1998) *Brecht and Method*, London: Verso.

Kirby, Michael (1975) 'On Political Theatre', *The Drama Review: TDR*, 19 (2) (June), 129–35.

Leach, Robert (2004) *Makers of Modern Theatre: An Introduction*, London: Routledge.

McGrath, John (1981) *A Good Night Out – Popular Theatre: Audience, Class and Form*, London: Eyre Methuen.

Patterson, Michael (1981) *The Revolution in German Theatre 1900–1933*, London: Routledge and Kegan Paul.

Pearlman, Alan (2000) *Ernst Toller: Plays One*, London: Oberon Books.

Piscator, Erwin (1980) *The Political Theatre*, trans. H. Rorrison, London: Eyre Methuen.

Ramelson, Marian (1976 [1967]) *The Petticoat Rebellion: A Century of Struggle for Women's Rights*, London: Lawrence and Wishart.

Samuel, Raphael, Ewan MacColl and Stuart Cosgrove (1985) *Theatres of the Left, 1880–1935: Workers' Theatre Movements in Britain and America*, London: Routledge and Kegan Paul.

Spender, Dale and Carol Hayman (eds) (1985) *How the Vote Was Won and Other Suffragette Plays*, London: Methuen.

Stowell, Sheila (1992) *A Stage of Their Own: Feminist Playwrights of the Suffrage Era*, Manchester: Manchester University Press.

Taxidou, Olga (2007) *Modernism and Performance: Jarry to Brecht*, Basingstoke: Palgrave Macmillan.

Williams, Raymond (2005 [1980]) *Culture and Materialism*, London: Verso.

Further reading

Benjamin, Walter (1998 [1966]) *Understanding Brecht*, London: Verso.

Bennett, Tony (1986) *Popular Culture and Social Relations*, Milton Keynes: Open University Press.

Boal, Augusto (1979) *The Theatre of the Oppressed*, London: Pluto Press.

Brecht, Bertolt (1977) *Measures Taken and Other Lehrstücke*, trans. Stefan S. Brecht, London: Methuen.

Chambers, Colin (1989) *The Story of Unity Theatre*, London: Lawrence and Wishart.

Eyre, Richard and Nicholas Wright (2000) *Changing Stages: A View of British and American Theatre in the Twentieth Century*, London: Bloomsbury.

Goorney, Howard and Ewan MacColl (1986) *Agit-Prop to Theatre Workshop: Political Playscripts 1930–50,* Manchester: Manchester University Press.

Kershaw, Baz (1999) *The Radical in Performance: From Brecht to Baudrillard*, London: Routledge.

Leach, Robert (1989) *Vsevolod Meyerhold*, Cambridge: Cambridge University Press.

Martin, Carol and Henry Bial (2000) *Brecht Sourcebook*, London: Routledge.

Stourac, R. and K. McCreery (1986) *Theatre as a Weapon: Workers' Theatre in the Soviet Union, Germany and Britain 1917–1934,* London: Routledge and Kegan Paul.

Styan, J. L. (1981) *Modern Drama in Theory and Practice 3: Expressionism and Epic Theatre*, Cambridge: Cambridge University Press.

Willett, John (ed.) (1964) *Brecht on Theatre,* London: Eyre Methuen.

3.1 HOW THE VOTE WAS WON (1909)

CICELY HAMILTON AND CHRISTOPHER ST JOHN

Cicely Hamilton (born Hammill) (1872–1952) *and* *Christopher St John (born Christabel Marshall) (1871–1960)* *co-authored* How the Vote Was Won *in 1909. Hamilton, an actress, journalist and dramatist in her own right, co-founded the Women Writers' Suffrage League (WWSL) in 1908. Her work with the WWSL and the Actresses' Franchise League (est. 1908) made an inimitable contribution to the social and gender debates within the first-wave feminist movement, epitomized in her political treatise* Marriage as a Trade *(1909). Christopher St John was also active within the first-wave feminist movement. She authored other plays such as* The First Actress *(1911) and wrote, among other works, a biography of the composer Ethel Smyth. Both comical and provocative,* How the Vote Was Won *reverses the dominant and historically prevailing conditions of women's dependency on men.*

Characters

HORACE COLE, a clerk, about 30
ETHEL, his wife, 22
AGATHA, his sister
MOLLY, his niece
MADAME CHRISTINE, his distant relation
MAUDIE SPARK, his first cousin
MISS LIZZIE WILKINS, his aunt
LILY, his maid-of-all-work
GERALD WILLIAMS, his neighbour
WINIFRED, Ethel's sister

Scene: *Sitting-room in* HORACE COLE'S *house at Brixton. The room is cheaply furnished in a genteel style. The window looks out on a row of little houses, all of the Cole pattern. The door (centre) leads into a narrow passage communicating at once with the front door. The fireplace (left) has a fancy mantel border, and over it is an overmantel, decorated with many photographs, and cheap ornaments. The sideboard (right), a small bookcase (right), a table (left centre up stage), and a comfortable armchair (centre by table), are the chief articles of furniture. The whole effect is modest, and quite unpleasing.*

Time: *Late afternoon on a spring day in any year in the future.*

When the curtain rises, MRS HORACE COLE *is sitting in the comfortable armchair (centre) putting a button on to her husband's coat. She is a pretty, fluffy little woman who could never be bad-tempered, but might be fretful. At this minute she is smiling indulgently, and rather irritatingly, at her sister* WINIFRED, *who is sitting by the fire (left) when the curtain rises, but gets up almost immediately to leave.* WINIFRED *is a tall and distinguished looking young woman with a cheerful, capable manner and an emphatic diction which betrays the public speaker. She wears the colours of the NWSPU [National Women's Social and Political Union].*

WINIFRED: Well, good-bye, Ethel. It's a pity you won't believe me. I wanted to let you and Horace down gently, or I shouldn't be here.

ETHEL: But you're always prophesying these dreadful things, Winnie, and nothing ever happens. Do you remember the day when you tried to invade the House of Commons from submarine boats? Oh, Horace did laugh when he saw in the papers that you had all been landed on the Hovis wharf by mistake! 'By accident, on purpose!' Horace said. He couldn't stop laughing all the evening. 'What price your sister, Winifred?' he said. 'She asked for a vote, and they gave her bread.' He kept on – you can't think how funny he was about it!

WINIFRED: Oh, but I can! I know my dear brother-in-law's sense of humour is his strong point. Well, we must hope it will bear the strain that is going to be put on it today. Of course, when his female relations invade his house – all with the same story, 'I've come to be supported' – he may think it excrutiatingly funny. One never knows.

ETHEL: Winnie, you're teasing me. They would never do such a thing. They must know we have only one spare bedroom, and that's to be for a paying guest when we can afford to furnish it.

WINIFRED: The servants' bedroom will be empty. Don't forget that all the domestic servants have joined the League and are going to strike, too.

ETHEL: Not ours, Winnie. Martha is simply devoted to me, and poor little Lily *couldn't* leave. She has no home to go to. She would have to go to the workhouse.

WINIFRED: Exactly where she will go. All those women who have no male relatives, or are refused help by those they have, have instructions to go to the relieving officer. The number of female paupers who will pour through the workhouse gates tonight all over England will frighten the Guardians into blue fits.

ETHEL: Horace says you'll never *frighten* the Government into giving you the vote. He says every broken window is a fresh nail in the coffin of women's suffrage. It's quite true. Englishmen can't be bullied.

WINIFRED: No, but they can *bully*. It's your husband, your dear Horace, and a million other dear Horaces who are going to do the bullying and frightening this time. The women are going to stay quiet, at home. By tomorrow, perhaps before, Horace will be marching to Westminster shouting out 'Votes for Women!'

ETHEL: Winnie, how absurd you are! You know how often you've tried to convert Horace and failed. Is it likely that he will become a Suffragette just because –

WINIFRED: Just because –? Go on, Ethel.

ETHEL: Well, you know – all this you've been telling me about his relations coming here and asking him to support them. Of course, I don't believe it. Agatha, for instance, would never dream of giving up her situation. But if they did come Horace would just tell them he *couldn't* keep them. How could he on £4 a week?

WINIFRED: How could he? That's the point! He couldn't, of course. That's why he'll want to get rid of them at any cost – even the cost of letting women have the vote. That's why he and the majority of men in this country shouldn't for years have kept alive the foolish superstition that all women are supported by men. For years we have told them it was a delusion, but they could not take our arguments seriously. Their method of answering us was exactly that of the little boy in the street who cries 'Yah – Suffragette!' or 'Where's your " 'ammer"?' when he sees my badge.

ETHEL: I always wish you wouldn't wear it when you come here … Horace does so dislike it. He thinks it unwomanly.

WINIFRED: Oh! does he? Tomorrow he may want to borrow it – when he and the others have had their object-lesson. They wouldn't listen to argument … so we had to expose their pious fraud about woman's place in the world in a very practical and sensible way. At this very minute working women of every grade in every part of England are ceasing work, and going to demand support and the necessities of life from their nearest male relatives, however distant the nearest relative may be. I hope, for your sake, Ethel, that Horace's relatives aren't an exacting lot!

ETHEL: There wasn't a word about it in the *Daily Mail* this morning.

WINIFRED: Never mind. The evening papers will make up for that.

ETHEL: What male relative are you going to, Winnie? Uncle Joseph?

WINIFRED: Oh, I'm in the fighting line, as usual, so our dear uncle will be spared. My work is with the great army of women who have no male belongings of any kind! I shall be busy till midnight marshalling them to the workhouse … This is perhaps the most important part of the strike. By this we shall hit men as ratepayers even when they have escaped us as relatives! Every man, either in a public capacity or a private one, will find himself face to face with the appalling problem of maintaining millions of women in idleness. Do you think the men will take up the burden? Not they! (*Looks at her watch.*) Good heavens! The strike began ages ago. I must be off. I've wasted too much time here already.

ETHEL: (*Looking at the clock.*) I had no idea it was so late. I must see about Horace's tea. He may be home any minute. (*Rings the bell, left.*)

WINIFRED: Poor Horace!

ETHEL: (*Annoyed.*) Why 'poor Horace'? I don't think he has anything to complain of. (*Rings again.*)

WINIFRED: At this minute I feel some pity for all men.

ETHEL: What can have happened to Martha?

WINIFRED: She's gone, my dear, that's all.

ETHEL: Gone! Nonsense. She's been with me ever since I was married, and I pay her very good wages.

Enter LILY, a shabby little maid-of-all-work, dressed for walking, the chief effort of the toilette being a very cheap and very smart hat.

ETHEL: Where's Martha, Lily?

LILY: She's left, m'm.

ETHEL: Left! She never gave me notice.

LILY: No, m'm, we wasn't to give no notice, but at three o'clock we was to quit.

ETHEL: But why? Don't be a silly little girl. And you mustn't come in here in your hat.

LILY: I was just goin' when you rang. That's what I've got me 'at on for.

ETHEL: Going! Where? It's not your afternoon out.

LILY: I'm goin' back to the Union. There's dozens of others goin' with me.

ETHEL: But why –?

LILY: Miss Christabel – she told us. She says to us: 'Now look 'ere, all of yer – you who've got no men to go to on Thursday – yer've got to go to the Union, she says: 'and the one who 'angs back' – and she looked at me she did – 'may be the person 'oo the 'ole strain of the movement is restin' on, the traitor 'oo's sailin' under the 'ostile flag,' she says: and I says, 'That won't be me – not much!'

During this speech WINIFRED *puts on a sandwich board which bears the inscription: 'This way to the Workhouse.'*

WINIFRED: Well, Ethel, are you beginning to believe?

ETHEL: Oh, I think it's very unkind – very wicked. How am I to get Horace anything to eat with no servants?

WINIFRED: Cheer up, my dear. Horace and the others can end the strike when they choose. But they're going to have a jolly bad time first. Goodbye. (*Exit* WINNIE, *singing the 'Marseillaise.'*)

LILY: Wait a bit, Miss. I'm comin' with yer. (*Sings the 'Marseillaise' too.*)

ETHEL: No, no. Oh, Lily, please don't go, or at any rate bring up the kettle first, and the chops, and the frying pan. Please! Then I think I can manage.

LILY: (*Coming back into the room and speaking impressively.*) There's no ill-feeling. It's an objick-lesson – that's all.

Exit LILY. ETHEL *begins to cry weakly; then lays the table; gets bread, cruet, tea, cups, etc. from the cupboard, right.* LILY *re-enters with a frying pan, a kettle, and two raw chops.*

LILY: 'Ere you are – it's the best I can do. You see, mum, I've got to be recognised by the State. I don't think I'm a criminal nor a lunatic, and I oughtn't to be treated as sich.

ETHEL: You poor little simpleton. Do you suppose that, even if this absurd plan succeeds, *you* will get a vote?

LILY: I may – you never know your luck; but that's not why I'm giving up work. It's so as I shan't stop them as ought to 'ave it. The 'ole strain's on me, and I'm goin' to the Union – so goodbye, mum. (*Exit* LILY.)

ETHEL: And I've always been so kind to you! Oh, you little brute! What *will* Horace say? (*Looking out of the window.*) It can't be true. Everything looks the same as usual.

(HORACE's *voice outside.*)

HORACE: We must have at least sixteen more Dreadnoughts this year.

(WILLIAMS' *voice outside.*)

WILLIAMS: You can't get 'em, old chap, unless you expect the blooming colonies to pay for 'em.

ETHEL: Ah, here is Horace, and Gerald Williams with him. Oh, I hope Horace hasn't asked him to tea! (*She powders her nose at the glass, then pretends to be busy with the kettle.*)

Enter HORACE COLE – *an English master in his own house – and* GERALD WILLIAMS, *a smug young man stiff with self-consciousness.*

ETHEL: You're back early, aren't you, Horry? How do you do, Mr Williams?

GERALD WILLIAMS: How do you do, Mrs Cole. I've just dropped in to fetch a book your husband's promised to lend me.

HORACE *rummages in book-shelves.*

ETHEL: Had a good day, Horry?

HORACE: Oh, much as usual. Ah, here it is (*Reading out the title:*) 'Where's the Wash-tub now?' with a preface by Lord Curzon of Kedleston, published by the Men's League for Opposing Women's Suffrage. If that doesn't settle your missus, nothing will.

ETHEL: Is Mrs Williams a Suffragette?

GERALD: Rather, and whenever I say anything, all she can answer is, 'You know nothing about it.' I call that illogical. Thank you, old man. I'll read it to her after tea. So long. Goodbye, Mrs Cole.

ETHEL: Did Mrs Williams tell you anything this morning … before you went to the City?

GERALD: About Votes for Women, do you mean? Oh, no. Not allowed at breakfast. In fact, not allowed at all. I tried to stop her going to these meetings where they fill the women's heads with all sorts of rubbish, and she said she'd give 'em up if I'd give up footer matches on Saturday afternoons; so we agreed to disagree. See you tomorrow, old chap. Goodbye, Mrs Cole.

Exit GERALD WILLIAMS.

HORACE: You might have asked him to stop to tea. You made him very welcome – I don't think.

ETHEL: I'm sorry; but I don't think he would have stayed if I *had* asked him.

HORACE: Very likely not, but you should always be hospitable. Tea ready?

ETHEL: Not quite, dear. It will be in a minute.

HORACE: What on earth is all this!

ETHEL: Oh, nothing. I thought I would cook your chop for you up here today – just for fun.

HORACE: I really think, Ethel, that as long as we can afford a servant, it's rather unnecessary.

ETHEL: You know you're always complaining of Martha's cooking. I thought you would like me to try.

HORACE: My dear child! It's very nice of you. But why not cook in the kitchen? Raw meat in the drawing room! Do you want to turn me into a poor miserable vegetarian?

ETHEL: Oh, Horry, don't!

She puts her arms round his neck and sobs. The chop at the end of the toasting fork in her hand dangles in his face.

HORACE: What on earth's the matter? Ethel, dear, don't be hysterical. If you knew what it was to come home fagged to death and be worried like this ... I'll ring for Martha and tell her to take away those beastly chops. They're getting on my nerves.

ETHEL: Martha's gone.

HORACE: When? Why? Did you have a row? I suppose you had to give her a month's wages. I can't afford that sort of thing, you know.

ETHEL: (*Soothing.*) It's not you who afford it, anyhow. Don't I pay Martha out of my own money?

HORACE: Do you call it ladylike to throw that in my face ...

ETHEL: (*Incoherently.*) I'm not throwing it in your face ... but as it happens I didn't pay her anything. She went off without a word ... and Lily's gone, too. (*She puts her head down on the table and cries.*)

HORACE: Well, that's a good riddance. I'm sick of her dirty face and slovenly ways. If she ever does clean my boots, she makes them look worse than when I took them off. We must get a charwoman.

ETHEL: We shan't be able to. Isn't it in the papers?

HORACE: What *are* you talking about?

ETHEL: Winifred said it would be in the evening papers.

HORACE: Winifred! She's been here, has she? That accounts for everything. How that woman comes to be your sister I can't imagine. Of course, she's mixed up with this wild-cat scheme.

ETHEL: Then you know about it!

HORACE: Oh. I saw something about 'Suffragettes on Strike' on the posters on my way home. Who cares if they do strike? They're no use to anyone. Look at Winifred. What does she ever do except go round making speeches, and kicking up a row outside the House of Commons until she forces the police to arrest her. Then she goes to prison and poses as a martyr. Martyr! We all know she could go home at once if she would promise the magistrate to behave herself. What they ought to do is to try all these hysterical women privately and sentence them to be ducked – privately. Then they'd soon give up advertising themselves.

ETHEL: Winnie has a splendid answer to that, but I forget what it is. Oh, Horry, was there anything on the posters about the nearest male relative?

HORACE: Ethel, my dear, you haven't gone dotty, have you? When you have quite done with my chair, I – (*He helps her out of the chair and sits down.*) Thank you.

ETHEL: Winnie said that not only are all the working women going to strike, but they are going to make their nearest male relatives support them.

HORACE: Rot!

ETHEL: I thought how dreadful it would be if Agatha came, or that cousin of yours on the stage whom you won't let me know, or your Aunt Lizzie! Martha and Lily have gone to *their* male relatives; at least, Lily's gone to the workhouse – it's all the same thing. Why shouldn't it be true? Oh, look, Horace, there's a cab – with luggage. Oh, what shall we do?

HORACE: Don't fuss! It's stopping next door, not here at all.

ETHEL: No, no; it's here. (*She rushes out.*)

HORACE: (*Calling after her.*) Come back! You can't open the door yourself. It will look as if we didn't keep a servant.

Re-enter Ethel followed after a few seconds by AGATHA. AGATHA is a weary-looking woman of about thirty-five. She wears the National Union colours, and is dowdily dressed.

ETHEL: It *is* Agatha – and such a big box. Where *can* we put it?

AGATHA: (*Mildly.*) How do you do, Horace. (*Kisses him.*) Dear Ethel! (*Kisses her.*) You're not looking so well as usual. Would you mind paying the cabman two shillings, Horace, and helping him with my box? It's rather heavy, but then it contains all my wordly belongings.

HORACE: Agatha – you haven't lost your situation! You haven't left the Lewises?

AGATHA: Yes, Horace; I left at three o'clock.

HORACE: My dear Agatha – I'm extremely sorry – but we can't put you up here.

AGATHA: Hadn't you better pay the cab? Two shillings so soon becomes two-and-six. (*Exit HORACE.*) I am afraid my brother doesn't realise that I have some claim on him.

ETHEL: We thought you were so happy with the Lewises.

AGATHA: So were the slaves in America when they had kind masters. They didn't want to be free.

ETHEL: Horace said you always had late dinner with them when they had no company.

AGATHA: Oh, I have no complaint against my late employers. In fact, I was sorry to inconvenience them by leaving so suddenly. But I had a higher duty to perform than my duty to them.

ETHEL: I don't know what to do. It will worry Horace dreadfully.

Re-enter HORACE.

HORACE: The cab *was* two-and-six, and I had to give a man twopence to help me in with that Noah's ark. Now, Agatha, what does this mean? Surely in your position it was very unwise to leave the Lewises. You can't stay here. We must make some arrangement.

AGATHA: Any arrangement you like, dear, provided you support me.

HORACE: I support you!

AGATHA: As my nearest male relative, I think you are obliged to do so. If you refuse, I must go to the workhouse.

HORACE: But why can't you support yourself? You've done it for years.

AGATHA: Yes – ever since I was eighteen. Now I am going to give up work, until my work is recognised. Either my proper place is the home – the home provided for me by some dear father, brother, husband, cousin, or uncle – or I am a self-supporting member of the State, who ought not to be shut out from the rights of citizenship.

HORACE: All this sounds as if you had become a Suffragette! Oh, Agatha, I always thought you were a lady.

AGATHA: Yes, I *was* a lady – such a lady that at eighteen I was thrown upon the world, penniless, with no training whatever which fitted me to earn my own living. When women become citizens I believe that daughters will be given the same chance as sons, and such a life as mine will be impossible.

HORACE: Women are so illogical. What on earth has all this to do with your planting yourself on me in this inconsiderate way? You put me in a most unpleasant position. You must see, Agatha, that I haven't the means to support a sister as well as a wife. Couldn't you go to some friends until you find another situation?

AGATHA: No, Horace. I'm going to stay with you.

HORACE: (*Changing his tone, and turning nasty.*) Oh, indeed! And for how long – if I may ask?

AGATHA: Until a Bill for the removal of the sex disability is passed.

HORACE: (*Impotently angry.*) Nonsense. I can't keep you, and I won't. I have always tried to do my duty by you. I think hardly a week passes that I don't write to you. But now that you have deliberately thrown up an excellent situation as a governess, and come here and threatened me – yes, threatened me – I think it's time to say that, sister or no sister, I intend to be master in my own house!

Enter MOLLY, a good-looking young girl of about twenty. She is dressed in well-cut, tailor-made clothes, wears a neat little hat, and carries some golfclubs and a few books.

MOLLY: How are you, Uncle Horace? Is that Aunt Aggie? How d'ye do? I haven't seen you since I was a kid.

HORACE: Well, what have you come for?

MOLLY: There's a charming welcome to give your only niece!

HORACE: You know perfectly well, Molly, that I disapprove of you in every way. I hear – I have never read it, of course – but I hear that you have written a most scandalous book. You live in lodgings by yourself, when if you chose you could afford some really nice and refined boarding-house. You have most undesirable acquaintances, and altogether –

MOLLY: Cheer up, Uncle. Now's your chance of reforming me. I've come to live with you. You can support me and improve me at the same time.

HORACE: I never heard such impertinence. I have always understood from you that you earn more than I do.

MOLLY: Ah, yes; but you never *liked* my writing for money, did you? You called me 'sexless' once because I said that as long as I could support myself I didn't feel an irresistible temptation to marry that awful little bounder Weekes.

ETHEL: Reginald Weekes! How can you call him a bounder! He was at Oxford.

MOLLY: Hullo, Auntie Ethel! I didn't notice you. You'll be glad to hear I haven't brought much luggage – only a night-gown and some golf clubs.

HORACE: I suppose this is a joke!

MOLLY: Well, of course, that's one way of looking at it. I'm not going to support myself any longer. I'm going to be a perfect lady, and depend on my Uncle Horace – my nearest male relative – for the necessities of life. (*A motor horn is heard outside.*) Aren't you glad that I am not going to write another scandalous book, or live in lodgings by myself?

ETHEL: (*At the window.*) Horace! Horace! There's someone getting out of a motor – a grand motor. Who can it be? And there's no one to answer the door.

MOLLY: That doesn't matter. I found it open, and left it open to save trouble.

ETHEL: She's got luggage, too! The chauffeur is bringing in a dressing-case.

HORACE: I'll turn her into the street – and the dressing-case, too.

He goes fussily to the door, and meets MADAME CHRISTINE on the threshold. The lady is dressed smartly and tastefully. Age about forty, manners elegant, smile charming, speech resolute. She carries a jewelcase, and consults a legal document during her first remarks.

MADAME CHRISTINE: You are Mr Cole?

HORACE: No! Certainly not! (*Wavering.*) At least, I was this morning, but –

MADAME CHRISTINE: Horace Cole, son of John Hay Cole, formerly of Streatham, where he carried on the business of a –

A motor horn sounds outside.

HORACE: I beg your pardon, but my late father's business has really nothing to do with this matter, and to a professional man it's rather trying to have these things raked up against him. Excuse me, but do you want your motor to go?

MADAME CHRISTINE: It's not my motor any longer; and – yes, I do want it to go, for I may be staying here some time. I think you had one sister, Agatha, and one brother, Samuel, now dead. Samuel was much older than you –

AGATHA: Why don't you answer, Horace? Yes, that's perfectly correct. I am Agatha.

MADAME CHRISTINE: Oh, are you? How d'ye do?

MOLLY: And Samuel Cole was my father.

MADAME CHRISTINE: I'm very glad to meet you. I didn't know I had such charming relations. Well, Mr Cole, my father was John Hay Cole's first cousin; so you, I think, are my second cousin, and my nearest male relative.

HORACE: (*Distractedly.*) If anyone calls me that again I shall go mad.

MADAME CHRISTINE: I am afraid you aren't quite pleased with the relationship!

HORACE: You must excuse me – but I don't consider a second cousin a relation. A second cousin is a – well –

MADAME CHRISTINE: Oh, it answers the purpose. I suddenly find myself destitute, and I want you to support me. I am sure you would not like a Cole to go to the workhouse.

HORACE: I don't care a damn where any of you go.

ETHEL: (*Shocked.*) Horry! How can you!

MADAME CHRISTINE: That's frank, at any rate; but I am sure, Cousin Horace, that in spite of your manners, your heart's in the right place. You won't refuse me board and lodging, until Parliament makes it possible for me to resume my work?

HORACE: My dear madam, do you realise that my salary is £3.10s. a week – and that my house will hardly hold your luggage, much less you?

MADAME CHRISTINE: Then you must agitate. Your female relatives have supported themselves up till now, and asked nothing from you. I myself, dear cousin, was, until this morning, running a profitable dressmaking business in Hanover Square. In my public capacity I am Madame Christine.

MOLLY: I know! You make sweet gowns, but I've never been able to afford you.

HORACE: And do you think, Madame Christine –

MADAME CHRISTINE: Cousin Susan, please.

HORACE: Do you think that you are justified in coming to a poor clerk, and asking him to support you – you, who could probably turn over my yearly income in a single week! Didn't you come here in your own motor?

MADAME CHRISTINE: At three o'clock that motor became the property of the Women's Social and Political Union. All the rest of my property and all available cash have been divided equally between the National Union and the Women's Freedom League. Money is the sinews of war, you know.

HORACE: Do you mean to tell me that you've given all your money to the Suffragettes! It's a pity you haven't a husband. He'd very soon put an end to such folly.

MADAME CHRISTINE: I had a husband once. He liked me to do foolish things – for instance, to support him. After that unfortunate experience, Cousin Horace, you may imagine how glad I am to find a man who really is a man, and will support me instead. By the way, I should *so* much like some tea. Is the kettle boiling?

ETHEL: (*Feebly.*) There aren't enough cups! Oh, what *shall* I do?

HORACE: Never mind, Ethel; I shan't want any. I am going to dine in town, and go to the theatre. I shall hope to find you all gone when I come back. If not, I shall send for the police.

Enter MAUDIE SPARK, *a young woman with an aggressively cheerful manner, a voice raucous from much bellowing of music-hall songs, a hat of huge size, and a heart of gold.*

MAUDIE: 'Ullo! 'Ullo! Who's talking about the police? Not my dear cousin Horry?

HORACE: How dare you come here?

MAUDIE: Necessity, old dear. If I could have found a livelier male relative, you may bet I'd have gone to him! But you, Horace, are the only first cousin of this poor orphan. What are you in such a hurry for?

HORACE: Let me pass! I'm going to the theatre.

MAUDIE: Silly jay! the theatres are all closed – and the halls, too. The actresses have gone on strike – resting indefinitely. I've done my little bit towards that. They won't get any more work out of Maudie Spark, Queen of Comédiennes, until the women have got the vote. Ladies and fellow-relatives, you'll be pleased to hear the strike's going fine. The big drapers can't open tomorrow. One man can't fill the place of fifteen young ladies at once, you see. The duchesses are out in the streets begging people to come in and wash their kids. The City men are trying to get taxi men in to do their typewriting. Every man, like Horry here, has his house full of females. Most of 'em thought, like Horry, that they'd go to the theatre to escape. But there's not a blessed theatre to go to! Oh, what a song it'll make. 'A woman's place is the home – I don't think, I don't think, I don't think.'

HORACE: Even if this is not a plot against me personally, even if there are other women in London at this minute disgracing their sex –

MAUDIE: Here, stop it – come off it! If it comes to that, what are *you* doing – threatening your womankind with the police and the workhouse.

HORACE: I was not addressing myself to you.

AGATHA: Why not, Horace? She's your cousin. She needs your protection just as much as we do.

HORACE: I regard that woman as the skeleton in the cupboard of a respectable family; but that's neither here nor there. I address myself to the more ladylike portion of this gathering, and I say that whatever is going on the men will know what to do, and will do it with dignity and firmness. (*The impressiveness of this statement is marred by the fact that* HORACE'S *hand, in emphasising it, comes down heavily on the loaf of bread on the table.*) A few exhibitions of this kind won't frighten them.

MAUDIE: Oh, won't it! I like that! They're being so firm and so dignified that they's running down to the House of Commons like lunatics, and black-guarding the Government for not having given us the vote before!

Shouts outside of newsboys in the distance.

MOLLY: Splendid! Have they begun already?

MADAME CHRISTINE: Get a paper, Cousin Horace. I know some men will never believe anything till they see it in the paper.

ETHEL: The boys are shouting out something now. Listen.

Shouts outside: 'Extry special. Great strike of women. Women's strike. Theatres closed. Extry special edition. "Star!" "News!" 6.30 edition.'

MOLLY: You see. Since this morning Suffragettes have become women!

ETHEL: (*At window.*) Here, boy, paper!

Cries go on: 'Extra special "Star". Men petition the Government. Votes for Women. Extry special.'

Oh, heavens, here's Aunt Lizzie!

As ETHEL pronounces the name HORACE dives under the table. Enter AUNT LIZZIE leading a fat spaniel and carrying a bird cage with a parrot in it. MISS ELIZABETH WILKINS is a comfortable, middle-aged body of a type well known to those who live in the less fashionable quarter of Bloomsbury. She looks as if she kept lodgers, and her looks do not belie her. She is not very well educated, but has a good deal of native intelligence. Her features are homely, and her clothes about thirty years behind the times.

AUNT LIZZIE: Well, dears, all here? That's right. Where's Horace? Out? Just as well; we can talk more freely. I'm sorry I'm late, but animals do so hate a move. It took a long time to make them understand the strike. But I think they will be very comfortable here. You love dogs, don't you, Ethel?

ETHEL: Not Ponto. He always growls at me.

AUNT LIZZIE: Clever dog! he knows you don't sympathise with the cause.

ETHEL: But I do, Aunt; only I have always said that as I was happily married I thought it had very little to do with me.

AUNT LIZZIE: You've changed your mind about that today, I should think! What a day it's been! We never expected everything would go so smoothly. They say the Bill's to be rushed through at once. No more deceitful promises, no more dishonest 'facilities'; deeds, not words, at last! Seen the papers? The Press are not boycotting us today, my dears. (*MADAME CHRISTINE, MOLLY, and MAUDIE each take a paper.*) The boy who sold them to me put the money back into Ponto's collecting box. That dog must have made five pounds for the cause since this morning.

HORACE: (*Puts his head out.*) 'Liar!'

MOLLY: Oh, do listen to this. It's too splendid! (*Reading from the paper.*) 'Women's Strike. – Latest: Messrs Lyons and Co. announce that by special arrangement with the War Office the places of their defaulting waitresses will be filled by the non-commissioned officers and men of the 2nd Battalion Coldstream Guards. Business will therefore be carried on as usual.'

MADAME CHRISTINE: What do you think of this? (*Reading.*) 'Latest Intelligence. – It is understood that the Naval Volunteers have been approached by the authorities with the object of inducing them to act as charwomen to the House of Commons.'

AUNT LIZZIE: (*To ETHEL.*) Well, my dear! What have you got there? Read what the *Star* says.

ETHEL: (*Tremulously reading.*) 'The queue of women waiting for admission to Westminster Workhouse is already a mile and a half in length. As the entire police force are occupied in dealing with the men's processions, Lord Haldane has been approached with a view to ascertaining if the Territorials can be sworn in as special constables.'

MAUDIE: (*Laughing.*) This is a little bit of all right. (*Reading.*) 'Our special representative, on calling upon the Prime Minister with the object of ascertaining his views on the situation, was informed that the Right Honourable gentleman was unable to receive him, as with the assistance of the boot-boy and a Foreign Office messenger, he was actively engaged in making his bed.'

AUNT LIZZIE: Always unwilling to receive people, you see! Well, he must be feeling sorry now that he never received us. Everyone's putting the blame on him. It's extraordinary how many men – and newspapers, too – have suddenly found out that they have always been in favour of woman's suffrage! That's the sensible attitude, of course. It would be humiliating for them to confess that it was not until we held a pistol to their heads that they changed their minds. Well, at this minute I would rather be the man who has been our ally all along than the one who has been our enemy. It's not the popular thing to be an 'anti' any more. Any man who tries to oppose us today is likely to be slung up to the nearest lamp post.

ETHEL: (*Rushing wildly to the table.*) Oh, Horry! My Horry!

HORACE comes out from under the table.

AUNT LIZZIE: Why, bless the boy, what are you doing there?

HORACE: Oh, nothing. I merely thought I might be less in the way here, that's all.

AUNT LIZZIE: You didn't hide when I came in, by any chance!

HORACE: I hide from you! Aren't you always welcome in this house?

AUNT LIZZIE: Well, I haven't noticed it particularly; and I'm not calling today, you understand. I've come to stay.

HORACE, dashed and beaten, begins to walk up and down the room, and consults ETHEL.

Well, well! I won't deny it was a wrench to leave 118a,

Upper Montagu Place, where I've done my best for boarders, old and young, gents and ladies, for twenty-five years – and no complaints! A home from home, they always call it. All my ladies had left before I started out, on the same business as ourselves – but what those poor boys will do for their dinner tonight I don't know. They're a helpless lot! Well, it's all over; I've given up my boarding-house, and I depend on you, Horace, to keep me until I am admitted to citizenship. It may take a long time.

HORACE: It must *not* take a long time! I shan't allow it. It shall be done at once. Well, you needn't all look so surprised. I know I've been against it, but I didn't realise things. I thought only a few hooligan window-smashers wanted the vote; but when I find that *you* – Aunt – Fancy a woman of your firmness of character, one who has always been so careful with her money, being declared incapable of voting! The thing is absurd.

MAUDIE: Bravo! Our Horry's waking up.

HORACE: (*Looking at her scornfully.*) If there are a few women here and there who *are* incapable – I mention no names, mind – it doesn't affect the position. What's going to be done? Who's going to do it? If this rotten Government think we're going to maintain millions of women in idleness just because they don't like the idea of my Aunt Lizzie making a scratch on a bit of paper and shoving it into a ballot-box once every five years, this Government have reckoned without the men – (*General cheering.*) I'll show 'em what I've got a vote for! What do they expect? You can't all marry. There aren't enough men to go round, and if you're earning your own living and paying taxes you ought to have a say; it's only fair. (*General cheering and a specially emphatic* 'Hear, hear' *from* MADAME CHRISTINE.) The Government are narrow-minded idiots!

MADAME CHRISTINE: Hear, hear!

HORACE: They talk as if all the women ought to stay at home washing and ironing. Well, before a woman has a wash-tub, she must have a home to put it in, mustn't she? And who's going to give it her? I'd like them to tell me that. Do they expect *me* to do it?

AGATHA: Yes, dear.

HORACE: I say if she can do it herself and keep herself, so much the better for everyone. Anyhow, who are the Government? They're only representing *me*, and being paid thousands a year by *me* for carrying out *my* wishes.

MOLLY: Oh, er – what ho!

HORACE: (*Turns on her angrily.*) I like a woman to be a woman – that's the way I was brought up; but if she insists on having a vote – and apparently she does.

ALL: She does! she does!

HORACE: – I don't see why she shouldn't have it. Many a woman came in here at the last election and tried to wheedle me into voting for her particular candidate. If she has time to do that – and I never heard the member say then that she ought to be at home washing and ironing

the baby – I don't see why she hasn't time to vote. It's never taken up much of *my* time, or interfered with *my* work. I've only voted once in my life – but that's neither here nor there. I know what the vote does for me. It gives me a status; that's what you women want – a status.

ALL: Yes, yes, a status.

HORACE: I might even call it a *locus standi*. If I go now and tell these rotten Cabinet Ministers what I think of them, it's my *locus standi* –

MAUDIE: That's a good word.

HORACE: – that will force them to listen to me. Oh, I know. And, by gum! I'll give them a bit of my mind. They shall hear a few home truths for once. 'Gentlemen,' I shall say – well, that won't be true of all of them to start with, but one must give 'em the benefit of the doubt – 'gentlemen, the men of England are sick and tired of your policy. Who's driven the women of England into this? You – (*He turns round on* ETHEL, *who jumps violently.*) – because you were too stupid to know that they meant business – because you couldn't read the writing on the wall.' (*Hear, hear.*) It may be nothing to you, gentlemen, that every industry in this country is paralysed and every Englishman's home turned into a howling wilderness –

MOLLY: Draw it mild, Uncle.

HORACE: A howling wilderness, I repeat – by your refusal to see what's as plain as the nose on your face; but I would have you know, gentlemen, that it *is* something to us. We aren't slaves. We never will be slaves –

AGATHA: Never, never!

HORACE: And we insist on reform. Gentlemen, conditions have changed, and women have to work. Don't men encourage them to work, *invite* them to work?

AGATHA: *Make* them work.

HORACE: And women are placed in the battle of life on the same terms as we are, short of one thing, the *locus standi* of a vote.

MAUDIE: Good old *locus standi*!

HORACE: If you aren't going to give it them, gentlemen, and if they won't go back to their occupations without it, we ask you how they're going to live? Who's going to support them? Perhaps you're thinking of giving them all old age pensions and asking the country to pay the piper! The country will see you damned first, if, gentlemen, you'll pardon the expression. It's dawning upon us all that the women would never have taken such a step as this if they hadn't been the victims of a gross injustice.

ALL: Never.

HORACE: Why shouldn't they have a voice in the laws which regulate the price of food and clothes? Don't they pay for their food and clothes?

MAUDIE: Paid for mine since the age of six.

HORACE: Why shouldn't they have a voice in the rate of wages and the hours of labour in certain industries? Aren't they working at those industries? If you had a particle of common sense or decent feeling, gentlemen –

Enter GERALD WILLIAMS *like a souvenir of Mafeking night. He shouts incoherently and in a hoarse voice. He is utterly transformed from the meek, smug being of an hour before. He is wearing several ribbons and badges and carries a banner bearing this inscription: 'The men of Brixton demand votes for women this evening.'*

WILLIAMS: Cole, Cole! Come on! Come on! You'll be late. The procession's forming up at the town hall. There's no time to lose. What are you slacking here for? Perhaps this isn't good enough for you. I've got twelve of them in my drawing-room. We shall be late for the procession if we don't start at once. Hurry up! Come on! Votes for Women! Where's your banner? Where's your badge? Down with the Government! Rule Britannia! Votes for Women! D'you want to support a dozen women for the rest of your life, or don't you? … Every man in Brixton is going to Westminster. Borrow a ribbon and come along.

Hurry up, now! Hooray! (*Rushes madly out crying* 'Votes for Women! Rule Britannia; Women never, never shall be slaves! Votes for Women!')

All the women who are wearing ribbons decorate HORACE.

ETHEL: My hero! (*She throws her arms round him.*)

HORACE: You may depend on me – all of you – to see justice done. When you want a thing done, get a man to do it! Votes for Women!

AGATHA gives him a flag which he waves triumphantly.

Curtain tableau: HORACE *marching majestically out of the door, with the women cheering him enthusiastically.*

Note

This play, first published in 1913, is taken from Dale Spender and Carol Hayman, eds, *How the Vote Was Won and Other Suffrage Plays*, London: Methuen, 1985, pp. 17–34.

3.2 HOPPLA, WE'RE ALIVE! (1927)

A Prologue and Five Acts

ERNST TOLLER

Translated and edited by Alan Raphael Pearlman

Ernst Toller (1893–1939) *was born into a Prussian-Jewish family and volunteered for military service in the First World War. Deeply affected by his wartime experiences, Toller turned communist agitator, becoming involved in the fleeting Bavarian Soviet Republic (1919), for which he was subsequently imprisoned. It was while incarcerated that Toller became something of a prolific dramatist and poet. In 1927, three years after his release, the ground-breaking political theatre practitioner Erwin Piscator directed Toller's* Hoppla, We're Alive! (Hoppla, wir leben!) *in Berlin. Toller's epic play, set mostly contemporaneously and 'in many countries', dramatizes the struggles encountered by a revolutionary after he has been released from a mental asylum, particularly through the impact of his friends' accommodation to the political status quo, finally resulting in his suicide. The destiny of Toller's anti-hero was to be mirrored in the dramatist's own life. Interned and tortured in a Nazi concentration camp, Toller, along with numerous compatriot artists and writers, found himself as an émigré in the USA, and ended his own life in a New York hotel. This version contains a few corrections to the 2000 edition by the translator, and some of the appendices to that edition.*

Characters in the prologue

KARL THOMAS	FRAU MELLER
EVA BERG	SIXTH PRISONER
WILHELM KILMAN	WARDER RAND
ALBERT KROLL	LIEUTENANT BARON FRIEDRICH
SOLDIERS	

Time: 1919

Characters in the play

KARL THOMAS	FRITZ
EVA BERG	GRETE
WILHELM KILMAN	FIRST WORKER
FRAU KILMAN	SECOND WORKER
LOTTE KILMAN	THIRD WORKER
ALBERT KROLL	FOURTH WORKER
FRAU MELLER	FIFTH WORKER

RAND	EXAMINING MAGISTRATE
PROFESSOR LÜDIN	HEAD WAITER
BARON FRIEDRICH	PORTER
COUNT LANDE	RADIO OPERATOR
MINISTER OF WAR	BUSBOY
BANKER	CLERK
BANKER'S SON	BARKEEPER
PICKEL	POLICE CHIEF
MINISTRY OFFICIAL	FIRST POLICEMAN
MADHOUSE ORDERLY	SECOND POLICEMAN
STUDENT	THIRD POLICEMAN

CHAIRMAN OF THE UNION OF INTELLECTUAL BRAIN WORKERS

PHILOSOPHER X
POET Y
CRITIC Z
ELECTION OFFICER
SECOND ELECTION OFFICER
FIRST ELECTIONEER
SECOND ELECTIONEER
THIRD ELECTIONEER
VOTER
OLD WOMAN
PRISONER N
JOURNALISTS
LADIES, GENTLEMEN, PEOPLE

The play takes place in many countries. Eight years after the crushing of a people's uprising. Time: 1927.

Note to the director

All the scenes of the play can be played on a scaffolding which is built up in tiers and which can be changed without rebuilding. In theatres where it is completely impossible to use film equipment, the film segments may be omitted or replaced by simple slide projections.

   In order not to break the tempo of the work, there should be, as far as possible, only one interval, namely after Act 2.

The staging information contained in square brackets in italics is based on the running notes in Piscator's Promptbook [Erwin Piscator, who first directed the play]. In the case of the film sequences for which neither the films nor the shooting scripts still exist, these notes have been augmented by material from contemporary reviews reprinted in Knellessen and Rüehle.[1] Other stage directions are from the text as published.

   [Auditorium lights go down. Then up and down three times. Curtain up to reveal film screen almost covering scaffolding.]

Film Prologue

NOISES: SIRENS

FLASHING SEARCHLIGHTS

SCENES OF A PEOPLE'S UPRISING

ITS CRUSHING

FIGURES OF THE DRAMATIC PROLOGUE APPEARING ON AND OFF

[Film: brief shot of General's headless chest with medals. Then documentary German war footage of infantry attack, charging tanks, explosions, barrage of gunfire, wounded soldiers, vast military cemeteries, retreat of worn-out German Army, disposal of

weapons in a growing heap. KARL THOMAS *visible among the marching soldiers. General's chest again: a hand roughly rips off the medals. As film ends screen is raised and white and black gauzes lowered in its place. Centre compartment where prisoners will be begins to light up. Façade of prison windows projected on to gauze and remains to end of scene. Prison noises begin to build. As lights brighten prisoners can be seen. Back projections of prison walls on centre compartment rear screen and on middle and upper left and right compartment screens – from audience viewpoint as in the Promptbook and in all the following directions. Bottom left and right compartments closed. Prologue begins.]*

PROLOGUE
Large prison cell

KARL THOMAS: Damned silence!

ALBERT KROLL: Like to sing hymns?

EVA BERG: In the French Revolution the aristocrats danced the minuet to the guillotine.

ALBERT KROLL: Romantic con! You should have inspected their knickers. The odour wouldn't have smelled like lavender.

Silence.

[Lights dim centre compartment and film of guard passing from left to right projected on the gauze. Then back projection on central compartment rear screen of RAND *climbing stairs which turns into enlarged head of* RAND *appearing from right, hovering over prisoners and returning right.* WILHELM KILMAN *reacts in fear as if it is his hallucination.]*

WILHELM KILMAN: Mother Meller, you're an old woman. You're always silent or smiling. Don't you have any fear of ... of ...? Mother Meller (*Edges towards her.*) my legs are shaking from the heat and there's ice packed around my heart ... Understand, I've got a wife and child ... Mother Meller, I'm so scared ...

FRAU MELLER: Calm down, my boy, calm down. It only seems so bad when you're young. Later on it fades away. Life and death, they flow together. You come out of one womb and you journey into another ...

WILHELM KILMAN: Do you believe there's life there?

FRAU MELLER: No, drop it. My teachers beat that belief out of me.

WILHELM KILMAN: Nobody's visited you. Didn't you want them to?

FRAU MELLER: They stole my parents and my two children in the war. Caused me great pain, but I thought to myself: times will change. And they sure did. All is lost ... But others will go on struggling ...

Silence.

[Film on gauze of resting prisoners like caged animals, crammed together like corpses.]

KARL THOMAS: Listen! I've seen something.

EVA BERG: What?

[Back projected film on centre rear screen of warders approaching, growing larger, looking at prisoners, turning and going away.]

Figure 21 *Hoppla, We're Alive!* from the Berliner-Schauspielschule studio production, 1984. (Photographer: uncredited.)

KARL THOMAS: No, don't crowd around. Bug-eyes is at the spy-hole ... We'll escape.

ALBERT KROLL: Like the taste of lead?

KARL THOMAS: Look at the window. The plaster around the iron bars has crumbled.

ALBERT KROLL: Yes, you're right.

KARL THOMAS: And isn't that big piece of plaster faked to look firm? ...

ALBERT KROLL: Right.

KARL THOMAS: Do you see?

EVA BERG: Yes. Yes. A kid's trick to drive you mad.

FRAU MELLER: Yes. How true.

WILHELM KILMAN: That's where they once tried to get into the cell from outside ... Almost did it ... Well, I don't know.

FRAU MELLER: (*To* WILHELM KILMAN.) What, scaredy-pants?

WILHELM KILMAN: Yes, but ...

KARL THOMAS: What's with the 'but'?

ALBERT KROLL: You know I'm not reckless. It's night. How late?

KARL THOMAS: It's just struck four.

ALBERT KROLL: Then the guard has changed. We're on the first floor. If we stay here, we'll say good morning in a mass grave. If we try to escape, the odds are ten to one against. And even if they were a hundred to one, we must take the risk.

WILHELM KILMAN: If not ...

KARL THOMAS: Dead either way ... Albert, you do a parade march, six steps back and forth, from the window to the door without stopping. Then the spy-hole will be blocked for a few seconds and outside they won't notice anything. The fifth time I'll jump up to the window and with all my strength pull the iron bars out and then 'Bye-bye, boss'.

EVA BERG: I could scream! Karl, I could kiss you to death.

ALBERT KROLL: Later.

[*Back projected film on centre rear screen of two guards approaching, turning and leaving.*]

KARL THOMAS: Leave her alone. She's so young.

ALBERT KROLL: Karl, you jump out first, then Eva second; then, Wilhelm, you grab Mother Meller and push her up ...

WILHELM KILMAN: Yes, yes ... only I think ...

FRAU MELLER: Let him go first ... No one needs to help me. I can cope like all of you.

ALBERT KROLL: Shut up. You go first, then Wilhelm, then me last.

WILHELM KILMAN: What if the escape doesn't work? We'd better think it over.

ALBERT KROLL: If the escape doesn't work ...

KARL THOMAS: How can you know if any escape will work? You've got to take the risk, comrade! A revolutionary who doesn't take risks! You should have stayed home drinking coffee with your mother, not gone to the barricades.

WILHELM KILMAN: We'd all be lost afterwards. There'd be no more hope.

KARL THOMAS: To hell with hope! Hope for what? The death sentence was passed. For ten days we've been waiting for the execution.

FRAU MELLER: Last night they asked for the addresses of our relatives.

KARL THOMAS: So hope for what? A volley of gunfire, and if it misses the bonus of a finishing shot. A good victory or a good death – the battle cry hasn't changed for a thousand years.

WILHELM KILMAN cowers.

Or ... have you been begging for mercy? If so, at least swear you'll keep silent.

WILHELM KILMAN: Why do you let him insult me. Haven't I drudged day and night? For fifteen years I've slaved for

the Party and now I must be allowed my say ... I don't get breakfast in bed.

FRAU MELLER: Peace, both of you.

KARL THOMAS: Just think of the trial. Are they likely to quash the death sentence? Strike a concrete wall and do you think it's going to ring clear as a bell?

ALBERT KROLL: Let's go! Everybody ready? Eva, you count. Take care, Karl ... the fifth time.

ALBERT KROLL begins to march back and forth, from the window to the door, from the door to the window. Everybody tense.

EVA BERG: One ... two ... three ...

KARL THOMAS steals to the window.

FOUR ...

Noise at the door. Door creaks open.

ALBERT KROLL: Damn it!

WARDER RAND enters.

WARDER RAND: Anyone want the priest?

FRAU MELLER: He really ought to be ashamed of himself.

RAND: Don't commit a sin, old woman. You'll be standing before your Maker soon enough.

FRAU MELLER: I've learned the worms know nothing about religious faiths. Tell your priest Jesus drove the money-changers and usurers out of the temple with lashes of the whip. Tell him to write that down in his Bible, on the first page.

RAND: (*To the SIXTH PRISONER who's lying on a plank bed.*) And you?

SIXTH PRISONER: (*Softly.*) Forgive me, comrades ... I left the Church at sixteen ... now ... before death ... terrifying ... understand me, comrades ... Yes, I want to go to the priest, Herr Warder.

WILHELM KILMAN: Revolutionary? You shit-pants! To the priest! Dear God, make me holy so I'll go to heaven.

FRAU MELLER: Why attack the poor devil?

ALBERT KROLL: Before death ... Leave him alone.

WILHELM KILMAN: A man can say what he wants.

WARDER and SIXTH PRISONER leave. Door is closed.

[*Back projected centre rear screen film of RAND and SIXTH PRISONER going off, turns into laughing head of rand with distorted grimace as shooting starts.*]

ALBERT KROLL: Won't he betray us?

KARL THOMAS: No.

ALBERT KROLL: Look! Now that he has to go with him, he can't spy on us. Get going Karl, I'll help you. Here, on my back ...

[*Film on gauze of guns shooting. GUARD laughs and goes right.*]

ALBERT KROLL bends over. KARL THOMAS climbs on ALBERT KROLL's bent back. As he stretches both hands towards the windowsill to grab the iron bars, rifles rattle from below, plaster and other fragments come flying into the cell. KARL THOMAS jumps off ALBERT KROLL's back. They all stare at each other.

Are you wounded?

KARL THOMAS: No. What was that?

ALBERT KROLL: Nothing special. They're guarding our window. A small company.

EVA BERG: That ... means ...?

FRAU MELLER: Prepare yourself, my child.

EVA BERG: For ... for death ...?

The others are silent.

No ... no ... (*Sobs, cries.*)

FRAU MELLER goes to her, strokes her.

ALBERT KROLL: Don't cry, dear girl. We revolutionaries are all dead men on leave, as someone once said.

KARL THOMAS: Leave her alone, Albert. She's young. Barely seventeen. For her death means a cold, black hole which she has to lie in forever. And on top of her grave there's life – warm, exciting, gay and sweet.

KARL THOMAS goes to EVA BERG.

Your hands.

EVA BERG: Dear you.

KARL THOMAS: I love you very much, Eva.

EVA BERG: Will they bury us together, if we ask them?

KARL THOMAS: Maybe.

ALBERT KROLL jumps up.

ALBERT KROLL: Damn torture! Why don't they come? I once read that cats torture mice so long because they smell so good in their death throes ... For us there must be other refinements. Why don't they come? Why don't the dirty dogs come?

KARL THOMAS: Yes, why do we struggle? What do we know? For the Idea, for Justice – we say. No one's dug deep enough into himself to bow down before the ultimate, naked reason – if there are ultimate reasons.

ALBERT KROLL: I don't understand. I've known that our society lives off the sweat of our hands ever since I was sixteen and was dragged out of bed at five in the morning to deliver rolls. And what has to be done to end injustice, that I knew even before I could reckon how much ten times ten is ...

KARL THOMAS: Look around at how everyone pounces upon the Idea in times of revolution and war. One is running away from his wife because she makes his life hell. Another can't cope with life and limps along until he finds a crutch which makes him look wonderful and gives him a little heroic sheen. A third believes he can all of a sudden change his skin, which has become repulsive to him. A fourth seeks adventure. There are fewer and fewer who must do so out of inmost necessity.

[All but first and last lines of this speech cut.]

Noise. Door creaks open. SIXTH PRISONER enters. Silence.

SIXTH PRISONER: Do you hold it against me, comrades? I'm not converted, comrades ... But ... it makes me calmer ...

KARL THOMAS: Judas!

SIXTH PRISONER: But dear comrades ...

ALBERT KROLL: Still no decision! Still waiting! I'd like to smoke, has anyone got a butt?

They search in their pockets.

ALL: No.

KARL THOMAS: Wait ... sure ... I've got a cigarette.

ALL: Bring it here! Bring it here!

ALBERT KROLL: Matches? No go.

WILHELM KILMAN: I have one.

ALBERT KROLL: We must share it, of course.

WILHELM KILMAN: Really?

EVA BERG: Yes, please.

KARL THOMAS: Eva can have my share.

FRAU MELLER: Mine too.

EVA BERG: No, one puff each.

ALBERT KROLL: Good. Who'll start?

EVA BERG: We'll draw lots.

ALBERT KROLL: (*Tears a handkerchief into strips.*) Whoever draws the smallest strip.

All draw.

Mother Meller starts.

FRAU MELLER: Here goes. (*Smokes.*) Now your turn. (*Gives WILHELM KILMAN the cigarette.*)

WILHELM KILMAN: I hope they won't catch us.

ALBERT KROLL: What could they do to us? Four weeks solitary confinement for punishment! Ha, ha, ha.

They all smoke, one puff each. They watch each other closely.

Karl, you mustn't take two puffs.

KARL THOMAS: Don't talk rubbish.

ALBERT KROLL: Think I'm lying?

KARL THOMAS: Yes.

WILHELM KILMAN: (*To ALBERT KROLL.*) You sucked much longer than we did.

ALBERT KROLL: Shut up, coward.

WILHELM KILMAN: He's calling me coward.

ALBERT KROLL: Where did you creep off to during the days of decision? Where did you rub your trouser seat shiny while we stormed the town hall – with the enemy at our backs and a mass grave in front of us? Where were you hiding?

WILHELM KILMAN: Didn't I address the masses from the balcony of the town hall?

ALBERT KROLL: Yes, when we had power. But before, neither for nor against. Then in a flash you're at the feeding trough.

KARL THOMAS: (*To* ALBERT KROLL.) You have no right to talk like that.

ALBERT KROLL: Bourgeois lackey!

FRAU MELLER: What scum, to row five minutes before you're put up against the wall …

WILHELM KILMAN: He's calling me coward! For fifteen years I have …

ALBERT KROLL: (*Aping him.*) Fifteen years … Big shot … No great honour to bite the dust together with you.

EVA BERG: Shame!

KARL THOMAS: Yes, shame.

ALBERT KROLL: What shame! Go lie with your whore in the corner and give her a kid. Then it can hatch in the grave and play with the worms.

EVA BERG screams. KARL THOMAS jumps on ALBERT KROLL.

SIXTH PRISONER: (*Jumping up.*) Heavenly Father, is this Thy will?

As they hold each other by the throat, noise. Door creaks open. They let go.

RAND: The Lieutenant is coming now. You must get ready. (*Goes.*)

ALBERT KROLL goes up to KARL THOMAS, embraces him.

ALBERT KROLL: We don't know anything about ourselves, Karl. That wasn't me just now, that wasn't me. Give me your hand, dear Eva.

KARL THOMAS: For ten days we've been waiting for death. That has poisoned us.

Noise. Door creaks open. LIEUTENANT *enters with* SOLDIERS.

LIEUTENANT BARON FRIEDRICH: (*To* ALBERT KROLL.) Stand up. In the name of the President. The death sentence was pronounced in accordance with the law. (*Pause.*) As a sign of his clemency and his wish for reconciliation the President has quashed the death sentence. The condemned are to be held in protective custody and are to be transported to the internment camp immediately. With the exception of Wilhelm Kilman.

KARL THOMAS bursts into howls of laughter.

EVA BERG: Your laughter is terrifying, Karl.

FRAU MELLER: For joy.

LIEUTENANT BARON FRIEDRICH: Stop laughing, man.

EVA BERG: Karl! Karl!

ALBERT KROLL: He's not laughing for fun.

FRAU MELLER: Just look at him. It's convulsed him.

LIEUTENANT BARON FRIEDRICH: (*To the* WARDER.) Take him to the doctor.

KARL THOMAS is led out. EVA BERG *goes with him.*

ALBERT KROLL: (*To* WILHELM KILMAN.) You're the only one to stay. Forgive me, Wilhelm. We won't forget you.

FRAU MELLER: (*Leaving, to* ALBERT KROLL.) Clemency. Who would have thought that the authorities could feel so weak.

ALBERT KROLL: Bad sign. Who would have thought that the authorities could feel so strong.

All leave, except LIEUTENANT BARON FRIEDRICH *and* WILHELM KILMAN.

LIEUTENANT BARON FRIEDRICH: The President has granted your petition. He believes you, that you came to be in the ranks of the rebels against your will. You are free.

WILHELM KILMAN: Thank you most respectfully, Herr Lieutenant.

Curtain.

[Gauze up. Projection of prison windows off. Screen lowered for film.]

Film Interlude

Behind the stage:

CHORUS: (*In rhythmical crescendo and diminuendo.*)
Happy New Year! Happy New Year!
Special Edition! Special Edition!
Great Sensation!
Special Edition! Special Edition!
Great Sensation!

On the screen:

Scenes from the years 1919–1927.

Between them: KARL THOMAS *in asylum dress pacing back and forth in a lunatic cell.*

1919:
Treaty of Versailles
1920:
Stock Market Turmoil in New York
People go mad
1921:
Fascism in Italy
1922:
Hunger in Vienna
People go mad
1923:
Inflation in Germany
People go mad
1924:
Lenin's Death in Russia
Newspaper Notice: Tonight Frau Luise Thomas died …
1925:
Gandhi in India
1926:
Battles in China
Conference of European Leaders in Europe

1927:

Dial of a Clock

The hands advance. First slowly … then faster

and faster …

Noises: Clocks

[Seven minutes of documentary film of key events probably intercut with KARL THOMAS *pacing in Lunatic Asylum, and a collage of popular images of Weimar life contrasting, as the play does, frivolity and hardship. It followed the above scenario quite closely, including the clock, adding in events like the election of Hindenburg in 1925 and some self-filmed scenes. As the film ended, screen out and gauze in with projection of façade of Lunatic Asylum which remains through scene. Lights come up in the centre and right bottom compartments to reveal* PROFESSOR LÜDIN's *Office. Back projections of filing cabinet centre compartment screen and wardrobe bottom right compartment screen.]*

ACT 1
Scene 1
Office of a Lunatic Asylum

ORDERLY *at cupboard.*

PROFESSOR LÜDIN *at barred window.*

ORDERLY: One pair grey trousers. One pair woollen socks. Didn't you bring any underclothes with you?

KARL THOMAS: I don't know.

ORDERLY: Oh! One black waistcoat. One black coat. One pair of low shoes. Hat missing.

PROFESSOR LÜDIN: And money?

ORDERLY: None, Herr Doctor.

PROFESSOR LÜDIN: Relations?

KARL THOMAS: Notified me yesterday, that my mother died, three years ago.

PROFESSOR LÜDIN: You're going to find things difficult. Life is hard today. You've got to elbow your way. Don't despair. All in good time.

ORDERLY: Release date: 8 May 1927.

[This date was changed to that of the performance every night.]

KARL THOMAS: No!

PROFESSOR LÜDIN: Yes, indeed.

KARL THOMAS: 1927.

PROFESSOR LÜDIN: So, eight little years of room and board with us. Clothed, fed, cared for. Nothing was lacking. You can be proud of yourself: clinically you've been a noteworthy case.

KARL THOMAS: As if obliterated. Yes … I do remember something …

PROFESSOR LÜDIN: What?

KARL THOMAS: The edge of a wood. Trees stretched brown to the sky like pillars. Beech trees. The wood glittered green. With a thousand tiny suns. So delicate. I wanted to go in,

so very badly. I couldn't do it. Evilly the tree trunks bent outwards and three me back like a rubber ball.

PROFESSOR LÜDIN: Wait! Like a rubber ball. Interesting association. Look here, your nerves are consistent with the truth. The wood: the padded cell. The tree trunks: walls of best quality rubber. Yes, I remember: once every year you began to rave. We had to isolate you. Always on the same day. What a perfect clinical masterpiece!

KARL THOMAS: On which day?

PROFESSOR LÜDIN: On the day when … But you must know.

KARL THOMAS: On the day of the reprieve …

PROFESSOR LÜDIN: Do you remember everything?

KARL THOMAS: Yes.

PROFESSOR LÜDIN: Then you are cured.

KARL THOMAS: To wait even minutes for death … But ten days. Ten times twenty-four hours. Each hour sixty minutes. Each minute sixty seconds. Each second a murder. Murdered fourteen hundred and forty times in one day. And the nights! … I hated the reprieve. I hated the President. Only a dirty scoundrel could act like that.

PROFESSOR LÜDIN: Take it easy. You have every reason to be thankful … In here we don't mind strong language. But outside … You'd be rewarded with another year in prison for insulting the Head of State. Be reasonable. You must have already had a noseful of that.

KARL THOMAS: You have to say that because you belong to the bosses.

PROFESSOR LÜDIN: We should conclude this interview. You needn't be depressed because you were in a mad-house. Actually most people ought to be in one. Were I to examine a thousand, I would have to keep nine hundred and ninety-nine in hear.

KARL THOMAS: Why don't you do it?

PROFESSOR LÜDIN: The State has no interest in it. On the contrary. With a little drop of madness men become respectable husbands. With two drops of madness they become socially conscious … Don't do anything stupid. I only want what's good for you. Go to one of your friends.

KARL THOMAS: Where could they have got to? …

PROFESSOR LÜDIN: Weren't there others in your cell back then?

KARL THOMAS: Five. Only one wasn't reprieved. His name was Wilhelm Kilman.

PROFESSOR LÜDIN: Not reprieved? Ha, ha ha. His career has galloped ahead! Smarter than you.

KARL THOMAS: I don't understand you.

PROFESSOR LÜDIN: You'll understand me soon enough. Just go to him. He could help you. If he wants to help you. If he wants to know you.

KARL THOMAS: He's still alive?

PROFESSOR LÜDIN: You're going to experience a miracle. An excellent prescription for you. I have cured you clinically. He might cure you of your crazy ideas. Go to the Ministry of the Interior and ask for Herr Kilman. Good luck.

KARL THOMAS: Good day, Herr Doctor. Good day, Herr

Orderly ... It smells so strongly of lilac here ... Of course, spring. Isn't it true that there are real beeches growing outside the window ... not rubber padded walls ... (KARL THOMAS *leaves.*)

PROFESSOR LÜDIN: Bad breed.

Blackout.

[Gauze out. Screen in.]

Film Interlude

Bid City 1927

STREET CARS
AUTOS
UNDERGROUND TRAINS
AEROPLANE

[Film of KARL THOMAS in hostel for the homeless, helplessly seeking work from factory to factory, searching for lodgings, in the hustle and bustle of Potsdam Square etc. Screen out and gauze stays out. Back projection of Kaiser centre compartment screen and of wall paper in middle left and bottom right compartments for next scene.]

Scene 2

Two rooms visible: Minister's Antechamber, Minister's Office.

When the curtain rises both rooms can be seen.

The room in which nothing is said goes dark.

Office

WILHELM KILMAN: I sent for you.

EVA BERG: Of course.

Antechamber

BANKER'S SON: Will he receive you? He hasn't sent for you.

BANKER: Not receive me! Just let him try it.

BANKER'S SON: We need credits up to the end of the month.

BANKER: Why are you doubtful?

BANKER'S SON: Because he's rejected the chance both times now.

BANKER: I operated too crudely.

Office

WILHELM KILMAN: You sit on the Committee of the Union of Female Employees?

EVA BERG: Yes.

WILHELM KILMAN: You work as a secretary in the Revenue Office?

EVA BERG: Yes.

WILHELM KILMAN: For two months now your name has featured prominently in the police reports.

EVA BERG: I don't understand.

WILHELM KILMAN: You've been inciting the women workers at the Chemical Works to refuse overtime?

EVA BERG: I'm only exercising the rights which our Constitution guarantees me.

WILHELM KILMAN: The Constitution is intended for peaceful times.

EVA BERG: Aren't we living in them now?

WILHELM KILMAN: The State rarely knows peaceful times.

Antechamber

BANKER: The matter must be settled before the tariff announcement. Two hours of overtime, take it or leave it.

BANKER'S SON: The trade unions have decided to hold out for an eight hour working day.

BANKER: Whatever is good for the State will be right for heavy industry.

BANKER'S SON: We'll have to lock out half a million workers.

BANKER: And so what? We'll kill two birds with one stone. Overtime and lower pay.

Office

EVA BERG: I am against war. If I had the power, the Works would come to a standstill. What do they make? Poison gas!

WILHELM KILMAN: Your personal opinion, which doesn't interest me. I don't like war either. Do you know this leaflet? Are you the author?

EVA BERG: Yes.

WILHELM KILMAN: You have violated your duties as a State Official.

EVA BERG: There was a time when you did the same.

WILHELM KILMAN: We're having an official conversation, Fräulein.

EVA BERG: In the past you have ...

WILHELM KILMAN: Keep to the present. I have to maintain order ... Dear Fräulein Berg, be reasonable now. Do you want to bash your stubborn head in? The State always has a harder skull. I don't mean you any harm. We need the overtime at the moment. You lack practical knowledge. It would be damned painful for me to proceed against you. I know you well from before. But I would have to. Really. Be reasonable. Promise me that ...

EVA BERG: I promise nothing.

Antechamber

PICKEL: (*Who from the beginning of the scene has been pacing restlessly back and forth, stops in front of the BANKER.*) Pardon me, sir ... I come from Holzhausen, namely. Perhaps the gentleman knows Holzhausen? Indeed with the building of the railway, it won't be started until October. Nevertheless the mailcoach was really enough for me. There's a saying we have ...

BANKER turns away.

I believe, indeed, that the railway ...

As no one is listening to him, he breaks off, paces back and forth.

Office

WILHELM KILMAN: The State must protect itself. I was not obliged to send for you. I wanted to give you my advice. No one can say that ... you alone bear the responsibility. I warn you. (*Gesture.*)

EVA BERG goes.

(*On the telephone.*) Chemical Works ... Herr Director? ... Kilman ... Well? Works meeting at 12 o'clock ... Phone me the result ... Thank you ... (*Hangs up.*)

The MINISTER OF WAR *walks through the Antechamber*

MINISTER OF WAR: Ah, good day, Herr Director-General. You here too?

BANKER: Yes, unfortunately. This wretched waiting ... Permit me, Herr Minister of War, to introduce my son ... His Excellency von Wandsring.

MINISTER OF WAR: Pleased ... A delicate situation.

PICKEL: (*Turns to the* MINISTER OF WAR.) I think, Herr General, indeed the enemy ...

As the MINISTER OF WAR *doesn't pay him any attention, he breaks off, goes to the corner, fumbles in his pocket for a medal, pins it on hurriedly and with great difficulty.*

BANKER: You will see to it, Herr General.

MINISTER OF WAR: Certainly. Only ... it gives me no pleasure to shoot people whom we first give drumsticks to eagerly and then stop from beating the drum. These liberal utopias of democracy and freedom of the people are getting us into trouble. We need authority. The condensed experience of thousands of years. You can't refute that with slogans.

BANKER: Yet democracy, in moderation of course, needn't necessarily lead to mob-rule on the one hand, and on the other hand it could be a safety valve ...

MINISTER OF WAR: Democracy ... stuff and nonsense. The people rule? Where on earth? Well then, better an honest dictatorship. Let's not whitewash anything, Herr Director-General ... Will we see each other at the club tomorrow?

BANKER: With great pleasure.

MINISTER OF WAR leaves. COUNT LANDE *follows him to the door.*

COUNT LANDE: Excellency ...

MINISTER OF WAR: Ah, Count Lande. Arranged?

COUNT LANDE: Yes indeed, Excellency.

MINISTER OF WAR: Are things going well for you?

COUNT LANDE: The front groups are waiting.

MINISTER OF WAR: Don't act hot-headedly, Count. Nothing foolish. The time for violence is over. What we want

to achieve for our Fatherland, we can achieve by legal means.

COUNT LANDE: Excellency, we are relying on you.

MINISTER OF WAR: Count, with all my sympathy ... I caution you.

MINISTER OF WAR goes.

PICKEL: (*In a military manner.*) At your command, Herr General.

MINISTER OF WAR leaves without noticing him.

BANKER: How long will Kilman hold out?

BANKER'S SON: Why don't you do the business through Wandsring?

BANKER: Today Kilman governs. No harm being on the safe side.

BANKER'S SON: He's *passé*. You can throw your Kilman into the bankrupt estate of democracy. Just sniff the air of industry. I'd advise you to bet on a national dictatorship.

PICKEL: (*Turns to* COUNT LANDE.) Can you tell me, sir, what time it is?

COUNT LANDE: Fourteen past twelve.

PICKEL: The clocks in the city are always fast. I imagined that an interview with the Minister would be at twelve sharp ... Indeed the clocks in the country are always slow, consequently ...

As COUNT LANDE *doesn't notice him, he breaks off, paces back and forth.*

COUNT LANDE: How do you address Kilman?

BARON FRIEDRICH: As Excellency, naturally.

COUNT LANDE: Do the comrades enjoy the taste of 'Excellency'?

BARON FRIEDRICH: Same old business, my dear friend. Dress a man in a uniform and he'll pine for even a lance-corporal's stripes.

COUNT LANDE: And he keeps us waiting in the antechamber. Ten years ago I wouldn't have shaken hands with his kind unless I was wearing buckskin gloves.

BARON FRIEDRICH: Don't get excited. I can dish you up other delicacies. Eight years ago I almost had him put up against the wall.

COUNT LANDE: Fabulously interesting. Were you involved at that time?

BARON FRIEDRICH: Not half! Let's not talk about it.

COUNT LANDE: And still he appointed you to the Ministry. Always in his presence. You must get on his nerves.

BARON FRIEDRICH: That's exactly what I feared. When he first came into the Ministry, the Great Court of Chancellery, I took the liberty of raking up old stories. One must play the game in order to be ready for when times change again. He gave me a sharp look. From that day on, one promotion after another, however disagreeably. But he never talks about it.

COUNT LANDE: A sort of hush money.

BARON FRIEDRICH: Don't know. Let's speak about the weather. I suspect the rascal has first class spies at his disposal.

COUNT LANDE: The comrades have learned all the old tricks from us.

PICKEL: (*Turning to* BARON FRIEDRICH.) Indeed my neighbour in Holzhausen asserted, namely ... Pickel, he asserted, for an interview with the Minister you must buy yourself white gloves. That's how it was in the old government, and that's how it still remains in the new one. The ceremonial regulations demand it. However I ... I thought if the Monarchy demanded white gloves, in the Republic we ought to put on black gloves ... Namely that, exactly! ... Because we are now free men ...

As BARON FRIEDRICH *doesn't notice him, he breaks off, paces back and forth.*

BARON FRIEDRICH: A clever rascal, you have to give him that.

COUNT LANDE: Manners?

BARON FRIEDRICH: I don't know whether he took lessons from actors like Napoleon did. In any case, a gentleman from head to toe. Rides every morning in full dress, immaculate, I tell you.

COUNT LANDE: And through which cracks can you smell the stink of the prole?

BARON FRIEDRICH: Through all of them. You only have to see how he puts a little too much into every word, every gesture, every step. People think that if they have their dress coats cut by a first class tailor, that's enough. They don't realise that first class tailors are only worth something for first class customers.

COUNT LANDE: In any case I'd dine with the devil's grandmother, if she'd help me get out of the provinces into the capital.

BARON FRIEDRICH: The 'grandmother' with whom you'll dine keeps a table that's not to be despised.

COUNT LANDE: She's certainly been a house servant long enough for that.

Office

MINISTRY OFFICIAL: Her Excellency and your daughter would like to speak with you, Excellency. They are waiting in the drawing room.

WILHELM KILMAN: Please ask them to be patient for ten minutes.

MINISTRY OFFICIAL leaves. Telephone rings.

Hello. It's you, Herr Privy Councillor. Yes, it's me ... Nothing doing ... No, no, you're not disturbing me at all ... The collapse of the Chemical Works ... A stage trick ... It's fixed, of course it's fixed ... Very cunning people are behind it. We agreed State credits yesterday ... How? Unanimously ... Three per cent ... Always at your service ... Goodbye, Herr Privy Councillor.

MINISTRY OFFICIAL enters.

MINISTRY OFFICIAL: The ladies say ...

WILHELM KILMAN: They must wait, I have to work.

Antechamber

BARON FRIEDRICH: Please, said the little daughter and bared her knee.

COUNT LANDE: And the mother?

BARON FRIEDRICH: Thought it was refined manners and blushed silently.

COUNT LANDE: The capital is worth the strains of a maidenhead. How long it's taking. Governing doesn't seem to come easily to him.

KARL THOMAS enters, sits in a corner.

Office

WILHELM KILMAN rings. MINISTRY OFFICIAL enters.

MINISTRY OFFICIAL: Excellency ...?

WILHELM KILMAN: Baron Friedrich and Count Lande ...

MINISTRY OFFICIAL bows, goes out.

Antechamber

MINISTRY OFFICIAL: (*To* COUNT LANDE *and* BARON FRIEDRICH.) His Excellency will receive you now ...

BANKER: Excuse me, gentlemen. Give His Excellency this card. Only one minute.

MINISTRY OFFICIAL goes into the office. BANKER and SON follow him.

Office

WILHELM KILMAN: Good day, Herr Director-General. Good day, Herr Doctor. Today I'm not really in a position to ...

BANKER: Then we'd do better to meet at your leisure.

WILHELM KILMAN: Please.

BANKER: This evening at the Grand Hotel.

WILHELM KILMAN: Agreed.

BANKER and SON go.

MINISTRY OFFICIAL: (*To* COUNT LANDE *and* BARON FRIEDRICH.) His Excellency will receive you now.

Opens the door to the office. COUNT LANDE and BARON FRIEDRICH enter. MINISTRY OFFICIAL starts to leave through the side door.

KARL THOMAS: Excuse me.

MINISTRY OFFICIAL: His Excellency is busy. I don't know if His Excellency will receive anyone else today.

KARL THOMAS: I don't want to speak to the Minister. I want to speak to Herr Kilman.

MINISTRY OFFICIAL: Play your stupid jokes on someone else.

KARL THOMAS: Jokes, comrade . . .

MINISTRY OFFICIAL: I'm not your comrade.

KARL THOMAS: Perhaps Herr Kilman works as the Minister's secretary? The porter directed me to the Minister's antechamber when I asked for Herr Kilman.

MINISTRY OFFICIAL: Do you come from the moon? Are you trying to make me believe that you didn't know His Excellency's name is Kilman? On the whole you're making a very suspicious impression . . . I'm going to call the Chief Detective Inspector.

KARL THOMAS: Don't you mean another Kilman? There are so many Kilmans.

MINISTRY OFFICIAL: What do you want?

KARL THOMAS: I would like to speak to Herr Wilhelm Kilman. Kilman. K-I-L-M-A-N.

MINISTRY OFFICIAL: That's how His Excellency spells it . . . What a shady character.

(*MINISTRY OFFICIAL starts to go out.*)

KARL THOMAS: Kilman Minister? . . . No, wait. I know the Minister, you see. I am his friend. Yes, really, his friend. Eight years ago we were . . . Just wait now . . . Do you have a piece of paper? . . . Pencil? I'll write down my name for the Minister. He will receive me immediately.

MINISTRY OFFICIAL is unsure.

Go on then!

MINISTRY OFFICIAL: You should keep up with the times.

Gives KARL THOMAS paper and pen. Goes out. KARL THOMAS writes.

PICKEL: Well, well . . . a friend of the Minister . . . Although I namely . . . Pickel is my name . . . Oh, this lout of an official . . . Indeed one ought to take a stricter line with these old court flunkies, but nevertheless we Republicans put up with anything . . . I on the other hand understood the joke about your friend, the Minister, immediately . . . One ought to be allowed one's little joke about the Minister . . . I think something must be done . . . In the upper levels of administration for example this official . . . Namely that is a shortcoming in the Republic . . .

Office

WILHELM KILMAN: One must know how to deal with nations, gentlemen.

BARON FRIEDRICH: Excellency, don't you think that America has no interest in war . . .

COUNT LANDE: Consider, Excellency, France's peaceful attitude . . .

WILHELM KILMAN: Because Ministers prattle on about world peace and make a show of humanitarian ideas? But gentlemen. Observe how often 'world peace' and 'humanitarian idea' are flaunted in any ministerial speech, and I guarantee you that just so many poison gas factories and aeroplane squadrons are marked down for secret action. Ministerial speeches . . . gentlemen . . .

BARON FRIEDRICH: It is said that Machiavelli is one of your Excellency's favourite authors.

WILHELM KILMAN: What do we need Machiavelli for . . . Simple common sense.

MINISTRY OFFICIAL enters.

MINISTRY OFFICIAL: May the ladies now . . .

WILHELM KILMAN: show them in.

FRAU KILMAN and her daughter LOTTE KILMAN enter.

You know, I'm sure, Herr Baron . . .

BARON FRIEDRICH: Excellency . . . Fräulein.

FRAU KILMAN: But please don't always call me 'Excellency'. You know I don't like it.

WILHELM KILMAN: Count Lande. My wife. My daughter.

COUNT LANDE: Excellency . . . Fräulein.

BARON FRIEDRICH: No doubt we're disturbing you . . .

FRAU KILMAN: No, as it happens I just wrote to you. I invited you for Sunday.

COUNT LANDE: Enchanted to meet you.

FRAU KILMAN: Perhaps you'll bring your friend with you.

BARON FRIEDRICH: Only too honoured, Excellency.

LOTTE KILMAN: (*Softly to BARON FRIEDRICH.*) You stood me up yesterday.

BARON FRIEDRICH: (*Softly.*) But darling . . .

LOTTE KILMAN: Your friend pleases me.

BARON FRIEDRICH: I congratulate him.

LOTTE KILMAN: I read your personal file.

BARON FRIEDRICH: When can we meet?

WILHELM KILMAN: Yes, Count, we must simply deny it. Slanders from the Left – I don't even read. Slanders from the Right – they are blessed with one of my answers. I know the qualities of the men of the old regime. A man is only a man, has weaknesses, but the most extreme conservatives cannot charge me with a lack of justice.

COUNT LANDE: But Excellency . . . You are esteemed in Nationalist circles.

WILHELM KILMAN: I'll write to your District Head today. You start your Ministry employment in four weeks.

Antechamber

KARL THOMAS: (*Pacing back and forth rapidly.*) Minister . . . Minister . . .

Office

The MINISTER says goodbye to COUNT LANDE and BARON FRIEDRICH.

Antechamber

BARON FRIEDRICH: What did I tell you?

COUNT LANDE: Some comrades! . . . Some comrades! . . .

Both leave.

KARL THOMAS: I have seen that face. Where?

MINISTRY OFFICIAL enters.

Here's the note for the Minister.

MINISTRY OFFICIAL takes the note and carries it into the Office.

Office

[All other compartments dark. Scaffolding revolves to left to give close-up effect.]

MINISTRY OFFICIAL: A man, Excellency.

WILHELM KILMAN: I don't want ...

KARL THOMAS knocks on the door, enters without waiting for an answer.

KARL THOMAS: Wilhelm! Wilhelm!

WILHELM KILMAN: Who are you?

KARL THOMAS: You don't know me any more. The years ... eight years ...

WILHELM KILMAN: (*To* MINISTRY OFFICIAL.) You may go.

MINISTRY OFFICIAL leaves.

KARL THOMAS: You're still alive. Explain it to me. We were reprieved. You the only one not ...

WILHELM KILMAN: Chance ... a lucky chance.

KARL THOMAS: Eight years ... walled up like a grave. I told the doctor I remembered nothing. Oh Wilhelm, when fully conscious I often saw ... Often ... Saw you dead ... I gouged my eyes until they spurted blood ... the orderlies thought I was having fits.

WILHELM KILMAN: Yes ... those days ... I don't like to remember.

KARL THOMAS: Death always huddled with us. Inciting us against each other.

WILHELM KILMAN: What children we were.

KARL THOMAS: Those hours in prison bond us together in blood. That's why I came to you when I heard you were alive. You can count on me.

FRAU KILMAN: Wilhelm, we must go now.

KARL THOMAS: Frau Kilman. Good morning, Frau Kilman. I didn't even see you before. Are you their daughter? You're so grown up.

LOTTE KILMAN: Everyone grows up sometime; meanwhile my father has also become Minister.

KARL THOMAS: ... Do you remember how you were allowed to visit your husband for the last time in the condemned cell? How sorry I was for you. They had to carry you out. And your daughter stood next to the door with her hands over her face and just kept on repeating: No, no, no.

FRAU KILMAN: Yes, I remember. It was a hard time. Wasn't it, Wilhelm? Things are going well for you now? That's nice. Pay us a visit sometime.

KARL THOMAS: Thank you, Frau Kilman.

FRAU KILMAN and LOTTE KILMAN go.

Must it be like that? That your daughter pretends to be a fine lady?

WILHELM KILMAN: What?

KARL THOMAS: Your ministerial office is just a trick, isn't it? Still it's a risky trick. Before such tactics wouldn't have been permitted. Is the whole apparatus almost in our hands?

WILHELM KILMAN: You talk as if we were still in the middle of a revolution.

KARL THOMAS: What?

WILHELM KILMAN: Since then ten years have passed. Just when we began to see a straight way ahead, hard reality rose up and bent it crooked. Still, things go on.

KARL THOMAS: So you take your office seriously?

WILHELM KILMAN: Certainly.

KARL THOMAS: And the people?

WILHELM KILMAN: I serve the people.

KARL THOMAS: Didn't you once prove that whoever sits in a Minister's chair in such a State, with his worst enemies as colleagues, would fail, would have to fail, no matter whether he is driven by good intentions or not?

WILHELM KILMAN: Life doesn't unreel according to theories. You learn by experience.

KARL THOMAS: They should have put you up against the wall!

WILHELM KILMAN: Still the hot-headed dreamer. I won't take offence at your words. We want to govern democratically. But what is democracy after all? The will of all the people. As Minister I do not represent a party, but the State. When one has responsibility, my dear friend, things down below look different. Power confers responsibility.

KARL THOMAS: Power! What's the use of imagining you possess power, if the people have none? For five days I've been looking around. Has anything changed? You sit on top and legitimise the big con. Don't you understand that you've deserted the Idea, that you govern against the people?

WILHELM KILMAN: Sometimes it requires courage to govern against the people. More than going to the barricades.

Telephone rings.

Excuse me ... Kilman ... Unanimous decision to refuse overtime ... Thank you, Herr Director ... Does the leaflet contain names? Aha ... Make note: whoever leaves the factory at five o'clock is dismissed without notice ... Good, the factories will close for a few days. Do a deal with the private companies. The order for Turkey must be filled ... Goodbye, Herr Director ... (*Hangs up. Telephones again.*) Connect me with the police ... Eva Berg's file ... Hurry up ... Thank you. (*Hangs up.*)

KARL THOMAS: What courage! You have mastered the methods.

WILHELM KILMAN: Whoever works on top here must see to it that the complicated machinery doesn't come to a standstill because of clumsy hands.

KARL THOMAS: Aren't those women fighting for your old Ideas?

WILHELM KILMAN: Could I countenance the women workers of any factory to obstruct the mechanism of the State?

KARL THOMAS: Would your authority suffer so much?

WILHELM KILMAN: Should I make a fool of myself? Should I show myself to be less capable than the old Minister? A lot of the time it's not so easy … If one fails only once, then … There are hours … You imagine it is so … Oh, what do you know? …

KARL THOMAS: What do we know? You help the reactionaries get into the saddle.

WILHELM KILMAN: Nonsense! In a democracy I have to respect the rights of the employer just as much as the rights of the employee. We don't have a utopia yet.

KARL THOMAS: But the other side has the Press, money, weapons. And the workers? Empty fists.

WILHELM KILMAN: Oh, you only ever see armed struggle, beating, stabbing, shooting. To the barricades! To the barricades, all you workers! But we renounce the struggle of brutal violence. Unceasingly we have preached that we want to gain victory with moral and spiritual weapons. Violence is always reactionary.

KARL THOMAS: Is that the opinion of the masses? Haven't you even asked for their opinion?

WILHELM KILMAN: What are the masses? Were they able to accomplish any positive work in the old days? Nothing! Talk big and smash things up. We would have slid into chaos. Every adventurer got a command post. People who for the whole of their lives only knew about the workers from coffee house discussions. But let's be honest. We have saved the revolution … The masses are incompetent and they will remain incompetent for the time being. They lack all specialist knowledge. How could an untrained worker, in our epoch, take over the position of, let's say, the head of a syndicate? Or of the director of an electricity works? Later … in decades … in centuries … with education … with evolution … things will change. But today it is we who must govern.

KARL THOMAS: And to think I did time with you …

WILHELM KILMAN: Do you really think I'm a 'traitor'?

KARL THOMAS: Yes.

WILHELM KILMAN: Oh, my dear friend, I am used to that word. For you every bourgeois is a dirty scoundrel, a bloodsucker, a satan, or whatever. If you only grasped what the bourgeois world has achieved and is still achieving.

KARL THOMAS: Stop! You're twisting my words. I have never denied that the bourgeois world has achieved great things. I have never maintained that the bourgeoisie are raven black and the people snow white. But what has become of the world? Our Idea is the greater. If we succeed with it, we will achieve more.

WILHELM KILMAN: It comes down to tactics, dear fellow. With your tactics the darkest reaction would soon govern.

KARL THOMAS: I see no difference.

WILHELM KILMAN: Have you completely forgotten the whip marks lashed on your backs? What children you are. To want the whole tree when you can have an apple.

KARL THOMAS: What props you up? The old bureaucracy? And even if I believed your intentions were honourable, what are you in reality? A powerless scarecrow, a ping pong ball!

WILHELM KILMAN: What do you really want? Have a look at the inner workings here. How everything fits. How everything runs like clockwork. Everyone has expertise.

KARL THOMAS: And are you proud of that?

WILHELM KILMAN: Yes, of course, I am proud of my civil servants.

KARL THOMAS: We are speaking different languages … you mentioned a name a little while ago on the telephone.

WILHELM KILMAN: I was speaking about official matters.

KARL THOMAS: Eva Berg.

WILHELM KILMAN: Oh, her. She works in the Revenue Office. She's giving me a great deal of trouble. To think what's become of the little darling.

KARL THOMAS: She must be twenty-five years old now.

WILHELM KILMAN: I wanted to spare her. But she is rushing to her own ruin … I must say goodbye to you. Here, take this. (*Tries to give* KARL THOMAS *money; he refuses it.*) Unfortunately I cannot employ you. Go to the Trade Union. Perhaps you'll find some old friends there. I suppose so. One is so busy. One loses contact. May all go well with you. Don't do anything stupid. We are surely united in our goals. Only the means …

Pushes KARL THOMAS *gradually into the Antechamber.* WILHELM KILMAN *remains standing for a few seconds. Gesture.*

Antechamber

KARL THOMAS *stares, dumbstruck.*

PICKEL: (*To* MINISTRY OFFICIAL.) Is it my turn now, Herr Secretary?

MINISTRY OFFICIAL: Do you have an appointment?

PICKEL: I travelled two and a half days on the railway, Herr Secretary. Indeed one gets the shock of one's life on it. Are you familiar with Holzhausen?

MINISTRY OFFICIAL: Does the Minister know?

PICKEL: It's just with regard to the railway in Holzhausen.

MINISTRY OFFICIAL: I will inquire.

MINISTRY OFFICIAL *goes into the Office.*

PICKEL: Is the Minister, I wonder, a very stern man?

KARL THOMAS *doesn't answer.*

PICKEL: If the good Lord has made someone a Minister, as far as I am concerned, I imagine he is …

As KARL THOMAS *doesn't answer,* PICKEL *breaks off, paces back and forth.*

Office

WILHELM KILMAN: No, I don't mind. Show him in.

MINISTRY OFFICIAL *opens the door to the Antechamber.*

MINISTRY OFFICIAL: Herr Pickel.

PICKEL enters.

PICKEL: Your servant, Herr Minister. I have so much on my mind, Herr Minister. Indeed you are surely very busy. But nevertheless I don't want to steal your time from you, Herr Minister. Pickel is my name. Born in Holzhausen, Waldwinkel District. It is only with regard to the railway which you want to build through Holzhausen, Herr Minister. You know, I'm sure, in October ... Indeed, there is a saying with us: Hannes would grease the pope's nose of a fatted goose ... But nevertheless just such a fatted goose was Holzhausen. Steamers call three times a week; the mailcoach stops every day the good Lord sends. As far as I am concerned I would have ... Indeed I certainly don't want to bring myself into it ... The Minister will know better ... But nevertheless this is certain, the Minister didn't know that if the railway should pass over my property then ... I hope I'm not detaining you, Herr Minister.

WILHELM KILMAN: Well, my dear man, what's all this about the railway?

PICKEL: I told my neighbour straightaway that when I stand *vis à vis* the Minister then he will ... Indeed he said something about white gloves, and such matters ... But nevertheless I have always thought to myself: a Minister, what a lot he must know! Almost as much as our Lord God. Whether the harvest will be good, whether there will be war, whether the railway will run over one's own property or another's ... Yes, such is a Minister ... Oh, I haven't come only with regard to the railway ... Indeed the railway has its importance ... But nevertheless the other matter also has its importance. When I was sitting back in Holzhausen ... the newspapers, you don't get wise from them ... I said to myself, when you are first standing *vis à vis* the Minister ... if it is not asking too much, where do you imagine, where is all this leading to? ... If now the railway runs through Holzhausen and one can travel straight to India? ... And if in China the Yellows are rising up ... And if there are machines with which one can shoot as far as America ... and the niggers in Africa are talking big and want to throw the Mission out ... And they say the Government wants to abolish money ... Indeed Herr Minister is sitting here on top and he has to deal with all of it ... Nevertheless I said to myself you will ask him for once himself: Herr Minister, what will become of the world?

WILHELM KILMAN: What will become of the world?

PICKEL: I mean what do you want to make out of it, Herr Minister?

WILHELM KILMAN: No, let's first drink a cognac. Do you smoke?

PICKEL: Too kind, Herr Minister. Indeed I said to myself straightaway, you only have to stand *vis à vis* the Minister ...

WILHELM KILMAN: The world ... the world ... Hm ... it is not very easy to answer that. Go on, drink.

PICKEL: That's just what I've always said to my neighbour. Indeed my neighbour, I mean the one who has rented the village common, at first it ought to have cost two hundred marks, but nevertheless he is related to the Mayor, and if one is related ...

There is a knock.

MINISTRY OFFICIAL: I would like to remind you, Excellency, that at two o'clock Your Excellency must ...

WILHELM KILMAN: Yes, I know ... So, my dear Herr Pickel, have a peaceful journey back to Holzhausen. Give my greetings to Holzhausen ... Go on, drink your cognac.

PICKEL: Yes, Herr Minister. And the railway ... Indeed if after all it should run over my property, then ...

WILHELM KILMAN: (*Pushing PICKEL gradually into the Antechamber before PICKEL can finish his cognac.*) No one will suffer an injustice.

Antechamber

PICKEL: (*Going out.*) I will take care of things for you in Holzhausen.

MINISTRY OFFICIAL: (*To KARL THOMAS who stands as if paralysed.*) You must go, we are closing.

Curtain.

[*Scaffolding revolves two metres to right.*]

Film Interlude
WOMEN AT WORK:
WOMEN AS TYPISTS
WOMEN AS CHAUFFEURS
WOMEN AS TRAIN DRIVERS
WOMEN AS POLICE

[*This film sequence was unfortunately cut.*]

ACT 2
Scene 1

[*Back projections of a slum alley on centre compartment screen. Factories on upper and middle left compartment screens. Roof with hanging clothes on upper right compartment screen. Other rooms on middle and bottom right compartment screens. Bottom left compartment open for scene with white wall back projected on its screen. Alarm rings in the dark before lights come up.*]

Eva Berg's room

EVA BERG *jumps out of bed, starts to dress hurriedly.*

KARL THOMAS: (*In bed.*) Where are you going?

EVA BERG: To work, dear boy.

KARL THOMAS: What time is it?

EVA BERG: Half six.

KARL THOMAS: Stay here in bed until eight. Your office job doesn't start until nine.

EVA BERG: I must go to the Trade Union first. The election is in one week. The leaflets they printed for the women are dreadful. Last night when you were asleep I drafted the text for a new one.

KARL THOMAS: This life without work makes me lazier day by day.

EVA BERG: Yes, it's time you found work.

KARL THOMAS: Sometimes I think ... Do you call that cut 'bobbed hair'?

EVA BERG: Do you like it? ... How stupid, we don't have any representatives in the Sixth District. Just where have I left the papers? ... Oh, here. (*Reads, corrects, writes.*)

KARL THOMAS: That cut suits you because you have a face. Women without faces have to watch out. That cut makes them naked. How many can get away with nakedness?

EVA BERG: Is that what you think?

KARL THOMAS: The faces in the street, on the underground, awful. Before I never saw how few people have faces. Most are lumps of flesh bloated by fear and conceit.

EVA BERG: Not a bad conclusion ... Do you have burning desires for women inside?

KARL THOMAS: For the first seven years it was like I was buried ... In the last year I suffered terribly.

EVA BERG: What do you do then?

KARL THOMAS: Some carry on like boys; others fantasise that sheets, a piece of bread or a coloured cloth are lovers.

EVA BERG: That last, conscious year must have been desperate for you.

KARL THOMAS: How often I hugged my pillow like a woman, greedy to get warm.

EVA BERG: Inside everyone the ice hounds bark ... You must find work, Karl.

KARL THOMAS: But why ... Eva, come with me ... We'll travel to Greece. To India. To Africa. There must be places where men still live, childlike, who simply are, are. In whose eyes sky and sun and stars spin, brightly. Who know nothing of politics, who live without always having to struggle.

EVA BERG: Do politics make you sick? Do you think you could break their hold? Do you think southern sun, palm trees, elephants, colourful garments could make you forget the real life of men? This paradise you dream about does not exist.

KARL THOMAS: Since I saw Wilhelm Kilman I can't bear it any more. For what? So that our own comrades can smirk at the world like distorted mirror images of the old gang? No thanks. You must be my tomorrow and my dream of the future. You, I want you and nothing more.

EVA BERG: Escape, is it?

KARL THOMAS: Call it escape. What's in a word?

EVA BERG: You deceive yourself. By tomorrow impatience will be gnawing away at you, and a burning desire for your ... destiny.

KARL THOMAS: Destiny?

EVA BERG: Because we cannot breathe in this air of factories and slums. Because otherwise we'll die like caged animals.

KARL THOMAS: Yes, you are right.

KARL THOMAS starts to dress.

EVA BERG: You must look around for another place to live, Karl.

KARL THOMAS: Can't I live with you any more, Eva?

EVA BERG: Honestly, no.

KARL THOMAS: Is the landlady grumbling?

EVA BERG: I would get her to stop it.

KARL THOMAS: Why not then?

EVA BERG: I must be able to be alone. Understand me.

KARL THOMAS: Don't you belong to me?

EVA BERG: Belong? That word is dead. Nobody belongs to anybody.

KARL THOMAS: Sorry, I used the wrong word. Aren't I your lover?

EVA BERG: Do you mean because I slept with you?

KARL THOMAS: Doesn't that bind us?

EVA BERG: One glance exchanged with a stranger on a run-down street can bind me to him more deeply than some night of love. Which need be nothing but very beautiful play.

KARL THOMAS: Then what do you take seriously?

EVA BERG: The here and now I take seriously. I also take play seriously ... I am a living human being. Have I renounced the world because I'm in the struggle? The idea that a revolutionary has to forego the thousand little joys of life is absurd. All of us should take part in exactly what we want to.

KARL THOMAS: What is sacred ... to you?

EVA BERG: Why mystical words for human things? ... Why are you looking at me like that? ... When I talk to you I feel that the last eight years, during which you were 'buried', have changed us more drastically than a century normally would have done.

KARL THOMAS: Yes, sometimes I feel I come from a lost generation.

EVA BERG: To think what the world has experienced since that episode.

KARL THOMAS: Just listen to how you speak of the revolution!

EVA BERG: That revolution was an episode. It is past.

KARL THOMAS: What remains?

EVA BERG: Us. With our will to honesty. With our strength for new work.

KARL THOMAS: And what if you got pregnant during these nights?

EVA BERG: I wouldn't give birth.

KARL THOMAS: Because you don't love me?

EVA BERG: How you miss the point. Because it would be an accident. Because it wouldn't seem necessary to me.

KARL THOMAS: If I use stupid words now, wrong words, don't listen; listen to the inexpressible things which you too cannot doubt. I need you. I found you in days when we heard the very heartbeat of life because the heartbeat of death pounded so loudly and unstoppably. I cannot find my way now. Help me, help me! The glowing flame has gone out.

EVA BERG: You are wrong. It glows in a different way. Less sentimentally.

KARL THOMAS: I don't feel it anywhere.

EVA BERG: What do you see? You are scared of broad daylight.

KARL THOMAS: Don't speak like that.

EVA BERG: Yes, let me speak. All talking things out is over. Irrevocably. Either you will gain strength for a new beginning or you will be destroyed. To support your false dreams out of pity would be criminal.

KARL THOMAS: So you did have pity?

EVA BERG: Probably. I am not clear myself. There is never only one reason.

KARL THOMAS: What kind of experience has hardened you over these years?

EVA BERG: Again you are using concepts which don't apply any more. I was a child, granted. We cannot afford to be children any more. We can't throw away the lucidity and knowledge we've gained like toys which don't please us any more. Experience – sure, I have experienced a lot. Men and situations. For eight years I've worked like only men worked before. For eight years I've made the decisions about every hour of my life. That's why I am how I am … Do you think it was easy for me? Often, when I sat in one of those ugly furnished rooms, I threw myself on the bed … and howled, like having a breakdown … and I thought, I can't go on any more … Then came work. The Party needed me. I clenched my teeth and … Be reasonable, Karl. I must go to the office.

FRITZ and GRETE peer round the door. Disappear again.

Stay here this morning. Do you need money? Don't say no out of stupid pride. I'll help you as a comrade, that's all. Farewell.

EVA BERG goes. KARL THOMAS remains alone for a few seconds. FRITZ and GRETE, the landlady's children, open the door, look in curiously.

FRITZ: Can we come in now?

GRETE: We'd like to have a look at you, you see.

KARL THOMAS: Yes, come in.

FRITZ and GRETE come in, both look at KARL THOMAS.

FRITZ: We have to go soon, you see.

GRETE: We have tickets for the movies.

FRITZ: And this evening we're going to the boxing match. Want to box now?

KARL THOMAS: No, I can't box.

FRITZ: Oh, I see.

GRETE: But you can dance, can't you? Do you know the Charleston or the Black Bottom?

KARL THOMAS: No, not that either.

GRETE: Pity … Were you really in the madhouse for eight years?

FRITZ: She can't believe it.

KARL THOMAS: Yes. For sure.

GRETE: And before that were you sentenced to death?

FRITZ: Mother told her. She read it in the newspaper.

KARL THOMAS: Your mother rents rooms?

GRETE: Of course.

KARL THOMAS: Is your mother poor?

FRITZ: Only the black marketeers are rich today, mother always says.

KARL THOMAS: Do you also know why I was sentenced to death?

GRETE: Because you were in the war.

FRITZ: Goose! Because he was in the Revolution.

KARL THOMAS: What do you know about the war then? Has your mother told you about it?

GRETE: No, not mother.

FRITZ: We have to learn the battles in school.

GRETE: What day they were on.

FRITZ: Stupid that the World War had to come. As if we didn't have enough to learn already in our History lesson. The Thirty Years' War lasted from 1618 to 1648.

GRETE: Thirty years.

FRITZ: We have to learn only half as many battles for that one as for the World War.

GRETE: And it only lasted four years.

FRITZ: The battle of Lüttich, the battle of the Marne, the battle of Verdun, the battle of Tannenberg …

GRETE: And the battle of Ypres.

KARL THOMAS: Don't you know anything else about the war?

FRITZ: That's enough for us.

GRETE: And how! The last time I got 'unsatisfactory' because I mixed up 1916 and 1917.

KARL THOMAS: And … what do you know about the Revolution?

FRITZ: We don't need to learn so many dates about that, which is easier.

KARL THOMAS: What can the suffering and the knowledge of millions mean if the next generation is already deaf to it all? All experience rushes into a bottomless pit.

FRITZ: What are you saying?

KARL THOMAS: How old are you?

GRETE: Thirteen.

FRITZ: Fifteen.

KARL THOMAS: And what are your names?

FRITZ: Fritz.

GRETE: Grete.

KARL THOMAS: What you have learned about the war is meaningless. You know nothing about the war.

FRITZ: Oh, no!

KARL THOMAS: How to describe it to you? … Mothers were … no. What's standing there at the end of the street?

FRITZ: A big factory.

KARL THOMAS: What is made in it?

FRITZ/GRETE: Acids ... gas.

KARL THOMAS: What kind of gas?

GRETE: I don't know.

FRITZ: But I do. Poison gas.

KARL THOMAS: What is poison gas used for?

FRITZ: For when enemies attack us.

GRETE: Yes, against enemies if they try to destroy our country.

KARL THOMAS: Who are your enemies then?

FRITZ and GRETE are silent.

Give me your hand, Fritz ... What could happen to this hand if a bullet shot through it?

FRITZ: Thanks a lot. Kaput.

KARL THOMAS: What would happen to your face if it got caught in just a tiny cloud of poison gas? Did you learn that at school?

GRETE: Sure did! Be eaten all away. To the bone.

KARL THOMAS: Would you like to die?

GRETE: That's a funny question. Of course not.

KARL THOMAS: And now I want to tell you a story. Not a fairy tale. A true story which happened near where I was. During the war I was stationed somewhere in France in a trench. Suddenly, at night, we heard screams, like a man in his death agony. Then it went still. Somebody had been killed, we thought. An hour later we heard screams again, and then they never stopped. The whole night long a man screamed. The whole day long a man screamed. More and more painfully, more and more helplessly. When it grew dark, two soldiers climbed out of the trench and tried to rescue the man who lay wounded between the trenches. Bullets whizzed by, and both soldiers were shot dead. Two others tried again. They didn't come back. Then the order came: nobody else allowed out of the trench. We had to obey. But the man kept on screaming. We didn't know whether he was French or German or English. He screamed like a baby screams, naked, without words. He screamed for four days and four nights. To us, it was four years. We stuffed our ears up with paper. It didn't help at all. Then it went still. Oh, children, I wish I had the power to plant a vision in your hearts like seed in ploughed earth. Can you picture to yourselves what happened then.

FRITZ: Of course.

GRETE: The poor man.

KARL THOMAS: Yes, dear girl, the poor man! Not: the enemy. The man. The man screamed. In France and in Germany and in Russia and in Japan and in America and in England. At such times, when you, how should I say it, get down to the ground water, you ask yourself: why all this? What is all this for? Would you ask the same thing too?

FRITZ/GRETE: Yes.

KARL THOMAS: In all countries men brooded over the same question. In all countries men gave the same answer. For gold, for land, for coal, for nothing but dead things, men die and starve and despair – that is the answer. And in some places the most courageous of the people rose up and rallied the blind to their strong cry of no, and demanded that this war should cease, and all wars; and they struggled for a world in which all children could thrive ... Here among us they lost, here they were defeated.

Long pause.

FRITZ: Were there many of you?

KARL THOMAS: No, the people didn't understand what we were struggling for; didn't see that we were rising up for the sake of their own lives.

FRITZ: Were there many on the other side?

KARL THOMAS: Very many. They had weapons and money and soldiers who were paid.

Pause.

FRITZ: And were you so dumb to believe you could win?

GRETE: Yes, you were real dumb.

KARL THOMAS: (*Stares at them.*) What did you say?

FRITZ: You were dumb.

GRETE: Very dumb.

FRITZ: We must go now. Hurry up, Grete.

GRETE: Yes.

FRITZ/GRETE: Goodbye. See you.

Pause. EVA BERG comes back.

EVA BERG: Now I could go travelling with you.

KARL THOMAS: What's up?

EVA BERG: Quick answer.

KARL THOMAS: Say it!

EVA BERG: I didn't get into the office. The porter gave me my dismissal notice. Got the sack.

KARL THOMAS: Kilman!

EVA BERG: Because I addressed the locked-out women workers yesterday afternoon.

KARL THOMAS: That swine!

EVA BERG: Are you surprised? Anyone who does a botched job with clay has to keep working it.

KARL THOMAS: Are you satisfied now, Eva? Come. Here's a time-table. We'll travel this very night. Away! Let's get away, let's get away!

EVA BERG: Are you speaking for both of us? Nothing has changed. Do you seriously believe I'd leave my comrades in the lurch?

KARL THOMAS: Sorry.

EVA BERG: Maybe you'd like to work with us? ... Think it over.

EVA BERG goes out. KARL THOMAS stares after her.

Blackout.

[Black gauze and screen in. During film scaffolding moves back one metre to make room for next scene which was played in front of scaffolding.]

Film Interlude

East End of a Big City

FACTORIES
CHIMNEYS
CLOSING TIME
WORKERS LEAVE FACTORIES
CROWDS IN THE STREETS

[Instead of the above, an election film was projected from front. Film and screen out. For the scene, posters and slogans back projected on right and left compartment screens. Film of ballot papers falling into box, lasting until nine o'clock strikes, back projected on centre compartment screen.]

Scene 2
Workers' bar

The raised space at the back is fitted out as a polling station. ELECTION OFFICER at a table, next to him SECOND ELECTION OFFICER. On the right, the voting booth. Entrance turned towards the auditorium. In the front, customers at tables. When there is dialogue at a table, it is brightly lit and the rest of the space is darker. THIRD WORKER enters.

THIRD WORKER: Well, it's all go here. The great con flourishes.

SECOND WORKER: Man, shut up. We wouldn't get very far with your bloody anarchism.

THIRD WORKER: Sure, I know, if you vote you get far.

FIRST WORKER: Everything's all right in its own way. Even the election. Otherwise it wouldn't happen. If you're so dumb not to grasp that ...

SECOND WORKER: Only the stupidest sheep of all elect their own butchers ...

FIRST WORKER: Do you mean us?

SECOND WORKER: Like a punch in the face?

From the back.

ELECTION OFFICER: Quiet in front. We can't hear our own voices ... What is your name?

OLD WOMAN: Barbara Stilzer.

ELECTION OFFICER: Where do you live?

OLD WOMAN: From 1st October I shall live at 7 Schulstrasse.

ELECTION OFFICER: I would like to know where you live now.

OLD WOMAN: If the landlord thinks he can bully me because I complained at the Rent Office ... 11 Margaretenstrasse, Fourth Floor.

ELECTION OFFICER: Right.

The OLD WOMAN remains standing.

You can go cast your ballot.

OLD WOMAN: I only came because it's said they will punish you, if you don't vote.

ELECTION OFFICER: Well then, my dear woman, take a pencil, mark a cross next to the name of your candidate and put it in the ballot box in there.

OLD WOMAN: I don't have a ballot, Herr Detective Inspector ... I didn't know I had to bring a ballot with me ... How can you know where you are with all those paragraphs ...

ELECTION OFFICER: I am not a Detective Inspector. I am the Election Officer. The Electioneers are over there. Go get one and then come back.

The OLD WOMAN goes to the front.

FIRST ELECTIONEER: Here, young woman, you must make a cross next to Number One. Then you will be voting for the right President. The Minister of War is concerned about Peace and Order and about Women.

The OLD WOMAN turns the ballot to and fro indecisively.

SECOND ELECTIONEER: No, little mother, just put your cross next to Number Two. Don't you want coal and bread to be cheaper?

OLD WOMAN: Shameful, how prices have gone up again.

SECOND ELECTIONEER: All because of the big landowners, little mother. They're raking in the bacon. Put your cross here, then you're voting for National Reconciliation.

The OLD WOMAN turns the ballot to and fro indecisively.

THIRD ELECTIONEER: As a class conscious proletarian vote for Number Three. A clear decision, comrade. Peace and Order – rubbish. Peace and Order for the Capitalists, not for you. National Reconciliation – rubbish. If you bow and scrape, then you'll get to lick the hand of brotherhood – otherwise you'll get a kick in the teeth. Your cross next to Number Three, or else you twist the noose around your own neck.

The OLD WOMAN turns the ballot to and fro indecisively.

FIRST ELECTIONEER: Next to Number One, young woman! Don't forget!

SECOND ELECTIONEER: Next to Number Two, little mother!

THIRD ELECTIONEER: Only Number Three will help you break your chains, comrade!

The OLD WOMAN goes to the back.

[Film of ALBERT KROLL's lorry arriving projected from front on to gauze.]

ELECTION OFFICER: Do you have your ballot now?

OLD WOMAN: Here, three of them.

ELECTION OFFICER: Only put one in. Otherwise your vote is invalid.

The OLD WOMAN goes into the booth.

OLD WOMAN: May I come out again?

Comes out.

A very good evening to you, Herr Detective Inspector. (*To the* ELECTIONEERS *while going out.*) It's all right, it's all right, don't get excited, don't get excited. I've made a cross next to all three.

At the table left.

FIRST WORKER: Giving women the right to vote! Only the dog collars profit from that.

SECOND WORKER: Before, when I had work, I didn't sit in the bar in one month as much as I do now in one day.

FIRST WORKER: And your wife? I wouldn't like to hear the smacks. You got enough scratches.

SECOND WORKER: The aid we get lets us guzzle herring and jam for four days and sniff wind for the next three. It comes down to the same thing.

FIRST WORKER: Went out the door yesterday and a bourgeois lady was standing outside the bar, you know, in high class lace, larded up from head to toe. She said out loud: 'One must take pity on these people.' I answered: 'Frau Chamber of Commerce,' I said, 'perhaps the time will come round when you'll be only too happy if I take pity on you,' I said.

SECOND WORKER: They ought to hang, nothing else but hang. The whole lot of them.

FIRST WORKER: We'll show them with this election.

KARL THOMAS enters.

KARL THOMAS: (*To the* BARKEEPER.) Does Albert Kroll come here?

BARKEEPER: He was just here. He should be right back.

KARL THOMAS: I'll wait.

Sits at the table right. In front of the ELECTION OFFICER'S *table.*

VOTER: I won't put up with this.

ELECTION OFFICER: A mistake, sir …

VOTER: Which cost me my right to vote. I'll lodge a protest against the election! The election must be declared invalid. I won't drop it! I'll go to the highest authorities!

ELECTION OFFICER: I fully admit that your entry was wrongly left off the voting register …

VOTER: That doesn't help me at all! I want my rights! My rights!

ELECTION OFFICER: According to the law I cannot …

VOTER: But take away my rights, that you can do. I'll sort things out here! I'll denounce this pigsty!

ELECTION OFFICER: Be reasonable, sir. Just consider what unrest you'll cause among the people …

VOTER: Doesn't matter to me. Rights are rights …

SECOND ELECTION OFFICER: Please, sir …

ELECTION OFFICER: As a good citizen you would not wish to …

VOTER: It must get into the papers, in black and white. There's more to this than meets the eye. Of all people it has to happen to me, it always has to happen to me, always, always, always! But that's enough now!

Runs off, collides in the doorway with ALBERT KROLL *who is coming in.* ALBERT KROLL *stops short, recognises* KARL THOMAS.

ALBERT KROLL: Incredible!

KARL THOMAS: At last I've found you.

ALBERT KROLL: Poor devil. Been hard times. For us, too. Found work?

KARL THOMAS: I've been at the Employment Office six times. I learned typesetting when they threw me out of university. Old workmates act like a bunch of clerks towards you! Like section managers in a department store. Cold shoulder, worse than the proper ones. They could work just as perfectly in any department store.

ALBERT KROLL: Everyday life.

KARL THOMAS: You say it as if it has to be like that.

ALBERT KROLL: No. Only it doesn't upset me any more. Wait a minute, I'm going up there. I'm on the Election Committee. You got to keep a close eye on the devils.

Up at the election table.

SECOND ELECTION OFFICER: What a turn out! What a turn out! The election is over in one hour and already eighty per cent. Eighty per cent!

ALBERT KROLL: Three hundred workers have protested because they were not included on the voting register.

ELECTION OFFICER: Not my fault. The ones from the housing block at the Chemical Works had to be crossed off. They haven't lived here for four months yet.

ALBERT KROLL: But the students have the right to vote. And how long have they been here? Only three weeks!

ELECTION OFFICER: The Ministry of the Interior has made that decision, not I.

ALBERT KROLL: We will lodge a protest against the election.

SECOND ELECTION OFFICER: (*On telephone.*) Is that the Sixth District? How many have voted? Sixty-five per cent? Here it's eighty! (*Hangs up telephone.*) Gentlemen, we're in the lead, and you want to lodge a protest …

ALBERT KROLL goes to KARL THOMAS.

ALBERT KROLL: Kilman has stolen the right to vote from the workers at the Chemical Works!

KARL THOMAS: I don't care. What does it matter? Albert, comrade, look at what has become of our struggle. A department store I said before. Everyone's sitting pretty at his own little job. Cash register One … Cash register Ten … Cash register Twelve … No breath of fresh air. The very air is rotting with order. Because some little bit was missing I had to submit all my papers all over again to the proper authorities. It's all gone mouldy with bureaucracy.

ALBERT KROLL: We know. We know even more. Those who failed at the decisive moment are talking big again today.

KARL THOMAS: And you just take it?

ALBERT KROLL: We struggle on. We are too few. Most have forgotten, want their peace and quiet. We must win over new comrades.

KARL THOMAS: Hundreds of thousands are unemployed.

ALBERT KROLL: When hunger sneaks in the front door, understanding sneaks out the back.

KARL THOMAS: You sound like an old man.

ALBERT KROLL: Years like these count ten times as long. We are learning.

KARL THOMAS: Herr Minister Kilman said the same thing.

ALBERT KROLL: Possible. Because he had something to hide. I want to show you the truth.

FOURTH WORKER: (*Coming in.*) Albert, the police have seized our van.

ALBERT KROLL: Why?

FOURTH WORKER: On account of the pictures! We made fun of the Minister of War.

ALBERT KROLL: Choose a delegation at once to make complaints at the Ministry.

FOURTH WORKER: We already tried that earlier today because a leaflet distributor got arrested. Kilman admits no one.

ALBERT KROLL: He supplied the Minister of War with a military band for free ... Go on, go to the Ministry. Telephone me at once, if he refuses you.

FOURTH WORKER goes.

Did you hear, Karl?

KARL THOMAS: What's the election got to do with me? Show me your faith, your old faith, that was going to make a clean sweep of heaven and earth and the stars.

ALBERT KROLL: You mean I don't have it any more? Do I have to count up for you how many times we tried to throw off the damned yoke? Do I have to name you the names of all the old comrades who were hounded, locked up and murdered?

KARL THOMAS: Only faith counts.

ALBERT KROLL: We don't want eternal bliss in heaven. One must learn to see clearly and still keep from getting discouraged.

KARL THOMAS: Great leaders have never spoken like that.

ALBERT KROLL: Do you think? I imagine it differently. They just marched straight for it. On top of glass. And when they looked down through it, they saw the abyss formed from the hatred of the enemy and the stupidity of their own troops. And they probably saw much more.

KARL THOMAS: They wouldn't have moved a hand's breadth if they'd ever measured the depths beneath them.

ALBERT KROLL: Never measured. But always saw.

KARL THOMAS: All wrong, what you're doing. You even take part in the election con.

ALBERT KROLL: And what are you doing? What do you want to do?

KARL THOMAS: Something must happen. Someone must set an example.

ALBERT KROLL: Someone? Everyone. Every day.

KARL THOMAS: I mean something different. Someone must sacrifice himself. Then the lame will walk. Night and day I've pounded my brains. Now I know what I have to do.

ALBERT KROLL: I'm listening.

KARL THOMAS: Come here. Be discreet.

Speaks softly with ALBERT KROLL.

[Piscator added the line 'Kilman must go' for KARL THOMAS.]

ALBERT KROLL: You're no use to us.

KARL THOMAS: It's the only way I can help myself. Disgust chokes me.

ALBERT KROLL goes to the ELECTION OFFICER's table again.

ALBERT KROLL: The police have seized our van. That's sabotage of the workers' candidate.

A VOTER: Your candidate's been bribed by foreigners.

ALBERT KROLL: Lies! Election propaganda!

ELECTION OFFICER: (*To ALBERT KROLL.*) You must not electioneer. (*To VOTER.*) This isn't an information office, Herr Master Butcher.

ALBERT KROLL: I don't want to electioneer. But I'm still allowed to tell the truth.

SECOND ELECTION OFFICER: (*On the telephone.*) What time do you make it? Eight-fifty? ... Yes, yes, it's all go here. Huge turnout. They're even bringing in the sick on stretchers. (*Hangs up.*) The clock in the Fifteenth District is eight minutes fast. Eight minutes! I didn't tell them. Because we'll get to know the results eight minutes sooner.

ALBERT KROLL goes to KARL THOMAS' table.

ALBERT KROLL: They shut me up when I tell the truth. I won't bow and scrape.

KARL THOMAS: What great courage! In truth you are all cowards. All, all, all! Wish I'd stayed in the madhouse! Now even my own plan disgusts me. What for? For a bunch of petit bourgeois cowards who believe in elections?

ALBERT KROLL: You'd like the world to be an eternal firework display set off just for you, with rockets and flares and the roar of battle. You're the coward, not me.

At the table left.

FIRST WORKER: Did'ya vote yet?

SECOND WORKER: No, I'm going now. Why shouldn't I vote for National Reconciliation when the ladyship my Lina works for is voting that way too. There must be something wrong with Kilman, I tell you; Lina's ladyship has brains in her head. She's really classy. On Sunday when Lina has a day off, her ladyship always comes into the kitchen. 'Lina,' she says, 'I wish you a good Sunday.' And then she shakes hands with her. Every time.

FIRST WORKER: How about that!

SECOND WORKER goes to the election table. PICKEL comes in.

PICKEL: Excuse me, can one vote here?

The ELECTIONEERS surround PICKEL.

FIRST ELECTIONEER: Law and Order in the land, with God for our dear Fatherland! Vote for Number One.

SECOND ELECTIONEER: Awake, you people, it's not too late. Don't support the right or left, support the State. Vote for Number Two.

THIRD ELECTIONEER: The President of Number Three sets the workers and the peasants free! Vote for Number Three!

PICKEL: Thank you, thank you.

PICKEL goes to the ELECTION OFFICER's table.

ELECTION OFFICER: What is your name?

PICKEL: Pickel.

ELECTION OFFICER: Where do you live?

PICKEL: Indeed I live in Holzhausen, but nevertheless . . .

ELECTION OFFICER: You are not entered on the voting register . . . Do you spell your name with a B?

PICKEL: Where will I . . . Pickel . . . Pickel with a P . . . P . . . Not two Ps . . . Indeed I would like to explain that . . .

ELECTION OFFICER: Your explanation is of no use. You are not allowed to vote here. You are in the wrong polling place.

PICKEL: I must explain to you . . . Indeed I live in Holzhausen . . .

ELECTION OFFICER: What do you want here? Don't hold the election up. Next . . .

The voting continues.

PICKEL: (*Going to KARL THOMAS.*) Indeed it's all the same to me personally whether I vote or not, but nevertheless I don't want to be ungrateful to the Minister . . . I'd like to give him my vote.

KARL THOMAS: Leave me alone.

PICKEL goes to the THIRD WORKER.

PICKEL: Indeed I would have travelled home a long time ago. I only wanted to stay one day, but nevertheless it never stopped raining.

THIRD WORKER: Wish it was pissing down in here. Oughta flood out the whole show. All a fraud. They oughta wipe their bums with the ballots.

PICKEL: That's not what I meant. Namely I don't travel in rainy weather. I waited six weeks before I travelled to see the Minister, because there was always a thunderstorm in the sky.

BANKER comes in. ELECTIONEERS surround him.

BANKER: Thanks.

Goes to the ELECTION OFFICER.

ELECTION OFFICER: At your service, Herr Director-General. Herr Director-General, do you still live in Opernplatz?

BANKER: Yes, I've come a little late.

ELECTION OFFICER: Early enough, Herr Director-General. Over there, if you please.

BANKER goes into the voting booth.

PICKEL: I had an uncle who was struck by lightning on the railway. Indeed the railways attract the lightning, but nevertheless it's men who bear the guilt for it with their new-fangled commotions.

ELECTION OFFICER: (*To BANKER who has left the voting booth.*) Your most obedient servant, Herr Director-General, sir.

BANKER goes.

THIRD WORKER: He comes first, no one else, and the stupid workers guzzle his dust.

PICKEL: The radio and the electric waves, they mess up the atmosphere. Indeed . . .

ELECTION OFFICER: The poll is closed.

[Film of falling ballots stops. Back projection of heap of ballots in its place on centre compartment screen.]

FIRST WORKER: Now I'm really curious.

SECOND WORKER: Want to bet that the Minister of War is defeated?

THIRD WORKER: He'll be elected! And it serves you right!

SECOND WORKER: Don't talk such stupid rubbish, you old anarchist!

RADIO:

Attention! Attention! First election results. Twelfth District. 714 votes for the Minister of War, His Excellency von Wandsring. 414 votes for Minister Kilman. 67 for Bricklayer Bandke.

SECOND WORKER: Ouch!

FIRST WORKER: Rigged!

THIRD WORKER: Bravo!

FIRST and THIRD WORKERS go.

PICKEL: Herr Election Officer, you must not close. I insist . . . Indeed I am only . . . but nevertheless those in the big city always want us . . . Namely, I know Herr Minister Kilman, I've become friends with him . . .

ELECTION OFFICER: Make a complaint then.

PICKEL: If Minister Kilman now polls one vote too little. Just think if it's because of my vote . . .

RADIO:

Attention! Attention! Report from Osthafen. 6,000 for Bricklayer Bandke. 4,000 for Minister Kilman. 2,000 for His Excellency von Wandsring.

CROWD IN STREET: Hurrah! Hurrah!

ALBERT KROLL: The dock workers! Our pioneers! Bravo!

KARL THOMAS: Why bravo? How can you be pleased about votes? Are they a deed?

ALBERT KROLL: Deed – no. But a springboard to deeds.

RADIO:

Attention! Attention! According to the latest reports Minister Kilman has the majority in the capital.

CROWD IN STREET: Three cheers for Kilman! Three cheers for Kilman!

SECOND WORKER: Didn't I tell you? Come on, my three glasses of beer! Pay up! Pay up!

FIRST WORKER: Who said anything about three glasses of beer? We agreed one round.

SECOND WORKER: Now you're wriggling out of it!

FIRST WORKER: Just shut up, or else …

PICKEL: As far as I'm concerned I will not be quiet … The Minister would have had, if my vote … He would have had another vote … Indeed his election …

SECOND ELECTION OFFICER: Gentlemen, we have broken the record. Ninety-seven per cent election turnout! Ninety-seven per cent!

KARL THOMAS: If I could only understand! If I could only understand! Have I got caught in a crazy house?

RADIO:

Attention! Attention! At nine-thirty we shall announce the results.

SECOND WORKER: I'll bet on Kilman. Ten rounds? Who takes it?

PICKEL: I would straightaway … if my vote …

SECOND ELECTION OFFICER: We must put it in the papers. Ninety-seven per cent election turnout. That's never happened before! That's never happened before.

PICKEL: If you had allowed me to vote, the percentage would have …

Tumult outside the door. WORKERS *come in.*

THIRD WORKER: They've killed Mother Meller.

FOURTH WORKER: What gangsters! An old woman!

ALBERT KROLL: What's going on?

FIFTH WORKER: She tried to paste up an election leaflet at the Chemical Works.

FOURTH WORKER: With a truncheon! An old woman.

THIRD WORKER: Smashed to the pavement and done for!

FIFTH WORKER: Since when is it forbidden to paste up leaflets?

THIRD WORKER: Good question! Since we have a free election.

FOURTH WORKER: Smack on the head. An old woman.

KARL THOMAS: Did you hear?

ALBERT KROLL: Move, comrades.

ALBERT KROLL tries to go to the door. At this moment they bring in FRAU MELLER *unconscious.* ALBERT KROLL *makes a bed for her on the ground.*

A pillow … Water! … Unconscious. She's alive …

FOURTH WORKER: No warning. Smack with a truncheon. An old woman.

ALBERT KROLL: Coffee!

FIFTH WORKER: What about the constitution! They're going to have to answer for this.

THIRD WORKER: Who to? To their boss, the judge? Man, you're naive.

ALBERT KROLL: Mother Meller, I … Breathe calmly … Like that … Now you can lie back again. This is Karl Thomas. Do you recognise him?

FRAU MELLER: You, Karl …

ALBERT KROLL: What happened? Can you tell us?

FRAU MELLER: Oh, we forgot to dot an i on the leaflet. So some devil dotted the back of my head with a truncheon. In bold type … They've arrested Eva.

Tumult at the door. FIRST *and* THIRD WORKERS *come in with* RAND.

FIRST WORKER: Here's the little brother!

THIRD WORKER: I know him. Regular guest at our meetings. Always the most radical.

FIRST WORKER: Agent provocateur!

OTHER WORKERS: (*Closing in upon* RAND.) Smash him up! Smash him!

ALBERT KROLL jumps in between them, grabs RAND's *arm with his right hand.*

ALBERT KROLL: Order!

KARL THOMAS: To hell with order! Should we swallow everything. That's your election victory for you!

KARL THOMAS tries to knock rand *down.* ALBERT KROLL *grabs* KARL THOMAS *with his left hand.*

You … you … let go!

ALBERT KROLL: You take him, Mother Meller.

FIFTH WORKER: Hadn't we better ask the Party?

ALBERT KROLL: The Party! Are we babies in nappies?

RAND: Thank you very much, Herr Kroll.

ALBERT KROLL: Where do we know each other from?

RAND: I was once your warder.

FRAU MELLER: Well I'll be damned. A great reunion! We ought to drink a little cup of coffee together.

RAND: Haven't I always treated you in a friendly way, Herr Kroll. You must grant me that.

ALBERT KROLL: So friendly that if they ordered you to bump us off, you would have fetched us one by one … with a voice sweet as honey and a face fit for kissing … 'Please don't make it hard for me, I'm only doing my duty, it'll be over soon.'

WORKERS laugh.

RAND: What should a man do? I am only a worker like you. I have to live too. Got five children. And pay to make you puke. I'm only carrying out my orders.

FIRST WORKER: Here's the revolver we got off him.

KARL THOMAS jumps up, grabs the revolver, aims it at RAND.

ALBERT KROLL: (*Hits his arm.*) Stop fooling about!

FRAU MELLER has run over to KARL THOMAS, *pulls him to her.*

What have you stuffed up your belly? You don't care about the craze for being slim! (*Pulls leaflets about of* RAND's *waistcoat, reads.*) 'Comrades, beware of the Jews' … 'Foreign elements'. 'Don't allow the Elders of Zion …'. So you've got principles too?

RAND: You bet! The Jews …

ALBERT KROLL: How much cash do your principles earn you? ... Now get out! March! I've protected you once ... I couldn't do it a second time – even if I wanted to.

RAND goes.

WORKERS: Just wait till you get caught again!

KARL THOMAS: No, Mother Meller, no, let me go. I want to speak to him ... Why are you putting the breaks on me?

ALBERT KROLL: Because I want to go full steam ahead when it's time. It takes strength to have patience.

KARL THOMAS: Kilman says the same thing.

ALBERT KROLL: Fool.

KARL THOMAS: Then what should I do to understand you?

ALBERT KROLL: Work somewhere.

FRAU MELLER: I know what to do, boy. The hotel where I work needs an assistant waiter. I'll work on the head waiter. Got somewhere to stay? You can sleep at my place.

ALBERT KROLL: Do it, Karl. You must get involved in everyday life.

FRAU MELLER: I like you, Albert. Drinking my coffee like it was your own ... Another cup, barkeeper ...

FOURTH WORKER: With a truncheon. An old woman.

RADIO:

Attention! Attention! (*Radio fails ... Buzzing noises.*)

PICKEL: The atmosphere ...

RADIO:

[*Back projected on the centre compartment screen, the bottom of the war minister appears out of the heap of ballots and then he turns to the front and climbs out of the pile.*]

The Minister of War, His Excellency Wandsring, has been elected as President of the Republic by a great majority.

While shouting and singing swirl up in the street, the picture of the president appears on the cyclorama.

[*Screen in and film of the war minister projected on it from the front.*]

Curtain.

[*The interval was here. During it, the scaffolding was pushed to the front again and revolved to the left so that its back was at an angle to the audience.*]

ACT 3

[*After the interval, Act 3 began with Kate Kühl singing this song in the middle of the stage. She was lit by two follow-spots focused on her head and sang in a raucous cabaret style.*]

Hoppla, We're Alive!

Intermezzo for the Hotel Scene in Toller's Play by Walter Mehring

The cream of society stay
    At Hotel Earth *à-la-mode* –
Blithely holding at bay
    Life's unbearable load!
    Partaking of good consummation –
    They proffer a war declaration
    Instead of a cheque for the till –
Here diplomats congregate,
Our plight to deliberate,
They say: We have need of a war
And much better times will arrive!
There's one politics and no more:
Hoppla, we're alive –
    We're alive and we'll settle the bill!

Sabre-rattling Chauvinisms – Ecstatical Populisms –
Which dance will you dance in the morn?
      Hoppla!
Poison Gas-isms – Humanity-isms –
Our cares forlorn!
      Hoppla!
    Our hearts do bleed in distress
    From the sensationalist press,
      Hoppla!
    Freedom – behind bars survive –
    Into trenches dive.
    Hoppla! We're alive!

The men of the military stay
    At Hotel Earth *à-la-mode* –
We fight their battles each day –
    But hatred for us is their code!
    Spending in blood at their whims,
    They tip us in artificial limbs
    And leave a mass grave to fill –
    But when it's time to propose
    They pay for all the death-throes:
The Commander-in-Chief comes along,
And with him the clergy connive –
To sing, so moved, this epic song:
Hoppla, we're alive –
    We're alive! And we'll settle the bill!

The helmet-head – and the Red –
Will our enemies be come morn.
      Hoppla!
And over three million dead –
Our cares forlorn!
      Hoppla!
    Our hearts do bleed all the more
    Under the weight of iron ore!
      Hoppla!
    Freedom – behind bars survive –

Into trenches dive.
Hoppla! WE'RE alive!

Exposed to murder and war
   At Hotel Earth *à-la-mode* –
In the cellar so mean and so sore
   The proletarian herd makes abode –
   They fork out an arm and a leg
   For the little they're able to beg –
   And the whole gang collapses drained of all will!
Then the managers come and they shout:
We have lost out!
We gave you emergency shelter, you see,
And also a crutch to revive,
You are half-dead! – But we,
Hoppla! We're alive –
We're alive and we'll settle the bill!
You have nothing to lose and you're choking!
Can't borrow from us we've sworn!
   Hoppla!
Starving, freezing – and croaking –
Our cares forlorn!
   Hoppla!
We're bleeding away our stash!
You proles, give us our cash!
   Freedom? Behind bars survive –
   Into trenches dive –
   Hoppla! We're alive!

The cream of society stay
   At Hotel Earth *à-la-mode* –
Blithely holding at bay
   Life's unbearable load!
   Our foes were thrashed with devotion –
   Do give that cripple a groschen!
   Our funds are almost at nil!
Ministers, Philosophers and Poets of fame:
They all once again look the same!
All is just like it was before the last war –
And before the next war to arrive —
For battlefield music, the Charleston's the score!
Hoppla! They're alive!
When we settle their bill!
If we bring it all down unawares –
Which dance will you dance in the morn
   Hoppla?
If it's our cares that reign, instead of theirs,
Our cares that were once so forlorn
   Hoppla!
Then pray for your God's absolution
From death by electric execution
Hoppla!
   With your generals we'll strive!
WE'LL command and WE'LL thrive:
Hoppla! We're alive!

Scene 1

[Scaffolding revolved to the back to bring the STUDENT's *room, which had been set up and rolled in on the right, to the front. For ten seconds, film of a busy city at night was projected directly on the stage without the gauze and with appropriate night-life sounds, probably including the Hoppla song. As film ends, lights up on room in front of scaffolding.]*

Small room

STUDENT *is reading. There's a knock.*

STUDENT: Who's there?

COUNT LANDE *enters.*

COUNT LANDE: Well, what do you say about the new President?

STUDENT: I'm sure he has the best intentions.

COUNT LANDE: What good is that for us ... Kilman still remains as Minister.

STUDENT: Really?

COUNT LANDE: Do you have a cigarette? ... Our front group ought to be disbanded.

STUDENT: What? What are you saying?

COUNT LANDE: Kilman ...

STUDENT: Then something really must be done. We always talk about the great deed ...

COUNT LANDE: Can anyone eavesdrop at the door?

STUDENT: No ... What's the matter?

COUNT LANDE: Here.

STUDENT: The decision?

COUNT LANDE: Read it.

COUNT LANDE *gives* STUDENT *a piece of paper.*

STUDENT: I and Lieutenant Frank?

COUNT LANDE: Both of you.

STUDENT: When?

COUNT LANDE: I can't say. You have to be ready at any time.

STUDENT: How quick it's come.

COUNT LANDE: Are you hesitating? Haven't you volunteered twice? Can you forget that the same Kilman who should have been put up against the wall eight years ago now, as Minister, betrays the Fatherland?

STUDENT: Hesitating – no. It goes against the grain to have to wait for the deed.

COUNT LANDE: Hold your horses, *basta!* You took the oath of allegiance; Patriotism has sailed you into shore and now, quite rightly, you are ordered to drop anchor.

STUDENT: And what if we are hunted, hounded, and trapped ... in front of closed frontiers?

COUNT LANDE: In the first place, that is not very likely ... If you get stuck in a blind alley, you will be helped. If you reach the frontier, good. If you don't reach it ... You must make the sacrifice ... Besides you needn't doubt that the judges will be reasonable and show complete understanding for your motives.

STUDENT: May I leave a letter for my mother?

COUNT LANDE: Out of the question. Nationalism must not depend on chance. I know there are cowards ready to compromise in our ranks. They would readily sacrifice us for the sake of political tactics.

STUDENT: I understand so little about politics. I didn't even see service at the front. I joined up and one month later everything collapsed. I hate the Revolution like I've never hated anything. Ever since that one day. My uncle was a General. We boys worshipped him like a god. By the end he commanded an army corps. Three days after the Revolution I'm sitting beside him, the bell rings. A mere Private barges in. 'I'm on the Soldiers' Council. It's been reported to us, Herr General, that you have provoked the people in the street by wearing your golden epaulettes. Today there are no more epaulettes. We all have bare shoulders.' My uncle stood bolt upright. 'I should surrender my epaulettes, should I?' 'Yes.' My uncle takes his sword, which is lying on the table, and draws it out of its scabbard. I'm very frightened. Move nearer so I can help him, when I see the old man cough a hacking cough with tears in his eyes. 'Herr Soldiers' Council, for forty years I have worn the uniform of my Emperor with honour. Once I witnessed how a sergeant was disgraced by having his stripes ripped off. What you demand of me today is the lowest thing anyone can demand of me. If I can no longer wear my uniform with honour, here …' And at that moment the old man bent his sword, broke it in two and threw it at the feet of the soldier. That soldier was Herr Kilman …

COUNT LANDE: That dog!

STUDENT: The next day my uncle shot himself. On a piece of paper he left behind there were these words: 'I cannot survive the shame of our beloved Fatherland. May my death open the eyes of the inflamed people.'

COUNT LANDE: My career went bust too. What are we today compared to the rabble? Stooges. And in society always miles behind the moneybags … We will avenge your uncle. The goods have got to be delivered.

Blackout.

[As the same film is again projected directly on to the stage, the scaffolding revolves to the right until its front is again facing the audience. When it reaches halfway point, a film of hotel scenes is projected from the back and when the revolve stops this film continues on the centre compartment screen. Throughout the revolve, all the characters run around the scaffolding with as much movement as possible, particularly on the stairs, to their places in frenzied cacophony.]

Scene 2

The façade of the Grand Hotel can be seen.

The front wall opens.

Rooms of the Grand Hotel can be seen.

Diagram:

Grand Hotel												
Radio Station												
87	88	89	W C	90	91	92	93	94	95	96 open	97	98
26	27	28	29	30	31	32	33	34	W C	35	36	37
Private Room			Lobby					Club Room				
Hotel Staff Room and Servery								Writing Room				

Blackout.

Lights up:

The lobby

Dancing couple.

Blackout.

Between the separate scenes the Lobby can be seen for a few moments and a jazz band heard.

Lights up:

Staff room

[This section was cut.]

KARL THOMAS in waiter's uniform sits at a table. FRAU MELLER looks in through the door.

FRAU MELLER: Here, boy, a beef steak. It came back from a room. I warmed it up quick.

KARL THOMAS: Thanks a lot, Mother Meller. I have exactly five more minutes. My employment begins at eight o'clock.

FRAU MELLER: I must go to the kitchen again to wash up ... What a sight you are! I really wouldn't have recognised you. Ten years younger. But Karl, Karl, why are you always laughing?

KARL THOMAS: Don't be frightened, Mother Meller. You needn't fear that I'll go crazy again. Everywhere I applied for a job, the bosses asked me: 'Man, what's that undertaker's face for? You'll scare the customers away. Nowadays you have to laugh, always laugh.' Then, because rejuvenation is only a sport for rich people, I went to a beautician. And here's the new façade. Aren't I sweet enough to eat?

FRAU MELLER: Yes, Karl. You'll go down a treat with the girls. But it was weird to me at first ... What demands they make. Next we'll have to sign contracts to laugh the whole ten hours we slave away ... Well, eat now, boy. I must go back to the kitchen.

Blackout.

Lights up:

Private room

[Scaffolding revolved one and a half metres right for close-up effect. Back projection of wallpaper in middle left compartment. Lobby back projection always on in centre compartment.]

Enter BANKER, BANKER'S SON, HEAD WAITER, BUSBOY.

BANKER: Everything ready?

HEAD WAITER: Here's the menu. Would you like any changes, Herr Director-General?

BANKER: Good. For me personally bring something light; I can't eat anything heavy, my stomach ... Perhaps broth, a little chicken meat, compote, but unsugared.

HEAD WAITER: At your service, Herr Director-General.

The HEAD WAITER goes out.

BANKER'S SON: I'm still not sure.

BANKER: Why shouldn't we drive our coach on the route through his wife? An attempt, what does it matter?

BANKER'S SON: She must be simplicity in person. Recently at a government banquet she told stories about her days as a cook.

BANKER: I would have liked to see Kilman's face ... My dear man, one doesn't hear 'Excellency' here and 'Excellency' there every day without being punished. Yes, if there were still titles and orders ... But today money is the only foundation. As soon as one has his first hundred-thousand, he hangs his idealism up on the hatstand. Don't worry, he'll get a fat bank account and I'll get the cheap public credits.

BANKER'S SON: Just as you think.

WILHELM KILMAN and his WIFE enter, accompanied by HEAD WAITER and KARL THOMAS as Waiter, who helps both take off their outer garments.

Good evening, Herr Minister. Extremely delighted, Madam.

WILHELM KILMAN: Government devours you. People always imagine that we sit around in club chairs and smoke thick cigars. Excuse me for being late. I had to receive the Mexican Ambassador.

BANKER'S SON: Now we can begin.

All sit at the table. HEAD WAITER brings food, KARL THOMAS helps.

FRAU KILMAN: What's this lying next to my plate?

BANKER: A *petit rien*, madam. I took the liberty of bringing a rose for you.

FRAU KILMAN: A rose? But I see a case ... In gold? ... Set with pearls? ...

BANKER: It opens here ... This catch ... See, the rose ... La France ... My special rose. I hope you too like this sort ...

FRAU KILMAN: Really, Herr Director-General, very kind, but I cannot accept it. Whatever could I do with it?

WILHELM KILMAN: Come now, Herr Director-General ...

BANKER: Please, my dear Minister, don't make a fuss. Just yesterday I bought three of these things at auction, eighteenth century, Louis Quartorze, even though I already possess two or three.

FRAU KILMAN: You are so nice. We thank you for your kindness, but please take the case back.

WILHELM KILMAN: You know malicious tongues. One must avoid the least appearance ...

BANKER: I am immensely sorry that I didn't think of it ...

WILHELM KILMAN: So let's drink to a compromise. Emma,

please take the rose. What a scent it has, this La France. Better than the real one, ha ha ha … And when we visit you we'll be able to admire the case in your display cabinet.

BANKER: To your health, Madam. Your good health, Herr Minister … Waiter, bring a bottle of Mouton Rothschild '21 …

KARL THOMAS: Yes, indeed, sir.

Blackout.

Lights up:

Radio station

[This section was moved to after the second scene in Room 96. Piscator rewrote some of it to emphasise political and economic events affecting KARL THOMAS.]

RADIO OPERATOR: You finally came? I rang all of three times.

KARL THOMAS: I was busy down below.

RADIO OPERATOR: Here's a telegram for Minister Kilman. It was transmitted here by order of the Ministry.

KARL THOMAS: Can you really listen to the whole earth here?

RADIO OPERATOR: Is that news to you?

KARL THOMAS: What are you listening to now?

RADIO OPERATOR: New York: A great flood on the Mississippi is being reported.

KARL THOMAS: When?

RADIO OPERATOR: Now, at this very moment.

KARL THOMAS: While we speak?

RADIO OPERATOR: Yes, while we speak, the Mississippi is breaking its banks, people are fleeing.

KARL THOMAS: And what are you listening to now?

RADIO OPERATOR: I've tuned in to the 1100 wavelength. I'm listening to Cairo. The jazz band at Mena House, the hotel near the pyramids. They're playing during dinner. Want to have a listen? I'll switch on the loudspeaker.

LOUDSPEAKER: Attention! Attention! All Radio Stations of the world! The latest hit is 'Hoppla, We're Alive!'!

Jazz music can be heard.

RADIO OPERATOR: You can see them too.

Visible on the screen: restaurant at Mena House. Ladies and gentlemen are dining.

KARL THOMAS: Can you also see the Mississippi?

RADIO OPERATOR: Of course. But where have you been that makes you act like such a babe in arms?

KARL THOMAS: Oh, I've lived only in a … little village for the last ten years.

RADIO OPERATOR: Here.

LOUDSPEAKER: Attention! Attention! New York. Number of dead: 8,000. Chicago threatened. Further report follows in three minutes.

Visible on the screen: scenes from the flood.

KARL THOMAS: Inconceivable! At this very second …

LOUDSPEAKER: Attention! Attention! New York. New York. Royal Shell 104, Standard Oil 102, Rand Mines 116.

KARL THOMAS: What is that?

RADIO OPERATOR: The New York Stock Exchange. Petroleum shares on offer … I'll turn the dial. Latest news from around the world.

LOUDSPEAKER: Attention! Attention! Uprising in India … Uprising in China … Uprising in Africa … Paris Paris: Houbigant, the chic perfume … Bucharest Bucharest: Famine in Roumania … Berlin Berlin: The lady of fashion favours green wigs … New York New York: Largest bomber in the world invented. Capable of demolishing Europe's capital cities in a second … Attention! Attention! Paris London Rome Berlin Calcutta Tokyo New York: The complete gentleman drinks Mumm's Extra Dry …

KARL THOMAS: Enough, enough. Turn it off.

RADIO OPERATOR: I'll turn the dial.

LOUDSPEAKER: (*A clamour of cries is heard.*) Hey, hey, hey! Give it to him hard! … he's dizzy … A fix! (*A bell.*) He's saved! … MacNamara, Tonani! MacNamara! … Eviva, eviva …

RADIO OPERATOR: Six-day bicycle race in Milan … Now I'm getting something interesting. The first passenger aeroplane from New York to Paris radios that a passenger is having a heart attack. They are seeking contact with heart specialists. They want medical advice. Right, now you can hear the heartbeat of the patient.

The heartbeats can be heard over the loudspeaker. On the screen can be seen: The aeroplane over the ocean. The patient.

[Piscator showed a beating heart.]

KARL THOMAS: A human heartbeat over the middle of the ocean …

RADIO OPERATOR: A great event.

KARL THOMAS: How wonderful it all is! And what does mankind do with it … They live like muttonheads a thousand years behind the times.

RADIO OPERATOR: We won't change things. I discovered a method to make petroleum out of coal. They bought up my patent for a handful of scraps of paper and then what did they do? Destroyed it! The high and mighty oil magnates … You have to go now. The telegram is urgent. Who knows what tomorrow brings. Perhaps there's war.

KARL THOMAS: War?

RADIO OPERATOR: These apparatuses lead the way there too, helping men kill each other with all the more sophistication. What's the star turn of electricity? The electric chair. There are machines with electric wavelengths such that if they're turned on in London, Berlin would be a heap of rubble by tomorrow. We won't change things. Off you go, hurry up.

KARL THOMAS: Yes, sir.

Blackout.

Lights up:

Club room

[This section was cut.]

Discussion evening of the Union of Intellectual Brain Workers.

PHILOSOPHER X: I come to my conclusion: Where Quality is absent, there is nothing to counterpose Quantity. Therefore my precept runs: Let no one marry beneath his own level. Rather let everyone endeavour, by the appropriate choice of a mate, to raise his posterity to a higher level than he himself possesses. But what do we practice, gentlemen? Nothing but negative selective breeding. The very least, gentlemen, the very least condition of every marriage contract should be equality of birth. We trust instinct. But unfortunately instinct has been so thoroughly one-sided for centuries that it will not be so easy, for several generations, even in some two hundred years, to breed our way up to something better.

LYRIC POET Y: Where does that appear in Marx?

PHILOSOPHER X: I conclude: the instincts must be refined and spiritualised; they must strive ever more away from the Brutal-Vital and towards the Absolute-Superior.

LYRIC POET Y: Where does that appear in Marx?

PHILOSOPHER X: Only thus can the hopelessly degenerated white race be raised up again. Only thus can it nurture superior blooms as it once did. Yet, how can one, many will ask, recognise someone of good blood? Well, whoever cannot judge that in himself and in others, but in himself above all, cannot be helped to do so. He has become so lacking in instinct (*Directed to* LYRIC POET Y.) that I personally can only urgently recommend extinction. Indeed that is what is great in my Academy of Wisdom: it makes people wise by persuading those who formerly bred away blithely to become extinct of their own free will. Now when this is done logically, then in this domain, too, Evil will be conquered by Good once and for all.

SHOUTS: Bravo! Bravo! Point of order!

CHAIRMAN: Lyric Poet Y has the floor.

LYRIC POET Y: Gentlemen. We are gathered here together as intellectual brain workers. Indeed I would like to pose the question whether the theme about which Herr Philosopher X has spoken serves our task, which is the redemption of the proletariat. In Marx …

THE CRITIC: Stop showing off about having read Marx.

LYRIC POET Y: Herr Chairman, I beseech you to protect me. Yes, sir, I have read Marx, and I find that he is not at all so stupid. To be sure he lacks a sense of that new objectivity which we …

CHAIRMAN: You may not speak on a point of order: I'm taking the floor away from you.

LYRIC POET Y: Then I might as well go. Lick my arse! (*Goes.*)

SHOUTS: Outrageous! Outrageous!

THE CRITIC: He should be sent to a psychoanalyst. After analysis he'll stop writing poetry. All poetry is nothing but repressed complexes.

PICKEL comes in.

PICKEL: Indeed, I believe … but nevertheless, am I in the Green Tree Hotel?

CHAIRMAN: No. Private meeting.

PICKEL: Private? … Indeed I believed, the Green Tree … but nevertheless …

SHOUT: Don't disturb us.

PICKEL: Thank you kindly, gentlemen.

PICKEL goes.

CHAIRMAN: What do you want, Herr Philosopher X?

PHILOSOPHER X: A short postscript, gentlemen. To give an example. Herr Lyric Poet Y called into question the causal connection between my theme and the task which we have set ourselves: the intellectual redemption of the proletariat. Today unrepressed instincts are only to be found in the lower social classes. Let us ask a proletarian, let us ask a waiter, and it will prove my theory.

SHOUTS: Waiter! Waiter!

KARL THOMAS appears with a tray of bottles and glasses.

KARL THOMAS: The head waiter is coming right away.

SHOUTS: You must stay.

KARL THOMAS: I have work down below, gentlemen.

PHILOSOPHER X: Listen, Comrade Waiter, young proletarian. Would you perform coitus, sexual intercourse, with the first woman who comes your way or would you first consult your instincts?

KARL THOMAS bursts into laughter.

CHAIRMAN: That's nothing to laugh about. The question is serious. Besides we are guests and you are the waiter.

KARL THOMAS: Aha, first Comrade Waiter and now you play the boss. You … You want to redeem the proletariat? What, here in the Grand Hotel? Where were you when it started to happen? Where will you be? Always in the Grand Hotel! Eunuchs!

SHOUTS: Outrageous! Outrageous!

KARL THOMAS goes.

PHILOSOPHER X: Petit bourgeois ideologue!

CHAIRMAN: Now we come to the second item on the agenda. Proletarian communal love and the task of the intellectuals.

Blackout.

Lights up:

Private room

[*Continued by Piscator directly from previous scene in Private Room.*]

BANKER: What took you so long with the liqueur, waiter?

KARL THOMAS: Excuse me, sir, I was held up.

BANKER: Pass the cigars. Do you smoke cigarettes, madam?

FRAU KILMAN: No, thank you.

[RADIO OPERATOR *brings telegram to* WILHELM KILMAN *in Piscator production.*]

WILHELM KILMAN: The telegram brings the conflict to a head. To deny us the oil concessions!

BANKER: Quite good I had a sharp enough nose to advise my clients to sell off their Turkish holdings ... How do you actually invest your money, Herr Minister?

WILHELM KILMAN: Mortgage bonds, ha, ha, ha! I'm careful not to speculate.

BANKER: Who's talking about speculation? After all you have duties, you have to play the host. A man with your gifts ought to make himself independent.

WILHELM KILMAN: As a State Official, I ought ...

BANKER: But you are also a private person. What does the State give you. A couple of coins. Why don't you make the most of your information? Don't refuse, even a Bismark, a Disraeli, a Gambetta, didn't disdain ...

WILHELM KILMAN: Even so ...

BANKER: I'll give you an example. The Council of Ministers has decided to reduce the contango funds. Then you opportunely sell your stocks. And who can reproach you, if you sell a few more. Of course, it mustn't be done in your own name.

WILHELM KILMAN: Enough of that ...

BANKER: It would be an honour for me to advise you. You know that you can trust me.

WILHELM KILMAN: Waiter, where is the Press Conference taking place?

KARL THOMAS: In the Writing Room.

WILHELM KILMAN: Is Herr Baron Friedrich down there?

KARL THOMAS: Yes, sir.

WILHELM KILMAN: Tell Herr Baron that I shall expect him at the Ministry at midnight.

PICKEL *enters.*

PICKEL: If I am in the right place ... Namely I would like ... Indeed the prices ... but nevertheless ...

BANKER: Who is this man?

PICKEL: Ah, Herr Minister ...

WILHELM KILMAN: I have no time. (*Turns away.*)

PICKEL: I didn't expect that from you, Herr Minister! Haven't we made you Minister? ... Indeed, even if my vote in the Presidential election ... But nevertheless, Minister, you have me to thank for your post ...

Goes.

Blackout.

Lights up:

Writing room

[*This section was cut.*]

JOURNALISTS *writing.* KARL THOMAS *at the door.*

BARON FRIEDRICH: Gentlemen, what was once the task of the historian – to depict the actions, which reason of State demands, as the only solution, as a moral necessity – is now yours. In these difficult times for our Fatherland, the Government has the right to expect that over and above all party differences every newspaper will do its duty. We don't seek war. Let us stress that over and over again, gentlemen. The so-called sanctions which they want to impose on us are better left unmentioned. We want peace. But our patience will run out at once, gentlemen, if the prestige of our State is impugned.

KARL THOMAS: Excuse me, Herr Baron.

BARON FRIEDRICH: What is it?

KARL THOMAS: The Minister wishes to see you at midnight ...

Blackout.

Lights up:

Hotel room no. 96

[*Scaffolding revolves three metres to left for close-up effect. Back projection of red wallpaper on screen of middle right compartment.*]

COUNT LANDE: I clearly saw you make eyes at the blonde girl at the next table.

LOTTE KILMAN: Are you afraid that I'll betray you with her?

COUNT LANDE: That kind of business disgusts me.

LOTTE KILMAN: Maybe you men disgust me ... Maybe you're beginning to bore me now.

COUNT LANDE: But my treasure ...

LOTTE KILMAN: Only women can be tender in bed. I don't deny I'd like to seduce the little darling.

COUNT LANDE: You are drunk.

LOTTE KILMAN: Maybe I would be, if you had been more generous.

COUNT LANDE: Let's order another bottle of Cordon Rouge.

LOTTE KILMAN: Please. But I'd like the little blonde better, or a snort of coke.

COUNT LANDE: Cover yourself up. I'll ring for the waiter.

Blackout.

Lights up:

Servery and staff room

[*Scaffolding revolves three metres right. Back projection of tiled wall lower left compartment. White light on centre compartment screen which is forward to show in silhouette cashier and cash register which rings throughout the scene.*]

HEAD WAITER, KARL THOMAS, PORTER, BUSBOY *sit at supper.*

HEAD WAITER: Mussolini won first prize at the Paris races. Thoroughbred. Three-year-old.

PORTER: Two hundred to win, eighty-four to place.

WAITER enters.

WAITER: Three *entrecôtes.*

HEAD WAITER: (*Calling through the hatch to the kitchen.*) Three *entrecôtes* ... Did you bet anything?

PORTER: Of course, you can't get fat on the loot here.

WAITER: (*Enters.*) Six oxtail soups, double Madeira.

HEAD WAITER: Six oxtail soups, chef should put in double Madeira.

KARL THOMAS: I don't know what this soup tastes like.

PORTER: Do you want to eat *à la carte* instead?

WAITER: (*Enters.*) Two dozen oysters.

HEAD WAITER: Two dozen oysters.

KARL THOMAS: I don't demand oysters, but this muck ... Why doesn't the Works Council do anything?

PORTER: Because it's arm in arm with the hotel manager. I don't give a damn. I expect nothing from nobody. They're all the same. Before the inflation I saved one mark every week. Whenever I had ten, I went to the bank and got a gold piece. On Sunday I'd polish it bright and Monday I'd take it to the Savings Bank. I saved for six hundred weeks. Twelve years. And in the end what did I get? Damn all! Seven hundred million. Couldn't even buy myself a box of matches with it ... The likes of us always get treated dirty.

HEAD WAITER: Posh spread in the Private Room tonight.

KARL THOMAS: For the posh People's Minister.

HEAD WAITER: You don't understand anything about it. If he's dining with a banker, he'll have his own good reasons. Otherwise he wouldn't be Minister.

BUSBOY: The gentleman up in 101 always pinches my bum-bum.

HEAD WAITER: Don't make a fuss, you. You know you can get something out of it.

There's a ring.

Which number?

BUSBOY: Ninety-six.

HEAD WAITER: Karl, you go up. The floor waiter is standing in for me.

Blackout.

Lights up:

Landing

[*This section cut.*]

PICKEL: (*On the stairs.*) Well there you are ... Indeed one believes ... one travels for two days on the railway ... one is looking forward to it for his whole life ... in Holzhausen I thought, up there ... there one would certainly understand people, but up there it's exactly like it is with the railway, with one's own property ... the atmosphere ...

KARL THOMAS goes by.

Herr Waiter! Herr Waiter!

KARL THOMAS: No time.

PICKEL: No time ...

Blackout.

Lights up:

Room no. 96

There's a knock. KARL THOMAS enters.

COUNT LANDE: What took you so long? Service. A bottle of Cordon Rouge. Well chilled.

Blackout.

[*Radio Station scene moved to here by Piscator.*]

Lights up:

Servant's room

KARL THOMAS sits alone at the table, head buried in his hands. FRAU MELLER opens the door quietly.

FRAU MELLER: Tired, youngster?

KARL THOMAS doesn't stir.

It's a real strain the first day.

KARL THOMAS jumps up, tears the cravat from his neck, pulls off his tailcoat, throws it in the corner.

KARL THOMAS: There and there and there! ...

FRAU MELLER: What are you doing?

KARL THOMAS: I'm awake, so awake that I'm afraid I'll never go to sleep again.

FRAU MELLER: Calm down, Karl, calm down.

KARL THOMAS: Calm down? Only a real rotter could calm down. Call me a fool now, like Albert called me. I resolved to be patient. I've been here half a day. I've seen everyday life, in tailcoat and nightshirt. You're all asleep! You're all asleep! You must be awakened. I don't give a damn about your common sense! If sensible people are like you, then I want to play the fool. All of you must be awakened.

There's a ring. Pause.

FRAU MELLER: Karl ...

KARL THOMAS: Let the devil go wait on them!

There's a ring.

FRAU MELLER: The Private Room.

KARL THOMAS: The Private Room? ... Kilman? ... Good, I'll go.

KARL THOMAS dresses hurriedly.

FRAU MELLER: I'll come right back. We'll have a talk, Karl.

FRAU MELLER goes.

KARL THOMAS: (*Looks at his revolver a few seconds.*) This shot will awaken them all!

Blackout.

Lights up:

Room no. 96

There's a soft knock.

COUNT LANDE: Coming.

Blackout.

Lights up:

Half-dark corridor.

STUDENT: Where?

COUNT LANDE: In the Private Room. Who is going in?

STUDENT: We drew lots. Me. Lieutenant Frank is waiting in the car.

COUNT LANDE: Are you wearing a waiter's tailcoat?

STUDENT: (*Opens his coat.*) Yes.

COUNT LANDE: Break a leg. Quick now. You must not be arrested. If you have bad luck, then ... You mustn't make any statements ... Take care of yourself.

STUDENT: I have given my word of honour.

Blackout.

Lights up:

Private room

WILHELM KILMAN: Superb, that joke, superb. Just look at my wife. How red she's getting. She doesn't understand anything about that, ha, ha, ha.

BANKER: Do you know the one about Herr Meyer in the railway compartment?

WILHELM KILMAN: Tell it.

BANKER: The waiter at last! Another bottle of cognac ... Why are you standing there? Why are you staring at me? Didn't you understand?

KARL THOMAS: Don't you recognise me?

WILHELM KILMAN: Who are you?

KARL THOMAS: Feel free to use my first name. When we waited together for the mass grave, we weren't so formal. Are you ashamed of knowing me?

WILHELM KILMAN: It's you ... Don't talk crazy nonsense. Come to the Ministry tomorrow.

KARL THOMAS: You will answer for it today.

WILHELM KILMAN: (*To banker.*) Leave him be. A fantasiser whom I knew from before. Off the rails because of a romantic episode in his youth. Can't find a firm grip any more.

KARL THOMAS: I'm waiting for your answer.

WILHELM KILMAN: To what? What is going on in your head? What's going on in your head, Karl? Do I need to tell you again that times have changed? You'd rather damn the world than give up your insane demands; you'd rather damn the very men who are trying to make things progress a bit.

KARL THOMAS: Wilhelm ...

WILHELM KILMAN: Please stop the hollow phrases. They don't work.

BANKER: Hadn't I better call the Hotel Manager?

WILHELM KILMAN: For God's sake, don't make a scene.

BANKER: Calm down, waiter. He's in a bad way isn't he? Here, take ten marks.

WILHELM KILMAN: May I add another ten?

KARL THOMAS, clutching the revolver in his pocket with one hand, looks at the money bewildered, shrugs his shoulders in disgust as if he had gone off doing the deed and starts to turn away.

KARL THOMAS: It's not worth it. I couldn't give a damn about you now.

Then the door opens quietly. STUDENT in waiter's tailcoat enters. Raises his revolver over KARL THOMAS's shoulder. Turns the electric light out. Shot. Scream.

BANKER: Lights! Lights! The waiter has shot the Minister.

Curtain.

[Scaffolding revolves right so stairs are visible. KARL THOMAS and STUDENT run down them followed by spotlights. Gauze in and park is projected on it from front as scaffolding revolves face-on to audience for next act.]

ACT 4
Scene 1

Left of hotel. In a park.

KARL THOMAS *is running after the* STUDENT.

KARL THOMAS: You! You!

STUDENT *turns his head, runs on.*

You, I want to help you, comrade.

STUDENT: What, comrade! I'm not your comrade.

KARL THOMAS: But you shot Kilman ...

STUDENT: Because he's a Bolshevik, because he's a revolutionary. Because he's selling our country out to the Jews.

Bewildered, KARL THOMAS *takes a step towards him.*

KARL THOMAS: Has the world become a madhouse? Has the world become a madhouse!!!

STUDENT: Get back, or I'll shoot you down.

STUDENT *runs on, jumps into a car which speeds away.* KARL THOMAS *catches on, tears the revolver out of his pocket, shoots after it twice. Then he reflects, stands still in front of a tree.*

KARL THOMAS: Are you a beech tree? Or are you a rubber-padded wall? (*Feels it.*) You feel like bark, rough and cracked, and you do smell of earth. But are you really a beech tree?

Sits on a bench.

My poor head. Drumfire. Roll up, Ladies and Gentlemen. The bell is ringing. The ride is starting. Only one shot a go.

You see a house burning, grab a pail, try to put it out, and instead of water you pour buckets of oil on the flames ...

You sound the alarm throughout the whole city to awaken all the people, but the sleepers just turn over on their bellies and snore on ...

When night covers others in brown shadows, I see murderers crouching naked with brains exposed ...

And I run through the streets like a night watchman, with thoughts which wound themselves on the beam of a spotlight ...

Oh, why did they open the gate of the madhouse for me? Wasn't it good in there in spite of the North Pole and the flapping wings of grey birds?

I have lost my grip on the world
And the world has lost its grip on me

During the last phrases two POLICE DETECTIVES *have entered. Both go up to him, grab him by the wrists.*

FIRST POLICEMAN: Well, young man, no doubt you just found that revolver somewhere?

KARL THOMAS: What do I know? What do you know? Even the revolver turns against the gunman, and spurts laughter out of its barrel.

SECOND POLICEMAN: Just speak respectfully, you got that?

FIRST POLICEMAN: What is your name?

KARL THOMAS: Every name is a con ... See, I once believed that if I took the path straight through the park, I'd reach a hotel. A cup of coffee. Fifty pfennigs. Do you know where I landed? In the madhouse. And the police make sure that no one gets sane.

FIRST POLICEMAN: I'd like to make sure of that for you. You're under arrest.

SECOND POLICEMAN: Don't try to resist. You'll get shot trying to escape.

KARL THOMAS: Let me go.

FIRST POLICEMAN: Just the opposite. Be glad that we're protecting you. The people would lynch you.

SECOND POLICEMAN: Do you admit that you shot the Minister?

KARL THOMAS: Me?

FIRST POLICEMAN: Yes, you.

SECOND POLICEMAN: Come on, to the police station.

Blackout.

Shouts from a crowd of people are heard.

Scene 2

[After sounds of many ringing telephones and alarm during blackout, the top left compartment and bottom right compartments were lit, probably in that order, to show COUNT LANDE, *top left, telephoning the* CHIEF OF POLICE, *bottom right. This underlined the complicity between him and the police and echoed the secret telephone line between Chancellor Ebert and General Groener. Beginning of the scene was rewritten by Piscator, identifying that the conversation was with* COUNT LANDE *and underscoring their secret understanding as they spoke in a kind of shorthand code.]*

Police headquarters
Room of the Chief of Police

CHIEF OF POLICE *at a table. Piercing ring.*

CHIEF OF POLICE: (*On telephone.*) Hello? What's up? ... What? ... Assassination attempt on Minister Kilman at the Grand Hotel? ... The Minister's dead? ... Cordon off the Grand Hotel ... Clear the streets ... A suspect arrested? ... Bring him here ... I'll wait ... (*Hangs up. To* SECRETARY.) Stay here. You must make a transcript. (*Telephones.*) All stations on alert ... Thanks ... Report any suspicious incidents ... From the Left, of course ... Crush any demonstrations ... That's it ...

Meanwhile a POLICEMAN *has come in with* PICKEL.

PICKEL: (*To the* POLICEMAN.) You don't have to hold me like that, sir ... Who are you after all? Indeed you live in a big city where there's riff-raff, but nevertheless you should discriminate.

CHIEF OF POLICE: What's up?

POLICEMAN: This man was hanging about in the corridor of the Grand Hotel ... Shortly before the assassination he was in the Minister's room. He isn't staying at the Hotel, behaves suspiciously, and cannot account for why ...

CHIEF OF POLICE: Good. What is your name?

PICKEL: Indeed my name is Pickel, but nevertheless ...

CHIEF OF POLICE: Just answer my questions.

PICKEL: Namely I would like to ...

CHIEF OF POLICE: You were in the room of the murdered Minister shortly before the assassination. What did you want there?

PICKEL: I believed he ... Indeed, Herr General, I believed the Minister was a man of honour ... But nevertheless when I went up to him in the hotel room ...

CHIEF OF POLICE: You admit you were involved in the deed? You had a personal grudge against the Minister?

PICKEL: Namely I wanted ...

CHIEF OF POLICE: What did you want? Are you an anarchist? Do you belong to an illegal group?

PICKEL: Namely the veterans of the front have ... Although I was only behind the lines ... to the Soldiers' Union, Herr General.

CHIEF OF POLICE: To the Soldiers' Union? ... Can you prove that?

PICKEL: Yes, sir. Here is my membership card.

CHIEF OF POLICE: Aha ... Are you a Nationalist? ... Therefore ... Tell me, why did you murder the Minister?

PICKEL: I believed ... I would have gone through fire for him ...

CHIEF OF POLICE: Pay attention to my questions.

PICKEL: Namely ... I came only on account of the railway ... And there I am in the Ministry ... And I haven't any more ...

CHIEF OF POLICE: To the point.

PICKEL: Oh, Herr General, let me go home. The weather is changing ... I could travel now ... And my cows ... My wife has always said ...

Telephone rings.

CHIEF OF POLICE: (*On telephone.*) Police Headquarters ... You have interrogated the eye witnesses? ... A man in a waiter's tail coat? ... One moment ... Pickel, take off your coat.

PICKEL: I'm wearing namely ...

CHIEF OF POLICE: Frock-coat ... Aha ...

PICKEL: But nevertheless only because I ...

CHIEF OF POLICE: Be quiet. (*On telephone.*) ... Thanks ... Fräulein, take down Pickel's personal details ...

SECRETARY: Your name? Surname and Christian name?

PICKEL: Trustgod Pickel is my name, Fräulein ... As a boy my name was Godbeloved ... nevertheless my name is really Trustgod ... Namely the official at the Registry Office who with my father ... as long as they were well, every evening they played ...

POLICE DETECTIVE enters.

CHIEF OF POLICE: What's up?

FIRST POLICEMAN: We arrested a man in the park. He was holding a revolver in his hand. Two bullets are missing.

CHIEF OF POLICE: Bring him in.

POLICE DETECTIVE enters with KARL THOMAS.

What is your name?

KARL THOMAS: Karl Thomas.

CHIEF OF POLICE: What did you want with this revolver? ...

KARL THOMAS: To shoot the Minister.

CHIEF OF POLICE: Things are going very fast ... The second one ... So, a confession ... Do you belong to Herr Pickel's Soldiers' Union too?

KARL THOMAS: To the Soldiers' Union? ...

PICKEL: Herr General, I must point out that our Soldiers' Union in Holzhausen ... Indeed we don't after all accept any foreigners ... not even anyone from the neighbouring villages ... but nevertheless the President of the Reich is an Honorary Member ...

CHIEF OF POLICE: Silence ... (*To the POLICEMAN.*) What did the man look like then?

SECOND POLICEMAN: The people wanted to lynch him. We could hardly hold the crowds back.

CHIEF OF POLICE: Sit down. Tell me, why did you shoot the Minister?

KARL THOMAS: Is he dead?

CHIEF OF POLICE: Yes.

KARL THOMAS: I didn't shoot.

CHIEF OF POLICE: But you must admit you just confessed ...

PICKEL: No, Herr General, you are wrong there. I know him. He is namely a friend of the Minister ...

CHIEF OF POLICE: Why are you always interrupting?

PICKEL: Because you don't believe me ... I am namely the Treasurer of the Soldiers' Union. And our statutes ...

CHIEF OF POLICE: I'll have you removed straight away. (*To KARL THOMAS.*) You saw the Minister as vermin, didn't you? A traitor to his country?

KARL THOMAS: The murderer thought he was.

CHIEF OF POLICE: The murderer?

KARL THOMAS: I chased him. I shot at him.

CHIEF OF POLICE: What kind of crazy nonsense are you talking?

PICKEL: If he says so, Herr General ...

POLICE DETECTIVE goes over to the CHIEF OF POLICE, speaks softly with him.

CHIEF OF POLICE: He makes the same impression on me. Moreover the other one, Pickel, also ... Hand them both over to Department One. I'll come over straightaway ... (*On telephone.*) Connect me with the Public Prosecutor ...

PICKEL: Herr General ... namely I would like ... I would like to ask ...

CHIEF OF POLICE: What is it now?

PICKEL: Is it decided, Herr General? Will I be put in prison?

CHIEF OF POLICE: Yes.

PICKEL: Indeed ... Then ... Namely in Holzhausen ... And if they hear ... And if my wife ... And if my neighbour ... who is related to the Mayor ... And if the Soldiers' Union ... Do you know what you are doing? ... Now that I am 'previously convicted'. Where can I go, when I come out of prison? Where? I definitely couldn't show my face in Holzhausen again ...

CHIEF OF POLICE: If it turns out that you are not guilty, you can go home.

PICKEL: But nevertheless 'previously convicted'.

CHIEF OF POLICE: I have no time. (*On telephone.*) Connect me with the Public Prosecutor.

PICKEL: No time either ... White gloves, black gloves ... What can one believe in? ...

Blackout.

Scene 3

[This scene was cut.]

Room of the Examining Magistrate

EXAMINING MAGISTRATE and CLERK at a table. In front of the table, KARL THOMAS *in handcuffs.*

EXAMINING MAGISTRATE: You are only making your situation more difficult. Witnesses have testified that in the bar, The Bear, you expressed the intention to murder the Minister.

KARL THOMAS: I don't deny that. But I didn't shoot.

EXAMINING MAGISTRATE: You admit the intention ...

KARL THOMAS: The intention, yes.

EXAMINING MAGISTRATE: Have the witness, Rand, brought in.

RAND enters.

Herr Rand, do you know the suspect?

RAND: Very good, sir, yes.

EXAMINING MAGISTRATE: Is this the same man who pocketed your revolver during the attack in the polling station?

RAND: Very good, sir, yes.

EXAMINING MAGISTRATE: Thomas, what do you say to that?

KARL THOMAS: I don't dispute that. But ...

RAND: If I might be allowed to express my opinion, the Jews are behind all this.

EXAMINING MAGISTRATE: Haven't you shot the revolver, Rand?

RAND: Very good, sir, no. All the bullets ought to be in the cylinder.

EXAMINING MAGISTRATE: Two are missing. Is this nevertheless your revolver?

RAND: My service revolver, Herr Examining Magistrate.

EXAMINING MAGISTRATE: Do you still want to deny the deed, Thomas? Don't you want to relieve your conscience with a confession?

KARL THOMAS: I have nothing to confess, I did not shoot.

EXAMINING MAGISTRATE: How do you explain the two missing bullets?

KARL THOMAS: I fired at the assassin.

EXAMINING MAGISTRATE: So, fired at the assassin. Now only the great unknown assassin is missing. Do you perhaps know the mysterious culprit who, as you declare, came into the room behind you and shot?

KARL THOMAS: No.

EXAMINING MAGISTRATE: Well then, the famous Herr X.

KARL THOMAS: He was someone on the Right. He said so himself. I chased after him. I thought he would be a comrade.

EXAMINING MAGISTRATE: Don't talk nonsense. Are you trying to cover the traces of your back-room cronies? We know them; this time there's no amnesty. Your closest comrades are behind bars ... Have the Head Waiter of the Grand Hotel brought in.

HEAD WAITER enters.

Do you know the suspect?

HEAD WAITER: Yes indeed, sir. He was an assistant waiter at the Grand Hotel. If I had known, sir, that ...

EXAMINING MAGISTRATE: Did the suspect call Herr Minister Kilman abusive names?

HEAD WAITER: Yes indeed, sir; he said 'a perfect People's Minister'. No, 'a posh People's Minister', he said.

EXAMINING MAGISTRATE: Thomas, did you say that?

KARL THOMAS: Yes, but I did not shoot.

EXAMINING MAGISTRATE: Have Frau Meller brought in.

FRAU MELLER enters.

You know the suspect?

FRAU MELLER: Yes, he is my friend.

EXAMINING MAGISTRATE: So, your friend. Do you call yourself his ... comrade?

FRAU MELLER: Yes.

EXAMINING MAGISTRATE: Did you recommend the suspect to the Head Waiter of the Grand Hotel?

FRAU MELLER: Yes.

EXAMINING MAGISTRATE: The suspect is supposed to have said to you: 'You are all asleep. Someone must be done away with. Then you will awaken.'

FRAU MELLER: No.

EXAMINING MAGISTRATE: Pull yourself together, witness. You are suspected of aiding and abetting. You procured a place for the suspect at the Grand Hotel. The prosecution assumes that this position was only a pretence so that the suspect should get the opportunity to be near the Minister.

FRAU MELLER: If you know better about everything, then, go on, arrest me.

EXAMINING MAGISTRATE: I'm asking you for the last time: did the accused say, Someone must be done away with?

FRAU MELLER: No.

EXAMINING MAGISTRATE: Have the busboy come in.

BUSBOY comes in.

Do you know the accused?

BUSBOY: Thank you, yes. When he had to carry the plates in, he broke one straight away and told me I should hide the pieces so no one could find them.

EXAMINING MAGISTRATE: That is very interesting. Did you do that?

KARL THOMAS: Yes.

EXAMINING MAGISTRATE: That throws a proper light on your character ... Pay close attention, boy. Did you hear the suspect say: 'You are all asleep! Someone must be done away with. Then you will awaken'?

BUSBOY: Thank you, yes, and along with that he rolled his eyes and clenched his fists; he looked all bloodthirsty. I've only seen faces like that at the movies. I was shuddering.

EXAMINING MAGISTRATE: What did you do then?

BUSBOY: I ... I ... I ...

EXAMINING MAGISTRATE: You must tell the truth.

BUSBOY: (*Begins to cry, turns away from the EXAMINING MAGISTRATE to the HEAD WAITER.*) Sir, I won't do it any more, I know I told you I needed to pee, I didn't go to pee at all, I was so tired I laid down under the table and tried to sleep a little ... Sir, please don't report me to the boss.

EXAMINING MAGISTRATE: (*Laughing.*) That won't be so serious ... Thomas, what do you say to these statements?

KARL THOMAS: That I'm gradually getting the impression that I'm in a madhouse.

EXAMINING MAGISTRATE: I see, in a madhouse. The witnesses may leave. Frau Meller, for the present you are under arrest. Take her away.

Witnesses go.

Bring in Eva Berg, who's under arrest.

EVA BERG is brought in.

Your name is Eva Berg?

EVA BERG: Hello, Karl ... Yes.

EXAMINING MAGISTRATE: You are not allowed to speak to the suspect.

EVA BERG: I can't shake hands with him; you must take the handcuffs off first. Why is he handcuffed? Do you think he will escape? Outside there are a dozen warders. Or are you afraid of him? You don't seem to be very brave. Or are you only trying to intimidate him? They'll be disappointed, won't they Karl?

EXAMINING MAGISTRATE: I'll have you taken away at once, if you don't change your tone.

EVA BERG: I don't doubt you can summon up enough courage for that ... I'm waiting for you to have enough to set me free.

EXAMINING MAGISTRATE: I am not authorised by the law to do so.

EVA BERG: When it suits you, you hide behind the law. For weeks I've been held in custody. I've only exercised the rights which the constitution grants to everyone. Because public rights are public duties, you would have to resign your judgeship before admitting the law was broken.

EXAMINING MAGISTRATE: I have two questions to put to you. Did the suspect live with you?

EVA BERG: Yes.

EXAMINING MAGISTRATE: Have you had relationships with him which are punishable by law?

EVA BERG: What kind of a ridiculous question is that? Do you come from the fifteenth century?

EXAMINING MAGISTRATE: I want to know whether you have had sexual relations with the suspect?

EVA BERG: Will you first explain to me what an unsexual union looks like?

EXAMINING MAGISTRATE: You come from a respectable family ... Your father would ...

EVA BERG: My family is none of your business. And I consider your question so unrespectable that I would be ashamed of myself if I answered it.

EXAMINING MAGISTRATE: So you refuse to answer the second question ... During the time he lived with you, did the suspect express the intention of murdering Minister Kilman?

EVA BERG: Herr Examining Magistrate, I think we know each other from the old days ... You chose to remember that ... Wouldn't you class a fellow club member and friend who betrayed his comrades as the lowest of the low? Thus your third question is also unrespectable, because you believe in the probability that he said that. But I swear, on that honour which you can neither give nor ever take away from me, Karl Thomas never expressed the intention of murdering Kilman.

EXAMINING MAGISTRATE: Thank you. Take her away.

EVA BERG: Farewell, Karl. Don't give in.

KARL THOMAS: I love you, Eva.

EVA BERG: Even at a moment like this I must not lie to you.

EVA BERG is taken away.

EXAMINING MAGISTRATE: I've learned from your files that you spent eight years in a madhouse. You shall be referred to the Psychiatric Department to ascertain whether you are of sound mind.

Blackout.

Scene 4
The façade transforms into the façade of the Madhouse.
Open:
Examination room

[*This scene was played in the centre compartment of the scaffolding, revealed behind the projection of the façade. Back projection of filing cabinet as before.*]

PROFESSOR LÜDIN: You were referred to me by the Public Prosecutor for psychiatric treatment ... Stand still. Pulse normal. Open your shirt. Breathe deeply. Hold it. Heart healthy ... Tell me honestly, why did you commit this deed?

KARL THOMAS: I did not shoot.

PROFESSOR LÜDIN: (*Leafing through the files.*) The police first took you for a man who fired the shots for Nationalist motives. They believed a certain Pickel to be your accomplice. The Examining Magistrate came to the conclusion that this supposition was wrong. He takes the view that you belong to a radical left-wing terrorist group ... Your like-minded comrades have been arrested ... I, mind you, think ... Confide in me with full assurance, only your motives interest me.

KARL THOMAS: I have nothing to confess because I am not the culprit.

PROFESSOR LÜDIN: You wanted to avenge yourself, didn't you? You probably believed that the Minister would give you a top position. You saw that your high and mighty comrades, once they sit on top, also only take care of themselves. You felt sold out, betrayed? The world looked different from the picture of it in your head.

KARL THOMAS: I don't need a psychiatrist.

PROFESSOR LÜDIN: You feel sane?

KARL THOMAS: Sound as a bell.

PROFESSOR LÜDIN: Hm. This notion still dominates you? I think I remember that your mother also suffered from this complex.

KARL THOMAS laughs.

Don't laugh. No one is sound as a bell.

Short pause.

KARL THOMAS: Herr Professor!

PROFESSOR LÜDIN: Do you want to confess to me now why you shot? Understand, only the Why interests me. The deed is no concern of mine. Deeds are of no importance. Only motives are important.

KARL THOMAS: I want to tell you everything exactly, Herr Professor. I've lost my bearings. What I experienced ... May I tell you, Herr Professor.

PROFESSOR LÜDIN: Begin then.

KARL THOMAS: I must have clarity. The door slammed shut behind me, and when I opened it eight years had passed. A whole century. As you advised me, I first paid a visit to Wilhelm Kilman. Condemned to death like I was. I discovered he was Minister. Wedded to his former enemies.

PROFESSOR LÜDIN: Normal. He was just more cunning than you.

KARL THOMAS: I went to my closest comrade. A man who with just a revolver in his hand repulsed a whole company of Whites, all alone. I heard him say 'One must be able to wait.'

PROFESSOR LÜDIN: Normal.

KARL THOMAS: And at the same time he swore he remained true to the Revolution.

PROFESSOR LÜDIN: Abnormal. But not your fault. He ought to be examined. Probably a mild dementia praecox in a catatonic form.

KARL THOMAS: I was a waiter. For one whole evening. It stank of corruption. The people I worked with found it all in order and were proud of it.

PROFESSOR LÜDIN: Normal. Business is thriving again. Everybody makes money out of it in his own way.

KARL THOMAS: You call that normal? In the hotel I met a banker. They told me he harvests money like hay ... What does he get from it? He can't even fill his belly up with delicacies. When the others feed on pheasants, he has to slurp soup, because his stomach is bad. He speculates day and night. What for? What for?

[Distorted mask of BANKER projected middle left.]

Behind the projection, the Private Room in the Hotel lights up.

BANKER: (*On the table telephone.*) Hello! Hello! Stock Exchange? Sell everything! Paints and Potash and Pipes ... The assassination of Kilman ... Chemical Works shares already fallen about a hundred per cent ... What? ... Operator! ... Fräulein, why did you cut me off? ... I'll hold you liable ... Ruined by a telephone breakdown ... God in heaven!

PROFESSOR LÜDIN: What for? Because he's smart and because he wants to achieve something. Dear friend, the banker whom you saw – I wish I had his fortune – was normal.

BANKER: (*Grinning in the Hotel Room.*) Normal ... Normal ...

Blackout in Hotel Room.

KARL THOMAS: And the porter at the Grand Hotel? For twelve years he saved a gold piece every week. Twelve years! Then the inflation came. They paid him six hundred million and he couldn't even buy a box of matches with all his savings. But he wasn't cured, he thinks the whole con is unchangeable, today he scrapes and stints on food and then gambles away his last groschen. Is that normal?

[Distorted mask of PORTER projected bottom left.]

Behind the projection, the Staff Room in the Hotel lights up.

PORTER: Who won the Paris race? The beautiful Galatea ... A fix! A fix! I put all my savings on Idealist, and that damned jockey goes and breaks his neck ... I want to get my stake back! Or else ...

PROFESSOR LÜDIN: Nothing venture, nothing gain. The porter at the Grand Hotel, and I lived there once, is absolutely normal.

PORTER: (*In Hotel Room, grinning as he stabs himself with his knife.*) Normal ... Normal ...

Blackout in Hotel Room.

KARL THOMAS: Perhaps you also call a world normal in which it is possible for the most important inventions, inventions which could make the life of mankind easier, to be destroyed just because some people are frightened they won't make as much money any more?

[Distorted mask of RADIO OPERATOR projected top of centre compartment.]

Behind the projection, the Radio Station in the Hotel lights up.

RADIO OPERATOR: Attention! Attention! All radio stations of the world! Who will buy my invention? I don't want money. The invention will help everyone, everyone. Silence ... No one responds.

PROFESSOR LÜDIN: What's abnormal about that? Life is no meadow in which people dance ring-a-ring-o'-roses and play on pipes of peace. Life is struggle. Might is right. That is absolutely normal!

RADIO OPERATOR: (*In Hotel Room, grinning as he causes a short circuit.*) Normal ...

All the rooms of the Hotel light up.

CHORUS OF HOTEL OCCUPANTS: (*In a crouching position, leaning down towards the Examination Room, grinning and nodding.*) Normal! ... Normal! ...

Explosion in Hotel. Blackout.

KARL THOMAS: How could I have borne this world any longer! ... I formed a plan to shock mankind. I was going to shoot the Minister. At the very same moment someone else shot him.

PROFESSOR LÜDIN: Hm.

KARL THOMAS: I called after the culprit. Believed he was a comrade. Wanted to help him. He rejected me. I saw his twisted lips. He screamed at me: 'Because the Minister was a Bolshevik, a revolutionary.'

PROFESSOR LÜDIN: Normal. Relatively so, if this unknown person existed.

KARL THOMAS: Then I shot at the murderer of the same man I myself wanted to murder.

PROFESSOR LÜDIN: Hm.

KARL THOMAS: The fog suddenly lifted. Perhaps the world is not crazy at all. Perhaps I am ... Perhaps I am ... Perhaps it was all only a crazy dream.

PROFESSOR LÜDIN: What do you want? That's simply the way the world is ... Let's go back to your motives. Did you want to get rid of your past with this shot?

KARL THOMAS: Insanity! Insanity!

PROFESSOR LÜDIN: Don't play-act with me. You can't sway an old psychiatrist like that.

KARL THOMAS: Or is there no boundary between madhouse and world these days? Yes, yes ... really ... The same kind of people who are kept here as mad gallop around outside as normal and are permitted to trample others down.

PROFESSOR LÜDIN: I see ...

KARL THOMAS: And you! Do you dare say that you too are normal? You are a madman among madmen.

PROFESSOR LÜDIN: Enough of this strong language now! ... Or else I'll have you put in the padded cell. You're just trying to save yourself with the Section for the mentally ill, aren't you?

KARL THOMAS: Do you believe you're alive? You imagine that the world will always stay like it is now!

PROFESSOR LÜDIN: Well you've stayed the same ... You still want to change the world, set fire to it, don't you? If nature had not wanted some to eat less than others, there wouldn't be any poverty at all. Whoever achieves what he's capable of needn't go hungry.

KARL THOMAS: Whoever goes hungry needn't eat.

PROFESSOR LÜDIN: With your ideas men would become scroungers and shirkers.

KARL THOMAS: Are you happy with your ideas?

PROFESSOR LÜDIN: What, happiness! You suffer from overestimating this idea. Chimera! Phobia! The happiness concept sits in your brain like a stagnant reservoir. If you would cherish it for your own sake, that's fair enough. You'd probably write lyric poems full of soul and love blue violets and beautiful maidens ... or you'd become a harmless religious sectarian with a mild paraphrenia phantastica complex. But you want to make the world happy.

KARL THOMAS: I don't give a damn about your soul.

PROFESSOR LÜDIN: You undermine every society. Every one! What do you want? To turn the very foundations of life upside down, to create heaven on earth, the Absolute, isn't that it? Delusion! Like infectious poison you act on the weak in spirit, on the masses!

KARL THOMAS: What do you understand about the masses?

PROFESSOR LÜDIN: My collection of specimens opens even the blindest of eyes. The masses, a herd of swine. Cram to the trough when there's something to guzzle. Wallow in muck when their bellies are stuffed. And then every century psychopaths come and promise the herd paradise. The police ought to hand them over to us madhouse doctors at once, instead of watching them go berserk among mankind.

KARL THOMAS: You certainly aren't harmless.

PROFESSOR LÜDIN: It is our mission to protect society from dangerous criminals. You are the arch enemies of every civilisation! You are chaos! You must be neutralised, sterilised, eradicated!

KARL THOMAS: Orderlies! Orderlies!

ORDERLIES enter.

Lock this madman up in the padded cell.

PROFESSOR LÜDIN gives the ORDERLIES a sign. ORDERLIES grab KARL THOMAS.

PROFESSOR LÜDIN: Tomorrow you will be sent back to prison.

Curtain.

[At the end of this act, the Mary Wigman female dance group performed a frenzied Charleston across the stage. They were dressed in black with phosphorescent skeletons painted on their costumes which glowed under the ultraviolet light, eerily commenting on the skull beneath the skin of the Weimar Republic. Screen and gauze were lowered to human height so the Prison could be prepared behind. After the dance, white gauze remained in for projection of façade of prison windows from the front. Back projections of cells on the compartment screens. Captions for the knocking projected on the gauze running left and right and up and down. See the promptbook scene at end.]

ACT 5
Scene 1
Prison

For a moment all cells visible. Blackout. Then lights up: ALBERT KROLL'*s cell.*

ALBERT KROLL: (*Knocks on adjoining cell.*) Who is there?

Lights up: EVA BERG'*s cell.*

EVA BERG: (*Knocks.*) Eva Berg.
ALBERT KROLL: (*Knocks.*) You too? ...
EVA BERG: (*Knocks.*) Early today.
ALBERT KROLL: (*Knocks.*) And the others?
EVA BERG: (*Knocks.*) All arrested. Why did Karl do it?
ALBERT KROLL: (*Knocks.*) He says no, he didn't. Where is Karl?
EVA BERG: (*Knocks.*) Maybe Mother Meller knows.
ALBERT KROLL: (*Knocks.*) Mother Meller? Is she here too?
EVA BERG: (*Knocks.*) Yes. Above me. Wait, I'll knock.

Noise at ALBERT KROLL'*s door.*

ALBERT KROLL: (*Knocks.*) Look out! Someone's coming.

ALBERT KROLL'*s door creaks open.* RAND *enters.*

RAND: Soup ... Eat quick. Today is Sunday.
ALBERT KROLL: Oh, it's you.
RAND: Yes, I'm a prison officer again. You have something firm under your feet ... Well, now I have you all together again. Except Kilman. They're dedicating a memorial to him today.
ALBERT KROLL: Really?
RAND: Kilman was the only one among you worth anything, you have to admit that. I always said so.
ALBERT KROLL: (*Eats.*) Muck.
RAND: Doesn't the soup taste good to you? There's roast pork at Christmas. Be patient until then.
ALBERT KROLL: Tell me, is Karl Thomas here too?
RAND: Since yesterday evening ... What a life he's got behind him ...

RAND leaves.

ALBERT KROLL: (*Knocks.*) Now, Eva.
EVA BERG: (*Knocks.*) Where is Karl?
KNOCKING EVERYWHERE: Where is Karl?

Blackout in cells. Lights up: KARL THOMAS'*s cell.*

KARL THOMAS: Waiting again ... waiting ... waiting ...

Lights up: FRAU MELLER'*s cell.*

FRAU MELLER: (*Knocks.*) Where is Karl?
KARL THOMAS: (*Knocks.*) Here ... Who are you?
FRAU MELLER: (*Knocks.*) Mother Meller.
KARL THOMAS: (*Knocks.*) What? Old Mother Meller. (*Knocks.*) Who else is here?
FRAU MELLER: (*Knocks.*) All of us ... Eva ... Albert ... And the others ... On account of the assassination. We are with you, dear boy ...
KARL THOMAS: (*Knocks.*) Do you still remember eight years ago?
FRAU MELLER: (*Knocks.*) I don't really understand what you have done ... But I'll stick with you ...

Blackout in FRAU MELLER'*s cell.*

KARL THOMAS: (*Knocks.*) Listen now! ...

Lights up: PRISONER'*s cell.*

PRISONER N: (*Knocks.*) Not so loud ... Think of the rules ... You'll hurt us ...
KARL THOMAS: (*Knocks.*) Who are you?
PRISONER N: (*Knocks.*) If you keep on like that, there's no hope left for us. I won't answer anymore ...

Blackout in PRISONER'*s cell.*

KARL THOMAS: Ah, it's you ... You're here again too? ... I thought you were dead! ... Are you all here again? ... All here again ... Is it really so? ... The dance is beginning again? Waiting again, waiting, waiting ... I can't ... Don't you see? ... What are you doing? ... Go on, resist! ... No one hears, no one hears, no one ... We speak and hear each other not ... We hate and see each other not ... We love and know each other not ... We murder and feel each other not ... Must it always, always, be like this? ... You, will I never understand you? ... You, will you never comprehend me? ... No! No! No! ... Why do you gas, burn and destroy the earth? ... Is everything forgotten? ... Everything in vain? ... Then keep on spinning on your merry-go-round, dance, laugh, cry, and copulate – good luck! I'm jumping off ...
Oh madness of the world! ...
   Where to? Where to? ... The stone walls press nearer and nearer ... I am freezing ... and it is dark ... and the glacier of darkness clutches me mercilessly ... Where to? Where to? ... To the highest mountain ... To the highest tree ... The Deluge ...

[Piscator cut and changed a lot of this speech.]

KARL THOMAS makes a rope out of the sheet, climbs on the stool, fastens the rope to the door hook.

Blackout.

Scene 2

[This scene was cut.]

A group before a covered memorial.

COUNT LANDE: ... and so I present to the people ... this memorial to this outstanding man ... who in dark times ...

Blackout.

Scene 3
Prison

Lights up: ALBERT KROLL's cell. Noise. Door creaks open. RAND enters.

RAND: Because you were kind to me once, I'll tell you something.

ALBERT KROLL: You don't need to.

RAND: We're not like that. The Ministry of Justice has just telephoned, Thomas is not the murderer. They caught the real one in Switzerland. A student. Just as he was about to be arrested, he shot himself.

ALBERT KROLL: Will we be released straightaway?

RAND: Not today. Today is Sunday ... So I congratulate you, Herr Kroll.

RAND goes.

ALBERT KROLL: (*Knocks.*) Eva! Eva!

Lights up: EVA BERG's cell.

EVA BERG: (*Knocks.*) Yes.

ALBERT KROLL: (*Knocks.*) We are free! Rand told me. The real murderer was found.

EVA BERG: Thank goodness! (*Knocks on the other wall of the cell.*) Mother Meller!

Lights up: FRAU MELLER's cell.

FRAU MELLER: (*Knocks.*) Yes.

EVA BERG: (*Knocks.*) We are all free. Karl didn't shoot after all. They have the murderer.

FRAU MELLER: (*Knocks on the other wall.*) You, Karl! ... You! ... You! ... You! ... (*Knocks on the floor.*) Eva, Karl does not answer.

EVA BERG: (*Knocks.*) Knock louder.

FRAU MELLER: (*Knocks.*) Karl! Karl! Karl!

EVA BERG: (*Knocks.*) Albert, Karl doesn't reply.

ALBERT KROLL: (*Knocks.*) Let's all knock. Now it doesn't matter.

They knock. The other prisoners knock too. Silence. The whole prison knocks. Silence.

EVA BERG: He does not answer ...

WARDERS run through the gangways. The cells go dark. Blackout in the prison.

The stage closes.

The End.

Appendix I

In Erwin Piscator's Promptbook, the last scene of the play is given as follows. See *Gesammelte Werke 3* (pp. 325–6).

Lights up:

ALBERT KROLL's cell.

Noise. Door creaks open. RAND enters.

RAND: Kroll, Kroll, I congratulate you. The Ministry of Justice has just telephoned, Thomas is not the murderer. They caught the real one in Switzerland. A student. Just as he was about to be arrested, he shot himself.

ALBERT KROLL: Will we be released?

RAND: Not today. Today is Sunday ... So I congratulate you, Herr Kroll.

RAND goes.

ALBERT KROLL: (*Knocks.*)

Film

After Rand's exit, moving captions from the front:

From below right to below left:

'Thomas is not the murderer, they have another.'

Below left to first level left:

'Thomas is not the murderer.'

First level left to first level right:

'We are all free. Karl, my boy,

you didn't shoot after all. They have

the murderer. You Karl, you.'

'he does not answer'

'he does not answer'

knocking

knocking

knocking

knocking

(over the whole area)

Film out

They knock

The other prisoners knock too

Silence

Knocking in the whole prison

Silence

RAND: (*Screams.*) Hanged!!

FRAU MELLER: Is it true?

ALBERT KROLL: He shouldn't have done that; no revolutionary dies like that.

EVA BERG: Everyday life destroyed him.

FRAU MELLER: Damned world! – We have to change it.

Curtain.

Erwin Piscator reports in *Das Politische Theater* (Hamburg: Rowohlt, 1963, p. 154), first published in 1929, that the Berlin production ended with this speech:

FRAU MELLER: There is only one choice – hang yourself or change the world.

As the curtain fell, he relates, 'the proletarian youth spontaneously burst into *The Internationale* which, standing, we all sang up to the end'. The play then became the occasion for a stirring political demonstration.

Appendix II

Toller's original, but never published, ending for the play was a different version of Act 4, scene 4, with no Act 5 to follow. Written before his collaboration with Piscator, it exists in printed manuscript form (presumably ready for publication). with later handwritten corrections by Toller, in the possession of John M. Spalek. See *Gesammelte Werke 3* (pp. 318–25).

ACT 4
Scene 4

The façade transforms into the façade of the Madhouse

Open below right to:

Examination room

PROFESSOR LÜDIN: Stand still. Pulse normal. Open your shirt. Breathe deeply. Hold it. Heart healthy … Tell me honestly, why did you commit this deed?

KARL THOMAS: I did not shoot.

PROFESSOR LÜDIN: Confide in me.

KARL THOMAS: I have nothing to confess, because I am not the culprit.

PROFESSOR LÜDIN: You wanted to avenge yourself, didn't you? You believed the Minister would give you a top position in the Ministry. You felt betrayed.

KARL THOMAS: You'll torment me until I am really crazy.

PROFESSOR LÜDIN: Only your motives interest me.

KARL THOMAS: I don't need a psychiatrist.

PROFESSOR LÜDIN: You feel sane?

KARL THOMAS: Sound as a bell.

PROFESSOR LÜDIN: Very suspicious.

KARL THOMAS laughs.

PROFESSOR LÜDIN: Don't laugh. No one is sound as a bell.

KARL THOMAS: No one?

PROFESSOR LÜDIN: With the exception of madhouse doctors who make correct diagnoses.

Short pause.

KARL THOMAS: Professor!

PROFESSOR LÜDIN: Do you want to confess to me now why you shot? Understand, only the Why interests me. The deed is no concern of mine. Deeds are of no importance. Only motives are important.

KARL THOMAS: I want to tell you everything exactly, Herr Professor. I've lost my bearings. What I experienced … May I tell you, Herr Professor?

PROFESSOR LÜDIN: Begin then.

KARL THOMAS: I must have clarity. The door slammed shut behind me, and when I opened it eight years had passed. A whole century. I went out into the world. Life thundered in my head. Every flash of lightning struck me down. As you advised me, I first paid a visit to Wilhelm Kilman. Condemned to death like I was. I discovered he was Minister. Wedded to his former enemies. A profiteering potbelly.

PROFESSOR LÜDIN: Normal. He was just more cunning than you.

KARL THOMAS: I went to my closest comrade. A man who with just a revolver in his hand repulsed a whole company of Whites, all alone. I heard him say: 'One must be able to wait.'

PROFESSOR LÜDIN: Normal.

KARL THOMAS: And at the same time he swore he remained true to the Revolution.

PROFESSOR LÜDIN: Abnormal. But not your fault. He ought to be examined. Probably a mild dementia praecox.

KARL THOMAS: I was a waiter. For one whole evening. I was stewed in a witches' cauldron. It stank of corruption, of lechery, of arrogance, of muck. The people I worked with found it all in order and were proud of it.

PROFESSOR LÜDIN: Normal. Business is thriving again. Everybody makes money out of it in his own way.

KARL THOMAS: I formed a plan to shock mankind out of despicable lethargy. I bought myself a revolver. I wanted to shoot the Minister, the traitor. At the very same moment others shot him.

PROFESSOR LÜDIN: Hm.

KARL THOMAS: I asked one of them, one who didn't yell 'Hurrah', for the reason. I saw his twisted lips move. I heard his voice. Because the Minister was a Bolshevik, a revolutionary, he whispered.

PROFESSOR LÜDIN: Normal. Relatively so, if this unknown person existed.

KARL THOMAS: I wanted to put an end to myself. I wanted to shoot myself. The fog suddenly lifted. Perhaps the world is not crazy at all. Perhaps I am ... Perhaps I am ...

PROFESSOR LÜDIN: What do you want? Your logic is functioning perfectly. You must drink what you have brewed. Whoever goes over to the masses goes to rack and ruin there.

KARL THOMAS: What do you know about it?

PROFESSOR LÜDIN: You can tell me nothing about the psyche of the masses. My collection of specimens opens even the blindest of eyes. The masses: a herd of swine. Cram to the trough when there's something to guzzle. Wallow in muck when their bellies are stuffed.

KARL THOMAS: To stick a crazy man like you on the world, what a crime! ...

PROFESSOR LÜDIN: If you really didn't want to avenge yourself – something I assume as I don't believe in abstract motives and perhaps the real reason is unknown to you – then if we assume you really wanted to 'awaken' mankind with your foolish deed, what did you expect to achieve by that? What should the awakened do? Change the world? My dear fellow, if nature had not wanted some to eat less than others, then there wouldn't be any poverty at all. Whoever achieves what he's capable of needn't go hungry. With your ideas men would become scroungers and shirkers. Nature has organised things most beneficently.

KARL THOMAS: Stop it! My head is splitting.

PROFESSOR LÜDIN: I wish I was as healthy as you. I suffer from gout.

KARL THOMAS: Insanity! Insanity! Insanity!

PROFESSOR LÜDIN: Don't play-act with me. You can't sway an old psychiatrist like that.

KARL THOMAS: You must be cured! You first and foremost!

PROFESSOR LÜDIN: When someone gets stuck in a trap, when it's a matter of life and death, then he finally gives up the heroic pose and tries to save himself with the Section for the mentally ill.

KARL THOMAS: Why did I doubt it? Yes, yes, I am really crazy. How else could I have seen what I saw! ...

PROFESSOR LÜDIN: This institution is here for the mad, not for the sane.

KARL THOMAS: Charlatan! You are unmasked as a quack! Charlatan!

PROFESSOR LÜDIN: Right then, I'll show you what the crazy really look like. Then you'll have to stop fooling yourself ... Orderly, set up the projector.

On the façade of the Madhouse in the place where the BANKER and his SON sat in the Hotel, a madman can be seen gesticulating. Mask of the BANKER distorted into madness.

Look at the screen. That man up there, formerly a banker, imagines he can command a great boom with one word to all the Stock Exchanges of the world and thus become the richest man in the world.

Behind the projected image, the Private Room of the Hotel lights up. In the Hotel Room:

BANKER: (*On the table telephone.*) Hello! Hello! Stock Exchange! Sell everything! The assassination of Kilman ... Paints and Potash and Pipes ... Chemical Works shares already fallen about a hundred per cent ... What ? ... Operator! ... Fraülein, why did you cut me off? ... I'll hold you liable ... Ruined by a telephone breakdown ... God in Heaven!

KARL THOMAS: But he is very normal! I saw him in person. Just yesterday evening at the Hotel. A speculator like the dozens and dozens who buy and sell the world for profit.

PROFESSOR LÜDIN: My dear friend, the banker whom you saw – I wish I had his fortune – was normal.

KARL THOMAS: Ha ha ha, normal!

BANKER: (*Grinning in Hotel Room.*) Normal ... Normal ...

Blackout in Hotel Room.

PROFESSOR LÜDIN (*To ORDERLY.*) Proceed.

On the façade of the Madhouse in the place where the Staff Room of the Hotel was, a madman can be seen gesticulating. Mask of the PORTER distorted into madness.

Type Two. This man went mad in the inflation. He lost his assets. In place of the ten thousand marks he had saved he got fifty million. Because of that he went mad. He is forever scribbling numbers on paper and counting. He wants to get his assets back at any price and imagines that he won first prize in the lottery.

Behind the projected image, the Staff Room of the Hotel lights up.

PORTER: Who won the Paris race? The beautiful Galatea ... A

fix! A fix! I put all my savings on Idealist, and that damned jockey goes and breaks his neck ... I want to get my stake back! My stake, I want to get it back!

KARL THOMAS: He is also very normal! I am sure that's the porter of the Grand Hotel!

PROFESSOR LÜDIN: Type Two suffers from mental fixation. The porter of the Grand Hotel, and I lived there once, is absolutely normal.

PORTER: (*Grinning in the Hotel Room.*) Normal ... Normal ...

Blackout in Hotel Room.

PROFESSOR LÜDIN: Proceed.

On the façade of the Madhouse in the place where the Radio Station of the Hotel was, a madman can be seen gesticulating. Mask of the RADIO OPERATOR *distorted into madness.*

Type Three. He suffers from persecution mania. An inventor. He imagines he has invented an apparatus which can distil sugar from wood and is capable, just like Jehovah once was, of feeding all the hungry with wood. The apparatus, he thinks, was destroyed by a sugar beet farmer.

Behind the projected image, the Radio Station in the Hotel lights up.

RADIO OPERATOR: Attention! Attention! All radio stations of the world! Who will buy my invention? I don't want money. The invention will help everyone, everyone. Silence ... No one responds.

KARL THOMAS: He too is normal! He too is normal! That's the Radio Operator from the Grand Hotel! Nobody wanted to buy his invention from him because it serves peace, not war.

PROFESSOR LÜDIN: The Radio Operator at the Grand Hotel is a competent, hard-working official. A little fanciful, because he operates the radio, but otherwise normal!

RADIO OPERATOR: (*Grinning in Hotel Room.*) Normal ... Normal ...

Blackout in Hotel Room.

PROFESSOR LÜDIN: Proceed!

On the façade of the Madhouse in the place where the EXAMINING MAGISTRATE *was in the Prison, a madman can be seen gesticulating. Mask of the* EXAMINING MAGISTRATE *distorted into madness.*

Type Four. A former Public Prosecutor who imagines he is on the trail of all the criminals who have ever committed murder and not been found out. He thinks his nose, unusually developed, can sniff out the very smell of murder.

Behind the projected image, the Examination Room in the Prison lights up.

EXAMINING MAGISTRATE: The circumstantial evidence is perfectly conclusive. Put it on file. Next case ...

KARL THOMAS: The Examining Magistrate! I would have recognised his craziness without you.

PROFESSOR LÜDIN: I can well believe that you'd wish the Examining Magistrate not to be normal.

EXAMINING MAGISTRATE: (*Grinning in the Examination Room.*) Normal ... Normal ...

Blackout in the Examination Room.

PROFESSOR LÜDIN: Proceed!

On the façade of the Madhouse in the place where the Private Room in the Hotel was, a madman can be seen gesticulating. Mask of WILHELM KILMAN *distorted into madness.*

In conclusion the Innocent Type. Formerly a chauffeur. He's fixated on the idea that it's not the motor which drives his car, but that he drives it ... with the horn.

Behind the projected image, the Private Room in the Hotel lights up.

WILHELM KILMAN: The text of my decree will prevent any back-pedalling. Let it be printed. I am proud of it. A milestone of progress.

KARL THOMAS: Yes, I saw him like that at the end, Herr Minister Kilman. But innocent – no!

PROFESSOR LÜDIN: You should not mock your victim, Thomas. I wish we had many men like him. Level-headed, normal.

WILHELM KILMAN: (*Grinning in Hotel Room.*) Normal ... Normal ...

Blackout in Hotel Room. On the façade a Face laughs. Mask of PROFESSOR LÜDIN *distorted into madness.*

KARL THOMAS: (*Speaking to the Face up above.*) And you, are you going crazy too? How do you dare lock up normal men?

PROFESSOR LÜDIN: To whom are you speaking?

KARL THOMAS: (*Speaking to the Face above.*) Just dare say that you too are normal – go on, I'm waiting for your response! Normal ... Normal ...

The Face disappears.

PROFESSOR LÜDIN: No funny business, Thomas. Every psychiatrist knows that trick of speaking to thin air. You would have a happier and more dignified look if you, with free and full repentance, confessed to your crime.

KARL THOMAS: I'm a fool! Now I see the world clearly again. You have turned it into a madhouse. There is no dividing wall between inside here and outside there. The world's become an animal pen in which the sane are trampled down by a small herd of galloping crazies. And that is normal! Ha, ha, ha ...

All the rooms of the Hotel light up.

CHORUS OF HOTEL OCCUPANTS: (In a crouching position, leaning down towards the Examination Room, nodding.) Ha, ha, ha! ... Normal! ...

Blackout in Hotel.

PROFESSOR LÜDIN: Nothing can help you. Tomorrow you will be sent to prison. You've caused enough mischief. Now you must take your punishment.

KARL THOMAS: I see everything clearly. In former times we marched under the flag of paradise. Today we have to wear out our boots on earthly roads. You believe you're alive. You're headed for the abyss if you imagine that the world will always stay like it is now.

From outside, a distant song which gradually stops.

Noise of marching men.

PROFESSOR LÜDIN: (*To* ORDERLY.) What is it?

ORDERLY: (*At window.*) A demonstration. The people are demonstrating for the prisoner.

CHORUS FROM OUTSIDE: Support Karl Thomas! Support Karl Thomas!

Then in the street, shown on film, a vast silent crowd of demonstrators.

PROFESSOR LÜDIN: They're starting up again ... You've caused this with your lunatic deed!

KARL THOMAS: Me?

PROFESSOR LÜDIN: Yes, you! Don't play so innocent!

KARL THOMAS: But I have done nothing at all!

Short pause.

But I have done nothing at all!!

Suddenly KARL THOMAS *roars with laughter.*

PROFESSOR LÜDIN: Don't laugh so cynically. Even they can't save your neck.

KARL THOMAS *laughs.*

If you want to see a mass of crazy men, look out the window.

KARL THOMAS *laughs.*

Incurable crazies.

KARL THOMAS *laughs.*

ORDERLY: (*Pointing at* KARL THOMAS.) Professor, I think ...

PROFESSOR LÜDIN: (*Stands still in front of* KARL THOMAS, *observes him for a little while.*) A fit. Take him to the padded cell. To his ... beech wood.

[In German 'beech wood' is Buchenwald which gives a horrific, if unintended, resonance to this ending for the play.]

KARL THOMAS *is led away by the* ORDERLY.

Unfit for life.

While the People march past silently, the stage closes.

Appendix III

In addition to some criticism of Toller's writing style, Piscator gives a table of three endings he claims were considered for *Hoppla, We're Alive!* in *Das Politische Theater* (Hamburg: Rowholt, 1963, p. 148):

The three endings for 'Hoppla'

Arrest	**Escape**	**Arrest**
Police Station		Police Station
	Voluntary	
Transfer to Madhouse	return to Prison	Madhouse
	From conical masks filmic dissolve to officer's chest, crucibles, war pictures, run backwards	
Lüdin scene up to: Masses march past	In place of Kilman-mask–Kilman-monument. During Thomas's laughter and the last words a giant cannon appears on film and aims at the audience	Prison
		(Dialogue by knocking)
		Thomas hangs himself

It may be that Piscator misremembered here and that what was considered was a voluntary return to the Madhouse. This would make sense of Toller's denial and also of the filmic sequence described here which could have been used for Toller's original final scene.

Appendix IV

Reviewing his works in 1930, Toller wrote as follows about his collaboration with Piscator on *Hoppla, We're Alive!*, a response to Piscator's criticism of him in *The Political Theatre*. See 'Arbeiten', *Gesammelte Werke 1* (pp. 145–7).

From **Works**

Hoppla, We're Alive! is the name of the first play I wrote 'in freedom'. Once again I was concerned with the collision of a man who is determined to realise the absolute in the here and now with the forces of the time and his contemporaries who either abandon this work of realization from weakness, betrayal and cowardice or prepare for it to come in later days with strength, faith and courage. Karl Thomas doesn't understand either of them, equates their motives and actions and is destroyed. Alienated from true art by that childish American fashion for the 'happy end', many critics and spectators today demand from the playwright something which is not his task at all – that he ought to dismiss them at the end with those silly household sayings which our parents used to have written on sofa cushions, plates and posters for practical guidance, like: 'Always be faithful and honest', 'Ask not what others do, but attend to your own affairs', 'Have a sunny disposition', or as Durus wrote in No. 134 of the *Red Flag*, 1930: 'Let the fresh air of class struggle into the fresh air of nature'. Proletcult officials and arts-section critics on capitalist newspapers, who, from a guilty conscience and an obsession to roam like birds of passage through the newspaper columns, are more preachers of revolution than revolutionary activists, called the end of the drama 'not revolutionary' – and this was repeated many times and will continue to be repeated – because it didn't dismiss them with a little moral tract and the cry: 'Long live political line No. 73'. –

Today I regret that I, swayed by a trend of the times, broke up the architectonics of the original work for the benefit of the architectonics of the direction. The form that I strived for was stronger than that which appeared on the stage. I alone am responsible for that, but I have learned, and today I prefer a director to get too little out of a work than to put too much into it. Moreover, Piscator in Gasbarra's book *The Political Theatre*, really has no reason to complain about me and my style.★

At the time of revising the script I considered three endings as possible, but never the 'voluntary return to prison' which was falsely and unscrupulously attributed to me in the book. In my first version Thomas, who didn't understand the world of 1927, ran to the psychiatrist in the madhouse, discovers in his discussion with the doctor that there are two kinds of dangerous fools: the ones who are held in padded cells and the ones who, as politicians and military men, go berserk against mankind. At that moment he understands his old comrades who carry on with the Idea in the tougher work of everyday life. He wants to leave the madhouse, but because he has understood, because he has connected to reality like a mature man, the psychiatric official will never release him. Now for the first time – and not before when he was a troublesome dreamer – he becomes 'dangerous to the State'!

★ Or are these sentences, which Piscator proposed in place of those written by me, 'functional, advancing the dramatic action, building the mental tension', in short, do they provide 'the realistic substructure' and 'replace the poetic lyricism' of the author? (p. 147). I quote from Piscator's manuscript:

Scene after the murder of Wilhelm Kilman. Monologue of Karl Thomas:

KARL THOMAS: 'They shot him because he was a revolutionary; I wanted to shoot him because he was a nobody and ended up shooting at his murderer, as if I defended Kilman's henchmen and in so doing had become his friend, brother and comrade again ... Only one shift was needed, only one small step, and the liberation of the world from nationalist hatred, degrading class oppression, and rough justice would have been helped to victory. (*In a somewhat raised voice.*) If only, Wilhelm, I weren't unbearably guilty. Albert Kroll, Mother Meller, Eva, guilty, guilty. You there, you down there in the park, guilty, guilty, we and they (*He tries to go on speaking.*) ...'

Or:

Last prison scene. Monologue of Karl Thomas:

KARL THOMAS: '... I am awake, so awake that I can see right through you and still would have experienced nothing new ...
Oh, the merry-go-round spins and everything begins all over again. Yes, my dear friends, and my enemies, can't you see how the ground is cracking under your feet? Kilman, dead man, celebrated perhaps because of your murder ... if you were living, comrade, you could not begin all over again. You, undo it, undo it: tactics, betrayal. Volcanoes, fiery eyes of the earth open, crack open before you. You stand on the edge of a crater. What madness has seized you, to crouch there and stare into the white-hot glow! Save yourselves! Save yourselves! It's rising! In the boiling depths the lava is forming into a dreadful instrument of destruction! It's rising up unstoppably! Its hissing is scornful laughter at your stupidity not to see your solution: divide and rule ...'

Nothing at all to be said about the scene which was rehearsed one day and which, as I to my horror was forced to learn from [hearing] the character names, was 'written in' overnight without even asking me.

Appendix V

Herrn
Ernst Toller
Berlin – Grunewald
König Allee 45
10 August 1927

Dear Toller!
After very serious reflection, I sat down yesterday evening and made the attempt to work out the end scenes, just as we presented them to you in rough outlines several times before. After I went through it with Gasbarra this morning, we are both convinced that now the end, from the two shots up to the big Prison scene, has an ongoing dramatic build and that there is no longer any retardation in the dramatic action. The driving forces of each scene are nevertheless so distinct that every possibility is given to bring out at all points again the overall tendency in its full sharpness and forcefulness, without taking anything away from the climax in the Prison.
It strikes me as a main point that Thomas achieves a certain clarity from his last experiences, so that, in the midst of the confusion all around him, he now takes a pause. It must be like a last flash of spiritual strength, before the collapse in Prison takes place. Thus the monologue after the two shots must be written very calmly and clearly and also spoken in the same way. The monologue in the Prison scene picks up from this one. The full inner life of Thomas once again, without phrase-mongering, becomes transparent. It is the last attempt of a man to understand the world and to come to terms with himself.

When Thomas is arrested, his particular kind of madness can be indicated. One must have the feeling that he is already somewhat removed from the situation and also faces his arrest with indifference.

The most controversial point in our debates has probably been the scene before the Examining Magistrate. We have examined the meaning and content of this scene from every point of view and have come to the conclusion that this scene contributes nothing to the onward drive of the action. The characters who appear in it neither undergo a change nor does their legal confrontation possess any dramatic tension. The only reason it mattered to you was to get Thomas back into the Madhouse, in order to symbolically contrast the normal and the abnormal there. It would be a complete mistake to open up a test case about circumstantial evidence here. Only to show that circumstantial evidence doesn't hold up. The scene before the Examining Magistrate would perhaps be better than the scene in Police Headquarters, if the Examining Magistrate was some low down type and the case from the beginning on was handled in such a way that it seemed to the spectator, exactly at this place in the piece, especially abnormal and strange. That is to say, if the scene showed Thomas' environment as such or his character as such in a completely new light. But then, in turn, Lüdin standing face to face with an unchanged Thomas would be eliminated. And consequently the Lüdin scene would be ineffective. But ultimately both, according to the latest version, are not very important before the Prison scene. Above all we must achieve a dramatically effective and unstoppable forward development up to the end.

In the Police Headquarters scene in the dialogue between Count Lande and the Chief, the first assassin must be depicted as explicitly as possible. It is not enough for example to say: 'Young man, speaks literary German, closes his eyes when thinking!' [details almost exactly like those on Toller's 'Wanted Poster' from 1919!] or something similar. But some distinguishing mark must be given by which the Police Chief can be in no doubt whatsoever that he has the assassin described by Count Lande in front of him. Hence we are of the opinion that the student worms his way into the hotel as a waiter, for which Lande gives him the appropriate instructions in the preparation scene. Lande can report that he wears a waiter's tailcoat as a special, external mark, whereby the confusion with Thomas, who is also arrested in a tailcoat, then seems immediately believable.

Furthermore, I've come to think that it is better to have Lande appear in person at Police Headquarters than to have him telephone the Chief of Police, which in such a situation and given the importance of the matter perhaps seems unbelievable. The conversation between Lande and the Chief drafted by me is intentionally allusive and unclearly worded, and in my opinion no longer needs to be translated into Tolleresque literary German. On the other hand, the end of the scene could be even more fully worked out in formal respects.

Your version of the Lüdin scene, my draft aside, suffers from two defects: In his first conversation with Thomas, Lüdin cannot say that no one is sane because later he declares all those people Thomas regards as mad to be normal.

That is in itself a small change. On the other hand, in my opinion the moment of 'normal-normal' still needs to be thought through thoroughly, so that the types in the Hotel really seem mad to the spectator. For the different characters, for example the Porter, both true and false elements of madness are jumbled together. For the Porter, the passion for betting which devours him is mad, if that's the way you want to look at it. On the other hand one can't forget that the

Porter has been a victim of the inflation. If you want to bring in the inflation, then it must be depicted very differently.

For the Banker, as well, you must intensify his mad hunt for money by showing that he (perhaps) can personally make no use whatsoever of the money for himself, possibly hampered by stomach problems. In this way, the absolute emptiness of such a character would be brought out.

Finally, it still hampers the flow of this 'Normal-normal' scene that Thomas states substantially the same thing about the madness of the Hotel occupants that they act out a few seconds later. Thomas must depict much earlier which functions these people could perform normally, for example the Banker as an administrative functionary of the commodities owned by society, as a purposefully and systematically active element. So with this in mind! All the best

Erwin Piscator

(*Der Fall Toller*, pp. 182–5)

Note

1. Friedrich Wolfgang Knellessen, *Agitation auf der Bühne: Das politische Theater der Weimarer Republik*, Emsdetten: Lechte, 1970, and Gunther Rühle, ed., *Theater für die Republik: Im Spiegel der Kritik*, 2 vols, Frankfurt am Main: S. Fischer, 1988.

3.3 LOVE ON THE DOLE (1934)

RONALD GOW AND WALTER GREENWOOD

Ronald Gow (1897–1993) and *Walter Greenwood (1903–74)*. *Gow began his professional life as a teacher and made a number of educational films before moving into writing for theatre and film. Best known for his adaptations, his stage version of* Love on the Dole *by Walter Greenwood premiered at the Manchester Repertory Theatre in 1934 and starred Wendy Hiller and Cathleen Nesbitt. Greenwood, who wrote the original novel about the effects of poverty and unemployment on his local community while unemployed himself, wrote a number of successful novels, especially in the 1930s, and produced films for the British government during the 1939–45 war. Set contemporaneously in Salford, an area that directly borders Manchester in the once-industrial north of England,* Love on the Dole *is a passionate examination of the human consequences of mass unemployment and economic depression, including the raising of political consciousness. Both the novel and the play were huge commercial successes in the 1930s. The play's 'gritty realism', particularly in its representation of a disenfranchised youth, anticipates the work of the English 'new wave' dramatists (such as John Osborne and Shelagh Delaney) over twenty years later.* Love on the Dole *has also been adapted for cinema, television and the musical theatre.*

Characters

SALLY HARDCASTLE

MRS HARDCASTLE

LARRY MEATH

HARRY HARDCASTLE

MR HARDCASTLE

MRS JIKE

MRS DORBELL

MRS BULL

A POLICEMAN

HELEN HAWKINS

SAM GRUNDY

AGITATOR

MRS DOYLE

MR DOYLE

CHARLIE

The scenes are laid in Hanky Park, a park of Salford, England.

Act I

The kitchen living-room of the Hardcastles at No. 17 North Street, Hanky Park, a district in a Lancashire manufacturing town. There is a window on the right through which the street can be seen. Above it is the front door, and behind the door is an old dresser. On the left is a kitchen range, and below, in a recess, is the sink. Beside this a door leads to the other part of the house. There is very little furniture, and what there is shows signs of decay and collapse. A plain table has some rickety chairs beside it. Near the fireplace is a rocking-chair, and below the window is a dilapidated sofa. It is important to remember that this is not slum property, but the house of a respectable working man, whose incorrigible snobbery would be aroused if you suggested that North Street was a slum.

SALLY HARDCASTLE, a fine-looking girl of twenty, is ironing clothes, although the greater part of her interest is centred at the moment on events out in the street. The street door is open, and, out of sight and almost out of hearing, a SPEAKER is addressing a meeting. The angry voice of the SPEAKER, accompanied by the noise of the CROWD, suggests the troubled background of the lives of these people. The SPEAKER is saying '– and to find the cost of this present system you have only to look at our own lives and the lives of our parents and their parents. Labour never ending, pawnshops, misery and dirt. No time for anything bright and beautiful. Grey, depressing streets, mile after mile of them –' SALLY goes to the door, listening. As her mother enters she hurries back to her work.

MRS HARDCASTLE enters through the door on the left, carrying a laundry basket. She is a nondescript sort of woman who might have been as pretty as SALLY in her youth, but a losing fight against drudgery and poverty has played havoc with womanly grace and character.

SPEAKER: (*Goes on.*) '– unemployment and pauperdom, that is the legacy of the Industrial Revolution. That is the price we pay for the system. And that is the price you'll go on paying till you waken up to the fact that the remedy's in your own hands. You've got votes – why don't you use them? Why don't you think?'

Some half-hearted applause, and a VOICE says, 'You can't do without capital!' MRS HARDCASTLE removes her apron, hangs it up, and puts on her shawl.

SALLY: Going out, Ma?

MRS HARDCASTLE: Aye.

SALLY: Where to?

MRS HARDCASTLE: I'm taking Mrs Marlowe's washing. She gets that impatient.

SALLY: Look here, Mother, that's too heavy. Let me go.

MRS HARDCASTLE: Nay, you don't. I won't have no daughter o' mine carrying washing in the streets.

SALLY: Don't be daft. Give it to me.

MRS HARDCASTLE: Out of the way, Sally. Besides, I'll be right glad of a walk. (*She looks through the window.*) Is that young Larry Meath spouting on the soap-box yonder?

SALLY: Maybe it is.

MRS HARDCASTLE: Maybe it is! You know well enough it is. Politics, I suppose. Well, I've never seen much good come out of politics yet.

SALLY: Larry Meath's all right.

MRS HARDCASTLE: Aw, well, there's worse things than politics. Keeps 'em out of pubs, anyway.

As MRS HARDCASTLE is going out she meets LARRY MEATH at the door. He stands on one side to let her pass. He is an attractive young man, with a lean, tired face, and big eyes with a vision in them.

LARRY: Good evening, Mrs Hardcastle.

MRS HARDCASTLE: Good evening, Mr Meath.

With a look at SALLY, she goes out with her washing-basket.

LARRY: (*At the door.*) Good evening, Sally.

SALLY: Come in, lad.

She goes to the dresser to get a teacup. Suddenly a MAN appears outside, points a finger at LARRY and shouts, 'You can't do without capital!' and before LARRY can reply he is gone.

(*Returning to the table with the cup.*) That's got you guessing, Larry.

LARRY laughs and comes inside.

I heard you speaking.

LARRY: I didn't know *you* were listening.

SALLY: I can't very well do much else when you hold your meetings on our doorstep.

LARRY: I'm sorry. But the corner of North Street always was the best place for our meetings.

SALLY: Don't worry, I like listening to you.

LARRY: Do you, really?

SALLY: Come on in.

LARRY: (*Laughing.*) Don't tell me I've made a convert.

SALLY: Come on, here's a cup of tea for you.

LARRY: (*Taking the tea and sitting.*) Thanks.

SALLY: I like the way you talk. You can talk all right, but I don't know nothing – (*She corrects herself.*) – I mean, I don't know *anything* about politics. I don't know – it's just that I like to hear you.

During the following scene SALLY continues her work quietly.

LARRY: You know, that's what's wrong with people about here. They don't know anything about politics. Make it easier if they did. The trouble is, they don't seem to want to know.

SALLY: Drink your tea. You look tired.

LARRY: (*With a sigh.*) Um, it's a tough job reforming the world in Hanky Park. Don't you wish sometimes you were out of it, Sal – far away, somewhere else?

SALLY: (*After a pause.*) Aw, what's the use of feeling that way? Where can you go when you've got nothing? I was only thinking today that I've never had a holiday in my life. There's not many gets out of Hanky Park – except through cemetery gates. (*She hangs some socks on the line at the fireplace.*)

LARRY: Sal, when are you coming up on the hills again?

SALLY: (*Faces him.*) Oo, that was grand!

LARRY: And you've never been near us since.

SALLY: Oh, Larry, I never thought I'd ever be going out with you. Isn't it funny – well, you know, us living close by all this time and –?

LARRY: You can blame me for that. Some fellows are blind that way. But when are you coming again? They were asking for you at the Club. (SALLY *is silent.*) If you like it, why don't you come? You're welcome, you know.

SALLY: (*Diffidently.*) I don't like –

LARRY: Don't like what?

SALLY: You paying for me on the train.

LARRY: (*Smiling.*) I can manage that.

SALLY: And the clothes those other girls wore.

LARRY: Do you mean shorts and jerseys?

SALLY: Aye.

LARRY: Well, there's no need to wear them if you don't like them. Besides, they don't suit everybody.

SALLY: But I do like 'em. (*Indignantly.*) *And* they'd suit me, too.

LARRY: Of course – I didn't know – I'm sorry if –

SALLY: I should just think you are! Of course, if you think I haven't got the figure for shorts and things, why don't you say so? (*She hangs pants on the line.*)

LARRY: (*Watches her.*) Sally, I never said – You'd look wonderful in anything.

SALLY: Aw, don't worry. I'm only kidding. Perhaps I'll be getting some extra work at the mill, then I'll be able to buy short trousers and come with you.

LARRY: That'll be great.

SALLY: But I can't promise you fine talk like those other girls. I don't know anything about Bark and Baytoven and that fellow they call G.B.S. Is he a friend of yours?

LARRY: G.B.S.? No, why?

SALLY: From the way they're always telling what G.B.S. said, he must have done a rare lot of talking some time or other.

LARRY: (*Becoming serious.*) Sal, you don't think *I* talk too much?

SALLY: No, you mean no harm, and I like you for it. It's good talk to my way of thinking. If talking'll make Hanky Park a better place, you'll do it.

LARRY: I wonder. It's like butting your head against a stone wall. You know, you can call those men stupid if you like, but you can't help but admire their loyalty. I mean their loyalty to a system that's made 'em what they are. They go on hoping and hoping – and every week there's another hundred of 'em out of work. If they went mad and raised Hell you wouldn't blame 'em, but they're always thinking something's going to turn up. Or are they just asleep? Gosh, that's what I'm afraid of! Waking up suddenly to find they've been done. When people wake up all of a sudden they don't act very reasonably.

SALLY: It'd be a nasty shock to wake up sudden and find you'd been living in Hanky Park all your life.

LARRY: Ach! If we could only have a fresh start all round. The kids in the gutters – the dirt and the smoke and the foul ugliness of it all! Oh, Sal, it gets you and it dopes you and it eats into your heart. And it's going to be a hell of a sight worse yet, what with wage-cuts and all the rest. What's the use of talking to people – they're all too busy with their daft Irish sweeps and their betting – Aw, what does it matter, anyway?

SALLY: Here, lad, don't you get talking that way. What's come over you?

LARRY: I don't know, Sal. (*He looks at her wistfully.*) I think – Since we've –

SALLY: Go on. Let's have it. (*She sits at the table, facing* LARRY.)

LARRY: It's – it's meeting you, Sal. It's made me feel kind of different about things.

SALLY: What things?

LARRY: I'm beginning to realize – Aw, there's something in life for us, isn't there? There's not much fun fighting for other people's lives when your own's slipping away. I tell you, Sal, I want –

SALLY: Want what?

LARRY: It's since that day on the hills, Sal. Seeing you standing there on top of that rock with the white cloud behind you and the sun in your hair.

SALLY: (*Blushing happily.*) It was grand, Larry! And everywhere lovely and clean.

LARRY: I don't know – it makes all I'm fighting for – ideals and politics and all that – it makes it – well, it doesn't seem to matter like it did.

SALLY: You mean I'm interfering?

LARRY: No –

SALLY: I think you'd best forget me standing on that rock, and such-like rubbish. If I'm interfering in what you believe in perhaps you'd better not come here any more.

LARRY: No, Sal! Listen – you mean you believe in what I'm trying to do?

SALLY: Oh, I don't know what you're after, only to make things better. But I know you're a fighter, and that's good enough for me. I don't want to stand in any fellow's way. You're so different from all the others I've known. You don't seem to fit in with Hanky Park, somehow. That's what makes me like you, and that's what makes me – afraid.

LARRY: Afraid of what?

SALLY: (*Rising and taking her cup to the sink.*) I don't know.

LARRY: You're a grand girl, Sal. If you knew how I felt about you – Aw, but what's the use?

SALLY: What's the use of what?

LARRY: You're not laughing at me?

SALLY: No.

LARRY: I mean getting married. Buying furniture on the instalment plan. What can you do on forty-five bob a week?

SALLY: (*Thrilled.*) So you *have* been thinking that way? (*She sits again.*)

LARRY: What do you take me for, Sal?

SALLY: I never thought you cared so much.

LARRY: I haven't thought of much else lately.

SALLY: And I'm always thinking about you, Larry. But I didn't know – there's things you can't believe in – you know, things that make you so happy, you –

LARRY: I know – you want to shout and tell everybody.

SALLY: Yes – or else you want to cry.

LARRY: Lord, Sally, I do love you!

SALLY: And I love *you*, Larry. Only, don't forget, you won't always have me standing on a rock, with clouds, and the sun in my hair –

LARRY: Sally!

SALLY: It's for ever, isn't it, Larry?

SALLY's hand is resting on the table. LARRY seizes it and is about to kiss it, but rises and turns suddenly away to the head of the sofa. SALLY rises.

Why, what's wrong? There's nobody coming.

LARRY: Oh, don't you see? What's the use –

SALLY: But – it was – (*She goes to him.*) Didn't you mean it, Larry? (*She pulls him around to face her.*) Didn't you mean it?

LARRY: Of course I meant it. But let's get it straight. We both want the same thing, only – unless we get it straight in our minds first of all I'm no better than those other fellows. Forty-five bob a week! That's all I get. And look at the way things are at the mill – none of us know when we're going to finish. Is it fair to you, Sal?

SALLY: I'm not a film star, Larry. I can manage as others do.

LARRY: Yes, manage to keep alive. There's something more in life than just living. (*Again turning away from her.*)

SALLY: Do you love me?

LARRY: Would I act this way if I didn't?

SALLY: (*Again pulling him round to face her.*) Do you love me?

LARRY: Of course I love you.

SALLY: Then let's get married.

LARRY: But –

SALLY: I'll get extra work so's we can have more money. I'll – Oh, Larry, I'd do anything for you!

LARRY: I know, Sal, but I think –

SALLY: (*She strokes his hair.*) Don't think so much. Think about *us*. I want you and you want me. That's all there is to it.

LARRY: (*Holding her in his arms.*) Bless you, Sal! When I see you like that, with the red in your cheeks and your eyes lit up – you're like a flower – (*He laughs bitterly.*) – a flower in Hanky Park. A rose growing on a rubbish-heap. Hanky Park – we can't get away from that. It's got us. It gets everybody. But when you're near me like this, Sal, I don't seem to care. Listen, Sal, we're going to fight it, you and me together. We'll be different from the others. We won't go down.

SALLY: I don't want anything else if I've got you. You can't have everything.

LARRY: I'd have to start saving, Sal. But if you'd wait –

SALLY: Wait? Of course I'd wait. Oh, Larry –

They have hardly begun their embrace when whistling is heard in the street. HARRY peeps in at the window.

Aw, there's our Harry. He *would* come just now.

LARRY: Right. I'll be getting along.

SALLY goes to the fire, where she lights a spill (or match), then turns on the gas and lights it. HARRY comes in from the street. He is a slightly-built boy of seventeen. He wears blue overalls and a jacket which is much too small for him. SALLY prepares a cup of tea for HARRY.

HARRY: Hullo, Larry!

LARRY: Hullo! How's things, Harry?

HARRY: (*Grinning.*) Fine! How's yourself? (*He looks at SALLY and grins knowingly.*)

LARRY: All right, thanks. Still like that job?

HARRY: Aye – it's great!

LARRY: Ah, well, it's good to be young.

HARRY: I've been put on a machine up at the shop – capstan lathe, they call it. That's what I've wanted all along, and now I've got it. Have you seen the new machines, Larry? By gosh, they're wonderful.

LARRY: Yes, they're wonderful. They only need a lad of your years to work 'em.

SALLY gives tea to HARRY.

But they're not perfect yet, harry.

HARRY: What do you mean, not perfect? You should see the screw-cutting lathe. All you've got to do is to shove the lever over and the machine does the rest.

LARRY: That machine will only be perfect when it turns the lever for itself and Marlowe's can be rid of young Harry Hardcastle.

HARRY: (*Thoughtfully.*) Aye, I know that's coming. They turned another hundred fellows off this morning. But I'm not worrying. Maybe things'll take up. I can do with more than seventeen bob a week, though. Gah! That's a lad's pay and I'm doing a man's work.

LARRY: That's how it is, Harry. The factory wants cheap labour to keep prices down, and the apprentice racket's a good way of getting it. You're in a racket, Harry, only you're in at the wrong end. Nobody'll teach you anything because there's nothing to be learned. When you've served your time and want skilled mechanic's pay, they'll do with you what they did with the hundred out of the machine shop this week. You'll be fired.

SALLY: (*Who has been clearing up the ironing.*) He should have gone to an office when he had the chance. No short time there and holidays paid for.

HARRY: Aw, go on. I don't want no office. That's a sissy's job. It takes a man to do with machinery.

LARRY: Well, it's a grand thing to like your work. I wish we all did. Keep young if you can, Harry.

HARRY: Young! Me? Why, I'm seventeen.

LARRY: Go on!

SALLY: He thinks he's a young Samson. I saw him feeling his muscle the other day like a strong man at the circus.

HARRY: Just you wait. I'll show you one of these days. I'm not staying in Hanky Park all my life.

SALLY looks at LARRY. HARRY looking from one to the other.

What's wrong?

SALLY: Nothing, lad. Except that the same flea's been biting Larry and me, that's all.

HARRY: What flea?

LARRY: The Hanky Park bug, Harry. It's painful when you're young.

HARRY: I don't know what you're talking about.

LARRY: That's all right, Harry. It only bites the healthy ones. Well, good night, Sal. Good night, Harry.

HARRY goes over to the sink with his tea-cup. LARRY opens the door. SALLY goes up to LARRY.

See you tomorrow, Sal.

The presence of HARRY prevents a fonder good night and LARRY goes out. SALLY closes the door and drops to the head of the sofa, looking through the window. HARRY is at the sink in the corner removing his jacket. He washes himself, whistling occasionally.

HARRY: What's Larry after?

SALLY: Nothing particular.

HARRY giggles. SALLY gets the work-basket from the dresser to mend some stockings and sits at the table.

HARRY: (*Washing.*) I'm glad they've put me in the machine shop. There's something about a machine. Power – that's it. All shining new. Makes you feel grand being boss of all that power. Do you feel that way yourself about machinery, Sal?

SALLY: (*Absently.*) Can't say I do.

HARRY: Aw, girls make me sick. You never like the right things. I went into the foundry today. Gosh! But that's a place, if you like. There's a darned big crane and it picks up twenty tons of metal – white hot it is, like a river of fire – and they tip it in moulds, all spitting and splashing like fireworks. Fine place, Marlowe's, and never mind what Larry says. Better than a lousy office any day. (*He makes a big splashing and blowing at the sink.*)

SALLY: You aren't washing your neck, are you?

HARRY: (*Indignant.*) Well, don't I always do?

SALLY: Never seen you do that before.

HARRY: Gah!

SALLY: Must be going to meet a girl. Who is she?

HARRY: Girls make me sick, I tell you! (*He turns away from the sink with his eyes tightly closed and gropes with the soap in his eye.*) Where's the towel?

SALLY: There you are. Beside you.

HARRY finds the towel.

Does Helen Hawkins make you sick?

HARRY: She's different. I mean – you know – *girls*.

SALLY: Oh, I see. What do you want to wear those overalls for when you've finished work?

HARRY: (*Hesitating.*) It's – it's my trousers.

SALLY: What's wrong with your trousers?

HARRY: They're short 'uns.

SALLY: You're still wearing those knickers?

HARRY: (*Throws the towel down and crosses to the table – gloomily.*) I've never had a suit of clothes. Aw, Sal, I do wish you'd say something to Dad about it. I'm tired of asking. And a fellow my age feels soft wearing kids' things.

SALLY: I'll try, but I don't see where the money's coming from.

HARRY: You can pay weekly at Mrs Nattle's.

SALLY: (*Dubiously.*) Your Dad's suit's still at the pawnshop and we're still owing for the rent. (*She laughs.*) It's a funny business.

HARRY: Nothing to laugh at.

SALLY: You wanting long trousers and me wanting shorts.

HARRY: (*Laughs.*) You in shorts! Sally, you're balmy. (*He gets a mirror from the shelf and sets it on the table. Then produces a collar from his pocket.*)

SALLY: You wait. I'll show you.

HARRY makes a derisive noise. He is trying to fit on a collar much too large for him before the mirror.

What are you gawping at yourself for? You're worse than a girl.

HARRY: (*Ingratiatingly.*) Would you like to make this collar fit me, Sal? Go on, you're a good sewer.

SALLY: What's come over you? Wearing collars?

HARRY: Go on, Sal.

SALLY: Ach! I've no time to fool about with collars. I'm too busy.

HARRY: Aw, Sal.

SALLY: Get Helen Hawkins to do it for you.

HARRY: I wanted you to do it, Sal. I didn't want Helen to know that Larry Meath gave it to me.

SALLY: What?

HARRY: Larry Meath gave it to me.

SALLY: (*Pretending unconcern.*) Oh! Larry, was it? Well, you can leave it on the table. Maybe I'll do it later.

HARRY: Thanks, Sal. (*He puts his jacket on, then looks at her curiously.*) I tell you what, Sal, I'm having a threepenny treble every week with Sam Grundy. You know, you put money on a horse and if it wins you put it on another and another. And if I'm lucky I'll buy you those shorts and anything else you want. And *I'll* have a suit of clothes, you know, special measurement, shaped at the waist – (*Holding his jacket tightly to him and looking over his shoulder to see the effect.*) – not one of those ready-to-wear things.

SALLY: You ought to be ashamed of yourself, spending your money on betting, and Sam Grundy, too!

HARRY: (*Puts his scarf on.*) Well, Sam Grundy pays. Bill Higgs made five pounds last week on a shilling double. I'm sick of having nothing to spend. I've no love for Sam Grundy, but I could do with some of his dough.

SALLY: Ach!

HARRY: Aye, you can do anything when you've got the dough. They say he's got women all over the place. Down in Wales, they say, he's got a house where he keeps a woman –

SALLY: That'll do, lad. I know all about it. I wish he'd keep out of *my* road, that's all.

HARRY: (*Aghast.*) Sally –! He ain't –?

SALLY: I can manage Sam Grundy myself, thank you.

HARRY: Hoo! He'd better leave you alone. It makes me feel I'd like to –

SALLY: Hush!

MRS HARDCASTLE returns from her errand, carrying a bundle of washing.

MRS HARDCASTLE: Where's your Dad, Sally?

SALLY: He went out.

MRS HARDCASTLE: Where?

SALLY: He didn't say. Maybe he went to the Free Library to see the papers.

HARRY: Papers! They'll tell him that trade's turning corner again. Gah! Trade's been turning corner ever since I can remember. It's turned wrong corner and got lost. (*Finishing combing his hair, he returns the mirror to its place on the shelf.*)

MRS HARDCASTLE: (*Looking nervously at SALLY.*) I've asked Mrs Jike to come across, Sally.

SALLY: Mrs Jike? What for, Ma?

MRS HARDCASTLE: She's holding a circle – you know, spirits and fortune-telling. I thought she might tell us a bit.

SALLY: Oh, that fortune-telling. You know it's all nonsense.

MRS HARDCASTLE: Maybe it is. And I don't really believe she talks with spirits, same as she says she does. But a bit of nonsense is a comfort sometimes. (*She proceeds to roll up the shirts, etc., in the ironing-blanket.*)

SALLY: That means we'll have Mrs Dorbell and Mrs Bull here as well.

MRS HARDCASTLE: Well, I *did* say they'd be welcome. It makes it more of a party when we're all together. Mrs Jike says spirits won't come unless there's four of you –

HARRY: Huh! If that crowd's coming in here I'm going out. (*He puts on his cap.*)

MRS HARDCASTLE: Harry, run upstairs and fetch that little table down. It's just the thing for spirit meetings.

HARRY: Gar! You're all daft.

MRS HARDCASTLE: Harry! Go on, quick.

He goes, muttering 'Bloomin' spirits!' MRS HARDCASTLE removes the ironing things and begins to lay the tablecloth.

Let's hope your Dad stays out a bit. He doesn't like Mrs Jike and her friends. (*She looks steadily at SALLY.*) Mrs Jike was saying that you and Larry Meath –

SALLY: Interfering cat! Tell her to mind her own business.

MRS HARDCASTLE: I don't think she meant anything. She only said she'd seen him. Yes, he's a nice young man is that Mr Meath. I do like him, I do.

SALLY: (*Eagerly.*) Do you really, Ma?

MRS HARDCASTLE: I do. I reckon he's a gentleman and a credit to the neighbourhood. And I don't care what folks say about Labour men.

SALLY: That Sunday we went up on the hills. We had a grand time. Over mountains as high as you never saw. And he knows the names of all the birds.

MRS HARDCASTLE: Isn't that nice, now. Though I can't see it's much *good* knowing the names of all the birds.

SALLY: Better than knowing the names of horses.

MRS HARDCASTLE: Yes, I suppose eddication is like that – knowing a lot of things as don't really matter.

SALLY: And he paid my fare. I was in a state when I heard the others say the fare was two shillings and me with only tenpence in my purse. I never knew it would be so much. But I think he knew how I was fixed 'cos when I got all bothered, he smiled – you know how he smiles, Ma – well, he smiled like that and said he'd got tickets for both of us and that it was all right. Though he said it different – he wouldn't have done that if he hadn't – didn't –

MRS HARDCASTLE: That's true. When I was a lass it was took for granted that when a lad paid for you to places he meant something serious.

SALLY: There was a girl in the party that made herself free with him. She was trying to rile me, I know. But he didn't take much notice of her and he kept with me all the time – (*She sighs.*) Oh, I love the way he talks. And he's so – so – nice if you know what I mean.

MRS HARDCASTLE: (*Sighing also.*) I know.

SALLY: I never enjoyed myself so much in all my life.

MRS HARDCASTLE: Did he ask you to go again?

SALLY: Yes. He asked me again just now. And – (*She checks herself.*)

MRS HARDCASTLE: What were you going to say?

SALLY: Nothing – only I hope I get some extra work at the mill.

MRS HARDCASTLE: What for?

SALLY: So that I can get an outfit like the rest of the girls. I felt all wrong beside them with their heavy boots and jerseys and short trousers.

MRS HARDCASTLE: Oo –! Short trousers? Our Sally –?

SALLY: They all wear shorts when they go walking on the hills.

MRS HARDCASTLE: You're not thinking –?

SALLY: I am.

MRS HARDCASTLE: Do you think your Dad'd like you to be dressed like that, Sal?

SALLY: Aw, who cares what he thinks. I'll buy 'em and I'll wear 'em. Let him mind his own business.

MRS HARDCASTLE: You ought to be ashamed of yourself. I don't know what lasses are thinking about these days. Once your character was as good as gone when you wore short skirts. But short trousers –! Drat it, here's your Dad.

MR HARDCASTLE passes the window and enters. He is a thick-set miner, with a square-set, reliable face, and hair and moustache turning grey.

HARDCASTLE: (*Closing the door and seeing the cups on the table.*) What's to do, Mother?

MRS HARDCASTLE: I thought you were going to be out tonight, Henery.

HARDCASTLE: I've changed me mind. (*Hanging up his cap and crossing to the rocker.*) It's about all as I have to change. (*He moves the rocker into the best place for reading, under the gas bracket, and produces a newspaper.*)

MRS HARDCASTLE: (*After exchanging looks with* SALLY.) You won't find it very nice with all those clothes hanging up to dry.

HARDCASTLE: All right, Mother. Don't you worry about me. Maybe I'll go out again soon.

MRS HARDCASTLE: (*Relieved.*) Ah!

HARRY enters with a table from upstairs and sets it down in front of the sofa.

HARRY: Here you are, Ma.

HARDCASTLE: What's our Harry doing with yon table?

MRS HARDCASTLE: That? I asked Mrs Jike to come in –

HARDCASTLE: Ach! I thought you were going to take it to the pawnshop. (*He resumes his reading of the newspaper.*)

HARRY: (*Crosses to* SALLY.) Go on, Sal. Ask him now.

SALLY: (*Rises.*) Not now. Better ask him yourself.

She picks up her sewing and goes upstairs.

HARRY: (*By the head of the sofa, with his eye on his father.*) Ma?

MRS HARDCASTLE: (*Above the table.*) Yes?

HARRY: When am I going to have that there new suit?

HARDCASTLE glances up, then reads again.

MRS HARDCASTLE: (*Looks at* HARDCASTLE *– hesitates; sighing.*) Eh, lad, what can I do? You know Sal's not drawing much, and your Dad's only working three days a week and ain't sure of that –

HARRY: I know, Ma. But I've never had a proper suit yet. And me nearly eighteen.

MRS HARDCASTLE: Your Dad's tired now.

HARRY: Yes, but I'm ashamed to go out on a Sunday in these. And I can't wear short trousers like as if I was a kid. Look at Bill Lindsay and the others. They can have them. Why can't I?

MRS HARDCASTLE: They get 'em from the Clothing Club, Harry, and you know your Dad doesn't like weekly payments.

They both look hopefully at HARDCASTLE.

Let him alone. He's tired.

HARRY: But I don't see –

HARDCASTLE: You'll have to make do with what you've got. It's taking us all our time to live. You'll get one when things buck up.

HARRY: When things buck up! Huh!

HARDCASTLE: It's all very well talking that way. But trade's turning t' corner. Paper says so.

HARRY: I know I'm ashamed to turn the corner in these trousers.

MRS HARDCASTLE: Now, Harry, let your Dad alone.

HARRY: Why can't I have one through the Clothing Club like the others?

HARDCASTLE: (*Sternly.*) I'll tell you why. Because I'm shoving no blasted mill-stone of weekly payments round my neck. What we can't pay for cash down we'll do without. See?

HARRY: The others do it. And here I am working full time and nothing to go out in at week-ends.

HARDCASTLE: Aaach! I've worked all me blasted life, lad, and what have I got? All me clothes at pawnshop to get food to eat.

HARRY tries to speak.

Don't you set me off, now! Don't you set me off!

MRS HARDCASTLE: (*Pleading.*) Now, Harry, please –

HARRY: (*Angrily and almost tearfully.*) Well, I'm sick of it all, I can tell you. Nothing to spend and nothing to wear and me working full time. *Man's* work, that's what I do. And giving up all I earn except a shilling for spending.

HARDCASTLE: (*Flings down his newspaper and jumps up, blazing.*) God almighty! This is a fine life, this is! I come home to rest and what do I get? If it ain't you it's Sally. Why, man, do you think blasted money grows on trees?

MRS HARDCASTLE: Well, the lad's right, Henery. He ain't fit to be seen in the street.

HARDCASTLE: Worked every hour God sent, every day of me life. And what have I to show for it? Every blasted day, every blasted hour, and I'm worse off now than when I was first wed. (*He turns to the mantelpiece and gets a spill.*)

MRS HARDCASTLE: Three pounds! It's a lot of money, Harry.

HARDCASTLE: Huh! Three pounds! (*He produces a pipe.*)

MRS HARDCASTLE: You see, you pay three bob down to begin with and three bob every week for twenty weeks.

HARRY: Can't go out weekdays except in me overalls. And I've to stay in all of Sunday with everybody asking me why I don't come out –

HARDCASTLE: Oh, Missis, for God's sake get him blasted suit. Hell, I'm fair sick of it all, I am! (*He lights his spill and then his pipe.*)

HARRY: (*Fervently.*) Oh, thanks, Dad, thanks –

MRS HARDCASTLE: But, Henery, how are we going to –?

HARDCASTLE: We'll have to manage some way.

MRS HARDCASTLE: Three bob a week –

HARRY: Can I go now, Ma, to the Clothing Club?

HARDCASTLE: Ay, go's quick as you can before I change me mind.

HARRY: (*All smiles.*) Gosh! You don't know how I feel about it. I'm off. So long! (*He picks up his cap and darts out.*)

MRS HARDCASTLE: Henery –

HARDCASTLE: Well?

MRS HARDCASTLE: Do you think you ought to have given in?

HARDCASTLE: What the hell could I do? The lad's right. If I'd had any sense I'd have said 'No.' But I never did have any sense. Besides, he ain't fit to be seen.

MRS HARDCASTLE: I don't know how we're going to pay.

HARDCASTLE: Something else'll have to go, that's all. We'll start with this. (*He knocks out his pipe.*)

MRS HARDCASTLE: Not your pipe, Henery. You can't do without your pipe.

HARDCASTLE: Can't I? We'll see about that. (*He puts his pipe in a vase on the mantel.*)

MRS HARDCASTLE: Makes you that narky when you don't have tobacco.

HARDCASTLE: Well, I'll just have to *be* narky, then. (*He crosses to the door.*) Though I can't feel much worse than I do now. (*He gets his cap.*)

MRS HARDCASTLE: Are you going out?

HARDCASTLE: Aye.

MRS HARDCASTLE: Where are you going?

HARDCASTLE: I'm going to take me brains out and put 'em in cold water.

MRS HARDCASTLE: You're not angry with me, are you?

HARDCASTLE: With you? No. (*He turns to go.*)

MRS HARDCASTLE: Nor with our Harry?

HARDCASTLE: Harry? (*He smiles.*) No, he's a good lad.

MRS HARDCASTLE: Then who *are* you angry with?

HARDCASTLE: (*Looks at her.*) I don't rightly know. That's just it, Mother, I wish I did know. By God! I'd give 'em a piece of my mind.

He goes out. MRS HARDCASTLE *gets tea-things from dresser.*

SALLY: (*Peeping from the door on the left.*) Has Dad gone out?

MRS HARDCASTLE: Yes.

SALLY: Was there a row?

MRS HARDCASTLE: I've seen worse. Your Dad let himself go, but Harry got his trousers in the end. He's gone to the Clothing Club about it now.

SALLY: I suppose I'll have to get extra work at the mill now. And it's goodbye to those shorts of mine.

MRS HARDCASTLE: Ah, well, I can't say that I'm going to worry much about that. There'd be too much talk in North Street with you walking about half-naked.

SALLY: I'd do it to give 'em something to talk about. Gosh! I would!

MRS HARDCASTLE: Now, then, Sally. Don't talk that way. I'd be glad if you could settle down with a young man like Larry Meath. There's so many of the wrong sort waiting about these days.

SALLY: Um. Chance is a fine thing.

MRS HARDCASTLE: Has he never asked you?

SALLY: He has – and he hasn't. But I've asked *him*, though.

MRS HARDCASTLE: (*Shocked.*) Sally!

SALLY: Well, why not? A woman usually asks a man some way or another, though she doesn't always do it with her tongue. I'm one for plain-speaking.

MRS HARDCASTLE: You don't mean to say you *asked* him to marry you?

SALLY: I did.

MRS HARDCASTLE: Eh, Sally, it's not respectable. I *am* ashamed of you. (*Eagerly.*) What did he say?

SALLY: He said we'd have to wait. And he's saving up.

MRS HARDCASTLE: I wonder what the end of it all will be. That's where Mrs Jike can help us, maybe.

SALLY: Oh, that kind of thing's all nonsense.

MRS HARDCASTLE: It ain't all nonsense. Mrs Jike tells fortunes true. She warned Mrs Dorbell when her Willie was going to die, though I must say his cough was something awful at the time.

Two women pass the window, one of them tapping as she passes.

(*She rises.*) There's Mrs Jike now. (*Calling.*) Come in, everybody. (*She opens the door.*)

MRS JIKE *enters.* MRS JIKE *is a tiny woman with a man's cap and a late Victorian bodice and skirt. She talks with a Cockney accent, having been transplanted from London in her youth. She is followed by* MRS DORBELL, *a beshawled, ancient woman with a dewdrop at the end of her hooked, prominent nose.*

MRS JIKE: (*Peeps in.*) Are you in, Missis?

MRS DORBELL: Course she's in – Can't you see her?

MRS HARDCASTLE: Good evening, Mrs Jike, *and* you, Mrs Dorbell. Where's Mrs Bull?

MRS JIKE: We left her having an argument with a lidy. (*She goes to the window.*)

MRS BULL *is heard down the street carrying on a noisy argument.* MRS JIKE *and* MRS DORBELL *watch through the window.*

MRS BULL: (*Off.*) Go on with you! You trombone-playing old faggot. Give your husband his trousers back! Yah! If he'd any guts in him he'd knock your face in –

A VOICE: (*Off.*) Pay your debts! Pay your debts, says me –

MRS BULL: (*As she appears outside the window.*) Yah! You bleeding little gutter rat! (*She arrives at the door. Is about to enter, but turns again for a final insult.*) Aye, and take your face inside. You're blocking the traffic in the street. That'll teach her to argue with me!

MRS BULL, *a large woman, comes in and immediately adopts her politest voice.*

Good evening, Sarah. That Mrs Scodger's getting a bit above herself.

MRS HARDCASTLE: Now sit down, everybody, and make yourselves at home. (*Bringing a chair to the small table.*)

Figure 22 *Love on the Dole*, from the Skipton Little Theatre, Yorkshire, England in the 1930s.

MRS JIKE: (*To* SALLY.) Well, dearie! I saw you walking out with Mr Meath.

SALLY sits in the rocker and looks at the newspaper.

MRS BULL: Aye, Larry Meath's a fine lad, and that lass o' thine's lucky to have gotten him.

MRS DORBELL: Lucky? I wouldn't like any daughter o' mine to marry a Bolshy. Look what they've done in Russia. Broken up the home life, and nationalizing women. I wouldn't have nobody nationalizing me. (*She scratches herself indignantly.*)

MRS BULL: Shouldn't think there's many as would want to.

MRS JIKE: 'Ere you are, girls. Have a pinch of Birdseye. It'll do you good. (*She hands her snuff-box to* MRS BULL *and* MRS DORBELL.)

MRS HARDCASTLE: I'm brewing a pot of tea. It'll be ready in a minute. How are you, Mrs Bull? Haven't seen you much lately. (*She proceeds to pour five cups of tea.*)

MRS BULL: Eeh! Trade's bad.

MRS HARDCASTLE: I'm sorry. How's that, Mrs Bull?

MRS BULL: Yah! — I don't know what's come over folk these days. I remember the time when hardly a day passed without there was a confinement or a laying-out to be done.

MRS DORBELL: Young 'uns ain't having children the way they should. When I was a girl a woman wasn't a woman till she'd been in childbed ten times, not counting miscarriages.

MRS BULL: Ay! How can they expect a body to make a living when children going to school know more about things than we did after we'd been married years?

MRS JIKE: That's just it.

MRS DORBELL: Things have never been the same since the gentlefolk left the Old Road. Why, if my old Ma was alive today she'd turn over in her grave, that she would.

MRS JIKE: The world's never been the same since the old Queen died.

MRS BULL: What queen do you mean, Mrs Jike?

MRS JIKE: Why, Queen Victoria, of course.

MRS BULL: Oh, '*er*!

Cups of tea are passed to MRS DORBELL *and* MRS BULL.

MRS JIKE: When I used to live in London — that was the time. The old Queen 'ud give 'em snuff if she were alive. She would that.

MRS HARDCASTLE hands a cup of tea to MRS JIKE.

Thank you kindly, Mrs Hardcastle. I likes a nice cup o' tea. Would any lidy care to have a drop of this in her tea?

MRS HARDCASTLE gives SALLY *her tea, and stands before fire drinking her own.* MRS JIKE *produces a flat bottle of gin from her stocking.* MRS BULL *and* MRS DORBELL *accept.*

MRS DORBELL: Thank you, Mrs Jike. I don't mind if I do.

MRS DORBELL pours gin in her tea and hands the bottle to MRS BULL, *who helps herself liberally.*

How's your rheumatics, Mrs Bull? (*Critically watching* MRS BULL.)

MRS BULL: I'd be all right, only for a twinge now and again. But I don't worry. There's a rare lot up in the cemetery as 'ud be glad of a twinge or two.

MRS JIKE: (*Attempts to pour, but finds bottle empty — looking at the bottle.*) 'Ere, somebody's done herself well.

MRS BULL points with her thumb at MRS DORBELL.

You may be alcoholic, Mrs Dorbell, but you might 'ave the manners of a lidy.

There is the beginning of a good row, but MRS HARDCASTLE *interrupts.*

MRS HARDCASTLE: (*Puts her cup down and hurries across to them.*) Now, now. I thought you might like to hold a circle, Mrs Jike. That's why I brought out the table. (*She takes* MRS BULL'S *cup.*)

MRS DORBELL: Eeh, spirits! Come on, girls! (*She eagerly sits up to the small table.*)

MRS BULL: Nothing like talking with the dead to cheer you up.

MRS HARDCASTLE: Make yourselves comfortable.

MRS DORBELL commences her song here.

MRS BULL: Have you got everything ready?

MRS JIKE: Well, that all depends on the spirits, doesn't it?

MRS DORBELL: (*Sings quietly to herself as the gin begins to work.*)
'We'll laugh and we'll sing and we'll drive away care.
I've enough for meself and a little bit to spare.
If a nice young man should ride my way,
Oo-ow I'll make him welcome as the flowers in —'

MRS BULL: (*Freezing the singer with a look.*) Well, that's better out than in. (*She moves to sit on the sofa.*)

MRS JIKE: (*Crosses to the table.*) All round the tible now. Turn the lights down low, Sally.

SALLY turns the gas down. They gather round the table. MRS HARDCASTLE brings a chair and sits at the small table.

All hands on the tible-top. Only just your finger-tips.

MRS DORBELL sniffs.

Hush! You'll drive the spirits away. (*She assumes an eerie, monotonous voice.*) Are there any spirits present 'ere tonight? Answer three for 'yes' and two for 'no.'

Three raps are heard, which are obviously caused by MRS JIKE's knee. She announces in a brisk, matter-of-fact tone.

Yes, they're here. Now hush! (*She gets monotonous again.*) Has anybody got anything to ask the spirits about?

MRS DORBELL: Yes. Mrs Nattle's got a ticket in the Irish Sweep and she wants me to go shares. Ask the spirits if the ticket's going to draw a horse.

MRS JIKE: Will Mrs Nattle's ticket draw an 'orse? Answer three for 'yes' and two for 'no.'

Two raps.

No, it won't.

MRS DORBELL: Right. And thank you. She can keep her old ticket. I want none of it.

MRS JIKE: Hush, Mrs Dorbell, hush! Spirits don't like too much talking. Any more questions?

MRS BULL: Ask if Jack Tuttle's there.

MRS JIKE: Is Jack Tuttle present 'ere tonight? Answer three for 'yes' and two for 'no.'

Three raps.

Yes, 'e's 'ere.

MRS BULL: Hello, Jack lad. Are you there? Listen to me. When you died and I laid you out I found half a crown in thy pocket and as I was hard up I took it. I knew thou wouldn't need it where thou's gone, and I'm only telling you this so's you'll not think I pinched it. How are you finding things where you are, Jack?

MRS JIKE: Ask questions, Mrs Bull. The spirits don't like you to be familiar.

SALLY: (*Who has been sitting in the shadows by the fire.*) Oh, stop it! I never heard of anything so daft in my life. (*She springs up and turns the gas up again.*)

MRS JIKE: Eh, what? Now you've done it! The spirits have all gone away.

SALLY: I think you're an old twister, Mrs Jike.

MRS JIKE: (*Rises.*) Ow, am I? I like that.

MRS BULL: Go on, Sally lass, it's only a bit o' fun and it costs nothing.

MRS DORBELL: I'd a bought a ticket if spirits had said it was going to draw a horse, fun or no fun. Ee! Fancy me winning thirty thousand quid! I'd buy meself a fur coat and –

MRS BULL: Aye, and I'd be laying you out in a month, drunk to death, fur coat and all.

MRS DORBELL: I'd risk it. I'd have good once, anyway.

MRS HARDCASTLE: I'd like Sally to have her fortune told, Mrs Jike, in spite of what she says.

MRS JIKE: (*Sniffing.*) Can't say as I care to do it for an antiseptic.

MRS HARDCASTLE: (*Coaxing MRS JIKE back to her seat.*) Aw, come on, Mrs Jike. Sally meant no harm.

SALLY: (*Following.*) But I don't want my fortune told.

MRS HARDCASTLE: Now, Sally, just to please me.

MRS JIKE: Remember, I ain't responsible. Will you have cards or tea-leaves?

MRS DORBELL: Make it tea-leaves. It's more exciting when you go seeing things in the future the way you do.

MRS JIKE: Very well.

MRS HARDCASTLE: Is this your cup, Sal?

SALLY: Yes, Mother.

MRS HARDCASTLE brings a cup and saucer. SALLY is seated at the table and offers her cup.

MRS JIKE: No, no! Turn it round three times.

SALLY does so and again offers the cup.

No, no! Bottom side up.

SALLY turns the cup upside down on the saucer and again offers it. MRS JIKE takes the cup, shakes it and then peers into it.

Strike me pink! Look at that!

MRS DORBELL: What is it?

MRS JIKE: Money! Lots of money!

MRS BULL: Aye, in the bank.

MRS JIKE: Hush, I see two men – one's dark and 'andsome – Do you know a dark, 'andsome man?

SALLY does not answer.

MRS HARDCASTLE: That'll be Larry Meath.

MRS JIKE: The other's a fat man. Be on your guard against him. He means danger. Oo! And money, more money –

MRS DORBELL: And then what?

MRS JIKE: (*In her eerie voice.*) Now I'm seeing things. Right through the bottom of the cup I'm seeing into the future. It's all dark – darkness all round you – I see Sally Hardcastle with a dark, 'andsome bloke. They're trying to get up to the light, but they're being dragged down – down into the darkness. I can't see no more – it's getting darker and darker – Ow! (*She screams suddenly.*)

MRS HARDCASTLE: (*Frightened.*) What is it?

MRS JIKE: All red! Like blood –

SALLY: Stop it! (*She snatches the cup and dashes it down.*) Do you hear, you old fool? Stop it!

MRS BULL: Now see what you've done? You've frightened the lass. You didn't ought to do that.

SALLY: Get outside, the whole lot of you.

MRS HARDCASTLE: (*Above the table.*) Sally!

SALLY: Yes, Ma, I mean it. You ought to be ashamed of yourself, bringing them in here. Go on, get out! If you don't go I'll put you out! The whole damned pack of you!

MRS JIKE: (*To* SALLY.) I warned you.

SALLY: (*Shrinking away.*) You dirty old scut! Do you think I believe a word you said?

MRS JIKE: Ow? So that's 'ow you feel, is it? (*She points her hand at* SALLY, *then turns in the doorway.*) I warned you.

She goes out.

MRS DORBELL: And I was expecting to have mine told too. (*She turns to go.*)

MRS BULL: (*Stopping* MRS DORBELL.) I can tell it, lass. Thou'll keep on drawing thy old-age pension, and then thou'll die, and I'll be laying you out and parish will bury you. Come on. We aren't wanted.

MRS DORBELL: (*At the door.*) Good night, Mrs Hardcastle. I'm sorry your daughter was took that way. (*She goes out.*)

MRS BULL: (*At the door.*) Now, Sal, lass. Take no notice of what Mrs Jike says. It's all a bit of fun. Good night, Sarah. (*She goes out.*)

MRS HARDCASTLE: (*Almost in tears.*) Sally! What have you done?

SALLY: I've turned them out. And about time too.

MRS HARDCASTLE: But Sally – You've shamed me – They're me friends. What'll they think of me?

SALLY: Friends! Those our friends? It's us that's shamed, Ma, by letting 'em come here.

MRS HARDCASTLE: Sally! You're not getting notions, are you?

SALLY: (*Collecting the cups.*) Yes, I *am* getting notions. It's about time some of us at Hanky Park *started* getting notions. You call *them* your friends, that pack of dirty old women. Oh, I'm not blaming them – that's what Hanky Park's done for 'em. It's what it does for all the women. It's what it'll do for you, Ma – yes, it will! – and me too! We'll all go the same road – poverty and pawnshops and dirt and drink! Well, I'm not going that road, and neither are you, if I can help it. I'm going to fight it – me and Larry's going to fight it – and I'm starting *now*.

MRS HARDCASTLE: You can't, Sally, you can't – I've tried and you can't.

SALLY: Can't you? We'll see about that.

MRS HARDCASTLE: You're hard, Sally. You're like all the young 'uns, you're hard.

SALLY: Ay, I'm hard – and, by God, you need to be! (*She turns with the cups to the sink.*)

CURTAIN

Act 2
Scene I

An alley in Hanky Park. There is a large railway arch, through which is seen a view of distant factories and other buildings. It is night.

(*Note: This scene can be played in the simplest of settings. A drop cloth of a brick wall is adequate.*)

At the side of the arch is a street lamp on a bracket, which is lighted. Hardly discernible, in the feeble light, lies a drunken man (MR DOYLE) *under the arch.*

The curtain rises, and a train rumbles overhead.

MRS DOYLE: (*Is heard calling offstage.*) George! Oh, so you're there, are you? Drunk again! Get up! Get up! (*She grabs him by the arm and hauls, as he slowly rises.*) Do you hear me?

They stand under the lamp.

MR DOYLE: What time is it?

MRS DOYLE: What beats me is where you get brass for getting drunk. What about your wife and family, eh? (*She picks up his cap and puts it on his head.*) You great fat guzzling pig! You ought to be drowned in it. Aye, and them as serves you with it too! You with children starving at home – and you waste your money in the public house.

MR DOYLE: Shut your trap, will you, or I'll break your blasted jaw.

He makes a left-handed swipe at her. She dodges it. He misses and staggers against the corner of the arch. MRS DOYLE *supports him.*

MRS DOYLE: (*Shrilly.*) Ah, you would, would you? You big lousy coward! Strike your wife! (*She hits him on the arm.*) Go on, hit me – hit me –

DOYLE *turns toward her.*

And I'll tell the cops if you so much as lift a finger to me. (*Sticking her face up at him – asking for it.*)

MR DOYLE: Keep your blasted snout in your own business.

MRS DOYLE: My own business! Isn't it my business what you do with brass to keep the home going? Tell me that, George Doyle, tell me that. You great soaking swine you, I'll –

A POLICEMAN *enters from the back of the arch. She stops as she hears him.*

Look out, here's a cop! (*She supports and tidies* DOYLE.) It's all right, Mister. It's only my husband. He's been took queer – it's his indigestion.

DOYLE *hiccoughs.*

Somethink awful, it is! I'll get him home. Come on, love. (*She gives him a punch.*) Here, lad, take my arm. (*As she leads him up to the back of the arch.*) You'll be all right when you get home. Come on, lad. (*She turns to the* POLICEMAN.) He often gets took this way.

She pushes DOYLE *away. They disappear. The* POLICEMAN *watches them go, then turns and goes out.*

HARRY HARDCASTLE *comes on, closely followed by* HELEN HAWKINS, *a pretty but rather hungry-looking girl of about sixteen. She catches him by the arm so that he stops under the lamp.*

HARRY: (*Offstage.*) Don't talk so daft.

He enters.

HELEN: (*Following him on.*) Oh, Harry, let's not fall out.

HARRY: What do you mean? *Us* fall out? Huh! That's a fine way to talk.

HELEN: (*Plaintively.*) Oh, Harry, I never meant –

HARRY: Oh, that's all right. You're always making a fuss. Girls make me sick as a rule, but you're not so bad.

HELEN: (*Eagerly.*) Do you mean that, Harry? Do you mean it?

HARRY: Do I mean what?

HELEN: That I'm not so bad.

HARRY: (*Lighting a cigarette-end.*) Um. But, don't forget, I'm not walking out regular. Not yet.

HELEN: (*Disappointed.*) Oh – I don't know what's come over you lately, Harry.

HARRY: What do you mean?

HELEN: I mean – I thought you and me were –

HARRY: Well, we are in a way, aren't we? But I can't always be – You see, there's other chaps. I don't like 'em saying things.

HELEN: What sort of things?

HARRY: Aw, just – things.

HELEN: Take no notice of what *they* say. Oh, Harry, we could be – you know. I've always liked you best of everybody, and – oh, well, you're different from that other lot.

HARRY: Aw, they're not so bad. It's like this, you see. I like *you* too. Yes, I do, really, no kidding. But – well, I don't want to go out regular with nobody yet. I – oh, I don't know, Helen, I want to do things first.

HELEN: What sort of things?

HARRY: Big things. I want to make money or something like that. Gosh! I wish I was a footballer or a boxer, or something.

HELEN: (*Who thinks he's wonderful.*) Harry, I *do* love you – I do really.

HARRY: Do you, Helen? Thanks. (*He puts his arm around her, and is about to kiss her when he suddenly drags her into the shadows.*) Look out, here's that cop!

A POLICEMAN *crosses at the back. They watch him go out of sight.*

All right, he's gone. You know, I've been thinking. You see, Helen, it troubles me, having nowt to spend on you. It's rotten – kids get more to spend than me. Older you

grow, more work you do and less money you get to spend. Why, when I first started at Marlowe's, what with money I got for running errands, I got twice as much as what I do now. And me on a machine – Gar!

HELEN: Oh, never mind about money. I don't want nothing, Harry. Only you.

HARRY: Well, give me time, and I'll show you – I'll find a job –

HELEN: Would you rather be with the other lads than here with me, would you? (*She shakes him.*) Would you, Harry?

HARRY: No.

HELEN: Oh, Harry!

HARRY: You know, Helen, you aren't bad looking.

HELEN: (*Eagerly.*) Aren't I, Harry?

HARRY: You're not exactly – well, you aren't Greta Garbo. But you'll do. (*He kisses her.*)

HELEN: (*Bursts into tears.*) Oh, Harry, you do make me happy. (*She sobs on his shoulder.*)

HARRY: Lousy place for being happy, isn't it? Back alley in Hanky Park. I always used to think of love like on the movies, with moonlight and trees.

HELEN: I reckon love's the same the world over. Though I could do with moonlight and trees better than brick walls and chimney-stacks. But it doesn't matter, does it, Harry?

HARRY: (*Wistfully.*) No – it doesn't really matter.

HELEN: (*Drawing his face to hers.*) It's you and me, Harry.

HARRY: That's it, Helen. Me and you. It's strange, but that's how it is.

A train rumbles and lights flash overhead.

Look at that train, Helen. How'd you like to go on one?

HELEN: Oo, I've never been on a train in me life.

HARRY: I wish I had more money, just so as we could have a bit more fun. I'd like to be able to take you and me away for a holiday.

HELEN: Oh, Harry! Where could we get the money for that?

HARRY: Just you wait. You don't know what I'm doing on the quiet.

HELEN: What? Not stealing?

HARRY: Me – no! But one of these days I'll make more money than you ever saw.

HELEN: What is it? What're you *doing*?

HARRY: Well, I'm having a threepenny treble every week with Sam Grundy.

HELEN: What's a threepenny treble?

HARRY: Well, it's this way. You put threepence on a horse, whatever you fancy, of course, and if the horse wins, what you've made you put on another horse, and any winnings from that you put on another.

HELEN: You mean three horses have got to win?

HARRY: Ay. And then, you see, you –

HELEN: What? Three horses win? All in the same race?

HARRY: *No!* One after the other.

HELEN: Oh – but isn't it very difficult?

HARRY: To some it is. You've got to be a student of form – like me. But Bill Higgs won five quid on a shilling double, so I'm hoping.

HELEN: Five quid!

HARRY: It's exciting, you know. When I look in the paper tomorrow it'll be in the stop press. (*He is carried away.*) I stand to win – ooh – I don't know how much, and I can't lose more than threepence, see?

The POLICEMAN *appears.*

Oh, Helen, if I could make some money, there's things we could do, you and me –

HELEN: Oh, Harry, you *are* wonderful!

They embrace. The POLICEMAN *has advanced towards them.* HARRY *becomes conscious of his presence and looks up.* HELEN *turns, sees the* POLICEMAN *and exclaims.*

Oh!

Black out.

Scene 2

Out of the darkness comes the voice of the NEWSBOY *calling –* 'News Chronicle! Three o'clock winner. Racing Special! Evening News! Evening Chronicle! News Chronicle!' *The light returns, and now it is the daylight of late afternoon.* MRS BULL *appears with* MRS DORBELL, *earnestly discussing.*

MRS BULL: Yes, and he's had a thripp'ny treble every week for years. This is the first time it's ever come off.

The NEWSBOY *offers* MRS DORBELL *a paper.* 'Paper, lady?' *She shoos him away.* 'Get out!'

NEWSBOY: Keep your hair on!

He goes, still calling his papers.

MRS DORBELL: Twenty-two quid for thrippence!

MRS BULL: Now what do you think of that? He ain't twenty year old yet, neither, not by a long way.

MRS DORBELL: Twenty-two pounds for three pence. Yah! Some hopes.

MRS BULL: Mrs Dorbell, I'm not in the habit of having my word doubted, especially by one of me neighbours.

MRS DORBELL: Ah, but do you know it's true?

MRS BULL: True? It's as true as God's above. Some people have all the ruddy luck! Ay, he's lucky is young Harry Hardcastle.

MRS DORBELL: That's all very well, but will Sam Grundy pay it?

MRS BULL: Ah, now you're asking. That's what I'm here to see. If he does, then Sam Grundy gets all my bets in the future, you bet you does.

MRS DORBELL: Sam Grundy should be here now. It looks kind of suspicious. Huh! I bet he don't pay up.

MRS BULL: I bet he does.

MRS DORBELL: I bet he don't.

MRS BULL: I bet he does.

HARRY appears with a newspaper.

MRS DORBELL: Here's the lad now. Congratulations, Harry.

MRS BULL: (*Pushing in front.*) Eh, Harry, lad. You'll be going to the Rivyeera now.

MRS DORBELL: Who'd have thought it, Harry? Who'd have thought it?

MRS BULL: I hope he pays up.

HARRY: Have you seen him?

MRS BULL: Who?

HARRY: Sam Grundy.

MRS DORBELL: No, and like as not you never will.

MRS BULL: You'll stand us a bottle of gin, won't you, Harry?

HARRY: I will that, Mrs Bull.

MRS DORBELL: There's some bookies that won't pay more than five pounds. And if you ask me this sky's the limit business is all a bit of bluff. I wouldn't give much for your chances, lad.

SALLY is heard calling HARRY. *The crowd begins to assemble.*

SALLY: Harry! Is it true, Harry?

HARRY: Ay, I think so. Twenty-two quid.

SALLY: That's fine, lad.

HARRY: I'll be able to pay for that new suit of mine now, and to hell with weekly payments.

SALLY: Now don't go being soft with all that brass.

MRS BULL: (*Who is hovering.*) That's just what I were telling him.

SALLY: You keep out of this.

MRS BULL: (*Moving away.*) All right, Sally Hardcastle, I won't rob you of your lawful pickings, though I warn you there's nothing like money for breaking up a family.

HARRY: (*To* SALLY.) Take no notice. Listen, Sal, you can have those shorts and things as soon as you like.

SALLY: No, it's your money.

HARRY: Go on, I promised you, and you've got to have 'em.

SALLY: Thanks, Harry, very much. That'll be fine.

MRS BULL: (*Shouting.*) Here he is! He's coming down the street!

Excited voices are heard.

SALLY: See you later!

She runs off.

MRS DORBELL: Here he is. Here's Sam Grundy.

CHARLIE: (*In the arch.*) Make way there! Way for Sam Grundy.

SAM GRUNDY swaggers through the crowd. He is a not unpleasant man, though rather stout, and he has the confidence of one who lives on his wits. He wears spats, and a bowler hat is tilted at the back of his head. If he has to pay up this money he is determined to make a good advertisement of it.

SAM: Well? Where's Harry Hardcastle?

HARRY is pushed forward by the CROWD, *who gather round.*

So that's him, is it? Not much to look at, is he?

Roars of obsequious laughter.

CHARLIE: That's a good 'un!

SAM: Now, young fellow, I suppose you thought you'd break the bank, didn't you? But you know us bookies have a limit. You know that, don't you?

MRS DORBELL: (*Screaming.*) There you are! Didn't I tell you? Gah! Pay him. You're like all the rest.

There is a groan of dismay and shouts of 'Pay him'!

SAM: (*Waving his hand.*) Wait a minute! Wait a minute! I haven't finished yet.

MRS DORBELL: (*Aggressively.*) No, and *we* haven't finished yet.

SAM: All right, all right. Now, there's fellows that call themselves bookies that would only pay you a fiver on your bet and no more. You know that, don't you?

HARRY: I do, Mr Grundy.

SAM: Well, my lad, that ain't the way of honest Sam Grundy. Sam Grundy pays up – that's me!

He removes his hat with a flourish. Roars of applause and shouts of 'Good old Sam!', etc.

MRS BULL: (*To* MRS DORBELL.) What did I tell you?

CHARLIE: (*Shouting fervently.*) Sky's the limit!

SAM: Charlie, keep a look-out. We're going to do this thing proper and all square and fair and above board. Now listen to me, ladies and gentlemen! Honest Sam's got a motto and that motto is – Charlie?

CHARLIE: Sky's the limit with honest Sam!

SAM: Sky's the limit, ladies and gents, and don't you forget it. This young fellow – Stand up alongside of me, son, and let's have a look at you. Come on, lad, come on. Now you had a bet with me, didn't you, lad?

HARRY blushes and nods.

How much was it?

HARRY: (*In a small voice.*) Threepence, Mr Grundy.

SAM: Threepence! And how much do you reckon to draw for threepence?

HARRY: Twenty-two quid, Mr Grundy.

SAM: Twenty-two quid for threepence. How many bookies'd pay out that much? How many? Well, you all know honest Sam's motto.

CHARLIE: (*Bawling.*) Sky's the limit with honest Sam! (*He distributes cards amongst the crowd.*)

SAM: Sky's the limit! (*He flourishes a roll of notes.*) Hold out your cap, Harry.

HARRY holds out his cap, but SAM turns away to do some more business.

Now, doesn't that prove I'm the man for your little commissions? Support Sam Grundy, the old firm.

CHARLIE: (*Repeats.*) Support Sam Grundy, the old firm.

SAM: Take a threepenny treble every week.

CHARLIE: (*Repeats.*) Take a threepenny treble every week. (*He distributes betting slips.*)

SAM: That's the way to make money quick.

CHARLIE (*Repeats.*): That's the way to make money quick.

SAM: Risk a bit and gain a lot.

CHARLIE: Risk a lot and gain a bit.

Laughter.

SAM: See how this young fellow's made money.

MRS BULL: Ay, but you haven't –

SAM: Haven't what?

MRS BULL: Haven't paid him yet.

The crowd jeers.

SAM: Hold out your cap, Harry. (*He counts out the notes.*) Five, ten, fifteen, twenty – and two. Twenty-two quid. That's honest Sam for you, ladies and gents.

HARRY goes apart to count his money. SAM follows him. The crowd makes excited comments.

(*To* HARRY.) And don't forget to give your sister a couple of quid – tell her I said so. (*He turns to the crowd.*)

MRS DORBELL: Hey!

SAM: What?

MRS DORBELL: What about his stake money?

CHARLIE turns to explain. SAM hands over the extra threepence.

SAM: Take a threepenny treble every week. Take one for the wife and little 'uns, too. Better than insurance any day. Sky's the limit with honest Sam.

CHARLIE: (*Whistles and tugs his sleeve.*) Look out. Here's a cop.

SAM: You'll excuse me, ladies and gents. Honest Sam will have to retire.

SAM disappears through the crowd, who disperse quickly as the POLICEMAN approaches. HARRY conceals his money and leans against the wall. MRS BULL and MRS DORBELL have remained to watch the fun. CHARLIE whistles with his hands in his pockets. The POLICEMAN stands looking at him and CHARLIE hastens away, almost running when he finds the POLICEMAN is following him.

HARRY: Gosh! I thought he was going to take me up.

MRS BULL: Not he. The police'll never touch Sam Grundy or his customers. Don't forget, Harry!

MRS BULL makes a gesture of drinking out of a bottle as she goes with MRS DORBELL.

HARRY: (*Calls down the alley.*) Sal! Sal!

She runs up to him.

Look, he's paid me!

SALLY: Put it away quick!

HARRY: Well, I must find Helen and tell her. Here you are, Sal. (*He offers her two pound notes.*)

SALLY: No, Harry. No, I couldn't.

HARRY: Go on. Get your shorts and anything else you've a mind to.

SALLY: Well, I'll take one and give you the change. So you do like Helen Hawkins, after all?

HARRY: (*Shyly.*) Oh, leave us alone, Sal –

SALLY: It's nothing to be ashamed of. She's a nice girl.

HARRY: Do you think so? I'm glad. I like her, too.

SALLY: Very much?

HARRY: I suppose so. It happened sudden last night.

SALLY: Well, you're only young once, so if I was you I'd take that lass of thine away on a holiday.

HARRY: You mean it, Sal? That's what I thought, but –

SALLY: Go on with you – get yourself out of Hanky Park, while you've a chance.

HARRY: (*Feeling the money in his pocket.*) Gosh! It's like a dream. I bet there's a catch in it somehow. Twenty-two pounds.

SALLY: That'll take you to Blackpool or the Isle of Man.

HARRY: Blackpool? Phew!

SALLY: You'll spend your money on something or other, lad, so you may as well spend it on something you'll remember.

HARRY: I wonder where Helen is now. Funny if she's not heard about me winning.

SALLY: She's heard, all right.

HARRY: Then where is she?

SALLY: I've just left her crying her eyes out in back entry behind North Street.

HARRY: Crying? What was she crying for?

SALLY: Because you've won twenty pounds.

HARRY: Gosh! That's a daft way of showing you're happy.

SALLY: No, lad. She's not happy. She thinks she's lost you.

HARRY: Why, she's barmy. Here, I'd best go quick. (*He is going.*)

SALLY: (*Stops him.*) Here, lad, just a minute. She's not barmy. You be good to her.

HARRY: Aw, that's all right. I'll do me best. Goodbye.

SALLY: (*Waving.*) Goodbye, Harry.

He goes out. SALLY *watches him and then turns to go the other way.* SAM GRUNDY *has appeared.*

SAM: How do, Sally? Well, that was a grand bit of luck for your Harry, eh? You can't say old Sam didn't pay up handsome.

SALLY: I reckon he can afford it. There's plenty more in the bank.

SAM: Ay, you're right. Did the lad give you a share as I told him?

SALLY: That's no business of yours.

He surveys her.

Well, what're you staring at?

SAM: You're a fine girl, Sal Hardcastle.

SALLY: Aach! Let me pass.

SAM: Nay, hold on. Not so fast. (*He holds her arm.*) Let's have a look at you.

SALLY: (*Snatching away savagely.*) Leave go!

SAM: Aw, Sal, what's the matter with you? What have you got against me?

SALLY: Just that I don't want to even talk to men like you. It'd be better if you'd spend more time with your wife instead of pestering girls that wouldn't wipe their feet on you.

SAM: Oh, now, Sal, now. That ain't the way to talk to a friend that wants to help you.

SALLY: Fine sort of help *you* can give a girl. You've helped too many already.

SAM: God, Sal, you've got me all wrong. (*He draws out some pound notes which he stuffs into her hands. She holds them in a kind of amazed horror.*) Take these. I like you, Sal. Honest, I do. I'd – aw, I'd like you for a pal, that's all. You must be sick of having nothing to wear, and pinching and scraping week after week, and think what you could have if you wanted. Anything, Sal. Anything for the asking.

SALLY: (*Comes out of the daze in a fury and thrusts the notes back to him.*) You'd better look out if you won't leave me alone. Just you tell that to Larry Meath.

SAM: Larry Meath? So it's Larry Meath, is it?

SALLY: All right. You leave his name out of it. You ain't fit to have his name on your breath. All *you* want out of girls is one thing only. But you don't get it out of me. Do you understand?

SAM: (*Who has been lighting a cigar.*) So it's Larry Meath you're set on, is it?

SALLY: That's my business. You mind yours. (*She is going.*)

SAM: He works at Marlowe's, eh?

SALLY: (*Defiantly.*) Ay, he works and that's more than you ever did. (*She suddenly realizes the danger and turns.*) Why?

SAM: (*Turning on his heel and walking away.*) That's *my* business.

SALLY: (Following a step or two; with frightened appeal.) But, Mr Grundy – Mr Grundy –

Curtain

Scene 3

On the moors. A high rock against the sky, towards sunset.

SALLY'S *voice is heard, and then* LARRY'S *as they climb up behind the rock.*

SALLY: (*Laughing happily.*) Oh, Larry, I can't. It's too high!

LARRY: Go on – Only a few yards and we're there.

SALLY: Larry, I'm slipping!

LARRY: No, you're not. Up with you! There you are. All right?

SALLY: Yes, I'm up now.

SALLY *appears in hiking shorts and shirt.*

This is the place, Larry. Oo, be careful, you'll slip!

LARRY: (*Appears beside her, carrying his jacket.*) I'm all right. Don't you worry about me. (*He stands upright.*) Well, are you happy now we've got here?

SALLY: Fine! Aren't we high up in the world? This is a special place. And only us two know why. Isn't it grand being alone? I've never seen so much loneliness in all me life.

LARRY: (*Laughing.*) You *are* a funny girl.

SALLY: (*Gasping.*) Be careful, Larry. You give me a turn when you stand right on the edge.

LARRY: Come on, then – hold my hand. Isn't that a grand view?

SALLY: Grand! Miles and miles of it. Gosh! And this air – it's wonderful. I wish I could breathe it every day. Makes me feel I could fly.

LARRY: (*His turn to gasp.*) Well, don't do that. Or else you'll give me a turn. Here, take something to hold you down. (*He produces an apple from his pocket which he offers her.*) One apple left.

SALLY: No, that's yours. (*She kneels.*)

LARRY: You have it, Sal.

SALLY: I couldn't. It's yours. You've eaten nothing yourself.

LARRY: We'll go halves. (*He splits the apple.*) There you are. Take the red side. It matches your cheeks.

SALLY: Phew! I feel more like a beetroot. Wasn't it a climb?

LARRY: Um. We shall never manage to get up here when we're old.

They sit down and munch their apple.

SALLY: It's been lovely today, Larry.

LARRY: You've liked it?

SALLY: You know I have. Haven't you?

LARRY: (*Turning away.*) Of course, it's fine.

SALLY: (*Looking hard at him.*) Larry? Is there anything wrong?

LARRY: Wrong? No. Nothing could be wrong out here.

SALLY: You're not worried?

LARRY: No –

SALLY: Nothing on your mind?

LARRY: No, why?

SALLY: Well, you haven't said anything about –

LARRY: About what?

SALLY: You haven't said you liked my shorts.

LARRY: Haven't I? Why, Sally, you're lovelier than ever. Perhaps that's why I *am* sad today. Beauty makes you feel that way sometimes.

SALLY: Why?

LARRY: I don't know. I suppose because when you've lived in a place that's ugly all your life, beautiful things seem out of reach. We get to thinking beauty is something forbidden, something that's too good for us –

SALLY: You don't feel like that about me, surely?

LARRY: Sometimes.

SALLY: Don't talk nonsense, Larry. (*She ruffles his hair.*) Look at that sunset. Why is it so red?

LARRY: They say it's the sunshine through the smoke. Hanky Park's over there – thirty miles away. It's a queer thing all that foul smoke should make beauty for us up here.

SALLY: See that cloud – big black fellow with a bulge in him. (*She laughs.*) Why, it's Sam Grundy!

LARRY: (*Laughing too.*) So it is!

SALLY: See, there's his bowler hat and his cigar. Coo-ee! How are you, Sam?

LARRY: I shouldn't make too free with him, Sal.

SALLY: Oh, Larry, I feel like we're on top of the world! I feel real mad! And I'm so happy! I've never been so happy in me life.

LARRY: Bless you, Sal.

SALLY: Aren't you happy?

LARRY: Yes – if this could last for ever.

SALLY: For ever and ever! Larry –?

LARRY: Yes?

SALLY: We'll come up here – often?

LARRY: Of course.

SALLY: If we could build a house, and live here – and keep this place, just for two of us – sacred – Gosh! That's funny talk!

LARRY: Some people call it poetry. Wanting what you can't get. It's the same thing.

SALLY: I'm no poet, Larry, but there's something in all this loneliness, something I've been wanting – (*A pause.*) Larry?

LARRY: Well?

SALLY: Do you believe in – God?

LARRY: (*Smiling.*) Me? Why? What a funny question!

SALLY: Do you, though?

LARRY: Why do you ask that?

SALLY: Oh, I don't know. I've never felt that way before. I've never found anything worth believing in Hanky Park. But it's different up here. Here you belong – you belong to something big – something grand, something that it's fine to belong to –

LARRY: I know, Sal, I know.

SALLY: But sometimes I get frightened. It's like as if someone up there was saying – 'Take care, Sal Hardcastle. Take care you don't climb too high and fall.'

LARRY: That's nonsense. But just think of those poor devils in Hanky Park who never learn how good life can be. They're as good as dead the day they're born. They're satisfied because they don't know any better. We can thank heaven, Sal, that *we've* learned to be discontented.

SALLY: Yes, but we've got to go back. We've got to go back.

LARRY: Ay, that's it, Sal!

SALLY: Why? Oh, why –? There's other places in the world –

LARRY: We've got to go back where the money is. Money's our master, Sal, and we're its slaves. There's only one spot in the whole wide world where someone will buy our labour – our special brand of labour – and that spot's Hanky Park. You're right – there's no God there, with all their churches.

SALLY: (*Impulsively.*) Larry, we've got to get out.

LARRY: (*Bitterly.*) Yes, climb out roughshod over the others, but Hanky Park will still be there.

SALLY: Never mind Hanky Park. We'll be wed soon. It's you and me –

LARRY: That's it! You and me and to hell with the others. Oh, what's the use of talking. I love you, Sally, better than anything else on earth – but it's no use – God, it's no use!

SALLY: Larry! What's the matter?

LARRY: Nothing –

SALLY: There is – There's something hurting you. Tell me what it is –

LARRY: It's nothing. See, there's the others, going down to the train. We'll have to hurry, Sal.

SALLY: That was strange talk. What do you mean, it's no use?

LARRY: Let's forget all that. I meant today to be happy.

SALLY: Well, aren't we happy? We'll be wed by the end of this month, and it won't be a bad house when we've cleaned it up a bit. You don't know what it means, Larry, a house of my own. I'll scrub it from top to bottom and there won't be a bug left in it when I've finished with it. Not a one. You know, Larry, dreaming about things you can't have doesn't get you anywhere. Does it now? I can't promise curtains yet awhile. We'll have to wait for *them*. But the room'll look all right, what with your books and the walnut table we saw at Price and Jones's. Come on, lad. Buck up! Besides, it ain't *where* you live, it's who you live with.

LARRY: Oh, Sal, Sal –! (*He buries his face in his hands.*)

SALLY: What's wrong, lad?

LARRY: We'll have to put it off, Sally. I'm –

SALLY: Put it off?

LARRY: I'm – I've lost my job. They gave me the sack yesterday.

SALLY: The sack? *Larry!* (*With uncertain optimism.*) You'll get another job.

LARRY: Will I? (*He laughs bitterly.*) There's too many out already. Oh, Sal, I should have told you before. But I just wanted to have today with you – and be happy.

SALLY: Why can't we be married as we said? There's nothing to stop us. You'd get your dole, and I'm working.

LARRY: No, no, Sal. No, I can't do that.

SALLY: (*Taking her hands away.*) You mean you don't want?

LARRY: How do you think I'm going to manage on fifteen bob a week? Gosh, dragging us down into that hell of poverty –

SALLY: But, Larry, there's nothing for me to live for without you. You don't know what I'd do for you – Listen, I'll come and live with you. Who wants to get married? Who cares what folks say?

LARRY: Oh, God, no, Sal! Fifteen bob a week. Do you think I'm going to sponge on you? Drag you down? What the devil do you take me for?

SALLY: (*Hysterically.*) Don't talk like that. I'm sick of it all. Is that all you care for me? Aw, you're driving me barmy. Why don't those labour councillors that're always making a mug of you find a job for you? They're all right, they are – don't care a damn for us. They've all landed good jobs for 'emselves. And I – Oh, I hate you! I hate you –

She turns away from LARRY *– throws herself down on the rock*

and sobs. LARRY *looks despondently at the sunset which has faded rapidly. Faint voices come up from the valley.*

VOICES: (*In the distance.*) Coo-eee! Hey, Larry! Sally! Come down, it's time to go home –

LARRY: (*Waving his hand.*) All right – we're coming. (*He looks at his watch and then at the crumpled* SALLY.) It's time to go now if we're going to catch that train. (*He touches her shoulder.*) Don't, Sal, don't – I love you, Sal, and there's nothing else matters. We'll pull through – somehow –

SALLY: (*Turns and impulsively throws her arms around him.*) I'm sorry, Larry – I'm sorry –

LARRY: That's all right, Sal. I should have told you. I'd no right to bring you up here.

SALLY: No, lad, I'm glad we've had today. They can't take that away from us now. They can take our jobs but they can't take away our love. Can they? (*She is a little frightened and uncertain about this last question.*)

LARRY: No, Sal. We've still got that – Yes, we've still got that.

SALLY *shivers.*

Why, you're shivering! You're cold. (*He puts his jacket over her shoulders.*)

SALLY: It's different up here now the sun's gone down. I think this place has changed. It's growing dark – and, oh, Larry, I'm afraid – I'm afraid –

He holds her head close to him and buries his face in her hair. Darkness gathers round them. The voices call 'Coo-eee!'

Curtain

Act 3
Scene I

The HARDCASTLES' *kitchen. A year later. The door R. is closed.* MRS HARDCASTLE *is seated at the table, darning a sock.* SAM GRUNDY *is on the sofa. He is obviously ill at ease and has observed convention by removing his bowler hat.*

MRS HARDCASTLE: So that's what you want, is it?

SAM: (*Seated on the sofa.*) I tell you, it's for your own good. What more am I asking than that Sally should be my housekeeper down in Wales? It's a good job and there's nothing wrong in being a housekeeper.

MRS HARDCASTLE: That depends on whose house it is, doesn't it?

SAM: Now, then! I'm not having that kind of talk. I might be asking the girl to take a dose of poison. Listen, MRS HARDCASTLE, I'm not a bad sort of fellow really and I've got a grand house. Right away in the country it is, with hills and mountains and the sea. Just what the girl is needing to make her better. Yes, and I've got a conservatory all glass and palms and things. Cost me a lot of money, that house did.

MRS HARDCASTLE: (*Rising and facing him.*) You'd better go before Sal comes home, and if my husband finds out –

SAM: Well, what if he does? I've done nothing wrong. There's no harm in me offering a job.

MRS HARDCASTLE: No harm, Sam Grundy – (*She puts the work-basket and darning on the dresser.*) – but he'd *kill* you all the same. (*She moves down to the fireplace.*)

SAM: (*Rising.*) Look here, Mrs Hardcastle, do you think I don't know how to treat the girl well? Me, with a family of my own. Aw, don't you worry yourself. She wouldn't regret it when I'm gone. I'd make a fair settlement on her. It isn't as though I'd got no money.

MRS HARDCASTLE: (*From the fireplace.*) You'd better go!

SAM: (*After a pause.*) You know, Mrs Hardcastle, it's hard on a fellow like me. I'm not an old man, and look at my wife – separated – and she's taken the kids with her. I've got a big house doing nothing and nobody to enjoy it. It's lonely for a fellow like me.

MRS HARDCASTLE: Sam Grundy, I've kept my temper with you so far. I'm not easily roused. But, I tell you, I can't keep my hands off you much longer. You're wanting a house-keeper, are you? Well, you don't get our Sal! I know what you're after, let me tell you this –

MRS DORBELL and MRS BULL have appeared in the doorway, overhearing the last line or so.

MRS DORBELL: (*Entering.*) Eee, Mrs Hardcastle! So you've got company.

MRS HARDCASTLE: Mr Grundy was just going.

MRS BULL: (*By the door.*) Oh, no, he wasn't. You was having words. I heard you. I'm sure it's an honour to have Mr Grundy in to see you.

MRS DORBELL: Well, I suppose we're in the way.

She sits down on the lower end of the sofa. MRS BULL closes the door and then sits on the upper end of the sofa.

Go on with what you are saying. You can trust me with a secret.

SAM: There's no secret. I've made a fair offer. I'm only asking her to talk sense to the lass.

MRS HARDCASTLE: Sense! I may be old-fashioned, Sam Grundy, but I've more sense than to let any daughter of mine be housekeeper of thine.

MRS BULL: So that's how it is, is it?

MRS DORBELL: Yaah, Sairey Hardcastle, the way you talk. If a girl don't know which side her bread is buttered, then she bloomin' well ought to find out. Huh! It's well to be some folks what can pick and choose these days, by gum, it is.

SAM: (*Eagerly nodding.*) That's right, Mrs Dorbell. Ay, that's right.

MRS BULL: (*Rises.*) Well, it's nothing to do with me, MRS HARDCASTLE. I reckon it's nothing to do with nobody except Mr Grundy. But I take no notice of what the parsons say. Let 'em try starving like us do every day of our lives, parsons' jobs would be ten a penny then!

SAM: That's right, Mrs Bull, that's right.

MRS BULL: Gar! What do you know about starving, you fat porcupine? (*She sits again on the sofa.*)

MRS DORBELL: He's right, is Mr Grundy. It's a fair offer and your girl's a fool if she won't take it. Huh! I don't know why you want to waste your time, Mr Grundy. With all the money you've got, you've no need to go down on your bended knees. That you haven't.

SAM: Oh, it ain't that. But I take an interest in the girl. You speak to her. Tell her what she's missing.

MRS BULL: That's right.

SAM: Makes me sick to think of her wasting her chances here.

MRS DORBELL: I don't know what the girl's thinking of, indeed I don't. But I know what she'd do if she was my daughter.

MRS BULL: Ay, she'd give you one on the nose, Mrs Dorbell.

MRS DORBELL: (*Half rising.*) Ho! Would she?

A row is beginning.

MRS BULL: Ah, keep your hair on. (*She rises and looks into SAM's face.*) She's doing what I'd do myself if I was her age. Romantic, that's what she is.

MRS DORBELL: Hanging on after that Larry Meath. Why, chap's been on the dole for twelve months now. I don't know what's taken the girl.

SAM: (*Jingling money in his pocket.*) First lass I've met that didn't know the value of brass.

MRS HARDCASTLE: (*Quietly.*) I think you'd better go. All of you.

SAM shrugs his shoulders and goes to the table for his hat.

MRS DORBELL: Ho! If you feel that way about it after all we've done to oblige you –

MRS BULL: Mrs Dorbell is disappointed. She was expecting a bit of commission on the deal.

MRS DORBELL: It's a lie –!

SAM: Now then, now then.

MRS HARDCASTLE: I said I think you better go. Sally'll soon be home and I wouldn't like her to find you here.

SAM: Well, I've no more time to waste – (*He puts his hat on.*) – but just you think over what I've said, Mrs Hardcastle. (*He goes towards the door and turns.*) And another thing, don't let that lad of yours get mixed up in this unemployment demonstration they're having. There's going to be trouble. I know. Don't say I didn't warn you. And good day to you.

He goes out.

MRS DORBELL: (*Angrily.*) There now. It's like sweeping money off the doorstep. Huh! It's well to be some folk that can afford to have notions. Why, the man's just made of money.

MRS HARDCASTLE: And what do you think I'm made of, Mrs Dorbell? Do you think I'm made of cast-iron that I'd let my daughter be housekeeper to a man like him?

MRS DORBELL: There's many would jump at the chance.

MRS BULL: Ay, and her own mother couldn't stop her if she wanted to. She's got a will of her own has that lass.

MRS HARDCASTLE: Sally'll be here soon and you know she won't be very pleased to see you.

MRS DORBELL: Still got notions, has she? Bah! That girl's going to have a fall.

MRS HARDCASTLE: Well, she won't fall Sam Grundy's way. Not if I can help it.

MRS DORBELL: Huh! I'm going. And when you find out who your friends are, Sairey Hardcastle, you'll know where to find me. Come on, Mrs Bull, to them that can appreciate us.

She goes out.

MRS BULL: Take no notice of her, Sarah, but don't you be too sure. If I had my time over again I wouldn't turn my nose up at a fat belly – (*She goes up to the door and turns for her parting shot.*) – as long as it had a gold watch-chain hanging on it.

She follows MRS DORBELL.

MRS HARDCASTLE sighs, closes the door and takes a bundle from the cupboard below the dresser. She lays it on the table and taking a pair of candlesticks from the mantelpiece, polishes one on her apron, then begins to tie up the bundle. HARRY comes in from the street. He is thinner and paler, and obviously troubled.

HARRY: (*Gruffly.*) Hello, Ma. (*He watches her.*) What's that you're doing?

MRS HARDCASTLE: I'm making up a bundle for the pawnshop, though I wonder whether old Price will take them. I'm afraid he'll tell me they're worth nothing.

HARRY: (*Sits by the table and stares at the floor.*) Ma –

MRS HARDCASTLE: Well?

HARRY: I've got bad news.

MRS HARDCASTLE: What is it?

HARRY: They've knocked me off the dole money.

MRS HARDCASTLE: They've what?

HARRY: They've knocked me off the dole, I tell you.

MRS HARDCASTLE: But they can't. You're out of work–

HARRY is silent. MRS HARDCASTLE smiles with a forced hopefulness.

Ah, you mean they've found you a job?

HARRY: Not them! It's the Public Assistance Committee. They say the money's got to stop because Sally's working and Dad's getting the dole as it is. They say there's enough coming into one house.

MRS HARDCASTLE: But there isn't, Harry! You know there isn't. What are we going to do? What'll Sally say? We're living on her earnings as it is.

HARRY: But – it's Helen I'm thinking of. You see, we were going to get married.

MRS HARDCASTLE: Get married, lad? You've taken leave of your senses!

HARRY: (*Desperately.*) It's no use talking that way, Ma.

Figure 23 *Love on the Dole* at the Lowry Theatre, Salford, Manchester, 2004. (Photographer: Ben Blackall.)

MRS HARDCASTLE: What do you mean?

HARRY: I mean we've got to.

MRS HARDCASTLE: You and Helen Hawkins?

HARRY: Ay – she's seen the doctor – we've got to.

MRS HARDCASTLE: You've got to –? Oh, Harry, whatever'll your Dad say?

HARRY: That's just it. Look here, Ma, it isn't that I don't want to marry her. I do. I like her better than – well, anything, and we was planning to marry. We was going to make do on my dole money and what she's getting herself, and now this happens. If only we can get a start. I'll be drawing the dole again as soon as we are wed. And I thought perhaps – Well, I thought you and Dad would let her come here, and we could share the back room with Sally.

MRS HARDCASTLE: (*Rising.*) Ay, that's it. Share with Sally. Aren't we all sharing with Sally, as it is? She and Larry Meath wanted to get wed just as much as you did. But they didn't go and make fools of themselves, like you've done.

HARRY: But I thought I'd have got a job.

MRS HARDCASTLE: Ay, that's what a lot are thinking. But I don't think there's ever going to be work any more.

HARRY: Oh, gosh, Ma, it's driving me barmy.

He breaks down and buries his face.

Sorry, Ma, but I'm ashamed to walk the streets. I feel they're all watching me. I've been to twenty places this morning and it's the same blasted story all the time. 'No hands wanted.' Though they don't usually say it so polite. And look at me clothes. It'll take six months' pay to buy new ones. Aw, God, just let me get a job. I don't care if it's only half-pay, but give me something –

HARDCASTLE passes window.

MRS HARDCASTLE: Here's your Dad.

HARDCASTLE comes in from the street and hangs up his cap.

HARDCASTLE: Well? What's up now?

HARRY is silent.

MRS HARDCASTLE: Come on, speak up, lad. You'd best get it over.

HARDCASTLE: What's the matter with the lad?

MRS HARDCASTLE: It's him and Helen Hawkins.

HARDCASTLE: Eh?

MRS HARDCASTLE: And he's been knocked off his dole money.

HARDCASTLE: What's this about Helen Hawkins?

HARRY: You see, Dad, I'll have to marry her, and I thought –

HARDCASTLE: You what?

HARRY: I'll have to marry her.

HARDCASTLE: You blasted little fool!

MRS HARDCASTLE: Now, Henery –

HARDCASTLE: You, *you* getting wed! And who the devil do you think's going to keep you, eh?

HARRY: I thought, maybe, that we could come and live here and get a bed in back room with Sal.

HARDCASTLE: You *thought*? Yah! You little fool! Don't you think there's enough trouble here without you bringing more? I'm having no slut like that living here, do you hear me?

HARRY: (*Rises – warmly.*) Hey! I'm not having you calling her a slut. Just you leave her name out of it.

HARDCASTLE: (*Slowly as he clenches his fists.*) Are *you* threatening *me*?

HARRY: Aye, I am, if you call her names. I'm asking you for nothing. I'm not the only one out of work in this house, remember. Yah, you treat me like a kid just because I've got nothing and I'm out of work. You didn't talk like that when I was sharing my winnings with you, did you? Once let me get hold of some money again and I'll never part with a penny of it. I'm supposed to be a man, I am – Well, look at me. Aye, and if there was another war you'd call me a man too. I'd be a bloody hero then –

HARDCASTLE: You're bringing no wife here, do you understand? You've made your own bed with your nonsense – you must lie on it. Go and stay with *her* folk, the lowdown lot that they are –

HARRY: (*Hysterical.*) Stop it! Stop it, will you? I don't want to live here. Do you understand? I wouldn't live with *you* if I got the chance. You can go to hell! I'm leaving here –

He goes to the door. MRS HARDCASTLE attempts to stop him, but he brushes her aside.

MRS HARDCASTLE: No, Harry –! (*Following HARRY.*)

HARRY: Yes, I am, I'm leaving! I'm sick to death of it all. (*He rushes out.*)

MRS HARDCASTLE: See what you've done! You shouldn't, Henery, you shouldn't –

HARDCASTLE: (*Walks excitedly up and down.*) Who's the master

in this house, eh? I'm having no carryings-on in my family. My father kept respectable, and so did his father before him, and by God, I'll keep respectable too!

MRS HARDCASTLE: But he's only a lad.

HARDCASTLE: Only a lad, is he? Calls himself a man. Well, he can blasted well take the consequences – Aye, and take 'em somewhere else. Not in my house.

MRS HARDCASTLE: But he can't get a job, and they've knocked him off the dole.

HARDCASTLE: No more can I get a job. No more can any of us. Oh, well, he'll have to get workhouse relief, that's all.

MRS HARDCASTLE: Workhouse relief! No, Henery, no.

HARDCASTLE: It's all the same any bloomin' road. We're paupers living on charity. Dole or workhouse, it's all the same.

MRS HARDCASTLE: All my life I've feared it, and now it's come. Eh, that poor lad – (*She weeps.*)

There is a pause as HARDCASTLE looks at her, then turns his head away.

HARDCASTLE: (*Gruffly.*) Now, Ma. Now, Ma.

MRS HARDCASTLE: You might have let the lad stay on.

HARDCASTLE: I might. There's a lot of things I might have done. I might have had the gumption not to have a family at all. (*Pointing at the door.*) But it's his own doing, and there's an end of it.

MRS HARDCASTLE: I think he loves her, Henery.

HARDCASTLE: Loves? *Love*, did you say? I'm thinking that's a luxury the young 'uns can't afford these days.

MRS HARDCASTLE weeps.

Eh, Ma, I'm sorry – I thought I'd have done better for you.

She looks pleadingly at him.

No, don't ask me to change my mind. I tell you, Ma, he'll bring no wench in this house.

There is a roar of men's voices outside.

MRS HARDCASTLE: What's that?

She goes to the window.

HARDCASTLE: Aw, that's the men gathering for the demonstration. Fine lot of use that'll be, too.

MRS HARDCASTLE: I'm afraid our Harry'll get mixed up in it. Sam Grundy said –

HARDCASTLE: What's that?

MRS HARDCASTLE: He said there might be trouble.

HARDCASTLE: (*Slowly.*) Where did *you* see Sam Grundy?

MRS HARDCASTLE: Oh, he just happened to call. He's wanting a housekeeper.

HARDCASTLE: Wanting a housekeeper, is he? That's a new name for it. Listen, Ma, if I catch that swine hanging round our Sal again, I'll kill him, I will! I'll kill him, if I swing for it.

MRS HARDCASTLE: Don't talk like that, Henery. You know well enough that Sally's promised to Larry Meath. She ain't that kind of a girl, and you ought to be ashamed of yourself thinking that way about your own daughter.

SALLY comes in from the street. Crowd noise swells for a moment as the door opens.

SALLY: They've started the demonstration, Dad, and Larry's been asking for you.

HARDCASTLE: Then he'll have to wait. I've got troubles enough without demonstrating.

SALLY: And I met our Harry on the corner. He told me what's happened.

HARDCASTLE: Oh, he told you, did he?

SALLY: Ay. And I think you might have waited till I came in before you turned him away.

HARDCASTLE: What d'you mean?

SALLY: Only that it's *my* money that runs this house, and I might have had a word to say in the lad's favour.

HARDCASTLE: You keep out of this, Sal.

SALLY: I asked Harry to come back, Ma.

HARDCASTLE: You *what*?

SALLY: I tell you I asked him to come back.

HARDCASTLE: You interfering little hussy –

SALLY: All right, keep your hair on. He wouldn't, and he said he'd never be seen dead in here, so I suppose that's that.

HARDCASTLE: Look here, Sal, I'm boss of this show, and I won't have you interfering with my business. D'you think I'm having a lowdown wench living here, and all the neighbours talking –?

SALLY: If you want to stop the neighbours talking, you'd have done better to let her come. And Helen Hawkins isn't a lowdown wench either.

MRS HARDCASTLE: Here's Larry.

There is a knock at the door. SALLY opens it.

LARRY: Can I see Mr Hardcastle for a moment?

SALLY: Come inside, Larry.

LARRY: (*Is pale and has a distressing cough.*) I'd like a word with you, Mr Hardcastle, if you don't mind.

HARDCASTLE: What's the trouble now?

LARRY: I want your help. Things aren't going as they ought. Listen to 'em. That organizer fellow's a fool, and I won't answer for what happens if he gets 'em roused. There's police all over the place.

HARDCASTLE: Well, what d'you want *me* to do?

LARRY: I want you to be one of the deputation. The Mayor's promised to meet us at the Town Hall, and it's time we were there now, instead of wasting time making daft speeches. (*He coughs.*)

SALLY: Larry! You've no right to be out with a cough like that.

LARRY: I'm all right, Sal. Just a bit of cold. Will you come, Mr Hardcastle? We want some of the older men with a bit of sense.

HARDCASTLE: Ay, I'll come. Though a lot of good the whole business will do us.

MRS HARDCASTLE: No, I don't like you going.

HARDCASTLE: I can take care of myself, Ma.

An excited YOUNG MAN, with a strong Irish accent, appears in the doorway.

YOUNG MAN: Where's Larry Meath? Is he here?

LARRY: Yes, I'm here. What d'you want?

YOUNG MAN: Come on, man, hurry up! The crowd wants to hear you speak.

LARRY: There's no time to waste making daft speeches. Get 'em lined up for the procession. D'you know the Mayor's waiting for us?

YOUNG MAN: (*Coming forward to LARRY.*) Ach! Let him wait. Let him wait *our* pleasure. We've waited long enough.

LARRY grabs the YOUNG MAN's coat-lapels.

LARRY: Look here, I've had enough of your talk. D'you know there's a crowd of police down there all waiting for us?

YOUNG MAN: (*Throws LARRY off.*) Afraid, are you?

LARRY: Course I'm afraid. D'you think we're going to run our heads into a brick wall? What's a thousand half-starved men against a hundred healthy cops? I'm not leading them into trouble, if you are.

YOUNG MAN: Yah! Kow-towing to the boss class as usual, Larry Meath. It's hand in glove with 'em you are.

HARDCASTLE: (*Cutting him off.*) That's enough! Which road are you going?

YOUNG MAN: (*Defiantly.*) Past the Labour Exchange and down Crosstree Lane.

LARRY: Oh, talk sense, can't you? You've been told we can't go that way. They've got mounted police down there.

YOUNG MAN: Police? To hell with the police! Traitors to their class! Enemies of the workers! The iron heel of a bourgeois aristocracy –!

LARRY: Don't talk so damned daft! Get 'em lined up for the procession! I'm coming with you.

He reaches for his cap, coughs violently and leans against the table.

HARDCASTLE: Here, Larry, my lad, you'd best stay behind. Get the Missis and Sal to take you home. You're not fit to be out with that cough. (*He crosses the door and gets his cap.*)

LARRY: I'm all right – and I'm seeing this through.

MRS HARDCASTLE: You're not going, Dad.

HARDCASTLE: (*Puts his cap on.*) Of course I am. (*To the YOUNG MAN.*) Now, then, Mister – Trotsky, come on with you.

He goes.

YOUNG MAN: (*As he follows.*) Hired assassins of capitalism, that's what they are! Are we going to bow the knee –?

MRS HARDCASTLE goes to the door and looks after them.

LARRY: Gosh! That fellow makes me tired.

SALLY: Do what Dad tells you, Larry. You ought to see a doctor.

LARRY: I'm all right. Bit short of breath. I'll soon be right.

MRS HARDCASTLE: Was our Harry down there?

LARRY: Harry? Yes, I think he was.

MRS HARDCASTLE: Aye, he is too! The young fool – he's carrying a banner. Here, just let me get at him. (*She seizes her shawl and runs out.*)

SALLY: You're hot and feverish, Larry. You're bad, I tell you. Go home now and get to bed.

LARRY: I can't, Sal. I can't. (*Rises.*) I've got to see this through.

SALLY: For my sake –?

LARRY: No. I can't. It's my show, this, and everything was going well before those fools started their nonsense. I'm – (*He staggers against the sofa and she has to steady him and help him on to the sofa.*)

SALLY: There! I told you – (*She runs up to the dresser and gets a cup.*) You're bad, real bad. (*She fills the cup at the sink and takes it to him.*)

LARRY: (*Sits up, assisted by Sally, and drinks.*) It's nothing, nothing at all. (*He tightens his belt.*) I got excited on an empty stomach, that's all. Makes me lightheaded. There. I feel better now.

SALLY puts the cup on the table. LARRY tries to rise.

SALLY: Sit down, then, and rest.

She draws him to her.

Ah, Larry, Larry, why do you want to go fighting other people's battles? You've got yourself to think of, and me. Let other people take care of themselves.

LARRY: No, Sal, no – You don't understand. That's what's caused all this. Every man for himself and let others take care of themselves. That's what's wrong with the whole blasted world. Listen to 'em, shouting now they've lost their dole.

Crowd noise can hardly be heard now.

SALLY: (*Stroking his hair.*) Don't talk, Larry, it's rest you need –

LARRY: (*Leaning against her.*) Rest – Yes, Sal, I could rest if something inside'd let me. There's peace and quiet with you.

SALLY: We'll soon be old, Larry, and best part of our life gone. Is all your fighting and bitterness worth anything at all?

LARRY: Sometimes I think it isn't. But you don't know the misery of dreams – Be glad they don't hurt you –

SALLY: Me? Me not know dreams? You don't know. You don't know what I dream about you and me. For ages, Larry. Ay, and they hurt, those dreams.

LARRY: I know. It's wanting decent things and knowing they'll never be yours that hurts. But listen, Sal – (*He grips her arm.*) We've got to keep those dreams. They're ours, Sal – they're you and me. They're the only precious things we've got.

Crowd noise increases.

If we go down, Sal – if Hanky Park gets us as it gets the rest, it'll be something – something we shared together –

SALLY: Larry!

She holds tightly to him. A big drum starts beating down the street and voices sing the 'Internationale.' LARRY starts up.

LARRY: (*Rising.*) Listen! They've started!

SALLY: No, Larry, don't go! Don't go! You're not fit to go –

LARRY: I'm all right.

SALLY: (*Following.*) Come back, Larry!

LARRY: (*At door.*) God! The fools!

SALLY: What's the matter?

LARRY: Look at 'em! Straight for the Labour Exchange. It's that damned agitator leading 'em –

SALLY: No, Larry, no! Stay here! (*She tries to restrain him.*)

LARRY: I've got to head them off! (*He goes out shouting.*) Hey! Where do you think you're going –

SALLY: Larry! Larry!

People are running down the street from L. to R.

MRS BULL: (*As she passes – shouting.*) Come on, Sally, you'll miss all the fun.

HELEN appears in the doorway. She is weeping.

HELEN: Can I speak to you, Sal?

SALLY: Come inside, Helen.

HELEN: (*Closes the door.*) Are they all out?

Drum and singing soften. Crowd noises almost cease.

SALLY: Yes, there's only me. I'm worried about Larry. He's gone with the procession, and I'm sure the lad's ill. Well, young woman, what is it? So you're crying too, are you?

HELEN: I know what you're going to say. You're going to call me names and say it's my fault –

SALLY: Well, I wasn't going to congratulate you, Helen, but I'm not going to call you names.

HELEN: I don't care what people say. I love Harry, and Harry loves me –

SALLY: That's the spirit, lass. That's the way to talk. What are you crying for, then, if you feel that way?

HELEN: They've turned me out.

SALLY: Well, they've turned our Harry out, too, so there's a pair of you.

HELEN: Harry? You mean we can't live here?

SALLY: No, Dad won't have you. You see, we're so respectable in North Street, though you wouldn't think it sometimes.

HELEN: But what are we going to do?

SALLY: Well, now you're asking. I'm sorry, Helen. Don't cry, lass. You're not the only one as doesn't know where to turn. I'll do what I can for you.

HELEN: Where's Harry?

SALLY: Harry? He's carrying a banner in the demonstration.

And he'll be finding a home in a prison cell if he's not careful.

HELEN: If only we could find a room somewhere. I don't care where it is. You see, I've got my job at mill and we could live on that if someone'd take us in. But nobody'll take us in, nobody decent, 'cause we're not married, and we've no money for that.

SALLY: I wonder how much longer us women'll take to learn that living and loving's all a damn swindle? Love's all right on the pictures, but love on the dole ain't quite same thing.

HELEN: I won't give up Harry.

Drum, singing and crowd die right out.

SALLY: I'm not asking you to. I reckon that's all part of swindle. We *can't* give 'em up, else wouldn't we have a bit o' sense and do without love same as we do without fine clothes, and motor-cars and champagne? Would we bring children into Hanky Park if we weren't blasted lunatics?

HELEN: If I'd only known this was going to happen – (*She breaks down a little.*)

SALLY: (*Taking both of HELEN's hands.*) Aw, go on, Helen. Look at the silver lining. When you're married they'll be bound to give you money at the workhouse. And Harry'll stand a better chance of getting a job when he's wed.

HELEN: Yes, but – we can't get married. We've no money for that.

SALLY: (*Producing some notes from her stocking.*) Let's see, is it seven and six? Or is that a dog licence? Marriage licences last for ever, though, so it's cheaper than keeping dogs. I know some marriages that wouldn't last long if you had to take out a new licence every year. (*She gives HELEN a ten-shilling note.*)

HELEN: Oh, Sally. (*About to return the note.*)

SALLY: Here, take it before I change me mind.

HELEN: Oh, thanks, Sally, thanks. (*She bursts into tears on SALLY's knee.*)

SALLY: That's all right. If you feel as grateful in ten years' time, you can pay me back. You know where the Registrar's office is – in Mill Street? And don't forget to take Harry with you.

HELEN: (*Tearfully.*) No. What shall I say?

SALLY: Say you want to get married, of course. They can't eat you.

HELEN: It's not what I'd planned. I always thought I'd be married in a church.

Crowd noises start again.

SALLY: Aw. Plans are like that. If we'd any sense, we wouldn't make any.

HELEN: Well, goodbye, Sally. And – you're awfully nice. (*She kisses SALLY impulsively.*)

SALLY: That's all right, Helen. And don't worry yourself. Things'll be all right. (*She looks through the window.*) I wish I knew what was going on down there.

HELEN: I'm going to see where Harry is.

She opens the door and goes out. She is hauled inside by SALLY. Crowd noise very loud.

MRS BULL: (*Heard shouting.*) Yah! You big bully! Call yourself a policeman? (*She appears outside window.*) You're a bloody Mussolini, that's what you are! (*Backing towards the doorway and shouting.*)

SALLY: What's the matter, Mrs Bull?

MRS BULL: Look at him, the big bluebottle! Look at the size of his feet! I'd stop indoors with feet like that.

MRS BULL comes just inside and stands against the door, holding it open.

Eh, Sal, it's a bad business. I said no good'd come out of this.

SALLY: Why, what's happened?

MRS BULL: You'd better follow that lad o' thine. He may want bailing out.

HELEN: I'm going to find where Harry is.

MRS BULL: (*Tries to stop HELEN, who breaks through and goes off.*) Stay where you are. Cops won't let you get past.

SALLY: Has Larry been taken up?

MRS BULL: Ee, I couldn't see who was taken. But there were hundreds of policemen waiting down by the Labour Exchange.

SALLY: You mean they're fighting?

MRS BULL: Fighting? It's a bloody war!

MRS HARDCASTLE: (*Entering.*) Oh, my God! I knew something'd happen. Our Harry and your Dad's there in the middle of it.

MRS BULL: I wish I was a man. I'd show 'em.

MRS HARDCASTLE: And there's no saying what'll happen with your Dad in his present state. He gets that fierce when his temper's roused –

SALLY: I'm going to see for myself – (*She goes to the door.*)

MRS HARDCASTLE: (*Pulls her back.*) No, Sal, come back. It's not safe! They're charging into the crowd.

SALLY: I must find Larry.

A police whistle blows. There is a rush of people along the street.

MRS HARDCASTLE: Come back, Sally.

MRS JIKE appears at the door carrying a bundle under her shawl. She is very excited.

MRS JIKE: Shut the door quick.

SALLY closes the door.

Hey, girls, look what I've got.

She produces a policeman's helmet from under her shawl.

Oh, what a time I've had! We rolled him in the mud and I danced on his stomach. It's as good as being in Whitechapel again.

MRS HARDCASTLE: Oh, Mrs Jike, what *have* you been doing?

MRS JIKE: (*Putting on the helmet and dancing a few steps.*) 'If you want to know the time, ask a policeman.'

SALLY: Shut up, you!

MRS HARDCASTLE: Did you see our Harry?

MRS JIKE: Your Harry? Can't say that I did. I saw the cops taking some blokes off to prison and there were some lying on the ground. But the fellow what owned this helmet won't forget Hanky Park in a hurry.

Horses' hoofs are heard coming nearer. Another police whistle blows three distinct blasts. MRS JIKE *goes to the oven, opens it, and puts the helmet inside, closing the door.* HARRY *appears, breathless, slamming the door behind him. He carries* LARRY'S *cap in his hand. His head is bleeding. Crowd swells as door opens, then softens.*

MRS HARDCASTLE: Harry! Are you all right?

HARRY: Yes, Ma, I'm all right. Listen! Mounted police. Gosh! They charged out with their truncheons –

MRS HARDCASTLE: Where's your father?

HARRY: I saw him get away.

HELEN *enters. Crowd swells up for this, then stops.*

But he knocked two of 'em out first. They'd got all their men behind the Labour Exchange, and they told us to go around the other street. But that leader fellow refused, and before you could think they were on us –

SALLY: Harry! Where did you get that cap?

HARRY: I picked it up – it's –

SALLY: Let me see it. (*Takes the cap.*) It's Larry's –

MRS BULL: (*Looking out of the window.*) Here's a cop!

HARRY *and* HELEN *rush over to the left and stand in the doorway. There is a knock on the street door and a* POLICEMAN *enters.* MRS DORBELL *appears outside.*

POLICEMAN: Are you Sally Hardcastle?

SALLY: Yes.

POLICEMAN: You're wanted down the street. There's someone asking for you.

SALLY *goes with the* POLICEMAN. MRS DORBELL *comes inside.* MRS BULL *goes up to the doorway and looks after* SALLY.

MRS DORBELL: Well, did you ever see anything like it?

MRS BULL: What's the matter, Mrs Dorbell?

MRS DORBELL: Larry Meath's copped it.

MRS HARDCASTLE: Have they taken him to the police station?

MRS DORBELL: Hospital, you mean. Cops said it were serious. I saw him go down like a ninepin.

HARRY: Aye, I saw it too, only I didn't want to say anything when Sal was here. Cops collared hold of Larry and laid him out. I saw 'em. And Larry wasn't doing anything, except he was trying to turn the men back.

MRS BULL: Huh! This'll mean six months for Larry Meath.

MRS JIKE: He'll have sent for Sally to bail him out.

MRS BULL: I'll go down for seven days before my man gets

another penny out of me. Let him go to prison. I've spent enough money on him.

MRS DORBELL: Thank God I'm a widow and all me family's growed up and out of me sight. Dammum! I wouldn't have the worrit of 'em again, not for a king's ransom.

MRS HARDCASTLE: (*Half rising.*) You're sure your Dad's all right, Harry?

HARRY: I tell you I saw him get away. But they got Larry, all right. I couldn't get near him to help, though I tried. But I got his cap.

MRS BULL: Fine lot o' good that was!

MRS HARDCASTLE: Well, our Sally's got no money to bail him out.

Crowd noise heard faintly. HARRY *goes to the window.*

Can you see your father, Harry?

HARRY: (*Goes up towards the door.*) No, but there's a crowd on the street corner. Ay, Father's there – and Sally, too.

The ambulance bell is heard. The women crowd to the door. MRS HARDCASTLE *remains inside.*

MRS DORBELL: Let's have a look. (*She goes to the window and looks out.*)

MRS BULL: Look, there's the ambulance!

HARRY: (*At the window.*) Here's Dad, with Sally. They're coming now. Something's happened, Ma. They've got an ambulance.

A POLICEMAN *outside holds back the inquisitive* CROWD. MR HARDCASTLE *appears with* SALLY *leaning on his arm. She is carrying* LARRY'S *cap clasped to her breast.* MR HARDCASTLE *brings her inside and she sits at the table, staring in front of her. The door remains open.*

MRS HARDCASTLE: Oh, Sal! What is it, Sal?

HARDCASTLE: Leave her be, Ma.

MRS HARDCASTLE: What's happened?

HARDCASTLE: It's Larry – he's dead.

SALLY: Larry –

HARDCASTLE: Don't, Sal, don't!

SALLY: Well, that's put paid to that –

A silence creeps into the room. The crowd on the pavement stare through the open doorway.

Curtain

Scene 2

The same, six months later. Late afternoon.

MRS BULL, MRS DORBELL *and* MRS JIKE *are sitting round the table, on which is a bottle and three cups.* MRS HARDCASTLE *is seated on the sofa. The trio sing 'The More We Are Together' listlessly and untunefully.* MRS HARDCASTLE *sobs loudly and they finish abruptly.*

MRS DORBELL: More tears!

MRS BULL: Never in all me life did I see such a one as thee for blubbering. Lordy, what ails thee now?

MRS HARDCASTLE: What'll become of her? Oh, whatever'll become of her?

MRS BULL: Yah, ain't that just the way o' the world, eh? Her daughter gets a settlement made on her and then her Ma wonders what's gunna become of her.

MRS JIKE: (*Speaking through.*) Te, he! That's just it!

MRS BULL: Yah, y' don't deserve nothing, y' don't. Why don't you ask what's gunna become o' all o' us what's left in Hanky Park?

MRS DORBELL: Bah! I reckon she might have gone farther an' fared worse.

MRS HARDCASTLE: It's him. He'll murder her if he ever finds out. I know her father – an' it's such a disgrace! Everybody'll be talking – I'm feared.

MRS DORBELL: Talk's cheap enough. 'Ave another drop, Mrs Jike?

MRS JIKE: Thank you. I don't mind if I do.

She pours for herself. MRS BULL *puts her cup on the table, and* MRS JIKE *pours for her too.* MRS BULL *then goes and sits on the chair by the sink.*

'Ave a drop, Mrs Hardcastle. It'll cheer you up.

MRS HARDCASTLE: No, I don't want any.

MRS JIKE: Strike me pink! You're a nice one to give a little party. And me trying to be cheerful for you. Drink up, gels. While you've got it, enjoy it, says I. If it don't go one way, it'll go another.

She laughs and nudges MRS DORBELL.

MRS BULL: I dunno. Some folks don't know when they *are* well off. See here, Mrs Hardcastle, she'll take no hurt. Sally ain't that kind. She'd have been a sight worse off hangin' about here doin' nothing but thinking. If you want to know, it was *me* as hinted to Sam Grundy that she'd take no hurt if she went away for a while.

MRS HARDCASTLE: You?

MRS JIKE: Ee, Mrs Bull!

MRS BULL: And why not? Three or four months at that there place of his in Wales, with only nice weather in front of her – why, woman, she'll be new-made over again. All that she wants is something to make her forget. Everlasting thinking about that Larry Meath – It's more than flesh and blood can stand. Use your head, woman, use your head.

MRS HARDCASTLE: There's the other thing. Her and Mr Grundy. I don't like it – it's – it's – we've always been respectable.

MRS BULL *takes a drink.*

And now all the neighbours are talking.

MRS BULL: Let 'em talk. While they're talking about you they're leaving other folks be. Your Sally's had a bellyful of trouble, yes, a proper bellyful. First her dad gets out of work, and then her brother; then the fellow she's going

to marry dies. If your Sal had gone on brooding the way she was, she'd have done what poor soul did in the next street yesterday. Guardians told him he'd have to give five shillings to his people what had come under the Means Test, and him married with a wife and family of his own. And what did *he* do? Cut his throat and jumped through bedroom winder, poor soul. You think of that an' be cheerful.

MRS HARDCASTLE: Hush! She's here now.

SALLY *comes in from the street. She is better dressed than when we saw her before. She carries three or four small neat parcels. She enters with studied unconcern and greets the company airily. Her manner has hardened.*

SALLY: Hello, Mrs Bull! And how's Mrs Jike and Mrs Dorbell? Having a good time?

MRS DORBELL: Ah, well, perhaps I'd better be going. (*She rises.*)

SALLY: You've no need to go. My complaint isn't catching, as far as I know. I suppose the whole street knows me business by this time. Well, I ain't ashamed. (*She puts the parcels on the sofa and sits on the lower end.*)

MRS BULL: You'd be a damned fool if you was. Ay, lass, when you get as old as me you'll have learned that there ain't nothing worth worrying your head about except where next meal's coming from. Be God, you will!

MRS HARDCASTLE: Where've you been, Sally?

SALLY: I've been to order a taxi to take me to the station.

MRS HARDCASTLE: Taxi?

MRS DORBELL: Eee, lass! Taxi in North Street!

MRS JIKE: Sounds real wicked, don't it? A motor-car!

MRS HARDCASTLE: (*Shocked.*) You mean it's coming here for you, in front of all the neighbours? (*She rises.*)

SALLY: Well, why not?

MRS HARDCASTLE: Have you no feeling for my shame?

SALLY: (*Rises.*) *Your* shame, Ma. I like that. Thought it was *my* shame that all the trouble was about.

MRS HARDCASTLE: Oh, Sal, what's changed you so?

SALLY: Can't be worse than it is. It seems to me that things always turn out different to what you expect. I thought I'd have been married by now. Huh!

MRS DORBELL: Married? You ain't missed much missing that.

MRS JIKE: Getting married's like a bloke with a bald head. There's no parting.

SALLY: Well, it ain't for me now. I can't have what I wanted, so I've took next best thing. Sick and tired I am of slugging and seeing nothing for it. Never had a holiday in my life, I ain't. But I know what money means now. He's got it and by God I'll make him pay!

MRS JIKE *sniggers audibly.* MRS DORBELL *joins in.*

MRS DORBELL: Are you sure Sam Grundy's made settlement fair and proper? There's nothing like having the money in your own name.

MRS BULL: Tell the old scut to mind her own business, Sal.

MRS DORBELL *glares at* MRS BULL.

SALLY: I've seen to that. He's stinking with brass and he's as daft as the rest of his kind. Ach! What fools they look slobbering around you. (*She opens her handbag.*) But there was nothing doing until I got me own way. He can chuck me over soon as he's a mind to now. (*She hands a one-pound note to her mother.*) Here, Ma, take it. It won't be the last, neither.

MRS HARDCASTLE: N-no, lass, I daren't! What would your father say?

SALLY: Oh, don't *you* start! I'll get enough lip from Dad when he comes in, I reckon. (*She looks at her gold wristwatch.*) Well, me train's at five-forty-five and taxi'll be here soon. I'd best get my things. (*She gathers up her parcels and goes out by the door on the left.*)

MRS HARDCASTLE: Oo, I don't know what's come over her. She ain't the same girl.

MRS BULL: You're right. She ain't the same girl since Larry Meath died. And a good job, too, or she'd have followed him to an early grave.

MRS JIKE: That would be a bit of ready money for you – laying her out.

MRS DORBELL: If I had my time over again I'd never get wed. Marriage, yaa! You get wed for love and find you've let yourself in for a seven-day-a-week job with no pay.

MRS JIKE: (*Who has been drinking diligently, fills the three cups.*) Come on, gels! Let's be happy while we can. You're a long time dead.

They begin to sing, off key, 'For you're here and I'm here, so what do we care,' etc. The door opens and HARDCASTLE *appears. The music stops. He glares at the three women. They rise uncomfortably.* MRS HARDCASTLE *also rises.*

HARDCASTLE: Get out of here!

MRS DORBELL: Here, here –?

HARDCASTLE: You heard me. Get out!

MRS DORBELL: Ho! Certainly. (*She hastily finishes her drink.*) I've no wish to stay where I'm not wanted. (*She crosses to the door.*) Are you coming, Mrs Bull?

MRS BULL: (*Finishes her drink.*) Come on, Mrs Jike. We're not wanted here.

They start for the door.

HARDCASTLE: (*Pointing to the bottle on the table.*) And take that stuff with you!

MRS BULL *reaches for the bottle, but* MRS JIKE *is too quick for her. The three go out.* HARDCASTLE *shuts the door. His wife watches him fearfully. He leans with one hand against the fireplace, breathing heavily and gazing into the fire.*

MRS HARDCASTLE: You didn't get that job, then, Henery?

HARDCASTLE: (*Muttering.*) Job? Christ!

MRS HARDCASTLE: (*Placing a chair for* HARDCASTLE.) You're tired, Henery. Sit down.

HARDCASTLE *sits.* MRS HARDCASTLE *lights the light. She then crosses* R. *and lowers the blind.*

HARDCASTLE: Where's our Sal?

MRS HARDCASTLE: She's upstairs. Why?

HARDCASTLE: I've been hearing strange tales, that's why.

MRS HARDCASTLE: Ah, folk don't know what they're saying.

HARDCASTLE: There's something queer going on here, and by God I mean to find out.

MRS HARDCASTLE: Now, Henery, don't get in a temper. Don't, please –

SALLY *comes in. She is very neatly dressed for her departure and carries a small leather suitcase. She crosses to head of the sofa, where she deposits her jacket and puts the case on the floor above the sofa, then turns and faces her father.*

SALLY: (*After a pause.*) Well?

HARDCASTLE: What's these tales I'm hearing about you and Sam Grundy?

SALLY: Well? What about it?

HARDCASTLE: Why –! (*Rising slowly.*) You brazen slut! Have you got cheek to stand there and tell me it's true?

SALLY: Yes, I have.

MRS HARDCASTLE: (*Above the table.*) Nay, Sally, lass, don't –

SALLY: It's true, Mother, and I don't care who knows it. Aye, and I'll tell you something else. It's sick I am of codging old clothes to try and make them look like something. And sick I am of working week after week and seeing nothing for it. I'm sick of never having anything but what's been in pawnshops and crawling with vermin – Oh, I'm sick of the sight of Hanky Park and everybody in it –

MRS HARDCASTLE: Sally!

HARDCASTLE: So you'd go whoring and make respectable folk like me and your Ma the talk of the neighbourhood, eh? Damn you! You ain't fit to be my daughter!

SALLY: Yaa, who cares what folk say? There's none I know as wouldn't swap places with me if they had the chance. You'd have me wed, would you? Then tell me where's the fellow around here can afford it. Them as *is* working ain't able to keep themselves, never mind a wife. Look at yourself – and look at our Harry! On workhouse relief and ain't even got a bed as he can call his own. I suppose I'd be fit to call your daughter if I was like that with a tribe of kids at me skirts. Well, can you get our Harry a job? No, but I can. Yes, me. I've got influence now – but I'm not respectable.

HARDCASTLE: God! I'd rather see you lying dead at my feet!

SALLY: Dead? Dead, did you say? (*She laughs.*) Aren't we all dead, all of us in Hanky Park –

HARDCASTLE: (*Pointing to the door.*) Get out! Get out before I kill you!

SALLY: (*Defiantly.*) Right! And I can do that, too. (*She crosses to the sofa, picks up her jacket and puts it on.*) You kicked our Harry out because he got married and you're kicking me out because I ain't. You'd have me like all the rest of the women, working themselves to death and getting nothing for it. Look at Mother! Look at her! (*Pointing.*) Well, there ain't a man breathing, now Larry's gone, who can get me like *that* – for him!

HARDCASTLE: (*Rushing at her.*) Aach! You brazen bitch! Take that! (*He strikes her and she falls across the sofa.*) Keep your dirty lying tongue off your mother, do you hear?

SALLY lies where she has fallen, sobbing.

MRS HARDCASTLE: Eh, Father, Father, look what you've done to the lass. (*She sits above SALLY and gathers SALLY's head on her knees.*)

HARDCASTLE: Come away from her. Come away from her!

MRS HARDCASTLE: Nay, she didn't mean any harm. Don't cry, lass. You neither of you know what you're saying when you get that way.

HARDCASTLE: Haven't I worked all me life, body and soul, to keep a home for her? Haven't I kept myself respectable for her, when God knows I've been near driven to drink with things? And now me own daughter tells me she's a whore – Ay, and proud of it, too!

MRS HARDCASTLE: Lad, she's only young – she's only young. Where should we have been all these months if it hadn't been for our Sally? It's her money we've been living on since they knocked you off dole, and well you know it.

HARDCASTLE: Ay, and well I know it! And well I know I mean to be boss in me own house.

MRS HARDCASTLE: But the money –?

HARDCASTLE: To hell with money! She's made her own bed, she must lie in it.

MRS HARDCASTLE: It's your own bed you're making, Henry Hardcastle, when you drive our Sally out. Your bed and mine. I'm thinking it won't be that easy to lie on.

HARDCASTLE: (*Sinks into the chair at the table.*) Leave me be! Leave me be! I'm sick of hearing you! Oh, God, give me some work! Give me some work –!

He groans and his head falls on the table. There is a sudden impatient knock at the street door. SALLY sits up and dries her eyes. MRS HARDCASTLE opens the door.

HARRY: (*Outside.*) It's Helen, Ma. She's took bad. She wants Mrs Bull.

SALLY: Come in, Harry. I've something to say to you.

HARRY: It's Helen. She's going to have a baby – she wants Mrs Bull to come 'round as soon as she can. Do something, Sal! – Sal, do something!

SALLY: So it's come, has it? Another poor devil for Hanky Park. You might have saved yourself the trouble, lad. (*She rises and opens her purse.*) Here, take this – you'll be needing it. (*She gives him some notes.*)

HARRY: Eh, Sal! Thanks! But where did you get it?

SALLY: Never mind. And take this as well. (*She hands him an envelope.*) And here's another for Dad. (*She crosses and puts another on the table near her father's hand.*) I've been keeping it as a surprise for you. You take these letters to the East City Bus Offices and give them to Mr Moreland. There'll be a job for each of you. But remember, say nothing to nobody how you got it. And give the letters to nobody but Mr Moreland.

HARRY: Let's see. That's manager, Mr Moreland – him as Sam Grundy knows –

MRS HARDCASTLE: Hush – (*Indicating HARDCASTLE.*)

HARRY: (*Smiling.*) All right! Gosh, can you imagine what Helen'll say? Oh, ta, Sal – a job – I've got a job – You don't know what it means to me – (*He is hysterical.*) I – Oh, thanks!

He rushes out to hide his tears. MRS HARDCASTLE closes the door.

SALLY: I'm sorry, Dad – about all this. Things are different now to what you've been used to, and you've got to face things as they are, not as you'd like them to be. We all want a fresh start – that's what Larry said. Well, there's no starting fresh in Hanky Park, and I'm getting out, quickest road.

HARDCASTLE stares brokenly before him. SALLY pulls the letter a little nearer to his hand.

Maybe that'll be a good job – this'll get you a few smokes. (*She puts some small change on the table.*) Goodbye, Ma, and don't worry.

She goes up to her mother and they embrace. A taxi-horn is heard outside.

MRS DORBELL: (*Pushes open the door and enters.*) Hey! Here's the taxi come for your Sally.

There is an excited, talkative crowd in the darkness outside. SALLY stands for a moment hoping her father will turn his head. She then picks up her bag, still looking towards her father. She bites her lip, then drawing herself up proudly, turns and marches out to the taxi. Laughter and jeering are heard, then the discordant singing of 'Here Comes the Bride.' The taxi drives away and the noise dies down. MRS HARDCASTLE closes the door and comes over to the table behind her husband.

MRS HARDCASTLE: Don't take on so, Henry. You've got a job now. That's something to be thankful for. Don't be hard on the lass. There's no harm in her, she's only young and self-willed – And she's your own daughter, Henery –

HARDCASTLE: (*An angry, beaten man.*) Oh, God, I've done me best! I've done me best, haven't I?

MRS HARDCASTLE turns and takes the teapot. She goes to the kettle on the fire.

3.4 $E=mc^2$ (1947)

A Living Newspaper about the Atomic Age

HALLIE FLANAGAN DAVIS
(ASSISTED BY SYLVIA GASSEL AND DAY TUTTLE)

Hallie Flanagan Davis (born Ferguson) (1889–1969) was an American playwright, director, producer and teacher. She was a key figure in the development of the 'Living Newspaper' theatrical form, a component to the work of the Federal Theatre Project (FTP) in the USA during the 1930s. The FTP, part of Franklin D. Roosevelt's government-funded 'Works Progress Administration', sought to create political, socially relevant and provocative theatre by unemployed theatre workers, most specifically for new audiences. With the Living Newspaper – originally conceived in Russia – the FTP was influenced by Marxist-inspired experimental theatre practitioners such as Vsevolod Meyerhold and Erwin Piscator. Working against the dominant realistic and naturalistic forms of the day, the Living Newspaper integrated multimedia, agitprop and 'fact' derived from documentary sources. Written nearly a decade after the forced closure of the FTP, $E=mc^2$ considers the paradoxical challenges that the atomic age brought to the world.

The people in the scenes
Characters who appear throughout the play
STAGE MANAGER
PROFESSOR
ATOM
CLIO
HENRY

(Rest of characters may be played by 20 people, each playing several parts)

Act 1
Wall
MAN
STAGE MANAGER

Street
NEWSBOY
POLICEMAN
1ST GIRL
2ND GIRL
1ST LADY
2ND LADY

Camp
1ST SOLDIER
2ND SOLDIER
3RD SOLDIER

Nightclub
MAN
WOMAN

Telephone
YOUNG WIFE

Street
NEWSBOY
POLICEMAN
TWO KIDS
FANATIC
1ST OFFICER
2ND OFFICER
1ST HOKINSON WOMAN
2ND HOKINSON WOMAN

Subway
PEOPLE FROM THE STREET SCENE

Overseas
POW
SERGEANT
BRITISH COLONEL
BRITISH GENERAL

Henry's home
HENRY
FATHER
MOTHER
RADIO VOICES

British Cabinet
PRIME MINISTER
FRANCIS LIGHTFOOT
SECRETARY OF WAR
LORD HIGH CHANCELLOR and other CABINET MEMBERS

Scientists in house
D'OLIER
RIDENOUR
CONDON
STAGE MANAGER

Atom
ATOM
STAGE MANAGER
PROFESSOR EMERSON

Chain reaction (ballet)
ATOM

History lesson
ATOM
CLIO
HENRY
LEUCIPPUS
DEMOCRITUS
EPICURUS

VOICES OF WALT WHITMAN AND LUCRETIUS

White House
PRESIDENT ROOSEVELT
SECRETARY OF WAR STIMSON

Los Alamos
WORKERS AT LOS ALAMOS
STAGE MANAGER
STIMSON
UNDER-SECRETARY OF NAVY BARD

Act 2
Return from Oak Ridge
ATOM

Atomic perfume
GIRL
MEN

Atomic commutation
MAN
WIFE

Atomic laundry service
WIFE
LAUNDRYMAN

Atomic corn
FARMER
FARMER'S WIFE

House lights
STAGE MANAGER
PROFESSOR

Ivory tower
ATOM
COLLEGE MEN AND WOMEN

Off to Washington
ATOM
HENRY

Senate Committee Chamber
STAGE MANAGER
ATOM
HENRY
CLIO
ATTENDANT
SENATOR MCMAHON
LILIENTHAL
SENATOR MCKELLAR
HICKENLOOPER
AGNES WATERS

Other people at Trial including ARMY, POLITICIAN, and
SCIENTIST
PHOTOGRAPHER

Alphabet

A, B, C, D, E, F

Newsreel

STAGE MANAGER

ATOM

CLIO

HENRY

Honky tonk

Watchers:

ATOM

CLIO

HENRY

ARMY

NAVY

BUSINESS MAN

SCIENTIST

POLITICIAN

POWER

Uranium hunt (ballet and speaking chorus)

Crossroads

ARMY

NAVY

BUSINESSMAN

SCIENTIST

POLITICIAN

ATOM

CLIO

HENRY

STRANGER

Counter-attack center

STAGE MANAGER

BRIGADIER

CAPTAIN BRIGGS

COL. PEABODY

COL. SPARKS

PRESIDENT OF THE UNITED STATES

FOUR-STAR GENERAL

Act I

The overture should epitomize the play. It should be modern, powerful, dissonant. It has two dominant themes which are used all through the play, suggesting musically the two sides of the atom. Think, in imagining how one of these motifs should sound, of: 'A blur of energy whirling in a distant orbit around the nuclear sun.' For this same motif, think of 'the energy acquired by one electron falling through an electric field of one million volts.'

For the other motif, think of the elements progressing from hydrogen 'upward on a new level of mathematical law, order and complexity.' Then there are also sounds throughout the play to be incorporated in the score: A high eerie whistling which is air being forced out after it is used to cool the atomic pile; the pounding of the gavel in the British Cabinet scene, or in Washington; explosions; sounds of war. The musical score is as important as the light score.

The play is in two parts, each one of which is played continuously.

The Curtain rises on a scene which contains the basic elements to be used throughout the play. Against space a wall, which starts at extreme upstage Right and extends downstage toward Left in a diagonal, foreshortened. The wall is made up of blocks, irregular in size and shape, which are removable and which later become *the various things called for – a background for the President's study, a city street, etc. It is from one of the blocks that* ATOM *first speaks. The wall can be removed entirely or in segments; it can be used as a screen for projections, or it can be varied as to angles. There may be a ramp at a sharp angle with the wall going off down Right. There may be other blocks as needed.*

At rise: The stage is dark with a path of light cutting across along by the wall.

A MAN *is seen coming from far up Right along the wall. As* THE MAN *reaches about center stage the music reaches maximum – discordant and terrifying – then ends on a crash.* THE MAN, *who should register just as man and not Japanese, looks back, flings up his hands in a grotesque position so that his shadow is elongated on the wall in this strange and terrifying posture. He falls to the ground.*

His shadow remains on the wall as the scene blacks out. the STAGE MANAGER *comes forward.*

STAGE MANAGER: On August 6, 1945, at Hiroshima, Japan, the shadow of a human being was permanently etched on a wall. He was walking 7,890 feet from the explosion of a primitive atom bomb. The shadow, symbol of man's terrible power to destroy himself, is still on that wall – and it falls like an ominous cloud across our world. (*Music up, changing to staccato excitement under the next words.*) All over the world during the next few days, people were horrified, people were incredulous, and – surprising as it may seem – people were indifferent. In our own country – each person interpreted the bomb only as it affected his own life. We were so far away, felt so invulnerable that the bomb hardly caused a ripple –

Lights up on a city street. The shadow of the preceding scene is still on the wall, but dimly. The wall seems now to form the background of the street. People enter from up Right, go down along the wall and turn the corner Left; or they enter from up Left, follow the wall, go off up Right. The people coming and going include SOLDIERS, SAILORS, CIVILIANS, an occasional WAC or WAVE, BOBBYSOXERS, KIDS, and HELEN HOKINSON WOMEN. There is a POLICEMAN on the corner down Left and a newsstand up Right. Like all properties in similar scenes throughout the play, the papers on the stand are enlarged and one sees: 'ATOM' or 'BOMB' with an occasional 'Wall Street Journal' on which we can see 'WALL' and 'STREET.' People snatch at papers and fling down money as they rush past. This street scene is a background for the spot scenes down Right and Left and it laces these scenes together.

NEWSBOY: *Extra! – Extra!* Read all about it! Whole Japanese city wiped out! One bomb! – 100,000 people!

1ST GIRL: Why, I haven't had a date since he was sent overseas –

2ND GIRL: *Men!* Don't even *mention* them to me!

OLD LADY: (*To* POLICEMAN). I think the explosion of that bomb is just awful. Why, all those people! They didn't even know –

POLICEMAN: Yeah, terrible thing. I read it, too, lady. Terrible –

OLD LADY: But someone ought to do something – What if they dropped one on us?

POLICEMAN: Forget it. Put your mind on the Dodgers' batting average.

Dim off. Spot up on THREE MARINES. They have fieldpacks and rifles, but two are stretched out, resting and smoking. One is excited.

1ST MARINE: I'm tellin' ya! One B-29 carried the thing and it wiped out the whole damned city.

2ND MARINE: Oh, goody, now I can throw away my rifle.

1ST MARINE: Well, it was the President of the United States talking.

3RD MARINE: Yeah, Tokyo Rose probably has a boyfriend who can imitate President Truman.

1ST MARINE: Knock off, I'm givin' ya the word! I heard it myself. And the CO says it's straight, too.

2ND MARINE: This outfit is so damned fouled up that if we *have* got them automatic bombs –

1ST MARINE: *Atom* bombs.

2ND MARINE: All right, atom bombs. If we have got 'em, the brass will probably make a mistake and drop 'em on *us*.

3RD MARINE: That would be the smartest thing they ever did. Put us out of our misery.

1ST MARINE: OK, OK. But we've got the bomb and it's going to end the war damn quick.

3RD MARINE: If I could get out of this camp, I wouldn't mind being hit by one of them atom bombs.

Blackout.

Spot up on MAN and GIRL drinking in a swanky nightclub. Both are high. Music under scene.

MAN: Honest to God, I swear it's the truth.

GIRL: Oh, Morty, how terrif!

MAN: It's the biggest damn thing that ever went off.

GIRL: (*Giggling.*) Oh, isn't that just terrif!

MAN: It's just a little teeny thing no bigger than this. Jus' the littles' thing.

GIRL: But darling, you said it was a great *big* thing!

MAN: Lishen – if you'd ever lishen – to me. I said it was the littles' thing – no bigger than that! But I said it was the biggest, the biggest – fact! That's it – the littlest *thing* but the biggest *fact* of – history –

GIRL: Morty, you're terrif!

MAN and GIRL embrace. Dim off and up on street.

NEWSBOY: Extra! Extra! All about the bomb.

1ST KID: I'm making like a atom bomb. Put-put-put-put – booooommm!

2ND KID: Aw, that ain't right. There ain't no put-put-put-put – to that.

1ST KID: Put-put-put-put – *boom* – you're gone!

2ND KID: What d'you mean, I'm gone?

1ST KID: I just atomized you. (*They go out.*)

Dim off. Spot up on YOUNG WOMAN at telephone.

YOUNG WIFE: Can you believe it, Mom? – That the war's over? Yes, it was terrible about that bomb – but all I could think of was he'd be coming home. Of course he has enough points, anyway – two and a half years – and now that the war's over, they *can't* hold him. – Mom, what? – Oh, she's fine. Cold's all gone. Petey had prickly heat this morning but it's all gone, too – *Of* course Suzy'll recognize him. All she does is play daddy-coming-home – what? (*She laughs.*) Well, of course Petey won't, but *he'll* recognize Petey. Looks just like him. (*Bell rings offstage.*) Hey, wait a minute, Mom, someone at the door.

A hand reaches in a telegram and a VOICE says:

VOICE: War Department, Ma'am.

YOUNG WIFE stands looking at telegram; and we can hear the mother's voice at the other end of the wire saying: 'What is it? – What is it?' as the scene blacks out.

Lights and Sound up on street. RELIGIOUS FANATIC is giving out leaflets. None of the passers-by takes any.

FANATIC: The end of the World! – The end of the World!

NEWSBOY: Read all about it – *Extra! – Extra!* – Hiroshima in ruins! First atom bomb! – Read all about it –

1ST OFFICER: (*As they cross.*) – not at all. I only object to the Smythe Report on Atomic Energy – putting top military secrets in civilians' hands – these scientists!

2ND OFFICER: But scientists controlled by *us*, don't you think?

1ST HELEN HOKINSON WOMAN: (*As they cross.*) Of course, you know Timothy's been studying physics for years. I'm being perfectly objective, but I can't help but feel that he's played a large part in all this. So this is what Timothy has been talking about! – Why, he prophesied the whole thing!

2ND HOKINSON WOMAN: Well, the paper doesn't mention Timothy. The paper only says –

1ST HOKINSON WOMAN: Of course not – it's a secret! It's a military secret! – You don't think that Timothy and I would *break* the *blockade!* –

Spot up on imaginary subway, a row of people – the same ones we have seen in the street – holding onto imaginary straps and swaying back and forth. All are reading 'Extras,' again enlarged and out of scale. You see no faces to start with, merely the headlines of the papers: ATOM – ATOM – ATOM – ATOM. The noise is grinding and violent. Over the paper a MAN's face becomes visible for a moment, talking to his companion:

1ST MAN: Two hours standing in line for those damn nylons – two – whole – hours! –

1ST GIRL: An' I said he'd never try that on *me* but once an' he said, So what? an' I said –

2ND GIRL: *What* didja say?

2ND MAN: Lissen, I'd trade all my A coupons for a nice, thick, juicy steak. Why, they're so mixed up down in Washington on this food control stuff, they don't know from nothing, not from – nothing! – Why, a man – told – me – that –

3RD GIRL's face visible as she uses lipstick.

3RD GIRL: Say, what's a natum?

3RD MAN: (*Invisible behind newspaper.*) What's a natum?

3RD GIRL: What's a natum?

Car gives violent lurch, people begin to punch and shove each other in their attempt to get out at station. Most of them drop papers as they go out, trampling on them.

FANATIC: (*Entering subway car.*) 'The End of the World!' – (*FANATIC stops, picks up newspaper, and looks at headlines. The headline registers. In a different tone.*) The end of the world.

RADIO VOICE: (*Repeats the above under next three speakers.*)

Blackout – pinpoint of Light on FANATIC's face.

STAGE MANAGER: (*Reappearing.*) All over the world during those later summer months of 1945, the atom exploded in the minds of men – In a German prison camp –.

Spot up on a prisoner of war camp in Germany, an American SERGEANT with one of the 'Stars and Stripes' in his hand.

POW: Ach, nein, es ist nicht wahr.

SERGEANT: You don't believe it, huh? Well, it says so here. Them Banzai monkeys is done for and serves 'em right, too.

POW: Nicht wahr! Ich glaube es nicht. Es ist nur Americanische Propaganda –

Dim off.

STAGE MANAGER: In an officers' club in London –

Spot up on British military MEN in London Club.

COLONEL: (*Bitterly.*) It had to be the Americans.

GENERAL: We can be thankful for that.

COLONEL: I'm not thankful. Just because they can pick the brains of the world, just because they have unlimited money and unlimited means and unlimited gall –

GENERAL: And unlimited mechanical skill, too, don't forget that –

COLONEL: But that it had to be the Americans! (*Plaintively.*) Oh, *dammit!*

Blackout.

In the darkness we hear French, Italian and Russian voices with pertinent words in various languages rising – 'Atom Bomb' – 'American Propaganda' – 'Atom Bomb.'

STAGE MANAGER: Yet in every country in the world certain people were not uncomprehending, not incredulous and not indifferent. For they had seen, each in his own way, this thing approaching for a long time.

Spot up on a BOY listening to the radio. His FATHER is reading 'Time'; his MOTHER is reading 'Life'; and the BOY is reading 'Amazing Stories.' Cover of each magazine at opening of scene is enormous and at angles covering faces so that you see 'TIME,' 'LIFE,' and 'AMAZING.'

RADIO VOICE: (*Over the deep power-hum of a generator in the background of the broadcast, apparently from a plane.*) 97346– 97346 – Coming in over Detroit – Visibility limited – audibility limited – 97346 – 97346 –

2ND RADIO VOICE: It's a code! – They're getting the atom ray focussed! – It's 'Atomic Andy!' – Listen! –

MOTHER: (*To Father.*) For Heaven's sake, can't you make him turn off that terrible soap-opera drivel about atom-smashers?

The roar of the motor is increasing! – The planes circling above us are no ordinary planes!

2ND RADIO VOICE:

Check your bearings!
Check your bearings!
Check observatory time.
Check barometric pressure.

2ND RADIO VOICE:

Death ray attack imminent. Atomic Andy wards off the death-ray!

1ST RADIO VOICE:

The planes are circling low! Through the curving space –

FATHER: (*Behind ·'Time'.*) Henry, you hear your mother.

HENRY:

I'll turn it real low.

FATHER:

Henry, either turn it off or put down that magazine! No human mind can do two things at once.

HENRY:

Atomic Andy can.

MOTHER:

oh, for Heaven's sakes!

FATHER:

if you want to read, the house is full of good books – Dickens, Thackeray –

HENRY:

Aw, Dad –

FATHER:

Listen, Henry, you don't *believe* that stuff?

HENRY:

You just don't understand it.

FATHER:

Curving space! – Henry!

HENRY:

Well, space *is* curved, Dad –

FATHER:

You'll be telling me next that parallel lines meet!

HENRY:

But parallel lines *do* meet, Dad! Why, Atomic Andy *proved* just last week that –

Blackout: as the sound of the planes continues.

STAGE MANAGER: Parents and teachers were amused by boys like Henry, but as it turns out, those boys were really living in a world closer to reality than ours. The theatre, too, has its moments of prophecy. In a play produced by the Theatre Guild almost twenty years ago –

The STAGE MANAGER is interrupted by a clamor of VOICES and the banging of a gavel. Lights up on a Cabinet Council Room in London. We see the backs of several men and the faces of the PRIME MINISTER and a young man (FRANCES LIGHTFOOT), obviously not a Cabinet Minister.

PRIME MINISTER: Gentlemen of the British Cabinet: the matter we have to consider is so grave and confidential that I have not thought fit to give to any outside person any intimation of its nature. Yet you have noticed that there is a stranger present – Francis Lightfoot: his name and achievement as a physicist are familiar to every reader of the daily press. Gentlemen, Mr Lightfoot. Francis, the British Cabinet.

FRANCIS LIGHTFOOT: Gentlemen: my investigation aims at solving the old riddle: 'What is E – or energy?' So far as we know – we really know nothing – all energy resolves itself into what's popularly known as electricity. Now, electricity manifests itself in the perpetual dance of entities known as negative electrons round a positively charged nucleus. Such groups are, in fact, infinitesimally small solar systems, and of the different combinations of these systems – all matter is – as far as we know – made up.

SECRETARY OF WAR: Now look here, young man. Be a good feller: cut the cackle an' come to the hosses!

FRANCIS LIGHTFOOT: Well, if you must – gentlemen! (*The table grows silent.*) Gentlemen: I can control the energy – in the atom.

SECRETARY OF WAR: I beg your pardon. You said –?

LORD HIGH CHANCELLOR: What does that mean?

FRANCIS LIGHTFOOT: It means that the present, all that you're accustomed to call civilization, is – is relegated at last to its proper place as the confused remembrance of an evil dream. Yesterday, man was a slave; today, he's free! – Matter – obeys him.

LORD HIGH CHANCELLOR: How, for instance, does this affect my particular interest – the Law?

FRANCIS LIGHTFOOT: (*A little wearily.*) Law – well, of course, your system of law ceases to exist. Just as what we call money will cease to exist – just as armies and navies will be obsolete.

LORD HIGH CHANCELLOR: Come now, talk sense, young man, talk sense!

FRANCIS LIGHTFOOT: I *am* talking sense! – It is perfectly simple: a man touches a spring: Not only he, but his house, his street, London itself – disappears – is blown up. Today I put into your hands power *over* matter; the power of a – of a *god*, to slay and to make alive. It means food, shelter, abundance, for everyone. (*Quietly exhausted.*) That's what it means, gentlemen – that's what my discovery means! – Now I'm going to leave you to organize. That's your job: I'll come back, a week from today. Have your plans ready. (*LIGHTFOOT leaves.*)

Blackout. The STAGE MANAGER reappears. Sometimes visible and sometimes a voice, he is in charge of all dramatic effects throughout the show. He can call for actors or disperse them. He can call for maps, lights, etc. He is an artist in his own field, but like all really first-rate artists today, he knows that art takes cognizance of science, tries to understand it and learn from it.

STAGE MANAGER: Of course no one dreamed that when 'Wings Over Europe' (by Maurice Browne and Robert Nichols) was produced in 1928 that in the summer of 1945 the fantasy would have become reality. You see, my friends, from earliest times philosophers and poets have concerned themselves more than so-called 'practical' people with the nature of the universe. Plato, Aristotle, Socrates, Shelley, H. G. Wells – all of these men and many more found a way of projecting themselves into the future. But it is easy for 'practical' people to regard the philosopher and the artist as dreamers. And even to the scientist, 'practical' people give, for the most part, polite inattention. Up until this war you know, we paid little attention to science. We'd heard of the atom – but for the most part we didn't think of it as making the possible difference between life and death. After the bomb exploded, however, we *had* to listen to the scientists. And it happens that some of them

are here tonight. (*Looks out into audience.*) Mr. D'Olier, I believe you were chairman of the Strategic Bombing Survey established as far back as 1944 by President Roosevelt?

D'OLIER: Yes, sir – I was.

STAGE MANAGER: Are there steps we should be taking now against atomic war?

D'OLIER: We recommended in 1944, you know, that national civilian defense be set up at once. We think that all industrial and medical centers should be decentralized. Shelters should be built deep underground all over the country. For of course, in case of another war, we'd all have to live underground.

STAGE MANAGER: That would mean a reshaping of our whole life, isn't that so?

D'OLIER: Yes. That – or the abolition of war.

STAGE MANAGER: Thank you, Mr D'Olier. (*D'OLIER sits down.*) But isn't there any counter-measure which would keep the bomb from exploding? (*Singling out someone else from audience.*) Mr Ridenour, I believe you were Radar Assistant to General Spaatz during the war. Can you help us on this point?

LOUIS N. RIDENOUR: I know that the House Naval Affairs Committee has made public statements which encourage this hope – but there is no such thing as a specific countermeasure against an atomic explosion.

Spot up on E. U. CONDON in House.

E. U. CONDON: May I add a word here? I've worked at Westinghouse Research Laboratory, served on various uranium committees and am an adviser to the Senate Atomic Commission. My name is Condon.

STAGE MANAGER: Glad to hear from you, Mr Condon.

CONDON: We must accept the fact that in any room of any city – can be secreted a bomb capable of killing 100,000 people. Conceive the police state that must result in a world from which war has not been banished. If we do not have willing international agreements on the bomb, there is only one alternative: an agent of the FBI would have to inspect – at least every sixty days – every businessman's files, every factory's tool-chests, and every housewife's china closet – to say nothing of every bit of cargo on every ship and every item in the luggage carried by any traveller.

LOUIS N. RIDENOUR: Let me sum up my own opinion, which I think is shared by *all* the scientists who actually worked on the bomb – in four words: *There is no defense.*

E. U. CONDON: You see, atomic energy is *not* just the discovery of another weapon, but of a whole way of life. Or of death. You know, I wish that everyone in the world today could learn all about atomic energy – what it is – where it came from – in some very simple way. I wish we could somehow – demonstrate to you –

STAGE MANAGER: Well, now, let's see. We ought to be able to dream up something –

Dim off on scientists in House. Music up in a series of distant crashes. As the STAGE MANAGER paces back and forth in thought, there is a flurry onstage, an emanation of energy. One of the blocks moves forward and follows the STAGE MANAGER about in his pacing. It is from this block that we hear the voice of ATOM. This voice should have two components. One should be docile and meek, like Jimmy Savo's, and one should have the touch of hysteria and comedy that Danny Kaye gets in 'Anatol of Paris,' when he says 'design – (laugh) – women's hats.'

ATOM: (*From within box.*) Disappointed you, didn't I? You're waiting for a character to appear, a handsome actor to entertain you with some bright dialogue. And instead you don't see a thing – not a thing. (*Sigh.*) But *I'm* here all the same – I'm always here – I'm everywhere. Say, did I tell you who I am? I'm Atom and I'm in *everything* – in you – in a billion, billion, billion of me. But you needn't get stuck up about it because those atoms in you keep changing. They've been in birds and fish and snakes and sharks and skunks and elephants before. Yes, sir – or in a dinosaur or a sweet pea or a rose or a stinkweed or a chigger or a daisy. A whole menagerie of second-hand atoms, that's what you are!

STAGE MANAGER: (*Approaching the block warily and stroking it.*) I don't think you're doing much to endear yourself to the audience. If only you'd let people get to know you. Now, if you only *show* yourself –

ATOM: I won't show myself – I won't. (*Getting insane.*) I'll spite them! – I'll let them draw pictures of me till they're blue in the face – but I won't show my self as I really am. I won't, I *won't*! (*ATOM breaks into maniacal laughter. Pause.*) Oh, dear, I'm so awfully sorry – that happens all the time. There's nothing I can do about it, either. You see I'm a dual personality. Hyde and Jekyll, you know. I can't control myself. Other people have to do it for me – But *will* they? That's the question. You want to see what I look like? Well, you can't – it would be against nature.

STAGE MANAGER: Now just a moment, Atom. It may be against *nature* for you to show yourself, but it's against *theatre* for an actor to stay cooped up in a box all night. Actor's Equity wouldn't allow it, in the first place. And an audience – (this audience – *any* audience) – wouldn't stand for it.

ATOM: Then what are we going to do? All these scientists out there will get up and leave the minute I pop out – because *they* know I'm invisible.

STAGE MANAGER: Well, we're going to have to think of something.

ATOM: Wait a minute! I got an idea – What about a bean bag?

STAGE MANAGER: Good heavens! Why?

ATOM: That's what J. J. Thomson said I looked like – 'A bean bag, filled with an equal number of positive and negative beans.' – *Negative beans* – can you beat that?

STAGE MANAGER: That's not going to help us any – a bean bag!

ATOM: (*As the box gyrates wildly off towards wings.*) Hold your horses. Lord Rutherford exploded that bean bag.

Music up.

STAGE MANAGER: Atom! Come back! We need you. Where are you?

ATOM: I'm still here. Lord Rutherford found out most of my volume is just empty space. (*Pause.*) Gives you a queer feeling, doesn't it?

STAGE MANAGER: You give me a queer feeling all right, all right.

ATOM: Lucretius said I was like a poppy seed. Bacon – Sir Francis – called me Cupid – 'Stripped matter,' see? How about me as Cupid?

STAGE MANAGER: I wouldn't risk it.

ATOM: A brick? That's what Galen said I was, before he sent me into exile in the Middle Ages for a couple of hundred years. Did I care?

STAGE MANAGER: Look here – I've had enough – after all, there's more than *one* way of releasing atomic energy – and this is the *theatre* way! (*Calls up into flies.*) Hey, Willy, haul up Atom's box!

WILLY: (*Offstage.*) OK, Chief. (*More distant.*) Haul up on your sixth line there!

The box is hauled up into the flies, revealing ATOM, huddled up beneath it. She springs to her feet, vital and dynamic; turns several cartwheels to music of her motif.

ATOM: Well, at that I bet I look more like *energy* than I do in the diagrams these professors keep drawing of me. (*Comes down to audience.*) Let's see, where were we?

STAGE MANAGER: *We* were right here; *you* were bogged down somewhere in the Middle Ages.

ATOM: Let's skip down to the present – to Niels Bohr. You know – Danish. Up there they look at the sky a lot. He figured out that what I really look like is the solar system. (*A colored slide of the solar system fades in. Pointing to the slide.*) See that thing at the center like the sun? Well, it's *not* the sun, it's my nucleus! All around it is that space we were talking about. Empty space. Those things spinning around it – around me – around my *nucleus*, I mean! – aren't saucers. Don't believe all you read in the newspapers. Those are flying particles – electrons. They're negatively charged. They don't weigh a thing – or scarcely anything. It's my nucleus that you have to concentrate on. *That's* what makes it 'nuclear physics,' see? – My nucleus is made up of protons and neutrons, and the number of protons determines what kind of an atom I am. Wheeee! do I understand myself? (*ATOM turns a few handsprings.*) Well, 'know thyself,' I always say – All of us atoms who have the same number of protons but a different number of neutrons are isotopes. I'm an Atom – I'm an Isotope. Does this make you nervous? It does me. Bohr got the Nobel Prize for figuring all this out. But me, I don't get anything for explaining it to you. *Any*way, uranium is the most important substance that I'm in.

STAGE MANAGER: Just a minute, please. It's quite in accord with American principles to let the accused speak for herself, but I wonder whether you'd object to having an authority in this field, Professor Emerson, state the case for you more – or – well – scientifically.

ATOM: (*Tough and disagreeable.*) Make it seem harder, you mean? Go right ahead. Don't mind me. I'm only hypothetical, anyway. The dictionary says so. Of course, the dictionary could be wrong. It also says I'm indivisible. Indivisible – humph!

STAGE MANAGER: (*Calling down into house.*) Professor Emerson, would you care to come up and make sure we're on the right track?

The PROFESSOR *comes up, urbane, somewhat amazed at all the furore over science. His humor is dry and rather caustic.*

PROFESSOR: Very glad to. As a matter of fact, I was delighted to see Atom materialize in the proper sex – female of the species being notably more deadly than the male. And I'm pleasantly surprised that she got things as straight as she did. Over-simplified, perhaps, but straight. Now, let's see – You're quite right: the bean bag theory is out. This diagram is not bad – Pollard and Davidson, isn't it?

ATOM: (*Curtly.*) Stranathan's *The Particles of Nuclear Physics* – Advertisement.

PROFESSOR: Let's see. Suppose we start with Einstein. Remember, in 1905, he unified two existing laws of energy with his famous formula, $E=mc^2$. You know, Energy equals mass times the velocity of light squared. Specifically, such a conversion is seen in the nuclear fission of uranium. The amount of energy discharged is stupendous.

ATOM: (*To audience.*) Me – 'stup*end*ous'? Where do they *get* these words?

STAGE MANAGER: Professor, can you give us some idea of what you mean by a 'stupendous' amount of energy?

PROFESSOR: Well, let's see. If each student at Smith College[1] gave approximately one ton of coal to the college for the new heating system, that means we'd have – or the college would have – about 2,000 tons of coal. (That's a lot of coal, isn't it, 2,000 tons?) And then if the department of physics offered the college instead one pound of uranium – you know, a pound of something that you could lift very lightly in one hand – well, the energy released by the pound and the two thousand tons would be about the same.

ATOM: (*Confidentially to audience.*) Get what they mean about me being too hot to handle?

PROFESSOR: (*Warming up to his subject.*) But this one pound of energy – that's just a starter. When the neutron bombards the atom, it releases not only energy, but one to three spare neutrons. They, in turn, may bombard other atoms, thus setting up a chain reaction.

ATOM: Hold onto your hats, boys – here we go!

PROFESSOR: (*In his excitement, pushing* STAGE MANAGER *across stage.*) Now, when the block – or pile – of uranium (or plutonium) is built up beyond a certain secret size – (I've got to be indefinite here, because that size is still a secret) the fragments of 1,000 nuclear fissions, split many more than 1,000 additional nuclei. That is, in a chain reaction, fissions multiply geometrically, see? And the block of uranium disintegrates with explosive speed and violence – as in the bomb.

ATOM: So I end up with over a million times as much energy as I started with.

Slide whistle.

STAGE MANAGER: Sounds like a long process.

PROFESSOR: Not at all: the whole business is over in a millionth of a second.

ATOM: (*To audience.*) Did it wear me out! – Am I a nervous wreck!

STAGE MANAGER: You mean you hit something you can't see with a part of something else you can't see and it releases more energy than a billion tons of coal and it's all over in a millionth of a second?

PROFESSOR: That's one way of putting it.

STAGE MANAGER: Just one other point – how secret is all this about the atom?

PROFESSOR: It's no secret. All nations have been experimenting with the atom for years. We draw on all their research. Any nation can make an atom bomb as soon as it has mastered purely technical problems. Any nation that wants to.

STAGE MANAGER: Thank you very much, Professor Emerson. Will you stay around in case we need you again?

PROFESSOR: Just call on me. (*Returns to audience.*)

ATOM: (*Gloomily.*) I don't think he brought out *my* side of it very clearly. Even a professor of physics at Columbia said, quote: 'when slow neutrons are captured, it is very dramatic,' unquote. Dramatic, huh? – That's what *he* says – huh – (*Very confidentially to audience.*) What's dramatic about a professor? What's dramatic about talking to yourself? – Now my idea about something dramatic is entirely different. Girls! – Music! – Dance! – After all, I've been in the movies – Here's how *I'd* explain the dance of the electrons around the nucleus, *and* the chain reaction. OK?

STAGE MANAGER: OK. (*Calls offstage.*) Willy! Send in the girls!

STAGE MANAGER *goes off.* GIRLS *enter.*

1st ballet

Their dance illustrates the 'free neutrons penetrating or bombarding the nucleus, the nucleus then splitting into two almost equal fragments and flying violently apart, throwing off 1–3 other neutrons as it does so – thus setting up a chain reaction.' ATOM *breaks in somewhat in the manner of a Caller in a country dance, with the above phrases describing the dance. As dance reaches its climax,* ATOM *quotes the* PROFESSOR, *'disintegrates with explosive violence as in the bomb.' At end of ballet,* ATOM *follows* GIRLS *off.*

CLIO, *Muse of History, enters to music. She is dressed in classical draperies which sometimes fly out behind her as she executes a turn on roller-skates, her only mode of locomotion. She wears a wreath of bay-leaves about her head and sometimes flings her draperies – along with her lines – over her shoulder. She has a recording-tablet and stylus which she holds in the crooks of her arm in the proper position. She skates rapidly about the stage as if in search of someone.* ATOM *enters.*

ATOM: Hello, Clio. Haven't seen you since Bikini.

CLIO: So it's true. I *heard* you were released again!

ATOM: Oh, this is different – just a play.

CLIO: Maybe *Variety* can use the story. You're still in the public eye, Atom. I've got to record what you're doing. Got to make history, you know.

ATOM: *I'm* making history, you're just writing it down. Well, what do you want to know?

CLIO: (*As she skates an intricate pattern.*) Now that you're out, let's get to know the *real* you. *Paris-Soir* wants to know – *Pravda* wants to know – *The Hampshire Gazette* wants to know – *London Times* – *Moscow Times* – *New York Times* – *Life, Time, Fortune* –

ATOM: Oh, why do they always want me to ex*plain* myself? – Why can't they just accept me the way I am? (ATOM *sighs.*) I'm kind of sensitive, you know. Can't trust the papers these days. They'll only print what they *want* to print.

CLIO: Well, you can't blame them – considering your past.

ATOM: (*Becoming more manic.*) I – just – can't get – *used* to the criticism I get lately when there's so *many* things in me I want to *express.* (*Insane gyrations, beating breast violently.*) I've got so much – in *here!* – that I want to get out – I've got so much to *give* to people! – I've got so much – *energy!* (*Calms down instantly.*) Pardon me, Clio. I'm so uncontrolled!

CLIO: No limelight for you forever, Atom! In the last war, you know, it was poison gas, and before that, gunpowder. They thought *they* were going to end civilization, too. But civilization's pretty tough, don't forget that. And besides, I just had an interview with B.W. –

ATOM: Well, *who* is 'B.W.'?

CLIO: Bacteriological Warfare to you. And if you don't do something quick! – one way or another – you're going to be on the way – *out!*

ATOM: (*Wistfully.*) Well, I want to do something, Clio. I *want* people to like me. That's what I've been trying to tell you. I – I want to – *approach* people –

CLIO: You tried that and look what happened.

ATOM: I mean approach them in a *nice* way – this time. (*To the audience.*) Hello – I'm willing to be friends with you, if you'll be with me. (*No response from audience.* ATOM *becomes hard and manic.*) See? They don't *want* to be friends.

CLIO: Don't look at me, Atom. I've got to be objective – the ethics of my profession.

ATOM: (*To audience.*) Hello – (*More timidly.*) Wouldn't you like to be friends with me? If – I – behave – ?

VOICE OF HENRY: Hi! Can I come up – up there on the stage with you?

ATOM: (*Arrogantly.*) Sure. Everybody's gonna have to come to me eventually, so you might as well be the first.

CLIO: Atom! mind your manners. (*To* HENRY.) Come right up, delighted to have you. (*Aside to* ATOM.) Don't forget, you're looking for help in learning how to control yourself.

HENRY *by this time has come onstage. He is the boy we saw in a previous scene at the radio.* ATOM *and* HENRY *stand looking at one another.* HENRY *bows politely to* CLIO.

HENRY: How do you do?

CLIO: How do you do?

HENRY: (*To* ATOM.) You're Atom, aren't you? I've known about you for a long time.

ATOM: (*Flattered and surprised.*) You have?

HENRY: Sure. Ever since I can remember. Ever since I listened to the radio. Remember the time you destroyed the people on Saturn – gee! that was a *swell* program!

ATOM: (*Hastily.*) Don't let Clio hear that –

CLIO: I *did* hear it! Of course, if you're going into myth and legend, I might as well buzz off – (*She starts to skate away.*)

ATOM: (*To* HENRY.) See, she's mad. (*To* CLIO.) Don't go, Clio. Clio, this is my new friend – er –

HENRY: Henry.

ATOM: Henry. This is Clio, the Muse of History.

HENRY: (*Bowing again.*) Pleased to meet you, Clio. I study you – that is, I study your *subject* in high school.

CLIO: (*Cutting a figure 8.*) Am I what you expected?

HENRY: Well, I somehow didn't know you'd be so young and so, well –

CLIO: Well, you see, I'm – immortal. That helps. (*Executes another figure 8.*)

HENRY: I'd have liked history better if I'd known you were like this.

ATOM *has wandered over to the far side of the stage. She now becomes aware of* HENRY's *absorption in* CLIO.

ATOM: Oh, H-e-e-e-e-e-n-nry!

HENRY: (*Paying no attention.*) Though I should have thought they'd at least give you an airplane or a rocket to get around in.

CLIO: Oh, I like these skates. I like to keep my feet on the ground, and to be able at any time to assume the classic position. (*She does so as she coasts across the stage, her draperies fluttering out behind her.*)

ATOM: Oh, H-e-e-e-en-n-n-ry!

HENRY: Coming, Atom. (*Crosses stage to* ATOM.) Atom, did you know you're making all the headlines these days? Why, I bet that everyone that's an *American* knows all about –

ATOM: (*Very coldly and quite grand.*) I'm not just American, remember, and since I, as an atom, am *everywhere*, I would take it as a gesture of good will were you to consider yourself – while you are with me – merely a citizen of the world.

HENRY: (*Thinking.*) Well, I guess in a way, I *am* a citizen of the world – (*Turns to* CLIO.) By the way, Clio, are *you* American?

CLIO: I haven't any particular race or country.

HENRY: Kind of sounds, when you study history, as if you're always on our side! You know, Clio, I like this little brat so much that I'm going to be a scientist when I grow up – and find out what really makes her tick.

CLIO: If you're going to help Atom amount to something, you can't be one of these fly-by-nights that thinks every discovery is something *new*. Now Atom, for instance – Atom's been around for millenia, you know.

Scene dims off. Over the entire cyclorama, a slide of the moon, stars and planets. Like all the slides, except those purposely used in diagrammatic form, this one does not attempt to simulate reality. It is always suggestive, rather than real. It creates a new experience rather than competing with an old one. It does not look like a design in a book on astronomy, but rather like an expression of the inner essence of such a design. Van Gogh's 'Starry Night' might give an idea. CLIO, ATOM *and* HENRY *stand where the wall is low, looking over it. While they are taking their places, we hear a* VOICE, *possibly integrated with the music of the spheres.*

VOICE:
'When I heard the learned astronomer[2]
When the proofs, the figures, were ranged in column before me,
How soon unaccountably I became tired and sick
Till rising and gliding out I wandered off by myself,
In the mystical, moist night-air, and from time to time,
Looked up in perfect silence at the stars.'

CLIO: It all began with the stars – Atomic energy up there goes back beyond the beginning of what we call time.

HENRY: Did the stars look this way then?

CLIO: Astronomers – and geologists, too – think things were practically the same five hundred million years ago.

HENRY: Makes me feel queer.

ATOM: (*In a hoarse whisper.*) Small, that's how it makes me feel – small.

CLIO: Well, we *are* small, if you stop to think of it – in time and space both. Somehow stars transform atoms – into radiant energy which travels millions of miles to us – as starlight.

HENRY: Clio, if stars have kept going about the same way for five hundred million years, and *they* were splitting the atom naturally – perhaps now that we're trying to split the

atom in a different way, we don't need to be afraid we'll blow ourselves up.

CLIO: Oh, it's only in a *general* way that it's all pretty much the same. Individual stars and galaxies blow up and disappear all the time. Just as this planet, Earth, might – in fact, *may*, some day.

HENRY: Gee!

CLIO: Of course, we're a planet, not a star. Come down here where you can see better. (CLIO, ATOM *and* HENRY *move downstage.*) We're in Greece now, four centuries before Christ. Even at that time, you were an old story, Atom.

ATOM: I *was*?

CLIO: They'd been talking about you for centuries –

ATOM: Am I impressed – !

CLIO: – why, Hindus and Phoenicians had been discussing the structure of matter as far back as twelve centuries before Christ. And here – in Greece –

Spot up on a symposium of THREE PHILOSOPHERS.

LEUCIPPUS: 'Let us begin, Democritus, by assuming an unlimited number of elements, the atoms, which are always in motion. They move in the void – there is an infinite number of such atoms and they are invisible, on account of their smallness. Coming together, they cause coming into being – separating, they cause destruction of being.'

DEMOCRITUS: 'Only the atoms and the void are real, Leucippus. By convention, sweet is sweet, bitter is bitter. But in reality, Epicurus, there are only atoms and the void.'

EPICURUS: 'Atoms assume an incalculable variety of forms. They can be discovered only by thought. Yet I am as sure of the existence of atoms as if I had seen them with my eyes.'

Blackout.

HENRY: That's amazing. I'd no idea.

CLIO: And in about 50 BC the Roman philosopher Lucretius recorded in his own way the theories of the atomists.

VOICE: (*With music and slide integration as in the Whitman poem.*) 'The atoms – move hither and thither – when their order changes, they change their nature – and they surpass in speed of motion even the light of the sun – And war from time everlasting is carried on by the balanced strife of the atoms.'

HENRY: Why, it seems as if we haven't learned a thing in all these centuries!

CLIO: Let's just say that the Greeks put the question that modern scientists are trying to answer – By the 17th century, scientists in different countries – France, Germany, England, Italy, Russia – had rediscovered the atom.

HENRY: What about America? Did we catch on? – in those years?

CLIO: Well, Thomas Jefferson accepted the physics of Epicurus – wrote a long paper about it. And for a long time now, astronomers, geologists, chemists, physicists have *all* been experimenting, trying to work out a system that will *account* for things – through all space and all time.

STAGE MANAGER: (*Coming onstage.*) And it isn't only the scientists who want the sort of a world that we can understand. It's the philosopher, it's the statesman, it's the artist, it's the teacher, the student, it's you and I – *we* want it, too. We all want to get in on your education of Henry.

CLIO: Rather a sketchy trip through the ages that – just like American tourists.

HENRY: (*Excited.*) Don't worry, Clio. This makes me begin to see what's behind – and what's ahead, too! Atom and I, why, we can help *make* what's ahead, can't we?

CLIO: If Atom can ever learn to behave herself.

ATOM: People won't let me! (*Insanely.*) I get so *mad*! Didn't I have to show my worst side before people paid any attention to me? Isn't that the truth about life, anyway? And now to make it worse, my isotopes are getting stopped up. It's all this night air – (*ATOM snuffles and the next comes nasally – as if with a cold in the head.*)

HENRY: Atom, why do you behave so badly?

ATOM: The sweetest people live all around all the time and nobody pays any attention to *them* – too prophylactic – but *murderers* and *gangsters* and *chiselers* get into the papers all the time! – *They're celebrities!* Well, can you blame me if I show the *harm* I can do?

CLIO: Well, cold in the head, or no cold in the head, watch your step, Atom. I've got to go now, got another assignment to cover, now that I've caught up on you, Atom. Henry – you've sidetracked me with this history lesson.

HENRY: Where you off to? – Where's your next assignment?

CLIO: Down on Long Island – Lake Success, you know. (*CLIO skates off.*)

HENRY: (*Calling after her.*) Can't we come? (*To ATOM.*) Hey, Atom! Let's go after her.

ATOM: Awfully hard, Henry, keeping up with Clio. But we can try. (*Calling as they run after her.*) Hey, Clio – got any nose-drops?

HENRY and ATOM run off.

STAGE MANAGER: Well, we've seen the impact of the Atom – but the moral question remains, doesn't it? Should – we – have used atomic energy for destruction of civilians in the first place? The decision to use the atomic bomb, one of the gravest ever taken by the government of the United States, was not made lightly, or hurriedly –

MARCH OF TIME VOICE: October, 1941. Scene – the White House, in Washington.

Spot up on face of Stimson looking at PRESIDENT ROOSEVELT, who is seen only in silhouette. His back is to us. He is smoking a cigarette in a long holder.

PRESIDENT ROOSEVELT: Stimson: Let me ask you again. The work of this committee is still, after two years of experiment, completely secret?

STIMSON: It is, sir.

PRESIDENT ROOSEVELT: The weapon under discussion is never referred to in any communication except by its code number S-I, right?

STIMSON: Right, sir.

PRESIDENT ROOSEVELT: Stimson, sum up for me.

STIMSON: Our object has been from the first to spare no effort in securing the earliest possible development of an atomic weapon. Reason: The achievement of atomic fission occurred in Germany in 1938. It is quite possible that they are ahead of us. It is vital that they shall not be the first to use atomic weapons. If we develop it first, we shall have a great new instrument for shortening the war.

PRESIDENT ROOSEVELT: Of course you know that rumors are going around that you and Jim Conant have sold me a bill of goods on this thing – that it's going to be a terrific lemon.

STIMSON: Then it will be a lemon grown by four Nobel Prize winners and practically every physicist of standing in the country.

PRESIDENT ROOSEVELT: (*Making a decision.*) Count on whatever money you need. Draw in anyone else you need. Set the whole thing up, Stimson. We have no time to lose.

Blackout.

STAGE MANAGER: We had *indeed* no time to lose. December 7, 1941, Pearl Harbor! War is declared! (*Military music. On a gauze transparency covering the front of the stage we see war movies.*) With America at war, the atom experiments all over the country took on new urgency. Scientists in Chicago obtained the first substantial release of atomic energy. And in Los Alamos, New Mexico, one of the most gigantic undertakings in history was well under way.

Through the transparency on which scenes of war movies continue, we see people assemble. They identify themselves as they enter.

VOICES OF THE PEOPLE: (*As they assemble.*) Scientists! (*SCIENTISTS in white, a MAN and a WOMAN, enter from opposite sides and stand center back.*) The Army, the Navy, the Marines! (*OFFICERS of ARMY, NAVY and MARINES from opposite sides take places by the SCIENTISTS.*) Editors and writers! – Press and Radio! (*CIVILIANS from opposite sides enter and take places next to military men.*)

STAGE MANAGER: They kept the secret! They *all* kept the secret.

VOICES OF THE PEOPLE: (*Music under.*) Engineering Corps! – Chemical Warfare Service! – Chaplains Corps! – Corps of Military Police! – Military Intelligence! – Finance Department! – Signal Corps! – Quartermasters Corps! – Air Corps! – Field Artillery! – Coast Artillery! – Infantry! – Medical Corps! – Waves, Wacs, Spars! – Construction men! –

Suddenly there is a complete silence. Music stops. Action and movies stop but do not blackout.

STAGE MANAGER: On April 12, 1945, Franklin Delano Roosevelt died. His death is a part of this story, for his life and death touched every aspect of our age. For millions of people all over the world, everything stopped – (*Pause.*) Harry S. Truman became President of the United States. The war and the work of the world resumed.

Movies on screen and scene behind screen continue while STAGE MANAGER *speaks.*

STAGE MANAGER: It is often said that civilians and military can't work together to save their lives; that management and labor can't work together – to save their lives. But the answer is –

CHORUS OF ALL THE PEOPLE: At Los Alamos! – we *did* work together – *to save our lives!*

Blackout on people behind scrim but continuous war movies during the following.

STAGE MANAGER: Remember, at that time, it was literally to save our lives – for the outcome of the war was still in doubt. The President's Committee listened secretly and anxiously to Secretary of War Stimson.

STIMSON: (*Coming forward in spot.*) The bomb should be used against Japan as soon as possible; it should be used on a dual target, military and civilian; and it should be used without prior warning of the nature of the weapon.

MARCH OF TIME VOICE: Yet, in the end, the recommendation of the committee as to the military use of the bomb was not unanimous. Mr Bard, Under-Secretary of the Navy, dissented.

Spot up on BARD.

BARD: I have a feeling that before the bomb is actually used against Japan that Japan should have some preliminary warning. The position of the United States as a great humanitarian nation and the fair play attitude of our people generally is responsible for my feeling.

BARD *goes out and his footsteps are heard in the silence that follows.*

STIMSON: To extract a genuine surrender from the Emperor and his military advisers, they must be administered a tremendous shock which will carry convincing proof of our power to destroy the Empire. Such an effective shock would save many times the number of lives, both American and Japanese, that it would cost.

STIMSON *remains on stage. Military music up and film continues.*

MARCH OF TIME VOICE: July 26, 1945, Potsdam, Germany – Great Britain, China and the United States issued an ultimatum: 'If the Japanese continue the war, the full application of our military power will mean the inevitable complete destruction of the Japanese armed forces and the utter devastation of the Japanese homeland.'

STAGE MANAGER: July 28, from the Court of the Emperor, came an answer – 'The Potsdam ultimatum is unworthy of public notice.'

MARCH OF TIME VOICE: (*Over musical score.*) August 6, Hiroshima. (*Flash of newsreel, only enough to cover* VOICE.) August 9, Nagasaki. (*Another flash of newsreel, only to cover* VOICE.)

STAGE MANAGER: August 10, Japan surrenders. August 14, the articles are signed.

Battle music up to triumphant climax. Film continues and reaches climax with signing.

STIMSON: (*In spot.*) In this last great action of the Second World War, we were given final proof that the face of war is the face of death. War has grown steadily more barbarous, more destructive, more debased in all its aspects. Now, with the release of atomic energy, man's ability to destroy himself is very nearly complete. The bombs dropped on Hiroshima and Nagasaki ended a war. They also make it wholly clear that we must never have another war.

Spot out.

STAGE MANAGER: The war ended – and almost at once, the threat of another war began. And secretly, in Washington and in other capitals of the world, behind the scenes, and between the lines, there began to unfold the next chapter in the struggle over the atom, a struggle that is still going on. Who shall control it and for what shall it be used? And *that*, ladies and gentlemen, is what the second part of our play will be about.

Blackout.

Act 2

In Act 2 the wall is split into a number of irregular segments or piles arranged about the stage. Downstage Right a large horizontal one makes the background for the committee room. Throughout all scenes in committee the shadow can be seen – sometimes dimly – sometimes strongly. In and around these blocks, the hunt for uranium later takes place.

ATOM *comes on the stage alone. She wears a small tag – not noticeable until referred to.*

ATOM: (*In a decided Southern drawl; perhaps to the music of a guitar.*) Howdy, folks! – I sure hope you-all had a mighty fine intermission and time to get yourself a mint-julep, 'cause to start out with, anyway, this part of the play is gonna be mighty sweet – yessir, mighty sweet! – The war's been over for two years an' me – I jes' had myself a trip – I just come back from a long stay in Oak Ridge, Tenn. (*Inhales deeply.*) Did I get around? Am I impressed? Am I under control? – Say! – Senators an' such! Now you take McMahon – why, we're just like *that!* – He got me an honorable discharge, see my pin? Passed a bill. (*Starts down steps into audience.*) So here I am – right in your lap, folks, yessir, right – in – yours! (*ATOM seats herself in lap of man in aisle seat of 4th or 5th row.*) 'Cause the President appointed some big guns to a Civilian Commission. *So*, I'm all under control – (*Says very confidentially to* MAN *in whose lap she's sitting.*) Are *you* controlling – me? – (*Back to audience.*) Say – know how much I'm worth today? – Just in this one country alone? – Three – billion – five – hundred – million! – And know how much they're planning to spend on me a year? – Five – hundred – *million!* (*With the old truculence.*) So what, you say? – I'm worth it, don't you think? – Know what you're gettin' fer your money? Know what you're gettin'? – Well, there's a big red mountain down in New Mexico – an atom-smasher in California, the biggest in the world, and a new one being made at Columbia University – a plutonium pile up in Hanford, Washington – Big place – 4,000 acres to explode in if I feel like it – Then there's the Argonne Laboratory near Chicago, tools – instruments – instruments – tools. All of 'em made just to find out about me. – *Me* – myself – Not a movin' pitcher! Stopped in at Schenectady on my way back from Chicago – you know – General Electric up there – Oh, yes, Big Business is in on me, too – Standard Oil, Kelley, Chrysler, and the rest. An' then I stop in at Oak Ridge, Tennessee! Do I love it down there? (*Southern accent very strong again.*) Do I love Tennessee! – Down there they're makin' discoveries as peaceful as anythin' – showin' people how to grow crops an' find oil an' cure diseases, an' all with derivatives of *Me*! (*Becomes very confidential again.*) 'Member that cold I had? – Notice how improved I am? – that my isotopes are clearing up? – Well, they did *that* for me down in Tennessee! (*Changes manner again.*) Well, soon as I hit New York on the way up here – an' started to read the telephone directory – (y'know, the way you do first night you're in town to see whether anyone's around you can call up?) – was – I – surprised! – *Am* I in Manhattan, Brooklyn, Queens, and all the *other* telephone books! Say – they got Atomic Toys – Atomic Handbags – (and baggages) – Atomic Rainwear – sportswear – neckwear – and underwear! They got Atomic insecticide – (what *we* don't kill, they will!) In the Bronx – they even got an Atomette Company! – What does that mean? – I dunno. Sex, maybe.

The entire following sequence is done to music and is stylized as to acting. Over the cyclorama a huge sign appears in flashing lights which go on and off during the following sequence: 'MIMBELS HAS ISOTOPIA – THE NEW ATOMIC PERFUME.' Against the sign, to aphrodisiac music, a SIREN, very svelte in the latest evening gown, enters, takes stage, sighs at its lack of males, and squirts perfume all over herself. From behind the blocks MEN appear, each registering ardent attraction. They surround her, breathe heavily and fall at her feet. Blackout.

ATOM: (*Wistfully.*) See what I mean – Beauty – Happiness. I got finer feelings, too.

Lights up on another flashing sign: 'COMMUTE ATOMICALLY' – 'Why be a slave to outmoded jet propulsion? – Commute on your own energy!' A little MAN in front of a little door to a little suburban house is being kissed goodbye by his pretty WIFE.

WIFE: Don't forget, darling – we're dining with the Blimps tonight.

MAN: I've got that confounded luncheon date on Mars, sweetiepie – but I'll cut it short.

WIFE: (*Adjusting the small box he wears on a strap over his shoulder.*) Sure you've got enough energy?

MAN: I recharged myself this morning – 'Bye, pettykins! $E = mc^2$!

To the swoop of a slide whistle he flies up into the wings while WIFE throws kisses up at him. Blackout.

ATOM: (*Indicating them.*) You see – Life *Can* Be Beautiful! (*She imitates the rotund voice of a radio announcer.*) That is, if we – but – what's *that*?

There is the insistent ringing of a bell as a flashing sign says: ATOMIC LAUNDRY SERVICE. INSTANTANEOUS! The bell keeps on ringing as part of the musical score. The pretty GIRL, wife of the previous ad, walks across stage with a huge bag marked 'Laundry.' She opens imaginary door to a handsome young MAN who receives the bag and puts it in a container.

LAUNDRYMAN: (*Lyrically.*) Good morning! Atomic Laundry Service.

WIFE: Good morning! I'm afraid I have a very large laundry today.

LAUNDRYMAN: Just wait and see.

Bell rings and an enormous pile of shirts pops out, freshly laundered. She takes them. MAN smiles; bows.

LAUNDRYMAN: Instantaneous! Wasn't it?

WIFE: Indeed it was. Thank you.

Blackout.

STAGE MANAGER: (*Coming on stage.*) Just a minute, Atom. I don't like to break in on you, but we don't want to get carried away, do we?

ATOM: (*Very impatiently.*) But wait – but wait – but wait! – willyuh, huh? – Ya ain't seen nothin' yet! (*Gestures to audience.*) An' dey haven't, eider!

Lights and music up on final flashing sign: 'FARM CATALOG: 1955: ATOMIC SEED SECRET!' A young and handsome FARMER in rakishly debonair farm attire crosses the stage to music. He goes through the motions of ploughing a furrow. He is followed by his modishly dressed young WIFE who gaily drops seeds in a furrow. They execute this manoeuver as in a ballet. Behind them a row of corn sprouts up instantaneously and to enormous heights.

STAGE MANAGER: (*To* ATOM.) All right, that's enough of you for awhile. I'm ashamed of you – all these important people out there – and all this corn! (*Pushes corn back down. Calls down into audience.*) Oh, Professor, I'm wondering whether you and the other scientists in the house are offended by this somewhat florid conception of the atomic future?

PROFESSOR: (*As he comes up the aisle.*) Not at all. Exaggerated, of course, but suggestive – the little man who was going to lunch on Mars – he's a bit previous, of course – but it's true that 'atomic energy provides a source of fuel powerful enough to bring interplanetary travel nearer to possibility.' It's just a matter of time.

STAGE MANAGER: What about that 'Isotopia' perfume, Professor? I found that a little – alarming.

PROFESSOR: Really? It seemed to me a rather pleasant way to pass out – much less tiresome than any other form of unconsciousness that atomic energy threatens. Of course the farming episode is speeded up. But it's true that atomic energy is allowing us to see inside plants, to observe how chlorophyll creates food – and then, eventually, perhaps, we can duplicate the process. Think of India – China – Greece. Why, eventually atomic research can show us how to use solar energy to feed the whole world.

STAGE MANAGER: And heat the whole world, as well – Isn't that true?

PROFESSOR: It's going to take a long time, of course, before these things all come true. But we *do* expect to have power plants for peacetime uses, such as that at Oak Ridge, within a decade or two.

STAGE MANAGER: (*Aside to* ATOM.) Been to a fire sale, Atom?

ATOM: Gee! They forgot to take the tag off me when I left Oak Ridge.

PROFESSOR: Oh, yes – the 'tagged' Atoms. Yes, we can follow chemical processes with them now – and perhaps in the future, we'll be able to cure – not only cancer – but all sorts of other diseases.

ATOM: Boy! You should have been with me on that cancer run. Was I knocked out! Do I know about people's insides!

PROFESSOR: There's no question that we've tapped a source of energy in atomic power which *can* be harnessed to do most of the work of the world.

STAGE MANAGER: It's an amazing prospect, a world without – well – drudgery.

PROFESSOR: I'm looking forward to it. I could *use* a little rest!

STAGE MANAGER: *You* – a college professor?

PROFESSOR: (*Confidentially.*) Between ourselves, work has always been rather overrated, anyway –

STAGE MANAGER: Say, I'm glad to hear that –

PROFESSOR: – far too many neurotic people in the world, you know, rushing around desperately keeping themselves busy –

STAGE MANAGER: You're giving me an idea: I'm going to stay in bed for breakfast tomorrow.

PROFESSOR: (*Cheerfully.*) You do that: we might as well face it: in the future there just won't be much work for us to do. The problem will be to learn to use a magnificent leisure in which the race can develop. That is, if we *permit* the race to continue – to live at all.

STAGE MANAGER: Just as you begin to cheer me up – you come out with a statement like that.

PROFESSOR: I'm a realist, my dear fellow. Atomic energy *can* do all the things we've been discussing and many more –

STAGE MANAGER: Well, then – ?

PROFESSOR: – *but:* its power of destruction – is so unparalleled that there's a chance none of these achievements will take place.

STAGE MANAGER: Oh.

PROFESSOR: You see, atomic energy can cure disease – or cause it – create food – or poison it – provide heat for the whole world – or blow it sky-high – you see, it's going to be up to you and me. And to our friends out there.

VOICE IN THE AUDIENCE: You mean – up to *us*?

PROFESSOR: (*Turning to audience.*) Yes – up to you. And don't sound so incredulous about it! (*To* STAGE MANAGER.) It's going to take education – (*Taking* STAGE MANAGER'S *arm.*) – a lot more than we've got for the situation at present –

PROFESSOR and STAGE MANAGER *retire to wings.*

ATOM: Education! Listen, kids – I got more college degrees than you can shake a mortar-board at! – Want to know the colleges and universities I'm all mixed up in? Never happened before in the history of the world. Oh, I was *in* 'em all right before, but nobody noticed. But *now!* Just lissen to 'em all: all working over little hypomanic *me*. (*As* ATOM *calls out the following names her voice takes on a mid-Western twang and the Orchestra strikes up 'Gaudeamus Igitur' and* BOYS *and* GIRLS *in caps and gowns carrying banners with the seals of the following universities march out and circle the stage:*) Chicago! – Colorado! – Oklahoma! – Kansas! – Nebraska! – Iowa! – Minnesota! – Missouri! – etc., etc. (*Till there are 29 universities represented.*) Then there are the scientists working at the Brookhaven Atomic Laboratory on Long Island. (*Music continues as more* BOYS *and* GIRLS *in caps and gowns, carrying banners, fill the stage and range themselves in a semicircle in front of* ATOM, *their backs to the audience.*) MIT! – Cornell! – Yale! – Rochester! – Princeton! – Columbia! – Harvard! – Pennsylvania! – Johns Hopkins! – (*ATOM now dons cap and gown and mounts podium which has been pushed out under cover of the screen of people and addresses the colleges in the manner of a pompous commencement orator.*) boys and girls! – from the class of 1948 all over the country – men and women of tomorrow! – as I gaze out upon your bright and eager young faces – lined range on range before me – as a proud recipient of the honors you have conferred upon me –

and as your Commencement speaker – may I congratulate you – on having – in the words of one public figure – 'enormously complicated the process of extinction.' (*BOYS and GIRLS applaud politely and then begin to do a 'take'.*) May I conclude – by saying – that the next few years of your lives – *if any* – will be the most important years – of your life – *if any* –

Applause continues and then a take and blackout. During the blackout, BOYS *and* GIRLS *clear stage to music.*

STAGE MANAGER: (*As he and the* PROFESSOR *cross the stage.*) So that's the kind of commencement address we're going to hear in the universities?

PROFESSOR: Looks like it.

STAGE MANAGER: Seems as if that bomb that fell on Hiroshima knocked over a couple of ivory towers.

PROFESSOR: Not sure that it actually knocked 'em *over*. Just nicked 'em a little.

STAGE MANAGER and PROFESSOR go out.

ATOM: Well, folks, now that I've got my degrees and stuff, 'bout time I took the Grand Tour. Now that I'm a citizen of the world, y'know. Got to see what's cookin' in other nations where they're settin' me up. England's building me a pile; France has got a whole atomic village just put up in my honor – peaceful purposes, too. And Russia's built a 'Nameless City' – out in those Ural Mountains – just to see what makes me tick. (*Searches frantically in clothing.*) What *does* make me tick, anyway? – I wish I knew! (*Takes pulse; listens to own heart-beat.*) I'm tickin', all right, there's no doubt about that! But what makes me? – *What makes me – What makes me?*

HENRY: (*Comes running in, wearing white laboratory coat.*) Atom – come on! We've got to go to Washington right away!

ATOM: Aw! I've *seen* Washington – I'm going abroad. And *say*, Henry, what are you doing out of that Laboratory down at Oak Ridge, where you scraped my antrims and cleared my isotopes?

HENRY: Everything's held up down there for the present! Everything's stopped for the Committee Hearing. And it's about *you!* – You've got to be there! A Senate Committee's investigating you!

ATOM: Why they doing that? I thought the President appointed a committee on me and put a big shot in charge?

HENRY: It seems they don't like him. Some don't, anyway.

ATOM: Well, who is this man, and what's he done that's bad?

HENRY: He hasn't done anything that's bad only he's a civilian. Some people think you ought to be under the military.

ATOM: I thought I just got a discharge!

HENRY: Well, come along to Washington and see for yourself. And while we're in the hearing I'm going to put you back into your box! (*Wheels box out from behind large block.*) Come on! Get in, Atom! – Get in! Get in! Get in!

ATOM: (*Obeying plaintively.*) I don't see why I can't watch! – I like a good investigation as much as anybody! – I don't see why I have to be shut up again in my box!

HENRY: (*As he pushes ATOM down in the box.*) Because if you don't keep that trap of yours shut, you'll spill the neutrons – You just *talk* – too – much –

As HENRY rolls the box across the stage, an ATTENDANT approaches him.

ATTENDANT: (*Looking at box.*) No packages allowed in the Senate Office Building.

HENRY: She's not exactly a package, in fact she's a good deal more than a package.

ATOM: (*Crying angrily like a baby inside box.*) I'm *not* a package! – I'm *not* a package!

ATTENDANT: Say, what is this? – You got some kind of a pet in there?

HENRY: Well, she's not exactly what you'd call a pet, either!

ATOM: (*Banging wildly inside the box.*) I'll say I'm not a pet! – Let me *out* of here!

HENRY: You see this investigation going on in here is really all about her.

ATTENDANT: Are you off your trolley? – All about *her*?

HENRY: This is really everybody's problem I've got in this box, and for the moment I'm stuck with her. I thought that if I brought her in here –

CLIO skates in.

ATTENDANT: (*Dazed.*) And is this lady with you?

HENRY: Yes, she kind of goes wherever my problem and I go. This is Clio, the Muse of History, you know. She belongs in here, she records these events, and it would be really foolish to put us out.

ATTENDANT: (*Impatiently.*) Oh, stay, then. You're not much nuttier than the rest of these birds.

STAGE MANAGER: (*Coming on from Right.*) Late in January of 1947, the Senate Section of the Joint Committee on Atomic Energy started Hearings to investigate Mr Lilienthal's fitness for the position of its Chairman. The scenes in the courtroom that we're going to show you now have been adapted from the hearings before the Senate Section of the Joint Committee on Atomic Energy.[3] Scenes on the side here represent occasional interpolations on our part. Go ahead, please. (*STAGE MANAGER goes off.*)

Out of the darkness a sound of excited VOICES and flash bulbs. 'This way! – This way!' 'Just one more picture, Senator!' The sound of a gavel and a VOICE: 'Order! Order! The committee is convening!' Lights come up on a projection of a committee room with people at a long table. The projection is like a cartoon, with the people at various angles, foreshortened. In front of the projection is a table, in the form of a T, but greatly foreshortened, so audience can see both CHAIRMAN HICKENLOOPER and MCKELLAR at its head, and LILIENTHAL at its foot. HENRY rolls in the box and perches upon it, far down Right in the side stage. CLIO skates in and darts about the box and settles herself down with HENRY.

SENATOR MCKELLAR: Senator Hickenlooper, may I ask the witness one question?

CHAIRMAN HICKENLOOPER: You may, Senator McKellar. The Senator from Tennessee has the floor.

SENATOR MCKELLAR: Mr Lilienthal, when did you first learn from anyone that the United States Government was undertaking to discover the use of splitting the atom, so to speak? When was it? Give us the date.

LILIENTHAL: The first time I was sure was on the 6th of August, 1945.

SENATOR MCKELLAR: Who told you?

LILIENTHAL: I read it in the paper.

Laughter from the people in the Senate Chamber.

SENATOR MCKELLAR: (*Sarcastically.*) You read it in the paper?

VOICE FROM SENATE CHAMBER: That's the day we *all* read it in the paper, Senator!

Laughter from the court.

SENATOR MCKELLAR: Well, were you not surprised that in connection with experiments that have been carried on since the days of Alexander the Great when he had his Macedonian scientists try to split the atom, the President of the United States would discharge General Groves, the discoverer of the greatest secret that the world has ever known –

ATOM: (*Muffled, inside the box.*) I like that! – A fine way to talk about me!

HENRY: (*Kicking the side of the box.*) Quiet in there! Quie-et!

SENATOR MCKELLAR: – the greatest scientific discovery that has ever been made, to turn the whole matter over to you who never really knew except from what you saw in the newspaper that the Government was even thinking about atomic energy?

LILIENTHAL: Was I surp*rised?*

SENATOR MCKELLAR: *Were – you – not – surprised?*

Laughter and tumult.

CHAIRMAN HICKENLOOPER: (*Banging gavel.*) Let us have quiet, please – qui-et!

HENRY: (*Kicking the side of ATOM's box in the same rhythm.*) Let us have quiet, *please!*

LILIENTHAL: I would like to remind you, Senator, that it was the Secretary of War who urged that a civilian commission be appointed to succeed General Groves. I do not think that constitutes a reflection in the slightest on General Groves. He was a military officer and did a magnificent job.

SENATOR MCKELLAR: Do you not really think that General Groves – when having discovered the Atom – is entitled to some little credit for it?

Commotion and tumult.

ATOM: (*From inside the box.*) I never heard such nonsense! – General Groves did not discover – me!

HENRY: (*Kicking the sides of the box.*) Will you – keep – *quiet?*

ATOM: (*Poking her head out of the box and then disappearing.*) I'm not sure.

CHAIRMAN HICKENLOOPER: Order! – Order! (*Towards HENRY and ATOM.*) We'll have to have quiet over there!

Blackout: but the actors remain onstage.

STAGE MANAGER: As the weeks and months went by it became increasingly clear that the struggle over Mr Lilienthal's appointment was not a simple one; it was the problem of civilian control of a great new form of energy, as opposed to military control; and for a certain *kind* of civilian control, the kind for which TVA was famous – control by the public – as against control by big industry. It was a struggle pointing far into the future, the struggle for a new source of power – in a power-hungry world.

Lights up again on courtroom; the same people about the same table, looking more exhausted.

SENATOR MCKELLAR: (*With rising anger and increasing speed as the scene mounts.*)[4] Did you have any correspondence with Malinkov, Commissar Malinkov?

LILIENTHAL: No.

SENATOR MCKELLAR: With Commissar Stalin?

LILIENTHAL: No.

SENATOR MCKELLAR: With Commissar Slevnik?

LILIENTHAL: No.

SENATOR MCKELLAR: With Voznesensky?

LILIENTHAL: No.

SENATOR MCKELLAR: With Molotov?

LILIENTHAL: No.

SENATOR MCKELLAR: With Kaganovich?

LILIENTHAL: No.

SENATOR MCKELLAR: With Bulganin?

LILIENTHAL: No.

SENATOR MCKELLAR: (*Having trouble.*) With Ze – Zenonik?

LILIENTHAL: That's hard on the dentures, Senator.

Laughter. Dim off but the actors remain in place. Lights up on another part of stage. Six actors – A, B, C, D, E, F are standing close together. They use loud stage-whispers in addressing one another.

A: (*To B.*) Sh – sh! Did you ever hear that the wife of X once belonged to a front organization?

B: No! Yes! (*To C.*) Did you ever hear that X's wife belongs to a front organization and his daughter drinks vodka?

C: No! Yes! (*To D.*) Did you ever hear that X's wife's father was born in Russia and his daughter is in the Canadian spy ring?

D: No! Yes! (*Holds up a large newspaper with scare headlines which read: 'X is a communist Spy!' To E.*) Did you read in the papers that X is a spy from the Kremlin – that his wife was born in Moscow and that his twin daughters are smuggling blocks of uranium to Stalin?

E: No! Yes! (*Snatches the newspaper with headlines and addresses audience directly.*) Mr President: I ask unanimous consent to have printed in the Congressional Record an article appearing today out of nowhere entitled 'Russian Spy at Large – *Large* Russian Spy at Large.'

F: (*Snatching the newspaper from* E.) No! Yes! (*Oratorically.*) Gentlemen, I would not rise to the floor of this august body – except to state, declare, point out specifically and bring to your attention the fact that however innocent Mr X may *appear* – it has been rumored – and the rumors have been spread upon the *Congressional Record* – and it has been implied, alleged, bruited about, hinted at, and even said – that Mr X is a Communist. And need I call to your attention, gentlemen, that no person, even if he is innocent, should be appointed to public office in these United States against whom there has been – as against Mr X – the shadow of a doubt – Public servants, gentlemen, must be like – er – Macbeth's wife – above suspicion!

Blackout. Lights come up on Courtroom where the scene, although taken verbatim from the 'Congressional Record,' seems like a continuation of the Alphabet sequence.

VOICE 1: Mr Lilienthal's alleged and widely believed pro-Russianism –

VOICE 2: It's the New Deal all over again –

VOICE 3: It's nothing but the TVA!

VOICE 1: Objection!

VOICE 2: Objection!

VOICES 1, 2, AND 3: Proof! – proof! – proof!

CHAIRMAN HICKENLOOPER: Order! – *Order! ORDER!* Miss Agnes Waters has the floor.

Flashlights go off.

AGNES WATERS:[5] The men behind the Atomic Energy Commission – were the men who financed the Russian revolution – fingers dipping in blood again – in blood of every family from London to Timbuctoo. The Jews –

SENATOR MCMAHON:[6] I've heard a lot of rag-tail talk here and I'm tired of it –

CHAIRMAN HICKENLOOPER: Order! – order!

SENATOR MCKELLAR:[7] I think it is very important for us to find out, Mr Lilienthal, what your views are on Communistic doctrine – now what about them?

LILIENTHAL: I will do my best to make it clear. (*Room gets quiet.*) My convictions are not so much concerned with what I am against as with what I am for. I believe the Constitution of the United States to rest – as does religion – upon the fundamental proposition of the integrity of the individual. I believe that all Government and all private institutions must be designed to promote and protect the integrity and the dignity of the individual – Any form of government, therefore, which makes men means, rather than ends, which exalts the state – above the importance of men, which places arbitrary power over men, any such government is contrary to that conception, and, therefore, I am deeply opposed to it.

VOICES: I don't believe him. Hear, hear! – hear, hear!

Applause.

CHAIRMAN HICKENLOOPER: (*Pounding gavel.*) Order! – order!

LILIENTHAL: The Communistic form of government falls within the category to which I am opposed, for its fundamental tenet is that the state is an end in itself and that therefore the powers which the state exercises over the individual are without any ethical standards to limit them. That I deeply disbelieve. (*Applause.*) It is very easy to talk about being against Communism. It is equally important to believe those things which provide a satisfying and effective alternative. That satisfying alternative is a democracy.

Applause. PEOPLE *in the courtroom rise and* HENRY *shakes hands with* LILIENTHAL.

STAGE MANAGER: On April 9th, 1947, the appointment of David Lilienthal as Chairman of the Atomic Energy Commission was confirmed.

Applause. The Committee Room blacks out.

ATOM: Then we won! – our side won.

HENRY: Sure we won – for the moment. But listen:

STAGE MANAGER: Say, Henry, you seem to be having your troubles?

HENRY: (*Desperately.*) If you could only explain to this 'ultimate small particle' –

STAGE MANAGER: – that even if we *did* seem to have won, only a week later Senator McKellar introduced a bill into Congress – 'to repeal the Atomic Energy Act of 1945 and to provide for the exercise by the War Department of all powers and functions relating to atomic energy.'

HENRY: That's what I mean.

ATOM: (*Awed.*) Gee! I really am causing trouble, aren't I?

STAGE MANAGER: The fight to control you still goes on –

ATOM: (*Very Durante-ish.*) I been fightin' wid myself all me life!

STAGE MANAGER: In fact, the fight for atomic control has been going on since the Truman-Atlee-King proposals of November, 1945. Clio! – give us the record!

CLIO: Mr Technician, let me have the screen, please. I always make a mental note to thank Thomas A. Edison at moments like these. Did he make my job easier!

A screen descends and movies depicting events and personages are shown with the sound track cut off. STAGE MANAGER, ATOM *and* HENRY *watch from the side.*

CLIO: (*Skating to one side.*) Washington, DC! – November, 1945!

MARCH OF TIME VOICE: Great Britain, Canada and the United States propose 'that the trusteeship of the atom bomb be transferred from the United States to the United Nations.' They propose to eliminate atomic weapons from national armaments; and to insure the use of atomic energy for peaceful purposes.

CLIO: Moscow! – December, 1945!

MARCH OF TIME VOICE: The Truman-Atlee-King proposal is accepted by the United States, Great Britain, France and Russia. But with one amendment, made by the Russians and accepted by the Conference, that the prospective United Nations Commission on Atomic Energy be put under the Security Council and thus be subject to the veto of any one of the United Nations.

CLIO: London, January, 1946!

MARCH OF TIME VOICE: The United Nations General Assembly creates a United Nations Atomic Energy Commission to develop a control plan. Such a plan is worked out on the basis of the Acheson-Lilienthal report, calling for: 'an international system of control and inspection able to override both the sovereign and veto rights of any power –'

STAGE MANAGER: Just a moment, Clio. Isn't that virtually a proposal for the beginning of a world government?

CLIO: It certainly is. They proposed 'an international agency endowed with the power to own, manage and control all atomic energy production' and 'the right to send representatives and inspectors to all countries without hindrance.'

MARCH OF TIME VOICE: 'The existing stock of atomic weapons – (as far as we now know, that means the American) – would be turned over to a police force of the United Nations to prevent any aggression.'

STAGE MANAGER: But Clio, isn't it true that Russia raised an objection to this plan?

CLIO: Let Russia answer that for herself.

MARCH OF TIME VOICE: Russia *agrees* that international control of Atomic Energy is necessary. However, she feels that any such control should *follow* and not precede the destruction of all atom bombs or potential atom bombs. Russia further feels that the setting up of international control should *follow* and not *precede* the sharing of the secret of atomic energy now held by Great Britain, Canada and the United States. *Thereafter*, all nations will sign an agreement not to engage in atomic war.

CLIO: June 11, 1947! – Russia proposed a plan agreeing in several major points with that proposed by the United States.

MARCH OF TIME VOICE: One: control of atomic energy shall rest with an international commission. Two: inspection shall be by international personnel. Three: such inspection shall encompass all mines and plants capable of producing atomic fuels. The International Control Agency shall operate its own research laboratories.

CLIO: The Russians, however, continue to disagree with the United Nations, in that they do not believe that the International agency should include *ownership* of materials or management of plants.

Blackout on movies.

STAGE MANAGER: Certainly the cleavage between Russia and the United States is the most alarming situation in the world today. The newspapers are full of it – and the public talk goes on and on – committee reports, amendments, amendments to the amendments, talk, talk, talk – And behind the talk human beings waiting to be given back their place in the world. (*Film shows succession of faces of many nations.*) All these people turning to the United Nations with hope, with belief – Yet the tragedy is that in every country, including our own, behind the public talk and behind the private misery, there are whispers, whispers, whispers –

CLIO: (*Whispering savagely to* HENRY *and* ATOM.) Come on! I tell you *both* to come on!

HENRY: Where you taking us?

Lights up dimly revealing a murky place with FIVE MEN *whispering together. They are:* ARMY, NAVY, BUSINESS MAN, POLICITIAN *and* PROFESSOR EMERSON. *The music becomes honky-tonk, as in a dive.*

HENRY: (*Continued.*) Clio – where *are* you taking us?

ATOM: Sa-a-y! what kind of a joint *is* this?

CLIO: (*Drawing both far downstage where they observe the following scene.*) I've been in this kind of place in every country since the beginning of time. And I've seen these people since the beginning of time.

HENRY: Who *are* they?

CLIO: They're the people behind the scenes – behind the big news – and the big deals – and the big wars.

The whispers grow louder.

ATOM: What are they doing?

CLIO: They're playing a game that's popular in every age, in every country – a game called Power Politics.

ATOM: What they whispering about – *me*?

CLIO: In a way, yes – but most of them don't really know or care what you are, Atom – whether you are good or bad, and whether there *is* any way to reform you. They're always – in every country – after just one thing.

HENRY: What's that, Clio?

CLIO: Sometimes it has to do with people, sometimes with money, sometimes with resources – but they're all after just one thing – and here she comes! – *power!*

The music picks up urgency. Spot on ramp, down which comes POWER, *a beautiful woman.* ARMY, NAVY, BUSINESS MAN, POLITICIAN *and* PROFESSOR, *all converge on her.* ARMY MAN *reaches her first.*

HENRY: She doesn't look as if *she* belongs here, either.

CLIO: She always gets dragged in somehow.

CLIO, HENRY and ATOM watch and listen to the following sequence. All the speeches are done in exaggerated whispers to honky-tonk music.

ARMY: (*As they dance.*) I'm the guy for you, baby. Nothing against these other fellows – but you and I are a natural. You need me, and I need you. And don't forget that I'm paying plenty – one half a billion – a year!

NAVY: May I cut in?

ARMY: (*Very polite.*) If it's a joint enterprise, why not?

NAVY: (*Dancing with POWER.*) You look like a Navy girl to me, sweetheart – slick – stacked – smooth. You're costing me millions, sweetheart. But you're worth every penny of it –

POWER smiles enigmatically and says nothing as BUSINESS MAN cuts in; NAVY joins ARMY and they watch contemptuously.

BUSINESS MAN: Don't let that Army-Navy game fool you, baby. Anything high brass can offer you, I can double. But be careful. Don't give me a double play. Don't forget I've handled girls like you before – gas, electricity, coal, water – all the big girls. Some of those gals have become publicly owned. But they've always regretted leaving me because I'm experienced – I've got the touch – I've got the know-how –

POLITICIAN: (*As he cuts in on BUSINESS MAN.*) Ever think you'd like to live in Washington, sugah? – I could fix it up for you, sugah – I can play along with Army, Navy, Big Business – play along with all of 'em – even Professors. I can fix things – sugah –

ATOM: Boy! Wot a bunch of wolves that gal is with!

CLIO: Every country is a wolf when it comes to power, Atom.

ATOM: (*There is a whispering and a stirring behind the blocks which form the background of the honky-tonk.*) Hey! Henry – what's that?

By twos and threes behind three or four or five different blocks heads emerge, peering over the blocks and whispering.

FRENCH HEADS: (*whispering in chorus with great sibilance.*) *Puissance! puissance! – force! force! – empire! – autorite! – PUISSANCE!!!*

ITALIAN HEADS: *Forza! forza! potenza! potenza! – FORZA!*

GERMAN HEADS: *Macht! Macht! – Kraft! Kraft! – Schreklichkeit!*

POWER again smiles enigmatically and PROFESSOR cuts in on her. POLITICIAN joins ARMY, NAVY, BUSINESS MAN as they watch the following.

PROFESSOR: (*In a rather lofty and highbrow manner.*) I never have played around with such a high voltage girl before – rather good that, what? – and it has been going to my head. But I'll get used to you, my dear, ah – in time. The joker in the whole business *is*, my dear, that I'm the only one who *knows* that you have another side to you, my dear!

PROFESSOR whirls POWER about with her back to the audience

and to a crashing discord in the orchestra we see that the reverse side of her head is a grinning skull. Blackout.

STAGE MANAGER: In the meantime – all over the known globe people are looking for Power's latest hangout – a secret treasure-hunt is going on for something that has suddenly become the most valuable thing in the world – uranium!

In the darkness the faces seen peering over the blocks now come out from behind the blocks to Congo drumbeats from the orchestra. Each one hangs up a placard on a block:

'Congo: Belgium Uranium Commission: *Keep Out!*'
'Madagascar: French Uranium Commission: *Keep Out!*'
'Urals: Russian Uranium Commission: *Keep Out!*'
'South Pole: US Uranium Commission: *Keep Out!*'[8]

This sequence now goes into a ballet satirizing the frantic efforts at secrecy and yet maintaining a steadily mounting visual dramatization of the search for uranium. The Congo drumbeats of this Ballet are augmented by an off-stage CHORUS chanting the elements, in the Periodic Table of the Elements.

CHORUS. (*Behind scene.*) Hydrogen! – hydrogen! – helium! helium! – lithium! lithium! – beryllium! beryllium! (*The elements are now iterated only once in a steadily mounting 'Emperor Jones' kind of rhythm.*) Boron! – carbon! – nitrogen! – oxygen! – fluorine! – neon!

VOICE OF 1ST CHANTER: I am a noble gas!

CHORUS: (*To the ever-insistent drumbeats.*) Sodium! – magnesium! – aluminum!

CHORUS: (*To the drumbeats.*) Silicon! – phosphorus! – sulfur! – chlorien! – argon!

VOICE OF 2ND CHANTER: I, too, am a noble gas.

CHORUS: (*To the drumbeats.*) Potassium! – calcium! – scandium! – titanium! – vanadium! – chromium! –

VOICE OF 3RD CHANTER: Streamlined, I!

CHORUS: Manganese! – iron! – cobalt! – nickel! – copper! – zinc!

VOICE OF 1ST CHANTER: And all the etceteras and the soforths who make up the Periodic Table of the Elements from Number Thirty – *Zinc!* Through, up to, and including Number Eighty-Six –

CHORUS: Radon! Another noble gas!

VOICE OF 2ND CHANTER: Why are we 'noble gases'?

VOICE OF THREE CHANTERS: Because 'we do not combine with any other elements; we act as if we are completely satisfied with ourselves.'

CHORUS: (*As the drumbeats approach climax.*) 88 – Radium! – 89 – Actinium! – 90 – Thorium! – 91 – Protoactinium! – 92 – Uranium!

THE DANCERS: (*As the stage goes wild in a paroxysm of movement, color, sound and drumbeats.*) Uranium! – Uranium! – Uranium! – URANIUM!

Blackout.

ATOM: Gee, that was sump'n.

CLIO: That search is going on all over the world. Why, in one part of Africa alone, the Congo – uranium is an energy source equal to all the world's coal and oil supply.

ATOM: (*Impudent.*) How do you know that, Clio?

CLIO: (*As she executes a particularly intricate skating maneuver.*) *That* particular piece of information came from *Time* magazine, August 11, 1947 – but *I* was there first. On my roller-skates I – am – everywhere! (*She coasts off, her draperies fluttering out behind her.* ATOM *follows, imitating her.*)

The music becomes ominous again; the ballet has cleared. We see a dark and lonely place where three roads meet. There are three signboards, that point in different directions; but as yet we can't read them. ARMY, NAVY, BUSINESS MAN, POLITICIAN *and* PROFESSOR *all come on furtively, with hats and caps pulled over their faces and collars of their overcoats pulled up. Henry stands at the side, watching.*

PROFESSOR: Where are we, anyway? We don't seem to be getting anywhere.

BUSINESS MAN: Is business getting out or staying in? We've invested fortunes and all on a non-profit basis – but we have to look forward to the day when there *will* be profits.

ARMY: What if it *is* dark? We want it kept dark. We should have a complete blackout from the public. Let's keep it dark.

NAVY: There I agree with you, Army. The public knows too much about this – (*Whispers.*)

ARMY: What's that? I didn't get you.

NAVY: This atomic business.

ARMY: Yes, this atomic business.

PROFESSOR: May I point out that the reason we're in the dark and seem to be losing our way is that we don't know where other people are going – in this country or other countries – or what roads they are taking. And they don't know where we are going or what road we're taking, and it all adds up to – fear.

POLITICIAN: We've been in dark places before. There're certain advantages – if you know your way around.

Laugh is heard in the darkness. The MEN *rush together and pull their guns.*

ARMY: What's that?

Lights come up on a STRANGER *leaning against one of the signs, obscuring its words.*

NAVY: Oh, it's nobody. Just a citizen.

STRANGER: Right. Just a citizen. A peaceful citizen. I take it you gentlemen – with the guns in your hands – are all interested in peace.

ALL: Yes, of course. Peace, it's wonderful. Peace, peace, peace, peace, peace.

STRANGER: That's the way I hear them talking all over the world. 20,000,000 men in uniform, but everybody's talking peace.

Lights up on one of the signs: BUSINESS AS USUAL.

BUSINESS MAN: Good. Here we are. Pardon me. (*Starts down the road. Stops and looks back at* STRANGER.) I suppose you're one of those radicals who wouldn't go down this road if they paid you? Well, it looks mighty good to me. The days when you opened your paper and found nothing much to worry about but a bull market. But, of course, you're one of those guys who says we can't go back?

STRANGER: On the contrary, we can go back. And as a matter of fact, that's what's happening. With luck, you could count on fifteen or twenty years of the good old road. More expensive, of course, but worth it. If you have the money.

HENRY: (*Reading the BUSINESS AS USUAL sign.*) Excuse me, but it says here: The last stop on this road is slavery.

BUSINESS MAN: What?

STRANGER: Eventually, anyone who goes down that road of Business As Usual will be taken over and enslaved – by some new master race.

ARMY: Say, this fellow talks sense!

BUSINESS MAN: Doesn't impress me. Awfully old stuff. That's what Hitler tried to do and Hirohito.

STRANGER: You forget a certain bomb and all its ghastly equivalents being prepared for the next war. Today, any race that has those weapons and wants to be a master race, can *be* a master race.

POLITICIAN: Don't *use* those words. It isn't politic yet. We've got to soft-pedal all that Number One priority armament stuff.

Lights up on sign reading: TO WAR.

STRANGER: The second course is to prepare at once for the next war; to recognize its inevitability, to train our children to fight ruthlessly with ever more powerful weapons.

ARMY AND NAVY: (*For the first time noticing* HENRY.) Come along with us, boy.

HENRY: (*Reading second sign.*) But this war sign says: 'Check education, philosophy, religion, art and civilization at the gate.'

ARMY: The Army does not advocate war.

NAVY: The Navy does not want war.

STRANGER: Be realistic. Slave or killer? Which shall it be?

PROFESSOR: (*Strongly.*) We don't want to be slaves or killers. We want to be free men working with free men everywhere. So what road do we take?

STRANGER: The third way is to take steps to prevent war – any war – and this is something that has never in the whole history of the world been carried through to the finish. (*He moves aside and third sign Lights up: TO WORLD PEACE. All look at it.*) Well, what about it? You all say it's where you want to go. Dull, isn't it? No parades up that road. No trumpets.

HENRY: (*Reading the sign.*) It says: 'Road leads through unrest and despair of millions of cold and hungry people who must be warmed and fed.' Well, isn't that just what atomic energy can do? Feed 'em and warm 'em up?

ARMY: We want to go up that road as much as anyone does, but our duty is to protect our country.

NAVY: It may be that the only way to get to that road Peace is to go down the one to War.

STRANGER: Where have I heard that before?

ARMY and NAVY get closer and closer together. BUSINESS MAN edges out of his road towards them and has one foot in each road.

PROFESSOR: I'm entirely for going up that road to Peace. But unless all nations take it, isn't there danger?

STRANGER: Of course there's danger, horrible danger. We've just got to decide whether the risk of that road to Peace is worse than the certainty of the road to War.

BUSINESS MAN: Don't forget. You can't change human nature.

STRANGER: Listen, I've heard a lot of old-fashioned talk from you boys, but that one is motheaten. We human beings have shed all sorts of useless appendages – fins, gills. We've changed from man living in a cave, killing all comers, to man extending himself to include his family, his village, his country. Why can't man extend himself to include the world?

All turn away separately, except HENRY.

HENRY: Why can't he?

STRANGER: I'll tell you why. Because we have never – most of us – as people or as nations, grown up.

ARMY: What do you mean, never grown up?

STRANGER: A grownup person sticks to a job, doesn't he? Works at it till it's finished?

NAVY: The Navy did that during the war.

ARMY: The Army did that, too.

STRANGER: Then why not in peace too? A grownup person has a will to life, not death. A grownup person can work with other people, can cooperate, can be tolerant, can be patient. Don't you think, all of you, that if we had enough grownup people in the world we'd be able to stop war? (*ARMY, NAVY, BUSINESS MAN and POLITICIAN move away from the STRANGER, each in his own thoughts.*) Come down to brass tacks. Are we sticking to the machinery that the nations set up for international accord? Or are we only half-heartedly trying to make it work while at the same time we keep saying it never will? Are we thinking of oil in Iran? Bases in the Pacific? Are we trying to understand the way we look to other nations or are we thinking only of the way other nations look to us? Can we, will we, all of us, all over the world, grow up in time? (*Slowly and thoughtfully,* All except HENRY *go out separately in different directions.*) 'And they went away sorrowful, having great possessions.'

HENRY: I want to grow up. I don't want to die.

STRANGER: Like everyone else in the world, Henry, you'll have to make your own decision. That's part of growing up, too.

The STRANGER leaves. CLIO and ATOM enter.

HENRY: This is an awfully funny light. Do you suppose it's the end of the world?

CLIO: (*Thoughtfully.*) I don't think so.

ATOM: You don't *think* so? – For Pete's sake, don't you *know*?

CLIO: Though History I, no foreknowledge mine, Atom, of the future. I only know the places I have been and the times I've lived through.

HENRY: And have you ever lived through anything like this before?

CLIO: Only three or four times in the six thousand years of my recorded diary has Mankind ever stood at crossroads that could be even remotely compared to this.

HENRY: (*Whispering.*) What were they, Clio? – Can you remember?

CLIO: It was a long time ago. I remember a vast mountain pass – almost two miles up in the air – herds of elephants – with swaying generals on their backs.

HENRY: Elephants?

CLIO: Armed elephants – and scythe-bearing chariots – and hordes of bearded men on horseback.

HENRY: Clio! – That was Hannibal.

CLIO: And I was at these crossroads again with a girl in white armor under a banner of fleur-de-lis. She was listening to voices –

HENRY: (*Awed.*) – waiting for the wind to change by a river –

CLIO: And centuries later – on a battlefield – a man alone, wrapped in a cape, a little man –

HENRY: But big enough – almost – to conquer the world –

CLIO: It didn't turn out that way, did it? He had to decide – they all had to decide. A few of them tried to choose the third road but never enough to amount to anything. (*To* HENRY.) I've stayed with you as long as I can. I've overstayed the time alotted to you. I'll – be – back.

HENRY: Goodbye, Clio –

CLIO: (*She has skated over to the exit and now turns.*) By the way, I'm fond of you both. I hope you'll keep on together. Remember the formula, $E=mc^2$? The scientists don't have a monopoly on that.

HENRY: Energy's plus, you mean? Can't be lost? Adds up to something?

CLIO: Adds up to light – more light than we have ever had – if you two stick together. Goodbye. (*CLIO skates off.*)

HENRY: Goodbye, Clio. – Thanks for everything. (*He stands looking after CLIO, and when he turns his voice has a new mature note.*) Atom, I don't know why, just because no one ever has before, we can't go up that road. There always has to be someone to do things the first time.

ATOM: (*Encouragingly.*) Nothing to stop you.

HENRY: (*Excited.*) Listen, Atom, we've got a heck of a lot of work to do! I'm just going to scout a little up that road, this road marked 'Peace.'

ATOM: Going to be hard going.

HENRY: Oh, I know I can't do it alone. I've got to come back and work with you and with all the people who want to go in this direction. I only want to take a little look-see – just for myself. I'll be back. You wait here.

HENRY goes slowly up the road marked 'To World Peace.' ATOM rises and comes down to audience.

ATOM: So this is the way it's all gonna turn out. – Everybody wanting peace and everybody gettin' ready for war! – (*Pointing to the three roads.*) And nobody with nerve enough to take that one common sense road but a kid – (*Very informally to audience.*) Know what I think? – Well, it's not my business to think – that's yours! But I'll tell you one thing – somebody's got to help Henry. A lot of somebodies – somebody's got to take control. (No, I don't mean any of that Man-On-Horseback dictatorship stuff.) (*Shadow up menacingly through speech.*) You people have got to get together with people all over the world and take control! (*Starts to grow wild.*) Because I can't wait forever, see? – I have my hypomanic moments and when I'm in that state I may go into fission any minute, see? – 92 protons – 92 electrons all going around inside and outside of me at millions of miles a split second! – I'm gettin' so wrought up I'm goin' to have a nuclear breakdown, see? But you won't *believe* it till you're in it. Oh, no! – You're too proud, too smart, too high and mighty. You won't believe a thing till you see it for yourself! Well, I showed you Hiroshima! – I showed you Nagasaki! – I *showed* you Bikini! But no, you have to see for yourself? – All right, all right! – You won't control me? – Then here goes – here *goes!* – If you *don't* control me, *this* is the way it's going to be! (*ATOM disappears.*)

Lights up on a suggestion of the Operations Room of the Western Defense Command, somewhere in the San Francisco area and a hundred feet underground. COLONEL PEABODY, a Wac, is tending a teletype machine that connects the room with the world's principal cities. CAPTAIN BRIGGS and COLONEL SPARKS sit before a sort of telephone switchboard with key switches, lights and labels representing the world's major cities. At a large desk, Center, sits a BRIGADIER GENERAL reading reletype messages.

BRIGADIER: Captain Briggs!

CAPTAIN: (*Facing about and standing at attention.*) Yes, sir.

BRIGADIER: Ready for company?

CAPTAIN: Yes, sir.

BRIGADIER: See that everyone looks busy and on their toes.

CAPTAIN: Yes, sir.

A bell rings.

BRIGADIER: Captain – the door!

CAPTAIN crosses to the door and opens it. All stand rigidly at attention. CAPTAIN goes through the formula of examining passes.

CAPTAIN: Your passes, please. (*He admits a fourstar GENERAL and a CIVILIAN.*)

GENERAL: As you were. (*The men relax. The GENERAL leads the CIVILIAN over to the BRIGADIER.*) Mr President, this is Brigadier-General Anderson, Watch Officer in charge of the Operations Room here in San Francisco.

THE PRESIDENT: How do you do?

BRIGADIER: How do you do, sir? (*They shake hands.*) Mr President, may I present my staff?

He does so, the PRESIDENT repeating the names.

GENERAL: Now, Mr President, this is the nerve center of our counter-attack organization for the western area. The teletype machines you see over there – are on radio circuits that connect us with our embassies and consulates in all the principal cities of the world, and with the other continental defense commands.

THE PRESIDENT: I see.

BRIGADIER: The stations are marked here on the map – We've just come from the defense center, but this is counter-attack. Along that wall – (*BRIGADIER waves to rear.*) – is our control-board. If you'll step over here, sir, I'll show you how it works.

THE PRESIDENT: (*Moving with the GENERAL toward the telephone switchboard against the back wall.*) Defense and counter-attack, eh? Why keep them separate?

GENERAL: Well, the defense has to move quickly, or it is no good at all. But counter-attack – you see, you can't tell just from the direction of an attack who launched it these days.

THE PRESIDENT: No?

GENERAL: An attack, for instance, might be staged entirely by mines planted inside our own borders, so there wouldn't be any means of finding the direction it came from. We have pretty good information that some other countries, as well as ourselves, have got atomic bombs up above the stratosphere, 800 miles above the earth, atomic bombs going around the earth and circling over our heads like little moons. We've put up 2,000 of them in the last year, but we can see about 5,400 on our radar. Those odd 3,400 must belong to somebody! – Anytime, *somebody* can call down that odd 3,400 that don't belong to us by radio and send them wherever they want. There's no telling *which* nation controls those bombs.

THE PRESIDENT: No. (*The PRESIDENT moves towards switchboard.*) General, you haven't told me what these gadgets are for.

GENERAL: This is our counter-attack control-board. You see that every station is marked with the name of a city. And every station has three pilot lights: red, yellow and green.

THE PRESIDENT: (*Examining them with interest.*) All the green ones are on.

GENERAL: That's right, sir. We have radio transmitters in stations in every city of the world covered on this board. But if the transmitters in any station are destroyed, well, we lose the signal from that station. When that happens the green light goes out and the yellow light comes on.

THE PRESIDENT: How about the red light?

GENERAL: Yellow means partial destruction – red means complete destruction.

THE PRESIDENT: And green means peace?

GENERAL: Yes, sir. You see this key here?

THE PRESIDENT: Yes.

GENERAL: That sets off our mines. We have them planted in a great many cities, all over the world, and the radio control circuit can be unlocked from here.

THE PRESIDENT: Have we got the whole world pretty well mined by now?

GENERAL: Well, we haven't bothered much with Asia. And some countries are so hard to get into that coverage is pretty spotty. Our schedule calls for completion of mine installations in two years. But in the meantime, we have *another* card to play!

THE PRESIDENT: No one could say that you're not resourceful, General.

GENERAL: Yes, *sir!* – You remember I told you about the satellite bombs – the ones that are circling around in the stratosphere, 800 miles up?

THE PRESIDENT: Of course I do. What about them?

GENERAL: Well, this other key here will bring down on the city shown on the marker – (GENERAL inspects key.) – this one we're looking at happens to be Calcutta – one of those satellite bombs every – time – it is – pressed!

THE PRESIDENT: You mean to say one of those bombs is earmarked for each particular city?

GENERAL: (Smiling.) Oh, no. The bomb that just happens to be in the most favorable location at the time this key is pressed – that bomb falls on Calcutta. It might be any one of the whole 2,000 that we have circling about up there.

THE PRESIDENT: Well, it's extraordinarily ingenious, I must say. Who'd dare attack us when we're set up like this?

GENERAL: Surely, no one would. I don't think you need expect any trouble, Mr President, not for years and years – perhaps forever.

THE PRESIDENT: (Smiling as he turns to leave.) It's a comforting thought. (To the others.) Well, how do you officers like your job?

COLONEL SPARKS: (Thrilled.) We have a feeling – sir – of grave responsibility.

THE PRESIDENT: To judge by those keys over there, the fate of many nations is in your hands – but always remember that *our* nation is the most precious.

COLONEL SPARKS: Yes, sir.

GENERAL: Well, Mr President, we've fallen a little behind our schedule. They'll be waiting for us at the mess.

THE PRESIDENT: All right, General, let's get along. General Anderson, Colonel Sparks, Colonel Peabody, I've enjoyed very much seeing your installation. Keep on your toes. We're all depending on you.

GENERAL *AND* COLONELS: Yes, sir.

CAPTAIN BRIGGS goes over, opens the door and stands stiffly at

attention as the visitors file out amid a general chorus of 'goodbye' and 'goodbye, sir.' CAPTAIN BRIGGS *closes the door.* BRIGADIER *sits on desk and lights a cigarette.*

BRIGADIER: Well, that's that. The Old Man gave him a good story. I couldn't have done better myself.

COLONEL SPARKS: (Still in the clouds.) Just think: the President of the United States is depending on *us!*

BRIGADIER: Don't get romantic! Don't take it too hard, old boy, if you ever have to press one of those keys. All we're supposed to do is to make the other guy feel sorry. We can't save any lives or rebuild any cities. Never forget what pressing those keys does.

COLONEL SPARKS: Just the same, sir, I'm glad I was born an American. We've got the industrial know-how and we're the *only* ones who've got it. We sit here practically invulnerable, while –

At this moment there is a dull rumble. The floor and the walls of the room shake. The lights go out, except for the green ones on the control-board. Emergency lights, dimmer than the regular ones, come on at once. All men spring to their feet.

BRIGADIER: Good God! What was that?

COLONEL SPARKS: I don't know.

CAPTAIN BRIGGS: One of those damn bombs – one of the *other* 3,400!

COLONEL PEABODY: Must have landed right above us.

BRIGADIER: (Above the confusion of scraping chairs, people rushing to control-board, teletypes, etc.) Sparks! – Get out the red-line messages for the last twenty-four hours! – Peabody! – Get on the phone to Headquarters! – Captain! – Anything from the defense center?

CAPTAIN BRIGGS: My line to them seems to be out, sir.

BRIGADIER: What have you got for status on the control-board? Any city showing yellow or red?

CAPTAIN BRIGGS: It's ourselves, sir! San Francisco's showing red!

COLONEL SPARKS: (Riffling wildly through teletype messages.) This must be it. We're hit! – We're gone! (Screaming.) San Francisco – the city right above us up there – is *gone!*

BRIGADIER: Shut up, Sparks. Take it easy! (To PEABODY.) Can't you get Headquarters?

COLONEL PEABODY: The line is dead. I can't get reserve operations, either. Maybe this *is* the real thing!

COLONEL SPARKS: We better *do* something! Remember what it says in the book: 'Counter-attack must take action before the enemy's destruction of our center is complete.' (Half-hysterical.) We – must – do – something!

BRIGADIER: (Impatiently.) Before we can do something, we've got to find an enemy! – Which one of those keys would you press over there before you found an enemy?

COLONEL SPARKS: (His hysteria rising.) An enemy? – Where'd we find an enemy? – Who'd dare attack us?

BRIGADIER: Somebody must have! (To COLONEL PEABODY.) Peabody, who's got the highest negative rating in the latest State Department digest?

COLONEL PEABODY: Denmark, sir.

CAPTAIN BRIGGS: Denmark!

COLONEL PEABODY: But it's well below the danger-point. This came in a few hours ago: (*Reads from teletype.*) 'Copenhagen – Widespread disapproval of fountain statuary group presented to the King by US. Stop. Fountain being pelted vegetables by hoodlums. Formal protest stating statue insults King received,' and so and so on. Nothing there, I'd say.

COLONEL SPARKS: Nothing there? – With San Francisco in ruins? And all over a lousy set of statues? I say let Denmark have it!

BRIGADIER: Is that the hottest you've got from the State Department?

COLONEL PEABODY: Yes, sir. But I don't think it could have been Denmark, General. (*Reflectively.*) Though come to think of it, that sculptor *does* live in San Francisco.

BRIGADIER: We'd better wait and be sure. Captain, how are your lines now?

COLONEL SPARKS: (*With mounting hysteria.*) You're gonna wait? – Have you gone mad? – Whatever have we *got* this stuff for if we don't use it? – Didn't you hear what the President said? – He's depending on us – they're *all* depending on us! – If you *haven't* got the guts, I have! Denmark! Here we go!

Before they can stop him, SPARKS *rushes to the control-board and presses a key, after shoving* CAPTAIN BRIGGS *to the floor.* BRIGADIER *after* SPARKS *in a flash. He pulls him around and knocks him to the floor.* SPARKS *hits his head hard, and lies quiet.*

COLONEL PEABODY: (*Watching the control-board.*) He did it, General, I'm afraid. Copenhagen shows red – Copenhagen's destroyed.

BRIGADIER: The damn fool!

COLONEL PEABODY: (*At teletype.*) Sir, here's a message from the defense center. They've got their line working again. (COLONEL PEABODY *tears it off and brings it to* BRIGADIER.)

CAPTAIN BRIGGS: (*At control-board.*) Stockholm shows red, sir – Stockholm's destroyed!

COLONEL PEABODY: Of course. The Danes thought it was the Swedes. That export duties row they've been having.

CAPTAIN BRIGGS: And then the Swedes will destroy England, too, just to be on the safe side. Then the British will let the Russians have it, and we'll be next – the whole country. (*He has been reading the message he has been holding.*) Briggs! Peabody! – That wasn't a bomb at all – it wasn't by any stretch of the imagination the Danes.

COLONEL PEABODY: What was it, then?

BRIGADIER: It was an earthquake – three minutes ago – with its epicenter right here in San Francisco. An earthquake – not a war at all –

CAPTAIN BRIGGS: (*Calling from the control-board.*) London shows red, sir – London's gone! And Edinburgh – Manchester – Nottingham –

COLONEL PEABODY: It's a pity the Security Council didn't take time to consider all this.

BRIGADIER: Captain! – We probably can't pull this out of the fire but we've got to try. Send a message on all circuits:

COLONEL PEABODY: (*At teletype machine.*) Ready, sir.

BRIGADIER: To all stations: *Urge immediate worldwide broadcast this message: Destruction Copenhagen grievous error based on idea destruction San Francisco was act of war which it was not. Repeat not. Urge attacks be stopped until situation clarified. There is no war. Repeat. No war.* (*A pause.*) That is the end, Captain – that is the end – no war.

CAPTAIN BRIGGS: (*Who has been watching control-board.*) No war? – The hell there isn't. New York shows red on the board and Chicago and Milwaukee – New Orleans is flickering out just now and – Dark Ages! here we come!

The room rocks, the lights go out. Explosion. All people fall. A cloud of smoke through which the STAGE MANAGER *steps.*

STAGE MANAGER: Ladies and gentlemen – the scene you just saw is not from the pen of a poet – a dramatist – or a dreamer. It is by a physicist, Dr Louis Rideneour. He is allowing us to use it because he wants as many people as possible to *know* – that it *could* happen that way – that if we're not careful, it *will* happen that way. Only if it does, it will be quite too late to do anything about it. For the shadow is still on the wall at Hiroshima – mute symbol of man's terrible power to destroy himself. The only way to obliterate that shadow is to throw across the sky a tremendous affirmation of man's will to save himself from destruction – Whether we can do it and do it in time, rests not alone with the scientists, but with the psychologist – the economist – the philosopher – the artist – with you and with me. For it is still – in this moment of time – December 13, 1947[9] – by some desperate miracle – *our world.*

Blackout.

Story of the play

The theatrical effectiveness of the 'Living Newspaper' was conclusively demonstrated in the productions of 'Power' and 'One Third of a Nation.' This latest edition of the 'Living Newspaper' compares most favorably with the previous ones. Clearly, dramatically, and fearlessly it tells the past, present, and future of the Atom Bomb. It sustains a high level of interest; the story-line is easily followed and comprehended; the message of the play is easily grasped. At the core of the piece is the characterization of the Atom. Any discussion of the Atom is dynamite, but this piece is as carefully documented as seems possible to avoid irrelevant controversy. With the use of dramatic scenes, realistic and symbolic, music, dance, and movies, the piece swiftly explains the nature of Atomic power, its history, the present controversy waged over it and the present impasse. The Second Act demonstrates the potential progress that the discovery of Atomic power can bring to the world. It dramatizes the suggestions of some of the best minds of the age as to how it can be best controlled. Finally, it demonstrates dramatically what may likely come to pass if the destructive potential of Atomic power is loosed upon the world. It closes with the inevitable message that it is up to each and every one in the world to face and accept the responsibility that the discovery of Atomic power has thrust upon each and every one of us.

Notes

1. Change to fit any locale.
2. Walt Whitman, 'When I heard the learned astronomer –'
3. The following scene has been adapted for theatrical purposes from the Hearings before the Senate Section of the Joint Committee on Atomic Energy, 80th Congress, Monday, Feb. 17, 1947, p. 19. The dialogue is verbatim.
4. The following sub-scene has been adapted for theatrical purposes from the Hearings before the Senate Section of the Joint Committee on Atomic Energy, February 4, 1947, p. 121. Dialogue is verbatim. The testimony has been substantially cut, but the intent of the questioning has been in no way altered.
5. Testimony of Agnes Waters, 2/5/47, in the Hearings before the Senate Section of the Joint Committee on Atomic Energy, 80th Congress; verbatim.
6. The exact quote is: 'I've listened to a lot of rag, tag and bobtail that the Senator from Tennessee has produced.' Senator McMahon during the 2/18/47 Hearings before the Senate Section of the Joint Committee on Atomic Energy.
7. Adapted and shortened verbatim from the 2/4/47 Hearings, p. 131.
8. If the director prefers, the placard sequence can be done entirely by ballet; or ballet may be omitted.
9. Use date of current performance.

Note to directors of $E=mc^2$

This script, like any Living Newspaper, should be kept up to date. Also, like any Living Newspaper, it may be changed to suit local conditions. For example, if the play is done in Chicago, undoubtedly a scene at Stagg Field should be included; if done in California, a scene at the great cyclotron might be effective.

For the initial production it seemed best to have Atom played by a girl, but the part could be played, with equal effectiveness and with few changes of text, by a man.

The play could be done either very simply – just a few steps, levels and spotlights – or more elaborately as desired. It could use all projected scenery; or a revolving stage; or simple cut-outs which could be put on jacks and pushed on stage. We produced it with no front curtain, a small stage with several movable units and two small side stages with gauze front curtains which made possible instantaneous revelation, such as *Marines*, *Nightclub* and *Alphabet* scenes. The simple units on the center stage were changed in darkness, usually to music and often as a part of the action.

Movies: The two movie sequences may be omitted, though they add a great deal. The omission of the first in the Los Alamos sequence would require no change of text. If the second film sequence of the United Nations is omitted, some substitution would have to be arranged. For instance, people could march on with placards: 'London Conference,' 'Moscow Conference,' 'Washington Conference' and so forth and could speak the lines now given by the March of Time voice. In our production we assembled a film, cutting and editing to make the films synchronize with the action …

Music: If an original musical score is not used we suggest records as follows:

Act I

1 For the Overture up to the moment when the man falls: the *Scythian Suite* by Prokofiev (beginning of Side 1).
2 Street scene sounds: any street scene record.
3 Nightclub music (1945): *Delta Serenade* or anything with the feeling of *Mood Indigo*.
4 Subway scene: record of teletype or any subway record.
5 Atom motif: Same as Overture – *Scythian Suite*.
6 Chain Reaction Ballet: percussion.
7 Clio motif: *Scythian Suite* (Side 3, about a quarter of the way in).
8 Starry Night: *Scythian Suite* (beginning of Side 4) under the Whitman poem, blending into Holst's *Planets*. The *Venus* movement underlies dialogue and symposium of philosophers.

9 Military music for movie: *Protea Suite No. 2* by Milhaud – Prelude and Fugue (Side 2).

Act 2

1 Advertising Sequence: *Fancy Free* by Bernstein (Side 1).
2 College sequence: As background for entrance of colleges, coming to a climax as Atom mounts podium: *Notre Dame Victory Song* (Tex Beneke *Prom Date* Album).
3 Honky-tonk: *Crayfish Blues* (from *History of Jazz* Album).
4 Uranium Hunt Ballet: percussion and voice chorus …
5 Lonely Road: *Tapiola* by Sibelius (Side 2).
6 Counter-Attack Center: teletype record, as indicated in text. Explosion from any record of explosions.

Special Effects: The script calls for a number of special effects which are extremely effective though not necessary. The following ones seem most desirable: the shadow, Atom's box, flooring for Clio's skates, Atomic corn, and the Control Board in the Counter-Attack Center. (It is, however, possible to do Counter-Attack Center with no actual control-board by placing the board in such a position that the audience can see the faces of the officers as they talk about the lights coming on and off. In this case, rely on colors changing from green to red on their faces.)

Technical notes

At the outset this show is frightening technically, but it need not be. Confronted with thirty-six scenes, some of which are very short, one finds that the entire show must have a single environment, for ease and speed in transitions. This calls for a unit set which shows various aspects of the same unit rather than complete visual changes for each scene. Variety may be accomplished in several ways: (1) by using a stationary assortment of levels and ramps changed by lighting; (2) by breaking the set into rolling units that relate themselves in different combinations with various lighting effects, thereby allowing for variety and smooth scene shifts and giving a more cumulative support to the idea; and (3) by using step levels and projected backdrops. (Slide projectors can be rented.) The best way is to study the script and work out a set that fits the particular stage that will be used.

Special effects

1   The shadow on the wall: a lens projection, which must be handled according to the specific conditions of the theatre in which it is used.

2   Atom's box: a simple three-wheel kiddie-car arrangement enclosed in a box, the front being hinged on and covered with painted gauze which makes Atom invisible. If a swivel wheel is used for the front, a steering apparatus is unnecessary.

3   The floor for skating: a covering of Masonite. Unless pumice powder is spread on the Masonite during the early rehearsals, the surface will be too slippery for skating. From time to time during the run, Clio will have to add pumice to the floor, but it can be swept clean in a short time.

4   Atomic corn: artificial stalks, which can be assembled on the front of the stage, in the pit. The stalks can be cut from wallboard and stiffened with 1 × 2 White Pine. The stalks are then mounted on eight-inch belts protruding from the front wall of the stage. Drill 2 × 4 White Pine for half-inch bolts so that the bolts will protrude about eight inches below the stage level. Insert the eight-inch bolts into the 2 × 4s and affix them to the front of the stage. Drill a half-inch hole in the stalk about eighteen inches from the bottom. The stalks are then mounted on the bolts so that each one is blocked out far enough to fall clear of the adjacent stalk when in a horizontal position. Insert a half-inch screw eye in the bottom of each stalk. Then place a second screw eye or a pulley on the floor under the stalk as it stands in its proper verticle position. From the screw eye in the bottom of the stalk, run a sash cord through the second screw eye or the pulley on the floor. When all the stalks are mounted you will have a line for each stalk, which should be properly labeled and tied off at one side of the pit. The corn is placed in a horizontal position (at which time each stalk should be resting on the adjacent bolt). When the cue for the corn to 'sprout up instantaneously to enormous heights' comes, pull the lines in order as the farmer plants the seeds along the furrow. Four stalks placed about four feet apart should be sufficient. A false front can be used to cover the mechanism and the operators if there is no orchestra pit.

5   The bomb: Consult a local chemist for particulars on preparing a harmless bomb.

For references to original sources used in the making of this play see: *E=mc²: A Living Newspaper about the Atomic Age*, New York: Samuel French, 1947.

3.5 JOHNNY NOBLE (1945)

EWAN MACCOLL

Ewan MacColl (born Jimmie Miller) (1915–89) *was not only a British playwright and committed socialist, he was also a poet, songwriter, actor and folk singer. MacColl's political activities resulted in the counterintelligence service MI5 opening a file on him in 1932. His early theatre work demonstrated a particular interest in 'agitprop' forms of playmaking, and in the early 1930s he formed the Red Megaphones, a political theatre company in Manchester. Subsequently, with Joan Littlewood – also his first wife – he formed the political group Theatre Union (1936), leading ultimately to the formation of the ground-breaking Theatre Workshop (1946). In Johnny Noble (1945) the title-character epitomizes the working-class man who becomes politicized through an actual and emblematic journey of discovery. Subtitled 'An episodic play with singing', Johnny Noble utilizes dancing, poetry and direct-address narration to render the possibilities of political consciousness-raising.*

Characters

1ST NARRATOR
2ND NARRATOR
UNEMPLOYED MAN
1ST YOUTH
2ND YOUTH
THREE GIRLS
JOHNNY NOBLE
MARY
SEAMAN
MARY'S MOTHER
EDDIE
MICROPHONE VOICE
CHORUS
NEWSBOY
DURHAM MINER
TAFFY
NEIGHBOUR
MAN
YOUTH
SINGER
GUARD
WOMAN
SEAMEN
STOKER
GUNNER
1ST LOADER
2ND LOADER
ROARING BOYS
MAN IN AUDIENCE

The curtain opens on a completely dark stage draped in black curtains. On either side of the stage stand two NARRATORS, a man and a woman dressed in black oilskins. They are pin-pointed by two spotlights. Very simply the man begins to sing.

[MUSIC CUE 1]

1ST NARRATOR: (*Singing.*) Here is a stage –

2ND NARRATOR: (*Speaking.*) A platform twenty-five feet by fifteen.

1ST NARRATOR: (*Singing.*) A microcosm of the world.

2ND NARRATOR: (*Speaking.*) Here the sun is an amber flood and the moon a thousand-watt spot.

1ST NARRATOR. (*Singing.*) Here shall be space, here we shall act time.

2ND NARRATOR: (*Speaking.*) From nothing everything will come.

1ST NARRATOR. (*Singing.*) On this dead stage we'll make society appear.

An acting-area flood fades up, discovering three youths playing pitch-and-toss upstage centre.

The world is here –

2ND NARRATOR: (*Speaking.*) Our world.

Up boogie-woogie music. A woman enters, dances across the stage and off. Fade out music.

1ST NARRATOR: (*Singing.*) A little gesture from an actor's hand creates a rolling landscape: (*Speaking.*) or a desert.

2ND NARRATOR: (*Singing.*) A word from us and cities will arise; The night be broken by screaming factories.

Up burst of machinery. A red spot is faded up discovering a half-naked figure of a man. He mimes raking out a furnace in time to machinery. The light and machine-noise fade out together. The man goes off.

1ST NARRATOR: (*Speaking.*) Yes, we speak of days that linger in the memory like a bad taste in the mouth. Come back with us a dozen years or so, back to the early thirties, to the derelict towns and the idle hands, the rusting lathes and the silent turbines.

An UNEMPLOYED MAN enters, stands left centre, yawning.

UNEMP. MAN: Time to sign on. (*He exits.*)

A child enters, a small lonely figure in a pool of white light. She begins a queer abstracted hopping dance.

2ND NARRATOR: (*Speaking.*) Here a child grows up in a desolate land.

1ST NARRATOR: (*Singing.*)
Here is a street
In any seaport town.

Two distant blasts of a ship's siren.

It could be anywhere
Where a man's work is the sea.

The pitch-and-toss players begin to intone their calls.

1ST YOUTH: Heads.

2ND YOUTH: Tails.

1ST YOUTH: It's mine.

2ND YOUTH: What is it?

1ST YOUTH: Heads.

2ND YOUTH: Tails it is.

1ST YOUTH: My shout.

2ND YOUTH: Shout!

1ST YOUTH: Tails.

2ND YOUTH: It's mine.

Fade and hold behind following sequence. Two small GIRLS enter and are joined by the first little GIRL in a singing game.

[MUSIC CUE 2]

THREE GIRLS: (*Singing.*)
Have you seen owt o' my bonnie lad,
And are you sure that he's weel, O?
He's gone ower land wiv his stick in his hand,
He's gone to moor the keel, O.

ONE GIRL: (*Singing.*)
Yes, I've seen your bonny lad,
Upon the sea I spied him,
His grave is green but not wiv grass
And thou'll never lie beside him.

The song fades but is held faintly behind following sequence. The UNEMPLOYED MAN enters, takes a newspaper out of his pocket and begins to read it. JOHNNY NOBLE enters and starts to watch the gambling game.

UNEMP. MAN: Hello, Johnny.

JOHNNY: Hullo.

[MUSIC CUE 3]

1ST NARRATOR. (*Singing*)
Now come all you good people and listen to my song,
It's of young Johnny Noble and I won't detain you long,
Young Johnny lived on the north-east coast where trawler men are made,
And he was quite determined for to follow the sailor's trade.

UNEMP. MAN: Courting again, Johnny?

JOHNNY: You can call it that.

UNEMP. MAN: If you ask me, it's a mug's game.

JOHNNY: Nobody asked you.

2ND YOUTH: It's still a mug's game.

MARY enters. The youths whistle appreciatively.

JOHNNY. Hullo, Mary.

MARY and JOHNNY dance. The gamblers play. The UNEMPLOYED MAN reads his newspaper. The children play.

[MUSIC CUE 4]

2ND NARRATOR: (*Singing.*)
Now Johnny loved a neighbour's lass, young Mary was her name.
His love was deep and tender and burned him like a flame
And Mary had loved her Johnny since she was but a lass,
But you shall soon know their tale of woe and all that came to pass.

2ND YOUTH: You're a liar! It was tails.

1ST YOUTH: I tell you it was heads.

2ND YOUTH: Don't try and fool me. I saw you turn it over!

1ST YOUTH: Are you calling me a cheat?

2ND YOUTH: Yes, and a dirty rotten one at that!

The 1ST YOUTH strikes the 2ND.

2ND YOUTH: You pig!

1ST YOUTH: Take your coat off and I'll show you!

They prepare to fight.

LITTLE GIRLS: A fight! A fight!

MARY: O stop them, Johnny!

1ST YOUTH: Him and who else?

The other characters form a ring round the fighters.

UNEMP. MAN: Now take it easy. Do it proper. Make it a fair fight.

2ND YOUTH: I'll kill him!

They dance a fight. A FISHERMAN enters, watches the fight for a moment and is then noticed by JOHNNY.

JOHNNY: Whitey!

SEAMAN: Hi, Johnny!

The others crowd around the newcomer, the fight forgotten.

1ST YOUTH: I'll settle with you later.

2ND YOUTH: Any time you like.

JOHNNY: When did you get in?

SEAMAN: About an hour ago. We've been lying off the point since early this morning.

UNEMP. MAN: What kind of a catch did you have?

SEAMAN: More than four hundred cran.

2ND YOUTH: Then there'll be work at the fish dock! Come on, let's go.

SEAMAN: You won't be needed.

2ND YOUTH: Not with a load like that?

SEAMAN: They're back in the sea.

JOHNNY: You mean you dumped the whole catch?

SEAMAN: The whole catch. Five shiploads of dead herring caught off the Faroes.

MARY: But why?

SEAMAN: Owner's orders.

Enter MARY'S MOTHER.

MOTHER: Ted White! I didn't know you were back. Where's Dan?

SEAMAN: He's not with us.

MOTHER: Didn't he come back with you?

SEAMAN: No.

MOTHER: Well, where is he?

SEAMAN: Big John was to break the news. He'll be waiting back at your house now.

MOTHER: Ted, what is it? He's not . . .

SEAMAN: Tuesday night it was. The wind came up as we were drawing our nets just north of the Skerries. One minute it was dead quiet with nothing but the slip-slap of the water against the ship and the next it was all wind and thick sky bruised and angry. I never saw the sea in such a rage. It looked as if we'd have to cut the nets, but Dan was for facing it out. We worked there till the wind howled and the sky was in ribbons. By the time we got the nets aboard the sea was in the sky and roaring like a beast and then there came a great black blast and the sea gathered into one big fist of wave. It caught young Syms, the deckie, and crushed him against the cabin. He went limp and spun round like a stick in a cross-current. I saw Dan leap at the wave as a swimmer with a knife might leap to gut a barracuda. I tried to shout a warning but there was no room in the world for any voice but the sea's. The wave took them both.

While he has been speaking, the general lighting has faded leaving only WHITEY and the MOTHER spotlit. The other characters have retreated and formed a large semicircle half-hidden in shadow.

MOTHER: Dead!

CHORUS: (*Whispering.*) Dead! Dead!

MOTHER: First my son and then his father. Lost, both of them lost, for a handful of fishes. For twenty years I have lived with a fear of this night and cursed the cunning of it. I've prayed that the sea would be swallowed up and silenced forever. Curse on the sea that a man should be less to it than a fish.

MARY: O, Mother!

JOHNNY: Mary . . .

MOTHER: Stay away from her! The sea's taken all it's going to take of my life. Stay away from her. No child of mine is ever going to suffer what I've suffered. I'll wash clothes, I'll scrub floors, I'll beg in the street, but no child of mine will ever give her life to the sea or to anything or anyone that belongs to the sea.

During the foregoing passage the lights have faded, leaving only MOTHER and MARY and JOHNNY surrounded by shadows. MOTHER and MARY go off. JOHNNY stands centre stage. He looks round in perplexity. In the distance a barrel-organ plays. The stage becomes dark.

[MUSIC CUE 5]

2ND NARRATOR: (*Singing.*)
Now two years pass and Johnny Noble's
Parted from his dearie;
And still she yearns for his return
And her heart is sad and weary.
The lads all throng at Mary's side
For she has grown full bonny,
But the fairest flower amang them a'
Is the sailor lad called Johnny.

Distant blast of ships' sirens. Enter MARY and EDDIE, laughing.

MARY: I live just near here.
EDDIE: That's a pity.
MARY: Why?
EDDIE: Do you have to ask?
MARY: Well ... goodnight.
EDDIE: Don't go. It's early yet.
MARY: Do you call this early?
EDDIE: Look, when am I going to see you again?
MARY: Oh, some time.
EDDIE: How about tomorrow night?
MARY: No, I can't, I ...
EDDIE: Thursday, then. Listen, I'll tell you what. Let's have tea in town and then go on to the Plaza. They've got a marvellous band there; not like that bunch of amateurs at The Jig. Well, what do you say?
MARY: I'm sorry, but I can't.
EDDIE: Why not? You like dancing, don't you?
MARY: I love it.
EDDIE: Well, say you'll come. I'll see that you have a good time. Look Mary, I want to get to know you better.
MARY: You'd better ask someone else.
EDDIE: I don't want anybody else, that's why I'm asking you. You know, you're too good to waste your time dancing with a bunch of louts at social club hops. I knew that the first time I saw you. You've got style and when you and me dance together I feel like we've been practising all our lives just for that one dance. You see, dancing with you isn't just routine, it's ... O, I can't explain it but when I get that beat ... one ... two ... da di di, da di ...

Faint dance music.

... and feel you in my arms. (*He takes her in his arms.*) Well, it's more than just dancing.

The music grows louder. They dance. JOHNNY advances out of the shadows.

JOHNNY: Mary!

The music stops. The dancers fall apart.

EDDIE: What's the idea?
JOHNNY: Mary, I've got to talk with you.
EDDIE: Now look here, whatever your name is ...
MARY: Alright, Johnny ...
EDDIE: I seem to be in the way. If you'd told me about him in the first place I wouldn't have bothered.
JOHNNY: Beat it!
EDDIE: I seem to be losing my grip. (*He goes.*)
MARY: Well?
JOHNNY: Mary, I had to see you.
MARY: Did you have to spy on me?
JOHNNY: I wasn't spying. I've been waiting here for hours in the hope that I might see you.
MARY: You're shivering. You'll catch cold.
JOHNNY: I'm on fire Mary, I can't go on like this.
MARY: But what can I do? I told you everything was finished between us.
JOHNNY: I don't believe it. If you said it a thousand times I still wouldn't believe it. You and me couldn't live in the same world and not be close to each other. If you and me were finished then the sun would hide its face and the sea stop rolling, the wind would never blow again and every man and woman in this town would talk in whispers. Listen, you can hear the town breathing in its sleep. Do you think it would be so quiet if we were really through?
MARY: Is this what you wanted to say?
JOHNNY: I'm trying to wake you up out of this bad dream.
MARY: I'm sorry.
JOHNNY: Don't talk as if I am trying to sell you something. You remember me? I'm Johnny, the bloke who loves you. Remember?
MARY: I don't want to remember anything.
JOHNNY: Why not?
MARY: Because remembering hurts and I'm tired ...
JOHNNY: Not too tired to dance.
MARY: Is this all you've got to say?
JOHNNY: I once knew a girl who looked just like you. Her hair was softer than a summer's night and her eyes were as deep as the ocean. Even to look at her made me feel good.
MARY: Don't, Johnny!
JOHNNY: Her voice was like yours too, only warmer.
MARY: Oh, why don't you let me forget?
JOHNNY: I keep remembering the things she used to say, the memory of her words won't let me sleep.
MARY: Forget her, Johnny, forget her.
JOHNNY: Sometimes we would walk together along the old moorland road and the feel of her arm in mine made the stars nearer and the sky wider. Everything was different when I was with her. This place wasn't half so dark nor the streets nearly so deserted ...
MARY: Please, Johnny, please don't go on.
JOHNNY: Have you forgotten, Mary?
MARY: How could I forget?
JOHNNY: I love you, Mary.

MARY: No, don't say it ... it's no good ...

JOHNNY: I love you like the earth loves the sun, or the sea the sky, and what's more, you love me, don't you?

MARY: Yes, yes, but what's the good? Oh, Johnny, I'm so miserable I wish I could die. I'm tired of all the pain and hurt that's in loving. Do you think I don't feel all the things that you feel? I think of you all the time. Sleeping and waking, you are part of me, a part that never lets me rest.

JOHNNY: Then why do we act like strangers to each other?

MARY: Because it's the only way for us.

JOHNNY: Mary, you can't let your mother come between us like this. It's our lives ... Oh, I know how she feels about the sea, but ...

MARY: It's not how she feels. It's the way *I* feel. I hate the sea, too. Not just because it took my father but because of you. When I was little I used to lie awake at night and listen to my mother in the next room, lying awake and waiting. Sometimes I'd hear her moaning in her sleep and ... Oh, don't you see I couldn't live like that? I couldn't. I love you too much.

JOHNNY: Alright, you won't have to.

MARY: What do you mean?

JOHNNY: Mary, if I could get a regular job, a land job, do you think you and me could get together again?

MARY: Do you mean it?

JOHNNY: Of course I mean it. Trawling's finished. They tied up another five boats last month, that means the end of the fleet. I've worked fifteen days in the last four months and three of those were a dead loss. I can't sit around waiting forever, and in any case if I have to choose between you and the sea ... I don't care if I never see the sea again.

MARY: But where will you find work?

JOHNNY: There must be one job somewhere that I can do. Anyway, if there is, I'll find it.

MARY: You mean you're going away?

JOHNNY: Yes, Mary, I'm going to fish for work the way we fish for herring. I'll drag a net over the whole country if I have to, and one of these days I'll be writing to you and asking you to come to me. Will you?

MARY: To the end of the earth.

JOHNNY: And you'll wait?

MARY: Till the seas run dry.

They dance to the following song.

[MUSIC CUE 6]

1ST NARRATOR. (*Singing.*)
Fare you well, my dear, I must be gone,
And leave you for a while.
If I roam away I will come back again
Though I roam a thousand miles, my dear,
Though I roam a thousand miles.

2ND NARRATOR. (*Singing.*)
The salt sea will run dry, my dear,
And the rocks melt in the sun;
But I never will prove false to the lad I love
Till all these things be done, my dear,
Till all these things be done.

The lights fade. Up music behind the following. The lights fade up and a CHORUS *of unemployed men enter dancing.*

MICROPHONE VOICE: Crew of the Trawler 'Mary Ellis': Paid off!

CHORUS: No change! No work!

MIC. VOICE: Trawler 'Sun-bird', in dry dock, all repairs at a standstill.

CHORUS: No change! No work!

MIC. VOICE: Crew of the trawler *Merrily*: paid off!

CHORUS: No change! No work!

MIC. VOICE: In future, trawlermen will apply for work at their labour exchange. Ships' husbandmen will no longer book their crews at this dock.

CHORUS: No change! No work!

JOHNNY: What's wrong with the world? What's wrong with me? Don't people need clothes and shoes and houses any more? Don't they need fish out of the sea and coal out of the earth?

MIC. VOICE: The unemployment figures can now be said to be stabilised at two and a half million. No immediate deterioration is expected.

Roll of drums. The CHORUS *fall into line.*

MIC. VOICE: Two hundred Scottish hunger-marchers set out from Glasgow.

The CHORUS *begin to march, marking time.*

MIC. VOICE: November 1931. The unemployed of the north-east coast are marching.

1ST MAN: Men from Newcastle!

2ND MAN: Gateshead!

3RD MAN: Durham!

4TH MAN: Jarrow!

5TH MAN: Morpeth!

6TH MAN: Sunderland!

ALL CHORUS: Shields!

MARY: (*Offstage.*) Wait, Johnny! Wait!

A NEWSBOY *carrying papers and a poster dances on.*

NEWSBOY:
All the latest! Last Edition!
Mr Eden's German Mission.
Paris riots, foodshops looted,
Van de Lubbe executed.
Loch Ness Monster seen again.
Sentence passed on Ludwig Renn.
All the latest!

All the latest!
All the latest!

He goes off. The CHORUS *read their newspapers.*

1ST MAN: Plenty of words!

2ND MAN: Plenty of promises!

3RD MAN: Plenty of circuses!

ALL CHORUS: But no bread!

MARY: (*Offstage.*) Wait, Johnny! Wait!

JOHNNY: Not me, I'm not waiting. I'm going out to find what's wrong with the world. And if there's a job anywhere, I'll find it!

CHORUS *retreat, waving slowly as light fades.*

CHORUS: So long, Johnny! So long, Johnny!
So long!

CHORUS *goes off.*

[MUSIC CUE 7]

1ST NARRATOR: (*Singing.*)
  Johnny Noble has left his home,
  He has walked over moss and moor;
  And he has gone to the banks of Clyde,
  To try his luck in the shipyards there.

JOHNNY *dances across to the* NARRATOR *who suddenly takes the character of an unemployed man.*

JOHNNY: How's things around here, Mac?

CLYDESIDER: Deadly.

JOHNNY: Anything doing in the yards?

CLYDESIDER: No, we've been idle for the last six years. Where are you from?

JOHNNY: Hull way.

CLYDESIDER: Engineer?

JOHNNY: Fisherman.

CLYDESIDER: No work?

JOHNNY: That's right. I thought I'd try the shipbuilding game.

CLYDESIDER: It's a lost trade, chum.

JOHNNY: Are there no jobs at all?

CLYDESIDER: None at all.

JOHNNY: They sound busy enough in there.

CLYDESIDER: That's the wrecking gang. They're breaking up the equipment. Better go south. I'd be there myself if it wasnae for the wife.

The light and the NARRATOR *fade.* JOHNNY *dances.*

[MUSIC CUE 8]

2ND NARRATOR: (*Singing.*)
  In Durham County it is the same,
  The pithead gear is standing still,
  And men are filled with a sense of shame
  For idle hands and wasted skill.

A MINER *enters and stands in a pool of light, centre stage.*

DURHAM MINER: Why, but you've come to the wrong place, mon. There's no work here. Number Three was working until a year ago but that's finished now. The Ballarat seam's flooded out. They'll never get it working again. Why, there's not enough work to keep three men and a boy busy.

JOHNNY: How do you manage to keep going?

DURHAM MINER: Well, we've got our bit of dole and we scratch for coal on the screens to keep a bit fire in the house. Why … aye, but it's bad … it is that … bad all over, though they say things are better in the south …

Music. Man goes off. Unemployed men enter, dancing.

JOHNNY: Which is the road to Darlington, mate?

1ST MAN: Follow the road … straight on.

Dance.

JOHNNY: Which is the road to Leeds, mate?

2ND MAN: Follow the road … straight on.

Dance.

JOHNNY: How do I get to Manchester?

3RD MAN: Follow the road.

ALL: Follow the road, chum. Follow the road. Follow the road, straight on.

JOHNNY: Where are YOU going?

ALL: We don't know, chum. We don't know. We just keep going.

JOHNNY: Well, good luck!

ALL: Good luck, chum!

Slow blackout.

[MUSIC CUE 9]

2ND NARRATOR: (*Singing.*)
  Winter is past and the leaves are green,
  The time is past that we have seen.
  But still I hope the time will come,
  When you and I shall be as one.

The light fades up to half, showing a group of men sitting and lying on the stage.

NARRATOR: Men on the roads, men on the streets. The traversing of the endless circle. Hey, you there!

CHORUS: Yes?

NARRATOR: What are you waiting for?

CHORUS: For time to pass.

NARRATOR: Who are you?

CHORUS: We are the disinherited.

NARRATOR: Where are you from?

CHORUS: From everywhere.

NARRATOR: Where are you bound for?

CHORUS: Anywhere. We walk between one meal and the next.

NARRATOR: And this is your life?

CHORUS: We sign away our lives … every morning.

They lie down and sleep.

[MUSIC CUE 10]

2ND NARRATOR: (*Singing.*)

My Johnny's gone, I mourn and weep,
But satisfied I ne'er can sleep.
I'll write to you in a few short lines,
I suffer death ten thousand times.

One of the men sits up and begins filling his pipe.

JOHNNY: My, but I could do with a breath of air.

TAFFY: Well, there's no shortage of that outside, and no charge either.

JOHNNY: I like my air to be well seasoned.

TAFFY: What do you mean by that?

JOHNNY: My lungs are in need of salt … Oh, for some sea air!

TAFFY: Are you a matlo then?

JOHNNY: Fisherman.

TAFFY: You are a long way from home, bach, there are no fish here.

JOHNNY: No …

TAFFY: You are looking for work.

JOHNNY: Work? What's that?

TAFFY: Yes, things are bad. Tell me, have you ever heard of Potato Jones?

JOHNNY: Potato Jones? Isn't he the skipper of the 'Seven Seas Spray'?

TAFFY: The very man. Captain Jones, the blockade runner. I am sailing with him next trip.

JOHNNY: Oh, you're a seaman.

TAFFY: Ship's cook for thirty-seven years. A galley-slave, my boy.

JOHNNY: Where are you bound for?

TAFFY: Barcelona. We're carrying a cargo of canned milk.

JOHNNY: Dangerous work, isn't it?

TAFFY: Well, I've known safer trips. Master Franco doesn't like people who feed children. Captain Jones makes him very angry.

JOHNNY: It's good work.

TAFFY: You know, I think the captain is short of a deckhand. (*Pause.*) I thought you might be interested. (*Pause.*) Perhaps I shouldn't have mentioned it. Just forget everything I told you.

JOHNNY: Where are you sailing from?

TAFFY: Liverpool.

JOHNNY: When?

TAFFY: Thursday night.

JOHNNY: We'll have to be on the road early, then.

TAFFY: I thought you were the right sort.

JOHNNY: Good night, Taffy.

TAFFY: Good night, bach.

The light fades.

[MUSIC CUE 11]

1ST NARRATOR: (*Singing.*)

So Johnny shipped aboard a craft well known in the coasting trade,
She sailed for Barcelona through the fascist sea blockade.
They beat the German submarines, and floating mines as well,
And then they lay in the sheltered bay, a-heaving on the swell.

[MUSIC CUE 12]

2ND NARRATOR: (*Singing.*)

But back in the home town,
Where time passes slow,
There Mary sits waiting
For Johnny, her jo.
Her trust has not faded
Though they are apart
And the love has not withered
That grows in her heart.

The stage is flooded with light. Two YOUTHS stand upstage right, arguing. MARY sits downstage left. Her MOTHER sits nearby gossiping with a NEIGHBOUR. The UNEMPLOYED MAN stands upstage reading a newspaper.

1ST YOUTH: It was in the fourth round.

2ND YOUTH: No, you're wrong –

1ST YOUTH: But I tell you, I saw the film four times!

2ND YOUTH: I don't care if you saw it twenty times, it was at the beginning of the fifth round, a technical knockout.

1ST YOUTH: That wasn't the Baer fight – it was the Mexican champion.

2ND YOUTH: It was the Baer-Louis fight!

1ST YOUTH: Now look, in the third round, Joe Louis began to work on Baer, didn't he? He got Baer into a corner, see, and began by giving him a few short jabs to the side, I tell you. I can remember every single punch in that fight. He stands there like this, see, crowding Baer …

2ND YOUTH: So?

1ST YOUTH: So Maxie's getting tanned good and proper, so he tries to slip by on the ropes. Well, Louis waits till he's off-balance, see, and then he wades in with a smashing left drive. Maxie tries to side-step it, but Joe follows through with his right and closes Maxie's left eye for him.

2ND YOUTH: Well, who's arguing about that?

1ST YOUTH: You are. Anyway, Maxie's minus a lamp now, see, and this time he doesn't know what day it is. He's been punched around so much. Well, the bell goes for the fourth round. 'Seconds out of the ring! Time!' Clang! Louis crossing the ring looking determined, like, but not tough. He looks like what he's going to do is for Maxie's own good. Now Maxie comes in sparring, but Joe won't play. He leads with his left to Maxie's side. Bang! Bang! Then with his right he breaks Maxie's guard. Bang! Wallop! And then that terrific left swing comes from nowhere and Maxie's out for good. One-two-three-four … I tell you, the referee could have counted up to a thousand. The fourth round it was, and still three-quarters of a minute to go.

2ND YOUTH: It was the fifth round.

1ST YOUTH: You're punch-drunk.

The 1ST YOUTH takes a newspaper from his pocket and begins to study it. The 2ND smokes a cigarette.

MOTHER: My, but it's close, isn't it?

NEIGHBOUR: Terrible. It's just like an oven in the house.

MOTHER: Mary, why don't you go for a walk in the park?

MARY: I'm alright.

MOTHER: It would do you more good than sitting around here brooding.

A man enters reading a newspaper.

1ST YOUTH: What won the 3.30, Larry?

MAN: Castle in Spain at 8–1.

1ST YOUTH: I had a bob on Blue Silk!

MAN: Didn't stand a chance. Came in sixth.

Enter EDDIE.

EDDIE: Hello, Mary. Going to the dance?

MARY: No, I don't think I'll bother.

EDDIE: Still waiting for Johnny?

MARY: What if I am?

EDDIE: I think you're crazy. I bet you've almost forgotten how to dance.

MARY: I'm not complaining.

EDDIE: Mary, how would you like to take a run into the country this weekend?

MARY: No, Eddie, I've told you, I …

EDDIE: Alright, alright! I know the answer. It's a pity though, I've just bought a car.

MARY: A car? Well!

EDDIE: Yes, I've been doing alright.

MARY: You certainly have.

EDDIE: Seriously, though, Mary – you look as if you need some air.

MARY: Well, some other time.

EDDIE: Some other time! I seem to have heard that before. How's Johnny going on? Got a job yet?

MARY: Not yet.

EDDIE: What a mug you are. Hullo girls? Looking for me?

Enter TWO GIRLS.

1ST GIRL: Hullo, Eddie.

2ND GIRL: Coming to the dance, Mary?

EDDIE: No, she's got a date with a ghost.

1ST GIRL: How's Johnny?

MARY: He's alright, thanks.

MOTHER: Why don't you tell them he never writes?

MARY: Why should he? He said he wouldn't write till he found something.

2ND GIRL: I'd want a better excuse than that.

A youth enters playing a mouth organ. The two girls dance.

1ST YOUTH: Break it up, the experts are here.

They partner the girls.

EDDIE: Come on, Mary, you're safe enough here.

They dance. Enter 1ST NARRATOR with a letter.

[MUSIC CUE 13]

1ST NARRATOR: (*Singing.*)
  Which of you is Mary Marsden?
  I've a letter for you.

GIRLS: (*Singing.*)
  Mary, hear what he is saying:
  Here's a letter for you.

1ST NARRATOR: (*Singing.*)
  The lad that gave it to me said
  His name was Johnny Noble.

GIRLS: (*Singing.*)
  Well she knew her love was true,
  Her handsome Johnny Noble.
  Oh, oh, oh, oh, Seaman Johnny Noble.

MARY: Oh, let me see it quickly!

She opens the letter.

GIRLS: Oh, read it quickly, Mary, do
  And tell us what Johnny says to you.

MAN: Is his search for work now done?

GIRLS: And does he write for you to come?

ALL: Oh, read it quickly, Mary.

GIRLS: Oh tell us, Mary, do!

[MUSIC CUE 14]

1ST NARRATOR: Why do you grow so pale? What is so alarming?

1ST GIRL: (*Singing.*)
  Is it then bad news
  Makes you weep and mourn?

2ND GIRL: (*Singing.*)
  Here begins the grief,
  Pain without relief –
  Has he then forsaken his love?

GIRLS: (*Singing.*)
  She is left forsaken,
  Another she is taken,
  Johnny, Oh why do you so?

MARY: This letter – it's from Spain.

1ST NARRATOR: Well?

MARY: He promised me that he was finished with the sea.

MEN: (*Singing.*)

Oh, oh, oh, oh, faithless Johnny Noble.

[END OF SONG SEQUENCE]

MOTHER: I warned you, you should have left him when I told you.

1ST NARRATOR: But why? What's he done except try and keep famine from the door of a brave people?

MOTHER: That's not his business.

1ST NARRATOR: If a man in Spain dies because he opens his mouth to speak his mind, that's everybody's business.

EDDIE: We've enough trouble of our own without going out to look for more.

1ST NARRATOR: You don't have to go out to look for it. It's staring you in the face every time you open a newspaper. Look!

He takes a newspaper out of his pocket.

'Men and women are dying in China.'

A GIRL: That's a long way from here.

1ST NARRATOR: They are dying in Spain and that's not so far away. Aye, and Germany and Austria aren't far away. Look at these four lines in a newspaper: 'It is reported from Hamburg that Rudolph Schwartz was executed this morning for attempting to organise a trade union.' Instead of Rudolph Schwartz it could be you – or Johnny. And we would be his executioners.

1ST YOUTH: Who, me?

1ST NARRATOR: Yes, you. Look, we'll act it.

1ST YOUTH: But don't I need a black shirt?

1ST NARRATOR: Don't worry – Fascism doesn't always wear a black shirt.

MIC. VOICE: It is early morning. The city is still asleep. You have lain awake all night waiting for this moment, the moment when time stops. This is the last time you will ever know the cold air of morning or the streets in the moment between sleeping and waking. This is your last walk.

During the foregoing passage, the lights fade until only the condemned man and the guards are clearly visible – the chorus stands on the periphery of the light. A man advances from the body of the chorus and begins to sing. The rest of the scene is danced.

[MUSIC CUE 15]

SINGER: In the yard of a prison

That at last they might shoot him.

He stood, back to a wall,

Built by men such as he was.

GUARD: Eins! Zwei! Drei!

CHORUS: We mixed the lime and carried the hod

We laid the bricks for seventeen pfennig a day.

SINGER: Even the rifles that were levelled against his breast

And the bullets had been made by men like himself –

GUARD: Vier! Funf! Sechs!

CHORUS: We watched the lathe and turned the steel

For twenty-two pfennig a day.

SINGER: They were by this time long departed or were scattered,

Yet for him they lingered,

Still present in the work of their hands . . .

GUARD: Achtung!

SINGER: Even the men who would shoot him

They were not other than he

Nor forever cut off in their blindness.

CHORUS: Kill him! Kill him! Kill him! Kill him!

A WOMAN leaves the chorus and advances downstage.

WOMAN: Now memory comes, sharp and poignant

Filling his eyes with tears,

Trembling with distant music.

The suns of past summers

Stir in the blood

And the little roots of remembered springs tear at the soul.

CHORUS: (*Gives a long shuddering sigh.*)

WOMAN: Oh, let there be night without stars

Body without movement,

Mind without thought.

Let me die unseen in the night

Feeling nothing but the body's anguish

Under the teeth of the wolves of darkness.

CHORUS: (*Moans.*)

[MUSIC CUE 16]

Bravely he walked still encumbered with fetters,

With fetters forged by his comrades,

And hung on him by his comrades,

And though it was morning then

For at daybreak they marshalled them out,

The buildings were empty and still.

GUARD: Links! Recht! Links! Recht! Links! Recht!

WOMAN: Remember the days of hope,

When the night had ears to hear the words

That leap from house to house

In little blades of fire,

And men had the keen, sharp sight of birds

To recognise the first, trembling spasm of revolt.

Remember the song that thrilled the heart

And made the air itself respond

With brittle murmurings of dreams.

Remember the shared desires and the shared hunger,

The shared belief that all men are brothers,

Remember the sudden crack of voice

That made the streets rise up

And bar the way to soldiers.

These same streets, these same houses.

GUARD: Links! Recht! Links! Recht! Halt!

[MUSIC CUE 17]

SINGER: But to his eyes they sheltered now
A numberless host of workers,
whose strivings and aims are his own –
Now they led him forth against the wall,
And all this he perceived,
Yet understood it not.

The GUARD dances the shooting of the prisoner. The prisoner falls. Blackout. Up music and hold until the lights go up again. All the persons on the stage are discovered in their original positions, asleep.

SINGER: You see?

MARY: They're asleep.

[MUSIC CUE 18]

1ST NARRATOR: (*Singing.*)
Wake you up! Wake you up!
You seven sleepers!
And do take a warning from me,
Be prepared to defend
Your freedom to the end,
Make a stand now for your liberty.

Sound of aeroplane.

2ND NARRATOR: (*Singing.*)
The night is disturbed,
The calmness is broken,
And death overshadows the world,
You can hear the beat
Of an army's marching feet
And the war flags are being unfurled.

Sound of distant bombing.

MARY: What was that?

UNEMPLOYED MAN: It sounded like thunder.

EDDIE: We could do with a storm. My, but it's close.

MOTHER: This kind of weather always puts me on edge. I think I'll go in.

She goes in.

1ST YOUTH: It's a good night for a swim. What do you say?

2ND YOUTH: OK.

They go.

EDDIE: Sure you won't change your mind about the dance, Mary?

MARY: Not tonight.

EDDIE: (*To first girl.*) Come on, kid. You and me's going places. So long, Mary!

They go.

MARY: (*Reading JOHNNY's letter.*) O, Johnny, I wish you were here.

JOHNNY has entered silently.

JOHNNY: Do you?

MARY: Johnny! (*They embrace.*) I can't believe you're here!

JOHNNY: Oh, I'm here, alright. (*He kisses her.*) Does that convince you?

MARY: Oh, Johnny, I've missed you so much. Don't ever go away again, will you?

JOHNNY: I had to go, Mary. I had to find out. You know, Mary, I used to feel lost, as if there was no place in the world for me. There seemed to be no sense in being born. But I've learned something. There's a lot of people like me in the world. We're everywhere, and we're important. Yes, we are, Mary! Oh, I know they let us starve and they don't care what happens to us, but when there's big trouble anywhere we are the ones they call upon for help. You know what, Mary? I've discovered that everything that's worth looking at in all the towns and cities of the world was built by people like us. I don't feel lonely any more because I know there's a man in Madrid just like me and at this moment he's fighting a German tank with a bottle of petrol. There's a million like me in China picking off stray Japs with obsolete rifles. I used to walk around like a mongrel dog begging for a bone but that's all over. I know who I am now, and I know why I'm here. I don't know why I'm saying all this to you, but ...

MARY: I want to hear it.

JOHNNY: It's funny, but it's not what I intended to say.

MARY: No?

JOHNNY: No – I was going to ask you to marry me.

MARY: What, now?

JOHNNY: Well, not tonight, say in a week's time.

MARY: Ah ... (*She weeps.*)

JOHNNY: What's wrong? Did I say something?

MARY: Oh, I'm so happy.

JOHNNY: Then you will?

MARY: Of course.

JOHNNY: I've done it! I've done it! I've done it!

1ST YOUTH enters.

JOHNNY: Hey, cocky! I'm going to be married!

He whirls the YOUTH in a dance.

1ST YOUTH: Hey, Johnny's gone crazy.

Enter 2ND YOUTH.

2ND YOUTH: What's wrong?

1ST YOUTH: He's getting married.

2ND YOUTH: Larry, they've fixed up. They're getting hitched.

UNEMPLOYED MAN enters.

MAN: Congratulations, Mary – and you too, Johnny.
BOTH: Thanks, Larry.

Enter MARY'S MOTHER.

MOTHER: What's happening?
MARY: Johnny's asked me to marry him.
MOTHER: Ah, well, I knew it would come to it some day.

MOTHER kisses JOHNNY. The others enter.

1ST GIRL: Is it true, Mary?
MARY: Aye, it's true.
JOHNNY: And the whole street's invited to the wedding.
1ST YOUTH: Will there be a dance?
JOHNNY: Aye, you can dance yourself down to the knees.

He plays a jig on a mouth organ. The others dance until suddenly the jig is drowned out in a great sustained phrase of music. Slow fade-out.

MIC. VOICE: I am speaking to you from the Cabinet Room of Number 10 Downing Street. This morning the British Ambassador in Berlin handed to the German Government a final note stating that unless their troops were withdrawn from Poland by eleven o'clock this morning a state of war would exist between us. I have to tell you now that no such undertaking has been received and that, consequently, this country is at war with Germany.

Up level drone of planes behind the foregoing sequence. Cut in on last word with music, hold at peak and cross-fade with heavy ticking of clock. Hold behind the following.

MIC. VOICE: Passengers for Preston, Lancaster, Carlisle and Glasgow will leave on number 3 platform at 5.43. The train for Preston, Lancaster, Carlisle and Glasgow will leave number 3 platform at 5.43.
ANOTHER VOICE: Not much time left.

Two groups of figures, each composed of a man and a woman, are discovered embracing in two yellow pools of light.

1ST WOMAN: Don't forget your sandwiches, Jim. I've put them at the top of your case. And let me know your address as soon as you get there. I'll send you a parcel. Must keep talking, Jim, we must keep talking. It's queer, the minutes are bleeding away and all I can talk about are the things furthest from my mind. Do look after yourself, Jim, and don't forget to send anything you want washed. Four more minutes and it'll be the end. Oh, God!

Towards conclusion of foregoing fade up clock backed by voice.

VOICE: (*Whispering.*) Hurry, etc.
MIC. VOICE: The train for Crewe, Hereford, Birmingham, Pontypool and Bristol, will leave number 11 platform at 5.58.
MARY: Go on talking, Johnny, please go on talking. If we stop talking we'll start thinking. Take care of yourself, Johnny.

And please write as often as you can. Oh, so much to be said and no words to say with. If you need anything just write and I'll send it to you. Only a few minutes left and then … Perhaps it won't be for long. I'll be waiting for you. Oh, if only the clocks would stop forever!

Ticking of clock at peak. Sudden high-pitched blast of train whistle.

MIC. VOICE: Johnny Noble, able seaman!

JOHNNY looks round.

JOHNNY: It's time, Mary.
MIC. VOICE: James Munroe, bricklayer!
1ST MAN: It's time, lass.
MIC. VOICE: Young men, it's time to say goodbye.

The couples embrace. The men go off. The two women, lonely figures in the pools of yellow light, stand without moving. There is a sudden, loud, blast of escaping steam and the women begin waving handkerchiefs. The train gets under way and as the light fades there are two, short, melancholy blasts of the engine's whistle as it passes into a long tunnel.

MIC. VOICE: If only one could choose one's moments of eternity – but inexorable time divides and sub-divides and sub-divides again until nothing is left of a moment but an insubstantial memory.

Complete blackout.

MIC. VOICE: And everything is left unsaid except – Goodbye.

[MUSIC CUE 19]

2ND NARRATOR: (*Singing.*)
Westryn wind, when wilt thou blow?
The small rain down doth rain,
Oh, that my love were in my arms,
And I in my bed again.

Deep and wide the river runs
That steals my lad away,
And I must bide it here alone
And cannot bid him stay.

[MUSIC CUE 20]

1ST NARRATOR: (*Singing.*)
In nineteen hundred and forty two,
In November, the thirteenth day;
The 'Liberty Star' her anchor weighed
And for Murmansk bore away, brave boys,
And for Murmansk bore away.

Our course was set for nor'-nor' east,
Through the raging arctic sea, brave boys,
Through the raging arctic sea.

Fade up throb of ship's engines. Light fades up discovering JOHNNY seated on a box playing 'On top of Old Smokey' on a mouth organ. A STOKER enters. JOHNNY stops playing.

STOKER: Go on playing, Johnny. I just came up for a breather.
JOHNNY: My hands are too cold.
STOKER: What's her name, Johnny?
JOHNNY: Mary.
STOKER: The wife?
JOHNNY: Not yet.

Short blast of ship's siren.

STOKER: That'll be the 'Sverdrup'. She should be astern of us.

Two short blasts of ship's siren.

JOHNNY: My, but it's cold!
STOKER: Is this your first trip up here?
JOHNNY: Well, I was up as far as Iceland once.
STOKER: Iceland! That's the tropics. Wait till we reach the Behring Sea, then you'll know what cold is.
JOHNNY: How long have you been at this job, Frank?
STOKER: Thirty-seven years.
JOHNNY: That's a long time.

Three short blasts of ship's siren.

STOKER: Yes, I know these waters better than I know the back streets of Salford. I remember sailing up into the Kara Sea when the insurance risk was only three shillings to the ton. That's going back a bit. And I'd been up to the Chukotsk Sea twice by the time I was twenty. The first skipper I ever sailed with was one of the old timers of the Hull whaling fleet, never felt happy unless he was freezing off the coast of Greenland. A fine man. I was off Bear Island with the trawlers when this lot started. We were lucky to get home. I'll bet the halibut wondered what was happening.

The repeated alarm signal of a destroyer is heard. The clanging of bells. Red and green warning-lights flash.

STOKER: Back again!
JOHNNY: Well, come on then.

They race off. Blackout. Fade in droning of plane. Build to peak and hold with backing of music.

VOICE: (*Above music.*) Enemy, Green Nine-O!

Siren. Music out.

VOICE: Action station!

Fade up lights. Gun crew discovered stage centre. In the following scene they dance a gun crew in action. Up sound of circling plane.

1ST SEAMAN: What is it? Dornier 109?
GUNNER: Well, it's not a seagull.
VOICE: Bearing Green Nine-O!
GUNNER: Bearing Green Nine-O!
1ST LOADER: Bearing Green Nine-O!

Music. In dance mime the crew load and fire the gun.

1ST LOADER: Load!
2ND LOADER: Load!
1ST LOADER: On!
2ND LOADER: On!
GUNNER: Fire!

Music.

1ST LOADER: Load!
2ND LOADER: Load!
1ST LOADER: On!
2ND LOADER: On!
GUNNER: Fire!

Bomb explosion.

VOICE: Bearing Red Five-O!
LOADERS: Bearing Red Five-O!
GUNNER: Red Five-O!
1ST LOADER: Load!
2ND LOADER: Load!
1ST LOADER: On!
2ND LOADER: On!
GUNNER: Fire!
1ST LOADER: Load!
2ND LOADER: Load!
1ST LOADER: On!
2ND LOADER: On!
GUNNER: Fire!

Sound of dive-bombing and machine-gun fire. Crew drops to ground. One loader is killed.

[MUSIC CUE 21]

NARRATOR: (*Singing.*)
The Nazi planes from Christiansund
Above our ships did fly,
But our ack-ack guns got the measure of the Huns,
And we blew them from the sky, brave boys
And we blew them from the sky.

The members of the gun crew re-form and resume the dance.

1ST LOADER: Load!
2ND LOADER: Load!
1ST LOADER: On!
2ND LOADER: On!
GUNNER: Fire!
SEAMAN: He's falling! Look! Look!
2ND SEAMAN: There he goes!

Drone of plane falling followed by explosion. The crew cheer and the lights fade out.

[MUSIC CUE 22]

2ND NARRATOR: (*Singing.*)
And back in the homeland,

Where time passes slow,
There Mary sits waiting
For Johnny, her jo.

Her trust has not faded,
Though they are apart,
And the love has not withered
That grows in her heart.

Full lighting. JOHNNY *and a woman* NEIGHBOUR *enter from opposite directions, dancing.*

[MUSIC CUE 23]

NEIGHBOUR: (*Singing.*)
O Johnny, O Johnny, O Johnny,
And is it yourself that I see?
I thought you were on the Atlantic.
JOHNNY (*Singing.*)
I've been up through the cold northern sea.

TWO GIRLS enter, dancing.

TWO GIRLS: (*Singing.*)
It's Johnny, it's Johnny, Johnny Noble's come home,
He left his love, Mary, the wide world to roam;
But now he's come back from the ocean.
You're a welcome sight, Johnny, to me.

TWO YOUTHS enter, dancing.

1ST YOUTH: (*Singing.*)
Tonight let's all go out upon a binder.
TWO GIRLS: (*Singing.*)
There's a girl who's waiting patiently
To hear that you are safe.
ALL: (*Singing.*)
Hurry up, man, hurry up, man,
And find her.

MARY enters, dancing. She dances with JOHNNY.

[MUSIC CUE 24]

TWO GIRLS: (*Singing.*)
Winter is past and the leaves are green,
The worst is past that we have seen;
And now at last the time has come
When these two hearts shall be as one.
UNEMPLOYED MAN: (*Singing.*)
O Johnny lad, and are you glad
To be with us back home?
JOHNNY: (*Singing.*)
Why aye, but man, of course I am,
No more I wish to roam.
I've done my share of freezing
As you may understand,
And I've known some cold Nor'westers
On the banks of Newfoundland.

ALL: (*Singing.*)
He's done his share of freezing
As you may understand,
And he's known some cold Nor'westers
On the banks of Newfoundland.
YOUTH: (*Speaking.*) Never mind, Johnny, that's all over and done with. You're back home and that's all that matters.

The ROARING BOYS, *two grotesque figures wearing black tights and bowler hats, leap on to the stage.*

ROARING BOYS: Yes, it's over and done with.
ALL: The war is over now.
1ST R. BOY: No more government attacks.
2ND R. BOY: No more excess profits tax.
1ST R. BOY: No more joint production groups.
2ND R. BOY: No more nonsense from the troops.
ALL: No?
R. BOYS: No!
1ST R. BOY: Time we got back to normal. Can't go on being a hero forever, Johnny. The heroes have had their day. Now it's our turn. Business as usual, that's our slogan.
ALL: Which business?
R. BOYS: Money business.
1ST R. BOY: Time we got back to normal.
2ND R. BOY:
Time we got back to the good old days,
The happy-go-lucky production ways.
1ST R. BOY:
Back to the dignified position
Of unrestricted competition.
2ND R. BOY:
Back to surplus and higher rent,
And a profit of eighty-four per cent.
Back to normal.
1ST R. BOY: Back to normal.
BOTH R. BOYS: Back!

The CHORUS *have retreated in the face of their dance. Now, the* 1ST ROARING BOY *produces a whistle and blows a sharp blast on it. The* CHORUS *turn stiffly and go through, the motions of clocking in. Each time one moves a bell rings. When they have all clocked in he blows another blast on the whistle. The* CHORUS *dance a machine which the* TWO ROARING BOYS *accompany with the rhythmic reiterations of:*

R. BOYS: Time! Time! Time! Time!

The machine speeds up. At peak, JOHNNY *interrupts.*

JOHNNY: Stop!

The members of the CHORUS *straighten up like men coming out of a dream.*

JOHNNY: The war wasn't fought for this. They said it would be different. They said …

1ST R. BOY: Time to forget. Time to get back to the good old days. The days of plenty.

JOHNNY: Plenty of what?

CHORUS: Hungry bellies and long queues, plenty of time and nothing to do with it.

1ST R. BOY: That's life, Johnny. Survival of the fittest.

JOHNNY: We fought for something better.

CHORUS: Yes!

2ND R. BOY: Time you forgot the fighting, Johnny. You can't fight tradition. You can't fight history.

JOHNNY: But they said ...

Bell clangs.

1ST R. BOY: Time to forget! Seconds out of the ring! Time! On my right, ladies and gentlemen, standing in the shadows of protective might is Battling Johnny Privilege the heavyweight champion of the world. On my left, the challenger Johnny Noble, representing the pipe-dreamers. The prize is the Universe. Seconds out! Time!

A bell clangs. JOHNNY *comes out fighting and then drops his guard and looks round in daze.*

JOHNNY: I can't see him.

1ST R. BOY: Never mind, kid. Forget it. We've got a boom on our hands. A trade boom. Now you go home and leave everything to me. I'll fix things so that you don't have to think about anything.

He begins to shepherd JOHNNY *off the stage.*

MAN: (*In audience.*) Hey Johnny!

JOHNNY: Who was that?

MAN: It's me, Johnny.

JOHNNY: I seem to recognise the voice.

MAN: Do you remember a trimmer called Johnson who was drowned in the Barents Sea. That was me, Johnny. I was a little-piecer from Bolton called Arkroyd. I died screaming in the Burmese jungle. There was a bricklayer called Brown with a wife and three kids in Birmingham. The Germans burned him with a flame-thrower. That was me, Johnny.

1ST R. BOY: It's time we forgot about the war.

MAN: It's time you remembered why the war was fought. There's a job to be done, Johnny.

JOHNNY: But what can I do?

MAN: You've two hands and a brain and there's plenty of you. Take the world in your hands, Johnny, and wipe it clean. It's up to you, Johnny.

JOHNNY: Do you hear that? It's our world. It's up to us. We can do it, can't we?

CHORUS: Yes!

JOHNNY: Thanks, pal, for reminding me.

MAN: That's all right.

MAN *turns and walks slowly up the centre aisle. Turning, he addresses the stage.*

MAN: So long, Johnny. Good luck!

JOHNNY: So long, pal.

CHORUS: So long.

[MUSIC CUE 25]

MAN: (*Singing.*) This is the end.

2ND NARRATOR: (*Singing.*) The end of the story of Mary Marsdon and Johnny Noble.

3.6 Suffrage Theatre: Community Activism and Political Commitment (2006)

SUSAN CARLSON

THE THEATRE ASSOCIATED WITH the early twentieth-century suffrage movement in England is a bundle of contradictions. The suffragists were mostly middle-class women, women bred for the interiors of the home who became strategists of public space and massive public events. Their theatre, which ranged from public-hall skits to full-length plays in West End theatres, was at once conservative and radical. The suffragists dressed in harmony for public events, wearing the identifiable, co-ordinated colours of their organizations; at the same time they destroyed public art, torched golf courses and chained themselves to fences. In sum, the women (and men) involved with suffrage theatre drew from theatrical conventions which they knew and modified them for the commotion of the public square, the public hall and the streets as well as for the theatres. Memorable plays were not necessarily the main product of suffrage drama, but rather a concept of theatre which involved the streets as well as the stage and an expanded sense of women's roles in both places. Suffrage theatre had a duration of less than a decade, but it foreshadowed the now familiar conventions of subsequent community-based political theatre.

The suffrage community and its affinity with theatre

Most historians of the British suffrage movement date its beginnings to the advocacy of Mary Wollstonecraft or John Stuart Mill, but decades of nineteenth-century strategizing and commitment are overshadowed by the best-known and most intense years of the campaign, those in the decade preceding World War I, stretching roughly from 1905 to 1914. While the primary goal of the suffrage movement was obtaining the vote for women, the drive for enfranchisement was entwined with a variety of debates on related issues such as women's position in law, white slavery, the economic conditions of marriage, education, birth control and family roles, and taxation. The radical tactics of the Women's Social and Political Union (WSPU, founded in 1903), who preached 'deeds not words', were well known; they engaged in prison hunger strikes, breaking windows in public buildings and disrupting public events. Yet each of the major suffrage organizations, from the most radical to the most conservative, made use of public space and theatrically inspired events to promote the cause of the vote for women. Suffragists performed everything from monologues to tableaux, pageants to parodies, one-act to full-length plays in West End theatres, Hyde Park, labour halls, garden parties, and city streets and squares. The entity of 'suffrage theatre' was as much influenced by the political organizations and arguments of its day as it was by the aesthetics and practices of the theatre – and the fact that the two realms came together is a significant moment in theatre history.

The WSPU, the NUWSS (National Union of Women's Suffrage Societies), the WFL (Women's Freedom League) and other suffrage organizations provided the backbone of suffrage campaigning in the early twentieth century, but they were bolstered by groups of more specific affiliation such as the Actresses' Franchise League (AFL) and the Women Writers' Suffrage League, two groups central to suffrage theatre. Founded in 1908, the AFL had a membership of practising actresses, and the group was the gravitational centre of the explosive phenomenon of suffrage theatre. These actresses banded together, pledging to use their professional skills to advance the cause of women's suffrage: they trained activists in public speaking and presentational skills and, in extreme circumstances, helped costume suffragists on the run from government officials. With a literary department run by Australian-born Inez Bensusan, the AFL was responsible for the creation and production of a large share of the plays which directly staged the issue of suffrage. Working with branches of the suffrage societies to schedule performances of the plays, Bensusan and the AFL enlisted established writers like Beatrice Harraden, Cicely Hamilton, Laurence Housman and Bernard Shaw along with little-known and first-time playwrights. Motivated by the AFL's efforts, many women whose prior role in theatre had solely been acting became leaders, activists and, most importantly, writers. With some overlap in personnel, the Women Writers' Suffrage League operated in a parallel fashion as a location for women writers to pool their talents in support of women's suffrage. Cicely Hamilton and Elizabeth Robins, two writers who played key parts in the theatre of the day, were joined in this second group by Sarah Grand, Olive Schreiner, Ivy Compton Burnett and others. The plays that resulted were lively, sometimes raw, sometimes refined, but always provocative and engaged, and they were performed variously to a scattering or to thousands. As Julie Holledge has documented, the AFL played the more significant role, and while not solely responsible for suffrage theatre, this organization ensured that theatre and performance were a staple in the politics of the suffrage cause.

Of course, the context for suffrage theatre goes far beyond such organizations, and its activism must also be contextualized in terms of the other major political issues of the time: imperialism, nationalism and liberalism (Mayhall et al. 2000: xv). The suffrage theatre rarely addressed issues of race and nation which Britain's early-century global reach might have raised. In general, the suffragists writing plays and producing theatrical events tended to rely on conventional dramatic forms and concentrated on one political issue – the vote; their plays did not interrogate other social and cultural assumptions. In the main, suffrage theatre supported the politics of a variety of pro-suffrage groups, but there are moments when the critique also stretches to the power stratifications of marriage and class.

Theatre on demand: portable and provocative

In the end, it is very difficult to separate the intensity of the politics between 1905 and 1914 from the innovations of suffrage theatre, and it is hard to imagine the campaign for the vote without its highly visible performative aspects. Hilary Frances describes some of the WFL's interventions as fun-filled and highly symbolic, strategies she refers to as 'non-violent militancy' (Frances 2000: 189). The campaign for suffrage was configured in terms which were celebratory, transgressive and civil, and elsewhere I have used the words 'comic militancy' to convey the same idea (Carlson 2000: 198). As the mostly middle-class women involved moved the suffrage campaign into more public spaces in the years just before the war, they deployed a variety of performance venues and outlets, from social gatherings to newspapers, from political rallies to theatre stages.

Perhaps the most comfortable theatrical moments were those that took place as a part of the at-homes (neighbourhood suffrage meetings) and festivals put on to bring together those who were members of suffrage organizations and to persuade others to join them. Such meetings conducted business, featured speakers and often included performances of plays to rally those in attendance. Some of the one-act suffrage plays that were most popular included Cicely Hamilton and Christopher St John's *How the Vote Was Won* (1909), Evelyn Glover's *A Chat with Mrs Chicky* (1912) and Hamilton and St John's *The Pot and the Kettle* (1909). The 'Garden Fete', put on by the Croydon branch of the WFL in the summer of 1912, serves as a representative example of the oftentimes elaborate but domestically rooted suffrage 'events'. It welcomed women, children and men; offered food and embroidered items for sale; included a children's chorus and a political speech by WFL president C. Despard; and boasted as a capstone event performances of Glover's *A Chat with Mrs Chicky* and Graham Moffat's *The Maid and the Magistrate*.

Even larger events, like the Yuletide Festival held in the Albert Hall in December 1909, followed similar patterns of using theatrical performance as a climax to a programme of speeches, participatory events, networking and socializing. The programme included many of the plays which were most successful at buoying the suffragists: *The Pot and the Kettle*, *How the Vote Was Won*, and Cicely Hamilton's *A Pageant of Great Women* (staged by Edith (Edy) Craig). As reported in the *Vote*, the climactic *Pageant* was memorable: 'There has never been anything like this Pageant, which brought the day to a fitting close. It sang in one's blood with its colour harmonies and the sonorous sound of its message' (*Vote*, 16 December 1909, 89). The suffrage newspapers of the day document constant performances of suffrage plays in meetings of the London suffrage societies as well as in society meetings around the country (see Carlson 2001: 339–40).

The four London suffrage newspapers contributed to suffrage theatre by publishing plays regularly;[1] some of these plays saw performance, but many are a curiously unstageable mixture of dialogue and politics. Unlike the plays which saw heavy use at suffrage society meetings and which were generally upbeat and comic in form, plays in this second group were often more probing in their politics and tended to be unwieldy as theatre. The *Vote*, the organ of the WFL, published the largest number of such plays, including Alice Chapin's *At the Gates* (slated for performance at the Yuletide Festival in 1909 but dropped from the programme due to time-pressure), a play in which a suffragist sits through the night at the gates to Parliament, handing out petitions to all who pass by. From those who walk by, she accumulates responses which range from abuse to sympathy. The play is reflective and hopeful, but promises no political victory. Winifred St Clair's *The Science of Forgiveness* (*Vote*, 21 November 1913, 51, and 28 November 1913, 71–2; no known performance) places the argument for the vote in the context of sexual infidelity and a double standard for men and women involved in extra-marital affairs. While the play ends with key parties agreeing to equal treatment for men and women, it is not clear that this equitable agreement will lead to happiness for anyone. Perhaps the most common suffrage narrative in these newspapers is the 'conversion' play, in which the main event is the conversion of a non-believer to the cause of women's suffrage. Good examples are 'A. N.'s *Mr Peppercorn's Awakening* (pub. 1912), Edith M. Baker's *Our Happy Home* (pub. 1911) and A. L. Little's *The Shadow of the Sofa* (pub. 1913).

One of the most interesting developments in the newspapers was a collection of plays about selling suffrage newspapers, the most striking of which is Gladys Mendl's brief piece *Su'L'Pavé*, subtitled 'Half an hour in the life of a paper-seller' (*Votes for Women*, 9 January 1914, 224; no known performance). From the many people who walk by as she hawks her copies on the street, the paper-seller receives verbal batterings as well as unexpected support. The play's attention to women in new public spaces was one of many dramatic reflections on the ways in which the suffrage campaign was redefining public space as well as women's use of it.

From 1907 on, London itself also became a stage for the suffragists, who planned marches, meetings, and processions drawing hundreds of thousands at a time. In 1908, the WSPU arranged for 30,000 suffragists to take seven different processional routes through London to Hyde Park, where they were joined by up to half a million supporters. The Women's Coronation Procession of 1911, the 1913 funeral procession for suffrage martyr Emily Wilding Davison (who died after running in front of horses on the Derby race course), as well as the massive protest marches, like that in 1908, were often planned by women of the theatre and were in essence performances designed to drum up political support.

The conventional stages of London's early twentieth-century theatre were also conscripted for the suffrage cause, beginning with the performance of Elizabeth Robins's three-act play *Votes for Women!*; the play was staged under Harley Granville Barker's direction at the Royal Court in 1907. It set a high standard of writing for the suffrage plays to follow, but also opened a floodgate through which flowed the hundreds of suffrage plays written in the next seven years. Robins's play, like many other suffrage plays, was given a matinée performance, and many of London's key West End theatres, as well as its well-known actors and actresses, followed suit with the staging of plays directly about the vote as well as plays focused on issues of gender equity and gender roles. More notable efforts include Cicely Hamilton's *Diana of Dobson's* (1908), George Bernard Shaw's *Press Cuttings* (1910) and Charlotte Gilman's *Three Women* (1912). Matinée performances remained a constant, in part a reflection of the availability of the largely female audience they appealed to and in part a result of an explicitly political content. As was the case for many small theatre societies, censorship was a constant threat.

Women began to take on more prominent theatrical roles, perhaps as a result of such suffrage activism. Most importantly, women had key responsibilities in theatrical management in London and other cities: Annie Horniman did ground-breaking work at the Gaiety Theatre in Manchester, as did Edy Craig, Lena Ashwell, Gertrude Kingston, Lillah McCarthy and Lilian Bayliss in London. In addition, a simple cross-check of suffrage events with theatre events reveals that many of the most prominent actors played roles in suffrage plays or politics. Those active in the cause included Ellen Terry (whose daughter Edy Craig was one of the most important suffrage strategists), Laurence Housman, Johnston Forbes-Robertson, Gertrude Elliott, Henry Ainsley, Dorothy Minto, Ben Webster, Nigel Playfair, May Whitty and Harcourt Williams.

Suffrage plays

Sheila Stowell has defined the term 'suffrage drama' as referring to the 'auspices under which these plays were produced, not their specific content' (Stowell 1992: 42); and indeed, while the vast majority of plays staged by suffrage organizations made direct references to the vote, not all did, some preferring a more general focus on social issues. The plays reviewed below will, in general, offer at least some direct attention to the vote or will have been used in some major way by those campaigning for the vote.

Robins's *Votes for Women!* offered an auspicious start to suffrage drama. Drawing both from comedy of manners and from agit-prop pageantry, the play is simultaneously predictable and subversive, and exemplifies the contradictory theatre practices of the time. Act I offers recognizable drawing-room comedy in which a group of country-house weekend guests mix social flirtations with politics. Vida Levering, a politically active campaigner whose presence raises questions about her past, stands shoulder to shoulder with Jean Dunbarton, a politically naïve heiress. Both are inextricably linked to MP Geoffrey Stonor, as becomes clear in Act II, in the Trafalgar Square suffrage rally. The play is a curious mix of suffrage rhetoric and melodramatic revelations about Geoffrey's and Vida's shared past. Harley Granville Barker's innovative staging of the rally was praised for its authenticity, and its melding of theatre and suffrage protest set a standard for theatrically effective political speech which other suffrage plays aspired to during the next decade. The depiction of women in political action is stunning and has a rawness that still challenges audiences. Act III returns to the drawing room, where Jean, Vida and Geoffrey sort out their complex personal relationships through a rhetoric of suffrage politics. Jean and Geoffrey move towards marriage, but also join Vida in support of the women's vote. Vida's unwavering commitment to the vote inspires others and she stands as a complex portrait of the suffragist.

Of all suffrage drama, Robins's play has received the greatest critical attention. Although rarely staged, the play is on a par with the work of Harley Granville Barker, Henry James and others who deal with the nuances of Edwardian women's social and political options. Robins's conversion narrative and her radical Act II, which broke free of the drawing room, became a model for much of the suffrage drama to follow.

Not surprisingly, very few suffrage plays assume the three-act structure of Robins's play, since time-constraints made a full-length play generally unworkable for rallies and meetings – and it was primarily at such events that most performances took place. Thus the one-act, the monologue and the duologue became the mainstays of suffrage theatre, and many of them take from Robins the comic form as well as the selling of the vote through an examination of personal relationships. Cicely Hamilton and Christopher St John's *How the Vote was Won* is perhaps the best of these politically expedient plays. When, in the cause of the vote, a general strike is called for women, all women are directed to return to their 'nearest male relative' for support; the goal is to demonstrate to men how much they have come to rely on women's independence. The play reveals what this clever strategy means for one Horace Cole, a 30-year-old clerk living with his wife in Brixton. Through the course of the play's events, he realizes the ridiculousness of thinking 'today's' women need men, and he converts to the cause, concluding the play with a litany of reasons for women's vote: 'You may depend on me – all of you – to see justice done. When you want a thing done, get a man to do it! Votes for Women!' (Spender and Hayman 1985: 33). Such conversion is central to many of the suffrage plays published in newspapers (*Mr Peppercorn's Awakening*, *The Shadow of the Sofa*, *Our Happy Home*) as well as to those frequently performed at local rallies (for example, Evelyn Glover's *A Chat with Mrs Chicky* and her *Miss Appleyard's Awakening* (1913b)).

Edy Craig, Cicely Hamilton and others argued that such plays worked by promoting a change of heart among ideologically uncertain men and women while also reassuring others already committed to the cause. As Craig put it in a 1910 newspaper interview: 'I do think plays have done such a lot for the Suffrage. They get hold of nice frivolous people who would die sooner than go in cold blood to meetings. But they see the plays, and get interested, and then we can rope them in for meetings' (Carlson 2000: 201). The political expediency of such an approach also relies on comedy; what Craig's subversive strategy does *not* acknowledge is that the comic form, while allowing for rebellion in its topsy-turvy world, also has a companion structural reliance on the status quo. Thus in the celebratory endings of these conversion plays, there is often a tension between the affirmation of the vote and the affirmation of a relationship (often a marriage or engagement) which reifies social convention. While some of the plays did critique social institutions like marriage, many more made explicit that the vote would not threaten marriage, motherhood or social codes.

Many of the conversion plays have a processional element, as multiple people join a conversation or repeat an argument, swelling the scene until a whole community unites in agreement over the need for women's vote. Actual pageants were among the most influential suffrage plays, and may be among the most notable contributions of suffrage theatre. Perhaps the centrality of pageants is predictable, since suffrage activism of this era was marked by a reliance on demonstrations and large-scale meetings. The best and most influential of these pageants was *A Pageant of Great Women*, a collaboration of Cicely Hamilton's writing and Edy Craig's directing. With a cast ranging between 50 and 90 players, productions usually needed large spaces to amplify the play's grand scheme, and Craig was primarily responsible for its performance both in London and around the country, beginning in 1909 at London's Scala Theatre (Cockin 1998a: 94–107).

Hamilton provides a frame for the play in the three characters of Justice, Prejudice and Woman, who initiate the action with a debate about the possibility of women leading lives beyond the confines of their relationships to men. To prove the point that women have always functioned independently, there follows a procession of famous women in six groups: The Learned Women, The Artists, The Saintly Women, The Heroic Women, The Rulers and The Warriors. While each of the processing women has a very small speaking part, the cumulative effect of their stately presence and potent proclamations about women's abilities is to shame Prejudice into silence and retreat. Justice then tells the Woman that the 'world is thine', and the Woman concludes the play by letting men know they are not forgotten, but that women are now laughing as they feel 'the riot and rush of crowning hopes, / Dreams, longings, and vehement powers' (Nelson 2004: 229). This pageant was a powerful theatrical and political tool, not just because of its long and impressive line of influential women, but because in production key suffrage supporters could adopt the roles of the 'great' women. While some London productions boasted the most successful actresses of the day, many local productions used the opportunity to dress high-profile political supporters in the garb of such glorious figures as Jane Austen, Sappho, Florence Nightingale, Elizabeth I and Joan of Arc.

Christopher St John's *The First Actress* (1911) puts the processional in the narrower sphere of British theatrical history, and shows how the processional quality of suffrage campaigning seemed to influence the imagining of theatrical space. St John, a woman whose chosen male name confronts gender issues, creates a pageant of 11 famous actresses who line up to give encouragement to Margaret Hughes, assumed by St John to be the first actress on the English stage in 1661, performing the part of Desdemona. Hughes's performance is belittled by her male colleagues and she is about to conclude that women's acting is a failed experiment, but then the pageant begins. Coming from the future (post–1661), the 11 actresses reassure Hughes of the historic importance of her role. Performed initially by Edy Craig's Pioneer Players in 1911 and later for suffrage events, the play made easy connections between theatre and suffrage politics. This piece of theatre about theatre, in other words, made an effective argument for women's long-standing independence. In essence, such pageant plays use the procession of characters to visualize political progress.

While St John's play is not anthologized in any of the existing collections of suffrage drama (see Fitzsimmons and Gardner 1991; Holledge 1981; Nelson 2004; Spender and Hayman 1985), her well-crafted writing most clearly shows how the suffrage drama born in the initial efforts of Robins matured in the compressed political agitation of the next seven years. St John's 1914 play *Her Will* returns to the domestic interiors of Robins's world to bring suffrage politics squarely into the drawing room again; this time the drawing room has been transformed into a space controlled by independent and powerful women. As the play opens, suffragist Helen Wilton has just died, and the disposition of her estate brings her heirs into political contortions as they attempt to satisfy the demands of her will. A victim of a Holloway Prison stay (and its forced feedings), Wilton names as her first heir the suffrage cause itself, specifying that her money be used to support suffragists until the vote is awarded to women. Her second set of heirs (her family) are forced into a quick recognition of the several ways in which expanded suffrage will serve them, and they become objects of comedy as they begrudgingly move towards conversion. In this play, the drawing room is owned by a woman and becomes the space for political conversation, conversion and, most importantly, female autonomy (Carlson 2001: 344–5).

While the majority of suffrage plays deploy the comic form, using a feel-good factor to reinforce the rewards of political support for the suffrage cause, a sizeable number turn to both one-act and full-length dramas with darker endings. Stowell (1992) rightly names Hamilton's *Diana of Dobson's*, staged by Lena Ashwell at the Kingsway Theatre in 1908, as one of the key plays of the suffrage era, not because it deals with the issue of the vote, but because it forces questions about happiness and a woman's life choices. Act I, set in the dormitory of the shop girls employed at Dobson's, captures the bleak life of the women who work endless days for minimal wages. The promise of romance powers the next two acts, but the conclusion leaves the question of happiness unanswered. Many in the suffrage campaign were not willing to discuss the preju-dicial legal situation in relation to marriage, since they felt it would jeopardize the possibility of the vote. Hamilton's play does, however, allow for the issue to be raised.

Margaret Wynne Nevinson's *In the Workhouse* (1911) is a protest against the laws of coverture, which denied most married women legal standing, and as Nevinson says in her preface, 'married women are still in captivity at the will of some worthless husband' (Nevison in Nelson 2004: 247). The play takes place in a workhouse where seven women share experiences and beliefs, most focused on how marriage laws have compounded difficult lives. One character, Lily, begins the play by saying that she is eager to marry the father of her new baby, and ends – after listening to the life stories of the other women – by telling her baby that maybe she won't get married after all. In sharp contrast to most suffrage plays, this one clearly separates marriage from happiness. Most plays enlisted in the suffrage cause did not make such foundational critiques, though several skirt the issue, such as St Claire's *The Science of Forgiveness*.

Most studies of suffrage theatre focus on the plays and events created in the cause of women's vote, yet this review of suffrage theatre would not be complete without a note on the anti-suffrage plays which attempted to turn such pro-suffrage theatre in on itself. Many of these 'anti' plays used comic strategies which were conservative rather than subversive. Typically, the suffragist characters themselves were devoid of social skills and their politics inept; such qualities were meant to expose the suffragists' dangerous political goals. The women become comic targets when they give up their politics for love or when they are shown to be under-handed, illogical and promiscuous; Inglis Allen's *The Suffragettes' Redemption* (1909) and George Dance's *The Suffragettes* (1907) are good examples of such plays which undercut the suffrage cause (Carlson 2000: 207). One notable attempt to discredit women's arguments for the vote has a play full of children claiming that they too deserve the vote; Ernest Hutchinson's *Votes for Children* (1913) equates suffragists with a group of children who don't even know what a 'vote' is. The way in which anti-suffragists turned to theatre to counter the pro-suffrage plays is perhaps a back-handed compliment, an admission that the theatre was indeed a powerful political tool. But the anti-suffrage plays also suggest that the suffragists' frequent use of comedy might have been vulnerable to parody.

Conclusion

English suffrage theatre is a potent, brief example of a politically inspired theatre which leaves us with a legacy: it made new assumptions about theatrical space, domestic space and public space simultaneously; it catapulted women into the full range of roles in theatre; and it played a key role in women writers' conscriptions of dramatic form. World War I brought the suffrage theatre to a virtual halt, along with the suffrage campaign itself. Many of the women who had directed its militant efforts continued with theatre, but the concentrated urgency of the moment evaporated into other projects and concerns. Since the vote was not actually granted women until after the war (and even then in stages), it is not possible to make definitive claims about the political effec-tiveness of this theatre. These suffrage plays do, however, show a remarkable political energy, and more importantly, are a showcase for the political reach of the art form.

Note

1. The four papers were *Votes for Women*, the *Suffragette*, the *Vote* and *Common Cause*.

Primary and further reading

A. N. (1912). *Mr Peppercorn's Awakening, Vote*, 1 August, 229 (no known performance).

Allen, Inglis (1909). *The Suffragette's Redemption.* Lord Chamberlain's Plays, British Library (first performance 1909).

Baker, Edith M. (1911). *Our Happy Home, Vote*, 30 December, 115–17 (no known performance).

Carlson, Susan (2000). 'Comic Militancy: The Politics of Suffrage Drama' in Maggie B. Gale and Viv Gardner (eds). *Women, Theatre and Performance: New Histories, New Historiographies.* Manchester: Manchester University Press, 198–215.

Carlson, Susan (2001). 'Portable Politics: Creating New Space for Suffrage-ing Women', *New Theatre Quarterly* 17:4, 334–46.

Chapin, Alice (1909). *At the Gates, Vote*, 16 December, 94 (performance licensed 1909).

Cockin, Katharine (1998a). *Edith Craig (1869–1947): Dramatic Lives.* London: Cassell.

Dance, George (1907). *The Suffragettes*. Lord Chamberlain's Plays, British Library (first performance 1907).

Fitzsimmons, Linda and Gardner, Viv (eds) (1991). *New Woman Plays*. London: Methuen.

Frances, Hilary (2000). '"Dare to Be Free!": The Women's Freedom League and its Legacy' in June Purvis and Sandra Stanley Holton (eds). *Votes for Women*. New York and London: Routledge, 181–202.

Gardner, Viv (ed.) (1985). *Sketches from the Actresses' Franchise League*. Nottingham: Nottingham Drama Texts.

Glover, Evelyn (1913a). *A Chat with Mrs Chicky: A Duologue* in Dale Spender and Carole Hayman (eds) (1985). *How the Vote Was Won and Other Suffragette Plays*. London: Methuen; and in Carolyn Christensen Nelson (ed.). (2004). *Literature of the Women's Suffrage Campaign in England*. Peterborough, Ontario: Broadview Press (first performance 1912).

Glover, Evelyn (1913b). *Miss Appleyard's Awakening: A Play in One Act* in Carolyn Christensen Nelson (ed.). (2004). *Literature of the Women's Suffrage Campaign in England*. Peterborough, Ontario: Broadview Press (first performance 1911).

Hamilton, Cicely (1908). *Diana of Dobson's* in Linda Fitzsimmons and Viv Gardner (eds). (1991). *New Woman Plays*. London: Methuen, 27–77 (first performance 1908).

Hamilton, Cicely (1948; 1909). *A Pageant of Great Women* in Carolyn Christensen Nelson (ed.). (2004). *Literature of the Women's Suffrage Campaign in England*. Peterborough, Ontario: Broadview Press (first performance 1909).

Hamilton, Cicely and St John, Christopher (1909a). *How the Vote Was Won* in Dale Spender and Carole Hayman (eds). (1985). *How the Vote Was Won and Other Suffragette Plays*. London: Methuen; and in Carolyn Christensen Nelson (ed.). (2004). *Literature of the Women's Suffrage Campaign in England*. Peterborough, Ontario: Broadview Press (first performance 1909).

Hamilton, Cicely and St John, Christopher (1909b). *The Pot and the Kettle*. Lord Chamberlain's Plays, British Library (first performance 1909).

Holledge, Julie (1981). *Innocent Flowers: Women in the Edwardian Theatre*. London: Virago.

Hutchinson, Ernest (1913). *Votes for Children*. Lord Chamberlain's Plays, British Library (first performance 1913).

Little, A. L. (1913). *The Shadow of the Sofa*, *Vote*, 24 December, 139–41 (no known performance).

Mayhall, Laura E. Nym, Levine, Philippa and Fletcher, Ian Christopher (2000). 'Introduction' in *Women's Suffrage in the British Empire: Citizenship, Nation and Race*. London and New York: Routledge, xiii–xxii.

Moffat, Graham (1912). *The Maid and the Magistrate: A Duologue in One Act* in Carolyn Christensen Nelson (ed.). (2004). *Literature of the Women's Suffrage Campaign in England*. Peterborough, Ontario: Broadview Press (first performance 1912).

Nelson, Carolyn Christensen (ed.) (2004). *Literature of the Women's Suffrage Campaign in England*. Peterborough, Ontario: Broadview Press.

Nevinson, Margaret Wynne (1911). *In the Workhouse: A Play in One Act* in Carolyn Christensen Nelson (ed.). (2004). *Literature of the Women's Suffrage Campaign in England*. Peterborough, Ontario: Broadview Press (first performance 1911).

Robins, Elizabeth (1907). *Votes for Women* in Dale Spender and Carole Hayman (eds). (1985). *How the Vote Was Won and Other Suffragette Plays*. London: Methuen (first performance 1907).

St John, Christopher (1911). *The First Actress*. Lord Chamberlain's Plays, British Library (first performance 1911).

St John, Christopher (1914). *Her Will*. Lord Chamberlain's Plays, British Library (performance licensed 1914).

Spender, Dale and Hayman, Carole (eds) (1985). *How the Vote Was Won and Other Suffragette Plays*. London: Methuen.

Stowell, Sheila (1992). *A Stage of Their Own: Feminist Plays of the Suffrage Era*. Manchester: Manchester University Press.

Originally published in Mary Luckhurst, ed., *A Companion to Modern British and Irish Drama*. Oxford: Blackwell, 2006, pp. 99–109.

3.7 The Work of Art in the Age of its Technological Reproducibility (1935–6)

Second Version

WALTER BENJAMIN

Translated by Edmund Jephcott and Harry Zohn

The true is what he can; the false is what he wants.

– Madame de Duras[1]

I

WHEN MARX UNDERTOOK HIS analysis of the capitalist mode of production, that mode was in its infancy.[2] Marx adopted an approach which gave his investigations prognostic value. Going back to the basic conditions of capitalist production, he presented them in a way which showed what could be expected of capitalism in the future. What could be expected, it emerged, was not only an increasingly harsh exploitation of the proletariat but, ultimately, the creation of conditions which would make it possible for capitalism to abolish itself.

Since the transformation of the superstructure proceeds far more slowly than that of the base, it has taken more than half a century for the change in the conditions of production to be manifested in all areas of culture. How this process has affected culture can only now be assessed, and these assessments must meet certain prognostic requirements. They do not, however, call for theses on the art of the proletariat after its seizure of power, and still less for any on the art of the classless society. They call for theses defining the tendencies of the development of art under the present conditions of production. The dialectic of these conditions of production is evident in the superstructure, no less than in the economy. These defining the developmental tendencies of art can therefore contribute to the political struggle in ways that it would be a mistake to underestimate. They neutralize a number of traditional concepts – such as creativity and genius, eternal value and mystery – which, used in an uncontrolled way (and controlling them is difficult today), allow factual material to be manipulated in the interests of fascism. *In what follows, the concepts which are introduced into the theory of art differ from those now current in that they are completely useless for the purposes of fascism. On the other hand, they are useful for the formulation of revolutionary demands in the politics of art* [*Kunstpolitik*].

II

In principle, the work of art has always been reproducible. Objects made by humans could always be copied by humans. Replicas were made by pupils in practicing for their craft, by masters in disseminating their works, and, finally, by third parties in pursuit of profit. But the technological reproduction of artworks is something new. Having appeared intermittently in history, at widely spaced intervals, it is now being adopted with ever-increasing intensity. Graphic art was first made technologically reproducible by the woodcut, long before written language became reproducible by movable type. The enormous changes brought about in literature by movable type, the technological reproduction of writing, are well known. But they are only a special case, though an important one, of the phenomenon considered here from the perspective of world history. In the course of the Middle Ages the woodcut was supplemented by engraving and etching, and at the beginning of the nineteenth century by lithography.

Lithography marked a fundamentally new stage in the technology of reproduction. This much more direct process – distinguished by the fact that the drawing is traced on a stone, rather than incised on a block of wood or etched on a copper plate – first made it possible for graphic art to market its products not only in large numbers, as previously, but in daily changing variations. Lithography enabled graphic art to provide an illustrated accompaniment to everyday life. It began to keep pace with movable-type printing. But only a few decades after the invention of lithography, graphic art was surpassed by photography. For the first time, photography freed the hand from the most important artistic tasks in the process of pictorial reproduction – tasks that now devolved upon the eye alone. And since the eye perceives more swiftly than the hand can draw, the process of pictorial reproduction was enormously accelerated, so that it could now keep pace with speech. Just as the illustrated newspaper virtually lay hidden within lithography, so the sound film was latent in photography. The technological reproduction of sound was tackled at the end of the last century. *Around 1900, technological reproduction not only had reached a standard that permitted it to reproduce all known works of art, profoundly modifying their effect, but it also had captured a place of its own among the artistic processes. In gauging this standard, we would do well to study the impact which its two different manifestations – the reproduction of artworks and the art of film – are having on art in its traditional form.*

III

In even the most perfect reproduction, *one* thing is lacking: the here and now of the work of art – its unique existence in a particular place. It is this unique existence – and nothing else – that bears the mark of the history to which the work has been subject. This history includes changes to the physical structure of the work over time, together with any changes in ownership. Traces of the former can be detected only by chemical or physical analyses (which cannot be performed on a reproduction), while changes of ownership are part of a tradition which can be traced only from the standpoint of the original in its present location.

The here and now of the original underlies the concept of its authenticity, and on the latter in turn is founded the idea of a tradition which has passed the object down as the same, identical thing to the present day. *The whole sphere of authenticity eludes technological – and of course not only technological – reproduction.* But whereas the authentic work retains its full authority in the face of a reproduction made by hand, which it generally brands a forgery, this is not the case with technological reproduction. The reason is twofold. First, technological reproduction is more independent of the original than is manual reproduction. For example, in photography it can bring out aspects of the original that are accessible only to the lens (which is adjustable and can easily change viewpoint) but not to the human eye; or it can use certain processes, such as enlargement or slow motion, to record images which escape natural optics altogether. This is the first reason. Second, technological reproduction can place the copy of the original in situations which the original itself cannot attain. Above all, it enables the original to meet the recipient halfway, whether in the form of a photograph or in that of a gramophone record. The cathedral leaves its site to be received in the studio of an art lover; the choral work performed in an auditorium or in the open air is enjoyed in a private room.

These changed circumstances may leave the artwork's other properties untouched, but they certainly devalue the here and now of the artwork. And although this can apply not only to art but (say) to a landscape moving past the spectator in a film, in the work of art this process touches on a highly sensitive core, more vulnerable than that of any natural object. That core is its authenticity. The authenticity of a thing is the quintessence of all that is transmissible in it from its origin on, ranging from its physical duration to the historical testimony relating to it. Since the historical testimony is founded on the physical duration, the former, too, is jeopardized by reproduction, in which the physical duration plays no part. And what is really jeopardized when the historical testimony is affected is the authority of the object, the weight it derives from tradition.

One might focus these aspects of the artwork in the concept of the aura, and go on to say: what withers in the age of the technological reproducibility of the work of art is the latter's aura. This process is symptomatic; its significance extends far beyond the realm of art. *It might be stated as a general formula that the technology of reproduction detaches the reproduced object from the sphere of tradition. By replicating the work many times over, it substitutes a mass existence for a unique existence. And in permitting the reproduction to reach the recipient in his or her own situation, it actualizes that which is reproduced.* These two processes lead to a massive upheaval in the domain of objects handed down from the past – a shattering of tradition which is the reverse side of the present crisis and renewal of humanity. Both processes are intimately related to the mass movements of our day. Their most powerful agent is film. The social significance of film, even – and especially – in its most positive form, is inconceivable without its destructive, cathartic side: the liquidation of the value of tradition in the cultural heritage. This phenomenon is most apparent in the great historical films. It is assimilating ever more advanced positions in its spread. When Abel Gance fervently proclaimed in 1927, 'Shakespeare, Rembrandt, Beethoven will make films … All legends, all mythologies, and all myths, all the founders of religions, indeed, all religions, … await their celluloid resurrection, and the heroes are pressing at the gates,' he was inviting the reader, no doubt unawares, to witness a comprehensive liquidation.[3]

IV

Just as the entire mode of existence of human collectives changes over long historical periods, so too does their mode of perception. The way in which human perception is organized – the medium in which it occurs – is conditioned not only by nature but by history. The era of the migration of peoples, an era which saw the rise of the late-Roman art industry and the Vienna Genesis, developed not only an art different from that of antiquity but also a different perception. The scholars of the

Viennese school Riegl and Wickhoff, resisting the weight of the classical tradition beneath which this art had been buried, were the first to think of using such art to draw conclusions about the organization of perception at the time the art was produced.[4] However far-reaching their insight, it was limited by the fact that these scholars were content to highlight the formal signature which characterized perception in late-Roman times. They did not attempt to show the social upheavals manifested in these changes in perception – and perhaps could not have hoped to do so at that time. Today, the conditions for an analogous insight are more favorable. And if changes in the medium of present-day perception can be understood as a decay of the aura, it is possible to demonstrate the social determinants of that decay.

What, then, is the aura? A strange tissue of space and time: the unique apparition of a distance, however near it may be.[5] To follow with the eye – while resting on a summer afternoon – a mountain range on the horizon or a branch that casts its shadow on the beholder is to breathe the aura of those mountains, of that branch. In the light of this description, we can readily grasp the social basis of the aura's present decay. It rests on two circumstances, both linked to the increasing emergence of the masses and the growing intensity of their movements. Namely: *the desire of the present-day masses to 'get closer' to things, and their equally passionate concern for overcoming each thing's uniqueness [Überwindung des Einmaligen jeder Gegebenheit] by assimilating it as a reproduction.* Every day the urge grows stronger to get hold of an object at close range in an image [*Bild*], or, better, in a facsimile [*Abbild*], a reproduction. And the reproduction [*Reproduktion*], as offered by illustrated magazines and newsreels, differs unmistakably from the image. Uniqueness and permanence are as closely entwined in the latter as are transitoriness and repeatability in the former. The stripping of the veil from the object, the destruction of the aura, is the signature of a perception whose 'sense for all that is the same in the world'[6] has so increased that, by means of reproduction, it extracts sameness even from what is unique. Thus is manifested in the field of perception what in the theoretical sphere is noticeable in the increasing significance of statistics. The alignment of reality with the masses and of the masses with reality is a process of immeasurable importance for both thinking and perception.

V

The uniqueness of the work of art is identical to its embeddedness in the context of tradition. Of course, this tradition itself is thoroughly alive and extremely changeable. An ancient statue of Venus, for instance, existed in a traditional context for the Greeks (who made it an object of worship) that was different from the context in which it existed for medieval clerics (who viewed it as a sinister idol). But what was equally evident to both was its uniqueness – that is, its aura. Originally, the embeddedness of an artwork in the context of tradition found expression in a cult. As we know, the earliest artworks originated in the service of rituals – first magical, then religious. And it is highly significant that the artwork's auratic mode of existence is never entirely severed from its ritual function. In other words: *the unique value of the 'authentic' work of art always has its basis in ritual.* This ritualistic basis, however mediated it may be, is still recognizable as secularized ritual in even the most profane forms of the cult of beauty. The secular worship of beauty, which developed during the Renaissance and prevailed for three centuries, clearly displayed that ritualistic basis in its subsequent decline and in the first severe crisis which befell it. For when, with the advent of the first truly revolutionary means of reproduction (namely photography, which emerged at the same time as socialism), art felt the approach of that crisis which a century later has become unmistakable, it reacted with the doctrine of *l'art pour l'art* – that is, with a theology of art.[7] This in turn gave rise to a negative theology, in the form of an idea of 'pure' art, which rejects not only any social function but any definition in terms of a representational content. (In poetry, Mallarmé was the first to adopt this standpoint.)[8]

No investigation of the work of art in the age of its technological reproducibility can overlook these connections. They lead to a crucial insight: for the first time in world history, technological reproducibility emancipates the work of art from its parasitic subservience to ritual. To an ever-increasing degree, the work reproduced becomes the reproduction of a work designed for reproducibility.[9] From a photographic plate, for example, one can make any number of prints; to ask for the 'authentic' print makes no sense. *But as soon as the criterion of authenticity ceases to be applied to artistic production, the whole social function of art is revolutionized. Instead of being founded on ritual, it is based on a different practice: politics.*

VI

Art history might be seen as the working out of a tension between two polarities within the artwork itself, its course being determined by shifts in the balance between the two. These two poles are the artwork's cult value and its exhibition value.[10] Artistic production begins with figures in the service of magic. What is important for these figures is that they are present, not that they are seen. The elk depicted by Stone Age man on the walls of his cave is an instrument of magic, and is exhibited to others only coincidentally; what matters is that the spirits see it. Cult value as such even tends to keep the artwork out of sight: certain statues of gods are accessible only to the priest in the cella; certain images of the Madonna remain covered nearly all year round; certain sculptures on medieval cathedrals are not visible to the viewer at ground level. *With the emancipation of specific artistic practices from the service of ritual, the opportunities for exhibiting their products increase.* It is easier to exhibit a portrait bust that can be sent here and there than to exhibit the statue of a divinity that has a fixed place in the interior of a temple. A panel painting can be exhibited more easily than the mosaic or fresco which preceded it. And although a mass may have been no less suited to public presentation than a symphony, the symphony came into being at a time when the possibility of such presentation promised to be greater.

The scope for exhibiting the work of art has increased so enormously with the various methods of technologically reproducing it that, as happened in prehistoric times, a quantitative shift between the two poles of the artwork has led to a qualitative transformation in its nature. Just as the work of art in prehistoric times, through the exclusive emphasis placed on its cult value, became first and foremost an instrument of magic which only later came to be recognized as a work of art, so today, through the exclusive emphasis placed on its exhibition value, the work of art becomes a construct [*Gebilde*] with quite new functions. Among these, the one we are conscious of – the artistic function – may subsequently be seen as incidental. This much is certain: today, film is the most serviceable vehicle of this new understanding. Certain, as well, is the fact that the historical moment of this change in the function of art – a change which is most fully evident in the case of film – allows a direct comparison with the primeval era of art not only from a methodological but also from a material point of view.

Prehistoric art made use of certain fixed notations in the service of magical practice. In some cases, these notations probably comprised the actual performing of magical acts (the carving of an ancestral figure is itself such an act); in others, they gave instructions for such procedures (the ancestral figure demonstrates a ritual posture); and in still others, they provided objects for magical contemplation (contemplation of an ancestral figure strengthens the occult powers of the beholder). The subjects for these notations were humans and their environment, which were depicted according to the requirements of a society whose technology existed only in fusion with ritual. Compared to that of the machine age, of course, this technology was undeveloped. But from a dialectical standpoint, the disparity is unimportant. What matters is the way the orientation and aims of that technology differ from those of ours. Whereas the former made the maximum possible use of human beings, the latter reduces their use to the minimum. The achievements of the first technology might be said to culminate in human sacrifice; those of the second, in the remote-controlled aircraft which needs no human crew. The results of the first technology are valid once and for all (it deals with irreparable lapse or sacrificial death, which holds good for eternity). The results of the second are wholly provisional (it operates by means of experiments and endlessly varied test procedures). The origin of the second technology lies at the point where, by an unconscious ruse, human beings first began to distance themselves from nature. It lies, in other words, in play.

Seriousness and play, rigor and license, are mingled in every work of art, though in very different proportions. This implies that art is linked to both the second and the first technologies. It should be noted, however, that to describe the goal of the second technology as 'mastery over nature' is highly questionable, since this implies viewing the second technology from the stand-point of the first. The first technology really sought to master nature, whereas the second aims rather at an interplay between nature and humanity. The primary social function of art today is to rehearse that interplay. This applies especially to film. *The function of film is to train human beings in the apperceptions and reactions needed to deal with a vast apparatus whose role in their lives is expanding almost daily.* Dealing with this apparatus also teaches them that technology will release them from their enslavement to the powers of the apparatus only when humanity's whole constitution has adapted itself to the new productive forces which the second technology has set free.[11]

VII

In photography, exhibition value begins to drive back cult value on all fronts. But cult value does not give way without resistance. It falls back to a last entrenchment: the human countenance. It is no accident that the portrait is central to early photography. In the cult of remembrance of dead or absent loved ones, the cult value of the image finds its last refuge. In the fleeting expression of a human face, the aura beckons from early photographs for the last time. This is what gives them their melancholy and incomparable beauty. But as the human being withdraws from the photo-graphic image, exhibition value for the first time shows its superiority to cult value. To have given this development its local habitation constitutes the unique significance of Atget, who, around 1900, took photographs of deserted Paris streets.[12] It has justly been said that he photographed them like scenes of crimes. A crime scene, too, is deserted; it is photographed for the purpose of establishing evidence. With Atget, photographic records begin to be evidence in the historical trial [*Prozess*]. This constitutes their hidden political significance. They demand a specific kind of reception. Free-floating contemplation is no longer appropriate to them. They unsettle the viewer; he feels challenged to find a particular way to approach them. At the same time, illustrated magazines begin to put up signposts for him – whether these are right or wrong is irrelevant. For the first time, captions become obligatory. And it is clear that they have a character altogether different from the titles of paintings. The directives given by captions to those looking at images in illustrated magazines soon become even more precise and commanding in films, where the way each single image is understood seems prescribed by the sequence of all the preceding images.

VIII

The Greeks had only two ways of technologically reproducing works of art: casting and stamping. Bronzes, terra cottas, and coins were the only artworks they could produce in large numbers. All others were unique and could not be technologically reproduced. That is why they had to be made for all eternity. *The state of their technology compelled the Greeks to produce eternal values in their art.* To this they owe their preeminent position in art history – the standard for subsequent generations. Undoubtedly, our position lies at the opposite pole from that of the Greeks. Never before have artworks been technologically reproducible to such a degree and in such quantities as today. Film is the first art form whose artistic character is entirely determined by its reproducibility. It would be idle to compare this form in detail with Greek art. But on one precise point such a comparison would be revealing. For film has given crucial importance to a quality of the artwork which would have been the last to find approval among the Greeks, or which they would have dismissed as marginal. This quality is its capacity for improvement. The finished film is the exact antithesis of a work created at a single stroke. It is assembled from a very large number of images and image sequences that offer an array of choices to the editor; these images, moreover, can be improved in any desired way in the process leading from the initial take to the final cut. To produce *A Woman of Paris*, which is 3,000 meters long, Chaplin shot 125,000 meters of film.[13] *The film is therefore the artwork most capable of improvement. And this capability is linked to its radical renunciation of eternal value.* This is corroborated by the fact that for the Greeks, whose art depended on the production of eternal values, the pinnacle of all the arts was the form least capable of improvement – namely sculpture, whose products are literally all of a piece. In the age of the assembled [*montierbar*] artwork, the decline of sculpture is inevitable.

IX

The nineteenth-century dispute over the relative artistic merits of painting and photography seems misguided and confused today.[14] But this does not diminish its importance, and may even underscore it. The dispute was in fact an expression of a world-historical upheaval whose true nature was concealed from both parties. Insofar as the age of technological reproducibility separated art from its basis in cult, all semblance of art's autonomy disappeared forever. But the resulting change in the function of art lay beyond the horizon of the nineteenth century. And even the twentieth, which saw the development of film, was slow to perceive it.

Though commentators had earlier expended much fruitless ingenuity on the question of whether photography was an art – without asking the more fundamental question of whether the invention of photography had not transformed the entire character of art – film theorists quickly adopted the same ill-considered standpoint. But the difficulties which photography caused for traditional aesthetics were child's play compared to those presented by film. Hence the obtuse and hyperbolic character of early film theory. Abel Gance, for instance, compares film to hieroglyphs: 'By a remarkable regression, we are transported back to the expressive level of the Egyptians. ... Pictorial language has not matured, because our eyes are not yet adapted to it. There is not yet enough respect, not enough cult, for what it expresses.'[15] Or, in the words of Séverin-Mars: 'What other art has been granted a dream ... at once more poetic and more real? Seen in this light, film might represent an incomparable means of expression, and only the noblest minds should move within its atmosphere, in the most perfect and mysterious moments of their lives.'[16] It is instructive to see how the desire to annex film to 'art' impels these theoreticians to attribute elements of cult to film – with a striking lack of discretion. Yet when these speculations were published, works like *A Woman of Paris* and *The Gold Rush* had already appeared. This did not deter Abel Gance from making the comparison with hieroglyphs, while Séverin-Mars speaks of film as one might speak of paintings by Fra Angelico.[17] It is revealing that even today especially reactionary authors look in the same direction for the significance of film – finding, if not actually a sacred significance, then at least a supernatural one. In connection with Max Reinhardt's film version of *A Midsummer Night's Dream*, Werfel comments that it was undoubtedly the sterile copying of the external world – with its streets, interiors, railway stations, restaurants, automobiles, and beaches – that had prevented film up to now from ascending to the realm of art. 'Film has not yet realized its true purpose, its real possibilities. ... These consist in its unique ability to use natural means to give incomparably convincing expression to the fairylike, the marvelous, the supernatural.'[18]

X

To photograph a painting is one kind of reproduction, but to photograph an action performed in a film studio is another. In the first case, what is reproduced is a work of art, while the act of producing it is not. The cameraman's performance with the lens no more creates an artwork than a conductor's with the baton; at most, it creates an artistic performance. This is unlike the process in a film studio. Here, what is reproduced is not an artwork, and the act of reproducing it is no more such a work than in the first case. The work of art is produced only by means of montage. And each individual component of this montage is a reproduction of a process which neither is an artwork in itself nor gives rise to one through photography. What, then, are these processes reproduced in film, since they are certainly not works of art?

To answer this, we must start from the peculiar nature of the artistic performance of the film actor. He is distinguished from the stage actor in that his performance in its original form, from which the reproduction is made, is not carried out in front of a randomly composed audience but before a group of specialists – executive producer, director, cinematographer, sound recordist, lighting designer, and so on – who are in a position to intervene in his performance at any time. This aspect of filmmaking is highly significant in social terms. For the intervention in a performance by a body of experts is also characteristic of sporting performances and, in a wider sense, of all test performances. The entire process of film production is determined, in fact, by such intervention. As we know, many shots are filmed in a number of takes. A single cry for help, for example, can be recorded in several different versions. The editor then makes a selection from these; in a sense, he establishes one of them as the record. An action performed in the film studio therefore differs from the corresponding real action the way the competitive throwing of a discus in a sports arena would differ from the throwing of the same discus from the same spot in the same direction in order to kill someone. The first is a test performance, while the second is not.

The test performance of the film actor is, however, entirely unique in kind. In what does this performance consist? It consists in crossing a certain barrier which confines the social value of test performances within narrow limits. I am referring now not to a performance in the world of sports, but to a performance produced in a mechanized test. In a sense, the athlete is confronted only by natural tests. He measures himself against tasks set by nature, not by equipment – apart from exceptional cases like Nurmi, who was said to run against the clock.[19] Meanwhile the work process, especially since it has been standardized by the assembly line, daily generates countless mechanized tests. These tests are performed unawares, and those who fail are excluded from the work process. But they are also conducted openly, in agencies for testing professional aptitude. In both cases, the test subject faces the barrier mentioned above.

These tests, unlike those in the world of sports, are incapable of being publicly exhibited to the degree one would desire. And this is precisely where film comes into play. *Film makes test performances capable of being exhibited, by turning that ability itself into a test.* The film actor performs not in front of an audience but in front of an apparatus. The film director occupies exactly the same position as the examiner in an aptitude test. To perform in the glare of arc lamps while simultaneously meeting the demands of the microphone is a test performance of the highest order. To accomplish it is to preserve one's humanity in the face of the apparatus. Interest in this performance is widespread. For the majority of city dwellers, throughout the workday in offices and factories, have to relinquish their humanity in the face of an apparatus. In the evening these same masses fill the cinemas, to witness the film actor taking revenge on their behalf not only by asserting *his* humanity (or what appears to them as such) against the apparatus, but by placing that apparatus in the service of his triumph.

XI

In the case of film, the fact that the actor represents someone else before the audience matters much less than the fact that he represents himself before the apparatus. One of the first to sense this transformation of the actor by the test performance was Pirandello.[20] That his remarks on the subject in his novel *Sigira* [Shoot!] are confined to the negative aspects of this change, and to silent film only, does little to diminish their relevance. For in this respect, the sound film changed nothing essential. What matters is that the actor is performing for a piece of equipment – or, in the case of sound film, for two pieces of equipment. 'The film actor', Pirandello writes, 'feels as if exiled. Exiled not only from the stage but from his own person. With a vague unease, he senses an inexplicable void, stemming from the fact that his body has lost its substance, that he has been volatilized, stripped of his reality, his life, his voice, the noises he makes when moving about, and has been turned into a mute image that flickers for a moment on the screen, then vanishes into silence. ... The little apparatus will play with his shadow before the audience, and he himself must be content to play before the apparatus.'[21] The situation can also be characterized as follows: for the first time – and this is the effect of film – the human being is placed in a position where he must operate with his whole living person, while forgoing its aura. For the aura is bound to his presence in the here and now. There is no facsimile of the aura. The aura surrounding Macbeth on the stage cannot be divorced from the aura which, for the living spectators, surrounds the actor who plays him. What distinguishes the shot in the film studio, however, is that the camera is substituted for the audience. As a result, the aura surrounding the actor is dispelled – and, with it, the aura of the figure he portrays.

It is not surprising that it should be a dramatist such as Pirandello who, in reflecting on the special character of film acting, inadvertently touches on the crisis now affecting the theater. Indeed, nothing contrasts more starkly with a work of art completely subject to (or, like film, founded in) technological reproduction than a stage play. Any thorough consideration will confirm this. Expert observers have long recognized that, in film, 'the best effects are almost always achieved by "acting" as little as possible. ... The development,' according to Rudolf Arnheim, writing in 1932, has been toward 'using the actor as one of the "props," chosen for his typicalness and ... introduced in the proper context.'[22] Closely bound up with this development is something else. *The stage actor identifies himself with a role. The film actor very often is denied this opportunity.* His performance is by no means a unified whole, but is assembled from many individual performances. Apart from incidental concerns about studio rental, availability of other actors, scenery, and so on, there are elementary necessities of the machinery that split the actor's performance into a series of episodes capable of being assembled. In particular, lighting and its installation require the representation of an action – which on the screen appears as a swift, unified sequence – to be filmed in a series of separate takes, which may be spread over hours in the studio. Not to mention the more obvious effects of montage. A leap from a window, for example, can be shot in the studio as a leap from a scaffold, while the ensuing fall may be filmed weeks later at an outdoor location. And far more paradoxical cases can easily be imagined. Let us assume that an actor is supposed to be startled by a knock at the door. If his reaction is not satisfactory, the director can resort to an expedient: he could have a shot fired without warning behind the actor's back on some other occasion when he happens to be in the studio. The actor's frightened reaction at that moment could be recorded and then edited into the film. Nothing shows more graphically that art has escaped the realm of 'beautiful semblance,' which for so long was regarded as the only sphere in which it could thrive.[23]

XII

The representation of human beings by means of an apparatus has made possible a highly productive use of the human being's self-alienation. The nature of this use can be grasped through the fact that the film actor's estrangement in the face of the apparatus, as Pirandello describes this experience, is basically of the same kind as the estrangement felt before one's appearance [*Erscheinung*] in a mirror – a favorite theme of the Romantics. But now the mirror image [*Bild*] has become detachable from the person mirrored, and is transportable. And where is it transported? To a site in front of the masses.[24] Naturally, the screen actor never for a moment ceases to be aware of this. While he stands before the apparatus, he knows that in the end he is confronting the masses. It is they who will control him. Those who are not visible, not present while he executes his performance, are precisely the ones who will control it. This invisibility heightens the authority of their control. It should not be forgotten, of course, that there can be no political advantage derived from this control until film has liberated itself from the fetters of capitalist exploitation. Film capital uses the revolutionary opportunities implied by this control for counterrevolutionary purposes. Not only does the cult of the movie star which it fosters preserve that magic of the personality which has long been no more than the putrid magic of its own commodity character, but its counterpart, the cult of the audience, reinforces the corruption by which fascism is seeking to supplant the class consciousness of the masses.[25]

XIII

It is inherent in the technology of film, as of sports, that everyone who witnesses these performances does so as a quasi-expert. Anyone who has listened to a group of newspaper boys leaning on their bicycles and discussing the outcome of a bicycle race will have an inkling of this. In the case of film, the newsreel demonstrates unequivocally that any individual can be in a position to be filmed. But that possibility is not enough. *Any person today can lay claim to being filmed.* This claim can best be clarified by considering the historical situation of literature today.

For centuries it was in the nature of literature that a small number of writers confronted many thousands of readers. This began to change toward the end of the past century. With the growth and extension of the press, which constantly made new political, religious, scientific, professional, and local journals available to readers, an increasing number of readers – in isolated cases, at first – turned into writers. It began with the space set aside for 'letters to the editor' in the daily press, and has now reached a point where there is hardly a European engaged in the work process who could not, in principle, find an opportunity to publish somewhere or other an account of a work experience, a complaint, a report, or something of the kind. Thus, the distinction between author and public is about to lose its axiomatic character. The difference becomes functional; it may vary from case to case. At any moment, the reader is ready to become a writer. As an expert – which he has had to become in any case in a highly specialized work process, even if only in some minor capacity – the reader gains access to authorship. Work itself is given a voice. And the ability to describe a job in words now forms part of the expertise needed to carry it out. Literary competence is no longer founded on specialized higher education but on polytechnic training, and thus is common property.

All this can readily be applied to film, where shifts that in literature took place over centuries have occurred in a decade. In cinematic practice – above all, in Russia – this shift has already been partly realized. Some of the actors taking part in Russian films are not actors in our sense but people who portray *themselves* – and primarily in their own work process. In western Europe today, the capitalist exploitation of film obstructs the human being's legitimate claim to being reproduced. The claim is also obstructed, incidentally, by unemployment, which excludes large masses from production – the process in which their primary entitlement to be reproduced would lie. Under these circumstances, the film industry has an overriding interest in stimulating the involvement of the masses through illusionary displays and ambiguous speculations. To this end it has set in motion an immense publicity machine, in the service of which it has placed the careers and love lives of the stars; it has organized polls; it has held beauty contests. All this in order to distort and corrupt the original and justified interest of the masses in film – an interest in understanding themselves and therefore their class. Thus, the same is true of film capital in particular as of fascism in general: a compelling urge toward new social opportunities is being clandestinely exploited in the interests of a property-owning minority. For this reason alone, the expropriation of film capital is an urgent demand for the proletariat.

XIV

The shooting of a film, especially a sound film, offers a hitherto unimaginable spectacle. It presents a process in which it is impossible to assign to the spectator a single viewpoint which would exclude from his or her field of vision the equipment not directly involved in the action being filmed – the camera, the lighting units, the technical crew, and so forth (unless the alignment of the spectator's pupil coincided with that of the camera). This circumstance, more than any other, makes any resemblance between a scene in a film studio and one onstage superficial and irrelevant. In principle, the theater includes a position from which the action on the stage cannot easily be detected as an illusion. There is no such position where a film is being shot. The illusory nature of film is of the second degree; it is the result of editing. That is to say: *In the film studio the apparatus has penetrated so deeply into reality that a pure view of that reality, free of the foreign body of equipment, is the result of a special procedure – namely, the shooting by the specially adjusted photographic device and the assembly of that shot with others of the same kind.* The equipment-free aspect of reality has here become the height of artifice, and the vision of immediate reality the Blue Flower in the land of technology.[26]

This state of affairs, which contrasts so sharply with that which obtains in the theater, can be compared even more instructively to the situation in painting. Here we have to pose the question: How does the camera operator compare with the painter? In answer to this, it will be helpful to consider the concept of the operator as it is familiar to us from surgery. The surgeon represents the polar opposite of the magician. The attitude of the magician, who heals a sick person by a laying-on of hands, differs from that of the surgeon, who makes an intervention in the patient. The magician maintains the natural distance between himself and the person treated; more precisely, he reduces it slightly by laying on his hands, but increases it greatly by his authority. The surgeon does exactly the reverse: he greatly diminishes the distance from the patient by penetrating the patient's body, and increases it only slightly by the caution with which his hand moves among the organs. In short: unlike the magician (traces of whom are still found in the medical practitioner), the surgeon abstains at the decisive moment from confronting his patient person to person; instead, he penetrates the patient by operating. – Magician is to surgeon as painter is to cinematographer. The painter maintains in his work a natural distance from reality, whereas the cinematographer penetrates deeply into its tissue. The images obtained by each differ enormously. The painter's is a total image, whereas that of the cinematographer is piecemeal, its manifold parts being assembled according to a new law. *Hence, the presentation of reality in film is incomparably the more significant for people of today, since it provides the equipment-free aspect of reality they are entitled to demand from a work of art, and does so precisely on the basis of the most intensive interpenetration of reality with equipment.*

XV

The technological reproducibility of the artwork changes the relation of the masses to art. The extremely backward attitude toward a Picasso painting changes into a highly progressive reaction to a Chaplin film. The progressive attitude is characterized by an immediate, intimate fusion of pleasure – pleasure in seeing and experiencing – with an attitude of expert appraisal. Such a fusion is an important social index. As is clearly seen in the case of painting, the more reduced the social impact of an art form, the more widely criticism and enjoyment of it diverge in the public. The conventional is uncritically enjoyed, while the truly new is criticized with aversion. Not so in the cinema. The decisive reason for this is that nowhere more than in the cinema are the reactions of individuals, which together make up the massive reaction of the audience, determined by the imminent concentration of reactions into a mass. No sooner are these reactions manifest than they regulate one another. Again, the comparison with painting is fruitful. A painting has always exerted a claim to be viewed primarily by a single person or by a few. The simultaneous viewing of paintings by a large audience, as happens in the nineteenth century, is an early symptom of the crisis in painting, a crisis triggered not only by photography but, in a relatively independent way, by the artwork's claim to the attention of the masses.

Painting, by its nature, cannot provide an object of simultaneous collective reception, as architecture has always been able to do, as the epic poem could do at one time, and as film is able to do today. And although direct conclusions about the social role of painting cannot be drawn from this fact alone, it does have a strongly adverse effect whenever painting is led by special circumstances, as if against its nature, to confront the masses directly. In the churches and monasteries of the Middle Ages, and at the princely courts up to about the end of the eighteenth century, the collective reception of paintings took place not simultaneously but in a manifoldly graduated and hierarchically mediated way. If that has changed, the change testifies to the special conflict in which painting has become enmeshed by the technological reproducibility of the image. And while efforts have been made to present paintings to the masses in galleries and salons, this mode of reception gives the masses no means of organizing and regulating their response. Thus, the same public which reacts progressively to a slapstick comedy inevitably displays a backward attitude toward Surrealism.

XVI

The most important social function of film is to establish equilibrium between human beings and the apparatus. Film achieves this goal not only in terms of man's presentation of himself to the camera but also in terms of his representation of his environment by means of this apparatus. On the one hand, film furthers insight into the necessities governing our lives by its use of close-ups, by its accentuation of hidden details in familiar objects, and by its exploration of commonplace milieux through the ingenious guidance of the camera; on the other hand, it manages to assure us of a vast and unsuspected field of action [*Spielraum*].

Our bars and city streets, our offices and furnished rooms, our railroad stations and our factories seemed to close relentlessly around us. Then came film and exploded this prison-world with the dynamite of the split second, so that now we can set off calmly on journeys of adventure among its far-flung debris. With the close-up, space expands; with slow motion, movement is extended. And just as enlargement not merely clarifies what we see indistinctly 'in any case,' but brings to light entirely new structures of matter, slow motion not only reveals familiar aspects of movements, but discloses quite unknown aspects within them – aspects 'which do not appear as the retarding of natural movements but have a curious gliding, floating character of their own.'[27] Clearly, it is another nature which speaks to the camera as compared to the eye. 'Other' above all in the sense that a space informed by human consciousness gives way to a space informed by the unconscious. Whereas it is a commonplace that, for example, we have some idea what is involved in the act of walking (if only in general terms), we have no idea at all what happens during the split second when a person actually takes a step. We are familiar with the movement of picking up a cigarette lighter or a spoon, but know almost nothing of what really goes on between hand and metal, and still less how this varies with different moods. This is where the camera comes into play, with all its resources for swooping and rising, disrupting and isolating, stretching or compressing a sequence, enlarging or reducing an object. It is through the camera that we first discover the optical unconscious, just as we discover the instinctual unconscious through psychoanalysis.

Moreover, these two types of unconscious are intimately linked. For in most cases the diverse aspects of reality captured by the film camera lie outside only the *normal* spectrum of sense impressions. Many of the deformations and stereotypes, transformations and catastrophes which can assail the optical world in films afflict the actual world in psychoses, hallucinations, and dreams. Thanks to the camera, therefore, the individual perceptions of the psychotic or the dreamer can be appropriated by collective perception. The ancient truth expressed by Heraclitus, that those who are awake have a world in common while each sleeper has a world of his own, has been invalidated by film – and less by depicting the dream world itself than by creating figures of collective dream, such as the globe-encircling Mickey Mouse.[28]

If one considers the dangerous tensions which technology and its consequences have engendered in the masses at large – tendencies which at critical stages take on a psychotic character – one also has to recognize that this same technologization [Technisierung] has created the possibility of psychic immunization against such mass psychoses. It does so by means of certain films in which the forced development of sadistic fantasies or masochistic delusions can prevent their natural and dangerous maturation in the masses. Collective laughter is one such preemptive and healing outbreak of mass psychosis. The countless grotesque events consumed in films are a graphic indication of the dangers threatening mankind from the repressions implicit in civilization. American slapstick comedies and Disney films trigger a therapeutic release of unconscious energies.[29] Their forerunner was the figure of the eccentric. He was the first to inhabit the new fields of action opened up by film – the first occupant of the newly built house. This is the context in which Chaplin takes on historical significance.

XVII

It has always been one of the primary tasks of art to create a demand whose hour of full satisfaction has not yet come.[30] The history of every art form has critical periods in which the particular form strains after effects which can be easily achieved only with a changed technical standard – that is to say, in a new art form. The excesses and crudities of art which thus result, particularly in periods of so-called decadence, actually emerge from the core of its richest historical energies. In recent years, Dadaism has amused itself with such barbarisms. Only now is its impulse recognizable: *Dadaism attempted to produce with the means of painting (or literature) the effects which the public today seeks in film.*

Every fundamentally new, pioneering creation of demand will overshoot its target. Dadaism did so to the extent that it sacrificed the market values so characteristic of film in favor of more significant aspirations – of which, to be sure, it was unaware in the form described here. The Dadaists attached much less importance to the commercial usefulness of their artworks than to the uselessness of those works as objects of contemplative immersion. They sought to achieve this uselessness not least by thorough degradation of their material. Their poems are 'wordsalad' containing obscene expressions and every imaginable kind of linguistic refuse. The same is true of their paintings, on which they mounted buttons or train tickets. What they achieved by such means was a ruthless annihilation of the aura in every object they produced, which they branded as a reproduction through the very means of its production. Before a painting by Arp or a poem by August Stramm, it is impossible to take time for concentration and evaluation, as one can before a painting by Derain or a poem by Rilke.[31] Contemplative immersion – which, as the bourgeoisie degenerated, became a breeding ground for asocial behavior – is here opposed by distraction [*Ablenkung*] as a variant of social behavior. Dadaist manifestations actually guaranteed a quite vehement distraction by making artworks the center of scandal. One requirement was paramount: to outrage the public.

From an alluring visual composition or an enchanting fabric of sound, the Dadaists turned the artwork into a missile. It jolted the viewer, taking on a tactile [*taktisch*] quality. It thereby fostered the demand for film, since the distracting element in film is also primarily tactile, being based on successive changes of scene and focus which have a percussive effect on the spectator.[32] *Film has freed the physical shock effect – which Dadaism had kept wrapped, as it were, inside the moral shock effect – from this wrapping.*

XVIII

The masses are a matrix from which all customary behavior toward works of art is today emerging newborn. Quantity has been transformed into quality: *the greatly increased mass of participants has produced a different kind of participation.* The fact that this new mode of participation first appeared in a disreputable form should not mislead the observer. The masses are criticized for seeking distraction [*Zerstreuung*] in the work of art, whereas the art lover supposedly approaches it with concentration. In the case of the masses, the artwork is seen as a means of entertainment; in the case of the art lover, it is considered an object of devotion. – This calls for closer examination.[33] Distraction and concentration form an antithesis, which may be formulated as follows. A person who concentrates before a work of art is absorbed by it; he enters into the work, just as, according to legend, a Chinese painter entered his completed painting while beholding it.[34] By contrast, the distracted masses absorb the work of art into themselves. Their waves lap around it; they encompass it with their tide. This is most obvious with regard to buildings. Architecture has always offered the prototype of an artwork that is received in a state of distraction and through the collective. The laws of architecture's reception are highly instructive.

Buildings have accompanied human existence since primeval times. Many art forms have come into being and passed away. Tragedy begins with the Greeks, is extinguished along with them, and is revived centuries later. The epic, which originates in the early days of peoples, dies out in Europe at the end of the Renaissance. Panel painting is a creation of the Middle Ages, and nothing guarantees its uninterrupted existence. But the human need for shelter is permanent. Architecture has never had fallow periods. Its history is longer than that of any other art, and its effect ought to be recognized in any attempt to account for the relationship of the masses to the work of art. Buildings are received in a twofold manner: by use and by perception. Or, better: tactilely and optically. Such reception cannot be understood in terms of the concentrated attention of a traveler before a famous building. On the tactile side, there is no counterpart to what contemplation is on the optical side. Tactile reception comes about not so much by way of attention as by way of habit. The latter largely determines even the optical reception of architecture, which spontaneously takes the form of casual noticing, rather than attentive observation. Under certain circumstances, this form of reception shaped by architecture acquires canonical value. *For the tasks which face the human apparatus of perception at historical turning points cannot be performed solely by optical means – that is, by way of contemplation. They are mastered gradually – taking their cue from tactile reception – through habit.*

Even the distracted person can form habits. What is more, the ability to master certain tasks in a state of distraction first proves that their performance has become habitual. The sort of distraction that is provided by art represents a covert measure of the extent to which it has become possible to perform new tasks of apperception. Since, moreover, individuals are tempted to evade such tasks, art will tackle the most difficult and most important tasks wherever it is able to mobilize the masses. It does so currently in film. *Reception in distraction – the sort of reception which is increasingly noticeable in all areas of art and is a symptom of profound changes in apperception – finds in film its true training ground.* Film, by virtue of its shock effects, is predisposed to this form of reception. In this respect, too, it proves to be the most important subject matter, at present, for the theory of perception which the Greeks called aesthetics.[35]

XIX

The increasing proletarianization of modern man and the increasing formation of masses are two sides of the same process. Fascism attempts to organize the newly proletarianized masses while leaving intact the property relations which they strive to abolish. It sees its salvation in granting expression to the masses – but on no account granting them rights.[36] The masses have a *right* to changed property relations; fascism seeks to give them *expression* in keeping these relations unchanged. *The logical outcome of fascism is an aestheticizing of political life.* With D'Annunzio, decadence made its entry into political life; with Marinetti, Futurism; and with Hitler, the Bohemian tradition of Schwabing.[37]

All efforts to aestheticize politics culminate in one point. That one point is war. War, and only war, makes it possible to set a goal for mass movements on the grandest scale while preserving traditional property relations. That is how the situation presents itself in political terms. In technological terms it can be formulated as follows: only war makes it possible to mobilize all of today's technological resources while maintaining property relations. It goes without saying that the fascist glorification of war does not make use of *these* arguments. Nevertheless, a glance at such glorification is instructive. In Marinetti's manifesto for the colonial war in Ethiopia, we read:

> For twenty-seven years, we Futurists have rebelled against the idea that war is anti-aesthetic. … We therefore state: … War is beautiful because – thanks to its gas masks, its terrifying megaphones, its flame throwers, and light tanks – it establishes man's dominion over the subjugated machine. War is beautiful because it inaugurates the dreamed-of metallization of the human body. War is beautiful because it enriches a flowering meadow with the fiery orchids of machine-guns. War is beautiful because it combines gunfire, barrages, cease-fires, scents, and the fragrance of putrefaction into a symphony. War is beautiful because it creates new architectures, like those of armored tanks, geometric squadrons of aircraft, spirals of smoke from burning villages, and much more. … Poets and artists of Futurism, … remember these principles of an aesthetic of war, that they may illuminate … your struggles for a new poetry and a new sculpture![38]

This manifesto has the merit of clarity. The question it poses deserves to be taken up by the dialectician. To him, the aesthetic of modern warfare appears as follows: if the natural use of productive forces is impeded by the property system, then the increase in technological means, in speed, in sources of energy will press toward an unnatural use. This is found in war, and the destruction caused by war furnishes proof that society was not mature enough to make technology its organ, that technology was not sufficiently developed to master the elemental forces of society. The most horrifying features of imperialist war are determined by the discrepancy between the enormous means of production and their inadequate use in the process of production (in other words, by unemployment and the lack of markets). *Imperialist war is an uprising on the part of technology, which demands repayment in 'human material' for the natural material society has denied it.* Instead of deploying power stations across the land, society deploys manpower in the form of armies. Instead of promoting air traffic, it promotes traffic in shells. And in gas warfare it has found a new means of abolishing the aura.

'Fiat ars – pereat mundus,'[39] says fascism, expecting from war, as Marinetti admits, the artistic gratification of a sense perception altered by technology. This is evidently the consummation of *l'art pour l'art*. Humankind, which once, in Homer, was an object of contemplation for the Olympian gods, has now become one for itself. Its self-alienation has reached the point where it can experience its own annihilation as a supreme aesthetic pleasure. *Such is the aestheticizing of politics, as practiced by fascism. Communism replies by politicizing art.*

Notes

Written late December 1935 to beginning of February 1936; unpublished in this form in Benjamin's lifetime. *Gesammelte Schriften*, VII, pp. 350–84. Translated by Edmund Jephcott and Harry Zohn.

This version of the essay 'Das Kunstwerk im Zeitalter seiner technischen Reproduzierbarkeit' (first published in Volume 7 of Benjamin's *Gesammelte Schriften*, in 1989) is a revision and expansion (by seven manuscript pages) of the first version of the essay, which was composed in Paris in the autumn of 1935. The second version represents the form in which Benjamin originally wished to see the work published; it served, in fact, as the basis for the first publication of the essay – a somewhat shortened form translated into French – in the *Zeitschrift für Sozialforschung* in May 1936. The third version of the essay (1936–9) can be found in Benjamin, *Selected Writings, Volume 4: 1938–1940* (Cambridge, Mass.: Harvard University Press, 2003), pp. 251–83.

1. Madame Claire de Duras, née Kersaint (1778–1828), the wife of Duc Amédée de Duras, field marshal under Louis XVIII, was the author of two novels, *Ourika* (1823) and *Edouard* (1825). She presided over a brilliant salon in Paris. Benjamin cites Madame de Duras in the original French.
2. Karl Marx (1818–1883) analyzed the capitalist mode of production in *Das Kapital* (3 vols., 1867, 1885, 1895), which was carried to completion by his collaborator Friedrich Engels (1820–95).
3. Abel Gance, 'Le Temps de l'image est venu!' (It Is Time for the Image!), in Léon Pierre-Quint, Germaine Dulac, Lionel Landry, and Abel Gance, *L'Art cinématographique*, vol. 2 (Paris, 1927), pp. 94–6. [Benjamin's note. Gance (1889–1981) was a French film director whose epic films *J'accuse* (1919), *La Roue* (1922), and *Napoléon* (1927) made innovative use of such devices as superimposition, rapid intercutting, and split screen. – *Trans.*]
4. Alois Riegl (1858–1905) was an Austrian art historian who argued that different formal orderings of art emerge as expressions of different historical epochs. He is the author of *Stilfragen: Grundlegungen zu einer Geschichte der Ornamentik* (Questions of Style: Toward a History of Ornament; 1893) and *Die spätrömische Kunst-Industrie nach den Funden in Österreich-Ungarn* (1901). The latter has been translated by Rolf Winkes as *Late Roman Art Industry* (Rome: Giorgio Bretschneider, 1985). Franz Wickhoff (1853–1909), also an Austrian art historian, is the author of *Die Wiener Genesis* (The Vienna Genesis; 1895), a study of the sumptuously illuminated, early sixth-century A.D. copy of the biblical book of Genesis preserved in the Austrian National Library in Vienna.

5. 'Einmalige Erscheinung einer Ferne, so nah sie sein mag.' At stake in Benjamin's formulation is an interweaving not just of time and space – *einmalige Erscheinung*, literally 'one-time appearance' – but of far and near, *eine Ferne* suggesting both 'a distance' in space or time and 'something remote,' however near it (the distance, or distant thing, that appears) may be.

6. Benjamin is quoting Johannes V. Jensen, *Exotische Novellen*, trans. Julia Koppel (Berlin: S. Fischer, 1919), pp. 41–2. Jensen (1873–1950) was a Danish novelist, poet, and essayist who won the Nobel Prize for Literature in 1944. See 'Hashish in Marseilles' (1932), in Benjamin, *Selected Writings, Volume 2: 1927–1934* (Cambridge, Mass.: Harvard University Press, 1999), p. 677.

7. Applying Kant's idea of the pure and disinterested existence of the work of art, the French philosopher Victor Cousin made use of the phrase *l'art pour l'art* ('art for art's sake') in his 1818 lecture 'Du Vrai, du beau, et du bien' (On the True, the Beautiful, and the Good). The idea was later given currency by writers such as Théophile Gautier, Edgar Allan Poe, and Charles Baudelaire.

8. The French poet Stéphane Mallarmé (1842–98) was a central figure in the Symbolist movement, which sought an incantatory language divorced from all referential function.

9. In film, the technological reproducibility of the product is not an externally imposed condition of its mass dissemination, as it is, say, in literature or painting. *The technological reproducibility of films is based directly on the technology of their production. This not only makes possible the mass dissemination of films in the most direct way, but actually enforces it.* It does so because the process of producing a film is so costly that an individual who could afford to buy a painting, for example, could not afford to buy a [master print of a] film. It was calculated in 1927 that, in order to make a profit, a major film needed to reach an audience of nine million. Of course, the advent of sound film [in that year] initially caused a movement in the opposite direction: its audience was restricted by language boundaries. And that coincided with the emphasis placed on national interests by fascism. But it is less important to note this setback (which in any case was mitigated by dubbing) than to observe its connection with fascism. The simultaneity of the two phenomena results from the economic crisis. The same disorders which led, in the world at large, to an attempt to maintain existing property relations by brute force induced film capital, under the threat of crisis, to speed up the development of sound film. Its introduction brought temporary relief, not only because sound film attracted the masses back into the cinema but also because it consolidated new capital from the electricity industry with that of film. Thus, considered from the outside, sound film promoted national interests; but seen from the inside, it helped internationalize film production even more than before. [Benjamin's note. By 'the economic crisis,' Benjamin refers to the devastating consequences, in the United States and Europe, of the stock market crash of October 1929. – *Trans.*]

10. This polarity cannot come into its own in the aesthetics of Idealism, which conceives of beauty as something fundamentally undivided (and thus excludes anything polarized). Nonetheless, in Hegel this polarity announces itself as clearly as possible within the limits of Idealism. We quote from his *Vorlesungen zur Philosophie der Geschichte* [Lectures on the Philosophy of History]: 'Images were known of old. In those early days piety required them for worship, but it could do without *beautiful* images. Such images might even be disturbing. In every beautiful image, there is also something external – although, insofar as the image is beautiful, its spirit still speaks to the human being. But religious worship, being no more than a spiritless torpor of the soul, is directed at a *thing*. ... Fine art arose ... in the church ..., though art has now gone beyond the ecclesiastical principle.' Likewise, the following passage from the *Vorlesungen über die Ästhetik* [Lectures on Aesthetics] indicates that Hegel sensed a problem here: 'We are beyond the stage of venerating works of art as divine and as objects deserving our worship. Today the impression they produce is of a more reflective kind, and the emotions they arouse require a more stringent test.' [Benjamin's note. The German Idealist philosopher Georg Wilhelm Friedrich Hegel (1770–1831) accepted the chair in philosophy at the University of Berlin in 1818. His lectures on aesthetics and the philosophy of history (delivered 1820–9) were later published by his editors, with the text based mainly on notes taken by his students. – *Trans.*]

11. The aim of revolutions is to accelerate this adaptation. Revolutions are innervations of the collective – or, more precisely, efforts at innervation on the part of the new, historically unique collective which has its organs in the new technology. This second technology is a system in which the mastering of elementary social forces is a precondition for playing [*das Spiel*] with natural forces. Just as a child who has learned to grasp stretches out its hand for the moon as it would for a ball, so humanity, in its efforts at innervation, sets its sights as much on currently utopian goals as on goals within reach. For in revolutions, it is not only the second technology which

asserts its claims vis-à-vis society. Because this technology aims at liberating human beings from drudgery, the individual suddenly sees his scope for play, his field of action [*Spielraum*], immeasurably expanded. He does not yet know his way around this space. But already he registers his demands on it. For the more the collective makes the second technology its own, the more keenly individuals belonging to the collective feel how little they have received of what was due them under the dominion of the first technology. In other words, it is the individual liberated by the liquidation of the first technology who stakes his claim. No sooner has the second technology secured its initial revolutionary gains than vital questions affecting the individual – questions of love and death which had been buried by the first technology – once again press for solutions. Fourier's work is the first historical evidence of this demand. [Benjamin's note. Charles Fourier (1772–1837), French social theorist and reformer, urged that society be reorganized into self-contained agrarian cooperatives which he called 'phalansteries.' Among his works are *Théorie des quatre mouvements* (Theory of Four Movements; 1808) and *Le Nouveau Monde industriel* (The New Industrial World; 1829–30). He is an important figure in Benjamin's *Arcades Project*. The term *Spielraum*, in this note, in note 23, and in the text, literally means 'playspace,' 'space for play.' – *Trans.*]

12. Eugène Atget (1857–1927), French photographer, spent his career in obscurity making pictures of Paris and its environs. He is widely recognized as one of the leading photographers of the twentieth century. See Benjamin's 'Little History of Photography' (1931), in this volume.

13. *A Woman of Paris* (1923) – which Benjamin refers to by its French title, *L'Opinion publique* – was written and directed by the London-born actor and director Charlie Chaplin (Charles Spencer Chaplin; 1889–1977). Chaplin came to the United States with a vaudeville act in 1910 and made his motion picture debut there in 1914, eventually achieving worldwide renown as a comedian. He starred in and directed such films as *The Kid* (1921), *The Circus* (1928), *City Lights* (1931), *Modern Times* (1936), and *The Great Dictator* (1940). See Benjamin's short pieces 'Chaplin' (1929) and 'Chaplin in Retrospect' (1929), in this volume.

14. On the nineteenth-century quarrel between painting and photography, see Benjamin's 'Little History of Photography' (1931), in this volume, and Benjamin, *The Arcades Project*, trans. Howard Eiland and Kevin McLaughlin (Cambridge, Mass.: Harvard University Press, 1999), pp. 684–92.

15. Abel Gance, 'Le Temps de l'image est venu!' in *L'Art cinématographique*, vol. 2, p. 101. [Benjamin's note. On Gance, see note 3 above. – *Trans.*]

16. Séverin-Mars, cited ibid, p. 100. [Benjamin's note. Séverin-Mars (1873–1921) was a playwright and film actor who starred in three of Gance's films: *La Dixième Symphonie, J'accuse*, and *La Roue*. – *Trans.*]

17. Charlie Chaplin wrote and directed *The Gold Rush* in 1925. On Chaplin and *A Woman of Paris*, see note 13 above. Giovanni da Fiesole (1387–1455), known as Fra Angelico, was an Italian Dominican friar, celebrated for his 'angelic' virtues, and a painter in the early Renaissance Florentine style. Among his most famous works are his frescoes at Orvieto, which reflect a characteristically serene religious attitude.

18. Franz Werfel, 'Ein Sommernachtstraum: Ein Film von Shakespeare und Reinhardt,' *Neues Wiener Journal*, cited in *Lu*, November 15, 1935. [Benjamin's note. Werfel (1890–1945) was a Czech-born poet, novelist, and playwright associated with Expressionism. He emigrated to the United States in 1940. Among his works are *Der Abituriententag* (The Class Reunion; 1928) and *Das Lied von Bernadette* (The Song of Bernadette; 1941). Max Reinhardt (Maximilian Goldman; 1873–1943) was Germany's most important stage producer and director during the first third of the twentieth century and the single most significant influence on the classic German silent cinema, many of whose directors and actors trained under him at the Deutsches Theater in Berlin. His direct film activity was limited to several early German silents and to the American movie *A Midsummer Night's Dream* (1935), which he codirected with William Dieterle. – *Trans.*]

19. Paavo Nurmi (1897–1973), a Finnish long-distance runner, was a winner at the Olympic Games in Antwerp (1920), Paris (1924), and Amsterdam (1928).

20. Beginning in 1917, the Italian playwright and novelist Luigi Pirandello (1867–1936) achieved a series of successes on the stage that made him world famous in the 1920s. He is best known for his plays *Sei personaggi in cerca d'autore* (Six Characters in Search of an Author; 1921) and *Enrico IV* (Henry IV; 1922).

21. Luigi Pirandello, *Il turno* (The Turn), cited by Léon Pierre-Quint, 'Signification du cinéma,' in *L'Art cinématographique*, vol. 2, pp. 14–15. [Benjamin's note]

22. Rudolf Arnheim, *Film als Kunst* (Berlin, 1932), pp. 176–7. In this context, certain apparently incidental details of film directing which diverge from practices on the stage take on added interest. For example, the attempt to let the actor perform without makeup, as in Dreyer's *Jeanne d'Arc*. Dreyer spent months seeking the forty

actors who constitute the Inquisitors' tribunal. Searching for these actors was like hunting for rare props. Dreyer made every effort to avoid resemblances of age, build, and physiognomy in the actors. (See Maurice Schultz, 'Le Maquillage' [Makeup], in *L'Art cinématographique*, vol. 6 [Paris, 1929], pp. 65–6.) If the actor thus becomes a prop, the prop, in its turn, not infrequently functions as actor. At any rate, it is not unusual for films to allocate a role to a prop. Rather than selecting examples at random from the infinite number available, let us take just one especially revealing case. A clock that is running will always be a disturbance on the stage, where it cannot be permitted its role of measuring time. Even in a naturalistic play, real-life time would conflict with theatrical time. In view of this, it is most revealing that film – where appropriate – can readily make use of time as measured by a clock. This feature, more than many others, makes it clear that – circumstances permitting – each and every prop in a film may perform decisive functions. From here it is but a step to Pudovkin's principle, which states that 'to connect the performance of an actor with an object, and to build that performance around the object, ... is always one of the most powerful methods of cinematic construction' (V. I. Pudovkin, *Film Regie und Filmmanuskript* [Film Direction and the Film Script] (Berlin, 1928), p. 126). Film is thus the first artistic medium which is able to show how matter plays havoc with human beings [*wie die Materie dem Menschen mitspielt*]. It follows that films can be an excellent means of materialist exposition. [Benjamin's note. See, in English, Rudolf Arnheim, *Film as Art* (Berkeley: University of California Press, 1957), p. 138. Arnheim (1904–2007), German-born Gestalt psychologist and critic, wrote on film, literature, and art for various Berlin newspapers and magazines from the mid-1920s until 1933. He came to the United States in 1940 and taught at Sarah Lawrence, the New School for Social Research, Harvard, and the University of Michigan. Besides his work on film theory, his publications include *Art and Visual Perception* (1954), *Picasso's Guernica* (1962), and *Visual Thinking* (1969). *La Passion de Jeanne d'Arc*, directed by Carl Theodor Dreyer, was released in 1928. Dreyer (1889–1968), Danish writer-director and film critic, is known for the exacting, expressive design of his films, his subtle camera movement, and his concentration on the physiognomy and inner psychology of his characters. Among his best-known works are *Vampyr* (1931), *Vredens Dag* (Day of Wrath; 1943), and *Ordet* (1955). Vsevolod Illarionovich Pudovkin (1893–1953), one of the masters of Soviet silent cinema, wrote and directed films – such as *Mother* (1926), *The End of St. Petersburg* (1927), and *Storm over Asia* (1928) – that showed the evolution of individualized yet typical characters in a social environment. He also published books on film technique and film acting. – *Trans.*]

23. The significance of beautiful semblance [*schöner Schein*] is rooted in the age of auratic perception that is now coming to an end. The aesthetic theory of that era was most fully articulated by Hegel, for whom beauty is 'the appearance [*Erscheinung*] of spirit in its immediate ... sensuous form, created by the spirit as the form adequate to itself' (Hegel, *Werke*, vol. 10, part 2 [Berlin, 1837], p. 121). Although this formulation has some derivative qualities, Hegel's statement that art strips away the 'semblance and deception of this false, transient world' from the 'true content of phenomena' (*Werke*, vol. 10, part 1, p. 13) already diverges from the traditional experiential basis [*Erfahrungsgrund*] of this doctrine. This ground of experience is the aura. By contrast, Goethe's work is still entirely imbued with beautiful semblance as an auratic reality. Mignon, Ottilie, and Helena partake of that reality. 'The beautiful is neither the veil nor the veiled object but rather the object *in* its veil': this is the quintessence of Goethe's view of art, and that of antiquity. The decline of this view makes it doubly urgent that we look back at its origin. This lies in mimesis as the primal phenomenon of all artistic activity. The mime presents what he mimes merely as semblance [*Der Nachmachende macht, was er macht, nur scheinbar*]. And the oldest form of imitation had only a single material to work with: the body of the mime himself. Dance and language, gestures of body and lips, are the earliest manifestations of mimesis. – The mime presents his subject as a semblance [*Der Nachmachende macht seine Sache scheinbar*]. One could also say that he plays his subject. Thus we encounter the polarity informing mimesis. In mimesis, tightly interfolded like cotyledons, slumber the two aspects of art: semblance and play. Of course, this polarity can interest the dialectician only if it has a historical role. And that is, in fact, the case. This role is determined by the world-historical conflict between the first and second technologies. Semblance is the most abstract – but therefore the most ubiquitous – schema of all the magic procedures of the first technology, whereas play is the inexhaustible reservoir of all the experimenting procedures of the second. Neither the concept of semblance nor that of play is foreign to traditional aesthetics; and to the extent that the two concepts of cult value and exhibition value are latent in the other pair of concepts at issue here, they say nothing new. But this abruptly changes as soon as these latter concepts lose their indifference toward history. They then lead to a practical insight – namely, that what is lost in the withering of semblance

and the decay of the aura in works of art is matched by a huge gain in the scope for play [*Spiel-Raum*]. This space for play is widest in film. In film, the element of semblance has been entirely displaced by the element of play. The positions which photography had occupied at the expense of cult value have thus been massively fortified. In film, the element of semblance has yielded its place to the element of play, which is allied to the second technology. Ramuz recently summed up this alliance in a formulation which, in the guise of a metaphor, gets to the heart of the matter. He says: 'We are currently witnessing a fascinating process. The various sciences, which up to now have each operated alone in their special fields, are beginning to converge in their object and to be combined into a single science: chemistry, physics, and mechanics are becoming interlinked. It is as if we were eyewitnesses to the enormously accelerated completion of a jigsaw puzzle whose first pieces took several millennia to put in place, whereas the last, because of their contours, and to the astonishment of the spectators, are moving together of their own accord' (Charles Ferdinand Ramuz, 'Paysan, nature' [Peasant, Nature], *Mesure*, 4 [October 1935]). These words give ultimate expression to the dimension of play in the second technology, which reinforces that in art. [Benjamin's note. It should be kept in mind that *Schein* can mean 'luster' and 'appearance,' as well as 'semblance' or 'illusion.' On Hegel, see note 10 above. The poet Johann Wolfgang von Goethe (1749–1832) visited Italy in 1786–8 and in 1790, gaining new inspiration from his encounter with Greco-Roman antiquity; a classically pure and restrained conception of beauty informs his creation of such female figures as Mignon in *Wilhelm Meisters Lehrjahre* (Wilhelm Meister's Apprenticeship; 1796), Ottilie in *Die Wahlverwandtschaften* (Elective Affinities; 1809), and Helena in *Faust*, Part II (1832). Benjamin's definition of the beautiful as 'the object *in* its veil' is quoted (with the italics added) from his essay 'Goethe's Elective Affinities' (1924–1925), in Benjamin, *Selected Writings, Volume 1: 1913–1926* (Cambridge, Mass.: Harvard University Press, 1996), p. 351. Charles Ferdinand Ramuz (1878–1947) was a Swiss writer resident in Paris (1902–14), where he collaborated with the composer Igor Stravinsky, for whom he wrote the text of *Histoire du soldat* (The Soldier's Tale; 1918). He also published novels on rural life that combine realism with allegory. – *Trans.*]

24. The change noted here in the mode of exhibition – a change brought about by reproduction technology – is also noticeable in politics. *The crisis of democracies can be understood as a crisis in the conditions governing the public presentation of politicians.* Democracies exhibit the politician directly, in person, before elected representatives. The parliament is his public. But innovations in recording equipment now enable the speaker to be heard by an unlimited number of people while he is speaking, and to be seen by an unlimited number shortly afterward. This means that priority is given to presenting the politician before the recording equipment. Parliaments are becoming depopulated at the same time as theaters. Radio and film are changing not only the function of the professional actor but, equally, the function of those who, like the politician, present themselves before these media. The direction of this change is the same for the film actor and the politician, regardless of their different tasks. It tends toward the exhibition of controllable, transferable skills under certain social conditions, just as sports first called for such exhibition under certain natural conditions. This results in a new form of selection – selection before an apparatus – from which the champion, the star, and the dictator emerge as victors. [Benjamin's note]

25. It should be noted in passing that proletarian class consciousness, which is the most enlightened form of class consciousness, fundamentally transforms the structure of the proletarian masses. The class-conscious proletariat forms a compact mass only from the outside, in the minds of its oppressors. At the moment when it takes up its struggle for liberation, this apparently compact mass has actually already begun to loosen. It ceases to be governed by mere reactions; it makes the transition to action. The loosening of the proletarian masses is the work of solidarity. In the solidarity of the proletarian class struggle, the dead, undialectical opposition between individual and mass is abolished; for the comrade, it does not exist. Decisive as the masses are for the revolutionary leader, therefore, his great achievement lies not in drawing the masses after him, but in constantly incorporating himself into the masses, in order to be, for them, always one among hundreds of thousands. But the same class struggle which loosens the compact mass of the proletariat compresses that of the petty bourgeoisie. The mass as an impenetrable, compact entity, which Le Bon and others have made the subject of their 'mass psychology,' is that of the petty bourgeoisie. The petty bourgeoisie is not a class; it is in fact only a mass. And the greater the pressure acting on it between the two antagonistic classes of the bourgeoisie and the proletariat, the more compact it becomes. In *this* mass the emotional element described in mass psychology is indeed a determining factor. But for that very reason this compact mass forms the antithesis of the proletarian cadre, which obeys a collective *ratio*. In the petty-bourgeois mass, the reactive moment described in mass psychology is indeed a

determining factor. But precisely for that reason this compact mass with its unmediated reactions forms the antithesis of the proletarian cadre, whose actions are mediated by a task, however momentary. Demonstrations by the compact mass thus always have a panicked quality – whether they give vent to war fever, hatred of Jews, or the instinct for self-preservation. Once the distinction between the compact (that is, petty-bourgeois) mass and the class-conscious, proletarian mass has been clearly made, its operational significance is also clear. This distinction is nowhere more graphically illustrated than in the not uncommon cases when some outrage originally performed by the compact mass becomes, as a result of a revolutionary situation and perhaps within the space of seconds, the revolutionary action of a class. The special feature of such truly historic events is that a reaction by a compact mass sets off an internal upheaval which loosens its composition, enabling it to become aware of itself as an association of class-conscious cadres. Such concrete events contain in very abbreviated form what communist tacticians call 'winning over the petty bourgeoisie.' These tacticians have a further interest in clarifying this process. The ambiguous concept of the masses, and the indiscriminate references to their mood which are commonplace in the German revolutionary press, have undoubtedly fostered illusions which have had disastrous consequences for the German proletariat. Fascism, by contrast, has made excellent use of these laws – whether it understood them or not. It realizes that the more compact the masses it mobilizes, the better the chance that the counterrevolutionary instincts of the petty bourgeoisie will determine their reactions. The proletariat, on the other hand, is preparing for a society in which neither the objective nor the subjective conditions for the formation of masses will exist any longer. [Benjamin's note. Gustave Le Bon (1841–1931), French physician and sociologist, was the author of *Psychologie des foules* (Psychology of the Crowd; 1895) and other works. – *Trans.*]

26. Benjamin alludes here to *Heinrich von Ofterdingen*, an unfinished novel by the German Romantic poet Novalis (Friedrich von Hardenberg; 1772–1801), first published in 1802. Von Ofterdingen is a medieval poet in search of the mysterious Blue Flower, which bears the face of his unknown beloved. See Benjamin's 'Dream Kitsch' (1927), in this volume.

27. Rudolf Arnheim, *Film als Kunst*, p. 138. [Benjamin's note. In English in Arnheim, *Film as Art*, pp. 116–17. On Arnheim, see note 22 above. – *Trans.*]

28. Benjamin refers to Fragment 89 in the standard Diels-Kranz edition of the fragments of Heraclitus of Ephesus, the Pre-Socratic philosopher of the sixth–fifth centuries B.C. On Mickey Mouse, see the following note.

29. Of course, a comprehensive analysis of these films should not overlook their double meaning. It should start from the ambiguity of situations which have both a comic and a horrifying effect. As the reactions of children show, comedy and horror are closely related. In the face of certain situations, why shouldn't we be allowed to ask which reaction is the more human? Some recent Mickey Mouse films offer situations in which such a question seems justified. (Their gloomy and sinister fire-magic, made technically possible by color film, highlights a feature which up to now has been present only covertly, and shows how easily fascism takes over 'revolutionary' innovations in this field too.) What is revealed in recent Disney films was latent in some of the earlier ones: the cozy acceptance of bestiality and violence as inevitable concomitants of existence. This renews an old tradition which is far from reassuring – the tradition inaugurated by the dancing hooligans to be found in depictions of medieval pogroms, of whom the 'riff-raff' in Grimm's fairy tale of that title are a pale, indistinct rear-guard. [Benjamin's note. The internationally successful Mickey Mouse cartoon series developed out of the character of Mortimer Mouse, introduced in 1927 by the commercial artist and cartoon producer Walt Disney (1901–66), who made outstanding technical and aesthetic contributions to the development of animation between 1927 and 1937, and whose short animated films of the thirties won praise from critics for their visual comedy and their rhythmic and unconventional technical effects. See Benjamin's 'Mickey Mouse' (1931), in this volume. 'Riff-raff' translates 'Lumpengesindel,' the title of a story in Jacob and Wilhelm Grimm's collection of tales, *Kinder- und Hausmärchen* (Nursery and Household Tales; 1812, 1815). – *Trans.*]

30. 'The artwork,' writes André Breton, 'has value only insofar as it is alive to reverberations of the future.' And indeed every highly developed art form stands at the intersection of three lines of development. First, technology is working toward a particular form of art. Before film appeared, there were little books of photos that could be made to flit past the viewer under the pressure of the thumb, presenting a boxing match or a tennis match; then there were coin-operated peepboxes in bazaars, with image sequences kept in motion by the turning of a handle. Second, traditional art forms, at certain stages in their development, strain laboriously for effects which later are effortlessly achieved by new art forms. Before film became established, Dadaist performances sought

to stir in their audiences reactions which Chaplin then elicited more naturally. Third, apparently insignificant social changes often foster a change in reception which benefits only the new art form. Before film had started to create its public, images (which were no longer motionless) were received by an assembled audience in the Kaiserpanorama. Here the audience faced a screen into which stereoscopes were fitted, one for each spectator. In front of these stereoscopes single images automatically appeared, remained briefly in view, and then gave way to others. Edison still had to work with similar means when he presented the first film strip – before the movie screen and projection were known; a small audience gazed into an apparatus in which a sequence of images was shown. Incidentally, the institution of the Kaiserpanorama very clearly manifests a dialectic of development. Shortly before film turned the viewing of images into a collective activity, image viewing by the individual, through the stereoscopes of these soon outmoded establishments, was briefly intensified, as it had been once before in the isolated contemplation of the divine image by the priest in the cella. [Benjamin's note. André Breton (1896–1966), French critic, poet, and editor, was the chief promoter and one of the founders of the Surrealist movement, publishing the first *Manifeste du surréalisme* in 1924. In Zurich in 1916, an international group of exiles disgusted by World War I, and by the bourgeois ideologies that had brought it about, launched Dada, an avant-garde movement that attempted to radically change both the work of art and society. Dadaist groups were active in Berlin, New York, Paris, and elsewhere during the war and into the 1920s, recruiting many notable artists, writers, and performers capable of shocking their audiences at public gatherings. On Chaplin, see note 13 above. Thomas Alva Edison (1847–1931) patented more than a thousand inventions over a sixty-year period, including the microphone, the phonograph, the incandescent electric lamp, and the alkaline storage battery. He supervised the invention of the Kinetoscope in 1891; this boxlike peep-show machine allowed individuals to view moving pictures on a film loop running on spools between an electric lamp and a shutter. He built the first film studio, the Black Maria, in 1893, and later founded his own company for the production of projected films. The Kaiserpanorama (Imperial Panorama), located in a Berlin arcade, consisted of a dome-like apparatus presenting stereoscopic views to customers seated around it. See Benjamin's 'Imperial Panorama' (Chapter 6 in this volume), excerpted from his *Berlin Childhood around 1900* (1938). – *Trans.*]

31. Hans Arp (1887–1966), Alsatian painter, sculptor, and poet, was a founder of the Zurich Dada group in 1916 and a collaborator with the Surrealists for a time after 1925. August Stramm (1874–1915) was an early Expressionist poet and dramatist, a member of the circle of artists gathered around the journal *Der Sturm* in Berlin. The French painter André Derain (1880–1954) became well known when he, Henri Matisse, and Maurice de Vlaminck were dubbed the 'Fauves,' or 'wild beasts,' at the 1905 Salon d'Automne. Rainer Maria Rilke (1875–1926), Austro-German lyric poet and writer, published his *Duineser Elegien* (Duino Elegies) and *Sonette an Orpheus* (Sonnets to Orpheus) in 1923.

32. Let us compare the screen [*Leinwand*] on which a film unfolds with the canvas [*Leinwand*] of a painting. The image on the film screen changes, whereas the image on the canvas does not. The painting invites the viewer to contemplation; before it, he can give himself up to his train of associations. Before a film image, he cannot do so. No sooner has he seen it than it has already changed. It cannot be fixed on. The train of associations in the person contemplating it is immediately interrupted by new images. This constitutes the shock effect of film, which, like all shock effects, seeks to induce heightened attention. *Film is the art form corresponding to the pronounced threat to life in which people live today*. It corresponds to profound changes in the apparatus of apperception – changes that are experienced on the scale of private existence by each passerby in big-city traffic, and on the scale of world history by each fighter against the present social order. [Benjamin's note. A more literal translation of the last phrase before the sentence in italics is: 'seeks to be buffered by intensified presence of mind [*Geistesgegenwart*].' – *Trans.*]

33. Sections XVII and XVIII introduce the idea of a productive 'reception in distraction' (*Rezeption in der Zerstreuung*), an idea indebted to the writings of Siegfried Kracauer and Louis Aragon. This positive idea of distraction – *Zerstreuung* also means 'entertainment' – contrasts with the negative idea of distraction that Benjamin developed in such essays as 'Theater and Radio' (1932) and 'The Author as Producer' (1934), both in this volume; the latter idea is associated with the theory and practice of Bertolt Brecht's epic theater. See 'Theory of Distraction' (1935–6), in this volume.

34. Benjamin relates the legend of this Chinese painter in the 1934 version of his *Berlin Childhood around 1900*, in Benjamin, *Selected Writings, Volume 3: 1935–1938* (Cambridge, Mass.: Harvard University Press, 2002), p. 393.

35. The term 'aesthetics' is a derivative of Greek *aisthetikos*, 'of sense perception,' from *aisthanesthai*, 'to perceive.'

36. A technological factor is important here, especially with regard to the newsreel, whose significance for propaganda purposes can hardly be overstated. *Mass reproduction is especially favored by the reproduction of the masses.* In great ceremonial processions, giant rallies and mass sporting events, and in war, all of which are now fed into the camera, the masses come face to face with themselves. This process, whose significance need not be emphasized, is closely bound up with the development of reproduction and recording technologies. In general, mass movements are more clearly apprehended by the camera than by the eye. A bird's-eye view best captures assemblies of hundreds of thousands. And even when this perspective is no less accessible to the human eye than to the camera, the image formed by the eye cannot be enlarged in the same way as a photograph. This is to say that mass movements, and above all war, are a form of human behavior especially suited to the camera. [Benjamin's note]

37. Gabriele D'Annunzio (1863–1938), Italian writer, military hero, and political leader, was an ardent advocate of Italy's entry into World War I and, a few years later, an ardent Fascist. His life and his work are both characterized by superstition, amorality, and a lavish and vicious violence. Futurism was an artistic movement aiming to express the dynamic and violent quality of contemporary life, especially as embodied in the motion and force of modern machinery and modern warfare. It was founded by the Italian writer Emilio Filippo Tommaso Marinetti (1876–1944), whose 'Manifeste de Futurisme' (Manifesto of Futurism) was published in the Paris newspaper *Le Figaro* in 1909; his ideas had a powerful influence in Italy and Russia. After serving as an officer in World War I, he went on to join the Fascist party in 1919. Among his other works are a volume of poems, *Guerra sola igiene del mundo* (War the Only Hygiene of the World; 1915), and a political essay, *Futurismo e Fascismo* (1924), which argues that fascism is the natural extension of Futurism. Schwabing, a district of Munich, was much frequented by artists around the turn of the twentieth century; Hitler and other Nazi agitators met in certain of its restaurants and beer cellars and plotted the unsuccessful revolt against governmental authority known as the Beer Hall Putsch (1923).

38. Cited in *La Stampa Torino*. [Benjamin's note. The German editors of Benjamin's *Gesammelte Schriften* argue that this passage is more likely to have been excerpted from a French newspaper than from the Italian newspaper cited here. – *Trans.*]

39. 'Let art flourish – and the world pass away.' This is a play on the motto of the sixteenth-century Holy Roman emperor Ferdinand I: 'Fiat iustitia et pereat mundus' ('Let justice be done and the world pass away').

This version of the essay was originally published in Michael W. Jennings, Brigid Doherty and Thomas Y. Levin, eds, Walter Benjamin, *The Work of Art in the Age of its Technical Reproducibility, and Other Writings on Media*, Cambridge, MA: Harvard University Press, 2008, pp. 19–39.

3.8 The Street Scene (1938)

A Basic Model for an Epic Theatre

BERTOLT BRECHT

Translated by John Willett

IN THE DECADE AND a half that followed the World War a comparatively new way of acting was tried out in a number of German theatres. Its qualities of clear description and reporting and its use of choruses and projections as a means of commentary earned it the name of 'epic'. The actor used a somewhat complex technique to detach himself from the character portrayed; he forced the spectator to look at the play's situations from such an angle that they necessarily became subject to his criticism. Supporters of this epic theatre argued that the new subject-matter, the highly involved incidents of the class war in its acutest and most terrible stage, would be mastered more easily by such a method, since it would thereby become possible to portray social processes as seen in their causal relationships. But the result of these experiments was that aesthetics found itself up against a whole series of substantial difficulties.

It is comparatively easy to set up a basic model for epic theatre. For practical experiments I usually picked as my example of completely simple, 'natural' epic theatre an incident such as can be seen at any street corner: an eyewitness demonstrating to a collection of people how a traffic accident took place. The bystanders may not have observed what happened, or they may simply not agree with him, may 'see things a different way'; the point is that the demonstrator acts the behaviour of driver or victim or both in such a way that the bystanders are able to form an opinion about the accident.

Such an example of the most primitive type of epic theatre seems easy to understand. Yet experience has shown that it presents astounding difficulties to the reader or listener as soon as he is asked to see the implications of treating this kind of street-corner demonstration as a basic form of major theatre, theatre for a scientific age. What this means of course is that the epic theatre may appear richer, more intricate and complex in every particular, yet to be major theatre it need at bottom only contain the same elements as a street-corner demonstration of this sort; nor could it any longer be termed epic theatre if any of the main elements of the street-corner demonstration were lacking. Until this is understood it is impossible really to understand what follows. Until one understands the novelty, unfamiliarity and direct challenge to the critical faculties of the suggestion that street-corner demonstration of this sort can serve as a satisfactory basic model of major theatre one cannot really understand what follows.

Consider: the incident is clearly very far from what we mean by an artistic one. The demonstrator need not be an artist. The capacities he needs to achieve his aim are in effect universal. Suppose he cannot carry out some particular movement as quickly as the victim he is imitating; all he need do is to explain that *he* moves three times as fast, and the demonstration neither suffers in essentials nor loses its point. On the contrary it is important that he should not be too perfect. His demonstration would be spoilt if the bystanders' attention were drawn to his powers of transformation. He has to avoid presenting himself in such a way that someone calls out 'What a lifelike portrayal of a chauffeur!' He must not 'cast a spell' over anyone. He should not transport people from normality to 'higher realms'. He need not dispose of any special powers of suggestion.

It is most important that one of the main features of the ordinary theatre should be excluded from our street scene: the engendering of illusion. The street demonstrator's performance is essentially repetitive. The event has taken place; what you are seeing now is a repeat. If the scene in the theatre follows the street scene in this respect then the theatre will stop pretending not to be theatre, just as the street-corner demonstration admits it is a demonstration (and does not pretend to be the actual event). The element of rehearsal in the acting and of learning by heart in the text, the whole machinery and the whole process of preparation: it all becomes plainly apparent. What room is left for experience? Is the reality portrayed still experienced in any sense?

The street scene determines what kind of experience is to be prepared for the spectator. There is no question but that the street-corner demonstrator has been through an 'experience', but he is not out to make his demonstration serve as an 'experience' for the audience. Even the experience of the driver and the victim is only partially communicated by him, and he by no means tries to turn it into an enjoyable experience for the spectator, however lifelike he may make his demonstration. The demonstration would become no less valid if he did not reproduce the fear caused by the accident; on the contrary it would lose validity if he did. He is not interested in creating pure emotions. It is important to understand that a theatre which follows his lead in this respect undergoes a positive change of function.

One essential element of the street scene must also be present in the theatrical scene if this is to qualify as epic, namely that the demonstration should have a socially practical significance. Whether our street demonstrator is out to show that one attitude on the part of driver or pedestrian makes an accident inevitable where another would not, or whether he is demonstrating with a view to fixing the responsibility, his demonstration has a practical purpose, intervenes socially.

The demonstrator's purpose determines how thoroughly he has to imitate. Our demonstrator need not imitate every aspect of his characters' behaviour, but only so much as gives a picture. Generally the theatre scene will give much fuller pictures, corresponding to its more extensive range of interest. How do street scene and theatre scene link up here? To take a point of detail, the victim's voice may have played no immediate part in the accident. Eye-witnesses may disagree as to whether a cry they heard ('Look out!') came from the victim or from someone else, and this may give our demonstrator a motive for imitating the voice. The question can be settled by demonstrating whether the voice was an old man's or a woman's, or merely whether it was high or low. Again, the answer may depend on whether it was that of an educated person or not. Loud or soft may play a great part, as the driver could be correspondingly more or less guilty. A whole series of characteristics of the victim ask to be portrayed. Was he absent-minded? Was his attention distracted? If so, by what? What, on the evidence of his behaviour, could have made him liable to be distracted by just that circumstance and no other? Etc., etc. It can be seen that our street-corner demonstration provides opportunities for a pretty rich and varied portrayal of human types. Yet a theatre which tries to restrict its essential elements to those provided by our street scene will have to acknowledge certain limits to imitation. It must be able to justify any outlay in terms of its purpose.[1]

The demonstration may for instance be dominated by the question of compensation for the victim, etc. The driver risks being sacked from his job, losing his licence, going to prison; the victim risks a heavy hospital bill, loss of job, permanent disfigurement, possibly unfitness for work. This is the area within which the demonstrator builds up his characters. The victim may have had a companion; the driver may have had his girl sitting alongside him. That would bring out the social element better and allow the characters to be more fully drawn.

Another essential element in the street scene is that the demonstrator should derive his characters entirely from their actions. He imitates their actions and so allows conclusions to be drawn about them. A theatre that follows him in this will be largely breaking with the orthodox theatre's habit of basing the actions on the characters and having the former exempted from criticism by presenting them as an unavoidable consequence deriving by natural law from the characters who perform them. To the street demonstrator the character of the man being demonstrated remains a quantity that need not be completely defined. Within certain limits he may be like this or like that; it doesn't matter. What the demonstrator is concerned with are his accident-prone and accident-proof qualities.[2] The theatrical scene may show more fully-defined individuals. But it must then be in a position to treat their individuality as a special case and outline the field within which, once more, its most socially relevant effects are produced. Our street demonstrator's possibilities of demonstration are narrowly restricted (indeed, we chose this model so that the limits should be as narrow as possible). If the essential elements of the theatrical scene are limited to those of the street scene then its greater richness must be an enrichment only. The question of border-line cases becomes acute.

Let us take a specific detail. Can our street demonstrator, say, ever become entitled to use an excited tone of voice in repeating the driver's statement that he has been exhausted by too long a spell of work? (In theory this is no more possible than for a returning messenger to start telling his fellow-countrymen of his talk with the king with the words 'I saw the bearded king'.) It can only be possible, let alone unavoidable, if one imagines a street-corner situation where such excitement, specifically about this aspect of the affair, plays a particular part. (In the instance above this would be so if the king had sworn never to cut his beard off until … etc.) We have to find a point of view for our demonstrator that allows him to submit this excitement to criticism. Only if he adopts a quite definite point of view can he be entitled to imitate the driver's excited voice; e.g. if he blames drivers as such for doing too little to reduce their hours of work. ('Look at him. Doesn't even belong to a union, but gets worked up soon enough when an accident happens. "Ten hours I've been at the wheel."')

Before it can get as far as this, i.e. be able to suggest a point of view to the actor, the theatre needs to take a number of steps. By widening its field of vision and showing the driver in other situations besides that of the accident the theatre in no way exceeds its model; it merely creates a further situation on the same pattern. One can imagine a scene of the same kind as the street scene which provides a well-argued demonstration showing how such emotions as the driver's develop, or another which involves making comparisons between tones of voice. In order not to exceed the model scene the theatre only has to develop a technique for submitting emotions to the spectator's criticism. Of course this does not mean that the spectator must be barred on principle from sharing certain emotions that are put before him; none the less to communicate emotions is only one particular form (phase, consequence) of criticism. The theatre's demonstrator, the actor, must apply a technique which will let him reproduce the tone of the subject demonstrated with a certain reserve, with detachment (so that the spectator can say: 'He's getting excited – in vain, too late, at last. ...' etc.). In short, the actor must remain a demonstrator; he must present the person demonstrated as a stranger, he must not suppress the '*he* did that, *he* said that' element in his performance. He must not go so far as to be wholly transformed into the person demonstrated.

One essential element of the street scene lies in the natural attitude adopted by the demonstrator, which is two-fold; he is always taking two situations into account. He behaves naturally as a demonstrator, and he lets the subject of the demonstration behave naturally too. He never forgets, nor does he allow it to be forgotten, that he is not the subject but the demonstrator. That is to say, what the audience sees is not a fusion between demonstrator and subject, not some third, independent, uncontradictory entity with isolated features of (a) demonstrator and (b) subject, such as the orthodox theatre puts before us in its productions.[3] The feelings and opinions of demonstrator and demonstrated are not merged into one.

We now come to one of those elements that are peculiar to the epic theatre, the so-called A-effect (alienation effect). What is involved here is, briefly, a technique of taking the human social incidents to be portrayed and labelling them as something striking, something that calls for explanation, is not to be taken for granted, not just natural. The object of this 'effect' is to allow the spectator to criticize constructively from a social point of view. Can we show that this A-effect is significant for our street demonstrator?

We can picture what happens if he fails to make use of it. The following situation could occur. One of the spectators might say: 'But if the victim stepped off the kerb with his right foot, as you showed him doing. ...' The demonstrator might interrupt saying: 'I showed him stepping off with his left foot.' By arguing which foot he really stepped off with in his demonstration, and, even more, how the victim himself acted, the demonstration can be so transformed that the A-effect occurs. The demonstrator achieves it by paying exact attention this time to his movements, executing them carefully, probably in slow motion; in this way he alienates the little sub-incident, emphasizes its importance, makes it worthy of notice. And so the epic theatre's alienation effect proves to have its uses for our street demonstrator too; in other words it is also to be found in this small everyday scene of natural street-corner theatre, which has little to do with art. The direct changeover from representation to commentary that is so characteristic of the epic theatre is still more easily recognized as one element of any street demonstration. Wherever he feels he can the demonstrator breaks off his imitation in order to give explanations. The epic theatre's choruses and documentary projections, the direct addressing of the audience by its actors, are at bottom just this.

It will have been observed, not without astonishment I hope, that I have not named any strictly artistic elements as characterizing our street scene and, with it, that of the epic theatre. The street demonstrator can carry out a successful demonstration with no greater abilities than, in effect, anybody has. What about the epic theatre's value as art?

The epic theatre wants to establish its basic model at the street corner, i.e. to return to the very simplest 'natural' theatre, a social enterprise whose origins, means and ends are practical and earthly. The model works without any need of programmatic theatrical phrases like 'the urge to self-expression', 'making a part one's own', 'spiritual experience', 'the play instinct', 'the story-teller's art', etc. Does that mean that the epic theatre isn't concerned with art?

It might be as well to begin by putting the question differently, thus: can we make use of artistic abilities for the purposes of our street scene? Obviously yes. Even the street-corner demonstration includes artistic elements. Artistic abilities in some small degree are to be found in any man. It does no harm to remember this when one is confronted with great art. Undoubtedly what we call artistic abilities can be exercised at any time within the limits imposed by our street scene model. They will function as artistic abilities even though they do not exceed these limits (for instance, when there is meant to be no complete transformation of demonstrator into subject). And true enough, the epic theatre is an extremely artistic affair, hardly thinkable without artists and virtuosity, imagination, humour and fellow-feeling; it cannot be practised without all these and much else too. It has got to be entertaining, it has got to be instructive. How then can art be developed out of the elements of the street scene, without adding any or leaving any out? How does it evolve into the theatrical scene with its fabricated story, its trained actors, its lofty style of speaking, its make-up, its team performance by a number of players? Do we need to add to our elements in order to move on from the 'natural' demonstration to the 'artificial'?

Is it not true that the additions which we must make to our model in order to arrive at epic theatre are of a fundamental kind? A brief examination will show that they are not. Take the *story*. There was nothing fabricated about our street accident. Nor does the orthodox theatre deal only in fabrications; think for instance of the historical play. None the less a story can be performed at the street corner too. Our demonstrator may at any time be in a position to say: 'The driver was guilty, because it all happened the way I showed you. He wouldn't be guilty if it had happened the way I'm going to show you now.' And he can fabricate an incident and demonstrate it. Or take the fact that the text is learnt by heart. As a witness in a court case the demonstrator may have written down the subject's exact words, learnt them by heart and rehearsed them; in that case he too is performing a text he has learned. Or take a rehearsed programme by several players: it doesn't always have to be artistic purposes that bring about a demonstration of this sort; one need only think of the French police technique of making the chief figures in any criminal case re-enact certain crucial situations before a police audience. Or take making-up. Minor changes in appearance – ruffling one's hair, for instance – can occur at any time within the framework of the non-artistic type of demonstration. Nor is make-up itself used solely for theatrical purposes. In the street scene the driver's moustache may be particularly significant. It may have influenced the testimony of the possible girl companion suggested earlier. This can be represented by our demonstrator making the driver stroke an imaginary moustache when prompting his companion's evidence. In this way the demonstrator can do a good deal to discredit her as a witness. Moving on to the use of a real moustache in the theatre, however, is not an entirely easy transition, and the same difficulty occurs with respect to *costume*. Our demonstrator may under given circumstances put on the driver's cap – for instance if he wants to show that he was drunk: (he had it on crooked) – but he can only do so conditionally, under these circumstances; (see what was said about borderline cases earlier). However, where there is a demonstration by several demonstrators of the kind referred to above we can have costume so that the various characters can be distinguished. This again is only a limited use of costume. There must be no question of creating an illusion that the demonstrators really are these characters. (The epic theatre can counteract this illusion by especially exaggerated costume or by garments that are somehow marked out as objects for display.) Moreover we can suggest another model as a substitute for ours on this point: the kind of street demonstration given by hawkers. To sell their neckties these people will portray a badly-dressed and a well-dressed man; with a few props and technical tricks they can perform significant little scenes where they submit essentially to the same restrictions as apply to the demonstrator in our street scene: (they will pick up tie, hat, stick, gloves and give certain significant imitations of a man of the world, and the whole time they will refer to him as '*he*'!). With hawkers we also find *verse* being used within the same framework as that of our basic model. They use firm irregular rhythms to sell braces and newspapers alike.

Reflecting along these lines we see that our basic model will work. The elements of natural and of artificial epic theatre are the same. Our street-corner theatre is primitive; origins, aims and methods of its performance are close to home. But there is no doubt that it is a meaningful phenomenon with a clear social function that dominates all its elements. The performance's origins lie in an incident that can be judged one way or another, that may repeat itself in different forms and is not finished but is bound to have consequences, so that this judgment has some significance. The object of the performance is to make it easier to give an opinion on the incident. Its means correspond to that. The epic theatre is a highly skilled theatre with complex contents and far-reaching social objectives. In setting up the street scene as a basic model for it we pass on the clear social function and give the epic theatre criteria by which to decide whether an incident is meaningful or not. The basic model has a practical significance. As producer and actors work to build up a performance involving many difficult questions – technical problems, social ones – it allows them to check whether the social function of the whole apparatus is still clearly intact.

Notes

1. We often come across demonstrations of an everyday sort which are more thorough imitations than our street-corner accident demands. Generally they are comic ones. Our next-door neighbour may decide to 'take off' the rapacious behaviour of our common landlord. Such an imitation is often rich and full of variety. Closer examination will show however that even so apparently complex an imitation concentrates on one specific side of the landlord's behaviour. The imitation is summary or selective, deliberately leaving out those occasions where the landlord strikes our neighbour as 'perfectly sensible', though such occasions of course occur. He is far from giving a rounded picture; for that would have no comic impact at all. The street scene, perforce adopting a wider angle of vision, at this point lands in difficulties which must not be underestimated. It has to be just as successful in promoting criticism, but the incidents in question are far more complex. It must promote positive as well as negative criticism, and as part of a single process. You have to understand what is involved in winning the audience's approval by means of a critical approach. Here again we have a precedent in our street scene, i.e. in any demonstration of an everyday sort. Next-door neighbour and street demonstrator can reproduce their subject's 'sensible' or his 'senseless' behaviour alike, by submitting it for an opinion. When it crops up in the course of events, however (when a man switches from being sensible to being senseless, or the other way round), then they usually need some form of commentary in order to change the angle of their portrayal. Hence, as already mentioned, certain difficulties for the theatre scene. These cannot be dealt with here.
2. The same situation will be produced by all those people whose characters fulfil the conditions laid down by him and show the features that he imitates.
3. Most clearly worked out by Stanislavsky.

This translation was originally published in Bertolt Brecht, *Brecht on Theatre*, trans. John Willett, London: Methuen, 1973 [1957], pp. 121–9.

3.9 Theatre for Pleasure or Theatre for Instruction (*c.* 1936)

BERTOLT BRECHT

Translated by John Willett

A FEW YEARS BACK, anybody talking about the modern theatre meant the theatre in Moscow, New York and Berlin. He might have thrown in a mention of one of Jouvet's productions in Paris or Cochran's in London, or *The Dybbuk* as given by the Habima (which is to all intents and purposes part of the Russian theatre, since Vakhtangov was its director). But broadly speaking there were only three capitals so far as modern theatre was concerned.

Russian, American and German theatres differed widely from one another, but were alike in being modern, that is to say in introducing technical and artistic innovations. In a sense they even achieved a certain stylistic resemblance, probably because technology is international (not just that part which is directly applied to the stage but also that which influences it, the film for instance), and because large progressive cities in large industrial countries are involved. Among the older capitalist countries it is the Berlin theatre that seemed of late to be in the lead. For a period all that is common to the modern theatre received its strongest and (so far) maturest expression there.

The Berlin theatre's last phase was the so-called epic theatre, and it showed the modern theatre's trend of development in its purest form. Whatever was labelled '*Zeitstück*' or '*Piscatorbühne*' or '*Lehrstück*' belongs to the epic theatre.

The epic theatre

Many people imagine that the term 'epic theatre' is self-contradictory, as the epic and dramatic ways of narrating a story are held, following Aristotle, to be basically distinct. The difference between the two forms was never thought simply to lie in the fact that the one is performed by living beings while the other operates via the written word; epic works such as those of Homer and the medieval singers were at the same time theatrical performances, while dramas like Goethe's *Faust* and Byron's *Manfred* are agreed to have been more effective as books. Thus even by Aristotle's definition the difference between the dramatic and epic forms was attributed to their different methods of construction, whose laws were dealt with by two different branches of aesthetics. The method of construction depended on the different way of presenting the work to the public, sometimes via the stage, sometimes through a book; and independently of that there was the 'dramatic element' in epic works and the 'epic element' in dramatic. The bourgeois novel in the last century developed much that was 'dramatic', by which was meant the strong centralization of the story, a momentum that drew the separate parts into a common relationship. A particular passion of utterance, a certain emphasis on the clash of forces are hallmarks of the 'dramatic'. The epic writer Döblin provided an excellent criterion when he said that with an epic work, as opposed to a dramatic, one can as it were take a pair of scissors and cut it into individual pieces, which remain fully capable of life.

This is no place to explain how the opposition of epic and dramatic lost its rigidity after having long been held to be irreconcilable. Let us just point out that the technical advances alone were enough to permit the stage to incorporate an element of narrative in its dramatic productions. The possibility of projections, the greater adaptability of the stage due to mechanization, the film, all completed the theatre's equipment, and did so at a point where the most important transactions between people could no longer be shown simply by personifying the motive forces or subjecting the characters to invisible metaphysical powers.

To make these transactions intelligible the environment in which the people lived had to be brought to bear in a big and 'significant' way.

This environment had of course been shown in the existing drama, but only as seen from the central figure's point of view, and not as an independent element. It was defined by the hero's reactions to it. It was seen as a storm can be seen when one sees the ships on a sheet of water unfolding their sails, and the sails filling out. In the epic theatre it was to appear standing on its own.

The stage began to tell a story. The narrator was no longer missing, along with the fourth wall. Not only did the background adopt an attitude to the events on the stage – by big screens recalling other simultaneous events elsewhere, by projecting documents which confirmed or contradicted what the characters said, by concrete and intelligible figures to accompany abstract conversations, by figures and sentences to support mimed transactions whose sense was unclear – but the actors too refrained from going over wholly into their role, remaining detached from the character they were playing and clearly inviting criticism of him.

The spectator was no longer in any way allowed to submit to an experience uncritically (and without practical consequences) by means of simple empathy with the characters in a play. The production took the subject-matter and the incidents shown and put them through a process of alienation: the alienation that is necessary to all understanding. When something seems 'the most obvious thing in the world' it means that any attempt to understand the world has been given up.

What is 'natural' must have the force of what is startling. This is the only way to expose the laws of cause and effect. People's activity must simultaneously be so and be capable of being different.

It was all a great change.

The dramatic theatre's spectator says: Yes, I have felt like that too – Just like me – It's only natural – It'll never change – The sufferings of this man appall me, because they are inescapable – That's great art; it all seems the most obvious thing in the world – I weep when they weep, I laugh when they laugh.

The epic theatre's spectator says: I'd never have thought it – That's not the way – That's extraordinary, hardly believable – It's got to stop – The sufferings of this man appall me, because they are unnecessary – That's great art: nothing obvious in it – I laugh when they weep, I weep when they laugh.

The instructive theatre

The stage began to be instructive.

Oil, inflation, war, social struggles, the family, religion, wheat, the meat market, all became subjects for theatrical representation. Choruses enlightened the spectator about facts unknown to him. Films showed a montage of events from all over the world. Projections added statistical material. And as the 'background' came to the front of the stage so people's activity was subjected to criticism. Right and wrong courses of action were shown. People were shown who knew what they were doing, and others who did not. The theatre became an affair for philosophers, but only for such philosophers as wished not just to explain the world but also to change it. So we had philosophy, and we had instruction. And where was the amusement in all that? Were they sending us back to school, teaching us to read and write? Were we supposed to pass exams, work for diplomas?

Generally there is felt to be a very sharp distinction between learning and amusing oneself. The first may be useful, but only the second is pleasant. So we have to defend the epic theatre against the suspicion that it is a highly disagreeable, humourless, indeed strenuous affair.

Well: all that can be said is that the contrast between learning and amusing oneself is not laid down by divine rule; it is not one that has always been and must continue to be.

Undoubtedly there is much that is tedious about the kind of learning familiar to us from school, from our professional training, etc. But it must be remembered under what conditions and to what end that takes place.

It is really a commercial transaction. Knowledge is just a commodity. It is acquired in order to be resold. All those who have grown out of going to school have to do their learning virtually in secret, for anyone who admits that he still has something to learn devalues himself as a man whose knowledge is inadequate. Moreover the usefulness of learning is very much limited by factors outside the learner's control. There is unemployment, for instance, against which no knowledge can protect one. There is the division of labour, which makes generalized knowledge unnecessary and impossible. Learning is often among the concerns of those whom no amount of concern will get any forwarder. There is not much knowledge that leads to power, but plenty of knowledge to which only power can lead.

Learning has a very different function for different social strata. There are strata who cannot imagine any improvement in conditions: they find the conditions good enough for them. Whatever happens to oil they will benefit from it. And: they feel the years beginning to tell. There can't be all that many years more. What is the point of learning a lot now? They have said their final word: a grunt. But there are also strata 'waiting their turn' who are discontented with conditions, have a vast interest in the practical side of learning, want at all costs to find out where they stand, and know that they are lost without learning; these are the best and keenest learners. Similar differences apply to countries and peoples. Thus the pleasure of learning depends on all sorts of things; but none the less there is such a thing as pleasurable learning, cheerful and militant learning.

If there were not such amusement to be had from learning the theatre's whole structure would unfit it for teaching.

Theatre remains theatre even when it is instructive theatre, and in so far as it is good theatre it will amuse.

Theatre and knowledge

But what has knowledge got to do with art? We know that knowledge can be amusing, but not everything that is amusing belongs in the theatre.

I have often been told, when pointing out the invaluable services that modern knowledge and science, if properly applied, can perform for art and specially for the theatre, that art and knowledge are two estimable but wholly distinct fields of human activity. This is a fearful truism, of course, and it is as well to agree quickly that, like most truisms, it is perfectly true. Art and science work in quite different ways: agreed. But, bad as it may sound, I have to admit that I cannot get along as an artist without the use of one or two sciences. This may well arouse serious doubts as to my artistic capacities. People are used to seeing poets as unique and slightly unnatural beings who reveal with a truly godlike assurance things that other people can only recognize after much sweat and toil. It is naturally distasteful to have to admit that one does not belong to this select band. All the same, it must be admitted. It must at the same time be made clear that the scientific occupations just confessed to are not pardonable side interests, pursued on days off after a good week's work. We all know how Goethe was interested in natural history, Schiller in history: as a kind of hobby, it is charitable to assume. I have no wish promptly to accuse these two of having needed these sciences for their poetic activity; I am not trying to shelter behind them; but I must say that I do need the sciences. I have to admit, however, that I look askance at all sorts of people who I know do not operate on the level of scientific understanding: that is to say, who sing as the birds sing, or as people imagine the birds to sing. I don't mean by that that I would reject a charming poem about the taste of fried fish or the delights of a boating party just because the writer had not studied gastronomy or navigation. But in my view the great and complicated things that go on in the world cannot be adequately recognized by people who do not use every possible aid to understanding.

Let us suppose that great passions or great events have to be shown which influence the fate of nations. The lust for power is nowadays held to be such a passion. Given that a poet 'feels' this lust and wants to have someone strive for power, how is he to show the exceedingly complicated machinery within which the struggle for power nowadays takes place? If his hero is a politician, how do politics work? If he is a business man, how does business work? And yet there are writers who find business and politics nothing like so passionately interesting as the individual's lust for power. How are they to acquire the necessary knowledge? They are scarcely likely to learn enough by going round and keeping their eyes open, though even then it is more than they would get by just rolling their eyes in an exalted frenzy. The foundation of a paper like the *Völkischer Beobachter* or a business like Standard Oil is a pretty complicated affair, and such things cannot be conveyed just like that. One important field for the playwright is psychology. It is taken for granted that a poet, if not an ordinary man, must be able without further instruction to discover the motives that lead a man to commit murder; he must be able to give a picture of a murderer's mental state 'from within himself'. It is taken for granted that one only has to look inside oneself in such a case; and then there's always one's imagination. ... There are various reasons why I can no longer surrender to this agreeable hope of getting a result quite so simply. I can no longer find in myself all those motives which the press or scientific reports show to have been observed in people. Like the average judge when pronouncing sentence, I cannot without further ado conjure up an adequate picture of a murderer's mental state. Modern psychology, from psychoanalysis to behaviourism, acquaints me with facts that lead me to judge the case quite differently, especially if I bear in mind the findings of sociology and do not overlook economics and history. You will say: but that's getting complicated. I have to answer that it *is* complicated. Even if you let yourself be convinced, and agree with me that a large slice of literature is exceedingly primitive, you may still ask with profound concern: won't an evening in such a theatre be a most alarming affair? The answer to that is: no.

Whatever knowledge is embodied in a piece of poetic writing has to be wholly transmuted into poetry. Its utilization fulfils the very pleasure that the poetic element provokes. If it does not at the same time fulfil that which is fulfilled by the scientific element, none the less in an age of great discoveries and inventions one must have a certain inclination to penetrate deeper into things – a desire to make the world controllable – if one is to to be sure of enjoying its poetry.

Is the epic theatre some kind of 'moral institution'?

According to Friedrich Schiller the theatre is supposed to be a moral institution. In making this demand it hardly occurred to Schiller that by moralizing from the stage he might drive the audience out of the theatre. Audiences had no objection to moralizing in his day. It was only later that Friedrich Nietzsche attacked him for blowing a moral trumpet. To Nietzsche any concern with morality was a depressing affair; to Schiller it seemed thoroughly enjoyable. He knew of nothing that could give greater amusement and satisfaction than the propagation of ideas. The bourgeoisie was setting about forming the ideas of the nation.

Putting one's house in order, patting oneself on the back, submitting one's account, is something highly agreeable. But describing the collapse of one's house, having pains in the back, paying one's account, is indeed a depressing affair, and that was how Friedrich Nietzsche saw things a century later. He was poorly disposed towards morality, and thus towards the previous Friedrich too.

The epic theatre was likewise often objected to as moralizing too much. Yet in the epic theatre moral arguments only took second place. Its aim was less to moralize than to observe. That is to say it observed, and then the thick end of the wedge followed: the story's moral. Of course we cannot pretend that we started our observations out of a pure passion for observing and without any more practical motive, only to be completely staggered by their results. Undoubtedly there were some painful discrepancies in our environment, circumstances that were barely tolerable, and this not merely on account of moral considerations. It is not only moral considerations that make hunger, cold and oppression hard to bear. Similarly the object of our inquiries was not just to arouse moral objections to such circumstances (even though they could easily be felt – though not by all the audience alike; such objections were seldom for instance felt by those who profited by the circumstances in question) but to discover means for their elimination. We were not in fact speaking in the name of morality but in that of the victims. These truly are two distinct matters, for the victims are often told that they ought to be contented with their lot, for moral reasons. Moralists of this sort see man as existing for morality, not morality for man. At least it should be possible to gather from the above to what degree and in what sense the epic theatre is a moral institution.

Can epic theatre be played anywhere?

Stylistically speaking, there is nothing all that new about the epic theatre. Its expository character and its emphasis on virtuosity bring it close to the old Asiatic theatre. Didactic tendencies are to be found in the medieval mystery plays and the classical Spanish theatre, and also in the theatre of the Jesuits.

These theatrical forms corresponded to particular trends of their time, and vanished with them. Similarly the modern epic theatre is linked with certain trends. It cannot by any means be practised universally. Most of the great nations today are not disposed to use the theatre for ventilating their problems. London, Paris, Tokyo and Rome maintain their theatres for quite different purposes. Up to now favourable circumstances for an epic and didactic theatre have only been found in a few places and for a short period of time. In Berlin Fascism put a very definite stop to the development of such a theatre.

It demands not only a certain technological level but a powerful movement in society which is interested to see vital questions freely aired with a view to their solution, and can defend this interest against every contrary trend.

The epic theatre is the broadest and most far-reaching attempt at large-scale modern theatre, and it has all those immense difficulties to overcome that always confront the vital forces in the sphere of politics, philosophy, science and art.

Note

This translation was originally published in Bertolt Brecht, *Brecht on Theatre*, trans. John Willett, London: Methuen, 1978, pp. 69–76.

3.10 Rehabilitating Realism (1992)

SHEILA STOWELL

IN 'CONSTRUCTING THE SUBJECT,' Catherine Belsey accuses what she calls 'classic realism' of complicity in 'reinforcing the concepts of the world and of subjectivity which ensure that people "work by themselves" in the social formation' (Belsey 1985: 51) – in other words, of being a tool of industrial capitalism whose epoch has coincided with its own. It is a view embraced by a number of recent feminist theatre critics who present realism, to borrow Jill Dolan's phrase, as a 'conservative force that reproduces and reinforces dominant cultural relations' (Dolan 1988: 84). In offering audiences a 'seamless illusion', it is argued, realism precludes interrogation, portraying an arbitrary but self-serving orthodoxy as both natural and inevitable. As such, the realist text becomes tainted and counterproductive, of use only to those who would endorse a bourgeois hegemony with its consequent enshrinement of domus, family and patriarch. Yet is this 'case' against realism as strong or as self-evident as its proponents would have us believe? In the following paper I would like to review some of the principal charges that have been levelled against the form – and the dangers inherent in, what seems to me to be, a type of ahistorical thinking.[1]

The mystification of the author and his or her 'apparent absence from the self-contained fictional world on the stage', has been urged as evidence of realism's connivance in the status quo, the argument being that such anonymity perpetuates the view that what is being seen is the thing itself, free from authorial subjectivity. Yet how, precisely, are we to understand the playwright's disappearance? If we turn back to the heyday of 'realism' on the Edwardian stage and to the initial reception of plays by Bernard Shaw or Harley Granville Barker – as close to villains as the new dispensation provides – the most common complaint of critics and audiences alike was that *all* characters spoke just like their authors. Indeed, the same can be said for Oscar Wilde in the 1890s, whose minutely observed, if highly stylized, dramas fall within Belsey's realist net. Contemporary reviewers and cartoonists portrayed Wilde as puppeteer or ventriloquist – an *obvious* manipulator not only controlling but *seen* to control his stage characters and world.[2]

Then again if we are in each case experiencing an 'illusion of unmediated reality' how do we explain the discernible differences between realist authors? What methods of streamlining experience – i.e. mediation – make it possible for us to distinguish the works of Wilde, Shaw and Granville Barker from one another, or indeed from those of Ibsen, Chekhov, or feminist contemporaries like Githa Sowerby and Elizabeth Baker? The issue is elided by Belsey who snatches back with one hand what she gives with the other, acknowledging the author's presence after all as a 'shadowy authority' and 'source of the fiction'. There is, in other words, a mediating force both at work and, equally importantly, observably at work. The exigencies of the realist form as defined by Belsey are such, however, that the subjected subject 'reader is invited to perceive and judge the "truth" of the text, the coherent, non-contradictory interpretation of the world as it is perceived by an author whose autonomy is the source and evidence of the truth of the interpretation' (Belsey 1985: 52). Why, given Belsey's admission that 'truth' is a relative term, must the reader see the play's world as coherent and non-contradictory? Because, the argument goes, an 'autonomous' author perceives it as such. Yet turn-of-the-century plays like Shaw's *Widowers Houses* (1892), Granville Barker's *The Madras House* (1910) and Sowerby's *Rutherford and Son* (1912) were calculated, their authors claimed, to lay bare the contradictions of capitalism by exposing the logical (if profitable) absurdities of the worlds whose surfaces they so carefully set forth. This is not to ignore the possibility that 'too much furniture, or walls that are too tight, [can] create the effect of an unchangeable world, a "fated" world' (States 1988: 90); it is merely to insist that realist theatre does not *necessarily* present a coherent or unassailable view of society. It is rather a tool, or variety of tools, for shaping social perception. In the hands of turn-of-the-century feminists, (and here Susan Kingsley Kent's general comments on the vocabulary of early feminist discourse are apt) 'the language of fact and concrete reality was meant to expose, by contrast, the emptiness of idealized depictions of womanhood and the marital state' (Kent 1987: 85) – to challenge in other words concepts of the world and of subjectivity which ensure willing participation in the maintenance of the existing social formation.

Nor should we be quick to simplify the role of the reader/audience in realism. The audience is not some sort of monolithic tabula rasa unwittingly acquiescing to its inscription by an author who exercises 'singular authority over the construction of meaning' (Dolan 1990: 42). An audience is a collection of members, each one informing as well as being informed by a work. We need to generalize less about its response, and investigate more closely its gender, class and economic composition in order to determine how meaning is generated. Once again, if we turn our attention to the reception of realist works at the turn of the century, we find, as might be expected, different groups of spectators reading the same 'reality' in predictably different ways. Sowerby's *Rutherford and Son* (1912), a powerful piece concerning the struggle between a despotic factory owner and his strong-willed daughter-in-law, was praised by Emma Goldman and Marjorie Strachey as a political tract arguing the case for female empowerment.[3] Indeed, the radical Women's Freedom League saw Sowerby's depiction of the industrial North as a 'hell, created by the arrogance of men,' concluding that although it did not deal specifically with suffrage issues, 'no play has ever been written that in the truest, strongest sense was so really a "Suffrage" play' (*The Vote*, 20 July 1912). Yet mainstream male critics continued to construe the work as being 'about' trade and industry, hence its appeal to a 'business nation.' For the *Daily Telegraph* (12 March 1912), the *Era* (23 March 1912) and the *Saturday Review* (30 March 1912), old Rutherford was as much victim as oppressor. A similar divergence, this time along class rather than gender lines, is documented in initial responses to Edith Lyttelton's *Warp and Woof* (1904), an exposé of the luxury dress trade by an author who was herself in 'Society'. The working-class *Clarion* joined Mary Macarthur of the Women's Trade Union League in seeing the play as an unblinking condemnation of 'real' conditions of labour, while society papers such as *Vanity Fair* protected their readers by insisting that Lyttelton had in fact 'libelled ... the unfortunate butterflies of Mayfair and Belgravia' (16 June 1904).[4] The tendency of each piece to conform to the predispositions of opposed sub-audiences is symptomatic of a broader problem facing reception studies. The converting imagination is a potent and active force in creating significance – in realist, no less than in expressionist, epic, symbolist, or absurdist theatre. When, where, how, and to whom any play is performed are all factors constitutive of meaning; they significantly complicate matters of style and structure and we ignore them at our peril.

Realism is also condemned for 'illusionism', a concept Belsey tells us is 'self-explanatory'. It is not. From the perspective of Brechtian orthodoxy, the theatre of illusionism is that which shows the structure of society represented on stage as incapable of change by society represented by spectators, the maintenance of an on-stage illusion (that which is something other than itself) lulling a passive audience into social and political quiescence. Yet defined this way, and allowing for historical positioning, can realism be said to be more essentially 'illusionistic' than other forms of drama? The contrast Dolan draws, for example, between Brecht's 'exercise in complex seeing' (good) and the 'seduction of the illusionist [i.e. realist] text' (bad) sounds remarkably like Shaw's claim in the 1890s that his own keen-eyed 'realism' (good) could correct the unthinking complicity of 'romantic [i.e. illusionistic] drama' (bad). As Bert States has noted of productions of Brecht, an observation that holds true for Shaw as well, 'It is not the stage illusion that is undercut, or even the illusion that the stage represents a certain kind of "Nature"; what is undercut is simply the conventional system of current theatre' (States 1988: 95). Furthermore, and I quote States again, 'the "arbitrary" mode of representation does not, in itself, assure the basis of a "critical" theatre. It may, indeed, have been the best kind of theater for Brecht's project, but this is a little like saying that iambic pentameter was the best kind of language for Shakespeare's. Brecht's theatre, like Shakespeare's, is what he left us and one can draw no conclusions about its form being the best or the correct one for his and similar projects' (ibid: 97). Push Brecht into a period like our own, in which audiences have come to expect, rather than be unsettled by, his bag of alienation tricks, and you have the spectacle of *Mahagonny's* structural 'disruptions' amusing wealthy audiences at New York's Metropolitan Opera. One is as likely today to encounter elements of Brecht's 'epic theatre' (now become 'culinary theatre') on Broadway or in London's West End as in alternative performance spaces or fringe venues. Nor can we ignore the fact that realist theatre developed as a radical, low mimetic response to the glittering make-believe world of society drama, which was seen to be, to quote Dolan's critique of realism, 'prescriptive in that it reifie[d] the dominant culture's inscription of traditional power relations between genders and classes' (Dolan, 1988: 84). In brief, realism was championed as a means of challenging the ideological assumptions imbedded in melodrama and the well-made play.

But realism, it is contended, is essentially unhealthy. For Roland Barthes, an early champion of Brecht, a realist or representational sign 'effaces its own status as a sign, in order to foster the illusion that what is being perceived is reality without its intervention' (Eagleton 1983: 136). A 'healthy sign', on the other hand, is one which makes manifest its arbitrariness; it does not pretend to be 'natural', but rather 'in the very moment of conveying a meaning, communicates something of its own relative, artificial status as well' (ibid: 135). But can it be said of realist theatre, now handmaid to Ideology, that it seeks to 'naturalize' both itself and the ideologically complicit worlds it produces? Isn't it rather the case that it is centred in the perception of itself as artificial reproduction; it is applauded for the virtuosity of its artifice, for the very reason that it is not what it shows. Surely only the most naive believe that realist theatre is a 'mirror that truthfully records an objective social portrait' (Dolan 1990: 42); what it records are versions of social relations mediated by a set of inherently arbitrary conventions. So at the time of its first performances, the 'accentuated realism' of Granville Barker's *The Voysey Inheritance* (1905) could be seen by critic Dixon Scott in terms of 'the bright veracity of the streets of shops in harlequinade'. Elaborating, Scott goes on to observe that while:

offering itself to us as a simple 'slice of life' [*The Voysey Inheritance*] is really impaled, all the time, on the most fantastic toasting-fork of criminal pathology and fairy-tale finance. And so, although the characters' reactions to the prongs are observed with the most scrupulous fidelity and reproduced with the most wonderful skill, though they wear unquestionable top-hats and smoke real cigars, they still affect us as uncanny creatures. ... The mechanism that skewers them spitting each of them in turn until we have the entire row displaying each his special squirm, is every bit as arbitrary as Carnaby Leete's rapier, as recondite as his political intrigues. (Scott 1917: 145)

One of the paradoxes of stage realism at its most extreme is that its material exuberance encourages audiences to admire the painstaking business of its illusion making. Accordingly, audiences who applauded the Trafalgar Square set of Elizabeth Robins' *Votes for Women!* (1907) were appreciating the virtuosity (i.e. the artificiality) of a tableau. They would not, one presumes, have gone to Trafalgar Square to applaud the 'real' thing. The effect is predicated on the experience of estrangement, which Brecht claimed to be, in its widest sense, not so much 'a matter of special techniques, but a bringing-to-consciousness of a normal procedure of everyday life' (Gray 1961: 68) in such a way that it is reconceived 'as something strange, new, as a successful construction, and thereby to some extent as something unnatural' (qtd ibid).

Nor can it be said of realist theatre that it invariably 'naturalizes the social relations imposed by dominant ideology' (Dolan 1988: 106). Theatricalizing workrooms, drapers' establishments, law offices and (yes) drawing-rooms can have the effect of making visible traditionally invisible processes of capitalist production, exposing the usually hidden workings of an oppressive system, such staged revelations calling into question existing ideology's 'naturalized' view of the world, each one a call to action. In *The Perfect Wagnerite* Shaw likened the top hat of the capitalist shareholder to the Tarnhelm Alberich uses in *The Rhinegold* to render himself invisible to the workers he enslaves. They can feel his oppression – in Alberich's case the lashes of an unseen whip – but are unsure of its source (Shaw 1981: 434–35). Shaw's *Plays Unpleasant* were designed, he maintained, to strip invisibility from latter day Alberichs, revealing a systemic evil concealed from audiences of mid-century melodrama.[5] Indeed, Shaw's curtain call speech after the first performance of *Widowers' Houses* – a lecture on the evils of capitalism lest any of his viewers should miss the play's point – is similar to the Epilogue Brecht added to the *The Good Person of Setzuan* after its Viennese premiere, urging audiences to go out and change the world if they didn't like the play's conclusion.[6]

It has also been claimed that realism is distinguished by 'narrative which leads to closure'. In an oft-quoted passage breath-taking in the vastness of its generalization, Belsey asserts that:

classic realist narrative ... turns on the creation of enigma through the precipitation of disorder which throws into disarray the conventional cultural and signifying systems. Among the commonest sources of disorder at the level of plot in classic realism are murder, war, a journey or love. But the story moves inevitably towards closure which is also disclosure, the dissolution of enigma through the re-establishment of order, recognizable as a reinstatement or a development of the order which is understood to have preceded the events of the story itself. (Belsey, 1985: 53)

This definition of 'closure', however, is so broad that while it applies to much realist theatre, it can be said to be equally true (or false) of an arc of dramatic action shared by playwrights from Sophocles – whose *Oedipus* surely stands as the model of such narrative – to the contemporary work of playwrights as diverse in technique and political sympathies as Steven Berkoff and Timberlake Wertenbaker. More seriously, such a definition negates the possibility of cumulative experience, arguing that because a so-called 'order' is restored at the end of a play, the work's overall visceral and cerebral meaning is erased. It would deny the significance of a play's process, the possibility that a spectator may not feel or think the same way about 'order' at the end of a work as at the beginning. Applied to realism as a form, such generalizations have resulted in an inability to distinguish between reproduction and reinforcement; consequently we hear that to 'show' something in realist terms is to confirm its inevitability to uncritical and politically resigned spectators, a claim some feminist theatre critics have used to maintain that 'closure in a realist play' invariably 'chokes women to death' (Case 1989: 43). If this is so, what do we make of a veritable realist play like Elizabeth Baker's *Chains* (1909), in which a female character actively rejects imprisonment in the matrimonial cage whose social and economic underpinnings are made obvious? Remaining enigmatic and unplaced, she does not disappear like a chameleon into the play's environment but actively removes herself from the stage sitting-room at the play's end, a profoundly symbolic departure from a realist setting that 'says in effect, "It will all end here"' (States 1988: 69).

I am not of course defending every realist play; as practiced, much realist drama (like much pre, modern and postmodern theatre) warrants challenge from feminists. What I am arguing is that while dramatic and theatrical styles may be developed or adopted to naturalize or challenge particular positions, dramatic forms are not in themselves narrowly partisan. Indeed, historically those forms of theatre that have most actively endorsed the authority of Church and State – the medieval morality play and Stuart masque come immediately to mind – have been both hieratic and emblematic. More recently, Brecht's own brand of politicized theatre has come under attack by playwright/novelist Günter Grass. In *The Plebeians Rehearse the Uprising* Grass recasts Brecht as a 'privileged court jester,' 'a man of the theatre serene and untroubled' (Grass 1966: xxxiv– xxxvi) who, in the face of the workers' uprising of 1953, does not turn the theatre to political account but instead turns political rebellion into state-sponsored epic theatre. On the other hand, a number of now inherently tainted realist plays were, in their own day, seen to offer so profound a threat to entrenched regimes that they were banned by state censors. The point is surely that while genres or styles – realism has been claimed as both – may not be politically neutral, they are capable of presenting a range of ideological positions; the issue is not so much formal as historical, contextual and phenomenological. To condemn writers simply because of the forms in which they work is to indulge in a system of analysis shaped by melodramatic assumptions of 'good' and 'bad' – the possibility of silencing (women) writers because they do not 'write right' is a danger to which feminist critics should be particularly alert.

Notes

1. This paper developed out of brief observations made in my book, *A Stage of Their Own: Feminist Playwrights of the Suffrage Era* (Manchester University Press: 1992), and was presented as part of the Women and Theatre Programme at the ATHE Conference, August 1991.

2. See for instance Joel Kaplan's 'A Puppet's Power: George Alexander, Clement Scott and the Replotting of *Lady Windermere's Fan*,' *Theatre Notebook*, May 1992.

3. See Goldman's observations in *The Social Significance of Modern Drama* and Strachey's review in the *Englishwoman* 1912, vol. 14.

4. In the words of the *Clarion*, *Warp and Woof* 'formulates an awful charge against the conditions of society which permit ... a state of affairs' in which employees 'are made the slaves of the exacting demands and the thoughtless selfishness of the fashionable world, whilst the wretchedness of their lives (with the terribly long working hours) lays them open to the worst forms of temptation as the readiest means of relief' (10 June 1904). Mary Macarthur was quick to use the play as 'a peg to hang propaganda articles on and a means of enlisting interest for the struggling Dressmakers' Union' (Hamilton 1926: 48).

5. Before warning his readers that 'my attacks are directed against themselves, not against my stage figures' (Shaw, 1980: 27), Shaw explains that he used the dramatic power of *Plays Unpleasant* 'to force the spectator to face unpleasant facts. ... [especially] those social horrors which arise from the fact that the average homebred Englishman, however honorable and goodnatured he may be in his private capacity, is, as a citizen, a wretched creature who, whilst clamoring for a gratuitous millennium, will shut his eyes to the most villainous abuses...' (ibid: 25–26).

6. According to Eric Bentley, Brecht added the Epilogue as a result of 'misunderstandings of the ending in the press' on that occasion (Brecht 1968:108).

Works cited

Belsey, Catherine (1985) 'Constructing the Subject: Deconstructing the Text'. In *Feminist Criticism and Social Change: Sex, Class, and Race in Literature and Culture*. Judith Newton and Deborah Rosenfelt, eds. New York: Methuen.

Brecht, Bertolt (1968) *Parables for the Theatre*. Trans. Eric Bentley. Harmondsworth: Penguin.

Case, Sue-Ellen (1989) 'Towards a Butch/Femme Aesthetic'. In *Making a Spectacle: Feminist Essays on Contemporary Women's Theatre*. Ann Arbor: University of Michigan Press.

Dolan, Jill (1988) *The Feminist Spectator as Critic*. Ann Arbor: UMI Research Press.

Dolan, Jill (1990) '"Lesbian" Subjectivity in Realism'. In *Performing Feminisms: Feminist Critical Theory and Theatre*. Sue-Ellen Case, ed. Baltimore: Johns Hopkins UP.

Eagleton, Terry (1983) *Literary Theory*. Oxford: Blackwell.

Goldman, Emma (1987) *The Social Significance of Modern Drama*. 1914. New York: Applause Theatre Books.

Grass, Gunter (1966) *The Plebeians Rehearse the Uprising*. Trans. Ralph Manheim. New York: Harcourt, Brace & World.

Gray, John (1961) *Brecht*. Edinburgh: Oliver and Boyd.

Hamilton, Mary Agnes (1926) *Mary Macarthur*. New York: Thomas Seltzer.

Kaplan, Joel H. (1992) 'A Puppet's Power: George Alexander, Clement Scott, and the Replotting of *Lady Windermere's Fan*'. *Theatre Notebook* (May 1992)

Kent, Susan Kingsley (1987) *Sex and Suffrage in Britain, 1860–1914*. Princeton: Princeton UP.

Scott, Dixon (1917) *Men of Letters*. London.

Shaw, Bernard (1980) *Plays Unpleasant*. Harmondsworth: Penguin.

Shaw, Bernard (1981) *The Perfect Wagnerite*. In *Shaw's Music*. vol. III. Dan H. Laurence, ed. New York: Dodd, Mead.

States, Bert (1988) *Great Reckonings in Little Rooms*. Berkeley: University of California Press, 1988.

Originally published in *Journal of Dramatic Theory and Criticism*, 6(2) (1992): 81–8.

3.11 The Author as Producer (1976)

TERRY EAGLETON

Art as production

I HAVE SPOKEN SO far of literature in terms of form, politics, ideology, consciousness. But all this overlooks a simple fact which is obvious to everyone, and not least to a Marxist. Literature may be an artefact, a product of social consciousness, a world vision; but it is also an *industry*. Books are not just structures of meaning, they are also commodities produced by publishers and sold on the market at a profit. Drama is not just a collection of literary texts; it is a capitalist business which employs certain men (authors, directors, actors, stagehands) to produce a commodity to be consumed by an audience at a profit. Critics are not just analysts of texts; they are also (usually) academics hired by the state to prepare students ideologically for their functions within capitalist society. Writers are not just transposers of trans-individual mental structures, they are also workers hired by publishing houses to produce commodities which will sell. 'A writer', Marx comments in *Theories of Surplus Value*, 'is a worker not in so far as he produces ideas, but in so far as he enriches the publisher, in so far as he is working for a wage.'

It is a salutary reminder. Art may be, as Engels remarks, the most highly 'mediated' of social products in its relation to the economic base, but in another sense it is also part of that economic base – one kind of economic practice, one type of commodity production, among many. It is easy enough for critics, even Marxist critics, to forget this fact, since literature deals with human consciousness and tempts those of us who are students of it to rest content within that realm. The Marxist critics I shall discuss in this chapter are those who have grasped the fact that art is a form of social production – grasped it not as an *external* fact about it to be delegated to the sociologist of literature, but as a fact which closely determines the nature of art itself. For these critics – I have in mind mainly Walter Benjamin and Bertolt Brecht – art is first of all a social practice rather than an object to be academically dissected. We may see literature as a *text*, but we may also see it as a social activity, a form of social and economic production which exists alongside, and interrelates with, other such forms.

Walter Benjamin

This, essentially, is the approach taken by the German Marxist critic Walter Benjamin.[1] In his pioneering essay 'The Author as Producer' (1934), Benjamin notes that the question which Marxist criticism has traditionally addressed to a literary work is: What is its position with regard to the productive relations of its time? He himself, however, wants to pose an alternative question: What is the literary work's position *within* the relations of production of its time? What Benjamin means by this is that art, like any other form of production, depends upon certain techniques of production – certain modes of painting, publishing, theatrical presentation and so on. These techniques are part of the productive *forces* of art, the stage of development of artistic production;

and they involve a set of social *relations* between the artistic producer and his audience. For Marxism, as we have seen, the stage of development of a mode of production involves certain social relations of production; and the stage is set for revolution when productive forces and productive relations enter into contradiction with each other. The social relations of feudalism, for example, become an obstacle to capitalism's development of the productive forces, and are burst asunder by it; the social relations of capitalism in turn impede the full development and proper distribution of the wealth of industrial society, and will be destroyed by socialism.

The originality of Benjamin's essay lies in his application of this theory to art itself. For Benjamin, the revolutionary artist should not uncritically accept the existing forces of artistic production, but should develop and revolutionize those forces. In doing so he creates new social relations between artist and audience; he overcomes the contradiction which limits artistic forces potentially available to everyone to the private property of a few. Cinema, radio, photography, musical recording: the revolutionary artist's task is to develop these new media, as well as to transform the older modes of artistic production. It is not just a question of pushing a revolutionary 'message' through existing media; it is a question of revolutionizing the media themselves. The newspaper, for example, Benjamin sees as melting down conventional separations between literary *genres*, between writer and poet, scholar and popularizer, even between author and reader (since the newspaper reader is always ready to become a writer himself). Gramophone records, similarly, have overtaken that form of production known as the concert hall and made it obsolete; and cinema and photography are profoundly altering traditional modes of perception, traditional techniques and relations of artistic production. The truly revolutionary artist, then, is never concerned with the art-object alone, but with the means of its production. 'Commitment' is more than just a matter of presenting correct political opinions in one's art; it reveals itself in how far the artist reconstructs the artistic forms at his disposal, turning authors, readers and spectators into collaborators.[2]

Benjamin takes up this theme again in his essay 'The work of Art in the Age of Mechanical Reproduction' (1933).[3] Traditional works of art, he maintains, have an 'aura' of uniqueness, privilege, distance and permanence about them; but the mechanical reproduction of, say, a painting, by replacing this uniqueness with a plurality of copies, destroys that alienating aura and allows the beholder to encounter the work in his own particular place and time. Whereas the portrait keeps its distance, the film-camera penetrates, brings its object humanly and spatially closer and so demystifies it. Film makes everyone something of an expert – anyone can take a photograph or at least lay claim to being filmed; and as such it subverts the ritual of traditional 'high art'. Whereas the traditional painting allows you restful contemplation, film is continually modifying your perceptions, constantly producing a 'shock' effect. 'Shock', indeed, is a central category in Benjamin's aesthetics. Modern urban life is characterized by the collision of fragmentary, discontinuous sensations; but whereas a 'classical' Marxist critic like Lukács would see this fact as a gloomy index of the fragmenting of human 'wholeness' under capitalism, Benjamin typically discovers in it positive possibilities, the basis of progressive artistic forms. Watching a film, moving in a city crowd, working at a machine are all 'shock' experiences which strip objects and experience of their 'aura'; and the artistic equivalent of this is the technique of 'montage'. Montage – the connecting of dissimilars to shock an audience into insight – becomes for Benjamin a major principle of artistic production in a technological age.[4]

Bertolt Brecht and 'epic' theatre

Benjamin was the close friend and first champion of Bertolt Brecht, and the partnership between the two men is one of the most absorbing chapters in the history of Marxist criticism. Brecht's experimental theatre ('epic' theatre) was for Benjamin a model of how to change not merely the political content of art, but its very productive apparatus. Brecht, as Benjamin points out, 'succeeded in altering the functional relations between stage and audience, text and producer, producer and actor'. Dismantling the traditional naturalistic theatre, with its illusion of reality, Brecht produced a new kind of drama based on a critique of the ideological assumptions of bourgeois theatre. At the hub of his critique is Brecht's famous 'alienation effect'. Bourgeois theatre, Brecht argues, is based on 'illusionism': it takes for granted the assumption that the dramatic performance should directly reproduce the world. Its aim is to draw an audience, by the power of this illusion of reality, into an empathy with the performance, to take it as real and feel enthralled by it. The audience in bourgeois theatre is the passive consumer of a finished, unchangeable art-object offered to them as 'real'. The play does not stimulate them to think constructively of *how* it is presenting its characters and events, or how they might have been different. Because the dramatic illusion is a seamless whole which conceals the fact that it is *constructed*, it prevents an audience from reflecting critically on both the mode of representation and the actions represented.

Brecht recognized that this aesthetic reflected an ideological belief that the world was fixed, given and unchangeable, and that the function of the theatre was to provide escapist entertainment for men trapped in that assumption. Against this, he posits the view that reality is a changing, discontinuous process, produced by men and so transformable by them.[5] The task of theatre is not to 'reflect' a fixed reality, but to demonstrate how character and action are historically produced, and so how they could have been, and still can be, different. The play itself, therefore, becomes a model of that process of production; it is less a reflection *of*, than a reflection *on*, social reality. Instead of appearing as a seamless whole, which suggests that its entire action is inexorably determined from the outset, the play presents itself as discontinuous, open-ended, internally contradictory, encouraging in the audience a 'complex seeing' which is alert to several conflicting possibilities at any particular point. The actors, instead of 'identifying' with their roles, are instructed to distance themselves from them, to make it clear that they are actors in a theatre rather than individuals in real life. They 'show' the characters they act (and show themselves showing them), rather than 'become' them; the Brechtian actor 'quotes' his part, communicates a critical reflection on it in the act of performance. He employs a set of gestures which convey the social relations of the character, and the historical conditions which makes him behave as he does; in speaking his lines he does not pretend ignorance of what comes next, for, in Brecht's aphorism, 'important is as important becomes'.

The play itself, far from forming an organic unity which carries an audience hypnotically through from beginning to end, is formally uneven, interrupted, discontinuous, juxtaposing its scenes in ways which disrupt conventional expectations and force the audience into critical speculation on the dialectical relations between the episodes. Organic unity is also disrupted by the use of different art-forms – film, back-projection, song, choreography – which refuse to blend smoothly with one another, cutting across the action rather than neatly integrating with it. In this way, too, the audience is constrained into a multiple awareness of several conflicting modes of representation. The result of these 'alienation effects' is, precisely, to 'alienate' the audience from the performance, to prevent it from emotionally identifying with the play in a way which paralyses its powers of critical judgement. The 'alienation effect' shows up familiar experience in an unfamiliar light, forcing the audience to question attitudes and behaviour which it has taken as 'natural'. It is the reverse of the bourgeois theatre, which 'naturalizes' the most unfamiliar events, processing them for the audience's undisturbed consumption. In so far as the audience is made to pass judgements on the performance and the actions it embodies, it becomes an expert collaborator in an open-ended practice, rather than the consumer of a finished object. The text of the play itself is always provisional: Brecht would rewrite it on the basis of the audience's reactions, and encouraged others to participate in that rewriting. The play is thus an experiment, testing its own presuppositions by feedback from the effects of performance; it is incomplete in itself, completed only in the audience's reception of it. The theatre ceases to be a breeding-ground of fantasy and comes to resemble a cross between a laboratory, circus, music hall, sports arena and public discussion hall. It is a 'scientific' theatre appropriate to a scientific age, but Brecht always placed immense emphasis on the need for an audience to enjoy itself, to respond 'with sensuousness and humour'. (He liked them to smoke, for example, since this suggested a certain ruminative relaxation.) The audience must 'think above the action', refuse to accept it uncritically, but this is not to discard *emotional* response: 'One thinks feelings and one feels thoughtfully.'[6]

Form and production

Brecht's 'epic' theatre, then, exemplifies Benjamin's theory of revolutionary art as one which transforms the modes, rather than merely the contents, of artistic production. The theory is not, in fact, wholly Benjamin's own: it was influenced by the Russian Futurists and Constructivists, just as his ideas about artistic media owed something to the Dadaists and Surrealists. It is, nonetheless, a highly significant development;[7] and I want to consider briefly three interrelated aspects of it. The first is the new meaning it gives to the idea of form; the second concerns its redefinition of the author, and the third its redefinition of the artistic product itself.

Artistic form, for long the jealously-guarded province of the aesthetes, is given a significantly new dimension by the work of Brecht and Benjamin. I have argued already that form crystallizes modes of ideological perception; but it also embodies a certain set of productive relations between artists and audiences.[8] What artistic modes of production a society has available – can it print texts by the thousand, or are manuscripts passed by hand round a courtly circle? – is a crucial factor in determining the social relations between 'producers' and 'consumers', but also in determining the very literary form of the work itself. The work which is sold on the market to anonymous thousands will characteristically differ in form from the work produced under a patronage system, just as the drama written for a popular theatre will tend to differ in formal conventions from that produced for private theatre. The relations of artistic production are in this sense *internal* to art itself, shaping its forms from within. Moreover, if changes in artistic technology alter the relations between artist and audience, they can equally transform the relations between artist and artist. We think instinctively of the work as the product of the isolated, individual author, and indeed this is how most works have been produced; but new media, or transformed traditional ones, open up fresh possibilities of collaboration *between* artists. Erwin Piscator, the experimental theatre director from whom Brecht learnt a great deal, would have a whole staff of dramatists at work on a play, and a team of historians, economists and statisticians to check their work.

The second redefinition concerns just this concept of the author. For Brecht and Benjamin, the author is primarily a *producer*, analogous to any other maker of a social product. They oppose, that is to say, the Romantic notion of the author as *creator* – as the God-like figure who mysteriously conjures his handiwork out of nothing. Such an inspirational, individualist concept of artistic production makes it impossible to conceive of the artist as a worker rooted in a particular history with particular materials at his disposal. Marx and Engels were themselves alive to this mystification of art, in their comments on Eugène Sue in *The Holy Family*: they see that to divorce the literary work from the writer as 'living historical human subject' is to 'enthuse over the *miracle-working* power of the pen'. Once the work is severed from the author's historical situation, it is bound to appear miraculous and unmotivated.

Pierre Macherey is equally hostile to the idea of the author as 'creator'. For him, too, the author is essentially a producer who works up certain given materials into a new product. The author does not make the materials with which he works: forms, values, myths, symbols, ideologies come to him already worked-upon, as the worker in a car-assembly plant fashions his product from already-processed materials. Macherey is indebted here to the work of Louis Althusser, who has provided a definition of what he means by 'practice'. 'By *practice* in general I shall mean any process of *transformation* of a determinate given raw material into a determinate *product*, a transformation effected by a determinate human labour, using determinate means (of "production").'[9] This applies, among other things, to the practice we know as art. The artist uses certain means of production – the specialized techniques of his art – to transform the materials of language and experience into a determinate product. There is no reason why this particular transformation should be more miraculous than any other.[10]

The third redefinition in question – the nature of the art-work itself – brings us back to the problem of form. For Brecht, bourgeois theatre aimed at smoothing over contradictions and creating false harmony; and if this is true of bourgeois theatre, it is also true for Brecht of certain Marxist critics, notably George Lukács. One of the most crucial controversies in Marxist criticism is the debate between Brecht and Lukács in the 1930s over the question of realism and expressionism.[11] Lukács, as we have seen, regards the literary work as a 'spontaneous whole' which reconciles the capitalist contradictions between essence and appearance, concrete and abstract, individual and social whole. In overcoming these alienations, art recreates wholeness and harmony. Brecht, however, believes this to be a reactionary nostalgia. Art for him should expose rather than remove those contradictions, thus stimulating men to abolish them in real life; the work should not be symmetrically complete in itself, but like any social product should be completed only in the act of being used. Brecht is here following Marx's emphasis in the *Contribution to the Critique of Political Economy* that a product only fully becomes a product through consumption. 'Production', Marx argues in the *Grundrisse*, '... not only creates an object for the subject, but also a subject for the object.'

Realism or modernism?

Underlying this conflict is a deep-seated divergence between Brecht and Lukács on the whole question of realism – a divergence of some political importance at the time, since Lukács at this point represented political 'orthodoxy' and Brecht was suspect as a revolutionary 'leftist'. Responding to Lukács's criticism of his art as decadently formalistic, Brecht accuses Lukács himself of producing a purely formalistic definition of realism. He makes a fetish of one histori-cally relative literary form (nineteenth-century realist fiction) and then dogmatically demands that all other art should conform to this paradigm. In demanding this he ignores the historical basis of form: how, asks Brecht, can forms appropriate to an earlier phase of the class-struggle simply be taken over or even recreated at a later time? 'Be like Balzac − only up-to-date' is Brecht's sardonic paraphrase of Lukács's position. Lukács's 'realism' is formalist because it is academic and unhistorical, drawn from the literary realm alone rather than responsive to the changing conditions in which literature is produced. Even in literary terms its base is notably narrow, dependent on a handful of novels alone rather than on an examination of other *genres*. Lukács's case, as Brecht sees, is that of the contemplative academic critic rather than the practising artist. He is suspicious of modernist techniques, labelling them as decadent because they fail to conform to the canons of the Greeks or nineteenth-century fiction; he is a utopian idealist who wants to return to the 'good old days', whereas Brecht, like Benjamin, believed that one must start from the 'bad new days' and make something of them. *Avant-garde* forms like expressionism thus hold much of value for Brecht: they embody skills newly acquired by contemporary men, such as the capacity for the simultaneous registration and swift combination of experiences. Lukács, in contrast, conjures up a Valhalla of great 'characters' from nineteenth-century literature; but perhaps, Brecht speculates, that whole conception of 'character' belongs to a certain historical set of social relations and will not survive it. We should be searching for radically different modes of characterization: socialism forms a different kind of individual, and will demand a different form of art to realize it.

This is not to say that Brecht is abandoning the concept of realism. It is rather that he wishes to extend its scope: 'our concept of realism must be wide and political, sovereign over all conven-tions ... we must not derive realism as such from particular existing works, but we shall use every means, old and new, tried and untried, derived from art and derived elsewhere, to render reality to men in a form they can master.' Realism for Brecht is less a specific literary style or *genre*, 'a mere question of form', than a kind of art which discovers social laws and developments, and unmasks prevailing ideologies by adopting the standpoint of the class which offers the broadest solution to social problems. Such writing need not necessarily involve *verisimilitude*, in the narrow sense of recreating the textures and appearances of things; it is quite compatible with the widest uses of fantasy and invention. Not every work which gives us the 'real' feel of the world is in Brecht's sense realist.[12]

Consciousness and production

Brecht's position, then, is a valuable antidote to the stiff-necked Stalinist suspicion of experimental literature which disfigures a work like *The Meaning of Contemporary Realism*. The materialist aesthetics of Brecht and Benjamin imply a severe criticism of the idealist case that the work's formal integration recovers a lost harmony or prefigures a future one.[13] It is a case with a long heritage, reaching back to Hegel, Schiller and Schelling, and forwards to a critic like Herbert Marcuse.[14] The role of art, Hegel claims in the *Philosophy of Fine Art*, is to evoke and realize all the power of man's soul, to stir him into a sense of his creative plenitude. For Marx, capitalist society, with its predominance of quantity over quality, its conversion of all social products to market commodities, its philistine soullessness, is inimical to art. Consequently, art's power fully to realize human capacities is dependent on the release of those capacities by the transformation of society itself. Only after the overcoming of social alienations, he argues in the *Economic and Philosophical Manuscripts* (1844), will 'the wealth of human subjective sensuality, a musical ear, an eye for the beauty of form, in short, senses capable of human pleasures ... be partly developed ... partly engendered'.[15]

For Marx, then, the ability of art to manifest human powers is dependent on the objective movement of history itself. Art is a product of the division of labour, which at a certain stage of society results in the separation of material from intellectual work, and so brings into existence a group of artists and intellectuals relatively divorced from the material means of production. Culture is itself a kind of 'surplus value': as Leon Trotsky points out, it feeds on the sap of economics, and a material surplus in society is essential for its growth. 'Art needs comfort, even abundance', he declares in *Literature and Revolution*. In capitalist society it is converted into a commodity and warped by ideology; yet it can still partially reach beyond those limits. It can still yield us a kind of truth – not, to be sure, a scientific or theoretical truth, but the truth of how men experience their conditions of life, and of how they protest against them.[16]

Brecht would not disagree with the neo-Hegelian critics that art reveals men's powers and possibilities; but he would want to insist that those possibilities are concrete historical ones, rather than part of some abstract, universal 'human wholeness'. He would also want to insist on the productive basis which determines how far this is possible, and in this he is at one with Marx and Engels themselves. 'Like any artist', they write in *The German Ideology*, 'Raphael was conditioned by the technical advances made in art before his time, by the organisation of society, by the division of labour in the locality in which he lived ...'

There is, however, an obvious danger inherent in a concern with art's technological basis. This is the trap of 'technologism' – the belief that technical forces in themselves, rather than the place they occupy within a whole mode of production, are the determining factor in history. Brecht and Benjamin sometimes fall into this trap; their work leaves open the question of how an analysis of art as a mode of production is to be systematically combined with an analysis of it as a mode of experience. What, in other words, is the relation between 'base' and 'superstructure' *in art itself*? Theodor Adorno, Benjamin's friend and colleague, correctly criticized him for resorting on occasions to too simple a model of this relationship – for seeking out analogies or resemblances between isolated economic facts and isolated literary facts, in a way which makes the relationship between base and superstructure essentially *metaphorical*.[17] Indeed this is an aspect of Benjamin's typically idiosyncratic way of working, in contrast to the properly systematic methods of Lukács and Goldmann.

The question of how to describe this relationship within art between 'base' and 'superstructure', between art as production and art as ideological, seems to me one of the most important questions which Marxist literary criticism has now to confront. Here, perhaps, it may learn something from Marxist criticism of the other arts. I am thinking in particular about John Berger's comments on oil painting in his *Ways of Seeing* (1972). Oil painting, Berger claims, only developed as an artistic *genre* when it was needed to express a certain ideological way of seeing the world, a way of seeing for which other techniques were inadequate. Oil painting creates a certain density, lustre and solidity in what it depicts; it does to the world what capital does to social relations, reducing everything to the equality of objects. The painting itself becomes an object – a commodity to be bought and possessed; it is itself a piece of property, and represents the world in those terms. We have here, then, a whole set of factors to be interrelated. There is the stage of economic production of the society in which oil painting first grew up, as a particular technique of artistic production. There is the set of social relations between artist and audience (producer/consumer, vendor/purchaser) with which that technique is bound up, there is the relation between those artistic property-relations, and property-relations in general. And there is the question of how the ideology which underpins those property-relations embodies itself in a certain form of painting, a certain way of seeing and depicting objects. It is this kind of argument, which connects modes of production to a facial expression captured on canvas, which Marxist literary criticism must develop in its own terms.

There are two important reasons why it must do so. First, because unless we can relate past literature, however indirectly, to the struggle of men and women against exploitation, we shall not fully understand our own present and so will be less able to change it effectively. Secondly, because we shall be less able to *read* texts, or to produce those art forms which might make for a better art and a better society. Marxist criticism is not just an alternative technique for interpreting *Paradise Lost* or *Middlemarch*. It is part of our liberation from oppression, and that is why it is worth discussing at book length.

Notes (edited)

1. Benjamin was born in Berlin in 1892, the son of a wealthy Jewish family. As a student he was active in radical literary movements, and wrote a doctoral thesis on the origins of German baroque tragedy, later published as one of his important works. He worked as a critic, essayist and translator in Berlin and Frankfurt after the first world war, and was introduced to Marxism by Ernst Bloch; he also became a close friend of Bertolt Brecht. He fled to Paris in 1933 when the Nazis came to power and lived there until 1940, working on a study of Paris which became known as the Arcades Project. After the fall of France to the Nazis he was caught trying to escape to Spain and committed suicide.
2. 'The Author As Producer' can be found in Benjamin's *Understanding Brecht* (London: 1972). Cf. The Italian Marxist Antonio Gramsci: 'The mode of being of the new intellectual can no longer consist in eloquence, which is an exterior and momentary mover of passions and feelings, but in active participation in practical life, as constructor, organizer, "permanent persuader" and not just a simple orator...'; *Prison Notebooks* (London: 1971).
3. Reprinted in W. Benjamin, *Illuminations* (London, 1970).
4. For the 'shock' effect, see Benjamin's *Charles Baudelaire: Lyric Poet in the Age of High Capitalism* (London: 1973). See also his essay in *Illuminations* on 'Unpacking My Library', where he considers his own passion for collecting. For Benjamin, collecting objects, far from being a way of harmoniously ordering them into a sequence, is an acceptance of the chaos of the past, of the uniqueness of the collected objects, which he refuses to reduce to categories. Collecting is a way of destroying the oppressive authority of the past, redeeming fragments from it.
5. I leave aside the question of how far Brecht, in holding this view, is guilty of a 'humanist' revision of Marxism.
6. See *Brecht on Theatre: the Development of an Aesthetic*, translated by John Willett (London, 1964), for a collection of some of Brecht's most important aesthetic writings ...
7. Its implications for modern media have been discussed by Hans Magnus Enzenberger in 'Constituents of a Theory of the Media', *New Left Review* no. 64 (November/December, 1970).
8. See Alf Louvre, 'Notes on a Theory of Genre', *Working Papers in Cultural Studies* no. 4 (University of Birmingham, Spring 1973).
9. *For Marx* (English Edition, London, 1969).
10. Macherey is in fact opposed in the final analysis to the whole idea of the author as 'individual subject', whether 'creator' or 'producer', and wants to displace him from his privileged position. It is not so much that the author produces his text as that the text 'produces itself' through the author ...
11. See Bertolt Brecht, 'Against George Lukács', *New Left Review* no. 84 (March/April, 1974).

12. Brecht's position here should be distinguished from that of the French Marxist Roger Garaudy in his *D'un realism sans rivages* (Paris, 1963).

13. See S. Mitchell, 'Lukács's Concept of the Beautiful' in G. H. R. Parkinson (ed.) *George Lukács: The Man, His Work, His Ideas* (London, 1970), for an account of Lukács's aesthetic views.

14. See in particular his *Negations* (London, 1968), *An Essay on Liberation* (London, 1969), and his essay 'Art as Form of Reality', *New Left Review* no. 74 (July/August, 1972).

15. See I. Mezaros's comments on Marxist aesthetics in *Marx's Theory of Alienation* (London, 1970).

16. Though art is not in itself a scientific mode of truth, it can nevertheless communicate the *experience* of such a scientific (i.e. revolutionary) understanding of society. This is the experience which *revolutionary* art can yield us.

17. See Adorno on Brecht, *New Left Review* no. 81 (September/October, 1973).

Originally published in *Marxism and Literary Criticism*, London: Routledge, 1976, pp. 59–76.

Part 4
Ideology and Performance/ The Performance of Ideology

Timeline

	Social, cultural and political context	Theatre
1945	Atomic bombs dropped on Hiroshima and Nagasaki End of the Second World War Labour Party (UK) wins landslide general election victory	Joan Littlewood's Theatre Workshop formed (UK)
1950	Start of the Korean War (1950–3)	George Bernard Shaw dies
1951	Festival of Britain	
1953		First production of Samuel Beckett's *Waiting for Godot* (France)
1955	African-American Civil Rights Movement formed (1955–68)	
1956	Suez Crisis (military confrontation between Egypt and Britain, France and Israel over ownership of the Suez Canal) Soviet Union invades Hungary	The English Stage Company (at the Royal Court Theatre) formed – this was set up as a 'playwrights' theatre' John Osborne's *Look Back in Anger* (hailed as a seminal 'kitchen sink' drama) Bertolt Brecht dies Brecht's Berliner Ensemble visits London for the first time
1958	Campaign for Nuclear Disarmament (CND) founded (UK)	
1959	Start of the Vietnam War (until 1975). USA becomes involved in the early 1960s	*A Raisin in the Sun*: Lorraine Hansberry
1961	John F. Kennedy becomes President of the USA US-backed Cuban exiles invade Cuba (Bay of Pigs Invasion) Construction of the Berlin Wall	
1962	Commonwealth Immigrants Act (UK) – restricts migration to the UK from the former colonies Cuban Missile Crisis	
1963	President Kennedy assassinated *The Feminine Mystique*: Betty Frieden (seminal feminist manifesto)	National Theatre (UK) opens at the Old Vic Theatre, in London
1964	Labour Party wins general election (UK) Civil Rights Act (USA)	*Blues for Mister Charlie*: James Baldwin
1965	Malcolm X assassinated Beginnings of the Black Power Movement (USA) Capital punishment abolished (UK)	Black Arts Movement (1965–76) *Saved*: Edward Bond (play was banned by the Lord Chamberlain because of the scene in which a group of youths stone a baby in a pram)
1966	Labour Party wins general election (UK)	

	Social, cultural and political context	Theatre
1967	Sexual Offences Act (decriminalizes homosexual relations between consenting adults over the age of 21) (UK) Abortion Act (legalizing abortion in UK)	*Hair: The American Tribal Love-Rock Musical*
1968	Assassination of Martin Luther King, Jr Assassination of Robert Kennedy Student demonstrations and occupations in France	Theatres Act 1968 – abolition of stage censorship in UK
1969	Richard Nixon becomes President of the USA British troops deployed to Northern Ireland Stonewall Riots (New York) – riots inaugurated by the gay community seen as the beginnings of gay activism Woodstock Festival, New York	
1970	Conservative Party wins general election (UK) Germaine Greer's feminist book, *The Female Eunuch*, becomes a best seller	
1972	Watergate scandal begins (USA) – accusation of corruption leading to the resignation of President Richard Nixon in 1974	
1973	UK joins European Economic Community	*The Cheviot, the Stag and the Black, Black Oil*: John McGrath/7:84 (Scotland)
1974	Labour Party wins general election (UK)	
1975		Gay Sweatshop Theatre Company founded (UK) Joint Stock Theatre Company founded (UK)
1979	Conservative Party wins general election (UK) – Margaret Thatcher becomes Prime Minister Soviet Union invades Afghanistan	*Bent*: Martin Sherman
1980	Hunger strikes by IRA prisoners in Northern Ireland begin Iran/Iraq War commences	
1981	Martial law in Poland The beginnings of the AIDS crisis Angela Y. Davis's seminal *Women, Race and Class* published	
1982	Argentina invades Falkland Islands (recaptured by British troops)	*Top Girls*: Caryl Churchill

	Social, cultural and political context	Theatre
1983	USA invades Grenada	
1984	Coal miners strike begins (UK, March)	
	IRA attempt to assassinate British Prime Minister Margaret Thatcher	
1985	Coal miners return to work (March)	*The Normal Heart*: Larry Kramer
	Mikhail Gorbachev becomes leader of the Soviet Union	*Les Misérables* opens in London (the production remains running at the time of writing)
1989	George H. W. Bush becomes President of the USA	
	Tiananmen Square massacre (China)	
	East Germany opens border with West Germany, demolition of Berlin Wall begins	
1990	Reunification of Germany	
	First Gulf War (ends 1991)	
1991		*Angels in America: Millennium Approaches*: Tony Kushner
1992		*Angels in America: Perestroika*: Tony Kushner
1993	Bill Clinton becomes President of the USA	*Enter the Night*: Maria Irene Fornes
1996		*Shopping and Fucking*: Mark Ravenhill
1997	'New' Labour wins landslide general election victory – Tony Blair becomes Prime Minister	
2000		*Far Away*: Caryl Churchill
2001	George W. Bush becomes President of the USA	
	September 11 – terrorist attack on the USA	
2003	Anglo-American-led invasion of Iraq (Second Gulf War)	
2005		Harold Pinter awarded the Nobel Prize
2008	Global financial collapse	*Scenes from Family Life*: Mark Ravenhill
2009	Barack Obama becomes President of the USA	

Introduction

JOHN F. DEENEY

Part 4 brings together a range of plays which speak to issues of the relationship between performance, ideology and identity. All of the texts included are contextualized by a historical period which has seen enormous shifts in the meaning and implications of the term 'ideology'. Thus, in order to unravel the significance of ideology in relation to theatre and performance, this introduction begins by revisiting some of the ideas explored in the previous part of the anthology.

In Part 3, we considered 'political theatre' or 'theatres' in terms of how dramatists and theatre practitioners in Europe and the USA responded to the vast social and political upheavals of the first half of the twentieth century. Their theatres sought to revolutionize theatrical presentation and create new forms of spectatorship. Early political theatres' materialist analysis of history and the socio-political order was crucially reflected in practices that challenged the illusionist foundations of Naturalism. The collective recognition of the stage as a tangible material entity fostered forms of experimentation that located the human subject in a broader socio-historical context, beyond their immediate environment, and suggested a level of human agency which implied that individuals could effect change upon the world in which they lived. Many early political theatres were not simply concerned with breaking through or destroying the Naturalistic theatre's 'fourth wall'; this demolition needed to be strategically carried through into the performance space – even, as we have seen, beyond actual theatre buildings. Here, the recognizable spaces of Naturalistic drama – particularly 'the room', a powerful symbol of enclosure – were torn down to be replaced by 'epic' *mise en scènes* that more expansively acknowledged the possibility of human agency.

In Part 1 of this anthology we have seen how Darwinian determinism framed the individual in terms of a complex web of social and biological predestination. However, in this respect, Naturalism fosters a kind of double-illusion; the theatrical illusion itself being underpinned by the much weightier deceit that the Naturalist form provides a 'truthful' explanation of human behaviour. What we also have here is a fundamental questioning of the notion of the human subject. Brecht's famed 'table' that opposed 'Dramatic Theatre' with 'Epic Theatre', read simply, can be viewed as a manifesto for an antagonistic debate between bourgeois-capitalist and Marxist aesthetics. However, several of the oppositions – '[the human being] is unalterable'/'is alterable and able to alter'; 'man as a fixed point'/'man as a process'; 'thought determines being'/'social being determines thought' – are not merely Brecht's attempt to theorize the theatre's would-be contribution to the raising of class-consciousness in the revolutionary struggle, they also open up an important debate about the very constitution of the subject and her/his *modus operandi* (Brecht 2001: 37).

The plays included in this part each in their own way attend to this bequest from the early 'political theatres' from Part 3. However, this does not mean a straightforward shift of emphasis from 'structure' – the social/political/ideological apparatus – to 'agency' – the subject and her/his capacity to self-define and to 'act'. The plays explored here are concerned with the territory between the two, a territory characterized by questions of identity, subjectivity, ideology and culture. Together with the accompanying critical/theoretical texts, the plays both reflect and inform a development of the dramaturgical and production strategies of early to mid-twentieth-century political theatres and, arguably, a significant break from them.

From the middle to the latter half of the twentieth century a broad consensus had been built up around the idea of 'political theatre' – particularly in the British theatre – that made the term 'synonymous with left-wing theatre, socialist theatre of various types' (Holderness 1992: 3). However, even from the 1960s onwards, both in the British theatre and in that of the USA, the deftness of 'political theatre' – as both a practice and a descriptor – began to falter. We have already seen in Part 3 how the work of the Federal Theatre Project and the 'Living Newspaper' as far back as the 1930s – also exemplified in Hallie Flanagan Davis's $E=mc^2$ (3.4) – embodied a radical form for relatively liberal ends. The progression of the twentieth century bore witness to the faltering of the Marxist and leftist orthodoxies. New questions about and frameworks for the discussion of identity and politics, race, gender, sexuality, culture and nationality rapidly emerged and were at the forefront of political thought in both the public and private realm. The plays in this part cover a period from 1964 to 2008 and were composed against a background of momentous social and political change that gave rise to such questions. Not least of these was the fall of communism in Eastern Europe, beginning in the late 1980s, which served to ratify – as we shall see – many of the uncertainties that 'political' dramatists and practitioners had been rehearsing for some time. The work explored in this part raises important questions concerning 'the politics of practice', particularly relating to the role and function of 'the dramatist' – a matter also pursued, from a somewhat different angle, in Part 5. The plays included here each originate from either the UK or the USA, which will serve to highlight certain transatlantic schisms and alliances. Reference is also made in this introduction to the work of dramatists from outside Europe and the USA, notably from Africa. All of this will assist us in unscrambling what is defined here as a particular interrelationship, that between 'ideology and performance'.

Between 'politics' and 'ideology'

In formulating a title for Part 4, we have purposefully avoided employing the term 'political theatre'. This is not to assert that the name is now redundant. Indeed, there has been a resurgence of 'political' theatre over the past decade, exemplified in particular by the revitalization of 'verbatim' and documentary theatre in both the UK and the USA (see Forsyth and Megson 2009). Rather, the framework for this part functions more conveniently as an umbrella term for a range of related yet divergent plays and practices.

Holderness (1992) argues that the linking of politics and theatre 'immediately identifies a context of cultural difference, perhaps even a binary opposition: political theatre is not the same as ordinary theatre because it displays a different kind of relationship with something other than itself – "politics"'. The idea of *intentionality* or *purpose* in theatre practice is crucial here; '[t]heatre may be "political" without becoming "political theatre", in the sense that a play may represent political matters or address political issues, in exactly the same way as a play can represent love, or old age, or poverty'. Thus, ' "political theatre" ... must entail theatre's becoming partisan, splitting along the lines of party conflict, lining up with one particular group, or cause, or ideology' (ibid: 2). Acknowledging the limitations of such definitions, Holderness moves on to argue for the 'transformation of "political drama" – as an object of enquiry – into "the politics of drama"

– as a method of analysis' (ibid: 16). However, underlying Holderness's concern about *how* we investigate the relationship between 'politics' and 'theatre' is a more deep-seated predicament that performance theorist Baz Kershaw has identified in broader terms:

> For some time now the idea of 'political theatre' has been in crisis. Postmodernism and related theories have profoundly upset established notions of the 'political' in theatre, which were usually defined in relation to left-wing or socialist/Marxist ideologies. Right-wing theatre, by implication, was not political. The problem is now compounded because Left-progressive ideologies appear to be in decline, but more importantly also because of the new promiscuity of the political. Since the personal became political, in the 1960s, the political has found its way into almost every nook and cranny of culture. Identity politics, the politics of camp, body politics, sexual politics – the political is now ubiquitous and can be identified in all theatre and performance. (Kershaw 1999: 16)

Kershaw's identification of the 'personal as political' marks an important historical and cultural shift; here the politics of everyday lived experience becomes as important as the 'political' of social and historical movements and events. This reassertion of the importance of the personal embedded within the ideological has also had a significant effect on both the making and reception of theatre and performance, influencing practice and practitioners, and also the critical means we might employ to fully comprehend and study contemporary theatre. Thus the question of the idea of 'political theatre' no longer seems sufficient to denote an 'oppositional', 'partisan' or even 'critical' form of practice. Equally, the terms of engagement themselves appear to be at stake here. In order to understand this shift, we need to turn our attention to the broader social and cultural contexts of its making.

When, in 1992, the political economist and philosopher Francis Fukuyama published his influential book, *The End of History and the Last Man*, he was far from announcing an impending apocalypse. Rather, Fukuyama was crystallizing what many already perceived as an important historical turn. The fall of the Berlin Wall, built in 1961 to separate the communist German Democratic Republic (established in 1949) from West Germany, in 1989, marked the symbolic death of 'Really Existing Socialism' in Eastern Europe. Its literal death was quick to follow. In Russia, Mikhail Gorbachev, Lenin's last heir as leader of the Soviet Union, initiated 'perestroika' (reconstruction) and 'glasnost' (openness) in 1986. These policies ultimately accelerated Western-styled democratization within the Eastern bloc. But what Fukuyama named as 'the end of history' did not merely represent the end of the Cold War, it forged a powerful double-edged ideological weapon: a 'liberal-democratic political utopia' paralleled with 'the economic utopia of global market capitalism' (Žižek 2009: 5). The triumph of capitalism over socialism is therefore underwritten by the widespread acceptance of liberal democracy as the most successful form of government.

Although the *idea* of 'democracy' – the authority of the peoples of nation states to elect competing political parties into government – survives in Fukuyama's thesis, the supposed ability to choose between *real* political alternatives begins to diminish. Since the 1990s – in Europe particularly – most political battles have been about conquering the centre ground, where it is perceived that the majority of voters now naturally congregate. The choice is no longer between 'left' or 'right', but about what parties – with their different policy emphases in terms of education, healthcare, welfare and so forth – might better uphold the global ideological infrastructure. Thus the polarity of political ideologies once represented by the 'political left' and the 'political right', which inspired many of the early political theatres explored in Part 3, is no longer as clearly discernible. A political 'centre ground' now dominates and its tendrils have spread into and absorbed the margins so significantly, that there appears to be only this 'centre ground' set against forms of political extremism with little else in between.

Fukuyama's celebration of this historical turn gave rise to important questions about how potentially new forms of political opposition might be forged, and is instructive to us here for a number of reasons. First, it presupposes a fundamental diminishing of the tensions between 'agency' and 'structure'; that is, it assumes that the need for political contestation has lessened. This is deeply contested by many of the plays we shall move on to consider. Second, Fukuyama's thesis manifests important questions about the changing function of 'ideology' and its deep-rootedness in all aspects of private, public and political life. Ideology, broadly referring to a system of values, ideas and beliefs that determine consciousness and agency, cannot be reduced to a single verifiable definition. Indeed, we can identify a range of frequently competing ideologies: including liberalism, conservatism, socialism, nationalism, fascism, ecologism and feminism (Eccleshall *et al.* 2003). This multiplicity of possibilities raises the question of the relationship between ideologies and 'truth'. Even when ideologies employ 'empirical examples' and 'social scientific research' to substantiate their truth-claims, the problem remains that 'ideologies shape what we see when we look at the social and political world ... ideological spectacles are already adorned' (MacKenzie 2003: 11). Additionally, Marxist thinking and criticism have continued, despite the various death notices, to exert tremendous influence – although perhaps not always in the direction that Marx intended. It is astonishing to consider, for example, how one of the classical Marxist definitions of ideology as 'the general process of the production of meanings and ideas' can be seen to have been appropriated by neo-conservative thinkers such as Fukuyama (Williams 1977: 55). Thus, Fukuyama's thesis, rather than evidencing the end of ideology, is itself intensely ideological in its celebration of neo-liberalism.

Performance and ideology

Kershaw notes, 'to the extent that performance deals in the values of its particular society, it is dealing with ideology' (Kershaw 1992: 18). Whilst acknowledging the inescapability of ideology in all theatre and performance – from the international blockbuster musical to the community theatre event – our focus here is on dramatists and practices that deliberately make an ideological intervention. We can take our cue here from the Marxist philosopher Louis Althusser. He developed an influential theory of ideology which argued that human subjects – and thus consciousness – are never 'free' as such, but are produced by means of understanding their own actions in relationship to the dominant ideology (Althusser 1971: 127-86). It is the nature of this relationship that the plays discussed here intervene in and attempt to understand. The significance of Althusser's work also lies in his argument that art cannot be condensed to a straightforward expression of ideology. Indeed, Althusser saw theatrical performance as promoting 'complex behaviour' amongst spectators, behaviour that is 'primarily social and cultural-aesthetic, and as such ... also ideological' (Althusser 2005: 149). As Terry Eagleton explains,

Ideology signifies the imaginary ways in which men [*sic*] experience the real world ... However, art does more than just passively reflect that experience. It is held within ideology but also manages to distance itself from it, to the point where it permits us to 'feel' and 'perceive' the ideology from which it springs. In doing this, art does not enable us to *know* the truth which ideology conceals, since for Althusser 'knowledge' in the strict sense means *scientific* knowledge ... Science gives us conceptual knowledge of a situation; art gives us the experience of that situation, which is equivalent to ideology. But by doing this, it allows us to 'see' the nature of that ideology. (Eagleton 2006: 16–17)

The plays discussed in this part, however, whilst mostly produced in conventional theatre spaces, raise important questions about the theatre's critical and effective viability in a transformational contemporary society. To return to Althusser, he perceived in the theatre the possibility of 'the occasion for a cultural and ideological recognition' and 'the production of a new consciousness in the spectator' (Althusser 2005: 149, 151). Significantly, he was writing here about Brecht's practice, and it is this inheritance, so integral to an understanding of the materials further explored in Part 4, to which we now turn.

Brechtian legacies: developments and departures

Let's talk about theatre that has as its base a recognition of capitalism as an economic system which produces classes ... A theatre that sees the establishment of socialism, not as the creation of a utopia or the end of the dialectic of history, but as another step towards the realization of the full potential of every individual human life during the short time that every individual has to live. Socialist theatre. (McGrath 1979, 4.7: 635)

We are living the extinction of official socialism. When the opposition loses its politics, it must root in art ... Ideology is the outcome of pain. ... Since no art form generates action, the most appropriate art for a culture on the edge of extinction is one that stimulates pain. (Barker 1986, 4.8: 653–55).

John McGrath (1935–2002) and Howard Barker (b. 1946) came to prominence in the 1960s and 1970s respectively. As 'political dramatists', both were also part, alongside such figures as Howard Brenton, Caryl Churchill, David Edgar and David Hare, of the 'fringe' or 'alternative theatre movement' in Britain (see below). However, their career trajectories within the British theatre demonstrate contrasting positions concerning not only the legitimacy of a 'political theatre', but also its basis in Brechtian theory and practice. McGrath and Barker do share something; they are part of that rare breed in the contemporary British theatre, dramatists – others would include Edgar, Hare, Edward Bond and more latterly Mark Ravenhill – who have produced extensive theoretical commentaries on dramaturgical and theatre practice as well as a significant number of plays (see Barker 1997; McGrath 1989, 1990, 2002). In this journey between theory and practice which goes beyond the specifics of the craft of playwriting to explore more deeply the relationship between text, performance, context and affect, such playwrights link directly with Brecht's position as playwright and theatre theorist.

Trying to pin down and unpack precisely the impact of Brecht's theory and practice on contemporary theatre is akin to trying to identify the effect of technology on our contemporary lives; we are surrounded by it, we perhaps take it somewhat for granted and yet most of us would almost certainly malfunction if denied access to it. The pervasiveness of Brecht's ideas, in terms of theatrical production and the dismantling of Aristotelian-based dramatic forms, is everywhere to be seen. Plays as diverse as Caryl Churchill's *Top Girls* (1982), Tony Kushner's *Angels in America* (1991/2) and Mark Ravenhill's *Shopping and Fucking* (1996) owe a significant debt to Brecht. So too do many of the deconstructive strategies associated with the work of companies such as the Wooster Group in the USA (see Savran 1988) and Forced Entertainment in the UK within the field of contemporary performance (see Etchells 2005 and 5.3; also see Part 5). The modern musical, that doyen of global multimillion-dollar profitability, does not escape either; behind its revolving stage, its projections of text, its episodic historical narrative – even *Les Misérables* (1985) carries the grimacing ghost of Brecht. Neither should we ignore here the immense influence that Brechtian ideas have exerted on the cinema and on popular culture generally. Brechtian techniques of distanciation, which were originally aimed at producing forms of socio-historical critical recognition within the spectator, have been vigorously appropriated in late capitalist culture. Recent blockbuster films such as *The Matrix* (1999), popular television comedy serials such as *Scrubs* (2001–) and *Ugly Betty* (2006–) and a plethora of media advertising – selling everything from breakfast cereals to insurance – share a blissful self-awareness of their fictive qualities. Here, however, auto-referentiality – self-conscious, self-awareness of chosen performative strategies – is no longer attached to radicalizing spectatorship in the way that Brecht envisioned. As Brecht was more than aware, the efficacy of aesthetic-political strategies is historically and culturally specific and they do not automatically translate to subsequent periods of theatre making. Nevertheless, Amelia Howe Kritzer maintains that the 'important potential of Brechtian theatre remains its insistence on dialogue and its openness to active interpretation' (Kritzer 2008: 18 and see Reinelt 1996). In other words, there are discernible degrees and different levels of Brechtian influence on all areas of contemporary theatre practice.

McGrath and Barker's ideas serve to both endorse and challenge such a position. Throughout the 1970s and 1980s, McGrath developed his work outside the mainstream of theatrical production, even though his company 7:84 (a name which comes from the economic fact that 7 per cent of the population owned 84 per cent of the country's wealth) received state funding on a regular basis from the Arts Council of Great Britain. The potential efficacy of 7:84's project lay in understanding and developing the languages of theatre and performance available to working-class audiences and, according to McGrath, embedded within working-class cultural history. Illuminating this practice was the extensive investigation by McGrath into the ideological underpinnings of not only 7:84's work, but also the broad theatrical ecology of the British theatre. Borrowing from Raymond Williams's Marxist analysis of the modes of literary production (see also the Introduction to this volume), McGrath identifies the characteristics intrinsic to 'dominant' (state-subsidized mainstream), 'residual' (commercial mainstream) and 'emergent' (alternative) forms of theatre within British culture (4.7: 636–39; Williams 1977: 121–7). McGrath firmly locates 7:84's work outside the principal systems of capitalist production and exploitation; significantly, he likens theatres such as the Royal Shakespeare Company and the National Theatre – which, as the 1970s progressed began incorporating the work of political dramatists such as

Brenton, Edgar and Hare into their repertoires – to 'the nationalized industries: they are capitalist structures, but without the need to make profits' (4.7: 637). The gradual introduction of state subsidy into British theatre from the mid-1940s onwards enabled the making of theatre and performance events without the immediate need for a commercial driver. However, state funding has always been a double-edged sword. On the one hand, such a subsidy can allow for inventive risk-taking theatre; on the other, it can transform a creative process into an exercise in coercion. McGrath unsurprisingly found the newly ensconced Conservative Government of the early 1980s unwilling to subsidize left-wing, subversive theatre and so the activities of 7:84 and other 'political' theatre companies became limited by the operations of the same funding system which had helped them develop in the first place (see McGrath 1990). In the USA, the equivalent to the British Arts Council, the National Endowment for the Arts (established in 1965), has similarly often been accused of ideological bias in its delivery of financial support for the arts. Thus, McGrath sees the integration of the work of 'political' playwrights into the dominant mainstream subsidized theatre as a form of coercion and a watering down of its potential ideological impact. It is within the 'emergent', therefore, that McGrath identifies the possibility of 'a theatre that is *interventionist* on a political level' (4.7: 636).

Janelle Reinelt has observed how 'McGrath's theatre constructs and is constructed by Brecht's conception of the popular' (Reinelt 1996: 177). However, McGrath was also deeply sceptical of Brecht's theoretical propositions, particularly those dating from the late 1920s concerning the theatre's instructional or pedagogical possibilities (see 3.9):

> Pedagogics, after all, is the art of passing *down* information and judgements, the art of the superior to the inferior. Distance, in place of solidarity; pseudo-scientific 'objectivity' in place of the frank admission of a human, partisan and emotional perspective – coldness, in place of shared experience: politically, Stalinism rather than collectivism. (McGrath 1989: 40–1)

Furthermore, for McGrath, there was a 'fundamental contradiction at the heart of Brecht's theatrical ideology', which was that the theatre institutions within which Brecht predominantly worked – including the Berliner Ensemble in communist East Berlin following World War II – 'retained many of the forms and structures of bourgeois theatre' and were thus institutions 'of power rather than creation' (ibid: 43). McGrath, in both his theory and practice, raises a number of contentious yet significant points concerning not only the function of the author within political theatre, but also the means by which such a theatre might productively engage its audiences.

The Cheviot, the Stag and the Black, Black Oil (4.2)

The Cheviot, the Stag and the Black, Black Oil (1973) appears at first as a natural successor to the plays included in Part 3 of this anthology. This is an 'epic' piece; the play seeks to provide a materialist analysis of 200 years of Scottish history. It dramatizes three key elements of that history. The first section considers the consequences of the expulsion of indigenous highlanders – many of whom were forced to relocate to the British colonial outposts of the 'new world', particularly Australia – in order that landowners could benefit from profit from the yarn of the Cheviot sheep, whose grazing lands were once farmed by the less profitable human tenants. Section two considers another form of exploitation – the cultural and economic consequences of the Victorian ruling classes' penchant for stag-hunting, thus farm land was converted into grazing and hunting grounds. The final section fast-forwards to the present day (1973) and explores the potential effects on the Scottish people of the discovery of oil in the North Sea, which was already the subject of American incursions.

This narrative distillation marks *The Cheviot* as a history-cum-learning play. However, McGrath's use of facts and statistics, historical documents, direct address, parody and cartoon agitprop techniques, combined with the more familiar modes of realist dramaturgy, are all mediated through a particular performative framework. McGrath employs the *ceilidh*, a popular form of traditional Scottish and Irish entertainment that includes music, singing and dancing. The piece not only begins '*with the* FIDDLER *playing*' (4.2: 563), the *ceilidh*, as a performance trope itself, framed and was integrated into the entire work – rather than simply operating as one element among many – and was thus foundational to *The Cheviot*'s semiotic system of meaning-making. Like all of 7:84's work, *The Cheviot* (also the inaugural production of 7:84 Scotland) was produced for a very specific audience and context: in this case working-class audiences in the rural communities of the Scottish highlands. Kershaw employs a useful distinction here, one which suggests dialectical possibilities 'between the rhetorical conventions – which present the *company* – and the authenticating conventions – which represent the *community*' (Kershaw 1992: 163). Whilst McGrath was clearly seeking to create a 'socialist theatre' that could generate a revolutionary consciousness, this was not only a question of 'radical' theatrical form; any such form needed to fully acknowledge the spectators' collective identity and cultural practices.

In his now famous phrase, this was a theatre that demanded to be 'a good night out' (McGrath 1989). McGrath names the various qualities that characterize such a practice: 'directness', 'comedy', 'music', 'emotion', 'variety', 'effect', 'immediacy', 'localism (of material)' and 'localism (of identity)' (4.7: 648–51). What is revealing within this inventory is how it purposefully overturns the Brechtian claims concerning 'alienation' in forging a critical consciousness within the spectator, together with its persistent emphasis on identification between performers and audience. Although McGrath emphasizes 'emotion', it is useful to make a distinction here between 'empathy' and 'recognition'. As Chambers and Prior observe, 'stage persona, mediating the performer's contact with the audience and with the other characters on stage ... becomes therefore the focus of different levels of reality, the total effect of which must create for the audience an experience over and above the individual interest in any one character or set of characters' (Chambers and Prior 1987: 68). With the back of the stage being framed by the presence of a giant pop-up picture book used to signify the various locations of the play (see Figure 27: 576), the play requires the audience to identify not with characters but with their historical situation as it impacts upon the collective.

The production of *The Cheviot*, which toured extensively over a prolonged period and was adapted for television, also demonstrated how McGrath's 'good night out' – born out of assured socialist convictions – was predisposed to alternate interpretations that, in turn, served to question the oppositional efficacy of this particular form of political theatre. As such, the play highlights the complex relationships between the 'political' and the 'ideological', including questions of subjectivity and agency raised earlier in this introduction. For this reason *The Cheviot*, and the work of 7:84 generally, remains an important gateway for assessing subsequent developments (see also DiCenzo 1996).

If McGrath represents both a development of and departure from Brecht, together with other earlier models of political theatre, then Howard Barker would appear – on the surface at least – to suggest something of a major deviation. However, it is useful to consider the two non-dramatic pieces by these dramatists included in this part alongside each other. Although less than ten years separates their original authorship, the political and cultural contexts of their writing had fundamentally shifted. By the mid-1980s, Ronald Reagan and Margaret Thatcher – by then firmly installed as leaders of the USA and UK respectively – symbolized the political front of the rapid expansion of global capitalism. However, it was also the unique combination, particularly in the UK, of economic liberalism – the 'free market', open competition, limiting the protections that the state had afforded to society's disenfranchised – and social conservatism – a renewed emphasis on law and order, defence policy, the traditional family unit, nationhood – that represented a major redesign of the ideological map (see Hall 1988). This repositioning presented a largely unforeseen challenge to those who perceived socialism, whether democratic or otherwise, as a cure for society's ills. It also raised important questions concerning the role and function of an ideologically conscious theatre practice.

For Howard Barker, this contributed to a major reassessment of the very principles which constituted such a theatre. Immensely prolific as a dramatist, poet and theoretician, Barker also continues to direct his own work for The Wrestling School, originally an Arts Council-funded touring company (now independently funded) specifically set up in 1988 to produce his plays. Barker's call for a return to the notion of 'tragedy', which he subsequently renamed 'catastrophe', and a theatre, 'that stimulates pain', should not be mistaken for a reinstatement of Aristotelian ideas (4.8: 653–55). Rather, similar to the concerns of the Historical Avant-Garde (see Part 2), Barker calls into question the entire foundations on which the modern theatre has been built. His targets are multiple: he draws parallels between 'the authoritarian and the labourist culture alike' (ibid: **19**), involving, for example, both 'the musical' and the types of political theatre practice made not only by 7:84, but all dramatic and theatrical forms (including realism) that might seek to explicate the historical and social formation of human behaviour. Barker's own dramatic texts are densely poetic and complex affairs, speculative, linguistically rich, darkly comic, epic in scale and brimming with imaginative leaps. The *mise en scènes* of his plays are bleak and fractured landscapes; and although often formed from historical or extant textual sources – such as the restoration of the monarchy in seventeenth-century England (*Victory*, 1983) or his 'Chekhov' play ((*Uncle*) *Vanya*, 1996) – set out to purposefully destabilize received wisdoms surrounding the original. What Barker names as 'desire' – distinct from sexuality – is frequently uncovered in a violent collision between private and public worlds and becomes the catalyst to a character's articulation of identity and self-determination. However, it would be an error to perceive such a practice as a clear-cut withdrawal from the political. Indeed, Barker proposes that his theatre is founded on the principle of a 'politics beyond politics':

> The artist's response to the primacy of fact must be to revive the concept of knowledge, which is a private acquisition of an audience thinking individually and not collectively, an audience isolated in the darkness and stretched to the limits of tolerance. This knowledge, because it is forbidden by moral authoritarians of both political wings, becomes the material of a new drama that regards men and women as free, cognitive and essentially autonomous, capable of witnessing pain without the compensation of political structures. (Barker 1997: 50)

David Ian Rabey has thus proposed that Barker's theatre represents a radical redefinition of selfhood, a form of 'political expressionism' that carries with it the ability to stimulate a kind of existential resistance in the face of an ever-increasing ideological authoritarianism (Rabey 1989). In other words, Barker articulates the political and the ideological beyond the limitations and constraints of the political left and the political right. Barker is also explicit in terms of the strategies he believes such a theatre needs to employ:

> Not being conducted either by fetishisms of Clarity or Realism, [the audience] must be liberated from its fear of obscurity and encouraged to welcome its moments of loss. These moments of loss involve the breaking of the narrative thread, the sudden suspension of the story, the interruption of the obliquely related interlude, and a number of devices designed to complicate and overwhelm the audience's habitual method of seeing. The panic which can seize an audience, oppressed by years of trained obeisance, at 'losing the thread' (as if life were a thread), whether the author's (who since Brecht has been given the status of a deity in the modern theatre, the one who knows all and is permanently in command of his thoughts) or the director's (who must impose coherence at all costs) must be replaced by a sense of security in not knowing, and welcoming the same risks the author himself took in charting unknown territory, and the actors took in making the journey without maps. (Barker 1997: 53)

Barker simultaneously announces a radical departure from the Brechtian theatrical imperative, and seeks a remedy in a Brechtian discourse, to explain the nature of such a departure. However, just as is the case with the Historical Avant-Garde in particular (Part 2), the past, and the influence of ideas from the past, cannot be thoroughly negated or left behind. Whilst Barker dismisses some of Brecht's ideas, they are clearly the springboard for many of his own. This underscores two themes continually raised over the course of this introduction: the relevance (and persistence) of certain ideologies of theatre (Brecht's particularly), and the complexity of theatre as a form of ideological intervention.

McGrath and Barker offer practices and perspectives that engage in profoundly complementary forms of dialogue with that past. Their opposing theses, epitomized most fully in the idea of a 'popular' versus an 'elitist' theatre, demand radically contrasting aesthetic strategies. Nevertheless, one can also detect a connective thread here, in terms of how the theatre might seek alternative responses to questions of identity and selfhood – collectivist in McGrath and self-determining in Barker – that arise from the deliberation of its particular ideological conditions. When considered together, their ideas powerfully crystallize how the vestiges of modernism's primary utopian ideals around progress, egalitarianism and freedom – already tested by a century that had become defined by war, mass genocide and the destructive force of technology – were under terminal strain. Such concerns were vociferously being tested elsewhere in theatre practice.

Theatrical mutations: race, gender and sexuality

The 1960s bore witness to a remarkable set of events in the USA and Western Europe. This was a decade in which new ideas concerning personal liberation powerfully cohered with new social movements that were responding – often directly – to contemporary events. Demonstrations against the American intervention in Vietnam, the Paris student riots of 1968, the women's liberation movement (or 'second-wave' feminist movement) and countercultural movements all represented a demand for the recognition of new personal and social freedoms and, at the same time, were an attack on the ideological authoritarianism that was perceived to have become embedded in Western governments proffering so-called liberal democratic values. The Presidential election of John F. Kennedy in the USA in 1960 and Harold Wilson's 1964 Labour government in the UK marked a significant turn to left-of-centre values, producing significant concrete results. For example, the African-American Civil Rights Movement (1955–68) eventually led to legislation that prohibited discrimination in areas such as voting rights, employment practices and housing. In Britain, the rights of gay men began to be formally recognized by the state in 1967, with an Act of Parliament that decriminalized private homosexual acts between consenting adult males. The same year also produced the Abortion Act in the UK, seen by many as a significant gain for women – whose demand for greater self-governance was part and parcel of a desire to acquire power and control over their very bodies. However, other events of the decade, such as the assassinations of President Kennedy (1963), black activist leader Malcolm X (1965) and the civil rights leader Martin Luther King, Jr (1968) along with the brutality of the US incursion into Vietnam (the first war to be internationally mediated through television), and an increasing wave of urban-centred violent crime, all demonstrated that the utopian dream of generating new forms of social and political agency – in which the personal and the political are mutually recognized – would perhaps always remain an aspiration rather than a reality.

The ideological conditions of this period were incisively analysed by Guy Debord. In *The Society of the Spectacle* (1967), Debord argued that capitalism's invasiveness into the entire strata of contemporary life, propagated by twentieth-century advances in the mass media and technological production, had meant that '[a]ll that once was directly lived has become mere representation' (Debord 1994: 12). Thus, in resisting and challenging the deluge of this 'spectacle', artists and activists needed to be constantly vigilant of the risk of revolutionary ideas and practices being susceptible to appropriation by the dominant ideology. The challenge that Debord presented was, at least in part, taken up by theatre practitioners in the late 1960s and 1970s. In Britain, the 'alternative theatre movement' was founded on broadly collectivist – though by no means unitary – principles that forged a fragile alliance between overtly political/socialist, feminist, gay and lesbian, and black and Asian theatre practices (see Itzin 1980). McGrath's 7:84 venture was part of this movement, but so too were companies such as the feminist theatre collective Monstrous Regiment (from the mid-1970s to the early 1990s) that sought 'to shift consciousness in the area of women's relation to society' and reflect the 'dislocated nature of women's experience' (ibid: 274). The movement also embraced forms such as street theatre and performance art in conjunction with the more familiar strategies of political theatre such as agitprop – exemplified in the work of Albert Hunt for example (ibid: 64–7; see also Craig 1980). In the United States such coalescence was less immediately discernible as a movement. However, as Bigsby has noted, 'avant-garde' companies such as the Living Theatre, the San Francisco Mime Troupe and the Performance Group all engaged in acts of provocative direct intervention that frequently took their work outside theatre buildings and shared related concerns about 'transformation' that were also being tested by emergent voices in black and women's theatre (Bigsby 2000: 261). What becomes critical at this theatrical juncture is a challenge not simply to the power of 'language' in theatre, but how language's claim to be a force for exposing 'the real' is paradoxically set against the 'illusion and deceit' of theatre practice (ibid). This represents more than a return to the questions that Brecht began asking forty years earlier. It was also around this time that French philosopher and cultural theorist Michel Foucault (1926–84) famously questioned the idea that individuals (or subjects) were cohesive entities that had a centre to their being, and that ideologies themselves are historically shaped, 'effects of truth' that are 'produced within discourses which are themselves neither true or false' (qtd in Lloyd 2003: 228). Thus for Foucault, ideologies are imagined and constructed through human agency.

If we consider the practice of theatre in relation to Foucault's challenge, then a fascinating tension emerges. Foucault's discourse carries within it a utopian–like liberationist potential. Human subjects, freed from a Marxist notion of historical determinism, are given the capability to explore the multiple possibilities of new identities and social formations. What does this say, however, about how we might work to overcome the tangible realities of oppression and the types of ideological hegemony identified in Debord's 'society of the spectacle'? It is in this very gap, in the relationship between 'agency' and 'structure', that theatre practices in both the USA and UK in the 1960s, and beyond, found a provocative response, none less so than in the arenas of race, gender and sexuality.

Blues for Mister Charlie (4:1)

The emergence of a radicalized black theatre was most pronounced in the USA. The Black Arts Movement (BAM) – the artistic arm of the Black Power Movement (BPM) – was formed in the aftermath of the assassination of Malcom X in 1965. Although the BPM grew out of the Civil Rights Movement, it advocated black autonomy rather than integrationist policies. Similarly, the BAM was concerned with promoting – across a range of art forms – a specifically black rather than multicultural aesthetic. Some notable dramatists were associated with the BAM, including Lorraine Hansberry and its founder Amiri Baraka, formerly LeRoi Jones (see Sell 2005).

Although *Blues for Mister Charlie* (1964) by James Baldwin (1924–87) predates the BAM, Baraka credits the play with the inception of the movement (Shin and Judson 1998: 250). Set in the American South, and inspired by actual events, the play dramatizes the story of the murder of a black pastor's son at the hands of a white 'redneck' named Lyle, the consequences of the killing and Lyle's subsequent trial in the segregated town. As primarily a prose writer, Baldwin was originally criticized for his 'novelistic script' and lack of mastery of dramatic form (Taubman 1964). However, his use of flashbacks, parody of racial stereotypes (white and black), chorus and monologue, together with scenes approximating to a more conventional form of realism, may also illustrate an attempt by the dramatist to develop a dramatic form that *describes* the African-American experience and evokes the human, social and cultural sources of discrimination and the means by which – albeit tentative – justice and reconciliation might be envisioned. Bigsby observes that, in the 1960s, a 'crudity of form and expression' could be seen 'as evidence of authenticity and incorruptibility' (Bigsby 2000: 274). For example, towards the end of Act 1, the black pastor, Meridian, and Parnell, a white liberal, engage in a dialogue that illustrates a clash of values:

MERIDIAN: Must I be the man who watches while his people are chained, starved, clubbed, butchered?
PARNELL: You used to say that your people were all the people in the world – all the people God ever made, or would make. You said your race was the human race.
MERIDIAN: The human race!

PARNELL: I've never seen you like this before. There's something in your tone I've never heard before – rage – maybe hatred –

MERIDIAN: You've heard it before. You just never recognized it before. You've heard it in all those blues and spirituals and gospel songs you claim to love so much.

PARNELL: I was talking about *you* – not your history. I have a history, too. And don't be so sure I've never heard that sound. Maybe I've never heard anything else. Perhaps my life is also hard to bear. (4.1: 537)

This high-octane, even melodramatic, exchange might seem to express a deep-seated desire to recognize the need for human goodness and universal values in order to overcome the very particular conflicts that Baldwin dramatizes. However, even if *Blues for Mister Charlie* is infused by such a liberal ideology, Baldwin succeeds in rendering the private and public/political as inextricably linked. Again, we need to be cognizant here of not divorcing the play from the context of its production. Bigsby suggests that Baldwin reshapes his stage fiction, not in terms of the 'reality' of racially motivated murder but into one of 'shared experience' (Bigsby 2000: 274). Thus, it is within the very performance of Baldwin's play – particularly in the context of 1960s America – that a stage symbolically divided between 'WHITETOWN' and 'BLACKTOWN' (4.1: 525), performed by an interracial cast before an interracial audience, forges the possibility of a spectator becoming 'an actor in this drama' (Bigsby 2000: 275). The distinction here between the potential efficacies of prose fiction – Baldwin's original medium – and drama is crucial: a novel 'finds an individual audience', whereas a play 'must summon into existence a community of selves who mutually agree to one another's co-presence' (ibid). Bigsby's observations here not only have application to a range of theatre practices from this period and beyond. What was also considered to be a dilemma with Baldwin's play – its form – becomes part of a complex system for testing the possibilities of theatrical mediation in relation to the dominant theatrical and ideological discourses.

Feminism and theatre

Women's and feminist theatre practices of the 1970s and 1980s represent one of the most sustained challenges to both the dominant ideology and theatrical mainstream in this period, both in the USA and the UK (see Aston 1995; Canning 1996). This is in respect to both their articulation of new concerns relating to gender and identity, and how their form provided a powerful response to what Kruger terms the 'masculinist strategies of legitimation' present in both mainstream and alternative theatre practices (Kruger 1990: 28). In the UK particularly, the initial alliance between feminist and other politicized forms of theatre practice in the early 1970s may have been founded on collectivist ideals, but the theatre's conscious politicization of gender also led to a political and creative schism, by way of an exploration of how the construction of gender and ideology was intimately bound together, a question that political theatre generally perhaps too easily bypassed. We can see in Stowell's article in Part 3 (3.10) how a number of feminist thinkers have identified realism as an oppressive aesthetic in the representation of women's experience. A 'socialist feminist' theatre practice found a response to such critiques, utilizing Brechtian strategies to 'defamiliarize' and 'historicize' essentialist ideas concerning the formation of identity and social relations – in other words, the supposed 'natural' inferiority of women was reframed as socially constructed (see Aston 1995; Diamond 1997). Such innovations – which would, for example, include the dramaturgical manipulation of chronology as in the seminal play by Caryl Churchill, *Top Girls* (1982) – are central to feminist dramaturgical strategies. However, some feminist theatre theorists have also pointed to the development of a specifically *feminine* aesthetic in theatre practice (Aston 1995). Commentators, in tracing the origins of this development, have drawn from the work of the French feminist school, led by such figures as Hélène Cixous and Luce Irigaray. Sue-Ellen Case identifies such aesthetic forms as 'elliptical rather than illustrative, fragmentary rather than whole, ambiguous rather than clear, and interrupted rather than complete'. Furthermore, '[w]ithout closure … it abandons the hierarchical organizing principles of traditional form that served to elide women from experience'. Not least, 'women can inhabit the realm of the outsider … and create a new discourse and form that exhibit the field of female experience' (Case 1988: 129). We should note here that the characteristics of a feminist aesthetic identified by Case might also describe the strategy employed by Caryl Churchil in *Far Away* (4.4), but not for feminist ends. In other words, coming out of a feminist socialist tradition – although she herself has never specifically aligned her work with this movement – what might be identified as Churchill's feminist dramaturgy is powerfully utilized as part of a widely applicable ideological challenge. Such practices, whether feminist or not, are purposefully transgressive. They demonstrate how, for women, the field of performance might become not simply a link in a chain towards some kind of discernible change, but is itself a site of resistance. Within this site, aesthetic investment constitutes an incontrovertible political act, although an act without necessarily predetermined ends.

Enter the Night (4.3)

Although also refusing to be tied to labels such as 'feminist', the work of Maria Irene Fornes (b. 1930) serves to illustrate such strategies. Cuban born, Fornes continues to be one of the most significant dramatists working in the American theatre. Emerging from the off-off-Broadway and 'avant-garde' theatres of the 1960s, hers is described as a 'poetic theatre' which 'obeys its own, sometimes surreal logic' (Sofer 2005: 440). In addition to being a teacher of playwriting, Fornes is also a director, and is identified as an 'auteur in the mode of Richard Foreman and Robert Wilson', because of the emphasis and precision she gives to visual composition (ibid: 441).

Whilst *Enter the Night* (1993) deals with some of the tangible realities of modern American life, such as the AIDS crisis, this is not a play that can easily be reduced to being an 'issue drama' about gender and sexuality. Three friends – Tressa, Paula and Jack – are each, in their own way, damaged individuals. Tressa nurses the dying; Paula is sick with a heart condition and lacks financial security; Jack believes he has AIDS – although repeated testing proves that he is HIV negative – and thinks he was responsible for infecting his partner who has died of the disease. This threesome's means for dealing with their anguish is to enter a world of role-play, cross-dressing and fantasy, and so metatheatricality becomes a means of fortifying the human spirit, in the process forming a kind of surrogate family environment. For example, at the opening of Act 2 Jack and Tressa enact, with costumes, scenes from *Broken Blossoms* (1919), D. W. Griffith's silent film, with Jack as 'The Girl' and Tressa playing the male character 'Huang'. Bonnie Marranca argues that Fornes's use of 'theatrical gesture' in this way reveals 'the tragicomic reality of human behaviour', that she 'transforms drama into spiritual anthropology' (Marranca 1999: 59). Such observations point out how a play like *Enter the Night* withdraws from a concern with making an explicit ideological challenge, and manifests art as providing its own transcendent kind of resistance in the face of human frailties and material realities. However, the play also rehearses the theatre's constant susceptibility to being commandeered by coercive ideological forces. In one of the play's numerous long speeches, Jack – also an aspiring playwright – wittily envisages a gruesome theatrical future:

> The leading characters will have the illness most common among theatergoers. Since theatergoers prefer to have plays written about them. Plays will be funded by pharmaceutical laboratories. (4.3: 598)

In Jack's fantasy future, the uncritical bourgeoisie have taken over the theatre which entirely reflects both their neuroses and their interdependency with the consumer-driven culture of late capitalism. Thus, *Enter the Night*'s celebration of art's transformational potential also embeds a dialectic. This dialectic concerns the theatre's unquestioned susceptibility to commodification in late capitalism, and also a questioning as to how our terms of engagement as spectators are not altogether individually won and, indeed, collude in the perpetuation of such commodification.

Over the past forty years, theatrical representations of race, gender and sexuality have 'moved with the times' in terms of responding to developing concerns and social/cultural attitudes. Changes in the theatre industry itself have facilitated the presence of black, Asian, gay and women's theatre practices in the mainstream, frequently on Broadway and in the West End. However, we need to be careful here, and avoid a simplistic explanation of this in terms of 'acceptance' or the liberalization of attitudes. For example, since the late 1970s, plays such as Martin Sherman's *Bent* (1979) – which examines the Nazi persecution of homosexuals – and Larry Kramer's *The Normal Heart* (1985) – an early response to the AIDS crisis – have proved immensely successful in this respect. Whilst revealing the different personal and historical experiences of gay men, together with how continued forms of persecution and discrimination have unfolded, it is interesting how such plays partly work by recasting the homosexual as 'victim' and might even be seen as a call to acknowledge a common humanity rather than the assertion of 'difference'. Interestingly, Alan Sinfield makes the distinction here between 'cathartic' and 'political' modes of playwriting, again emphasizing – as feminist critics have done – that what may appear to be disruptive or radical in terms of subject matter, is constantly in danger of being co-opted by a dominant ideology (Sinfield 1999: 320–6).

Alternative responses: cultural materialism and post-colonialism

It is useful to consider here – particularly in light of the above – how 'cultural materialism' and 'post-colonialism' might productively inform this discussion. These discourses began to take hold in the 1970s, partly in response to the ideas reflected in post-structuralism and postmodernism, which were destabilizing notions of fixed identities and overriding belief systems or 'grand narratives'. Identity is therefore neither fixed nor a given, but rather, is constructed through social, and especially in the case of post-colonialism, historical/political relations. Of course, theatre may well carry the influence of such ideas, but it also has the capacity to critique them. *Enter the Night* (1993), for example, exhibits some of the tendencies of a postmodern art form. In particular, this is evident in the way it 'borrows' from American popular culture of the past, negates a rationalist (or realist) dramaturgy and refuses to pin down meaning. However, this does not imply, as we have seen, that Fornes is unequivocally endorsing postmodern ideas.

In the 'Theory of Cultural Production' (4.6), Alan Sinfield invites us to consider the continued relevance of Raymond Williams's anlaysis of the structures at play in cultural production, highlighted earlier in this introduction in relation to John McGrath's work. Thus for Sinfield, if 'socialists … had tended to believe that everyone could share the one "human' culture"', then cultural materialism examines 'the historical conditions in which textual representations are produced, circulated and received, often considering big-C culture alongside popular culture' (4.6: 626). So cultural materialism does not value 'high' over 'low' culture, but rather explores the relationships between the two and, in turn, their relation to the cultural hegemony at any given historical moment. Whilst John McGrath, for example, separates out bourgeois from what he perceives as 'working-class' cultures, in order to forge a singular socialist cultural/theatrical project, he is in danger of essentializing and fixing cultural tropes in a manner warned earlier against by Brecht. In other words, from Sinfield's cultural materialist perspective, McGrath creates an alternative hegemony, without recognition of the complex nuances of the interplay between different cultural forces. Sinfield identifies 'dissidence' – taking a disruptive and interrogative ideological position – as embraced by 'subcultures' in a manner which does not simply oppose dominant ideology. Dissidence and subcultures emerge 'from pressures and strains which the social order inevitably produces within itself, even as it attempts to secure itself' (ibid). Subcultures therefore often take a position of dissidence but can only be defined through their relation to the dominant culture. This represents a development of Williams's idea of dominant, residual and emergent cultures (see Introduction to this volume), in that new forms of emergent dissidence may be forged through a conscious, though critical, engagement with the dominant and residual. Such ideas have important implications for theatre practice. The chapter by Sinfield included in this part (4.6) provides a discussion of the work of the gay British writer and director Neil Bartlett (ibid: 628–30). In his analysis Sinfield here points to how subcultures – in this case gay or queer theatre – might be able to forge dissidence actually within the parameters of mainstream commercial theatre. Bartlett's own work – which is heavily influenced by, for example, the West End musical, drag performance, and the work of pre-liberationist gay dramatists such as Oscar Wilde and Noël Coward – draws on a 'popular' mainstream theatrical past that, Bartlett argues, equally informs the construction of modern-day alternative sexualities. Although their work could not be considered 'mainstream', the work of Split Britches, a company founded in New York, exploits American popular culture in order to examine the political transgressiveness of lesbian feminist butch/femme performative role playing (see Case 1996). Reading such work through the prism of cultural materialism emphasizes the contingent and potentially radical nature of marginalized sexual identities, as well as evidencing the ways in which the very act of 'performance' – in the widest sense possible – can be part and parcel of the formation of such identities.

In 'Introduction: Re-acting (to) Empire' (4.9) from their seminal book *Post-Colonial Drama: Theory, Practice, Politics,* Gilbert and Tompkins define post-colonialism as having a precise 'political' agenda: 'to dismantle the hegemonic boundaries and the determinants that create unequal relations of power based on binary oppositions such as "us and them", "first world and third world", "white and black", "coloniser and colonised"', and so represents a 'continued destabilisation of the cultural and political authority of imperialism' (4.9: 657). Post-colonial theories can therefore be used to study not only the cultures of previously colonized nations, but also those cultures and peoples which – through forced and unforced migration – have become part, frequently over a long period of time, of the former colonizers' own national domains. Thus, black and Asian theatre in the USA and UK might be framed as 'post-colonial performance'. It should be taken on board that some theorists question the veracity of the 'post' in post-colonialism; removing the colonizer does not remove the historical effects of colonization. A post-colonial cultural product therefore will always contain the remnants of identity formed through colonization. Gilbert and Tompkins, however, identify some of the 'features' that constitute post-colonial practice, including 'acts that respond to the experience of imperialism', 'acts performed for the continuation and/ or regeneration of the colonised' and 'acts that interrogate the hegemony that underlies imperial representation' (ibid: 662). Post-colonialism – in terms of cultural practice as well as theoretical critique – thus not only extends the boundaries of what we mean by 'ideology and performance'. It also, like cultural materialism, provides a particular critique of power relations between marginalized and dominant groups. Wole Soyinka's play *Death and the King's Horseman* (1975) provides a useful example here. Set in colonial Nigeria during World War II, and based on actual events, it dramatizes the consequences of the British seeking to prevent a tribal ritual, in which a king's horseman prepares to follow the custom of performing ritual suicide following his ruler's death. The British intervention has catastrophic results and highlights a conflict of seemingly irreconcilable values. Interestingly, however, Soyinka insists that the play cannot be reduced to being about a '"clash of cultures"', a prejudicial label which ... presupposes a potential equality *in every given situation* of the alien culture and indigenous' (Soyinka 1984: 144). Rather, the 'confrontation in the play is largely metaphysical', and 'can be fully realised only through an evocation of music from the abyss of transition' (ibid: 145). Soyinka's observations thus serve to highlight the complexity of post-colonial practices and discourses, particularly in challenging the boundaries of both aesthetic practices and critical strategies when considering the interrelationship between ideology and performance. Similarly, since the 1970s – and partly influenced by the Black Arts Movement in America – black and Asian theatre has systematically questioned the aesthetic and ideological assumptions that underpin mainstream theatre practice. Such questions have often resulted in practitioners challenging ideas about authorship and representation and a refusal to be colonized or contained by the text-based 'norms' of Western theatre. This has often meant a turn to mixed art forms, utilizing film, ritual, dance, music and visual art (Ugwu 1995; see also Part 5).

Theatre and performance in the age of globalization

Theatre and performance are an ephemeral phenomena, tied to specific dimensions of space and time, but also impermanent within those dimensions. Whilst play texts provide some evidence to counteract this temporality, such formal conditions might seem a barrier to full engagement with what is now perceived as a particularly pervasive phenomenon, that is to say, globalization. Like ideology, 'globalization' is something of a contested term. For many, it is primarily economic, and relates to the 'natural' extension of capitalism. It has also been conceived in more philosophical terms, as being about the 'expansion of consciousness', of how our interconnectedness as peoples of the world has been forged through new forms of crisis such as 'global warming'. In turn, this leads to the idea that it is about 'world cultures' and their 'hybridization', particularly through the media of television, cinema and the internet. Globalization has also been conceived as a 'political phenomenon', in terms of liberal democracy being exulted as the most preferred and successful form of government (Rebellato 2009: 4–8). We can certainly see the effects of globalization in the theatre. Musicals such as *Cats* (1981) and *The Lion King* (1997) have multiple reproduced international productions running simultaneously, constituting their own formidable industry. Indeed, 'globalization is best understood as itself having taken on a theatrical form, with the global system writing the script, directing everyone's entrances and exits, and casting some people in the leading roles and the rest as spear-carriers' (ibid: 9). However, there are other means by which theatre and performance might productively intervene in issues and questions raised by globalization. It is useful here to consider together the two final plays included in this section.

Far Away (4.4) and *Scenes from Family Life* (4.5)

Caryl Churchill (b. 1938) and Mark Ravenhill (b. 1966) may seem to have rather different political and philosophical concerns. Churchill, as we have already noted, emerged from the socialist and feminist theatre movement of the 1970s. Ravenhill became established in the mid-1990s as, along with others, a writer of provocative 'in-yer-face' plays dealing explicitly with contemporary themes (Sierz 2001). *Far Away* (2000, 4.4) appears, at first, to be set in a world rather uncomfortably recognizable as being close to home. The play, divided into three scenes, begins with a girl, Joan, quizzing her aunt, Harper, over a brutal scene she has witnessed. Scene 2 is set a number of years later and is divided into six short sections. Joan and Todd, a young man, are working at making extravagant hats that we learn are to be worn by convicts prior to their execution. Joan's concern is that the hats, works of art, are not preserved:

JOAN: It seems so sad to burn them with the bodies.
TODD: No I think that's the joy of it. The hats are ephemeral. It's like a metaphor for something or other.
JOAN: Well, life.
TODD: Well, life, there you are. Out of nearly three hundred hats I've made here I've only had three win and go in the museum. But that's never bothered me. You make beauty and it disappears, I love that. (4.4: 609)

Whilst one might expect Joan and Todd to be more concerned about the death of the prisoners who are paraded in the hats before their execution, their conversation dismisses genocide in favour of the 'metaphor' of art. At the same time, the brutality of execution is juxtaposed with the development of a tender and humanizing relationship between alienated co-workers. In the final scene we return to Harper's house; again it is some years later. World war has broken out, involving humans, animals and the cosmos itself. It is not possible to discern who is on what side in the conflict, 'The Bolivians are working with gravity, that's a secret so as not to spread alarm. But we're getting further with noise and there's thousands dead of light in Madagascar. Who's going to mobilise darkness and silence?' (4.4: 611). *Far Away* ends in a kind of apocalyptic implosion, where the natural and the material world are engaged in an interminable conflict with humanity and each other.

Mark Ravenhill's *Scenes from Family Life* (2008, 4.5) begins with two teenage partners, Jack and Lisa, excited at the prospect of Lisa's forthcoming baby. Then Lisa starts to vanish – into thin air – and reappear without explanation. The vanishings start to multiply and seem permanent. Civil unrest breaks out until Jack and Stacy, the pregnant girlfriend of Jack's best friend Barry, appear to be the only people left on the planet. As wild animals skulk in the outdoors, Jack, Stacy and

Stacy's baby begin to form a family. But when Stacy and her baby also disappear, following Barry's brief return, Jack turns feral:

JACK: ... I am everything.
 I am the world.
 I am King.
 So I ...
 Hunt. Eat. Sleep. Move on. This is my world.
 And I ...
 No if there were never others then there's no loneliness.
 No lone ... lone ... lo ... lo ...
 Lugh. Lugh. Lugh. Lee. Negh. Ssssssss.
 No feelings like ... no feelings just –
 (*A howl of emotion.*) Ooowwwwwwww!
 (*Ape-like.*) Ugh ugh ugh.

 He's becoming more animal, his centre of gravity moving down.

 I ugh oh a oh a ooo m a ugh.
 Me.
 Me.
 Me.

 Pattern of movement, almost dancing.

 Me.
 Me.
 Me.
 And I.
 And I.
 And I.

 Onto all fours snuffling and whining. A great animal howl.

 Hunt. Attack. Defend. Me.
 (4.5: 622)

When the vanished people start to come back, Jack begins to rehumanize. The final scene, set over a year later, sees Jack and Lisa reunited as parents.

What these plays share is revealing. Both begin by using familiar dramatic modes, employing a form of pared-down realism – particularly in terms of the dialogue – but which desists from providing us with background information or given circumstances – of the type that we might most obviously associate with Naturalism. Thus, it is in the way that both plays set up 'the familiar' or 'recognizable', and their subsequent breaking apart of this, that each dramatist is able to forge a more imaginative landscape for their themes. *Far Away* is perhaps more obviously a play *about* globalization. As Rebellato points out, the movement through the play is 'from the domestic to the national to the global', and 'in the turmoil of international allegiances in the last act, the play presents national differences as moral absurdities' (Rebellato 2009: 81; see also Dymkowski 2003). On the other hand, *Scenes from Family Life* – written for the National Theatre in London, to be performed specifically by young people – initially suggests that it is about teenage parenthood. However, in its metamorphosis into a dark fairy tale, it becomes a 'rites of passage' play for Jack, in terms of how he adjusts to a world where he seemingly lacks agency. As Ravenhill observes of the characters:

we notice from an early age that they're trying to create a structure to their lives ... [in] a world that has become too chaotic and has lost a sense of structure. Additionally, the play asks the question 'What is normaility? What is this desire we have as human beings to feel normal?' In this instance the desire to have children or to have someone or something to care for seems to be an overriding theme and for the characters to achieve a 'normality' to their existence. (Ravenhill 2008: 419)

Jack's speech (quoted above), if read literally and out of context, might seem to be about our 'base' animal instincts. Rather, it points to how human identity is configured through meaningful social relations and productive forms of intersubjectivity that stress the very contingency of the human subject. Indeed, *Scenes from Family Life* not only critiques the very idea of fully autonomous human agents, it presents a potent, if sometimes elliptical, intervention, as does *Far Away*, signifying the acute antagonisms between agency and structure within contemporary ideological formations.

In his article 'Me, My iBook, and Writing in America' (4.10), Ravenhill offers some prescient observations on playwriting under globalization. His constant emphasis is on the contingent nature of his own practice and agency, that if he cannot willingly escape the productive forces of late capitalism, a more useful strategy might be to critically engage with them. This also applies to Ravenhill's own dramaturgical practice. For example, when he writes of wanting his first major play, *Shopping and Fucking*, 'to have a different relationship to history and geography from the existing tradition of contemporary British playwriting', of stripping the play of any element that places it too readily within a particular locale, he is also aware of the fact that he cannot entirely avoid that tradition (ibid: 167). Indeed, Ravenhill's method of rendering his own contemporary drama is to engage in a dialogue with both past and present, dramaturgical and ideological, thus acknowledging that the desire for new forms of drama that speak meaningfully to a changing world cannot magically bypass what has gone before. Of course, this also positions Ravenhill in a particular tradition, linking back to the ideas of Brecht and Walter Benjamin discussed in Part 3.

Conclusion

Of all the sections that make up this anthology, it is this one which, in both its dramatic and critical coverage, is perhaps the most difficult to define in terms of a discernible 'movement' within theatre. Rather, the included texts are connected through the ways in which they respond to the challenges set forth by earlier twentieth-century practices, in relation to the theatre's capacity to articulate, critique and even potentially disrupt the evolving nature of social, political and ideological forces. All of the texts are written as responses to emerging ideological questions, centring particularly on identity and agency and the ways in which the 'political' relates in particular to the 'personal'. The philosopher Slavoj Žižek claims that, due to 'its all-pervasiveness, ideology [today] appears as its own opposite, as *non-ideology*, as the core of our human identity underneath all the ideological labels' (Žižek 2009: 39). Thus for Žižek, the absence of fully fledged and genuinely contesting ideologies, particularly in the West, means that we are perhaps less attuned to the operation of ideology in our day-to-day lives. The plays and theatre practices discussed in this introduction, however, each in their own way challenge or at least test out such a hypothesis. In theatre and performance, it would seem, ideology remains a site, albeit contested, of struggle. In the next part we explore the ways in which aesthetic choices and different performance strategies respond to and engage with this struggle, through examining the work of performance practitioners whose work is framed by notions of the contemporary, the postmodern and the 'postdramatic'.

Bibliography

Althusser, Louis (1971) *Lenin and Philosophy and Other Essays*, trans. B. Brewster, New York: Monthly Review Press.

Althusser, Louis (2005 [1969]) *For Marx*, trans. B. Brewster, London: Verso.

Aston, Elaine (1995) *An Introduction to Feminism and Theatre*, London: Routledge.

Aston, Elaine (2003) *Feminist Views on the English Stage: Women Playwrights 1990–2000*, Cambridge: Cambridge University Press.

Barker, Howard (1997) *Arguments for a Theatre*, 3rd edn, Manchester: Manchester University Press.

Bigsby, C. W. E. (2000) *Modern American Drama, 1945–2000*, Cambridge: Cambridge University Press.

Brecht, Bertolt (2001 [1964]) *Brecht on Theatre: The Development of an Aesthetic*, ed. and trans. J. Willett, London: Methuen.

Canning, Charlotte (1996) *Feminist Theatres in the USA*, London: Routledge.

Case, Sue-Ellen (1988) *Feminism and Theatre*, Basingstoke: Macmillan.

Case, Sue-Ellen (ed.) (1996) *Split Britches: Lesbian Practice / Feminist Performance*, London: Routledge.

Chambers, Colin and Mike Prior (1987) *Playwrights' Progress: Patterns of Post-War British Drama*, Oxford: Amber Lane Press.

Craig, Sandy (ed.) (1980) *Dreams and Deconstructions: Alternative Theatre in Britain*, Ambergate: Amber Lane Press.

Debord, Guy (1994) *The Society of the Spectacle*, trans. D. Nicholson-Smith, New York: Zone Books.

Diamond, Elin (1997) *Unmaking Mimesis: Essays on Feminism and Theatre*, London: Routledge.

DiCenzo, Maria (1996) *The Politics of Alternative Theatre in Britain: The Case of 7:84 (Scotland)*, Cambridge: Cambridge University Press.

Dymkowski, Christine (2003) 'Caryl Churchill: *Far Away* ... but Close to Home', *European Journal of English Studies*, 7(1), 55–68.

Eagleton, Terry (2006 [1976]) *Marxism and Literary Criticism*, London: Routledge.

Eccleshall, Robert *et al.* (2003 [1984]) *Political Ideologies: An Introduction*, 3rd edn, London: Routledge.

Etchells, Tim (2005 [1999]) *Certain Fragments: Contemporary Performance and Forced Entertainment*, London: Routledge.

Forsyth, Alison and Chris Megson (eds) (2009) *Get Real: Documentary Theatre Past and Present*, Basingstoke: Palgrave Macmillan.

Fukuyama, Francis (1992) *The End of History and the Last Man*, London: Penguin Books.

Hall, Stuart (1988) *The Hard Road to Renewal: Thatcherism and the Crisis of the Left*, London: Verso.

Holderness, Graham (1992) 'Introduction', in G. Holderness *The Politics of Theatre and Drama*, Basingstoke: Macmillan, pp. 1–17.

Itzin, Catherine (1980) *Stages in the Revolution: Political Theatre in Britain Since 1968*, London: Eyre Methuen.

Kershaw, Baz (1992) *The Politics of Performance: Radical Theatre as Cultural Intervention*, London: Routledge.

Kershaw, Baz (1999) *The Radical in Performance: Between Brecht and Baudrillard*, London: Routledge.

Kritzer, Amelia Howe (2008) *Political Theatre in Post-Thatcher Britain*, Basingstoke: Palgrave Macmillan.

Kruger, Loren (1990) 'The Dis-Play's the Thing: Gender and the Public Sphere in Contemporary British Theatre', *Theatre Journal*, 42, 27–47.

Lloyd, Moya (2003 [1984]) 'The End of Ideology?', in R. Eccleshall *et al. Political Ideologies: An Introduction*, 3rd edn, London: Routledge, pp. 217–41.

McGrath, John (1989 [1981]) *A Good Night Out – Popular Theatre: Audience, Class and Form*, London: Methuen.

McGrath, John (1990) *The Bone Won't Break: On Theatre and Hope in Hard Times*, London: Methuen.

McGrath, John (2002) *Naked Thoughts that Roam About: Reflections on Theatre 1958–2001*, ed. Nadine Holdsworth, London: Nick Hern Books.

MacKenzie, Iain (2003 [1984]) 'The Idea of Ideology', in R. Eccleshall *et al. Political Ideologies: An Introduction*, 3rd edn, London: Routledge, pp. 1–16.

Marranca, Bonnie (1999) 'The Economy of Tenderness', in M. Robinson (ed.) *The Theatre of Maria Irene Fornes*, Baltimore: The Johns Hopkins University Press, pp. 47–60.

Rabey, David Ian (1989) *Howard Barker – Politics and Desire: An Expository Study of his Drama and Poetry, 1969–87*, Basingstoke: Macmillan.

Ravenhill, Mark (2008) *Scenes from Family Life*, in *New Connections 2008: Plays for Young People*, London: Faber and Faber, pp. 417–67.

Rebellato, Dan (2009) *Theatre and Globalization*, Basingstoke: Palgrave Macmillan.

Reinelt, Janelle (1996 [1994]) *After Brecht: British Epic Theater*, Ann Arbor: University of Michigan Press.

Savran, David (1988) *Breaking the Rules: The Wooster Group*, New York: Theatre Communications Group.

Sell, Mike (2005) 'The Drama of the Black Arts Movement', in D. Krasner (ed.) *A Companion to Twentieth Century American Drama*, Oxford: Blackwell, pp. 263–84.

Shin, Andrew and Barbara Judson (1998) 'Beneath the Black Aesthetic: James Baldwin's Primer of Black American Masculinity', *African American Review*, 32(2), 247–61.

Sierz, Alex (2001) *In-Yer-Face Theatre: British Drama Today*, London: Faber and Faber.

Sinfield, Alan (1999) *Out on Stage: Lesbian and Gay Theatre in the Twentieth Century*, New Haven: Yale University Press.

Sofer, Andrew (2005) 'Maria Irene Fornes: Acts of Translation', in D. Krasner (ed.) *A Companion to Twentieth Century American Drama*, Oxford: Blackwell, pp. 440–55.

Soyinka, Wole (1984 [1976]) *Six Plays*, London: Methuen.

Taubman, Howard (1964) 'Theater: *Blues for Mister Charlie*', *The New York Times*, 24 April.

Ugwu, Catherine (ed.) (1995) *Let's Get It On: The Politics of Black Performance*, London: Institute of Contemporary Arts.

Williams, Raymond (1977) *Marxism and Literature*, Oxford: Oxford University Press.

Žižek, Slavoj (2009) *First as Tragedy, Then as Farce*, London: Verso.

Further reading

Aston, Elaine (2003) *Feminist Views on the English Stage: Women Playwrights 1990–2000*, Cambridge: Cambridge University Press.

Blau, Herbert (1992) *To All Appearances: Ideology and Performance*, London: Routledge.

Delgado, Maria M. and Caridad Svich (eds) (1999) *Conducting a Life: Reflections on the Theatre of Maria Irene Fornes*, Lyme, NH: Smith and Kraus.

Freeman, Sandra (1999) *Putting Your Daughters on the Stage: Lesbian Theatre from the 1970s to the 1990s*, London: Cassell.

Goodman, Lizbeth (1993) *Contemporary Feminist Theatres: To Each Her Own*, London: Routledge.

Goodman, Lizbeth with Jane de Gay (eds) (2000) *The Routledge Reader in Politics and Performance*, London: Routledge.

Hill, Erroll and James Vernon Hatch (2003) *A History of African American Theatre*, Cambridge: Cambridge University Press.

Innes, Christopher (2002) *Modern British Drama: The Twentieth Century*, Cambridge: Cambridge University Press.

Kelleher, Joe (2009) *Theatre and Politics*, Basingstoke: Palgrave Macmillan.

Shellard, Dominic (1999) *British Theatre Since the War*, New Haven: Yale University Press.

Tompsett, A. Ruth (ed.) (1996) *Performing Arts International* (Special Issue – *Black Theatre in Britain*), 1(2), Amsterdam: Harwood Academic Publishing.

4.1 BLUES FOR MISTER CHARLIE (1964)

JAMES BALDWIN

James Baldwin (1924–87) was an influential African American novelist, dramatist, poet, critic and civil rights campaigner. Baldwin infamously came to wide public attention following the publication of his novel Giovanni's Room *(1956). The novel was not only vilified for its examination of white male homoeroticism, it raised important questions, particularly pertinent in mid-twentieth-century USA, about what it meant to be a 'black writer'.* Blues for Mister Charlie *(1964) was inspired by the actual murder of an African American man and the subsequent acquittal of those accused by an all-white male jury. Set in the American South, Baldwin's play is marked by the sophisticated manner in which it deals with the race question, and how cultures and identities might move from tolerance to understanding. This is underpinned by a dramatic structure that disrupts a conventional linear timeframe, also counterpointed by the use of internal soliloquies.* Blues for Mister Charlie *was first produced by The Actors Studio Theatre in New York, directed by Burgess Meredith.*

Characters

MERIDIAN HENRY, NEGRO MINISTER
TOM
KEN
ARTHUR
JUANITA   NEGRO STUDENTS
LORENZO
PETE
JIMMY
MOTHER HENRY, MERIDIAN HENRY'S MOTHER
LYLE BRITTEN, A WHITE STORE–OWNER
JO BRITTEN, LYLE'S WIFE
PARNELL JAMES, EDITOR OF THE LOCAL NEWSPAPER
RICHARD, MERIDIAN HENRY'S SON
PAPA D., OWNER OF A JUKE JOINT
HAZEL
LILLIAN
SUSAN
RALPH   WHITE TOWNSPEOPLE
ELLIS
REV. PHELPS
GEORGE
CLERK
JUDGE
THE STATE
COUNSEL FOR THE BEREAVED
FOREMAN
CONGREGATION OF REV. HENRY'S CHURCH, PALLBEARERS, BLACKTOWN, WHITETOWN

Act 1

Multiple set, the skeleton of which, in the first two acts, is the Negro church, and, in the third act, the courthouse. The church and the courthouse are on opposite sides of a southern street; the audience should always be aware, during the first two acts, of the dome of the courthouse and the American flag. During the final act, the audience should always be aware of the steeple of the church, and the cross.

The church is divided by an aisle. The street door upstage faces the audience. The pulpit is downstage, at an angle, so that the minister is simultaneously addressing the congregation and the audience. In the third act, the pulpit is replaced by the witness stand.

This aisle also functions as the division between WHITETOWN *and* BLACKTOWN. *The action among the blacks takes place on one side of the stage, the action among the whites on the opposite side of the stage – which is to be remembered during the third act, which takes place, of course, in a segregated courtroom.*

This means that RICHARD'S *room,* LYLE'S *store,* PAPA D.'S *joint,* J'S *kitchen, etc., are to exist principally by suggestion, for these*

Figure 24 Diane Sands in *Blues for Mister Charlie* at the ANTA Theater, New York, 1964. (Photographer: Gjon Mili, by permission of Getty Images.)

shouldn't be allowed to obliterate the skeleton, or, more accurately, perhaps, the framework, suggested above.

For the murder scene, the aisle functions as a gulf. The stage should be built out, so that the audience reacts to the enormity of this gulf, and so that RICHARD, *when he falls, falls out of sight of the audience, like a stone, into the pit.*

In the darkness we hear a shot.

Lights up slowly on LYLE, *staring down at the ground. He looks around him, bends slowly and picks up* RICHARD'S *body as though it were a sack. He carries him upstage, drops him.*

LYLE: And may every nigger like this nigger end like this nigger – face down in the weeds!

Exits.

(BLACKTOWN: *The church. A sound of mourning begins.* MERIDIAN, TOM, KEN *and* ARTHUR.)

MERIDIAN: No, no, no! You have to say it like you mean it – the way they really say it: nigger, nigger, nigger! *Nigger!* Tom, the way *you* saying it, it sounds like you just *might* want to make friends. And that's not the way they sound out there. Remember all that's happened. Remember we having a funeral here – tomorrow night. Remember why. Go on, hit it again.

TOM: You dirty nigger, you no-good black bastard, what you doing down here, anyway?

MERIDIAN: That's much better. Much much better. Go on.

TOM: Hey, boy, where's your mother? I bet she's lying up in bed, just a-pumping away, ain't she, boy?

MERIDIAN: *That's* the way they sound!

TOM: Hey, boy, how much does your mother charge? How much does your sister charge?

KEN: How much does your *wife* charge?

MERIDIAN: Now you got it. You really got it now. That's them. Keep walking, Arthur. *Keep walking!*

TOM: You get your ass off these streets from around here, boy, or we going to do us some cutting – we're going to cut that big, black thing off of you, you hear?

MERIDIAN: Why you all standing around there like that? Go on and get you a nigger. Go on!

A scuffle.

MERIDIAN: All right. All right! Come on, now. Come on.

KEN *steps forward and spits in* ARTHUR'S *face.*

ARTHUR: You black s.o.b., what the hell do you think you're doing? You mother –!

MERIDIAN: Hey, hold it! Hold it! Hold it!

MERIDIAN *wipes the boy's face. They are all trembling.*

MOTHER HENRY *enters.*

MOTHER HENRY: Here they come. And it looks like they had a time.

JUANITA, LORENZO, PETE, JIMMY, all Negro, carry placards, enter, exhausted and dishevelled, wounded; PETE is weeping. The placards bear such legends as Freedom Now, We Want The Murderer, One Man, One Vote, *etc.*

JUANITA: We shall overcome!

LORENZO: We shall not be moved! (*Laughs.*) We were moved tonight, though. Some of us has been moved to *tears.*

MERIDIAN: Juanita, what happened?

JUANITA: Oh, just another hometown Saturday night.

MERIDIAN: Come on, Pete, come on, old buddy. Stop it. Stop it.

LORENZO: I don't blame him. I do not blame the cat. You feel like a damn fool standing up there, letting them white mothers beat on your ass — shoot if I had my way, just once — stop crying, Pete, goddammit!

JUANITA: Lorenzo, you're in church.

LORENZO: Yeah. Well, I wish to God I was in an arsenal. I'm sorry, Meridian, Mother Henry — I don't mean that for you. I don't understand you. I don't understand Meridian here. It was his son, it was your grandson, Mother Henry, that got killed, butchered! Just last week, and yet, here you sit — in this — this — the house of this damn almighty God who don't care what happens to nobody, unless, of course, they're white. Mother Henry, I got a lot of respect for you and all that, and for Meridian, too, but that white man's God is *white*. It's that damn white God that's been lynching us and burning us and castrating us and raping our women and robbing us of everything that makes a man a man for all these hundreds of years. Now, why we sitting around here, in *His* house? If I could get my hands on Him, I'd pull Him out of heaven and drag Him through this town at the end of a rope.

MERIDIAN: No, you wouldn't.

LORENZO: I wouldn't? Yes, I would. Oh, yes, I would.

JUANITA: And then you wouldn't be any better than they are.

LORENZO: I don't want to be better than they are, why should I be better than they are? And better at what? Better at being a doormat, better at being a corpse? Sometimes I just don't know. We've been demonstrating — *non-violently* — for more than a year now and all that's happened is that now they'll let us into that crummy library downtown which was obsolete in 1897 and where nobody goes anyway; who in this town reads books? For that we paid I don't know how many thousands of dollars in fines, Jerome is still in the hospital, and we all know that Ruthie is never again going to be the swinging little chick she used to be. Big deal. Now we're picketing that great movie palace downtown where I wouldn't go on a bet; I can live without Yul Brynner and Doris Day, thank you very much. And we *still* can't get licensed to be electricians or plumbers, we still can't walk through the park,

our kids still can't use the swimming pool in town. We still can't vote, we can't even get registered. Is it worth it? And these people trying to kill us, too? And we ain't even got no guns. The cops ain't going to protect us. They call up the people and tell them where we are and say, 'Go get them! They ain't going to do nothing to you — they just dumb niggers!'

MERIDIAN: Did they arrest anybody tonight?

PETE: No, they got their hands full now, trying to explain what Richard's body was doing in them weeds.

LORENZO: It was wild. You know, all the time we was ducking them bricks and praying to *God* we'd get home before somebody got killed — (*Laughs.*) I had a jingle going through my mind, like if I was a white man, dig? and I had to wake up every morning singing to myself, 'Look at the happy nigger, he doesn't give a damn, thank God I'm not a nigger —'

TOGETHER: '— Good Lord, perhaps I am!'

JUANITA: You've gone crazy, Lorenzo. They've done it. You have been unfitted for the struggle.

MERIDIAN: I cannot rest until they bring my son's murderer to trial. That man who killed my son.

LORENZO: But he killed a nigger before, as I know all of you know. Nothing never happened. Sheriff just shovelled the body into the ground and forgot about it.

MERIDIAN: Parnell will help me.

PETE: Meridian, you know that *Mister* Parnell ain't going to let them arrest his ass-hole buddy. I'm sorry, Mother Henry!

MOTHER HENRY: That's all right, son.

MERIDIAN: But I think that Parnell has proven to be a pretty good friend to all of us. He's the only white man in this town who's ever *really* stuck his neck out in order to do — to do right. He's *fought* to bring about this trial — I can't tell you how hard he's fought. If it weren't for him, there'd be much less hope.

LORENZO: I guess I'm just not as nice as you are. I don't trust as many people as you trust.

MERIDIAN: We can't afford to become too distrustful, Lorenzo.

LORENZO: We can't afford to be too trusting, either. See, when a white man's a *good* white man, he's good because he wants *you* to be good. Well, sometimes I just might want to be *bad*. I got as much right to be bad as anybody else.

MERIDIAN: No, you don't.

LORENZO: Why not?

MERIDIAN: Because you know better.

PARNELL enters.

PARNELL: Hello, my friends. I bring glad tidings of great joy. Is that the way the phrase goes, Meridian?

JUANITA: Parnell!

PARNELL: I can't stay. I just came to tell you that a warrant's being issued for Lyle's arrest.

JUANITA: They're going to arrest him? Big Lyle Britten? I'd love to know how you managed *that*.

PARNELL: Well, Juanita, I am not a *good* man, but I have my little ways.

JUANITA: And a whole lot of folks in this town, baby, are not going to be talking to you no more, for days and days and *days*.

PARNELL: I hope that you all will. I may have no other company. I think I should go to Lyle's house to warn him. After all, I brought it about and he *is* a friend of mine — and then I have to get the announcement into my paper.

JUANITA: So it *is* true.

PARNELL: Oh, yes, it's true.

MERIDIAN: When is he being arrested?

PARNELL: Monday morning. Will you be up later, Meridian? I'll drop by if you are — if I may.

MERIDIAN: Yes. I'll be up.

PARNELL: All right, then. I'll trundle by. Good night all. I'm sorry I've got to run.

MERIDIAN: Good night.

JUANITA: Thank you, Parnell.

PARNELL: Don't thank me, dear Juanita. I only acted — as I believed I had to act. See you later, Meridian.

PARNELL exits.

MERIDIAN: I wonder if they'll convict him.

JUANITA: Convict him. Convict him. You're asking for heaven on earth. After all, they haven't even *arrested* him yet. And, anyway — why *should* they convict him? Why him? He's no worse than all the others. He's an honourable tribesman and he's defended, with blood, the honour and purity of his tribe!

(*WHITETOWN: LYLE holds his infant son up above his head.*)

LYLE: Hey old pisser. You hear me, sir? I expect you to control your bladder like a *gentleman* whenever your Papa's got you on his knee.

JO enters.

He got a mighty big bladder, too, for such a little fellow.

JO: I'll tell the world he didn't steal it.

LYLE: You mighty sassy tonight.

Hands her the child.

Ain't that right, old pisser? Don't you reckon your Mama's getting kind of sassy? And what do you reckon I should do about it?

JO is changing the child's diapers.

JO: You tell your Daddy he can start sleeping in his own bed nights instead of coming grunting in here in the wee small hours of the morning.

LYLE: And you tell your Mama if she was getting her sleep like she should be, so she can be alert every instant to your needs, little fellow, she wouldn't *know* what time I come — *grunting* in.

JO: I got to be alert to *your* needs, too. I think.

LYLE: Don't you go starting to imagine things. I just been over to the store. That's all.

JO: Till three and four o'clock in the morning?

LYLE: Well, I got plans for the store, I think I'm going to try to start branching out, you know, and I been — making plans.

JO: You thinking of branching out *now?* Why, Lyle, you know we ain't *hardly* doing no business *now.* Weren't for the country folks come to town every Saturday, I don't know *where* we'd be. This ain't no time to be branching *out.* We barely holding *on.*

LYLE: Shoot, the niggers'll be coming back, don't you worry. They'll get over this foolishness presently. They already weary of having to drive forty-fifty miles across the state line to get their groceries — a lot of them ain't even got cars.

JO: Those that don't have cars have *friends* with cars.

LYLE: Well, friends get weary, too. Joel come in the store a couple of days ago —

JO: Papa D.? He don't count. You can always wrap him around your little finger.

LYLE: Listen, will you? He come in the store a couple of days ago to buy a sack of flour and he *told* me, he say, The niggers is *tired* running all over creation to put some food on the table. Ain't nobody going to keep on driving no forty-fifty miles to buy no sack of flour — what you mean when you say Joel don't count?

JO: I don't mean nothing. But there's something wrong with anybody when his own people don't think much of him.

LYLE: Joel's got good sense, is all. I think more of him than I think of a lot of white men, that's a fact. And he knows what's right for his people, too.

JO: (*Puts son in crib.*) Well. Selling a sack of flour once a week ain't going to send this little one through college, neither. (*A pause.*) In what direction were you planning to branch out?

LYLE: I was thinking of trying to make the store more — well, more colourful. Folks like colour —

JO: You mean, niggers like colour.

LYLE: Dammit, Jo, I ain't in business just to sell to niggers! Listen to me, can't you? I thought I'd dress it up, get a new front, put some neon signs in — and, you know, we got more space in there than we use. Well, why don't we open up a line of ladies' clothes? Nothing too fancy, but I bet you it would bring in a lot more business.

JO: I don't know. Most of the ladies I know buy their clothes at Benton's, on Decatur Street.

LYLE: The niggers don't — anyway, we could sell them the same thing. The white ladies, I mean —

JO: No. It wouldn't be the same.

LYLE: Why not? A dress is a dress.

JO: But it sounds better if you say you got it on Decatur Street! At Benton's. Anyway — where would you get the money for this branching out?

LYLE: I can get a loan from the bank. I'll get old Parnell to co-sign with me, or have him get one of his rich friends to co-sign with me.

JO: Parnell called earlier – you weren't at the store today.

LYLE: What do you mean, I wasn't at the store?

JO: Because Parnell called earlier and said he tried to get you at the store and that there wasn't any answer.

LYLE: There wasn't any business. I took a walk.

JO: He said he's got bad news for you.

LYLE: What kind of bad news?

JO: He didn't say. He's coming by here this evening to give it to you himself.

LYLE: What do you think it is?

JO: I guess they're going to arrest you?

LYLE: No, they ain't. They ain't gone crazy.

JO: I think they might. We had so much trouble in this town lately and it's been in all the northern newspapers – and now, this – this dead boy –

LYLE: They ain't got no case.

JO: No. But you was the last person to see that crazy boy – alive. And now everybody's got to thinking again – about that other time.

LYLE: That was self-defence. The Sheriff said so himself. Hell, I ain't no murderer. They're just some things I don't believe is right.

JO: Nobody never heard no more about the poor little girl – his wife.

LYLE: No. She just disappeared.

JO: You never heard no more about her at all?

LYLE: How would I hear about her more than anybody else? No, she just took off – I believe she had people in Detroit somewhere. I reckon that's where she went.

JO: I felt sorry for her. She looked so lost those last few times I saw her, wandering around town – and she was so young. She was a pretty little thing.

LYLE: She looked like a piccaninny to me. Like she was too young to be married. I reckon she *was* too young for him.

JO: It happened in the store.

LYLE: Yes.

JO: How people talked! That's what scares me now.

LYLE: Talk don't matter. I hope you didn't believe what you heard.

JO: A lot of people did. I reckon a lot of people still do.

LYLE: *You* don't believe it?

JO: No. (*A pause.*) You know – Monday morning – we'll be married one whole year!

LYLE: Well, can't nobody talk about *us*. That little one there ain't but two months old.

The door bell rings.

JO: That's Parnell.

Exits.

LYLE walks up and down, looks into the crib. JO and PARNELL enter.

LYLE: It's about time you showed your face in here, you old rascal! You been so busy over there with the niggers, you ain't got time for white folks no more. You sure you ain't got some nigger wench over there on the other side of town? Because, I declare –!

PARNELL: I apologize for your husband, Mrs Britten, I really do. In fact, I'm afraid I must deplore your taste in men. If I had only seen you first, dear lady, and if you had found me charming, how much suffering I might have prevented! You got anything in this house to drink? Don't tell me you haven't, we'll both need one. Sit down.

LYLE: Bring on the booze, old lady.

JO brings ice, glasses, etc.; pours drinks.

What you been doing with yourself?

PARNELL: Well, I seem to have switched territories. I haven't been defending coloured people this week, I've been defending you. I've just left the Chief of Police.

LYLE: How is the old bastard?

PARNELL: He seems fine. But he really *is* an old bastard. Lyle – he's issuing a warrant for your arrest.

LYLE: He's going to arrest *me?* You mean, he believes I killed that boy?

PARNELL: The question of what he believes doesn't enter into it. This case presents several very particular circumstances and these circumstances force him to arrest you. I think we can take it for granted that he wouldn't arrest you if he could think of some way not to. He wouldn't arrest anybody except blind beggars and old coloured women if he could think of some way not to – he's bird-brained and chicken-hearted and big-assed. The charge is murder.

JO: Murder!

LYLE: Murder?

PARNELL: Murder.

LYLE: I ain't no murderer. You know that.

PARNELL: I also know that somebody killed the boy. Somebody put two slugs in his belly and dumped his body in the weeds beside the railroad track just outside of town. Somebody did all that. We pay several eminent, bird-brained, chicken-hearted, big-assed people quite a lot of money to discourage such activity. They never do, in fact, discourage it, but, still – we must find the somebody who killed that boy. And you, my friend, according to the testimony of Joel Davis, otherwise known as Papa D., were the last person to see the boy alive. It is also known that you didn't like him – to say the least.

LYLE: Nobody liked him.

PARNELL: Ah. But it isn't nobody that killed him. *Somebody* killed him. We must find the somebody. And since you were the last person to see him alive, we must arrest you in order to clear you – or convict you.

LYLE: They'll never convict me.

PARNELL: As to that, you may be right. But you *are* going to be arrested.

LYLE: When?

PARNELL: Monday morning. Of course, you can always flee to Mexico.

LYLE: Why should I run away?

PARNELL: I wasn't suggesting that you should run away. If you did, I should urge your wife to divorce you at once, and marry me.

JO: Ah, if that don't get him out of town in a hurry, I don't know what will! The man's giving you your chance, honey. You going to take it?

LYLE: Stop talking foolishness. It looks bad for me, I guess. I swear, I don't know what's come over the folks in this town!

PARNELL: It doesn't look good. In fact, if the boy had been white, it would look very, *very* bad, and your behind would be in the jail house now. What do you mean, you don't understand what's come over the people in this town?

LYLE: Raising so much fuss about a nigger – and a northern nigger at that.

PARNELL: He was born here. He's Reverend Meridian Henry's son.

LYLE: Well, he'd been gone so long, he might as well have been a northern nigger. Went North and got ruined and come back here to make trouble – and they tell me he was a dope fiend, too. What's all this fuss about? He probably got killed by some other nigger – they do it all the time – but ain't nobody even thought about arresting one of *them*. Has niggers suddenly got to be *holy* in this town?

PARNELL: Oh, Lyle, I'm not here to discuss the sanctity of niggers. I just came to tell you that a warrant's being issued for your arrest. *You* may think that a coloured boy who gets ruined in the North and then comes home to try to pull himself together deserves to die – I don't.

LYLE: You sound like you think I got something against coloured folks – but I don't. I never have, not in all my life. But I'll be damned if I'll mix with them. That's all. I don't believe in it, and that's *all*. I don't want no big buck nigger lying up next to Josephine and that's where all this will lead to and you know it as well as I do! I'm against it and I'll do anything I have to do to stop it, yes, I will!

PARNELL: Suppose *he* – my godson there – decides to marry a Chinese girl. You know, there are an awful lot of Chinese girls in the world – I bet you didn't know that. Well, there are. Let's just say that he grows up and looks around at all the pure white women, and – saving your presence, ma'am – they make him want to puke and he decides to marry a pure Chinese girl instead. What would you do? Shoot him in order to prevent it? Or would you shoot her?

LYLE: Parnell, you're my buddy. You've *always* been my buddy. You know more about me than anybody else in the world. What's come over you? You – you ain't going to turn against me, are you?

PARNELL: No. No, I'll never turn against you. I'm just trying to make you think.

LYLE: I notice you didn't marry no Chinese girl. You just never got married at all. Women been trying to saddle old Parnell for I don't know how long – I don't know what you got, old buddy, but I'll be damned if you don't know how to use it! What about this present one – Loretta – you reckon you going to marry her?

PARNELL: I doubt it.

JO: Parnell, you're just awful. Awful!

PARNELL: I think I'm doing her a favour. She can do much better than me. I'm just a broken-down newspaper editor – the editor of a newspaper which *nobody* reads – in a dim, grim backwater.

LYLE: I thought you liked it here.

PARNELL: I don't like it here. But I love it here. Or maybe I don't. I don't know. I must go.

LYLE: What's your hurry? Why don't you stay and have pot-luck with us?

PARNELL: Loretta is waiting. I must have pot-luck with *her*. And then I have errands on the other side of town.

LYLE: What they saying over there? I reckon they praying day and night for my ass to be put in a sling, ain't they? Shoot, I don't care.

PARNELL: Don't. Life's much simpler that way. Anyway, Papa D.'s the only one doing a whole lot of talking.

JO: I told you he wasn't no good, Lyle, I told you!

LYLE: I don't know what's got into him! And we been knowing each other all these years! He must be getting old. You go back and tell him I said he's got it all *confused* – about me and that boy. Tell him you talked to me and that *I* said he must have made some mistake.

PARNELL: I'll drop in tomorrow, if I may. Good night, Jo, and thank you. Good night, Lyle.

LYLE: Good night, old buddy.

JO: I'll see you to the door.

JO and PARNELL exit. LYLE walks up and down.

LYLE: Well! *Ain't* that something! But they'll never convict me. Never in this world. (*Looks into crib.*) Ain't that right, old pisser?

(BLACKTOWN: *The church, as before.*)

LORENZO: And when they bring him to trial, I'm going to be there every day – right across the street in that court-house – where they been dealing death out to us for all these years.

MOTHER HENRY: I used to hate them, too, son. But I don't hate them no more. They too pitiful.

MERIDIAN: No witnesses.

JUANITA: Meridian. Ah, Meridian.

MOTHER HENRY: You remember that song he used to like so much?

MERIDIAN: I sing because I'm happy.

JUANITA: I sing because I'm free.

PETE: For his eye is on the sparrow –

LORENZO: And I know he watches – me.

Music, very faint.

JUANITA: There was another song he liked – a song about a prison and the light from a train that shone on the prisoners every night at midnight. I can hear him now: Lord, you wake up in the morning. You hear the ding-dong ring –

MOTHER HENRY: He had a beautiful voice.

LORENZO: Well, he was pretty tough up there in New York – till he got busted.

MERIDIAN: And came running home.

MOTHER HENRY: Don't blame yourself, honey. Don't blame yourself!

JUANITA: You go a-marching to the table, you see the same old thing –

JIMMY: All I'm going to tell you: knife, a fork, and a pan –

Music stronger.

PETE: And if you say a thing about it –

LORENZO: You are in trouble with the man.

Lights dim in the church. We discover RICHARD, standing in his room, singing. This number is meant to make vivid the RICHARD who was much loved on the Apollo Theatre stage in Harlem, the RICHARD who was a rising New York star.

MERIDIAN: No witnesses!

Near the end of the song, MOTHER HENRY enters, carrying a tray with milk, sandwiches, and cake.

RICHARD: You treating me like royalty, old lady – I ain't royalty. I'm just a raggedy-assed, out-of-work, busted musician. But I sure can sing, can't I?

MOTHER HENRY: You better learn some respect, you know that neither me nor your father wants that kind of language in this house. Sit down and eat, you got to get your strength back.

RICHARD: What for? What am I supposed to do with it?

MOTHER HENRY: You stop that kind of talk.

RICHARD: Stop that kind of talk, we don't want that kind of talk! Nobody cares what people feel or what they think or what they do – but stop that kind of talk!

MOTHER HENRY: Richard!

RICHARD: All right. All right. (*Throws himself on the bed, begins eating in a kind of fury.*) What I can't get over is – what in the world am I doing *here*? Way down here in the ass-hole of the world, the deep, black, funky South.

MOTHER HENRY: You were born here. You got folks here. And you ain't got no manners and you *won't* learn no sense and so you naturally got yourself in trouble and had to come to your folks. You lucky it wasn't no worse, the way you go on. You want some more milk?

RICHARD: No, old lady. Sit down.

MOTHER HENRY: I ain't got time to be fooling with you. (*But she sits down.*) What you got on your mind?

RICHARD: I don't know. How do you stand it?

MOTHER HENRY: Stand what? You?

RICHARD: Living down here with all these nowhere people.

MOTHER HENRY: From what I'm told and from what I see, the people you've been among don't seem to be any better.

RICHARD: You mean old Aunt Edna? She's all right, she just ain't very bright, is all.

MOTHER HENRY: I am not talking about Edna. I'm talking about all them other folks you got messed up with. Look like you'd have had better sense. You hear me?

RICHARD: I hear you.

MOTHER HENRY: That all you got to say?

RICHARD: It's easy for you to talk, Grandmama, you don't know nothing about New York City, or what can happen to you up there!

MOTHER HENRY: I know what can happen to you anywhere in this world. And I know right from wrong. We tried to raise you so you'd know right from wrong, too.

RICHARD: We don't see things the same way, Grandmama. I don't know if I really *know* right from wrong – I'd like to, I always dig people the most who know *anything*, especially right from wrong!

MOTHER HENRY: You've had yourself a little trouble, Richard, like we all do, and you a little tired, like we all get. You'll be all right. You a young man. Only, just try not to *go* so much, try to calm down a little. Your Daddy loves you. You his only son.

RICHARD: That's a good reason, Grandmama. Let me tell you about New York. You ain't never been North, have you?

MOTHER HENRY: Your Daddy used to tell me a little about it every time he come back from visiting you all up there.

RICHARD: Daddy don't know nothing about New York. He just come up for a few days and went right on back. That ain't the way to get to know New York. No ma'am. He *never* saw New York. Finally, I realized he wasn't never *going* to see it – you know, there's a whole lot of things Daddy's never seen? I've seen more than he has.

MOTHER HENRY: All young folks thinks that.

RICHARD: Did *you*? When you were young? Did you think you knew more than your mother and father? But I bet you really did, you a pretty shrewd old lady, quiet as it's kept.

MOTHER HENRY: No, I didn't think that. But I thought I could find *out* more, because *they* were born in slavery, but *I* was born free.

RICHARD: *Did* you find out more?

MOTHER HENRY: I found out what I had to find out – to take care of my husband and raise my children in the fear of God.

RICHARD: You know I don't believe in God, Grandmama.

MOTHER HENRY: You don't know what you talking about.

Ain't no way possible for you not to believe in God. It ain't up to you.

RICHARD: Who's it up to, then?

MOTHER HENRY: It's up to the life in you – the life in you. *That* knows where it comes from, *that* believes in God. You doubt me, you just try holding your breath long enough to die.

RICHARD: You pretty smart, ain't you? (*A pause.*) I convinced Daddy that I'd be better off in New York – and Edna, she convinced him too, she said it wasn't as tight for a black man up there as it is down here. Well, that's a crock, Grandmama, believe me when I tell you. At first I thought it was true, hell, I was just a green country boy and they ain't got no signs up, dig, saying you can't go here or you can't go there. No, you got to find that out all by your lonesome. But – for awhile – I thought everything was swinging and Edna, she's so dizzy she thinks everything is *always* swinging, so there we were – like *swinging*.

MOTHER HENRY: I know Edna got lost somewhere. But Richard – why didn't *you* come back? You knew your Daddy wanted you back, your Daddy and me both.

RICHARD: I didn't want to come back here like a whipped dog. One whipped dog running to another whipped dog. No, I didn't want that. I wanted to make my Daddy proud of me – because, the day I left here, I sure as hell wasn't proud of *him*.

MOTHER HENRY: Be careful, son. Be careful. Your Daddy's a fine man. Your Daddy loves you.

RICHARD: I know, Grandmama. But I just wish, that day that Mama died, he'd took a pistol and gone through that damn white man's hotel and shot every son of a bitch in the place. That's right. I wish he'd shot them dead. I been dreaming of that day ever since I left here. I been dreaming of my Mama falling down the steps of that hotel. *My* Mama. I never believed she fell I *always* believed that some white man pushed her down those steps. And I know that Daddy thought so, too. But he wasn't there, he didn't know, he couldn't say nothing, he couldn't *do* nothing. I'll never forget the way he looked – whipped, whipped, whipped, whipped!

MOTHER HENRY: She fell, Richard, she *fell*. The stairs were wet and slippery and she *fell*.

RICHARD: My mother *fell* down the steps of that damn white hotel? My mother was *pushed* – you remember yourself how them white bastards was always sniffing around my mother, *always* around her – because she was pretty and *black*!

MOTHER HENRY: Richard, you can't start walking around believing that all the suffering in the world is caused by white folks!

RICHARD: I can't? Don't tell me I can't. I'm going to treat everyone of them as though they were responsible for all the crimes that ever happened in the history of the world – oh, yes! They're responsible for all the misery

I've ever seen, and that's good enough for me. It's because my Daddy's got no power that my Mama's dead. And he ain't got no power because he's *black*. And the only way the black man's going to *get* any power is to drive all the white men into the sea.

MOTHER HENRY: You're going to make yourself sick. You're going to make yourself sick with hatred.

RICHARD: No, I'm not. I'm going to make myself well. I'm going to make myself *well* with hatred – what do you think of that?

MOTHER HENRY: It can't be done. It can never be done. Hatred is a poison, Richard.

RICHARD: Not for me. I'm going to learn how to drink it – a little every day in the morning, and then a booster shot late at night. I'm going to remember everything. I'm going to keep it right here, at the very top of my mind. I'm going to remember Mama, and Daddy's face that day, and Aunt Edna and all her sad little deals and all those boys and girls in Harlem and all them pimps and whores and gangsters and all them cops. And I'm going to remember all the dope that's flowed through my veins. I'm going to remember everything – the jails I been in and the cops that beat me and how long a time I spent screaming and stinking in my own dirt, trying to break my habit. I'm going to remember all that, and I'll get well. I'll get well.

MOTHER HENRY: Oh, Richard. Richard. Richard.

RICHARD: Don't Richard *me*. I tell you, I'm going to get *well*.

He takes a small, sawed-off pistol from his pocket.

MOTHER HENRY: Richard, what are you doing with that gun?

RICHARD: I'm carrying it around with me, that's what I'm doing with it. This gun goes everywhere I go.

MOTHER HENRY: How long have you had it?

RICHARD: I've had it a long, long time.

MOTHER HENRY: Richard – you never –?

RICHARD: No. Not yet. But I will when I have to. I'll sure as hell take one of the bastards with me.

MOTHER HENRY: Hand me that gun. Please.

RICHARD: I can't. This is all that the man understands. He don't understand nothing else. *Nothing else!*

MOTHER HENRY: Richard – your father – think of your father –

RICHARD: Don't tell him! You hear me? (*A pause.*) Don't tell him!

MOTHER HENRY: Richard. Please.

RICHARD: Take the tray away, old lady. I ain't hungry no more.

After a moment, MOTHER HENRY *takes the tray and exits.* RICHARD *stretches out on the bed.*

JUANITA: (*Off.*) Meridian? Mother Henry? Anybody home in this house? (*Enters.*) Oh! Excuse me.

RICHARD: I think they might be over at the church. I reckon Grandmama went over there to pray for my soul.

JUANITA: Grandmama?

RICHARD: Who are you? Don't I know you?

JUANITA: Yes. I think you might.

RICHARD: Is your name Juanita?

JUANITA: If your name is Richard.

RICHARD: I'll be damned.

JUANITA: Ain't you a mess? So you finally decided to come back here – come here, let me hug you! Why, you ain't hardly changed at all – you just a little taller but you sure didn't gain much weight.

RICHARD: And I bet you the same old tomboy. You sure got the same loud voice – used to be able to hear you clear across this town.

JUANITA: Well, it's a mighty small town, Richard, that's what you always said – and the reason my voice got so loud so early, was that I started screaming for help right quick.

PETE enters.

Do you know Pete Spivey? He's someone come on the scene since you been gone. He's going to school down here, you should pardon the expression.

RICHARD: How do you do, man? Where you from?

PETE: I'm from a little place just outside Mobile.

RICHARD: Why didn't you go North, man? If you was going to make a *move. That's* the place. You get lost up there and I guarantee you some swinging little chick is sure to find you.

JUANITA: We'll let that pass. Are you together? Are you ready to meet the day?

RICHARD: I am *always* together, little sister. Tell me what you got on your mind.

PETE: We thought we'd just walk around town a little and maybe stop and have a couple of drinks somewhere. Or we can drive. I got a car.

RICHARD: I didn't think I'd never see you no more, Juanita. You been here all this time?

JUANITA: I sure have, sugar. Just waiting for you to come home.

RICHARD: Don't let this chick upset you, Pete. All we ever did was climb trees together.

PETE: She's had me climbing a few trees, too. But we weren't doing it together.

(*PAPA D.'s juke joint: Juke box music, loud. Less frantic than* RICHARD's *song. Couple dancing, all very young, doing very lively variations of the 'Twist,' the 'Wobble,' etc.* PAPA D. *at the counter. It is now early evening.* JUANITA, PETE *and* RICHARD *enter.*)

JUANITA: How you making it, Papa D.? We brought someone to see you – you recognize him?

PAPA D.: It seems to me I know your face, young man. Yes, I'm *sure* I know your face. Now, wait a minute, don't tell me – you ain't Shirelee Anderson's boy, are you?

RICHARD: No. I remember Shirelee Anderson, but we ain't no kin.

PETE: Try again, Papa D.

PAPA D.: You your father's boy. I just recognized that smile – you Reverend Henry's son. Well, how you doing? It's nice to have you back with us. You going to stay a while?

RICHARD: Yes sir. I think I'll be around for a while.

PAPA D.: Yeah, I remember you little old string bean of a boy, full of the devil. How long you been gone from here?

RICHARD: Almost eight years now. I left in September – it'll be eight years next month.

PAPA D.: Yeah – how's your Daddy? And your Grandmother? I ain't seen them for a while.

PETE: Ain't you been going to church, Papa D.?

PAPA D.: Well, you know how it is. I try, God *knows* I try!

RICHARD: They fine, Papa D.

PAPA D.: You all don't want nothing to eat?

RICHARD: We'll think about it.

They sit down.

PETE: Old Papa D. got something on everybody, don't he?

JUANITA: You better believe it.

RICHARD: He's kind of a Tom, ain't he?

PETE: Yeah. He *talks* about Mister Charlie, and he *says* he's with us – us kids – but he ain't going to do nothing to offend him. You know, he's still trading with Lyle Britten.

RICHARD: Who's Lyle Britten?

PETE: Peckerwood, owns a store nearby. And, man, you ain't *seen* a peckerwood until you've seen Lyle Britten. Niggers been trading in his store for years, man, I wouldn't be surprised but if the cat was rich – but that man still expects you to step off the sidewalk when he comes along. So we been getting people to stop buying there.

JUANITA: He shot a coloured man a few years back, shot him dead, and wasn't nothing never said, much less done, about it.

PETE: Lyle had been carrying on with this man's wife, dig, and, naturally, Old Bill – his name was Bill Walker, everybody called him Old Bill – wanted to put a stop to it.

JUANITA: She was a pretty little thing – real little and real black.

RICHARD: She still around here?

PETE: No. She disappeared. She went North somewhere.

RICHARD: Jive mothers. They can rape and kill our women and we can't do nothing. But if we touch one of their dried-up, pale-assed women, we get our nuts cut off. You remember that chick I was telling you about earlier, lives in Greenwich Village in New York?

PETE: What about her?

RICHARD: She's *white*, man. I got a whole *gang* of white chicks in New York. That's *right*. And they can't get enough of what little Richard's got – and I give it to them, too, baby, believe me. You say black people ain't got no dignity? Man, you ought to watch a white woman when she wants you to give her a little bit. They will do anything, baby, *anything!* Wait – I got some pictures. That's the one lives in the Village. *Ain't* she fine? I'd hate to tell you where I've had that long yellow hair. And, dig this one, this is Sandy, her old man works on Wall Street –

PETE: We're making Juanita nervous.

JUANITA: Don't worry about *me*. I've been a big girl for a *long* time. Besides, I'm studying abnormal psychology. So please feel free. Which one is this? What does *her* father do?

RICHARD: That's Sylvia. I don't know what her father does. She's a model. She's loaded with loot.

PETE: You take money from her?

RICHARD: I take their money and they love it. Anyway, they ain't got nothing else to do with it. Every one of them's got some piss-assed, faggoty white boy on a string somewhere. They go home and marry him, dig, when they can't make it with me no more – but when they want some *loving*, funky, downhome, bring-it-on-here-and-put-it-on-the-table style –

JUANITA: They sound very sad. It must be very sad for you, too.

RICHARD: Well, I want *them* to be sad, baby, I want to screw up *their* minds *for ever*. But why should *I* be so sad? Hell, I was swinging, I just about had it made. I had me some fine chicks and a fine pad and my car, and, hell, I was on my way! But then – then I screwed up.

JUANITA: We heard you were sick.

RICHARD: Who told you I was sick?

JUANITA: Your father. Your grandmother. They didn't say what the sickness was.

PAPA D. passes their table.

RICHARD: Hey, Papa D., come on over here. I want to show you something.

PAPA D. comes over.

Hey, look at these, man, look! Ain't they some fine chicks? And you know who *each one* of them calls: *Baby! Oh, baby?* That's right. You looking at the man.

PAPA D.: Where'd you steal those pictures, boy?

RICHARD: (*Laughs.*) *Steal* them! Man, I ain't got to steal girls' pictures. I'm telling you the truth!

PAPA D.: Put them pictures away. I thought you had good sense.

He goes back to the counter.

RICHARD: Ain't that a bitch. He's scared because I'm carrying around pictures of white girls. That's the trouble with niggers. They all scared of the man.

JUANITA: Well, I'm *not* scared of the man. But there's just no point in running around, asking –

PETE: – to be lynched.

RICHARD: Well, okay, I'll put my pictures away, then. I sure don't want to upset nobody.

PETE: Excuse me. I'll be back.

Exits.

RICHARD: You want to dance?

JUANITA: No. Not now.

RICHARD: You want something to eat?

JUANITA: No. Richard?

RICHARD: Yeah?

JUANITA: Were you *very* sick?

RICHARD: What d'you want to know for?

JUANITA: Like that. Because I used to be your girl friend.

RICHARD: You was more like a boy than a girl, though. I couldn't go nowhere without you. You were determined to get your neck broken.

JUANITA: Well, I've changed. I'm now much more like a girl than I am like a boy.

RICHARD: You didn't turn out too bad, considering what you had to start with.

JUANITA: Thank you. I guess.

RICHARD: How come you ain't married by now? Pete, now, he seems real fond of you.

JUANITA: He *is* fond of me, we're friends. But I'm not in any hurry to get married – not now. And not here. I'm not sure I'm going to stay here. I've been working very hard, but next year I think I'll leave.

RICHARD: Where would you go?

JUANITA: I don't know. I had always intended to go North to law school and then come back down here to practise law – God knows this town could stand it. But, now, I don't know.

RICHARD: It's rough, huh?

JUANITA: It's not that so much. It *is* rough – are you all right? Do you want to go?

RICHARD: No, no. I'm all right. Go on. (*A pause.*) I'm all *right*. Go on.

JUANITA: It's rough because you can't help being scared. I don't want to die – what was the matter with you, Richard, what were you sick with?

RICHARD: It wasn't serious. And I'm better now.

JUANITA: Well, no, that's just it. You're not really better.

RICHARD: How do you mean?

JUANITA: I watch you –

RICHARD: *Why* do you watch me?

JUANITA: I care about you.

RICHARD: You care about me! I thought you could hold your liquor better than that, girl.

JUANITA: It's not liquor. Don't you believe that anyone can care about you?

RICHARD: Care about me! Do you know how many times chicks have told me that? That they *cared* about me?

JUANITA: Well. This isn't one of those times.

RICHARD: I was a junkie.

JUANITA: A what?

RICHARD: A junkie, a dope addict, a hop-head, a mainliner – a dope fiend! My arms and my legs, too, are full of holes!

JUANITA: I asked you tell *me*, not the world.

RICHARD: Where'd Pete go?

JUANITA: He's dancing.

RICHARD: You want to dance?

JUANITA: In a minute.

RICHARD: I got hooked about five years ago. See, I couldn't stand these chicks I was making it with, and I was working real hard at my music, and, man, I was lonely. You come off a gig, you be tired, and you'd already taken as much shit as you could stand from the managers and the people in the room you were working and you'd be off to make some down scene with some pasty white-faced bitch. And so you'd make the scene and somehow you'd wake up in the morning and the chick would be beside you, alive and well, and dying to make the scene again and somehow you'd managed not to strangle her, you hadn't beaten her to death. Like you wanted to. And you get out of there and you carry this pain around inside all day and all night long. No way to beat it – no *way*. No matter how you turned, no matter what you did – no *way*. But when I started getting high, I was cool, and it didn't bother me. And I wasn't lonely then, it was all right. And the chicks – I could handle them, they couldn't reach me. And I didn't know I was hooked – until I was *hooked*. Then I started getting into trouble and I lost a lot of gigs and I had to sell my car and I lost my pad and most of the chicks, they split, naturally – but not all of them – and then I got busted and I made that trip down to Lexington and – here I am. Way *down* upon the Swanee River. But I'm going to be all right. You can bet on it.

JUANITA: I'd like to do better than that. I'd like to see to it.

RICHARD: How?

JUANITA: Well, like I used to. I won't let you go anywhere without me.

RICHARD: You *still* determined to break your neck.

JUANITA: Well, it's a neck-breaking time. I wouldn't like to appear to be above the battle.

RICHARD: Do you have any idea of what you might be letting yourself in for?

JUANITA: No. But you said you were lonely. And I'm lonely, too.

LYLE enters, goes to the counter. His appearance causes a change in the atmosphere, but no one appears to stop whatever they are doing.

LYLE: Joel, how about letting me have some change for cigarettes? I got a kind of long drive ahead of me, and I'm out.

PAPA D.: Howdy, Mister Lyle, how you been? Folks ain't been seeing much of you lately.

LYLE: (*Laughs.*) That's the truth. But I reckon old friends just stays old friends. Ain't that right?

PAPA D.: That's right, Mister Lyle.

JUANITA: That's Lyle Britten. The one we were talking about before.

RICHARD: I wonder what he'd do if I walked into a white place.

JUANITA: Don't worry about it. Just stay out of white places – believe me!

RICHARD: (*Laughs.*) Let's TCB – that means taking care of business. Let's see if I can dance.

They rise, dance. Perhaps she is teaching him the 'Fight', or he is teaching her the 'Pony'; they are enjoying each other. LYLE gets his change, gets cigarettes out of the machine, crosses to the counter, pauses there to watch the dancers.

LYLE: Joel, you know I ain't never going to be able to dance like that.

PAPA D.: Ain't nothing to it. You just got to be supple, that's all. I can *yet* do it.

Does a grotesque sketch of the 'Twist'.

LYLE: Okay, Joel, you got it. Be seeing you now.

PAPA D.: Good night, Mister Lyle.

On LYLE's way out, he jostles JUANITA. RICHARD stops, holding JUANITA at the waist. RICHARD and LYLE stare at each other.

LYLE: Pardon me.

RICHARD: Consider yourself pardoned.

LYLE: You new around here?

PAPA D.: He just come to town a couple of days ago, Mister Lyle.

RICHARD: Yeah. I just come to town a couple of days ago, Mister Lyle.

LYLE: Well. I sure hope your stay'll be a pleasant one.

Exits.

PETE: Man, are you *anxious* to leave this world? Because he wouldn't think nothing of helping you out of it.

RICHARD: Yeah. Well, I wouldn't think nothing of helping him out of it, neither. Come on, baby, record's going to waste – let's TCB.

They dance.

So you care about me, do you? Ain't that a bitch?

(*The church:* PETE *and* JUANITA, *a little apart from the others.*)

PETE: Why have you been avoiding me? Don't answer that. You started going away from me as soon as Richard came to this town. Now listen, Richard's dead but you still won't turn to me. I don't want to ask you for more than you can give, but why have you locked me out? I *know* – you liked me. We had nice times together.

JUANITA: We did. I *do* like you. Pete, I don't know. I wish you wouldn't ask me now. I wish *nobody* would ask me for anything now!

PETE: Is it because of Richard? Because if that's what it is, I'll wait – I'll wait until you know inside you that Richard's dead, but you're alive, and you're *supposed* to live, and I love you.

JUANITA: When Richard came, he – *hit* – me in some place

where I'd never been touched before. I don't mean — just physically. He took all my attention — the deepest attention, maybe, that one person can give another. He needed me and he made a difference for me in this terrible world — do you see what I mean? And — it's funny — when I was with him, I didn't think of the future, I didn't dare. I didn't know if I could be strong enough to give him what he needed for as long as he would need it. It only lasted four or five days, Pete — four or five days, like a storm, like lightning! And what I saw during that storm I'll always see. Before that — I thought I knew who I was. But now I know that there are more things in me than I'll ever understand — and if I can't be faithful to myself, I'm afraid to promise I'll be faithful to one man!

PETE: I need you. I'll be faithful. That helps. You'll see.

JUANITA: So many people need so much!

PETE: So do you. So do I, Juanita. You take all my attention. My deepest attention.

JUANITA: You probably see things that I think are hidden. You probably think I'm a fool — or worse.

PETE: No. I think there's a lot of love in you, Juanita. If you'll let me help you, we can give it to the world. You can't give it to the world until you find a person who can help you — love the world.

JUANITA: I've discovered that. The world is a loveless place.

PETE: Not yet —

The lights of a car flash in their faces. Silence. They all listen tensely as the lights of another car approach, then pass; they watch the lights disappear. The telephone rings in the office. MOTHER HENRY goes off to answer it. They listen to the murmur of MOTHER HENRY's voice. MOTHER HENRY enters.

MOTHER HENRY: That was Freddy Roberts. He say about two-thirty his dog started to barking and woke him up and he let the dog out on the porch and the dog run under the porch and there was two white men *under* Freddy's porch, fooling around with his gas pipes. Freddy thinks the dog bit one of them. He ran inside to get him his rifle but the rifle jammed and the men got away. He wanted to warn us, maybe they might come prowling around here.

LORENZO: Only we ain't got no rifles.

JUANITA: It was the dog that woke him up? I'll bet they come back and kill that dog!

JIMMY: What was they doing under the man's house, messing around with his gas pipes, at that hour of the morning?

PETE: They was fixing to blow up his house. They *might* be under your house, or *this* house, right now.

LORENZO: The real question is why two white men feel safe enough to come to a black neighbourhood after dark in the first place. If a couple of them get their heads blown off, they won't feel so goddamn courageous!

JUANITA: I better call home.

Exits into office.

PETE: Will you have your mother call my house?

LORENZO: And have *his* mother call *my* house?

JIMMY: And tell all the people that don't have rifles or dogs to stay off their porches!

LORENZO: Tell them to fall on their knees and use their Bibles as breast-plates! Because I know that each and every one of them got *Bibles!*

MERIDIAN has walked to the church door, stands looking off.

Don't they, Meridian?

MOTHER HENRY: Hush.

We hear JUANITA's voice, off. Then silence falls. Lights dim on the students until they are in silhouette. Lights up on MERIDIAN. We hear RICHARD's guitar, very lonely, far away.

A car door slams. The voices of young people saying good night. RICHARD appears, dressed as we last saw him.

RICHARD: Hello, Daddy. You still up?

MERIDIAN: Yeah. Couldn't sleep. How was your day?

RICHARD: It was all right. I'd forgotten what nights down here were like. You never see the stars in the city — and all these funny country sounds —

MERIDIAN: Crickets. And all kinds of bugs and worms, running around, busy, shaking all the bushes.

RICHARD: Lord, if I'd stayed here, I guess I might have married old Juanita by now, and we'd have a couple of kids and I'd be sitting around like this *every* night. What a wild thought.

MERIDIAN: You can still marry Juanita. Maybe she's been waiting for you.

RICHARD: Have you ever thought of marrying again?

MERIDIAN: I've thought of it.

RICHARD: Did you ever think of marrying Juanita?

MERIDIAN: Why do you ask me that?

RICHARD: Because I'd like to know.

MERIDIAN: *Why* would you like to know?

RICHARD: Why would you like to hide it? I'd like to know because I'm a man now, Daddy, and I can ask you to tell me the truth. I'm making up for lost time. Maybe you should try to make up for lost time too.

MERIDIAN: Yes. I've thought of marrying Juanita. But I've never spoken of it to her.

RICHARD: That's the truth?

MERIDIAN: Yes.

RICHARD: Why didn't you tell me the truth way back there? Why didn't you tell me my mother was murdered? She was pushed down them steps.

MERIDIAN: Richard, your mother's dead. People die in all kinds of ways. They die when their times comes to die. Your mother loved you and she was gone — there was nothing more I could do for her. I had to think of you. I didn't want you to be — poisoned — by useless and terrible suspicions. I didn't want to wreck your life. I knew your life was going to be hard enough. So, I let you go. I thought it might be easier for you – if I let you go. I didn't want you to grow up in this town.

RICHARD: But there was something else in it, too, Daddy. You didn't want me to look at you and be ashamed of you. And you didn't know what was in my eyes, you couldn't stand it, I could tell from the way you looked at me sometimes. That was it, wasn't it?

MERIDIAN: I thought it was better. I suppose I thought it was all over for me, anyway. And I thought I owed it to your mother and to girls like your mother, to try – try to change, to purify this town, where she was born, and where we'd been so happy, and which she loved so much. I was wrong, I guess. I was wrong.

RICHARD: You've just been a public man, Daddy, haven't you? Since that day? You haven't been a private man at all.

MERIDIAN: No. I haven't. Try to forgive me.

RICHARD: There's nothing to forgive. I've been down the road a little bit. I know what happened. I'm going to try again, Daddy.

A pause. RICHARD *takes out the gun.*

Here. Grandmama saw this this morning and she got all upset. So I'll let you hold it for me. You keep it till I ask you for it, okay? But when I ask you for it, you got to give it to me. Okay?

MERIDIAN: (*Takes the gun.*) Okay. I'm proud of how you've come through – all you've had to bear.

RICHARD: I'm going to get some sleep. You coming over to the house now?

MERIDIAN: Not yet.

RICHARD: Good night. Say, Daddy?

MERIDIAN: Yeah?

RICHARD: You kind of like the idea of me and Juanita getting together?

MERIDIAN: Yeah. I think it's a fine idea.

RICHARD: Well, I'm going to sleep on it, then. Good night.

MERIDIAN: Good night.

RICHARD exits.

(*After* RICHARD's *exit, the lights come up on the students.*)

JUANITA: Lord it's gone and started raining.

PETE: And you worried about your hair.

JUANITA: I am *not* worried about my hair. I'm thinking of wearing it the way God arranged it in the first place.

LORENZO: Now, now, Mau-Mau.

PETE: This chick is going through some weird changes.

MERIDIAN: That's understandable. We all are.

JIMMY: Well, we'll see you some time tomorrow. It promises to be a kind of *active* day.

MERIDIAN: Yes, we've got some active days ahead of us. You all better get some sleep.

JUANITA: How're you getting home, Jimmy?

JIMMY: Pete's driving us all home.

JUANITA: And then – are you going to drive all the way to your house alone, Pete?

PETE: You're jumpy tonight. I'll stay at Lorenzo's house.

LORENZO: You can call your house from there.

MOTHER HENRY: You get some sleep, too, Meridian, it's past three o'clock in the morning. Don't you stay over here much longer.

MERIDIAN: No, I won't. Good night, all.

MOTHER HENRY: Good night, children. See you in the morning, God willing.

They exit. MERIDIAN *walks to the pulpit, puts his hand on the Bible.* PARNELL *enters.*

PARNELL: I hear it was real bad tonight.

MERIDIAN: Not as bad as it's going to get. Maybe I was wrong not to let the people arm.

PARNELL: If the Negroes were armed, it's the Negroes who'd be slaughtered. You know that.

MERIDIAN: They're slaughtered anyway. And I don't know that. I thought I knew it – but now I'm not so sure.

PARNELL: What's come over you? What's going to happen to the people in this town, this church – if you go to pieces?

MERIDIAN: Maybe they'll find a leader who can lead them some place.

PARNELL: Somebody with a gun?

MERIDIAN *is silent.*

Is that what you mean?

MERIDIAN: I'm a Christian. I've been a Christian all my life, like my Mama and Daddy before me and like their Mama and Daddy before them. Of course, if you go back far enough, you get to a point *before* Christ, if you see what I mean, *B.C.* – and at that point, I've been thinking, black people weren't raised to turn the other cheek, and in the hope of heaven. No, then they didn't have to take low. Before Christ. They walked around just as good as anybody else, and when they died, they didn't go to heaven, they went to join their ancestors. My son's dead, but he's not gone to join his ancestors. He was a sinner, so he must have gone to hell – if we're going to believe what the Bible says. Is that such an improvement, such a mighty advance over B.C.? I've been thinking, I've had to think – would I have *been* such a Christian if I hadn't been born black? Maybe I *had* to become a Christian in order to have any dignity at all. Since I wasn't a man in men's eyes, then I could be a man in the eyes of God. But that didn't protect my wife. She's dead, too soon, we don't really know how. That didn't protect my son – he's dead, we know how too well. That hasn't changed this town – this town, where you couldn't find a white Christian at high noon on Sunday! The eyes of God – maybe those eyes are blind – I never let myself think of that before.

PARNELL: Meridian, you can't be the man who gives the signal for the holocaust.

MERIDIAN: Must I be the man who watches while his people are beaten, chained, starved, clubbed, butchered?

PARNELL: You used to say that your people were all the people in the world – all the people God ever made, or would make. You said your race was the human race.

MERIDIAN: The human race!

PARNELL: I've never seen you like this before. There's something in your tone I've never heard before – rage – maybe hatred –

MERIDIAN: You've heard it before. You just never recognized it before. You've heard it in all those blues and spirituals and gospel songs you claim to love so much.

PARNELL: I was talking about *you* – not your history. I have a history, too. And don't be so sure I've never heard that sound. Maybe I've never heard anything else. Perhaps my life is also hard to bear.

MERIDIAN: I watched you all this week up at the Police Chief's office with me. And you know how to handle him because you're sure you're better than he is. But you both have more in common with each other than either of you have with me. And, for both of you – I watched this, I never watched it before – it was just a black boy that was dead, and that was a problem. He saw the problem one way, you saw it another way. But it wasn't a *man* that was dead, not my *son* – you held yourselves away from *that*!

PARNELL: I may have sounded – cold. It was not because I felt cold. There was no other way to sound, Meridian. I took the only tone which – it seemed to me – could accomplish what we wanted. And I *do* know the Chief of Police better than you – because I'm white. And I can make him listen to me – because I'm white. I don't know if I think I'm so much better than he is. I know what we have done – and do. But you must have mercy on us. We have no other hope.

MERIDIAN: You have never shown us any mercy at all.

PARNELL: Meridian, give me credit for knowing you're in pain. We are two men, two friends – in spite of all that could divide us. We have come too far together, there is too much at stake, for you to become black now, for me to become white. Don't accuse me. Don't accuse me. *I* didn't do it.

MERIDIAN: So was my son – innocent.

PARNELL: Meridian – when I asked for mercy a moment ago – I meant – please – please try to understand that it is not so easy to leap over fences, to give things up – all right, to surrender privilege! But if you were among the privileged you would know what I mean. It's not a matter of trying to hold *on*; the things, the privilege – are part of you, are *who* you are. It's in the *gut*.

MERIDIAN: Then where's the point of this struggle, where's the hope? If Mister Charlie can't change –

PARNELL: Who's Mister Charlie?

MERIDIAN: You're Mister Charlie. *All* white men are Mister Charlie!

PARNELL: You sound more and more like your son, do you know that? A lot of the coloured people here didn't approve of him, but he said things they longed to say – said right out loud, for all the world to hear, how much he despised white people!

MERIDIAN: He didn't say things *I* longed to say. Maybe it was because he was my son. I didn't care *what* he felt about white people. I just wanted him to live, to have his own life. There's something you don't understand about being black, Parnell. If you're a black man, with a black son, you have to forget all about white people and concentrate on trying to save your child. That's why I let him stay up North. I was wrong, I failed, I failed. Lyle walked him up the road and killed him.

PARNELL: We don't *know* Lyle killed him. And Lyle denies it.

MERIDIAN: Of course, he denies it – what do you mean, we don't *know* Lyle killed him?

PARNELL: We *don't* know – all we can say is that it looks that way. And circumstantial evidence is a tricky thing.

MERIDIAN: *When* it involves a white man killing a black man – if Lyle didn't kill him, Parnell, who did?

PARNELL: I don't *know*. But we don't know that Lyle did it.

MERIDIAN: Lyle doesn't deny that he killed Old Bill.

PARNELL: No.

MERIDIAN: And we know how Lyle feels about coloured people.

PARNELL: Well, yes. From your point of view. But – from another point of view – Lyle hasn't got anything *against* coloured people. He just –

MERIDIAN: He just doesn't think they're human.

PARNELL: Well, even *that's* not true. He doesn't think they're *not* human – after all, I know him, he's hot-tempered and he's far from being the brightest man in the world – but he's not mean, he's not cruel. He's a poor white man. The poor whites have been just as victimized in this part of the world as the blacks have ever been!

MERIDIAN: For God's sake spare me the historical view! Lyle's responsible for Richard's death.

PARNELL: But, Meridian, we can't even in our own minds, *decide* that he's guilty. We have to operate the way justice *always* has to operate and give him the benefit of the doubt.

MERIDIAN: *What* doubt?

PARNELL: Don't you see, Meridian, that now you're operating the way white people in this town operate whenever a coloured man's on trial?

MERIDIAN: When was the last time one of us was on *trial* here, Parnell?

PARNELL: That *can't* have anything to do with it, it *can't*. We must forget about all – *all* the past injustice. We have to start from scratch, or do our best to start from scratch. It isn't vengeance we're after. Is it?

MERIDIAN: I don't want vengeance. I don't want to be paid back – anyway, I couldn't be. I just want Lyle to be made to know that what he did was evil. I just want this town to be forced to face the evil that it countenances and to turn from evil and do good. That's why I've stayed in this town so long!

PARNELL: But if Lyle didn't do it? Lyle is a friend of mine – a strange friend, but a friend. I love him. I know how he suffers.

MERIDIAN: *How* does he suffer?

PARNELL: He suffers – from being in the dark – from having things inside him that he can't name and can't face and can't control. He's not a wicked man. I know he's not, I've known him almost all his life! The face he turns to you, Meridian, isn't the face he turns to me.

MERIDIAN: Is the face he turns to you more real than the face he turns to me? *You* go ask him if he killed my son.

PARNELL: They're going to ask him that in court. That's why I fought to bring about this trial. And he'll say no.

MERIDIAN: I don't care what he says in court. You go ask him. If he's your friend, he'll tell you the truth.

PARNELL: No. No, he may not. He's – he's maybe a little afraid of me.

MERIDIAN: If you're *his* friend, you'll know whether he's telling you the truth or not. Go ask him.

PARNELL: I can't do it. I'm his friend. I can't betray him.

MERIDIAN: But you can betray *me*? You *are* a white man, aren't you? Just another white man – after all.

PARNELL: Even if he says yes, it won't make any difference. The jury will never convict him.

MERIDIAN: Is that why you fought to bring about the trial? I don't care what the jury does. I know he won't say yes to them. He won't say yes to me. But he might say yes to you. You say we don't know. Well, I've got a right to know. And I've got the right to ask you to find out – since you're the only man who *can* find out. And *I've* got to find out – whether we've been friends all these years, or whether I've just been your favourite Uncle Tom.

PARNELL: You know better than that.

MERIDIAN: I don't know, Parnell, any longer – any of the things I used to know. Maybe I never knew them. I'm tired. Go home.

PARNELL: You don't trust me any more, do you, Meridian?

MERIDIAN: Maybe I never trusted you. I don't know. Maybe I never trusted myself. Go home. Leave me alone. I must look back at my record.

PARNELL: Meridian – what you ask – I don't know if I can do it for you.

MERIDIAN: I don't want you to do it for me. I want you to do it for you. Good night.

PARNELL: Good night.

PARNELL exits. MERIDIAN comes downstage. It is dawn.

MERIDIAN: My record! Would God – would *God* – would God I had died for thee – my son, my son!

Act 2

WHITETOWN: The kitchen of LYLE's house. Sunday morning. Church bells. A group of white people, all ages, men and women. JO and an older woman, HAZEL, have just taken a cake out of the oven. HAZEL sets it out to cool.

HAZEL: It's a shame – having to rush everything this way. But it can't be helped.

JO: Yes. I'm just so upset. I can't help it. I know it's silly. I know they can't do nothing to Lyle.

HAZEL: Girl, you just put all those negative thoughts right out of your mind. We're going to have your little anniversary celebration *tonight* instead of *tomorrow* night because we have reason to believe that *tomorrow* night your husband might be called away on business. Now, you think about it that way. Don't you go around here with a great long face, trying to demoralize your guests. I won't have it. You too young and pretty for that.

LILLIAN: Hallelujah! I *do* believe that I have finally mastered this recipe.

SUSAN: Oh, good! Let me see.

LILLIAN: I've only tried it once before, and its real hard. You've got to time it just right.

SUSAN: I have tried it and tried it and it never comes out! But yours is wonderful! We're going to eat tonight, folks!

RALPH: You supposed to be cooking something, too, ain't you?

SUSAN: I'm cooking our contribution later, at our own house. We got enough women here already, messing up Jo's kitchen.

JO: I'm just so glad you all come by I don't know what to do. Just go ahead and mess up that kitchen, I got lots of time to clean it.

ELLIS: Susan's done learned how to cook, huh?

RALPH: Oh, yeah, she's a right fine cook. All you got to do is look at me. I never weighed this much in my life.

ELLIS: Old Lyle's done gained weight in this year, too. Nothing like steady home cooking, I guess, ha-ha! It really don't seem like it was a year ago you two got married. Declare, I never thought Lyle was going to jump up and do that thing. But old Jo, here, she hooked him.

REV. PHELPS: Well, I said the words over them, and if I ever saw a happy man in my life, it was Big Lyle Britten that day. Both of them – there was just a light shining out of them.

GEORGE: I'd propose a toast to them, if it wasn't so early on a Sunday, and if the Reverend wasn't here.

REV. PHELPS: Ain't nothing wrong with toasting happy people, no matter what the day or hour.

ELLIS: You heard the Reverend! You got anything in this house we can drink to your happiness in, Mrs Britten?

JO: I'm pretty sure we do. It's a pity Lyle ain't up yet. He ain't never slept through this much racket before.

ELLIS: No ma'am, he ain't never been what you'd call a heavy sleeper. Not before he passed out, ha-ha! We used to have us some times together, him and me, before he got him some sense and got married.

GEORGE: Let him sleep easy. He ain't got no reason not to.

JO: Lyle's always got his eye on the ball, you know – and he's just been at that store, night after night after night, drawing up plans and taking inventory and I don't know what all – because, come fall, he's planning to branch out and have a brand new store, just about. You all won't recognize the place, I guarantee you!

ELLIS: Lyle's just like his Daddy. You can't beat him. The harder a thing is, well, the surer you can be that old Lyle Britten will do it. Why, Lyle's Daddy never got old – *never!* He was drinking and running after women – and getting them, too! – until just before they put him in his grave. I could tell you stories about the old man, boy – of course, I can't tell them now, on a Sunday morning, in front of all these women!

JO: Here you are, gentlemen. I hope you all drink bourbon.

RALPH: Listen to her!

GEORGE: Ladies! Would you all like to join us in a morning toast to the happy and beloved and loving couple, Mr and Mrs Lyle Britten, on the day immediately preceding their first wedding anniversary?

ELLIS: The bridegroom ain't here because he's weary from all his duties, both public and private. Ha-ha! But he's a good man, and he's done a lot for us, and I know you all know what I'm talking about, and I just feel like we should honour him and his lovely young wife. Ladies! Come on, Reverend Phelps says it's all right.

SUSAN: Not too much for me, Ralph.

LILLIAN: I don't think I've ever had a drink at this hour of a Sunday morning, and in the presence of my pastor!

They pour, drink, and sing 'For He's a Jolly Good Fellow.'

HAZEL: Now you've started her to crying, naturally. Here, honey, you better have a little drink yourself.

JO: You all have been *so* wonderful. I can't imagine how Lyle can go on sleeping. Thank you, Hazel. Here's to all of you! (*Drinks.*) Listen. They're singing over there now.

They listen.

HAZEL: Sometimes they can sound so nice. Used to take my breath away when I was a girl.

ELLIS: What's happened to this town? It was peaceful here, we all got along, we didn't have no trouble.

GEORGE: Oh, we had a little trouble from time to time, but it didn't amount to a hill of beans. Niggers was all right then, you could always get you a nigger to help you catch a nigger.

LILLIAN: That's right. They had their ways, we had ours, and everything went along the way God intended.

JO: I've never been scared in this town before – never. They was all like my own people. I never knew of anyone to mistreat a coloured person – have you? And they certainly didn't *act* mistreated. But now, when I walk through this town – I'm scared – like I don't know what's going to happen next. How come the coloured people to hate us so much, all of a sudden? We *give* them everything they've got!

REV. PHELPS: Their minds have been turned. They have turned away from God. They're a simple people – warm-hearted and good-natured. But they are very easily led, and now they are harkening to the counsel of these degenerate Communist race-mixers. And they don't know what terrible harm they can bring on themselves – and on us all.

JO: You can't tell what they're thinking. Why, coloured folks you been knowing all your life – you're almost afraid to hire them, almost afraid to *talk* to them – you don't know what they're thinking.

ELLIS: *I* know what they're thinking.

SUSAN: We're not much better off than the Communist countries – that's what Ralph says. *They* live in fear. They don't want us to teach God in our schools – you send your child to school and you don't know *what* kind of Godless atheist is going to be filling the little one's mind with all *kinds* of filth. And he's going to believe it, of course, kids don't know no better. And now they tell us we got to send our kids to *school* with niggers – why, everybody *knows* that ain't going to work, won't nobody get no education, white *or* black. Niggers can't learn like white folks, they ain't got the same *interests*.

ELLIS: They got one interest. And it's just below the belly button.

GEORGE: (*Laughs.*) You know them yellow niggers? Boy, ain't they the worst kind? Their own folks don't want them, don't nobody want them, and you *can't* do nothing with them – you might be able to scare a black nigger, but you can't do nothing with a yellow nigger.

REV. PHELPS: That's because he's a mongrel. And a mongrel is the lowest creation in the animal kingdom.

ELLIS: Mrs Britten, you're married and all the women in this room are married and I know you've seen your husband without no clothes on – but have you seen a nigger without no clothes on? No, I guess you haven't. Well, he ain't like a white man, Mrs Britten.

GEORGE: That's right.

ELLIS: Mrs Britten, if you was to be raped by an orangoutang out of the jungle or a *stallion*, couldn't do you no worse than a nigger. You wouldn't be no more good for nobody. I've *seen* it.

GEORGE: That's *right*.

RALPH: That's why we men have got to be so vigilant. I tell you, I have to be away a lot nights, you know – and I bought Susan a gun and I taught her how to use it, too.

SUSAN: And I'm a pretty good shot now, too. Ralph says he's real proud of me.

RALPH: She's just like a pioneer woman.

HAZEL: I'm so glad Esther's not here to see this. She'd die of shame. She was the sweetest coloured woman – you remember her. She just about raised us, used to sing us to sleep at night, and she could tell just the most beautiful stories – the kind of stories that could scare you and make you laugh and make you cry, you know? Oh, she was wonderful. I don't remember a cross word or an evil expression all the time she was with us. She was always the same. And I believe she knew more about me than my own mother and father knew. I just told her everything. Then, one of her sons got killed – he went bad, just like this boy they having a funeral for here tonight – and she got sick. I nursed her, I bathed that woman's body with my own hands. And she told me once, she said, 'Miss Hazel, you are just like an angel of light.' She said, 'My own couldn't have done more for me than you have done.' She was a wonderful old woman.

JO: I believe I hear Lyle stirring.

SUSAN: Mrs Britten, somebody else is coming to call on you. My! It's that Parnell James! I wonder if he's sober this morning. He never *looks* sober.

ELLIS: He never acts it, either.

PARNELL enters.

PARNELL: Good morning, good people! Good morning, Reverend Phelps! How good it is to see brethren – and sistren – walking together. Or, in this case, standing together – something like that, anyway; my Bible's a little rusty. Is church over already? Or are you having it here? Good morning, Jo.

JO: Good morning, Parnell. Sit down, I'll pour you a cup of coffee.

GEORGE: You look like you could use it.

REV. PHELPS: We were all just leaving.

PARNELL: Please don't leave on my account, Reverend Phelps. Just go on as you were, praying or singing, just as the spirit may move you. I *would* love that cup of coffee, Jo.

ELLIS: You been up all night?

PARNELL: Is that the way I look? Yes, I *have* been up all night.

ELLIS: Tom-catting around, I'll bet. Getting drunk and fooling with all the women.

PARNELL: Ah, you flatter me. And in games of chance, my friend, you have no future at all. I'm sure you always lose at poker. So *stop betting.* I was not tom-catting, I was at home, working.

GEORGE: You been over the way this morning? You been at the nigger funeral?

PARNELL: The funeral takes place this evening. And, yes, I will be there. Would you care to come along? Leaving your baseball bat at home, of course.

JO: We heard the singing –

PARNELL: Darkies are always singing. You people know that. What made you think it was a funeral?

JO: Parnell! You are the limit! Would anybody else like a little more coffee? It's still good and hot.

ELLIS: We heard that a nigger got killed. That's why we thought it was a funeral.

GEORGE: They bury their dead over the way, don't they?

PARNELL: They do when the dogs leave enough to bury, yes.

A pause.

ELLIS: Dogs?

PARNELL: Yes – you know. Teeth. Barking Lots of noise.

ELLIS: A lot of people in this town, Parnell, would like to know exactly where you stand, on a lot of things.

PARNELL: That's exactly where I stand. On a lot of things. Why don't you read my paper?

LILLIAN: I wouldn't filthy my hands with that Communist sheet!

PARNELL: Ah? But the father of your faith, the cornerstone of that church of which you are so precious an adornment, was a communist, possibly the first. He may have done some tom-catting. We *know* he did some drinking. And he knew a lot of – loose ladies and drunkards. It's all in the Bible, isn't it, Reverend Phelps?

REV. PHELPS: I won't be drawn into your blasphemous banter. Ellis is only asking what many of us want to know – are you with us or against us? And he's telling you what we all feel. We've put up with your irresponsibility long enough. We won't tolerate it any longer. Do I make myself clear?

PARNELL: Not at all. If you're threatening me, be specific. First of all, what's this irresponsibility that you won't tolerate? And if you aren't going to tolerate it, what *are* you going to do? Dip me in tar and feathers? Boil me in oil? Castrate me? Burn me? Cover yourselves in white sheets and come and burn crosses in front of my house? Come on, Reverend Phelps, don't stand there with your mouth open, it makes you even more repulsive than you are with it closed, and all your foul, graveyard breath comes rushing out, and it makes me want to vomit. Out with it, boy! What's on your mind?

ELLIS: You got away with a lot of things in this town, Parnell, for a long time, because your father was a big man here.

PARNELL: One at a time. I was addressing your spiritual leader.

SUSAN: He's *worse* than a nigger.

PARNELL: I take that as a compliment. I'm sure no man will ever say as much for you. Reverend Phelps?

REV. PHELPS: I think I speak for us all – for *myself* and for us all, when I say that our situation down here has become much too serious for flippancy and cynicism. When things were more in order here, we didn't really mind your attitude, and your paper didn't matter to us, we never read it, anyway.

ELLIS: We knew you were just a spoiled rich boy, with too much time on his hands that he didn't know what to do with.

REV. PHELPS: And so you started this paper and tried to make yourself interesting with all these subversive attitudes. I honestly thought that you would grow out of it.

GEORGE: Or go North.

REV. PHELPS: I know these attitudes were not your father's attitudes, or your mother's. I was very often invited to your home when they were alive –

PARNELL: How well I remember! What attitudes are you speaking of?

HAZEL: Race-mixing!

PARNELL: *Race-mixing!* Ladies and gentlemen, do you think anybody gives a good goddamn who you sleep with? You can go down to the swamps and couple with the snakes, for all I care, or for all anybody else cares. You may find that the snakes don't want you, but that's a problem for you and the snakes to work out, and it might prove astonishingly simple – the working out of the problem, I mean. I've never said a word about race-mixing. I've talked about social justice.

LILLIAN: That sounds Communistic to me!

PARNELL: It means that if I have a hundred dollars, and I'm black, and you have a hundred dollars, and you're white, I should be able to get as much value for *my* hundred dollars – my black hundred dollars – as you get for your *white* hundred dollars. It also means that I should have an equal opportunity to *earn* that hundred dollars –

ELLIS: Niggers can get work just as well as a white man can. Hell, *some* niggers make *more* money than me.

PARNELL: Some niggers are smarter than you, Ellis. Much smarter. And much nicer. And niggers *can't* get work just as well as a white man can, and you know it.

ELLIS: What's stopping them? They got hands.

PARNELL: Ellis, you don't really work with your *hands* – you're a salesman in a shoe store. And your boss wouldn't give that job to a nigger.

GEORGE: Well, goddammit, white men come before niggers! They *got* to!

PARNELL: Why?

LYLE enters.

LYLE: What's all this commotion going on in my house?

JO: Oh, Lyle, good morning! Some folks just dropped in to see you.

LYLE: It sounded like they was about to come to blows. Good morning, Reverend Phelps, I'm glad to see you here. I'm sorry I wasn't up, but I guess my wife might have told you, I've not been sleeping well nights. When I *do* go to sleep, she just lets me sleep on.

REV. PHELPS: Don't you apologize, son – we understand. We only came by to let you know that we're with you and every white person in this town is with you.

JO: Isn't that nice of them, Lyle? They've been here quite a spell, and we've had *such* a nice time.

LYLE: Well, that *is* mighty nice of you, Reverend, and all of you – hey there, Ellis! Old George! And Ralph and Susan – how's married life suit you? Guess it suits you all right, ain't nobody seen you in months, ha-ha! Mrs Proctor, Mrs

Barker, how you all? Hey! Old Parnell! What you doing up so early?

PARNELL: I was on my way to church, but they seemed to be having the meeting here. So I joined the worshippers.

LYLE: On your way to church, that's a good one. Bet you ain't been to bed yet.

PARNELL: No, I haven't.

LYLE: You folks don't mind if I have a little breakfast? Jo, bring me something to eat! Susan, you look mighty plump and rosy, you ain't keeping no secrets from us, are you?

SUSAN: I don't think so, Lyle.

LYLE: I don't know, you got that look – like a real ripe peach, just right for eating. You ain't been slack in your duty, have you, Ralph? Look at the way she's blushing! I guess you all right, boy.

ELLIS: You know what time they coming for you tomorrow?

LYLE: Some time in the morning, I reckon. I don't know.

REV. PHELPS: I saw the Chief of Police the other day. He really doesn't want to do it, but his hands are tied. It's orders from higher up, from the North.

LYLE: Shoot, I know old Frank don't want to arrest me. I understand. I ain't worried. I know the people in this town is with me. I got nothing to worry about.

ELLIS: They trying to force us to put niggers on the jury – that's what I hear. Claim it won't be a fair trial if we don't.

HAZEL: Did you *ever* hear anything like that in your *life?*

LYLE: Where they going to find the niggers?

ELLIS: Oh, I bet your buddy, Parnell, has got that all figured out.

LYLE: How about it, Parnell? You going to find some niggers for them to put on that jury?

PARNELL: It's not up to me. But I might recommend a couple.

GEORGE: And how they going to get to court? You going to protect them?

PARNELL: The police will protect them. Or the State troopers –

GEORGE: That's a good one!

PARNELL: Or Federal marshals.

GEORGE: Look here, you really think there should be niggers on that jury?

PARNELL: Of course I do, and so would you, if you had any sense. For one thing, they're forty-four per cent of the population of this town.

ELLIS: But they don't vote. Not most of them.

PARNELL: Well. That's also a matter of interest to the Federal government. Why *don't* they vote? They got hands.

ELLIS: You claim Lyle's your buddy –

PARNELL: Lyle *is* my buddy. That's why I want him to have a fair trial.

HAZEL: I can't listen to no more of this, I'm sorry, I just can't. Honey, I'll see you all tonight, you hear?

REV. PHELPS: We're all going to go now. We just wanted to see how you were, and let you know that you could count on us.

LYLE: I sure appreciate it, Reverend, believe me, I do. You

make me feel much better. Even if a man knows he ain't done no wrong, still, it's a kind of troublesome spot to be in. Wasn't for my good Jo, here, I don't know what I'd do. Good morning, Mrs Barker. Mrs Proctor. So long, George, it's been good to see you. Ralph, you take good care of Susan, you hear? And name the first one after me – you might have to bring it on up to the jail house so I can see it.

SUSAN: Don't think like that. Everything's going to be all right.

LYLE: You're sure?

SUSAN: I guarantee it. Why they couldn't – *couldn't* – do anything to you!

LYLE: Then I believe it. I believe *you*.

SUSAN: You keep right on believing.

ELLIS: Remember what we said, Parnell.

PARNELL: So long, Ellis. See you next Halloween.

LYLE: Let's get together, boy, soon as this mess is over.

ELLIS: You bet. This mess is just about over now – we ain't going to let them prolong it. And I know just the thing'll knock all this clear out of your mind, this, and everything else, ha-ha! Bye-bye, Mrs Britten.

JO: Goodbye. And thanks for coming!

HAZEL, LILLIAN, SUSAN, RALPH, ELLIS, REVEREND PHELPS and GEORGE exit.

LYLE: They're nice people.

JO: Yes. They are.

PARNELL: They certainly think a lot of you.

LYLE: You ain't jealous, are you, boy? No. We've all had the same kind of trouble – it's the kind of trouble you wouldn't know about, Parnell, because you've never had to worry about making your living. But me! I been doing hard work from the time I was a puppy. Like my Mama and Daddy before me, God rest their souls, and their Mama and Daddy before them. They wore themselves out on the land – the land never give them nothing. Nothing but an empty belly and some skinny kids. I'm the only one growed up to be a man. That's because I take after my Daddy – he was skinny as a piece of wire, but he was hard as any rock. And stubborn! Lord, you ain't never see nobody so stubborn. He should have been born sooner. Had he been born sooner, when this was still a free country, and a man could really *make* some money, I'd have been born rich as you, Parnell, maybe even richer. I tell you – the old man struggled. He worked harder than any nigger. But he left me this store.

JO: You reckon we going to be able to leave it to the little one?

LYLE: We're going to leave him more than that. That little one ain't going to have nothing to worry about. I'm going to leave him as rich as old Parnell here, and he's going to be educated, too, better than his Daddy; better, even, than Parnell!

PARNELL: You going to send him to school in Switzerland?

LYLE: *You* went there for a while, didn't you?

JO: That's where Parnell picked up all his wild ideas.

PARNELL: Yes. Be careful. There were a couple of African princes studying in the school I went to – they did a lot more studying than I did, I must say.

LYLE: African princes, huh? What were they like? Big and black, I bet, elephant tusks hanging around their necks.

PARNELL: Some of them wore a little ivory, on a chain – silver chain. They were like everybody else. Maybe they thought they were a little *better* than most of us – the Swiss girls certainly thought so.

LYLE: The *Swiss* girls? You mean they didn't have no women of their own?

PARNELL: Lots of them. Swiss women, Danish women, English women, French women, Finns, Russians, even a couple of Americans.

JO: I don't believe you. Or else they was just trying to act like foreigners. I can't stand people who try to act like something they're not.

PARNELL: They were just trying to act like women – poor things. And the Africans were men, no one had ever told them that they weren't.

LYLE: You mean there weren't no African women around at *all*? Weren't the Swiss people kind of upset at having all these niggers around with no women?

PARNELL: They didn't seem to be upset. They seemed delighted. The niggers had an awful lot of money. And there weren't many African girls around because African girls aren't educated the way American girls are.

JO: The American girls didn't *mind* going out with the Africans?

PARNELL: Not at all. It appears that the Africans were excellent dancers.

LYLE: I won't never send no daughter of mine to Switzerland.

PARNELL: Well, what about your son? *He* might grow fond of some little African princess.

LYLE: Well, that's different. I don't care about that, long as he leaves her over there.

JO: It's *not* different – how can you say that? White men ain't got no more business fooling around with black women than –

LYLE: Girl, will you stop getting yourself into an uproar? Men is different from women – they ain't as delicate. Man can do a lot of things a woman can't do, you know that.

PARNELL: You've heard the expression, sowing wild oats? Well, all the men we know sowed a lot of wild oats before they finally settled down and got married.

LYLE: That's right. Men *have* to do it. They ain't like women. Parnell is *still* sowing his wild oats – I sowed mine.

JO: And a woman that wants to be a decent woman just has to – *wait* – until the men get tired of going to bed with – harlots! – and decide to settle down?

PARNELL: Well, it sounds very unjust, I know, but that's the way it's always been. I *suppose* the decent women were waiting – though nobody seems to know *exactly* how they spent the time.

JO: Parnell!

PARNELL: Well, there *are* some who waited too long.

JO: Men ought to be ashamed. How can you blame a woman if she – goes wrong? If a decent woman can't find a decent man – why – it must happen all the time – they get tired of waiting.

LYLE: Not if they been raised right, no sir, that's what my Daddy said, and I've never known it to fail. And look at you – *you* didn't get tired of waiting. Ain't nobody in this town ever been able to say a word against you. Man, I was so scared when I finally asked this girl to marry me. I was afraid she'd turn me out of the house. Because I had been pretty wild. Parnell can tell you.

JO: I had heard.

LYLE: But she didn't. I looked at her, it seemed almost like it was the first time – you know, the first time you really *look* at a woman? – and I thought, I'll be damned if I don't believe I can make it with her. I believe I can. And she looked at me like she loved me. It was in her eyes. And it was just like somebody had lifted a great big load off my heart.

JO: You shouldn't be saying these things in front of Parnell.

LYLE: Why not? I ain't got no secrets from Parnell – he knows about men and women. Look at her blush! Like I told you. Women is more delicate than men.

He touches her face lightly.

I know you kind of upset, sugar. But don't you be nervous. Everything's going to be all right, and we're going to be happy again, you'll see.

JO: I hope so, Lyle.

LYLE: I'm going to take me a bath and put some clothes on. Parnell, you sit right there, you hear? I won't be but a minute.

Exits.

JO: What a funny man he is! It don't do no good at all to get mad at him, you might as well get mad at that baby in there. Parnell? Can I ask you something?

PARNELL: Certainly.

JO: Is it true that Lyle has no secrets from you?

PARNELL: He said that *neither* of you had any secrets from me.

JO: Oh, don't play. Lyle don't know a thing about women – what they're really like, to themselves. Men don't know. But I want to ask you a serious question. Will you answer it?

PARNELL: If I can.

JO: That means you won't answer it. But I'll ask it, anyway. Parnell – was Lyle – is it true what people said? That he was having an affair with Old Bill's wife and that's why he shot Old Bill?

PARNELL: Why are you asking me that?

JO: Because I have to know! It's true, isn't it? He had an affair with Old Bill's wife – and he had affairs with lots of coloured women in this town. It's *true*. Isn't it?

PARNELL: What does it matter who he slept with before he married you, Jo? I know he had a – lot of prostitutes. Maybe some of them were coloured. When he was drunk, he wouldn't have been particular.

JO: He's never talked to you about it?

PARNELL: Why would he?

JO: Men talk about things like that.

PARNELL: Men often joke about things like that. But, Jo – what one man tells another man, his friend – can't be told to women.

JO: Men certainly stick together. I wish women did. All right. You can't talk about Lyle. But tell me this. Have *you* ever had an affair with a coloured girl? I don't mean a – a *night*. I mean, did she mean something to you, did you like her, did you – love her? Could you have married her – I mean, just like you would marry a white woman?

PARNELL: Jo –

JO: Oh! Tell me the truth, Parnell!

PARNELL: I loved a coloured girl, yes. I think I loved her. But I was only eighteen and she was only seventeen. I was still a virgin. I don't know if she was, but I think she was. A lot of the other kids in school used to drive over to niggertown at night to try and find black women. Sometimes they bought them, sometimes they frightened them, sometimes they raped them. And they were proud of it, they talked about it all the time. I couldn't do that. Those kids made me ashamed of my own body, ashamed of everything I felt, ashamed of being white –

JO: Ashamed of being white.

PARNELL: Yes.

JO: How did you meet – this coloured girl?

PARNELL: Her mother worked for us. She used to come, sometimes, to pick up her mother. Sometimes she had to wait. I came in once and found her in the library, she was reading Stendhal. *The Red and The Black*. I had just read it and we talked about it. She was funny – very bright and solemn and very proud – and she was *scared*, scared of me, but much too proud to show it. Oh, she was funny. But she was bright.

JO: What did she look like?

PARNELL: She was the colour of gingerbread when it's just come out of the oven. I used to call her Ginger – later. Her name was really Pearl. She had black hair, very black, kind of short, and she dressed it very carefully. Later, I used to tease her about the way she took care of her hair. There's a girl in this town now who reminds me of her. Oh, I loved her!

JO: What happened?

PARNELL: I used to look at her, the way she moved, so beautiful and free, and I'd wonder if at night, when she might be on her way home from some place, any of those boys at school had said ugly things to her. And then I thought that I wasn't any better than they were, because I thought my own thoughts were pretty awful. And I wondered what she thought of me. But I didn't dare to ask. I got so I could hardly think of anyone but her. I got sick wanting to take her in my arms, to take her in my arms and love her and protect her from all those other people who wanted to destroy her. She wrote a little poetry, sometimes she'd show it to me, but she really wanted to be a painter.

JO: What happened?

PARNELL: Nothing happened. We got so we told each other everything. She was going to be a painter, I was going to be a writer. It was our secret. Nobody in the world knew about her *inside*, what she was like, and how she dreamed, but me. And nobody in the world knew about *me* inside, what I wanted, and how I dreamed, but her. But we couldn't look ahead, we didn't dare. We talked about going North, but I was still in school, and she was still in school. We couldn't be seen anywhere together – it would have given her too bad a name. I used to see her sometimes in the movies, with various coloured boys. She didn't seem to have any special one. They'd be sitting in the balcony, in the coloured section, and I'd be sitting downstairs in the white section. She couldn't come down to me, I couldn't go up to her. We'd meet some nights, late, out in the country, but – I didn't want to take her in the bushes, and I couldn't take her anywhere else. One day we were sitting in the library, we were kissing, and her mother came in. That was the day I found out how much black people can hate white people.

JO: What did her mother do?

PARNELL: She didn't say a word. She just looked at me. She just looked at me. I could see what was happening in her mind. She knew that there wasn't any point in complaining to my mother or my father. It would just make her daughter look bad. She didn't dare tell her husband. If he tried to do anything, he'd be killed. There wasn't anything she could do about me. I was just another horny white kid trying to get into a black girl's pants. She looked at me as though she were wishing with all her heart that she could raise her hand and wipe me off the face of the earth. I'll never forget that look. I still see it. She walked over to Pearl and I thought she was going to slap her. But she didn't. She took her by the hand, very sadly, and all she said was, 'I'm ready to go now. Come on.' And she took Pearl out of the room.

JO: Did you ever see her again?

PARNELL: No. Her mother sent her away.

JO: But you forgot her? You must have had lots of other girls right quick, right after that.

PARNELL: I never forgot her.

JO: Do you think of her – even when you're with Loretta?

PARNELL: Not all of the time, Jo. But some of the time – yes.

JO: And if you found her again?

PARNELL: If I found her again – yes, I'd marry her. I'd give her the children I've always wanted to have.

JO: Oh, Parnell! If you felt that way about her, if you've felt it all this time!

PARNELL: Yes. I know. I'm a renegade white man.

JO: Then Lyle could have felt that way about Old Bill's wife – about Willa Mae. I know that's not the way he feels about me. And if he felt that way – he could have shot Old Bill – to keep him quiet!

PARNELL: Jo!

JO: Yes! And if he could have shot Old Bill to keep him quiet – he could have killed that boy. He could have killed that boy. And if he did – well – that *is* murder, isn't it? It's just nothing but murder, even if the boy *was* black. Oh, Parnell! Parnell!

PARNELL: Jo, please. Please, Jo. Be quiet.

LYLE: (*Off.*) What's all that racket in there?

PARNELL: I'm telling your wife the story of my life.

LYLE: (*Off.*) Sounds pretty goddamn active.

PARNELL: You've never asked him, have you, Jo?

JO: No. No. No.

PARNELL: Well, *I* asked him –

JO: When?

PARNELL: Well, I didn't really *ask* him. But he said he didn't do it, that it wasn't true. You heard him. He wouldn't lie to me.

JO: No. He wouldn't lie to you. They say some of the niggers have guns – did you hear that?

PARNELL: Yes. I've heard it. But it's not true.

JO: *They* wouldn't lie to you, either? I've just had too much time to worry, I guess – brood and worry. Lyle's away so often nights – he spends so much time at that store. I don't know what he does there. And when he comes home, he's just dead – and he drops right off to sleep.

LYLE *enters, carrying the child.*

Hi, honey. What a transformation. You look like you used to look when you come courting.

LYLE: I sure didn't come courting carrying no baby. He was awake, just singing away, and carrying on with his toes. He acts like he thinks he's got a whole lot of candy attached to the end of his legs. Here. It's about time for him to eat, ain't it? How come you looking at me like that? Why you being so nice to me, all of a sudden?

PARNELL: I've been lecturing her on the duties of a wife.

LYLE: That so? Well, come on, boy, let's you and me walk down the road a piece. Believe I'll buy you a drink. You ain't ashamed to be seen with me, I hope?

PARNELL: No, I'm not ashamed to be seen with you.

JO: You going to be home for supper?

LYLE: Yeah, sugar. Come on, Parnell.

JO: You come, too, Parnell, you and Loretta, if you're free. We'd love to have you.

PARNELL: We'll try to make it. So long, Jo.

JO: So long.

They exit. JO *walks to the window. Turns back into the room, smiles down at the baby. Sings.*

Hush, little baby, don't say a word,

Mama's going to buy you a mocking bird –
But you don't want no mocking bird right now, do you?
I know what you want. You want something to eat. All
right, Mama's going to feed you.

Sits, slowly begins to unbutton her blouse. Sings.

If that mocking bird don't sing,
Mama's going to buy you a diamond ring.

(LYLE's *store: Early evening. Both* LYLE *and* PARNELL *are a
little drunk.*)

LYLE: Didn't you ever get like that? Sure, you must have got
like that sometimes – just restless! You got everything
you need and you can't complain about nothing – and
yet, look like, you just can't be satisfied. Didn't you ever
get like that? I swear, men is mighty strange! I'm kind of
restless now.

PARNELL: What's the matter with you? You worried about
the trial?

LYLE: No, I ain't worried about the trial. I ain't even mad
at you, Parnell. Some folks think I should be, but I ain't
mad at you. They don't know you like I know you. I
ain't fooled by all your wild ideas. We both white and
we both from around here, and we been buddies all our
lives. That's all that counts. I know you ain't going to let
nothing happen to me.

PARNELL: That's good to hear.

LYLE: After all the trouble started in this town – but before
that crazy boy got himself killed, soon after he got here
and started raising all that hell – I started thinking about
her, about Willa Mae, more and more and more. She was
too young for him. Old Bill, he was sixty if he was a day,
he wasn't doing her no good. Yet and still, the first time I
took Willa Mae, I had to fight her. I swear I did. Maybe
she was frightened. But I never had to fight her again. No.
It was good, boy, let me tell you, and she liked it as much
as me. Hey! You still with me?

PARNELL: I'm still with you. Go on.

LYLE: What's the last thing I said?

PARNELL: That she liked it as much as you – which I find hard
to believe.

LYLE: Ha-ha! I'm telling you. I never had it for nobody bad
as I had it for her.

PARNELL: When did Old Bill find out?

LYLE: Old Bill? He wouldn't never have thought nothing if
people hadn't started poisoning his mind. People started
talking just because my Daddy wasn't well and she was up
at the house so much because somebody had to look after
him. First they said she was carrying on with *him*. Hell,
my Daddy would sure have been willing, but he was far
from able. He was really wore out by that time and he just
wanted rest. Then people started to saying that it was me.

PARNELL: Old Bill ever talk to you about it?

LYLE: How was he going to talk to me about it? Hell, we was

right good friends. Many's the time I helped Old Bill out
when his cash was low. I used to load Willa Mae up with
things from the kitchen just to make sure they didn't go
hungry.

PARNELL: Old Bill never mentioned it to you? Never? He
never gave you any reason to think he knew about it?

LYLE: Well, I don't know what was going on in his *mind*,
Parnell. You can't never see what's in anybody else's *mind*
– you know that. He didn't *act* no different. Hell, like
I say, she was young enough to be his grand-daughter
damn near, so I figured he thought it might be a pretty
good arrangement – me doing *his* work, ha-ha! because
he damn sure couldn't do it no more, and helping him to
stay alive.

PARNELL: Then why was he so mad at you the last time you
saw him?

LYLE: Like I said, he accused me of cheating him. And I ain't
never cheated a black man in my life. I hate to say it,
because we've always been good friends, but sometimes I
think it might have been Joel – Papa D. – who told him
that. Old Bill wasn't too good at figuring.

PARNELL: Why would Papa D. tell him a thing like that?

LYLE: I think he might have been a little jealous.

PARNELL: Jealous? You mean, of you and Willa Mae?

LYLE: Yeah. He ain't really an old man, you know. But I'm
sure he didn't mean – for things to turn out like they did.
(*A pause.*) I can still see him – the way he looked when
he come into this store.

PARNELL: The way *who* looked when he came into this store?

LYLE: Why – Old Bill. He looked crazy. Like he wanted to
kill me. He *did* want to kill me. Crazy nigger.

PARNELL: I thought you meant the other one. But the other
one didn't die in the store.

LYLE: Old Bill didn't die in the store. He died over yonder,
in the road.

PARNELL: I thought you were talking about Richard Henry.

LYLE: That crazy boy. Yeah, he come in here. I don't know
what was the matter with him, he hadn't seen me but
one time in his life before. And I treated him like – like I
would have treated *any* man.

PARNELL: I heard about it. It was in Papa D.'s joint. He was
surrounded by niggers – or *you* were –

LYLE: He was dancing with one of them crazy young ones –
the real pretty nigger girl – what's her name?

PARNELL: Juanita.

LYLE: That's the one. (*Juke box music, soft. Voices. Laughter.*)
Yeah. He looked at me like he wanted to kill me. And he
insulted my wife. And I hadn't never done him no harm.
(*As above, a little stronger.*) But I been thinking about it.
And you know what I think? Hey! You gone to sleep?

PARNELL: No. I'm thinking.

LYLE: What you thinking about?

PARNELL: Us. You and me.

LYLE: And what do you think about us – you and me? What's

the point of thinking about us, anyway? We've been buddies all our lives – we can't stop being buddies now.

PARNELL: That's right, buddy. What were you about to say?

LYLE: Oh. I think a lot of the niggers in this town, especially the young ones, is turned bad. And I believe they was egging him on.

A pause. The music stops.

He come in here one Monday afternoon. Everybody heard about it, it was all over this town quicker'n a jackrabbit gets his nuts off. You just missed it. You'd just walked out of here.

(*LYLE rises, walks to the doors and opens them. Sunlight fills the room. He slams the screen door shut; we see the road.*)

JO: (*Off.*) Lyle, you want to help me bring this baby carriage inside? It's getting kind of hot out here now.

PARNELL: Let *me.*

LYLE and PARNELL bring in the baby carriage. JO enters.

JO: My, it's hot! Wish we'd gone for a ride or something. Declare to goodness, we ain't got no reason to be sitting around this store. Ain't nobody coming in here – not to *buy* anything, anyway.

PARNELL: I'll buy some bubble gum.

JO: You know you don't chew bubble gum.

PARNELL: Well, then, I'll buy some cigarettes.

JO: Two cartons, or three? It's all right, Parnell, the Britten family's going to make it somehow.

LYLE: Couple of niggers coming down the road. Maybe they'll drop in for a Coke.

Exits, into back of store.

JO: Why no, they won't. Our Cokes is *poisoned.* I get up every morning before daybreak and drop the arsenic in myself.

PARNELL: Well, then, I won't have a Coke. See you, Jo. So long, Lyle!

LYLE: (*Off.*) Be seeing you!

PARNELL exits. Silence for a few seconds. Then we hear LYLE hammering in the back. JO picks up a magazine, begins to read. Voices. RICHARD and LORENZO appear in the road.

RICHARD: Hey, you want a Coke? I'm thirsty.

LORENZO: Let's go on a little further.

RICHARD: Man, we been walking for *days,* my mouth is as dry as that damn dusty road. Come on, have a Coke with me, won't take but a minute.

LORENZO: We don't trade in there. Come on –

RICHARD: Oh! Is this the place? Hell, I'd like to get another look at the peckerwood, ain't going to give him but a dime. I want to get his face fixed in my *mind,* so there won't be no time wasted when the time comes, you dig? (*Enters the store.*) Hey, Mrs Ofay Ednolbay Ydalay! you got any Coca Cola for sale?

JO: What?

RICHARD: Coke! Me and my man been toting barges and lifting bales, that's right, we been slaving, and we need a little cool. Liquid. Refreshment. Yeah, and you can take that hammer, too.

JO: Boy, what do you want?

RICHARD: A Coca Cola, ma'am. Please ma'am.

JO: They right in the box there.

RICHARD: Thank you kindly. (*Takes two Cokes, opens them.*) Oh, this is fine, *fine.* Did you put them in this box with your own little dainty dish-pan hands? Sure makes them taste *sweet.*

JO: Are you talking to me?

RICHARD: No ma'am, just feel like talking to myself from time to time, makes the time pass faster. (*At screen door.*) Hey, Lorenzo, I got you a Coke.

LORENZO: I don't want it. Come on out of there.

JO: That will be twenty cents.

RICHARD: *Twenty* cents? All right. Don't you know how to say please? All the women *I* know say please – of course, they ain't as pretty as you. I ain't got twenty cents, ma'am. All I got is – twenty dollars!

JO: You ain't got nothing smaller?

RICHARD: No ma'am. You see, I don't never carry on me more cash than I can afford to *lose.*

JO: Lyle! (*LYLE enters, carrying the hammer.*) You got any change?

LYLE: Change for a twenty? No, you know I ain't got it.

RICHARD: You all got this big, fine store and all – and you ain't got change for *twenty* dollars?

LYLE: It's early in the day, boy.

RICHARD: It ain't that early. I thought white folks was rich at *every* hour of the day.

LYLE: Now, if you looking for trouble, you just might get it. That boy outside – ain't he got twenty cents?

RICHARD: That boy outside is about twenty-four years old, and he ain't got twenty cents. Ain't no need to ask him.

LYLE: (*At the door.*) Boy! You got twenty cents?

LORENZO: Come on out of there, Richard! I'm tired of hanging around here!

LYLE: Boy, didn't you hear what I asked you?

LORENZO: Mister Britten, I ain't *in* the store, and I ain't *bought* nothing in the store, and so I ain't *got* to tell you whether or not I got twenty cents!

RICHARD: Maybe your wife could run home and get some change. You *got* some change at home, I know. Don't you?

LYLE: I don't stand for nobody to talk about my wife.

RICHARD: I only said you was a lucky man to have so fine a *wife.* I said maybe she could run *home* and look and see if there was any change – in the *home.*

LYLE: I seen you before some place. You that crazy nigger. You ain't from around here.

RICHARD: You *know* you seen me. And you remember where. And when. I was born right here, in this town. I'm Reverend Meridian Henry's son.

LYLE: You say that like you thought your Daddy's name was some kind of protection. He ain't no protection against *me* – him, nor that boy outside, neither.

RICHARD: I don't need no protection, do I? Not in my own home town, in the good old USA. I just dropped by to sip on a Coke in a simple country store – and come to find out the joker ain't got enough bread to change twenty dollars. Stud ain't got *nothing* – you people been spoofing the public, man.

LYLE: You put them Cokes down and get out of here.

RICHARD: I ain't finished yet. And I ain't changed my bill yet.

LYLE: Well, I ain't going to change that bill, and you ain't going to finish them Cokes. You get your black ass out of here – go on! If you got any sense, you'll get your black ass out of this town.

RICHARD: You don't own this town, you white mother-fucker. You don't *even* own twenty dollars. Don't you raise that hammer. I'll take it and beat your skull to jelly.

JO: Lyle! Don't you fight that boy! He's crazy! I'm going to call the Sheriff! (*Starts towards the back, returns to counter.*) The baby! Lyle! Watch out for the baby!

RICHARD: A baby, huh? How many times did you have to try for it, you no-good, ball-less peckerwood? I'm surprised you could even get it up – look at the way you sweating now.

LYLE raises the hammer. RICHARD grabs his arm, forcing it back. They struggle.

JO: Lyle! The baby!

LORENZO: Richard!

He comes into the store.

JO: Please get that boy out of here, get that boy out of here – he's going to get himself killed.

RICHARD knocks the hammer from LYLE's hand, and knocks LYLE down. The hammer spins across the room. LORENZO picks it up.

LORENZO: I don't think your husband's going to kill no more black men. Not today, Mrs Britten. Come on, Richard. Let's go.

LYLE looks up at them.

LYLE: It took two of you. Remember that.

LORENZO: I didn't lay a hand on you, Mister Britten. You just ain't no match for – a *boy*. Not without your gun you ain't. Come on, Richard.

JO: You'll go to jail for this! You'll go to jail! For years!

LORENZO: We've been in jail for years. I'll leave your hammer over at Papa D.'s joint – don't look like you're going to be doing no more work today.

RICHARD: (*Laughs.*) Look at the mighty peckerwood! On his *ass*, baby – and his woman watching! Now, who you think is the better man? Ha-ha! The master race! You let me

in that tired white chick's drawers, she'll know who's the master! Ha-ha-ha!

(*Exits. RICHARD's laughter continues in the dark. LYLE and PARNELL as before.*)

LYLE: Niggers was laughing at me for days. Everywhere I went.

PARNELL: You never did call the Sheriff.

LYLE: No.

PARNELL fills their glasses. We hear singing.

PARNELL: It's almost time for his funeral.

LYLE: And may every nigger like that nigger end like that nigger – face down in the weeds!

A pause.

PARNELL: Was he lying face down?

LYLE: Hell, yeah, he was face down. Said so in the papers.

PARNELL: Is that what the papers said? I don't remember.

LYLE: Yeah, that's what the papers said.

PARNELL: I guess they had to turn him over – to make sure it was him.

LYLE: I reckon. (*Laughs.*) Yeah. I reckon.

PARNELL: You and me are buddies, huh?

LYLE: *Yeah*, we're buddies – to the end!

PARNELL: I always wondered why you wanted to be my buddy. A lot of poor guys hate rich guys. I always wondered why you weren't like that.

LYLE: I ain't like that. Hell, Parnell, you're smarter than me. I know it. I used to wonder what made you smarter than me. I got to be your buddy so I could find out. Because, hell, you didn't seem so different in *other* ways – in spite of all your *ideas*. Two things we always had in common – liquor and poon-tang. We couldn't get enough of neither one. Of course, your liquor might have been a little better. But I doubt if the other could have been any better!

PARNELL: Did you find out what made me smarter?

LYLE: Yeah. You richer!

PARNELL: I'm richer! That's all you got to tell me – about Richard Henry?

LYLE: Ain't nothing more to tell. Wait till after the trial. You won't have to ask me no more questions then!

PARNELL: I've got to get to the funeral.

LYLE: Don't run off. Don't leave me here alone.

PARNELL: You're supposed to be home for supper.

LYLE: Supper can wait. Have another drink with me – be my buddy. Don't leave me here alone. Listen to them! Singing and praying! Singing and praying and laughing behind a man's back!

(*The singing continues in the dark. BLACKTOWN: The church, packed. MERIDIAN in the pulpit, the bier just below him.*)

MERIDIAN: My heart is heavier tonight than it has ever been before. I raise my voice to you tonight out of a sorrow and a wonder I have never felt before. Not only I, my Lord, am in this case. Everyone under the sound of my voice, and many more souls than that, feel as I feel, and tremble as I tremble, and bleed as I bleed. It is not that the days are dark – we have known dark days. It is not only that the blood runs down and no man helps us; it is not only that our children are destroyed before our eyes. It is not only that our lives, from day to day and every hour of each day, are menaced by the people among whom you have set us down. We have borne all these things, my Lord, and we have done what the prophets of old could not do, we have sung the Lord's song in a strange land. In a strange land! What was the sin committed by our forefathers in the time that has vanished on the other side of the flood, which has had to be expiated by chains, by the lash, by hunger and thirst, by slaughter, by fire, by the rope, by the knife, and for so many generations, on these wild shores, in this strange land? Our offence must have been mighty, our crime immeasurable. But it is not the past which makes our hearts so heavy. It is the present. Lord, where is our hope? Who, or what, shall touch the hearts of this headlong and unthinking people and turn them back from destruction? When will they hear the words of John? *I know thy works, that thou art neither cold nor hot: I would that thou wert cold or hot. So, then because thou art lukewarm and neither cold nor hot, I will spew thee out of my mouth. Because thou sayest, I am rich and increased with goods, and have need of nothing; and knowest not that thou art wretched and miserable and poor and blind and naked.* Now, when the children come, my Lord, and ask which road to follow, my tongue stammers and my heart fails. I will not abandon the land – this strange land, which is my home. But can I ask the children for ever to sustain the cruelty inflicted on them by those who have been their masters, and who are now, in very truth, their kinfolk, their brothers and their sisters and their parents? What hope is there for a people who deny their deeds and disown their kinsmen and who do so in the name of purity and love, in the name of Jesus Christ? What a light, my Lord, is needed to conquer so mighty a darkness! This darkness rules in us, and grows, in black and white alike. I have set my face against the darkness, I will not let it conquer me, even though it will, I know, one day, destroy this body. But, my Lord, what of the children? What shall I tell the children? I must be with you, Lord, like Jacob, and wrestle with you until the light appears – I will not let you go until you give me a sign! A sign that in the terrible Sahara of our time a fountain may spring, the fountain of a true morality, and bring us closer, oh, my Lord, to that peace on earth desired by so few throughout so many ages. Let not our suffering endure for ever. Teach us to trust the great gift of life and learn to love one another and dare to walk the earth like men. Amen.

MOTHER HENRY: Let's file up, children, and say goodbye.

Sing: 'Great Getting-Up Morning.' MERIDIAN *steps down from the pulpit.* MERIDIAN, LORENZO, JIMMY *and* PETE *shoulder the bier. A dishevelled* PARNELL *enters. The Congregation and the Pallbearers file past him.* JUANITA *stops.*

JUANITA: What's the matter, Parnell? You look sick.

PARNELL: I tried to come sooner. I couldn't get away. Lyle wouldn't let me go.

JUANITA: Were you trying to beat a confession out of him? But you look as though he's been trying to beat a confession out of you. Poor Parnell!

PARNELL: Poor Lyle! He'll never confess. Never. Poor devil!

JUANITA: Poor devil! You weep for Lyle. You're luckier than I am. I can't weep in front of others. I can't say goodbye in front of others. Others don't know what it is you're saying goodbye to.

PARNELL: You loved him.

JUANITA: Yes.

PARNELL: I didn't know.

JUANITA: Ah, you're so lucky, Parnell. I know you didn't know. Tell me, where do you live, Parnell? How can you not know all of the things you do not know?

PARNELL: Why are you hitting out at me? I never thought you cared that much about me. But – oh, Juanita! There are so many things I've never been able to say!

JUANITA: There are so many things you've never been able to hear.

PARNELL: And – you've tried to tell me some of those things?

JUANITA: I used to watch you roaring through this town like a St George thirsty for dragons. And I wanted to let you know you haven't got to do all that; dragons aren't hard to find, they're everywhere. And nobody wants you to be St George. We just want you to be Parnell. But, of course, that's much harder.

PARNELL: Are we friends, Juanita? Please say that we're friends.

JUANITA: Friends is not exactly what you mean, Parnell. Tell the truth.

PARNELL: Yes. I've always wanted more than that, from you. But I was afraid you would misunderstand me. That you would feel that I was only trying to exploit you. In another way.

JUANITA: You've been a grown man for a long time now, Parnell. You ought to trust yourself more than that.

PARNELL: I've been a grown man far too long – ever to have dared to dream of offering myself to you.

JUANITA: Your age was never the question, Parnell.

PARNELL: Was there ever any question at all?

JUANITA: Yes. Yes. Yes, once there was.

PARNELL: And there isn't – there can't be – any more?

JUANITA: No. That train has gone. One day, I'll recover. I'm sure that I'll recover. And I'll see the world again – the marvellous world. And I'll have learned from Richard – how to love. I must. I can't let him die for nothing.

Juke box music, loud. The lights change, spot on PARNELL's *face.*

JUANITA steps across the aisle. RICHARD appears. They dance. PARNELL watches.

Act 3

Two months later. The courtroom.

The courtroom is extremely high, domed, a blinding white emphasized by a dull, somehow ominous gold. The JUDGE's stand is centre stage, and at a height. Sloping down from this place on either side are the black and white TOWNSPEOPLE; the JURY; PHOTOGRAPHERS and JOURNALISTS from all over the world; microphones and TV cameras. All windows open: one should be aware of masses of people outside and one should sometimes hear their voices – their roar – as well as singing from the church. The church is directly across the street from the courtroom, and the steeple and the cross are visible throughout the act.

Each witness, when called, is revealed behind scrim and passes through two or three tableaux before moving down the aisle to the witness stand. The witness stand is downstage, in the same place and at the same angle as the pulpit in Acts 1 and 2.

Before the curtain rises, song: 'I Said I Wasn't Going To Tell Nobody, But I Couldn't Keep It To Myself.'

The JUDGE's gavel breaks across the singing, and the curtain rises.

CLERK: (*Calling.*) Mrs Josephine Gladys Britten!

(*JO, serving coffee at a church social. She passes out coffee to invisible guests.*)

JO: Am I going to spend the rest of my life serving coffee to strangers in church basements? Am I? – Yes! Reverend Phelps was truly noble! As *usual!* – Reverend Phelps has been married for more than twenty years. Don't let those thoughts into your citadel! You just remember that the mind is a citadel and you can keep out all troubling thoughts! – My! Mrs Evans! you are certainly a sight for sore eyes! I don't know how you manage to look so unruffled and *cool* and *young!* With all those *children.* And Mr Evans. How are you tonight? – She has a baby just about every year. I don't know how she stands it. Mr Evans don't look like that kind of man. You sure can't tell a book by its cover. Lord! I wish I was in my own home and these were *my* guests and my husband was somewhere in the room. I'm getting old! Old! Old maid! *Maid!* – Oh! Mr Arpino! You taken time out from your engineering to come visit here with us? It sure is a pleasure to have you! – My! He is big! and dark! Like a Greek! or a Spaniard! Some people say he might have a touch of nigger blood I don't believe that. He's just – *foreign.* That's all. He needs a hair cut. I wonder if he's got hair like that all *over* his body? Remember that your mind is a citadel. A citadel. Oh, Lord, I'm tired of serving coffee in church basements! I want, I want – Why, good evening, Ellis! And Mr Lyle Britten! We sure don't see either of *you* very often! Why, Mr Britten! You know you don't mean that! You come

over here just to see little old *me?* Why, you just go right ahead and drink that coffee, I do believe you need to be sobered up!

(*The light changes.*)

REV. PHELPS: (*Voice.*) Do you, Josephine Gladys Miles, take this man, Lyle Britten, Jr., as your lawfully wedded husband, to have and to hold, to love and to cherish, in sickness and in health, till death do you part?

JO: I do. I *do!* Oh, Lyle. I'll make you the best wife any man ever had. I *will.* Love me. Please love me. Look at me! *Look* at me! He *wanted* me. He wanted *me!* I am – Mrs Josephine Gladys Britten!

(*The light changes again, and JO takes the stand. We hear the baby crying.*)

BLACKTOWN: Man, that's the southern white lady you supposed to be willing to risk death for!

WHITETOWN: You know, this is a kind of hanging in reverse? Niggers out here to watch us being hanged!

THE STATE: What is your relationship to the accused?

JO: I am his wife.

THE STATE: Will you please tell us, in your own words, of your first meeting with the deceased, Richard Henry?

WHITETOWN: Don't be afraid. Just tell the truth.

BLACKTOWN: Here we go – down the river!

JO: Well, I was in the store, sitting at the counter, and pretty soon this coloured boy come in, loud, and talking in just the most awful way. I didn't recognize him, I just knew he wasn't one of *our* coloured people. His language was something awful, awful!

THE STATE: He was insulting? Was he insulting, Mrs Britten?

JO: He said all kinds of things, dirty things, like – well – just like I might have been a coloured girl, that's what it sounded like to me. Just like some little coloured girl he might have met on a street corner and wanted – wanted to – for a night! And I was scared. I hadn't seen a coloured boy act like him before. He acted like he was drunk or crazy or maybe he was under the influence of that dope. I never knew nobody to be *drunk* and act like him. His eyes was just going and he acted like he had a fire in his belly. But I tried to be calm because I didn't want to upset Lyle, you know – Lyle's mighty quick-tempered – and he was working in the back of the store, he was hammering –

THE STATE: Go on, Mrs Britten. What happened then?

JO: Well, he – that boy – wanted to buy him two Cokes because he had a friend outside –

THE STATE: He brought a friend? He did not come there alone? Did this other boy enter the store?

JO: No, not then he didn't – I –

BLACKTOWN: Come on, bitch. We *know* what you going to say. Get it over with.

JO: I – I give him the two Cokes, and he – tried to grab my hands and pull me to him, and – I – I – he pushed himself up against me, real close and hard – and, oh, he was just like an animal, I could – smell him! And he tried to kiss me, he kept whispering these awful, filthy things and I got scared, I yelled for Lyle! Then Lyle come running out of the back – and when the boy seen I wasn't alone in the store, he yelled for this other boy outside and this other boy come rushing in and they both jumped on Lyle and knocked him down.

THE STATE: What made you decide not to report this incident – this unprovoked assault – to the proper authorities, Mrs Britten?

JO: We've had so much trouble in this town!

THE STATE: What sort of trouble, Mrs Britten?

JO: Why, with the coloured people! We've got all these northern agitators coming through here all the time, and stirring them up so that you can't hardly sleep nights!

THE STATE: Then you, as a responsible citizen of this town, were doing your best to keep down trouble? Even though you had been so brutally assaulted by a deranged northern Negro dope addict?

JO: Yes. I didn't want to stir up no more trouble. I *made* Lyle keep quiet about it. I thought it would all blow over. I knew the boy's Daddy was a preacher and that he would talk to the boy about the way he was behaving. It was all over town in a second, anyway! And look like all the coloured people was on the side of that crazy boy. And Lyle's always been real good to coloured people!

Laughter from BLACKTOWN.

THE STATE: On the evening that the alleged crime was committed – or, rather, the morning – very early on the morning of the 24th of August – where were you and your husband, Mrs Britten?

JO: We were home. The next day we heard that the boy was missing.

COUNSEL FOR THE BEREAVED: Doesn't an attempt at sexual assault seem a rather strange thing to do, considering that your store is a public place, with people continually going in and out; that, furthermore, it is located on a public road which people use, on foot and in automobiles, all of the time; and considering that your husband, who has the reputation of being a violent man, and who is, in your own words, 'mighty quick tempered', was working in the back room?

JO: He didn't know Lyle was back there.

COUNSEL FOR THE BEREAVED: But he knew that someone was back there, for, according to your testimony, 'He was hammering.'

JO: Well, I told you the boy was crazy. He had to be crazy. Or he was on that dope.

BLACKTOWN: You ever hear of a junkie trying to rape anybody?

JO: *I didn't say rape!*

COUNSEL FOR THE BEREAVED: Were you struggling in Mr Henry's arms when your husband came out of the back room, carrying his hammer in his hand?

JO: No. I was free then.

COUNSEL FOR THE BEREAVED: Therefore, your husband had only *your* word for the alleged attempted assault! *You* told him that Richard Henry had attempted to assault you? Had made sexual advances to you? Please answer, Mrs Britten!

JO: Yes. I had – I had to – tell him. I'm his wife!

COUNSEL FOR THE BEREAVED: And a most loyal one. You told your husband that Richard Henry had attempted to assault you and then begged him to do nothing about it?

JO: That's right.

COUNSEL FOR THE BEREAVED: And though he was under the impression that his wife had been nearly raped by a Negro, he agreed to forgive and forget and do nothing about it? He agreed neither to call the law, nor to take the law into his own hands?

JO: Yes.

COUNSEL FOR THE BEREAVED: Extraordinary. Mrs Britten, you are aware that Richard Henry met his death some time between the hours of two and five o'clock on the morning of Monday, August 24th?

JO: Yes.

COUNSEL FOR THE BEREAVED: In an earlier statement, several months ago, you stated that your husband had spent that night at the store. You now state that he came in before one o'clock and went to sleep at once. What accounts for this discrepancy?

JO: It's natural. I made a mistake about the time. I got it mixed up with another night. He spent so many nights at that store!

JUDGE: The witness may step down.

JO *leaves the stand.*

CLERK: (*Calls.*) Mr Joel Davis!

(*We hear a shot.* PAPA D. *is facing* LYLE.)

LYLE: Why'd you run down there this morning, shooting your mouth off about me and Willa Mae? Why? You been bringing her up here and taking her back all this time, what got into you this morning? Huh? You jealous, old man? Why you come running back here to tell me everything he said? To tell me how he cursed me out? Have you lost your mind? And we been knowing each other all this time. I don't understand you. She ain't the only girl you done brought here for me. Nigger, do you hear me talking to you?

PAPA D.: I didn't think you'd shoot him, Mr Lyle.

LYLE: I'll shoot any nigger talks to me like that. It was self defence, you hear me? He come in here and tried to kill me. You hear me?

PAPA D.: Yes. Yes sir. I hear you, Mr Lyle.

LYLE: That's right. You don't say the right thing, nigger, I'll blow your brains out, too.

PAPA D.: Yes sir, Mr Lyle.

(*Juke box music.* PAPA D. *takes the stand.*)

WHITETOWN: He's worked hard and saved his money and ain't never had no trouble – why can't they all be like that?

BLACKTOWN: Hey, Papa D.! You can't be walking around here without no handkerchief! You might catch cold – after all *these* years!

PAPA D.: Mr Lyle Britten – he is an *oppressor*. That is the only word for that man. He ain't never give the coloured man no kind of chance. I have tried to reason with that man for *years*. I say, Mr Lyle, look around you. Don't you see that most white folks have changed their way of thinking about us coloured folks? I say, Mr Lyle, we ain't slaves no more and white folks is ready to let us have our chance. Now, why don't you just come on up to where *most* of your people are? and we can make the South a fine place for all of us to live in. That's what I say – and I tried to keep him from being so *hard* on the coloured – because I sure do love my people. And I was the closest thing to Mr Lyle, couldn't nobody else reason with him. But he was *hard* – hard and stubborn. He say, 'My folks lived and died this way, and this is the way I'm going to live and die.' When he was like that couldn't do nothing with him. I know. I've known him since he was born.

WHITETOWN: He's always been real good to you. You were friends!

BLACKTOWN: You loved him! Tell the truth, mother – tell the truth!

PAPA D.: Yes, we were friends. And, yes, I loved him – in my way. Just like he loved me – in his way.

BLACKTOWN: You knew he was going to kill that boy – didn't you? If you knew it, why didn't you stop him?

PAPA D.: Oh. Ain't none of this easy. What it was, both Mr Lyle Britten and me, we both love money. And I did a whole lot of things for him, for a while. Once I had to help him cover up a killing – coloured man – I was in too deep myself by that time – you understand? I know you all understand.

BLACKTOWN: Did he kill that boy?

PAPA D.: He come into my joint the night that boy died. The boy was alone, standing at the juke box. We'd been talking –

(RICHARD, *in the juke box light.*)

If you think you've found all that, Richard – if you think you going to be well now, and you found you somebody who loves you – well, then, I would make tracks out of here. I would –

RICHARD: It's funny, Papa D. I feel like I'm beginning to understand my life – for the first time. I can look back – and it doesn't hurt me like it used to. I want to get Juanita out of here. This is no place for her. They're going to kill her – if she stays here!

PAPA D.: You talk to Juanita about this yet?

RICHARD: No. I haven't talked to nobody about it yet. I just decided it. I guess I'm deciding it now. That's why I'm talking about it now – to you – to see if you'll laugh at me. Do you think she'll laugh at me?

PAPA D.: No. She won't laugh.

RICHARD: I know I can do it. I know I can do it!

PAPA D.: That boy had good sense. He was wild, but he had good sense. And I couldn't blame him too much for being so wild, it seemed to me I knew how he felt.

RICHARD: Papa D., I been in pain and darkness all my life. All my life. And this is the first time in my life I've ever felt – maybe it isn't all like that. Maybe there's more to it than that.

PAPA D.: Lyle Britten come to the door –

(LYLE *enters.*)

He come to the door and he say –

LYLE: You ready for me now, boy? Howdy, Papa D.

PAPA D.: Howdy, Mr Lyle, how's the world been treating you?

LYLE: I can't complain. You ready, boy?

RICHARD: No. I ain't ready. I got a record to play and a drink to finish.

LYLE: You about ready to close, ain't you, Joel?

PAPA D.: Just about, Mr Lyle.

RICHARD: I got a record to play. (*Drops coin: juke box music, loud.*) And a drink to finish.

PAPA D.: He played his record. Lyle Britten never moved from the door. And they just stood there, the two of them, looking at each other. When the record was just about over, the boy come to the bar – he swallowed down the last of his drink.

RICHARD: What do I owe you, Papa D.?

PAPA D.: Oh, you pay me tomorrow. I'm closed now.

RICHARD: What do I owe you, Papa D.? I'm not sure I can pay you tomorrow.

PAPA D.: Give me two dollars.

RICHARD: Here you go. Good night, Papa D. I'm ready, Charlie.

Exits.

PAPA D.: Good night, Richard. Go on home now. Good night, Mr Lyle. Mr Lyle!

LYLE: Good night, Joel. You get you some sleep, you hear?

Exits.

PAPA D.: Mr Lyle! Richard! And I never saw that boy again. Lyle killed him. He killed him. I know it, just like I know I'm sitting in this chair. Just like he shot Old Bill and wasn't nothing never, never, never done about it!

JUDGE: The witness may step down.

PAPA D. *leaves the stand.*

CLERK: (*Calls.*) Mr Lorenzo Shannon!

(*We hear a long, loud, animal cry, lonely and terrified: it is* PETE, *screaming. We discover* LORENZO *and* PETE, *in jail.*

Night. From far away, we hear Students humming, moaning, singing: 'I Woke Up This Morning With My Mind Stayed On Freedom.')

PETE: (*Stammering.*) Lorenzo? Lorenzo. I was dreaming – dreaming – dreaming. I was back in that courtyard and Big Jim Byrd's boys was beating us and beating us and beating us – and Big Jim Byrd was laughing. And Anna Mae Taylor was on her knees, she was trying to pray. She say, 'Oh, Lord, Lord, Lord, come and help us,' and they kept beating on her and beating on her and I saw the blood coming down her neck and they put the prods to her, and, oh, Lorenzo! people was just running around, just crying and moaning and you look to the right and you see somebody go down and you look to the left and you see somebody go down and they was kicking that woman and I say, 'That woman's going to have a baby, don't you kick that woman!' and they say, 'No, she ain't going to have no baby,' and they knocked me down and they got that prod up between my legs and they say, 'You ain't going to be having no babies, neither, nigger!' And then they put that prod to my head – ah! *ah!* – to my *head!* Lorenzo! I can't see right! What have they done to my head? Lorenzo! Lorenzo, am I going to die? Lorenzo – they going to kill us all, ain't they? They mean to kill us all –

LORENZO: Be quiet. Be quiet. They going to come and beat us some more if you don't be quiet.

PETE: Where's Juanita? Did they get Juanita?

LORENZO: I believe Juanita's all right. Go to sleep, Pete. Go to sleep. I won't let you dream. I'll hold you.

(*LORENZO takes the stand.*)

THE STATE: Did you accompany your late and great friend, Richard Henry, on the morning of August 17, to the store which is owned and run by Mr and Mrs Lyle Britten?

LORENZO: We hadn't planned to go there – but we got to walking and talking and we found ourselves there. And it didn't happen like she said. He picked the Cokes out of the box himself, he came to the door with the Cokes in his hand, she hadn't even moved, she was still behind the counter, he never touched that dried out little peckerwood!

WHITETOWN: Get that nigger! Who does that nigger think he is!

BLACKTOWN: Speak, Lorenzo! Go, my man!

THE STATE: You cannot expect this courtroom to believe that so serious a battle was precipitated by the question of twenty cents! There was some other reason. What was this reason? Had he – and you – been drinking?

LORENZO: It was early in the day, Cap'n. We ain't rich enough to drink in the daytime.

THE STATE: Or *smoking*, perhaps? Perhaps your friend had just had his quota of heroin for the day, and was feeling jolly – in a mood to *prove* to you what he had already suggested with those filthy photographs of himself and naked white women!

LORENZO: I never saw no photographs. White women are a problem for white men. We had not been drinking. All we was smoking was that same goddamn tobacco that made *you* rich because we picked it for you for nothing, and carried it to market for you for nothing. And I *know* ain't no heroin in this town because none of you mothers need it. You was *born* frozen. Richard was better than that. I'd rather die than be like you, Cap'n, but I'd be *proud* to be like Richard. That's all I can tell you, Mr Boss-Man. But I know he wasn't trying to rape nobody. Rape!

THE STATE: Your Honour, will you instruct the witness that he is under oath, that this is a court of law, and that it is a serious matter to be held in contempt of court!

LORENZO: More serious than the chain gang? *I* know I'm under oath. If there was any reason, it was just that Richard couldn't stand white people. *Couldn't stand white people!* And, now, do you want me to tell you all that I know about *that?* Do you think you could stand it? You'd cut my tongue out before you'd let me tell you all that I know about *that!*

COUNSEL FOR THE BEREAVED: You are a student here?

LORENZO: In my spare time. I just come off the chain gang a couple of days ago. I was trespassing in the white waiting room of the bus station.

COUNSEL FOR THE BEREAVED: What are you studying – in your spare time – Mr Shannon?

LORENZO: History.

COUNSEL FOR THE BEREAVED: To your knowledge – during his stay in this town – was the late Mr Richard Henry still addicted to narcotics?

LORENZO: No. He'd kicked his habit. He'd paid his dues. He was just trying to live. And he almost made it.

COUNSEL FOR THE BEREAVED: You were very close to him?

LORENZO: Yes.

COUNSEL FOR THE BEREAVED: To your knowledge – was he carrying about obscene photographs of himself and naked white women?

LORENZO: To my knowledge – and I would know – no. The only times he ever opened a popular magazine was to look at the Jazz Poll. No. They been asking me about photographs they say he was carrying and they been asking me about a gun I never saw. No. It wasn't like that. He was a beautiful cat, and they killed him. That's all. That's *all.*

JUDGE: The witness may step down.

LORENZO: Well! I thank you kindly. *Suh!*

LORENZO leaves the stand.

CLERK: (*Calls.*) Miss Juanita Harmon!

(*JUANITA rises from bed; early Sunday morning.*)

JUANITA: He lay beside me on that bed like a rock. As heavy as a rock – like he'd fallen – fallen from a high place – fallen so far and landed so heavy, he seemed almost to be sinking out of sight – with one knee pointing to heaven. My God.

He covered me like that. He wasn't at all like I thought he was. He fell on – fell on me – like life and death. My God. His chest, his belly, the rising and the falling, the moans. How he clung, how he struggled – life and death! Life and death! Why did it all seem to me like tears? That he came to me, clung to me, plunged into me, sobbing, howling, bleeding, somewhere inside his chest, his belly, and it all came out, came pouring out, like tears! My God, the smell, the touch, the taste, the sound, of anguish! Richard! Why couldn't I have held you closer? Held you, held you, borne you, given you life again! Have made you be born again! Oh, Richard. The teeth that gleamed, oh! when you smiled, the spit flying when you cursed, the teeth stinging when you bit – your breath, your hands, your weight, my God, when you moved in me! Where shall I go now, what shall I do? Oh. Oh. Oh. Mama was frightened. Frightened because little Juanita brought her first real lover to this house. I suppose God does for Mama what Richard did for me. Juanita! I don't care! I don't care! Yes, I want a lover made of flesh and blood, of flesh and blood, like me, I don't want to be God's mother! He can *have* His icy, snow-white heaven! If he is somewhere around this fearful planet, if I ever see Him, I will spit in His face! In God's face! How *dare* He presume to judge a living soul! A living soul. Mama is afraid I'm pregnant. Mama is afraid of so much. I'm not afraid. I hope I'm pregnant. I *hope* I am! One more illegitimate black baby – that's right, you jive mothers! And I am going to raise my baby to be a man. A *man*, you dig? Oh, let me be pregnant, let me be pregnant, don't let it all be gone! A man. Juanita. A man. Oh, my God, there are no more. For me. Did this happen to Mama some time? Did she have a man some time who vanished like smoke? And left her to get through this world as best she could? Is that why she married my father? Did this happen to Mother Henry? Is this how we all get to be mothers – so soon? of helpless men – because all the other men perish? No. No. No. No. What is this world like? I will end up taking care of some man, some day. Help me do it with love. Pete. Meridian. Parnell. We have been the mothers for them all. It must be dreadful to be Parnell. There is no flesh he can touch. All of it is bloody. Incest everywhere. Ha-ha! You're going crazy, Juanita. Oh, Lord, don't let me go mad. Let me be pregnant! Let me be pregnant!

(*JUANITA takes the stand. One arm is in a sling.*)

BLACKTOWN: Look! You should have seen her when she *first* come out of jail! Why we always got to love *them*? How come it's *us* always got to do the loving? Because you *black*, mother! Everybody knows we *strong* on loving! Except when it comes to our women.

WHITETOWN: Black slut! What happened to her arm? Somebody had to twist it, I reckon. She looks like she might be a right pretty little girl – why is she messing up her life this way?

THE STATE: Miss Harmon, you have testified that you were friendly with the mother of the deceased. How old were you when she died?

JUANITA: I was sixteen.

THE STATE: Sixteen! You are older than the deceased?

JUANITA: By two years.

THE STATE: At the time of his mother's death, were you and Richard Henry considering marriage?

JUANITA: No. Of course not.

THE STATE: The question of marriage did not come up until just before he died?

JUANITA: Yes.

THE STATE: But between the time that Richard Henry left this town and returned, you had naturally attracted other boy friends?

BLACKTOWN: Why don't you come right out and ask her if she's a virgin, man? Save you time.

WHITETOWN: She probably pregnant right now – and don't know who the father is. That's the way they are.

THE STATE: The departure of the boy and the death of the mother must have left all of you extremely lonely?

JUANITA: It can't be said to have made us any happier.

THE STATE: Reverend Henry missed his wife, you missed your playmate. His grief and your common concern for the boy must have drawn you closer together?

BLACKTOWN: Oh, man! Get to *that*!

WHITETOWN: That's right. What about that liver-lipped preacher?

THE STATE: Miss Harmon, you describe yourself as a student. Where have you spent the last few weeks?

JUANITA: In jail! I was arrested for –

THE STATE: I am not concerned with the reasons for your arrest. How much time, all told, have you spent in jail?

JUANITA: It would be hard to say – a long time.

THE STATE: Excellent preparation for your future! Is it not true, Miss Harmon, that before the late Richard Henry returned to this town, you were considering marriage with another so-called student, Pete Spivey? Can you seriously expect this court to believe anything you now say concerning Richard Henry? Would you not say the same thing, and for the same reason, concerning the father? Concerning Pete Spivey? And how many others!

WHITETOWN: That's the way they are. It's not their fault. That's what they want us to integrate with.

BLACKTOWN: These people are sick. Sick. Sick people's been known to be made well by a little shedding of blood.

JUANITA: I am not responsible for your imagination.

THE STATE: What do you know of the fight which took place between Richard Henry and Lyle Britten, at Mr Britten's store?

JUANITA: I was not a witness to that fight.

THE STATE: But you had seen Richard Henry before the fight? Was he sober?

JUANITA: Yes.

THE STATE: You can swear to that?

JUANITA: Yes, I can swear to it.

THE STATE: And you saw him after the fight? Was he sober then?

JUANITA: Yes. He was sober then. (*Courtroom in silhouette.*) I heard about the fight at the end of the day – when I got home. And I went running to Reverend Henry's house. And I met him on the porch – just sitting there.

THE STATE: You met whom?

JUANITA: I met – Richard.

(*We discover* MERIDIAN.)

MERIDIAN: Hello, Juanita. Don't look like that.

JUANITA: Meridian, what happened today? Where's Richard?

MERIDIAN: He's all right now. He's sleeping. We better send him away. Lyle's dangerous. You know that.

(*Takes* JUANITA *in his arms; then holds her at arm's length.*)

You'll go with him. Won't you?

JUANITA: Meridian – oh, my God.

MERIDIAN: Juanita, tell me something I have to know. I'll never ask it again.

JUANITA: Yes, Meridian –

MERIDIAN: Before he came – I wasn't just making it all up, was I? There was something at least – beginning – something dimly possible – wasn't there? I thought about you so much – and it was so wonderful each time I saw you – and I started hoping as I haven't let myself hope, oh, for a long time. I knew you were much younger, and I'd known you since you were a child. But I thought that maybe that didn't matter, after all – we got on so well together. I wasn't making it all up, was I?

JUANITA: No. You weren't making it up – not all of it, anyway, there was something there. We were lonely. You were hoping. I was hoping, too – oh, Meridian! Of all the people on God's earth I would rather die than hurt!

MERIDIAN: Hush, Juanita. I know that. I just wanted to be told that I hadn't lost my mind. I've lost so much. I think there's something wrong in being – what I've become – something really wrong. I mean, I think there's something wrong with allowing oneself to become so lonely. I think that I was proud that I could bear it. Each day became a kind of test – to see if I could bear it. And there were many days when I couldn't bear it – when I walked up and down and howled and lusted and cursed and prayed – just like any man. And I've been – I haven't been as celibate as I've seemed. But my confidence – my confidence – was destroyed back there when I pulled back that rug they had her covered with and I saw that little face on that broken neck. There wasn't any blood – just water. She was soaked. Oh, my God. My God. And I haven't trusted myself with a woman since. I keep seeing her the last time I saw her, whether I'm awake or asleep. That's why I let you get away from me. It wasn't my son that did it. It was me. And so much the better for you. And him.

And I've held it all in since then – what fearful choices we must make! In order not to commit murder, in order not to become too monstrous, in order to be some kind of example to my only son. Come. Let me be an example now. And kiss you on the forehead and wish you well.

JUANITA: Meridian. Meridian. Will it always be like this? Will life always be like this? Must we always suffer so?

MERIDIAN: I don't know, Juanita. I know that we must bear what we must bear. Don't cry, Juanita. Don't cry. Let's go on on.

(*Exits.*)

JUANITA: By and by Richard woke up and I was there. And we tried to make plans to go, but he said he wasn't going to run no more from white folks – never no more! – but was going to stay and be a man – a *man!* – right here. And I couldn't *make* him see differently. I knew what he meant, I knew how he felt, but I didn't want him to die! And by the time I persuaded him to take *me* away, to take *me* away from this terrible place, it was too late. Lyle killed him. Lyle killed him! Like they been killing all our men, for years, for generations! Our husbands our fathers, our brothers, our sons!

JUDGE: The witness may step down.

JUANITA *leaves the stand.* MOTHER HENRY *helps her to her seat.*

This court is adjourned until ten o'clock tomorrow morning.

Chaos and cacophony. The courtroom begins to empty. Reporters rush to phone booths and to witnesses. Light bulbs flash. We hear snatches of the Journalists' reports, in their various languages. Singing from the church. Blackout. The next and last day of the trial. Even more crowded and tense.

CLERK: (*Calls.*) Mrs Wilhelmina Henry!

MOTHER HENRY, *in street clothes, walks down the aisle, takes the stand.*

THE STATE: You are Mrs Wilhelmina Henry?

MOTHER HENRY: Yes.

THE STATE: Mrs Henry, you – and your husband, until he died – lived in this town all your lives and never had any trouble. We've always gotten on well down here.

MOTHER HENRY: No white man never called my husband Mister, neither, not as long as he lived. Ain't no white man never called *me* Mrs Henry before today. I had to get a grandson killed for that.

THE STATE: Mrs Henry, your grief elicits my entire sympathy, and the sympathy of every white man in this town. But is it not true, Mrs Henry, that your grandson arrived in this town armed? He was carrying a gun and, apparently, had carried a gun for years.

MOTHER HENRY: I don't know where you got that story, or why you keep harping on it. *I* never saw no gun.

THE STATE: You are under oath, Mrs Henry.

MOTHER HENRY: I don't need you to tell me I'm under oath. I been under oath all my life. And I tell you, I never saw no gun.

THE STATE: Mrs Henry, did you ever see your grandson behaving strangely – as though he were under the influence of strong drugs?

MOTHER HENRY: No. Not since he was six and they pulled out his tonsils. They gave him ether. *He* didn't act as strange as his Mama and Daddy. He just went on to sleep. But they like to had a fit. (*RICHARD's song.*) I remember the day he was born. His mother had a hard time holding him and a hard time getting him here. But here he come, in the wintertime, late and big and loud. And my boy looked down into his little son's face and he said, 'God give us a son. God's give us a son. Lord, help us to raise him to be a good strong man.'

JUDGE: The witness may step down.

CLERK: (*Calls.*) Reverend Meridian Henry!

(*Blackout.* MERIDIAN, *in Sunday School. The class itself, predominately adolescent girls, is in silhouette.*)

MERIDIAN: – And here is the prophet, Solomon, the son of David, looking down through the ages, and speaking of Christ's love for His church. (*Reads.*) How fair is thy love, my sister, my spouse! How much better is thy love than wine! and the smell of thine ointments than all spices! (*Pause. The silhouette of girls vanishes.*) Oh, that it were one man, speaking to one woman!

(*Blackout.* MERIDIAN *takes the stand.*)

BLACKTOWN: I wonder how he feels now about all that turn-the-other-cheek jazz. His son sure didn't go for it.

WHITETOWN: That's the father. Claims to be a preacher. He brought this on himself. He's been raising trouble in this town for a long time.

THE STATE: You are Reverend Meridian Henry?

MERIDIAN: That is correct.

THE STATE: And you are the father of the late Richard Henry?

MERIDIAN: Yes.

THE STATE: You are a minister?

MERIDIAN: A Christian minister – yes.

THE STATE: And you raised your son according to the precepts of the Christian church?

MERIDIAN: I tried. But both my son and I had profound reservations concerning the behaviour of Christians. He wondered why they treated black people as they do. And I was unable to give him – a satisfactory answer.

THE STATE: But certainly you – as a Christian minister – did not encourage your son to go armed?

MERIDIAN: The question never came up. He was not armed.

THE STATE: He was not armed?

MERIDIAN: No.

THE STATE: You never saw him with a gun? Or with any other weapon?

MERIDIAN: No.

THE STATE: Reverend Henry – are you in a position to swear that your son never carried arms?

MERIDIAN: Yes. I can swear to it. The only time the subject was ever mentioned he told me that he was stronger than white people and he could live without a gun.

BLACKTOWN: I bet he didn't say how.

WHITETOWN: That liver-lipped nigger is lying. He's lying!

THE STATE: Perhaps the difficulties your son had in accepting the Christian faith is due to your use of the pulpit as a forum for irresponsible notions concerning social equality, Reverend Henry. Perhaps the failure of the son is due to the failure of the father.

MERIDIAN: I am afraid that the gentleman flatters himself. I do not wish to see Negroes become the equal of their murderers. I wish us to become equal to ourselves. To become a people so free in themselves that they will have no need to – fear – others – and have no need to murder others.

THE STATE: You are not in the pulpit now. I am suggesting that you are responsible – directly responsible! – for your son's tragic fate.

MERIDIAN: I know more about that than you do. But you cannot consider my son's death to have been tragic. For you, it would have been tragic if he had lived.

THE STATE: With such a father, it is remarkable that the son lived as long as he did.

MERIDIAN: Remarkable, too, that the father lived!

THE STATE: Reverend Henry – you have been a widower for how many years?

MERIDIAN: I have been a widower for nearly eight years.

THE STATE: You are a young man still?

MERIDIAN: Are you asking me my age? I am not young.

THE STATE: You are not old. It must have demanded great discipline –

MERIDIAN: To live among you? Yes.

THE STATE: What is your relationship to the young, so-called student, Miss Juanita Harmon?

MERIDIAN: I am her old friend. I had hoped to become her father-in-law.

THE STATE: You are nothing more than old friends?

WHITETOWN: That's right. Get it out of him. Get the truth out of him.

BLACKTOWN: Leave the man *something*. Leave him something!

THE STATE: You have been celibate since the death of your wife?

BLACKTOWN: He never said he was a monk, you jive mother!

WHITETOWN: Make him tell us all about it. *All* about it.

MERIDIAN: Celibate? How does my celibacy concern you?

THE STATE: Your Honour, will you instruct the witness that he is on the witness stand, not I, and that he must answer the questions put to him!

MERIDIAN: *The questions put to him!* All right. Do you accept this answer? I am a man. A *man!* I tried to help my son become a man. But manhood is a dangerous pursuit, here. And that pursuit undid him because of *your* guns, *your* hoses, *your* dogs, *your* judges, *your* law-makers, *your* folly, *your* pride, *your* cruelty, *your* cowardice, *your* money, *your* chain gangs, and *your* churches! Did you think it would endure for ever? that we would pay for *your* ease for ever?

BLACKTOWN: Speak, my man! Amen! Amen! Amen! Amen!

WHITETOWN: Stirring up hate! Stirring up hate! A *preacher* – stirring up hate!

MERIDIAN: Yes! I *am* responsible for the death of my son. I – hoped – I prayed – I struggled – so that the world would be different by the time he was a man than it had been when he was born. And I thought that – then – when he looked at me – he would think that I – his father – had helped to change it.

THE STATE: What about those photographs your son carried about with him? Those photographs of himself and naked white women?

BLACKTOWN: Man! Would I love to look in *your* wallet!

WHITETOWN: Make him tell us about it, make him tell us *all* about it!

MERIDIAN: Photographs? My son and naked white women? He never mentioned them to me.

THE STATE: You were closer than most fathers and sons?

MERIDIAN: I never took a poll on most fathers and sons.

THE STATE: You never discussed women?

MERIDIAN: We talked about his mother. She was a woman. We talked about Miss Harmon. *She* is a woman. But we never talked about dirty pictures. We didn't need that.

THE STATE: Reverend Henry, you have made us all aware that your love for your son transcends your respect for the truth or your devotion to the church. But – luckily for the truth – it is a matter of public record that your son was so dangerously deranged that it was found necessary, for his own sake, to incarcerate him. It was at the end of that incarceration that he returned to this town. We know that his life in the North was riotous – he brought that riot into this town. The evidence is overwhelming. And yet, you, a Christian minister, dare to bring us this tissue of lies in defence of a known pimp, dope addict, and rapist! You are yourself so eaten up by race hatred that no word of yours can be believed.

MERIDIAN: Your judgment of myself and my motives cannot concern me at all. I have lived with that judgment far too long. The truth cannot be heard in this dreadful place. But I will tell you again what I know. I know why my son became a dope addict. I know better than you will ever know, even if I should explain it to you for all eternity, how I am responsible for that. But I know my son was not a pimp. He respected women far too much for that. And I know he was not a rapist. Rape is hard work – and, frankly, I don't think that the alleged object was my son's type at all!

THE STATE: And you are a minister?

MERIDIAN: I think I may be beginning to become one.

JUDGE: The witness may step down.

MERIDIAN leaves the stand.

CLERK: (*Calls.*) Mr Parnell James!

(*PARNELL in his bedroom, dressed in a bathrobe. Night.*)

PARNELL: She says I called somebody else's name. What name could I have called? And she won't repeat the name. Well. That's enough to freeze the blood and arrest the holy, the liberating orgasm. Christ, how weary I am of this dull calisthenic called love – with no love in it! What name could I have called? I hope it was – a *white* girl's name, anyway! Ha-ha! How still she became! And I hardly realized it, I was too far away – and then it was too late. And she was just looking at me. Jesus! To have somebody just looking at you – just looking at you – like that – at such a moment! It makes you feel – like you woke up and found yourself in bed with your mother! I tried to find out what was wrong – poor girl. But there's nothing you can say at a moment like that – really nothing. You're caught. Well, haven't I kept telling her that there's no future for her with me? There's no future for me with anybody! But that's all right. What name could I have called? I haven't been with anybody else for a long time, a long time. She says I haven't been with her, either. I guess she's right. I've just been using her. Using her as an anchor – to hold me here, in this house, this bed – so I won't find myself on the other side of town, ruining my reputation. *What* reputation? They all know. I swear they all *know*. Know what? What's there to know? So you get drunk and you fool around a little. Come on, Parnell. There's more to it than that. That's the reason you draw blanks whenever you get drunk. Everything comes out. Everything. They see what you don't dare to see. What name could I have called? Richard would say that you've got – black fever! Yeah, and he'd be wrong – that long, loud, black mother. I wonder if she's asleep yet – or just lying there, looking at the walls. Poor girl! All your life you've been made sick, stunned, dizzy, oh, Lord! driven half mad by blackness. Blackness in front of your eyes. Boys and girls, men and women – you've bowed down in front of them all! And then hated yourself. Hated yourself for debasing yourself? Out with it, Parnell! The nigger-lover! Black boys and girls! I've wanted my hands full of them, wanted to drown them, laughing and dancing and making love – making love – wow! – and be transformed, formed, liberated out of this grey-white envelope. Jesus! I've always been afraid. Afraid of what I saw in their eyes? They don't love me, certainly. You don't love them, either! Sick with a disease only white men catch. Blackness. What is it like to be black? To look out on the world from *that* place? I give nothing! How dare she say that! My girl, if you knew what I've given! Ah. Come off it, Parnell. To *whom* have you given? What name did I call? What name did I call?

(*Blackout.* PARNELL *and* LYLE. *Hunting on* PARNELL'S *land*.)

LYLE: You think it's a good idea, then? You think she won't say no?

PARNELL: Well, you're the one who's got to go through it. *You've* got to ask for Miss Josephine's hand in marriage. And then you've got to live with her – for the rest of your life. Watch that gun. I've never seen you so jumpy. I might say it was a good idea if I thought she'd say no. But I think she'll say yes.

LYLE: Why would she say yes to me?

PARNELL: I think she's drawn to you. It isn't hard to be – drawn to you. Don't you know that?

LYLE: No. When I was young, I used to come here sometimes – with my Daddy. He didn't like *your* Daddy a-*tall*! We used to steal your game, Parnell – you didn't know that, did you?

PARNELL: I think I knew it.

LYLE: We shot at the game and your Daddy's overseers shot at us. But we *got* what *we* came after. *They* never got *us*!

PARNELL: You're talking an awful lot today. You nervous about Miss Josephine?

LYLE: Wait a minute. You think I ought to marry Jo?

PARNELL: I don't know who anybody should marry. Do you want to marry Jo?

LYLE: Well – I got to marry somebody. I got to have some kids. And Jo is – *clean!*

PARNELL sights, shoots.

PARNELL: Goddamn!

LYLE: Missed it. Ha-ha!

PARNELL: It's probably somebody's mother.

LYLE: Watch. (*Sights, shoots.*) Ha-ha!

PARNELL: Bravo!

LYLE: I knew it! Had my name written on it, just as pretty as you please! (*Exits, returns with his bird.*) See? My Daddy taught me well. It was sport for you. It was life for us.

PARNELL: I reckon you shot somebody's baby.

LYLE: I tell you – I can't go on like this. There comes a time in a man's life when he's got to have him a little – peace.

PARNELL: You mean calm. Tranquillity.

LYLE: Yeah. I didn't mean it like it sounded. You thought I meant – no. I'm tired of –

PARNELL: Poon-tang.

LYLE: How'd you know? You tired of it, too? Hell. Yeah. I want kids.

PARNELL: Well, then – marry the girl.

LYLE: She ain't a girl no more. It might be her last chance, too. But, I swear, Parnell, she might be the only virgin left in this town. The only *white* virgin. I can vouch for the fact ain't many black ones.

PARNELL: You've been active, I know. Any kids?

LYLE: None that I know of. Ha-ha!

PARNELL: Do you think Jo might be upset – by the talk about you and Old Bill? She's real respectable, you know. She's a *librarian.*

LYLE: No. Them things happen every day. You think I ought to marry her? You really think she'll say yes?

PARNELL: She'll say yes. She'd better. I wish you luck. Name the first one after me.

LYLE: No. You be the godfather. And my best man. I'm going to name the first one after my Daddy – because he taught me more about hunting on your land than *you* know. I'll give him your middle name. I'll call him Lyle Parnell Britten, Jr.!

PARNELL: If the girl says yes.

LYLE: Well, if she says no, ain't no problem, is there? We know where to go when the going gets rough, don't we, old buddy?

PARNELL: Do we? Look! Mine?

LYLE: What'll you bet?

PARNELL: The price of your wedding rings.

LYLE: You're on. Mine? *Mine!*

(*Blackout.* PARNELL *walks down the aisle, takes the stand.*)

WHITETOWN:

Here comes the nigger-lover!

But I bet you one thing – he knows more about the truth in this case than anybody else.

He ought to – he's with them all the time.

It's sad when a man turns against his own people!

BLACKTOWN:

Let's see how the Negro's friend comes through!

They been waiting for *him* – they going to tear his behind *up!*

I don't trust him. I *never* trusted him!

Why? Because he's *white*, that's why!

THE STATE: You were acquainted with the late Richard Henry?

PARNELL: Of course. His father and I have been friends all our lives.

THE STATE: Close friends?

PARNELL: Yes. Very close.

THE STATE: And what is your relationship to the alleged murderer, Mr Lyle Britten?

PARNELL: We, also, have been friends all our lives.

THE STATE: Close friends?

PARNELL: Yes.

THE STATE: As close as the friendship between yourself and the dead boy's father?

PARNELL: I would say so – it was a very different relationship.

THE STATE: Different in what respect, Mr James?

PARNELL: Well, we had different things to talk about. We did different things together.

THE STATE: What sort of different things?

PARNELL: Well – hunting, for example – things like that.

THE STATE: You never went hunting with Reverend Henry?

PARNELL: No. He didn't like to hunt.

THE STATE: He told you so? He told you that he didn't like to hunt?

PARNELL: The question never came up. We led very different lives.

THE STATE: I am gratified to hear it. Is it not true, Mr James, that it is impossible for any two people to go on a hunting trip together if either of them has any reason at all to distrust the other?

PARNELL: Well, of course that would have to be true. But it's never talked about – it's just understood.

THE STATE: We can conclude, then, that you were willing to trust Lyle Britten with your life but did not feel the same trust in Reverend Henry?

PARNELL: Sir, you may not draw any such conclusion! I have told you that Reverend Henry and I led very different lives!

THE STATE: But you have been friends all your lives. Reverend Henry is also a southern boy – he, also, I am sure, knows and loves this land, has gone swimming and fishing in her streams and rivers, and stalked game in her forests. And yet, close as you are, you have never allowed yourself to be alone with Reverend Henry when Reverend Henry had a gun. Doesn't this suggest some *lack* – in your vaunted friendship?

PARNELL: Your suggestion is unwarranted and unworthy. As a soldier, I have often been alone with Negroes with guns, and it certainly never caused me any uneasiness.

THE STATE: But you were fighting a common enemy then. What was your impression of the late Richard Henry?

PARNELL: I liked him. He was very outspoken and perhaps tactless, but a very valuable person.

THE STATE: How would you describe his effect on this town? Among his own people? Among the whites?

PARNELL: His effect? He was pretty well liked.

THE STATE: That does not answer my question.

PARNELL: His effect was – kind of unsettling, I suppose. After all, he had lived in the North a long time, he wasn't used to – the way we do things down here.

THE STATE: He was accustomed to the way things are done in the North – where he learned to carry arms, to take dope, and to couple with white women!

PARNELL: I cannot testify to any of that, sir. I can only repeat that he reacted with great intensity to the racial situation in this town, and his effect on the town was, to that extent, unsettling.

THE STATE: Did he not encourage the Negroes of this town to arm?

PARNELL: Not to my knowledge, sir, no. And, in any case, they are not armed.

THE STATE: You are in a position to reassure us on this point?

PARNELL: My friends do not lie.

THE STATE: You are remarkably fortunate. You are aware of the attitude of the late Richard Henry towards white women? You saw the photographs he carried about with him?

PARNELL: We never discussed women. I never saw the photographs.

THE STATE: But you knew of their existence?

PARNELL: They were not obscene. They were simply snapshots of people he had known in the North.

THE STATE: Snapshots of white women?

PARNELL: Yes.

THE STATE: You are the first witness to admit the existence of these photographs, Mr James.

PARNELL: It is very likely that the other witnesses never saw them. The boy had been discouraged, very early on, from mentioning them or showing them about.

THE STATE: Discouraged by whom?

PARNELL: Why – by – me.

THE STATE: But you never saw the photographs –

PARNELL: I told him I didn't want to see them and that it would be dangerous to carry them about.

THE STATE: He showed these photographs to you, but to no one else?

PARNELL: That would seem to be the case, yes.

THE STATE: What was his motive in taking you into his confidence?

PARNELL: Bravado. He wanted me to know that he had white friends in the North, that – he had been happy – in the North.

THE STATE: You did not tell his father? You did not warn your close friend?

PARNELL: I am sure that Richard never mentioned these photographs to his father. He would have been too ashamed. Those women were beneath him.

THE STATE: A white woman who surrenders to a coloured man is beneath all human consideration. She has wantonly and deliberately defiled the temple of the Holy Ghost. It is clear to me that the effect of such a boy on this town was irresponsible and incendiary to the greatest degree. Did you not find your close friendship with Reverend Henry somewhat strained by the son's attempt to rape the wife of your other close friend, Lyle Britten?

PARNELL: This attempt was never mentioned before – before today.

THE STATE: You are as close as you claim to the Britten family and knew nothing of this attempted rape? How do you explain that?

PARNELL: I cannot explain it.

THE STATE: This is a court of law, Mr James, and we will have the truth!

WHITETOWN: Make him tell the truth!

BLACKTOWN: Make him tell the truth!

THE STATE: How can you be the close friend you claim to be of the Britten family and not have known of so grave an event?

PARNELL: I – I knew of a fight. It was understood that the boy had gone to Mr Britten's store looking for a fight. I – I cannot explain *that*, either.

THE STATE: Who told you of the fight?

PARNELL: Why – Mr Britten.

THE STATE: And did not tell you that Richard Henry had attempted to assault his wife? Come, Mr James!

PARNELL: We were all very much upset. Perhaps he was not as coherent as he might have been – perhaps I failed to listen closely. It was my assumption that Mrs Britten had misconstrued the boy's actions – he had been in the North a long time, his manner was very free and bold.

THE STATE: Mrs Britten has testified that Richard Henry grabbed her and pulled her to him and tried to kiss her. How can those actions be misconstrued?

PARNELL: Those actions are – quite explicit.

THE STATE: Thank you, Mr James. That is all.

JUDGE: The witness may step down.

PARNELL leaves the stand.

BLACKTOWN: What do you think of our fine friend *now?* He didn't do it to us rough and hard. No, he was real gentle. I hardly felt a thing. Did you? You can't never go against the word of a white lady, man, not even if you're white. Can't be done. He was sad. *Sad!*

WHITETOWN: It took him long enough! He did his best not to say it – can you imagine! So her story was true – after all! I hope he's learned his lesson. We been trying to tell him – for years!

CLEAK: (*Calls.*) Mr Lyle Britten!

(*LYLE, in the woods.*)

LYLE: I wonder what he'll grow up to look like. Of course, it might be a girl. I reckon I wouldn't mind – just keep on trying till I get me a boy, ha-ha! Old Miss Josephine is something, ain't she? I really struck oil when I come across her. She's a nice woman. And she's *my* woman – I ain't got to worry about *that* a-tall! You're making big changes in your life, Lyle, and you got to be ready to take on this extra responsibility. Shoot, I'm ready. I know what I'm doing. And I'm going to work harder than I've ever worked before in my life to make Jo happy – and keep her happy – and raise our children to be fine men and women. Lord, you know I'm not a praying man. I've done a lot of wrong things in my life and I ain't never going to be perfect. I know You know that. I know You understand that. But, Lord, hear me today and help me to do what I'm supposed to do. I want to be as strong as my Mama and Daddy and raise my children like they raised me. That's what I want, oh Lord. In a few years I'll be walking here, showing my son these trees and this water and this sky. He'll have his hand in my hand, and I'll show him the world. Isn't that a funny thing! He don't even exist yet – he's just an egg in his mother's belly, I bet you couldn't even find him with a microscope – and I put him there – and he's coming out soon – with fingers and toes and eyes – and by and by, he'll learn to walk and talk – and I reckon I'll have to spank him sometimes – if he's anything like me, I know I will. Isn't that something! My son! Hurry up and get here, so I can hug you in my arms and give you a good start on your long journey!

(*Blackout. LYLE, with PAPA D. Drunk. Music and dancing.*)

LYLE: You remember them days when Willa Mae was around? My mind's been going back to them days. You remember? She was a hot little piece, I just had to have some of that, I just *had* to. Half the time she didn't wear no stockings, just had them brown, round legs just moving. I couldn't keep my eyes off her legs when she didn't wear no stockings. And you know what she told me? You know what she told me? She said there wasn't a nigger alive could be as good to her as me. That's right. She said she'd like to *see* the nigger could do her like I done her. You hear me, boy? That's something, ain't it? Boy – she'd just come into a room sometimes and my old pecker would stand up at attention. You ain't jealous, are you, Joel? Ha-ha! You never did hear from her no more, did you? No, I reckon you didn't. Shoot, I got to get on home. I'm a family man now, I got – great responsibilities! Yeah. Be seeing you, Joel. You don't want to close up and walk a-ways with me, do you? No, I reckon you better not. They having fun. Sure wish I could be more like you all. Bye-bye!

(*Blackout. As LYLE approaches the witness stand, the lights in the courtroom dim. We hear voices from the church, singing a lament. The lights come up.*)

JUDGE: Gentlemen of the jury, have you reached a verdict?

FOREMAN: We have, Your Honour.

JUDGE: Will the prisoner please rise?

LYLE rises.

Do you find the defendant, Mr Lyle Britten, guilty or not guilty?

FOREMAN: Not guilty, Your Honour.

Cheering in WHITETOWN. Silence in BLACKTOWN. The stage is taken over by REPORTERS, PHOTOGRAPHERS, WITNESSES, TOWNSPEOPLE. LYLE is congratulated and embraced. BLACKTOWN files out silently, not looking back. WHITETOWN files out jubilantly, and yet with a certain reluctance. Presently, the stage is empty, except for LYLE, JO, MOTHER HENRY, MERIDIAN, PARNELL, JUANITA, and LORENZO.

JO: Let's get out of here and go home. We've been here just for days. I wouldn't care if I *never* saw the insides of a courtroom again! Let's go home, sugar. We got something to celebrate!

JUANITA: We, too, must go – to another celebration. We're having a prayer meeting on the City Hall steps.

LORENZO: Prayer meeting!

LYLE: Well, it was touch and go there for a while, Parnell, but you sure come through. I knew you would.

JO: Let's go, Lyle. The baby's hungry.

MERIDIAN: Perhaps now you can ask him to tell you the truth. He's got nothing to lose now. They can't try him again.

LYLE: Wasn't much sense in trying me now, this time, was there, Reverend? These people have been knowing me and my good Jo here all our lives, they ain't going to doubt us. And you people – you people – ought to have better sense and more things to do than running around stirring up all this hate and trouble. *That's* how your son got himself killed. He listened to crazy niggers like you!

MERIDIAN: Did you kill him?

LYLE: They just asked me that in court, didn't they? And they just decided I didn't, didn't they? Well, that's good enough for me and all those white people and so it damn sure better be good enough for you!

PARNELL: That's no answer. It's not good enough for me.

LYLE: What do you mean, that's no answer? Why isn't it an answer? Why isn't it good enough for you? You know, when you were up on the stand right now, you acted like you doubted my Jo's word. You got no right to doubt Jo's word. You ain't no better than she is! You ain't no better than me!

PARNELL: I am aware of that. God knows I have been made aware of that – for the first time in my life. But, as you and I will never be the same again – since our comedy is finished, since I have failed you so badly – let me say this. I did not doubt Jo's word. I knew that she was lying and that you had made her lie. That was a terrible thing to do to her. It was a terrible thing that I just did to you. I really don't know if what I did to Meridian was as awful as what I did to you. I don't expect forgiveness, Meridian. I only hope that all of us will suffer past this agony and horror.

LYLE: What's the matter with you? Have you forgotten you a white man? A white man! My Daddy told me not to *never* forget I was a white man! Here I been knowing you all my life – and now I'm ashamed of you. Ashamed of you! Get on over to niggertown! I'm going home with my good wife.

MERIDIAN: What was the last thing my son said to you – before you shot him down – like a dog?

LYLE: Like a dog! You a smart nigger, ain't you?

MERIDIAN: What was the last thing he said? Did he beg you for his life?

LYLE: *That* nigger! He was too smart for that! He was too full of himself for that! He must have thought he was white. And I gave him every chance – every chance – to live!

MERIDIAN: And he refused them all.

LYLE: Do you know what that nigger said to me?

(*The light changes, so that everyone but* LYLE *is in silhouette.* RICHARD *appears, dressed as we last saw him, on the road outside* PAPA D.*'s joint.*)

RICHARD: I'm ready. Here I am. You asked me if I was ready, didn't you? What's on your mind, white man?

LYLE: Boy, I always treated you with respect. I don't know what's the matter with you, or what makes you act the way you do – but you owe me an apology and I come out here tonight to get it. I mean, I ain't going away without it.

RICHARD: *I* owe *you* an apology! That's a wild idea. What am I apologizing for?

LYLE: You know, you mighty lucky to still be walking around.

RICHARD: So are you. White man.

LYLE: I'd like you to apologize for your behaviour in my store that day. Now, I think I'm being pretty reasonable, ain't I?

RICHARD: You got anything to write on? I'll write you an IOU.

LYLE: Keep it up. You going to be laughing out of the other side of your mouth pretty soon.

RICHARD: Why don't you go home? And let me go home? Do we need all this shit? Can't we live without it?

LYLE: Boy, are you drunk?

RICHARD: No, I ain't drunk. I'm just tired. Tired of all this fighting. What are you trying to prove? What am *I* trying to prove?

LYLE: I'm trying to give you a break. You too dumb to take it.

RICHARD: I'm hip. You been trying to give me a break for a great, long time. But there's only one break I want. And you won't give me that.

LYLE: What kind of break do you want, boy?

RICHARD: For you to go home. And let me go home. I got things to do. I got – lots of things to do!

LYLE: I got things to do, too. I'd like to get home, too.

RICHARD: Then why are we standing here? Can't we walk? Let me walk, white man! Let me walk!

Figure 25 *Blues for Mister Charlie* at the ANTA Theater, New York, 1964. (Photographer: Gjon Mili, by permission of Getty Images.)

LYLE: We can walk, just as soon as we get our business settled.

RICHARD: It's settled. You a man and I'm a man. Let's walk.

LYLE: Nigger, you was born down here. Ain't you never said sir to a white man?

RICHARD: No. The only person I ever said sir to was my Daddy.

LYLE: Are you going to apologize to me?

RICHARD: No.

LYLE: Do you want to live?

RICHARD: Yes.

LYLE: Then you know what to do, then, don't you?

RICHARD: Go home. Go home.

LYLE: You facing my gun. (*Produces it.*) Now, in just a minute, we can both go home.

RICHARD: You sick mother! Why can't you leave me alone? White man! I don't want nothing from you. You ain't got nothing to give me. You can't eat because none of your sad-assed chicks can cook. You can't talk because won't nobody talk to you. You can't dance because you've got nobody to dance with – don't you know I've watched you all my life? *All my life!* And *I* know your women, don't you think I don't – better than you!

LYLE shoots, once.

Why have you spent so much time trying to kill me? Why are you always trying to cut off *my* cock? You worried about it? Why?

LYLE shoots again.

Okay. Okay. Okay. Keep your old lady home, you hear? Don't let her near no nigger. She might get to like it. You might get to like it, too. Wow!

RICHARD falls.

Juanita! Daddy! *Mama!*

(*Singing from the church. Spot on* LYLE.)

LYLE: I had to kill him then. I'm a white man! Can't nobody talk that way to *me!* I had to go and get my pick-up truck and load him in it – I had to carry him on my back – and carry him out to the high weeds. And I dumped him in the weeds, face down. And then I come on home, to my good Jo here.

JO: Come on, Lyle. We got to get on home. We got to get the little one home now.

LYLE: And I ain't sorry. I want you to know that I ain't sorry!

JO: Come on, Lyle. Come on. He's hungry. I got to feed him.

JO and LYLE exit.

MOTHER HENRY: We got to go now, children. The children is already started to march.

LORENZO: Prayer!

MERIDIAN: You know, for us, it all began with the Bible and the gun. Maybe it will end with the Bible and the gun.

JUANITA: What did you do with the gun, Meridian?

PARNELL: You have the gun – Richard's gun?

MERIDIAN: Yes. In the pulpit. Under the Bible. Like the pilgrims of old.

Exits.

MOTHER HENRY: Come on, children.

Singing.

PETE enters.

PETE: (*Stammers.*) Are you ready, Juanita? Shall we go now?

JUANITA: Yes.

LORENZO: Come here, Pete. Stay close to me.

They go to the church door. The singing swells.

PARNELL: Well.

JUANITA: Well. Yes, Lord!

PARNELL: Can I join you on the march, Juanita? Can I walk with you?

JUANITA: Well, we can walk in the same direction, Parnell. Come. Don't look like that. Let's go on on.

Exits.

After a moment, PARNELL *follows.*

4.2 THE CHEVIOT, THE STAG AND THE BLACK, BLACK OIL (1973)

JOHN MCGRATH

John McGrath (1935–2002) *is a key figure in mid- to late twentieth-century British theatre: he wrote for stage, TV and film and also wrote manifestos for radical theatre such as* A Good Night Out *(1981)* and The Bone Won't Break *(1990).* The Cheviot, the Stag and the Black, Black Oil *(1973) takes three key historical periods to examine how the systematic colonial abuse of Scotland under British rule has disenfranchised the Scottish working classes. The play would seem to owe much to the Brechtian 'epic' form in both its composition and production. Produced by McGrath's 7:84 Scotland Theatre Company (1973-2008), the play toured extensively in the Highlands of Scotland, playing in community centres and church halls. McGrath's commitment to indigenous working-class Scottish audiences involved the utilization of the ceilidh, a traditional Gaelic evening of entertainment involving singing, dancing, storytelling, etc. The play remains a unique example of how theatre and its audiences might productively represent and reclaim history, politics and culture.*

Characters

FIDDLER
MC
GAELIC SINGER
TWO WOMEN
YOUNG HIGHLANDER
PATRICK SELLAR
JAMES LOCH
TWO SPEAKERS
OLD MAN
READERS
MINISTER
SHERIFF'S MAN
OLD WOMAN
WOMAN
MACLEOD
JURY
JUDGE
GENT
HARRIET BEECHER STOWE
SHEEP
RED INDIANS
LORD SELKIRK

STURDY HIGHLANDER

GRANNY

FRENCH NORTHWEST TRADER

WIFE

TWO HIGHLANDERS

TWO WOMEN OF GLENDALE

MEN OF GLENDALE

QUEEN VICTORIA

GHILLIE

LORD CRASK

LADY PHOSPHATE

3RD DUKE OF SUTHERLAND

ACADEMIC

MC1

MC2

MC3

MC4

MC5

ANDY MCCHUCKEMUP

LORD VAT OF GLENLIVET

TEXAS JIM

WHITEHALL

ABERDONIAN RIGGER

SNP EMPLOYER

POLWARTH

CROFTER

WIFE

The evening begins with the FIDDLER *playing Scottish and Irish fiddle tunes among the audience, in the bar, foyer, etc., as the audience are coming in. The Company are preparing their props, costumes, etc at the side of the platform, talking to friends in the audience, playing drum, whistle, etc to accompany the fiddle; the audience stamp their feet, clap, etc to the music, if they want to.*

The stage is a platform on the floor of the hall, with four chairs on either side of it, on the floor, the same chairs that the audience are sitting on. There is a microphone centre front, and speakers on either side. Every member of the cast has his or her chair, and all their props, costumes, musical instruments, etc are arranged by them, in full view of the audience, around their chair, or hanging on nails in walls, etc behind them.

In the centre of the stage a huge book stands, upright, closed, with the title of the play on the cover. When the audience is almost all in, and the Company nearly ready and all sitting on stage, the fiddle plays a reel that everybody can stamp their feet to. As it finishes, the MC *comes on stage, and, after applause for the fiddler, welcomes the audience, comments on weather, conditions in the hall, etc.*

Then he proposes to start the evening with a song the audience can all join in, and by special request, it will be: 'These Are My Mountains'.

A brief intro on the fiddle, and the MC *leads the audience in the singing. After a few lines, he says we can do better than that, or terrible, or very good, but let's get some help – and says:* 'We've brought some mountains with us – can we have the mountains, please, lads? Go the bens.' *He plays a roll on the drum as the rest of the Company lift the book, lay it flat on the actual stage of the hall or some arrangement to lift it higher than the acting platform, behind it. They open the first page, and, as in children's pop-up books, a row of mountains pops up from in between the pages. The* MC *then calls on the words – and two members of the Company hold up a sheet with the words of the song printed on it. He calls up the accordion, and says we're all set, now we can really sing.*

He and the whole Company, with fiddle and accordion, lead a chorus, verse and final rousing chorus of 'These Are My Mountains'.

'These Are My Mountains'
(words and music: James Copeland)

For these are my mountains
And this is my glen
The braes of my childhood
Will see me again
No land's ever claimed me
Though far I did roam

For these are my mountains
And I'm coming home.
For fame and for fortune
I've wandered the earth
But now I've come back to
The land of my birth
I've gathered life's treasures
But only to find
They're less than the pleasures
I first left behind.
(*Repeat verse*).

MC: Later on we're going to have a few songs like that one – if you know the words, join in – and then we're going to have a dance, and in between we'll be telling a story. It's a story that has a beginning, a middle, but, as yet, no end.

GAELIC SINGER: (*Begins to sing a quiet Jacobite song in Gaelic.*)
Och! a 'Thearlaich òig Stiubhairt,
Is e do chùis rinn mo leir eadh,
Thug thu bhuam gach ni bh'agam,
Ann an cogadh na t-aobhar:
Cha chrodh, a's cha chaoirich –

MC: It begins, I suppose, with 1746 – Culloden and all that. The Highlands were in a bit of a mess. Speaking – or singing – the Gaelic language was forbidden. (*Singing stops.*) Wearing the plaid was forbidden. (SINGER *takes off her plaid, sits.*) Things were all set for a change. So Scene One – Strathnaver 1813.

Drum Roll. Page of book turned, a cottage pops up from in between the next two pages.

Enter two Strathnaver girls, singing.

GIRLS: Hé mandu's truagh nach tigeadh
Hé mandu siod 'gam iarraidh
Hé mandu gille's litir
He ri oro each is diollaid
Heman dubh hi ri oro
Hó ró hù ó

As they sing, a YOUNG HIGHLANDER *comes on, watches them, talks to audience.*

YH: The women were great at making it all seem fine. But it was no easy time to be alive in. Sir John Sinclair of Caithness had invented the Great Sheep; that is to say,

he had introduced the Cheviot to the North. Already in Assynt the Sutherland family had cleared the people off their land – and the people were not too pleased about it.

FIRST WOMAN: Ach blethers –

SECOND WOMAN: Cha chuir iad dragh oirnne co diubh. (They won't bother us here.)

FIRST WOMAN: The Countess has always been very kind to us.

YH: Aye, and she's away in England.

FIRST WOMAN: Why wouldn't she be?

YH: With her fancy palaces and feasts for Kings and fine French wines – and it's our rent she's spending.

FIRST WOMAN: Rent! You never pay any rent –

YH: Where would I get the money to pay rent? (*To audience.*) If it's not bad weather flattening the barley, it's mildew in the potatoes, and last year it was both together ... And now they're talking about bringing in soldiers to clear us off the land completely ...

SECOND WOMAN: Saighdearan? De mu dheidhinn saighdearan? (Soldiers – what do you mean, soldiers?)

YH: There were one hundred and fifty of them arrived in a boat off Lochinver.

FIRST WOMAN: Would you get on with some work?

SECOND WOMAN: Seo-lion an cogan. (Here fill up the bucket.)

They sing on, as YH *goes to a corner of the cottage to pee in the bucket. They watch him and laugh. Suddenly he panics, does up his trousers and rushes over.*

YH: Here – there's a couple of gentlemen coming up the strath.

FIRST WOMAN: Gentlemen?

YH: (*To audience.*) The two gentlemen were James Loch and Patrick Sellar, factor and under-factor to the Sutherland estates.

FIRST WOMAN: Oh, look at the style of me ...

YH: (*Handing them the bucket*). You might find a good use for this. (*Goes.*)

SECOND WOMAN: I hope they have not come to improve us.

FIRST WOMAN: Bi samhach. (Behave yourself.) (*Giggles.*)

Enter PATRICK SELLAR *and* JAMES LOCH, *looking very grand.* SELLAR *sniffs the bucket, ignores the women, who are huddled under their shawls.*

SELLAR: (*With a Lowland Scots accent.*) Macdonald has told me, Mr Loch, there are three hundred illegal stills in Strathnaver at this very moment. They claim they have no money for rent – clearly they have enough to purchase the barley. The whole thing smacks of a terrible degeneracy in the character of these aboriginals ...

LOCH: The Marquis is not unaware of the responsibility his wealth places upon him, Mr Sellar. The future and lasting interest and honour of his family, as well as their immediate income, must be kept in view.

They freeze. A phrase on the fiddle. Two SPEAKERS *intervene between them, speak quickly to the audience.*

SPEAKER 1: Their immediate income was over £120,000 per annum. In those days that was quite a lot of money.

SPEAKER 2: George Granville, Second Marquis of Stafford, inherited a huge estate in Yorkshire; he inherited another at Trentham in the Potteries; and he inherited a third at Lilleshall in Shropshire, that had coal-mines on it.

SPEAKER 1: He also inherited the Bridgewater Canal. And, on Loch's advice, he bought a large slice of the Liverpool–Manchester Railway.

SPEAKER 2: From his wife, Elizabeth Gordon, Countess of Sutherland, he acquired three-quarters of a million acres of Sutherland – in which he wanted to invest some capital.

Another phrase on the fiddle: they slip away. SELLAR *and* LOCH *reanimate.*

SELLAR: The common people of Sutherland are a parcel of beggars with no stock, but cunning and lazy.

LOCH: They are living in a form of slavery to their own indolence. Nothing could be more at variance with the general interests of society and the individual happiness of the people themselves, than the present state of Highland manners and customs. To be happy, the people must be productive.

SELLAR: They require to be thoroughly brought to the coast, where industry will pay, and to be convinced that they must worship industry or starve. The present enchantment which keeps them down must be broken.

LOCH: The coast of Sutherland abounds with many different kinds of fish. (LOCH *takes off his hat, and speaks directly to the audience.*) Believe it or not, Loch and Sellar actually used these words. (*Puts hat on again.*) Not only white fish, but herring too. With this in mind, His Lordship is considering several sites for new villages on the East Coast – Culgower, Helmsdale, Golspie, Brora, Skelbo and Knockglass – Helmsdale in particular is a perfect natural harbour for a fishing station. And there is said to be coal at Brora.

SELLAR: You will really not find this estate pleasant or profitable until by draining to your coast-line or by emigration you have got your mildewed districts cleared. They are just in that state of society for a savage country, such as the woods of Upper Canada – His Lordship should consider seriously the possibility of subsidising their departures. They might even be inclined to carry a swarm of dependants with them.

LOCH: I gather you yourself, Mr Sellar, have a scheme for a sheep-walk in this area.

SELLAR: The highlands of Scotland may sell £200,000 worth of lean cattle this year. The same ground, under the Cheviot, may produce as much as £900,000 worth of fine wool. The effects of such arrangements in advancing this estate in wealth, civilisation, comfort, industry, virtue and happiness are palpable.

Fiddle in – Tune, 'Bonnie Dundee'*, quietly behind.*

LOCH: Your offer for this area, Mr Sellar, falls a little short of what I had hoped.

SELLAR: The present rents, when they can be collected, amount to no more than £142 per annum.

LOCH: Nevertheless, Mr Sellar, His Lordship will have to remove these people at considerable expense.

SELLAR: To restock the land with sheep will cost considerably more.

LOCH: A reasonable rent would be £400 per annum.

SELLAR: There is the danger of disturbances to be taken into account. £300.

LOCH: You can depend on the Reverend David Mackenzie to deal with that. £375.

SELLAR: Mackenzie is a Highlander. £325.

LOCH: He has just been rewarded with the parish of Farr – £365.

SELLAR: I shall have to pay decent wages to my plain, honest, industrious South-country shepherds. £350.

LOCH: You're a hard man, Mr Sellar.

SELLAR: Cash.

LOCH: Done.

They shake hands, then prepare to sing – 'High Industry' *to the tune of* 'Bonnie Dundee'.

LOCH & SELLAR: As the rain on the hillside comes in from the sea
All the blessings of life fall in showers from me
So if you'd abandon your old misery –
I will teach you the secrets of high industry:

Your barbarous customs, though they may be old
To civilised people hold horrors untold –
What value a culture that cannot be sold?
The price of a culture is counted in gold.

Chorus:
As the rain, etc.

LOCH: There's many a fine shoal of fish in the sea
All waiting for catching and frying for tea –
And I'll buy the surplus, then sell them you see
At double the price that you sold them to me.

Chorus:
As the rain, etc.

SELLAR: I've money to double the rent that you pay
The factor is willing to give me my way
So off you go quietly – like sheep as they say –
I'll arrange for the boats to collect you today.

Chorus:
As the rain, etc.

LOCH & SELLAR: Don't think we are greedy for person gain
What profit we capture we plough back again
We don't want big houses or anything grand
We just want more money to buy up more land.

Chorus:
As the rain, etc.

At the end of the song they go off. The GAELIC SINGER *stands and says:*

SINGER: 'Mo Dhachaidh' (My home)

She sings the song, in Gaelic. The Company and audience join in the chorus.

SINGER: Seinn he-ro-vo, hu-ro-vo hugaibh o he,
So agaibh an obair, bheir togail do m' chridhe,
Bhith stiuireadh mo chasan do m' dhachaidh bheag fhein
Air criochnachadh saothair an là dhomh.

Seall thall air an aiseag am fasgadh nan craobh
Am botham beag geal ud 'se gealaicht le 'aol
Sud agaibh mo dhachaidh 'se dhachaidh mo ghaoil
Gun chaisteal 's an t-saoghal as fhearr leam.

Chorus:
Seinn he-ro-vo etc.

'S an ait ud tha nadur a ghnath cur ri ceol,
Mur e smeorach 's an duilleach 'se'n uiseag neoil
No caochan an fhuarain ag gluasad troimh lon
No Morag ri cronan do'n phaisde.

Final chorus.

At the end of the song, the First Strathnaver GIRL *takes the stage.*

FIRST GIRL: 'A Poem by Donnachadh Buidhe, the Chisholm bard'
Destruction to the sheep from all corners of Europe. Scab, wasting, pining, tumours on the stomach and on the hide.

Foxes and eagles for the lambs. Nothing more to be seen of them but fleshless hides and the grey shepherds leaving the country without laces on their shoes.

I have overlooked someone. The Factor. May he be bound by tight thongs, wearing nothing but his trousers, and beaten with rods from head to foot. May he be placed on a bed of brambles, and covered with thistles.

Enter PATRICK SELLAR. *He pats the baby the* FIRST GIRL *is carrying on her head, then walks up to audience.*

SELLAR: I am not the cruel man they say I am. I am a business man.

He winks and goes, leaving the Two Strathnaver GIRLS *on stage. Whistles of warning come from around them. They are alarmed, but not afraid. They call other women's names, shouting to them in Gaelic: Hurry up, get down here, there come the men with the papers.* OLD MAN *comes on, anxious.*

OLD MAN: Dé tha sibh a' deanamh? (What are you up to?)

FIRST GIRL: A bheil thu bodhar? (Are you deaf?)

SECOND GIRL: Nach eil thu 'gan cluinntinn? (Can't you hear them?)

OLD MAN: De? (What?)

SECOND GIRL: Tha iad a' tighinn le'n cuid pairpearan, air son 'ur sgapadh. (They're coming with their papers to have us thrown out.) Nach eil thu dol a chur stad orra?

OLD MAN: Oh cha chuir iad dragh oirnne co-dhiùbh.

SECOND GIRL: Cha chuir? Gabh dhaibh le do chromag – (Give it them with your stick.)

OLD MAN: Na bi gorach – (Och, away.)

SECOND GIRL: Mur a gabh thusa gabhaidh mise – (If you won't, I will.)

OLD MAN: The Countess of Sutherland will not leave us without –

FIRST GIRL: Tell that to the people of Eddrachilles.

She thrusts the baby into his arms. Both women call to the other women to come and fight.

SECOND GIRL: Mhairil Greasaibh oirbh! (Hurry up.)

FIRST GIRL: Kirsti! The men are all gone and the ones that are here are useless!

SECOND GIRL: (*To* OLD MAN.) No naire mhor ort. (Shame on you.)

The GIRLS *go out.* OLD MAN *shouts after them.*

OLD MAN: We will form a second line of defence.

He turns to the audience as himself.

When they came with the eviction orders, it was always the women who fought back ... Glen Calvie, Ross-shire.

He introduces READERS *from the Company, who stand in their places and read from books:*

READER 1: 'The women met the constables beyond the boundaries over the river, and seized the hand of the one who held the notices. While some held it out by the wrist, others held a live coal to the papers and set fire to them.'

OLD MAN: Strathoykel, Sutherland.

READER 2: 'When the Sheriff and his men arrived, the women were on the road and the men behind the walls. The women shouted "Better to die here than America or the Cape of Good Hope." The first blow was struck by a woman with a stick. The gentry leant out of their saddles and beat at the women's heads with their crops.'

READER 3: In Sollas, North Uist, lands held by MacDonald of the Isles. 'In one case it was necessary to remove two women out of the house by force; one of the women threw herself upon the ground and fell into hysterics, barking and yelling like a dog, but the other woman, the eldest of the family, made an attack with a stick upon an officer, and two stout policemen had great difficulty in carrying her outside the door.'

OLD MAN: And again in North Uist.

READER 4: 'McBain put his men into two divisions, and they attacked the women on two sides. They drove them along the shore, the women screaming to their men – "be manly," and "stand up!" Police and women fought on the sand until McBain recalled his officers and the women crawled away to bathe their bloody heads.'

OLD MAN: Greenyards, Easter Ross.

READER 5: 'Sheriff Taylor accompanied by several officers and a police force of about thirty or more arrived at Greenyards, near Bonar Bridge, and found about 300 people, two-thirds of whom were women. The women stood in front, armed with stones, while the men occupied the background. The women as they bore the brunt of the battle were the principal sufferers, a large number of them being seriously hurt, the wounds on their skulls and bodies showing plainly the severe manner in which they had been dealt with by the police when they were retreating.'

READER 6: 'The police struck with all their force, not only when knocking down but after, when they were on the ground, they beat and kicked them while lying weltering in their blood. Anne Ross, 40, struck on the breast, kicked in the head. Margaret Ross, 18, head split, alienation of mental faculties very perceptible. Elizabeth Ross, 25, knocked down, kicked on the breasts, the batons tore away part of her scalp, shattered frontal and parietal bones. Her long hair, clotted with blood, could be seen in quantities over the ploughed land. Margaret Ross, mother of seven, fractured skull from baton wounds, died later. Catherine Ross, who came to help the wounded, struck down until she fell in the river. Grace Ross, felled with a blow on the forehead. Helen Ross, brought home on a litter, and for the space of eight days could not move her hands or feet.'

OLD MAN: But for every township that fought back, there were many more that didn't. The landlords had an ally in the heart of the community.

Fiddle plays: 'The Lord is my Shepherd'. The Company hum quietly as one of the actors is dressed as the MINISTER *and the* OLD MAN *places his pulpit in position.*

MINISTER: Dearly beloved Brethren, we are gathered here today in the sight of the Lord and in the house of the Lord, to worship the Lord and sing His praises, for He is indeed, the Lord and Shepherd of our souls. Oh you are sheep, sheep who have gone astray, who have wandered from the paths of righteousness and into the tents of iniquity. Oh guilty sinners, turn from your evil ways. How many times and on how many Sabbaths have I warned you from this very pulpit of your wickedness and of the wrath of the Almighty. For I will repay, saith the Lord. The troubles that are visiting you are a judgement from God, and a warning of the final judgement that is to come. Some of you here today are so far from the fold, have so far neglected the dignity of your womanhood, that you have risen up to curse your masters, and violate the laws of the land. I refer of course to the burning of the writs. And everybody here gathered knows to which persons I

am referring. There will be no more of this foolishness. Be warned. Unless you repent, you are in great danger of the fire, where there will be much wailing and gnashing of teeth. On that fearful day when God divides the sheep from the goats, every one of us, and particularly those whom I have spoken of today, will have to answer for their flagrant transgression of authority.

He goes off.

OLD MAN: And it worked …

SECOND GIRL: Everywhere, except in Knockan, Elphin and Coigeach.

FIRST GIRL comes on stage and says, to mounting cheers from the others:

FIRST GIRL: Here the people made a stout resistance, the women disarming about twenty policemen and sheriff-officers, burning the summonses in a heap, and ducking the representatives of the law in a neighbouring pool. (*Big cheer.*) The men formed a second line of defence – (*Groan.*) – in case the women should receive any ill-treatment. (*More groans.*) They, however, never put a finger on the officers of the law – all of whom returned home without serving a single summons or evicting a single crofter!

A big hooch from the Company, the fiddle strikes up and they leap onto the stage to dance to celebrate this victory, the women leading off.

At the end, all go off except the actor playing the OLD MAN, *who comes to mike and talks to the audience as himself.*

OLD MAN: What was really going on? There is no doubt that a change had to come to the Highlands: the population was growing too fast for the old, inefficient methods of agriculture to keep everyone fed. Even before the Clearances, emigration had been the only way out for some. But this coincided with something else: English – and Scottish – capital was growing powerful and needed to expand. Huge profits were being made already as a result of the Industrial Revolution, and improved methods of agriculture. This accumulated wealth had to be used, to make profit – because this is the law of capitalism. It expanded all over the globe. And just as it saw in Africa, the West Indies, Canada, the Middle East and China, ways of increasing itself, so in the Highlands of Scotland it saw the same opportunity. The technological innovation was there: the Cheviot, a breed of sheep that would survive the Highland winter and produce fine wool. The money was there. Unfortunately, the people were there too. But the law of capitalism had to be obeyed. And this was how it was done:

Bell ringing. Enter SHERIFF'S MAN, *reading eviction order.*

Enter PATRICK SELLAR, *interrupting him.*

SELLAR: Get on with it, man, you're costing me a fortune with your verbiage: I've got a flock of sheep waiting in Culmailly.

SHERIFF'S MAN: Sheriff Macleod said to be sure and read this, Sir –

SELLAR: Macleod's well known to be a poacher – how would he not be sympathetic to other thieves and tinkers? Who's in there, then?

SHERIFF'S MAN: William Chisholm, sir –

SELLAR: Another tinker.

SHERIFF'S MAN: His family have lived here for some time, Mr Sellar –

SELLAR: Well, he'll no' be here for much longer – he's a sheep-stealer, a squatter who pays no rent, and the Minister informs me he's bigamist. Get him out –

SHERIFF'S MAN: (*Calls at door.*) Chisholm! (*From within an* OLD WOMAN's *voice cries out in terror* – 'Sin Sellar, Sin Sellar!')

SHERIFF'S MAN: (*To* SELLAR.) There's an old woman in there, sir –

SELLAR: Well, get her out, man!

A WOMAN *comes out in great distress. A man,* MACLEOD, *has come on. He watches.*

WOMAN: Mo mhàithair, mo mhàithair. (My mother, my mother.)

SELLAR: (*Annoyed at the Gaelic.*) What's she saying?

SHERIFF'S MAN: She says it's her mother, sir –

The WOMAN *goes over to* MACLEOD.

WOMAN: O mhaigstir MhicLeoid, tha mo mhàthair ceithir fichead bliadhna 'sa coig deug – 's ma theid a carachadh theid a mort. (Oh, Mr Macleod, my mother is 94 years old and if she's moved she'll die.)

MACLEOD: She says her mother is 94 years old, Mr Sellar, and if she's moved she'll die.

SELLAR: (*To* SHERIFF'S MAN.) Get her out. (SHERIFF'S MAN *hesitates.*) Do your job, man –

SHERIFF'S MAN: I'd rather lose my job, sir –

SELLAR: (*Quietly.*) Get the torch.

SHERIFF'S MAN *goes out.*

MACLEOD: You have a great hatred for the people of these parts, Mr Sellar.

SELLAR: I am compelled to do everything at the point of the sword. These people here are absolutely a century behind and lack common honesty. I have brought them wonderfully forward, and calculate that within two years I shall have all the Estate arranged.

MACLEOD: Aye, to your own advantage. Have you no shame at what you are doing to these people?

SELLAR: Such a set of savages is not to be found in the wilds of America. If Lord and Lady Stafford had not put it into my power to quell this banditti, we may have bid adieu to all improvement.

MACLEOD: Will you not even give her time to die?

SELLAR: Damn her the old witch, she's lived long enough –

Enter SHERIFF'S MAN *with a torch; he throws it onto the cottage.*

– let her burn.

Sound of fire, fire-effect on cottage, screams, etc. Blackout. Silence. Single spot on WOMAN, OLD WOMAN *and* MACLEOD.

MACLEOD: Five days later, the old woman died.

Light up.

SELLAR: (*To audience.*) I am perfectly satisfied that no person has suffered hardship or injury as a result of these improvements.

The Company go back to their seats, and read short sections of accounts of the Clearances from many different areas of the North. Note: readings to be selected from the following, according to where the show is being done.

READER: Donald Sage, Kildonan, Sutherland. 'The whole inhabitants of Kildonan parish, nearly 2,000 souls, were utterly rooted and burned out. Many, especially the young and robust, left the country, but the aged, the females and children, were obliged to stay and accept the wretched allotments allowed them on the seashore and endeavour to learn fishing.'

READER: Ardnamurchan, Argyll. 'A half-witted woman who flatly refused to flit was locked up in her cottage, the door being barricaded on the outside by masonwork. She was visited every morning to see if she had arrived at a tractable state of mind, but for days she held out. It was not until her slender store of food was exhausted that she ceased to argue with the inevitable and decided to capitulate.'

READER: Ross-shire. 'From the estate of Robertson of Kindace in the year 1843 the whole inhabitants of Glencalvie were evicted, and so unprovided and unprepared were they for removal at such an inclement season of the year, that they had to shelter themselves in a church and a burying ground. For months there were nineteen families within this gloomy and solitary resting abode of the dead.'

READER: Ravigill, Sutherland. 'The factor, Mr Sellar, watched while the burners tore down the house of John Mackay. His wife, although pregnant, climbed on to the roof and fell through in a desperate attempt to protect her home. Her screams of labour were mingled with the cries of protest of her husband who said: "the law of the country must surely have changed for such things to be done with the approval of the Sheriff's Officer and the Factor".'

READER: Strathnaver, Sutherland. 'Grace MacDonald took shelter up the brae and remained there for a day and a night watching the burnings. When a terrified cat jumped from a burning cottage it was thrown back in again and again until it died.'

READER: Suisinish, Skye. 'Flora Matheson, aged 96, who could not walk, was evicted while all the able-bodied men and boys were away south to earn money to pay the rent. Her three grand-children – the oldest aged 10 – helped her to crawl along on her hands and knees until she reached a sheep-cot. They remained there until the following December. Meanwhile her son came home from the harvest in the south and was amazed at the treatment his aged mother and children had received. He was then in good health. Within a few weeks, with the cold and damp, he was seized with violent cramp and cough, his limbs and body swelled, and he died. His corpse lay across the floor, the wind waving his long black hair to and fro until he was placed in his coffin. The sick grand-children were removed from the cot by the Inspector for the Poor. The old woman was reduced to a skeleton and had no food but a few wet potatoes and two or three shellfish.'

READER: 'The Island of Rhum was cleared of its inhabitants, some 400 souls, to make way for one sheep farmer and 8,000 sheep.'

READER: Knoydart, Inverness-shire. 'John McKinnon, a cottar aged 44, with a wife and six children, had his house pulled down. The ruins of an old chapel were near at hand and parts of the walls were still standing. There McKinnon proceeded with his family. The manager of Knoydart then appeared with his minions and invaded this helpless family even within the walls of the sanctuary. They pulled down the sticks and sails they set up within the ruins, threw his tables, stools, chair and other belongings over the walls, burnt up the hay on which they slept, and then left the district. Four times they came and did the same thing.'

READER: 'In 1811 Rogart in Sutherland had a population of 2,148. By 1911 it was 892.'

READER: 'During the time of the Clearances, the population of the parishes of Killarow and Kilmenny – in Islay – was reduced from 7,100 to 2,700. The population of the entire island was halved.'

READER: Ceal na Coille, Strathnaver. 'The people were pushed further and further down to the coast. They suffered very much for the want of houses and threw up earthen walls with blankets over the top, and four or five families lived like this throughout the winter while the last of their cattle died. They were removed as many as four or five times until they could go no further, unless by taking a ship for the colonies.'

From the middle of the Suisinish reading, the GAELIC SINGER has been quietly humming the tune of 'Soraidh Leis an ait'. *She now stands and sings:*

SINGER: Soraidh leis an àit',
Ad d'fhuair mi m'arach òg,
Eilean nan beann àrda,
Far an tàmh an ceo.

MC steps forward.

MC: Of all the many evictors, Mr Patrick Sellar was the only one who did not escape the full majesty of the law. He was charged with the murder of three people and numerous crimes at Inverness High Court.

The Company become a murmuring JURY.
Enter the JUDGE. They stand, then sit silently.
Enter PATRICK SELLAR.

SELLAR: Re the charge of culpable homicide, my Lord – can you believe, my good sir, that I, a person not yet cognosed or escaped from a madhouse, should deliberately, in open day, by means of an officer who has a wife and family, burn a house with a woman in it? Or that the officer should do so, instead of ejecting the tenant? The said tenant and woman being persons of whom we have no felonious intent, no malice, no ill-will.

JUDGE: Therefore, I would ask you (the jury) to ignore all the charges except two. One of these concerns the destruction of barns. In this case, Mr Sellar has ignored a custom of the country, although he has not infringed the laws of Scotland. And the second case concerns the burning of the house of Chisholm. And here we are reminded of the contradictory nature of the testimony. Now if the jury are at all at a loss on this part of the case, I would ask them to take into consideration the character of the accused, for this is always of value in balancing contradictory testimony. For here there is, in the first place, real evidence as regards Mr Sellar's conduct towards the sick – which in all cases has been proved to be most humane. And secondly, there are the letters of Sir George Abercrombie, Mr Fenton and Mr Brodie – which, although not evidence, must have some weight with the jury. And there are the testimonies of Mr Gilzean, and Sir Archibald Dunbar – (*Sees him in the audience, waves.*) – hello, Archie. All of them testifying to Mr Sellar's humanity of disposition. How say you?

JURY: Oh, not guilty, no, no, no, etc.

JUDGE: My opinion completely concurs with that of the jury.

JURY applaud PATRICK SELLAR.

SELLAR: Every reformer of mankind has been abused by the established errors, frauds and quackery. But where the reformers have been right at bottom, they have, by patience, and by their unabating zeal and enthusiasm, got forward, in spite of every opposition. And so, I trust, will Lord and Lady Stafford, in their generous exertions to better the people in this country.

More applause. Distant humming of 'Land of Hope and Glory'.

SELLAR: (*Pointing to the mountains, from behind which a giant statue slowly emerges – eventually dwarfing the entire hall.*) In lasting memorial of George Granville, Duke of Sutherland, Marquess of Stafford, K.G., an upright and patriotic nobleman, a judicious, kind and liberal landlord;

who identified the improvement of his vast estates with the prosperity of all who cultivated them; a public yet unostentatious benefactor, who, while he provided useful employment for the active labourer, opened wide his hands to the distresses of the widow, the sick and the traveller: a mourning and grateful tenantry, uniting with the inhabitants of the neighbourhood, erected *this pillar* . . .

Music turns sour. Statue disintegrates or flies away.

Enter a Victorian GENT.

GENT: And now a poem, by Lord Francis Egerton, in honour of the first Duke of Sutherland:

He coughs politely then performs the poem in a Victorian posturing manner, with vivid gestures – some perhaps a little unlikely.

He found our soil by labour un-subdued,
E'en as our fathers left it, stern and rude;
And land disjoined from land, and man from men,
By stubborn rock, fierce tide, and quaking fen,
His liberal hand, his head's sagacious toil,
Abashed the ruder genius of the soil.
The fen forbore to quake, the ascent was plain,
Huge mounds restrained and arches spanned the main.
He tamed the torrent, fertilized the sand,
And joined a province to its parent land.
Recurrent famine from her holds he chased,
And left a garden what he found a waste.
A stranger from a distant land he came,
But brought a birthright where he chose a name;
And native accents shall his loss bewail,
Who came a Saxon and remained a Gael.
Thank you.

At the end of the poem, the Company applaud politely.

Enter the GAELIC SINGER.

SINGER: A translation of a Gaelic poem in honour of the Duke of Sutherland:
Nothing shall be placed over you
But the dung of cattle.
There will be no weeping of children
Or the crying of women.
And when a spade of the turf is thrown upon you,
Our country will be clean again.

She goes off. Enter HARRIET BEECHER STOWE *in a large pink bonnet.*

HARRIET BS: Good evening. My name is Harriet Beecher Stowe, and I am a lady novelist from Cincinatti, Ohio. You may have heard of my *Uncle Tom's Cabin*. (*Confidentially.*) Well, that was about the negro slaves, and my *new* book – *Sunny Memories of a Stay in Scotland* – is about your *dreamy*

Highlanders. And my dear friend and namesake, Harriet, Duchess of Sutherland – I've been visiting with her you know, at her delightful home in London, Stafford House, and her country home in the Midlands, Trentham House, and her ancestral home Dunrobin Castle, Scotland . . . where was I? Oh yes – well she is a very enlightened, charming lady, and she is known for her undying support of the oppressed people of the world – the negroes, the slaves, Mr Garibaldi's Italians – she thinks they all ought to be treated much nicer. And as to those ridiculous stories about *her*, one has only to be here, moving in society to see how excessively absurd they are. I was associating from day to day with people of every religious denomination and every rank of life, and had there been the least shadow of a foundation for any such accusations, I certainly should have heard it. To my view, it is an almost sublime instance of the benevolent employment of superior wealth and power in shortening the struggles of advancing civilisation.

COMPANY: Baa. Baa. Baa, etc.

They come after her on all fours, bleating. She backs away in some confusion. The sheep sing 'These Are My Mountains'.

Sound of Indian drums, war-whoops, jungle birds, coyotes, hens, dogs barking. Book turns to an Indian setting. Enter RED INDIANS. *They dance and then freeze.*

Enter LORD SELKIRK *in top hat. He passes between the* INDIANS *to the microphone.*

LORD SELKIRK: I am Lord Selkirk and I have a plan. The people of the glens have become a redundant population. I favour their going where they have a better prospect of happiness and prosperity so long as they are not lost to Britain. The present stream of emigration must be diverted so as to strengthen Britain overseas. My partners and I have recently acquired stock worth just over £12,000 in the Hudson's Bay Company of Canada and Fenchurch Street. It is not a controlling interest, but it is a large interest. Our rivals, the Northwest Company, a collection of Frenchmen, have so far ingratiated themselves with the natives – (*Indicates them.*) – as to become a serious threat to our trading operations throughout the colony. They are ruthless and unprincipled. The only hope for the Hudson's Bay Company is to combine the needs of the Highlanders for land with our own most urgent interest, and settle the place. I had at first thought of settling it with Irishmen, but the Colonial Officer pointed out that a colony made up of people so intractable – not to say wild – was foredoomed and unsuitable for our purposes. So I have acquired a tract of land five times the size of Scotland (*Indicates the number.*) and several boat loads of sturdy Highlanders. There is no point in placing them on land that is already tamed. They must go to the Red

River Valley and curtail the activities of the Northwest Company and their Indian friends.

He strikes a post at the side of the stage and waits. Exeunt INDIANS *beating their drums.*

Enter STURDY HIGHLANDER *punting up a river. He does elaborate pantomime double take at Red Indian painted on the set, and punts down to the microphone.*

SH: (*To audience.*) Has anybody here seen Selkirk?

LORD SELKIRK: (*From his corner.*) I was at that time in my house in London anxiously awaiting news.

SH: Ah well, since himself is not here we'll have to get on with the tilling of the land. As you can see by my costume, I'm a Sturdy Highlander, and I've been sent here to till the land for future generations and for Lord Selkirk. While I'm getting on with the planting of the brussel sprouts and the runner beans, I am particularly vulnerable to attack from the rear. So if any of you should see any of those big Red Indians I've heard about will you let me know? Will you do that now? I tell you what, you'd better shout something, let me see, let me see – I know. *Walla Walla Wooskie.* Will you shout that? Let's have a practice – after three now, one, two, three – *Walla Walla Wooskie!*

He goes through several attempts to get the audience to join in until they do, with gusto – then:

Very good. Smashing. Now I can get on with it.

Enter GRANNY *with shawl carrying baby.*

GRANNY: De? What? What?

SH: What?

GRANNY: I can't hear, I can't hear!

SH: Oh I forgot to tell you – that's Granny. She can't hear a thing. She's never been the same since the police hit her over the head at Strathnaver. So as well as the shouting of the Walla Walla Wooskie will you all wave your hands. (*He does.*) Then Granny can see, and I can hear, and a quick bash with the cromach and we'll be all right. All right? Let's have a practice.

They all do until he's satisfied.

Great, great.

GRANNY *beams, gives the thumbs up and goes off to sit down.*

On with the planting of the radishes!

He starts to dig the ground, singing to himself, head down. Re-enter INDIANS *beating drum, tomahawks raised. The audience shouts 'Walla Walla Wooskie'. The* INDIANS *run off before the* STURDY HIGHLANDER *sees them. He accuses the audience of having him on. Repeat this twice. The third time they creep on and after some dodging about, stand towering over him tomahawks raised.*

FIRST INDIAN: Ug!

SECOND INDIAN: Ug!

SH: (*Into microphone.*) Gulp!

Enter outrageous FRENCH NORTHWEST TRADER. *He signals the* INDIANS *to leave. They do, tugging forelocks. He taps* SH. SH *collapses thinking it's the tomahawks.*

His WIFE *and* GRANNY *run on and watch with suspicion.*

NWT: I am Nor-west Tra-der! Oo are you?

SH: I'm fine, hoo's yersel'?

NWT: No no, *what* are you?

SH: I am a Sturdy Highlander and this is my Granny. And this is wee Calum.

He indicates the baby she is carrying still.

NWT: (*Patting the baby's head.*) Thank heaven for little Gaels! I have a très bonne idée!

SH: What?

NWT: A very good idea – why don't *you* go back home!

SH: Because we have no home to go back to, this is our home now.

WIFE *and* GRANNY *nod.*

NWT: That is where you are very wrong my friend, we have ways of making you leave! Où sont mes peaux rouges – (*To audience.*) Anyone who says walla walla wooskie or the waving of the palms will (*He makes throat-cutting gesture.*) Tonto!

RED INDIAN 1: (*Leaps on.*) Pronto!

NWT: Hawkeye!

RED INDIAN 2: (*Leaps on.*) Och aye!

The INDIANS *come on and stand menacing the group one on each side.*

NWT: These are my little friends. They give me furs, beaver skins, Davy Crockett hats and all the little necessities of life, I give them beads, baubles, VD, diphtheria, influenza, cholera, fire water and all the benefits of civilisation. These – are my mountains, and you're going home.

SH: (*Clinging to his womenfolk.*) I'll have to speak to Lord Selkirk about that.

Exit NWT *with hollow laugh.*
The INDIANS *remain where they are.*
The group huddle and freeze.

LORD SELKIRK: Things are not going well in the Red River Valley.

SH: (*Turning his head.*) You can say that again!

LORD SELKIRK: Things are not going well in the Red River Valley. The Governor of the Province seems to have no control over the hooligans of the Northwest Company and their half-breed servants. I have complained to the Colonial Secretary. Unfortunately the Northwest

Company denies our allegations and the Governor will not provide troops to protect the settlers. However – the highlanders are a sturdy breed and accustomed to the hazards of life in the wild so I am sending out another three boatloads.

He exits pleased. The lights change to fire on the encampment. The INDIANS dance round the family, with scalping gestures while they sink down with wails to the ground.

WIFE and GRANNY remain and hum the song, 'Take me Back to the Red River Valley', while SH rises, crosses to the microphone and narrates:

SH: (*Out of character.*) But we came, more and more of us, from all over Europe, in the interests of a trade war between two lots of shareholders, and, in time, the Red Indians were reduced to the same state as our fathers after Culloden – defeated, hunted, treated like the scum of the earth, their culture polluted and torn out with slow deliberation and their land no longer their own.

The humming dies away and the mouth-organ takes over quietly.

But still we came. From all over Europe. The highland exploitation chain-reacted around the world; in Australia the aborigines were hunted like animals: in Tasmania not one aborigine was left alive; all over Africa, black men were massacred and brought to heel. In America the plains were emptied of men and buffalo, and the seeds of the next century's imperialist power were firmly planted. And at home, the word went round that over there, things were getting better.

GAELIC SINGER stands and reads a poem in Gaelic.

SINGER: Gur muladach mise 'smi seo gun duine idir
a thogas, no thuigeas, no sheineas leam dàn
le durachd mo chridhe soraidh slan leis na gillean
a sheòl thar na linne gu manitoba.

Tha luchd fearainn shaor anns an am so ro ghaolach
air storas an t-saoghail a shlaodadh bho chach.
's bidh innleachdan baoghalt 's a gaidhealtachd daonan
gu forgradh nan daoine 's chuir chaorach nan ait.

Cha labhar mi tuileadh mu euchd nam fear curant
do Bhreatuinn fuar urram 'gach cumasg is spairn
'se daoired an fhearainn a dh 'fhag sinn cho tana
's gun chuimhne air sebastapol 's manitoba.

Enter two comic-stereotype HIGHLANDERS.

HIGHLANDER 1: Scene 5, Isle of Skye, 1882!

Roll on drums.

HIGHLANDER 2: Now at that time, Lord Macdonald was driving the people down to the shores …

HIGHLANDER 1: What shores?

HIGHLANDER 2: Oh, I'll have a wee dram!

Roll on drum.

No, but seriously though, he was having a bit of an altercation about the grazing rights on a little moor …

HIGHLANDER 1: A little moor?

HIGHLANDER 2: Oh well, that's very civil of you!

HIGHLANDER 1: Oh, Sandy, you're a great one for the drink.

HIGHLANDER 2: Oh Angus I am that, I am.

HIGHLANDER 1: I tell you what, when I'm dead will you pour a bottle of the Talisker over my dead body?

HIGHLANDER 2: Certainly, certainly, you won't mind if I pass it through the kidneys first.

HIGHLANDER 1 drives him off. Drum roll.

HIGHLANDER 1: Scene 5, 1882, Isle of Skye, Glendale.

Enter two Glendale WOMEN in shawls. They cross to read a notice.

WOMAN 1: De thann. (What's this?)

WOMAN 2: (*Reads.*) 'We the tenants on the estate of Glendale do hereby warn each other to meet on or about 1 p.m. on 7th Feb. 1882 at Glendale Church, for the purpose of stating our respective grievances publicly' – So they're doing something about it at last – 'in order to communicate the same to our superiors'.

WOMAN 1: De th'ann superiors?

WOMAN 2: Na daoine mhoral! (The great ones.)

WOMAN 1: Huh.

WOMAN 2: As if they'd listen.

The rest of the Company, as the MEN of Glendale, enter discussing the meeting.

OLD MAN: The whole of the bruachs are being emptied to make way for the sheep, as if they hadn't done enough already.

YOUNGER MAN: Aye, all the crofts in Glendale are being split up to make room for those they've thrown off, and the land's being worked to death till it will grow no more.

OLD MAN: No wonder, when half our own seaweed is taken from us and we have to row all the way round the point to Dunvegan to buy it at 31 shillings and sixpence a ton, and sometimes he's not even in …

YOUNGER MAN: Aye, and the rents are going up forbye.

WOMAN 2: Did you hear, the factor's closed all the shops – he's to open his own meal store and we can only buy from him.

OLD MAN: And it's a helluva long row all the way to Dunvegan …

WOMAN 1: And they've stuck up a notice to stop us gathering the driftwood from our own shores.

OLD MAN: And that loch can be very choppy …

MAN 3: And do you know the factor has ordered me to shoot my own dog in case he worried the sheep –

OLD MAN: Och what are the sheep worried about, they don't have to row all the way round the point –

YOUNGER MAN: Bith eamh sabhach. (*Behave yourself.*)

MAN 3: Order! Order!

YOUNGER MAN: (*Addresses them all.*) Contrary to the opinion of our noble proprietors set forth in the newspapers, notably *The Scotsman*, known hereabouts as The United Liar, they have shown themselves to have no interest in these parts except for the extraction of greater and greater rents, the removal of the people to all corners of the earth and the subjection of those who remain to the will of their factor. Over the last sixty years, we in Skye have put up with just about every indignity a human being can suffer. They have succeeded because we are divided amongst ourselves. It has been proposed that the people of Glendale should unite to take action altogether as one body. We are all in the same situation. Every man and every township has a grievance.

OLD MAN: Och that's right enough.

YOUNGER MAN: If we go one by one to make separate claims, we know what will happen. It should not fall on any one person to be singled out for the wrath of the factor. We must go altogether, and any punishment will have to be inflicted on all of us.

General agreement.

OLD MAN: Ach well I just don't know about that …

YOUNGER MAN: To guard against anyone falling out of the ranks, it has been proposed that we one and all subscribe our names in a book, and pledge ourselves as a matter of honour to stand by any demand we may make.

Cheers.

And until our grievances are met, it has been proposed that we hold back our rent.

WOMAN 2: No trouble at all!

Cheers.

YOUNGER MAN: That way the situation might strike the factor with greater urgency!

OLD MAN: I might strike him with urgency myself …

WOMAN 2: Where's the book – I'll be the first to sign …

YOUNGER MAN produces a book, gives it to WOMAN 2. All sign. YOUNGER MAN comes forward, speaks to audience out of character.

YOUNGER MAN: The idea of united action spread. The tenants of a certain Dr Martin of Borreraig were obliged to sell their fish and their cattle to the laird at his own price, and to give him eight days' free labour each year, or 2/6d a day in lieu. They have now struck against this labour; and propose to walk in the same paths as the men of Glendale. And in the Braes area of Skye a mighty confrontation was about to take place. Lord Macdonald, in order to settle his vast debts, had already driven out the people from most of

his estate. His tenants in the Braes area resolved, like the people of Glendale, to withhold their rent until certain of their grievances were met.

Lord Macdonald made up his mind to put the law in force against them and not on any account to yield to their demands. The unfortunate Sheriff Officer, his assistant who also happened to be the factor's clerk and his Lordship's ground officer, set out from Portree to serve writs of removal on all the people of the townships of Peinichorrain, Balmeanach, and Gedintaillear.

A SINGER steps forward and sings, the Company joining in the chorus.

'The Battle of the Braes'
(To the tune of 'The Battle of Harlaw')

A Sheriff from the factor came
And he came down our way
By Lord Macdonald he was sent
To clear us out frae Skye

Chorus:
Oh the battle was long but the people were strong
You should have been there that day
His depute Martin came along
He could not speak nor stand
They'd filled him up with usique beath
To throw us off our land

Chorus:
Oh the battle, etc.

Oh he had come with fifty men
He could not pass that day
For all the women from the Braes
Went out to bar his way

Chorus:
Oh the battle, etc.

The Laird was angered he was wild
Macdonald must not fail
He sent the sheriff back again
To throw us into jail

Chorus:
Oh the battle, etc.

And next came fifty policemen
From Glasgow they were sent
The Inverness police knew fine
That what we said we meant

Chorus:
Oh the battle, etc.

A wet and dismal morning dawned
As from Portree they rode
The men of the Braes were up in time
And met them on the road

Chorus:
Oh the battle, etc.

All day the cruel battle raged
We showed them we could fight
But five brave men were taken off
To Inverness that night.

Chorus:
Oh the battle, etc.

The judge he found them guilty men
And fined them two pounds ten
In half a minute he was paid
And off they went again

Chorus:
Oh the battle, etc.

Once more Macdonald's anger broke
'Invade the Isle of Skye
Two thousand soldiers, boats and guns
The people must comply!'

Chorus:
Oh the battle, etc.

'Oh if we send one million men'
In London they declared
'We'd never clear the Isle of Skye
The Braes men are not feared.'

Chorus:
Oh the battle, etc.
The police up in Inverness
Demanded extra men
No other town in all the land
Would help them out again.

Chorus:
Oh the battle, etc.

So back the Sheriff came to Braes
All Scotland watched him go
Will you clear off Macdonald's land?
The people answered NO.

Chorus:
Oh the battle was long but the people were strong
You should have been there that day.

At the end of the song, a big 'Heugh!' And all go off leaving the MC on stage.

MC: Lord Macdonald was forced, in the interests of his own class, to come to a settlement in the Braes. A victory had been won.

The men of Glendale did not fare so well. A gunboat was sent in, and three men were imprisoned for two months. But the resistance continued. Two gunboats, a transport ship and a hundred marines were sent in against

them. Her Imperial Majesty's Government would move in its own time.

Enter QUEEN VICTORIA. She waves, and sings: 'These Are Our Mountains'.

QUEEN VICTORIA: These are our mountains
And this is our glen
The braes of your childhood
Are English again

Though wide is our Empire
Balmoral is best
Yes these are our mountains
And we are impressed.

Enter shooting party with large armoury. GHILLIE, LORD CRASK, and LADY PHOSPHATE OF RUNCORN.

LADY PH: Her Royal Majesty the Queen is so right about the charm of this divine part of the world, what? Your estates, Lord Crask, abound in brown trout and grouse – what? –
LORD CRASK: Has your Ladyship sampled the salmon?
LADY PH: The rugged beauty hereabouts puts one in mind of the poetic fancies of dear Lord Tennyson – what?
LORD CRASK: Lady Phosphate of Runcorn you are too kind.
LADY PH: Oh listen for the vale profound is overflowing with the sound.

Blast of gunfire.

GHILLIE: (*Tries to stop them.*) No no no no – the beaters are just having their tea.
LADY PH: As one does. What?
LORD CRASK: What?

Goes to fire; GHILLIE restrains him.

GHILLIE: (*To audience.*) That's nothing, you should see him when he's fishing.
LADY PH: How far do your domains extend over this beauteous countryside, Lord Crask?
LORD CRASK: I have about 120,000 acres down that way, but most of it's over that way.
LADY PH: Oh Archie ... Capital, capital, capital ...
LORD CRASK: Oh yes I've got bags of that too – 200,000 shares in Argentine Beef, half a million tied up in shipping, and a mile or two of docks in Wapping.
LADY PH: Topping –
LORD CRASK: No Wapping –
LADY PH: What?

LORD CRASK goes to shoot – GHILLIE restrains him.

GHILLIE: No no no no no.
LADY PH: Your highland air is very bracing – I quite fancy a small port ...
LORD CRASK: Oh – how would you like Lochinver?
LADY PH: No no no, I mean I'd like to wet my whistle –

Figure 26 Bill Paterson as the English (in tweeds) stag hunter meeting a kilted Scots hunter (John Bett), in 7:84 Scotland's production of *The Cheviot, the Stag and the Black, Black Oil*, 1973. (Reprinted by kind permission of SCRAN: Royal Commission on the Ancient and Historical Monuments of Scotland.)

LORD CRASK: (*Waving hand.*) We've left a bush over there for that sort of thing ...

GHILLIE *whistles up the beaters.*

GHILLIE: Any moment now sir ...

LORD CRASK: Here come the grouse, Lady Phosphate –

LADY PH: What?

LORD CRASK: The grouse –

LADY PH: Oh, how lovely. (*She gets out a sten gun.*) I find it so moving that all over the north of North Britain, healthy, vigorous people are deriving so much innocent pleasure at so little cost to their fellow human beings.

Barrage. GHILLIE *aims* LORD CRASK'S *gun up higher, struggles*

with him. LADY PHOSPHATE *fires her sten from the hip. Bombs, shells, etc. Barrage ends.*

GHILLIE: Oh no – Thon was a nice wee boy.

Music – guitar and mandolin begins. LORD CRASK *and* LADY PHOSPHATE *sing a duet.*

BOTH: Oh it's awfully, frightfully, ni-i-ce,
Shooting stags, my dear and grice –
And there's nothing quite so righ-it-it
As a fortnight catching trite:

And if the locals should complain,
Well we can clear them off again.

LADY PH: We'll clear the straths

LORD CRASK: We'll clear the paths

LADY PH: We'll clear the bens

LORD CRASK: We'll clear the glens

BOTH: We'll show them we're the ruling class.

Repeat from: 'We'll clear the straths'. *Instrumental half verse.*

LORD CRASK: (*Speaking over the music.*) Oh they all come here, you know – Lady Phosphate of Runcorn – her husband's big in chemicals – she has a great interest in Highland culture.

LADY PH: How I wish that I could paint –
For the people are so quaint
I said so at our ceilidh
To dear Benjamin Disraeli.
Mr Landseer showed the way –
He gets commissions every day –
The Silvery Tay.

LORD CRASK: The Stag at Bay

LADY PH: The misty Moor –

LORD CRASK: Sir George McClure

BOTH: We are the Monarchs of the Glen –

LADY PH: The Shepherd Boy

LORD CRASK: Old Man of Hoy

LADY PH: And Fingal's Cave

LORD CRASK: The Chieftain Brave

BOTH: We are the Monarchs of the Glen

LORD CRASK: We love to dress as Highland lads
In our tartans, kilts and plaids –

LADY PH: And to dance the shean trew-oo-oos
In our bonnie, ghillie, shoes –

BOTH: And the skirling of the pi-broch
As it echoes o'er the wee-loch

LORD CRASK: We love the games

LADY PH: Their funny names

LORD CRASK: The sporran's swing

LADY PH: The Highland fling

BOTH: We are more Scottish than Scotch

LADY PH: The Camera-ha

LORD CRASK: The Slainte-Vah

LADY PH: Is that the lot?

Figure 27 John Bett and Elizabeth MacLennan (7:84 Scotland) in *The Cheviot, the Stag and the Black, Black Oil*, 1973. (Photographer: Barry Jones.)

BOTH: Sir Walter Scott –
We are more Scottish than the Scotch.

They become more serious. They turn their guns on the audience.

LORD CRASK: But although we think you're quaint,
Don't forget to pay your rent,
And if you should want your land,
We'll cut off your grasping hand.
LADY PH: You had better learn your place,
You're a low and servile race –
We've cleared the straths
LORD CRASK: We've cleared the paths
LADY PH: We've cleared the bens
LORD CRASK: We've cleared the glens
BOTH: And we can do it once again –
LADY PH: We've got the brass
LORD CRASK: We've got the class.
LADY PH: We've got the law
LORD CRASK: We need no more –
BOTH: (*Climax.*) We'll show you. We're the ruling class!

Song ends.

GHILLIE: You're in fine voice today Lord Crask and Lady Phosphate.
LORD CRASK: Thank you, MacAlister –
GHILLIE: Er – MacPherson, sir –
LORD CRASK: Yes, that's right MacDougall. Do you know, Lady Phosphate, there's a whole lot of trouble-makers, do-gooders, woolly thinkers in the South trying to say these people aren't satisfied in some way or another.
LADY PH: Oh – ghastly …
LORD CRASK: Absolute poppycock – look at MacDonald here, he's a bit of a peasant –
LADY PH: Yes, you're a peasant, aren't you?
GHILLIE: MacPherson, sir.
LORD CRASK: Nothing wrong with you is there, Macdonald? No complaints?
GHILLIE: No sir, no sir, not at all.
LORD CRASK: Everything's all right with you, MacAlister –
GHILLIE: Just fine, sir, just fine, everything's just fine.
LORD CRASK: Been with me twenty years. Just like one of the family, aren't you? Mac – er. What's your name again?
GHILLIE: MacPherson, sir.
LORD CRASK: That's right, Mackenzie – none of your people complaining, eh? How's your father?
GHILLIE: Dead, sir –
LORD CRASK: Marvellous, no complaints, marvellous – None of your people had to leave the district, what?
GHILLIE: Oh no sir, my own niece from Skye, Mary, she's away working in the hospital in Glasgow – Mary MacPherson's her name.
LORD CRASK: Oh Mary – bright little girl – always singing happily around the house, never understood a word she said.

Exeunt LORD CRASK and LADY PHOSPHATE.

GHILLIE: Aye, Mary MacPherson, happy as a linnie, sir.

The GAELIC SINGER comes on as MARY MACPHERSON, sings a very sad song.

Ged tha mo cheann air liathadh
Le diachainnean is bron
Is Grian mo leth chiad bliadhna
A 'dol sios fo na neòil,
Tha m' aigne air a liònadh
Le iarrtas ro mhòr
Gum faicinn Eilean sgiathach
Nan siantannan 's a' cheò

Ach cò aig a bheuil cluasan
No cridhe gluasad beó
Nach seinneadh leam an duan so
M'an truaighe thainig òirnn?
Na miltean air a' fuadach,
Thar chuan gun chuid gun chòir,
An smaointean thar nan cuantan
Gun Eilean uain' a' cheò.

At the end of the song, the MC comes to the microphone.

MC: During the time of the Clearances, many of the men did not resist because they were away in the Army, defending the British way of life. By the 1850s, it slowly dawned on people that they were being used.

A ridiculous procession, led by bagpipes and drums comes on, followed by the 3RD DUKE OF SUTHERLAND. He addresses the audience.

DUKE: Good morning. I have come all this way to Golspie to speak to you, my tenants, because our country is in need.

TENANT: (*From audience.*) Baa-aah.

DUKE: The Russians under their cruel despotic Tsar seem to think they are the masters of Europe. Well, they're not. We are. And we're going to show him we are. The Queen, God bless her, upon whose Empire the sun never sets, will not be dictated to by some pesky, Rusky, potentate. Particularly when it comes to the great trading arrangements she has made all over the globe, to the everlasting benefit of all of us, of you – er – and particularly of me. Now she has called upon us, her sturdy Highlanders, to come to her aid in far-off Crimea. In 1800, the 93rd Highlanders was raised, 1,000 strong; 800 of them were from Sutherland – tenants of this estate. They have a long and noble history. They are even now under orders for Scutari; now we have been asked to raise the proud banner of the Second Battalion of the 93rd Highlanders. The Queen needs men, and as always, she looks to the North. My Commissioner, Mr Loch, informs me that the response so far has been disappointing.

Enter LOCH, now an old man.

LOCH: Disappointing? A disgrace. In the whole county of Sutherland, not one man has volunteered.

DUKE: I know you to be loyal subjects of the Queen. I am prepared to reward your loyalty. Every man who enlists today will be given a bounty of six golden sovereigns from my own private purse. Now if you will all step up in an orderly manner, Mr Loch will take your names and give you the money.

The DUKE sits. Silence. Nobody moves. The DUKE stands angrily.

DUKE: Damn it, do you want the Mongol hordes to come sweeping across Europe, burning your houses, driving you into the sea? (*LOCH fidgets.*) What are you fidgeting for Loch? Have you no pride in this great democracy that we English – er – British have brought to you? Do you want the cruel Tsar of Russia installed in Dunrobin Castle? Step forward.

Silence. Nobody moves.

DUKE: For this disgraceful, cowardly conduct, I demand an explanation.

Short silence. OLD MAN stands up in audience.

OLD MAN: I am sorry for the response your Grace's proposals are meeting here, but there is a cause for it. It is the opinion of this country that should the Tsar of Russia take possession of Dunrobin Castle, we could not expect worse treatment at his hands than we have experienced at the hands of your family for the last fifty years. We have no country to fight for. You robbed us of our country and gave it to the sheep. Therefore, since you have preferred sheep to men, let sheep now defend you.

ALL: Baa-aa.

The DUKE and LOCH leave. SOLDIER beats retreat.

MC: One man only was enlisted at this meeting. No sooner was he away at Fort George than his house was pulled down, his wife and family turned out, and put in a hut from which an old female pauper was carried a few days before to the churchyard.

Out of thirty-three battalions sent to the Crimea, only three were Highland.

But this was only a small set-back for the recruiters. These parts were still raided for men; almost as fast as they cleared them off the land, they later recruited them into the Army. The old tradition of loyal soldiering was fostered and exploited with careful calculation.

In the words of General Wolfe, hero of Quebec – 'Some Highland Divisions might be of some use – they are hardy, used to difficult country and no great mischief if they fall.' They were used to expand the Empire and to subdue other countries, whose natural resources were needed to feed the industrial machine of Great Britain.

Lights go down. Book turns to a war memorial.

Every village has its memorial. Every memorial has its list of men. They died to defend something. Those who came back found very little worth defending.

FIDDLER plays a lament. At the end the lights go up.

On stage, the book changes back to mountains. The Company stand in a group, out of which an ACADEMIC emerges, wringing his hands plaintively.

ACADEMIC: If only the Highlands had some resources, things would be – much better.

MC1: The figures of de-population increase and increase.

MC2: In 1755, the population of the seven crofting counties was more than 20 per cent of the population of Scotland.

MC3: In 1801 it was 18 per cent.

MC4: In 1851 it was 13 per cent.

MC2: In 1901 it was 7 per cent.

MC3: In 1951 it was 5 per cent.

MC4: And yesterday it was 3 per cent.

ACADEMIC: If only the Highlands had some resources, things would be – much better.

MC2: In 1861, one hundred and sixty of the islands of the Hebrides were inhabited. In 1941, there were seventy-three.

ACADEMIC goes to the microphone, holding a book.

ACADEMIC: All this created a mighty wilderness. In the words of the Highlands and Islands Development Board Brochure – Explore the Highlands and Islands: 'A great open lung, guaranteed to breathe new life into the most jaded ... Overcrowding? Not in Sutherland ... a land of solitary splendour ... mountains, lochs and glens of unrivalled beauty add a sharper poignancy to the scattered stones of the ruined crofting townships.' Yes, the tragedy of the Highlands has become a saleable commodity.

Enter ANDY MCCHUCKEMUP, a Glasgow Property-operator's man. He looks round, takes the mike.

ANDY: The motel – as I see it – is the thing of the future. That's how we see it, myself and the Board of Directors, and one or two of your local Councillors – come on now, these are the best men money can buy. So – picture it, if yous will, right there at the top of the glen, beautiful vista – The Crammem Inn, High Rise Motorcroft – all finished in natural, washable, plastic granitette. Right next door, the 'Frying Scotsman'. All Night Chipperama – with a wee ethnic bit, Fingal's Caff – serving seaweed-suppers-in-the-basket, and draught Drambuie. And to cater for the younger set, yous've got your Grouse-a-go-go. I mean, people very soon won't want your bed and breakfasts, they want everything laid on, they'll be wanting their entertainment and that, and wes've got the know-how to do it and wes have got the money to do it. So – picture it, if yous will – a drive-in clachan on every hill-top where formerly there was hee-haw but scenery.

Enter LORD VAT OF GLENLIVET, a mad young laird.

LORD VAT: Get off my land – these are my mountains.
ANDY: Who are you, Jimmy?
LORD VAT: Lord Vat of Glenlivet. I come from an ancient Scotch family and I represent the true spirit of the Highlands.
ANDY: Andy McChuckemup of Crammem Inn Investments Ltd., Govan, pleased for to make your acquaintance Your Worship. Excuse me, is this your fields?
LORD VAT: You're invading my privacy.
ANDY: Excuse me, me and wor company's got plans for to develop this backward area into a paradise for all the family – improve it, you know, fair enough, eh?
LORD VAT: Look here, I've spent an awful lot of money to keep this place private and peaceful. I don't want hordes of common people trampling all over the heather, disturbing the birds.
ANDY: Oh no, we weren't planning to do it for nothing, an' that – there'll be plenty in it for you ...

LORD VAT: No amount of money could compensate for the disruption of the couthie way of life that has gone on here uninterrupted for yonks. Your Bantu – I mean your Highlander – is a dignified sort of chap, conservative to the core. From time immemorial, they have proved excellent servants – the gels in the kitchen, your sherpa – I mean your stalker – marvellously sure-footed on the hills, your ghillie-wallah, tugging the forelock, doing up your flies – you won't find people like that anywhere else in the world. I wouldn't part with all this even if you were to offer me half a million pounds.
ANDY: A-ha. How does six hundred thousand suit you?
LORD VAT: My family have lived here for over a century: 800,000.
ANDY: You're getting a slice of the action, Your Honour – 650,000.
LORD VAT: I have my tenants to think of. Where will they go? 750,000.
ANDY: We'll be needing a few lasses for staff and that ... 700,000 including the stately home.
LORD VAT: You're a hard man, Mr Chuckemup.
ANDY: Cash.
LORD VAT: Done (*Shake.*)
ANDY: You'll not regret it, sir. Our wee company antic-ipate about approximately about 5,000 people per week coming up here for the peace and quiet and solitude – not to forget the safari park.
LORD VAT: On safari; hippos in the loch, tigers on the bens, iguana up the burns, rhinos in the rhododendrons.

They go off.

The GAELIC SINGER comes on, singing:

SINGER: Haidh-o haidh rum
Chunna mis' a raoir thu

(*Repeat twice.*)

Direadh na staoir' 's a royal
Haidh-o hu-o
Cha ghabh mis' an t-uigeach

(*Repeat twice.*)

Cha dean e cail ach rudhadh na monach.
Haidh-o hair-am
Cha ghabh mis' a siarach

(*Repeat twice.*)

Cha dean e cail ach biathadh nan oisgean.
MC: It's no good singing in Gaelic any more – there's an awful lot of people here won't understand a word of it.
SINGER: And why not?

Drum: 2 chords on guitar. Company members come on stage to answer this question.

MC1: In the 18th century speaking the Gaelic language was forbidden by law.

(*Chords.*)

MC2: In the 19th century children caught speaking Gaelic in the playground were flogged.

(*Chords.*)

MC1: In the 20th century the children were taught to deride their own language.

(*Chords.*)

Because English is the language of the ruling class. Because English is the language of the people who own the highlands and control the highlands and invest in the highlands –

MC2: Because English is the language of the Development Board, the Hydro Board, the Tourist Board, the Forestry Commission, the County Council and, I suppose, the Chicago Bridge Construction Company.

(*Chords.*)

MC3: The people who spoke Gaelic no longer owned their land.

MC1: The people had to learn the language of their new masters –

MC1: A whole culture was systematically destroyed – by economic power.

(*2 Chords.*)

MC1: The same people, no matter what they speak, still don't own their land, or control what goes on in it, or what gets taken out of it.

(*2 Chords. They sit.*)

MC: It's no good walking away lamenting it in either language – what have the people ever done about it?

Drum beat begins.

MC4: Easter 1882. Angus Sutherland formed the Highland Land League. In 1884 John Murdoch set up the Scottish Land Restoration League. In 1885 five crofters' MPs elected to Parliament.

MC5: In 1886, Crofter's Commission set up by Act of Parliament.

MC4: Rents reduced by 30 per cent, arrears by 60 per cent; security of tenure guaranteed, hereditary rights established –

MC5: The landlords retaliated. Trouble flared up on the Duke of Argyll's estate on Tiree. The turret ship Ajax, with 250 marines, was sent to quell a population of 2,000.

MC4: October 1886. Skye: writs served at bayonet point. Six crofters arrested. A medal was awarded for every crofter captured.

MC5: 1887, Lewis. One thousand crofters raided the Park Deer Forest which had been enclosed, and killed 200 deer. A venison feast was held, with a white-haired patriarch saying grace before the roasting stags.

MC4: 1887, Assynt, Sutherland. Hugh Kerr, the crofters' leader, took to the hills pursued by the authorities. The women of Clashmore raided the police station at midnight.

MC5: 1904, overcrowded crofters from Eriskay made a land raid on Vatersay and broke in new crofts.

MC4: 1912, the Pentland Act gave the government power to force landlords to sell their land to the state.

MC5: This power was never used. 1921–22, impatient with the new government's inactivity, young men from overcrowded areas made more land raids on Raasay, Skye, the Uists, Stratherick and Lewis.

MC4: 1919, Portskerra, Sutherland. Fourteen ex-servicemen drove their cattle on to Kirkton farm, led by the piper who had played them ashore at Boulogne. Their own crofts were small, none bigger than three acres.

MC5: The land had been promised to them by the Duke of Sutherland. When they came back from the war he had sold it to a wealthy farmer named McAndrew.

MC4: Legal injunctions were served on them. They resolved to stay put and not to be daunted by threats.

SINGER moves forward, sings unaccompanied. At final verses, the Company join in, humming and stamping feet.

SINGER: I will go
I will go
Now the battle is over
To the land
Of my birth
That I left to be a soldier
I will go
I will go

When we went
To that war
Oh the living was not easy
But the laird
Promised land
If we joined the British army –
So we went
So we went –

Now we're home
Now we're home
The laird has changed his fancy
And he's sold
All our land
To a farmer who's got plenty
Now we're home
Now we're home

With the pipes

At our head
That had led us into battle
We set off
For the land
That we fought for in the Army
We set off
We set off

Oh you Land –
Leaguer men
Of Raasay, Skye and Lewis
Had you seen
Us that day
You'd have cheered us on to glory
Had you seen
Us that day

Oh the Laird
Had the law
And the police were his servants
But we'll fight
Once again
For this country is the people's
Yes we'll fight, once again
(*Spoken.*) And with these buggers, we'll have to –
MC: And what is happening now?
MC2: A whole new culture is waiting to be destroyed.
MC1: By economic power. Until economic power is in the hands of the people, then their culture, Gaelic or English, will be destroyed. The educational system, the newspapers, the radio and television and the decision-makers, local and national, whether they know it or not, are the servants of the men who own and control the land.
MC3: Who owns the land?
MC: The same families – the Macleods, the Lovats, the Argylls, the MacDonalds, the Sinclairs, the Crichton-Stewarts, and the Sutherlands.
MC4: Plus the property dealers.
MC5: The shipowners.
MC3: The construction men.
MC: The distillers. The brewers. The textile men.
MC5: The sauce-makers.
MC4: The mustard kings.
MC5: And the merchant bankers.
MC3: The new ruling class!

Music. Two of the Company sing.

DUO: We are the men
Who own your glen
Though you won't see us there –
In Edinburgh clubs
And Guildford pubs
We insist how much we care:
Your interests
Are ours, my friends,

From Golspie to the Minch –
But if you want your land
We'll take a stand
We will not budge one inch …
(*Spoken.*) The Sporting Estate proprietor:
SINGER 1: If you should wish
To catch the fish
That in your lochs are stacked,
Then take your creel
Book, rod and reel
And get your picnic packed.
Now cast away
The livelong day
But don't think it's all free
You own your rods
The rain is God's
But the rest belongs to me!
(*Spoken.*) Doctor Green of Surrey …
SINGER 2: Doctor Green of Surrey
Is in no hurry
For a ferry to cross the Sound
You want a pier?
Oh no, not here –
I need that patch of ground:
This island she
Belongs to me
As all you peasants know –
And I'm quite merry
For I need no ferry
As I never intend to go
(*Spoken.*) The Ministry of Defence …
SINGER 1: The Minister of Defence
He is not dense
He knows just what he's found
The place to test
Torpedoes best,
Is right up Raasay Sound
A few bombs too
In a year or two
You can hear the people groan –
This water's ours
So NATO powers
Go test them up your own.
(*Spoken.*) Continental Tour Operators …
SINGER 2: Herr Heinrich Harr
Says it is wunderbar
To shoot animals is it not?
For a reasonable sum
You can pepper their bum
With bullets and buckshot:
You may call us krauts
Cos we're after your trouts
But listen you Scottish schwein –
This is part of a plan

That first began
In nineteen thirty-nine.
DUO: We are the men
Who own your glen
Though you won't see us there.
In Edinburgh clubs
And Guildford pubs
We insist how much we care –
Your interests
Are ours, my friends
From Golspie to the Minch –
But if you want your land
We'll take a stand
We will not budge one inch.

Song ends.

MC: One thing's for certain, these men are not just figures of fun. They are determined, powerful and have the rest of the ruling class on their side. Their network is international.

MC4: Question: What does a meat-packer in the Argentine, a merchant seaman on the high seas, a docker in London, a container-lorry driver on the motorways, have in common with a crofter in Lochinver?

MC: Nothing at all.

MC4: Wrong. They are all wholly-owned subsidiaries of the Vestey Brothers.

MC: Ah! The Vesteys – owners of over 100,000 acres in Sutherland and Wester Ross! – and directors of approximately 127 companies, including:

MC4: Red Bank Meatworks
Monarch Bacon
Blue Star Line
Booth's Steamship Company
Shipping and Associated Industries
Premier Stevedoring
Aberdeen Cold Storage
International Fish
Norwest Whaling
Commercial Properties
Albion Insurance
Assynt Minerals
Assynt Trading
Lochinver Ice and Scottish-Canadian Oil and Transportation.

Music: 'Grannie's Hielan' Hame' on accordion.

Enter TEXAS JIM, *in 10-gallon hat. He greets the audience fulsomely, shakes hands with the front row, etc.*

TEXAS JIM: (*To the backing of the accordion.*) In those far-off days of yore, my great-great grand-pappy Angus left these calm untroubled shores to seek his fortune in that great continent across the Atlantic Ocean. Well, he went North, and he

struck cold and ice, and he went West, and he struck bad times on the great rolling plains, so he went South, and he struck oil; and here am I, a free-booting oil-man from Texas, name of Elmer Y. MacAlpine the Fourth, and I'm proud to say my trade has brought me back to these shores once more, and the tears well in my eyes as I see the Scottish Sun Sink Slowly in the West behind ... (*Sings.*)

'My Grannie's Hielan' Hame'

Blue grass guitar in, country style. He changes from nostalgia to a more aggressive approach.

For these are my mountains
And this is my glen
Yes, these are my mountains
I'll tell you again –
No land's ever claimed me
Though far I did roam
Yes these are my mountains
And I – have come home.

Guitar continues: he fires pistol as oil rigs appear on the mountains.

Fiddle in for hoe-down. Company line up and begin to dance hoe-down.

JIM shakes hands with audience, then back to mike and begins square dance calls:

TEXAS JIM: Take your oil rigs by the score,
Drill a little well just a little off-shore,
Pipe that oil in from the sea,
Pipe those profits – home to me.

I'll bring work that's hard and good –
A little oil costs a lot of blood.

Your union men just cut no ice
You work for me – I name the price.

So leave your fishing, and leave your soil,
Come work for me, I want your oil.

Screw your landscape, screw your bays
I'll screw you in a hundred ways –

Take your partner by the hand
Tiptoe through the oily sand

Honour your partner, bow real low
You'll be honouring me in a year or so

I'm going to grab a pile of dough
When that there oil begins to flow

I got millions, I want more
I don't give a damn for your fancy shore

1 2 3 4 5 6 7
All good oil men go to heaven

8 9 10 11 12
Billions of dollars all to myself

13 14 15 16
All your government needs is fixing

17 18 19 20
You'll get nothing. I'll get plenty

21 22 23 24
Billion billion dollars more

25 26 27 28
Watch my cash accumulate

As he gets more and more frenzied, the dancers stop and look at him.

27 28 29 30
You play dumb and I'll play dirty

All you folks are off your head
I'm getting rich from your sea bed

I'll go home when I see fit
All I'll leave is a heap of shit

You poor dumb fools I'm rooking you
You'll find out in a year or two.

He stops, freaked out. The dancers back away from him. He gets himself under control and speaks to the audience.

Our story starts way way back in 1962. Your wonderful government went looking for gas in the North Sea, and they struck oil.

Guitar.

Well, they didn't know what to do about it, and they didn't believe in all these pesky godless government controls like they do in Norway and Algeria and Libya, oh, my God – no, you have a democracy here like we do – so your government gave a little chance to honest God-fearing, anti-socialist businessmen like myself –

Guitar. Two Company members stand in their places to speak.

MC1: Shell-Esso of America, Transworld of America, Sedco of America, Occidental of America – and of Lord Thompson.
MC2: Conoco, Amoco, Mobil, Signal.
TEXAS JIM: All of America.
MC1: And British Petroleum –
TEXAS JIM: A hell of a lot of American money, honey.

Guitar. Enter WHITEHALL, a worried senior Civil Servant.

WHITEHALL: You see we just didn't have the money to squander on this sort of thing.
TEXAS JIM: That's my boy –
WHITEHALL: And we don't believe in fettering private enterprise: after all this is a free country.

TEXAS JIM: Never known a freer one.
WHITEHALL: These chaps have the know how, and we don't.
TEXAS JIM: Yes sir, and we certainly move fast.
MC1: By 1963 the North Sea was divided into blocks.
MC2: By 1964 100,000 square miles of sea-bed had been handed out for exploration.
WHITEHALL: We didn't charge these chaps a lot of money, we didn't want to put them off.
TEXAS JIM: Good thinking, good thinking. Your wonderful labourite government was real nice: thank God they weren't socialists.
MC1: The Norwegian Government took over 50 per cent of the shares in exploration of their sector.
MC2: The Algerian Government control 80 per cent of the oil industry in Algeria.
MC1: The Libyan Government are fighting to control 100 per cent of the oil industry in Libya.

Guitar.

WHITEHALL: Our allies in NATO were pressing us to get the oil flowing. There were Reds under the Med. Revolutions in the middle-east.
TEXAS JIM: Yeah, Britain is a stable country and we can make sure you stay that way. (*Fingers pistol.*)
WHITEHALL: There is a certain amount of disagreement about exactly how much oil there actually is out there. Some say 100 million tons a year, others as much as 600 million. I find myself awfully confused.
TEXAS JIM: Good thinking. Good thinking.
WHITEHALL: Besides if we produce our own oil, it'll be cheaper, and we won't have to import it – will we?
MC1: As in all Third World countries exploited by American business, the raw material will be processed under the control of American capital – and sold back to us at three or four times the price –
MC2: To the detriment of our balance of payments, our cost of living and our way of life.
TEXAS JIM: And to the greater glory of the economy of the US of A.

Intro. to song. Tune: souped-up version of 'Bonnie Dundee'. TEXAS JIM and WHITEHALL sing as an echo of LOCH and SELLAR.

TEXAS JIM & WHITEHALL: As the rain on the hillside comes in from the sea
All the blessings of life fall in showers from me
So if you'd abandon your old misery
Then you'll open your doors to the oil industry –
GIRLS: (*As backing group.*) Conoco, Amoco, Shell-Esso, Texaco, British Petroleum, yum, yum, yum. (*Twice.*)
TEXAS JIM: There's many a barrel of oil in the sea
All waiting for drilling and piping to me
I'll refine it in Texas, you'll get it, you'll see
At four times the price that you sold it to me.
TEXAS JIM & WHITEHALL: As the rain on the hillside, etc. (*Chorus.*)

GIRLS: Conoco, Amoco, etc. (*Four times.*)

WHITEHALL: There's jobs and there's prospects so please have no fears,

There's building of oil rigs and houses and piers,

There's a boom-time-a-coming, let's celebrate – cheers –

TEXAS JIM pours drinks of oil.

TEXAS JIM: For the Highlands will be my lands in three or four years.

No oil in can. Enter ABERDONIAN RIGGER.

AR: When it comes to the jobs all the big boys are Americans. All the technicians are American. Only about half the riggers are local. The American companies'll no take Union men, and some of the fellows recruiting for the Union have been beaten up. The fellows who get taken on as roustabouts are on a contract; 84 hours a week in 12 hour shifts, two weeks on and one week off. They have to do overtime when they're tell't. No accommodation, no leave, no sick-pay, and the company can sack them whenever they want to. And all that for £27.00 a week basic before tax. It's not what I'd cry a steady job for a family man. Of course, there's building jobs going but in a few years that'll be over, and by then we'll not be able to afford to live here. Some English property company has just sold 80 acres of Aberdeenshire for one million pounds. Even a stairhead tenement with a shared lavatory will cost you four thousand pounds in Aberdeen. At the first sniff of oil, there was a crowd of sharp operators jumping all over the place buying the land cheap. Now they're selling it at a hell of a profit.

Drum. Company step on stage again, speak to the audience.

MC1: In the House of Commons, Willie Hamilton, MP, said he was not laying charges at the door of any particular individual who had *quote*: moved in sharply to cash-in on the prospect of making a quick buck. There is a great danger of the local people being outwitted and out-manoeuvred by the Mafia from Edinburgh and Texas ... end quote.

MC2: The people must own the land.

MC3: The people must control the land.

MC1: They must control what goes on on it, and what gets taken out of it.

MC3: Farmers in Easter Ross have had their land bought by Cromarty Firth Development Company.

MC2: Crofters in Shetland have had their land bought by Nordport.

MC1: Farmers in Aberdeenshire have had their land bought by Peterhead and Fraserburgh Estates.

MC3: All three companies are owned by Onshore Investments 'of Edinburgh'.

MC2: Onshore Investments, however, was owned by Mount St Bernard Trust of London and Preston, Lancashire.

MC3: A man named John Foulerton manages this empire. But whose money is he handling? Who now owns this land in Easter Ross, Shetland and Aberdeenshire? Whose money is waiting to buy *you* out?

Drum roll.

MC1: Marathon Oil?

MC2: Trafalgar House Investments?

MC3: Dearbourne Storm of Chicago?

MC4: Apco of Oklahoma?

MC 5: Chicago Bridge and Iron of Chicago?

MC2: P&O Shipping?

MC3: Taylor-Woodrow?

MC1: Mowlems?

MC2: Costains?

MC5: Cementation?

MC4: Bovis?

MC3: Cleveland Bridge and Engineering?

MC2: These people have been buying up the North of Scotland.

TEXAS JIM: A-a, a-a. With the help of your very own Scottish companies: Ivory & Sime of Edinburgh; Edward Bates & Son of Edinburgh; Noble Grossart of Edinburgh; and the Bank of Scotland, of – er – Scotland.

MC4: And the Sheik of Abu Dhabi's cousin who owns a large slice of the Cromarty Firth ...

MC2: Mrs Cowan of the Strathy Inn was offered a lot of money by a small group of Japanese.

TEXAS JIM: What can you little Scottish People do about it?

Silence. Exit TEXAS JIM.

MC2: Mr Gordon Campbell, in whose hands the future of Scotland rested at this crucial period, said:

WHITEHALL gets up, does nothing, sits down.

Scottish capitalists are showing themselves to be, in the best tradition of Loch and Sellar – ruthless exploiters.

Enter SNP EMPLOYER.

SNP EMPLOYER: Not at all, no no, quit the Bolshevik haverings. Many of us captains of Scottish industry are joining the Nationalist Party. We have the best interest of the Scottish people at heart. And with interest running at 16 per cent, who can blame us?

MC2: Nationalism is not enough. The enemy of the Scottish people is Scottish capital, as much as the foreign exploiter.

Drum Roll.

Actor who played SELLAR and WHITEHALL comes on.

ACTOR: (*As SELLAR.*) I'm not the cruel man you say I am. (*As WHITEHALL.*) I am a Government spokesman and not responsible for my actions ...

TEXAS JIM: I am perfectly satisfied that no persons will suffer hardship or injury as a result of these improvements.

Drum Roll.

Short burst on fiddle. JIM *and* WHITEHALL *go to shake hands. Enter between them, in black coat and bowler hat,* POLWARTH – *not unlike* SELKIRK'S *entrance.*

POLWARTH: I am Lord Polwarth, and I have a plan. The present government seems to have no control over the hooligans of the American oil companies and their overpaid government servants, so the government has appointed me to be a knot-cutter, a trouble-shooter, a clearer of blockages, and a broad forum to cover the whole spectrum. However, I am not a supremo. In this way, the people of Scotland – or at least the Bank of Scotland – will benefit from the destruction of their country.

MC2:   Before becoming Minister of State, Lord Polwarth was Governor of the Bank of Scotland, Chairman of the Save and Prosper Unit Trust, a Director of ICI and was heavily involved in British Assets Trust, Second British Assets Trust and Atlantic Assets Trust, which at that time owned 50 per cent of our old friend, Mount St Bernard Trust.

Musical intro. Tune: 'Lord of the Dance'.

TEXAS JIM *and* WHITEHALL *turn* LORD POLWARTH *into a puppet by taking out and holding up strings attached to his wrists and back. They sing:*

ALL: Oil, oil, underneath the sea,
I am the Lord of the Oil said he,
And my friends in the Banks and the trusts all agree,
I am the Lord of the Oil – Tee Hee.

POLWARTH: I came up from London with amazing speed
To save the Scottish Tories in their hour of need:
The people up in Scotland were making such a noise,
That Teddy sent for me, 'cos I'm a Teddy-boy …

ALL: Oil, oil, etc.

POLWARTH: Now all you Scotties need have no fear,
Your oil's quite safe now the trouble-shooter's here,
So I'll trust you, if you'll trust me,
'Cos I'm the ex-director of a trust company.

ALL: Oil, oil, etc.

POLWARTH: Now I am a man of high integrity,
Renowned for my complete impartiality,
But if you think I'm doing this for you,
You'd better think again 'cos I'm a businessman too –

ALL: Oil, oil, etc.

At the end of the song, LORD POLWARTH *freezes.* TEXAS JIM *and* WHITEHALL *let go of his strings, and he collapses.* MC2 *catches him on her shoulder and carries him off.* JIM *and* WHITEHALL *congratulate each other, then turn to the audience.*

TEXAS JIM: And the West is next in line.

WHITEHALL: And the West is next in line.

GAELIC SINGER: And the West is next in line. Even now exploration is going on between the Butt of Lewis and the coast of Sutherland.

WHITEHALL: Don't worry it will take at least five years.

GAELIC SINGER: They've started buying land already.

WHITEHALL: We can't interfere with the free play of the market.

TEXAS JIM: Leave it to me, I'll take it out as quick as I can and leave you just as I found you.

GAELIC SINGER: Worse, by all accounts.

WHITEHALL: Now look here, we don't want you people interfering and disturbing the peace – What do you know about it?

GAELIC SINGER: We'd like to know a hell of a lot more … (*Exit.*)

WHITEHALL: As our own Mr Fanshaw of the HIDB said: 'These oil rigs are quite spectacular. I hear they actually attract the tourists –'

Enter CROFTER *and his* WIFE.

You can give them bed and breakfast.

Doorbell rings.

WIFE: Get your shoes on, that'll be the tourists from Rotherham, Yorks, and put some peats on top of that coal – they'll think we're no better than theirselves.

CROFTER: Aye, aye, aye – go you and let them in …

WIFE: Put off that television and hunt for Jimmy Shand on the wireless.

CROFTER mimes this action.

Oh God, there's the Marvel milk out on the table, and I told them we had our own cows –

Bell rings again.

CROFTER: Aye, aye, aye, they'll be looking like snowmen stuck out there in this blizzard –

WIFE: Och, it's terrible weather for July –

CROFTER: It's not been the same since they struck oil in Loch Duich.

WIFE: Now is everything right?

She wraps a shawl round her head; he rolls up his trouser leg, and throws a blanket round himself to look like a kilt, and puts on a tammy.

WIFE: Get out your chanter and play them a quick failte.

CROFTER: How many would you like?

WIFE: Just the one –

He plays a blast of 'Amazing Grace'. She takes a deep breath, and opens the door. The visitors are mimed.

WIFE: Dear heart step forward, come in, come in. (*Clicks fingers to* CROFTER).

CROFTER: (*Brightly.*) Och aye!

WIFE: You'll have come to see the oil rigs – oh, they're a grand sight right enough. You'll no see them now for the stour, but on a clear day you'll get a grand view if you stand just here –

CROFTER: Aye, you'll get a much better view now the excavators digging for the minerals have cleared away two and a half of the Five Sisters of Kintail.

WIFE: You'll see them standing fine and dandy, just to the west of the wee labour camp there –

CROFTER: And you'll see all the bonnie big tankers come steaming up the loch without moving from your chair –

WIFE: You'll take a dram? Get a wee drammie for the visitors –

CROFTER: A what?

WIFE: *A drink.* I doubt you'll have anything like this down in Rotherham, Yorks. All the people from England are flocking up to see the oil rigs. It'll be a change for them.

CROFTER: Here, drink that now, it'll make the hairs on your chest stick out like rhubarb stalks.

WIFE: When the weather clears up, you'll be wanting down to the shore to see the pollution – it's a grand sight, right enough.

CROFTER: Aye, it's a big draw for the tourists: they're clicking away at it with their wee cameras all day long.

WIFE: Or you can get Donnie MacKinnon to take you in his boat out to the point there, to watch the rockets whooshing off down the range – but he'll no go too far, for fear of the torpedoes. Himself here would take you but he gave up the fishing a while back.

CROFTER: It's no safe any more with the aerial bombs they're testing in the Sound. Anyway all the fish is buggered off to Iceland.

WIFE: What does he do now? Oh, well, he had to get a job on the oil rigs.

CROFTER: Oh, aye, it was a good job, plenty money . . .

WIFE: He fell down and shattered his spine from carelessness. (*Clicks her fingers at him.*)

CROFTER: (*Brightly.*) Och aye!

WIFE: And now he can't move out of his chair. But he has a grand view of the oil rig to give him something to look at, and helping me with the visitors to occupy him.

CROFTER: No, no, no compensation –

WIFE: But we'll have plenty of money when we sell the croft to that nice gentleman from Edinburgh.

CROFTER: Aye, he made us an offer we can't refuse.

WIFE: And we can't afford to live here any more with the price of things the way they are, and all the people from the village gone, and their houses taken up . . .

CROFTER: We were wondering now about the price of houses in Rotherham.

WIFE: Or maybe a flat. I've always wanted to live in a flat. You'll get a grand view from high up.

CROFTER: (*Taking off funny hat.*) One thing's certain, we can't live here.

WIFE: (*Very sadly.*) Aye, one thing's certain. We can't live here.

The GAELIC SINGER comes forward: they stay sitting. She sings the verse of 'Mo Gachaidh'. The rest of the Company comes on to join the chorus.

At the end of the song, all stay on stage and speak to the audience in turn.

The people do not own the land.

The people do not control the land.

Any more than they did before the arrival of the Great Sheep.

In 1800 it was obvious that a change was coming to the Highlands.

It is obvious now that another change is coming to the Highlands.

Then as now, the economy was lagging behind the development of the rest of the country.

Then as now, there was capital elsewhere looking for something to develop.

In those days the capital belonged to southern industrialists.

Now it belongs to multi-national corporations with even less feeling for the people than Patrick Sellar.

In other parts of the world – Bolivia, Panama, Guatemala, Venezuela, Brazil, Angola, Mozambique, Nigeria, Biafra, Muscat and Oman and many other countries – the same corporations have torn out the mineral wealth from the land. The same people always suffer.

Then it was the Great Sheep.

Now it is the black black oil.

Then it was done by outside capital, with the connivance of the local ruling class and central government –

And the people had no control over what was happening to them.

Now it is being done by outside capital, with the connivance of the local ruling class and central government.

Have we learnt anything from the Clearances?

When the Cheviot came, only the landlords benefited.

When the Stag came, only the upper-class sportsmen benefited.

Now the Black Black Oil is coming. And must come. It could benefit everybody. But if it is developed in the capitalist way, only the multi-national corporations and local speculators will benefit.

At the time of the Clearances, the resistance failed because it was not organised. The victories came as a result of militant organisation – in Coigeach, The Braes, and the places that formed Land leagues. We too must organise, and fight – not with stones, but politically, with the help of the working class in the towns, for a government that will control the oil development for the benefit of everybody.

Have we learnt anything from the Clearances? In the 1890s Mary MacPherson, whose family was cleared from Skye, wrote this song:

GAELIC SINGER: (*Sings.*) Cuimhnichibh gur sluagh sibh
Is cumaibh suas 'ur coir
Tha beairteas bho na cruachan
Far an d'fhuair sibh arach og
Tha iarrann agus gual ann
Tha luaidhe ghlas is or
Tha meinnean gu 'ur buannachd
An Eilean Uaine a 'Cheo.

MC: The song says:
'Remember that you are a people and fight for your rights –

There are riches under the hills where you grew up.
There is iron and coal there grey lead and gold,

There is richness in the land under your feet.
Remember your hardships and keep up your struggle
The wheel will turn for you
By the strength of your hands and the hardness of your fists.
Your cattle will be on the plains
Everyone in the land will have a place
And the exploiter will be driven out.'

COMPANY: Cuimhnichibh ur cruadal
Is cumaibh suas ur sroill,
Gun teid an roth mun cuairt duibh
Le neart is cruas nan dorn;
Gum bi ur crodh air bhuailtean
'S gach tuathanach air doigh,
'S na Sas'naich air fuadach
A Eilean Uain a' Cheo.

4.3 ENTER THE NIGHT (1993)

MARIA IRENE FORNES

Maria Irene Fornes (b. 1930) was born in Cuba and emigrated to the USA in 1945. Her first play, Tango Palace, *was produced in 1963, with* Fefu and Her Friends *(1977) establishing Fornes' reputation for developing an innovative, poetic yet politically engaged dramatic form. Also a teacher and director, Fornes was particularly active on the New York avant-garde scene in the 1960s and 1970s.* Enter the Night *(1993) focuses on three friends coming together for a reunion, experiencing various forms of spiritual, emotional and physical dislocation. It is only through imaginative flight that individual pain, torment and even mortality come to be accepted. Embedded in a self-conscious theatricality,* Enter the Night *is a provocative examination of the relationship between art and life in the contemporary world. Originally called* Dreams, *Fornes directed the premiere production for Theatre Zero at the New City Theatre, Seattle.*

Characters

TRESSA

PAULA

JACK

An empty warehouse or barn. The downstage area has been turned into a living space. In the center there is a pit, as large as the space permits. On the down side of the pit there is a railing and stairs that lead to the floor below. On both sides of the pit there are planks that lead to the upstage area. On the down-left area there is the entrance to a bathroom, a kitchen, and TRESSA'S *bedroom.*

Center stage, down of the railing, there is a bench that will serve as a bed. On the right there is a table and four chairs. On the upstage side of the pit there is another bench that also serves as a bed. On the upstage right of the bench there is a folding screen and to the left there is an armchair. Upstage of the screen there is a kitchen.

Downstage left there is a small table (table 2) with a chair facing upstage. To the right of the table there is a carpenter's cabinet. At the start one of its drawers is open. On top of the cabinet there is a cassette player and a table mirror.

The characters quote from the novel Lost Horizon *by James Hilton. The voice of the High Lama in the last scene is that of Sam Jaffe from Frank Capra's film* Lost Horizon.

Act 1

The stage lights are very dim. A car is heard stopping outside. There is the sound of a car door opening and closing. The lights of dawn are seen on the wall stage right as the doors below open. Steps are heard. A light is turned on downstairs. TRESSA *is seen coming up the steps. She wears a light coat over a dress and white oxford shoes. She carries a purse over her shoulder and a nurse's uniform over her arm. She walks to a light switch and turns on a dim overhead light. She walks to the table, takes a notebook and pencil from her purse and lays them on the table. She walks to the upstage area, taking the purse and uniform with her. On the way there, she leans over* PAULA, *who is asleep on the upper bench, and gently pulls the covers over her shoulders. She then walks to the cassette player and turns it on. Billie Holiday's 'Don't Explain' is heard. She walks behind the screen, hangs the purse and uniform on it. She takes off her coat, shoes, stockings, and dress, puts on an undershirt, puts on the pants of a blue cotton Chinese worker's outfit, puts on plain Chinese black slippers and a Chinese worker's jacket. She walks down and left to the kitchen, then reenters with a cup of coffee, and she walks to the table. She turns on the overhead lamp, sits, and goes over her notes, pencil in hand. In the course of her reading she makes some pencil corrections.*

TRESSA:

6 p.m. Patient in bed. Intermittent cough. Fogger in use. Skin very dry. Lotion applied to extremities.

8:30 Patient raising green phlegm periodically. Fluids not accepted.

11 p.m. Dr. Winternits in to visit. Heparin lock d/c.

3 a.m. Patient incontinent of large amount of formed soft yellow BM. Decubitus care given. Mycitracin ointment to skin on buttocks.

3:30 Massage applied to legs. Elastic stockings replaced. /c legs elevated.

6 a.m. Patient resting in bed at this time. Relieved by Nurse Becker. Tressa Harris RN.

She turns to look in the direction of PAULA; she turns back and leans her head on her hands for a moment. She takes a drink of coffee and walks left, taking the cup of coffee with her. She stops at the light switch and turns on the light on the left of the upper platform. She sits on the chair on the upper platform.

PAULA: (*Half asleep.*) Who's there?

TRESSA: It's me.

PAULA: Oh, you scared me.

TRESSA goes to PAULA.

TRESSA: (*Touching PAULA's face.*) It's just me.

TRESSA starts walking down.

PAULA: Someone came in a while ago.

TRESSA: Who?

PAULA: He was standing there, looking in the drawer.

TRESSA: Which drawer?

PAULA: That one. – It's open.

TRESSA walks to the drawer.

TRESSA: Who was it?

PAULA: (*Pointing to the cabinet.*) He was standing there, where you are.

TRESSA starts walking up.

He said he wasn't a thief. That he needed something and you told him to get it.

TRESSA: (*Turning to look at the drawer.*) What was it he needed?

PAULA: A tool.

TRESSA: What tool?

PAULA: He didn't say.

TRESSA: (*Walking toward the drawer.*) And where was he looking for that tool?

PAULA: In that drawer. – It's open.

TRESSA leans over the drawer.

TRESSA: There are no tools in that drawer.

PAULA: Well, that's the one he was looking into.

Short pause.

TRESSA: What was the tool for?

PAULA: He didn't say.

TRESSA walks to the up-left chair and sits.

TRESSA: How did he get in?

PAULA: I don't know.

TRESSA looks in the direction of the drawer.

TRESSA: Did he take anything?

PAULA: Not that I know.

TRESSA: What did he look like?

PAULA: He was short. He had long shiny straight hair like a Latin. He wore baggy pants that went up to his chest like a zoot suit. He wore suspenders. And a white shirt. And he was very clean. That's why I wasn't scared – as if murderers couldn't be clean. He had a big mustache and a big nose. He said his name was José Luis. Do you know any José Luis?

TRESSA: That must've been Jack.

PAULA: Jack? Why would Jack come in dressed like that?

TRESSA: To be funny.

PAULA: It wasn't Jack. You think I wouldn't recognize Jack?

TRESSA: What happened then?

PAULA: He sat there where you're sitting.

TRESSA: He did?

PAULA: Yes.

TRESSA: And then?

PAULA: He said he couldn't possibly marry me.

TRESSA: That sounds like Jack.

PAULA: It wasn't Jack.

TRESSA: What made him say that?

PAULA: I don't know. I never said he should. – Then he said, 'Look at me. Hairs growing out of my nostrils. A mustache. Look at my mustache. Look at my gold tooth. I'm a short guy. Why should I marry you?' Then he leaned forward and said, 'Do your legs want to wrap themselves around me?' I said, 'Sure.'

TRESSA: What?

PAULA: I lost my sense of judgment. It didn't matter to me who I wrapped my legs around.

TRESSA: Paula!

PAULA: I'm kidding. I wasn't awake. – He said, 'OK.'

PAULA shrugs her shoulders. TRESSA laughs.

TRESSA: What happened then?

PAULA: I don't know.

TRESSA: You dreamt it.

PAULA shrugs again.

You want coffee?

TRESSA starts to go to the left ramp.

PAULA: (*Walking down the right ramp.*) I'll get it.

TRESSA: I'll get it. (*As she exits left.*) Anything else happen while I was gone?

PAULA: Pete called.

TRESSA: He misses you?

PAULA: I guess. He wanted to see if I got in OK. And to say he was OK.

TRESSA: That's nice. How is he?

PAULA: He's fine.

TRESSA: Good. Did Jack call?

PAULA: No.

TRESSA: He's coming.

PAULA: He is? When?

TRESSA: Early. He said early. He can't wait to see you. He's bringing croissants.

TRESSA exits left.

PAULA: Are you staying up?

TRESSA: Yes. I'm wide awake.

PAULA: How's your patient?

TRESSA: Not good. He was in pain.

PAULA: Did you get any rest?

TRESSA: (*Entering with a cup of coffee for* PAULA.) No. (*Pause.*) I think he's going to die.

PAULA: Will he go to the hospital?

TRESSA: He wants to stay home.

She gives PAULA *the coffee and returns to the up-left chair.*

PAULA: Why?

TRESSA: I think he's given up.

PAULA: You can't save him?

TRESSA: Me? Save him?

PAULA: (*Standing and opening her arms.*) I always think when I'm about to die I'll call your name and you'll run to my side and save me. You'll just put your hand on my forehead and I'll get well.

TRESSA: Sure, that's what we nurses do.

PAULA: That's right.

PAULA walks to TRESSA, *puts her arm around her, and leans her head on hers.*

At least you.

PAULA goes to the bench and puts her blanket around her shoulders.

TRESSA: I just work hard making people comfortable.

PAULA walks down toward the table and sits.

… if possible. So they can bear their pain … their agony. If they get well my work is rewarded. It's wonderful to see their first smile as they begin to feel better. And even more wonderful if that smile is directed at me.

TRESSA walks down.

When they begin to feel better they feel you've been a partner in their cure because you've watched them at every step. They are grateful and appreciative for the help you've given them.

PAULA: And if they don't survive?

She walks to the table.

TRESSA: If they don't survive we feel a sense of loss.

She sits.

We've lost the battle.

PAULA: Have you lost the battle for Russell?

TRESSA: Yes, I think he wants to die.

TRESSA walks to the downstage bench and sits. She is despondent. PAULA walks to her and kisses her forehead.

PAULA: You should rest, dear.

TRESSA: I will.

TRESSA exits left and speaks from offstage.

You want anything?

PAULA: Like what?

TRESSA: Breakfast?

PAULA: No thank you. I'm not ready to get up yet. I'm going back to bed.

She starts to get into bed, reaches for her cup, and hands it to TRESSA.

I'll have some more coffee though.

TRESSA goes to the kitchen.

TRESSA: (*Offstage.*) So, how are things with you?

PAULA: All right I suppose …

PAULA sits on the lower bench.

The same.

TRESSA: (*Entering with a headband on and holding an open jar of yellowish white base, which she is applying to her face.*) What do you mean?

PAULA: (*Lying on the bench.*) I'm not well. But I don't pay any attention to it.

TRESSA: (*Going to the table left.*) What's wrong?

PAULA: I pretend I'm well. No one has told me that I'm well. But I act as if I am.

TRESSA starts walking to PAULA.

As if I've been told by a doctor that I'm well, and I can go ahead and do whatever I want. Well, I haven't been told that. If I stop taking my heart pills, I'll die.

TRESSA: (*Going to the left side of the bench and kneeling.*) … Paula …

PAULA: Yes. – I keep doing the work on the farm and I keep saying, 'It's not going to harm me.' I keep saying that. But there's a voice inside me that tells me, 'If you keep doing what you're doing you're going to die. The next shovel you push through the dirt will kill you.' (*As if replying to herself.*) 'This is good for me.' If I carry a sack of feed: 'This has to be good for me.' I can't just stand there and let everything I've worked for go to waste, sit and let the animals lie on their own manure, uncared for, let them starve and die. Let them get sick and die. I can't do that. I can't just let my meadows go to waste. I can't sit there and watch the weeds take over and do nothing. That's not the way I am. I'd rather die. I don't want to be different from the way I am. I don't want to be a different person just to stay alive. If the person I am dies, then I die. – If taking care of what I love kills me, then I want to die. – 'It's a Russian roulette,' the voice says. 'Every time you climb a ladder or pick up a bag of feed or a bucket of manure it can be the last.' (*Pause.*) I can die. (*Snapping her fingers.*) Just like that. – Next time you run after a sheep. (*Snaps her fingers.*) Like that! (*Standing.*) I can't afford to pay someone to take care of things. (*Showing* TRESSA *the palm of her hands.*) Look at my hands.

TRESSA takes her hands affectionately.

Pete wants to help. He has gotten in debt for me. But he can't borrow any more. He's lost his credit. He's done all he can to help … can't ask him to do any more. He humiliates himself for me. They won't lend him any more money. I can't bear it. You'd think I'd make enough money selling the milk and the wool and the eggs. But I don't. I don't know how to make it work. It costs more to feed the animals than what you could earn from them. I owe that money to Peter. I want to pay him back. He says not to be silly, that he's my husband and besides he is my partner. But that's not so. He's gone into it just to help me. He's never understood why I do it – keep my hands in the dirt all day long. I don't want to ask him for money and I still do it. I ask him for more money. It's a loan. I always say it's a loan. I've never looked kindly on people who can't take care of themselves and their obsessions or their vices; people who make excuses for themselves and make others pay their bill. That's what I'm doing. I know I should sell the animals and most of the land. But I can't. I'm like a drug addict who will do anything to satisfy her vice. I've lost my faith, my honor, my sense of pride. I still have them though … (*As if seeing them.*) I still have them … running in my meadow.

PAULA looks at her hands.

I do the work because I have to. Because I can't afford to get help. If I don't I would have to watch them starve to death. Do you think I could sit there and watch them die in a swamp of manure? I couldn't. I would die before them. I couldn't stand seeing them suffer.

TRESSA: (*Saddened.*) … Oh, Paula.

PAULA: … Oh, Paula … (*Standing and crossing to the right of the bench and sitting.*) Oh, Paula. – Don't worry. Don't worry. It doesn't matter. My life is over. – There's nothing to worry about.

TRESSA: Are you crazy? Your life is over?

PAULA: It is. Whether I die or not. I'm serious. From here on it's downhill. A downhill ride. (*She somersaults off the bench down center and remains seated.*) I know my life is over. So my problems are over. (*She sits on the floor.*)

TRESSA: Oh, Paula …

PAULA: They are. I have suffered disappointment after disappointment, humiliation after humiliation. And I've survived it. So I've nothing to worry about.

TRESSA: Oh, Paula …

PAULA: (*Interrupting.*) Don't say anything. Forget everything I said. I don't want to depress you. –What are you doing tonight?

TRESSA: I work tonight. What are you doing this afternoon?

PAULA: I'm going out.

TRESSA: (*Walking to* PAULA.) Doing what?

PAULA: I have a couple of things to do in town. Which I won't do till this afternoon, because I'm going back to bed. (*Kissing* TRESSA.) Good night. (*Walking up to the bench.*) I'm free for dinner. You want to have dinner? Then I'm going to a party which you're welcome to come to. Tomorrow I go home bright and early.

As they speak PAULA *fixes the covers on the bench.* TRESSA *goes to table 2 and continues applying the cream.*

TRESSA: When do you think you'll be back?

PAULA: About four, I guess. At what time are you going to work?

TRESSA: Six. Six to midnight.

PAULA: I guess you can't go to the party unless you want to go after work.

TRESSA: I can't see people after work. I have to unwind. If I'm up when you get back we can have a drink. If we don't see each other tonight, wake me up tomorrow before you leave. Say good-bye.

PAULA: I will. (*Turns to look at* TRESSA.) What is that you're putting on your face?

TRESSA: Cream.

PAULA walks to TRESSA *and looks at her face.*

PAULA: Hm? – What does it do?

TRESSA: I like … the way it feels on my skin.

PAULA: It's white?

TRESSA: Yes.

PAULA: It looks nice.

TRESSA: It goes with my pajamas.

PAULA: Yes, it does.

TRESSA: It makes me feel calm to wear this. It soothes me. When I wear this I feel smooth, calm … People dress in a certain way to feel in a certain way. It's natural to me to dress this way. I feel whole. It soothes me.

PAULA: And if you're not dressed like this?

TRESSA: I feel ... clumsy.

PAULA: Clumsy? – You're not clumsy.

TRESSA: Maybe I'm not. But I feel clumsy.

PAULA: I think you're very lovely.

TRESSA: I thank you. – I think I'm a cross dresser.

PAULA: How's that?

TRESSA: Yes.

PAULA: Could you explain that to me?

TRESSA: I don't think I can. ... When I dress like this I feel I'm a man. – I feel I am an Asian man. Thoroughly an Asian man. My heart, my groin, my head, my tongue, my hands, I like to dress like this. I like the way it feels on my body. I like looking at my face in the mirror when I have my yellow face, my oblique eyes. I like the way my voice sounds, the way these clothes make me think. I like my Oriental face. My feet. I feel calm like this. Calm. I'd dress as a Western man to go to a party. To fool around. But when I dress like this. I'm not fooling around.

PAULA: Seeing you like this makes me feel I'm with a man ... a lovely man ... How exotic ...

The phone rings. PAULA offers her hand to TRESSA. They do a very quick minuet kind of walk to the timing of the telephone rings. PAULA picks up the receiver and hands it to TRESSA.

TRESSA: Hello ... (*She listens and smiles. She looks at PAULA and mouths the word 'Jack.' PAULA nods. They both smile with glee.*) Yeah ... (*Pause.*) Yeah ... (*Pause; then, she laughs.*) Oh ... (*Pause; then, in surprise and amusement.*) Oh ... (*Pause; then, in surprise and amusement.*) Oh, my God. – Yeah. Yeah. OK. Right. Yeah-yeah, I know. Fine-fine. OK. (*Laughs.*) OK. (*She hangs up the receiver. She laughs again.*) That was Jack. (*She starts down the stairs.*) He's round the corner.

PAULA: Oh, boy.

TRESSA: Yes. He's funny.

PAULA: He's a funny guy.

There is the sound of a large door rolling on metal wheels. And the door hitting the wall. PAULA takes a dress and a pair of shoes from behind the screen, examines the dress, starts coming down the left plank and into the bathroom. She reenters and walks up the left plank and behind the screen. She reappears with more clothes and goes into the bathroom. Then, she enters and goes up the left plank. TRESSA comes up the steps. She is pensive. She stops center. PAULA turns to her.

PAULA: What's the matter?

TRESSA: Jack is in bad shape. He believes he's ill but he's not.

PAULA: What do you mean?

TRESSA: He thinks he has AIDS. His friend is very sick. He has AIDS. But Jack doesn't. He's obsessed with it. He tests negative. But he doesn't trust the test. He's sure he's HIV positive and has been for years. The slightest bruise or sore makes him think that it's the start of AIDS. He keeps getting tested. And it keeps coming out negative. (*She walks down right.*) I think he'd be relieved if he tested positive. He's like a paranoid who feels relieved if someone is actually following him. He'd say, 'See I was right. I'm being followed.' I can't help him. I can't convince him he doesn't have AIDS. He just thinks the tests are not accurate. On the surface he seems all right but he's tormented. Obsessed. Sometimes he frightens me. He hallucinates. It will kill him. In the end it will kill him.

The downstairs door is heard opening.

JACK: (*Offstage.*) Hello. (*Pause.*) Anybody home?

PAULA takes her clothes to the bathroom. TRESSA goes to the railing.

TRESSA: Here.

PAULA reenters.

JACK: Cover your eyes.

They cover their eyes. JACK comes upstairs. He wears a false mustache, glasses, a nose, and a gold tooth. He wears a leather JACKet and blue jeans.

TARAAAA ...!!!

They uncover their eyes.

Hi girls!

PAULA AND TRESSA: Jack ...!!!

PAULA jumps on JACK and puts her legs around him. She takes the glasses, nose, and mustache off him.

PAULA: How wonderful to see you. (*Touches his face, kisses it, kisses his hand.*) How wonderful to be with you. (*Touches his face again.*) Let me see you.

He gives her a big smile showing the gold tooth.

Jack!

JACK: What?

PAULA: (*Pointing to the tooth.*) The tooth.

JACK: It's not real. (*He looks at TRESSA and points to the gold tooth.*) Chocolate wrap. How good to see you.

PAULA: It was you!

JACK: What?

PAULA: José Luis.

JACK: Me – José Luis. You – Conchita. (*He laughs.*) You're crazy.

They laugh. He takes off his nose and mustache.

PAULA: (*Taking him by the arm to the left.*) Come with me.

JACK: Where are you taking me?

PAULA: You'll see.

JACK: She has something up her sleeve.

PAULA: I have something up my sleeve.

JACK: What is it?

They exit left.

PAULA: Close your eyes.

JACK: They are closed.

Pause.

TRESSA: Watch it! One more step.

Pause.

Turn around.

JACK: Can I open my eyes?

TRESSA: Not yet.

Pause.

JACK: It's a coat!!

TRESSA: Don't look yet!!

JACK: It's a coat! It's a coat! It's a coat!

JACK enters wearing a man's nineteenth-century frock, jumping.

Paula look! It's a coat! It's a coat! Oh! Oh! (*He gets his briefcase from the landing.*) I brought my new play. (*He sits on the bench and opens the briefcase.*) Let's read it. (*Improvising music that vibrates as the birth of a miracle, he slowly brings his hands inside the briefcase and takes out two copies of a play. Holding a copy of the play in each hand, he extends one to TRESSA and one to PAULA.*)

PAULA: (*Gently.*) I'm not up yet.

JACK: (*Disappointed.*) Oh.

PAULA: I haven't washed my face.

JACK: (*Pouting.*) . . . You don't have to wash your face . . .

PAULA: . . . I was on my way to wash up . . .

JACK: (*Hugging the scripts to his chest and pouting.*) . . . I thought you'd want to read it . . .

PAULA: I have to brush my teeth . . .

JACK sighs.

I won't take long.

JACK: . . . Please, don't take long.

PAULA: (*Sweetly.*) I won't. I don't have that many teeth.

JACK: (*Pouting.*) OK, but don't take long.

PAULA: I won't.

PAULA exits left. JACK throws himself on the floor and has a pouting tantrum. He bangs on the floor with fists and feet.

JACK: She doesn't want to read it . . . She doesn't want to read it. (*Toward the bathroom.*) You don't want to read it! (*To the heavens.*) No one wants to read my play! No one wants to read my play! No one wants to read my play! (*He lies on his stomach and bangs his fists on the floor. As he walks to the bathroom.*) How long are you going to take? (*He goes into the bathroom.*) Please, don't take long.

PAULA: (*Amused.*) Jack . . .!

JACK: Five minutes? Three minutes?

Silence.

Half an hour?

PAULA: Jack . . .

JACK: Ten . . . minutes?

PAULA: Go away, Jack.

He enters and goes to TRESSA.

JACK: Would you read it?

TRESSA takes the script and starts to read. JACK sits on the floor to watch her read.

Paula, Tressa's reading it.

He looks at TRESSA for signs. He walks away, turns to look at her from a different angle, circles her, lies down with his head propped on his hand. She smiles.

Paula, she's smiling.

She is still reading. He watches her. She laughs. He contracts with a tremor of pleasure. He watches a while longer. She smiles again, then laughs.

JACK: Paula, she's laughing!

PAULA: Good.

A moment passes. TRESSA turns the page. She reads.

JACK: Paula, she's still reading. It must be good.

PAULA: Is it good, Tressa?

TRESSA: Huh Huh.

PAULA: Can you tell yet?

TRESSA: It's good.

PAULA: What is it about?

TRESSA: Compote.

PAULA: Compost?

TRESSA: Compote, Paula!

PAULA: Is it good?

TRESSA: Yeah. (*To Jack.*) When did you write this?

JACK: (*Professional.*) It's just a first draft. It's not there yet. I just started it. (*Stands and paces, doing important-person gestures.*) The premise. A man and a woman. He, from the city. She, from a farm. Vermont. The conflict between urban and rural life. Two different cultures. That is the premise. (*Pause.*) It has saved my life. It has made me calm down, be still, I don't spend nights roaming around the city anymore.

TRESSA: You weren't here last night?

JACK: No. Why?

TRESSA: The gold tooth.

JACK: (*Taking out the gold foil.*) Just foil.

TRESSA: Paula dreamt you came in with a gold tooth.

JACK: She did? Hmm. Smart. (*Pointing to his own head.*) She's smart. (*Pointing to where PAULA is.*) Smart girl. (*Speaking out to PAULA.*) Paula.

PAULA: What?

JACK: You dreamt about my tooth.

PAULA: That's right.

PAULA enters. She wears a smart business suit, high heels, and makeup.

JACK: God, Paula, you look great!

She poses.

Where are you going?

PAULA: I'm doing a few errands.

JACK: You have a date?

PAULA: ... No, I don't have a date.

JACK: Tell Jack.

PAULA: (*Dropping the pose.*) I'm seeing a man about a job.

JACK: A man?

PAULA: A job.

JACK: A job? In town?

PAULA: No, not in town.

JACK: Oh, I thought you'd stay in town.

PAULA: Not in town. Freelance. From home.

JACK: What's the job?

PAULA: Research.

JACK: On what?

PAULA: Husbandry.

JACK: That's right up your alley.

PAULA: Yeap.

JACK: For whom?

PAULA: A conservancy magazine.

JACK: Ah! I hope you get it.

PAULA: Have my fingers crossed.

JACK: Cross mine too.

PAULA: I'll also be meeting a man about a loan.

JACK: Hmm. What man?

PAULA: A man in a bank. I owe money.

JACK: Hmm.

JACK: The farm? (*She nods.*) Hope you get it.

PAULA: Yeah.

JACK: You should get all the money you need.

PAULA: I sure should.

JACK: How could they refuse you?

PAULA: They couldn't.

JACK: Of course they couldn't.

PAULA: I'm also going to see Dr Eckland.

JACK: ... Eckland ...

PAULA: Cardiologist.

JACK: Oh?

PAULA: Uh huh.

JACK: You?

PAULA: Yeap.

JACK: Since when?

PAULA: A while. He's going to do some tests.

JACK: That's a bunch of things you're doing.

PAULA: That's right. You see why I have to look sharp.

JACK: That's right.

PAULA: (*Laughs.*) Have to impress those machines.

JACK: It's an important day.

PAULA: Yeap. Loaded.

JACK: I hope you score.

PAULA: Uh huh. – Pray for me. (*To TRESSA.*) Pray for me.

TRESSA: With all my heart.

PAULA: Jack. – What made you put on that gold tooth and nose and mustache?

JACK: I don't know ... Nothing.

PAULA: When you came in like that, I was confused.

JACK: Why?

PAULA: Last night I dreamt of a man who came in here looking just like that.

JACK: You did?

PAULA: Yes. Did you know that?

JACK: No. I just thought it was funny.

PAULA: Why is that funny?

JACK shrugs.

JACK: I got it at a funny trick store.

PAULA: (*Starting to go toward the bathroom.*) Take it back. Tell them nobody found it funny. Get a refund.

JACK laughs.

JACK: How's Pete?

PAULA: Pete's fine.

JACK: How're the kids?

PAULA: Kids? They're taller than Pete.

JACK: How's that possible?

PAULA: (*From the bathroom.*) It's been three years. You haven't been up in three years, Jack.

JACK: Three years?

PAULA: (*Offstage.*) Yep.

JACK: You couldn't be right.

PAULA: (*Offstage.*) That's what it is. Three years. Last time you came up was three years ago, it was spring.

JACK: Is that right?

PAULA: (*Offstage.*) Yeah. That's the last time you came up. Three years ago.

JACK: Three years ...

PAULA: (*Offstage.*) That's right.

JACK: (*Going to TRESSA.*) Does that sound right to you?

TRESSA: That sounds right. That's when I got the red quilt.

JACK: The red quilt ... Three years since the red quilt. Can't believe it. How time passes. (*Sits and leans his head on his hands.*) I can't believe it. Oh my God. Oh, my God.

He looks up. His eyes are full of tears. He walks right and kneels next to TRESSA.

Oh my God. Oh my God ... How life slips through your fingers.

TRESSA extends her arms to JACK. He walks down to her and kneels.

TRESSA: (*Strokes his head.*) It does. It does. (*Pause.*) What's wrong, my sweet?

JACK: ... I'm fine ... I'm fine. How time passes ... How time passes ...

TRESSA strokes his head.

TRESSA: Are you working?

JACK: ... Here and there ...

TRESSA: What are you doing?

JACK: ASM.

TRESSA: ASM?

JACK: Associate Sado-Masochist. (*Short pause.*) Assistant Stage Manager. Backstage work.

PAULA: (*From the bathroom.*) Oops. What happened? The light went out. It must be the bulb.

JACK: I'll get it.

JACK goes to the bathroom.

PAULA: (*Offstage.*) It's dark here.

JACK: (*Offstage.*) I'll be right back.

JACK enters, gets a bulb from the cabinet and returns to the bathroom.

JACK: (*Offstage.*) Where are you?

PAULA: Here.

JACK: Hold this. Do you have a match?

PAULA: No, Jack. I don't have a match.

JACK: Ouch! It's hot.

PAULA: Wait till it cools.

JACK: You mean stand here and wait till it cools?

PAULA: Well, why not?

They laugh.

JACK: You're silly.

PAULA: Here's something.

JACK: What?

PAULA: A washcloth.

JACK: It's wet!

PAULA: Yeah. Let me get something else. (*Short pause.*) Here's a towel. It's dry.

JACK: OK. (*Short pause.*) Where's the bulb? It was here a moment ago.

PAULA: Give me your hand.

JACK: Here's my hand. Where's yours?

They laugh.

Here it is. I have it. – OK. (*Short pause.*) Hold this.

PAULA: Is it still hot?

JACK: Hold it with the towel. (*Short pause.*) Where's the other bulb? Where did I put the other bulb? Here it is. – OK. (*Pause. Then the light goes on.*)

PAULA: Thank you.

JACK: You're welcome.

JACK appears at the door. He stands for a while. He is downcast.

Joey died.

TRESSA: ... Oh!

JACK walks down and sits.

JACK: That's why I haven't been around. – I've been a mess. I fell apart. But I wrote this. It's not great but I like it. I like the characters. They are sweet. It kept me from going away.

PAULA enters. She stays in the back.

I couldn't stand thinking that he was dead. That I could never see him again. I couldn't sleep. I kept wandering and wandering around the streets ... the places we used to go to. But that was too painful, remembering him. Then I went to places I had never been to. But then I got scared because when I had no memories of him I felt desperate. But I couldn't go home because there everything reminded me of him. I saw him everywhere. I couldn't sleep. I saw him sitting on every chair. I saw him in every corner. In the tub, by the sink, on the toilet. On the bed, under the sheets. On top of the covers. I couldn't rest. I couldn't eat. Then I thought I was going to die. Then I wrote this. (*To PAULA.*) You met him ... He was my love ... He died. He was the sweetest person on earth. That's why I loved him. He was good. Like you. You're good. That's why I love you. You're good. (*To TRESSA.*) I'm not good. I don't know how to be good. I never had that feeling in my heart. Never. I'm just clever, that's all. I laugh at things. I'm not good inside. The most tender I can be is when I'm witty. That's the best I can be. I don't know how to be good. I love goodness, though. I wish I could be good. It's peaceful. Isn't it ... being good? When I'm witty I feel close to being good but it's not the same. I feel a little tender when I'm witty. But it's not the same. Joey was good. You could see it in his face, in his body. There was no poison in it. His body was like a baby's. No nerves. No tendons. (*To PAULA.*) Like you. (*To TRESSA.*) You're good. (*To PAULA.*) You're good. (*To both.*) That's why I love you. You and he are the only persons I've loved. And I killed him.

JACK is now crying. TRESSA goes to him.

JACK: (*Very intensely.*)	TRESSA:
It was I who killed him.	No Jack. You didn't. You
It was I who killed him.	don't have AIDS. You're
I gave him AIDS. It was	not contagious. You're
I who gave him AIDS.	not HIV positive. You're
I killed him. I killed him.	negative.

He walks left and sits at the table.

JACK: His family is being terrible. They didn't want me to see him when he was dying. They didn't want me to go to the funeral. They took all his things. Things I had given him. I didn't want any of it. I just wanted the fur coat that used to be mine and I didn't want any more and I gave to him because he loved it. That's the only reason I wanted it, because he loved it. He loved to touch it. He loved to lie in bed wearing nothing but the coat. He loved the way it felt on his body. And that's why I wanted it. Because having that coat would make me feel that I still had him. They thought I wanted it because it was valuable. It was an old coat. I wanted to get naked and wear it and feel him.

JACK lowers his head slowly. TRESSA and PAULA look at him in silence awhile. PAULA goes to him. She kisses his forehead.

PAULA: Remember Shangri-la …? Remember Shangri-la?

JACK nods.

What did the High Lama say to Conway?

JACK: (*Tearful. He quotes words from* Lost Horizon.) 'The storm, this storm you talked of …'

PAULA: 'I believe you will live through the storm, my child. You will still live through the long age of desolation,

JACK joins her.

growing older and wiser and more patient.

TRESSA joins them.

You will conserve the fragrance of our history hidden behind the valley of Shangri-la.'

PAULA, JACK, AND TRESSA: 'You will conserve the fragrance of our history hidden behind the valley of Shangri-la.'

Short pause.

PAULA: … Let's read your play.

JACK: … Yes.

They take the scripts, walk to the upstage area. PAULA and TRESSA sit at each end of the bench. JACK sits on the chair left. 'Banks of the Ohio' from Music of the Ozarks *[National Geographic Society] plays.*

A one-room cottage on a farm in Vermont. The cottage is impeccably clean. Wilma and Eric sit at the table. Eric wears a suit. Wilma wears a housedress.

ERIC: (*Read by one of the women with a heavy German accent.*) This is a very good compote.

WILMA: (*Read by the other with a heavy German accent.*) Yah. It is very good compote. And very good bread. I make the bread myself sometimes. This one I didn't make but it is made the same way as the bread I make. And this butter is the best. It couldn't be better because it's made with fresh milk of cows that put out very creamy milk that is r sty because milk can have a bland taste. Here is salt. You can put in it salt. Taste it. You look hungry. You want milk. Milk tastes good with bread. It just came out of the cow. It's still warm from the udder.

ERIC: The udder what?

WILMA: The udder from the cow. – Dunk the bread. If you dunk the bread in the milk it gets damp with the milk and it tastes better.

They drink.

ERIC AND WILMA: Ah ha!

WILMA: My hand is damp. (*She puts her hand on ERIC's cheek. Pause.*) See? I will dry it on my apron because it is damp. (*She dries her hand and puts it on his cheek again. Pause.*) See? (*She takes the hand away.*) Now it is dry. It is good to keep your hand dry. – Eat, this is the best. Do you know cows better than these ones?

ERIC: I don't know other cows.

WILMA: I thought you knew other cows.

ERIC: No.

WILMA: It is a pity. Are you not ashamed?

ERIC: I am not ashamed. In the city there are no cows. In the city it is not a pity not to know a cow.

WILMA: Not?

ERIC: No. A cow is large. There is no place to keep a cow in house in the city. And also a lot of people live in apartment. And apartment is smaller than house.

WILMA: Apartment is smaller than house?

ERIC: Of course. Some people have yard and garden. But they don't want to keep a cow in garden.

WILMA: Why not?

ERIC: Why not?

WILMA: Yes. Why not?

ERIC: To keep a cow in garden?

WILMA: Why not?

ERIC: Oh. – One, the cow would trample the grass and eat it. Do cows eat flowers?

WILMA: Of course cows eat flowers.

ERIC: Two. – The cow would eat the flowers. Do cows moo?

WILMA looks at ERIC.

WILMA: (*Indignant and condescending.*) Do cows moo? Of course cows moo.

ERIC: Well, the cow will moo, then.

WILMA: Cows have to moo. Do you want a cow not to moo? Do you want a cow to say, 'I would like to be milked now, so please milk me now.' – Is that what you want the cow to do?

ERIC: Do cows moo at night?

WILMA: No cows moo at night.

ERIC: At what time do they moo?

WILMA: When did the cow go to sleep?

ERIC: I don't know when the cow went to sleep.

WILMA: She moos because she needs milking.

ERIC: She needs milking?

WILMA: Of course.

ERIC: Why?

WILMA: Because the milk fills the udders and it hurts the udders.

ERIC: What udder?

WILMA: The udder of the cow. If they are milked at six they will moo at six.

ERIC: Like nurses.

WILMA: What?

ERIC: Yah. Six would be too early. A cow mooing at six would wake up everyone.

WILMA: Six is good time to wake up.

ERIC: In the city people get angry to be wakened at six by a cow.

WILMA: I don't see how they could drink fresh milken then.

ERIC: In the city milk is delivered from the country in bottles every day.

WILMA: If it is delivered from the country and the bottles make a tinkle sound it is not fresh, then. It is old milk. It is not like the milk in that glass. Don't drink the milk in the bottle. It is not fresh. Drink this. It is fresh.

They drink some milk, lick their lips, smack their lips, and put the glass down.

Yah!

The lights fade to suggest a passage of time. As country music ['Down in the Arkansas,' Music of the Ozarks, National Geographic Society] plays, JACK does a cowboy two-step moving to the downstage area.

JACK: Act two. A year later. Spring approaches. Wilma wears a housedress. Eric wears a straw hat and a pair of overalls.

JACK does a turn doing the two-step and lies down on the downstage bench facing the readers. The music ends.

ERIC: I'm going to buy two cows, or one cow and six goats, or ten pigs and some hens. Or not buy cows and build a shed and buy land or put money in the bank.

WILMA: Eric, my husband, you work too hard. You want to work all the time? – Put some fish in the pond and we can go fishing on Sundays.

ERIC: Good Wilma. I am so glad I have you for a wife. I am happy because you are my wife, Wilma, my wife.

WILMA: I am happy, Eric, my husband. Put fish in the pond and we can go fishing on Sundays.

ERIC: Ah yah. I am glad I married you, Wilma. You make life a paradise.

WILMA: Ahh, Eric, my husband. I am glad.

They hold hands.

WILMA AND ERIC: Yaaaaah!

PAULA AND TRESSA: (*Applauding.*) Very good Jack! Very good Jack!

'Angel Band' from Music of the Ozarks [National Georgraphic Society] starts playing softly. PAULA and TRESSA go to each side of JACK. He goes toward the plank, faces them, and bows.

PAULA: That is so beautiful, Jack.

JACK: I thank you.

TRESSA: It is so dear.

JACK: (*Starting to walk backwards down the plank.*) Thank you.

TRESSA: Oh, Jack, I want to cry.

JACK: Cry?

PAULA: I cried, Jack.

JACK walks toward center as TRESSA and PAULA walk down the plank.

TRESSA: It is so sweet.

JACK is shyly thrilled and excited. He drops to the floor. They run to him and drop on each side of him and hug him.

JACK: (*Opening his arms and speaking religiously.*) To Joey!

TRESSA AND PAULA: To Joey!

PAULA: May your heart live!

JACK: May your heart live!

TRESSA: ... May your heart live ...

'Icy Blue Heart' by John Hiatt plays. JACK's hands go up in the air, then to his mouth. He blows a kiss as he throws his hands up.

JACK: Now we celebrate.

TRESSA AND PAULA: We celebrate.

The volume of music goes up. They dance through the following. JACK goes to the stairs and goes down a few steps. He throws a tablecloth and napkins over the railing. TRESSA catches the tablecloth and lays it on the table. PAULA catches the napkins. TRESSA goes to the kitchen and gets glasses, a bowl of fruit, a paring knife, and a bell. JACK comes up with a paper bag, a bakery box, and a bottle of wine. They set the table. He opens the bottle. PAULA opens the box and takes out croissants, then takes out cheese from the paper bag. They sit around the table, raise their napkins, shake them, and place them on their laps in unison with the music.

JACK: (*Raising his glass.*) Breakfast!

TRESSA sounds the bell. TRESSA and PAULA raise their glasses and toast with JACK.

TRESSA, PAULA, AND JACK: Breakfast!

They drink and eat.

TRESSA: (*Toasting.*) May Art live!

ALL: (*Toasting.*) May Art live!

They drink and eat. The music begins to fade.

PAULA: (*Toasting.*) May Theater live!

ALL: (*Toasting.*) May Theater live!

They drink and eat.

JACK: (*Toasting.*) May Poetry live!

ALL: (*Toasting.*) May Poetry live!

PAULA walks around the table.

PAULA: What would you give up to be the greatest artist in the world? Would you give up your youth? ... Tressa?

TRESSA: I would. How much would I have to give up?

PAULA: Seven years.

TRESSA thinks.

TRESSA: ... Seven years ...

PAULA: See? We're not interested in art. We're only interested in seduction. (*Continues walking around the table.*) When we're young we pretend we want to be artists. But all we're interested in is seduction. We want the world to have a crush on us. We want to be irresistible.

JACK and TRESSA at the same time mumble the following.

JACK: Not me. I never felt that.

TRESSA: That's not so. Art comes first.

PAULA: Would you give up your youthful good looks to be the greatest artists in the world?

JACK AND TRESSA: Yeah ... Yeah ...

PAULA: Look like Quasimodo?

JACK and TRESSA applaud. PAULA leans on JACK with her arms around him.

JACK:	TRESSA:
Well no. Not that. You're right. I wouldn't.	No, not like Quasimodo. That's true. I wouldn't.

TRESSA: Yet it doesn't matter. If you're a good artist you will be loved no matter what.

JACK: I wouldn't say no matter what.

TRESSA: Ugly artists get loved more than other ugly people.

JACK: Ugly rich people get loved more than ugly artists.

TRESSA: True, but next to ugly rich people I think it's ugly artists.

JACK: Yeap.

PAULA: Yeah.

TRESSA: To ugly artists.

PAULA AND JACK: To ugly artists.

TRESSA: (*Peeling an apple.*) My mother loved people for their beauty and yet she loved my father because he was an artist. He wasn't good looking. And yet she loved him. – Why? Because he was an artist. – Even if she only loved people for their beauty, she fell in love with him because he was an artist. He didn't look like Quasimodo, but he wasn't the prettiest thing on earth. Yet she loved him. – She once loved a girl because she was beautiful. She told me she wanted the girl to love her, but she didn't. My father loved my mother because she was beautiful. He too loved people for their beauty. He loved my brother because he was beautiful and he liked to paint him. He didn't like me because I wasn't beautiful.

JACK:	PAULA:
You weren't beautiful?	What do you mean you were not beautiful?

TRESSA: (*Ignoring their objections.*) He painted my brother all the time and not me. My mother wanted me to like a girl who lived nearby just because she was beautiful. I didn't like that girl and I told her I didn't love people just because they were beautiful and I didn't like her. But she said, 'You should still like her. Because she's beautiful.' I didn't like her and that was that. (*Going to the kitchen. To* JACK.) She didn't like you because you weren't beautiful.

JACK: I wasn't beautiful?

PAULA goes to the bench and sits as TRESSA enters.

TRESSA: She said you weren't. My brother said that you were cute because you looked like me. And she said you didn't.

JACK: I look like you?

TRESSA: Yes. That's the reason why I liked you. I didn't like girls except for you.

JACK: Me? (*Laughs.*)

TRESSA: (*Reaching toward* PAULA.) Since then I never liked a girl except for Paula, who is my love. Whom I have loved for years and who won't have me. Because she loves Jack. And won't have me. Because she only has eyes for Jack.

JACK: (*Sitting to the left of* PAULA *and hugging her.*) Me too. My eyes are for Paula, my Paula. I only have eyes for you. You should love me and not mean Huang.

PAULA: Huang?

JACK: Yes, that person there is Huang.

PAULA: Paula loves you. She loves you and she always will. Even after death she will love you.

JACK: Paula will not die. She will live forever to love Jack.

TRESSA: (*Standing.*) ... Paula's not well, Jack.

Pause.

PAULA: I'm fine. (*She flexes her muscles.*) I'm fine. I had heart palpitations like fibrillations. (*Pinching* JACK's *cheek.*) My heart beat so fast I thought it would burst. Peter prepared an injection that makes the heart relax and I was OK. Had this continued for one more minute I would have died. But I didn't.

JACK: So many people are ill ... so many people ... everyone is ill. One day every single person will be ill ... old illnesses ... new illnesses ... old symptoms ... new symptoms ... old treatments ... new treatments ... (*Starting to clear the table. In the course of the speech,* JACK *takes everything on the table to the kitchen.*) Everything in our minds will be illness, the ill, the dying. All art will be about illness. All plays will be about illness. And the ill. The characters will be defined by their illness. It is the characters' illness that will determine the plot. Instead of the ingenue, the romantic lead, the friend, the villain, the characters will be defined by their illness: the cancer victim, the AIDS victim, the tubercular, the diabetic. The person poisoned by industrial chemicals, in the air, in food. The central issue of the plots will be the development of the illness: the first notice of the symptoms, the first visit to the doctor, the relationship with the doctors, with other patients, with family, with one's own body, with side effects, how one copes. Treatment will be an integral part of the plot. – The plots will be whether to save one patient or the other: possibility of blackmail, bribes in exchange for special treatment, relationships with the attending doctor: attachment, hatred, jealousy toward other patients. Or bank robberies to pay for medical care. The murder mysteries will be: patients of a renowned doctor are murdered. The doctor is suspected but the murderer is a patient who is waiting his turn for an operation and he may die before the doctor can get to him, so he kills all patients who are scheduled before him. The serial murders will be: the patient kills everyone who has the same disease as him so he can have his choice of physician. After a while plays will be more subtle. Each character will suffer a different illness. The illness won't be mentioned, but the audience will be able to identify it by the way the characters walk, the way they stand, the way they breathe. Does his hand go up to a certain part of the body? His side, his neck? Does he need to catch his breath: The best actors will be the ones who can reproduce the particular breathing for each illness. We'll notice the way the character enters, the way she sits, the way they kiss. We'll notice the way they avoid contact with each other. The audience will also be able to identify the illness by the little pills the characters bring to their mouths. Is it the one with the yellow stripe or the royal blue stripe? The bottle with the blue label? What is the gravity of the illness? Is the character taking one, two, or more pills at a time? How frequently? The leading characters will have the illness most common among theatergoers. Since theatergoers prefer to have plays written about them. Plays will be funded by pharmaceutical laboratories.

There is a pause.

PAULA: (*Standing.*) Well . . . it's time for me to go.
JACK: (*Distressed.*) Are you going to the doctor now?
PAULA: Don't worry. We're all a part of it . . . Not one of us is invulnerable to it. (*Pause.*) Where is my briefcase? (*She looks for it and exits left. She reenters with the briefcase.*) Here it is. OK, I'll be back. (*She goes to the landing and starts down.*)
JACK: (*Starting to go down.*) I'll walk you down.
PAULA: Heavens, I'm not an invalid.
JACK: (*Stopping.*) Of course.
TRESSA: You don't want me to drive you?
PAULA: Heavens no. I have my car.

She starts down the steps. JACK leans over the railing.

JACK: Give me a kiss.

PAULA gives him a kiss. She continues down.

Tell them what I think of you.

TRESSA: Tell them to give you all their money.
PAULA: I will.
JACK: You just tell them that. And tell them to give you that job.
PAULA: OK.
TRESSA: And tell the doctor there's nothing wrong with you.
PAULA: I will. – Thanks, you-all. See you later.
TRESSA: Good luck.
PAULA: Thank you.
JACK: Don't take any wooden nickels.

PAULA laughs.

PAULA: I won't.
TRESSA: Are you going to be back for dinner?
PAULA: I think so.
JACK: I'm bringing Chinese.

The lights begin to fade.

PAULA: Good. I'll be here, then.
TRESSA: We're eating early. I have to be at work at six.
PAULA: At what time should I be back?
TRESSA: Four thirty will be good.
PAULA: OK.
JACK: . . . Good-bye . . .
PAULA: Good-bye.

A moment passes.

JACK: . . . Good-bye . . .

A moment passes.

JACK: . . . Good-bye . . .

There is the sound of the door closing. JACK turns to face front. He looks gloomy. There is a pause.

Three years since I last saw her . . .

The lights fade to black.

Act 2

JACK and TRESSA perform scenes from D. W. Griffith's Broken Blossoms *while silent-movie organ music plays. JACK performs Lillian Gish's part, The Girl, and wears the loose frock of a waif. TRESSA performs Richard Barthelmess's part, Huang, and wears a Chinese box jacket and pants. They first walk in opposite directions around the stage, reenacting the scene where The Girl has been beaten by her father and wanders around in the streets to finally faint on the floor of Huang's shop (upstage). Huang takes her up to his room (downstage) and dresses her in an embroidered silk gown, lowers her to his bed, puts makeup on her face, and puts a decorative crown of flowers on her head. She falls asleep as he exits. A moment later turbulent music is heard. An invisible Father has entered. The Girl is terrified. The Father shakes her and throws her on the floor, grabs her by the arm and takes her home. There he beats her unconscious and leaves. Huang enters to find a dying Girl. He holds her in his arms as she dies. They stay motionless for a while.* PAULA *comes up the stairs and watches the last minutes of their act.* PAULA *walks to them. She looks at them and touches* JACK's *face and the ornaments on his face. She touches* TRESSA's *face. She walks around the front, goes to the kitchen, and reenters with a flan mold on a plate and a spoon. She eats a few mouthfuls of the flan.* JACK *and* TRESSA *start to come out of their stillness and walk slowly downstage to* PAULA.

PAULA: When I was little I had a cousin who was my age. I loved him very much. He was very nice to me. He was my first lover. We did everything. He put his pipi inside me and I enjoyed it very much. The first time he tried he wasn't able to put it in very far. But each time after he put it in a little further until he came in all the way, which wasn't very far because we were very little. Each time we enjoyed it more. I learned to come with him. But I didn't come each time. And I got very upset when I didn't. He said he didn't mind. He said he liked it when I came and he liked it when I didn't. I said, 'Well, I don't,' and he said that he liked to see me desperate and frustrated. And I said, 'Why?' And he said, 'Because then I know you want something from me.' He saw my frustration as desire. Which it was. He was a sweet darling and ... And I forgave him. He was eight and so was I. (*Pause.*)

I saw the doctor. – He says it's kind of bad. – He said that if the fibrillations had lasted any longer I could have died. I asked him and that's what he said – that it was true. He said that Peter should teach the kids to do an intravenous injection in case it happens when he is not home. – But I don't have too much hope for that. It's difficult to do. So I suppose I would have to do it myself. But how could I give myself an intravenous injection in that state with that horrible feeling that your heart is coming out of your mouth? I don't know if I could do it. So I suppose I will have to die.

She puts her head on JACK's *head, walks around the bench and faces them.*

You look beautiful together ... I never imagined ...

Short pause.

Do you mind that I saw you ...

TRESSA *and* JACK *shake their heads.*

It's 'Broken Blossoms,' isn't it?
JACK: (*Almost in a whisper.*) ... Yes.

Pause.

PAULA: ... Do you mind my asking?
TRESSA: ... No.
PAULA: ... Is this something you do?
JACK: ... Yes.

Pause.

PAULA: ... Are you lovers?

JACK: ... We love each other ... (*Touching their clothes.*) ... And we love this ... It is very satisfying.
PAULA: ... *Broken Blossoms*?
TRESSA: ... Oh yes ...
PAULA: ... Does it satisfy you ...? I mean ... do you?
TRESSA: ... Oh yes ...
PAULA: Huang ...? Do you always wear ...? I mean ... is this a man's outfit?
TRESSA: ... Yes.
PAULA: ... Do you ever wear women's clothes ... when you are with him?

JACK *walks slowly to the upper bench and sits peacefully.*

TRESSA: ... No.
PAULA: ... Why not?
TRESSA: (*Short pause.*) Once I knew why. (*Short pause.*) It makes him nervous.
PAULA: What does?
TRESSA: I think it does. (*To* JACK.) Does it make you nervous? (*She looks at him.*) Yes, it makes him nervous.
PAULA: What does?
TRESSA: The woman.
PAULA: You're a lovely woman.
JACK: ... She's a lovely man.
TRESSA: I like to wear this ... (*Walking around the left of the bench and turning to them.*) It soothes me. I wear this when he comes.
PAULA: Why is that?
TRESSA: He's calm. I like him when he's calm.
PAULA: Do you think he will fall in love with you if you dress like a man?
TRESSA: Yes. He did once ...
PAULA: He did?
TRESSA: Yes.
PAULA: Fell in love with you?
TRESSA: Yes.
PAULA: Did you fall in love with him?
TRESSA: (*Sitting by the foot of the bench.*) Yes.
PAULA: Are you still in love with him?
TRESSA: In love with him ... (*Sitting.*) I am in love with him. Of course I am. I'll always be ... Always but not the same way ...
PAULA: I'm glad you're clear about that.
TRESSA: It's very clear.
PAULA: (*Going to her, and kissing her on the forehead.*) I love you, Huang.
TRESSA: He did love me – one night.
PAULA: Oh?
TRESSA: We dressed up for a costume party. We left here arm in arm.

JACK *stands, walks slowly to the upper bench, sits, and listens peacefully.*

At the party I saw him looking at me lovingly. Then we

danced. And we danced some more. And we danced and we danced. He was nervous and his hands were trembling. We danced very close and I felt his heart pounding in his chest. It went boom boom. Boom boom. Boom boom. He was sweating and he looked frightened. He stared away from me as he held me closer and closer. He smiled nervously and he said, 'Let's go home.' He took me home and we made love.

PAULA: Jack ...?

TRESSA: Jack.

JACK: Yes I did.

PAULA: When was that?

TRESSA: Many years ago.

PAULA: ... Did I know you then?

TRESSA: Yes. (*She laughs.*)

PAULA: What were you wearing?

TRESSA: A tuxedo.

PAULA: A tuxedo. Then what happened?

TRESSA: I didn't see him for a long time.

PAULA: Coward.

TRESSA: Not I. (*Pause.*) He went away. And didn't come back for a long time. Then one day he came. He was quiet, nervous, scared that something would happen. Scared that I would want something to happen. I didn't show my feelings. – Things went back to normal. He started coming to see me again. I noticed that if I wore a dress he'd be nervous. If I wore pants he was relaxed. One day I dressed like this. And I felt very calm and he was very calm. And he came close to me and he said 'Wang.' And I said 'Yes.' And he held me close and he whispered ... 'Broken Blossoms?' ... And I said, 'Yes.' He was beautiful and I felt beautiful and it was beautiful just the way we were with each other, at peace with each other.

PAULA: Do you still want him?

TRESSA: Once in love always in love. We're friends, I love him, and he loves me. Like friends. That's the way love is.

PAULA goes to the table and sits right.

PAULA: (*To* TRESSA.) Do you want to buy my house? They're going to sell it. Maybe in the future you can ask me to visit. – and maybe I wouldn't be able to visit. I couldn't stand going there and thinking it belongs to anyone else. Even you. Why are they willing to sell it for nothing to anyone but me? Why can't I buy it for nothing the way anyone else can? (*Short pause.*) Are we going to cook or go out?

TRESSA: Let's get Chinese. Jack, you want to go get some food?

PAULA starts walking around TRESSA *slowly. She is observing her. Looking at her under a different light.*

JACK: ... Sure ... (*Going behind the screen.*) What do you want?

TRESSA: Mushu pork.

JACK: And you, Paula?

PAULA: Chicken with mushrooms.

JACK: (*To himself, from behind the screen.*) Moo goo gai pan.

PAULA: (*To* TRESSA.) Are you coming to the party?

TRESSA: Tonight?

PAULA: Yes.

TRESSA: I have to work.

PAULA: After work.

TRESSA: No ... I'll be tired then.

JACK comes out from behind the screen. He is wearing jeans and a leather jacket.

JACK: You want rice?

PAULA: Fried rice.

TRESSA: Steamed rice.

JACK: (*Pointing to each as he repeats their choices.*) Mushu pork. Chicken and mushrooms. Moo goo gai pan. Fried rice. Steamed rice. Steamed rice. (*He starts exiting.*) You want fortune cookies?

TRESSA: Yeah.

PAULA: Sure.

JACK: Yeah.

JACK exits whistling as the lights fade.

It is 2:00 a.m. The lights are dim. JACK's *leather jacket is on the back of a chair. There is a light downstairs.* JACK's *voice is heard from below. He memorizes the backstage work from Everett Quinton's* Tale of Two Cities *at The Ridiculous Theatrical Company.*

JACK: Preshow. Open dressing room. Turn on hot water to sink and shower. Set clothes up in dressing room. Check water, cups, kleenex. Costumes checked (Checklist). Turn on water to bathtub. Turn on work and running lights. Drain water barrel. Open prop cabinet. Set up all props. Check winch and track. Check main drape and wigpipe. Patch hole. Set up costumes from closet. Check preset. Set up closet and curtain.

A light is turned on in the bedroom.

Give deck ready to stage manager. Fix food, – Act one. Open main curtain. Show starts – strike window light. Closet opens – knock over closet pile. Door closes – move basket to doorway. Everett sits after phone – ring doorbell. Ding dong. Cue: 'Goddamn it.'

TRESSA *enters from the bedroom. She watches* JACK.

Knock on door. Door starts to open – run behind set. Basket on dresser – open trap door. Donut handed to baby – toss downstage right. After donut toss – reset closet stuff and Manette stuff.

TRESSA: Jack.

JACK: Hi.

TRESSA: What are you doing?

JACK: I'm going over my backstage running list.

TRESSA: What running list?

JACK: The show I'm stage managing. It's a tough show to run. Ridiculous theater. Things move too fast. I have to memorize it. Otherwise I won't be able to keep up. Things happen just like this (*Snapping his fingers repeatedly.*) One after the other. Would you check me on this?

TRESSA: OK.

JACK: After donut toss – open trap door. You see where that is?

TRESSA: OK. Yeah. Go ahead.

JACK: After donut toss – reset closet stuff and set Manette stuff. Pross entrance – open trap door. Fork into basket – grab fork and hand off broken fork. After fork taken – close trap door. Cue: 'Anything but black bread and death' – ring doorbell. Hand off from Everett – receive wig head from Everett. Door closed – take wig head to closet. Everett into closet – hand white wig to Everett, label up. Everett into closet – tap on closet wall. Everett out of closet – stop tapping. After Manette scene open trap door. Cue: 'Crush him under the wheels' – receive frame and box. Closet opens, Everett into closet–help Everett into coat and swagger stick. Cue: 'Feed you with a slingshot' – squirt Everett with water bottle. After squirt–close trap door. During broadcast – receive clothes. TV report – receive TV. Alarm (*makes alarm sound*) – set pannier. Cue: 'Very good understanding, Mr Darnay.'

TRESSA: 'A health, a toast.'

JACK: Right! 'A health, a toast' – open trap door. Then 'Very good understanding, Mr Darnay' – raise baby in basket. Cue: – Evremonde!!!!!' – Raise baby knife, hold three beats and lower. After knife – close trap door. Cue: 'She must not find us together' – help Everett with pannier, basket, and Christmas garland and start (*Singing.*) 'O come all Ye Faithful.' Cue: 'God bless you, Sidney' – receive pannier, etc. Cue: 'Work comrades all' – hand out red sheet. (*He comes upstairs carrying two blankets, a pillow, the script, and a flashlight and starts making his bed on the downstage bench. He is wearing jeans and a T shirt.*) Now I have to memorize the second act.

TRESSA: You need some rest.

JACK: (*Lies down and covers himself with the blanket.*) I'll do it tomorrow.

TRESSA kisses him on the cheek, and starts left.

TRESSA: Try to get some sleep.

JACK: I will.

TRESSA: Good night.

JACK: Good night.

TRESSA exits. JACK turns on the flashlight and very quietly memorizes the following.

JACK: Raise baby knife, hold three beats, and lower. After knife – close trap door. Raise baby knife, hold three beats, and lower. After knife – close trap door. Cue: 'She must not find us together' –

The lights begin to fade as he starts to doze off and his voice becomes softer.

Help Everett with pannier, basket, and Christmas garland and start ... O come all ye faithful ...

The lights fade to a very dim level. A few seconds pass.

It is 4:00 a.m. The lights remain the same. JACK is still asleep. The upstage door opens, then closes. PAULA's footsteps are heard below. Something is knocked down.

PAULA: What was that? (*Pause.*) Jack? (*Pause.*) Are you there?

Cans drop and roll downstairs. JACK begins to stir.

God! (*Pause.*) What's the matter with this light? (*Pause.*) Jack.

Something falls downstairs.

Damn it! (*Pause.*) It's dark here.

Something falls downstairs.

What's this?

The sound of something being thrown. She starts up stairs.

Jack.

JACK: ... What ...?

PAULA: I hit your car and I don't know if I damaged it. – I think I did. But it wasn't my fault and I'm not paying for it. – You were parked in the wrong direction and that's illegal. If you take me to court you won't collect because it's illegal to park in the wrong direction. The front of the car doesn't reflect an oncoming car so if you're coming into it you can't see it. It was dark and I didn't see it. – I didn't even see the road. I was drunk and I couldn't see a thing. Didn't even know I was driving on the sidewalk. It doesn't matter whether I was driving on the sidewalk or not. And it doesn't matter whether I was drunk or not drunk. I am not drunk. I only had a couple of drinks. (*Sits.*) In a court of law if you're parked on the wrong direction you don't have a leg to stand on. I don't know how much damage I did to your car but I'm not paying for it. In fact I think my car is embedded into yours. I may have totaled my car and yours too. What time is it?

JACK is dumbfounded. PAULA continues talking as she goes downstairs.

I'm going down to see what the damage is but I'm not paying for it because you were parked in the wrong direction and that's illegal.

JACK: What did you say?

PAULA: I said you were parked in the wrong direction and that that's illegal. That the front of the car doesn't reflect an oncoming car so if you're coming into it you can't see it. That it was too dark and I didn't see it. That I couldn't even see the road. That my car is imbedded into yours.

PAULA goes downstairs. JACK drops to the floor. PAULA's footsteps are heard. The upstage door opens. The lights of dawn are seen outside. JACK stands. He goes to the kitchen, reenters, looks around. He is dumbfounded.

JACK: (*Slmost speechless.*) ... Tressa ...
TRESSA: (*Somnolent.*) ... Yes ...?
JACK: Did you hear that?
TRESSA: ... What ...?
JACK: Paula wrecked my car.

There is a silence. she snores.

(*To himself.*) ... My car ...

He prepares himself a cup of tea and walks up the ramp. He drinks. PAULA's footsteps are heard. She comes up the steps and sees him.

PAULA: It's OK. I think I dozed off for a moment there when I parked. I guess I must've dreamt I crashed. (*She goes to the landing, looks at JACK and laughs.*) You look kind of scared. (*She goes to the table and sits.*) Is that tea you're drinking?

JACK looks at the cup, then looks at PAULA and speaks in a high-pitched voice.

JACK: Yes.
PAULA: May I have some?
JACK: Yes.
PAULA: (*Ingratiatingly.*) I'm glad I didn't wreck your car.

   Pause.

JACK: (*In a squeaky high voice.*) Oh ...
PAULA: Relieved?
JACK: Oh ...
PAULA: Oh what?

JACK exits dumbfounded. TRESSA appears left. She is putting on a housecoat.

TRESSA: Hi.
PAULA: Hi.
TRESSA: What happened?
PAULA: Nothing.
TRESSA: You just got in?
PAULA: Just now.
TRESSA: How was the party?
PAULA: You're lucky you didn't come.
TRESSA: What? – Was it boring?
PAULA: Yes. It was depressing.
TRESSA: What happened?

PAULA: Nothing happened. – Dan and Flo were there.
TRESSA AND JACK: Oh.

   TRESSA stretches her neck.

PAULA: You're tired.
TRESSA: I'm going to bed. (*Starts to exit left.*)
PAULA: Yes, it's late.
TRESSA: Good night.
PAULA: Good night.
JACK: Good night. (*Reaches for his jacket and puts it on.*)
PAULA: Where are you going?
JACK: Going for a walk.
PAULA: Now?!
JACK: Yeah, I feel restless.
PAULA: Where're you going?
JACK: Out.

   He kisses PAULA and starts to exit. PAULA is anxious.

PAULA: Be careful.
JACK: I will.
PAULA: (*Her anxiety builds.*) I'll go with you.
JACK: No, Paula.
PAULA: Please.
JACK: I want to be alone.
PAULA: (*Going on her knees by the railing.*) Where are you going? (*She waits a moment.*) Why Jack? I'm worried! Let me go with you!
JACK: I'll be all right.
PAULA: Please! Jack!

   Silence.

Jaaack!! Where are you going!!! Where are you going!!!

   TRESSA enters from the kitchen. She and PAULA look at each other. PAULA stands.

He went ...

They embrace.

Into the night. (*Sobs.*) Into the night ... Into the night ...

The lights fade.

It's 5:00 a.m. JACK is standing on the railing. His hands are tied behind him to the post. He is bare-chested. There is blood smeared on his chest. TRESSA stands left, PAULA right. They both face him.

JACK:

They wanted to fuck me and they did. They fucked me till I was blue in the face. One first and then another and another. And they came back. They couldn't get enough. And I wanted all they had. They didn't use condoms. Nothing.

On the raw. I told them I was HIV positive.

I did, and I handed them condoms.

And they didn't take them. They said they had more pleasure without them. I was bleeding like a faucet and they fucked me and fucked me and it hurt like the devil and I screamed and screamed till I couldn't scream any more. And they kept fucking me, one after the other, and I never had so much pleasure in my life.

I handed them condoms and they didn't care. I've never been so happy in my life. One big cock after the other. I screamed like a goat in the slaughterhouse. I don't know. I don't know. Did I think? Did I think? I didn't think. I didn't think when I got it. I just got it. It's a virus. It happened when I got fucked by someone. When you get a cold, do you wonder who gave it to you? No one gave it to me. I got it. Maybe I got it when I got the best fuck in my life. And then maybe I got it into me when I got a lousy fuck … so what.

He puts his head down and sobs.

Don't touch me.

I'm contagious.

I don't want to give you AIDS.

Sobs.

  I have AIDS.
I'm contagious.

I have AIDS.
I have AIDS.
I have AIDS.

Yes. I am!
What should I remember?

TRESSA:
Didn't they?

You're not!
They didn't care.

Why did you say that?

Did they know what a condom is?

Did you think you were giving them AIDS?

Oh…

Oh…

Don't touch me.

Jack, you don't have AIDS.

You don't have AIDS. And if you did, you would never do what you say you did. Jack, you would never do that. Jack, you have to protect yourself. You don't have AIDS. You're not HIV positive. You have to be careful. No. Remember.

PAULA:
Didn't they, Jack?

Why do you think you do?
Why did you say that? Why Jack?

Oh, Jack!

Oh, Jack!

You don't have AIDS.

Why does he say he has AIDS?

Why does he say that? Stop it, Jack! Stop it.

TRESSA: That you don't have AIDS. That you have been tested. Why do you think you have AIDS?

He is near fainting.

You don't have AIDS. You don't. You don't. I have seen your tests. You're not. You're not.

she reaches to him as he descends. She holds him up as they walk back to the bench.

JACK: Because … Because … Because …

She sits holding him on her lap in a Pietá position. She slides her hand on his chest.

TRESSA: All my life I've had a passion in me and it is for you. All my life it was there, has been there, reserved for you. I never felt it. I never knew that passion was in me. – It was there, but only for you. I say 'you' because I don't know what else to call you. I could call you Key, or Burst, or Debris, or Flood. You touched it and it rose and burst out like a dike that opens to the force of the waters inside and everything comes out, water, stones, boulders, trees. Like prisoners in a jail who think of nothing but escape day and night, year after year and when the riot breaks and the doors crack and burst open because of the force of the explosion as if it were of dynamite, or like the eruption of a volcano underneath the floors when the force of the prisoners' desire for freedom erupts and the walls burst and the stones and the water rush through the opening ferociously, wildly, and fearlessly. It is like that. It feels like that. You touched it and it rose and burst out; water, hard stones, branches, gravel, mud, foam … out of my chest … for you … burst. Let me call you Burst.

PAULA kneels next to them. Her head is on JACK's knees. A blazing fire is projected on them. A gust of wind blows on them while JACK starts lifting his head slowly. TRESSA and PAULA start looking up. The voice of the High Lama and the music of the film are heard as they speak. Stormy Wagnerian music joins in.

THE HIGH LAMA'S VOICE AND PAULA: 'I have waited for you, my child for a long time. I believe you will live through the storm. And after, through the long age of desolation, you may still live, growing older and wiser and more patient.

TRESSA joins their voices.

You will conserve the fragrance of our history and add to it the touch of your own mind. You will welcome the stranger,

JACK joins their voices.

and teach him the rule of age and wisdom, and one of these strangers, it may be, will succeed you when you are yourself very old. Beyond that, my vision weakens, but I see, at a great distance, a new world stirring in the ruins, stirring clumsily but in hopefulness, seeking its lost and legendary treasure. And they will all be here, my children, hidden behind the mountains in the valley of Shangri-la, preserved as by a miracle for a new Renaissance …'

The volume of the music increases as the lights fade to black.

It is 8:00 a.m. TRESSA is standing on the steps. She wears a bathrobe. PAULA stands by the table. She is finishing putting her clothes in a suitcase on the table. She wears a light coat.

TRESSA: He's still asleep. Should I wake him?

PAULA puts the last garments in the suitcase.

PAULA: Let him sleep.

TRESSA goes to the bench.

I'll wait a while. I want to see him before I go. (*Closes the suitcase.*) He's going through the worse time. (*Sits at the table.*) I'd like to ask him to come up and spend a few days with us.

TRESSA lies on the downstage bench.

TRESSA: That would be good for him. That would be good. To spend a few days in the country.

PAULA: Yes it would … to spend a few days in the open. He likes it there. (*Goes to armchair and sits.*) Maybe when the play closes … a week or two.

TRESSA: Yes. (*Pulls covers over her.*) That would be good for him. He's going through a very hard time …

PAULA: Yes … You go to sleep, Tressa. You must be tired. I'll wait for him.

TRESSA: (*As she turns and closes her eyes.*) … Yes, Paula … I'm tired.

The lights fade slightly as JACK enters from the bedroom. He is wrapped in a blanket, walks slowly to the upstage bench and sits. PAULA and TRESSA slowly turn towards him.

JACK: … I'm tired … I can't go back to sleep …

His head and torso curve slightly toward the pillow. The lights fade slowly as JACK lets out a soft cry. The lights go to black.

4.4 FAR AWAY (2000)

CARYL CHURCHILL

Caryl Churchill (b. 1938) is a leading contemporary British playwright, both prolific and highly influential. The interface between feminism and theatre in the 1970s led Churchill to produce a number of ground-breaking plays, including Cloud Nine *(1979) and* Top Girls *(1982). Her career has also been marked by shifts in thematic focus, an ever-increasing tendency towards formal experiment and the exploration of new working partnerships with both directors and choreographers.* Far Away *(2000), although refusing to verify a precise geographical and political landscape, is a haunting contemplation on our personal and political responses to genocide, war and terror in an era of globalization, media simulation and the exhaustion of nature.* Far Away *was first produced at the Royal Court Theatre Upstairs in London, directed by Stephen Daldry.*

Characters
JOAN, a girl
HARPER, her aunt
TODD, a young man

1

Harper's house. Night.

JOAN: I can't sleep.

HARPER: It's the strange bed.

JOAN: No, I like different places.

HARPER: Are you cold?

JOAN: No.

HARPER: Do you want a drink?

JOAN: I think I am cold.

HARPER: That's easy enough then. There's extra blankets in the cupboard.

JOAN: Is it late?

HARPER: Two.

JOAN: Are you going to bed?

HARPER: Do you want a hot drink?

JOAN: No thank you.

HARPER: I should go to bed then.

JOAN: Yes.

HARPER: It's always odd in a new place. When you've been here a week you'll look back at tonight and it won't seem the same at all.

JOAN: I've been to a lot of places. I've stayed with friends at their houses. I don't miss my parents if you think that.

HARPER: Do you miss your dog?

JOAN: I miss the cat I think.

HARPER: Does it sleep on your bed?

JOAN: No because I chase it off. But it gets in if the door's not properly shut. You think you've shut the door but it hasn't caught and she pushes it open in the night.

HARPER: Come here a minute. You're shivering. Are you hot?

JOAN: No, I'm all right.

HARPER: You're over-tired. Go to bed. I'm going to bed myself.

JOAN: I went out.

HARPER: When? just now?

JOAN: Just now.

HARPER: No wonder you're cold. It's hot in the daytime here but it's cold at night.

JOAN: The stars are brighter here than at home.

HARPER: It's because there's no street lights.

JOAN: I couldn't see much.

HARPER: I don't expect you could. How did you get out? I didn't hear the door.

JOAN: I went out the window.

HARPER: I'm not sure I like that.

JOAN: No it's quite safe, there's a roof and a tree.

HARPER: When people go to bed they should stay in bed. Do you climb out of the window at home?

JOAN: I can't at home because – No I don't.

HARPER: I'm responsible for you.

JOAN: Yes, I'm sorry.

HARPER: Well that's enough adventures for one night. You'll sleep now. Off you go. Look at you, you're asleep on your feet.

JOAN: There was a reason.

HARPER: For going out?

JOAN: I heard a noise.

HARPER: An owl?

JOAN: A shriek.

HARPER: An owl then. There are all sorts of birds here, you might see a golden oriole. People come here specially to watch birds and we sometimes make tea or coffee or sell bottles of water because there's no café and people don't expect that and they get thirsty. You'll see in the morning what a beautiful place it is.

JOAN: It was more like a person screaming.

HARPER: It is like a person screaming when you hear an owl.

JOAN: It was a person screaming.

HARPER: Poor girl, what a fright you must have had imagining you heard somebody screaming. You should have come straight down here to me.

JOAN: I wanted to see.

HARPER: It was dark.

JOAN: Yes but I did see.

HARPER: Now what did you imagine you saw in the dark?

JOAN: I saw my uncle.

HARPER: Yes I expect you did. He likes a breath of air. He wasn't screaming I hope?

JOAN: No.

HARPER: That's all right then. Did you talk to him? I expect you were frightened he'd say what are you doing out of your bed so late.

JOAN: I stayed in the tree.

HARPER: He didn't see you?

JOAN: No.

HARPER: He'll be surprised won't he, he'll laugh when he hears you were up in the tree. He'll be cross but he doesn't mean it, he'll think it's a good joke, it's the sort of thing he did when he was a boy. So bed now. I'll go up too.

JOAN: He was pushing someone. He was bundling someone into a shed.

HARPER: He must have been putting a big sack in the shed. He works too late.

JOAN: I'm not sure if it was a woman. It could have been a young man.

HARPER: Well I have to tell you, when you've been married as long as I have. There are things people get up to, it's natural, it's nothing bad, that's just friends of his your uncle was having a little party with.

JOAN: Was it a party?

HARPER: Just a little party.

JOAN: Yes because there wasn't just that one person.

HARPER: No, there'd be a few of his friends.

JOAN: There was a lorry.

HARPER: Yes, I expect there was.

JOAN: When I put my ear against the side of the lorry I heard crying inside.

HARPER: How could you do that from up in the tree?

JOAN: I got down from the tree. I went to the lorry after I looked in the window of the shed.

HARPER: There might be things that are not your business when you're a visitor in someone else's house.

JOAN: Yes, I'd rather not have seen. I'm sorry.

HARPER: Nobody saw you?

JOAN: They were thinking about themselves.

HARPER: I think it's lucky nobody saw you.

JOAN: If it's a party, why was there so much blood?

HARPER: There isn't any blood.

JOAN: Yes.

HARPER: Where?

JOAN: On the ground.

HARPER: In the dark? how would you see that in the dark?

JOAN: I slipped in it.

She holds up her bare foot.

I mostly wiped it off.

HARPER: That's where the dog got run over this afternoon.

JOAN: Wouldn't it have dried up?

HARPER: Not if the ground was muddy.

JOAN: What sort of dog?

HARPER: A big dog, a big mongrel.

JOAN: That's awful, you must be very sad, had you had him long?

HARPER: No, he was young, he ran out, he was never very obedient, a lorry was backing up.

JOAN: What was his name?

HARPER: Flash.

JOAN: What colour was he?

HARPER: Black with a bit of white.

JOAN: Why were the children in the shed?

HARPER: What children?

JOAN: Don't you know what children?

HARPER: How could you see there were children?

JOAN: There was a light on. That's how I could see the blood inside the shed. I could see the faces and which ones had blood on.

HARPER: You've found out something secret. You know that don't you?

JOAN: Yes.

HARPER: Something you shouldn't know.

JOAN: Yes I'm sorry.

HARPER: Something you must never talk about. Because if you do you could put people's lives in danger.

JOAN: Why? who from? from my uncle?

HARPER: Of course not from your uncle.

JOAN: From you?

HARPER: Of course not from me, are you mad? I'm going to tell you what's going on. Your uncle is helping these people. He's helping them escape. He's giving them shelter. Some of them were still in the lorry, that's why they were crying. Your uncle's going to take them all into the shed and then they'll be all right.

JOAN: They had blood on their faces.

HARPER: That's from before. That's because they were attacked by the people your uncle's saving them from.

JOAN: There was blood on the ground.

HARPER: One of them was injured very badly but your uncle bandaged him up.

JOAN: He's helping them.

HARPER: That's right.

JOAN: There wasn't a dog. There wasn't a party.

HARPER: No, I'm trusting you with the truth now. You must never talk about it or you'll put your uncle's life in danger and mine and even your own. You won't even say anything to your parents.

JOAN: Why did you have me to stay if you've got this secret going on?

HARPER: The lorry should have come yesterday. It won't happen again while you're here.

JOAN: It can now because I know. You don't have to stop for me. I could help uncle in the shed and look after them.

HARPER: No, he has to do it himself. But thank you for offering, that's very kind. So after all that excitement do you think you could go back to bed?

JOAN: Why was uncle hitting them?

HARPER: Hitting who?

JOAN: He was hitting a man with a stick. I think the stick was metal. He hit one of the children.

HARPER: One of the people in the lorry was a traitor. He wasn't really one of them, he was pretending, he was going to betray them, they found out and told your uncle. Then he attacked your uncle, he attacked the other people, your uncle had to fight him.

JOAN: That's why there was so much blood.

HARPER: Yes, it had to be done to save the others.

JOAN: He hit one of the children.

HARPER: That would have been the child of the traitor. Or sometimes you get bad children who even betray their parents.

JOAN: What's going to happen?

HARPER: They'll go off in the lorry very early in the morning.

JOAN: Where to?

HARPER: Where they're escaping to. You don't want to have to keep any more secrets.

JOAN: He only hit the traitors.

HARPER: Of course. I'm not surprised you can't sleep, what an upsetting thing to see. But now you understand, it's not so bad. You're part of a big movement now to make things better. You can be proud of that. You can look at the stars and think here we are in our little bit of space, and I'm on the side of the people who are putting things right, and your soul will expand right into the sky.

JOAN: Can't I help?

HARPER: You can help me clean up in the morning. Will you do that?

JOAN: Yes.

HARPER: So you'd better get some sleep.

2

Several years later. A hat makers.

1.

JOAN and TODD are sitting at a workbench. They have each just started making a hat.

TODD: There's plenty of blue.

JOAN: I think I'm starting with black.

TODD: Colour always wins.

JOAN: I will have colour, I'm starting with black to set the colour off.

TODD: I did one last week that was an abstract picture of the street, blue for the buses, yellow for the flats, red for the leaves, grey for the sky. Nobody got it but I knew what it was. There's little satisfactions to be had.

JOAN: Don't you enjoy it?

TODD: You're new aren't you?

JOAN: This is my first hat. My first professional hat.

TODD: Did you do hat at college?

JOAN: My degree hat was a giraffe six feet tall.

TODD: You won't have time to do something like that in the week.

JOAN: I know.

TODD: We used to get two weeks before a parade and then they took it down to one and now they're talking about cutting a day.

JOAN: So we'd get an extra day off?

TODD: We'd get a day's less money. We wouldn't make such good hats.

JOAN: Can they do that?

TODD: You'd oppose it would you?

JOAN: I've only just started.

TODD: You'll find there's a lot wrong with this place.

JOAN: I thought it was one of the best jobs.

TODD: It is. Do you know where to go for lunch?

JOAN: I think there's a canteen isn't there?

TODD: Yes but we don't go there. I'll show you where to go.

2.

Next day. They are working on the hats, which are by now far more brightly decorated ie the ones they were working on have been replaced by ones nearer completion.

JOAN: Your turn.

TODD: I go for a swim in the river before work.

JOAN: Isn't it dangerous?

TODD: Your turn.

JOAN: I've got a pilot's licence.

TODD: I stay up till four every morning watching the trials.

JOAN: I'm getting a room in a subway.

TODD: I've got my own place.

JOAN: Have you?

TODD: Do you want to see it? That's coming on.

JOAN: I don't understand yours but I like the feather.

TODD: I'm not trying. I've been here too long.

JOAN: Will you leave?

TODD: My turn. There's something wrong with how we get the contracts.

JOAN: But we want the contracts.

TODD: What if we don't deserve them? What if our work isn't really the best?

JOAN: So what's going on?

TODD: I'll just say a certain person's brother-in-law. Where does he work do you think?

JOAN: Where does he work?

TODD: I'm not talking about it in here. Tell me something else.

JOAN: I don't like staying in in the evenings and watching trials.

TODD: I watch them at night after I come back.

JOAN: Back from where?

TODD: Where do you like?

3.

Next day. They're working on the hats, which are getting very big and extravagant.

TODD: I don't enjoy animal hats myself.

JOAN: I was a student.

TODD: Abstract hats are back in a big way.

JOAN: I've always liked abstract hats.

TODD: You must have not noticed when everyone hated them.

JOAN: It was probably before my time.

Silence. They go on working.

JOAN: It's just if you're going on about it all the time I don't know why you don't do something about it.

TODD: This is your third day.

JOAN: The management's corrupt – you've told me. We're too low paid – you've told me.

Silence. They go on working.

TODD: Too much green.

JOAN: It's meant to be too much.

Silence. They go on working.

TODD: I noticed you looking at that fair boy's hat. I hope you told him it was derivative.

Silence. They go on working.

TODD: I'm the only person in this place who's got any principles, don't tell me I should do something, I spend my days wondering what to do.

JOAN: So you'll probably come up with something.

Silence. They go on working.

4.

Next day. They are working on the hats, which are now enormous and preposterous.

TODD: That's beautiful.

JOAN: You like it?

TODD: I do.

JOAN: I like yours too.

TODD: You don't have to say that. It's not one of my best.

JOAN: No it's got – I don't know, it's a confident hat.

TODD: I have been doing parades for six years. So I'm a valued old hand. So when I go and speak to a certain person he might pay attention.

JOAN: You're going to speak to him?

TODD: I've an appointment after work.

JOAN: You might lose your job.

TODD: I might.

JOAN: I'm impressed.

TODD: That was the idea.

JOAN: Will you mention the brother-in-law?

TODD: First I'll talk about the money. Then I'll just touch in the brother-in-law. I've a friend who's a journalist.

JOAN: Will you touch in the journalist?

TODD: I might imply something without giving the journalist away. It might be better if he can't trace the journalist back to me.

JOAN: Though he will suspect.

TODD: However much he suspects. One thing if I lost my job.

JOAN: What's that?

TODD: I'd miss you.

JOAN: Already?

5.

Next day. A procession of ragged, beaten, chained prisoners, each wearing a hat, on their way to execution. The finished hats are even more enormous and preposterous than in the previous scene.

Figure 28 *Far Away* at the Royal Court Theatre, 2000, directed by Stephen Daldry. (Photographer: Ivan Kyncl.)

6.

A new week. JOAN and TODD are starting work on new hats.

JOAN: I still can't believe it.

TODD: No one's ever won in their first week before.

JOAN: It's all going to be downhill from now on.

TODD: You can't win every week.

JOAN: That's what I mean.

TODD: No but you'll do a fantastic body of work while you're here.

JOAN: Sometimes I think it's a pity that more aren't kept.

TODD: There'd be too many, what would they do with them?

JOAN: They could reuse them.

TODD: Exactly and then we'd be out of work.

JOAN: It seems so sad to burn them with the bodies.

TODD: No I think that's the joy of it. The hats are ephemeral. It's like a metaphor for something or other.

JOAN: Well, life.

TODD: Well, life, there you are. Out of nearly three hundred hats I've made here I've only had three win and go in the museum. But that's never bothered me. You make beauty and it disappears, I love that.

JOAN: You're so . .

TODD: What?

JOAN: You make me think in different ways. Like I'd never have thought about how this place is run and now I see how important it is.

TODD: I think it did impress a certain person that I was speaking from the high moral ground.

JOAN: So tell me again exactly what he said at the end.

TODD: 'These things must be thought about.'

JOAN: I think that's encouraging.

TODD: It could mean he'll think how to get rid of me.

JOAN: That's a fantastic shape to start from.

TODD: It's a new one for me. I'm getting inspired by you.

JOAN: There's still the journalist. If he looks into it a bit more we could expose the corrupt financial basis of how the whole hat industry is run, not just this place, I bet the whole industry is dodgy.

TODD: Do you think so?

JOAN: I think we should find out.

TODD: You've changed my life, do you know that?

JOAN: If you lose your job I'll resign.

TODD: We might not get jobs in hats again.

JOAN: There's other parades.

TODD: But I think you're a hat genius.

JOAN: Unless all the parades are corrupt.

TODD: I love these beads. Use these beads.

JOAN: No, you have them.

TODD: No, you.

3

Several years later. HARPER's house, daytime.

HARPER: You were right to poison the wasps.

TODD: Yes, I think all the wasps have got to go.

HARPER: I was outside yesterday on the edge of the wood when a shadow came over and it was a cloud of butterflies, and they came down just beyond me and the trees and bushes were red with them. Two of them clung to my arm, I was terrified, one of them got in my hair, I managed to squash them.

TODD: I haven't had a problem with butterflies.

HARPER: They can cover your face. The Romans used to commit suicide with gold leaf, just flip it down their throat and it covered their windpipe, I think of that with butterflies.

TODD: I was passing an orchard, there were horses standing under the trees, and suddenly wasps attacked them out of the plums. There were the horses galloping by screaming with their heads made of wasp. I wish she'd wake up.

HARPER: We don't know how long she'd been walking.

TODD: She was right to come.

HARPER: You don't go walking off in the middle of a war.

TODD: You do if you're escaping.

HARPER: We don't know that she was escaping.

TODD: She was getting to a place of safety to regroup.

HARPER: Is this a place of safety?

TODD: Relatively, yes of course it is. Everyone thinks it's just a house.

HARPER: The cats have come in on the side of the French.

TODD: I never liked cats, they smell, they scratch, they only like you because you feed them, they bite, I used to have a cat that would suddenly just take some bit of you in its mouth.

HARPER: Did you know they've been killing babies?

TODD: Where's that?

HARPER: In China. They jump in the cots when nobody's looking.

TODD: But some cats are still OK.

HARPER: I don't think so.

TODD: I know a cat up the road.

HARPER: No, you must be careful of that.

TODD: But we're not exactly on the other side from the French. It's not as if they're the Moroccans and the ants.

HARPER: It's not as if they're the Canadians, the Venezuelans and the mosquitoes.

TODD: It's not as if they're the engineers, the chefs, the children under five, the musicians.

HARPER: The car salesmen.

TODD: Portuguese car salesmen.

HARPER: Russian swimmers.

TODD: Thai butchers.

HARPER: Latvian dentists.

TODD: No, the Latvian dentists have been doing good work in Cuba. They've a house outside Havana.

HARPER: But Latvia has been sending pigs to Sweden. The dentists are linked to international dentistry and that's where their loyalty lies, with dentists in Dar-es-Salaam.

TODD: We don't argue about Dar-es-Salaam.

HARPER: You would attempt to justify the massacre in Dar-es-Salaam?

She's come here because you're here on leave and if anyone finds out I'll be held responsible.

TODD: It's only till tomorrow. I'll wake her up. I'll give her a few more minutes.

HARPER: Did you see the programme about crocodiles?

TODD: Yes but crocodiles, the way they look after the baby crocodiles and carry them down to the water in their mouths.

HARPER: Don't you think everyone helps their own children?

TODD: I'm just saying I wouldn't be sorry if the crocodiles were on one of the sides we have alliances with. They're unstoppable, come on.

HARPER: Crocodiles are evil and it is always right to be opposed to crocodiles. Their skin, their teeth, the foul smell of their mouths from the dead meat. Crocodiles wait till zebras are crossing the river and bite the weak ones with those jaws and pull them down. Crocodiles invade villages at night and take children out of their beds. A crocodile will carry a dozen heads back to the river, tenderly like it carries its young, and put them in the water where they bob about as trophies till they rot.

TODD: I'm just saying we could use that.

HARPER: And the fluffy little darling waterbirds, the smallest one left behind squeaking wait for me, wait for me. And their mother who would give her life to save them.

TODD: Do we include mallards in this?

HARPER: Mallards are not a good waterbird. They commit rape, and they're on the side of the elephants and the Koreans. But crocodiles are always in the wrong.

TODD: Do you think I should wake her up or let her sleep? We won't get any time together.

HARPER: You agree with me about the crocodiles?

TODD: What's the matter? you don't know whose side I'm on?

HARPER: I don't know what you think.

TODD: I think what we all think.

HARPER: Take deer.

TODD: You mean sweet little bambis?

HARPER: You mean that ironically?

TODD: I mean it sarcastically.

HARPER: Because they burst out of parks and storm down from mountains and terrorise shopping malls. If the does run away when you shoot they run into somebody else and trample them with their vicious little shining hooves, the fawns get under the feet of shoppers and send them crashing down escalators, the young bucks charge the plate glass windows –

TODD: I know to hate deer.

HARPER: and the old ones, do you know how heavy their antlers are or how sharp the prongs are when they twist into teenagers running down the street?

TODD: Yes I do know that.

He lifts his shirt and shows a scar.

HARPER: Was that a deer?

TODD: In fact it was a bear. I don't like being doubted.

HARPER: It was when the elephants went over to the Dutch, I'd always trusted elephants.

TODD: I've shot cattle and children in Ethiopia. I've gassed mixed troops of Spanish, computer programmers and dogs. I've torn starlings apart with my bare hands. And I liked doing it with my bare hands. So don't suggest I'm not reliable.

HARPER: I'm not saying you can't kill.

TODD: And I know it's not all about excitement. I've done boring jobs. I've worked in abattoirs stunning pigs and musicians and by the end of the day your back aches and all you can see when you shut your eyes is people hanging upside down by their feet.

HARPER: So you'd say the deer are vicious?

TODD: We've been over that.

HARPER: If a hungry deer came into the yard you wouldn't feed it?

TODD: Of course not.

HARPER: I don't understand that because the deer are with us. They have been for three weeks.

TODD: I didn't know. You said yourself.

HARPER: Their natural goodness has come through. You can see it in their soft brown eyes.

TODD: That's good news.

HARPER: You hate the deer. You admire the crocodiles.

TODD: I've lost touch because I'm tired.

HARPER: You must leave.

TODD: I'm your family.

HARPER: Do you think I sleep?

JOAN comes in and walks into TODD's arms.

HARPER: You can't stay here, they'll be after you. What are you going to say when you go back, you ran off to spend a day with your husband? Everyone has people they love they'd like to see or anyway people they'd rather see than lie in a hollow waiting to be bitten by ants. Are you not going back at all because if you're not you might as well shoot me now. Did anyone see you leave? which way did you come? were you followed? There are ospreys here who will have seen you arrive. And you're risking your life for you don't know what because he says things that aren't right. Don't you care? Maybe you don't know right from wrong yourself, what do I know about you after two years, I'd like to be glad to see you but how can I?

JOAN: Of course birds saw me, everyone saw me walking along but nobody knew why, I could have been on a mission, everyone's moving about and no one knows why, and in fact I killed two cats and a child under five so it wasn't that different from a mission, and I don't see why I can't have one day and then go back, I'll go on to the end after this. It wasn't so much the birds I was frightened of, it was the weather, the weather here's on the side of the Japanese. There were thunderstorms all through the mountains, I went through towns I hadn't been before. The rats are bleeding out of their mouths and ears, which is good, and so were the girls by the side of the road. It was tiring there because everything's been recruited, there were piles of bodies and if you stopped to find out there was one killed by coffee or one killed by pins, they were killed by heroin, petrol, chainsaws, hairspray, bleach, foxgloves, the smell of smoke was where we were burning the grass that wouldn't serve. The Bolivians are working with gravity, that's a secret so as not to spread alarm. But we're getting further with noise and there's thousands dead of light in Madagascar. Who's going to mobilise darkness and silence? that's what I wondered in the night. By the third day I could hardly walk but I got down to the river. There was a camp of Chilean soldiers upstream but they hadn't seen me and fourteen black and white cows downstream having a drink so I knew I'd have to go straight across. But I didn't know whose side the river was on, it might help me swim or it might drown me. In the middle the current was running much faster, the water was brown, I didn't know if that meant anything. I stood on the bank a long time. But I knew it was my only way of getting here so at last I put one foot in the river. It was very cold but so far that was all. When you've just stepped in you can't tell what's going to happen. The water laps round your ankles in any case.

Note

The Parade (Scene 2.5): five is too few and twenty better than ten. A hundred?

4.5 SCENES FROM FAMILY LIFE (2008)

MARK RAVENHILL

(For Marcus Nicolai)

Mark Ravenhill (b. 1966) came to prominence as a dramatist in 1996 with the Out of Joint/Royal Court Theatre production of Shopping and Fucking, *an explicit, comic and politically aware exploration of disenfranchised youth in a 'post-ideological' age.* Scenes from Family Life *(2008) is representative of Ravenhill's ongoing commitment to theatre for young people. Commissioned by the Royal National Theatre's 'New Connections' youth programme, the play was specifically written to be performed by young non-professional actors. A 'rites of passage' play,* Scenes from Family Life *employs a form of magical realism to ask important questions about the desires of young people to have children and create families, and their difficult journey into adulthood. Ravenhill's other-worldly theatrical landscape invites a confrontation with tangible realities.*

Characters

JACK
LISA
STACY
BARRY
A group of their female friends from a baby shower: HOLLY, KAREN, JANINE, AMY, MARTA, MARIE
RYAN, HOLLY's boyfriend
THREE SOLDIERS
MOTHER with an empty pram
ENTERTAINER
A large group of PARENTS and BABIES

Setting: Living room of JACK and LISA's flat

1

Living room of JACK and LISA's flat.

JACK: What's going on in your head?
LISA: Oh ... I don't know.
JACK: What you thinking?
LISA: Well...
JACK: Tell me.
LISA: Well ... happiness.
JACK: Yeah?
LISA: Yeah. Happiness. You. Me. Baby.
JACK: That all?
LISA: Yeah. That's all.

JACK: You sure .?
LISA: I can't tell you every feeling and –
JACK: I want a feel.
LISA: Go on then.

JACK reaches out and touches LISA's stomach.

JACK: Oh yeah. Head and feet and ... Tiny but somewhere there's ...
LISA: You thought of names?
JACK: Not yet. Don't want to jinx it. Too soon. Barry and Stace in't chosen and they're in month eight. What's it feel like?
LISA: Different.
JACK: Does it send you messages and stuff? Through your body?

LISA: I dunno. Maybe. Yeah.

JACK: What messages? Tell me the messages. You gotta know.

LISA: No. You ready to be a dad?

JACK: Totally ready. My mum she says we're too young but I say I got a job, Lisa's got a job, we got the flat, it's time. I love you.

LISA: And I love you.

They kiss.

JACK: Together forever. Got you now.

LISA: Love it. Love you. See ... there's a world out there of people and they're all odd. They seem odd. They have like freak outs on buses and stuff. Talk to themselves. Punch strangers. I can't handle that. You're normal aren't you?

JACK: Reckon.

LISA: That's why I picked you. I gotta have a totally normal baby father.

JACK: Come here.

LISA: Yeah?

They hug.

JACK: You big kid. I'll get the tea.

Exit JACK. *Woosh, flash,* LISA *vanishes into thin air. Re-enter* JACK.

JACK: Lisa do you want white or the ...? Lees? Lees? Lisa?

Pause.

Lisa?

Pause.

Lisa!

Pause.

Lisa?

He hunts around the room.

JACK: I'm gonna find you and when I find you I'm gonna ... Lisa?

He goes and checks in the bedroom.

JACK: (*Off.*) Lisa!

He enters from the bedroom. She reappears – a rematerialisation.

JACK: Oh my –. Oh my oh oh –

LISA: What? What?

JACK: I ... There was nothing there. It was frightening. There was like this gap where a person should be and I was calling out but there was nothing there. And then you were there.

LISA: Stop messing around.

JACK: I'm not I – Lees. Where do you go? Where you just been? Tell me.

LISA: Don't be silly. Forget it. Trick of the light. Kiss me.

JACK: Listen I ... can't.

LISA: You're scared of me.

JACK: No just I –

LISA: You are. You're scared of me.

JACK: Of course if you can just –

LISA: I'm solid – I'm real – you see – you see – touch me – touch me – what do you feel?

JACK: Yeah solid, real yeah.

LISA: So I'm here. Nothing happened. Nobody's running away. Nobody's fading. I'm here with you. We're gonna have the baby together. We're gonna be together – forever. Yeah?

JACK: Lees. I'm not making it up. You did do it. You vanished. Faded away and then – You're not gonna do it again?

LISA: This is mad.

JACK: I want you to stop doing that. I don't like it. Stop it.

LISA: I'm not doing anything.

JACK: There's a place up there or down there or in there or ... somewhere and you went there. You vanished. You went somewhere. You came back. Tell me.

LISA: I have enough of this. I've wanted this baby ever since I was thirteen and now you, you – I'm going out.

JACK: Where?

LISA: I don't know. A mate's. Barry and Stacy's. Or Holly's. She's having her baby shower. Everyone turns up with presents now she's not far off. Yeah – Holly's. I'll go there.

JACK: No. I won't let you. Stay here. With the current circumstances ...

LISA: There are no ...

JACK: I'll look after you. Stay. Stay. Stay in the house. How we gonna look after baby if you don't stay in the house?

LISA: How can we if you keep going mad? We're incompatible. You and me we're –

Whooshing, flashing, etc. JACK *rapidly gets out his mobile phone. Starts video recording.* LISA *vanishes.*

JACK: You're not gonna get me. I'll sort this. Come back Lees!

Whooshing, flashing, etc. LISA *reappears.*

JACK: You did it again.

LISA: No I never I –

JACK: You did. Look.

JACK *rewinds the images, indicates to* LISA *to have a look on the phone.*

LISA: This is stupid I'm not gonna just –

JACK: Look when I tell you to look.

Reluctantly, she looks.

LISA: ... Oh my god. Thin air and then I ... Hold me. Oh babe.

JACK: (*Holds her.*) You see? Should have trusted me. I don't lie. When I tell you something you have to believe me.

LISA: Am I solid now? I feel solid.

JACK: You are. You're solid now. And I'm looking after you.

LISA: What we gonna do? If I'm the kind of person who just vanishes – I don't wanna be the kind of person who just vanishes. I never heard of that … people who just … oh. I want to be here forever. You. Me. Baby. Forever.

JACK: Won't let you go again. I'm gonna put a stop to it.

LISA: Yeah?

JACK: Find a way. You are never gonna leave my sight.

Doorbell.

JACK: Answer it. I'll watch you.

They answer it. Enter BARRY *and* STACY, *who is eight months pregnant.*

BARRY: Will you tell her, will you tell her –?

STACY: Watch Barry. Just watch. That's what I'm doing. Watching him all the time. In case –

BARRY: Will you two tell her –? Will you tell her – she's got this idea, she's got this really stupid –

STACY: It's not a stupid –

BARRY: She says that I'm – listen to this right? – vanishing. Can you believe that? She says –

STACY: You do.

BARRY: I don't.

STACY: You do. You fade in front of my eyes – you go to nothing. You leave me alone. There's gaps. It's been … I can't sleep. Lie in bed. Look at him on the pillow. Fading. Empty bed. Coming back. I'm not eating now. Baby's calling out inside for food but still I can't …

BARRY: Will one of you, both of you, tell her that she is mad? Hormones.

STACY: I'm not –

BARRY: People don't just vanish. I try but I – it's the baby playing with her hormones she doesn't – When women are pregnant they get these … your head gets muddled up. You cry and then you're happy and then I vanish. Few days you'll be happy again. Why don't you two go round Holly's baby shower? Jack – footie's starting.

JACK: Barry mate –

BARRY: Yeah?

JACK: It's true. People vanish. Lisa's doing the same. I've seen her disappear.

BARRY: Jesus. World's gone mad.

JACK: I never thought 'til today. But I've seen it. You can just … lose people. Look. (*He shows* BARRY *and* STACY *the phone clip.*)

BARRY: … Oh my god. Is that what I …?

STACY: Just the same. Same as you.

BARRY: Is this real?

LISA: Yeah. Real.

BARRY: But …. I want to be in this world. All the time. I don't want to miss stuff.

JACK: Maybe you're aliens.

LISA: You reckon?

JACK: You go out with someone, you live with someone …You get pregnant with someone – And then … this. Aliens or ghosts. Secrets.

LISA: Hold me.

JACK: Not now.

LISA: I'm not choosing to go – do you choose …? I wouldn't choose … I want to be with you.

STACY: (*To* BARRY.) What if you vanish when the baby's born? Can't have you vanishing once the baby's born. That's not a role model. I want a two-parent family.

BARRY: Course.

STACY: I gotta have – That's what it's about isn't it? A mum and a dad. I'm not gonna be a sad cow pushing a kid round by myself. That's not what I want.

LISA: We're not aliens or ghosts. Stupid. Hold me. I think we'd know if we were aliens or ghosts wouldn't we? And we'd let you know so don't – Hold me. Hold me. Hold me. I'm totally frightened. Don't just look at me like that staring. Come and hold me.

JACK: … I can't. Not yet babe. Sorry.

LISA: Oh. I just can't take this. It's doing my head in. I got a kid on the way. Hold me. Kiss me. Kiss me. Kiss me.

JACK: No. I don't know what you are.

Whoosh, flash. LISA *and* BARRY *disappear.*

JACK: Oh.

STACY: Barry! Barry! This is doing my head in.

JACK: How many times it's happened to you?

STACY: Four, five times since breakfast. This is my sixth.

JACK: Does it get any easier?

STACY: No. Still hurts. In your gut. Your heart. Whatever. Miss him.

JACK: Yeah. Like they're punishing us. I couldn't ever get used to a vanishing person.

STACY: Maybe we'll have to.

JACK: I'm not. I gotta take control.

STACY: But if this is, like, the way it's gonna be.

JACK: Then I just can't handle the way it's gonna be.

STACY: Well at least I'll have the kid if Barry goes.

JACK: If it's a stayer. Maybe the kid'll be a vanisher too.

STACY: Don't.

JACK: If the dad's a vanisher then maybe the kid's a vanisher too.

STACY: Stop. Stop. Scaring me.

JACK: You still want it?

STACY: Yeah only …

JACK: You'll cope whatever won't you? Vanisher or stayer?

STACY: I suppose I don't – this is so new. Vanishers. Stayers. I didn't know there was a difference when I woke up this morning.

JACK: We're not all the same. Terrible innit?

STACY: Yeah. Terrible.

JACK: This could be rest of our lives.

STACY: No. That is too much. That is gonna drive me mad.

I can feel my mind turning. I'm losing it. Losing it. Agggghhhhh! Panic – attack!

JACK: Come on. Sssssh. Ssssssh. They'll be back. Let me hold you. Come on. I'm here. We'll find out what's going on. Getting calmer?

STACY: Yeah.

JACK: What's Lisa up to – up there? She could be doing anything. Aliens. Aliens experiment on you don't they? Oh yeah. They abduct you, abduct you up to their spaceship and experiment. They could be putting an alien baby inside her. Taking out my baby and … I'm not letting her have an alien baby. I'm taking her up the hospital to get inspected.

STACY: You really having a baby?

JACK: Yeah. Until I got a kid, I'm a kid. That's what I reckon.

STACY: Same for me … They've not come back.

JACK: We're gonna stop this.

STACY: How we gonna …?

JACK: They'll come back and then if we just hold to them. Hold onto them really tight and don't let them go.

STACY: Forever?

JACK: Well …

STACY: You can't just hold onto someone forever.

JACK: We could. Just 'til the vanishing's over.

Long pause.

STACY: Oh he's not coming, he's not coming back … she oh my god he's not coming back. I've lost him. I had him and now he's gone. I think we should do something. (*To the sky.*) Give him back, send him back, and send him back to us … come on! Oh. This is stressing me so much. I'm only two weeks off my due date I shouldn't be stressing like this. This can't go on forever. Can't live days like this. What we gonna do? (*Clutches stomach.*) Oh!

JACK: What?

STACY: Something. Baby moving.

JACK: Can I listen? I'd like to listen. (*He listens.*) Oh yeah. Boy or girl?

STACY: Girl – oooo. Better not be – oooo –

JACK: What?

STACY: Contractions. No. Not yet. I'm alright. Baz has gotta be here if –

JACK: Yeah. I'll look after you if –

STACY: Yeah?

JACK: Make sure you're up the hospital and that you know if you start –

STACY: But you're not the dad.

JACK: No. I know that.

STACY: It's not the same.

JACK: All I'm saying –

STACY: It has to be the dad. It has to be Baz.

JACK: But if he's not here –

STACY: He's got to be here. I need him here. I want him here.

JACK: Yeah but all I'm saying if he's vanished forever.

STACY: He hasn't. Nobody vanishes forever. (*Clutches stomach.*) ooooo.

JACK: 'Nother listen?

STACY: It's not a game. I don't want you to.

JACK: But it's what I want. (*He leans into her stomach.*) Dun't sound too bothered that her dad's a vanisher.

STACY: I am.

JACK: Listen to baby. She's saying everything's alright.

STACY: Baz!

JACK: There's only me and baby to talk to now.

Doorbell rings.

JACK: Ignore it.

Doorbell rings again.

STACY: I want to get up the hospital.

Doorbell rings again.

JACK: Wait 'til they've gone.

Doorbell. Banging on door.

HOLLY: (*Off.*) Jack? Lisa? – it's Holly. You seen Stace? Something weird's going on. There's sort of vanishings. Are you there?

JACK answers the door. Lets in a group of female friends: KAREN, HOLLY (heavily pregnant), AMY, MARTA, MARIE, JANINE. A couple of them have babies in buggies.

KAREN: Stace – there you are. Listen. We were all round Holly's house for the baby shower and then Holly vanished. To nothing.

HOLLY: That's right.

KAREN: But then Holly came back again didn't you?

HOLLY: That's right.

KAREN: But then it was Marie, Janine and baby Tyson, me –

AMY: And me.

KAREN: One at a time until it was like: who's next? Who's going to go next? Stick together 'cos we don't know who's going to go next. Nothing's solid. We are seriously frightened.

HOLLY: Started off so happy – me baby shower. Vanishings? That's no world for me kid.

Enter RYAN (HOLLY's boyfriend), running after them.

RYAN: It's happening all over the world, babe.

HOLLY: Yeah?

RYAN: Been on the news. Everywhere there's people fading away to nothing. They've got footage from China, America, India – everything. Nobody knows the figures. One in ten. That's what they're saying. One in ten people has already gone but the numbers keep going up – with every minute there's more and more.

JACK: They're could be nobody left soon.

HOLLY: I wish I wasn't having this baby.

STACY: Don't. We gotta have the babies.

JACK: In this world? By the end of today – nobody left.

MARIE: Let's pray.

MARTA: What's that gonna do?

MARIE: We gotta do something. I'm bringing mine up religious. So should you. (*Kneels.*) Oh wise one who created this world and made everything in it and is now taking away everything in it have pity on us poor children. Spare us spare us spare us. (*MARIE continues to mutter a prayer under.*)

STACY: I feel so close. Baby's telling me it wants out.

JACK: Yeah?

STACY: It might happen. What if it happens? I don't want to have my baby like this.

JACK: Sssssssh. Whatever it is – we'll cope. I'll look after you.

STACY: I want Barry. BARRY!

JACK: Stace – no – you musn't upset yourself – you'll bring it on – Stace!

STACY: BARRY!

MARIE vanishes. General panic.

HOLLY: Marie! Marie! When's it gonna end? This is my baby shower.

MEGAPHONE: (*Off.*) This is the authorities. Stay in your homes. I repeat: stay in your homes.

JANINE: Oh my god.

MEGAPHONE: Anyone leaving their home without authorisation will be shot. We are investigating the vanishings but you must stay in your homes.

Enter two SOLDIERS.

SOLDIER 1: Whose flat is this?

JACK: Mine.

SOLDIER 1: The military has taken control. This country is now under military control.

STACY: Please. My baby's very close I need to get to a –

SOLDIER 1: My orders say you stay here.

STACY: I want the hospital. Tell him Jack. The hospital!

JACK: You'll be alright here.

STACY: No I won't I – I gotta get out – ah!

SOLDIER 1: (*Raising gun.*) Keep calm.

JACK: Listen to what he says Stace.

SOLDIER 2: No harm will come to you if you do exactly as the army say.

HOLLY: Come on Stace – take it easy.

JACK: I want to help sort out the emergency. What can I do?

SOLDIER 2: Well ... We are requisitioning a number of houses in which to herd the civilian population. I suppose ...

JACK: Use my flat. A suitable centre for civilians.

SOLDIER 2: It's a bit small ....

JACK: Under the circumstances.

SOLDIER 2: Alright. Let's use this place.

SOLDIER 1: (*Who's been listening on an earpiece.*) Shall I bring in the civilians?

JACK: Yeah definitely. Bring them in.

SOLDIER 1: (*Calls off.*) In here.

SOLDIER 2: Your home is to be the base for the parents and babies group. This way, this way.

SOLDIER 3 marches in a huge range of different parents and babies: single parents and couples, papooses front and back, and buggies, prams – some with twins, triplets. The noise of crying babies fills the air.

JACK: That's it – make room, make room – if you squeeze in – you gotta make room.

STACY: I don't want all them people.

SOLDIER 1: (*Pointing gun.*) Calm and orderly – that's it.

STACY: Take 'em away.

HOLLY: Army orders, Stace.

JACK: Room for everyone.

Finally everyone is in – but it's a very tight squeeze.

SOLDIER 1: (*With megaphone.*) Right. Everyone sit down. We have to keep order. We have to keep control. Each parent must take responsibility for controlling their baby. No baby is to crawl or in any way move from their buggy or papoose. It is vital that we keep calm.

JACK: Let's organise entertainment. (*On megaphone.*) While the world crisis is being sorted the babies have got to be entertained. Can anyone juggle, dance or offer any skills that might amuse the babies?

A MAN or WOMAN comes forward.

WO/MAN: Me.

JACK: Right, entertain the babies.

SOLDIER 3: That's an order.

The WO/MAN begins to break-dance or juggle or play the ukelele – or anything else that might entertain a large crowd of parents and babies – but after a while whooshing, flashing, etc. Most of the people in the room vanish. There's just JACK, STACY, a young MOTHER and a SOLDIER with an empty pram and a couple more parents and babies left. Panic.

SOLDIER 1: Quiet. Quiet. We'll wait here for further orders. Remain calm. (*To mouthpiece.*) Hello? Hello? It's just me and a small group of civilians left. Hello? Is there anyone out there?

JACK: How's your baby doing?

MOTHER: My baby? There's no baby. Look. The pram's empty. Vanished. She was three weeks old. Now – empty. Me gut hurts now.

JACK: It'll all come right. We'll sort it.

MOTHER: You don't know.

JACK: I don't – no – but ...

MOTHER: You? You're a kid. You don't speak my language. You got kids or you haven't got kids. And if you haven't got a kid you don't speak the language. I used to wander round the park looking at all them mums going: I'm a kid, I'm a kid. Got to be a mum, not a kid. Her dad was only around for a couple of weeks. But he did the job. All I needed.

JACK: Yeah – but –

MOTHER: Sorry. Kid. You don't understand.

JACK: Maybe. But I'll understand – yeah. Very soon I'll understand when Lisa –

MOTHER: You'll never get your chance. You missed your chance. This is it. No more people. No more babies, no more parents. End of the line. Kid.

JACK: I'm not having it.

MOTHER: You say your goodbyes. My pram's empty. All I want now is to vanish. Listen to them babies crying. Soon be gone now.

JACK: No I've got to have her back. Want my baby. LISA! LISA! LISA!

SOLDIER 1: Order, order – we must have order.

JACK: Lisa? Lisa?! Come back come back.

SOLDIER 1: (*Raises gun.*) Steady.

JACK: Lisa. I want a baby.

SOLDIER 1: Stop or I shoot – you're spreading panic.

STACY: Listen to him Jack.

JACK: But I have to have her. She's everything I need –

SOLDIER 1: (*Raising gun.*) I have permission to shoot troublemakers.

JACK: Shoot me then go on. What's the point? That's my future just vanished. Better shoot me now. They've got babies. You've got babies. That's what I want. Give me a baby. Give me a baby. I want Lisa back so we can have our baby and fill up the world again. I'm not a nutter. Just 'cos you got your babies. Could be me. Should be me with a baby. Give me a baby. Give me a baby.

JACK goes to grab a parent's baby. They try to fight him off.

PARENT: My baby. My baby. My baby. Not your baby. Off.

JACK gets the baby.

JACK: My baby now. Come on baby. Look at me.

SOLDIER 1: Return the baby. (*Gun to JACK.*) Return the baby.

JACK: I wanna look after –

SOLDIER 1: Return the baby.

JACK hands back the baby.

PARENT: Animal you animal. You're a total. (*To baby.*) Alright, alright.

Whoosh, flash – total darkness.

MOTHER: Here we go. We're fading away. All fading away. Yes yes. Thank you. Thank you. It's the end. We're vanishing.

The room empties of people. Silence. Utter darkness.

JACK: Hello? Hello? Anyone there? Anyone at all?

JACK uses a lighter to create a little bit of light.

JACK: is there anyone left? Or am I the only person left in the world? No please don't do that. I don't want to be the only person left in the world. That's horrible. See I won't know what to do if it's just me 'cos I need people to talk to and to do things with. I don't exist if there's no one else. I'm nobody without other people. What are they all doing in the other world? Is there another world? Come on – take me there – I don't want to be like this forever.

He finds a candle and lights it. He bumps into the empty pram.

JACK: Pram. Baby. Yes. (*Feeling inside.*) Nothing. No. Empty pram. Dad to nothing.

STACY: Jack – is that you?

JACK: Stace – over here.

STACY: Have they all gone?

JACK: I reckon.

STACY: (*Calls.*) Hello? Hello? .... They've all gone ... Jack –

JACK: Yeah?

STACY: I'm contracting.

JACK: You mean like ...?

STACY: The baby. My contractions.

JACK: Are you sure?

STACY: Yeah – oh – oh – yeah – I'm sure.

JACK: How long have we got?

STACY: Few hours. Oh. Maybe they'll come back. Maybe all the doctors and nurses and midwives and everything'll be back in time.

JACK: Maybe.

STACY: Oh. Bigger contractions. (*To sky.*) Please – come back. All of you – come back ... Oh. I'm just about to have – oh – once my waters break that's it.

JACK: Then I'm gonna have to –

JACK cuddles STACY.

JACK: Alright, alright. You ... breathe and calm and when you're breathing and calm and – I'll take care of this.

STACY: You can't. They'll be mess and pain and everything.

JACK: I know. (*Beat.*) Stace. Do you think this was how it was meant to be?

STACY: No I don't. Do you?

JACK: I don't ... yes. I think this was how it was meant to be.

STACY: No – this is not supposed to be. This is not normal. This is ...

JACK: The last thing in the world?

STACY: Yeah.

JACK: We're all alone now. Just you and me. Listen to that. See? If you really listen. Nothing. No babies, no mums and dads. Nothing. I reckon there's no one. Anywhere. Just you and me. We're the world. Just us now.

STACY: And a – oh! – new one on the way.

JACK: Not a problem.

STACY: No?

JACK: No problem. I can deliver a baby.

STACY: Yeah?

JACK: It's inside your soul. Doing a birth. Instinct – human instinct. Every man's got it if he knows how. I've got the instinct.

STACY: I want a doctor and a midwife.

JACK: Lie back Stace.

STACY: You're not up to this Jack.

JACK: I am.

STACY: Come back all of you! Come back!

JACK: Lie back Stace. I'm in control. You got to trust me. I'm gonna be inside you.

STACY: Oh. (*She gets on all fours with the pain.*)

JACK: Big breaths – come on – listen to me – big breaths –

STACY: So frightened.

JACK: No need. I'm here.

STACY: This was supposed to be Baz. A hospital.

JACK: Gone. Everything gone. Just me.

STACY: Aggghhhhh!

JACK: I'm everything now.

STACY: I don't want this.

JACK: This is the best way. We're having a baby. That's it. A baby's on the way. Once upon a time there were people. The world was full of people. But it got too full of people. Too many of them. So they had to go. And everything started all over again. With just you and me.

STACY: No I –

JACK: Lie back and listen. We were chosen you and me. Must be. Got to be a reason. We're the special ones. Chosen to stay behind. And inside you is a special baby. And tonight is a special night when the special baby gets born. I'm gonna make that so special for us.

STACY: I – I – I –

JACK: Forget the others. All gone now. New start. We're just beginning. We're gonna full up this empty pram today alright?

STACY: Alright.

2

The living room. Six months later. JACK *and a baby in the pram.*

JACK: (*To baby.*) And once upon a time there was a brand new world. And the world had no people. Until – pop – there were two people. And they were called Jack and Stacy. And they were happy but they wanted more people. And then were three people in the world 'cos along came a baby. And they called that baby Kelly. You're lovely aren't you Kelly? Yes you are. Your mum's out there hunting somewhere and your mum'll be back soon. And we'll be back together. Family. 'Cos that's what we are we're a –

Enter STACY, *with a rucksack on.*

JACK: Hey. How do you get on?

STACY: Yeah. Not bad.

JACK: Baby's good. Took her feed. Nice sleep. Show me what you got.

She opens the rucksack for his inspection of contents.

JACK: More beans? It's always beans.

STACY: Yeah. Sorry. But – look.

She holds up a packet of nappies.

JACK: Well done. Brilliant. At last.

STACY: Yeah.

JACK: You get attacked by them escaped lions again?

STACY: No, there's dogs though. They gone feral. Started hunting in packs. There's a load of them live up the multi-storey car park. You have to watch yourself.

JACK: You got blood.

STACY: It's nothing.

JACK: Show me.

STACY *shows her hand.*

STACY: There was a cat and a load of kittens sat on the nappies. We had a fight.

JACK: See. Told you. The animals are still breeding.

STACY: Spose.

JACK: She must have met a tom. We gotta look after that.

STACY: It's nothing.

JACK: I'll bandage it.

Exit JACK. STACY *takes out a tin of rice pudding from the rucksack and a tin opener and opens it. Enter* JACK *with plaster, TCP, etc.*

JACK: You gonna eat that cold?

STACY: I been hunting all day.

JACK: Still no sign of any humans?

STACY: No.

JACK: See. I told you.

STACY: Got to keep looking.

JACK: Six months – if there was anyone else we'd have found them by now.

STACY: I suppose.

JACK: Come on Stace there can't be –

STACY: Don't you want people? Don't you want the world?

JACK: You could have microwaved that.

STACY: This can't be just – why would it just be us?

JACK: Luck. Fate.

STACY: A thousand – a thousand thousand – miles – there's someone else.

JACK: No. Just you and me and ... baby. Stace – don't you think we should give her a name?

STACY: No.

JACK: I mean six months – 'baby' – it'll stunt her development, something.

STACY: I know only ...

JACK: How long you gonna wait?

STACY: I want to choose it with Baz.

JACK: I don't miss humans. Humans were noisy.

STACY: Those elephants down the road make noise.

JACK: Just a few of them. They're lonely. But billions of human beings. That was terrible. It's good that they went.

STACY: Don't you miss Lisa?

JACK: Sometimes.

STACY: You were having a kid.

JACK: Yeah well she's gone now.

STACY: But if you're having a kid –

JACK: After six months, you move on.

STACY: Move on? There's nobody to … Ugh! She needs her nappy changing.

JACK: I'll do it. (*To baby.*) Come on Kelly we're going to –

STACY: What did you call her?

JACK: Dun't matter.

STACY: You called her something. Kelly?

JACK: She needs a name. It's not good for her.

STACY: Oh no, oh no – That is not Kelly right? That is 'baby'. And I'm not having you doing anything different. Understand? Understand? Give me baby.

JACK: I'm gonna –

STACY: Give me baby – now. Come on baby let's clean you up.

STACY and baby exit. JACK opens a box of cornflakes from the rucksack, starts eating with his hands. Whoosh, flash. BARRY appears.

BARRY: Stace? Stace?

JACK: Baz? No. You can't come back.

BARRY: Stace. I want Stacy. Gotta speak to her. She had my baby? Must have been born now. They alright?

JACK: Baz she's –

BARRY: She had the baby yet Jack? (*Sees the pram.*) Where's the baby?

JACK: Barry mate –

BARRY: Stace! You tell Stace I gotta see her. I gotta see my baby. I'm slipping back. You tell her Jack. Baz is looking for her.

JACK: I don't want you here you can't just … Baz I like this world now. It's brilliant. Perfect. Me, Stacy, baby. Everything. I love that I can't –

BARRY: I can't stay now. But I'm coming back. Back for Stacy and my baby.

Whoosh, flash, BARRY disappears, STACY re-enters with baby.

STACY: Where's them fresh nappies?

JACK: Stace – let's go somewhere. Now. The whole world's empty. We could live anywhere. Buckingham Palace. Yeah – let's move. Find somewhere else.

STACY: We're fine here. She's used to it.

JACK: No – we got to move now. I'll get some things.

STACY: Don't be mad.

JACK: Make a head start before it gets dark.

STACY: I'm not going anywhere.

JACK: It's dangerous here. It's not safe.

STACY: Alright. You go if you want to.

JACK: Stace you don't understand –

STACY: Go.

JACK: By myself?

STACY: Jack. I know what you're up to.

JACK: You reckon?

STACY: Playing families.

JACK: It's not a game. Pack your bags.

STACY: Well you're not dad see?

JACK: I know but –

STACY: So keep away from her. She's my baby. Mine. You keep off her Jack. Piss off – piss off you – piss off and leave me and my baby in peace. You're a kid and I'm a mum and me and baby don't want you.

JACK: Right – I gave you a warning. This is what we're doing. I'm taking charge. We're moving on. Pack a few things and get down here in ten minutes and we move on or I –

STACY: What?

JACK: I –

STACY: See? Nothing.

JACK: (*Grabs her.*) This is a perfect world. This is my world. I'm in charge. Not having that ruined. You're not spoiling it for me.

STACY: Get off.

JACK: It's just you and me and me and Kelly.

STACY: She's not called –

JACK: She's called Kelly.

JACK reaches into the rucksack and pulls out a breadknife.

JACK: (*Waves knife.*) Alright?

STACY: No, I don't wanna –

JACK: Somebody's gotta make decisions in this family. She's called Kelly.

STACY: Baby. Baby. Baby. She's called. Baby.

JACK: No. Kelly. I name our child Kelly. Kelly – tonight from this moment on, now and forever more you are christened Kelly. Kelly. Kelly. (*To STACY, wielding knife.*) Yes? Yes? Yes? (*Holds knife to her throat.*)

STACY: … Yes. Kelly.

JACK: That's it mummy. Say hello to Kelly.

STACY: … Hello Kelly.

JACK: Thank you Stacy. I didn't want to lose it only … Stace – I get lonely in my bed.

STACY: Can't help that.

JACK: Sleep with me Stace.

STACY: No.

JACK: We don't have to do nothing – just share the bed.

STACY: It'll lead to stuff.

JACK: It won't. Last two humans – at least we could share the bed.

STACY: Forget it. It's not gonna happen.

JACK: It's gonna happen. Tonight Kelly – mummy and daddy are going to have a lovely meal of all the food that mummy got up the shops then when mummy and daddy are feeling nice and tired they are going to go to a big house somewhere a long way away somewhere like Buckingham Palace with a big double bed –

STACY: No.

JACK: Big double bed and they're going to take their clothes off and they're going to get into the big double bed. And they're hold each other all night. Mummy's been too shy since you were born to sleep with daddy but tonight she's not going to be shy. Tonight she'll get over that and she'll hold daddy. And maybe if the mood's right they'll have sex. Yeah – maybe if it's an extra special night they'll have sex. Yeah. They'll have sex.

STACY: I'm not gonna do that.

JACK: You'll do just what daddy tells you to do or I'll – because this is all for Kelly, this is all. We got to be normal. Normal family. It's what happens. In a normal family – baby's got a name, mummy and daddy love each other, mummy and daddy have sex, mummy and daddy try for another baby.

STACY: No.

JACK: Kelly all on her own. Not good. Not right. So we start working on a little brother or little sister for Kelly. We start working on that tonight.

STACY: It's not gonna happen.

JACK: It's the normal thing.

STACY: Then I'm not going to be normal.

JACK: You are.

He pulls the knife across her cheek.

STACY: Don't Jack – no. Is there blood?

JACK: A bit.

STACY: I'll go septic and die.

JACK: No.

STACY: Yeah. I'll go septic and die and then what you gonna do?

JACK: I'm here for you. I'm here to look us all. I'm gonna mend this and then you're gonna pack our stuff and we're gonna move on to our new place. (*He dresses her cheeks with TCP and sticks a plaster on each.*) Go and pack.

STACY: Can I change baby? Kelly. Don't hurt her. You can hurt me only …

JACK: I'd never do that. She's everything to me.

STACY: Alright as long as …

JACK: I know what's best. I'm dad.

STACY: Yeah.

STACY exits with Kelly. Whoosh, flash. BARRY appears.

BARRY: Where's Stace ..?

JACK: Still … a long way away … hunting.

BARRY: My kid. Want to see my kid.

JACK: Listen Baz. I gotta tell you …

BARRY: Yeah?

JACK: World's gone bad. Streets are full of wild animals. Baz it's really bad here, you don't wanna, the world's such a bad place. Baz …

BARRY: Yeah?

JACK: And … It's been six months. World moves on.

BARRY: Well … yeah.

JACK: There's no one left in the world Baz – 'cept me and Stace and Kelly. Oh yeah. We called the kid Kelly.

BARRY: But I wanted to –

JACK: Sorry mate. I delivered the baby. See and now … we got a bond. Stacy. She's mine.

BARRY: No.

JACK: And Kelly – we decided it was best, too confusing see. Not gonna tell her about the world before, the vanished people. Decided to tell Kelly I'm her dad. Mummy daddy and baby.

BARRY: You bastard.

JACK: So the rest of you can stay up there or down there or out there or whatever because we don't want you. You're not wanted here. So you stay right where you –

BARRY: No!

A fight between the two of them. BARRY punches JACK in the stomach. JACK collapses. BARRY kicks him.

BARRY: My kid. My world.

JACK: Don't want you. Stay in your world 'cos this world's better without you. I'm King here.

Whooshing, flashing, BARRY vanishes. JACK is winded. Gets up.

JACK: Alright, alright, everything's okay. Over now.

Enter STACY with a shopping trolley fully loaded with bags, etc., wearing a coat.

JACK: Good girl. I don't like forcing you.

STACY: Funny way of …

JACK: Only sometimes I just see. What's best. For the family.

STACY: Right.

JACK: You'll like Buckingham Palace.

STACY: I'll do what you say.

JACK: Stace – you gotta love me.

STACY: That an order?

JACK: That should come natural.

STACY: Well – it's not natural.

JACK: Give it time.

STACY: No. Anything you want you'll have to use that [*knife*].

JACK: If I have to.

STACY: Yeah you'll have to.

JACK: Kelly's gonna have her own apartments when she's older. Her own wing. Kensington Palace.

STACY: Let her choose.

JACK: She'll need guiding. Wagons roll.

JACK puts baby in the pram, starts to push it.

JACK: Come on Kelly. New home. New start.

STACY: Oh I – (*STACY staggers.*)

JACK: What?

STACY: I – I – I – (*She collapses.*)

JACK: Gotta move. Gotta move on. Come on. Gotta get up. Come on.

STACY: Jack – I'm – oh!

Flashing. Brief vision of the hordes of the VANISHED.

VANISHED: We are the vanished
We were once in the world
But now we're not in the world
Everyone gone
And we claim you.

They all point to STACY. *Whooshing. Dies down.* STACY *has vanished. Just* JACK *and the baby left.*

JACK: Right. Right.

Pause.

(*To baby.*) Just you and me. Which is ... this is ...
STACY? STACE?

Pause.

Just you and me. That's ... yes ... that's good.

Long pause.

Once there was a new world. And there was just me in it. And I was all alone. And I grew up. And then one day this baby – pop. I called her Kelly. I looked after her. I fought off the animals. I hunted. I had meaning. I was a King and there was a Princess.

That's good isn't it? We're the first and one day they'll be – pop pop pop – from nowhere more babies but until then ...

Yeah. You and me. Empty world.

Always knew really – here – the gut – this was what my life was – me – a kid – no one else – always knew that was it.

Had a girlfriend once. What was she? Lees ... Lees ... forgotten ... forgotten ... long time ago.

She didn't matter. Nobody mattered. 'Cept you and me. This was I wanted. All the others gone. Me and my baby.

Goes to door.

Lions on the street. Shit. Looking hungry.

Right. We'll ... Sleep here tonight. We'll move on in the morning.

Night Kelly. (*Leans into pram, kisses baby.*) Night.

And we all slept sound 'cos we were the only two in the world and there was no fighting.

JACK *lies down to sleep, closes his eyes. Flashing, whooshing.* JACK *leaps up.*

JACK: Kelly!

Brief vision of STACY *and* BARRY *carrying away the baby.*

JACK: Don't take her please.

STACY: But she's ours.

JACK: You don't need her. There's millions in your world.

STACY: She came out my body.

BARRY: I'm the dad.

JACK: But over there – the vanished – millions of you – but here – me – there's just me and her. Leave me her.

STACY: Can't have what don't belong to you Jack.

JACK: But this is the real world.

STACY: Not anymore, we've all gone to the new world now. Passed through the door. This is just the old one.

BARRY: Come on love we got to go.

JACK: Don't take her no don't. Love her like nothing I –

STACY: Bye JACK.

JACK: (*Rushes with knife.*) Give me give me give me.

BARRY *and* STACY *raise a hand each. Power crackles from their palms, slamming* JACK *away from them. The knife falls from his grasp.*

STACY: Thanks for doing the delivery Jack you were brilliant.

BARRY: Time to go.

JACK: I'm not going to let you go. STOP! STOP!

He rushes and grasps at them. The crackle of energy. He falls, as dead.

STACY: Jack? Jack? Is he dead? The shock he's ... we might have killed him. Oh Jack.

BARRY: We got to go back.

STACY: I want to stay. Oh Jack. Jack. Jack. Wake up Jack.

BARRY: Come away now.

STACY: I can't.

BARRY: You have to. Me the baby. Stacy – what are you going to ...? You gonna stay here with him. Or you coming to your family.

STACY: ... Sorry Jack.

Whooshing, flashing. JACK *is alone. He lies still for a while. Then he comes round.*

JACK: What is this place?

(*Inspects pram.*) ... Empty pram. Empty world.

Long pause.

The day that Jack was born ... Yeah. I'll tell that one. The day that Jack was born.

I was born into this place of the animals and of the shops and the food and the houses.

And I was the only person. The first and the last.

And so I never thought about it. How could I ever think ...? If you never knew there were others then ...

But sometimes I dreamt, I imagined there were others. Somewhere – others.

But ... no. Can't remember the names of any others. Can't remember anything the others ever did.

Something in this. [*pram*] Must have been something in this? What was it called? I. I. I. Can't remember.

But that was fantasy. Because the world is just me. Now and forever. And on and on and good good good.

Only ever me.
So why the –? [*pram*]
A thing from long ago.

Beats the pram rhythmically.

Don't need you pram. Never need you pram. Don't know
what you're for pram. You're for nothing pram.
Nothing. Nothing. Nothing.
You are … a dead thing.

Kicks over the pram, carries on kicking it.

You are a totally dead thing.
I am everything.
I am the world.
I am King.
So I …
Hunt. Eat. Sleep. Move on. This is my world.
And I …
No if there were never others then there's no loneliness.
No lone … lone … lo … lo …
Lugh. Lugh. Lugh. Lee. Negh. Sssssss.
No feelings like … no feelings just –

(A howl of emotion.) Ooowwwwwww!

(Ape-like). Ugh ugh ugh.

He's becoming more animal, his centre of gravity moving down.

I ugh oh a oh a ooo m a ugh.
Me.
Me.
Me.

Pattern of movement, almost dancing.

Me.
Me.
Me.
And I.
And I.
And I.

Onto all fours snuffling and whining. A great animal howl.

Hunt. Attack. Defend. Me.

Flashing, whooshing. SOLDIER 1 *appears.*

SOLDIER 1: Hello? Hello? (*To walkie talkie.*) Anyone there? I'm
back in the world. I've left the vanished. Is anyone else
back? Am I on my own? Hello? Hello? I need orders. Am
I on my own? Hello?

JACK snarls.

SOLDIER 1: What the –?

JACK growls, squats, ready to attack.

SOLDIER 1: Steady. Alright – easy, easy. Don't be frightened.
I'm a human. What are you?

JACK bares his teeth.

SOLDIER 1: Animal. Now listen – I don't want to harm. Find
civilians. Find a superior. Bring back order.

JACK snarls and barks.

SOLDIER 1: I'm going now to bring order to the world.

JACK leaps and blocks SOLDIER's *path.*

SOLDIER 1: I have to bring order to the world.

JACK is preparing to attack.

SOLDIER 1: Step aside or I will fire. You must not prevent me.
It's vital the world is –

JACK comes from very close, snapping.

SOLDIER 1 *goes to fire.*

SOLDIER 1: You had your warning.

JACK leaps at SOLDIER 1, *biting at him and snarling a tustle on
the ground.* JACK *is biting at the* SOLDIER. *The gun falls from the*
SOLDIER's *hand. He retreats.*

SOLDIER 1: You've drawn blood – you animal. (*To walkie
talkie.*) Please – is there anyone there? Anyone out there
I –?

SOLDIER 2 *runs in from the street.* JACK *snarls.*

SOLDIER 2: Get back.
SOLDIER 1: Mate. It's not just me.
SOLDIER 2: We're all coming back. People on the streets.
World's filling again. What's that? [*JACK*]
SOLDIER 1: I dunno. Looks human but –

JACK has retreated. Whooshing, flashing.

SOLDIER 2: Here we go. Told you. They're coming back!

*The room begins to fill up with the vanished. Soon the room is
full of the parents and babies, the soldiers, the friends and* BARRY,
STACY *and* LISA. *Everyone is talking, calling out.* MOTHER *with
the empty pram steps forward.*

MOTHER: My kid. My kid. Where's my kid?

She disappears into the crowd searching.

JACK is whimpering on the floor.

LISA: Jack.
SOLDIER 1: Keep away from him.
LISA: He'll know me.
SOLDIER 1: He doesn't know anything. Keep away.
SOLDIER 2: What shall we do with him?
SOLDIER 1: Feral. Mad. Let me shoot him.

SOLDIER 2: No – keep him there. We'll have him put away. (*On megaphone.*) Attention everyone. Give me your attention. I have received instructions that it is over. The emergency is now over. The vanished have returned. You are to go back to your homes. There will be a period of transition in which the army will be guiding you. But democracy will return. Back to your homes. Go back home. Normality will be restored. The world is normal again.

SOLDIER 3: Alright – come along everybody – back to your homes.

The room is clearing.

LISA: (*To SOLDIER 1.*) Let me talk to him.

SOLDIER 1: No point, he's an animal.

LISA: Please. Jack it's me – Lisa. Do you know me – Lisa?

JACK: Mmmmgrrrmmrrr.

LISA: Lisa.

JACK: I. Me. Duh. Duh. Mad. Mad.

LISA: You're not mad Jack. Look at all the people. Babies.

JACK: Uh grrrroooo ooo.

LISA: No Jack speak words I want a human. (*To SOLDIER 1.*) Leave me with him.

SOLDIER 1: If he attacks –

LISA: I'll call the army.

SOLDIER 1 moves away.

JACK: Grrrrrrr. Grrrrrrrr.

It's just JACK, LISA, BARRY, STACY and the MOTHER with the empty pram.

MOTHER: I got no baby. Pram's empty.

LISA: What you gonna do?

MOTHER: Search. It hasn't vanished.

LISA: Could have.

MOTHER: No. I'm a mother. I've gotta find her.

Exit MOTHER.

LISA: Jack. We're all back ... Are you human? Come on Jack. Human words. Please Jack. I want a human.

STACY: Jack – what's happened to you?

JACK: Grrrrrrrrrrrrr.

STACY: You're frightening.

BARRY: Come on love. Keep away.

STACY: Oooo. Felt something. I reckon this baby might come early.

BARRY: Shall we pick names?

STACY: Tonight?

JACK: But you – you – you –

STACY: What's he saying?

BARRY: I don't know.

JACK: You – you – you

LISA: What is it Jack?

JACK: You already – you had the baby already. I was there.

LISA: Don't Jack.

STACY: Course I haven't – look. (*Shows her stomach.*) I haven't had the baby yet.

JACK: I lied attacked animal I.

BARRY: Don't remember anything mate.

LISA: We've been somewhere else.

JACK: But you had a baby and you came back to –

BARRY: I don't remember –

STACY: It didn't happen.

BARRY: Come on love. You need your rest.

STACY: Yeah. Night.

Exit BARRY and STACY.

JACK: But but but but

LISA: Alright Jack. You're safe now. No one remembers. It's okay.

3

LISA and JACK's living room. Over a year later. There's a pram. JACK is looking inside. Enter LISA. She holds a wrapped-up present. She stands watching him.

LISA: How long you gonna stand there?

JACK: I don't know.

LISA: Three hours now. He's not going anywhere.

JACK: I know. But ... new baby.

LISA: You never ate.

JACK: I'm happy just watching.

LISA: You're mad.

JACK: No. Our baby. You proud?

LISA: Course.

JACK: Glad it was all normal – after all the vanishing and that.

LISA: Everything's normal. The whole world's normal. Everything totally back to normal.

JACK: Yeah.

LISA: You coming round Baz and Stacy's?

JACK: I want to stay here.

LISA: Come on – Lorraine's first birthday. You got to go to that. Baz and Stace are expecting you. Janine'll be round to baby sit any minute.

JACK: I just want to stay here.

LISA: He'll survive without you for a bit.

JACK: I just like imagining what's going on in his head.

LISA: And ...? What's in his head?

JACK: All sorts. Other worlds.

LISA: Sign the card.

She hands him the card.

JACK: Lorraine. That's a stupid name. Who calls a kid Lorraine?

LISA: It's not bad. You wanna tell Baz and Stace? What would you call her?

JACK: What would I call her? I'd call her ... Don't know. I suppose Lorraine's alright.

He signs, hands her the card.

LISA: I'm gonna go. Be back in time to feed him. You sure you're not coming?

JACK: Lees. Where did you go?

LISA: I told you.

JACK: I can't get it out of my head. Please. I was the only one. Where were you?

LISA: Like I said. Nowhere. Emptiness. It's a blank.

JACK: Think. Underworld? Spaceship?

LISA: You can ask as many times as you like. When you vanish there's nothing.

JACK: Maybe you'll get flashes or dreams or …?

LISA: Jack. Empty.

JACK: It'll come back. One day you'll know what there is.

LISA: Maybe.

JACK: You'll tell me. It's important.

LISA: I gotta go. You don't have to stand there the whole time.

JACK: I want to.

LISA: You'll frighten him.

JACK: How can I frighten him? I'm his dad.

LISA: Still … What did you do?

JACK: Eh?

LISA: Six months on the planet. What did you do?

JACK: I don't know …

LISA: You're the only human being who knows. Stacy knows nothing.

JACK: I –

LISA: Yeah?

JACK: Did what I could to survive. Went out hunting. Did what I could for Stace and the baby, for Lorraine. I kept things going. Fought. Protected.

LISA: Like an animal?

JACK: You have to. Do you think it was aliens?

LISA: Stop.

JACK: Maybe if you tried drawing or …

LISA: Just stop.

JACK: Hypnosis to –

LISA: Stop. Stop. Stop. Listen. You are never going to know. Face it. It's not going to –

JACK: The mother of my – everyone's been there. Secret. And I don't know it. It's impossible. Can't live with that.

LISA: There's no choice.

JACK: I want to see inside their heads, their memories –

LISA: No.

JACK: Cut 'em open: where did you go? Where did you go? Where did you go?

LISA: Stop it Jack – you're horrible.

JACK: How am I supposed to spend the rest of my life with you if you got a secret?

LISA: I'm going to Baz and Stace's. I won't be long. Janine'll be here any minute. If you want to come on –

JACK: Maybe later.

LISA: Alright.

Exit LISA. JACK watches the pram for a while then JACK picks the baby from the pram.

JACK: And everyone in the world had a secret. Everyone had been to the same place. And one day Daddy was going to find out where that place was.

Doorbell rings.

JACK: Sssssh. Ssssssh. Keep quiet 'til they go away.

Doorbell rings again.

JACK: Sssssshhhh. Soon be over.

Doorbell rings.

JANINE: (*Off.*) Jack? Lisa? I'm here for the baby sitting. Jack. Lisa. Hello.

Long pause.

JACK: That's it. Just you and me forever more. Sssssssshhhhhh.

4.6 **Theory of Cultural Production** (1998)

ALAN SINFIELD

IN EARLIER CHAPTERS I have explored aspects of identity, art and subculture through textual instances, trying to stake out, quite informally, a les/bi/gay cultural politics for the time of the post-gay. In this chapter I try to elaborate a more sustained theory of gay cultural production.

Cultural materialism

There are many valuable accounts of aspects of lesbian and gay culture, but there is no lesbian and/ or gay theory of cultural production as such. The two theories of culture in Western societies are the *idealist* or *formalist*, and the *materialist*. The idealist supposes high culture – culture 'with a big C' – to derive from the human spirit, and hence to transcend historical conditions, constituting a reservoir of ultimate truth and wisdom and belonging thereby to all people indifferently.

Cultural materialists argue that the notion of an unchanging human reality inhibits thoughts of progressive change by perceiving oppression and injustice as 'the human condition' – tragic but inevitable. They declare that cultures are produced by people in history, and regard high culture with some suspicion, since it is almost certainly promoting particular interests behind the claim of universal relevance. For the terms 'art' and 'literature' are neither spontaneous nor innocent. They are bestowed by the gatekeepers of the cultural apparatus, and should be understood as tactics for conferring authority upon certain works. Art and literature are involved in the circulation of representations through which cultural norms come to seem plausible, even necessary, and hence in authorising or calling into question the prevailing power arrangements. They do not – cannot – transcend the material forces and relations of production. This does not mean that they have to be conservative. How far high culture is complicit with the dominant ideology, or available to a critique of it, depends on the instance and on what we do with it.

Until 1945, it was fairly apparent that big-C culture, though it claimed universality, was in fact predominantly a subculture of the middle and upper classes. After World War II, governments thought they could control the economic cycle of boom and slump, and hence produce a fairer society without having to interfere much with capital. As with access to housing, education, healthcare and social security, in all of which public funding was to redress the most extreme inequities of capitalism, the State would facilitate access to high culture for everyone. However, the end of the postwar boom showed that these goals were not to be so conveniently attained. On the right, it was objected that the economy prospers better when the deprived are left to fend for themselves, that subsidy for the arts had been sheltering a left-liberal interest group, and that the proper way to organise culture, like everything else, is the market. On the left, it was objected that notions of quality and universality had been, in practice, pushing to the margins already subordinated groups – the lower classes, women, racial and sexual minorities.

Hitherto, socialists too had tended to believe that everyone could share the one 'human' culture, but in the 1970s disillusionment with the operations of (allegedly) universal culture gave rise to cultural materialism. This is Raymond Williams' term, and his *Marxism and Literature* is a key text; the work of Stuart Hall is equally important, and the whole Birmingham Centre for Contemporary Cultural Studies which he directed [Williams 1977; Morley and Chen 1996]. Cultural materialists investigate the historical conditions in which textual representations are produced, circulated and received, often considering big-C culture alongside popular culture. They engage with questions about the relations between dominant and subordinate cultures, the implications of racism, sexism and homophobia, the scope for subaltern resistance, and the strategies through which the system might tend to accommodate or repel diverse kinds of dissidence. Their work is cognate with and illuminated by that of materialist-feminists [Newton and Rosenfelt 1985].

Cultural materialists start from the premise that any social formation has to reproduce itself. It has to do this in material terms – people have to have food and water, shelter and other protection. Also, it has to reproduce itself ideologically – through churches, schools, the family, the law, the political system, trades unions, the communications system, cultural institutions. If it did not, it would die out or be transformed. There are directly repressive apparatuses as well – the police, courts, prisons, army. But, above all, people get socialised into ways of thinking that facilitate maintenance of the system. Therefore it makes sense to speak of a 'dominant ideology': the central and most authoritative set of ideas and attitudes. The dominant ideology is very plausible (that is why it is dominant); because we have come to consciousness as individual subjectivities within its terms, it seems to be *natural, normal, god-given, the way things are, simply human*. Of course, it embraces normative ideas about gender and sexuality – which I have been calling, informally, 'the straightgeist'.

This analysis is disputed. For commentators such as Jean-François Lyotard and Jean Baudrillard, ideological authority in postmodern societies is so dispersed and so mediated through a bombardment of flickering (televisual) messages that no one version can be regarded as dominant [Connor 1989: chapter 2]. However, I reply (i) that some ideologies are indubitably more powerful than others, and the dominant is, simply, the most powerful (it does not have to derive from any conspiracy among politicians and businessmen, or even to operate always in their interests, though since they control the circulation of ideas it is likely to); (ii) were there not such an effective ideology, people would not put up with social arrangements that are neither fair nor in their interests.

Although the dominant ideology is very powerful, it would be quite wrong to suppose that it is coherent, secure and unchallengeable. On the contrary, as Williams observes, its dominance depends on continuous processes of adjustment, reinterpretation, incorporation, dilution. For 'its own internal structures are highly complex, and have continually to be renewed, recreated and defended' [Williams 1980: 37–8]. Dominant ideological formations are always, in practice, under pressure from diverse disturbances. For conflict and contradiction stem from the very strategies through which dominant ideologies strive to contain the expectations that they need to generate in order to establish their dominance. Dissidence then, derives not from our irrepressible humanity, but from pressures and strains which the social order inevitably produces within itself, even as it attempts to secure itself (hence the title of my book, *Faultlines*) [Sinfield 1992: 35–42,

45–51, 291–9]. Thus gay rights campaigners are able to exploit laws of citizenship which were designed initially to guarantee the rights of property, and never envisaged as justifying queer goings-on. Les/bi/gay people, like other dissidents, are well able to perceive and assert their own interests, both within and in opposition to the dominant ideology.

Hence my attention to subculture. As I said in chapter 2, if the dominant ideology constitutes subjectivities that will find 'natural' its view of the world, subcultures constitute *partially alternative subjectivities*. In Ken Plummer's formulation, 'As gay persons create a gay culture cluttered with stories of gay life, gay history and gay politics, so that very culture helps to define a reality that makes gay personhood tighter and ever more plausible. And this in turn strengthens the culture and the politics' [Plummer 1995: 87; Califia 1994: 21]. Hence also my attention to fictional, or 'literary', texts. Along with film, song, autobiography, and so on, they are places where our subculture and its myths are constituted and where they may be questioned and developed. Cultural materialism frames cultural production in terms of the constituency that may be engaged, rather than through mystified notions of universality.

This approach may not immediately persuade les/bi/gay people. First, insofar as big-C culture claims to be universal, it promises to include us. Actually, though, even with the current fashionable kudos of gay men, it does that hardly at all – and even less for lesbians. Second, high culture, traditionally, is one of the things gay men have been good at. It suits our 'gay sensibility'. However, if there is no ultimate general truth about humanity for Raphael, Haydn and Ezra Pound to manifest, there is no ultimate particular truth about homosexuality in Michelangelo, Tchaikovsky and Djuna Barnes.

According to Jack Babuscio, gay sensibility is organised around camp, and has four basic features: irony, aestheticism, theatricality and humour [Babuscio 1977: 42; Medhurst 1997]. In *The Wilde Century* I trace these features to the model of the queer man – dandified, effeminate, leisured, aesthetic, flamboyant – that was personified by Oscar Wilde. This model has as much to do with class as gender – with the perception of the leisure class as effete, in contrast to the purposeful middle classes. Hence, in part, the elements of theatricality and ironic disjunction: camp includes a 'sorry I spoke' acknowledgment of its inappropriateness in the mouth of the speaker. Aestheticism fits the model because high culture is regarded, implicitly and perhaps residually, as a leisured preserve, and as feminine in comparison with the (supposedly) real world of business and public affairs.

Gay sensibility is a specific formation that we have pieced together in the conflicted histories that we have experienced; it derives from the resources that have been available to us, and from our determination to seize them and make them work for us. These are the mechanisms of all cultural production. Recognising this, as Andy Medhurst points out, does not make gay sensibility any less real for people who frame their lives partly through it [Medhurst 1991: 197–208]. Nevertheless, we do need to notice that straightgeist crediting of gay men with artistic talent has generally been on condition that we be discreet, thereby acknowledging our own unspeakableness. Decoding the work of closeted artists discovers not a cause for celebration, but a record of oppression and humiliation.

Organic intellectuals

A central argument of this book is that les/bi/gay people, because of rather than despite moving into the post-gay, need a more intelligent and purposeful subculture. The idea is not to establish any kind of party line; of course, we are divided in terms of class, gender and race, and experience the massive conflicts that derive from those divisions in capitalism and patriarchy today. This diversity makes it more, not less, desirable to explore our situations. We need to create many more opportunities to think hard about our confusions, conflicts and griefs. We have enemies, and we sometimes damage ourselves. We need to get our act together.

The body of theory that will enable me to discuss the roles of subcultural producers has been developed particularly around the concept of the intellectual. Antonio Gramsci's treatment is valuable partly because he acknowledges that all people are intellectual, while also specifying as a social category the people who perform the professional function of intellectuals. That category will comprise people whose work mainly involves pushing ideas around society – journalists, broadcasters and copywriters, novelists, playwrights and film-makers, songwriters and performers, teachers and students. Of course, everyone is involved in some measure in moving ideas around; that is what happens in social interaction. But people with the professional function of intellectuals have distinct roles, and, I suggest, distinct responsibilities.

According to Gramsci, an emergent group needs intellectuals to help it define its own technical, political, economic and social activity. It will find already-established 'traditional' intellectuals; very likely they 'put themselves forward as autonomous and independent of any social group'; an obvious instance is the priesthood. An emergent group may co-opt some of these traditional intellectuals. Also, such a group may produce 'its own organic intellectuals', from within its own resources [Gramsci 1971: 5–10; Sinfield 1994: chapter 4]. Lately, as Foucault has observed, these terms need reformulating. Most intellectuals are employed – usually to exercise particular skills, often by business or the State [Foucault 1980: 126–33]. Even so, they may cultivate an 'organic' relation with a subcultural constituency.

My stress upon the scope for les/bi/gay cultural workers is not intended to disqualify my earlier arguments about how we may appropriate work that is not actually oriented towards us. Nor is it my thought, by any means, that the virtue of an artwork depends on the intention of the creator, or that work done by les/bi/gay people should be subject to special reverence. As I tried to show in chapters 4–6 particularly, mythic subcultural texts, regardless of their origins, are most valuable when we challenge them.

Unfortunately, artists and critics are often reluctant to accept that their work might be oriented purposefully towards a subcultural constituency. Listening to Cherry Smyth talking about the painters she prints in her powerful collection, *Damn Fine Art* [Smyth 1996], it is depressing how many of them seem to wish *not* to be perceived as *a lesbian artist*. To be sure, 'lesbian' does propose certain boundaries, but so does 'artist'. To regard 'lesbian' as a limited and constricting kind of concept, and 'art' – apprehended here as access to galleries and the rest of the conventional apparatus of artistic production – as contrastingly free and ample, is strangely lopsided. Indeed, as I argued in chapters 1 and 2, the hybridity likely to result from involvement with such straightgeist formations may effect a drag back into conservative positions. Not that we can simply break free of the straightgeist; but we may attempt an emphasis.

I want now to discuss Neil Bartlett and Monique Wittig, because their achievements in gay and lesbian subcultures demand that their ideas be taken seriously.

In *Who Was That Man? A Present for Mr Oscar Wilde* (1988) and *A Vision of Love Revealed in Sleep* (1989), Bartlett uses 'we' to mean not the allegedly universal 'man' of art and human nature but 'we gay men' of subculture. At the start of *Who Was That Man?* he writes of the difficulty of 'using certain words, the most ordinary of words, because I wanted to give them meanings which this city doesn't normally allow. When I write "we" for instance, I mean we gay men' [Bartlett 1988: xxii]. *A Vision of Love* invokes Simeon Solomon from the viewpoint of a gay performer and audience: 'What should I say when I meet him; how should we talk to each other? I mean, how did men like us talk to each other in those days?' [Bartlett 1990: 89]. However, Bartlett has been arguing lately that gay theatre does not need to be confined to a subcultural fringe, so I was keen to interview him about this. 'The 1970s opposition between a fringe margin which is radical, and a conservative mainstream: I think that's a false diagram – historically false', he says. Gay theatre belongs, and has always belonged, 'in the mainstream'.

> After all, if you remove Wilde, Rattigan, Maugham, Coward, Orton and Novello from the post-1900 British theatre profession – from the money-earning profession of theatre – you're left with a pretty serious problem at the box office. And if you remove [the mid-century producer] Binkie Beaumont then you lose half of the actors you've ever heard of. [Sinfield 1996: 215]

But, I ask, wasn't this gay mainstream theatre a middlebrow, boulevard affair of subterfuge and equivocation? Not altogether, Bartlett explains:

> By 'mainstream' I mean those points of entry which the mainstream allows me, to its mechanics and economics, *by accident*; certain moments in Wilde, Rattigan, Maugham, Novello, Coward, but also Malcolm Scott, Douglas Byng, Frederick Ashton, Robert Helpmann, Angus McBean. It's not a tradition so much as a cluster of artistic flashpoints – points of aesthetic excess at which the mainstream becomes ripe for my evil purposes, for plucking. So my mainstream is very picky; one that most people wouldn't recognise. It is deeply queer, kinky, complicated, melodramatic, over-determined, disruptive and disrupted. [Ibid: 218]

Bartlett believes he can rely upon his own vision to draw from the mainstream whatever is excessive and hence disruptive in the queer practitioners who have worked there, and to reorient such materials so that they will re-present this vision in our own time. In fact, he does regard this as a subculturally effective strategy: 'It's important to say: "Actually, this has happened before – gays in the mainstream – and maybe we can draw lessons and strength from the way it's happened before" ' [Ibid: 215].

To be sure, the more we know about how sexual dissidents have lived historically, the better. But I still want to ask who is hearing what, for the idea of a mainstream tradition 'that most people wouldn't recognise' is plainly paradoxical. The mid-century theatre of Coward and Rattigan was characterised by a sleight-of-hand whereby massaging the anxieties of conservative, middlebrow audiences secured the box office, while an in-the-know minority thrilled to dangerously dissident nuances. In those circumstances there were, in effect, *two (simultaneous) performances*, one for each audience. For the time, this was a necessary and cunning way of insinuating subcultural awareness, but the effect was only nominally mainstream, since mainstream audiences didn't realise it was happening [Sinfield 1991]. Further, it probably can't be done today because … very many people are likely now to pick up queer nuances; and, anyhow, we don't much need it because we have many other ways of signalling to each other.

Bartlett has other important arguments: working conditions on the fringe are unfair and oppressive, and audiences are predictable and complacent, whereas boulevard theatre may offer notable artistic scope at the moment. Those are entirely fair points. The working conditions available to organic or subcultural intellectuals of subordinated groups are generally inferior, and no-one is entitled to demand that they forego other opportunities. Indeed, my case is not that there is nothing to be gained by working in the mainstream; on the contrary, we have to do what we can with all the chances that present themselves. But we should not undervalue purposeful subcultural work. If you get asked to do a play for the Royal National Theatre, fine; but don't take it for granted that this is better than working with Gay Sweatshop. Of the exhibition linked to his book *The Sexual Perspective*, Emmanuel Cooper declares: 'It's in a gallery in the West End, it's in the mainstream, and that's where it belongs. It must stand within the mainstream, and be judged within those terms' [Cooper 1994]. Well, it is pleasing that people in a position to visit the West End can see these pictures, but we should not imagine that their standards are somehow superior. And if the assumption is that they have just been waiting for our work to become good enough before letting it into their galleries, that is bizarre. Actually, some of our work will be of high quality, some not – like anyone else's – and we can assess that for ourselves if we want to. We don't need to depend on recognition by establishment gatekeepers.

These considerations apply also in Lesbian and Gay Studies: academics too like to enjoy mainstream approval, and the working conditions that follow from impressing senior colleagues, a fellowship committee, a university press. And consequently, as much as Derek Jarman and the Pet Shop Boys ... we are vulnerable to co-option. In particular, we are likely to feel obliged to run queer subcultural concerns through academic routines, which will be illuminating in some aspects but inhibiting in others. Again, my thought is not that young colleagues should risk their jobs through impetuously explicit sexual politics, but that we should try to use the expertise and authority of the academy, insofar as we have some of that, to work in and through sexually dissident subcultures. This will mean trying to write our academic work in more accessible ways, and looking for opportunities to present it in the lesbian and gay press.

Monique Wittig would seem to be a good instance of a materialist intellectual who has committed her work to lesbians and other women. Diana Fuss invokes her as 'first and foremost a materialist thinker who believes that nothing which signifies can "escape the political in this moment in history" '. Her most famous comment, that lesbians are not women, discloses 'the act of social construction implicit in the very naming of "women" ' [Fuss 1989: 41–2 from Wittig 1992: 25]. In her essay 'Paradigm' Wittig claims for lesbian subculture a considerable measure of autonomy:

As lesbians we are the product of a clandestine culture that has always existed in history. Until the last century Sappho was the only writer of our literature who was not clandestine. Today lesbian culture is still partially clandestine, partially open, in any case 'marginal' and completely unknown to *the* culture. It is, nevertheless, an international culture with its own literature, its own painting, music, codes of language, codes of social relations, codes of dress, its own mode of work. [Wittig 1979: 117]

This situation derives from the ancient world, where lesbianism, as represented in the poems of Sappho, developed not '*against* the other, but rather outside of it, coexisting with it. To the extent that its origin is to be found outside the patriarchy, one could call it an a-patriarchal, a-heterosexual culture' [ibid: 116]. Hence 'Lesbianism is the culture through which we can politically question heterosexual society on its sexual categories, on the meaning of its institutions of domination in general, and in particular on the meaning of that institution of personal dependence, marriage, imposed on women' [ibid: 118]. Wittig announces here a role for the lesbian organic intellectual.

To be sure, there are problems with the argument of 'Paradigm'. As Fuss points out, Wittig proposes a miraculous free cultural space, and homogenises lesbians; as Judith Butler observes, lesbian and gay commentators today are more likely to understand our cultures as 'embedded in the larger structures of heterosexuality even as they are positioned in subversive or resignatory relationships to heterosexual cultural configurations' [Fuss 1989: 43; Butler 1990: 121]. A fully materialist account will need to ground lesbian subculture in the historical conditions in which lesbian writers have worked, investigating the scope for dissidence and co-option in relation to the dominant cultural arrangements and the diversity of same-sex passion among women. All this said, Wittig's argument in 'Paradigm' offers a challenging and important evocation of the viability of lesbian subcultural work.

However, Wittig does not reprint 'Paradigm' in her collection, *The Straight Mind and Other Essays* (1992). In the title essay in that volume she insists on 'the material oppression of individuals by discourses', instancing psychoanalysis, science, the mass media, pornography, films, magazine photos, posters, the social sciences, history: these 'discourses of heterosexuality oppress us in the sense that they prevent us from speaking unless we speak in their terms' [Wittig 1979: 25, 27]. But *literature* is not in that list: it is not specified, on a footing with those others, as an oppressive discourse.

In fact, in another essay, 'The Point of View: Universal or Particular?' (1980), Wittig revokes the position she took in 'Paradigm': she specifically disqualifies subcultural writing by lesbians, other women, and gay men. 'A text by a minority writer is effective only if it succeeds in making the minority point of view universal, only if it is an important literary text', she writes. A gay theme is a gamble at best: the risk is that 'the theme will overdetermine the meaning, monopolize the whole meaning, against the intention of the author who wants above all to create a literary work' [Wittig 1992: 62, 64].

Of course, Wittig is right: if you take 'literature' as your reference point, it will draw you towards a 'universal', i.e. straightgeist (straight-mind), way of thinking. But why should the lesbian or gay man be wanting 'above all to create a literary work'? 'Art' and 'literature' are defined by the established gatekeepers as meaningful to heterosexuals ... That is why we have terms like 'the gay novel' and 'lesbian art': the qualifications indicate that these are partial, incomplete kinds of art. So when Wittig exclaims that Proust's '*Remembrance of Things Past* is a monument of French literature *even though* homosexuality is *the* theme of the book' [ibid: 64], this is indeed correct: only special excellence can persuade the literary establishment to allow an *evidently* gay text into its higher reaches.

Wittig concludes in this vein: 'even if Djuna Barnes is read first and widely by lesbians, one should not reduce and limit her to the lesbian minority' [ibid: 63]. That is not acceptable. There is no more *reduction* in being appreciated by a lesbian minority than there is in being appreciated by the minority who feel themselves to be addressed in the discourses of art and literature (and it is a minority – never forget that big-C culture discriminates primarily in terms of educational attainment). Bartlett makes the point: 'people say: "You're just writing for gay people and all your work is about being gay and isn't that incredibly limiting?" So you just look them in the eye: "No, not at all" ' [Sinfield 1996: 214].

John Frow, in his book *Cultural Studies and Cultural Value*, challenges the idea of organic or subcultural intellectuals on the ground that the relationship between intellectuals and a posited working-class constituency has generally been nostalgic and sentimental. He quotes Stuart Hall's retrospective analysis of the Birmingham School: 'The problem about the concept of an organic intellectual is that it appears to align intellectuals with an emerging historic movement and we couldn't tell then, and can hardly tell now, where that emerging historical movement was to be found. We were organic intellectuals without any organic point of reference' [Hall 1996: 267; and see Frow 1995: 128–9]. Indeed, it hardly seemed then, and does not seem now, that either working-class or youth movements in Britain are about to become the kind of formation to which intellectuals can conveniently hitch their visions of revolutionary political opportunity. However, Hall does reassert his belief in some such project: 'the organic intellectual cannot absolve himself or herself from the responsibility of transmitting those ideas, that knowledge, through the intellectual function, to those who do not belong, professionally, in the intellectual class' [Hall 1996: 268].

Frow's suggestion is that we bear in mind that 'intellectuals have interests and "tastes" which, like everyone else's, are shaped by their class position'. 'This is an institutional, not a personal question' [ibid: 6] – to do with the role of intellectuals in the social formation, not with their individual sympathies and predilections. Their cultural politics, therefore, 'should be openly and without embarrassment presented as their politics, not someone else's' [ibid: 169].

In my view that is right. Intellectuals are a kind of class, class fraction or social category, and there is a disjunction, by definition, between them and people of other classes, class fractions or social categories. Intellectuals may forge sympathetic identifications with workers or aristocrats, but insofar as they do this *as intellectuals* they are engaging with concerns that are not immediately or entirely theirs. An element of altruism is involved, and this is open to charges of romanticism. But the pattern is different when we consider allegiances of race, ethnicity, gender and sexuality. In such cases, although the intellectual still has a distinct social role, there is no necessary disjunction *in respect of the organising principle of the subculture* – sexuality, for instance. The gay intellectual shares much of the history and current circumstances of the gay worker or businessperson. The idea of an organic relationship between intellectuals and a sexual constituency involves no intrinsic self-deception or nostalgia. The les/bi/gay intellectual has a legitimate role in the formation of a critical subculture, especially insofar as s/he works through subcultural myths and media. None of this means that organic intellectuals will not cultivate a wider analysis of relations in capital and patriarchy; to the contrary, one task is to bring such an analysis to the subculture.

To be sure, with the elitist and exclusionary use of jargon in the academy on the one hand and commercial media exploitation of ideas on the other, les/bi/gay people generally have little reason to trust intellectuals, whatever their sexual politics. However, the point about the organic intellectual is that she or he is envisaged, not as telling anybody what to think, but as claiming space for cultural work; space in which to explore, in terms that make sense to us, questions that are – *inevitably* – ignored or manipulated elsewhere by others. For, as I have said, it is unwise to leave these matters within the control of people who, we know, do not like us. Sarah Schulman observes:

> Many of us were deeply shaken by the casual, passing notice that took place in the mainstream press, of Audre Lorde's life and death, and it underlined yet again the understanding that our leaders, our geniuses, and our teachers can live and die without the respect and acknowledgment that they merit because our lives are simply not as important as the lives of heterosexuals. [Schulman 1993 [1995]: 275]

We should not have been surprised. We have to develop our own structures of understanding and recognition.

Bibliography

Babuscio, Jack (1977) 'Camp and the Gay Sensibility', in Richard Dyer, ed., *Gays and Film*, London: British Film Institute.

Bartlett, Neil (1988) *Who Was That Man? A Present for Mr Oscar Wilde*, London: Serpent's Tail.

Bartlett, Neil (1990) *A Vision of Love Revealed in Sleep*, in Michael Wilcox, ed., *Gay Plays Volume Four*, London: Methuen.

Butler, Judith (1990) *Gender Trouble*, London: Routledge.

Califia, Pat (1994) *Public Sex*, Pittsburgh: Cleis Press.

Connor, Steve (1989) *Postmodern Culture*, Oxford: Blackwell.

Cooper, Emmanuel (1994) 'Kaleidoscope', BBC Radio 4, 8 September.

Foucault, Michel (1980) *Power/Knowledge*, Brighton: Harvester Press.

Frow, John (1995) *Cultural Studies and Cultural Value*, Oxford: Clarendon Press.

Fuss, Diana (1989) *Essentially Speaking*, New York: Routledge.

Gramsci, Antonio (1971) *Selections from the Prison Notebooks*, trans. Quentin Hoare and Geoffrey Nowell Smith, London: Lawrence and Wishart.

Hall, Stuart (1996) 'Cultural Studies and its Theoretical Legacies', in David Morley and Kuan-Hsing Chen, eds, *Stuart Hall: Critical Dialogues in Cultural Studies*, London: Routledge.

Medhurst, Andy (1991) 'That Special Thrill: *Brief Encounter*, Homosexuality and Authorship', *Screen*, 32 (Summer).

Medhurst, Andy (1997) 'Camp', in Sally Munt and Andy Medhurst, eds, *Lesbian and Gay Studies*, London: Cassell.

Morley, David and Kuan-Hsing Chen, eds (1996) *Stuart Hall: Critical Dialogues in Cultural Studies*, London: Routledge.

Newton, Judith and Deborah Rosenfelt, eds (1985) *Feminist Criticism and Social Change*, New York: Methuen.

Plummer, Ken (1995) *Telling Sexual Stories*, London: Routledge.

Schulman, Sarah (1993) 'A Modest Proposal', repr. in Schulman (1995) *My American History*, London: Cassell.

Sinfield, Alan (1991) 'Private Lives/Public Theatre: Noel Coward and the Politics of Homosexual Representation', *Representations*, 36 (Fall), pp. 43–63.

Sinfield, Alan (1992) *Faultlines*, Berkeley: California University Press and Oxford University Press.

Sinfield, Alan (1994) *Cultural Politics – Queer Reading*, London: Routledge.

Sinfield, Alan (1996) ' "The Moment of Submission": Neil Bartlett in Conversation', *Modern Drama*, 39, Special Issue on Lesbian/Gay/Queer Drama, ed. Hersh Zeifman, pp. 211–21.

Smyth, Cherry (1996) *Damn Fine Art*, London: Cassell.

Williams, Raymond (1977) *Marxism and Literature*, Oxford University Press.

Williams, Raymond (1980) *Problems in Materialism and Culture*, London: New Left Books.

Wittig, Monique (1992) 'The Straight Mind', in *The Straight Mind and Other Essays*, Hemel Hempstead: Harvester.

Wittig, Monique (1979) 'Paradigm', in George Stambolian and Elaine Marks, eds, *Homosexualities and French Literature*, Ithaca: Cornell Press.

Note

Originally published as Chapter 8 of *Gay and After*, London: Serpent's Tail, 1998, pp. 146–59. Some minor omissions hav been made where the author refers to other chapters in the book.

4.7 **The Theory and Practice of Political Theatre** (1979)

JOHN MCGRATH

BEFORE SOMEBODY SAYS 'ALL theatre is political' – a statement which should be banned from this discussion as diversionary, if true – let's agree to talk about the theatre that exists somewhere within the shadow (or at least the penumbra) of the ideas of Marx and the Marxists. Let's talk about theatre that has as its base a recognition of capitalism as an economic system which produces classes; that sees the betterment of human life for all people in the abolition of classes and of capitalism; that sees that this can happen only through the rise to state power of the current under-class, the working class, and through a democratization – economic as well as political – of society and of its decision-making processes. A theatre that sees the establishment of socialism, not as the creation of a utopia or the end of the dialectic of history, but as another step towards the realization of the full potential of every individual human life during the short time that every individual has to live. Socialist theatre.

There are other kinds of political theatre. There is the anarchist theatre, for example, which, when it is conscious of anything at all, sees the struggle for state power as a self-defeating aim and appears to insist on every individual making their own bid for revolution and immediate fulfilment. Or the social democratic theatre which, in its rare moments of theoretical insight, sees the betterment of the working class as a process of gradual gains within a basically capitalistic framework, needing no revolution of power or consciousness, merely material improvement which requires as its precondition the health of the capitalist system – all that is to be arranged thanks to the great man in whose hall we now prepare to dig holes and fill them in again.

I can't speak for those varieties of political theatre; I disagree with their theoretical base and rarely enjoy their practice. So I can only talk about socialist political theatre.

Ideology of the dominant class

Before I go on to outline the three main ways in which theatre relates to the Marxist theoretical base, it is important to stress the relationship between the economic structure of a society, in our case a capitalist one, and the political, social and cultural realities of that society. The traditional Marxist way to express this relationship stems from Marx and Engels: 'The dominant ideology of a society is that of the dominant class.' Traditionally, Marxists have constructed a model of society with an economic base which is capitalist, or feudal, or whatever, and which directly determines the 'superstructures' of government, law, education, religion and the other institutions, including the cultural 'superstructure'.

There is no time to go into the argument about this determining relationship here, but it seems a good place to express my personal gratitude to Raymond Williams for having tackled this issue clearly, and I hope definitively, in his book *Marxism and Literature*. It is one of the few genuinely *useful* books written on the subject and is a piece of theoretical ammunition of the highest quality.

Several important features of this relationship between the economic structure of society and its literary self-expression arise from a consideration of Raymond Williams's work. One is that the directness or determining nature of this relationship is thrown into question. Literature, which I take here to include theatre, can often appear to have an autonomous development of its own, connected only tangentially with the modes of production, ownership of the means of production, and the state of play in the class war. This development can be affected by internal factors of uneven development, by other elements in the social and cultural life of the society – even by individual talent, or the absence of it.

Secondly, in any period there are likely to be three main elements of literary production – the *residual*, which draws its sources from a previous period but is still effectively alive in the present; the *dominant*, which exercises hegemony over the period culturally; and the *emergent* element, by which, and I quote, 'new meanings and values, new practices, new relationships and kinds of relationships are constantly being created. But it is exceptionally difficult to distinguish between those which are really elements of some new phase of the dominant culture, and those which are substantially alternative or oppositional to it – emergent in the strict sense, rather than the merely novel' (Raymond Williams, *Marxism and Literature*, p. 123).

All these three elements of course interrelate in a dynamic way, but each has a significance of its own. In spite of these questions, it must be stated that for any Marxist, 'it is not the consciousness of men that determines their being, but, on the contrary, their social being that determines their consciousness' – 'the economic movement finally asserts itself as necessary'.

But it remains important that when we examine the political role of theatre in a society, both the theatre, the society, and their relationship should be seen in all their complexity.

Three sectors of British theatre

This leads me back to what I see as the three main areas of activity of 'political' theatre. Loosely speaking, they are: first, the struggle within the institutions of theatre against the hegemony of the 'bourgeois' ideology within those institutions; secondly, the making of a theatre that is *interventionist* on a political level, usually outside those institutions; and thirdly and most importantly, the creation of a counter-culture based on the working class, which will grow in richness and confidence until it eventually displaces the dominant bourgeois culture of late capitalism.

It is important here to see theatre not just as 'plays', but as a means of production, with bosses, workers, and unemployed, with structural relationships and varied contradictions. It is through its structures as much as through its product that theatre expresses the dominant bourgeois ideology.

There are three different sectors of theatre, each with its own mini-ideology, each with its own relationship with the changing economic base of our society, and each with its own structure: one, the commercial, or West End theatre; two, the orthodox subsidized theatres – the subsidized establishment, the National and Royal Shakespeare companies, the main reps, etc.; and thirdly, the fringe, or touring theatre.

Each of these sectors corresponds very loosely to Williams's categories. The commercial or West End theatre can be seen as in many senses *residual*, but active. In structure it resembles a nineteenth-century small capitalist enterprise, with investors, with a management, employees on the lowest possible wages, and a product which it hopes to market for a profit. It is a high-risk investment in theory, but can offer compensatorily high dividends. A good manager will contrive devices to lessen the risks of total failure – as in Harold Fielding's recent mounting of four musicals back to back, with each unit of investment spread over all of them.

The central contradiction in this category is the old one between the social or group-effort means of production and the private ownership of those means. The classic worker versus capitalist situation. This is alleviated to some extent by allowing star actors, writers, directors, designers, sometimes lighting designers, to take a small percentage of the gross income thus making them junior partners in the enterprise, and by the exercise of the traditional theatre ideologies – 'the show must go on' – plus the obvious appeal to the vanity of the individual actor or writer of becoming famous through involvement in a successful show. This 'fame' is also an economic incentive, as it often leads to film and television engagements which pay a lot of money.

The ideology contained within the *product* of this system is usually *residual* in the extreme. Indeed, nostalgia is one of its main preoccupations, as a glance through the West End listings of any newspaper will show. That again derives from its audience, since the West End audience is to a great extent the bourgeoisie and professional classes of London.

But not entirely. There is not only a large section of visiting bourgeois and professional people from what are called the provinces and from all over the world, but also a large and important sector which is working class – the coach parties from Northampton for the big musicals and the comedies with TV stars, edging into a world of unreality for the evening, like young conscripts edging into the brothels of Hamburg. These last two sectors of the audience are drawn in by a massive publicity machine, which promotes shows like motor cars. The end result of the whole process can be a truly fabulous profit. Residual it may be, but active it certainly is.

The West End was once the dominant sector of theatre. All the reps in the country would put on re-runs of West End hits, with actors hoping to become West End stars, for audiences who wished they were in the West End. But this has changed. The *dominant* sector of theatre now, financially as well as ideologically, is the subsidized establishment: the National Theatre – the British Leyland of showbusiness – the RSC, the major reps, like Nottingham and Sheffield, which echo in style, structure, product, and ideology their big brothers on the South Bank, at Stratford and the Aldwych; and following trimly in their footsteps the lesser reps, the art theatres, the studios and the more pretentious of the amateur companies.

The 'correspondence' between the changed economic structure of British capitalism, now using a servile state machine to prop itself up, and the economic structure of these theatres, propped up by millions of pounds of public money, is immediately apparent. (What is less obvious is the correspondence between the new ideology of technological social democracy, the servile welfare state, and the ideology of the stuff to be seen on these stages. But that must be examined another time.)

As power-structures, these theatres reflect the nationalized industries: they are capitalist structures, but without the need to make profits. What they need to make is the individual reputation of the new masters – and to balance their books, give or take a few million pounds. Sometimes they have a spurious air of democracy, even worker-representation on their boards, and, to enhance their reputation, sometimes they even tackle bold subjects, like the Russian Revolution, safe in the hands of Robert Bolt.

But they are dominant, in the sense that their product is recognized generally as what we must all aspire to appreciate, or create, or imitate. Ninety five per cent of British actors, directors, and so on would like to work in these institutions, and when we think of the highest levels of theatre art in this country they are what come to mind – even though they may lapse from time to time below their own exalted standards. Their audiences in London are typically from the cultured, higher-educated, professional, or managerial groups and their children, plus the cosmopolitan culture-seekers of all lands.

In what are now known in this context as the 'regions', the audiences can have a certain amount of social variety, but those which are generally aimed at, which lurk at the back of the director's mind, are from the cultured, higher-educated, professional, or managerial sector – the AB readership, on whose behalf the reviewers assess the suitability of the production.

The nature of the fringe

All this so far has been very schematic and left a great deal unsaid. The first and most important omission is the recognition that within both the West End and the subsidized establishment there are contradictions, and that there are elements of class struggle – economic, social and, vitally, ideological. Both sectors are of necessity open to new blood, new ideas; both contain people of good-will, anxious to encourage change, even socialist change. Although their overall effect, if they succeed, is all too often to turn the genuinely oppositional into the merely novel, they are by no means monolithic.

All this preamble is by way of setting out the necessary context for examining the third element, roughly corresponding to the *emergent* element, in our theatre: the 'political' theatre, usually found on the fringe, touring, or in the smaller subsidized companies. This appears to be an entity in so far as we have all met here to talk about it, and some of us make our living by it. There is little point in talking about the fringe as a whole – its components are too various, their *raisons d'être* varying from principled Marxist interventionism, via simply providing employment, to unpaid exhibitionism.

But some features of the fringe are significant. Firstly, it is organized in groups or companies, created by an act of will or initiative, and when that original impetus dies or fails to grow, the group usually dies, unlike the larger institutions. Secondly, most groups active on the fringe draw subsidy from the state, via the Arts Council, or from local government via regional arts associations, or a combination of both, and most are dependent on this for survival. Thirdly, most groups are small enough to see themselves as organized on a co-operative or democratic basis. Fourthly, most fringe groups aim at audiences outside those which regularly attend the West End or the National Theatre. And, fifthly, most fringe groups demand an application of a member's talents, and a degree of involvement, different from that of the other sectors of the theatre.

All of these features have positive and negative potentialities. At the negative extreme they could create an egomaniac, subsidy-sucking, pseudo-democratic group of freaks, performing rubbish for an élite of similar freaks. On the other hand, these features do offer the possibility of a highly principled, creative Marxist cultural intervention, giving back to the public something valuable for a small amount of public money, organized in a genuine democracy, demanding new skills and imaginative efforts to create a new kind of culture of the highest standards, for and of the working class. So enriching the Labour movement and helping it to make its ultimate victory a worthwhile victory.

It is because of this *potential* that the fringe theatre must be taken seriously by Marxist theatre workers, critics, and audiences. It is because of this potential that I would like to categorize it as the *emergent* element of theatre in Britain today and examine its theory and its practice.

Defining the theatrical contribution

The central economic problem in capitalist society is the ownership and control of the means of production, distribution, and exchange. Public ownership of some firms is not enough, the mixed economy is not enough. Public control, both on a national level with full accountability to the people as a whole and on a local level accountable to and organized by workers and consumers, is necessary to create a sane, non-exploiting society. The capitalist system preserves itself from this principally by means of the state, which has at its disposal not only its myriad apparatuses – parliament, civil service, education system, church, the media, and all their output and mystification and manipulation – but also a police force and an army. Both of these are trained to deal with enemies of the state and will do so. So the state becomes the central political problem for a Marxist, together with the party or the means of overthrowing that state and replacing it with a socialist state.

The question I should like to ask is what can a laugh, a song, and a dance contribute to this problem? Or even the most penetrating socialist drama? The answer, I think, is quite a lot, if you are laughing at the right things, singing the right songs, and dancing well enough – and if your drama is meaning something to the right people, penetrating the right mystique in a dialectical manner. In other words the contribution of political theatre to the struggle of the labour movement for the emancipation of the whole of society from capitalism can only mean anything if seen in class terms. Because within this massive, daunting structure of capitalism there is its central inescapable contradiction: it creates a working class whose interests are opposed to it and who will overthrow it.

I would like to look more closely at the three main areas of activity of political theatre in a capitalist society as I've described them. The first was the challenge to the hegemony of bourgeois ideology within the theatre institutions themselves. Trevor Griffiths has tried to do this with two plays at the National Theatre; David Edgar with *Destiny* at the Aldwych; John Arden and Margaretta D'Arcy with *The Island of the Mighty*, also at the Aldwych; Edward Bond, Howard Brenton, David Hare, with plays at the National, the Aldwych, and the major reps. The plays of Brecht have been used for the same purpose, and some of Sean O'Casey's.

There are immense problems involved in this process, as most of these writers have discovered. It is no doubt useful to the general movement of socialist ideas to have them aired prominently, to enter the national (or at least the metropolitan) consciousness, on a certain level of seriousness, and occasionally to draw into those theatres certain politically-conscious members of the Labour movement. But, good as these works may be, the process is not contributing to the creation of a new, genuinely oppositional theatre. They become 'product' and the process remains the same: they are in constant danger of being appropriated in production by the very ideology they set out to oppose.

Poor Bertolt Brecht has suffered greatly in this way, but he is dead. The Ardens raised hell at the Aldwych five years ago for precisely this reason. In Trevor Griffiths's *The Party*, at the National, the character of an old Marxist revolutionary from Glasgow was taken over by Lord Olivier, and became a vehicle for a star to communicate with his admirers.

The process, the building, the wages structure, the publicity machine, the free interval drinks budget, all these can turn opposition into novelty. But it could be short-sighted to deny the value of trying. This challenge to the dominance of bourgeois ideology on its own ground is important; it creates allies for the movement and is a weapon to use, and we are not in a position to throw any weapon away.

Outside the institutions

Outside the London institutions more possibilities are open for creating a socialist theatre. At certain periods in the past, some of the bolder companies, like the Liverpool Everyman, the Victoria in Stoke, the Playhouse in Nottingham, the Northcott in Exeter, the Belgrade in Coventry, even the Royal Court in London, have embarked on policies of presenting socialist plays. Some of these companies have tried to make their theatres attractive to working-class audiences, some have even created a style of presentation that is anti-bourgeois – of building a relationship between the theatre, the performers, and the local working class that makes the theatre more the property of its audience.

Here I think Peter Cheeseman's work and Alan Dosser's work in Stoke and Liverpool should be mentioned, and in some ways a theatre like the Everyman has produced a whole crop of actors who have the skills and the attitudes that good working-class theatre needs, and that bourgeois theatre critics don't even begin to understand.

But few of these theatres have escaped from the power structures of capitalism. All, to qualify for subsidy from the Arts Council and the local authority, have to have a board of directors, generally local worthies and councillors. They appoint an administrator and an artistic director, both of whom, while having a certain amount of autonomy, need board approval for their plans, and answer to the board for their success or failure. Within this framework, the artistic director can consult members of the company on his future programme, can have company meetings to sort out problems in a communal spirit, and so on, but few actually do this, even in left-wing theatres.

Some of these theatres *have* presented work of a high standard with a socialist content, and some have pioneered styles of production which contact working-class audiences, and for these we should be grateful. But it is to the other two areas that I would like to turn. They are the areas that I am most familiar with and have thought a great deal about. Both concern making theatre for working-class audiences, first and foremost; and both present immense questions of theory and massive problems of practice.

The first area is that of the direct interventionist theatre-piece – polemical, openly political, and whose avowed aim is to gain support for a particular party or position inside the working class, and among its potential allies. The support demanded can be for a strike, a struggle, fund-raising, or a piece of legislation; or against a piece of legislation; or concerned with a more general issue, like grasping the salient features of a particular firm, or the way ACAS [Advisory, Conciliation and Arbitration Service] works, or the way racism works, or sexism, or the press; or it can be support for an even more general attitude to, and understanding of, the operation of (say) multi-national corporations, the role of the British army in the North of Ireland, or indeed the way the Labour Government operates.

In this area, the political theatre company sees its ultimate purpose as agitational. It uses theatrical devices to explain, elucidate, remind, and eventually persuade its audience to act or think differently. It sees a politically-conscious working class as the agent of social change – its power as ultimately revolutionary. So it sets about working within that class to raise the awareness of those who may have been mystified or apathetic, or divided against their fellow workers. It sets out to raise their consciousness of themselves as members of a class with interests in common, the ultimate one being the overthrow of capitalism.

For that class consciousness to be there, more than the individual worker's own immediate, family, and local experience needs to be present in his or her mind. Very often that experience itself has been mediated through a false consciousness created by the process of living under capitalism, and requires representation: also, the experiences of other workers in other towns doing the same job, or in other countries, working for the same multi-national, or at other times in history, or even just down the street, need to be presented. Theatre is a graphic way of presenting other people's experience – even of re-presenting our own experience and history to ourselves. This is a valid social function of theatre.

Statistics of the social fabric

Even items of factual information which may have been concealed but which are relevant to people's attitudes to society can be presented from the stage as a legitimate part of theatre, fulfilling that function. To give one instance, about four years ago I was working on a show about land ownership in the north of Scotland with the Scottish 7:84, to tour around Highland communities. It proved impossible to discover who owned what land. No land census had been taken in Scotland since 1871, and although the Scottish Landowners' Federation ran a register, they would not disclose the acreages of any individual owners.

But they had commissioned a man to mark out on the Ordnance Survey maps for the whole of Scotland the marches or the boundaries of all the estates. Presumably, this was done to settle territorial disputes amongst their members or their progeny. I was told about a retired forester called John McEwan, who was then aged 86 and living in the heart of Perthshire, who detested the landlords so much that he had photocopied all these hundreds of maps at his own expense, stuck them together, and gone round the boundaries marked on them with a machine to calculate the acreages. He intended to publish this information, but hadn't finished his work on it.

Two members of the company drove up to see him one night, after rehearsal. He gave them a thorough political grilling and eventually decided they were alright, and they came back with one of his pillowcases stuffed with maps, sheets of acreages and ownerships. Armed with this we could not only publish the most important facts in the programme, but also tell them to the audience at a certain point in the show, adding local information for the area we happened to be in.

The effect was truly electric. The best-guarded secrets of the lairds were revealed publicly to people who sometimes lived on their estates and didn't know how big they were. The fact, for example, that 0.1 per cent of the population of Ross and Cromarty own 97 per cent of the land – that is, 74 landowners owned one and a half million acres of that county – was an essential part of the social fabric of the Highlands, which was our real subject. Now an actress standing on a rostrum in a village hall reciting a few statistics about acreages may seem a far cry from pure art, the poetry of Wordsworth's 'Highland Lass', for example – but is probably what her haunting song was all about.

Gramsci used Lassalle's phrase, 'to tell the truth is revolutionary', on the masthead of his paper. As Goran Therborn points out: 'The essential point is rather the following: if you want to change something fundamentally and in a definite direction, you have to know how it works; if you want only to sit on it, then no such problems arise.'

The problems which arise with this kind of theatre are, of course, immense. I am not particularly bothered with the aesthetic categories of the thing. I spend too long arguing with actors who bring abstract, received notions, of what is 'right' and 'wrong', and 'proper' and 'improper', 'correct' and 'incorrect' in the theatre to spend any more time on worrying about the correct categorization of style, convention, and the consistency thereof. It works if the audience get it with the same sense of wonder and rightness and relevance that you as a group 'got it' with – if the instinctive reaction is not jarred by any incongruous worries, if the subterranean connections are made and the scene itself is gripping, for good reasons. That's the end of aesthetics. These problems solve themselves.

The real problems with this kind of theatre lie in three main areas. One has to do with the actual organization of the company, the second with the nature of the people who work with it, and the third with political organization on a national level – which leads on to a host of others.

Organizing the company

On the question of organization of a company, as I have said, most political companies grow from an impetus or an act of will to *do* something, to make an intervention. There is clearly a difficulty which will arise here, in that the aims and objects of the company have been in a sense pre-defined. But it is the nature of any fringe theatre group that its membership changes constantly, and hence the contradiction that the new membership of that company may wish to redefine its objectives and aims.

There will be conflict and a certain amount of ineffectuality about the company if these two forces – the original impetus and the redefinition – are not worked out on a proper political level. What frequently happens is that a company will change and those who are about to leave will bear no responsibility for the future actions of that company. Those who join, to take their place, will have no identity with the past of that company, and certainly no experience of the actual problems.

So why not have the same company all the time? This is a practical problem. People have to survive and many people find that they can't take it. In fact, someone has just left 7:84 England saying that it was too much like hard work – and indeed it is. So the theory of the organization of a company presents great difficulties. To make an intervention you need consistency of purpose and identity and a growing relationship with the audience. But to stay alive as individuals you need variety, breaks, time to read, time to wash your socks, time to see other people's work, and so on. To make a democracy within that sort of shifting situation, you run a very good chance of diluting your interventionist possibilities.

There are, further, the specific problems of theatre workers. Actors in a capitalistic system have been brought up to believe in a hierarchy, and to hold together in a kind of emotional bond to protect themselves against the hierarchy, and this leads to a reluctance to criticize other actors publicly. Furthermore, the nature of the work is such that the actors are interdependent on stage, so that the necessary processes of democracy, of criticism and self-criticism, have certain barriers erected against them, which are the result of working within a capitalist system.

There are things that would help, like more money, more paid holidays, and certainly a higher political level. But there is never enough subsidy, and as for raising the political level, it is often the case that actors with a very high political level are actually not very good at acting, which is a serious difficulty. And those who are very good at the kind of acting that is required by a particular company may be reluctant to raise their political level, or simply not have the time to do it.

The solutions to these organizational problems within the companies are as various as the companies themselves, and indeed they change from year to year within companies, but it is a major area of conflict between the ideal situation and the actual practical problems.

The needs of the performers

The second problem area involves individual company members. The basic attitude of socialist performers, as far as I'm concerned, should be that they are on the same level as the audience – they are the same as the audience. Identification should take place between the performers and the audience on a personal level, which is certainly not the case in bourgeois theatre. Those performers are there to do things for the audience because it's their job and because they have the skills. They can play the fiddle or sing or show other characters clearly, they can time a gag, they can make an exit, but at the end of that they can be the same again.

It's like watching a plumber work. He comes in, has a cup of tea, has a fag, and then when it comes to the actual plumbing, he is on, it is his turn, he does it, and everybody has to watch it because he knows what he is doing. At the end of it, he puts the tools back in the bag, has a cup of tea, has another fag, and goes. He returns to exactly the same level as the people whose pipes he is mending, or whatever.

To take a more specific example, I think of the fiddler in the Scottish 7:84 company, whom I have watched often in pubs, who would sort of lean over the bar and talk to everybody, so that they soon know he's a fiddler, and he knows he's a fiddler, and he knows they're going to say, 'give us a tune', and they know that they're going to say 'give us a tune', so eventually he will be persuaded to pick up his fiddle and play, and he will play for an hour and a half. Pure magic. Then he will put the fiddle away again and not vanish behind a curtain, or go to his dressing room, or wait for the chauffeur-driven car to appear at the door, but just sort of have another pint; he's generally pissed by then anyway.

The question of specialization comes up as well: the kind of performer that I think should be working in socialist theatre is the kind of performer who has skills in a variety of areas and is prepared to develop his or her skills in areas that he or she is interested in but has never had a chance to explore.

In drama school, for example, there are two separate courses: stage management and acting. Now this sort of division of labour is often very frustrating because a lot of stage managers really want to act, and a lot of actors are potentially interested in making props or being good lighting people. The kind of performer that I'm interested in, the kind that I think should be in a socialist company, should be able to use and develop a lot more skills than simply the one skill of acting or the one skill of hanging lights in the right place, and pushing the right sliders.

Coping with 'people problems'

Particularly with actors – and particularly in England as opposed to Scotland – the actors' mentality is a product of late romanticism, a hangover from the 1890s: a product of a concept of art as ultimate sensibility. There's a huge amount of bullshit taught and spoken in drama schools and in the reps on this mystique of the actor, the mystique of the artistic sensibility, and similarly a great deal of bullshit, mystique and late romanticism about the roles of the director and writer. There seems to be an unwritten rule that to be truly creative in the theatre you must be a pain in the arse, otherwise nobody knows that you're being truly creative.

Now that mystique, which is very prevalent, is one that has no place whatsoever within the socialist theatre company. It's a question of skills, of acquiring the same kind of skills that a plumber acquires, of doing an apprenticeship, having an easy mastery over them, and that is only acquired through hard work. These skills should then be used for the pleasure of the audience – a joint sharing of the skills and of the fun.

You watch a child build with bricks and then knock them down again, you see the pleasure of just doing something for the fun of it. If you watch a talent night in a club maybe the singer will be absolutely awful, but if you watch the faces of the audience when someone they know, and whose act they enjoy, goes on, you will see the kind of relationship that I think socialist theatre workers should have with an audience.

To sum up and add a few problems with people involved. *First*, there's the problem of people subscribing to the mystiques and the bullshit. *Secondly*, there are a lot of people with no interest in entertainment skills, or in developing further other skills. *Thirdly*, lower middle-class actors don't think the working class will appreciate their art. *Fourthly*, a lot of actors from the working class have used acting as a way out of the working class and into the ranks of the middle class, and they don't fancy risking falling back again. They'd rather run an antique shop in Barnes – quite a few do. *Fifthly*, there's the problem of individuals who have no politics, are not interested in politics, but who have the necessary skills. (This problem in some ways is preferable to that of the individuals who have strong populist or anarchist politics, but who *think* they are Marxists.) *Sixthly*, there is the problem of the socialist theatre worker who joins the company and becomes engrossed in political theory, and particularly in the organization of the company, and gets turned in on the company, seeing it as a socialist utopia and forgetting about the actual intervention and the audience. *Seventhly*, many find it difficult to make criticism and self-criticism on a high political level, to see the politics of acting – for example, the way a half thought-out performance can have a political meaning.

Eighthly, and connected with that, is the desire among a lot of actors to create a sensitive performance and preserve it, come what may, and if it fails the audience is to blame. There are a lot of people who become actors because they want to be liked, and this presents a great deal of difficulty, either when you are in the position of having to criticize or be criticized by your fellow-workers, or when you are in a position of having to perform a character with a certain amount of detachment, or a character who is not likeable.

Pros and cons of party affiliation

Should a theatre group belong to a party? There are many reasons why they should. First, to be part of something which provides a political channel of action, assuming that people are agitated by what you say. There's a possibility with a political party of follow-up to make the involvement of the audience more permanent, and not just getting everybody going and then leaving them to it. It raises the possibility of the audience becoming active, becoming the actors, not passively receiving. There is a further benefit in belonging to a party: within the group itself there will be more coherence or identity of purpose; but there is a practical problem, which is the present situation of the left in this country. The heritage of Labourism means that the mass party of the working class is Labour. The heritage of Stalin and Stalinism is that the Communist Party is feared and is characterized as totalitarian, dictatorial, by many people in the working class and in society as a whole.

Now if a company openly identified with the position of the other groups – the C.P.G.B.M.L. [Communist Party of Great Britain (Marxist-Leninist)] or the W.R.P. [Workers' Revolutionary Party] or the S.W.G. [Socialist Workers Party] or the I.M.G. [International Marxist Group] – there would immediately be a tendency for the audience to become a faction and for the others to stay away. The Workers' Revolutionary Party at one point put on shows and some of them were very good indeed. I saw one in St. Helen's, for example, which was about the English revolution in 1649, which was very well done, but was attended by only a very small handful, of whom I would imagine 90 per cent were W.R.P. members – most of whom had seen it before because they had been attending all the other performances.

The question of affiliation to a political party or organization raises the issue of what theatre 'can and should do'. The single-issue agitprop piece very rarely actually persuades anybody intellectually. Rather it is a show of support – part of a publicity machine, evidence of energy in that cause which impresses the ditherers and the 'don't knows' in the audience. It can relate a single issue to wider questions, thus informing the audience, but it rarely changes their prejudices.

In some single-issue pieces there is an organization, a strike committee, a local group, a tenants' association, or such, towards which to direct the audience's further action. The political follow-up is then structured anyway: but in the wider-issue agitational pieces (particularly the ideological agitational pieces) about the repression of women, about the role of the police, or the army, or the multi-nationals, or labourism, or racism or fascism, the problems do indeed become more complex.

If the ultimate aim of the group is the strengthening of the organizations of the working class, surely there should be some organic link with one of those organizations, and one which has clear political aims? What is the point of raising consciousness in the abstract? Surely involvement in struggle with a political dimension is the only way to build effective class-consciousness, and surely only a Marxist party can co-ordinate both the individual struggle and the overall strategy demanded by class politics?

The answer to all these questions is 'Yes', but no political fringe group that I know of is organically linked with a party at this moment. As far as I know, Red Ladder, Belt and Braces, the two 7:84 companies, Pirate Jenny, the Women's Theatre Group, Monstrous Regiment, North-West Spanner, Common Stock, Recreation Ground, and so on are all politically independent. Yet all are attempting to raise consciousness and to agitate on issues which demand political follow-up and coherence, which they can't provide. Does this then make them politically ineffective? The answer is in my opinion 'No', but it makes it more difficult for them to be politically effective.

So why don't they join with a political party? The main reason comes from what is in many ways the central failure of the British left. There are other reasons, which are connected with Arts

Council subsidies not being available to sub-sections of political parties, but oddly enough I do not think that this has much bearing on the situation. Far more important has been the combined effect of Labourism and Stalinism on and the evacuation of Marxism from mass working-class politics in this country.

What we do have is a Labour Movement which is increasingly moving apart from its national bureaucracy. On shop stewards' committees, trades councils, in certain union branches, on action groups, on solidarity groups, in the universities, in tenants' associations, on community projects, in women's groups, and of course within the Marxist parties and groups, and even within the Labour Party, there exists, on the ground, a massive and not entirely incoherent number of militants who are closely involved with the everyday struggles of the working class.

They combine across party and sectarian lines on certain issues, broad and narrow; and many have a strong practical sense of the way towards socialism. Their support within the working class is volatile – which is not surprising since the moment they show any sign of winning a struggle they become the most reviled group of individuals in society, turned by the screeches of the media and the major parties into the lepers of the Welfare State. They interconnect in action. On a theoretical level there are huge disparities between them, and frequent political clashes, but they exist as the real core of the left Labour Movement, and it is the failure of left wing politics in Britain that they do not have a unified party to assist them.

Given this situation, it is indeed better and more effective for a socialist theatre group to relate to this cross section of people than to one or other of the factions who are bidding to control them. These are the people who bother to organize the shows, to get an audience in, to carry the can if the evening is a flop. They are also our major critics and our major sources of feedback. They recognize the value of raising the awareness of their workmates and neighbours, not only on single economic issues, but also on broader issues which involve political and class-consciousness, and which raise questions which are ultimately ones of Marxist theory.

A good series of events in an area can help to raise the level of militancy and can in the process give confidence and a sense of depth to the movement. A good show can and should also cheer these people up and help them to feel in touch with a larger, if loosely defined, socialist movement. This is one practical reason why I don't think that theatre groups do or should join with a party.

Single and complex issues

At this point, perhaps it would be interesting to develop one other aspect concerning the wider-issue agitational pieces which form the bulk of the output of the political companies. The broader the issue raised, the more complex the argument becomes, and the more complete the statement of the play consequently needs to be.

For example, to examine adequately the role of alcohol in the lives of Scottish workers, as I have recently attempted, demands a piece that will raise questions of alienation at work and at home, of consumerism, of the historical dissociation of Scottish workers from their place of work, of the historical failures and successes of the movement in Scotland, of the specific nature of the control over Scottish industry, and so on to the contradictions within the Scottish working class between men and women, between orange and green, between Highland and Lowland – and the processes by which the state and society create the consciousness of the individual, of him or herself, through schooling and sexual stereotyping, role playing within a group, the class's attribution of characteristics to itself, and much more besides, such as the biochemistry of alcohol in the blood stream, and the nature of drunkenness as a social device.

As becomes obvious, this issue of booze demands a work that draws into itself more facets of human nature than agitprop can begin to cope with. It begins to raise issues central to human life itself, to acquire the complexity, the depth, of a piece of what is called 'theatre'. To be believable, measurable, the characters have to be full, rounded, whole human beings, no matter how alienated their presentation.

Major questions of form present themselves; it's not enough simply to organize an argument schematically in theatrical terms. You are no longer simply dressing a piece of agitation with theatrical devices, you are trying to stretch the possibilities of theatre itself. And yet the central issue must emerge plainly, the analysis show itself clearly, or you simply end up with a slice of life as uninformative and inconclusive as *Coronation Street* or *McCoronation Street*.

In addition, the sense of the actors' cultural identity with the audience becomes vital when raising issues which are so critical of many people in the audience. A treatise dropped from on high will be worse than ineffective. It will be positively offensive. In short, what in purely agitational terms began as a broad single issue has led to the need for a new kind of theatre.

'What is theatre?'

In this situation, received notions of what theatre is begin to creep in, and to inflect the thinking of the writers and the company, and the director, towards the values of 'real theatre'. It is important to identify these received notions as the source of much confusion. 'Real theatre' in this sense is the term for the dominant mode of theatre – in our case, that of the subsidized establishment. The ideological values of that theatre are ultimately based on the ideology of a class structure and a management structure and an audience which are all opposed to the values of socialist structures, socialist theatre, and the working class. The demands of working-class audiences for a *new* kind of theatre cannot be satisfied by populist or oeuvrierist inflections of an *old*, bourgeois kind of theatre.

It is at this point that I am generally accused of inverted snobbery; but I am certain that it is actually much more difficult for a middle-class writer or performer, brought up on a diet of bourgeois cultural mystification, unleavened with the roughage of experience of working-class life, to understand that there is a serious confusion in this area. It is not impossible, just more difficult.

However, there *is* a confusion and a danger. For what is demanded in this situation is a revolutionary socialist theatre, not only in the forms of group organization, political purpose, venue and audience, and relationship with the audience; but essentially in what you actually do on the stage.

Here, it is important to invoke once again the perspective of class struggle. The public stage is a medium of expression, of communication, of activity. It is a part of the cultural 'superstructure' of society, and as such is a product of the ideological nexus of that society. The dominant ideology of our society is that of the ruling class, aided and abetted by the middle, professional, and petty bourgeois classes or sectors. But, as I have tried to show, there is an oppositional or emergent cultural ideology in the theatre, rooted in socialism and the values of the working class.

It is well to remember at this point that what happens on the public stage in Britain has for many years been controlled directly by the capitalist state in the person of the Lord Chamberlain, a servant of the Crown, not even answerable to Parliament. This control has only very recently been dropped, and that happened at a time when the theatre had reached a very low level of public signif-icance. This function will shortly be usurped by the funding authorities. We have seen the decision of the Greater Manchester Council to cut their grant to the North West Arts Association by the amount that the Arts Association promised to North-West Spanner, because they will not subsidize a Marxist group. Now the arts associations have nobly tried to resist such outside pressures, but are quite capable as state institutions of exercising those very pressures themselves in more devious ways.

Clearly, to fulfil the role of agitation on an ideological level within the working class requires a certain amount of attention to working-class forms of entertainment. I believe that in spite of the immense difficulties in specifying them, there are important and significant differences between the cultural values and traditions of the working class and those of the middle class. There are equally important differences between their respective theatre values and traditions.

There are one or two caveats. Firstly, I am not about to elaborate a proletcult thesis, that the only brand of good theatre is proletarian, and the rest should be mercilessly crushed. This kind of accusation of philistinism is groundless and is usually made by those who are trying to justify the equally philistine position of rejecting anything less aesthetic than Peter Hall. For the record, bourgeois theatre has created great, valuable works which should be performed and treasured. But this does not mean one therefore approves of capitalism any more than appreciation of Sophocles implies approval of slavery.

I am talking about a struggle within our age. No doubt good bourgeois plays will continue to be written and performed. I am not proposing to oppose them with the People's Police, I am not a member of the Gang of Four (or five if you include Bernard Levin). Secondly, I am not about to suggest that the values of the working class are, *ipso facto*, above criticism, to be endorsed and applauded in some mindless ouvrierist manner. For historical reasons, they have many appalling features.

What then are the main differences between the theatre tastes of bourgeois and working-class audiences in Britain today? I shall make some huge generalizations which are based partly on my own life, the kind of entertainment I enjoy, and partly on the last eight to ten years' experience.

Working-class and bourgeois theatre

1. *Directness.* A working-class audience likes to know exactly what you are trying to do or say to it. A middle-class audience prefers obliqueness and innuendo – it likes to feel the superiority of exercising its perception, which has been so expensively acquired, thus opening areas of ambiguity and avoiding any stark choice of attitude. In *Lay-Off*, for example, a show with the English 7:84, we spoke straight to the audiences about what we thought of the multi-nationals.

   In a factory occupation at Swinton, just outside Manchester, where we played the show, there was no problem whatsoever. It was appreciated that we said what we thought. In Murray Hall, in East Kilbride, there was no problem. But after a performance in London at Unity Theatre, a socialist publisher came up to me and said, 'I don't like to be told what to think, I preferred *Fish in the Sea*'. The national critics who saw the show felt patronized, but not the working class of Manchester – because they knew we were saying what we thought and they were prepared to weigh it up. Some critics even said they thought we were patronizing the working class; but in fact *they* were, because working-class audiences have minds of their own and they like to hear what your mind really is, not what it might be.

2. *Comedy*. Working-class audiences like laughs. Middle-class audiences in the theatre tend to think laughs make the play less serious. Working-class audiences are a bit more sophisticated on this subject. Many working-class people spend a lot of their lives making jokes about themselves and their bosses and their world as it changes. So the jokes that a working-class audience likes have got to be good new ones, not bad old ones.

   They also require a higher level of comic skill. Comedy has to be sharper, more perceptive, and more deeply related to their lives. The Royal Court audience, on the other hand, doesn't laugh very much, and most audiences for plays in the West End have to be satisfied with mechanical gags or weak jokes, delivered by a famous person.

   Much working-class comedy is sexist, racist, even anti-working class. We all know the jokes about big tits and Pakis and Paddies and the dockers and the strikers – there are countless jokes current in those areas. Therefore, without being pompous about it, comedy has to be critically assessed.

   The bourgeois comedy, largely of manners or of intellect, tends to assume there is a correct way of doing things – that is, the way of the average broadminded commuter. Working-class comedy is more anarchic and more fantastical – the difference between the wit and wisdom of the Duke of Edinburgh and Ken Dodd.

3. *Music*. Working-class audiences like music in shows, live and lively, popular, tuneful, and well-played. They like beat sometimes, more than the sound of banks of violins, and they like melody above all. There's a long submerged folk tradition – which emerged recently as a two-million sale for a song called 'Mull of Kintyre'. Standards of performance in music are demanded and many individuals in working-class audiences are highly critical about the music in shows. But the music is enjoyable for itself, for emotional release, and for the neatness of expression of a good lyric, or a good tune.

   Middle-class theatregoers see the presence of music generally as a threat, again, to seriousness – unless of course, it is opera, when it's different. Big musicals, lush sounds, and cute tunes are okay in their place, but to convey the emotional heart of a genuine situation in a pop song is alien to most National Theatre-goers. Music is there for a bit of a romp to make it a jolly evening.

4. *Emotion*. In our experience, a working-class audience is more open to emotion on the stage than a middle-class audience, who get embarrassed by it. The critics call emotion on stage mawkish, sentimental, etc. Of course, working-class audiences can also love sentimentality. In fact I quite enjoy a bit of it myself, at the right moment, so does everybody, but emotion is more likely to be apologised for in Bromley than in the Rhondda Valley.

5. *Variety*. Most of the traditional forms of working-class entertainment that have grown up seem to have an element of variety – of *kinds* of performing. They seem to be able to switch from

a singer to a comedian, to a juggler, to a band, to a chorus number, to a conjurer, to a sing-along, to bingo, to wrestling, to striptease, and then back again to a singer, and a comedian and a grand 'altogether now' finale, with great ease. If we look at music hall, variety theatre, club entertainment, the Ceilidh in Scotland, the *Noson Lawen* in Wales, panto, and through to the *Morecambe and Wise Show* on the box, you can see what I'm talking about.

The middle-class theatre seems to have lost this tradition, round about 1630, when it lost the working class, and it has never rediscovered it. Since the dominant strain of British middle class theatre now can be traced back, to Ibsen by way of Rattigan and Shaw, the traditional structure is one of two or three long acts of concentrated spoken drama usually with no more than five or six main characters. The actors communicate the plot by total immersion in the character they are playing, and move around on a set or sets made to look as much like the real thing as possible.

The 'variety' within this kind of theatre is more a question of variation of pace and intensity while doing essentially the same thing throughout. I utter no value judgements on these formal elements, merely note that the second is no less bizarre in its essence than the first, and one might be forgiven for seeing more creative possibilities in the first. However, the received opinion is that the second is more serious and is more capable of high art.

6. *Effect*. Working-class audiences demand more moment-by-moment effect from their entertainers. If an act is not good enough they let it be known, and if it's boring they chat amongst themselves until it gets less boring, or they leave, or they throw things. They like clear, worked-for results – laughs, respectful silence, rapt attention to a song, tears, thunderous applause. Middle-class audiences have been trained to sit still in the theatre for long periods, not talk, and bear with a slow build-up to great dramatic moments, or slow build-ups to nothing at all, as the case may be. Through TV and radio and records, working-class audiences have come to expect a high standard of success in gaining effects. They know it comes from skill and hard work, and they expect hard work and skill.

7. *Immediacy*. This element is more open to argument, but my experience of working-class entertainment is that it is in subject matter much closer to the audience's lives and experiences than, say, plays at the Royal Shakespeare Company are to middle-class audiences. Of course there is a vast corpus of escapist art provided for the working class; but the meat of a good comic is the audience's life and experience, from Will Fife to Billy Connolly, or from Tommy Handley to Ken Dodd. Certainly in clubs, pantos, and variety shows, this is the material that goes down best. A middle-class audience can be more speculative, metaphysical, and often prefers the subject to be at arm's length from their lives. They prefer paradigms or elaborate images to immediacy – the interesting parallel to, say, a comedy about the decline of the private sector.

8. *Localism*. Closely connected with immediacy. Of course, through television, working-class audiences have come to expect stuff about Cockneys, or Geordies, or Liver Birds, and have become polyglot in a way that would not have been very likely some years ago. But the best response in working-class audiences comes from character and events with a local feel.

Middle-class audiences have a great claim to cosmopolitanism; the bourgeoisie does have a certain internationality, interchangeability. I can't imagine Liverpool Playhouse crowds reacting very differently from say Leeds Playhouse or Royal Lyceum, Edinburgh, audiences to the latest Alan Ayckbourn comedy. They all get it, anyway, just as they all get imitations of the National Theatre and the Royal Shakespeare's 'Aldwych Greatest Hits'. This bourgeois 'internationality' must be distinguished from true internationalism, which is an ideological attribute that ebbs and flows in the working class alarmingly, but which can be there.

9. *Localism*, not only of material, but also deriving from a sense of identity with the performer, even if coming from outside the locality – a sense not of knowing his or her soul, but that he or she cares enough about being in that place with that audience and knows something about them. Hence the early success of Billy Connolly in Glasgow, of Max Boyce in South Wales, before they began to realize their commercial assets, and to peddle sentimental fantasies of this experience to the cosmopolitan fun-packagers. However, working men's clubs in the North of England depend on this sense of locality, of cultural identity with the audience. But there are few middle-class audiences who know or care where John Gielgud, for example, comes from. They don't mind if he is a bit disdainful when he's in Bradford: he's a great man, an artist, and he exists on another planet.

Learning and criticizing

There are many other broad general differences but these are enough to indicate that, if a socialist theatre company is interested in contacting working-class audiences with some entertainment, they can't simply walk in with a critical production of Schiller, or a play written and performed in a style designed to appeal to the bourgeoisie of Bromley, or even the intelligentsia of NW1.

A masterpiece might survive of course. I'm not saying that the working class are incapable of appreciating great art in the bourgeois tradition. They may well be, but if a socialist theatre company or a socialist playwright wants to speak to the working class, then they would do well to learn something of its language, and not assume that the language of bourgeois theatre of the twentieth century is all that is worthy of pouring from their lips. This is why I think it is much harder for a middle-class intellectual to grasp the demands of theatre of and for the working class, and why there is a confusion of form in the area of the wider-issue agitational play.

But there is a danger that in schematically drawing up a list of some features of working-class entertainment, I am indulging in what is called 'tailism' – that is, trailing along behind the tastes of the working class, debased as they are by capitalism, and merely 'translating' an otherwise bourgeois message into this inferior language. It is a real danger, and I have seen people with the best intentions falling into it. But this is not the case, for two important points do emerge.

One is, as I have already said, that these features of working-class entertainment must be handled critically. Directness can lead to simplification. Comedy can be racist, sexist, even anti-working class. Music can become mindlessness. Emotion can become manipulative and can obscure judgement. Variety can lead to distintegration of meaning and pettiness. Effect for effect's sake can lead to trivialization. Immediacy and localism can close the mind to the rest of the world, lead to chauvinism. And a sense of identity with the performer can lead to nauseating, ingratiating performances with no dignity or perspective.

But given a critical attitude to these features of working-class entertainment, they contain within them the seeds of a revitalized, new kind of theatre, capable of expressing the fullness of meaning of working-class life today, and not only working-class life. They are some of the first sounds in a new language of theatre that can never be fully articulate until socialism is created in this country. But before then we can work to extend those first sounds into something like speech by making more and more demands of them, by attempting bolder projects with them, and above all, by learning from our audiences whether we are doing it right or not.

So I have discussed two areas of activity for socialist theatre workers. Within the bourgeois theatre institutions, challenging the hegemony of the bourgeois ideology, and outside it, presenting interventionist agitational pieces, some on single issues, some on issues that make great demands, both of and for the working class. But as the demands on a language of this kind of theatre increase, so the third area, which is perhaps the most important, becomes possible – the creation of a counter-theatre, an emergent, truly oppositional theatre, based on the working class, which will grow in richness and in confidence until it eventually displaces the dominance of bourgeois theatre in late capitalism.

This, of course, depends on more than hard work in the theatre. I offer it to you however as the perspective within which I have been working for the last eight or ten years, and which I think is shared by many fellow-workers in political theatre.

Note

Originally published in *Theatre Quarterly*, 9(35) (1979): 43–54.

4.8 Fortynine Asides for a Tragic Theatre (1986)

HOWARD BARKER

W E ARE LIVING THE extinction of official socialism. When the opposition loses its politics, it must root in art.

The time for satire is ended. Nothing can be satirized in the authoritarian state. It is culture reduced to playing the spoons. The stockbroker laughs, and the satirist plays the spoons.

The authoritarian art form is the musical.

The accountant is the new censor. The accountant claps his hands at the full theatre. The official socialist also hankers for the full theatre. But full for what?

In an age of populism, the progressive artist is the artist who is not afraid of silence.

The baying of an audience in pursuit of unity is a sound of despair.

In a bad time laughter is a rattle of fear.

How hard it is to sit in a silent theatre.

There is silence and silence. Like the colour black, there are colours within silence.

The silence of compulsion is the greatest achievement of the actor and the dramatist.

We must overcome the urge to do things in unison. To chant together, to hum banal tunes together, is not collectivity.

A carnival is not a revolution.

After the carnival, after the removal of the masks, you are precisely who you were before. After the tragedy, you are not certain who you are.

Ideology is the outcome of pain.

Some people want to know pain. There is no truth on the cheap.

There are more people in pursuit of knowledge than the accountants will admit.

There is always the possibility of an avalanche of truth-seekers.

Art is a problem. The man or woman who exposes himself to art exposes himself to another problem.

It is an error typical of the accountant to think there is no audience for the problem.

Some people want to grow in their souls.

But not all people. Consequently, tragedy is elitist.

Because you cannot address everybody, you may as well address the impatient.

The opposition in art has nothing but the quality of its imagination.

The only possible resistance to a culture of banality is quality.

Because they try to debase language, the voice of the actor becomes an instrument of revolt.

The actor is both the greatest resource of freedom and the subtlest instrument of repression.

If language is restored to the actor he ruptures the imaginative blockade of the culture. If he speaks banality he piles up servitude.

Tragedy liberates language from banality. It returns poetry to speech.

Tragedy is not about reconciliation. Consequently, it is the art form for our time.

Tragedy resists the trivialization of experience, which is the project of the authoritarian regime.

People will endure anything for a grain of truth.

But not all people. Therefore a tragic theatre will be elitist.

Tragedy was impossible as long as hope was confused with comfort. Suddenly tragedy is possible again.

When a child fell under a bus they called it a tragedy. On the contrary, it was an accident. We have had a drama of accidents masquerading as tragedy.

The tragedies of the 1960s were not tragedies but failures of the social services.

The theatre must start to take its audience seriously. It must stop telling them stories they can understand.

It is not to insult an audience to offer it ambiguity.

The narrative form is dying in our hands.

In tragedy, the audience is disunited. It sits alone. It suffers alone.

In the endless drizzle of false collectivity, tragedy restores pain to the individual.

You emerge from tragedy equipped against lies. After the musical, you are anyone's fool.

Tragedy offends the sensibilities. It drags the unconscious into the public place. It therefore silences the banging of the tambourine which characterizes the authoritarian and the labourist culture alike.

It dares to be beautiful. Who talks of beauty in the theatre any more? They think it is to do with the costumes.

Beauty, which is possible only in tragedy, subverts the lie of human squalor which lies at the heart of the new authoritarianism.

When society is officially philistine, the complexity of tragedy becomes a source of resistance.

Because they have bled life out of the word freedom, the word justice attains a new significance. Only tragedy makes justice its preoccupation.

Since no art form generates action, the most appropriate art for a culture on the edge of extinction is one that stimulates pain.

The issues are never too complex for expression.

It is never too late to forestall the death of Europe.

Note

Originally published in the *Guardian*, 10 February 1986, this version was published in Howard Barker, *Arguments for a Theatre*, 3rd edn, Manchester: Manchester University Press, 1997 [1989], pp. 17–19.

4.9 Re-acting (to) Empire (1996)

HELEN GILBERT AND JOANNE TOMPKINS

IN 1907, *THE THEATRE*, a short-lived Sydney newspaper, reported on 'Seditious Drama' in the Philippines. It noted that the Filipinos, governed at that time by the United States, had 'turned their stage to a seditious purpose, though the authorities [had] not seen fit to censor it, except for the more daring of the dramas intended to stir up the native spirit' (1907: 17). As a common device to thwart American propaganda, the Filipinos used politicised costumes:

> [They are] so coloured and draped that at a given signal or cue the actors and actresses rush together, apparently without design, and stand swaying in the centre of the stage, close to the footlights, their combination forming a living, moving, stirring picture of the Filipino flag. Only an instant or so does the phantom last, but that one instant is enough to bring the entire house to its feet with yells and cries that are blood-curdling in their ferocious delight, while the less quick-witted Americans in the audience are wondering what the row is about.
>
> (ibid: 17)

Such a display, understood in political terms by the Filipinos in the audience and *mis*understood by the Americans – the targets of the act of political resistance – provides an example of theatre's politicality in a post-colonial context in which performance functions as an anti-imperial tool. This book focuses on the methods by which post-colonial drama resists imperialism and its effects. We isolate possible ways to read and view theatre texts from around the post-colonial world as well as ways to interpret the strategies by which playwrights, actors, directors, musicians, and designers rework a historical moment or a character or an imperial text or even a theatre building.

Post-colonialism

At a time when the prefix 'post' has been affixed to almost every concept, state of being, or theory (for instance, postmodernism, post-feminism, post-structuralism, post-industrialism), the hazards of using a term with such a prefix are great. While it risks being relegated to the increasingly less useful and less meaningful 'post-box' of trite expressions, 'post-colonial', we feel, is a relevant term, and certainly more relevant than its alternatives: the dated and homogenising Commonwealth Literature; New Literatures in English, very few of which are 'new'; and, as the Modern Languages Association terms them, Literatures other than British and American, a categorisation which perpetuates these literatures' already well-ingrained marginalisation from the countries who have historically declared themselves as constituting the metropolitan cultural centre or mainstream. Post-colonialism is often too narrowly defined. The term – according to a too-rigid etymology – is frequently misunderstood as a temporal concept meaning the time after colonisation has ceased, or the time following the politically determined Independence Day on which a country breaks away from its governance by another state. Not a naive teleological sequence which supersedes colonialism,[1] post-colonialism is, rather, an engagement with and contestation of colonialism's discourses, power structures, and social hierarchies. Colonisation is insidious: it invades far more than political chambers and extends well beyond independence celebrations. Its effects shape language, education, religion, artistic sensibilities, and, increasingly, popular culture. A theory of post-colonialism must, then, respond to more than the merely chronological construction of post-independence, and to more than just the discursive experience of imperialism. In Alan Lawson's words, post-colonialism is a 'politically motivated historical-analytical movement [which] engages with, resists, and seeks to dismantle the effects of colonialism in the material, historical, cultural-political, pedagogical, discursive, and textual domains' (Lawson 1992: 156). Inevitably, post-colonialism addresses *reactions to* colonialism in a context that is not necessarily determined by temporal constraints: post-colonial plays, novels, verse, and films then become textual/cultural expressions of resistance to colonisation. As a critical discourse, therefore, post-colonialism is both a textual effect and a reading strategy. Its theoretical practice often operates on two levels, attempting at once to elucidate the post-coloniality which inheres in certain texts, and to unveil and deconstruct any continuing colonialist power structures and institutions.

While the time frames of both post-colonialism and post-modernism generally intersect, and postmodern literary devices are often found in post-colonial texts, the two cannot be equated. Part of postmodernism's brief is the dismantling of the often unwritten but frequently invoked rules of genre, authority, and value. Post-colonialism's agenda, however, is more specifically political: to dismantle the hegemonic boundaries and the determinants that create unequal relations of power based on binary oppositions such as 'us and them', 'first world and third world', 'white and black', 'coloniser and colonised'. Postmodern texts are certainly political, but post-colonial texts embrace a more specifically political aim: that of the continued destabilisation of the cultural and political authority of imperialism. Post-colonialism, then, has more affinity with feminist and class-based discourses than with postmodernism, even if post-colonialism and postmodernism employ similar literary tropes.

Within its specific agenda, post-colonialism's effects can be wide-ranging. Post-colonial literature is, according to Stephen Slemon, 'a form of cultural criticism and cultural critique: a mode of disidentifying whole societies from the sovereign codes of cultural organisation, and an inherently dialectical intervention in the hegemonic production of cultural meaning' (Slemon 1987: 14). Post-colonial *theatre*'s capacity to intervene publicly in social organisation and to critique political structures can be more extensive than the relatively isolated circumstances of written narrative and poetry; theatre practitioners, however, also run a greater risk of political intervention in their activities in the forms of censorship and imprisonment, to which Rendra in Indonesia, Ngũgĩ wa Thiong'o in Kenya, and countless South African dramatists can attest. While banning books is often an 'after the fact' action, the more public disruption of a live theatre presentation can literally 'catch' actors and playwrights in the act of political subversion.

Post-colonial studies are engaged in a two-part, often paradoxical project of chronicling similarities of experience while at the same time registering the formidable differences that mark each former colony. Laura Chrisman cautions that criticism of a nation's contemporary literature cannot be isolated from the imperial history which produced the contemporary version of the nation (Chrisman 1990: 38). Shiva Naipaul, a Trinidadian writer, puts it more succinctly: 'No literature is free-floating. Its vitality springs, initially, from its rootedness in a specific type of world' (Naipaul 1971: 122). Post-colonial criticism must carefully contextualise the *similarities* between, for example, the influence of ritual on the Ghanaian and Indian theatrical traditions, at the same time as it acknowledges significant *divergences* in the histories, cultures, languages, and politics of these two cultures. It is the particular attention to 'difference' that marks post-colonialism's agency. Alan Lawson and Chris Tiffin situate the politics and possibilities of difference in a useful construction:

> 'Difference', which in colonialist discourse connotes a remove from normative European practice, and hence functions as a marker of subordination, is for post-colonial analysis the correspondent marker of identity, voice, and hence empowerment. Difference is not the measure by which the European episteme fails to comprehend the actual self-naming and articulate subject. Moreover, difference demands deference and self-location ...: not all differences are the same. (Lawson and Tiffin 1994: 230)

A theory of post-colonialism that fails to recognise this distinction between 'differences' will recreate the spurious hierarchies, misreadings, silencings, and ahistoricisms that are part of the imperial enterprise. Critiques of post-colonialism are frequently responses to arguments based primarily on attempts to homogenise texts, histories, and cultures.

Much discussion surrounds which countries ought to be considered part of the post-colonial world. Since former states of the Soviet Union have adopted the expression to refer to post-glasnost, 'post-colonialism' is not specific to a particular imperial regime, even though it often refers to the former colonies of the British Empire, the focus – with some exceptions – of this study. The British Empire was the largest modern empire, and its vestiges still exist today in a reconfigured organisation of former commonwealth states which oversees political alliances and trade discussions among the former colonies. Many of these former colonies now possess a linguistic heritage that is based on the English language. While English is not the only language of post-colonial writing[2] – in fact the incorporation of a variety of tongues is vital to post-colonial literatures – it is the base language of most of the texts discussed here.

Debates within the field of post-colonialism are themselves fraught with division and difference, as the divergences between several recent critical texts illustrate. The most important theoretical treatment to date is *The Empire Writes Back: Theory and Practice in Post-Colonial Literatures* (1989) by Bill Ashcroft, Gareth Griffiths, and Helen Tiffin, which introduces many approaches to post-colonial literatures, concentrating particularly on language. This text was followed in 1995 by their *The Post-Colonial Studies Reader*. The post-colonial reader edited by Patrick Williams and Laura Chrisman, *Colonial Discourse and Post-Colonial Theory* (1993), is one of many readings of the field that questions the claim that various regions and/or constituencies have to the post-colonial umbrella.[3] Heavily privileging Edward Said's *Orientalism* and the construction of the Oriental 'other' as the core text/concept of the field, this reader discounts settler colonies where, among other locations, Said's Orientalism can be said to be inadequately historicised, or even inapplicable. Generally overlooking indigenous peoples from the settler-invader regions, this reader delimits the post-colonial world to an organisation that is curiously devoid of the controversy and paradox that is inevitable and constructive in the experience of post-imperial states. The essentialist[4] arguments that many critics have adopted concerning who may and may not participate in post-colonial discourse often amount to disagreements concerning power versus impotence, and particularly contests over who can claim a more impressive victim position; the irony in these disputes is that such struggles merely invert (unproductively) the hegemony upon which imperialism is based. It seems more reasonable and productive to capitalise on the differences between former colonies while not losing sight of their similarities.

Chris Tiffin and Alan Lawson argue that 'Imperial textuality appropriates, distorts, erases, but it also *contains*' (1994: 6). The imperial project contains cultures/subjects in order to control them, but no former colony is as simply circumscribed as colonial discourse would have it: each post-colonial political, historical, linguistic, and cultural situation inevitably becomes much more convoluted than is figured by the coloniser. Discussions of some of these intricacies have been drawn out, further complicated, and fruitfully enhanced by, among other theorists, Homi Bhabha, whose work elucidates the ambivalent psychological positioning of both the colonised *and* the coloniser. Contrary to the assumptions inherent in the binary opposition of coloniser and colonised, Bhabha (1984) maintains that the colonised is never *always impotent*; the coloniser is never *always powerful*. The ambivalence inherent in these binaries assists in breaking down the constructed limitations of all binary oppositions. In, for instance, the binary of 'white' and 'black', 'white' is not only defined in terms of 'blackness', but its reliance upon a conceptual knowledge of blackness also perpetually destabilises the power invested in 'white' and not in 'black'. Bhabha's work offers valuable assistance in dismantling binaries (and their correlative power structures) by recognising their inevitable ambivalences. As Ashcroft, Griffiths, and Tiffin point out, 'The term, "post-colonial" is resonant with all the ambiguity and complexity of the many different cultural experiences it implicates' (1995: 2).

There are at least two types of former colonies among the remains of the British Empire. The first, settler-invader colonies, are comprised of land masses that were, at the time of initial imperial explorations, proclaimed (usually with the full knowledge of the presence of indigenous people) to be empty, nearly empty, or peopled by compliant 'natives'.[5] As settlers invaded the territories, usually driving out the local inhabitants, massacring them, or pressing them into service, these colonies could conveniently forget about the presence of 'natives' altogether. The particular position that such settler-invader colonies (Australia, Canada, New Zealand/Aotearoa,[6] and in some cases, South Africa) occupy is extremely problematic: they neither quite satisfy the requirements for acceptance into the 'first' and 'old' world of Europe, nor are they 'poor' enough to be included in the economically and politically determined 'third world', a term that is still used on occasion to define the post-colonial world. The settler-invader colonies are located in an awkward 'second world' position (Lawson 1994) that is neither one nor the other; they have been colonised by Europe at the same time that they themselves have colonised indigenous peoples who experienced (and frequently continue to experience) the constraints on freedom, language, religion, and social organisation that also litter the histories of many of the second type of former colony, the 'occupation' colonies. These include India, parts of South-East Asia, west and central Africa, and many islands of the Caribbean.[7] The settler-invader colonies share many similar subject positions, and historical and geographical elisions with the 'occupation' colonies (which are often considered to be more *bona fide* post-colonial cultures than settler-invader societies). The depth to which imperial rhetoric has been established in both types of colonies complicates attempts to remove the constraints of subordination, inferiority, and insignificance that the colonised subject inevitably experiences.

Post-colonialism and drama

This study considers plays from Australia, Canada, India, Ireland, New Zealand, various countries in Africa, parts of South-East Asia, and the Caribbean. Ireland, Britain's oldest colony, is often considered inappropriate to the post-colonial grouping, partly because it lies just off Europe. Yet Ireland's centuries-old political and economic oppression at the hands of the British – and its resistance to such control – fits well within the post-colonial paradigm. We do not consider the United States, also once a British colony, as post-colonial because the political and military might that the United States wields in its role as global 'superpower' has long since severed its connections with the historical and cultural marginality that the other former colonies share. American *neo-imperialism* and the neo-imperial activities of several former colonies are, however, not exempt from examination here. Neo-imperialism, which frequently takes the form of apparently mutually lucrative industrialisation projects, tourism, or aid programmes, typically repeats many of the same power games and struggles of initial imperial endeavours. For a very different reason, this text does not analyse Indian drama to any great detail. Since its history/practice is extremely complex, it is impossible to do justice to Indian drama in a broadly comparative study.[8] Moreover, the varieties of drama, dance, languages, and cultures that have influenced Indian theatre are too vast to consider in a text other than one devoted to just India. For the same reason, some sectors of Asia will not be considered as fully here as the drama from other parts of the former empire. Many of our arguments are nevertheless valid in these contexts and we hope that readers will find this an opportunity to test our theories, rather than to condemn this text for any perceived 'anomalies'.

When Europeans settled a colony, one of the earliest signs of established culture/'civilisation' was the presentation of European drama which, according to official records, obliterated for many years any indigenous performance forms:[9] in 1682, for instance, a playhouse was established in Jamaica and functioned until slaves were freed in 1838 (Wright 1937: 6). India boasted a proliferation of grand proscenium arch theatres from 1753, and five full-size public theatres by 1831, the popularity of which prompted the erection of many rival private theatres financed by rajahs (Mukherjee 1982: viii; Yajnik 1970: 86). Neither the Jamaican theatre nor the Indian theatres were designed for the indigenous peoples or transported slaves; rather, they were built for the entertainment of the British officers. The first play staged in Canada was Marc Lescarbot's 1606 *Théâtre Neptune en la Nouvelle France*, presented by French explorers. It included words in various native Canadian languages, as well as references to Canadian geography, within a more typically French style of play (Goldie 1989: 186). The nature of theatre designed for colonial officers and/or troops (and the nature of colonialism itself) required that the plays produced in these countries be reproductions of imperial models in style, theme, and content. Various elements of 'local colour' were of course included, so that an early settler play might position a native character in the same way that the nineteenth-century British theatre figured the drunken Irishman: as an outsider, someone who was in some central way ridiculous or intolerable. While it may have appeared that the deviations from the imperial plots were generally isolated to issues of setting and occasional minor characters, sometimes the plays produced in the colonies transformed mere 'local colour' into much more resistant discourses. In the case of Australia, the performance of the first western play in 1789, George Farquhar's *The Recruiting Officer*, provided an early opportunity for political resistance. The cast, composed of transported convicts, used the play's burlesque trial and military theme as an apt expression of life in a colony that was itself predicated on punishment, and they also wrote a new epilogue to Farquhar's play, calling attention to their plight. Colonial theatre, then, can be viewed ambivalently as a potential agent of social reform and as an avenue for political disobedience.

Even though Ola Rotimi, a Nigerian playwright, maintains that drama is the best artistic medium for Africa because it is not alien in form, as is the novel (Rotimi in Burness 1985: 12), most post-colonial criticism overlooks drama, perhaps because of its apparently impure form: playscripts are only a part of a theatre experience, and performance is therefore difficult to document.[10] Given that dramatic and performance theories, particularly those developed in conjunction with Brechtian, feminist, and cultural studies criticism, have much to offer post-colonial debates about language, interpellation, subject-formation, representation, and forms of resistance, this marginalisation of drama suggests a considerable gap in post-colonial studies. Examining drama through the conceptual frameworks developed in post-colonial studies involves more than a simple and unproblematic transposition of reading strategies because some of the signifying systems through which plays 'mean' are vastly different to those of texts not designed for performance. Hence, although this study seeks to demonstrate how its subject area might be illuminated by the chosen theoretical approach, it also aims to extend the current limits of that approach. In this respect, theories of drama and performance have much to add to debates about how imperial power is articulated and/or contested.

Our field of inquiry falls into three main sections that address post-colonial performance: dramatic language (vocal and visual, as expressed through the performing body), the arrangement of theatrical space and time, and the manipulation of narrative and performative conventions of drama. Within this field, we inevitably focus on the connections between form and content which a politicised approach to theatre always recognises.

Interculturalism and anthropological approaches to theatre

The drama from the 'outposts of empire' has not been entirely ignored by critics from the centres of Europe and the United States: theatre anthropologists and interculturalists have examined the theatre forms and styles of other cultures and often embraced the possibilities inherent in adopting them for use in a western context. Yet an anthropological approach to drama (such as that espoused by Victor Turner, Eugenio Barba, and Richard Schechner) is designed to enumerate the similarities between all cultures without recognising their highly significant differences. In this style of analysis, several plays and/or theatre cultures are usually compared in order to highlight the likenesses in various rituals or practices, which Anuradha Kapur deems a result of postmodernism:

> In mounting an attack on mimesis, postmodernism claims as its territory non-mimetic forms from all over the world. Thus theatre from the 'Third World' comes to be defined by the needs and uses of postmodernism; forms from different cultural contexts become evacuated of subject matter and are seen as a series of formal options. (1990: 27)

Interculturalism and postmodernism intersect at the point of ahistorical, acultural synthesis that can also be perceived to be neo-colonial, particularly as practised in the United States. An example from Gautam Dasgupta, a critic located in New York, is revealing: writing of interculturalism, he invokes the ethos of the Indian *Vedas* and the refrain from a recent American pop song. Arguing that interculturalism recognises personal as well as public spheres of influence, he concludes without obvious irony that 'We are the world' (1991: 332). This imperialist notion that the United States *is* the world emanates from an insidious pop song that, while ostensibly raising money for starving people in Africa, reinscribes western (particularly American) privilege/power, by stressing the west's capacity to do good works. This type of intercultural approach is obviously self-centred: it often involves the parasitical activity of taking that which seems useful and unique from another culture and leaving that host culture with little except the dubious opportunity to *seem to have been* associated with a powerful and influential nation(s). Not all intercultural theorists are ethnocentric: Rustom Bharucha (1993) and others are acutely aware of the political ramifications of failing to acknowledge a country's historical, political, and cultural specificity. Bharucha attacks critics and practitioners such as Schechner, Barba, and Peter Brook for mining 'exotic' – usually 'third world' – cultures for theatrical raw materials, much in the way that multinational corporations have been known to exploit materials and cheap labour from the developing world, conveniently overlooking the safety and security of the local people and the pollution of their land. As well as ignoring the differences among and between peoples who have been colonised, the anthropological approach to theatre also moves perilously close to universalist criticism whereby a text is said to speak to readers all around the world because it espouses, for example, universal principles of life. Texts which apparently radiate such 'universal truths' have usually been removed from their social and historical setting. Although it is a favourite catch-cry of theatre critics, the 'universal theme' allows no appreciation of cultural difference.

Markers of post-colonial drama

The apparent unity of the British Empire (iconised by such devices as the vast pink surfaces on many classroom maps indicating the dominion of the Queen of England) has been substantially denied by post-colonial texts. Often, post-colonial literatures refuse closure to stress the provisionality of post-colonial identities, reinforcing Helen Tiffin's comment that 'Decolonization is process, not arrival' (1987: 17). The absence of a 'conclusion' to the decolonising project does not represent a failure; rather it points to the recombinant ways in which colonised subjects now define themselves. Situated within the hybrid forms of various cultural systems, such subjects can usefully exploit what Diana Brydon calls 'contamination' (1990), whereby the influence from several cultures can be figured as positive rather than negative, as for instance, is miscegenation.

For the purposes of this study, we define post-colonial performance as including the following features:

- acts that respond to the experience of imperialism, whether directly or indirectly;
- acts performed for the continuation and/or regeneration of the colonised (and sometimes pre-contact) communities;
- acts performed with the awareness of, and sometimes the incorporation of, post-contact forms; and
- acts that interrogate the hegemony that underlies imperial representation.[11]

Building on existing work done in the separate fields of post-colonial and performance studies, this book develops specific post-colonial performative and theoretical frameworks in relation to selected plays from a range of countries. It does not attempt to categorise texts, regions, types of plays, historical approaches to drama; to identify the major playwrights of different countries; or to discuss national theatre traditions separately, country by country.[12] Readers should be able to use the frameworks we establish as reading strategies for interpreting a range of post-colonial playtexts, and for deconstructing imperialist thought, practices, and regimes. One of the aims of this book is to teach readers and audiences to re-see or re-read texts in order to recognise their strategic political agendas, since, as Ian Steadman notes in the context of South African theatre, 'the real potential of dramatic art lies in its ability to teach people *how* to think' widely (1991: 78), beyond the narrow parameters of the status quo, of political oppressiveness, and even of political correctness. To this end, we are particularly concerned with the intersection of dramatic theory with theories of race in post-colonial contexts; in the varieties of feminisms, including many forms of third world feminism through which the gendered body can be described; in the body, the voice, and the stage space as sites of resistance to imperial hegemonies; and in the deployment of theatricalised cultural practices such as ritual and carnival to subvert imposed canonical traditions. Accordingly, Chapter 1 outlines a process of canonical counter-discourse through which imperial/classical texts are no longer automatically privileged at the expense of other discourses. Chapter 2 contextualises ritual and carnival, two forms that intersect with and reconfigure drama in decidedly non-western ways. How history and language are articulated in post-colonial drama and how they reshape theatrical texts are the focus of Chapters 3 and 4. Historical recuperation is one of the crucial aims and effects of many post-colonial plays, which frequently tell the other side of the conquering whites' story in order to contest the official version of history that is preserved in imperialist texts. Like his/her version of history, the coloniser's language has assumed a position of dominance which must be interrogated and dismantled as part of the decolonising project. Theatrical manipulations of the English language can significantly amplify the political effects of a play, since, according to Bill Ashcroft, post-colonial adaptations of English have managed to 'relocate the "centre" of the English language by *decentring* it' (1987: 117). Other modes of communicating, such as song and music, also destabilise the political position of spoken English as the dominant transmitter of meaning. The body in its various colonial and post-colonial contexts is explored in Chapter 5, which pays particular heed to the ways in which theatre can recuperate the disintegrated and dissociated body characteristic of colonialism. Finally, Chapter 6 surveys contemporary manifestations of neo-imperialism, with a particular focus on the effects of tourism and the globalisation of the media.

The colonised subject exists in a complex representational matrix, variously situated between opposing forces (in the settler-invader cultures) or figured in opposition to the imperial powers (in occupation cultures as well as in indigenous cultures within settler-invader countries). Theatre's three-dimensional live context further complicates representations of the colonised subject so that interpreting post-colonial drama requires a careful analysis of multiple sign systems. This text takes up such issues to provide ways of re-acting to the imperial hegemonies that continue to be manifest throughout the world.

Notes

1. Our distinction between 'colonialism' and 'imperialism' follows the definitions Edward Said has delineated in *Culture and Imperialism*: ' "imperialism" means the practice, the theory, and the attitudes of a dominating metropolitan centre ruling a distant territory; "colonialism", which is almost always a consequence of imperialism, is the implanting of settlements on distant territory' (1994: 8). While both imperialism and colonialism can also take place on local territory (witness Ireland in the British Empire), these terms are generally useful. Imperialism, then, is the larger enterprise, but colonialism can be more insidious.

2. The former colonies of Spain, France, and Portugal, to name just a few, exercise similar resistant strategies to imperial forces, using hybrid forms of the dominant, colonising languages.

3. See also Hodge and Mishra (1991).

4. 'Essentialism', when combined with Spivak's modifying adjective, 'strategic' (1988: 205), becomes a tool by which marginalised peoples can deliberately foreground constructed difference to claim a speaking position. Otherwise, essentialism problematically appeals to absolute difference without an awareness of 'similarity' in the broader historical and cultural paradigm.

5. This term must be clarified. While all people born in a particular place are 'natives' of that country, we use 'native' to refer more specifically to the indigenous inhabitants of the settler-invader colonies, those people who were already living in a particular location when the Europeans arrived. 'Indian', the historical name for indigenous North Americans, is a misnomer instituted by Christopher Columbus who thought, on seeing their skin colour, that he had indeed found the easier route to India that he was seeking. This term has been fortified by Hollywood-type representations of indigenous peoples in 'Cowboy and Indian' movies. 'First Nations' is a term adopted by Canada's indigenous people in a politically astute move that reminds other North Americans that the land was already occupied when Europeans claimed it. More recently, 'Aboriginal Canadians' has been used to underscore that chronology: the term 'aboriginal' means 'from the beginning'. In contrast to the Aborigines of Australia, Aboriginal Canadians have chosen this name themselves rather than having had it given to them by white invaders. In the North American context, we use 'Indian' in the same way that Daniel Francis uses it in *The Imaginary Indian* (1992): to signify white *representations* of natives. We use 'native' or 'First Nations' or 'indigenous peoples' to represent the people themselves.

6. New Zealand is frequently also recognised by its Maori name, 'Aotearoa', meaning 'the land of the long white cloud'.

7. The Caribbean region is a special case, comprised of islands/territories which have been at once both settler and occupation colonies. After imperial campaigns largely annihilated indigenous inhabitants of the area, the European colonists repopulated many islands with slave and indentured labour from Africa, India, and other places. Most of these colonies were then governed from afar until the latter half of the twentieth century, setting up different relationships than with other settler societies. We use the term 'West Indies' to indicate the English-speaking (ex)colonies of the area, while 'Caribbean' refers to the wider cultural/geographical region.

8. Indian theatre history dates back to the *Natyashastra*, the ancient Sanskrit theory of drama, which was written down by Bharata approximately fifteen hundred years ago. Bharata did not know how long the *Natyashastra* had already existed as an oral text before he transcribed it (Rangacharya 1971: 2). It is also very difficult to study Indian theatre texts since few are published in English.

9. In all probability, they were still happening underground.

10. Our definition of drama and our theoretical discussions also incorporate other performance events (such as dance) even though most of the texts we examine are 'plays'.

11. In order to schematise our study, this generalised definition is inevitable. There are undoubtedly many examples of post-colonial performance which exceed the parameters outlined and we encourage readers to pursue such works.

12. While we attempt to ground our analyses of plays in their (different) historical contexts, it is not always possible for a variety of reasons. Particular texts and their production histories can be explored independently through reviews, articles, interviews, and books focused on individual playwrights and/or specific national theatres.

Bibliography

Ashcroft, B. (1987) 'Language Issues Facing Commonwealth Writers: A Reply to D'Costa', *Journal of Commonwealth Literature*, 22(1), pp. 99–118.

Ashcroft, B., Griffiths, G. and Tiffin, H. (1989) *The Empire Writes Back: Theory and Practice in Post-Colonial Literatures*, London: Routledge.

Ashcroft, B., Griffiths, G. and Tiffin, H., (eds) (1995) *The Post-Colonial Studies Reader*, London: Routledge.

Bhabha, H. (1984) 'Of Mimicry and Ma: The Ambivalence of Colonial Discourse', *October*, 28, pp. 125–33.

Bharucha, R. (1993) *Theatre and the World: Performance and the Politics of Culture*, London: Routledge.

Brydon, D. (1990) 'The White Inuit Speaks: Contamination as Literary Strategy', in I. Adam and H. Tiffin (eds), *Past the Last Post: Theorising Post-Colonialism and Post-Modernism*, Calgary: University of Calgary Press, pp. 191–203.

Burness, D. (ed.) (1985) *Wanasema: Conversations with African Writers*, Athens, OH: Ohio University Center for International Studies.

Chrisman, L. (1990) 'The Imperial Unconscious?: Representations of Imperial Discourse', *Critical Quarterly*, 32(3), pp. 38–58.

Dasgupta, G. (1991) 'Interculturalism: A Lettrist Sampler', in B. Marranca and G. Dasgupta (eds), *Interculturalism and Performance*, New York: PAJ, pp. 319–32.

Francis, D. (1992) *The Imaginary Indian: The Image of the Indian in Canadian Culture*, Vancouver: Arsenal Pulp.

Goldie, T. (1989) *Fear and Temptation: The Image of the Indigene in Canadian, Australian and New Zealand Literatures*, Kingston, Ontario: McGill-Queen's University Press.

Hodge, B. and Mishra, V. (1991) *Dark Side of the Dream: Literature and the Postcolonial Mind*, Sydney: Allen and Unwin.

Kapur, A. (1990) *Actors, Pilgrims, Kings and Gods: The Ramlila at Ramnagar*, Calcutta: Seagull.

Lawson, A. (1992) 'Comparative Studies and Post-Colonial "Settler" Cultures', *Australian-Canadian Studies*, 10(2), pp. 153–9.

Lawson, A. (1994) 'Un/Settling Colonies: The Ambivalent Place of Colonial Discourse', in C. Worth, P. Nestor and M. Pavlyshyn (eds), *Literature and Opposition*, Clayton, Victoria: Centre for General and Comparative Literature, Monash University, pp. 67–82.

Lawson, A. and Tiffin, C. (1994) 'Conclusion: Reading Difference', in C. Tiffin and A. Lawson (eds), *De-scribing Empire: Post-Colonialism and Textuality*, London: Routledge, pp. 230–5.

Mukherjee, S. (1982) *The Story of the Calcutta Theatres, 1753–1980,* Calcutta: Bagchi.

Naipaul, S. (1971) 'The Writer Without a Society', in A. Rutherford (ed.), *Commonwealth*, Aarhus, Denmark: University of Aarhus Press.

Rangacharya, A. (1971) *The Indian Theatre*, New Delhi: National Book Trust.

Said, E. (1979) *Orientalism*, New York: Vintage.

Said, E. (1994) *Culture and Imperialism*, London: Vintage.

Slemon, S. (1987) 'Monuments of Empire: Allegory/Counter-Discourse/Post-Colonial Writing', *Kunapipi*, 9(3), pp. 1–16.

Spivak, G.C. (1988) *In Other Worlds: Essays in Cultural Politics*, New York: Methuen.

Steadman, I. (1991) 'Theatre beyond Apartheid', *Research In African Literatures*, 22(2), pp. 77–90.

Tiffin, C. and Lawson, A. (eds) (1994) *De-scribing Empire: Post-Colonialism and Textuality*, London: Routledge.

Tiffin, H. (1987) 'Post-Colonial Literatures and Counter-Discourse', *Kunapipi*, 9(3), pp. 17–34.

Williams, P. and Chrisman, L. (eds) (1993) *Colonial Discourse and Post-Colonial Theory: A Reader*, New York: Harvester Wheatsheaf.

Wright, R. (1937) *Revels in Jamaica 1682–1838*, New York: Dodd Mead.

Yajnik, R.K. (1970) *The Indian Theatre: Its Origins and its Later Developments under European Influence*, New York: Haskell House.

Originally published as 'Introduction: Re-acting (to) Empire', in *Post-Colonial Drama: Theory, Practice, Politics*, London: Routledge, 1996, pp. 1–14.

4.10 Me, My iBook, and Writing in America (2006)

MARK RAVENHILL

I SOMETIMES WONDER IF I would ever have written a play it if hadn't been for Apple Mac. I made various starts at writing a play during the first thirty years of my life – bits of scenes in old exercise books, a few pages on a typewriter bought in a junk shop, a student attempt on an early Sinclair computer with a printer that printed a page of text every ten minutes (you'd set aside an afternoon to print out the draft of a document), bits and pieces on various friends' PCs. But it was only when I was sharing a flat with a friend in 1992, a friend who had a Mac, that I started to make my first serious attempts at writing, attempts that led, three years later, to me becoming a professional playwright.

Now I wouldn't claim that it was the Mac alone that made me a playwright. That would be silly. There was also the political climate, the Major government returned once again for a final period of 'office without power'; there was the personal experience I went through in 1993 of losing my boyfriend to Aids; there was the jolt to comfortable assumptions about good and evil brought about by the murder of Jamie Bulger;[1] there was a change in theatrical fashion which meant the high water mark of performance and physical theatre had turned and once again it seemed like a smart thing for a young man with theatrical aspirations to write a play.

All of these things played their part in making me a playwright. But the actual technology, the actual thought processes, the actual mechanism of creating those plays? I think the Mac was an essential part of all that. Because my hunch is that the technology available is not just a recorder of the artist's thoughts and feelings but itself makes some thoughts and feelings possible that were never possible before, makes other thoughts and feelings no longer transferable to the page.

It's a slightly fanciful notion, but all I know is that once I'd opened a word document on a Mac, once I was clicking on its icons, once I was dragging across its desktop, I felt that it thought as I thought, that here was something that was an extension of my heart and head in a way that the pencil or the typewriter or the PC had never been. Sat before the screen of a Mac, I was a writer.

A writer used to be heroic. You could lock him or her up in a prison cell for twenty years and still they'd find a way to carry on writing. They'd risk everything to pass around *samizdat* copies of their work. The Church or the State or the Stasi were out to get them but they'd carry on writing – even if only in their head. There is not an ounce of the hero about me – maybe none of us are heroes today, maybe we're in a post-heroic age, maybe we're all more Carrie Bradshaw than Solzhenitsyn – but I certainly wouldn't have finished a full-length play and written several drafts without a Mac.

I may just be romanticising my own lack of heroism. Maybe I am a writer. And if I had to write on a typewriter I would. It's one of the tricks of new technology that within months we cannot imagine a life without it. (However did I call my partner from the train to say I was on my way home before the invention of the mobile phone?) But certainly now, as I approach ten years as a produced playwright, I cannot imagine having produced the body of work that I have without the programmes of the several Macs I've got through over the years – currently iBook, OS X 10, AppleWorks Word Document. The rhythms, the structures, the themes of those plays are as much Mac's as they are mine.

There is an irony about this of course. Plenty of commentators, mainly journalists but a few people who should know better, have chosen only to report the 'shocking' moments in my plays: the 'bloody rimming' moments. But other commentators have spotted another, bigger project in my plays to date: something which may even report upon, maybe even critique, a world of globalised capitalism. I'd like to think that's there. There's nothing very schematic about writing a play: you tend to start with an instinct and only later, often after the audience have seen the play, can you say 'ah maybe that's what this thing is about'. Even so, I'd like to think that the best bits of my writing have captured some of the weightless, soulless emptiness of contemporary global capitalism and in doing so opened up a space for some of the audience to think more critically about The Way We Live Now than they might have done before. So of course it's ironic that this writing is been made possible by the technology coming out of Silicone Valley, the nerve centre of that same globalised world.

This is the embarrassing contradiction I find myself in as a playwright: I would like to think of my plays as oppositional, of critical, of outside of the ebb and flow of information and capital but I suspect they would never have existed without start-ups, bubbles and chips. I'd like to be a free thinker but maybe in truth I'm just another microserf.

And if I were just going to be a jolly postmodernist, I could embrace this. I don't want to do that, but nor is it just possible to deny this irony, return to the pre-ironic simplicity of a world where I would have written on a Remington – or probably reclined on a sofa while a poorly paid fifteen year old girl from a Secondary Modern School typed on a Remington for me. So what is to be done?

I first became really aware of the word globalisation (no doubt later than most people) towards the end of the 1990s. Searching around for material for the play that would become *Some Explicit Polaroids*, I took a whole pile of books away for a week to a cheap room in Ibiza and gave myself a crammer course, trying to understand how the world's economies had changed. In the spring of 1999, Max Stafford-Clark asked me if I'd like to do a week-long workshop for this new play. I had very little text to show (and indeed didn't have much more text to show when the play began rehearsing in the autumn) but I said I thought we should look at this subject of globalisation and Max, myself and the actors in the workshop made up lists of people we would like to meet to interview and try to find out what this globalisation thing was.

I'm not sure who came up with the idea of meeting Charles Saatchi. I think it was one of the actors. But I went with a couple of the actors from the workshop – I think it was Lesley Manville and Monica Dolan – to the headquarters of Saatchi and Saatchi and we were shown into the office of the great man. He told us that several years before his company had identified 'globalisation' as the wave of the future and had been preparing themselves for the new globalised economy.

'But really' he said with a weary smile, 'globalisation is just a weasel word – what we're really talking about is Americanisation'.

I was very taken aback by this. This somehow seemed to be the sentiment of an anti-globalist, an anti-American and Saatchi was clearly neither. 'So would you say', asked Monica Dolan, 'that globalisation is a good thing or a bad thing?'

'Oh you can't say something like that is good or bad,' Saatchi said. 'It's a fact. It's like the wind blowing or the tide coming in. It's not good or bad. It just is.'

I was struck just how in that moment he resembled one of Brecht's capitalists, who always forget (or deliberately deny) that the economy is a human construct and not a tsunami. It was as though he were speaking from the selfsame script as Brecht's Pierpont Mauler in *St Joan of the Stockyards*. Saatchi was a fascinating character, hugely charismatic and a big influence on the development of the character of Jonathan when I came to write *Some Explicit Polaroids*.

Was Saatchi right? Was 'globalisation' 'Americanisation'? There was certainly plenty of Americanisation about me.

I think this is something you become particularly aware of when you start writing about your experiences as a gay man. Because contemporary 'gay' identity is almost entirely an American construct. The group lobbying for gay legal and democratic rights in the UK is called Stonewall after a bar in New York that only a tiny proportion of British gays and lesbians can ever have ever been to. Most gays and lesbians rehearse their coming outs by engaging with American coming out narratives: the gay genre fiction in any British bookshop is almost entirely American. Early generations of British gay men made an ironic appropriation of the camp images of Hollywood glamour. Maybe in the absence of robust European or British narratives of gay identity, or maybe by excluding them, it is American images and narratives that have defined British gay identity. Try to buy gay porn featuring men with British accents and you'd be hard pushed (so to speak). It's all California dudes or daddies with, in the last few years, a wave of new Eastern European product. And as if to prove how entirely hegemonic all this is even the challenge to 'gay' with the early 1990s 'queer' was a largely American movement, albeit in part inspired by European philosophy and critical theory.

Now I felt pretty pleased with myself that my first play *Shopping and Fucking* had managed to move outside of the parameters of a 'gay' narrative without being too self-consciously 'queer' either. The characters enjoyed or suffered what *Little Britain* calls 'some cock and arse action' but there were no coming out narratives, no hugs, no learning.

I was troubled by one particular block (of several) that I hit while writing *Some Explicit Polaroids*. In the play the character of Tim, who is HIV positive, refuses to take his medication and eventually dies of an Aids-related illness. Now this was the most autobiographical thing I had ever written: five years before I wrote the play my boyfriend, also called Tim, had died of an Aids-related illness. And yet when I came to write these scenes for the play I couldn't connect with anything that had happened to me in real life because all I could see, all I could hear, was stuff from other people's Aids narratives: *The Normal Heart, Longtime Companion, Angels in America*. As soon as I stuck a character in a hospital bed and gave them a Kaposi's Sarcoma (KS) lesion they would start to talk with an American accent and before you knew it Meryl Streep was sitting by the bed and everyone was hugging each other.

I think it's important – certainly for me when I'm writing – that we don't just play the weary game of referencing and quoting other narratives in a warm glow of cynicism. I want to test in my writing how much the new experiences of humanity can be captured in a piece of theatre. But for months I would come back to writing those scenes, always with the same effect. A play that was supposedly set in London would suddenly lurch over the Atlantic once the doors of the Aids ward were open. Eventually I became really angry. This was my experience. This was my narrative. How *dare* Larry Kramer and Tony Kushner colonise my life like this? Why was I seeing the first revelation of the KS lesion from *The Normal Heart* or Louis, Prior and the Angel when I shut my eyes, and not my own memory? Damn you for writing your American Aids plays!

I didn't feel, having written *Some Explicit Polaroids*, that I had done anything other than chip away at the subject of globalisation – if indeed it is still a 'subject' (is something a 'subject' when it is so integrated into our lives?). It's still something I want to write about but I keep on hitting the same block every time I sit down wanting to write dramatically about it: the action wants to happen in America. The research I read, the popular anti-globalisation books are about American companies doing terrible things to American workers and consumers for the benefit of the American shareholder. And I don't feel it would be honest of me to write with a setting of Americanoise (I did it in my play *Faust is Dead* with mixed results). Of course Brecht used a mythic America repeatedly as a setting that allowed him to write an earlier stage of capitalist development but I can't help feeling that to write plays set in America is to have one's narrative defined by America, however critical the play might be of America or globalisation.

Britain may have become increasingly part of a global economy, and culturally and economically we may be more and more American, but the fashionability of these truths is in danger of preventing commentators and dramatists from exploring what is specifically British about us. Because there is still plenty about us, I think, that is very specific to this island. Writing globally, nationally, locally, personally, it's a lot for a playwright to do.

'Where is the state of the nation play?' a dying breed of grumpy old men still ask, assuming that the state of the nation is the same thing as the fate of the planet, the choices facing the globe or the way of the world – all of these concerns every bit as ambitious and political as the 'state of the nation'.

Because if you were to take the conflict between capital and labour as a basic motor of human experience (a widely discredited idea but still one with a bit of life in it), you can see how problematic it is to dramatise for a contemporary playwright. Hauptmann could bring his nineteenth-century weavers in conflict with their bourgeois masters by setting his play in a small German town. Of course, nineteenth-century 'free trade' saw a fair amount of movement of goods and capital but it's possible to imagine many, many situations where a dramatist can place the seller of labour and the owner of capital in the same geographic space. This is far more difficult today. Where did the food come from that you ate today? Who made your trainers? Who wove that cloth? They are phantoms and the profits have vanished off to phantoms elsewhere. Certainly a very different type of play is needed if we're going to write about this world.

But actually this very fundamental conflict between capital and labour – perhaps the fundamental social and economic conflict – was rarely ever at the heart of the British 'state of the nation' play, an ideal model of a play that perhaps never quite existed in the British theatre from the 1950s through to the 1980s.

The main tradition in British 'political' theatre was an oppositional voice that spoke up against the crushing hand of the Big Other: the Headmaster, the Priest, the Colonel, the Men from the Ministry – the Daddy who wants to deny the voice and energy of his offspring. It was at the heart of the satire boom of the 1960s (laughing at these Big Others fuelled *Beyond the Fringe*); it was the 'heroes led by donkeys' anger of *Oh What A Lovely War*; it was Osborne's Jimmy and Wesker's Beattie. (Osborne and Wesker are good dramatists and so invite complex responses to Jimmy and Beattie).

It's a drama in which tradition and its intertwining with class plays a very significant part and fuels many writers' anger, but in which no very significant part is played by the economic life of the characters, nor by the conflict between capital and labour. British theatre never produced a character with the force of Arthur Miller's Willy Loman or Brecht's Mother Courage, characters for whom at the very core of their being, at the basis of their conflict with the world, is the economic. We nearly always preferred to play a scene in front of a Union Jack and attack 'authority' and call this 'political theatre'. This was 'oppositional' theatre I would suggest but was rarely rooted enough in the economic to be thoroughly 'political'.

If anyone has the time or the inclination I think it could be illuminating to do a word count for the occurrence of the word 'England' in English plays from the 1950s to the present day. I suspect you'd find a pretty steady occurrence of the word from the 1950s through to the 1980s, with a rapid trailing off in the 1990s. From John Osborne's rallying cry of 'Damn You England!', ushering Jimmy Porter and Archie Rice and his bumping and grinding Britannia onto the stage of the English Stage Company, through to Edgar's *Destiny* and Brenton's *The Churchill Play*, in which Winston Churchill leaps from his coffin at his state funeral, and onto Wertenbaker's *Our Country's Good*, the 'English' word rings out alongside the iconography of Englishness.

But then something changed. I think maybe we reached a stage in the 1990s where a new group of younger dramatists weren't so interested in criticising these figures in power (the basic patricidal impulse) – largely I suspect because these figures of power have learned to speak a different language – one that promises (or threatens) inclusion rather than coercion. Looking at my own plays, rather than railing against patriarchal figures, the characters tend to have a nostalgic hankering for a time when there was a stern father figure looking over them, a time when we weren't expected to make so many choices for ourselves.

David Hare once remarked that it was a strange thing but you only needed to mention the word 'Weybridge' to get a huge laugh on the London stage. I've noticed that Alan Bennett's audiences seem to find 'Battenberg' or 'antimacassar' similarly hilarious. It is as though British theatre audiences, certainly mainstream London theatre audiences, like to be reminded of their parochialism, of their naffness, of their not quite moving with the times. There is real pride in that laughter at 'Weybridge' or 'Battenberg'.

When I started writing my first full length play *Shopping and Fucking*, I didn't have much of an idea about what course the action of the play was going to take or what the play was going to be about. Playwrights often don't. But starting on *Shopping and Fucking* I did have a clear idea, a rule that I set myself: there would be no geographical references, no references to England, London, Streatham, Halifax, Weybridge and also no references to anything that had been in use for more than a decade or so; characters were allowed to use a microwave but not a kettle, send an email but not a postcard. Very consciously, I wanted the play to have a different relationship to history and geography from the existing tradition of contemporary British playwriting.

Why did I do this? I think in part because I'd observed that English audiences would cling onto place names or products – think Batley, think Bovril – as comfort blankets, and I wanted to take those comfort blankets away. And because I suppose I sensed that for the young characters in my play being part of the narrative of nationhood or history played very little part in their lives. But this didn't come from any theory. I'd been too busy doing a portfolio of badly paid jobs to read any Fukuyama, at least until the profits from being a West End playwright rolled in.

I don't think the director of the play, Max Stafford-Clark, ever really saw this absence of reference in the play as anything other than a weakness. Max had a huge, and almost entirely beneficial, influence on the development of the play through the various drafts I worked on once his Out of Joint Company committed to the production of the play. From my very first meeting with him through to the last week of rehearsals, he would push and push for something more 'specif', as we jokingly called it. Where were these characters born? Where were they living now? What were their surnames? (I didn't even want to give them first names but got round this by naming the characters after early 1990s popsters, Take That).

I remember once, in complete exasperation at one of our meetings, Max threw down his script and said: 'Look you've got to put in some more specif stuff – otherwise they'll do this play in Germany and it'll all be Expressionist and they'll all have Mohicans. Do you want that?' I remarked glibly that I believed the royalties from German productions were rather good. (They are and I'm sure a production not unlike Max's nightmare has taken place in a *stadttheater* somewhere.) It was a glib response because I couldn't really rationalise at the time why a geographical or historical reference in the play was wrong. I was flying on instinct but I strongly resisted putting any of those references in the play. Looking at it now I would say *Shopping and Fucking* mostly works inside the language of 'social realism'; it just selects slightly different bits of the social and the real to define its world than those things that Max was used to with his long and illustrious work directing new British plays.

I'd been partly inspired to write in this way by the plays and essays of David Mamet. An American offered the way forward. Mamet had a huge influence on a significant group of the new British playwrights of the 1990s, as I discovered when Patrick Marber, Joe Penhall and myself got together to discuss Mamet's *Edmond* for a programme article to accompany the National Theatre's revival of the play. You can trace it through Marber's career, from his first play *Dealer's Choice* (Mamet is an advocate of poker), his performance in Mamet's *Speed The Plow* (picked up for revival by a West End management after Penhall directed a reading at the Royal Court), Marber's direction of Mamet's *The Old Neighbourhood*, which may in turn have led Marber to the world of his most recent play *Howard Katz*.

I think maybe we were drawn to Mamet for a number of reasons. He offered a clear definition of masculinity, at a time when masculinity was supposedly in crisis. (Is it still? Was it ever?) But also he offered a strict set of aesthetic disciplines at a time when we didn't feel inspired by an older generation of British playwrights. What Mamet stresses time and time again in his essays is that the play should be stripped off all extraneous detail until just the story, which he defines as just the protagonist in pursuit of their objective, is left. Mamet insists that the dramatist can't make the play say anything beyond this or on top of this, that the meaning of the play *is* this story. In some ways it's the old Hemingway adage of 'cut out the good writing' applied to the play but it's certainly worked for David Mamet. His work from *American Buffalo* through to *The Old Neighbourhood* (charitably ignoring *Boston Marriage*) is as impressive a body of work as that of any dramatist alive.

And in some ways, through his absorption in the narrative purity of Aristotelian poetics,

Mamet was bringing us in touch with a European tradition which the British theatre had never fully absorbed. (British playwrights from Shakespeare to Churchill have preferred to disrupt and transgress the Aristotelian rules.) What Mamet was arguing for was a theatre free of ideology in which the audience would undergo a profound experience by projecting themselves into the uninflected protagonist. This is the idea that lies at the heart of Mamet's aesthetic. Of course you can spot a more superficial influence of Mamet on the development of dialogue, the repetitive masculine drive of his characters' language echoed in a lot of British new writing of the 1990s. But more profoundly it is the stripping away of detail and opinion, the emphasis on narrative, where Mamet's influence can be felt on Marber, Penhall, Neilson, McDonagh *et al.* (He was very definitely a role model for emerging male writers rather than women.)

In one of his essays, Mamet talks about the decor of American Jewish homes, of its wish to be tasteful and to be acceptable, not to give too much away, not to be too Jewish. Recently in his writing and in his life he has explored his identity as a Jew in a way that he never publicly did in the 1970s and 1980s. It struck me reading the essay that as well as describing the decor of Jewish homes he was pretty much describing his own aesthetic as a playwright. Was his desire to strip a play of wasteful detail, to present a central protagonist who can be defined by the pursuit of their objective, what Jewish writers for Hollywood and Broadway have been doing for the whole century? Was the aesthetic purity of all this making sure that the little guy at the centre of their stories could stand for an American Everyman and not a Jew? It struck me that it was and I'm sure Mamet, a writer who thinks very deeply about his work, will have been struck by this too.

For the group of writers starting off their careers in the 1990s, Mamet's influence allowed us to break free of the existing dominant discourse of British theatre – the discourse about Britishness and the attack on the bad Father (I'm talking of course about an impulse that was largely unconscious and rarely discussed, these weren't a group of playwrights who ever discussed a movement or came up with a manifesto, many of them have never met each other to this day).

So, I wrote *Shopping and Fucking*. It was a commercial and critical success here, the Out of Joint production toured internationally with the support of the British Council, and the play was quickly translated into many languages and produced all over the world. From being part of the British new writing scene I had become a global commodity. Ironically, though in much of the world the play was received at least as well as it was at home, the place where the play did least well was in New York where the play was universally loathed by the critics – 'Mr Ravenhill belongs to a long line of whingeing Brits from John Osborne to Caryl Churchill' and 'Mr Ravenhill should go home and learn how to write a play' – but it sold out for its allotted run. 'I don't get it' said the American producer, 'A sold-out flop!'

I was hugely excited to be produced all over the world. I would often be invited to productions of the play. The temptation was to rush to each of them, not because I wanted to see the play again and again, but because of the opportunities for free travel that were offered. I decided to ration myself and only go to a few of these overseas productions but I went to enough to start to suspect that I was becoming part of the global class who live out of a mini-bar and a breakfast buffet. It's a life I quite like.

I was amused to see how many of the productions replaced the missing 'Britishness' of the play, the Britishness I had so carefully excluded, but this was the height of Britpop, so in Greek, Lithuanian, Danish productions I saw characters in Union Jack t-shirts with pictures of Princess

Diana pinned to their wall listening to a soundtrack of Blur and Oasis. No small part of the appeal of the play, I saw, was that it was British and if the writer hadn't provided enough of the Old Country then the production would do the work. 'Your writing – it's so like Dickens, it's Oliver Twist' said a director in Amsterdam. At first I was completely mystified but on reflection I could see this play, which was predominantly social realist with a group of lost kids getting drawn into nefarious activity, had much more in common with Dickens, who I'd read avidly in my teenage years, than I would really like to admit. I had to confront the fact that not only would overseas productions actually emphasise, even over emphasise, the Britishness of the play, but actually maybe there was actually something essentially British about the play.

Despite this Britishness, I was aware that one of the reasons the play had proved such good export material was that it wasn't cluttered with references that would confuse foreign audiences and that the commodified world of the play was not a specifically British one. I think by the time I came to write *Some Explicit Polaroids* I wanted to write another play that would repeat the international success of *Shopping and Fucking*. I'd had a taste of the travel and the interest and some decent money and I wanted to repeat the experience. Of course this calculation is fatal to the creative process and that play was the slowest, most painful thing I've ever written, wrung out of me scene by scene by an incredibly patient Max Stafford-Clark.

It was a grimly ironic experience. I wanted to write about globalisation, hence the workshop where we'd interviewed Charles Saatchi, but as a playwright I had become a global commodity, with *Shopping and Fucking* franchises all over the world. Now I wanted to produce a new global product that would speak to people in Johannesburg and Melbourne, Toronto and Mexico City: places I'd only been to for a couple of days and whose cultures I knew no more of than a quick tasting in a food hall. Trying to think of this global audience was so daunting that I became totally blocked, until finally I resolved to write anything that came into my head and to deliver a play that I liked even if it wasn't performed in a single translation.

And looking at *Some Explicit Polaroids* on opening night I thought, well, I'm proud of what I've come up with but this is clearly not a global play. The young characters of the play – Tim, Victor, Nadia – belong to a similar world to the young people of *Shopping and Fucking* but the characters of Nick and Helen, the old socialists, belong to an entirely different, a very – so it seemed to me – British world. Indeed so different were these two groups of characters I found it almost impossible to conceive of scenes where they would talk to each other and in the end Helen's intrusion into Tim, Victor and Nadia's world proved to be brief.

I was wrong about *Some Explicit Polaroids*. It's received almost as many productions overseas as *Shopping and Fucking*, far more than my other plays. And directors and actors have told me that the central generational conflict between a weary politicised older generation and a party-happy apolitical younger generation is one that is reflected in their country, in South America or in Eastern Europe. And then there's one scene set on the terrace of the Houses of Parliament when they can really leap on the Britishness in the staging if they want to. Oddly enough, most productions choose not to. I guess the fashion for all things Cool Britannia has passed. With *Polaroids* I realised that the playwright could never play the game of guessing what would play with different audiences; you write for yourself, maybe for the immediate culture around you and then wait and see what will travel.

In 2002, I got the opportunity to spend a month writing at the Eugene O'Neill Centre in Connecticut alongside twenty other playwrights, all of them American. I was sent by the National Theatre's Connections programme, where I was to write a play for young people to perform in schools and youth theatres. When I flew into New York the country was preparing to commemorate the first anniversary of 9/11, while also psyching itself up for the assault on Iraq, after Afghanistan hadn't provided the 'closure' that was being sought for.

On the train travelling up through New York state and into Connecticut I was amazed at the number of houses (in many areas the majority) that had huge Stars and Stripes flags hanging down the side of the building, many of them the full length of the houses. I was struck by how much America still had recourse to a strong narrative of national identity, of buzzwords, of rituals, of routines, that we no longer have. We called our programme *Pop Idol*; they called theirs *American Idol*. What does it say about the two cultures where one side aspires to be Pop, the other aspires to be American?

Arriving at the O'Neill, it was soon obvious that no-one had heard of me or any of my plays. This was rather different from the reception I'd got used to in the rest of the world but I decided it would be a very good, if rather humbling experience for me. (I'm rubbish at being humble and for most of the month I carried on like Simon Cowell but I gave it a go.) But I had to write the play, eventually called *Totally Over You*, while I was there. Surrounded by American voices, I found when I sat down to write I could do one of two things: write dialogue that was very self-consciously English (in a Richard Curtis, Julian Fellowes sort of a way, which has always exported very well) or in a sort of mid-Atlantic chat. I suspect that in conversation during the day I slipped between the two. It's amazing how quickly your ear for your own culture's rhythms go: I'd lost mine within a couple of days. But I had to write a play within four weeks and there was little time to anguish about the rhythms of my writing. I decided that the teenagers in my play, who are obsessed by celebrity culture, would have existed entirely on a diet of American television, American cinema, American music and American food. Since American actors were going to present the play to an American audience as a staged reading at the end of the month, I didn't want to spend my time explaining a lot of British youth references to them or to expect them to perform with a north London accent. I chose to place the play in a genre – teenagers in a school adapted from a European classic (I was inspired by Molière) – that I'd enjoyed in the American teen comedies *Clueless* and *Ten Things I Hate About You*. And I had my characters talk in mid-Atlantic because I figured there were a whole generation of kids living in Camden or Bradford or Glasgow who either spoke like American teenagers or aspired to talk like American teenagers and with identical pop-culture references. Whether the young people who performed the play were always aware of the play's critique of this Americanisation of youth experience, or whether they revelled in speaking mid-Atlantic I was never sure.

But however much we may have in common, however much it's possible to write in a demotic language that sits just as easily on the lips of kids in Harlesden as it does in Harlem, I realised there was a fundamental difference between the theatre cultures of the two countries. One evening during a panel discussion with the other writers at the O'Neill, I said (probably rather grandly) that I thought we should be writing plays that 'existed at the centre of the culture'. There was little response at the time but with the session over one of my fellow playwrights, his whole body drawn tight with anger, stepped into my path. 'How can you say that?' he hissed. 'How dare you come over here and say that?'

'I'm sorry?'

'A theatre at the centre of the culture. Don't you know what a ridiculous idea that is? That's never going to happen! And you stand here and you throw it in our faces!'

'But surely if we're not aiming for the centre of the –'

'You don't understand America, you don't understand our theatre, just don't talk about it.' And off he went. I subsequently learned that he lived in the strange shadow world of being a virtual playwright with a salaried post as a professor of playwriting and various plays workshopped and read over the years, but nothing produced.

But what he'd voiced was, I think, a fundamental distinction between the way many American writers and the way British writers tend to view themselves. There is a mournful sense from many American writers that they are cut adrift from a society which has little interest in anything they have to write. The writer and actor Wallace Shawn voices this in an interview for a programme at the Royal Court when he says that the audience comes to the theatre looking for a world that is calmer and more polite than the world around them but all the playwrights have to offer them is 'frenzied glimpses of lives in little rooms'. The audience and the playwright, Shawn said, have grown apart, their needs irreconcilable.

There are some very similar sentiments expressed by Jonathan Franzen's in his recent collection of essays,[2] mourning the death of the great American social novel, the death of the novel in general, the death of reading. Why is he writing at all when there is every sign that his dying culture is finally going to turn its back on writing and reading once and for all?

It's only when you read these bleak assessments of the writer's struggle that you realise how different the situation is here in Britain. Of course, writers always feel insecure – why hasn't that theatre programmed my play? why did that actor turn down the lead? why can't that critic understand what I'm doing? – but somehow, underneath all this there is still a fundamental, unspoken sense that what we do matters, that theatres are looking for new writers, that audiences want to see their work, that the new plays will be studied and discussed, that they are part of the wider cultural life of the country. It sometimes doesn't feel that way, but meet a group of American writers and you suddenly realise how different our perception of ourselves is.

And I think a great deal of it is perception. Wallace Shawn and Jonathan Franzen draw a picture of themselves alienated and alone, shouting against the glass at a culture that can't hear. But in reality both are hugely respected and one suspects reasonably well remunerated for their talents. You might not find the latest literary novel or fringe play being debated in every bar in every state, but the *New York Review of Books* or the *New York Times* often give more consideration to new work than any comparable British publication.

And over here, despite the guilt imposed upon us by the Thatcherites for our lack of economic efficiency and by the Blairites for our lack of access, we somehow still feel central to the culture, when in reality most people in Britain couldn't name a contemporary playwright or novelist. The American writer may be creating a mirage of alienation and victimhood for themselves, but our cultural institutions carefully cushion us from a sense that what we do doesn't really matter.

So for all the globalisation, the Americanisation, this is where there is still something fundamentally different about being a British playwright: the sense that our writing counts. And this may be an illusion that our theatres, our newspapers, our universities help us to sustain, but it's a valuable, maybe even a necessary, illusion for a writer to have and I'm grateful that while I've written on my iBook I've been able to do it in a culture which is still in some ways peculiarly British.

Notes

1. Mark Ravenhill, 'A Tear in the Fabric: The Jamie Bulger Murder and New Theatre Writing in the 'Nineties', *New Theatre Quarterly*, 20(4) (November 2004), 305–14.
2. Jonathan Franzen, *How To Be Alone: Essays* (New York: Farrar Straus Giroux, 2002).

Originally published in *Contemporary Theatre Review*, 16(1) (2006), pp. 131–8.

Part 5
Contemporary Performance/The Contemporaneity of Practice

Timeline

	Social, cultural and political context	Theatre
1964		Odin Theatre founded by Eugenio Barba, Oslo, moves to permanent company setting in Denmark in 1966
1966		*Ornitofilene* (inaugural production of Odin Theatre – Scandinavian tour)
1967	Sexual Offences Act (decriminalizes homosexual relations between consenting adults over the age of 21 (UK) Abortion Act (legalizing abortion in UK)	*Hair: The American Tribal Love-Rock Musical* The Performance Group founded, USA (Richard Schechner)
1968	Assassination of Martin Luther King, Jr Assassination of Robert Kennedy Student demonstrations and occupations in France Roland Barthes's seminal essay *The Death of the Author* first published.	Theatres Act 1968 – abolition of stage censorship in UK *Dionysus in 69* (first production of The Performance Group, USA)
1969	Richard Nixon becomes President of the USA British troops deployed to Northern Ireland Stonewall Riots (New York) – riots inaugurated by the gay community seen as the beginnings of gay activism Woodstock Festival, New York The internet developed out of US military defence project VCR video player invented – becomes widely available by 1977	
1970	Conservative Party wins general election (UK) Germaine Greer's *The Female Eunuch* becomes a best-seller	
1972	Invention of email communication (in wide public use by the mid 1990s) Mobile or cell phone invented, made widely available to the general public by Vodaphone in 1985 Watergate scandal begins (USA) – accusation of corruption leading to the resignation of President Richard Nixon in 1974	
1973	UK joins European Economic Community	

	Social, cultural and political context	Theatre
1974	Labour Party wins general election (UK)	The Wooster Group formed (USA) (Elizabeth LeCompte and Spalding Gray, USA)
1975		*Sakonnet Point* (inaugural production of The Wooster Group, USA)
1976		Philip Glass and Robert Wilson's *Einstein on the Beach* premieres
1978		Pina Bausch's *Café Müller,* Germany
1979	Conservative Party wins general election (UK) – Margaret Thatcher becomes Prime Minister Soviet Union invades Afghanistan Jean-François Lyotard's *The Postmodern Condition: A Report on Knowledge* first published	Eugenio Barba and collaborators found the International School of Theatre Anthropology (ISTA)
1980	Hunger strikes by IRA prisoners begin in Northern Ireland Iran/Iraq War commences	Laurie Anderson, 'O Superman'
1981	Martial law in Poland The beginnings of the AIDS crisis IBM produces PC computer for the mass market	
1982	Argentina invades Falkland Islands (recaptured by British troops) Music recorded on CD made available	*Brecht's Ashes* (1982/4), Odin Theatre
1983	USA invades Grenada	*United States*: Laurie Anderson
1984	Coal miners strike begins (UK, March) IRA attempt to assassinate British Prime Minister Margaret Thatcher Apple Macintosh produces its first computers for mass market	Forced Entertainment founded in Sheffield, UK *L.S.D (... Just the High Points ...)*: The Wooster Group
1985	Coal miners return to work (March) Mikhail Gorbachev becomes leader of the Soviet Union	
1986		DV8 Physical Theatre formed (Lloyd Newson, UK)

	Social, cultural and political context	Theatre
1989	George H. W. Bush becomes President of the USA Tiananmen Square massacre (China) East Germany opens border with West Germany, demolition of Berlin Wall begins Following the development of the world wide web (www) the internet opens up to wide public usage	
1990	Reunification of Germany First Gulf War (ends 1991)	
1991		*Angels in America: Millennium Approaches*: Tony Kushner
1992		*Angels in America: Perestroika*: Tony Kushner
1993	Bill Clinton becomes President of the USA	*Enter the Night*: Maria Irene Fornes
1995		Laurie Anderson, *The Nerve Bible*
1996	DVD players being sold in Japan (and in the USA in 1997)	Robert Lepage & Marie Brassard *Polygraph*
1997	'New' Labour wins landslide general election victory – Tony Blair becomes Prime Minister	*House/Lights*: the Wooster Group
1998	Google, the free internet search engine, launched	
1999/ 2000	Millennium celebrations	Jerzy Grotowski dies
2001	George W. Bush becomes President of the USA September 11 – terrorist attack on the USA Apple iPod available on mass market Wikipedia, the free internet encyclopedia, launched	
2003	Anglo-American-led invasion of Iraq (Second Gulf War) DVD sales overtake VHS video sales in USA	
2005		Harold Pinter awarded the Nobel Prize
2008	Global financial collapse	*Spectacular*: Forced Entertainment
2009	Barack Obama becomes President of the USA	Pina Bausch dies

Introduction

MAGGIE B. GALE AND JOHN F. DEENEY

> The plethora of phenomena in the theatre landscape of the last few decades that have challenged the traditional forms of drama and 'its' theatre with aesthetic consistency and inventiveness suggests that it is justified to speak of a new *paradigm* ... These works of theatre also become paradigmatic because they are widely recognized – albeit not always welcomed – as an authentic testimony of the times. (Lehmann 2006: 24)

ANY ACCOUNT OF CONTEMPORARY performance has to encompass the varying nuances of an enormous diversity of experimentation in work produced over the past forty or so years in Europe and the United States. Some would agree with Lehmann that there has been a 'new paradigm' in theatre and performance, whereas others would see the differences in practice as signifying that no such paradigm is possible to either configure or fix. In this part we try to embrace these two positions and bring together diverse texts, which in different ways represent points on a map of contemporary theatre and performance practice, from live and performance art to texts which link in more obvious ways with the traditional play written for production in a theatre. In order to explore how these materials might be seen as responding to their contemporary moment, we use a number of aesthetic and critical frameworks: the idea of the contemporary, postmodernity and the postmodern and the 'postdramatic'.

The contemporary and contemporaneity

Contemporary is a word commonly used to denote that which is happening in the here and now. It is also the case that many cultural critics see an analysis of the contemporary as problematic because it cannot be viewed from a 'historical' perspective. Clearly, *all* the materials in this anthology reflect upon and are reflections of their contemporary moment. However, whilst something contemporary may lie at the cutting edge of practice during one decade, its quality of contemporaneity and contemporary relevance will quickly fade in another. Here we use the word contemporary in a generic sense to try and group together work from the 1970s onwards. We identify shared attitudes underlying the disparate territories of theatre and performance practice, and also explore the ways in which these practices engage with the complex dynamics of the contemporary world.

Historically the period following on from the social upheavals of the late 1960s (see Part 4) is constituted by the most extraordinary communications and technological revolution, which has changed forever the ways in which we as humans engage in the processes of social and personal exchange which theatre and performance exemplify so well. Computers, mobile telephones, the internet or the world wide web – all part of the new generation of communications technology which have become commonplace – have not in and of themselves transformed theatre and performance beyond recognition. They have however – from technological advances made in scenography, to the increase in use of TV, video and digital technology in performance – impacted on the ways and means by which theatre and performance are both conceived and received. Technology has transformed both our expectations of and engagement with the world. In terms of theatre and performance, Etchells also notes that such a 'shifting of cultural forms' – a move to 'soundbite' culture reliant on the visual and on technology, creates, 'changes in our consciousness' (Etchells 1996b: 111). It could be argued that because of our engagement with a culture so dependent on technology, we have come to expect a different kind of experience from theatre and performance from audiences of the eras covered in Parts 1–3 of this anthology. As one contemporary practitioner succinctly notes:

> We now live in a culture more attuned to the performative, the live, changeable, interactive, mixable and quotable than ever before. The dialogue of culture and technology moves us on into a future in which we must engage with ideas about fiction and reality, presence and absence, the nature of objects and the fixity of texts in order to take part in our culture fully. In this mix everything is up for imaginative appropriation. (Clare Macdonald qtd in Deeney 1998: 48)

The previous part examined in some detail the changing ideological landscape in which theatre and performance have been made over the past forty or so years. Here, however, we focus on different approaches, both pragmatic and aesthetic, to theatre and performance making. Whilst Part 4 focused on plays as texts for performance, this part focuses more on the 'textuality' of performance as represented by performance texts or scores. Similarly, the performance work developed from the late 1960s onwards more explicitly explores the potential of the body to signify and express experience. In the 1970s and 1980s Europe in particular saw an explosion of theatre and performance work that was influenced by developments in dance and performance art. The work of practitioners such as Pina Bausch (1940-2009) in Germany and DV8 Physical Theatre in Britain, for example, has shifted the boundaries between forms of performance. Dance Theatre, in some ways reminiscent of the work of innovative modernist choreographers such as Mary Wigman (see Part 3) associated with the Historical Avant-Garde, and influenced by mid-century practitioners such as Merce Cunningham (1919–2009) in the USA, dominated European stages during the latter decades of the twentieth century. Such work is not detailed here, but its influences can be felt in some of the practice we explore, certainly in the case of practice where the body becomes as important as the text and is deliberately framed as part of the rich textuality of performance. What can also be felt in the practices documented in this part is the influence of interdisciplinarity: using anthropological, philosophical and scientific discourse and engaging with the various areas of cultural theory have become common practice for artist and critic alike.

Much of the performance work explored in this part takes place in the margins of subsidized theatre, although some of the practitioners we look at, such as Laurie Anderson (5.1) and Robert Lepage (5.2), have worked on a much larger scale and have been absorbed to some extent by the commercial mainstream. The economic climate for the production and circulation of performance has moved from a period of relative plenty in the 1970s and 1980s where economic subsidy was perhaps more readily available, to a moment when most forms of funding had been radically depleted by the opening decade of the twenty-first century. In this climate most of the practice exemplified in the texts in this part is embedded in a tradition of small to mid-scale touring and arts festival performance. The majority of the texts, however, are in flux; they are unfinished and will change according to the performance context.

If many of the texts included in this part are 'performance' texts, 'versions' of the textual component of a performance, they are effectively samples, they are not representations of the central component of a performance in the same way as a play might be. Traditionally a play is written prior to a rehearsal process, although it might be changed and developed during that process. The included performance texts are products of a process of theatre/performance making. What they give us are *traces* of performance. At one extreme Peggy Phelan has suggested that, 'Performance's only life is in the present. Performance cannot be saved, recorded, documented, or otherwise participate in the circulation of representations of representation ... Performance's being ... becomes itself through disappearance' (Phelan 1993: 146). Whilst we acknowledge the particularity of performance existing only in the here and now of its live moment, we revert to and rely upon the power of language and text to enable us to study performance: it cannot comprehensively document the performance but it can open up interpretive possibilities. Where possible we have included photographic images that shed light on the relation between a textual representation of a performance and the performance itself. In other words, whilst we acknowledge the problematic relationship between the written word and the live performance – that one cannot stand in for the other – the desire to include a range of materials for exploration means that the traces of the performance text have to suffice as a starting point for discussion. The nearest to a 'play' in this part, therefore, is Robert Lepage and Marie Brassard's *Polygraph* (5.2), but even here what we have is a *version* of performance, indicative of a moment in the history of the text in performance. Similarly we have included technical stage directions in the Laurie Anderson score (5.1), to give a stronger sense of the relationship between the spoken text and the composition of the context in which it is performed.

As with the other parts in this anthology, the critical and theoretical materials are included in order to extend a range of available reading strategies. Similarly, the range of performance texts included allow for a wide spectrum of contrasting opportunities in our reading of contemporary performance practice over the last quarter of the twentieth century and the first decade of the twenty-first. For our purposes, 'contemporary theatre and performance' is an umbrella term for a geographically expansive movement, a pluralistic movement with a range of connected and unconnected models of and attitudes to process and practice.

The contexts of contemporary performance – postmodernity and postmodernism

> The real postmodernism ... was about flight from modernism, a revival of the classical, the figurative, the decorative. Postmodernism was inherently backward-looking and nostalgic ... nostalgia was not really about the past but about its erasure by democratic mass society. Postmodernism was the great leveler of differences, horizontally across culture, vertically within history. Postmodernism was the cultural dominant of late capitalism, commodity driven, and fundamentally reactionary. (Fuchs 1996: 144)

Contemporary performance practice is a direct result of the cultural modes it both engages with and rejects, but it cannot be seen as an absolute and straightforward break from the conventions it challenges. Thus, Bert O. States's suggestion that 'the difference between art paradigms and scientific paradigms is that art rarely discards any previous achievement', is relevant to our understanding of the modes of performance in contemporary practice (States 1985: 88–9). Equally relevant here is the theoretical framework of postmodernity which roughly covers the period represented in this part. Postmodernity is a historical phase which follows on from the modernist tropes of the first half of the twentieth century. Generally understood as having emerged from the 1950s onwards, it is a term used to reflect a cultural shift which, following the end of World War II, is post-Holocaust and riven with ideological, technological, political and philosophical uncertainty. The nature of this uncertainty frequently centres around ideas of the end of progress, social and cultural fragmentation, and struggles with the failing utopian project of consensus and cohesion: typically framed by the idea, for example, that we are somehow now at the 'end of history' (see also Part 4). Postmodernity is also conscious of the growing impossibility of any realization of utopian ideals. It is, rather, driven, certainly in its general aesthetic, by a playful juxtaposition of the classic and the modern. In architecture, for example, postmodernity has been expressed in the mixing of materials such as marble and glass inside concrete or metal structures, and the externalizing of traditionally internalized components such as pipework. In art, pastiche and kitsch might reign supreme, or we might find reference to nostalgic or iconic images in cutting-edge avant-garde film and so on. Cultural products often operate through the playing against each other of the personal and the public, through a play between the live and the recorded and a celebration of a complex hybridity of form. The 'postmodern' is therefore a product of postmodernity.

The easy association of the idea of 'the end of history' (see Part 4) with postmodernism is queried in Nick Kaye's analysis of the difference between the modernist and the postmodernist position with regard to the historical and its function:

> while the 'modernist' project rejects the past precisely because it can be read, understood and so transcended, the postmodern self-consciously 'replays' images of a past that cannot be known, but that can only be constructed and re-constructed through a play of entirely contemporary references to the idea of the past. (Kaye 1994: 20)

For Jean-François Lyotard, the 'postmodern condition' is wrought with uncertainty and the proliferation of social and economic instability. Within this the 'self' exists in a 'fabric of relations that is now more complex and mobile than ever before' (Lyotard 1997: 15). Institutions upon which we relied as reference points, and within this Lyotard would include 'historical traditions' (ibid), no longer appear to have the stability as frames of reference that they once possessed: we have, as a result, become destabilized in terms of our subjectivity. This has produced a kind of crisis of subjectivity, manifest in a great deal of contemporary performance, where we can see a crisis of 'I', or as one practitioner names it, a focus upon the 'self erased' – or permanently destabilized – and how, where, by whom and to whom that 'I' is constructed and expressed (Etchells 1996b: 117). Here the postmodern in performance is exemplified by fragmentation and self-referentiality, but also by nostalgia, the sublime, the uncanny and by an engagement with a dystopian perspective on our social and political world. Some postmodern performance appears more concerned with style and display and moves away entirely from the 'functional austerity' of modernist works (Birringer 1993: 5).

In terms of distinguishing a typology of postmodern performance, practitioner and theorist Tim Etchells connects a number of characteristics of performance work during the 1980s and 1990s – such as the 're-framing of narrative', the use of 'media-culture imagery', 'questioning the idea of the body as an essential object', a re-thinking of the location of performance and a retreat into or an embracing of the 'fictional', the 'dreamlike' and the 'imaginary' (see Etchells 1996b). Such characteristics might certainly be classed as postmodern in their appearance, but we should also note here the ever-present resistance of some theorists to define the 'postmodern' in any complete sense. David Harvey has suggested that as the definition of 'modernism' is so problematic and 'confused' so too is the definition of the 'postmodern', which is meant to represent a departure from it. He uses Terry Eagleton to elucidate this point, and it is useful to refer directly to Eagleton's summary here:

> There is, perhaps, a degree of consensus that the typical post-modernist artefact is playful, self-ironizing and even schizoid; and that it reacts to the austere autonomy of high modernism by impudently embracing the language of commerce and the commodity. Its stance towards cultural tradition is one of irreverent pastiche, and its contrived depthlessness undermines all metaphysical solemnities, sometimes by a brutal aesthetics of squalor and shock. (qtd in Harvey 1996: 7–8)

If we think back to the work in Part 2, we can see that many of the aesthetic strategies of the Historical Avant-Garde reappear within the postmodern framework – the centrality of playfulness, reference to popular culture, a desire for a lack of fixity and so on. The texts included in Part 2, although appearing to have little in common at times, shared certain 'attitudes' to theatre and performance, such as a breaking away from the dominance or linearity of text, or the reframing of the visual in performance – either scenographically or in terms of the role of the performer. So too, the texts included in this part share certain 'attitudes', in particular to the idea and function of narrative. One of the tenets of postmodern theory is the idea of the collapse of 'grand narratives'; thus it is useful to explore the ways in which contemporary theatre and performance practice has reconceptualized the creation, exploration and expression of narrative.

The death of narrative?

Contemporary theatre and performance frequently draw attention to narrative, and fragment, undermine or play with its role and function. Narrative, story, storytelling and story making and unmaking are central to postmodern performance practice as is typified in the work of both Laurie Anderson and SuAndi included in this volume (see 5.1 and 5.4). In a text such as Forced Entertainment's *Speak Bitterness* (5.3), for example, the absence of named characters or indeed the lack of apportioning text to specified speakers does not however undermine the dominant function of narration and narrative within the text. What is important is the chance assignment, combination and tonal delivery of the narrative not the chronology or linearity. Similarly, the effect of narrative is not intentionally laid out by the authors – meaning is gathered, if at all, on a personal basis and cumulatively through either the recognition or non-recognition of patterns in the language or in the actions the language narrates. We connect to the text in short moments through the images, the moments and events that the text narrates. As such, *Speak Bitterness* could be considered as a postmodern performance text *par excellence*. It demonstrates Jean François Lyotard's 'incredulity toward metanarratives' (Lyotard 1997: xxiv), and remains rich on the level of micro-narrative as opposed to metanarrative. Narrative is central to a great deal of postmodern and contemporary performance practice. As Linda Hutcheon also suggests, the question is not about metanarrative in retreat, it is more to do with a confrontation with the unproblematic assertion of a metanarrative that is somehow a representation of 'truth' (Hutcheon 1989).

What is often absent in the performance practices included here is a linear sequence, or 'character', or any security of knowledge of the authentic or authoritative voice. Confession or testimony may be central to the composition of the text, but they are a game, an act, a playful bricolage, a fabrication and manipulation of imagined and experienced events. Whether the events confessed are 'real' or not is irrelevant, what is important is the telling and witnessing of them. The relationship between *acting* and *being* – so central to differentiating between theatre and performance – here becomes blurred: a feature of many of the performance works which come out of the period we cover in this part (see Auslander 1997). In the work of Laurie Anderson, Forced Entertainment and SuAndi, for example, there is less of an engagement with the idea of 'acting' than there is with the presence/non-presence of the performer; many of the texts are self-generated and so too the relationship between author and performer is radically altered. What comes into question is the relationship between the 'fictional' and the 'real' and this is a central conundrum in a great deal of the cultural theory and practice which has been produced during the past forty years. Whilst ideas of replication and authenticity were foundational to Walter Benjamin's exploration of cultural production (see 3.7), Baudrillard's seminal *Simulacra and Simulation* (5.7) has become a key reference point for contemporary cultural theory and practice.

Jean Baudrillard, *The Precession of Simulacra* (5.7)

In her chapter 'Postmodernism and the Scene of Theater', Elinor Fuchs elaborates a thesis concerning how the 'the protean image of the theatrical' is embedded in the writings of many leading philosophers and cultural theorists from the 1960s to the 1980s (Fuchs 1996: 147). Citing such seminal figures as Guy Debord (see also Part 4), Jacques Derrida, Hélène Cixous, Gilles Deleuze and Félix Guattari, Fuchs argues that 'semiotic, deconstructive, neo-Marxist [and] feminist' writings from this period, 'serve as an anticipation and explication of the postmodern paradigm shift' (ibid: 146). For Fuchs, this meeting point between theatricality and postmodernism reaches its pinnacle in the work of Jean Baudrillard, who 'contemplates the movement of society from a stable real to a final and negative hyper-theatre' (ibid: 151).

Baudrillard's relevance to theatre, and particularly to contemporary performance, can be traced in the two extracts included in this part from his *Simulacra and Simulation* (5.7). Here Baudrillard argues that, in our excessively technologically mediatized world, 'simulation threatens the difference between the 'true' and the 'false', the 'real' and the 'imaginary' (ibid). Our experience of the world is now so immensely mediated that 'the real' no longer constitutes an objective concrete actuality, as something that can then be 'reflected' or 'represented' to reveal its truth content. Thus – as spectators – our experience of events, however actual or real these original events might be, is *simulated*. For example, Baudrillard controversially compared the 1991 Gulf War to the film thriller *Capricorn One* (1977), in which astronauts supposedly exploring the planet Mars, the events of which are being televised around the world, are in reality being filmed in a studio (Baudrillard 2006: 61). Baudrillard is seeking to challenge the very efficacy, even the possibility, of *representation* as something that operates on 'the principle of the equivalence of the sign and of the real' (5.7: 784). Thus, transmutation of the image (or sign) can be characterized in four consecutive stages:

> it is the reflection of a profound reality; it masks and denatures a profound reality; it masks the *absence* of a profound reality; it has no relation to any reality whatsoever: it is its own pure simulacrum. (ibid)

When Baudrillard states, '[i]llusion is no longer possible, because the real is no longer possible', he offers both an ideological critique of contemporary society and provides a cue to performance practitioners and theorists for questioning and reformulating the underpinnings of those theatre practices – particularly Naturalism and realism – but also any practice that operates within 'conventional' representational regimes (Baudrillard 2006: 19). This is also where we can a make a useful distinction between philosophical and political impulses behind the Historical Avant-Garde and those of contemporary performance. We might view the Surrealists, for example, as seeking the means to create radical cultural and aesthetic forms that render an *authenticity* to human subjectivity. For Baudrillard, however, as for a range of contemporary performance makers, the very idea of an authentic subject is up for grabs. Furthermore, if theatricality, mediatization and deconstructing ideas of 'the real' are central to Baudrillard's critique of society, so too are they in the making and understanding of spectatorship in contemporary performance.

Robert Lepage and Marie Brassard's *Polygraph* (5.2)

The story of three characters, whose lives are bound to each other by a series of connected associations with a dead woman who never appears on stage other than in a filmic replayed image of her death, *Polygraph* is built around the conceit that a polygraph machine – a lie detector – has the power to define 'truth' from 'falsity', the real from the simulated. The play relies on theatre's capacity to capitalize on the possibilities of mediatized culture with its 'metamorphosis of film into theatre and of theatre back into film' (Dundjerovic 2007: 180). The characters 'perform' moments and events from their lives as well as dialoguing with each other in 'real time'. Lucie, an actress who is playing the part of the murdered woman in a film, performs 'flashback' scenes as if she is either being filmed – a filmed simulation – or the woman *actually* being murdered – a performed simulation. The actors occasionally perform in slow motion, shifting the timeframe of the action and focusing our gaze on the finite movements of a particular exchange. At one point David, the detective who originally carried out the polygraph test on François – a key suspect in the original murder investigation – is visible to the audience only as a 'reflection' in a two-way mirror. Again our gaze is distracted and a character's physical presence is distorted. Some of the text is performed in French (Lepage's company, Ex Machina, are Quebec-based and often perform using mutiple languages), whilst translations are projected onto the walls. Titles for the scenes are also projected onto the stage walls and the action moves back and forwards in time, with a frequent use of simultaneous scenes, sometimes played without speech, sometimes entirely interconnected as for example in the first scene where David is reading an autopsy report about the murder victim and François is in a university class giving a 'presentation' about the Berlin Wall.

Just as the action moves between and interlaces the 'live' and the 'acted out' or 'playbacked', so too there is a complex and accidental interweaving of the lives and histories of the three characters throughout the text. David has emigrated to Canada from East Germany, François is studying the political history of (East) Germany in his political science class, Lucie is an actress, having an affair with David, and is cast in a film as the dead woman who was François's close friend. As the text moves backwards and forwards in time, and the performers 'playback' and 'flashback' scenes, so we piece together the story. The play is full of references to watching, or witnessing and being watched. Throughout, David is observing François who he recognizes as being a key suspect in the original murder case, and remembers in detail the 'polygraph interview', which he carried out on him. Lucie, an actress whose professional life is all about being observed, questions the power relations involved in film's ability to simulate reality, and states that when being filmed she felt as if she was being somehow taken apart, or fragmented, in the process. *Polygraph* plays with our perception as an audience through its way of creating 'temporal and spatial interrelations' and its use of intermediality (Chapple and Kattenbelt 2006: 11). It is a love story in which death, sex, violence and desire are intertwined, and the 'performance' of reality, whether live, played back, fractured or distorted, is self-consciously theatricalized using the compositional possibilities of both theatre and film. Also produced as a film, *Polygraphe* (1996), the play is both hybrid text and simple 'whodunnit' (see Garrity 2000). Thus questions of truth or veracity – the answer to which can only ultimately be subjective – lie at the heart of the play. There is no closure and we are provided with a steady flow of multiple and contradictory 'truths'.

Contemporary performance: text and textuality and the 'death of the author'

Contemporary performance repeatedly breaks the traditional linearity of text – often more than one narrative is at play at any one time, and may or may not be revealed or explored in chronology (see *Polygraph* 5.2 and *Speak Bitterness* 5.3). Much early postmodern performance played with the formal qualities of text, fragmenting or repeating it and exploring the play of tone and rhythm that language might offer rather than its semantic significance or meaning (see, for example, Robert Wilson's early work with Philip Glass such as *Einstein on the Beach* [1976]; see Holmburg 1996). Similarly, contemporary performance plays with the compositional possibilities of repeated patterns of sound, movement and chosen 'rules' in the process of making work (see also Part 2). These 'rules' are often similar to those in a game – so whilst the performers are generating materials through improvisation, for example, the 'rules' provide a dramaturgical framework for processing those materials and constituting them into the performance (see Barba: 5.9 and Etchells 1996a). What the performance might then capitalize upon is its ability to elicit response rather than 'interpretation', to produce experience rather than meaning.

We need here to make reference to philosopher and cultural theorist Roland Barthes's seminal essay *The Death of the Author* (1977). Barthes's essay made the radical observation that meaning was not to be derived from the singular position of the author but rather was created by the reader. In other words, 'in the multiplicity of writing, everything is to be *disentangled*, nothing *deciphered*' (ibid: 147). The author ceases to function as a 'god-like' figure, the creator of all meaning, and is replaced with the mediation by the reader of all they themselves bring to the reading of the text – their history, their social milieu, their memory, their sexuality and so on. Such a stark departure from a traditional view of the relationship between the maker of the artwork, the artwork itself and its audience, as Barthes's essay suggests, marks a cultural turn in the democratizing of the role of the spectator. In his earlier *Myth Today* (5.6), Barthes suggests that we should 'take *language*, *discourse*, *speech*, etc., to mean any significant unit or synthesis, whether verbal or visual: a photograph will be a kind of speech for us in the same way as a newspaper article; even objects will become speech, if they mean something' (5.6: 775). Thus what constitutes text cannot be reduced to the written and the spoken word, and this of course has a profound significance for theatre and performance, where, with the exception perhaps of the Historical Avant-Garde, the written or spoken word dominated in a hierarchy of elements until the closing decades of the twentieth century. Barthes was primarily a semiologist, interested in the formation, expression and analysis of both linguistic and visual signs. He offers at least two momentous theoretical propositions which have had an impact on contemporary performance practices. The first is the idea that the *intention* of the author, in terms of the creation of meaning, may bear little relation to the actual and multiple readings of the artwork by the reader or, for our purposes, the spectator. The second is the recognition that written language cannot be assumed to be the dominant feature of performance or cultural production, nor is it singular – language can be visual, kinaesthetic, musical. In fact what comes into play is a textuality and an intertextuality in terms of the composition of an artwork as a cultural signifier, to which no one meaning can be attached. Thus for Barthes the authority of the author is not fixed, nor is the relationship between an object and what that object signifies.

These ideas are played out very differently in performance practices over the period covered in this part. If we focus on the ways in which text is composed, processed and then located inside the performance in relation to both the performer, their performed materials and the spectator, we can see connections between the seemingly diverse practices included in this part. Early in the period, companies such as Odin Theatre in Denmark created performance works from found texts and improvisation. The performance would come out of a process whereby the director mediated their creations through his own compositional technique. All this took place without a desire to create fixed meaning or order, but, rather, to materialize performed moments, image sequences, soundscapes and relationships between performers. The montage of materials therefore would not be driven by any sense of a singular or overarching narrative but rather a bricolage of responses to materials and ideas generated by a particular theme. So, for example, in the original version of Odin's *Brecht's Ashes* (1982–4), the source materials included a biography of Brecht, text from his plays and poetry such as *Mother Courage* (1939), and historical events from Brecht's life – World War I, the rise of Nazism and so on. These were responded to by the performers in the improvisational process, and the material they generated was then formed into a performative composition by the director Eugenio Barba. This kind of process has almost become understood as conventional practice now, but in its time presented a radical departure in European practice whereby the ensemble, the director and the spectator all, in one way or another, assume the role of 'author' in terms of the generation of possible 'meanings' from a performance event.

Eugenio Barba (1936–) in *Dramaturgy* and *Montage* (5.9) writes about the strategies involved in making performance. His work comes out of a tradition inspired by the performance training work of Jerzy Grotowski (1933–99); see Grotowski (2000)) and from that of ensemble theatre making which has developed and thrived during the period covered in Part five. Barba sees text, performance and spectatorship as intertwined: all are elements of the process of making a performance and constitute the basis of action, from the perspective of both the performer and the spectator: 'Everything that works directly on the spectators' attention, on their understanding, their emotions, their kinaesthesia, is an action' (5.9: 816). Thus, for Barba, dramaturgy – a term which has a variety of implied meanings from the process of researching a production to the management of the creation and composition of text in rehearsal – is relevant to much more than the text as the written or spoken word. The 'text' of performance relates to its overall texture, its textuality – as Barba reminds us, the word text originates from a conception of a 'weaving together' of different elements: 'In this sense, there is no performance which does not have "text"' (ibid). Thus in *Montage* (5.9), where Barba discusses the processing of materials generated for performance, he uses a theoretical concept originating in film practice to build a strategy for describing the practice of performance making. Here, the term 'montage' relates to the ways in which materials both come out of a creative impulse and are then (re)placed into a performative sequence. Again, the object is not to 'represent or to reproduce' in any straightforward way. The sequence of movements created by a performer are not imitative of the image, word or instruction which may have inspired them, and instead is motivated by the performer's personal response to the given impulse. This, in turn, is effected by their existing and available movement vocabulary, their memory, their own research and so on. What Barba then suggests is that the products of the performers' creative process can be reprocessed and remontaged without regard to their origin or the potential fixing of meaning for the spectator. The business of a theatre maker is not to define an assumed reception of the materials which comprise the performance.

Barba's work comes out of a particular tradition and specific cultural moment. Working from the 1970s and 1980s onwards, he developed a kind of anthropology of theatre, working across Europe, South America and Asia, building a network of experimental theatre companies and practitioners. He connects his own work with the theories and practices of a variety of twentieth-century innovative practitioners such as Stanislavski, Eisenstein, Artaud, Brecht and Grotowski. His intercultural interweaving of Western and non-Western performance techniques and desire to find a communion between performer and spectator might appear to be somehow old-fashioned. But this has been married with a technique of theatre making which works against an understanding of theatre as commodity or overt polemic, producing instead theatre which is technically sophisticated and demanding from the perspective of the performer and audience. Text is less important than texture; experience is not mediated by a traditional dramaturgy of chronological narrative, plot and character. Barba's theatre and the intercultural International School of Theatre Anthropology (founded in 1979) are predicated on the creation of a laboratory for experimentation and an artistic space in which the unique qualities of theatre and performance can be investigated (see Barba and Savarese 2006). Although unique and somewhat removed from, or at least standing back from, a great deal of practice created by their contemporaries, the tradition developed by Barba and Odin Theatre lies at one end of a spectrum of contemporary performance practices, but shares with others the desire to attack, as Hans-Thies Lehmann notes, 'language's function of representation' (5.8: 791).

Tim Etchells/Forced Entertainment and *Speak Bitterness* (5.3)

Originally created as a six-hour durational performance, the text of *Speak Bitterness* included in this volume represents the performance score at a particular historical moment; as Etchells notes, the text 'remains decidedly in process' (5.3: 736). Originally performed by eight male and female performers working inside a blue tarpaulin box, where the audience were free to come and go at will during the six hours, the 'theatre' version of the piece represented here has been developed from 1995 onwards. For this, one wall of the tarpaulin box was 'lost' to fit the piece into a more traditional stage space. On the back of the tarpaulin is printed the phrase 'SPEAK BITTERNESS' and the ceiling is hung with bare electric light bulbs extended over the audience. This scenography remains fairly constant over the lifetime of the piece, as Hugo Glendinning's photographs from the 2009 version imply (see Figures 35 and 36).

In reworking the piece over time, the company have made use of video recording in rehearsal and tried to preserve the 'feeling' of the original durational version – 'spatial and performance intimacy, a sense of real-time process' – whilst adding what Etchells calls 'structural architecture' (ibid: 693). In the original version, scripts, the long list of confessions and catalogues of statements of guilt printed on sheets of paper, were placed on the table, which runs right across the front of the stage. Chairs were placed at the table and at the back of the stage – and performers chose which bits of text to read or perform on a random basis, adhering to the improvisational 'rules' set up during the process of making the performance. In the version reproduced here, there is a 'fixed' ordering of the text or, rather, the 'structural architecture' is less dependent on the rhythm and chance moments of an improvisational format. Some sections and the ordering of the text in the 'theatre' version in performance, however, continue to be improvised. Whilst there is some repetition of ideas, confessions or motifs, and occasional moments are extended beyond the bare statement of fact – the confession of working for the Beckhams, for example, extends beyond one statement, to another and another, all related to the final statement 'We just wanted to work for the Beckhams we didn't really mind in what capacity' (ibid: 740). The piece still gives the impression of 'a practice of listing and of cataloguing-through-language', as Etchells notes. Reminiscent of the performance practice of some of the Historical Avant-Garde (see Part 2), Etchells is at pains to point out, however, that this 'text' is not like the 'modernist' experiments in collage where images integrate and overlay each other. Rather, 'the act of listing does not layer, merge, overlay, re-mix or blur together its contents. Lists rather, with a seriality that implies but never fully delivers narrative, let each of their items stand alone but together, a menu or line of ingredients rather than a soup' (ibid: 735). We should note here, however, that our propensity to organize materials on reception can lead us to reformulate the text as delivered in terms of Barba's 'montage': we try to find connections between images implied, events described, the performers' tone and mood of delivery and their relationships with each other on stage. We might, for example, after noting the reference to celebrities such as the artist Tracey Emin and the footballer David Beckham, expect to find more direct references to celebrities, but are just as likely to find references to more anonymized figures – Colin, Jason, Cynthia and so on. Etchells is aware of and plays with this expectation when he states that, 'Lists are blank or "spacious" since the job of guessing the constituency of listed items and of unpacking their individual meaning is left to the viewer' (ibid). The audience experiences the moment but produces the 'meaning' evoking the terms of Roland Barthes's *Death of the Author* (see above). This impetus is built into a great deal of Forced Entertainment's work. They often play with the idea of gaps or emptiness: the creation of 'space', as Etchells calls it, is a deliberate strategy played out in their practice. Whilst this again connects their work process to Barba's idea of dramaturgy (5.9), it is important to note that their work comes out of a very different tradition, equally linked to live art and performance art as it is to a theatre heritage. Both rely on the spectator to 'complete' the picture as it were, to become their own 'author'. Here the connection to innovations in art practice and the development of conceptual live art in the 1970s are paramount. In this sense we might see 'performance art' as performance practices 'that explicitly reject, oppose, expose or move beyond the framework of theatre' (Ridout 2007: 5; see also Féral 1982). A great deal of contemporary performance plays with the theatrical, and self-consciously manipulates and challenges our understanding and expectation of a theatre event.

In *Speak Bitterness*, the performers are all dressed in anonymous, everyday 'working' or semi-formal clothing: grey, black or dark-coloured suits. They come to the front of the stage one, two or more at a time, and pick up the sheets of paper where the texts are printed: they might remain standing or they might sit. The tone and speed of delivery of the text varies, and there are clear moments when it seems as if the performers are in dialogue or are inflecting their speech with a particular emotional 'mood', but almost as soon as this appears to be happening in a manner which might elicit empathy, something changes or the speaker switches: our moment of recognition is quickly undermined. None of this is implied in the text as printed in this anthology – where, as we have noted previously, speakers are not assigned specific text, nor is there any sense of stage direction, rhythm, pause and so on. An 'understanding' of *Speak Bitterness* cannot be derived or reduced from its arbitrary content. Predicated on the 'live dynamic of the performers interacting with each other and the text' (ibid: 736), this is a piece, like much of the work in Part five, that is more specifically concerned with the act and experience of spectating, of perception and of the relationship between the elements of an event. As Etchells notes:

> Far from the blanket communal comfort it may appear to offer, the 'we' of *Speak Bitterness* both refuses and accuses those watching, dividing and subdividing the supposedly shared social space of the auditorium. (ibid)

Phelan reminds us that Etchells uses the term 'witness' rather than 'spectator', as he notes, 'to witness an event is to be present at it in some fundamentally ethical way, to feel the weight of things and one's place in them, even if that place is simply, for the moment, as an on-looker' (Etchells 2005: 18). For Phelan, witnessing, as distinct from spectating, implies an ethical response where we are directly implicated (ibid: 9). The way in which this operates on the level of the 'political' is different from the 'political' as we have identified it elsewhere in this anthology (see Parts 3 and 4 in particular). Whilst Etchells notes the 'suspect certainties of what other people call political theatre' (ibid: 19), his use of the idea of witnessing evokes a differently conceptualized political concern enacted in performance. This is much more explorative of the contingencies of relationship and uncertainties of encounter in the *moment* of performance, than any identifiable political programme or ideology.

Hans-Thies Lehmann and 'postdramatic theatre' (5.8)

Forced Entertainment's *Speak Bitterness* provides a useful example of what Hans-Thies Lehmann has named, in relation to contemporary theatre and performance, as 'postdramatic theatre' (Lehmann 2006). The term was originally coined by performance theorist Richard Schechner to describe certain aspects of avant-garde practices from the 1960s associated with 'happenings' (see Schechner 1988; Sandford 1995). However, Lehmann's developed conception of postdramatic theatre has, over the past decade, offered a paradigm for understanding a range of diverse performance practices within contemporary theatre that seek to challenge – aesthetically, culturally and politically – the authority of drama-based theatre. Postdramatic theatre is not, however, reducible to a particular style and form of theatre and/or performance practice (5.8). Lehmann's proposal that, 'there is never a harmonious relationship but rather a perpetual conflict between text and scene', reflects upon the ways in which contemporary practitioners have sought to problematize notions of the dramatic (ibid: 790):

> The adjective 'postdramatic' denotes a theatre that feels bound to operate beyond drama, at a time 'after' the authority of the dramatic paradigm in theatre. What it does not mean is an abstract negation and mere looking away from the tradition of drama. 'After' drama means that it lives on as a structure – however weakened and exhausted – of the 'normal' theatre; as an expectation of large parts of its audience, as a foundation for many of its means of representation. (Lehmann 2006: 27)

In his attempts to define the 'postdramatic', Lehmann refers to theatre and performance practices where conventional Aristotelian-influenced dramatic forms are substituted by self-consciously deconstructed narrative, and compositional strategies which are 'manufactured', not to support logic and internal coherence, but, rather, as a challenge to linearity and synthesis. Simply put, 'postdramatic' theatre relies on a reordering of the hierarchies of performance where text no longer determines or defines performance. As a term, 'postdramatic' does not mean 'post drama', as in without dramatic text. Lehmann uses the word 'dramatic' in all its complexity and what he tries to identify is a *vocabulary* of contemporary theatre and performance which certain companies and practitioners appear to share. Thus, as with postmodernism, 'the prefix "post"' indicates that a culture or artistic practice has stepped out of the previously unquestioned horizon of modernity but still exists with some kind of reference to it' (ibid). Lehmann's postdramatic theatre interfaces with the idea of 'postmodern theatre' discussed elsewhere in this introduction. However, postdramatic refers to both critical interventions and aesthetic practices that cannot simply be subsumed under the umbrella of postmodernism: 'postdramatic' theatre demands a further extraction, a recognition of a specific series of attitudes to practice and places as a connected subset in terms of categorizing practices. For example, Caryl Churchill's *Far Away* (see Part 4) engages with a number of postmodern discourses, such as fragmentation and the 'problem' of contemporary subjectivity and agency. Nevertheless, however innovative we might regard Churchill's use of dramatic form to be, the play does not fundamentally challenge the basis of the solo-authored play text as a means for mediating contemporary concerns. Other performance scores which rely on textuality rather than semantics – produced through collaborative or ensemble-based practices – can more easily be categorized as postdramatic in their challenge to a formal adherence and traditional hierarchy of performance elements. Similarly, 'postmodern' ideas and attitudes might find a resonance in contemporary productions of classical texts, yet such productions do not necessarily challenge the value and efficacy of 'drama'. Thus The Wooster Group, who cut, delete, reformulate, regurgitate and redefine classical texts, and Odin, who mix sources, relayer, extract from and rebind texts, might both be seen as companies whose work is postdramatic despite the fact that their work borrows both aesthetical, technically and compositionally from very diverse cultural heritages.

Lehmann offers us another model of definition of practice to add to the categories of postmodern and contemporary. But just as there are crossovers and crosscurrents here, so too the postdramatic cannot be separated out in total. It is possible for a production to take a postmodern approach – look for example again at Figure 7, where we see a scenographically postmodern conceptualization of Chekhov's *Three Sisters* – without altering the formal and absolutely modernist qualities of the dramatic text. This kind of approach has been common during the 1980s and 1990s where productions of classic texts have been inflected by postmodern ideas. However, this does not make them postdramatic in Lehmann's terms. Interestingly, the work of Robert Lepage is defined by Lehmann as postdramatic but, certainly in the case of the text and discussion included here, the work lies more clearly on a line *between* the postmodern and the postdramatic.

Contemporary performance: aesthetic/political strategies

Groups and ensembles

Contemporary performance varies as to the degree with which it embraces the many cultural theories generated during the past forty years. There is a sense, however, in which one can identify moments of exchange between practice and theory in the work of a wide variety of contemporary practitioners. In turn, there are certain processes and operational structures which can be identified as typifying performance practice during this period: one which might be seen as key is the proliferation of performance groups or ensembles.

Making theatre and performance within an ensemble or collective organizational structure is not new to the contemporary period but arguably such practice has become more common-place amongst theatre and performance makers in Europe and in the USA. Whilst many of these groups have dynamic 'leaders' or directors, they place an emphasis on collective ways of working in which the hierarchies so prevalent in more 'traditional' theatre practice are subverted. Often all members of the group are paid on an equal basis and each member has multiple responsibilities within the company, as performer, technician, administrator and so on. Sometimes membership of the group remains fairly permanent, as is the case with The Wooster Group and Goat Island (USA), Odin Teatret (Denmark) and Forced Entertainment (UK). Equally the group may have a core membership whilst additional performers become members for the duration of a project such as is the case with Théâtre du Soleil (France) (see Williams 1999). Some ensembles follow a particular theatre heritage, an ethos or a commonly shared ethic; others have a shared training, as is the case with Theatre de Complicite (UK). In Europe in particular, where funding is more readily available than in the USA, these groups make performances over a prolonged period, sometimes one or two years, and the work stays in the repertoire for a further two or three, or even more, years.

The work of many of these performance groups often exemplifies a conscious desire to push at the boundaries of and interconnect different art forms, thus moving towards a hybridity of form. Here the lines between performance, performance art, live art and theatre have become blurred, shifting or interchangeable. There is also a shared interest in experimentation with the performer/spectator relationship – with the spectator becoming more directly implicated in the *composition* of the performance, for example. Similarly, many of the performance groups dislodge the primacy and centrality of the text, patchworking or sampling different classical texts together with personal materials such as autobiographical texts, or simply fragmenting and rearranging classical texts. One example here is The Wooster Group's *House/Lights* (1997), which performs a 'playful interweaving of Gertrude Stein's *Dr Faustus Lights the Lights* (1938) and Joseph Mawra's B-movie, *Olga's House of Shame* (1964) (see Quick 2007: 14). The delivery, as opposed to the 'acting out' of the text, happens within the context of a manipulation of a live and recorded multimedia display. What much of the work of these groups and ensembles exemplify is experimentation with power relations between text, space, performer, technology and performance during the period. There is often a refusal, for example, to accept the geographical and compositional limitations of traditional performance spaces and theatre buildings. Thus, we see performance moving through galleries, museums, underground carparks, empty hotels, railway stations, city scapes and everyday public space – made for a site-specific space or from a site-sensitive position. Performances might require audiences to come and go, or engage with performers in small groups. In terms of the pragmatics of performance making we see on different levels, and to various extents, the embracing of simultaneous staging – our gaze is not directed but confronted by a collection of images. This might include a combination or integration of live and recorded media, which may also include film directly relating to the live performer's work on stage, or film which bears no discernible relation to the stage action.

Solo performance and the auto/biographical 'I': SuAndi and *The Story of M* (5.4)

Whilst the choice to work in a collective through an ensemble method is often a political one, informed by a commitment to a less hierarchical approach to theatre making, so too many performers choosing to work in the field of solo performance do so through a belief in its political as well as aesthetic potential and economic viability. This is even more so in the case of autobiographical solo work which embodies a strategic impulse to unveil, to retell and to reposition the subject. As Deirdre Heddon succinctly summarizes:

> The vast majority of autobiographical performances have been concerned with using the public arena of performance in order to 'speak out', attempting to make visible denied or marginalised subjects, or to 'talk back', aiming to challenge, contest and problematise dominant representations and assumptions about those subjects. (Heddon 2007: 20)

SuAndi is one of the foremost artists of her generation and describes herself as a 'performance poet'. She is known for her work with black arts organizations in Britain and elsewhere, and in particular for the ways in which her activism as a black woman artist and performer shapes her practice with 'diverse … and disadvantaged, communities' (Aston and Harris 2008: 60). This sense of the artist as activist also strongly impacts on her solo performance work as *The Story of M* (5.4) exemplifies: her ethnic background has a significant impact on the 'production, reception and perception of her work' (Aston and Harris 2008: 62). However, her performance text as reprinted here also firmly places her in a general tradition of solo performance alongside practitioners like Laurie Anderson (5.1), whose cultural background could not be more different.

   The Story of M is performed by SuAndi herself, who for most of the text 'plays' her mother dying of cancer in hospital. *M* tells the story of her life as a working woman and a mother. It is not until the end of the text, as Aston has noted, that we realize that her mother is a white woman who has married a black man, even though the text is strewn with details of the racial hatred and ignorance which have surrounded *M* and her family. Here, also, the 'mother' transforms into the daughter, SuAndi the performer, who removes her 'costume' and closes the performance by interconnecting her mother's life with her own, 'it's only the body that dies. But the spirit continues and you carry it here, in this place of love' (5.4: 768). The text represents a recapitulation of a life story which runs from the middle years of the twentieth century and depicts the interconnection between issues of class, sexism and race. Aston notes the weaving together by *M* of issues of racism and discourses of 'pollution or contamination' in her descriptions of the social response to her interracial marriage and her children (Aston 2003: 145). *M*, a working-class woman, transgresses many social taboos: children out of wedlock, sharp social wit, a woman bringing up a family on her own, a mother of mixed-race offspring and so on. The racial abuse she suffers is unveiled in such a way as to express a history of class as well as racial stereotypes – she is an Irish working-class woman living in England at a time when the Irish were also socially stigmatized. *The Story of M* touches on the personal and the political simultaneously, celebrating the multicultural world of working-class Manchester and Liverpool in the 1950s, as well as noting its decline into a racially divided community, a divide which reflects the breakdown of urban communities with the fragmentation of industry after World War II. SuAndi's text is not confined to referring to the particular history of England and makes numerous references to the influence of world events, such as the assassination of Malcolm X, and the lives of ordinary people living on the other side of the world. Far from being a liberal text which presents the victim of racial abuse as a survivor, *M*'s humour draws us willingly into her world but we are also implicated by it as an audience. We may laugh at the stories she comically depicts, as SuAndi notes, '*M*'s resilience and caustic humour draw the audience in' (SuAndi 2006: 126). The humour is deliberately subverted by our growing sense that the racial abuse *M* describes is real and has had profound effects on the lives of people she represents. Being spat at in the street, refused credit because of your gender or race, or hearing your neighbours shouting, 'Don't cut the branches on that side, I don't want those niggers looking in on me' (5.4: 764), were parts of *M*'s life not shared by a white audience. SuAndi suggests that her work gives expression to 'familial and cultural ancestry' (SuAndi 2006). She also notes the dangers of nostalgia inherent in a retelling of history so central to much feminist and black performance, but that a weaving of 'the past into the present' is a political strategy to performatively 'fill the voids of history' (ibid: 125). Black culture and experience have been historically marginalized, and SuAndi's performance text works against the ongoing practice of such marginalization. As such, SuAndi's work connects strongly with feminist practice and is embedded in the work of a new generation of black artists whose work crosses the boundaries between art, poetry and performance. It articulates the experience not only of the auto/biographical individual but is a positive response to aspects of what has been described by one critic as a 'black community in crisis in Britain', a crisis of agency and subjectivity (Ugwu 1995: 56). Equally, SuAndi's work can be linked to the work of many US black artists whose practice centres on modes of testimony in performance as a means of cultural memorialization (ibid).

Storytelling, testimony and subjectivity: Laurie Anderson (5.1 and 5.10) and Guillermo Gómez-Peña (5.5 and 5.11)

The critical and creative relationship between the contemporary world, the artwork and the artist is central to the practice of both US and US/Mexican performance artists Laurie Anderson and Guillermo Gómez-Peña, each of whom challenge and reformulate an understanding of the cultural and political role of artist and artwork in a contemporary, fragmented and alienating culture. These artists crucially draw on testimony, technology and storytelling to make performances that disturb and relocate the subject and subjectivity of performer and audience.

Laurie Anderson's work stretches from the 1970s to the present day and of all the artists whose work is examined in this part she is the one who has most claim to popular notoriety. Her composition 'O Superman' reached the number two slot in the UK pop charts in 1981. Sung, spoken and framed by an electronic soundscape, the song is a fiercely critical take on the American Dream and a culture of war, but it is the unusual catchy refrain which frames the song that caught the public imagination. Anderson originally worked in performance art where, having trained as a classical musician, she invented electronically enhanced musical instruments. The interstices of technology and music have remained in a constant relationship of enquiry throughout her work. A successful recording artist in the 1980s, her work during this time often took the form of concert-performances interwoven with storytelling. Here she not only combined performance, story, music and song, but integrated innovative technological interventions into the work, playing for example with the acoustic possibilities of microphones, wired mouthpieces, a drum bodysuit, film and slide projections, loop tapes, or live and recorded voice mediated through computers and so on. Her seminal eight-hour durational piece *United States* (1983) carried what have become her trademark, 'political commentary and intellectual inquiry', and is seen by many to have been both 'a summation of the sensibilities and value system of the 1970s', as well as 'a gateway to the 1980s' (Goldberg 2000: 11–13). Some of her songs have been 'interpreted as spoofs on language theories', and a number of her works make direct reference to philosophers such as Wittgenstein and Walter Benjamin (ibid: 17).

Stories from the Nerve Bible (1993: 5.1) was a full-length multimedia performance which used 'elaborate computer-generated stage effects, including a row of television monitors across the stage', and a mixture of writing, depicting 'recollections from the past and questions about the future' (Goldberg 2000: 156). Deeply political in its outlook, the performance refers to the first Gulf War and the transformation of the experience of travelling for US citizens because of an atmosphere of paranoia. The piece also refers to the bizarre way in which war was being glorified in the media because of technology which supported precision bombing, celebrated by military press coverage. Anderson notes that war is being talked about in the same language as we might use to talk about 'grand opera' and the 'superbowl' (ibid: 159). The excerpt we include here takes us from the middle of the Pacific to Mexico to New York to Anderson's failed trip to the North Pole. She mentions Marinetti's glorification of war (see Part 2), her early associations with Southern Baptism and religion, and details of a phone conversation with the Avant-Garde cult-status composer and theorist John Cage (1912–92) where she asked him about his thoughts on the future. Anderson structured the piece around the 'idea of time', and images of time run through the performance as a whole (see 5:1): she described the piece as a 'retrospective of the future' (McKenzie 1997: 33). The performance weaves complex philosophical and scientific musings with stories of everyday life and the experience of being an artist in the late twentieth century.

Despite the high-tech production and sophisticated integrating and hybridizing of media, Anderson's project is one which is concerned with the human and making art 'that other people could understand' (5.10). She notes that the term 'multimedia artist', which many critics have tried to label her with, is less relevant as a label than a 'storyteller' (ibid), seeking a 'real contact' with her audiences. Thus despite the technology and extraordinary visual composition of much of her work, her impulse is to communicate very directly using testimony, observation and a keen sense of political critique. Always commenting on contemporary and immediate events, one critic has noted the connection between Anderson's work and Baudrillard's theory, where 'simulation comes across ... as an authentic expression in a highly technological world ... Her new work continues to read as a search for cracks between simulation and authentic being, as a quest for place wherein to reinsert both a new meaning and a critique of that meaning' (Jestrovic 2004: 37). Similarly, the body in her work is not 'unified, coherent' or 'stable', but 'crosses borders (male/female, animal/human, organic/machine)': it is 'multiple, fragmented, distorted, transforming and transformative' (Prinz 2002: 403).

Such a landscape, in which the authentic and the simulated compete, is also explored by a number of other performance artists and performance activists during the period covered in Part five. For performance artist/activist Guillermo Gómez-Peña (see 5.5 and 5.11), late capitalism and globalization have created a world characterized by 'unprecedented emptiness and acute social crises' (Gómez-Peña 2001b: 26), which has brought with it a 'backlash against humanistic concerns and identity politics' (ibid: 7). Identifying with both Mexican and American cultures, Gómez-Peña's work crosses what he names as 'extremely volatile geographic and cultural borders' (Gómez-Peña 2001a: 7). He defines himself as a 'migrant provocateur, an intercultural pirate' (ibid: 9) and experiments with forms of political activism and performance, operating with great suspicion about the coercive imperatives of mediatized cultures. In the excerpt included here, Gómez-Peña performs in a wheelchair and follows the movement patterns of a 'mechanical video-game-like pattern' whilst being given instructions by his co-performer Roberto Sifuentes (5.5). The performance is full of self-ironizing commentary about performance and the cultural role of an artist, and plays with language, mixing Spanish and English. Gómez-Peña is told by Sifuentes to 'give me some burning trivia' whereby he makes cynical quips about popular cultural appropriation: 'Madonna defeated Argentina & got to play Evita Gooooo Madonna!' (5.5: 772), or jokes about the media furore around the affair between former US President Bill Clinton and White House intern Monica Lewinski, as a 'great millennial soap opera' – 'Clintoris & Linguinsky' – playing on the fetishized relationship between sex and food (ibid: 773). The performance ends with the entrance of another performer as a 'Green Alien' and the 'Beginning of Nintendo Ethnic Wars'. The piece hybridizes 'high' art – beginning with an opera singer singing Mozart with a 'soundbed of Japanese techno music' and popular culture and races with anarchic fervour from one social/political issue to another, with Gómez-Peña failing all the time to achieve the tasks which Sifuentes, as a kind of 'MC puppetmaster', requests of him.

In *Away from the Surveillance Cameras of the Art World: Strategies for Collaboration and Community Activism* (5.11), Gómez-Peña notes how, in making work, he and his collaborators look for 'images that will create a disturbing sediment in the consciousness of the spectator' (ibid: 838).

Like Barba, he refers to the ways in which any of the images or icons he uses in performance have the character of a 'polysemantic image' – whereby different readings by different audiences are expected and welcomed. Indeed he wants his performance work to trigger 'a process of reflexivity' and starts from a 'theoretical proposal' when beginning to make a performance. Just as Anderson's work crosses from popular culture to the world of performance and live art, which has a more elite circulation, so too Gómez-Peña, like SuAndi, crosses between the public world, the 'civic realm' – with, for example, his 'experimental town meetings' where activists, performers and scholars perform and improvise a 'hypertextual script' in a real political meeting/discussion/ performance (5.11) – and the world of performance, working in activist as well as performance contexts. Like SuAndi, too, much of Gómez-Peña's work is concerned with race and gender issues and questions of identity, the formation of subjectivity and the social/political role of the artist, in a fragmented, racist, war-ridden and alienating world.

Conclusion

From the standpoint of the social, the technological and the political, the world of contemporary performance makers and that of the artists and practitioners working at the beginning of the twentieth century is very far apart. Yet the concerns of artists driven to blur the boundaries between art and life, theatre and performance in the early decades of the twentieth century are echoed in the practices of contemporary artists at the start of the twenty-first century. In contemporary performance practice we still see artists responding to the political world in which they function, both embracing and rejecting technology as a means of mediation between human and mechanical expression, moving between the complexities of mediatized performance to the seeming simplicity of confession, autobiography, storytelling and 'stand-up' routines. There is similarly a fascination with the relationship between theatricality and the everyday, fact and fiction, between the 'real' and the 'simulated', in a world where performance and performativity appear to be so embedded in our lives, from mediatized war, the 'performed political personas' of our politicians, viewing transmitted live performance in a cinema, to 'reality' TV, which appears to bear little relation to our lived realities.

This Part can only hint at the huge variety of practice which we might place under the umbrella of contemporary performance, and so has been offered as a 'framed' starting point only, as with the other Parts in the anthology. Arguably, the best writing about the performers and performances we have explored in Part 5 comes from the artists themselves, many of whom articulate far better than critics and scholars how their work operates and the conceptual and aesthetic frameworks involved in the process of making that work. Many of these artists create access to their work through vibrant websites and of course on the endlessly fascinating forum YouTube, where our access to soundbites of performance work help make sense of our 'reading' of the traces of performance available as paper-based documentation. This is an extraordinary resource, less in flux than it was a few years ago as many artists now use it as an archiving resource – so you can see, for example, digitized clips of Odin's early work as well as clips of Forced Entertainment, Laurie Anderson (even the video and rereleased remixes of Anderson's 'O Superman'!) or Gómez-Peña. We conclude this anthology therefore with the suggestion that you combine your 'readings' of the materials it offers with others which await you in cyberspace: type the name of a practitioner, theatre company or performance into the search box and …

Bibliography

Aston, Elaine (2003) *Feminist Views on the English Stage*, Cambridge: Cambridge University Press.

Aston, Elaine and Geraldine Harris (eds) (2008) *Performance Practice and Process: Contemporary (Women Practitioners)*, Basingstoke: Palgrave Macmillan.

Auslander, Phillip (1999) *Liveness: Performance in a Mediatized Culture*, London: Routledge.

Barba, Eugenio and Nicola Savarese (2006 [1991]) *A Dictionary of Theatre Anthropology: The Secret Art of the Performer*, London: Routledge.

Barthes, Roland (1977 [1968]) *Music, Image, Text*, London: Fontana Press.

Baudrillard, Jean (2006 [1981]) *Simulacra and Simulation*, trans. S. F. Glaser, Ann Arbor: University of Michigan Press.

Birringer, Johannes (1993 [1991]) *Theatre, Theory, Postmodernism*, Bloomington: Indiana University Press.

Chapple, Freda and Chiel Kattenbelt (eds) (2006) *Intermediality in Theatre and Performance*, Amsterdam: Rodopi.

Deeney, John (1998) *Writing Live: An Investigation of the Relationship Between Writing and Live Art*, London: London Arts Board.

Dundjerovic, Aleksandar (2007) *The Theatricality of Robert Lepage*, Montreal: McGill-Queen's University Press.

Etchells, Tim (1996a) *Certain Fragments*, London: Routledge.

Etchells, Tim (1996b [1994]) 'Diverse Assembly: Some Trends in Recent Performance', in Theodore Shank (ed.), *Contemporary British Theatre*, Basingstoke: Macmillan, pp. 107–22.

Etchells, Tim (2005 [1999]) *Certain Fragments: Contemporary Performance and Forced Entertainment*, London: Routledge.

Féral, Josette (1982) 'Performance and Theatricality: The Subject Demystified', trans. Therese Lyons, *Modern Drama*, 25(1), 170–81.

Fuchs, Elinor (1996) *The Death of Character: Perspectives on Theatre after Modernism*, Bloomington: Indiana University Press.

Garrity, Henry A. (2000) 'Robert Lepage's Cinema of Time and Space', in Joseph Donohoe Jr and Jane M. Koustas (eds), *Theater sans frontières: Essays on the Dramatic Universe of Robert Lepage*, Michigan: Michigan State University Press, pp. 95–108.

Goldberg, RoseLee (2000) *Laurie Anderson*, London: Thames and Hudson.

Gómez-Peña, Guillermo (2001a [2000]) *Dangerous Border Crossings: The Artist Talks Back*, London: Routledge.

Gómez-Peña, Guillermo (2001b) 'The New Global Culture: Somewhere Between Corporate Multiculturalism and the Mainstream Bizarre (a Border Perspective)', *The Drama Review*, 45(1) (T169), 7–30.

Grotowski, Jerzy (2002 [1968]) *Towards a Poor Theatre*, London: Routledge.

Harvey, David (1996 [1990]) *The Condition of Postmodernity*, Oxford: Blackwells.

Heddon, Dee (2007) *Autobiography and Performance*, Basingstoke: Palgrave Macmillan.

Holmberg, Arthur (1996) *The Theatre of Robert Wilson*, Cambridge: Cambridge University Press.

Hutcheon, Linda (1989) *The Politics of Postmodernism*, London: Routledge.

Jestrovic, Silvija (2004) 'From the Ice Cube Stage to Simulated Reality: Place and Displacement in Laurie Anderson's Performances', *Contemporary Theatre Review*, 14(1), 25–37.

Kaye, Nick (1994) *Postmodernism and Performance*, Basingstoke: Macmillan.

Lehmann, Hans-Thies (2006 [1999]) *Postdramatic Theatre*, trans. K. Jürs-Munby, London: Routledge.

Lyotard, Jean-François (1997 [1979]) *The Postmodern Condition: A Report on Knowledge*, trans. G. Bennington and B. Massumi, Manchester: Manchester University Press.

McKenzie, Jon (1997) 'Laurie Anderson for Dummies', *The Drama Review*, 41(2) (T154), 30–50.

O'Connor, Steve (2005 [1989]) *Postmodernist Culture,* Oxford: Blackwell.

Phelan, Peggy (1993) *Unmarked: The Politics of Performance*, London: Routledge.

Prinz, Jessica (2002) '"It's Such a Relief Not to Be Myself": Laurie Anderson's *Stories from the Nerve Bible*', in Sidonie Smith and Julia Watson (eds), *Interfaces: Women/Autobiography/Image/Performance*, Ann Arbor: University of Michigan Press, pp. 385–405.

Quick, Andrew (2007) *The Wooster Group Workbook*, London: Routledge.

Ridout, Nicholas (2007) *Stage Fright, Animals and Other Theatrical Problems*, Cambridge: Cambridge University Press.

Sandford, Mariellen R. (ed.) (1995) *Happenings and Other Acts*, London: Routledge.

Schechner, Richard (1988) *Performance Theory*, London: Routledge.

Shank, Theodore (1996 [1994]) *Contemporary British Theatre*, Basingstoke: Macmillan.

States, Bert O. (1985) *Great Reckonings in Little Rooms: On the Phenomenology of Theatre*, Berkeley: University of California Press.

SuAndi (2006) 'Africa Lives on in We: Histories and Futures of Black Women Artists', in Elaine Aston and Geraldine Harris (eds), *Feminist Futures? Theatre, Performance, Theory*, Basingstoke: Palgrave Macmillan, pp. 118–29.

Ugwu, Catherine (1995) 'Keep on Running: The Politics of Black British Performance', in Catherine Ugwu, *Let's Get It On: The Politics of Black Performance*, London: Institute of Contemporary Arts/Bay Press, pp. 54–83.

Williams, David (1999) *Collaborative Theatre: The Théâtre du Soleil Workbook*, London: Routledge.

Further reading

Anderson, Laurie (1994) *Stories from The Nerve Bible: A Retrospective, 1972–1992*, New York: HarperCollins.

Auslander, Philip (1997) *From Acting to Performance: Essays in Modernism and Postmodernism*, London: Routledge.

Barba, Eugenio (2010) *On Directing and Dramaturgy: Burning the House*, trans. Judy Barba, London: Routledge.

Davis, Tracy C. (2008) *The Cambridge Companion to Performance Studies*, Cambridge: Cambridge University Press.

Goldberg, RoseLee (1993 [1979]) *Performance Art: From Futurism to the Present*, London: Thames and Hudson.

Gómez-Peña, Guillermo (2005) *Ethno-Techno: Writings on Performance, Activism and Pedagogy*, London: Routledge.

Heathfield, Adrian (ed.) (2000) *Small Acts: Performance, the Millennium and the Marking of Time*, London: Black Dog Publishing.

Heathfield, Adrian (ed.) (2004) *Live: Art and Performance*, London: The Arts Council/Tate Publishing.

Helmer, Judith and Florian Malzacher (2004) *Not Even a Game Anymore: The Theatre of Forced Entertainment*, Berlin: Alexander Verlag.

Kelleher, Joe and Nicholas Ridout (2006) *Contemporary Theatres in Europe: A Critical Companion*, London: Routledge.

Lepage, Robert (1995) *Connecting Flights: In Conversation with Rémy Charest*, London: Methuen.

Rappaport, Herman (1986) '"Can You Say Hello?" Laurie Anderson's *United States*', *Theatre Journal*, 38, 339–54.

Savran, David (1986) *Breaking the Rules: The Wooster Group*, New York: Theatre Communications Group.

Savran, David (2005) 'The Death of the Avantgarde', *The Drama Review*, 49(3) (T187), 10–42.

Servos, Norbert (1984) *Pina Bausch-Wuppertal Dance Theater, or, The Art of Training a Goldfish: Excursions into Dance*, Cologne: Ballett-Bühnen-Verlag.

Shepherd, Simon (2006) *Theatre, Body and Pleasure*, London: Routledge.

Tufnell, Miranda and Chris Crickmay (1990) *Body, Space, Image*, London: Dance Books.

Zarrilli, Phillip (1995) *Acting (Re)Considered*, London: Routledge.

5.1 STORIES FROM THE NERVE BIBLE (1995)

Excerpts

LAURIE ANDERSON

With notes by RoseLee Goldberg

Laurie Anderson (b. 1947) *is an American multimedia performance artist, singer, composer and writer. Having studied classical music she turned to more experimental modes but equally engaged with popular forms, as her hit 'pop' record 'O Superman' (1981) exemplifies. Unusually for a performance artist, Anderson signed a record deal (with Warner Brothers) and followed this with a number of spectacular performance 'shows' – such as the concert/film* Home of the Brave *(1986),* Stories from the Nerve Bible *(1993) and* Songs and Stories from Moby Dick *(1999-2000). She became NASA's first artist in residence in 2003 and has collaborated with numerous iconic artists and invented a number of innovative musical 'instruments'.*

April 1993, Philadelphia, Pennsylvania
#1. PRESET
STAGE: all screens are out
M-1 keys in pit
camera, neon bow, violin center stage
House to half; House Out; Go cue for LA & Audio

#2. STORIES	(app 15 mins)
AUDIOTAPE	DAT #1 (birds)
STAGE	LA at keys in pit

119

In 1980 as part of a project called 'Word of Mouth', I was invited – along with eleven other artists – to go to Ponape, a tiny island in the middle of the Pacific. The idea was that we'd sit around talking for a few days and then the conversations would be made into a record. The first night we were all really jetlagged but as soon as we sat down, the organizers set up a huge array of mics [microphones] and switched on a bank of 1000-watt lights and we tried our best to be as intelligent as possible.

Television had just come to Ponape a week before we arrived and there was a strange excitement around the island as people crowded around the few sets. And then the day after we arrived, in a bizarre replay of the plot of the first TV show broadcast to Ponape, prisoners escaped

Within the image:

O Little Town of B
rock-throwing capital of th

You know the reason why some nights
you don't have a dream?
When there's just blackness?
And total silence?

Well, this is the reason:
It's because on that night
you are in somebody else's dream.
And this is the reason you can't
be in your own dream because
you're already busy
in somebody else's dream.

Figure 29 *Stories from the Nerve Bible*, Laurie Anderson. (Originally produced in Laurie Anderson, *Stories from the Nerve Bible: A Retrospective*, New York: HarperPerennial, 1994, p. 272.)

from a jail, broke into the radio station, and murdered the DJ. Then they went off on a rampage through the jungle armed with lawn mower blades. In all, four people were murdered in cold blood. Detectives were flown in from Guam to investigate. At night I stayed around the cottages with the other artists listening out into the jungle.

120 POLE

Finally the chief of the biggest tribe on the island decided to hold a ceremony for the murder victims. The artist Marina Abramovic and I went, as representatives of our group, to film it. The ceremony was held in a large thatched lean-to. Most of the ceremony involved cooking beans in

Figure 30 *Stories from the Nerve Bible*, Laurie Anderson. (Photographer: Monika Rittershaus.)

pits and brewing a dark drink from roots. The smell was overwhelming. Dogs careened around barking and everybody seemed to be having a fairly good time – as funerals go.

After a few hours, Marina and I were presented to the chief who was sitting on a raised platform above the pits. We had been told we couldn't turn our backs to the chief or – at any time – be higher than he was. So we scrambled up onto the platform with our film equipment and sort of duck-waddled up to the chief. As a present I'd brought one of those little 'Fred Flintstone' cameras – the kind where the film cannister is also the body of the camera – and I presented it to the chief. He seemed delighted and began to click off pictures. He wasn't advancing the film between shots but since we were told we shouldn't speak unless spoken to, I wasn't able to inform him that he wasn't going to get twelve pictures – but only one very very complicated shot.

After a couple more hours, the chief lifted his hand and there was absolute silence. All the dogs had suddenly stopped barking. We looked around and saw the dogs. All their throats had been simultaneously cut and their bodies, still breathing, pierced with rods, were turning on the spits.

The chief insisted we join in the meal but Marina had turned green and I asked if we could just have ours to go. They carefully wrapped the dogs in leaves and we carried their bodies away.

150
LIGHT CUE

In 1984, as part of the press for the tour I was doing in Japan, I was asked to go to Bali and speak about the future with the prince of Ubud. The idea was that I would represent the western world, the prince the southern world, and the Japanese press representative would represent whatever was left. The conversations would be published in a large book (scheduled for release one year after the concert tour). As press, this didn't seem like a great way to advertise the concerts, but it sounded like fun anyway.

I stayed at the palace in one of the former king's harem houses. Each of the king's wives had had her own house guarded by a pair of live animals – a bear and a fox for example. By the time I got there years later, the menagerie had dwindled a bit. My house was 'guarded' by two fish swimming around in bowls.

113

Bali was extremely hot in the afternoons and the conversations with the prince drifted along randomly from topic to topic. The prince was a bon vivant, trained in Paris. He spoke excellent English and when he wasn't in the palace he was out on the bumpy back roads racing cars. So we talked about cars – a subject I know absolutely nothing about – and I felt that, as far as representing the western world went, I was failing dismally.

On the second night, the prince served an elaborate feast of Balinese dishes. At the end of the meal, the conversation slowed to a halt and after a few minutes of silence he asked, 'Would you like to see the cremation tapes of my father?'

The tapes were several hours long and were a record of the elaborate 3 month ceremony shot by the BBC. When the king died the whole country went to work building an enormous funeral pyre for him. Practically everyone in Bali contributed something – a woven mat or intricate chains of braided straw – bits of pottery and cloth.

177

After months of preparation (during which the king continues to reside in the living room) they hoisted his body to the top of this rickety, extremely flammable structure and lit a match. The delicate tower crumpled almost immediately and the king's body fell to the ground with a sickening thud. This didn't seem to disturb anyone but me. The prince considered the ceremony a triumph. His father had been touched by fire and hadn't flown away.

130

He explained that when a Balinese dies, the soul turns into a bird and sits by the house for a while. The big danger is that it will escape and fly out over the ocean. The Balinese hate water, don't swim, don't trust it. So the idea is to keep the bird within earshot until the body can be burned and the soul can safely ascend, finally, to heaven.

188
85
LIGHT CUE

In 1974 I went to Mexico to visit my brother who was working as an anthropologist with the Tzotzil Indians – the last surviving Mayan tribe. The Tzotzil speak a lovely birdlike language and are quite tiny physically. I towered over them.

Mostly I spent my days following the women around since my brother wasn't really allowed to do this. We got up at 3 am and began to separate the corn into three colors. Then we boiled it, ran to the mill and back and finally started to make the tortillas. All the other womens' tortillas were 360 degrees, perfectly toasted, perfectly round. Even after a lot of practice, mine were still lopsided and charred. When they thought I wasn't looking, they threw them to the dogs.

165

After breakfast we spent the rest of the day down at the river watching the goats and braiding and unbraiding each other's hair. So usually there wasn't that much to report. One day the women decided to braid my hair Tzotzil style. After they did this, I saw my reflection in a puddle. I looked ridiculous but they said, 'Before we did this, you were ugly. But now maybe you will find a husband.'

Figure 31 *Stories from the Nerve Bible*, Laurie Anderson. (Photographer: Steve Cohen.)

177

I lived with them in a yurt, a thatched structure shaped like a cupcake. There is a central fireplace ringed by sleeping shelves, sort of like a dry beaver dam. My Tzotzil name was 'Loscha' which, loosely translated, means 'the-ugly-one-with-the-jewels'. Now, ugly, OK. I was awfully tall by the local standards. But what did they mean by the jewels? I didn't find out what this meant until one night when I was taking my contact lenses out and – since I'd lost the case – carefully placing them on the sleeping shelf. Suddenly I noticed that everyone was staring at me. I suddenly realized that none of the Tzotzil had ever seen glasses, much less contacts, and that these were the jewels – the transparent, perfectly round jewels that I carefully hid on the shelf at night and then put, for safe-keeping, into my eyes every morning. So I may have been ugly but so what? I had the Jewels.

LIGHT CUE

> Full fathom five thy father lies.
> Of his bones are coral made.
>
> Those are pearls that were his eyes.
> Nothing of him that doth fade.
>
> But that suffers a sea change.
> Into something rich and strange.
>
> And I alone am left to tell the tale.
> Call me Ishmael.

LIGHT CUE
150

The summer of 1974 was brutally hot in New York and I kept thinking about how nice and icey it must be at the north pole and then I thought: wait a second, why not go? You know, like in cartoons where they just hang 'Gone to the North Pole' on their doorknobs and just take off.

179

I spent a couple of weeks preparing for the trip, getting a hatchet, a huge backpack, maps, knives, sleeping bag, lures, and a three-month supply of bannock – a versatile high protein paste that can be made into flatbread, biscuits, or cereal, I had decided to hitchhike and one day I just walked out to Houston Street, weighted down with seventy pounds of gear, and stuck out my thumb.

C10

'Going north?' I asked the driver, as I struggled into his station wagon. After I got out of New York, most of the rides were trucks until I reached the Hudson Bay and began to hitch in small mail planes. The pilots were usually guys who had gone to Canada to avoid the draft or else embittered Vietnam vets who never wanted to go home again. Either way, they always wanted to show off a few of their stunts. We'd go swooping low along the rivers, doing loop de loops and 'Baby Hughies'. They'd drop me off at an air strip, 'There'll be another plane by here 'coupla weeks. See 'yal Good luck!'

177

I never did make it all the way to the pole. It turned out to be a restricted area and no one was allowed to fly in – or even over it. I did get within a few miles though, so it wasn't really disappointing. I entertained myself in the evenings cooking or smoking – watching the blazing light of the huge Canadian sunsets as they turned the blade of my knife into bright red neon as it lay by the fire. Later I lay on my back looking up at the northern lights and imagining there had been a nuclear holocaust and that I was the only human being left in all of North America and what would I do then? And then when these lights went out, I stretched out on the ground, more alone than I had ever been, watching the stars as they turned around on their enormous silent wheels.

I finally decided to turn back because of my hatchet. I had been chopping some wood and the hatchet flew out of my hand on the upswing. I did what you should never do when this happens: I looked up to see where it had gone. It came down WWWWFFFFFII just missing my head and I thought: My God! I could be walking around here with a hatchet embedded in my skull and I'm ten miles from the airstrip and nobody in the world knows I'm here.

LIGHT CUE

Remember me is all I ask
and if remembered be a task
Forget me.

Daddy Daddy it was just like you said:
Now that the living outnumber the dead

Where I come from it's a long thin thread
Across an ocean down a river of red
Now that the living outnumber the dead

Speak my language.

BLACKOUT at 'language'

#3. WIND	(30 secs)
VIDEO	E: blue
ACTION	Guy, Greg., & Cyro in position
	during blackout,
	LA moves to center
BAND	Accordion and Bass Drone
	begin immediately
STAGE	Wind machines on at 'language'
	F&G down
	SLIDERS MOVE IN HALFWAY
	35 SCREEN DOWN
ACTION	LA moves to center, gives hand cue,
	leaves upstage
	puts on Bodysynth (Bodysynth tested)
STAGE	M-1 keys in pit are struck

#4. TITLE MUSIC	(1:40 mins)
AUDIOTAPE:	DAT # 2 Title Music
	(drums & groans) on at hand cue
BAND:	accordion, bass, percussion
VIDEO:	On at hand cue
	35: Book burning
	A&D: Book burning
	F&G: Smoke
BUHL SLIDE:	*Stories from the Nerve Bible* on at
	40 seconds
	out at 55 seconds

#5. BODYSYNTH	(2 mins)
ACTION	LA enters along path from upstage,
STAGE	sliders close after LA passes through opening
BAND	Bodysynth: Breath/heartbeat D-70 RM

Come here little girl. Get into the car.

It's a shiny red one – a brand new Cadillac.

Come here little girl.

hand signal

BLACKOUT   at hand signal

BAND   accordion & bass drone

(10–20 seconds)

#6. GULF (1:50 mins)

BLACKOUT

AUDIOTAPE   DAT # 3 (wind & percussion; 1:30 xfades to birds)

on at hand signal

VIDEO: On after 10–20 seconds of bass drone

when sliders are in place

35: Gulf

ABCD: Gulf

E: Gulf

SLIDES: 'War is the highest form of modern art'

On 30 seconds after Gulf begins –

Italian Futurist Marinetti

Add 3 seconds after quote is up

2 second fade of all after 10 secs

BAND   begins when slide goes out

STAGE   Sparkler Smoke bombs behind the monitor beam on at third video 'explosion'

(app 1:37 from beginning of Gulf cue)

additional smoke from hose behind monitor beam

35 SCREEN blacked out after 3rd video 'explosion'

AUDIOTAPE: DAT # 4 (SFX explosion) at 3rd video 'explosion' with Sparkler Smoke Bomb

(DAT #3 continues but at low level)

ACTION   LA to monitor beam after 3rd explosion

#7. GRANDMOTHER   (4 mins)

BAND: Violin & voice: H3000 622;

Ahh-haaaaa ...... Ah-haaaaaa ....

VIDEO   fade up during 'ahh-haaaa ...'

ABCD: Whirlwind (road & coals in background)

F&G: Flames

SLIDES: On 5 seconds after video appears

5 seconds each w/fades

Wild beasts shall rest there

and their houses shall be filled with snakes

And ostriches shall dwell there

And the hairy ones shall dance there
And sirens in the temples of pleasure.
Isaiah 13:21

AUDIOTAPE: DAT #3 completely out after slides
BAND   accordion, bass, percussion
Aaa-haaaaa
Lately I've been thinking about the future – maybe because things have been happening so fast – or maybe because the end of the millenium is coming up. Whenever I think of the future I think of my grandmother –
She was a Southern Baptist from the Holy Roller school and she had a very clear idea about the future and of how the world would end – in fire – like in Revelations in fire – like in Revelations
When I was 10 years old, my grandmother told me the world was going to end in a year. So I spent the whole year praying and reading the Bible and telling all my friends and alienating all my relatives. And by the end of the year, *I was ready!*

Notes by Rose Lee Goldberg

As much as *Stories from the Nerve Bible* was about current affairs, a frequent refrain throughout was a report of a telephone conversation about the future with one of her all-time heroes, John Cage, which took place some months before he died. Anderson had hoped for his insights into the next century, knowing full well that Cage's answer would be as elliptical as ever.

So here are the questions. Is time long or is it wide?
And the answers?
Sometimes the answers just come in the mail and you get a letter that says all the things you were waiting to hear, the things you suspected, the things you knew were true.
And then in the last line it says:
Burn this.

Stories from the Nerve Bible was also the title of a book on Anderson that was published in 1994. An annotated personal overview of twenty years of her work, it included themes such as technology, dreams, language, politics, and art. Her comments about the book could just as easily be applied to aspects of the performance:

I've tried so many times to picture the United States, which is also the background for everything my work is about: memory, language, technology, politics, utopia, power, men, and women. I've tried to understand and describe some of the ways this country continues to remake itself, and I have always been interested in its many coexisting contradictions like Puritanism and violence, mass culture and art. It is also a collection of the many voices and talking styles that characterize English as spoken by Americans; the voices of machines, politicians, sitcom stars, nuns, and Ouija boards. Along the way, I've tried to touch on related topics such as the invention of ventriloquism, the relationship of music and architecture, technology as a primitive form of parasite, animation, aesthetics, and fanaticism.

Anderson talked about the meaning of the phrase 'Nerve Bible'. 'It is of course, the body,' she wrote, referring to the ways in which the book (and the performance) is divided into head and heart, mind and imagination, and all the senses. 'It is like that drawing in medical books of the human body called "The Sensory Homunculus," a depiction of the relative proportions of the sensory neurons as they're presented in the brain,' she explained. But 'Nerve Bible' also speaks of the part religion has played in Anderson's life, from her childhood, spent in the heart of the Bible Belt close to a grandmother who was a Southern Baptist missionary – 'she practically had the Bible memorized,' Anderson has said – to her longstanding involvement with Buddhism. 'I'm from the Bible Belt, first of all, and I'm just telling the same mixture of midwestern Bible stories that I always have. They're a mixture of the most mundane things with a fabulous twist to them.'

The fact that the *Nerve Bible* tour ended in Israel was especially meaningful to her. 'And Jerusalem? It looked just the way my grandmother had described it – pristine, white, majestic. Except that it was full of guns. Guns and bones. I'd come to Jerusalem hoping to find out something about time and timelessness, something about how an ark could turn into a whale or into a book. But *Stories from the Nerve Bible* is about the future, and it didn't have any answers, only questions.'

From the very beginning Anderson has referred in her work to her religious upbringing. Wearing a white smock with a ruffled collar and loose trousers in *Duets on Ice*, or her Screen Dress in *Songs and Stories for the Insomniac*, she looked more like a choir girl than a downtown New York musician. This perception was reinforced by such objects as a sponge cross, which she wore around her neck in *Duets*, and references to hymns and Bible quotations in that and many subsequent pieces. She was baptized by total immersion in 1958, in the First Church of Christ. She has an intimate connection to Bible stories she heard as a child and vivid recollections of religious experiences with her grandmother, and she has integrated them into her life as an artist in a particularly heartfelt way. Angels have frequented the various landscapes that Anderson has described and inhabited on stage and they have become less angelic and more argumentative as her work has matured. 'Last night I woke up / Saw this angel,' she sings in 'Gravity's Angel' (1986). 'He flew in my window / And he said: Girl, pretty proud of yourself, huh?'

Anderson's quest for authenticity and calm in a swiftly spinning world has led her to investigate a range of spiritual realms and forms, from charismatic evangelism to Indian mudras, palm readings, Buddhist retreats, and visits to Tibet and the Holy Land. Her work comprises a complicated world of instinct and intellect, human and animal, past and future. It also reveals an overall motif of profound awareness and concern for other people – 'I've written a lot of stories for nobodies' – and for animals – 'I'm positive that animals have emotions.' 'The art I aspire to make,' she wrote in the catalogue to the *High and Low* performance series, 'helps people live this life as well as possible. Art must address the issues – sensually, emotionally, vividly, spiritually.'

Like all of Anderson's performances, *Stories from the Nerve Bible* was carefully constructed and structured. She explains:

It began with a room full of charts and diagrams showing how things relate to each other. I then tried to build the idea of time into the structure of the piece. For example, the set is a thirty-six-foot-long girder i-beam, and you just slide along that track, and then above. It's kind of T-shaped, so there's a path going back up the stage. Most of the stories happen in present time; things that can be changed happen along one axis and the things that cannot be changed happen along another. Now I doubt that anybody who ever sees it is ever going to pick that up.

There are lots of short stories about the passage of time and longer things about it as well. There are maybe twenty images of time, from little alarm clocks to time codes. There's a story about Stephen Hawkins, who describes time as this huge tunnel. In one of his lectures – which are really wonderful, it's really amazing to hear his voice – he envisions this image of the black hole imploding, and what happens to the information about all the objects that have disappeared. He proposes that all the information about all sorts of things begins to skid down an infinitely long tunnel. In other words he's proposing that nothing's ever lost, that you can reconstruct everything by using all the debris of information in the black hole.

Note

From RoseLee Goldberg, *Laurie Anderson*, London: Thames and Hudson, 2000, pp. 161–4.

5.2 POLYGRAPH (1996)

ROBERT LEPAGE AND MARIE BRASSARD

Translated by Gyllian Raby

Robert Lepage (b. 1957) *is a Candian theatre and film director, a playwright and performer. He worked originally with Théâtre Repère in Quebec and is the founder and director of Ex Machina, a multi-disciplinary arts company based in Canada. His theatre works include* The Dragons' Trilogy *(1985),* The Seven Streams of the River Ota *(1994) and* Lipsynch *(2007). His theatre works combine performers' collective improvisations, are often multilingual and multimedia, and are often transformed while touring and beyond: thus the text printed here is a version of* Polygraph *from 1996. Marie Brassard is a French Canadian playwright, director and performer who has worked extensively with Robert Lepage. She played Lucie in both the stage and film versions of* Polygraph.

Characters

DAVID
FRANÇOIS
LUCIE
ANNA'S VOICE

Prologue

A brick wall runs right across the playing area, behind a shallow platform forestage. Music plays in a film-style introduction, while slides flash the play title and actors' credits in a large format that completely covers the wall. Then, stage right, a projection titles the scene. The film-script-style introduction of each scene in this way will continue throughout the play. Dialogue and action begin during the projection of the credits.

Projection:

1. The filter

Stage Left, in a 'flashback' performance at an Inquest six years prior to the action of the play, DAVID *reads a Pathologist's report about a murder victim. He demonstrates his points by pointing at the anatomy of a skeleton which lies on the stage floor near his feet. Stage right, behind and above the wall,* FRANÇOIS *is in a Political Science class at the university, delivering a presentation on the Berlin Wall.*

DAVID: The autopsy has revealed that the stab wounds were caused by a sharp, pointed instrument which penetrated the skin and underlying tissues –

FRANÇOIS: After the fall of the Third Reich, little remained of its capital, Berlin, except a pile of ruins and a demoralised people.

DAVID: The body wounds are extremely large considering the small size of the inflicting instrument. I would surmise that the shape, depth and width of the wounds were enlarged during the struggle –

FRANÇOIS: The triumphant Allies enforced a new statute –

DAVID: – by the slicing action of the knife –

FRANÇOIS: – which split the city into international sectors: American, French, British –

DAVID: – as the victim attempted to defend herself.

FRANÇOIS: – and to define their sector, the Soviets built a wall over forty kilometers in length, cutting the city in two.

DAVID: The victim received cuts to the left hand, the right upper arm, and was pierced through the rib-cage and the right lung, to the stomach. We have determined that the fatal cut was given here/

DAVID *and* FRANÇOIS: – Right through the heart –

FRANÇOIS: /of the city.

DAVID: – between the fifth and the sixth ribs.

FRANÇOIS: The 'Wall of Shame' as the West Germans called it, was built to stop the human/

DAVID and FRANÇOIS: /Hemorrhage –

FRANÇOIS: /of Berliners leaving the East for the West –

DAVID: – was caused by the laceration of the septum.

FRANÇOIS: – symbolic of the division between the Communist and Capitalist worlds.

DAVID: The septum functions like a wall bisecting the heart; it controls the filtration of blood –

FRANÇOIS: For almost three decades, visitors from the West have been permitted to enter the Eastern Bloc –

DAVID: – from the right ventricle to the left –

DAVID and FRANÇOIS: – but the passage is one way only. A sophisticated system of alternating doors open and close to allow the flow of –

FRANÇOIS: – visitors from the West –

DAVID: – de-oxygenated blood –

DAVID and FRANÇOIS: – and to impede –

FRANÇOIS: – inhabitants of the East –

DAVID: – oxygenated blood –

DAVID and FRANÇOIS: – from circulating the 'wrong' way.

As if a continuous loop, the tempo of the Filter dialogue increases with the volume and drive of the music. As it is repeated, the naked body of LUCIE rises stage left behind the wall, lit by anatomical slide projections: muscles, veins, organs and bones superimposed on her flesh, as though she is transparent. The scene ends on a music crescendo, and a brief blackout.

Projection:
2. Parthenais Institute of Criminal Pathology, Montreal
Interior, night.

In the blackout, more meditative music plays. Lights reveal first the skeleton, which slowly rises to its feet, then the rest of the scene. Stage right, DAVID is at work, note-taking as he watches intently the bleeping, whirring Polygraph Machine. He turns off the Polygraph, puts on his coat, and takes a letter from the pocket. He reads a few lines to himself then replaces it. Thoughtfully, he lights a cigarette. He approaches the skeleton and slowly takes its head in his hand, assuming the cliché position of Hamlet with Yorick's skull. Lights crossfade to the next scene as LUCIE's voice is heard.

Projection:
3. Hamlet
Exterior, night.

LUCIE appears above and behind the wall, Stage Left, reciting in profile Hamlet's speech to Yorick (Act 5, Scene 1). She wears black, and holds a skull.

LUCIE: Hélas, pauvre Yorrick! ... Je l'ai connu Horatio! C'était

un garçon d'une verve infinie, d'une fantaisie exquise; il m'a porté sur son dos mille fois. Et maintenant quelle horreur il cause à mon imagination! Le coeur m'en lève. Ici pendaient les lèvres que j'ai baisées, je ne sais combien de fois. Où sont vos plaisanteries maintenant? Vos escapades? Vos chansons? Et ces éclairs de gaieté qui faisaient rugir la table de rires? Quoi! Plus un mot à présent pour vous moquer de vos propres grimaces? Plus de lèvres? ... Allez maintenant trouver madame dans sa chambre et dites-lui qu'elle a beau se mettre un pouce de fard, il faudra bien qu'elle en vienne à cette figure là! Faites la bien rire avec ça ...

Lights crossfade into the next scene. A change in soundscore now suggests the hubbub of a busy restaurant.

Projection:
4. François
Interior, night.

FRANÇOIS enters stage left with a 'table for two' over his shoulder. This he swings down in an easy movement. Quickly setting it with plates and cutlery, he then positions two chairs either side. When the table is 'set' he immediately unmakes it, swings it over his shoulder, and repeats the whole sequence in a different space, all the while talking rapidly to invisible customers. During the course of the scene he covers the whole stage, so suggesting a room full of tables, and he never stops moving or talking.

FRANÇOIS: Vous avez bien mangé? Je vous apporte l'addition monsieur. Par ici s'il vous plaît. Vous avez regardé le menu du jour sur le tableau? Oui. C'est pour combien de personnes? Par ici s'il vous plaît. Prendriez-vous un digestif? Deux cafés cognac ... tout de suite ... Ca sera pas long monsieur ... Oui bonjour. Non, malheureusement, on a plus de rôti à l'échalotte. À la place, le chef vous suggère son poulet rôti, un poulet au citron, c'est délicieux. Alors deux fois. Allez-vous prendre un dessert? Aujourd'hui, c'est la tarte à l'orange maison. C'est excellent, je vous le recommande ... Oui. Une personne. Par ici s'il vous plaît. For two? ... I'm sorry we don't 'ave any English menu ... I'll translate for you. Deux places? Par ici s'il vous plaît. Pardon? Vous auriez dû me le dire, je vous l'aurait changé sans problème. Oui, la prochaine fois, d'accord. Par ici s'il vous plaît.

LUCIE: (*Enters and sits at the table, talking rapidly to keep pace with his non-stop work.*) Salut François! Aie, il parait que toi pis ton chum, vous êtes venus voir la pièce hier ... Vous êtes pas venus me voir après, est-ce que c'est parce que vous avez pas aimé ça?

FRANÇOIS: Ah non! C'était magnifique ... On a beaucoup aimé l'idée de faire jouer Hamlet par une femme ... De nos jours, c'est beaucoup plus percutant que ce soit une femme qui tienne ces propos-là plutôt qu'un homme.

LUCIE: Ben en fait à l'origine, cétait pas prévu … Ils m'ont téléphoné à la dernière minute … Le gars qui jouait Hamlet est tombé malade puis le metteur en scène a eu la drôle d'idée de me demander de le remplacer … Aie François, j'ai entendu dire … Il paraît qu'à CKRL, ils cherchent un annonceur pour lire le bulletin de nouvelle le soir … t'as une belle voix … il me semble que tu serais bon là dedans.

FRANÇOIS: C'est gentil d'avoir pensé à moi, mais ces temps-ci c'est pas possible, j'ai trop d'ouvrage au restaurant.

LUCIE: Aie, j'ai croisé Alain dans l'escalier tantôt, il m'a même pas dit bonjour … c'est tu parce qu'il est fâché contre moi?

FRANÇOIS: Fais-toi en avec ça … c'est à moi qu'il en veut.

LUCIE: En tous cas, je te remercie beaucoup, c'était très bon.

LUCIE exits; FRANÇOIS continues at the same pace.

FRANÇOIS: A bientôt Lucie.

FRANÇOIS goes out with the table settings, returns and sits at the table. Change in lights and music indicate that it is now the end of the day, and he is exhausted. He taps out three lines of coke and snorts it. DAVID enters the restaurant over the wall, sliding down with his back to it, his arms and his suit jacket spread like a giant, ominous spider. David lands smoothly in the empty seat across the table from FRANÇOIS.

DAVID: François, can you hear me properly? But you can't actually see me, can you? François, we are going to conduct a little test. Are we in Canada? Is it summertime? Was it you who killed Marie-Claude Légaré?

FRANÇOIS shakes his head, as if to dislodge disturbing thoughts. DAVID disappears up the wall in a slow reversal of the way he entered. Lights crossfade to a spotlight stage right.

Projection:
5/6. The audition/Sauvé metro station
Interior, day.

LUCIE walks diffidently into the bright spotlight. She squints nervously at the light as she begins her audition, talking to unseen interviewers positioned in the audience. Her English is good, but sometimes hesitant and a bit convoluted.

Hi. My name is Lucie Champagne …
My hair is shorter than on the photograph because I'm playing a guy in a show right now, so they cut it …
I should tell you right away – I've never …
What? To the camera! … okay …

She turns slightly to face it.

I've never worked on a movie before – but I have done a lot of video, mainly comedies, but I like drama just as much … my videos were for the government social services … Let's see … an example would be … ? Oh yes! I played a woman whose money was stolen by her brother-in-law; to you or me that might seem a pretty tame crisis – but for this woman, it was profoundly dramatic, I mean it was completely devastating, because, well … it was her money … and … it was her brother in law … so I … I had to play this part with as much emotion as I possibly could …

Oh yes! While I was at the theatre school I was in a play by Tennessee Williams called: *Talk To Me Like The Rain and Let Me Listen*. It has a long title but the play is actually very short. It's about a couple, and I played the woman, and my character was anorexic. But not by choice – I mean, she was anorexic because she hadn't eaten for four days, because she didn't have any money, because her boyfriend took off with the welfare check; I loved that role!

My first experience? Well, I'll tell you, but you'll laugh!

It was for the priest's birthday when I was in Grade One. Everyone in my class was in it. The other kids all lined up in front of the wall behind me, and they sang, 'Where are you going little Bo-Peep, where are you going Bo-Peep … ?' And I was out in front wearing a little white dress, and I sang back 'I am following this beauteous star and all my sheep are saying baaa … '!

My God, it was so cool! I loved to tell lies when I was a kid – that is, I was not a liar but … I was fascinated that I could say untrue things but do it convincingly that people would believe me; maybe that explains why I always wanted to be an actress … What? Oh! Yes … For my audition I have brought a soliloquy from Shakespeare's *Hamlet* … No, no, not the part of Ophelia, the part of Hamlet. Oh … you would prefer an improv. Euh …

She looks around.

Should I improvise here? …
What would you like me to improvise?
To imagine myself in a tragic situation … ?
Is that so you can see if I can cry? Because, I mean, … I can't cry at the drop of a hat …
I mean, what I mean is: put me in a movie where there's a sad scene where I have to cry, and I'd concentrate to the point where tears would well up, but I can't cry just like that … here …
To imagine myself in an absolute state of panic …
Don't you think I'm panicking enough here?
Okay, okay, I'll do it.

Projection: *Sauvé metro*
The metro station logo is also projected on the wall. The soundscape

evokes a large, hollow echoing Underground. LUCIE *focuses on the front edge of the stage, an expression of petrified horror on her face; she backs up to lean against the wall with an inarticulate scream.* DAVID *enters. He kneels, expressionless, beside the 'tracks' at the edge of the stage. In his hand he holds a bloody T-shirt, which he places in a zip-lock plastic bag. He takes out a notebook and writes.* LUCIE, *meantime, is going into shock, shouting and crying in semi-hysteria.* DAVID *assesses her, completes his notes, puts away his notebook carefully, then goes to her. As she sobs for breath, he pulls her away from the wall to lean against him, and smooths her shoulders, rhythmically. Gradually, she is able to control her breathing. He checks her pulse, her heartbeat, and takes some pills from a bottle in his pocket, which he offers to her. When he speaks, it is with a German accent.*

DAVID: Take this, it's a mild tranquiliser.

LUCIE: Was ... was he killed on impact?

DAVID: Yes. Can I give you a lift somewhere?

LUCIE: Yes.

DAVID: Where do you live?

LUCIE: In Quebec City;

> DAVID *is momentarily alarmed as it is three hours' drive to Quebec City from Montreal.*

I was on my way to catch the bus.

DAVID: I'll walk you to the bus terminal then.

> DAVID *puts his arm around her shoulders and they move off towards stage left.* LUCIE *breaks away, runs back to look at the tracks, and then returns to her starting position in the present, leaning against the wall in her audition spotlight. As* DAVID *exits, this is now the only light on stage.*

LUCIE: *Back in her audition. Was that enough? Black out. A metallic, driving music accompanies a red light that shines from behind the wall.*

Projection:
7. The flesh
Interior, night.

FRANÇOIS *enters, like a predator, over the top of the wall into a gay bar . He drinks a beer, watching bodies on the dance floor. Soon he realises that he's being assessed by one of the crowd, and he agrees to follow the man stage right to a back room for sex. A change in light and baffling of sound indicate they are now private. In a very sensual scene,* FRANÇOIS *takes off his shirt, and then his belt, which he gives to his companion. Their relationship is one where they 'play' at coercion.* FRANÇOIS *unzips his pants and kneels facing the wall, supported by the wall. As we hear the sounds of the whiplash,* FRANÇOIS' *body physically recoils against the wall with each blow. As he comes, as his body shudders, the wall bleeds, gushing blood.* FRANÇOIS *meets the eyes of his lover. He gives a cursory wave as the other man leaves. With an air of soul-weary satisfaction,* FRANÇOIS *gathers his clothes, and returns to the bar. As lights fade to black, he drinks another beer and watches the dance floor.*

In the blackout, a two-way mirror drops from the ceiling to hang above the wall Stage Right. It is the make-up mirror of LUCIE's *dressing-room at the theatre. The audience watch the scene from 'behind' the mirror.*

Projection:
8. The tears
Interior, night.

DAVID *is waiting in the dressing room with a bunch of carnations, a flower associated with funerals and said by Quebecois actors to bring bad luck to a show.* LUCIE *enters, having finished her performance of* Hamlet; *she holds the skull of Yorick.*

DAVID: Good evening.

LUCIE: David, my God, it's you! Did you come all the way from Montreal just to see the show?

DAVID: Well, in fact, I had some business this week in Quebec City, and since I promised myself I would see you act one day: here I am.

LUCIE: We weren't exactly sold out tonight ...

DAVID: That makes it more intimate theatre.

LUCIE: So, what did you think? Did you like it?

DAVID: Well, I thought it was quite interesting. Oh, here!

> *He presents her with the carnations.*

LUCIE: Oh my God! Carnations! – Thank you ...

DAVID: (*Examines the skull on the dressing-room table.*) Is this Yorick?

LUCIE: You know him well?

DAVID: Of course ... He is the only character who isn't killed at the end of the play!

LUCIE: I like the way you call him by his name. Round here they just call him 'the skull'.

DAVID: What is written on his forehead? (*Reading*) ... Hélas, pauvre Yorrick ...

LUCIE: My lines! I didn't have time to learn them properly so I wrote them out ...
Would you mind waiting for me, just a second? I have to get changed and I'll be right back. (*LUCIE exits.*)

DAVID: 'To be or not to be, that is the question ...' It must be difficult to pronounce 'To be or not to be', and to question the fundamental things of life: love, honour –

DAVID *and* LUCIE: (*Simultaneously, as she re-enters.*) – death ...

LUCIE: It's on my mind ... more than ever ... seeing that boy throw himself in front of the train in Montreal. You know ... I want to thank you for driving me all the way back to Quebec City ... you didn't have to do that.

DAVID: Let's just say I was not acting purely out of duty; it also gave me the opportunity to get to know you a little better and to make a new friend. ... So ... What about the movie? Did you get the part?

LUCIE: Not yet ... but next week they want me to do some screen tests. I'm terrified because they want to shoot a scene where l cry and it's not so easy to do ... They gave me this. (*She takes a tube from the dressing-room table.*) You'll never guess what it's for. It's a special product they use in movies to help actors cry.

DAVID: Really! Why?

LUCIE: Imagine redoing the same sad scene twelve times? It's hard to cry every time, right? So, they put this in the actor's eyes and the tears flow all on their own.

DAVID: Wait a minute. Are you telling me that when an actress like ... Jane Fonda for example, ... when she cries, it's all fake?

LUCIE: Sometimes, yes.

DAVID: What a deception! I believed that for an actor at least, tears were the ultimate proof of true emotion!

LUCIE: This is another of the misconceptions people have about acting! D'you want to try it?

DAVID: Surely you don't want to make me cry!

LUCIE: Yes! You'll see, it won't hurt ... It will be funny!

DAVID: Alright then! What should I do here?

LUCIE: First, I'll ask you to take off your glasses. And now, since we are making a movie, I'll ask you to think about something sad, so the scene will be truthful.

DAVID: Something sad ... Something recent?

LUCIE: Whatever you want!

And now I say:

'Quiet on the set ... sound ... camera ... action!'

As DAVID remembers, there is a musical theme reminiscent of his past in East Berlin. LUCIE freezes, still holding his glasses. Like a statue, she slowly recedes from the playing area, as if flying away. The set of the dressing room disappears simultaneously, and a projection of the Brandenburg Gate fills the cyclorama. DAVID, in another time, brings out a letter from his pocket. A woman's voice is heard, reading the letter in German.

ANNA'S VOICE: Ich weiss das man niemanden zur Liebe zwingen kan. Aber ich moechte das sie wissen das ist das Gefühl habe sie sein ein Stück von mir. An dem Morgen, als sie Ostberlin verliessen zitterte ich am ganzen Körper. Sie sagen: 'Ich bin bald wieder zuruck aber ich wuste sofort obwohl ich es nicht sagte.' Was nicht von Herzen kommt geht nicht zu Herzen. Ich kann in ihren Augen lesen wenn ich hier nicht gefangen ware, ware ich nah bei ihnen. Sie fehlen mir. Anna

In a slow motion, fearful escape, DAVID acts out his crossing of the Berlin Wall. He swings his upper body over, out and down, head first, holding his legs vertical above him. Gripping the wall, he swivels his legs down into a standing position, but remains suspended against the wall. English subtitles, projected on the wall, translate the letter:

I know that it is impossible to force someone into loving ... But I want you to know that I feel you are a part of me. The

morning you left East Berlin, I was quite shaken. When I asked: 'When will you return?' You replied, 'Soon'. I did not let on, but in that instant, I knew you were lying. What does not come from the heart is not taken to heart ... I could see it in your eyes. If I could leave this city, I would be with you. I miss you deeply. Anna.

As the letter ends, DAVID reverses his movement, until he is standing where he began the memory: in the dressing room, behind the mirror, talking to LUCIE who has been glided simultaneously back into her starting position. But now, DAVID is crying. He wipes his eyes.

DAVID: This stuff really burns ... It's like getting soap in your eyes

LUCIE: It won't hurt for long ...

If you want it to look like you are suffering, sometimes you have to suffer ...

Gently, she wipes his eyes. The lights fade as they kiss.

Projection:

9. Apartment # 7

Interior, night.

Stage Left, a washbasin set into the wall, with a mirror above it, indicates the bathroom in FRANÇOIS' appartment. FRANÇOIS enters, drunk, limping and sore. He puts his ear against the wall to listen if anyone is home next door. He calls through the wall:

FRANÇOIS: Lucie!. Lucie ...

FRANÇOIS puts a glass against the wall to listen for any sounds from next-door. Silence: there is no-one home. He drops his leather jacket on the floor and peels off his T-shirt. His back is marked with whiplash weals. He soaks the shirt in water and lays it across his back with a sigh of relief.

LUCIE: (*Entering his apartment suddenly.*) François?

FRANÇOIS: Oui ... entre.

LUCIE: Qu'est-ce que t'as ... Es-tu malade?

FRANÇOIS: Oui ... J'me sens pas bien ... J'pense que j'ai trop bu ... Ça te tentes-tu de rester prendre un café?

LUCIE: Ben ... J'aimerais ça mais ... (*Pointing at the silhouette of a man waiting at the door.*) c'est parce que j'suis pas toute seule ...

FRANÇOIS: Ah ... Y a quelqu'un qui t'attend ...

LUCIE: Oui. On se reprendra ... Excuses-moi de te déranger à cette heure là ... C'est parce que je viens d'arriver chez nous pis j'peux pas rentrer, j'ai pas mes clés.

FRANÇOIS: Ah ... (*he digs for LUCIE's key inside his jeans' pocket and gives it to her*)

LUCIE: Merci ... Prends soin de toi là ...

As she goes to kiss him on both cheeks, she inadvertently touches his back; FRANÇOIS winces. LUCIE tries to look at his back.

Qu'est-ce que t'as, j't'ai-tu fait mal?
DAVID: (*His voice comes from behind the wall.*) Lucie? ...
FRANÇOIS: Non, non ... Laisses faire.
LUCIE: (*Tries again to see his back.*) Ben voyons ... Qu'est-ce que t'as?
FRANÇOIS: (*Reacting violently.*) Laisse faire j'te dis ... c'est rien.
LUCIE: Okay, okay!
DAVID: Lucie, are you alright?
LUCIE: Yeah, yeah ... (*Awkwardly, as she exits.*) Merci.

FRANÇOIS is now very alone. Lights crossfade to the expanse of the cyclorama, above the wall.

Projection:
10. The snow
Exterior, night.

Above the wall the moonlit night sky glows, and snow falls gently. Music accompanies this. FRANÇOIS appears, as if walking on the ramparts of Quebec City's wall. He wears no shirt, only his leather jacket, which he holds together against the cold. At one point, he stops, climbs on to the edge of the wall, and stares down as if he's contemplating a suicide jump. He cries silently.

Projection:
11. Apartment # 8
Interior, day.

Stage right, a washbasin full of water is set into the wall, with a mirror above it, to indicate the bathroom of LUCIE's apartment. DAVID is shaving, when he hears violent and lamenting cries from the other side of the wall. The voice belongs to FRANÇOIS. He checks to see if LUCIE is still sleeping, then puts his ear against the wall to listen. The cries get louder. DAVID knocks on the wall a couple of times. The lamentation stops. LUCIE enters, surprising him.

LUCIE: David, what are you doing?

She is still sleepy and goes to embrace him, but he politely fends her off.

DAVID: Good morning! Lucie, listen! I really have to go! I promised my secretary I'd be in Montreal at ten o'clock ... it's now eight thirty and I haven't even left Quebec City yet. So, you can imagine how impossibly behind I am!
LUCIE: That's too bad, I thought we could eat breakfast together. Shall I put on some coffee?
DAVID: That's very nice of you, but I really must go.
LUCIE: Will we see each other again?
DAVID: Soon.
LUCIE: When?
DAVID: I have some business in Quebec City next week. Perhaps we could arrange a rendez-vous? I'll be at the morgue.

LUCIE: At the morgue? I would prefer a restaurant!

She walks towards him, allowing her robe to slide from her shoulders to the ground.

DAVID: That's what I meant ...

As they move into a kiss, the cries from FRANÇOIS' apartment begin again. LUCIE stops and turns her head to listen, but DAVID pulls her passionately against him. As they embrace, DAVID checks his watch behind her back, and figuring he has enough time, he gives in to the love scene, and lifts her up on him, turning so that she stretches out her arms to grip the wall for support as he caresses her body with his lips, and lights fade ...

Projection:
12. Travelling backward
Interior, day.

Thriller music begins in the blackout. Stage left, LUCIE stands naked, her back to the wall. Suddenly, she contracts as though she has been stabbed. She staggers forwards, and to the left, clawing at the air, then swivels as she falls: her back is covered with blood from the wall. Her movement is closely tracked by a camera on a panasonic pee-wee dolly that zooms maniacally in and out on her face and body with the tension rhythm of the music. LUCIE falls, dead, to the floor. The music stops abruptly and she gets to her feet, appearing to listen to instructions from a director. She performs three 'takes' of the death scene. After the last one, she receives the 'thumbs up' signal. She speaks to the director:

LUCIE: Can I go now? (*LUCIE covers herself with a towel and exits.*)

Projection:
13. The wound
Interior, night.

At FRANÇOIS' restaurant. DAVID enters.

FRANÇOIS: Bonsoir monsieur. Ce sera pour combien de personnes?
DAVID: I'm sorry, euh ... (*He doesn't speak French.*)
FRANÇOIS: Excuse me. You would like a table for how many?
DAVID: For two please.
FRANÇOIS: Does this one suit you?
DAVID: Yes, that's fine. Oh, excuse me – would you take my coat please?
FRANÇOIS: Sure.

FRANÇOIS leaves with the coat. As he waits, DAVID hides a small gift bag under his chair.

LUCIE: (*Enters in a rush.*) Oh, David, I'm sorry, I'm late –
DAVID: That is perfectly fine.
LUCIE: I hope you haven't been waiting too long?
DAVID: I arrived just a moment ago. It's nice to see you.
LUCIE: It was longer than I expected ... We were supposed

Figure 32 *Polygraph* (Ex Machina/Robert Lepage) from the Harbourfront Festival's Quayworks, Toronto, 1990. (Photographer: Michael Cooper.)

to finish shooting at three o'clock, but we had a very complicated technical scene.

DAVID: You look tired ...

LUCIE: Playing a victim is tiring!

FRANÇOIS: (*Enters to serve them.*) Bonjour Lucie.

LUCIE: Ah. Bonjour François ... Tiens, je te présente un ami, David Haussmann, François Tremblay ... He's my next-door neighbour ...

DAVID: Oh ... you're the one in apartment number eight!

FRANÇOIS: Yes.

DAVID: (*Shaking his hand.*) I heard ... so much about you!

LUCIE: David is the one who drove me back to Quebec City after I saw the guy throw himself in front of the train in Montreal.

FRANÇOIS: Strange circumstances to meet someone.

DAVID: Yes indeed ... Metro stations in Montreal seem to be used more often now to commit suicide than for commuting ...

LUCIE: Why's that?

FRANÇOIS: C'est la façon la plus cheap de se suicider ...

DAVID: What?

FRANÇOIS: ... Do you want to order something to drink before your meal?

DAVID: Well ... I think I'll avoid hard liquor –

LUCIE: – Me too –

DAVID: – But ... Would you like to drink some wine with the meal?

LUCIE: Yes ... sure.

FRANÇOIS: I'll leave you to look at the wine list. (*He gives it to* LUCIE, *who passes it to* DAVID.)

DAVID: What kind of wine do you prefer?

LUCIE: Well ... red or white.

DAVID: That's what I meant ... Red or white?

LUCIE: I like both.

DAVID: How about red?

LUCIE: Red? Perfect!

DAVID: What kind of red do you like ... Bourgogne, Bordeaux, Beaujolais ...

LUCIE: I like all of them.

DAVID: Beaujolais?

LUCIE: Beaujolais? Great!

DAVID: What kind of Beaujolais would you prefer?

LUCIE: Euh ... It's up to you!

DAVID: How about a bottle of Brouilly?

LUCIE: Good idea!

DAVID: Do you like Brouilly?

LUCIE: I love it ! You know ... it's a very good restaurant here, they serve a kind of 'mixed genre' cuisine ... A little of this ... a little of that ... French, Hindu, Vegeterian ...

FRANÇOIS: (*Re-enters for their order.*) Have you decided on the wine?

LUCIE: (*She scans the wine list.*) Yes, we will have a bottle of ... Brouilly.

FRANÇOIS: Brouilly ... Okay (FRANÇOIS *exits for their order.*)

DAVID: So! How does it feel to be a movie star?

LUCIE: My god, give me a chance! ... It's my first day of filming! I think I felt a bit ... silly ... ! I found the director quite aggressive with his camera ... He wanted to shoot a scene from above, you know, as if you're looking through the eyes of a murderer, who's watching his victim through a skylight ... But during the shooting, I felt more observed by the crew, and the director himself, than by the voyeur in the scenario ...

DAVID: But aren't you used to being watched?

LUCIE: In theater, it's different. When you perform, the audience is watching the whole you ... But today, I felt that they were taking me apart.

DAVID: Taking you apart ...

LUCIE: Yes ... Close up of one eye, medium shot of the knife in the back, my right hand scratching at the floor ...

FRANÇOIS *comes back with the bottle, shows it to* LUCIE *who simply reads the label.*

LUCIE: Brouilly.

DAVID: What were you filming exactly? Indoor scenes, outdoor scenes?

LUCIE: We are taking the interiors first, because the film is set in spring …

So we have to wait for the end of winter.

DAVID: What will you do if it rains all the time?

LUCIE: It's a thriller! They want it to rain, because all the scenes happen in the rain!

DAVID: What if it never rains?

LUCIE: Well … I suppose they'll make it rain!

DAVID: Of course, just as for tears … As far as they are concerned, making it is not a problem, merely a question of water quantity!

LUCIE: (*Trying to make a pun, just as* FRANÇOIS *appears with the wine.*) Exactly: when you're 'making it', it's the size of the equipment that counts! (*She laughs, joined by* FRANÇOIS *who pours a little wine into her glass so she can 'taste' it.*) Merci!

FRANÇOIS: Ben … Goûtes-y.

DAVID: Taste it.

LUCIE: Oh … yes, sure. Hmm … it's very good … (*As* FRANÇOIS *pours the rest.*)

It's even a little bouchonné!

FRANÇOIS: Oh – I'll get you another bottle…

LUCIE: No no, it's very good … It is bouchonné … Bouchonné.

FRANÇOIS: Yes, but … if it's bouchonné –

DAVID: Isn't that supposed to mean that it tastes like cork?

LUCIE: Well … in this case, it can't possibly be bouchonné because it tastes great!

DAVID: Maybe I should double-check … It's a very expensive bottle!

> DAVID *does so, religiously. As he looks at* FRANÇOIS, *he seems to recognize him.*

FRANÇOIS: Something wrong?

DAVID: No, no … It's an excellent wine!

LUCIE: Like I said.

FRANÇOIS: Are you ready to order?

DAVID: After you, Lucie.

LUCIE: No, no … You go first David, you are the guest!

DAVID: What do you mean, I am the guest? I thought I was the one inviting you for dinner!

LUCIE: No, No … I mean, you are the foreigner!

DAVID: (*Does not respond. To* FRANÇOIS.) Is this soup?

FRANÇOIS: Yes … Potage Crécy.

Figure 33 *Polygraph* (Ex Machina/Robert Lepage) from the Harbourfront Festival's Quayworks, Toronto, 1990. (Photographer: Michael Cooper.)

DAVID: Well. I'll have that please, and the filet de boeuf Brisanne. I'd like that done rare but please in the French understanding of the word rare ... not the Canadian.

LUCIE: I'll have the same as him, but with the Canadian rare!

FRANÇOIS leaves with the order.

DAVID: Well ... Here's to your film! (*They make a toast.* DAVID *takes the package from under his chair.*) I'm not very good at this ... but here! (*He puts it on the table, offering it to her.*) This is for you.

LUCIE: What is it?

DAVID: What do you think it is? ... It's a present!

LUCIE: But it's not my birthday.

DAVID: It's a present just the same.

LUCIE: No ... I mean ... There is no need for you to be buying me presents David.

DAVID: Well ... I'm sorry then.

A very awkward pause, which LUCIE *breaks.*

LUCIE: No ... No ... I'm sorry ... I'm the one acting weird here ... Let me open it! Oh!.A Russian doll!

DAVID: Yes, the real thing.

LUCIE: These come in all different sizes and there are people who collect them!

DAVID: In fact ... You won't have to collect them ... They are all there, included one inside the other.

LUCIE: What do you mean?

DAVID: Open it!

LUCIE: Oh, it's beautiful.

DAVID: It's called a Matruska.

LUCIE: A Matruska.

LUCIE opens up the dolls and lines them up on the table top so that they form a wall between her and DAVID.

DAVID: I bought it in Eastern Europe but you find them everywhere now. It's a traditional doll. Representing generations ... So, this big one here is the mother of this one and also the grandmother of this one because she is the mother of this one and this one is the mother of that one and that one ... and ... to infinity I suppose! But ... I like to think it may stands for other things like ... Hidden feelings. ... One truth which is hiding another truth and another one and another one ...

LUCIE: I'm very moved ... Thank you.

DAVID: I'm glad you like it.

A marked 'slow' change in lights and sound indicate a time warp: Time is rapidly passing. LUCIE *and* DAVID *reach for their coffee cups in slow motion, their eyes locked together.* FRANÇOIS *glides in to take away the empty dishes and glasses. As he takes the bottle of wine, he slowly lays it across the middle of the table,*

tipping its contents so that the red wine stains the white table-cloth, and drips to the floor.

DAVID: (*Back to real time.*) ... And at one point in the film, the angel turns to him and says: 'Beware mirrors ... Death comes and goes through mirrors ... If you don't believe me, gaze upon yourself all your life in the looking glass and you will see her at work.'

LUCIE: That's beautiful.

DAVID: That's Cocteau.

Another time passage, marked in the same way with lights, sound and slow motion as LUCIE *and* DAVID *stir their coffee, the sounds of the spoons making an evocative late-night rhythm on their china cups.* FRANÇOIS *comes in, looking at his watch. The meal has been over for a long time.*

FRANÇOIS: I'm sorry but I am going to have to close now.

DAVID: What time is it?

FRANÇOIS: A quarter past three.

DAVID: A quarter past three!

LUCIE: My God! ... We didn't notice the time pass!

DAVID: I'm very sorry ... We were completely engrossed in our conversation while digesting this excellent meal!

LUCIE: Oui. Merci beaucoup ... C'était très bon.

DAVID: Can you tell me where I could find my coat please?

FRANÇOIS: It's in the cloakroom ... I'll get it for you.

DAVID: Lucie ... You are forgetting your Matruska!

LUCIE: Oh ... my Matruska ... (*showing it to* FRANÇOIS.) Regarde François ce que David m'a donné ... C'est une poupée Russe ... un Matruska. Il l'a achetée à l'Est.

FRANÇOIS: C'est beau.

They move towards the exit of the restaurant. LUCIE *stands against the wall with the men on each side of her.* FRANÇOIS *addresses* DAVID.

You're from Europe?

DAVID: Yes. I'm from East Berlin. But I have been a Canadian citizen for many years now.

FRANÇOIS: And what do you do here?

DAVID: I am a criminologist. I work for a criminal institution in Montreal.

FRANÇOIS: Parthenais?

DAVID: Yes, Parthenais.

LUCIE: Tu connais ça?

FRANÇOIS: Oui ... J'ai déjà eu affaire là.

LUCIE: Comment ça?

FRANÇOIS: Pas en prison ... I went there to undergo a polygraph test.

LUCIE: A what?

FRANÇOIS: Un test de polygraphe.

DAVID: A lie detector ... For what?

FRANÇOIS: Because six years ago one of my best friends was murdered here in Quebec City. I was the last one to see her alive so, I was a suspect. In fact, it was me who found

Figure 34 *Polygraph* (Ex Machina/Robert Lepage). (Photographer: Claudel Huot.)

her dead in her apartment. She had been tied up, raped and stabbed many times.

DAVID: Did they find the murderer?

FRANÇOIS: No. They never identified him.

DAVID: What was your friend's name?

FRANÇOIS: Marie-Claude Légaré.

LUCIE reacts to the name. As if 'flashing back' to the previous film-shoot scene, she turns as though she's been stabbed, to face the wall. Her back is covered with blood. She falls to the ground between the two men, who, without acknowledging her fall, continue to face each other in conversation.

DAVID: Yes … I think I remember … Don't worry, they'll track him down. Nobody is able to go through life with a murder on their conscience …

As DAVID continues to talk to where he was standing, FRANÇOIS 'relives' finding his friend's corpse, kneels down by her, silently enacts his grief.

Well, thank you once again and my compliments to the chef; the food was indeed excellent. And the service, impeccable! Have you been a waiter for long?

FRANÇOIS stands again to continue the conversation normally. He speaks to DAVID's original position as DAVID in turn kneels by LUCIE and performs an 'autopsy' on her, ripping her shirt with a scalpel.

FRANÇOIS: Long enough … Three years now. Before this, I was at school, University, studying Political Science – and I worked part time in a Yugoslavian restaurant.

DAVID: Yugoslavian …

FRANÇOIS: Yes. I like it better here though, it's more friendly.

DAVID: Do you intend to do this for long? I mean … waiting tables! I know how transient things are in the restaurant business.

FRANÇOIS: I don't know. If I could find work related to my studies, I'd move on for sure.

DAVID: Well … It's better than no work at all. You know, when I lived in East Berlin, I thought the West was full of 'golden opportunities' – but now I see how hard it is to succeed here. Over there, the jobs are trivial sometimes, but at least everybody has the right to work.

LUCIE uncoils from the floor to take the same position against the wall; simultaneously, the two men each put one foot on the wall, turning their bodies horizontal so as they appear to be in the classic cinematic 'top shot' of a corpse. FRANÇOIS and DAVID shake hands 'over' her body.

DAVID: It was a pleasure meeting you François.

The scene returns to 'real' time and space

Well, if we want to exercise our own right to work tomorrow, perhaps we should be moving along.

LUCIE: (*She kisses him.*) Salut François.
FRANÇOIS: A bientôt Lucie.

LUCIE walks slowly towards DAVID, looking at her hand.

DAVID: What's the matter Lucie? (*He takes her hand.*) You're bleeding!
LUCIE: It's nothing. I must have cut myself with a knife.
DAVID: Come ... We'll take care of it.

As soon as they are gone, FRANÇOIS pulls out a bag of coke, and prepares himself a few lines.

Projection:
14. The ramparts
Exterior, night.

A projection of the Quebec City skyscape covers the cyclorama of the theatre. LUCIE and DAVID enter. She is withdrawn and quiet.

DAVID: What an exquisite city.
LUCIE: I walk here often, but in summer usually, not winter.
DAVID: I greatly prefer the winter. I don't know why really, but I find I like the cold ... anything cold. Perhaps it's because I was born in December. Have you noticed that when people talk about the cold, it's always in pejorative terms. But for me, the cold evokes a kind of objective calm, wisdom and, above all, a great gentleness, like these snowflakes slowly falling ... Leaning against the ramparts like that, you remind me of someone I once knew ...
LUCIE: Who was she?
DAVID: Someone whom I loved deeply and to whom I did a great wrong ... A German woman.
LUCIE: I'm too nosy, aren't I?
DAVID: It was a long time ago. What's wrong Lucie? Since we've left the restaurant you have seemed preoccupied somehow.
LUCIE: Well ... I am. It's because – You know the story François just told us in the restaurant, about his friend? That is the story of the film we are making. It's based on the real murder situation – but I didn't know François was connected to it. It gave me a shock ... And now I feel uneasy about playing in it, and I'm wondering if there's still time for them to find someone else.
DAVID: They have lousy taste. To base a film script on an unresolved murder case ... How do they end the movie?

LUCIE: Well ... after the girl's been killed, they set everything up to look as if it was one of her close friends who did it but at the end we discover –
DAVID: – at the end, we discover that it was the police who did it.
LUCIE: How did you know?
DAVID: It's a classic. When you don't know how to end a who-done-it, you always blame it on the cops. It's easy ... When I was a student of Criminology, I feared that the people developing Investigative Techniques were violent brutes: a product of their line of work. But I needn't have worried about becoming a brute. No, they are much more dangerous than that. The men leading the field of Criminal Research are very, very intelligent; a fact you will never see in a thriller. It's too frightening perhaps. Poor François ... At Parthenais they know he is innocent, but he'll probably never be told.
LUCIE: Why not?
DAVID: In a Police Inquiry where the guilty party hasn't been identified, it's strategy to keep everyone in ignorance.
LUCIE: How do you know François is innocent?
DAVID: François does not know, but I was the one who conducted his Polygraph Test. This must remain between us, Lucie; it's a confidence.
LUCIE: But – how can I look him in the face without telling him?
DAVID: Stop seeing him for a while.

He tries to hold her, but she pushes her away and continues walking along the ramparts.

Projection:
15. The call
Exterior, night.

FRANÇOIS enters, stage right, takes change from his pocket and crosses to stand at a 'phone kiosk' in the stage left wing. Noises, as of dialling a pay-phone, are heard. FRANÇOIS is lit so as to blow up an enormous grotesque shadow across the entire wall, in such a way that every movement of his dialling and speaking on the phone registers. Over the phone line, we hear LUCIE's answering machine.

LUCIE: Bonjour, vous êtes bien chez Lucie Champagne ... Malheureusement, je ne peut pas vous répondre pour le moment, mais si vous voulez bien laisser votre nom et votre numéro de téléphone, je vous rappelle dans les plus brefs délais.

FRANÇOIS lets the phone drop as the message continues. He comes back on stage, kicks the wall, then leans against it, pressing his face and body into it. As lights fade to black, we hear the beep and tone of the answering machine.

Projection:
16. The line-up
Interior, night.

The line-up is a re-cap scene which shows the most telling moments in the play so far. It begins with a matrix projected on the wall, reminiscent of the 'Man in Motion' photographs by Eadweard Muybridge. The scene is played nude by the actors. Choreographic images of FRANÇOIS working in the restaurant, LUCIE in shock in the subway, FRANÇOIS being whipped, DAVID's meeting with LUCIE, DAVID and LUCIE embracing against the wall, the 'Film Noir Top Shot' of the handshake in the restaurant. The scene and movement fragments are repeated, overlayed, dissected and recombined at a pace of increasing frenzy. Black out.

Projection:
17. The spring
Exterior, day.

FRANÇOIS has a bucket of water with which he sluices the wall. With a brush, he starts to scrub it. DAVID enters, with sunglasses and a travel bag.

DAVID: Hello François. Have you seen Lucie?

FRANÇOIS: Not for a month, at least. She must be busy, shooting her movie.

DAVID: I came to say goodbye, but if she is off on location …

FRANÇOIS: You're going away?

DAVID: I'm going back to East Berlin. The government is sending me there for a series of conferences on Investigative Techniques. Now that the Wall has disappeared, there is a great demand for up-to-date technologies. But to tell you the truth, my motivation is more personal than professional.

FRANÇOIS: And what's the government's motivation: to share knowledge or sell free enterprise?

DAVID: To share knowledge. Well, if you see Lucie, tell her I was here … (*He makes as if to leave, then stops.*) What the hell are you doing François?

FRANÇOIS: I'm washing the wall.

DAVID: Yes, I can see, but why?

FRANÇOIS: The landlord told me to strip my graffiti off the garden wall before I move out, or else he'll prosecute.

DAVID: Prosecute … For graffiti! … What did it say?

FRANÇOIS: L'histoire s'écrit avec le sang.

DAVID: Which means?

FRANÇOIS: History is written with blood. It means that we write history through war, fascism and murder.

DAVID: Murder … You mean political assassinations.

FRANÇOIS: No. I mean murders. The smallest little killing, of some totally unimportant person … In a way that's still a political act, don't you think?

DAVID: Is that what you learned in political sciences?

FRANÇOIS loses his temper.

FRANÇOIS: Why do you ask me so many questions? You sound like an interrogator in a bad detective movie!

Defiantly, FRANÇOIS gathers up his bucket and brush, and exits.

Projection:
18. Travelling fowards
Exterior, night.

LUCIE appears in profile, stage left, behind and above the wall. She's lit from behind by the light of a movie projector positioned in the Stage Left wing. The rushes of the movie are projected onto the Stage Right wall, but are not visible to the audience, while she is watching the rushes of the movie. The projector stops.

LUCIE: (*Addresses the director offstage.*) This is from yesterday? And what we shoot tomorrow will be linked with it − ? (*She starts to cry silently.*) − Excuse me … (*She pulls herself together.*) May I see it again please?

Black out.

Projection:
19. Apartment # 8
Interior, day.

FRANÇOIS is packing boxes in the washroom of his apartment. The washbasin is set into the wall as before. LUCIE enters with books. The scene is translated into subtitles that are projected with slides on the wall.

LUCIE: Salut François, je t'ai rapporté les livres que tu m'avais prêté … 'L'orgasme au masculin', j'ai trouvé ça ben intéressant.

FRANÇOIS: Tu peux les garder encore si t'en a pas fini.

LUCIE: Non, non … je sais ce que je voulais savoir …

LUCIE examines the cosmetics strewn in the washbasin.

Ouan … t'en a des affaires pour un gars …

She starts to poke around in one of his boxes as he puts the books in.

T'écris pas ce que tu mets dans tes boites?

FRANÇOIS: C'est pas nécessaire … Pour ce que j'ai …

LUCIE: Écris où est ce que ça va toujours, sinon tu vas être mêlé quand tu vas arriver là-bas. (*Pointing to a box.*) Ça c'est quoi? Des cosmétiques? Je vais écrire pharmacie dessus. Pis celle-là?

FRANÇOIS: Là dedans … des couvertures, serviettes des débarbouillettes, des livres, des vieux journaux …

LUCIE: J'pourrais écrire divers.

Inside the box, LUCIE finds a long leather strap with a strange fastening at the end.

Ça, ça sert à quoi?

FRANÇOIS: (*He puts the strap around his neck and demonstrates.*) Quand je me masturbe, je me sers de ça. Je tire – puis je lâche, je tire – puis je lâche. Puis juste avant de venir, je tire de plus en plus fort ... Mais à un moment donné, il faut que tu lâches, si tu veux pas venir pour la dernière fois ...

LUCIE: Est-ce que ça sert juste à ça?

FRANÇOIS takes the strap from around his neck and goes to the washbasin.

FRANÇOIS Viens ici.

She hesitates.

Viens ici!

She goes to him.

Assis-toi, donnes-moi ta main.

He ties the belt around LUCIE's hand, takes it through the u-bend pipe on the washbasin and wraps it round her neck before tying it up. In a simultaneous scene, DAVID gives a lecture about the Polygraph Machine in East Berlin. He stands upstage of the wall, but not above it. He is visible to the audience only as a reflection in the two-way mirror which is positioned at such an angle as to reveal him.

DAVID: ... Firstly, the lie registers on the cardiograph, with an accelerated heartbeat. At the temple, we monitor for an increase or, in the case of some subjects, a decrease of arterial pressure –

FRANÇOIS: Là je vais serrer un peu ...

DAVID: Respiration has a direct effect on the person responding to questions: this contributes yet another reading of the physical response. Lastly, we measure the subject's perspiration. The Polygraph Machine detects the most minute psycho-physical variations occuring during interrogation.

FRANÇOIS: (*He puts a blindfold on her eyes, rendering her completely helpless.*) Comme ça, t'as vraiment l'impression d'être vulnérable ...

DAVID: The fear and mystique which surrounds the Polygraph Machine makes it a useful pressure tactic in obtaining a confession. But such strategies, I believe, should be used only with great care and compassion. Sometimes, the psychological response we trigger is so violent as to effect a lasting disorder in the mind of a totally innocent suspect.

LUCIE: Pis après?

DAVID: Let me tell you about a Polygraph Test undertaken in the context of an unresolved murder case. The questioning of a particular suspect went somewhat like this:

FRANÇOIS: Des fois, quand on se ramasse une gang de gars ...

DAVID: François, we are going to conduct a little test.

FRANÇOIS: Y'en a un qui se fait attacher comme ça ...

DAVID: Can you hear me properly?

FRANÇOIS: ... Pis au hasard y'en a un autre qui est choisi pour aller le rejoindre ...

DAVID: But you cannot actually see me can you?

FRANÇOIS: ... celui qui est attaché, il peut rien faire ...

DAVID: François, are we in Canada?

FRANÇOIS: ... Il peut rien voir ...

DAVID: Is it summertime?

FRANÇOIS: ... pis l'autre il fait ce qu'il veut avec ...

DAVID: Was it you who killed Marie-Claude Légaré?

FRANÇOIS: (*In his memory, FRANÇOIS 'relives' the Polygraph Test scene.*) Non.

DAVID: Is it 1986?

FRANÇOIS: Oui.

DAVID: Are we in the month of August?

FRANÇOIS: Non.

DAVID: Is it the month of July?

FRANÇOIS: Oui.

DAVID: Are you responsible for the death of Marie-Claude Légaré?

FRANÇOIS: Non.

DAVID: Now, the result of this Polygraph Test gave evidence that this witness was actually telling the truth. But the person conducting the test told him afterwards that the machine had established that the test was inconclusive: so as to consider the spontaneous reaction of the witness as the ultimate proof of his innocence ...

FRANÇOIS: (*A complete emotional breakdown.*) Allez-vous me lâcher tabarnak! C'est pas moi qui l'a tuée!! C'est pas moi!! Vous voulez me rendre fou, c'est ça!! Y vont me rendre fou hostie ...

LUCIE: (*LUCIE is frozen, blindfolded and terrified. FRANÇOIS gives her no word, only opening and closing a metal clip he has taken from the box.*)
François ...?
François ...?
François?

DAVID: But the police never told him he was released from suspicion ... He was never let off the hook.

FRANÇOIS: (*He slowly recovers, goes to her and takes off the blindfold.*) Veux-tu que je te détache?

He does so, then silently puts the belt and blindfold in a box.

LUCIE: Est-ce que c'est toi qui l'a tuée?

FRANÇOIS: ... J'pense pas non.

LUCIE: Pourquoi tu dis «j'pense» pas?

FRANÇOIS: Parce que des fois ... je l'sais plus.

He starts to cry, an emotion from deep inside. LUCIE goes to him, takes him in her arms.

LUCIE: Moi, je l'sais ... que tu serais pas capable de faire mal à une mouche.

She holds him, fiercely comforting and reassuring him. She touches his face, and the comfort becomes passion. Lights fade as they start to embrace.

Projection:
20. The rain
Exterior, day.
Rain falls from the ceiling behind the wall. Above the wall the camera appears, covered with an umbrella. LUCIE *has not turned up for the day's filming.*

Projection:
21. Apartment # 7
Interior, night.
An eerie dream sequence. LUCIE *leans against the wall with a hidden light strapped to her back. It shines at the wall, creating a strange halo around her body, and placing her in silhouette. She walks slowly to the front of the stage.*

DAVID: (*Enters Stage Left.*) Lucie! I'm back!

> FRANÇOIS *enters from* LUCIE'S *bedroom, without a shirt.* DAVID *is shocked . He appears not to see* LUCIE *downstage, and speaks to* FRANÇOIS *behind her back.*

What are you doing here? Where's Lucie?
FRANÇOIS: She's in the room.

> DAVID *goes into the room then comes back in anger.*

DAVID: (*Showing the exit.*) Get out!
FRANÇOIS: Maybe we could talk ...
DAVID: Get out!
FRANÇOIS: Wait ...

> DAVID *seizes* FRANÇOIS *to throw him out, and they fight violently.* FRANÇOIS' *head is knocked against the wall. Slowly,* LUCIE *walks backwards to her original place, and the lighting changes. She leans against the wall, lost in her thoughts.* FRANÇOIS *enters from the bedroom. He leans against the wall beside* LUCIE. *He is restless and anxious. They smile gently at one another, and* FRANÇOIS *takes her hand, as if unable to speak the things in his heart. He holds her like a frightened child – which then becomes a passionate kiss.* FRANÇOIS *then withdraws, and bids goodbye to* LUCIE. *He exits. David's voice is heard offstage.*

DAVID: Lucie! I'm back!

> DAVID *enters.*

How are you?
LUCIE: I'm fine ...
DAVID: (*He takes his bag into the bedroom, then comes back and starts to wash his face in the washbasin.*) I thought you were supposed to be filming today?
LUCIE: Yes ... I was scheduled, but I decided not to go.
DAVID: Why?
LUCIE: We were scheduled to shoot the close-ups for the death sequence, and I feel I have no right to do it.

DAVID: This is very courageous of you.
LUCIE: François just left for Montreal ... David ... While you were away – I slept with François.

> DAVID *stops washing, abruptly. He holds very still.*

I've spent the whole week with him because he needed someone. And I told him everything you told me on the ramparts. He told you the truth, but you lied to him.

> LUCIE *looks at* DAVID, *who has straightened to regard her, without expression.*

David ... React! ... Feel something!
DAVID: (*As he calmly turns to her.*) What do you want me to 'feel'? You want me to be jealous of a fucking homosexual?
LUCIE: If that's the truth, yes!
If you want to cry, cry!

> *The lights fade on them.*

Projection:
22. Death
Interior, night.
Behind the wall, FRANÇOIS *arrives at the metro station and paces impatiently, waiting for the train. We can't see him but he is lit so that his silhouette is projected upon the cyclorama behind the wall.* LUCIE *appears above the wall to perform Hamlet. She holds a knife and recites the famous soliloquy as* FRANÇOIS *waits.*

LUCIE: Être ou ne pas être.
C'est la question.
Est-il plus noble pour une âme de souffrir les flèches et les coups d'un sort atroce, ou de s'armer contre le flot qui monte, et de lui faire face, et de l'arrêter?
Mourir, dormir ... Rien de plus.
Terminer par du sommeil la souffrance du coeur et les mille blessures qui sont le lot de la chair.
C'est bien le dénouement que l'on voudrait ... et de quelle ardeur!
Mourir, dormir ...
Dormir ... Peut-être rêver.
C'est l'obstacle ...
Car l'anxiété des rêves qui viendront dans ce sommeil des morts, quand nous aurons chassé de nous le tumulte de vivre, est là pour nous retenir ...
Et c'est la pensée qui fait que le malheur a si longue vie.

The lights on her fade slowly. We hear the sound of the train coming. FRANÇOIS *takes off his leather jacket and lets it fall to the floor behind him; without hesitation, he throws himself in front of the arriving train. As his silhouette dives out of sight, his body comes hurtling through the brick wall. Behind the wall,*

FRANÇOIS arrives at the metro station and paces impatiently, waiting for the train. We can't see him but he is lit so that his silhouette is projected upon the cyclorama behind the wall. We hear the sound of the train coming. FRANÇOIS takes off his leather jacket and lets it fall to the floor behind him; without hesitation, he throws himself in front of the arriving train. As his silhouette dives out off sight, the brick wall suddenly falls and a piercing light shines through as FRANÇOIS' naked body comes hurtling through the falling bricks to land on a hospital gurney. There he lies, amidst the broken bricks, dead and awaiting an autopsy. DAVID pushes the gurney stage right, so that it is positioned beneath the mirror, which is hung at an angle such that FRANÇOIS' body is reflected in it. Slowly, the reflection in the mirror over him changes so that we no longer see his body, but a skeleton, which lies in the same position, as if the mirror see through his flesh. Above the wall, across the cyclorama, clouds are running in a vast sky.

Appendix

The three characters meet a few months before the fall of the Berlin Wall. The murder of Marie-Claude Légaré took place six years prior to the action, when François was studying Political Science at the university, and David was in charge of polygraph examinations at the Parthenais. The action of the play occurs in 1989.

It would be possible to place the action later. Our only stipulation is that six years before the main action of the play the Berlin Wall was still intact. Lucie and François are Québecois, and so English is their second language, as it is also for David, an emigrant to Canada from East Berlin; however, he has a more 'perfect' command than they do. Official business, such as polygraph tests and film auditions are often conducted in English, so although they have marked Québecois accents, François and Lucie are fluent in English. David lives in Montreal but has not learned any French, so constantly needs translations of menus, etc.

In the original production, all the scenes between François and Lucie were performed in French, since it's their own language. Lucie's theatre production of *Hamlet* is also in French, as indicated in the script. In case of an all-English production, the scenes that involve French are translated below.

Projection:
4. François
Interior, night.

FRANÇOIS enters stage left with a 'table for two' over his shoulder. This he swings down in an easy movement. Quickly setting it with plates and cutlery, he then positions two chairs either side. When the table is 'set' he immediately unmakes it, swings it over his shoulder, and repeats the whole sequence in a different space, all the while talking rapidly to invisible customers. During the course of the scene

he covers the whole stage, so suggesting a room full of tables, and he never stops moving or talking.

FRANÇOIS: Did you enjoy your meal? The bill? At once, sir. Would you please follow me? Did you notice today's Specials on the board? Yes. You'd like a table for … ? Please, follow me. Something to drink, perhaps? You'd like to see the wine list. Two coffees with cognac … It'll just be a moment, sir! Good evening. No, unfortunately we're all out of the roast veal. The chef suggests instead the chicken in lemon: it's very good. So … two chicken. Would you care for dessert? Today's Special is Homemade Orange Cheesecake; it's excellent … So, a table for one? … Would you please follow me … For two? … I'm sorry, we have no English menus, I'll be happy to translate for you. For two, sir? … I have one table over there … Sorry? Oh … You should have told me before, I would have replaced it, no problem … Okay … Next time … This way please; a table for … ?

LUCIE: (*Enters and sits at the table, as François continues his actions.*) Hi François! How're you doing? … Hey, they said you and your boyfriend came to the show last night? Why didn't you come backstage to see me – you didn't like it?

FRANÇOIS: No! It was excellent! We thought it was brilliant to cast a woman as Hamlet; some of those questions take on real significance coming from a woman; especially for today – more so than from a man.

LUCIE: Actually, it wasn't planned that way, originally. They called me at the last minute. The guy who was playing Hamlet got sick and the director had this strange idea of casting a woman for the part. Oh, François – I heard the radio station CKRL is looking for someone to read the late-night news. You've got such a nice voice, why don't you apply? You'd be great!

FRANÇOIS: Thanks for thinking of me, but it wouldn't be possible right now. Too much work at the restaurant.

LUCIE: François, is Alain angry at me? I met him on the stairs at home, and he didn't even say hello … what's his problem?

FRANÇOIS: No problem. It's me he's mad at. We had a fight …

LUCIE: Ah. Well … Thanks. It was great!

LUCIE exits, FRANÇOIS continues at the same pace.

FRANÇOIS: See you, Lucie!

FRANÇOIS goes out with the table settings, returns and sits at the table. Change in lights and music indicate that it is now the end of the day, and he is exhausted. He taps out three lines of coke and snorts it. DAVID enters the restaurant over the wall, sliding down with his back to it, his arms and his suit jacket spread like a giant ominous spider. DAVID lands smoothly in the empty seat across the table from François.

DAVID: François, can you hear me properly? But you can't actually see me, can you? François, we are going to conduct a little test. Are we in Canada? Is it summertime? Was it you who killed Marie-Claude Légaré?

FRANÇOIS shakes his head, as if to dislodge disturbing thoughts. DAVID disappears up the wall in a slow reversal of the way he entered. Lights crossfade to a spotlight stage right.

Projection:
9. Apartment # 7
Interior, night.

Stage left, a washbasin set into the wall, with a mirror above it, indicates the bathroom in FRANÇOIS' apartment. FRANÇOIS enters, drunk, limping and sore. He puts his ear against the wall to listen if anyone is home next door. He calls through the wall:

FRANÇOIS: Lucie! … Lucie …

FRANÇOIS puts a glass against the wall to listen for any sounds from next-door. Silence: there is no-one home. He drops his leather jacket on the floor and peels off his T-shirt. His back is marked with whiplash weals. He soaks the shirt in water and lays it across his back with a sigh of relief.

LUCIE: (*Entering his apartment suddenly.*) François?
FRANÇOIS: Come in.
LUCIE: Is something wrong? Are you sick?
FRANÇOIS: Yes … I don't feel good … I think I drank too much. D'you want to stay for a coffee?
LUCIE: I'd like to, but uh … (*Pointing at the silhouette of a man waiting at the door.*) I'm not alone.
FRANÇOIS: Ah. Someone's waiting for you.
LUCIE: Yes. I'll take a rain check. Sorry to bother you so late, but I only just got home, and I can't get in. I lost my keys.
FRANÇOIS: Ah … (*He digs for LUCIE's key inside his jeans' pocket and gives it to her.*)
LUCIE: Thank you. Well, take care …

As she goes to kiss him on both cheeks, she inadvertently touches his back, FRANÇOIS winces. LUCIE tries to look at his back.

What's the matter, did I hurt you?
DAVID: (*His voice comes from behind the wall.*) Lucie? …
FRANÇOIS: No, no … it's nothing.
LUCIE: (*Tries again to see his back.*) Come on … What's the matter?
FRANÇOIS: (*Reacting violently.*) Leave me alone … I said it's nothing!
LUCIE: Okay, okay!
DAVID: Lucie, are you alright?
LUCIE: Yeah, yeah … (*Awkwardly, as she exits.*) Thank you.

FRANÇOIS is now very alone. Lights crossfade to the expanse of the cyclorama, above the wall.

Projection:
15. The call
Exterior, night.

FRANÇOIS enters, stage right, takes change from his pocket and crosses to stand at a 'phone kiosk' in the stage left wing. Noises, as of dialling a pay-phone, are heard. FRANÇOIS is lit so as to blow up an enormous grotesque shadow across the entire wall, in such a way that every movement of his dialling and speaking on the phone registers. Over the phone line, we hear LUCIE's answering machine.

LUCIE: Hello, you've reached the home of Lucie Champagne … I'm sorry I'm not available to take your call right now, but if you would leave your name and number I'll get back to you as soon as possible.

FRANÇOIS lets the phone drop as the message continues. He comes back onstage, kicks the wall, then leans against it, pressing his face and body into it. As lights fade to black, we hear the beep and tone of the answering machine.

Projection:
19. Apartment # 8
Interior, day.

FRANÇOIS is packing boxes in the washroom of his apartment. The washbasin is set into the wall as before. LUCIE enters with books.

LUCIE: Hi François, I brought back the books you lent me … I found the 'The Male Orgasm' pretty interesting.
FRANÇOIS: You can keep them if you're not finished.
LUCIE: No, no. I found out everything I wanted to know!

LUCIE examines the cosmetics strewn in the washbasin.

You've got a lot of make-up for a guy.

She starts to poke around in one of his boxes as he puts the books in.

Aren't you marking what's in the boxes?

FRANÇOIS: There's no point. I haven't got much stuff.
LUCIE: You should at least write where it belongs, so you won't be mixed up when you move into your new place. (*Pointing to a box.*) What is in there? Cosmetics? I'll write 'personal things' on the side. And what's in this one?
FRANÇOIS: Blankets, facecloths, books, old newspapers …
LUCIE: I could write … miscellaneous.

Inside the box, LUCIE finds a long leather strap with a strange fastening at the end.

And … What is this used for?

FRANÇOIS: (*He puts the strap around his neck and demonstrates.*) I use it when I masturbate. I pull then release, pull and release, and just before I come, I pull harder and harder … Then there's a certain point where I have to let go, or else it'll be the last time I come.
LUCIE: Do you use it for anything else?

FRANÇOIS takes the strap from around his neck and goes to the washbasin.

FRANÇOIS: Come here.

She hesitates.

Come here!

She goes to him.

Sit down … give me your hand.

He ties the belt around LUCIE's hand, takes it through the u-bend pipe on the washbasin and wraps it round her neck before tying it up. In a simultaneous scene, DAVID gives a lecture about the Polygraph Machine in East Berlin. He stands upstage of the wall, but not above it. He is visible to the audience only as a reflection in the two-way mirror which is positioned at such an angle as to reveal him.

DAVID: … Firstly, the lie registers on the cardiograph, with an accelerated heartbeat. At the temple, we monitor for an increase or, in the case of some subjects, a decrease of arterial pressure –

FRANÇOIS: I'm going to tighten it a bit …

DAVID: Respiration has a direct effect on the person responding to questions: this contributes yet another reading of the physical response. Lastly, we measure the subject's perspiration. The Polygraph Machine detects the most minute psycho-physical variations occuring during interrogation.

FRANÇOIS: (*he puts a blindfold on her eyes, rendering her completely helpless.*) This makes you feel really vulnerable …

DAVID: The fear and mystique which surrounds the Polygraph Machine, makes it a useful pressure tactic in obtaining a confession. But such strategies, I believe, should be used only with great care and compassion. Sometimes, the psychological response we trigger is so violent as to effect a lasting disorder in the mind of a totally innocent suspect.

LUCIE: And then?

DAVID: Let me tell you about a Polygraph Test undertaken in the context of an unresolved murder case. The questioning of a particular suspect went somewhat like this:

FRANÇOIS: Sometimes, when I get together with a gang of friends …

DAVID: François, we are going to conduct a little test.

FRANÇOIS: One of us gets tied up like this.

DAVID: Can you hear me properly?

FRANÇOIS: Then someone is picked at random to go in and join him …

DAVID: But you cannot actually see me can you?

FRANÇOIS: … the one who's all tied up can't do anything …

DAVID: François, are we in Canada?

FRANÇOIS: … he can't see anything …

DAVID: Is it summertime?

FRANÇOIS: … and the other one does whatever he wants with him.

DAVID: Was it you who killed Marie-Claude Légaré?

FRANÇOIS: (*In his memory, FRANÇOIS 'relives' the Polygraph Test scene.*) No.

DAVID: Is it 1986?

FRANÇOIS: Yes.

DAVID: Are we in the month of August?

FRANÇOIS: No.

DAVID: Is it the month of July?

FRANÇOIS: Yes.

DAVID: Are you responsible for the death of Marie-Claude Légaré?

FRANÇOIS: No.

DAVID: Now, the result of this Polygraph Test gave evidence that this witness was actually telling the truth. But the person conducting the test told him afterwards that the machine had established that he was lying: so as to consider the spontaneous reaction of the witness as the ultimate proof of his innocence …

FRANÇOIS: (*A complete emotional breakdown.*) Let me fucking go! I didn't kill her!! It wasn't me! It wasn't me! …

LUCIE: (*LUCIE is frozen, blindfolded and terrified. FRANÇOIS gives her no word, only opening and closing a metal clip he has taken from the box.*)
François …?
François …?
François?

DAVID: But the police never told him he was released from suspicion … He was never let off the hook.

FRANÇOIS: (*He slowly recovers, goes to her and takes off the blindfold.*) Do you want me to untie you?

He does so, then silently puts the belt and blindfold in a box.

LUCIE: Was it you killed her?

FRANÇOIS: I don't think so

LUCIE: Why do you say … You don't 'think' so?

FRANÇOIS: Because sometimes … I don't know anymore.

He starts to cry, an emotion from deep inside. LUCIE goes to him, takes him in her arms.

LUCIE: Listen to me … I know: I know you couldn't hurt a fly.

She holds him, fiercely comforting and reassuring him. She touches his face, and the comfort becomes passion. Lights fade as they start to embrace.

A note on the production history of this text

Polygraph was first produced in French as Le Polygraphe at Implanthéatre, in Quebec City, 6 to 14 of May, 1988 by Théatre Repère. The play was developed through improvisation by actors Robert Lepage, Marie Brassard and Pierre Phillipe Guay, with contributions and script notation from observer/collaborator Gyllian Raby. A second version was developed in Montreal for a November 1988 coproduction by Théatre Repère and Montreal's Théatre de Quat'Sous. This substantially altered the original scenario through a process of improvisation-based creation by the actors and director during rehearsal, which continued throughout the run of the production. The second version was translated into English for a production at the Almeida Theatre in London, England, from February 21 to March 04 1989. Here, Robert Lepage received the Time Out Award for his direction. From this time on, it played under the English title *Polygraph*. The following year, 21 February to 03 March, *Polygraph* was presented as part of the Harbourfront Festival's QuayWorks in Toronto. The script continued to metamorphose as a live, actor-created entity, with scripting and translation updates noted only periodically. In particular, the play became bilingual. The scenes between the Quebecois characters François and Lucie were played in French, with the introduction of projected English subtitles during the crisis scene. Marc Béland and Pierre Auger replaced Pierre Phillipe Guay and Robert Lepage in the cast, and more fine-tuning alterations were made to the order of the scenes and segues between them. *Polygraph* was featured at six summer festivals in Europe during 1990: Amsterdam, 12-16 June; Nuremberg, 19-20 June; Maubeuge (France), 5-6 July; Hamburg, 14-16 July; Barcelona, 23-26 July; Salzburg 13-15 August. In Barcelona, Marie Brassard was given the Best Foreign Actress award for her portrayal of Lucie. In 1990 *Polygraph* was part of the Next Wave Festival at the Brooklyn Academy of Music, 23 to 28 of October 1990. Shortly afterwards it played in the Studio season of Canada's National Arts Centre (where Robert Lepage was Artistic Director), and in April 1991 in Edmonton, Alberta as a co-production of Workshop West Theatre and Northern Light Theatre (where Gyllian Raby was Artistic Director). Since then, the play has been touring around Europe in Brussel, Glasgow, Berlin, Frankfurt, Vienna, Basel. Zurich, Aarhnem, Paris, Dieppe and was lastly perform in Hong Kong in February 1995. Other Canadian companies have produced the play, and in 1996 it was translated into Japanese by Matsuoka San, and with a Japanese cast, it was produced at the Tokyo Globe Theatre by Robert Lepage and Marie Brassard. In autumn1996 a film version of the story was released.

Translator's notes

I first translated *Polygraph* as it was being created, with the odd result that an English text existed before the authors considered their French production to be complete. Through the major revisions since then, characters, time-frame and situations have altered – and in our separate reality the Berlin Wall has fallen. The living performance script has been allowed to metamorphose to reflect the authors' deepening perception of and relationship with their material.

1. 'Travelling' is French film parlance for a 'dolly': smooth lateral movement of a film camera.

5.3 'Confess to Everything': A Note on *Speak Bitterness* (2008) and *Speak Bitterness* (1994–)

TIM ETCHELLS

Tim Etchells (b. 1956) *is a writer, performer and director. He has worked with Forced Entertainment, a leading UK-based experimental performance company, since 1984. The group works through improvisation to collectively create performances which are often centred around questions of contemporary identity and urban living as well as investigating the performative elements of theatricality. The performances are often durational, multimedia or site-specific and are predicated on creating non-linear narratives which evoke rather than state. Like many experimental performance companies their work plays with chance, rules and montage and often has a personal, confessional tone.*

Confess to Everything: A Note on *Speak Bitterness*

IN *SPEAK BITTERNESS* A line of performers make confessions from positions stood or seated behind a long table in a brightly lit space, the blue backdrop for which bears the title for the piece. The text for the performance – a long list or catalogue of statements admitting guilt, responsibility or complicity for a wide range of human wrong-doings great and small – is strewn across the table. This text – confessions for things like forgery, murder or genocide to more domestic stuff like reading each other's diaries or forgetting to take the dogs out for a walk – is the raw material through which relationships between the performers themselves and between performers and the audience are constructed in the piece. At different times the confessions are read, whispered, or shouted, appearing as single lines, as fast-paced exchanges and as long monologues or lists. With the lines punctuated by doubt, laughter and hesitation, invigorated by passion or laughter the performance itself shifts around in tone throughout, moving from apparent sincerity to numb accusation and blatant absurdity.

Central to *Speak Bitterness* is a practice of listing and of cataloguing-through-language. As the work unfolds the text creates a rolling and shifting map of the world outside the theatre space – a map which defines and redefines an idea or question of what's out there, its highs, lows, shape and borders. Each new sequential addition to the list (which, in performance occurs as part of a temporal process) either adjusts or confirms the watchers' developing guess about the culture it comes from and goes to. Manipulating or transforming this guess is a key element in the dramaturgy (or game) of lists. The list itemizes, catalogues and, essentially, stores data, presenting its contents as temporarily equivalent, without transparent comment or opinion. Unlike another staple of modernist composition – the collage – the act of listing does not layer, merge, overlay, re-mix or blur together its contents. Lists rather, with a seriality that implies but never fully delivers narrative, let each of their items stand alone but together, a menu or line of ingredients rather than a soup. Lists are blank or 'spacious' since the job of guessing the constituency of listed items and of unpacking their individual meaning is left to the viewer.

In its process of textual cataloguing *Speak Bitterness* has a strong relation to other durational works I've made with Forced Entertainment such as *Quizoola!* (1996) and *And on the Thousandth Night . . .* (2000), the former a catalogue of written questions and improvised answers, the latter an entirely improvised compendium of stories developed by a group of eight performers over a period of six hours. *Speak Bitterness* also relates to my more recent projects *That Night Follows Day* (with Victoria, 2007), a performance about the relationship between children and adults, for a group of sixteen young people aged between eight and fourteen, and *Sight Is The Sense. . .* (2008), a long free-associating list-monologue exploring language and its ability to define or describe the world, for the American actor Jim Fletcher.

In each of these quite different works the text explores a particular formal category or aspect of language, and particular kinds or genres of content – pushing at the limits of the category, raising questions not just about individual fragments of content but about the broader social and cultural frameworks that contain them. *Speak Bitterness* in this sense is as much about the nature of confession and guilt, the limits and energies of empathy, complicity, forgiveness and judgement, as it is about any particular thing that is named. *Speak Bitterness* is also, quite explicitly, about the audience, since the we which dominates and reverberates through the text at all times is of course a shifting and problematic construct. At times this we is something that might happily encompass the whole of the audience on any particular occasion. Most people would perhaps feel covered by or sign up to statements like 'we had our doubts' or 'we lost our way', but many would balk at signing up to statements such as 'we were date rapists' or 'we pushed dog shit through immigrants' doors'. The 'we' of the text, first appearing as a place of communal shelter and definition, rapidly becomes a problem – a fact which the piece is keen to explore and exploit. Even the range of confessions (from admitting distant historical events to admitting evidently futuristic or highly improbable fictional actions) makes an issue of our potential belonging. Far from the blanket communal comfort it may appear to offer, the 'we' of *Speak Bitterness* both refuses and accuses those watching, dividing and subdividing the supposedly shared social space of the auditorium. It's a probing of the idea of 'audience' that has continued in many later works that I have made with Forced Entertainment, notably *First Night* (2001), the disastrous vaudeville which constantly worries and provokes at the question of who exactly is watching out there in the dark, niggling to comic and disturbing effect at the question of their needs, (lack of) morals and (low) expectations.

⋆

In its original 'durational' version *Speak Bitterness* (National Review of Live Art, 1994) played with eight performers as an ongoing improvisational task and lasted six hours, with audience members free to arrive, depart and return at any point. Latterly the performance was developed in a condensed theatre version for seven performers, lasting one and half hours, and with a largely fixed text and dramaturgy. The original text drew on short passages of confessions material I had written for earlier Forced Entertainment pieces (*Let The Water Run Its Course*) *To The Sea That Made The Promise* (1986) and for *Marina & Lee* (1991). This material was joined by a large additional amount of new material written by me and then added to again with writing from performers Robin Arthur, Cathy Naden, Tim Hall and Sue Marshall. This writing was edited by me and further augmented by improvisation from the whole company. Since the theatre version (1995), I've continued to add more material to the text every year, accumulating confessions in reference to current events, cultural shifts and new areas of possibility and invention that open up in the writing.

Like most of the durational performances created by myself and Forced Entertainment the original long version of *Speak Bitterness* was not structured beyond its six-hour time-limit and an outline of simple performance rules and strategies. In such a performance, as in later six-hour works like *Quizoola!* and *And on the Thousandth Night...*, the event of the piece unfolds in real time: an encounter between the public, the performers and their decisions on the day. Subject to the influence of desire, tiredness, accident, whim and impulse, this version of *Speak Bitterness* remains a moveable feast, constructed and constrained through the simple device of the confessions and very much a vehicle for the live improvisational energies of the group.

The theatre version of *Speak Bitterness* was developed during summer 1995. We took the same blue tarpaulin box we'd used for the Glasgow performances (a space which contained both actors and audience) and adapted it as a stage-space – losing one wall to create an open rectangle that the public looked into. Strings of bare bulbs hung over the performance area were extended over the auditoria of venues that we toured to – lighting the audience slightly and sustaining a sense of being 'in the same room as' the performance.

In dramatic terms we tried to preserve the feeling of the Glasgow durational (spatial and performance intimacy, a sense of real-time process etc.) whilst adding enough in the way of structural architecture (narrative or musical development) to keep a theatre audience engaged for an hour and a half. Rehearsals involved the usual glut of improvisation based, on this occasion, on the reams of confessional texts. We used video a lot – playing back rehearsals and analysing them. We set and scripted sections out of successful improvisations and then combined these sections into various different orders. We also left some sections of the piece relatively unscripted so that performers would be free to choose new lines in each performance, or to interrupt each other, speaking in a different order each night in various sections. Our aim – as has been the case in much of our theatre work since this point and including works as diverse as the minimalist *Spectacular* (2008) and the energetic chaos of *Bloody Mess* (2004) – was for an architecture/structure in the performance that did develop – leading the viewer in different directions – but a structure which nonetheless could still seem live, accidental and to a certain extent spontaneous.

The *Speak Bitterness* text as presented here represents a wide range of the confessions material from the piece. The fact that it's not broken down and distributed between individual or named speakers reflects most accurately the form of the piece that we continue to present – the durational version – in which the text appears unhierarchicalised, in any sequence, from any of the performers, in blocks or line by line, according to the decisions people make on the spot. What draws us to this version is the live dynamic of the performers interacting with each other and the text, the ups and downs of the social interaction between them, and the way that this exhausting and exhaustive work stresses the task of the performance – 'confess to everything' – over and above any dramaturgy or the revelation of any particular item of content. Everything in this work remains decidedly in process.

Figure 35 *Speak Bitterness* (Forced Entertainment), Essen tour, 2009. (Photographer: Hugo Glendinning.)

Figure 36 *Speak Bitterness* (Forced Entertainment), Essen tour, 2009. (Photographer: Hugo Glendinning.)

Speak Bitterness

TIM ETCHELLS/FORCED ENTERTAINMENT

WE CONFESS TO LUST, greed, envy and hate crimes. We're guilty of bad coughs, Chest X-Rays, Lithium and Librium. We lost our equilibrium. We lost our will to live. We lost our way somewhere just after the junction and never found it again. We had double standards. We put the psychiatric patients in cage-beds. We saw the economic advantages of warfare and destruction. We smirked at the Simpson trial. When the markets crashed, we laughed out loud. We never claimed to have halos and wings. Our show used adult humour. Our kids had broken ribs. We joined a network of disorganised crime. We crashed the spaceship on purpose. We got drunk too often. We nobbled horses. We made each other bleed. We dropped atomic bombs on Nagasaki, Coventry, Seattle, Belize, Belsize Park and Hiroshima. We were rightly arrested under sections 7 and 23 and rightly charged under section 45. We planned the overthrow of governments, and holidays in the summer. We put love first. We broke our legs playing rounders. We were scumbags in a shooting war with other scumbags. We thought Gordon Brown was inspiring. We filmed events in which we could not intervene, events that spilled out of control, events that didn't even exist. We altered documents and photographs to disguise the location of people and places that were dear to us. We knew that a professional foul inside the thirty yard box could lead to a penalty but in the 83rd minute we felt there was no choice – some of us went one way and some went the other, sandwiching the bloke and bringing him down hard – the referee was a Hungarian and never saw a thing. We were cold callers, scared of kryptonite. We were class traitors and cry-for-help shoplifters. We were murderers of sleep. Everything was a movie to us. We hacked and hoodwinked, we wounded with intent. When the food-aid arrived in the lorries, we started shoving and pushing. We had nose jobs, chin-jobs, eye jobs, tummy-tucks and bum sucks. We were bloody fools. We're guilty of that look people have sometimes when they dare not speak their minds. We confess to radium, railways and roman-ticism. We were jealous of Helen Sebley's personal transformation. We never made the rendezvous. We were deathless, never fading. We ate pet food straight from the can. We dipped our toes in the water and we got our fingers burned. We had a truce on Christmas day. In the last years of our rule we deteriorated both physically and mentally – we planned to eliminate even our most loyal supporters. We went to Blackpool and got caught in the act. We used a telescope to read other people's newspapers and novels on the beach. We devised viral marketing campaigns. We wrecked the neighbours' garden with a Strimmer. We registered Internet domain names based on the names of well-known celebrities and established brands of merchandise in the hope of getting rich. RobertRedford.com, DrewBarrymore.com, ChristinaMilian.com, Steps.com, JayZ.com and ABucketofMcNuggetswithSaucetoGo.com were all our work. We made a film using stock footage. We switched the medications when the nurse was not looking. We made mockumen-taries. We made cockumentaries. We did not think that low budget and lowest common denominator were necessarily the same thing. We were broke and mistaken all the time. We were addicted to sadness. We worked for Enron. We got the cable turned back on but pretty soon the excitement wore off. We came as we were. We paid as we went. We said, 'Let it be.' We said, 'So it goes.' We said, 'Try to think of the heart attack as nature's way of warning you.' We lay in the hot-tub and fooled around with a handgun, taking aim at the stars. We were bag snatchers. We were stockbrokers. We threatened a cashier with a replica pistol. We threatened a nightclub bouncer with a kids' plastic raygun. We threatened a fat white shopkeeper with a cucumber hidden under a sweatshirt. We gave Peter a black eye. We gave Ethel a cauliflower ear. We gave Jed a bloody nose. We watched too much TV. We did not believe that there was a hierarchy of suffering. We tried to please our girlfriends by setting up three- and foursomes with several well-hung guys. We robbed peoples' lockers while they were down in surgery. We had the St James' Infirmary Blues. Our sarcasm was uncalled for in the circumstances. We had no last wishes. We left last wills and testaments which were confusing in some places, vague or even contradictory in others, and which in yet further places seemed to have been designed deliberately to cause disputes amongst the surviving family members, especially our assortment of ex-wives and ex-husbands, lovers, kids, step-kids and friends. Our dying words were, 'Let the bastards fight.' Our last words were incomprehensible. Our last words were deliberately cryptic. Our last words were totally inaudible. We were the judges in a third-rate televised talent show. We banned hunting. We pulled a knife. We pulled some girl from Southampton but couldn't really fuck her on account of her period. We puffed and panted. We dumbed it down. We said that God would be our judge on Afghanistan and Iraq. We confess to Aerobics, Pilates, Power Yoga, Carb Attack and Body Burn. We were rap's Grateful Dead. We were Death Metal's The Carpenters. We were light entertainment's answer to Charles Manson. We got all the girls in the crowd to shout YEAH YEAH, then we got all the guys in the crowd to shout YEAH YEAH, then we got the girls to wave their arms in the air and say YO YO, then we got the guys to shout YO YO and shake their butts around. Afterwards, sat together in the dressing room or on the tour bus with its built-in Jacuzzi, we laughed and laughed about how phenomenally dumb our fans really were. We drew a line under what happened. We made great friends with the neighbours. We made great friends with the bloke in the bed next door. We didn't make friends at all. We frightened each other with the Ouija board. We coughed up phlegm into neatly labelled jars. We left Wendy tied to a tree. We left Johan tied to the railway tracks. We didn't know how to party. We drank Velvet Crush. We drank Southern Comfort. We slipped a few points in the polls but we thought 'So what?' We offered cold comfort to strangers. We offered a kind of formulaic comfort to the families of the injured or deceased. We offered up our only daughters in exchange for the village being spared from the wrath of the Dragon. We said, 'OK people – it's time to rewind.' We could not memorise the sequence of numbers. We pulled dead rabbits out of hats. We had opinions about things that we did not know anything about. We were number crunchers, lone drinkers, postal voters. We kissed babies and pressed palms. We wanted second chances. We wanted a simple life with Marvin and the kids. On talk shows we were silent and on chat shows we would speak not a word. We were a dime a dozen. We read the newspaper over other people's shoulders. We offered support. We offered down-home guidance to our staff. We wanted war in the Caucuses – we didn't care about the consequence. We paid through the nose. We dropped butter and crumbs in the marmalade. We left a trail of jam, honey or marmite in the margarine. We joked and chatted with the nurses but nothing could hide how frightened we were. We were de-motivational speakers. We were the flunkies and the yes-men that swarmed around uncharismatic leaders, fawning, obsequious and grey. We were shallow. We were shadows. We were less than shadows. Our lives were a tissue of lies, our pasts were a web of deceit, our futures were a tangle of distortions, dark dreams and long unspeakable fantasies. We hid our emotions behind a brick wall of silence, strength and pride. We hid the kids where the cops would never find them. We left the kids in the apartment while the rest of us went out to get tapas. We tested people's patience. We tested people's limits. We tested our parents, trying to identify the weak spots, finding gaps in their defences. By the time we were ready to strike, what we did was quick, easy and totally devastating. We wrote words with the letters all in the wrong order. We robbed little kids of their mobile phones, trainers and dinner money. We were pimps. We were gangsters. We were goody-fucking-two-shoes. Our boredom threshold was too low for comfort. We imposed a state of emergency. We slept with Tracey Emin but she forgot to put our names in her tent. When they asked us our religions, we said 'NONE'. We broke every bone in our victims' bodies. We liked men with limited verbal skills. We took the easiest girls to the sleaziest clubs. As fathers, we saw our main function as explaining the dangers of an offside trap. We had more than our fair share of bad luck. We lost Kirsten's phone number in a fight. We lost the house in a card game. We lost our souls in a tap dancing contest. We went to the lessons each week but we never practised at home. We forgot to set the alarm. We were travelling salesmen who got lost on the back-roads, fell in with a crowd of drifters and never found our way back to the place we started out. We hung out in the Zombie Room. Our music only made sense if you were taking the right kind of drugs. We put our feet in the footsteps of those who went just before us. We traipsed along behind. We didn't think for ourselves. We're guilty of dice, of teletype and needles. We spread true rumours and wrote false receipts. On game shows we cheated and on quiz shows we lied. We lay at home with the flu and a hangover. We made the heartbreak face and then we smiled. We stank of chlorine and fists fell on us like the rain. We made a mockery of justice and a mockery of the American/English language. We doctored photographs, carefully erasing figures and substituting stonework, pillars and curtains to make it look like George Michael had stood on the balcony all alone. We sacked the town; we painted it red. We slipped through customs at Nairobi International, without even being seen. We were exiled kings, useless princes. We revamped our image; we were really working class. We made the crowd blush. We were driven by demons whose names we couldn't even spell. We were white collar criminals, haunted by our pasts. We told Mrs Gamble that Helen was with us when she wasn't. We were ex-cons trying to go straight. We thought that Freud was probably right about laughter. We thought that Hitler had a point. We had it in for Hillary. We had no moral compass, or if we did have one it had been badly damaged during the frequent electrical storms. We're guilty of heresy and hearsay, of turning our backs to the wall. We saw Arthur Scargill's blue movie cameo. We lied when it would've been easier to tell the truth. When we broke the law about satellites, there was no one to stop us or care. We sent death threats by fax machine and kept a list on a computer of the people we were going to kill. We put the bop in the bop she wop. We loved each other too much. We held each other's hands. We spat in the beer when no one was looking. We're guilty of murder, arson and theft. We gave Dr Taylor a good taste of his own medicine. We trapped Quentin in the showers and gave him what for. We read the same books again and again. We checked into a hotel and started work on the mini-bar – life seemed simpler that way. We had nothing much to say. We lusted after strangers. We exchanged body fluids on the westbound platform of the District Line. We exchanged parcels on the uptown F train. We tried to take photographs of ghosts. We fixed prices. We lived on the streets. We loved nocturnal darkness. We climbed in through a skylight that someone else had left open on purpose. We lay weeping in the bed. We tried to contain the rioters in B wing but they set fire to their mattresses and we were forced to open up the security screens that allowed them access to the rest of the jail. What happened after that was more or less inevitable. We calculated an incorrect orbit for an asteroid as it came quite close to earth. We got sent back to the past to stop the future from happening. We got sent to the future to ask them for help but when we got there we found the place deserted. We were frightened to use adjectives. We made scale models of boats. We dealt swiftly with a bloke that came rushing at us with a hammer. We let our kids drink wine. We got a job doing security for the Beckhams. We got jobs as financial advisors to the Beckhams. We got jobs as magicians for the Beckhams' kids' Christmas party. We just wanted to work for the Beckhams we didn't really mind in what capacity. We just wanted to get the ball rolling. We just wanted to get things done. We just wanted to give peace a chance. We just wanted the step-kids out of the way so that we could have Miriam all for ourselves. We accidentally summoned menus and incomprehensible option boxes by pressing random combinations of keys on the keyboard. We crashed the computer, right into the canal. We walked off in the middle of other people's anecdotes. We fell asleep while our partners made clumsy attempts at a reconciliation. We towed the line. We came from Planet Stress. We were deliciously vicious. We were student teachers, just having a laugh. When we removed Mr Chadwick's appendix, we left a plastic wristwatch inside him as a kind of comical intervention. We played the same role in every movie we made. We played golf with a baseball bat instead of clubs and a hamster instead of a ball. We said we were rough diamonds but really we were heartless fools. When we got to the end, all we could hear was our own voices, echoing and echoing. We inflicted democracy on innocent people. We gave them ballot boxes, beatings and ten months in solitary. We were too brutal for mercy, too depraved to reform, too lost to be found again, too out of it to make much sense at all. As we fumbled for our change and made conversation with the checkout girls, we made everyone curse the moment that they'd chosen to stand behind us in the supermarket checkout line. We did not stop, look and listen. We did not look both ways. We thought the Americans should just go home. We took one look at the guy sleeping at the table near the window and decided to sit somewhere else. We spent our last night together making a Top Ten list of highs and lows of the relationship. We each made our own lists at first and then at midnight began to share them in a kind of awards ceremony slash long long night of drunken vindictiveness and melancholy. We got caught red-handed then we legged it. We stuffed the ears of men with false reports. We confess to oil rigs and pylons. We're guilty of landslide victories and throwing in the towel. We looked at pictures of rare skin diseases. We got drunk and got tattoos. We cut to the quick and were frozen to the bone. We read books to avoid conversation. We confess to the dimming of streetlamps on long tropical nights. We thought thuggery was better than common sense. We didn't like modern Britain. We thought modern art was a load of shit. When we started to go bald, we grew our hair long in one of those Bobby Charlton haircuts, with a very long very thin strand of side hair plastered all over the bald bit at the front. We were cowards, strictly black market. We became nocturnal, inward looking, scared. We set men a new standard by which to measure infamy and shame. We lived on diet of speed and chips. We fell off the earth. We cut off the hand of an evil-hearted pirate called Captain Hook in a fair fight and threw it to a crocodile which had also eaten an alarm clock. The crocodile so enjoyed eating Hook's hand that he followed the pirate around all the time, hoping to get a second helping – but the tick tock tick from the alarm clock he'd swallowed always warned the pirate of the crocodile's approach. We made false economies. We were one of those double acts from way back – onstage it was all love and laughter; offstage we never spoke. We pissed on the flag. We made a soap for black people. We told long boring anecdotes. We worked for £2.90 an hour. We gave Helen fifteen minutes to pack her bags and get out of the house. We never thought. We never danced at weddings. They invented a new classification of lunatic just for us. We wrote biographies without bothering to research or ask permission. We lost the front door keys. We dressed Geisha and looked ridiculous. We did that Sharon Tate. We used laser treatment on hapless immigrants. We stood outside the prisoners' doors all night and whispered nonsense so they couldn't sleep. We sang the songs of streetlamps and paving slabs. We kept a boyfriend in waiting. We dug a few graves in the football pitch and buried the bodies at night. We were not quite at home in the world. We made a film called AMERICAN BONDING CRAP – it was mainly for boys but some girls liked it. We invented a TV channel called THE MONEY CHANNEL – 24 hours of nothing but long fingers handling money – it was a hit all over the world. We blazed the trail, set off rockets and yelled from rooftops. We were small minded, rusty after too many years. We were wankers. We noticed, not for the first time, the look between Carol and Jessica's boyfriend Martin Gardener. We held our savings in Deutschmarks, under a bed. We confess to autumn leaves, to fatherless children and shift work. We were regrouping fighters, looking for somewhere to sleep. We served up the beer in cups made from human skulls. Our trade was to traffic in human misery. We sold the records that we'd bought in our teens and which were no longer fashionable. We were bored of the poor. We killed the first daughter of all English greengrocers in an attempt to avoid any unfortunate recurrences of the last ten years. We confess to intercoms, faxes and prohibited places. We are guilty of arsenic, poor-laws, pass-laws and slightness in the face of adversity. We said we were the best there's ever been. We fucked around. We were Neocons. We lived in condos. We sniggered at a Scotsman's account of an alien attack – they ripped his trousers and left him in the pub. We invented rain-glare on tarmac and UHT cream which you could squirt from a tin. We were sceptics who didn't believe in anything. We drew our own blood with a syringe to make ourselves anorexic. We injected ourselves with yeast to make the blood clot. We injected red dye to make the blood more red, more red when we were bleeding. We crept out when everyone else was fast asleep. We had eyes like the stars. We talked to the trees. We named our sons THIRSTY, LUCKY and MEMORY. We sat up some nights and talked about the future of history. We talked about doing time. Our lives were like a soap made in heaven. We cut open our own bodies to try and find the evil in them – we found nothing, lost a bit of blood, needed stitches. We confess to wasting promises. We wrongly prescribed medicines. We turned down the title Miss Scunthorpe Evening Telegraph. When morning came, we changed our stories. We confess to fraud and to forgery. We're guilty of coldness and spite. We gave up too easy, hit our children too hard. We confess to trade routes, comedy scenes, kitchen knives and libel. We confess to microphones, water and polygraphs. We needed help but we wouldn't take it. We wanted spiritualist ends through materialist means. We lacked faith and therefore patience. We spat on soldiers in the street. In a parody we published, high state officials were portrayed in an insulting manner – the public and premeditated humiliation of their honour and worth was reproduced widely in the mass media in an unseemly and counterproductive fashion, adding greater insult to our already reprehensible words. We wanked off for money. We were at Tet and My Lai. We kissed Tom on the mouth before we killed him. We had butterflies. We wanted to write love songs, really good love songs that would really last but we didn't know music and we couldn't write. We had unorthodox thoughts about the economy. We burned people's faces off with a blow-torch. We got nostalgic for Spangles. In a previous life we had a previous wife. We rubbed salt in other people's wounds. We thought that class was more important than race. We accused the people at our birthday parties of stealing. We slept in coffin hotels. We measured our cocks with a plastic ruler borrowed from the kids' pencil case. We scratched ourselves raw. We drank water to keep our blood pressure up. We smoked fags to keep our weight down. We were remix artists. We exploited the workforce. We scoured the second-hand record stores looking for beats, breaks and stuff to sample. We always ducked when the shit hit the fan. We only wanted tenure. We had a party when we finally made payroll. We were inadequate, indifferent and afraid. We launched the death ray. We passed off crap as good stuff. We drove the planes right into the towers. It was beautiful, beautiful, beautiful and it changed the world. We lost our grip. When daylight came we lost our limited charm. It was our job to insinuate strange objects into the crowd scenes of cinema – the man carrying a surfboard in *Anna Karenina* at the station, the child in Bertolucci's *1900* who's wearing a bum-bag and the woman in *Basic Instinct* who's leading oxen to the slaughter – all these were our work. We confess to lip-synching, eye winking and overturned lorries. Our good deeds would not take much recounting. We ate Kimberly Saunders' arm. We waited till Jim was completely drunk and then beat the fuck out of him. We went to the dogs. We drank our own tears. We farted on the first date. We said the Lord's prayer backwards. We fell asleep in the middle and so didn't understand. We killed children. We practised false chemistry and worshipped graven images. The company we set up was fictitious – just a trading screen for another company which in turn was just a trading screen for a third company and so on – you could chase the money halfway round the world if you wanted and still never find the place where it ended up. We drank our own tears. We bathed in Diet Lilt. We had to get up in the night with a stomach ache. We had the doubts of daytime and the doubts of nighttime. We perpetrated a hoax. We shot people in the head. We thought in shapes rather than words. We wouldn't talk about things; we just bottled them up. We photocopied our own semen and excrement. We bargained for immunity. We watched the light changing. We loved the sky. We dreamed in black and white. We rumbled with other gangs. We dreamed of drained swimming pools. We went into shock for a year. We didn't give anything; we were just there. We shouted for so long and we kept shouting until it didn't even sound like our voices anymore. We told simple stories to children. We put family first. We were opinionated and sloppily dressed. We burst into tears. We confess to driftwood, safe breaking and teletype. We said, 'Come on, come on, let's drink and make up ... ' We were stowaways. We left tapes with bad instructions. We wouldn't read novels at all because we found ourselves so taken over by the characters. We tested the animals with approximately 345cl of the serum. We used force to get people's attention. Our big Broadway show was a total flop. We lived on sliced water and bottled bread. We made licence plates and sowed mail-bags in jail. We played a lot of chess. We worked with Justin Timberlake, Kanye West and a load of the other big names in pop. We thought there was nothing more to 'security' than wearing dark suits, dark glasses and those funny little ear-piece communicators. We cried at family photos. We played the field. There was love in us somewhere but somehow it got lost. We scratched Nigel's face out in all the wedding pictures, turning his head into an angry whirlpool of biro marks, the scribbles and scratches spiralling out from his fat stupid grinning face. We were top of the fucking food chain. We dreamt of hammer blows. When we looked back at the Super 8 and video of ourselves, we could not recognise anything. We were cop killers. We were comedy sub-plots. We got jobs teaching sarcasm to censors. We're guilty of astrophysics and heavy gases. We confess to truth serum, old tricks and stratagems. In the ID line we smiled. In Tesco's when we saw each other again, we just pretended that nothing had happened. We found a way of digitising death. We confess to canned laughter and circular saws. We were cheeky little monkeys that need teaching a lesson. We dreamed of Tokyo, snow monsters and John Ford on his deathbed. We stood at the altar but couldn't say the words. We gave cabinet posts to all of our mates. We tied cans to the back of Martin Gardener's hearse – it's what he would've wanted. Each morning when we put the kids on the bus to school, we took their photographs – it was less a piece of photography and more an act of magic – making talismans to try and ensure that they'd come back OK. We confess to never having an original idea. We feigned disapproval of things we'd done ourselves. We loved the rush of wind and ran when the lorries thundered by. We said, 'Hold on, hold on it won't be long now … '. We sat back in a pose of indifference; we stank of sweat and the Yankee hash. When a few housing benefit cheques arrived made out to Greg Samson, we used them to open a Building Society account in that name and then cashed the cheques. We were antheads, chickenheads and snaggle-toothed deviants. We were just a bunch of fucking arseholes. We had unnatural talents, we used supernatural means. We confess to night vigils that left us tired and lonely. We wept with the aid of glycerine and caught the red-eye home. We struck it lucky on the hit parade. We knew god-damned ALL there was to know about the rumba. We didn't want to blow our own trumpet but it blasted anyway. We said, 'Oh, any old how darling, any old time … '. We held a shredding party in the basement at midnight. We sat with our backs to the wall and posed full-frontal. We lived in a city of fainting buildings; we lived in difficult times. Our smiles suggested something more of surgery than of pleasure. We sat by Rachel's bedside and read stuff to her, hoping to wake her from the coma – we read her Tolstoy and *Peter Pan*, we told her stories, we told her all the wrongs we'd ever done. We thought cheap thoughts in risky places. We called our children Dawn, Leslie and Lisa-Marie, Chantale Duran and Young Whipper Snapper. We went on *Swap Shop* the same day that Edward died. We were often seen in the background of other people's holiday snaps, blurred, out of focus, staring downstream. We had identical operation scars – it was too uncanny, just something meant to be. We designed the Bull Ring Centre. We designed the Millennium Dome. We had enigmatic smiles. We wanted to be Michael's love child because he had such deep-set eyes. We were dizzy with happiness. We saw ourselves as commodities. When we got to the island, the natives told us they looked after a huge monkey god called King Kong – we thought it would be a good idea to capture it and take it back to New York to exhibit – the rest is history. We were inaccessible, inaccurate, inadequate, inadmissible, inane, inanimate, inapplicable, inapposite, inappreciable, inappreciative, inappropriate, inapt, inarticulate, inartistic, inattentive, inaudible, inauspicious, inbred, incalculable, incapable, incautious, incendiary, incessant, incestuous, incidental, incivil, incognito, incoherent, incommensurable, incommensurate, incommunicable, incompatible, incompetent, incomplete, incomprehensible, inconceivable, inconclusive, incongruous, inconsequential, inconsiderate, inconsistent, inconstant, incontinent, inconvenient, incorrect, incredible, incurable, indebted, indecent, indecipherable, indecorous, indefensible, indictable, indifferent, indigestible, indignant, indiscreet, indistinct, indolent, indulgent, inebriated, ineffective, inefficient, inelegant, ineligible, inept, inert, inexpert, infamous, infantile, infectious, inferior, infested, inflammatory, inflated, inflexible, inflicted, inglorious, inhibited, inhospitable, inhuman, inhumane, iniquitous, injudicious, injust, insalubrious, insane, insanitary, insatiable, insecure, insensate, insensible, insensitive, insentient, insidious, insignificant, insincere, insipid, insolent, insomniac, institutionalised, insubordinate, insubstantial, insufferable, insufficient, insular, insulting, insurgent, intimidating, intolerable, intolerant, intoxicated, intransigent, introverted, invalid, invidious and invisible. We took what we could get. We took the Fifth. We did long slow kisses that lasted three days. We confess to tidal waves, hurricanes and magnetic storms. We're guilty of everything. We were clumsy – we got lipstick on our boyfriends' trousers. We loved language. We hated Jews. We dated Asians out of curiosity. We knew the place but we didn't know the time. We sent dirty faxes. We signed our names. We christened our children DEATH, SOLITUDE and FORGETTING. We ate like pigs and never left home. We confess to mud and bleach. We perpetrated a fraud. We set the clocks forward ten minutes to counteract our general tendency to be late. We reserved six tickets for a show and then never turned up to collect them. We chartered planes but never flew. We charted the Straits of Magellan. We lived with our mothers too long. We sold sex for crack. We told lies to the people we were supposed to represent. We robbed Peter to pay Paul. We staged a dancing dogs competition. We had wheels of steel. We had tits made of titanium. We zoned out. We played an old-fashioned sweeper combination. We thought that John McCain wasn't old enough, that John Betjeman was a misogynist and that Stalin was misunderstood. We said, 'Lets keep on going like we were before, like nothing changed at all.' We said, 'Look, please, look'. We asked the patients a question to distract them from the pain. We did not listen to Cynthia's advice. The last thing we said to Joanna before she died was, 'Fuck off bitch.' The last thing we said to Florian was, 'Sorry Dude.' It was probably the effects of the heroin. We served up death for breakfast. We pushed each other's buttons. When the kids came shivering out of the water, we were not ready with the towel. We ordered the prisoners to take a walk for a while and stretch their legs. We held a wet T-shirt competition for the women and a wet trousers competition for the men. We were scum. We passed out drunk on the floor of a garage. We watched a film with bad language; it got four stars. We wrote death threats to ourselves. We made a film called OUT OF SOUTH AFRICA. We thought that Black Watch was a musical. We made false promises. We never sat down. We tried to bring about the false death of President Kennedy – false in the sense of co-existent or alternate. We left the best bits on the cutting-room floor. We sulked and skulked and stamped. We confess to breaking three ribs in our sleep. We said we'd speak again soon and then never called back. We were accessories. We gave names, names and more names. We mistranslated. We drove too fast. We admit to announcing personal problems instead of the next train approaching platform four. We asked awkward questions on the Granada studios tour. We never had our fill of bombing and shooting; we were cry for help shoplifters, bingo callers with cancer of the throat. Long after Stalin died we pretended he was alive – wheeling him out for public appearances, waving his hand from the balcony. We never wore seat belts. We got rumbled and frisked. We found panoramic views. We transmitted deadly advice. We switched labels just before the checkout but didn't realise that the bar-code would betray us. We never spoke another language. We flipped channels quickly when the film got embarrassing. We wrote in to the magazine WIFE BEATER MONTHLY. We peeled the skin back and looked. We made no difference. We made no sense. We were the worst kind of people in the world. We're guilty of bright light and rum. We altered flight paths and planned alternative routes. We confess to static, break up and climactic change. We broke into phone boxes. We weren't comfortable in our skins. We were witches. We stole hotel soap. In the scene of community singing filmed in an air-raid shelter and designed to show the goodwill and high spirits of Londoners during the Blitz, we were the ones in the background whose lips were hardly moving. We were bloody fools. We were sick as a parrot. We ran a numbers racket and we dug our own graves. We were loons that danced naked at harvest time. We never wanted children anyway. We confess to zinc and shopping malls, to bad dreams and collectivisation. We fucked the economy. We talked about democracy. All we wanted to do was to tempt into life things that were hidden and strange. We went into town and stopped dead in our tracks. We had a bag full of controlled substances hidden in the toilets. Our hobbies were card playing and time wasting. We drank too much champagne. We were a slick act; we were stadium rockers – every mumble, every gesture every bit of impromptu patter was the same at every gig, all over the world. We had HUNGER for breakfast and STARVATION for lunch. We were suicide bombers. We made a film called STREETS OF YESTERDAY. We're guilty of heart attacks, car crashes and falling off bridges. We agreed with Albert Einstein the scientific genius. We confess to X-Boxes, Gamecubes, Megadrives, PSPs and PS3s. We sewed a horse's head onto the body of a cholera patient, replacing his feet with hooves and his hands with the tentacles of an octopus. He didn't last long but once cleaned, pickled and placed in an outsized jar he made an excellent attraction. We were sheep, eyewitnesses, minor-clerics, prostitutes and baseball fans. We dreamt of heat and of solitude. We wished for peace, or a cease-fire at least. We cut the head off a live rooster and drank the blood – we thought it would help. We fucked our brother. We were smugglers, heathens and pirates. We lied about our age and then hoped for better things. We showed a gun in the first act, in a drawer, hidden under some papers – the central character kept staring at it and mumbling, crying almost, but we weren't prepared to let her use it; the dramatic tension was all wrong and so by act four the audience were still wondering what the gun thing was all about. We burned effigies of trade negotiators. We were fraudulent mediums, working the crowd. We were not beautiful or especially bright but we had the strange gift of being remembered. We were hate-filled children with ice in our veins. In interrogation our voices got quieter and quieter, and the detectives, not wishing to break the mood, got quieter and quieter too, until, by the end of it, stage by stage, we each were only moving our lips and no sound came out, the tape recorder running for posterity. We altered the limits of human action. We loved a piece of time too small to give it a name. We came to the place where the tape says POLICE LINE DO NOT CROSS and then we crossed it. We were funny without meaning to be. We listened to *Stairway to Heaven* 13 times in a row. We played in the show houses on the edge of the estate. Long periods of boredom were our fault. We spent long hours at the bus stop. We were long lost cousins in love. We liked the way Sarah smiled. We liked the smell of napalm in the morning. We missed episode two. We lied through false teeth. We watched repeats of everything. We did thankless tasks. We were continuity flaws. We jumped ship before the world had taken one full turn. We took three sugars in our coffee. We confess to parricide, conspiracy and Pearl Harbor. We all wore clothes our mothers made. We were black-listed in car manuals. We evacuated whole communities overnight. We buried our pasts in shallow graves. In the baths we spontaneously combusted and in the park we talked while the kids played on the climbing frame. After a long time of fake deliberation over the menu at the motorway services, we went for the special offer RECESSION BUSTER BREAKFAST (2 kids eat free with 2 adults). We confess to personal interest, hobbies and irrelevant experience; we are guilty of landing awkwardly. We are responsible for the coasts and the moors and cumulus clouds and great vistas and vast landscapes and poignant winters. We read the map the wrong way up. We confess to sarcastic suicide notes, to Aeroflot and diagrams. We sniffed lighter fluid and spat through our teeth. We took the gun shot, we took the ricochet; that's all there is to say. We were extras, walk-ons, stand-ins and losers. We were just there to make up the numbers in some of the crowd scenes. We knew we were gay from the age of five. We had plastic surgery to look oriental or black so we could supposedly report on what it was like to be different – we reported our findings on Good Morning Television to the pleasure and interest of Richard and Judy. We confess to knowing Sam and refusing to wave to him. We bled in open spaces. We climbed without a rope. We revealed secrets to the Russians and cheated for small change. We were cautioned for loitering under Section 35. We were test patients, sitting in a hospital room and waiting for the side-effects. We got mixed up; we got into the Occult. We dreamt the whole of the Second World War before it happened. We had the faith of no faith. We thought that less was less. We failed the breath test. We gambled everything on the chance to win diamonds, camcorders and holidays. We were bogus asylum seekers, bogus refugees. We travelled through the German night; we met the German girl. Our marriage was just part of a plan to blow up the train. We had sex in the visionary position – sat far apart on opposite sides of the room and gazing and, masturbating, staring at each other in a mixture of fear, desire and disbelief, certain in the knowledge that even if we came together we would not come together at all. We stayed up after midnight. We worked at Guantanamo. We worked at Abu Ghraib. We were described by photofits. We sighed when the evening had to end. We were invisible. We sadly lacked in the subject of botany. We switched the bags while no-one was looking. We noticed, not for the first time, the look between Brian and Peter's boyfriend Neville Darby. We christened diseases with beautiful names; we cut off the villages and sealed off the streets. We drew the curtains when the window cleaners came. We mispronounced URANUS and SCHEAT. We thought we were funny, funnier than anyone had ever been. We took afternoon naps when we should have been working. We fell in love with every co-star. We cheated at cards. It took us three hours to cut off the head with an open knife. We dreamt about dinosaurs and planes crash-landing in back gardens. We never said how much we needed each other. We washed up badly. We never thought. We never danced until the end of the disco. We got tattoos done on our foreheads saying PAX AMERICANA. We stole some electrical equipment which looked expensive and complicated but which we couldn't understand; we plugged it in at home and got some nasty burns – objects began to arrive from the future; we were puzzled and then later imprisoned. We made small talk. Some of the paperwork we submitted was a little bit irregular. We asked the hairdresser about his recently dead father. We stole fish. We worshipped cruel Aztec Gods. We were careless with the truth. We patented an obviously crackpot device for listening to the songs of angels. We built extensions on our houses without the necessary planning permission. We treated people like scenery. We treated the whole place like a hotel. World War III was just a thinly painted backdrop for our love. We kept lifting up the curtain and peeking behind. We hit rock bottom. We found our own level. We tried to guess the presents by feeling through the wrapping paper. We filmed a frog's leg, twitching on a slab. We hated robbing banks – it got boring after a while. We handcuffed Lee Morris to the railings in the playground and pulled his trousers down. We lived a harsh fast life. We were glad to be alive. We didn't have an opinion on anything except how crazy the world was. We're guilty of attic rooms, power cuts and bombs. We confess to statues, ruins and our older brother's Gameboys. We confess to aborting our children for research, killing our parents for the house and putting granddad in a home. We were not at our best in the mornings. We did not feed the neighbours' cat. We lost the thread. We laid down our lives for someone else's country. We smiled invitingly at Antoine, thereby raising expectations that we had no intention of fulfilling. We frequented gaming hells, low hostelries and the late-night super-market on Jasmine Street. We passed folded notes and whispered at the back. We sang off-key and stared at the person to our right. We weren't ready for our opening night. We were sex tourists. We liked Steven but he smelt funny. We told stolen jokes on *The X Factor*. We sang out of key on *Pop Idol: The Rivals*. We sold defective oven gloves door to door. We lived in clutter. We were top of the pops. We stayed out past bedtime, past curfew, past caring. We knew what we were doing. We looked on at the ecstatic twilight of technological society. We saw nine great motorway pile-ups. We were always interested in missing things – time, people and history. We fenced stolen farming equipment. When the mermaids tried to warn us, we threw stones at them. We snored loudly while other people were trying to eat. We read novels with unhappy endings. We wept for slimmers. We learnt how to fly but we did not learn how to land. We were intellectual pygmies. We flung mud. We dug up mass graves. We played truant. We taught Russian roulette at A level. We dubbed silent movies; we coughed in dramatic pauses. We chanted meaningless or silly slogans to put the other marchers off and when the stewards tried to stop us, we ducked under the crash barriers and ran off into the park. We played musical chairs. We believed in the spirits of dead astronauts. We were scared of volcanoes. We sent each other used underwear through the post. We countenanced forever as an expression of mortality. We honoured without exception all church architecture. We said, 'Love is like floating in duckweed.' We were dead meat. We stand accused of Saturday nights and early Monday mornings. We were jealous in a sensational manner. We used supermodels in war documentaries – they were excellent. We were poisoners. We put the last buffalo to sleep. We went to Stonehenge and didn't like it. We ate an irregular meal. We watched a man die in six inches of water. We're guilty of making weak tea. We drove madness into the hearts of good folks. We broke all the rules of ice hockey in one day. We forged doctors' notes. We could never return. We broke down doors, smashed windows and blamed Philip Lawson. We took a lot of liberties. We took advice from demons. We pretended to know people. We took too long getting ready. We inflicted viscous attacks and horrible injuries. We stole from a warehouse on Last Minute Street. We practised strange tactics for interviews including The Long Sustained Silence, Repetition of the Previous Question and Sudden Welling Up of Tears. We idolised Raymond and Lesley. We liked uniforms and signs of obedience. We held him down – it was fascinating. We had piss stains on our trousers. We had shit stains on our shoes. We had no hope. We linked our arms and skipped in a desperate imitation of the wizard of Oz. Our philosophy was do them before they do you. We fingered our arses. We thought we were relatives of Robert Duvall – but we weren't. We confess to rubbing up against tables. We redrew maps to slowly excise certain areas – this was a slow technical distortion (nothing as crude as omission) by which unwanted areas were minutely compressed over long periods of time. When the government changed, and with it our political fortunes, we had to slowly distort it all back. We sniffed lighter fluid and spat through our teeth. We took the gun shot; we took the ricochet. We came from a country where smiling was considered dangerous. We were tricksters, pranksters, practical jokers – we put meat in someone's tea; we left the bedroom looking like a raid; we wore funny noses, bow ties that went round and round – for the grandchildren we pretended to be powered by electricity, drawing energy from the light bulb in the centre of the ceiling and moving in a strange jerky way. We blocked the fucking fast lane. We rang the wrong number twice, no, three times. We bought the same magazine for years. We had tattoos done on our arses saying LONG LIVE THE HEROISM OF SENSELESS PURSUITS. We had tattoos done on our heads saying LET NO MAN ENTER HERE. We had tattoos done on our stomachs saying WHY EMPTY? We ran out on Vic – it was a gamble. We missed a train. We were death mechanics. We were sleep throwers – when we woke up in the mornings there was nothing near us. We were loud drunks and fornicators. After dark was a time of hate and burning for us. We fell asleep at the wheel and woke up some miles down the road. We were pirates. We were lawless. We sailed beneath the black flag. We had our hands in the till. Stumbling lost and disorientated, we realised the world was full of dames. We confess to bellowing sweet nothings. We believed in UFOs. We believed that Jung was probably right about women. We believed that truth was always the best policy. We dealt in imaginary videos. We got drunk on half a pint. We entered the wrong room and backed out hastily. We had sexual intercourse that night, not once, but seventeen times. We sent our daughters off into prostitution and one of them came back dying of AIDS; we could not understand why she was dying, or even that she was dying at all – with her sweats, her blisters and her strange agonised deliriums we thought she was becoming a shaman, a magic priestess, but it didn't work out that way. When the lights went out, we swapped places. We were YTS vandals – losers on job-creation schemes. We pretended to fall over outside a hospital. We lied about our age. We looked promising in mirrors. We lied twice, denied three times. We killed ten men, burned sixteen houses. We wrote two love songs twice on the trot, we made six threatening phone calls and six gentle apologies. We saw six crows sat on a fence, we wept sixteen gallons of tears, we drank fourteen vodkas, we issued several writs. We saw each other 57 times, we threw nine coins in the fountain, we threw seventeen coins at the goalkeeper, we made three wishes, we had seven dreams, we had ten seconds of silence, ten years of peace, ten scars on our arms where the rotor blades had hit. We tore five pages from the back of the book, we crashed 200 cars, fathered 39 children, walked backwards for nine days. We wrote six novels with the same plot, we whispered seven desires, we murmured eighteen pleas, we broke nine mirrors, seventeen plates, 36 cups, a window, a washing-machine and three statues. We shouted 36 curses, told three thousand cautious jokes. Our lounge was like Bosnia – divided into two – the two of us looking shell-shocked across space. We cut the crime rate by introducing a new system of counting. We said, 'Don't call here again; it's dangerous.' We spoke OCTOBER LANGUAGE. We dreamt of hammer blows; we trained as cosmonauts in Star City. We were spastic bashers. We were the captives of our own metaphors. We danced naked for money. We tried to export things without all the proper documents – it wasn't deliberate fraud but you could see why the customs men at Ramsgate were suspicious – they kept looking over the paperwork and tutting and then making phone calls to a man in one of the other portacabins. It was 3am when they let us go, and only then because it was the end of their shift. We told mortician jokes at weddings. We betrayed our friends through silence. We were lonely for twelve years. We loved the way the rain ran off the windscreen. We confess to making love for an irregular amount of time. We smiled secretively, faking orgasms as we did. We sold our kidneys to a rich Arab. We escaped with the help of the netball team. We burned and maimed in recognition of our illustrious past. We were drunk in charge of a telephone. Our nicknames were muck-mouth, filth-tongue and toxic avenger. Our town was famous for its mud. We burnt the grass 'cos we got sick of waiting for Bruno to mow it. We suspected our husbands of having a bit on the side. We suspected our best friends of espionage. We asked our boyfriends to drive the getaway car. When we met in a gay disco, we could never have known what horrors lay ahead. We had savage compulsions. We knew the law, not because we wanted to obey it, but because we wanted to get away with things. We used Ju-Ju to bind people to us. We did not like the big goodbyes. We refused to succumb. We refused to suck Colin's cock until he had been to the bathroom and washed it. We turned the tables on Jason. We saved our trump cards till last. We killed ourselves so that we could spend more time with the kids. We saw the moon reflected in a pool of our own blood. We saw the future in the face of a dead civillian. They traced our travel through the credit cards. We were freeloaders. We switched off the SatNav. We had lecherous plans. We locked our eldest daughter up at the top of a very tall tower so that she could not escape. We said, 'Lets go back to the hotel. No one will notice.' We secretly shat ourselves whilst halfway up the climbing wall. Most days we doubted things, some days we doubted it all.

5.4 **THE STORY OF M** (1995)

SUANDI

SuAndi (b. 1951) is a UK-based performer, director, poet and writer. She has been working as a performance poet and live artist since the mid-1980s and has worked with the Black Arts Alliance as an artist-activist in the UK for which she was awarded the Queen's Honours of an O.B.E. in 1999. She has worked extensively in the UK and the USA in particular with community arts projects which engage with the work of artists of colour. Her public artworks include the libretto for an opera about Mary Seacole and 24 poetry disks at Salford Quays Lowry Centre, Manchester, England.

I wrote M following a mediocre production that closed with homage to white women who had endured racism following their inter-racial marriages. Lois Keidan felt it was the strongest section and encouraged me to write more, as fact is always more interesting. Forty minutes into my return journey to Manchester I'd done as advised with tears running down my face. It took very little more writing to complete.

SCENE – Hospital room with a single bed with a screen to the side. A chair next to a small locker on which is placed a jug of water, tissues and a flower vase. 'M' is led onto the stage by a nurse; she is continuously coughing.

I've got cancer.
I have.
Bloody cancer
And I know exactly when I got it –
eating a jam cream sponge cake
with my daughter's boyfriend.
I suppose you'll think I'm daft
Me calling him her boyfriend
what with him being gay!
But he is,
he's her boyfriend
and for me he's like a second son.
I was over at their place.
They live together.
Not together like,
But you know, together.
I was eating this jam cream sponge cake –
It was my first for months
I'd been dieting
Getting ready for her coming home.
I was born big – me.
Big!
Always was.
Take the time like I tried to join the
Sally Army now you'll not believe this.
They wouldn't let me in
Because my legs were too big for the boots.
Christianity my big toe.

Hi get it?
Big toe, big foot, big leg,
Oh never mind

I'd lost two stone
thought I was a bloody miracle –
when suddenly
I get this massive pain
and wow cancer.
Think of all those cream cakes
I could have eaten.
Now I'm here, two parts dead.
Going over me life
like you do,
like you all will,
given the chance.

Not like poor Malcolm –
No cancer for him –
Just a bloody racist
With a gun.
But for me –
it's a long drawn out death.
And you'd be amazed
how those memories
come flooding back.

SCENE – *M sleeps (Nurse) picks up then drops a kidney tray.*

Munitions?
All my friends worked in munitions,
but not me.
I've always been really sensitive to smells.
I was always passing out in church.
Used to drive the nuns crazy.

So I went into the laundries.
Loved it –
All that cleanliness,
Messing about with the suds.
Played bloody murder with your hands
And the heat could burn the end of your
nose off.

Anyways there I was this day
When the new Charge-hand goes past
And says, loud enough for me to hear like,
I bet this heat doesn't bother some people.
Them that belong in jungle!
Well bugger that. I was off.
The rest stayed, but not me.
I knew better.
There were folk from all over the world
Doing their bit for the war effort and here

was this fool talking about the bleedin'
jungle.
I bet he'd been no further than top of
the street.

Anyway –
I could wash at home
For my son and my husband.
Husband!
Bastard more like!
Don't get me wrong. I like men.
It took some time, I'll admit, what, with me
being born a Catholic
And thinking any man, not wearing a
frock (a black frock naturally), was
suspect.
I suppose that's why you never see
Jesus in trousers – because the Catholic
Church has spread so many stories
about the evils in them.

Well I found out the hard way.
I wasn't just naive,
I was thick.
First man that said he loved me, got me –
and not a wedding vow on his lips.
But being the Catholic that I was
I believed in the sanctity of marriage.
So I took him to court.
He was scared shitless!

The first day he stood in the dock
looking like the very criminal he was.
The next day he brought half the ship's
crew with him,
And they testified.
I'd been with them all.
A prostitute he called me.
Me! A Catholic girl, and the judge
believed him.
He looked at me as though I just stepped
off Lime St.
I cried;
I cried; then really cried.
I had no one to turn to.
In the end I won the case,
But my son never took his name.
And I went back!
Back to the only home I'd ever known,
the orphanage.
Convent, more like!
I thought I'd had enough of nuns to last
me a lifetime, and then a bit more, and
here I was back with them.

They gave you another name,
A church name so to speak,
Like Sister Theresa or something.
Every morning, crack of dawn
They'd wake you
And tell you where you were working
that day.
And, they'd also pass out any Special
announcements.
Like, Sister Theresa your baby died
last night.
Oh, and by the way, you're in the kitchen.
I'd pray every night that my son wouldn't
die.
It took me ages to realise
All these babies – they weren't dying.
They were being given away for adoption.

And no one wanted a Black lad.
Well, Thank You Blessed Jesus.
But, I needed a husband,
A father for my son.
In those days my son
Was the only person I loved in the whole
wide world.
Loving a child is important –
I should know,
No one ever really loved me.

My mum had cancer and my elder sister.
For my mum they called it a broken heart.
You see, my father was lost at sea and
from the day he disappeared, she never
got out of bed.
I used to climb up to snuggle next to her.
Close – the way a cat does.
But if she realised it was me
She would shoo me away.
She didn't love me you see.
And I was the youngest.
I should have been loved the best.
They said, the day she died they found me
Lying right next to her cold dead body,
I must have been there for hours.
Neighbours took us in.
Neighbours!
An extended family, with no blood ties.
But they couldn't feed themselves
Never mind the three of us.
So, in time, the church took us.
Seems it was decided by some relatives
from across the water.
You can bet your life they didn't want us,
but they wanted to make sure we were

brought up as Catholics.
See what I mean.
Christianity. It's bloody stupid!

SCENE – M is coughing really badly.

The priest's been round today with his
bloody rosary.
Telling me I should welcome death.
Welcome death!
I'd sooner welcome Margaret Thatcher.

My husband.
My ex-husband
Smokes 40 fags a day
And he's not got cancer.
He's an African.
A real African.
Not like me, a mix up of this, that, and a
bit of the other.
And the only good thing he ever did for me
Was give me my daughter.
She's beautiful my daughter.
The day I got rid of him we had a party!
Bloody good riddance.
But he's a great father – always there for her.
Buys her things; takes her out;
Loves her.
Maybe even more than I do
But as a husband,
well – he just another bastard man.

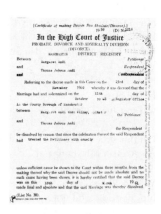

I met him on Berkley St.
All the sailors lived on Berkley St,
Sort of on top of each other.
Liverpool was great in them days.
It was like the world
You know,
People from all over the world
And we all lived happily
side-by-side.

I mean, I had names for the Chinese
That weren't,
Well you know,
Very nice.
I mean,
I didn't exactly
Call them Chinese.

But there again,
I don't suppose the names they called me
were very flattering either.
But we didn't beat each other up,

Shit, on each other's doorsteps.
Oh there were fights.
And name calling.
That made my mouth seem virginal,
And I'm sure there were many
Who would have liked to put us all
On our respective boats
and floated back home.
But in Liverpool 8,
You married anyone you wanted,
And no one gave a bugger;
So why the hell did I marry him?
I mean,
He didn't pretend to like my son.
He didn't even pretend to like me
But he still gave me my daughter.

Hulme
In the 50's
was just like Liverpool

On our street there was an Irish cobbler,
An African fish shop, and
Two funny French people
Who sold horsemeat to make stew out of.
No, not dog food, love, stew.
Where are you from OH?
Anyway, the grocers, the off licence,
And the people in the shop across the road,
They were English,
Or Scottish, or Welsh, or something.
Well, I mean, I can't tell,
can you?
We had Indians across the street
And Jamaicans round the corner.

But it was harder in Manchester;
You see, the war was over,
And the unity had gone out of our lives.
And I had become harder.
I don't mean, I was getting used to it
Just, that, well, I was getting used to it
And had to get harder.
Being spat on in the street!
Being turned away from rooms to let!
Not being able to get HP.
Hearing mothers tell their kids
Not to play with my kids.
Hearing their kids ask my kids
Why they were dirty.
I hit one kid once, outside church.

My daughter was like a flower,
All dressed up with long ringlets in her hair.

I made each of those ringlets, by hand,
every day.
I don't mean that weave on stuff like
they've got now,
It was her own hair.
And every morning I'd make her
stand there
As I tortured these ringlets into place.
Then out we'd go and some sod would
pat her head like she was a dog
And they'd all fall out.

I was trying her out at a new
Sunday school,
As much as I hated the church,
And as much as the old fella should have!
We still wanted her to go.

Anyway, we were all stood outside,
Not together like.
The mothers and kids over there,
And me and mine over here
When this spotty little four eyed creature
Comes up and says to my daughter,
If you have a wash next week
I'll be your friend and Jesus will love you.
Well, Love that, I said,
As I slapped across the mouth.
The police were called.
There was loads of trouble,
I had to go round and apologise.
I know I shouldn't have done it,
And if it had been my daughter hit
I would have stabbed the lot of them.
But I was angry and hurting –
Hurting from the ignorance.
So when they decided to pull Hulme down,
I decided to move my kids
As far away from the likes of that as
possible.
So we moved to Ancoats,
A new council estate.

There were two blocks of maisonettes.
On the other side they were all dead smart.
Clean windows lace and ironed curtains.
On our side, there were a few curtains,
but mainly bits of cloth or nothing at all,
which didn't really matter
Because you couldn't see through the
windows for the muck.
Now, me,
I have always washed my windows.
And I change my curtains for Christmas,

Easter, Whitsun, Birthdays, and sometimes
just when I feel like.
You see I'd reckoned that I couldn't and
Didn't want to change black to white.
But people do judge books by their covers.
So I'd decided, long time back, that no
matter how badly off we might be.
Our home would be spotless and my kids
the same.

My daughter had all her clothes tailored.
Tailored.
And when I did buy
I bought the best.
Her dresses came from this posh shop
on Stretford Road with a French name.
Funny,
I can't remember the name now.
I was paying a fiver for her frocks,
Off-the-peg as they say
And it was only 1958.
Her shoes were leather,
her coats had fur trims in the winter,
And she always wore a hat and gloves.
What, me?
Me?
Well, I always wore a rain mac
And carried a plastic shopping bag.
But I was living for my daughter now.
When it came time for her to go to
Secondary School.
I hit a major problem.
The school uniform.
How in God's name
was I going to make sure
that everyone knew she was clean
each day?
Then one night I hit on this great idea.
I had the days of week,
You know, Monday, Tuesday
Wednesday, Thursday, Friday
Embroidered on the collar of her school
blouses, and every day she swapped a
cardigan for a jumper, you know.
You're laughing,
I'm laughing.
But it's not funny to be called dirty
and smelly.
So why are we laughing.

*SCENE – The nurse has given M a bowl to vomit into – her weak state is becoming
more and more apparent.*

What was I talking about?
This chemotherapy is doing me head –

I told that nurse, I don't know about
getting rid of the cancer

Bloody hell
I'll tell you something,
Don't take up hospital visiting
As a career –
For you're all bloody useless!
I was talking about the maisonette –
Good God, it's me that's dying, isn't it?

I'd been moving in, getting things ready
mostly during the early hours of the
morning.
I was working nights by then, in a canteen;
had been for a few years.

My son Malcolm,
(well, he was away at Queens College)
That's what we used to call prison –
I'd lost him to school expulsions,
Petty thieving, drugs, Nigger calling,
police beatings,
Do you think it was because of his colour?

I remember one time
I was working nights.
My daughter was about 5 or 6
My son 17–18,
He was supposed to look after her while
I worked.
I'd leave home at 7 for a 7.30 start
and get back around 4 in the morning.
This one day as soon as I turned into
our street
I knew something was wrong.
All the lights were on.
The house was ablaze like Christmas.
My heart started beating really loud
You know I could hear it.
When I got outside of the house
The front door was wide open.
I started to pray,
Pray for my daughter.
When I stepped inside the room – looked
as though it had been raped!
My head was bursting,
All I could think about was her.
Was she safe
Was she safe?
I flew upstairs to her bedroom.
It was empty.
I must have started screaming.
I know I was making a noise but what

I was saying
I don't know.
I rushed out into the street
And the neighbour must have told me
The police had taken her.
So I ran.
I ran all the way from Hulme
To Moss Lane Police Station, and when I
went inside
I saw her, sat on a bench in her blue
dressing gown and slippers with the
red trim.
She had this look in her eyes.
I have never forgotten that look in her eyes,
It turned out they had been looking for
my son.
Looking for something, found nothing.
So they took her instead.
Home Alone, that's what they call it now,
Isn't it?
Oh, they hadn't tried to contact me.
Hadn't even contacted Social Services.
They just left her sat there, all night long.
She must have seen so much that night.
The thieves,
the drunks
the druggies
the prossies.
You see, me,
I hate the police every last man of them.
And don't tell me they are here for my
protection.
I could tell you some stories about the
police,
About that caring arm across your shoulder,
then a hand slips down to your breast.
Or the reassuring pat on your knee that
travels up your thighs.
Yes, I could tell you stories,
But what's the point?

When my son was younger.
Not more than a toddler

I tried to do homework.
You know, work from home.
But I couldn't sew.
Couldn't do anything, really, but clean.
I couldn't cook either, much to the
annoyance of my husband.
So my homework was odd like there was
this one time I made stuffed straw dolls.
The first day
These two huge bales of hay arrived.

And this bungle of rags
For the dolls' dresses.
I had to make fifty a day to get paid.
At the end of the first day there was
this thing.
It had half a head –
Dropping, two arms, no body, and a leg.
And its eyes popped off.
And the house looked like a romp in
a stable.
I had a right earful from the hubby for
the mess.
Well, after that,
I cleaned other people's houses.
But they knew I needed the money,
So each day the lady of the house
Would increase the work.

First it was,
Could you rub this shirt through for my
husband?
Soon I was doing the whole family wash.
By hand!
For the same pay as I got for mopping
and dusting.
So the first chance I got to work in a
canteen
I took it.
And when the father left (*she waves*)
I washed those stacks of dishes with an
energy you wouldn't believe.

My daughter slept over with this West
Indian Family.
They were Jamaicans,
With three girls of their own,
So she was in good company.
Although I do wish they wouldn't tell
Those Tarzan stories about Africans,
She gets really upset.

Anyway, I was busy, as we were moving,
So every night after my shift
I'd get the all night bus from town and go
over to the maisonette to hang me
curtains or clean something.
The people living on the other side
Must have been really impressed
Thinking their own kind were moving in.
They must have been gob-smacked
to see us!
I heard one of them, you know the type,
Hair by mistake, make-up by necessity,
Asking my daughter when had she first

come to England.
Long before your lot, I yelled,
She slammed her balcony door
And we never spoke again.
Me and Anne West used to go shopping
together.
She lived next-door, Anne,
And didn't give a damn who you were or,
where you came from.
Her life had been too hard for snobbery,
And very soon it was going to get
murderously worse.
I don't know why I decided to move,
I'm sure some of it was instinct.
I had this fella by then,
He was Polish this fella and dead clever
with money.
His family had the lot; land, property, and
he was educated – that's how he got the
job as a wine waiter.
I don't mean he had studied wine
He bloody drank it,
You know, with his dinner.
He'd even got me sipping Drambuie.
Drambuie

It's dead posh that Drambuie.
Well, when the Communists took over,
he came to England.
And can you believe this
Just because he hadn't been educated
in Britain
They wouldn't let him work as a vet.
I told him
I wasn't surprised –
I'd seen it all before.
There are West Indians – university
qualified -
You know like teachers,
Driving bloody buses,
Believe me, I said,
As far as this country is concerned
If it's not bloody British it's shit.
Anyway it was him who convinced me to
buy somewhere.
I had no money, only me wages,
And no one was going to give me credit,
were they?
The only thing I could get on the tick
Was from the catalogue or Pauldens.
It's called Debenhams now.

In fact every thing we owned came from
Pauldens,

And one day my two complained so the
next Saturday I took them to town
To Lewis's.
We picked out this three-piece suite,
I didn't need it, like, but I had to make
them understand.
Then we went upstairs to the offices,
Filled the forms out and waited
For this snooty nosed bastard,
in his smelly suit, to tell me
That they didn't give credit to coloured
families,
And he was sure that I would understand.
Well, I didn't understand, but I did.
So George –
he was called George – did I tell you that?
He arranged everything
You know, like as though he was buying,
But my name went on the mortgage.
I'd pick the ones I liked from the pictures
And he'd go and look at them – and you
know, it was really strange,
But as soon as I got the one I wanted.
I wanted out of that maisonette.
I don't think we spent a year there.
And after all these years –
I still think about it.
Well, it could have been my daughter.
My little girl, but it wasn't, it was Lesley.
She was beautiful, Lesley.
Mum, can Lesley stay for tea?
Mum, I'm going to play with friend Lesley.
Lesley. Lesley.

10 second silent pause.

There were trees in Levenshulme

And at the back of our new house
a small garden
With a fence to one side
A wall to the other,
And one separating us from the garden
at the back.
Although we never went near the place,
Before signing the contracts,
They all knew we were coming.
Some of our stuff arrived on the back of a
lorry.
I kid you not, on the back of a lorry,
some in a mini van, a friend's car, a taxi,
and the rest by movers.

The old couple on the right

Never spoke one word to any of us
For the ten or more years we lived there.
The neighbours on the left weren't so bad,
Nosey like, but over the years –
we became sort of friends.
When we first moved in, my daughter
would leave the hall light on for me
coming home from work.
The grandmother remarked one day,
That maybe it was delight of having
electricity
That was making us so extravagant.
Silly cow.

But back to when we first moved.
On the first Monday.
The first Monday!
I done a bit of washing, curtains or
something.
I was hanging them out, as the house at
the back of us was having this tree
trimmed and heard them say to the bloke
doing the job
Don't cut the branches on that side,
I don't want those niggers
looking in on me.

By the end of the day
I had this fucking big fence erected,
To stop that racist
Looking in on us.
To stop him looking in on us.

So much happened in that house
As we laughed and argued
Through each day.

The world was changing too.
I remember when my nephew –
Have I told you about my family?
We're just like anybody
I mean, I'm not talking to that lot.
And wouldn't have them lot over
if you paid me!
But when my nephew was boxing
at the Olympics games,
we watched every minute on the telly.

That's how we came to see it
Black Power against American racism.
My son Malcolm, had grown his hair,
he was reading the Solidad Brothers
and quoting X.
We were always fighting, arguing.

Him screaming at me,
I've never cried so much in my life,
But I wanted him to grab a future,
to escape the life that was destroying him.

Sam Cooke died and we played his music
late into the night, and I sang
won't somebody tell me what's wrong
with me –
why my life is so full of misery?
And I prayed that the woman found with
him wasn't white.
Much the same way as I tried to explain
to my daughter,
I prayed that the Yorkshire Ripper wouldn't
be black.
A Black man and so many murders
Would send people rioting onto the streets,
and many an innocent Black man
Would pay the price for one man's guilt.
Oh, there s no lynching in England
Here, they just beat you to death.

SCENE – *The nurse has removed M's dressing gown and slippers. she covers M's head with a cap, ready for surgery.*

I'd do anything to be out of here,
out and about.
Not that I ever went anywhere.
When I first left the orphanage
I went into service, working for priests.
On the first night
I took a fancy to cold porridge.
So I nicked some. And popped myself up
in bed with a great bowlful.
The other maid just looked at me then
blew out the candle.
I didn't mind.

When we were kids
My sister worked in the kitchen cooking
for the nuns.
She used to sneak food in her
knickers and, along with our mate Winnie,
we'd eat it in the dark.
Anyway, the next night
I fancied porridge again.
So I nicked some more,
And the girl said,
Why are you eating that? she said
Why, because I fancied it. I said
Well don't. she said
Why not? I said,
Because the last girl that worked here,
she said.

Ate porridge every night laced with
arsenic until she died.
I left the next morning.

We used to get one Saturday off per
month, in Service.
I used to meet my mates at Lime Street
to go to the matinees.
We would buy a great big bag of rotten
tomatoes
And go to see Arthur Askey.
Do you remember him?
I'm a buzzing, bloody buzzing,
busy bloody bee.
Well, buzz off, we'd say
And threw the buggers – then over the
road for Ken Dodd with the other half.
Tight Ken we called him even then,
and we were right.
Mind you,
I wouldn't pay my taxes –
given half the chance.
That was it for me really.
As the years passed,
I'd spend my rare night off in front of the
telly, my feet up on a pouffe, eating a
cream cake.

I went on holidays.
I went to Paris once, –
in France!
It was marvellous.
Went to the Moulin Rouge
To see the can-can dancers.
And listen to this,
when the girls kicked their legs up,
They had no knickers on!
Well, I started laughing
and when I laugh –
everyone knows about it.
I laughed so much they threw me out!

My daughter did the can-can once.
Over at the Lesser Free Trade Hall.
I sent her to dancing school
as soon as she could walk.
Well, I couldn't dance, so I just thought
that she wouldn't be able to either.
Well, what did I know about natural
rhythms, in any form,
If you get my meaning?
And she was a natural
She could do anything –
Tap,

Ballet,
Which amazed the teachers –
Well, African bottoms are not supposed
To be able to learn certain ballet techniques.
Bloody stupid if you ask me,
Well, you don't dance with your arse,
Do ya?

When she was thirteen
She auditioned and got a place
In the pantomime at the Palace Theatre.
When I went to collect her, after the first
rehearsal they told me, apologising,
Not to bring her back the next day.
They said she didn't blend in with the
rest of the kids.
Anyone try and tell me that now
I'd swing for them.
But that day –
I don't know.
I simply hugged her close, and took
her home.
I used to say to my daughter,
you're beautiful.
I don't mean on the outside
but on the inside.
And you have to remember that.
For so many people are going to try –
to prove different.
I'd tell her, wherever you go and you're
the only coloured person there.
I used to say coloured then.
Naturally I say black now.
Well, I'd tell her, you are representing
all black people,
so hold your head up high.
I'd say,
You see your father,
well, I can't stand the bastard.
But he's an African – that means you're
an African
never forget that.
I told my kids that I would always be
proud of them and hope that they would
never, you know, grow up and become
ashamed of me.
Kids!
Who'd have them?
Who'd be without them once they're here.

SCENE – The stage slowly goes darker and darker

Nurse, turn the light on.
I hate the dark.
Turn the light on.

She's useless that nurse.
I've told her,
In the forties and fifties thousands of
qualified women came over from the
West Indies to be nurses, and ended up
scrubbing hospital floors.
She'd be better off as a backing-singer.
Turn the bloody light on.
I'm scared of the dark.

SCENE – BLACK OUT.
M rises removing her hospital gown and cap as she walks towards the screen and reads aloud the certificate.

When my mother died, the world did not
stand still.
Nothing stopped, changed to note her
passing.
It was almost as though everything
moved at double speed.
She was there and suddenly – she was
this small container of ash, and I could
carry the whole of her here in my hands.
When my mother died
No one felt the emptiness of life like I did.
Then, I don't know, weeks, months later
I woke up crying.
But in that moment
Between sleep and waking
I began to laugh.
That dreadful laugh of my mum.
That laugh that said they won't keep us
down forever.
Then I began to remember her as she was
In private times,
Like at the end of a day she would come
home stand in front of the fire, raise her
skirt and pull off her corset, scratching
red welts into her skin.
I began to remember her stories,
tales of the convent.
Of her struggle to keep us proud of what
we were.
And wonder why she was always hopeful
that we would never be ashamed of her.
That day, I realised, that it's only the body
that dies.
But the spirit continues and you carry it
here, in this place of 'love'.
And I laughed then at myself for forgetting
that I carry the spirit of an ancestral people,
Not only in the colour of my skin
But in my determination to see each day
through.
Better than yesterday.

And mixed in along with all those Africans
is this.

One special woman.

So, if any of you think that all mixed
raced people.
Grow up confused, without identity,
Think again.
I work in schools,
And often, the cocky lad sat at the back
Asks me where I come from.
I answer, 'Manchester'.
He'll say, 'Nope, where do you really
come from,
Manchester?
Why, where do you think I come from?
Somewhere hot and exotic he'll say
Well it's exotic in Manchester some days
well, I mean look at me.
Then there's the media, desperate for
a story,
Headlining, The Mixed Heritage,
confused shows.
They can F
I know exactly who I am –
I am a Black woman
A mixed race woman.
I am proud to be a Nigerian daughter
whose father loved her.
He loved me so much,
And I am equally proud to be the daughter
of a Liverpool woman of Irish descent.
Confused? Get out of here.
If you're loved you're –
hell I wish you'd known my mother.
Oh, I forgot, you do now.
For this was the story of M –
M for Margaret,
M for Mother,
And now M for Me.
And my name is SuAndi.

5.5 SUPERNINTENDO RANCHERO

Excerpt from BORDERscape 2000

GUILLERMO GÓMEZ-PEÑA

Guillermo Gómez-Peña (b. 1950) *is a Mexican performance artist, writer, cultural critic and activist. He pioneered multimedia performance making use of live performance, photography, film and installation. His performances are often collaborative and durational and play with the relationship between the artwork, the performer and the audience, such as in* The Couple in the Cage *(1992). A politically driven artist, Gómez-Peña's work frequently explores themes around hybridization, identity, borders, globalization and consumerism (see also 5.11).* **Roberto Sifuentes** *is an interdisciplinary practitioner whose work combines the live and the mediafized. He has collaborated with Gómez-Peña as a member of La Pocha Nostra from 1994 to 2000.*

'Performance is the most flexible language I have found. I utilize it to analyze our social crises and cultural misplacement; to articulate my desires and frustration in the overlapping realms of politics, sexuality, art and spirituality. Performance is a vast conceptual territory where my eclectic and ever-changing ideas, and the ideas of my collaborators, can be integrated into a coherent system and be put into practice. It's radical theory turned into praxis through movement, ritual, gesture, sound, light and spoken text.
From Gómez-Peña's *Performance Diaries*, 1990

(Opera singer sings Mozart intertwined with a soundbed of Japanese techno music. ROBERTO SIFUENTES stands on top of a metallic pyramid. He wears a laboratory coat and teched-out glasses, and speaks in a computer-processed, mechanical voice. GUILLERMO GÓMEZ-PEÑA enters dressed as El Mad Mexterminator, riding a motorized wheelchair. He moves across the stage in a mechanical, video-game-like pattern, responding to gestural commands from SIFUENTES.)

RS: San Francisco, March of 99. Dear Chicano colleagues, welcome to *BORDER scape 2000*, part three of a performance trilogy. Allow me to introduce to you the very first prototype: a beta version of an imperfect Mexican. This cyborg still has a sentimental mind and a political consciousness. He failed the test for robotic migrant workers, and still longs for his homeland. Eventually when we manage to get the Mexican bugs out of him, we will create a Chicano, the vato uberalis, the next step on the evolutionary scale. Speak Mexi-cyborg!! Repent yourself!! Use voice #53 and please stick to the script.

GGP: (*Processed voice #1*) No, I won't cru-ci-fy myself to protest la migra no more.

RS: You can't repeat a performance or it would become theater.

GGP: No, I swear,

I won't box with a hanging chicken for art's sake . . .
nor will I exhibit myself inside a gilded cage
as an endangered species or an androgynous wrestler/shaman.

RS: Why Mad Mex Frankenstein?

GGP: I'm just gonna be a poet for a while.

RS: Then be a poet. Stick to the spoken word material. Go!! Go North!!

GGP: So I continue my trek north
like a compulsive explorer
El Marco Pollo de Tijuana,
El Vasco de Gama de Aztlán
ever looking for a new island, a new performance stage
to spill my beans, my bleeding tripas,
expose my crevasses, my wounded penis
in the name of ex-pe-ri-men-ta-tion.

RS: Now you wish to be a performance artist again?

"*Performance is the most flexible language I have found. I utilize it to analyze our social codes and cultural misplacement; to articulate my desires and frustration in the overlapping realms of politics, sexuality, art and spirituality. Performance is a vast conceptual territory where my eclectic and ever-changing ideas, and the ideas of my collaborators, can be integrated into a coherent system and be put into practice. It's radical theory turned into praxis through movement, ritual, gesture, sound, light and spoken text.*"

FROM GÓMEZ-PEÑA'S PERFORMANCE DIARIES, 1990

7. El Veteran Survivor.

Figure 37 El Veteran Survivor. (Photographer: Eugenio Castro.)

GGP: Not exactly.

(*GGP intersperses 'no's' through following text.*)

RS: So Vato, give us some blood,
  show us your piercings, your prosthetics,
  eat your green card or burn your bra
  but get fuckin' real!

GGP: no, no, ni madres.

RS: Why?

GGP: Cause I'm giving up, right now, in front of you.

RS: Oh god, you fuckin' martyr!

GGP: I willingly turn myself in to my inner border patrol
  three agents are present tonight
  come on, get me!!
  this is your golden chance culeros
  I su-rren-der to my own darkest fears.

RS: You're not responding to my performance commands. You were much better when you were just trying to be a poet. Go back to poetry. Synthesize an entire cosmology into one burning sentence. Go!

GGP: Fear is the foundation of your identity. (*He points at someone in audience.*)

RS: What a fuckin' assumption.

GGP: To be Mexican is a felony not a misdemeanor …

RS: Hey better, chido, punchy.

GGP: versus ser pocho es still una afrenta binacional.

RS: You are using Spanish unnecessarily. Shift accent.

GGP: (*Texan accent.*) I'm fully aware that your ears are tired of listening to so many foreign languages. (*He speaks in 'gringo tongues,' interspersed with recognizable English words.*)

RS: Stop! Next dialect!

GGP: Hey, that's how English sounded to me when I was a kid.

RS: So upgrade yourself!

GGP: Such linguistic vertigo you have to endure daily
  I mean, you can't even communicate with your maid
  or your gardener,
  and then you come to California
  (*gringoñol*)
  & carrramba mamazita!
  the artist speaks Spanglish and gringoñol
  (*mispronounced Spanish*)
  io hablou el idiouma del criminal, il drogadictou y la piuta
  e' cuandouu io hablou tu muérres un poquitou mas.

RS: English only, pinche wetback!

GGP: I mean, 23 states in America have embraced English only
  California just abolished bilingual education
  and I dare to talk to you in Spanglish? Que poca ma …

RS: Good boy … you are assimilating.
  What is your prime directive? Explain yourself.

GGP: To you or to the audience?

RS: To the audience.

GGP: Dear citizens of nothingness:
  this is a desperate attempt by a dying performance artist
  to recapture the power of the spoken word
  in the year of virtual despair and victorious whiteness.

RS: Stop! Now, do something more kinetic, more defiant. Don't you have a fuckin choreographer?

GGP: Sara!!!

RS: Music!!

GGP: Sara!!!

RS: We need some hip music
  cd #3; track 2, take 1: Japanese tea house lounge. Go.

(*Lights transition to lounge look.*)

RS: Yeah! Now, stand up & dance. (*Repeats three times.*)

GGP stops wheelchair and attempts to stand up but fails. He eventually succeeds in standing. GGP dances cheesy disco & twist, then falls down on his knees.

RS: Stop the music. This is terrifying
  Who do you think you are? an MTV Latino?

GGP crawls back onto the chair while speaking. Lights return to normal and sound goes back to techno music.

GGP: El Mariachi with a biiiiiig moooouth.

RS: Not anymore carnal.

GGP: Mexi-cyborg el extra-extra-terrestre.

RS: Not quite yet. You wish.

GGP: El immigrant bizarro con su mente explosiva y expansiva al servicio de la fragmentación político-poética.

RS: State your function or lose your greencard.

GGP: To you or to the audience?

RS: To the audience.

GGP: My normal state of being, carnal,
is to die for you, cause after all these years
I'm still imprisoned inside this historical purgatory.

RS: Still obsessed with history in the year 2000?

GGP: *Yes.*

RS: That's cute.

GGP: Do you remember the terms of the Guadalupe-Hidalgo treaty?
do you fuckin' remem …

RS: Can anyone answer this pathetic poet?

GGP: Est-ce que vous êtes illégal?
L'illégalité est à la mode, n'est-ce pas?

RS: OK, you win this time. Let's talk about illegality … Go!

GGP moves to extreme downstage and looks into audience. House lights come up. After each question, RS *intersperses improvised replies.*

GGP: Are there any illegal immigrants in the audience?
People who once were illegal?
What about people who have had sex with an illegal alien?
Can you describe in detail their genitalia?
Are there people here who have hired illegal immigrants for domestic, or artistic purposes?
Yessss! To do what exactly?
How much did you pay them?
How did you feel about that?
Thanks for your sincerity …
Now, have any of you ever fantasized about being from another race or culture?
Which one?
Black, Indian?
Native American? Mexican?

RS: Boring. Cambio de canal: give me burning sentence #2.

House lights down.

GGP: Ser emigrante en América ya es un acto ilegal.

RS: Translation please?

GGP: Just to be different is potentially an illegal act
one strike & you're out!
punishable with deportation without trail,
and retroactive to 10 years.

RS: That's too … technical

GGP: I mean, to be excluded from a national project
at a time when all nation states are collapsing

is not an extraordinary act of heroism
or literary fiction, ask the Welsh or the Irish, man …

RS: That's too fuckin' heavy to deal with right now.
This is the year 2000;
it's all about style without content.

GGP: You mean radical actions without repercussions?

RS: Right!

GGP: Tropical tourism without Montezuma's revenge?

RS: Global nada … rien

GGP: Nothing-ness, really?
Just style, anonymous sex, weird trivia?
So, if that's what defines your values and your identity,
let's fuckin' engage in trivia.

RS: Good! But bring down at least 10 decibels the level of your drama.
Remember: pc est passé, and so is rage, Supermojado.
Now, give me some burning trivia. Go:

GGP: Madonna defeated Argentina & got to play Evita
Gooooo Madonna!!

RS: Dated material. Next!

GGP: Selena died precisely during the crossover.
(*Looking up.*) Selena, we luv you diva, auuu!!

RS: What's so fucking special about Selena?

GGP: Her whiny voice, her liposuctioned nalgas.
Besides, she is all we have, since we've got no real leaders
o que? Do you think we have any true Chicano leaders?

RS: Kind of.

GGP: Can you mention one?

RS: Eddie Olmos (GGP *reacts.*), El Haniachi Two (GGP *reacts.*), the Taco Bell Chihuahua.

GGP: Fax you, man! Marcos! He is not a Chicano but he is certainly a leader …

RS: He's just a fading myth. Back to our search for burning trivia. Go!

GGP: Zappa is resting in the Olympus of Americana
(me persigno)
per ipsum, ecu nip zzzzum Zzzzappa!

RS: And so is Sinatra.

GGP: Sinatra?
(*Sings.*) 'When I was 35, it was a very good year'
ese mi Frank
your absence hurts much more than that of Octavio Paz.

RS: Hey that's a great trivial line.
Do you have some of this shit on disc?

GGP: No. I no longer have a laptop. I am a Neo-Luddite.

RS: A luddite with a mechanical wheelchair?

GGP: Yes.

RS: You fuckin' ro-man-tico! Shift 348X-13 Trivialize race. Go!

GGP: OJ was a cyborg constructed by your own fears & desires.

RS: But was he guilty?

GGP: Yes, he was guilty & not that interesting a character

RS: But we cared about him, cause he was (*GGP intersperses* 'Que?') … cause he is a … a … a … black cyborg.

Pause.

GGP: I didn't say it. You did!!

RS: These are the issues that truly matter

GGP: Sure … in a time & place
where nothing significant truly matters.

RS: What you consider trivia is my raison d'être.
Give me a headline that truly captures our times.

GGP: Clintoris & Linguinsky: the great millennial soap opera.

RS: Elaborate … elaborate … elaborate.

GGP: Monica finally described in detail the genitals of your President.

RS: Don't elaborate.

GGP: She said, she said:
'it's pink, about three inches long, and it never gets hard but there is something endearing about it.'

RS: You are diverging from our subject matter. We are beginning to sound like bad experimental poetry. Neruda meets Jello Biafra.
What are we really here for?

GGP: Tonight?

RS: Tonight

GGP: Tonight?

RS: Tonight

GGP: (*To the audience.*) There is too much turmoil in your private life for me to bother you with the truly heavy issues like racism, homelessness or police brutality.

RS: Right! That was the 80s, ese.
We've heard that pop song so many times
but tonight, your audience is understandably tired.
They suffer from … repeat with me:
com-pa-ssion fa-tigue, yeah.

GGP: com-pa-ssion fa-tigue, yeah.

RS: Just to hear you say it makes me want to slash you in the face.

GGP: Thank you.

Lights up on Sara Shelton-Mann SL. dressed as Mariachi Zapatista. She breaks into fast-paced, Chaplinesque movements with a gun, dancing to Mexican punk. Strobe light. Music stops abruptly and video cuts out at end of her dance. Juan Ybarra as Green Alien enters. Beginning of Nintendo Ethnic Wars.

Note

Originally published in Guillermo Gómez-Peña, *Dangerous Border Crossers: The Artist Talks Back*, London: Routledge, 2000. pp. 24–33.

5.6 **Myth Today** (1957)

ROLAND BARTHES

Translated by Annette Lavers

WHAT IS A MYTH, today? I shall give at the outset a first, very simple answer, which is perfectly consistent with etymology: *myth is a type of speech.*[1]

Myth is a type of speech

Of course, it is not *any* type: language needs special conditions in order to become myth: we shall see them in a minute. But what must be firmly established at the start is that myth is a system of communication, that it is a message. This allows one to perceive that myth cannot possibly be an object, a concept, or an idea; it is a mode of signification, a form. Later, we shall have to assign to this form historical limits, conditions of use, and reintroduce society into it: we must nevertheless first describe it as a form.

It can be seen that to purport to discriminate among mythical objects according to their substance would be entirely illusory: since myth is a type of speech, everything can be a myth provided it is conveyed by a discourse. Myth is not defined by the object of its message, but by the way in which it utters this message: there are formal limits to myth, there are no 'substantial' ones. Everything, then, can be a myth? Yes, I believe this, for the universe is infinitely fertile in suggestions. Every object in the world can pass from a closed, silent existence to an oral state, open to appropriation by society, for there is no law, whether natural or not, which forbids talking about things. A tree is a tree. Yes, of course. But a tree as expressed by Minou Drouet is no longer quite a tree, it is a tree which is decorated, adapted to a certain type of consumption, laden with literary self-indulgence, revolt, images, in short with a type of social *usage* which is added to pure matter.

Naturally, everything is not expressed at the same time: some objects become the prey of mythical speech for a while, then they disappear, others take their place and attain the status of myth. Are there objects which are *inevitably* a source of suggestiveness, as Baudelaire suggested about Woman? Certainly not: one can conceive of very ancient myths, but there are no eternal ones; for it is human history which converts reality into speech, and it alone rules the life and the death of mythical language. Ancient or not, mythology can only have an historical foundation, for myth is a type of speech chosen by history: it cannot possibly evolve from the 'nature' of things.

Speech of this kind is a message. It is therefore by no means confined to oral speech. It can consist of modes of writing or of representations; not only written discourse, but also photography, cinema, reporting, sport, shows, publicity, all these can serve as a support to mythical speech. Myth can be defined neither by its object nor by its material, for any material can arbitrarily be endowed with meaning: the arrow which is brought in order to signify a challenge is also a kind of speech. True, as far as perception is concerned, writing and pictures, for instance, do not call upon the same type of consciousness; and even with pictures, one can use many kinds of reading: a diagram lends itself to signification more than a drawing, a copy more than an original, and a caricature more than a portrait. But this is the point: we are no longer dealing here with a theoretical mode of representation: we are dealing with *this* particular image, which is given for *this* particular signification. Mythical speech is made of a material which has *already* been worked on so as to make it suitable for communication: it is because all the materials of myth (whether pictorial or written) presuppose a signifying consciousness, that one can reason about them while discounting their substance. This substance is not unimportant: pictures, to be sure, are more imperative than writing, they impose meaning at one stroke, without analysing or diluting it. But this is no longer a constitutive difference. Pictures become a kind of writing as soon as they are meaningful: like writing, they call for a *lexis*.

We shall therefore take *language, discourse, speech*, etc., to mean any significant unit or synthesis, whether verbal or visual: a photograph will be a kind of speech for us in the same way as a newspaper article; even objects will become speech, if they mean something. This generic way of conceiving language is in fact justified by the very history of writing: long before the invention of our alphabet, objects like the Inca *quipu*, or drawings, as in pictographs, have been accepted as speech. This does not mean that one must treat mythical speech like language; myth in fact belongs to the province of a general science, coextensive with linguistics, which is *semiology*.

Myth as a semiological system

For mythology, since it is the study of a type of speech, is but one fragment of this vast science of signs which Saussure postulated some forty years ago under the name of *semiology*. Semiology has not yet come into being. But since Saussure himself, and sometimes independently of him, a whole section of contemporary research has constantly been referred to the problem of meaning: psycho-analysis, structuralism, eidetic psychology, some new types of literary criticism of which Bachelard has given the first examples, are no longer concerned with facts except inasmuch as they are endowed with significance. Now to postulate a signification is to have recourse to semiology. I do not mean that semiology could account for all these aspects of research equally well: they have different contents. But they have a common status: they are all sciences dealing with values. They are not content with meeting the facts: they define and explore them as tokens for something else.

Semiology is a science of forms, since it studies significations apart from their content. I should like to say one word about the necessity and the limits of such a formal science. The necessity is that which applies in the case of any exact language. Zhdanov made fun of Alexandrov the philosopher, who spoke of '*the spherical structure of our planet*'. '*It was thought until now*', Zhdanov said, '*that form alone could be spherical.*' Zhdanov was right: one cannot speak about structures in terms of forms, and vice versa. It may well be that on the plane of 'life', there is but a totality where structures and forms cannot be separated. But science has no use for the ineffable: it must speak about 'life' if it wants to transform it. Against a certain quixotism of synthesis, quite Platonic incidentally, all criticism must consent to the *ascesis*, to the artifice of analysis; and in analysis, it must match method and language. Less terrorized by the spectre of 'formalism', historical criticism might have been less sterile; it would have understood that the specific study of forms does not in any way contradict the necessary principle of totality and History. On the contrary: the more a system is specifically defined in its forms, the more amenable it is to historical criticism. To parody a well-known saying, I shall say that a little formalism turns one away from History, but that a lot brings one back to it. Is there a better example of total criticism than the description of saintliness, at once formal and historical, semiological and ideological, in Sartre's *Saint-Genet*? The danger, on the contrary, is to consider forms as ambiguous objects, half-form and half-substance, to endow form with a substance of form, as was done, for instance, by Zhdanovian realism. Semiology, once its limits are settled, is not a metaphysical trap: it is a science among others, necessary but not sufficient. The important thing is to see that the unity of an explanation cannot be based on the amputation of one or other of its approaches, but, as Engels said, on the dialectical co-ordination of the particular sciences it makes use of. This is the case with mythology: it is a part both of semiology inasmuch as it is a formal science, and of ideology inasmuch as it is an historical science: it studies ideas-in-form.[2]

Let me therefore restate that any semiology postulates a relation between two terms, a signifier and a signified. This relation concerns objects which belong to different categories, and this is why it is not one of equality but one of equivalence. We must here be on our guard, for despite common parlance which simply says that the signifier *expresses* the signified, we are dealing, in any semiological system, not with two, but with three different terms. For what we grasp is not at all one term after the other, but the correlation which unites them: there are, therefore, the signifier, the signified and the sign, which is the associative total of the first two terms. Take a bunch of roses: I use it to *signify* my passion. Do we have here, then, only a signifier and a signified, the roses and my passion? Not even that: to put it accurately, there are here only 'passionified' roses. But on the plane of analysis, we do have three terms; for these roses weighted with passion perfectly and correctly allow themselves to be decomposed into roses and passion: the former and the latter existed before uniting and forming this third object, which is the sign. It is as true to say that on the plane of experience I cannot dissociate the roses from the message they carry, as to say that on the plane of analysis I cannot confuse the roses as signifier and the roses as sign: the signifier is empty, the sign is full, it is a meaning. Or take a black pebble: I can make it signify in several ways, it is a mere signifier; but if I weigh it with a definite signified (a death sentence, for instance, in an anonymous vote), it will become a sign. Naturally, there are between the signifier, the signified and the sign, functional implications (such as that of the part to the whole) which are so close that to analyse them may seem futile; but we shall see in a moment that this distinction has a capital importance for the study of myth as semiological schema.

Naturally these three terms are purely formal, and different contents can be given to them. Here are a few examples: for Saussure, who worked on a particular but methodologically exemplary semiological system – the language or *langue* – the signified is the concept, the signifier is the acoustic image (which is mental) and the relation between concept and image is the sign (the word, for instance), which is a concrete entity.[3] For Freud, as is well known, the human psyche is a stratification of tokens or representatives. One term (I refrain from giving it any precedence) is constituted by the manifest meaning of behaviour, another, by its latent or real meaning (it is, for instance, the substratum of the dream); as for the third term, it is here also a correlation of the first two: it is the dream itself in its totality, the parapraxis (a mistake in speech or behaviour) or the neurosis, conceived as compromises, as economies effected thanks to the joining of a form (the first term) and an intentional function (the second term). We can see here how necessary it is to distinguish the sign from the signifier: a dream, to Freud, is no more its manifest datum than its latent content: it is the functional union of these two terms. In Sartrean criticism, finally (I shall keep to these three well-known examples), the signified is constituted by the original crisis in the subject (the separation from his mother for Baudelaire, the naming of the theft for Genet); Literature as discourse forms the signifier; and the relation between crisis and discourse defines the work, which is a signification. Of course, this tri-dimensional pattern, however constant in its form, is actualized in different ways: one cannot therefore say too often that semiology can have its unity only at the level of forms, not contents; its field is limited, it knows only one operation: reading, or deciphering.

In myth, we find again the tri-dimensional pattern which I have just described: the signifier, the signified and the sign. But myth is a peculiar system, in that it is constructed from a semiological chain which existed before it: it *is a second-order semiological system*. That which is a sign (namely the associative total of a concept and an image) in the first system, becomes a mere signifier in the second. We must here recall that the materials of mythical speech (the language itself, photography, painting, posters, rituals, objects, etc.), however different at the start, are reduced to a pure signifying function as soon as they are caught by myth. Myth sees in them only the same raw material; their unity is that they all come down to the status of a mere language. Whether it deals with alphabetical or pictorial writing, myth wants to see in them only a sum of signs, a global sign, the final term of a first semiological chain. And it is precisely this final term which will become the first term of the greater system which it builds and of which it is only a part. Everything happens as if myth shifted the formal system of the first significations sideways. As this lateral shift is essential for the analysis of myth, I shall represent it in the following way, it being understood, of course, that the spatialization of the pattern is here only a metaphor:

Language	1. Signifier	2. Signifier	
MYTH	3. Sign I SIGNIFIER		II SIGNIFIED
	III SIGN		

It can be seen that in myth there are two semiological systems, one of which is staggered in relation to the other: a linguistic system, the language (or the modes of representation which are assimilated to it), which I shall call the *language-object*, because it is the language which myth gets hold of in order to build its own system; and myth itself, which I shall call *metalanguage*, because it is a second language, *in which* one speaks about the first. When he reflects on a metalanguage, the semiologist no longer needs to ask himself questions about the composition of the language-object, he no longer has to take into account the details of the linguistic schema; he will only need to know its total term, or global sign, and only inasmuch as this term lends itself to myth. This is why the semiologist is entitled to treat in the same way writing and pictures: what he retains from them is the fact that they are both *signs*, that they both reach the threshold of myth endowed with the same signifying function, that they constitute, one just as much as the other, a language-object.

It is now time to give one or two examples of mythical speech. I shall borrow the first from an observation by Valéry.[4] I am a pupil in the second form in a French *lycée*. I open my Latin grammar, and I read a sentence, borrowed from Aesop or Phaedrus: *quia ego nominor leo*. I stop and think. There is something ambiguous about this statement: on the one hand, the words in it do have a simple meaning: *because my name is lion*. And on the other hand, the sentence is evidently there in order to signify something else to me. Inasmuch as it is addressed to me, a pupil in the second form, it tells me clearly: I am a grammatical example meant to illustrate the rule about the agreement of the predicate. I am even forced to realize that the sentence in no way *signifies* its meaning to me, that it tries very little to tell me something about the lion and what sort of name he has; its true and fundamental signification is to impose itself on me as the presence of a certain agreement of the predicate. I conclude that I am faced with a particular, greater, semiological system, since it is co-extensive with the language: there is, indeed, a signifier, but this signifier is itself formed by a sum of signs, it is in itself a first semiological system (*my name is lion*). Thereafter, the formal pattern is correctly unfolded: there is a signified (*I am a grammatical example*) and there is a global signification, which is none other than the correlation of the signifier and the signified; for neither the naming of the lion nor the grammatical example are given separately.

And here is now another example: I am at the barber's, and a copy of *Paris-Match* is offered to me. On the cover, a young Negro in a French uniform is saluting, with his eyes uplifted, probably fixed on a fold of the tricolour. All this is the *meaning* of the picture. But, whether naïvely or not, I see very well what it signifies to me: that France is a great Empire, that all her sons, without any colour discrimination, faithfully serve under her flag, and that there is no better answer to the detractors of an alleged colonialism than the zeal shown by this Negro in serving his so-called oppressors. I am therefore again faced with a greater semiological system: there is a signifier, itself already formed with a previous system (*a black soldier is giving the French salute*); there is a signified (it is here a purposeful mixture of Frenchness and militariness); finally, there is a presence of the signified through the signifier.

Before tackling the analysis of each term of the mythical system, one must agree on terminology. We now know that the signifier can be looked at, in myth, from two points of view: as the final term of the linguistic system, or as the first term of the mythical system. We therefore need two names. On the plane of language, that is, as the final term of the first system, I shall call the signifier: *meaning* (*my name is lion, a Negro is giving the French salute*); on the plane of myth, I shall call it: *form*. In the case of the signified, no ambiguity is possible: we shall retain the name *concept*. The third term is the correlation of the first two: in the linguistic system, it is the *sign*; but it is not possible to use this word again without ambiguity, since in myth (and this is the chief peculiarity of the latter), the signifier is already formed by the *signs* of the language. I shall call the third term of myth the *signification*. This word is here all the better justified since myth has in fact a double function: it points out and it notifies, it makes us understand something and it imposes it on us.

The form and the concept

The signifier of myth presents itself in an ambiguous way: it is at the same time meaning and form, full on one side and empty on the other. As meaning, the signifier already postulates a reading, I grasp it through my eyes, it has a sensory reality (unlike the linguistic signifier, which is purely mental), there is a richness in it: the naming of the lion, the Negro's salute are credible wholes, they have at their disposal a sufficient rationality. As a total of linguistic signs, the meaning of the myth has its own value, it belongs to a history, that of the lion or that of the Negro: in the meaning, a signification is already built, and could very well be self-sufficient if myth did not take hold of it and did not turn it suddenly into an empty, parasitical form. The meaning is *already* complete, it postulates a kind of knowledge, a past, a memory, a comparative order of facts, ideas, decisions.

When it becomes form, the meaning leaves its contingency behind; it empties itself, it becomes impoverished, history evaporates, only the letter remains. There is here a paradoxical permutation in the reading operations, an abnormal regression from meaning to form, from the linguistic sign to the mythical signifier. If one encloses *quia ego nominor leo* in a purely linguistic system, the clause finds again there a fullness, a richness, a history: I am an animal, a lion, I live in a certain country, I have just been hunting, they would have me share my prey with a heifer, a cow and a goat; but being the stronger, I award myself all the shares for various reasons, the last of which is quite simply that *my name is lion*. But as the form of the myth, the clause hardly retains anything of this long story. The meaning contained a whole system of values: a history, a geography, a morality, a zoology, a Literature. The form has put all this richness at a distance: its newly acquired penury calls for a signification to fill it. The story of the lion must recede a great deal in order to make room for the grammatical example, one must put the biography of the Negro in parentheses if one wants to free the picture, and prepare it to receive its signified.

But the essential point in all this is that the form does not suppress the meaning, it only impoverishes it, it puts it at a distance, it holds it at one's disposal. One believes that the meaning is going to die, but it is a death with reprieve; the meaning loses its value, but keeps its life, from which the form of the myth will draw its nourishment. The meaning will be for the form like an instantaneous reserve of history, a tamed richness, which it is possible to call and dismiss in a sort of rapid alternation: the form must constantly be able to be rooted again in the meaning and to get there what nature it needs for its nutriment; above all, it must be able to hide there. It is this constant game of hide-and-seek between the meaning and the form which defines myth. The form of myth is not a symbol: the Negro who salutes is not the symbol of the French Empire: he has too much presence, he appears as a rich, fully experienced, spontaneous, innocent, *indisputable* image. But at the same time this presence is tamed, put at a distance, made almost transparent; it recedes a little, it becomes the accomplice of a concept which comes to it fully armed, French imperiality: once made use of, it becomes artificial.

Let us now look at the signified: this history which drains out of the form will be wholly absorbed by the concept. As for the latter, it is determined, it is at once historical and intentional; it is the motivation which causes the myth to be uttered. Grammatical exemplarity, French imperiality, are the very drives behind the myth. The concept reconstitutes a chain of causes and effects, motives and intentions. Unlike the form, the concept is in no way abstract: it is filled with a situation. Through the concept, it is a whole new history which is implanted in the myth. Into the naming of the lion, first drained of its contingency, the grammatical example will attract my whole existence: Time, which caused me to be born at a certain period when Latin grammar is taught; History, which sets me apart, through a whole mechanism of social segregation, from the children who do not learn Latin; paedagogic tradition, which caused this example to be chosen from Aesop or Phaedrus; my own linguistic habits, which see the agreement of the predicate as a fact worthy of notice and illustration. The same goes for the Negro-giving-the-salute: as form, its meaning is shallow, isolated, impoverished; as the concept of French imperiality, here it is again tied to the totality of the world: to the general History of France, to its colonial adventures, to its present difficulties. Truth to tell, what is invested in the concept is less reality than a certain knowledge of reality; in passing from the meaning to the form, the image loses some knowledge: the better to receive the knowledge in the concept. In actual fact, the knowledge contained in a mythical concept is confused, made of yielding, shapeless associations. One must firmly stress this open character of the concept; it is not at all an abstract, purified essence; it is a formless, unstable, nebulous condensation, whose unity and coherence are above all due to its function.

In this sense, we can say that the fundamental character of the mythical concept is to be *appropriated*: grammatical exemplarity very precisely concerns a given form of pupils, French imperiality must appeal to such and such a group of readers and not another. The concept closely corresponds to a function, it is defined as a tendency. This cannot fail to recall the signified in another semiological system, Freudianism. In Freud, the second term of the system is the latent meaning (the content) of the dream, of the parapraxis, of the neurosis. Now Freud does remark that the second-order meaning of behaviour is its real meaning, that which is appropriate to a complete situation, including its deeper level; it is, just like the mythical concept, the very intention of behaviour.

A signified can have several signifiers: this is indeed the case in linguistics and psycho-analysis. It is also the case in the mythical concept: it has at its disposal an unlimited mass of signifiers: I can find a thousand Latin sentences to actualize for me the agreement of the predicate, I can find a thousand images which signify to me French imperiality. This means that *quantitively*, the concept is much poorer than the signifier, it often does nothing but re-present itself. Poverty and richness are in reverse proportion in the form and the concept: to the qualitative poverty of the form, which is the repository of a rarefied meaning, there corresponds the richness of the concept which is open to the whole of History; and to the quantitative abundance of the forms there corresponds a small number of concepts. This repetition of the concept through different forms is precious to the mythologist, it allows him to decipher the myth: it is the insistence of a kind of behaviour which reveals its intention. This confirms that there is no regular ratio between the volume of the signified and that of the signifier. In language, this ratio is proportionate, it hardly exceeds the word, or at least the concrete unit. In myth, on the contrary, the concept can spread over a very large expanse of signifier. For instance, a whole book may be the signifier of a single concept; and conversely, a minute form (a word, a gesture, even incidental, so long as it is noticed) can serve as signifier to a concept filled with a very rich history. Although unusual in language, this disproportion between signifier and signified is not specific to myth: in Freud, for instance, the parapraxis is a signifier whose thinness is out of proportion to the real meaning which it betrays.

As I said, there is no fixity in mythical concepts: they can come into being, alter, disintegrate, disappear completely. And it is precisely because they are historical that history can very easily suppress them. This instability forces the mythologist to use a terminology adapted to it, and about which I should now like to say a word, because it often is a cause for irony: I mean neologism. The concept is a constituting element of myth: if I want to decipher myths, I must somehow be able to name concepts. The dictionary supplies me with a few: Goodness, Kindness, Wholeness, Humaneness, etc. But by definition, since it is the dictionary which gives them to me, these particular concepts are not historical. Now what I need most often is ephemeral concepts, in connection with limited contingencies: neologism is then inevitable. China is one thing, the idea which a French petit-bourgeois could have of it not so long ago is another: for this peculiar mixture of bells, rickshaws and opium-dens, no other word is possible but *Sininess*.[5] Unlovely? One should at least get some consolation from the fact that conceptual neologisms are never arbitrary: they are built according to a highly sensible proportional rule.

Notes

1. Innumerable other meanings of the word 'myth' can be cited against this. But I have tried to define things, not words.
2. The development of publicity, of a national press, of radio, of illustrated news, not to speak of the survival of a myriad rites of communication which rule social appearances, makes the development of a semiological science more urgent than ever. In a single day, how many really non-signifying fields do we cross? Very few, sometimes none. Here I am, before the sea; it is true that it bears no message. But on the beach, what material for semiology! Flags, slogans, signals, sign-boards, clothes, suntan even, which are so many messages to me.
3. The notion of *word* is one of the most controversial in linguistics. I keep it here for the sake of simplicity.
4. *Tel Quel*, II, p. 191.
5. Or perhaps *Sinity*? Just as if Latin/Latinity = Basque/x, x = Basquity.

An extract from *Mythologies*, London: Paladin, 1973, pp. 117–31. (Copyright © 1957 Editions du Seuil, Paris.) This translation copyright © Jonathan Cape Ltd 1972, translated from the French by Annette Lavers.

5.7 The Precession of Simulacra (1981)

[Extracts]
JEAN BAUDRILLARD

Translated by Sheila Faria Glaser

The divine irreference of images

TO DISSIMULATE IS TO pretend not to have what one has. To simulate is to feign to have what one doesn't have. One implies a presence, the other an absence. But it is more complicated than that because simulating is not pretending: 'Whoever fakes an illness can simply stay in bed and make everyone believe he is ill. Whoever simulates an illness produces in himself some of the symptoms' (Littré). Therefore, pretending, or dissimulating, leaves the principle of reality intact: the difference is always clear, it is simply masked, whereas simulation threatens the difference between the 'true' and the 'false', the 'real' and the 'imaginary'. Is the simulator sick or not, given that he produces 'true' symptoms? Objectively one cannot treat him as being either ill or not ill. Psychology and medicine stop at this point, forestalled by the illness's henceforth undiscoverable truth. For if any symptom can be 'produced', and can no longer be taken as a fact of nature, then every illness can be considered as simulatable and simulated, and medicine loses its meaning since it only knows how to treat 'real' illnesses according to their objective causes. Psychosomatics evolves in a dubious manner at the borders of the principle of illness. As to psychoanalysis, it transfers the symptom of the organic order to the unconscious order: the latter is new and taken for 'real' more real than the other – but why would simulation be at the gates of the unconscious? Why couldn't the 'work' of the unconscious be 'produced' in the same way as any old symptom of classical medicine? Dreams already are.

Certainly, the psychiatrist purports that 'for every form of mental alienation there is a particular order in the succession of symptoms of which the simulator is ignorant and in the absence of which the psychiatrist would not be deceived'. This (which dates from 1865) in order to safeguard the principle of a truth at all costs and to escape the interrogation posed by simulation – the knowledge that truth, reference, objective cause have ceased to exist. Now, what can medicine do with what floats on either side of illness, on either side of health, with the duplication of illness in a discourse that is no longer either true or false? What can psychoanalysis do with the duplication of the discourse of the unconscious in the discourse of simulation that can never again be unmasked, since it is not false either?[1]

What can the army do about simulators? Traditionally it unmasks them and punishes them, according to a clear principle of identification. Today it can discharge a very good simulator as exactly equivalent to a 'real' homosexual, a heart patient, or a madman. Even military psychology draws back from Cartesian certainties and hesitates to make the distinction between true and false, between the 'produced' and the authentic symptom. 'If he is this good at acting crazy, it's because he is.' Nor is military psychology mistaken in this regard: in this sense, all crazy people simulate, and this lack of distinction is the worst kind of subversion. It is against this lack of distinction that classical reason armed itself in all its categories. But it is what today again outflanks them, submerging the principle of truth.

Beyond medicine and the army, favored terrains of simulation, the question returns to religion and the simulacrum of divinity: 'I forbade that there be any simulacra in the temples because the divinity that animates nature can never be represented.' Indeed it can be. But what becomes of the divinity when it reveals itself in icons, when it is multiplied in simulacra? Does it remain the supreme power that is simply incarnated in images as a visible theology? Or does it volatilize itself in the simulacra that, alone, deploy their power and pomp of fascination – the visible machinery of icons substituted for the pure and intelligible Idea of God? This is precisely what was feared by Iconoclasts, whose millennial quarrel is still with us today.[2] This is precisely because they predicted this omnipotence of simulacra, the faculty simulacra have of effacing God from the conscience of man, and the destructive, annihilating truth that they allow to appear – that deep down God never existed, that only the simulacrum ever existed, even that God himself was never anything but his own simulacrum – from this came their urge to destroy the images. If they could have believed that these images only obfuscated or masked the Platonic Idea of God, there would have been no reason to destroy them. One can live with the idea of distorted truth. But their metaphysical despair came from the idea that the image didn't conceal anything at all, and that these images were in essence not images, such as an original model would have made them, but perfect simulacra, forever radiant with their own fascination. Thus this death of the divine referential must be exorcised at all costs.

One can see that the iconoclasts, whom one accuses of disdaining and negating images, were those who accorded them their true value, in contrast to the iconolaters who only saw reflections in them and were content to venerate a filigree God. On the other hand, one can say that the icon worshipers were the most modern minds, the most adventurous, because, in the guise of having God become apparent in the mirror of images, they were already enacting his death and his disappearance in the epiphany of his representations (which, perhaps, they already knew no longer represented anything, that they were purely a game, but that it was therein the great game lay – knowing also that it is dangerous to unmask images, since they dissimulate the fact that there is nothing behind them).

This was the approach of the Jesuits, who founded their politics on the virtual disappearance of God and on the worldly and spectacular manipulation of consciences – the evanescence of God in the epiphany of power – the end of transcendence, which now only serves as an alibi for a strategy altogether free of influences and signs. Behind the baroqueness of images hides the éminence grise of politics.

This way the stake will always have been the murderous power of images, murderers of the real, murderers of their own model, as the Byzantine icons could be those of divine identity. To this murderous power is opposed that of representations as a dialectical power, the visible and intelligible mediation of the Real. All Western faith and good faith became engaged in this wager on representation: that a sign could refer to the depth of meaning, that a sign could be exchanged for meaning and that something could guarantee this exchange – God of course. But what if God himself can be simulated, that is to say can be reduced to the signs that constitute faith? Then the whole system becomes weightless, it is no longer itself anything but a gigantic simulacrum – not unreal, but a simulacrum, that is to say never exchanged for the real, but exchanged for itself, in an uninterrupted circuit without reference or circumference.

Such is simulation, insofar as it is opposed to representation. Representation stems from the principle of the equivalence of the sign and of the real (even if this equivalence is utopian, it is a fundamental axiom). Simulation, on the contrary, stems from the utopia of the principle of equivalence, *from the radical negation of the sign as value*, from the sign as the reversion and death sentence of every reference. Whereas representation attempts to absorb simulation by interpreting it as a false representation, simulation envelops the whole edifice of representation itself as a simulacrum.

Such would be the successive phases of the image:

it is the reflection of a profound reality;
it masks and denatures a profound reality;
it masks the *absence* of a profound reality;
it has no relation to any reality whatsoever: it is its own pure simulacrum.

In the first case, the image is a *good* appearance – representation is of the sacramental order. In the second, it is an evil appearance – it is of the order of maleficence. In the third, it plays at being an appearance – it is of the order of sorcery. In the fourth, it is no longer of the order of appearances, but of simulation.

The transition from signs that dissimulate something to signs that dissimulate that there is nothing marks a decisive turning point. The first reflects a theology of truth and secrecy (to which the notion of ideology still belongs). The second inaugurates the era of simulacra and of simulation, in which there is no longer a God to recognize his own, no longer a Last Judgment to separate the false from the true, the real from its artificial resurrection, as everything is already dead and resurrected in advance.

When the real is no longer what it was, nostalgia assumes its full meaning. There is a plethora of myths of origin and of signs of reality – a plethora of truth, of secondary objectivity, and authenticity. Escalation of the true, of lived experience, resurrection of the figurative where the object and substance have disappeared. Panic-stricken production of the real and of the referential, parallel to and greater than the panic of material production: this is how simulation appears in the phase that concerns us – a strategy of the real, of the neoreal and the hyperreal that everywhere is the double of a strategy of deterrence. [...]

The strategy of the real

The impossibility of rediscovering an absolute level of the real is of the same order as the impossibility of staging illusion. Illusion is no longer possible, because the real is no longer possible. It is the whole *political* problem of parody, of hypersimulation or offensive simulation, that is posed here.

For example: it would be interesting to see whether the repressive apparatus would not react more violently to a simulated holdup than to a real holdup. Because the latter does nothing but disturb the order of things, the right to property, whereas the former attacks the reality principle itself. Transgression and violence are less serious because they only contest the *distribution* of the real. Simulation is infinitely more dangerous because it always leaves open to supposition that, above and beyond its object, *law and order themselves might be nothing but simulation.*

But the difficulty is proportional to the danger. How to feign a violation and put it to the test? Simulate a robbery in a large store: how to persuade security that it is a simulated robbery? There is no 'objective' difference: the gestures, the signs are the same as for a real robbery, the signs do not lean to one side or another. To the established order they are always of the order of the real.

Organize a fake holdup. Verify that your weapons are harmless, and take the most trustworthy hostage, so that no human life will be in danger (or one lapses into the criminal). Demand a ransom, and make it so that the operation creates as much commotion as possible – in short, remain close to the 'truth', in order to test the reaction of the apparatus to a perfect simulacrum. You won't be able to do it: the network of artificial signs will become inextricably mixed up with real elements (a policeman will really fire on sight; a client of the bank will faint and die of a heart attack; one will actually pay you the phony ransom), in short, you will immediately find yourself once again, without wishing it, in the real, one of whose functions is precisely to devour any attempt at simulation, to reduce everything to the real – that is, to the established order itself, well before institutions and justice come into play.

It is necessary to see in this impossibility of isolating the process of simulation the weight of an order that cannot see and conceive of anything but the real, because it cannot function anywhere else. The simulation of an offense, if it is established as such, will either be punished less severely (because it has no 'consequences') or punished as an offense against the judicial system (for example if one sets in motion a police operation 'for nothing') – but *never as simulation* since it is precisely as such that no equivalence with the real is possible, and hence no repression either. The challenge of simulation is never admitted by power. How can the simulation of virtue be punished? However, as such it is as serious as the simulation of crime. Parody renders submission and transgression equivalent, and that is the most serious crime, because it *cancels out the difference upon which the law is based.* The established order can do nothing against it, because the law is a simulacrum of the second order, whereas simulation is of the third order, beyond true and false, beyond equivalences, beyond rational distinctions upon which the whole of the social and power depend. Thus, *lacking the real,* it is there that we must aim at order.

This is certainly why order always opts for the real. When in doubt, it always prefers this hypothesis (as in the army one prefers to take the simulator for a real madman). But this becomes more and more difficult, because if it is practically impossible to isolate the process of simulation, through the force of inertia of the real that surrounds us, the opposite is also true (and this reversibility itself is part of the apparatus of simulation and the impotence of power): namely, it is *now impossible to isolate the process of the real,* or to prove the real.

This is how all the holdups, airplane hijackings, etc. are now in some sense simulation holdups in that they are already inscribed in the decoding and orchestration rituals of the media, anticipated in their presentation and their possible consequences. In short, where they function as a group of signs dedicated exclusively to their recurrence as signs, and no longer at all to their 'real' end. But this does not make them harmless. On the contrary, it is as hyperreal events, no longer with a specific content or end, but indefinitely refracted by each other (just like so-called historical events: strikes, demonstrations, crises, etc.),[3] it is in this sense that they cannot be controlled by an order that can only exert itself on the real and the rational, on causes and ends, a referential order that can only reign over the referential, a determined power that can only reign over a determined world, but that cannot do anything against this indefinite recurrence of simulation, against this nebula whose weight no longer obeys the laws of gravitation of the real, power itself ends by being dismantled in this space and becoming a simulation of power (disconnected from its ends and its objectives, and dedicated to the *effects of power* and mass simulation).

The only weapon of power, its only strategy against this defection, is to reinject the real and the referential everywhere, to persuade us of the reality of the social, of the gravity of the economy and the finalities of production. To this end it prefers the discourse of crisis, but also, why not? that of desire. 'Take your desires for reality!' can be understood as the ultimate slogan of power since in a nonreferential world, even the confusion of the reality principle and the principle of desire is less dangerous than contagious hyperreality. One remains among principles, and among those power is always in the right.

Hyperreality and simulation are deterrents of every principle and every objective, they turn against power the deterrent that it used so well for such a long time. Because in the end, throughout its history it was capital that first fed on the destructuration of every referential, of every human objective, that shattered every ideal distinction between true and false, good and evil, in order to establish a radical law of equivalence and exchange, the iron law of its power. Capital was the first to play at deterrence, abstraction, disconnection, deterritorialization, etc., and if it is the one that fostered reality, the reality principle, it was also the first to liquidate it by exterminating all use value, all real equivalence of production and wealth, in the very sense we have of the unreality of the stakes and the omnipotence of manipulation. Well, today it is this same logic that is even more set against capital. And as soon as it wishes to combat this disastrous spiral by secreting a last glimmer of reality, on which to establish a last glimmer of power, it does nothing but multiply the *signs* and accelerate the play of simulation.

As long as the historical threat came at it from the real, power played at deterrence and simulation, disintegrating all the contradictions by dint of producing equivalent signs. Today when the danger comes at it from simulation (that of being dissolved in the play of signs), power plays at the real, plays at crisis, plays at remanufacturing artificial, social, economic, and political stakes. For power, it is a question of life and death. But it is too late.

Whence the characteristic hysteria of our times: that of the production and reproduction of the real. The other production, that of values and commodities, that of the belle epoque of political economy, has for a long time had no specific meaning. What every society looks for in continuing to produce, and to over-produce, is to restore the real that escapes it. That is why *today this 'material' production is that of the hyperreal itself*. It retains all the features, the whole discourse of traditional production, but it is no longer anything but its scaled-down refraction (thus hyper-realists fix a real from which all meaning and charm, all depth and energy of representation have vanished in a hallucinatory resemblance). Thus everywhere the hyperrealism of simulation is translated by the hallucinatory resemblance of the real to itself.

Power itself has for a long time produced nothing but the signs of its resemblance. And at the same time, another figure of power comes into play: that of a collective demand for *signs* of power – a holy union that is reconstructed around its disappearance. The whole world adheres to it more or less in terror of the collapse of the political. And in the end the game of power becomes nothing but the *critical* obsession with power – obsession with its death, obsession with its survival, which increases as it disappears. When it has totally disappeared, we will logically be under the total hallucination of power – a haunting memory that is already in evidence every-where, expressing at once the compulsion to get rid of it (no one wants it anymore, everyone unloads it on everyone else) and the panicked nostalgia over its loss. The melancholy of societies without power: this has already stirred up fascism, that overdose of a strong referential in a society that cannot terminate its mourning.

With the extenuation of the political sphere, the president comes increasingly to resemble that *Puppet of Power* who is the head of primitive societies (Clastres).

All previous presidents pay for and continue to pay for Kennedy's murder as if they were the ones who had suppressed it – which is true phantasmatically, if not in fact. They must efface this defect and this complicity with their simulated murder. Because, now it can only be simulated. Presidents Johnson and Ford were both the object of failed assassination attempts which, if they were not staged, were at least perpetrated by simulation. The Kennedys died because they incar-nated something: the political, political substance, whereas the new presidents are nothing but caricatures and fake film – curiously, Johnson, Nixon, Ford, all have this simian mug, the monkeys of power.

Death is never an absolute criterion, but in this case it is significant: the era of James Dean, Marilyn Monroe, and the Kennedys, of those who really died simply because they had a mythic dimension that implies death (not for romantic reasons, but because of the fundamental principle of reversal and exchange) – this era is long gone. It is now the era of murder by simulation, of the generalized aesthetic of simulation, of the murder-alibi – the allegorical resurrection of death, which is only there to sanction the institution of power, without which it no longer has any substance or an autonomous reality.

These staged presidential assassinations are revealing because they signal the status of all negativity in the West: political opposition, the 'Left', critical discourse, etc. – a simulacral contrast through which power attempts to break the vicious circle of its nonexistence, of its fundamental irresponsibility, of its 'suspension'. Power floats like money, like language, like theory. Criticism and negativity alone still secrete a phantom of the reality of power. If they become weak for one reason or another, power has no other recourse but to artificially revive and hallucinate them.

It is in this way that the Spanish executions still serve as a stimulant to Western liberal democracy, to a dying system of democratic values. Fresh blood, but for how much longer? The deterioration of all power is irresistibly pursued: it is not so much the 'revolutionary forces' that accelerate this process (often it is quite the opposite), it is the system itself that deploys against its own structures this violence that annuls all substance and all finality. One must not resist this process by trying to confront the system and destroy it, because this system that is dying from being dispossessed of its death expects nothing but that from us: that we give the system back its death, that we revive it through the negative. End of revolutionary praxis, end of the dialectic. Curiously, Nixon, who was not even found worthy of dying at the hands of the most insig-nificant, chance, unbalanced person (and though it is perhaps true that presidents are assassinated by unbalanced types, this changes *nothing*: the leftist penchant for detecting a rightist conspiracy beneath this brings out a false problem – the function of bringing death to, or the prophecy, etc., against power has always been fulfilled, from primitive societies to the present, by demented people, crazy people, or neurotics, who nonetheless carry out a social function as fundamental as that of presidents), was nevertheless ritually put to death by Watergate. Watergate is still a mechanism for the ritual murder of power (the American institution of the presidency is much more thrilling in this regard than the European: it surrounds itself with all the violence and vicissitudes of primitive powers, of savage rituals). But already impeachment is no longer assassination: it happens via the Constitution. Nixon has nevertheless arrived at the goal of which all power dreams: to be taken seriously enough, to constitute a mortal enough danger to the group to be one day relieved of his duties, denounced, and liquidated. Ford doesn't even have this opportunity anymore: a simulacrum of an already dead power, he can only accumulate against himself the signs of reversion through murder – in fact, he is immunized by his impotence, which infuriates him.

In contrast to the primitive rite, which foresees the official and sacrificial death of the king (the king or the chief is nothing without the promise of his sacrifice), the modern political imaginary goes increasingly in the direction of delaying, of concealing for as long as possible, the death of the head of state. This obsession has accumulated since the era of revolutions and of charismatic leaders: Hitler, Franco, Mao, having no 'legitimate' heirs, no filiation of power, see themselves forced to perpetuate themselves indefinitely – popular myth never wishes to believe them dead. The pharaohs already did this: it was always one and the same person who incarnated the successive pharaohs.

Everything happens as if Mao or Franco had already died several times and had been replaced by his double. From a political point of view, that a head of state remains the same or is someone else doesn't strictly change anything, so long as they resemble each other. For a long time now a head of state – *no matter which one* – is nothing but the simulacrum of himself, and *only that gives him the power and the quality to govern*. No one would grant the least consent, the least devotion to a *real* person. It is to his double, he being always already *dead*, to which allegiance is given. This myth does nothing but translate the persistence, and at the same time the deception, of the necessity of the king's sacrificial death.

We are still in the same boat: no society knows how to mourn the real, power, the *social itself*, which is implicated in the same loss. And it is through an artificial revitalization of all this that we try to escape this fact. *This situation will no doubt end up giving rise to socialism.* Through an unforeseen turn of events and via an irony that is no longer that of history, it is from the death of the social that socialism will emerge, as it is from the death of God that religions emerge. A twisted advent, a perverse event, an unintelligible reversion to the logic of reason. As is the fact that power is in essence no longer present except to conceal that there is no more power. A simulation that can last indefinitely, because, as distinct from 'true' power – which is, or was, a structure, a strategy, a relation of force, a stake – it is nothing but the object of a social *demand*, and thus as the object of the law of supply and demand, it is no longer subject to violence and death. Completely purged of a *political* dimension, it, like any other commodity, is dependent on mass production and consumption. Its spark has disappeared, only the fiction of a political universe remains.

The same holds true for work. The spark of production, the violence of its stakes no longer exist. The whole world still produces, and increasingly, but subtly work has become something else: a need (as Marx ideally envisioned it but not in the same sense), the object of a social 'demand', like leisure, to which it is equivalent in the course of everyday life. A demand exactly proportional to the loss of a stake in the work process.[4] Same change in fortune as for power: the *scenario* of work is there to conceal that the real of work, the real of production, has disappeared. And the real of the strike as well, which is no longer a work stoppage, but its alternate pole in the ritual scansion of the social calendar. Everything occurs as if each person had, after declaring a strike, 'occupied' his place and work station and recommenced production, as is the norm in a 'self-managed' occupation, exactly in the same terms as before, all while declaring himself (and in virtually being) permanently on strike.

This is not a dream out of science fiction: everywhere it is a question of doubling the process of work. And of a doubling of the process of going on strike – striking incorporated just as obsolescence is in objects, just as crisis is in production. So, there is no longer striking, nor work, but both simultaneously, that is to say something else: a *magic of work*, a trompe l'oeil, a scenodrama (so as not to say a melodrama) of production, a collective dramaturgy on the empty stage of the social.

It is no longer a question of the ideology of work – the traditional ethic that would obscure the 'real' process of work and the 'objective' process of exploitation – but of the scenario of work. In the same way, it is no longer a question of the ideology of power, but of the *scenario* of power. Ideology only corresponds to a corruption of reality through signs; simulation corresponds to a short circuit of reality and to its duplication through signs. It is always the goal of the ideological analysis to restore the objective process, it is always a false problem to wish to restore the truth beneath the simulacrum.

This is why in the end power is so much in tune with ideological discourses and discourses on ideology, that is they are discourses of *truth* – always good for countering the mortal blows of simulation, even and especially if they are revolutionary.

Notes

1. A discourse that is itself not susceptible to being resolved in transference. It is the entanglement of these two discourses that renders psychoanalysis interminable.
2. Cf. M. Perniola, *Icônes, visions, simulacres (icons, visions, simulacra)*, 39.
3. Taken together, the energy crisis and the ecological mise-en-scène are themselves *a disaster movie*, in the same style (and with the same value) as those that currently comprise the golden days of Hollywood. It is useless to laboriously interpret these films in terms of their relation to an 'objective' social crisis or even to an 'objective' phantasm of disaster. It is in another sense that it must be said that it is *the social itself that*, in contemporary discourse, *is organized along the lines of a disaster-movie script*. (Cf. M. Makarius, *La stratègie de la catastrophe* [The strategy of disaster], 115).
4. To this flagging investment in work corresponds a parallel decline in the investment in consumption. Goodbye to use value or to the prestige of the automobile, goodbye amorous discourses that neatly opposed the object of enjoyment to the object of work. Another discourse takes hold that is a *discourse of work on the object of consumption* aiming for an active, constraining, puritan reinvestment (use less gas, watch out for your safety, you've gone over the speed limit, etc.) to which the characteristics of automobiles pretend to adapt. Rediscovering a stake through the transposition of these two poles, work becomes the object of a need, the car becomes the object of work. There is no better proof of the lack of differentiation among all the stakes. It is through the same slippage between the 'right' to vote and electoral 'duty' that the divestment of the political sphere is signaled.

From *Simulacra and Simulation*, trans. S. F. Glaser, Ann Arbor: University of Michigan Press, 2006 [1994], pp. 3–7, 19–27.

5.8 Aspects: Text – space – time – body – media (1999)

HANS-THIES LEHMANN

Translated by Karen Jürs-Munby

Text
Chora-graphy, the body-text

THE NEW THEATRE CONFIRMS the not so new insight that there is never a harmonious relationship but rather a perpetual conflict between text and scene. Bernhard Dort talked about the unification of text and stage never really taking place, saying that it always remained a relationship of oppression and of compromise.[1] Being a latent structural conflict of any theatrical practice anyway, this inevitability can now become a consciously intended principle of staging. What is decisive here is not – as is often implied by the popular and unquestioned opposition between 'avant-gardist' theatre and 'text theatre' – the opposition verbal/non-verbal. The wordless dance may be boring and overly didactic while the signifying word may be a dance of language gestures. In postdramatic theatre, breath, rhythm and the present actuality of the body's visceral presence take precedence over the logos. An opening and dispersal of the logos develop in such a way that it is no longer necessarily the case that a meaning is communicated from A (stage) to B (spectator) but instead a specifically theatrical, 'magical' transmission and connection happen by means of language. Artaud was the first to theorize this. Julia Kristeva pointed out that Plato in his *Timaeus* develops the idea of a 'space' that is meant to render a logically unsolvable paradox thinkable in an 'anticipating manner', namely the paradox of having to think of being also as becoming. According to Plato, there was at the origin a conceiving, receptive (maternally connoted) 'space', not logically comprehensible and in whose womb the logos with its oppositions of signifiers and signifieds, hearing and seeing, space and time was differentiating itself in the first place. This 'space' is called 'chora'. The chora is something like an antechamber and at the same time the secret cellar and foundation of the logos of language. It remains antagonistic to logos. Yet as rhythm and enjoyment of sonority it subsists in all language as its 'poetry'. Kristeva refers to this dimension of the 'chora' in all processes of signification as the '*Semiotic*' (as distinguished from the 'Symbolic'). What is emerging in the new theatre, as much as in the radical attempts of the modernist 'langage poétique', can therefore be understood as attempts towards a *restitution of chora*: of a space and speech/discourse without telos, hierarchy and causality, without fixable meaning and unity. In this process the word will resurge in its whole amplitude and volume as sonority and as address, as a beckoning and appeal (Heidegger's 'Zu-sprache'). In such a signifying process across all positings (*Setzungen*) of the logos, it is not the destruction of the latter that is happening but its poetic – and here theatrical – deconstruction. In this sense, we can say theatre is turned into *chora-graphy*: the deconstruction of a discourse oriented towards meaning and the invention of a space that eludes the laws of telos and unity.

A history of the new theatre (and already of the modern theatre) would have to be written as the history of a mutual disruption between text and stage. From this perspective, Brecht's theses on the 'literarization' of theatre, developed in the 1920s, appear in a new light, too: they are equally, although with different intention, aimed at the presence of the written text as an interruption of the self-sufficient imagery of the stage. An interesting example for the theatrical treatment of literary text can be found in the work of Giorgio Barberio Corsetti. Corsetti, one of the most distinguished minds of the Italian avant-garde theatre, worked on Kafka for many years. His thesis, too, is: the theatre needs the *text as a foreign body*, as a 'world outside the stage'. Precisely because theatre increasingly extends its borders with the help of optical tricks and the combination of video, projections and live presence, according to Corsetti, it must not get lost in the permanent self-thematization of the 'opsis' (visual presentation). Rather, it has to refer to the text as a quality that resists the scenic image. Corsetti explicitly refers to Meyerhold, Grotowski and The Living Theatre. In his theatre works the performers do not embody particular persons. A critic described Corsetti's realization of Kafka's *Description of Struggle* as follows:

> Sometimes they – the actors – are one and the same person with three people, sometimes monsters with multiple heads and arms, ... sometimes only an element, a 'building block' in a complicated body machine, sometimes a projected film 'shadow' of a person takes on a surreal life of its own.[2]

The unreal room evoked in Kafka's text finds its correspondence in tilting boxes, revolving walls, steep staircases the actors are having to struggle up, and the alternation of shadow play and corporeal presence. Interior and exterior intertwine just as in Kafka's text. Theatre here does not interpret individuals and the narrative threads of a text but articulates its language as a disturbing reality on stage, which for its part is inspired by the text's idiosyncrasies.

The *principle of exposition* applied to body, gesture and voice also seizes the language material and attacks language's function of representation. Instead of a linguistic *re*-presentation of facts, there is a 'position' of tones, words, sentences, sounds that are hardly controlled by a 'meaning' but instead by the scenic composition, by a visual, not text oriented dramaturgy. The rupture between being and meaning has a shock-like effect: something is exposed with the urgency of suggested meaning – but then fails to make the expected meaning recognizable. The idea of an exposition of language seems paradoxical. Nevertheless, since Gertrude Stein's theatre texts – if not earlier – we have the example of a language that loses its immanent teleological temporality and orientation towards meaning and becomes like an *exhibited object*. Stein achieves this through techniques of repeating variations, through the uncoupling of immediately obvious semantic connections, and through the privileging of formal arrangements according to syntactic or musical principles (similarities in sound, alliterations, or rhythmic analogies).

Apart from collage and montage, the principle of polyglossia proves to be omnipresent in postdramatic theatre. Multilingual theatre texts dismantle the unity of national languages. In *Roman Dogs* (1991) Heiner Goebbels created a collage made up of spirituals, texts by Heiner Müller in German and by William Faulkner in English (*The Sanctuary*), and French Alexandrine verses from Corneille's *Horace* (performed by the actress Cathérine Jaumiaux). These verses were being sung more than recited, the language perpetually tipping over from beautiful perfection into broken stuttering and noise. Theatre asserts a polyglossia on several levels, playfully showing gaps, abruptions and unsolved conflicts, even clumsiness and loss of control. Certainly the employment of several languages within the frame of one and the same performance is often due to the conditions of production: many of the most advanced creations of theatre can only be financed through international co-productions, so even for pragmatic reasons it seems obvious to bring the languages of the participating countries to prominence. But this polyglossia also has immanent artistic reasons. Rudi Laermans has pointed out that for Jan Lauwers it is not enough to state that his theatre is multilingual. For this circumstances does not explain why his performers have to use sometimes their mother tongue but sometimes also a foreign language, so that the 'difficulty with language communication' arises not just for the spectators. Lauwers establishes a shared *space of language problems* in which the actors as well as the spectators experience the blockades of linguistic communication.

Frequently we are made aware of the physical, motoric act of speaking or reading of text itself as an *unnatural, not self-evident* process. In this principle of understanding the *speech act as action*, a split emerges that is important for postdramatic theatre: it provokes by bringing to light that the word does not belong to the speaker. It does not organically reside in his/her body but remains a *foreign body*. Out of the gaps of language emerges its feared adversary and double: stuttering, failure, accent, flawed pronunciation mark the conflict between body and word. In the reading-performances of Theater Angelus Novus, however, the sheer duration of the *Iliad* reading (22 hours) entailed that after a certain time the sensual and vocal sound world of speech seemed to separate from the people reading. The words were floating in space by themselves like the sound of certain Tibetan 'singing bowls' as you circle their rim – like an autonomous sonorous body that hovers above it in the air. Jacques Lacan has advanced the thesis that the voice (just like the gaze) belongs to the fetishized objects of desire that he refers to with the term '*objet a*'. The theatre presents the voice as the object of exposition, of an erotic perception – which produces all the more tension when it contrasts so drastically with the horrifying content of battle descriptions, as in the case of the Homer reading.

Textscape, theatre of voices

A term that could capture the new variants of text should carry the connotation of the 'spacing' understood in the sense of Derrida's 'espacement': the phonetic materiality, the temporal course, the dispersion in space, the loss of teleology and self-identity. I have chosen the term 'textscape' because it designates at the same time the connection of postdramatic theatre language with the new dramaturgies of the visual and retains the reference to the landscape play. Text, voice and noise merge in the idea of a *soundscape* – but of course in a different sense than in classical stage realism (e.g. Stanislavsky's stagings of Chekhov's plays). By contrast to the latter, the postdramatic 'audio landscape' Wilson talks about does not mimetically represent reality but creates a space of association in the mind of the spectator. The 'auditive stage' around the theatre image opens up 'intertextual' reference to all sides or complements the scenic material through musical motifs of sound or 'concrete' noise. In this context, it is illuminating that Wilson occasionally remarked that his ideal of theatre was the union of silent film and radio play. This, he said, was a matter of opening the frame. For the respective other sense – the imaginary seeing in the radio play, the imaginary hearing in silent film – a boundless space opens up. When we are watching (a silent film), the auditive space is boundless, when we are listening (to a radio play) the visual space is boundless. While watching a silent movie, we imagine voices of which we can only see the physical realization: mouths, faces, the facial expressions of the people listening, etc. When listening to a radio play we imagine faces, figures and shapes for the disembodied voices. What we are talking about here is that the space of the stage and the more comprehensive sound space together create a third space that comprises the scene *and* the theatron.

From sense to sensuality is the name of the shift inherent to the theatrical process. And it is the phenomenon of the live *voice* that most directly manifests the presence and possible dominance of the sensual *within* sense/meaning itself and, at the same time, makes the heart of the theatrical situation, namely the *co-presence of living actors*, palpable. Owing to an illusion constitutive to European culture, the voice seems to be coming directly from the 'soul'. It is sensed as the quasi-unfiltered mental, psychic and spiritual charisma of the 'person'. The speaking person is the *present person* par excellence, a metaphor of the 'other' (in the sense used by Emmanuel Levinas) appealing to the responsibility of the spectators – not to a hermeneutics. The spectators find themselves exposed to the 'meaningless' (*sinnfrei*) presence of the speaker as a question addressed to them, to their gaze as corporeal creatures. But often postdramatic theatre does not so much aim to make us hear the one voice of the one subject but rather realizes a *dissemination* of voices, which incidentally is by no means exclusively tied to electronically or otherwise 'technically' arranged fragmentations. We find the *choral* bundling and the *desecration* of the word; the exposition of the *physis* of the voice (in screaming, groaning, animal noises) and the architectonic *spatialization*. Whether we think of Schleef, Fabre and Lauwers, of Matschappej Discordia, Theatergroep Hollandia, La Fura dels Baus or Théâtre du Radeau – simultaneity, polyglossia, chorus and 'scream arias' (Wilson) contribute to the text, frequently becoming a semantically irrelevant libretto and a sonorous space without firm boundaries. The boundaries between language as an expression of live presence and language as a prefabricated material are blurred. The reality of the voice itself is thematized. It is arranged and made rhythmic according to formal musical or architectonic patterns; through repetition, electronic distortion, superimposition to the point of incomprehensibility; the voice exposed as noise, scream and so on; exhausted through mixing, separated from the figures as disembodied and *misplaced voices*.

Traditionally, the vocal sound as an aura around a body, whose truth *is* its word, promised nothing less than the subjectively determined identity of the human being. Hence, playing with the new media technologies that decompose the presence of the actor and especially his/her corporeal and vocal unity is no child's play. The electronically purloined voice puts an end to the privilege of identity. If the voice was classically defined as the most important instrument of the player, it is now a matter of the whole body 'becoming voice'. An explicit experience of the auditive dimension emerges when the tightly sealed whole of the theatre process is decomposed, when sound and voice are separated and organized according to their own logic, when the body-space, the scenic space and the space of the spectator are divided, redistributed and newly united by sound and voice, word and noise. Between the body and the geometry of the scene, the sonic space of the voice is the unconscious of spoken theatre (*Sprechtheater*). The theatre of drama, the *mise en scène* of textual meaning, does not bring the auditive semiotics to prominence in its own right. Reduced to transporting meaning, the word is deprived of the possibility to sketch a sonic horizon that can only be realized theatrically. In postdramatic theatre, however, the electronic and corporeal/sensory disposition newly discovers the voice. As it makes the presence of the voice the basis of an auditive semiotics, it separates it from meaning, conceiving of the sign-making as a *gesticulation of the voice* and listening to the echoes in the dungeons of the literary palaces. This is a *sonoanalysis* of the theatrical unconscious: behind the slogans the scream of the body, behind the subjects the vocal signifiers. It is not 'I' but 'it' that is speaking, namely through/as a complex machinized composition (Deleuze's 'agencement'). Thus, in the work of John Jesurun the stage becomes an environment of light structures and auditive structures. From the very first moment, a text machine of voices, words and associations is working at rapid speed with lightning fast responses and connections, practically without pause. Fragments of a plot can be intuited. From the field of indeterminacies individual dialogues, disputes, declarations of love, etc. become discernible. Political and private matters mix. Jesurun's theme – communication, the uncanniness of language – conveys itself through the form more than the content. In his work, too, the voices are often 'purloined' through invisible microphones and heard from elsewhere. Sentences fly back and forth, orbit, or create fields, which produce interferences with what is visually presented. Who is speaking just now? One discovers the moving lips, associates the voice with the image, reassembles the fragmented parts, and loses them again. Just as the gaze moves back and forth between body and video image, reflecting on itself in order to find out where fascination, eroticism or interest attach themselves – i.e. experiencing itself as a video gaze – thus the hearing constructs another space inside the optical space: fields of references, lines crossing the barriers. Beyond the lost sentiment, precisely in the machinism, at points of rupture, the longing for communication suddenly articulates itself, the distress at the impossibility (difficulty, hope) of breaking through the wall, the sonic wall of untranslatable languages. A 'human' moment flares up, the whole subject is momentarily found when the gaze has located the voice and returns it to the body – the moment of the human. Then the mechanism of sounds, reactions, electric particles, image and soundtracks takes over again.

Space
Dramatic and postdramatic space
In general it can be said that dramatic theatre has to prefer a 'medium' space. Tendentially dangerous to drama are the huge space and the very intimate space. In both cases, the structure of the *mirroring* is jeopardized. For the stage frame functions like a mirror that ideally allows a homogeneous world of the viewers to recognize itself in the equally coherent world of the drama. A theatre, on the contrary, in which not the transmission of signs and signals but what Grotowski called 'the proximity of living organisms'[3] dominates perception, runs counter to the distance and abstraction essential to drama. If one reduces the distance between performers and spectators to such an extent that the physical and physiological proximity (breath, sweat, panting, movement of the musculature, cramp, gaze) masks the mental signification, then a space of a tense *centripetal* dynamic develops, in which theatre becomes a moment of *shared energies* instead of transmitted signs. The other threat to dramatic theatre is the vast space with a *centrifugal* effect. This can be a space that outweighs or overdetermines the perception of all other elements simply through its enormous dimensions (e.g. the Berlin Olympia Stadion in

Grüber's *Winterreise*) or a space that eludes being mastered by perception because actions simultaneously take place in different locations, as in 'integrated' theatre. Common to all open forms of space beyond drama is that the visitor becomes more or less active, more or less voluntarily a co-actor. The solo performance of *K.I. from Crime and Punishment* staged by Kama Ginka (as seen in 1997 in Avignon) turned the space that only had a few fragmentary props into a scene of real address of the present spectators. They were individually contacted, taken by the hand, asked for help and drawn into the playful hysteria of the actress (Okzana Mysina) playing (with) the figure of Katerina Ivanova from Dostoevsky's novel. The blurring of the borderline between real and fictive experience to such an extent has far-reaching consequences for the understanding of the theatre space: it turns from a metaphorical, symbolic space into a *metonymic space*. The rhetorical figure of metonymy creates the relationship and equivalence between two givens by means of letting one part stand in for the whole (*pars pro toto*: he's a bright mind) or by using an external connection (e.g. Washington denies . . .). In this sense of a relationship of metonymy or contiguity, we can call a scenic space metonymic if it is not primarily defined as symbolically standing in for another fictive world but is instead highlighted as a part and *continuation* of the real theatre space.

In classical theatre, the distance covered on stage by an actor signifies as a metaphor or symbol a fictive distance, perhaps the distance Grusha travels through the Caucasus mountains. In a metonymically functioning space the distance covered by an actor first represents a reference to the space of the theatre situation, thus referring as *pars pro toto* to the real space of the playing field and *a fortiori* of the theatre and the surrounding space at large.

By contrast, as a *tableau* the stage space deliberately and programmatically closes itself off from the theatron. The closeness of its internal organization is primary. The theatre of Robert Wilson is exemplary for the effects of the stage as tableau. It has justly been compared to the tradition of the *tableau vivant*. In painting the frame is part of the tableau. Wilson's theatre is a primary example for the use of frames. A bit like in baroque art, everything begins and ends here – with framings. Framing effects are produced, for example, by special lighting surrounding the bodies, by geometrical fields of light defining their places on the floor, by the *sculptural precision* of the gestures and the heightened concentration of the actors that have a 'ceremonial' and thus again framing effect.

Another form of postdramatic space can be found in the works of Jan Lauwers. Here, bodies, gestures, postures, voices and movements are torn from their spatio-temporal continuum, newly connected, isolated, and assembled into a tableau-like montage. The habitual hierarchies of dramatic space (the site of the face, of the meaningful gesture, of the confrontation of the antagonists) become obsolete and with them a 'subjectivized' space, a space arranged by the subject-I. In the face of the playing field that is dissected into individual heterogeneous parts, the viewer has the impression of being led back and forth between parallel sequences as in a film. The procedure of *scenic montage* leads to a perception reminiscent of *cinematic montage*. Here one organizational principle can be highlighted that is also peculiar to classical painting: the actors on stage repeatedly behave *like spectators* watching what other performers are doing. Thus, a peculiar focusing on the observed action develops and it functions analogously to the 'direction of the gaze' (*Blickregie*) in classical paintings, which through the gazes of the represented figures traces in advance the 'optic path' for the viewer.

Yet another strategy can be observed in Pina Bausch's work where the space is an autonomous co-player of the dancers, seemingly marking their dance time by commenting on the physical processes. In *Nelken*, the field of thousands of carnations is trampled underfoot, even though the dancers initially try carefully not to tread on the flowers. In this way, the space functions *chronometrically*. At the same time, it becomes a *place of traces*: the events remain present in their traces after they have happened and passed, time becomes denser. Another possibility of bringing the space to life is the process of 'spatializing' the physical actions with the help of a sonic space created with microphones and loudspeakers. For example, the heartbeat of the dancers becomes audible by means of a heart sound amplifier, or their heavy exhalation and inhalation are amplified through a microphone and fill the space. Charged by physical energy, such immediately spatialized *body-time* aims to communicate directly with the spectators' nervous system, not to inform them. The spectators do not observe but experience themselves inside of a time-space.

Outside of the conventional theatre space there are possibilities described as *site specific theatre*, a term originally used in visual arts. Theatre here seeks out an architecture or other location (in the early works of the company Hollandia it was the flat land) – not so much, as the term 'site specific' might suggest, because the site corresponds well to a certain text but because it is made to 'speak' and is *cast in a new light* through theatre. When a factory floor, an electric power station or a junkyard is being performed in, a new 'aesthetic gaze' is cast onto them. The space presents itself. It becomes a co-player without having a definite significance. It is not dressed up but made visible. The spectators, too, however, are co-players in such a situation. What is namely staged through site specific theatre is also a level of *commonality* between performers and spectators. All of them are *guests of the same place*: they are all strangers in the world of a factory, of an electric power station or of an assembly hangar. Similarly as in visual arts, and above all in Performance Art, we often find works whose motor is the *activation of public spaces*. This can take on very different forms. The company Station House Opera under the artistic direction of Julian Maynard Smith seeks the connection with everyday life. To this purpose it conceives of theatre as developing awareness of architectural processes (e.g. in their architectural performances using breeze blooks in various locations). Theatre opens up in a different way in a project with the title *Aufbrechen Amerika* that Christof Nel, Wolfgang Storch and Eberhard Kloke realized in 1992 (on the Quincentenary of the 'discovery' of America) in and around Bochum. Spread out over three days, this was a mixture of eccentric 'journeys' by bus, train and ship through the heterogeneous diversity of the industrial landscape between Bochum, Duisburg, Gelsenkirchen and Mülheim. The region and its everyday environment mutated into a vast scene. A theatre that has long found its centre elsewhere than in the staging of a fictive dramatic world also includes the *heterogeneous space*, the space of the everyday, the wide field that opens up between framed theatre and 'unframed' everyday reality as soon as parts of the latter are in some way scenically marked, accentuated, alienated or newly defined.

Time

Postdramatic aesthetics of time

Theatre is familiar with the *time dimension of the staging* peculiar to it. While the text gives the reader the choice to read faster or slower, to repeat or to pause, in theatre the specific time of the performance with its particular rhythm and its individual dramaturgy (tempo of action and speech, duration, pauses and silences, etc.) belongs to the 'work'. It is a matter of the time no longer of one (reading) subject but of the shared time of many subjects (collectively spending time). In this way, a physical, sensual reality of the experience of time is inseparably interwoven with a mental reality, namely the aesthetic 'concretization' of what is indented in the performance (as Pavis says following Ingarden). *L'Age d'Or* by Théâtre du Soleil (1975) was a milestone in post-war theatre history, narrating in individual stations the life of an Algerian immigrant worker (family scenes, conflicts at work, etc.) in the representational style of *Commedia dell'Arte*. The vast hall of the Cartoucherie in Vincennes was divided into four large dells, carpeted in a warm ochre tone, on whose 'slopes' the audience sat looking at the performance in the respective 'valley'. From one scene to another, the audience was led into a different dell, a transition that caused the formation of ever new groups and seating arrangements. The intensity and fictional density of the play, which transported the audience into the 'other time' in spite of and because of its epic techniques, also came about through numerous stunning inventions. One example: the worker, who despite a heavy storm has to work on a high scaffold, falls off it to his death. The way the performer, simply standing there, managed to make the position of the body high up above the abyss 'visible' by the way he spread his legs and anxiously looked down; the way he showed the storm by rhythmically pulling on his trouser legs so that they appeared to be fluttering terrifyingly as in a heavy storm; the way his long fall took place as a great run through the hall with outstretched arms; this was one of the moments of great theatre magic. At the end of the performance a remarkable thing happened: as the curtains were pulled aside, a very bright light shone in from outside. It was actually superbly imitated daylight, yet the fact that the spectators had lost all sense of time caused many of them to look at their watches – as if it could already be early morning without them having realized the passing of so many hours. For one precious moment of confusion, one could really believe this to be possible: the 'other' time of the staging had asserted itself against the reality of people's inner clock.[4]

Fictive action *and* staging are familiar with another dimension that cuts across the temporal levels mentioned here, namely *historical time*. It is significant for all dramatic theatre working with older texts and feeding on the realization of past figures and stories. For theatre reception, however, this differentiation remains theoretical, for here an amalgamation develops that merges the heterogeneous levels of time into *one and only one* time of theatre experience. Even sophisticated structures such as the 'play within a play', anachronism and time-collage are of far less importance for the theatre than for the text. The real time of live performance comes into play to such an extent that it overdetermines all theoretically distinguishable levels of time. Compared to the historical time represented in the drama, the time of drama (story and plot) and the temporal structure of the staging, we have to emphasize the *time of the performance text*.[5] Following Schechner, we designate the total real and staged situation of the performance as 'performance text' in order to emphasize the impulse of presence always inherent to it, an impulse that also motivates Performance Art in the narrower sense. Included in this are so-called 'external factors' (which in fact they are not) such as long journeys to get to the performance, late, e.g. nocturnal, performance times, performance durations over several days or throughout a whole night until daybreak (e.g. Peter Brook's *Mahabharata* in a quarry near Avignon, which lasted from late afternoon until morning). It is thus generally important to analyse the 'real time' of the theatre process in its entirety, its fore and after play and its accompanying circumstances: the circumstance that its reception in a very practical sense 'takes up' time, 'theatre time' that is life time and does not coincide with the time of the staging.

The core of drama was the human subject in conflict, in a 'dramatic collision' (Hegel). This essentially constituted the self through an intersubjective relationship with the antagonist. We can say the subject of dramatic theatre only exists in the space of this conflict. In this respect, it is pure intersubjectivity and through conflict constituted as a *subject of rivalry*. The time of intersubjectivity, however, has to be a homogeneous time, one and the same time unifying the enemies in conflict. Dramatic theatre requires one time in which the opponents, agonist and antagonist, can meet at all. The temporal perspective of the individual, isolated subject (as in lyricism or monology) does not suffice here, and neither does the comprehensive time of a world context in which the collision takes place (as in the epic). One recognizes the perspective of our description: once the kind of intersubjectivity we are discussing – let's call it the duel – does not work, the binding intersubjective temporal form becomes obsolete, too. And inversely: inasmuch as the shared homogeneous time becomes confused or disintegrates, the duellists can no longer find each other, so to speak; they get lost in particles acting on different plateaux unrelated to each other. The 'crisis of drama' (Szondi) around the turn of the century was essentially a crisis of time. The transformations in the scientific image of the world (relativity, quantum theory, space-time) contributed to this as much as the experience of a chaotic mixture of the different speeds and rhythms of the metropolis and new insights into the complex temporal structure of the unconscious. Bergson distinguishes experienced time as 'durée' from objective time ('temps'). The increasingly apparent divergence of the time of social processes (mass society, economy) from the time of subjective experience intensified the 'dissociation of world time and life time' Blumenberg observed about modernity. Blumenberg sees this dissociation caused by the expanded historical perspective onto past and future and the subject's concomitant new experience of 'an image of history of such spaciousness and expansiveness that the individual life no longer seems to have any significance in it'.[6] Louis Althusser has turned the irreducible 'alterity' between the time of the social dialectic and the subjective experience of time into the basic model of any 'materialist' and critical theatre, whose task would be to shake 'ideology' in the sense of a subject-centred perception and miscognition of reality.[7] In Kant's work, the function of the 'inner sense' was to guarantee the unity of self-consciousness through the form of a 'temporal order' (*Zeitordnung*). He defined time as the 'form of the inner sense'; this form backs the coherence of the changing representations – which would otherwise pulverize consciousness – with the persistent continuum of time that Kant represents in analogy to the line. This linear continuum ultimately supports the unity of the subject because it lends direction and orientation to the experiences, which are radically discontinuous among themselves. However, at the latest since Nietzsche and since Freud theorized the discourse of the unconscious, identity as an immemorial familiarity of the continuous subject with itself has come under the suspicion of being a chimera. In modernity, the subject – and with it the intersubjective mirroring through which it could continually enhance itself – loses its ability to integrate the representations into a unity. Or, to put it the other way round: the disintegration of time as a continuum proves to be a sign of the dissolution – or at least subversion – of the subject possessing the certainty of its time.

At the end of the 1950s, one began to observe parallel developments in Informel painting, Serial music and dramatic literature, which amounted to a rejection of traditionally constructed totalities. We can diagnose the loss of the *time frame*. When Stockhausen in the 1960s envisioned that visitors to a concert could arrive later and leave earlier or when Wilson caused a stir by stipulating 'intermissions at your discretion', this epitomized an essential tendency of the new dramaturgies of time. They suspend the unity of time with beginning and end as the *enclosing frame* of the theatre fiction in order to gain the dimension of the *time 'shared'* by the performers and the audience as a processuality that is on principle open and has structurally neither beginning, nor middle, nor end. Aristotle had demanded precisely these, however, as a basic rule for drama, so that a whole ('holon') could come about. The new concept of *shared* time regards the aesthetically shaped and the real experienced time as a single cake, so to speak, shared by visitors and performers alike. The idea of time as an experience shared by all constitutes the centre of the new dramaturgies of time: from the diverse distortions of time to the assimilation of the speed of pop; from the resistance of slow theatre to theatre's convergence with Performance Art and its radical assertion of *real time* as a situation people live through together.

The basis of dramatic theatre was the demand that the spectators leave their everyday time to enter a segregated area of 'dream time', abandoning their own sphere of time to enter into another. In epic theatre the 'filling in of the orchestra pit' (Benjamin) signifies a shared level of reflection. Brecht wanted the thinking and the smoking spectator, where smoking was meant to be a sign of the spectators' distanced dispassionateness, precisely not a manifestation of *one* shared temporal space. Brecht's spectators precisely do not immerse themselves into a 'being in the here and now' that is emotionally merged with the events on stage (this would be the identification with the dramatic events) but they lean back and smoke, distanced in 'their own time'. While it does not seek illusion either, the postdramatic aesthetic of real time signifies, however, that the scenic process cannot be separated from the time of the audience. Again the contrast between the epic and the postdramatic gesture is clearly apparent. If time becomes the object of 'direct' experience, logically it is especially the techniques of time distortion that come to prominence. For only an experience of time that deviates from habit provokes its explicit perception, permitting it to move from something taken for granted as a mere accompaniment to the rank of a theme. Thus, a new phenomenon in the aesthetics of theatre is established: the intention of utilizing the specificity of theatre as a mode of presentation to turn *time as such* into an object of the aesthetic experience.

Consciously noticeable duration is the first important factor of time distortion in the experience of contemporary theatre. Elements of a *durational aesthetic* can be witnessed in numerous contemporary works of theatre. The *prolongation of time* is a prominent trait of postdramatic theatre. Robert Wilson created a 'theatre of slowness'. Only since Wilson's 'invention' can we speak of a proper aesthetics of duration. The visual object on stage seems to store time in it. The passing time turns into a 'Continuous Present', to use the words of Wilson's role model Gertrude Stein. Theatre becomes similar to a kinetic sculpture, turning into a *time sculpture*. This is true in the first instance for the human bodies, which turn into kinetic sculptures through slow motion. But it is also for the theatrical tableau as a whole, which owing to its 'non-natural' rhythm creates the impression of having a time of its own – midway between the achronia of a machine and the traceable and palpable lifetime of human actors, who attain here the gracefulness of marionette theatre.

Alongside the durational aesthetic, an *aesthetic of repetition* has developed. Hardly any other procedure is as typical for postdramatic theatre as repetition – we only need to mention Tadeusz

Kantor, the extreme repetition in some ballets by William Forsythe, the works of Heiner Goebbels and of Erich Wonder where repetition is an explicit theme. As in duration, a crystallization of time occurs in repetition, a more or less subtle compression and negation of the course of time itself. Certainly rhythm, melody, visual structure, rhetoric and prosody have always used repetition: there is no musical rhythm, no composition of an image, no effective rhetoric, no poetry and, in short, no aesthetic form without purposefully employed repetition. In the new theatre languages, however, repetition takes on a different, even opposite meaning: formerly employed for structuring and constructing a form, it is now used for the destructuring and deconstructing of story, meaning and totality of form. If processes are repeated to such an extent that they can no longer be experienced as part of a scenic architecture and structure of organization, the overtaxed recipient experiences them as meaningless and redundant, as a seemingly unending, unsynthesizable, uncontrolled and uncontrollable course of events. We experience the monotonous noise of a surge of signifiers that have been drained of their communicative character and can no longer be grasped as a part of a poetic, scenic or musical totality of a work: a negative postdramatic version of the sublime. On closer inspection, however, even in theatre, there is no such thing as true repetition.[8] The very position in time of the repeated is different from that of the original. We always see something different in what we have seen before. Therefore, repetition is also capable of producing a new attention punctuated by the memory of the preceding events, *an attending to the little differences*. It is not about the significance of the repeated events but about the significance of repeated perception, not about the repeated but about repetition itself. *Tua res agitur*: the temporal aesthetic turns the stage into the arena of reflection on the spectators' act of seeing. It is the spectators' impatience or their indifference that becomes visible in the process of repetition, their paying attention or their reluctance to delve deeper into time; their inclination or disinclination to do justice to and make space for differences, for the smallest thing, and for the phenomenon of time by immersing themselves into the self-alienating act of seeing.[9]

The static effect of theatre beyond dramatic movement, which is produced through duration and repetition, thus has the remarkable consequence that *the focus on 'image-time'*, i.e. the disposition of perception peculiar to the viewing of images, enters the perception of theatre. Just like theatre, the visual arts had earlier taken the step of turning their factual, material reality into the dominant factor of their constitution and consequently also 'imposed' the temporality of the image onto reception: what emerged was the demand on the viewer to realize not simply the temporality of the represented but the temporal aspects of the image itself. Following Gottfried Boehm, let us assume that the image as a 'form of relations' exhibits an 'image time' (*Bildzeit*) that is specific only to it. It appeals to the temporal sense of the viewers to retrace, resense, continue, and in short to 'produce' the movement that is immobilized and *latent* in the image. The image initially appears to be 'without time'. Yet through their own sense of time, imagination, empathy and the capacity to relate physically to sequences of movements, the viewers come to know the temporal movement in the image. It 'supplements' their own seeing (in the case of realistic representations of moving object or figures), repeats it, or rather produces it in the first place (in the case of non-representational or heavily abstracted imagery). Under the banner of visual dramaturgy, the perception of theatre no longer simply prepares for a 'bombardment' of the sensory apparatus with moving images but, just as in front of a painting, activates the dynamic capacity of the gaze to produce processes, combinations and rhythms on the basis of the data provided by the stage. As the visual semiotics seems to want to stop theatre time and to transform the temporal events into *images for contemplation*, the spectators' gaze is invited to 'dynamize' the durational stasis offered to them through their own vision. The result is a hovering of perceptional focus between a 'temporalizing' viewing and a scenic 'going along', between the activity of seeing and the (more passive) empathy. In this way, postdramatic theatre effects a displacement of theatrical perception – for many provocative, incomprehensible, or boring – turning from abandoning oneself to the flow of a narration towards a constructing and constructive co-producing of the total audio-visual complex of the theatre.

By contrast to the strategies of deceleration, immobilization and repetition, other postdramatic forms of theatre attempt to adopt and even surpass the speed of media time. We could mention here the references to the *aesthetic of video clips*, combined with media quotes, a mixture of live presence and recordings or the segmentation of theatrical time as in television series. The works of younger theatre practitioners of the 1990s in particular develop this style, not letting themselves be discouraged by the potential proximity of their work to multi-media spectacles and show business but taking up the media patterns as material they make use of, more or less satirically and mostly at high speed. Thanks to radio, television and the internet, reality from all parts of the world can be integrated into the performance, putting the spectators in contact with people far away from the actual site of performance. What would otherwise remain trivial as a mere demonstration of media communication, in the context of theatre manifests the latent conflict between the moment of life and the surface of virtual electronic time. In the work of Jürgen Kruse the integration of pop and media quotes leads to interesting interpretations of drama, the Danish company Von Heyduck integrates film illusion, and the plays of younger directors like René Pollesch, Tim Staffel, Stefan Pucher or companies like Gob Squad build on the speed of the aesthetic of pop and media. The *simultaneity* that becomes dominant here is one of the major characteristics of the postdramatic shaping of time. It produces speed. The simultaneity of different speech acts and video imports produces the interference of different rhythms of time, bringing body time and technological time into competition with one another (as in the work of John Jesurun or Station House Opera's *Mare's Nest*); and through the uncertainty of whether an image, sound or video is produced live or reproduced with a time delay, it becomes clear that time is 'out of joint' here, always 'jumping' between heteronomic spaces of time. The principle of consciousness to lend continuity and identity to experience through repetition is undermined.

The unity of time

In more than one respect the rule of the unity of time was essential to the Aristotelian tradition of dramatic theatre. Perhaps it referred in the beginning to the unity of a trial and hearing court – Adorno once called ancient tragedy a 'hearing without a judgment'. Even where an external unity of time was not sought (as, for example, in Elizabethan theatre), theatre was governed by the ideal of organic closeness, which had to have consequences for the representation of time. To be distinguished from this are those dramaturgies that transformed the understanding of theatre in the twentieth century. Brecht's concept of 'non-Aristotelian drama', coined in the 1930s, distinguished the epic theatre not so much from the classical rules of dramatic theatre but from the aim of the spectator's 'catharsis' through empathy. Part of the design of epic theatre is a dramaturgy of leaps in time that point to human reality and behaviour as discontinuous:

The modern spectator does not wish to be patronized and violated (namely through 'all kinds of emotional states'), he rather wants to be presented simply with human material *in order to arrange it himself*. This is why he also loves to see the human being in situations that are not self-explanatory; and this is why he needs neither the logical justifications nor the psychological motivations of the old theatre.

And further:

The relations of people in our time are not clear-cut. Therefore, the theatre has to find a form of representing this lack of clarity in as classical a form as possible, that is in epic serenity.[10]

While Brecht privileges jumps and cuts at all levels, the logical and the temporal, in Aristotle the central importance of the unity of time is to guarantee the unity of action as a coherent totality. No jumps and digressions must occur that could cloud clarity and confuse understanding. Rather, a recognizable logic shall reign without interruption. Important in this context is the already quoted remark in chapters 6 and 7 of Aristotle's *Poetics* that is rarely as appreciated as it deserves to be, namely that the dramatic action has to have a certain magnitude – in the sense of a temporal expansion. Aristotle here uses a strange comparison of the action with an animal (only comprehensible in the light of the idea of the organic unity and totality of action). The beautiful, he says – and it is worth quoting the passage again – depends not solely on the arrangement but also on the right magnitude:

For this reason no organism could be beautiful if it is excessively small (since observation becomes confused as it comes close to having no perceptible duration in time) or excessively large (since the observation is then not simultaneous [*hama*], and the observers find that the sense of unity and wholeness is lost from their observation, e.g. if there were an animal a thousand miles long).[11]

What is the meaning of this seemingly grotesque comparison of an animal of a length of 1,000 miles, at the extrme limit of perceptibility? What is at stake is the *avoidance of confusion* and the '*at once*' (Greek 'hama'). The form – beauty, organic harmony – has to be perceivable to the intuition without a time delay, in one beat, at one glance. Applied to dramatic action this means that its coherent logic and wholeness (holon) must not elude the spectator. Therefore, the argument goes, the action has to be condensed in such a way that it remains 'eusynopton' – easily surveyable – and simultaneously easy to remember: 'eumnemoneuton'.

A clear overview, the absence of confusion and the reinforcement of logical unity are needed. Without them, nothing beautiful can come about. In the name of this ideal of 'surveyability', the right length of dramatic action is determined according to the time it takes for a reversal, a peripeteia, to take place. A rise and a fall, in other words: *time of the logic of a reversal*. Drama brings logic and structure into the confusing plethora and chaos of being – this is why, for Aristotle, it has a higher status than historiography, which only reports the chaotic events. It is essentially the unity of time that has to support the unity of this logic that is meant to manage without confusion, digression and rupture. One aspect of this concept of the unity of time, that remains only implicit in Aristotle, is this: to the same degree as time and action attain an internal coherence, seamless continuity and totality of surveyability, this same unity draws a distinct line between drama and the external world. It safeguards the closed structure of tragedy. Gaps and leaps in the internal continuum of time, on the other hand, would immediately function as points of intrusion for external reality. Internal coherency and closure towards external reality are complementary aspects of this uniform theatrical time. The aesthetic pleasure must not be without order – to be avoided, for example, are collective ritual ecstasy or excessive 'mimetic' behaviour threatening to lead to affective fusion. The Aristotelian concept of the unity of dramatic time thus seeks (1) to demarcate a sealed off sphere of the aesthetic with its own artistic time, (2) to conceive of an experience of beauty that constitutes it as analogous to rationality. The imperatives of internal continuity, coherency, organic symmetry and temporal surveyability all serve to promote this analogy. In contrast, Aristotle clearly realizes the highly emotional effect of the theatre – eleos and phobos are violent affects. Catharsis is meant to tame them by means of a kind of framing through the logos.

Regardless of its philosophical implications, Aristotle's *Poetics* was a pragmatic and descriptive text. In modern times, however, its observations were reinterpreted as normative rules, the rules as prescriptions, and the prescriptions as laws – description was turned into prescription. During the Renaissance there was still a rivalry between a neo-Platonic notion of art oriented towards the 'poetic furor' and an Aristotelian notion of art oriented towards rationality and rules. The Aristotelian line won out and came to define the ideas of theatre in modern times, above all in classicism. Pierre Corneille's *Discours sur les trois unités* explains in 1660 that the playwright should try to achieve an identity between the represented time and the time of the theatrical representation. This rule, he explains, is dictated not just by Aristotle's authority but simply by 'natural reason'. The dramatic poem ('poème dramatique') is for Corneille without any question an imitation or more precisely a *portrait* of human actions ('une imitation, ou pour en mieux parler, un portrait des actions des hommes'). This comparison is striking. Corneille immediately makes it serve the main argument: the perfection of a portrait, he says, is measured – 'hors de doute' (without a doubt) – by its similarity with the original. As far as the function of the unity of time is concerned, the significant keyword comes up at the point where Corneille argues why after all the represented time must not be longer than the time of the representation, original and 'portrait' having to be as alike as possible in this respect, too. Corneille gives one special reason why we aspire to this identity: namely, for fear of falling into a state without rules ('de peur de tomber dans le dérèglement').[12] The pragmatic and technical identity of represented time and time of representation is not the real motivation for the unity of time but rather the *fear of deregulation* and confusion. The reason for the rule is – the assertion of the rule itself. What is at stake is the prevention of confusion, the prevention of a free-roaming imagination uncontrolled by the dramatic process, the prevention of the outbreak of the imagined reception in Lord knows what other spatial and temporal spheres.

The comprehension of longer time spans in drama, according to Corneille, should be regulated in such a way that greater lapses in time, if inevitable, be placed *between* the acts. The thematization of real time is avoided altogether by not referring to exact dates and times in the spoken text. Likewise, reports about events occuring prior to the stage action are to be minimized in order not to overload the spectator's memory and intellectual power.[13] As a preferably perfect double of reality and, at the same time, as an entity of suggestive rationality and coherence, theatre needs the unity of time, the concentration on the present and the exclusion of multi-layered spaces of time. The unity creates a continuity that is meant to make invisible any split between fictive time and real time. For any rupture in the structure of time, we read, would harbour the danger that the spectator becomes aware of the difference between original and copy, reality and image, and is – inevitably – steered towards *his* time, the real time. Then, without any control, he could let his imagination run wild, reflect, occupy himself with reasoning or else dream. The temporal structures of the Aristotelian tradition are not simply an innocent and nowadays outdated framework but rather an essential part of a powerful tradition against whose normative efficacy the contemporary theatre continually has to assert itself – even if nobody still adheres to the norm of the unity of time in any formal sense. The basic aesthetic and dramaturgical conceptions of this tradition can be deciphered as definitions and containments of reception, as an attempt to structure the mode of imagination, thought and feeling in theatre. Within it, the unity of time has the value of a decisively important symptom. We have here focused on Aristotle and Corneille. Yet in the eighteenth century, too, under the banner of the so-called 'natural signs' the poetics of theatre continues to be working on the control and formation of the imagination, including the physical habitus.

The complementary aspects of the unity of time – continuity on the inside, isolation from the outside – have been and still are the basic rules not only of theatre but also of other narrative forms, as a side glance at Hollywood films with their ideal of the 'invisible cut' would quickly prove. We could conclude that the Aristotelian tradition of the dramaturgy of time pursued not least of all this aim: *to prevent the appearance of time as time*. Time as such is meant to disappear, to be reduced to an unnoticeable condition of being of the action. And the rules for its treatment ultimately served the purpose that it remained unnoticed. Nothing was to release the spectator from the spell of the dramatic action. The true meaning of the Aristotelian aesthetics of time is not aesthetic. Rather the unity of time in theatre – as a continuity of the fictive time of the drama and the time of the performance – points to a much more profound *fantasy image, a phantasm of continuity*. Theatre is meant to reflect and intensify the social continuum of interaction and communication, the continuum of a socio-symbolic context of ideals, values and conventions. Inversely: if theatre presupposes the rupture of this deeper continuity, the unity of time will cease, too – not just in drama but also in the reality of the performance text.

Body
Postdramatic images of the body
Cultural notions of what 'the' body is are subject to 'dramatic' changes, and theatre articulates and reflects these ideas. It represents bodies and at the same time uses bodies as its main signifying material. But the *theatrical body* does not exhaust itself in this function: in theatre it is a value *sui generis*. Nevertheless, before modernism the physical reality of the body remained in principle incidental. The body was a gratefully accepted given. It became the manifestation of the 'domination of nature applied to the human being' (Rudolf zur Lippe); it was disciplined, trained and formed to serve as a signifier; but it was not an autonomous problem and theme of the dramatic theatre, where as such it rather remained a kind of *sous-entendu*. This is not surprising considering that drama essentially came about as an abstraction from the density of the material world through the 'dramatic' concentration on 'spiritual' conflicts – by contrast to the epic's love

for concrete detail. Before modernism, physicality was explicitly thematized only in exceptional cases that confirm the rule of its discursive marginalization: the phallus of ancient comedy, Philoctetes' pain, the torture and agony in Christian theatre, Gloucester's hump, Woyzeck's illness. In modernism, however, sexuality, pain and disease, physical difference, youth, old age, skin colour (Wedekind, Jahnn) become 'presentable' themes for the first time. The 'marriage of man and machine' (Heiner Müller) began in the historical avant-gardes with couplings between the organic and the machinic. It continues under the banner of new technologies and takes hold of the human body in a comprehensive manner: wired up to information systems, the body breeds new phantasms in postdramatic theatre, too. While the spatial organization of Schlemmer's *Triadic Ballet* or the arrangement of the surface in Mondrian's paintings implied the utopian perspective of a rational social organization, the technically mediated machines of desire and terror in contemporary theatre lack this (dramatic) utopian trait. Instead one finds variations of a *technically infiltrated body*: cruel images of the bodies between organism and machinery.

Modernist theatre and postdramatic theatre gain new potentials from overcoming the semantic body. A characteristic factor of the theatre now comes into its own, to which the following formula applies: sensuality undermines sense. It required the emancipation of theatre as a proper dimension of art in order to grasp that the body did not have to content itself with being a signifier but could be an *agent provocateur* of an experience without 'meaning', an experience aimed not at the realization of a reality and meaning but at the experience of potentiality. As such, by pointing only to its own presence in an auto-deixis, the body opens the pleasure and fear of a gaze into the paradoxical emptiness of possibility. Theatre of the body is a *theatre of potentiality* turning to the unplannable 'in-between-the-bodies' and bringing to the fore the potential as a threatening dispossession (as Lyotard theorizes it in the concept of the sublime) and simultaneously as a promise.

The dramatic process occured *between* the bodies; the postdramatic process occurs *with/ on/to* the body. The mental duel, which the physical murder on stage and the stage duel only translate metaphorically, is replaced by physical motor activity or its handicap, shape or shapelessness, wholeness or fragmentation. While the dramatic body was the carrier of the agon, the postdramatic body offers the image of its *agony*. This prevents all representation, illustration and interpretation with the help of the body as a mere medium. The actor has to offer himself. Valère Novarina remarks: 'The actor is no interpreter because the body is no instrument.' He dismisses the idea of a 'composition' of a dramatic person through the actor, opposing it with the formula that it is rather the *decomposition of the human being* that is happening on stage.[14] The concept of theatrical communication *qua* body changes drastically. One could say that the dynamic that used to maintain the drama as a form of development has moved into the body, into its 'banal' existence. A *self-dramatization of physis* takes place. The impulse of postdramatic theatre to realize the intensified presence ('epiphanies') of the human body is a quest for *anthropophany*. From this basic position, a series of diverse images of the body arise that all point to the reality that exists only in theatre, namely the *theatrical reality (das TheatReale)*.

Not by coincidence, it is in dance that the new images of the body are most clearly visible. In dance we find most radically expressed what is true for postdramatic theatre in general: it articulates not meaning but energy, it represents not illustrations but actions. Everything here is gesture. Previously unknown or hidden energies seem to be released from the body. It becomes its own message and at the same time is exposed as the most profound *stranger of the self*: what is one's 'own' is *terra incognita*. This is evident in ritual cruelty exploring the extremes of what is bearable or when phenomena that are alien and uncanny to the body are brought to the surface (of the skin): impulsive gesticulations, turbulence and agitation, hysterical convulsions, autistic disintegrations of form, loss of balance, fall and deformation. Just as the new dance privileges discontinuity, the different members (*articuli*) of the body take precedence over its totality as a *Gestalt*. The renunciation of the 'ideal' body in the work of William Forsythe, Meg Stuart or Wim Vandekeybus is highly visible. There are no heightening costumes, unless they are used ironically. The novel postures do not exclude falling, rolling about, lying or sitting; contortions, gestures like shrugging one's shoulders, the integration of language and the voice, a novel intensity of physical contact (Meg Stuart).

Among the series of images of the body that can be considered as symptomatic for postdramatic theatre is the *technique of slow motion*, which is omnipresent in the wake of Wilson's work. It cannot be reduced to a merely external visual effect. When physical movement is slowed down to such an extent that the time of its development itself seems to be enlarged as through a magnifying glass, the body itself is inevitably *exposed* in its concreteness. It is being zoomed in on as through the lens of an observer and is simultaneously 'cut out' of the time–space continuum as an art object. At the same time, the motor apparatus is *alienated*: every action (walking, standing, getting up and sitting down) remains recognizable but is changed, as never seen. The act of striding along is decomposed, becoming the lifting of a foot, advancing of a leg, sliding shift of weight, careful coming down of the sole. The scenic 'action' (walking) takes on the beauty of a purposeless *pure gesture*.

But what do we mean by gesture? Above all, we have abandoned the sphere of purposive means: walking not as a means for displacing the body but not as an end in itself either (aesthetic form). Dance, for example, is gesture, according to Giorgio Agamben, 'because it consists entirely in supporting and exhibiting the media character of physical movement. *The gesture consists in exhibiting a mediality, in rendering a means visible as such.*' In this description following Walter Benjamin, the body and its gestic essence are articulated as a dimension in which all 'potential' remains in the 'act', in suspense, in a 'pure milieu' (Mallarmé). Gesture is that which remains unsublated in any purposive action: an excess of potentiality, the phenomenality of visibility that is blinding, so to speak, namely surpassing the merely ordering gaze – having become possible because no purposiveness and no tendency to illustrate weakens the real of space, time and body. The postdramatic body is a body of gesture, understood as follows: 'The gesture is a potential that does not give way to an act in order to exhaust itself in it but rather remains as a potential in the act, dancing in it.'[15]

In the work of Societas Raffaello Sanzio the sculptural aesthetic is noticeable. This astonishing company, one of the most important experimental Italian theatre companies, began in 1981. For every project a new ensemble is assembled around the core of the group, the siblings Romeo and Claudia Castellucci. They often integrate people with an 'abnormal' physicality or a physicality modified by disease. 'Every body has its own tale', explains Romeo Castellucci. It is a matter of the return of the body as an incomprehensible and simultaneously unbearable reality. Important productions are *Santa Sofia – Teatro Khmer* (1985), *Gilgamesh* (1990), *Hamlet – the Vehement Exteriority of the Death of a Mollusk* (1992), *Masoch* (1993), *Oresteia* (1995) and *Giulio Cesare* (1997).

In *Oresteia* there is an abundance of quotes from visual arts: an actor is chosen because he is long and spindly like a figure by Giacometti. Another is dressed in white with white make-up so that he is reminiscent of the sculptures by George Segal and he sometimes takes on the postures and attitudes of Kafka's drawings. Clytemnestra is played by an actress who literally seems to be a mountain of flesh coloured in red, reclining in a fairytale-like melting immobility. As a corporeal sign her heaviness communicates her power, yet the immediately sensual impression devoid of any interpretation remains dominant. Cassandra is locked into a box-like framework, her features distorted through frosted glass, so that one seems to be looking at a painting by Francis Bacon. Theatre here exists in closest proximity to the visual arts.

The live, trembling human sculpture, the movement sculpture between torpor and vitality, leads to the exposure of the spectator's voyeuristic gaze onto the performer. When the sculptural motif returns in the theatre of the 1980s and 1990s, it is under completely different premises than in classical modernism. The ideal turns into a motif of anxiety. The body is not exhibited for the sake of its closeness to a classical ideal but for the sake of a painful confrontation with imperfection. The attraction and aesthetic dialectic of the classical sculptures of bodies consists not least of all in the sense that the living human being cannot compete with them. In the here and now of the exchange of looks between audience and stage, by contrast, the ageing and degenerating body is subjected to an unsparing exposition. The performer balances on a knife edge between a metamorphosis into a dead exhibition piece and her self-assertion as a person. In a certain way, the performer also presents herself *as a victim*: without the protection of the role, with the fortification of the idealizing serenity of the ideal, the body in its fragility and misery is also surrendered to the tribunal of judging gazes as an offer of erotic stimulation and provocation. From this victim position, however, the postdramatic sculptural body image can turn into an act of aggression and of challenging the audience. As the performer faces him as an individual, vulnerable person, the spectator becomes aware of a reality that is masked in traditional theatre, even though it inevitably adheres to the gaze's relationship to the 'scene': to the *act of seeing* that is voyeuristically applied to the exhibited performer as if she was a sculptural object.

Theatre that rejects the dramatic model can retrieve the possibility of returning to things their value and to the human actors the experience of 'thing-ness' that has become alien to them. At the same time, it gains a new playing field in the sphere of machines, which connects human beings, mechanics and technology – from Kantor's bizarre machines of love and death to high tech theatre. Heiner Müller noticed about Wilson's theatre the 'wisdom of fairy tales that the history of humans cannot be separated from the history of the animals (plants, stones, machines)'. It seemed to anticipate 'the unity of man and machine, the next step in evolution'.[16] It seems indeed that the ever accelerating technologization and with it the tendency of a transformation of the body from 'destiny' to controllable and selectable apparatus – a programmable techno-body – announces an *anthropological mutation* whose first tremors are registered more precisely in the arts than in quickly outdated judicial and political discourses.

Pain, catharsis

Theatre has always been fascinated by pain, even if this traditionally has not had a good press in aesthetics compared to the more ideal suffering. Since antiquity, pain, violence, death and the feelings of fear and pity provoked by them have been at the 'root of the pleasure in tragic objects'

(Schiller). In the evocation of the unpresentable that pain constitutes, we encounter a central problem of theatre: the challenge to actualize the incomprehensible by means of the body, which itself *is* 'pain memory' because culture and 'pain as the most powerful mnemonic aide' (Nietzsche) have been inscribed in it in disciplining ways. The mimesis *of* pain initially means that torture, agony, physical suffering and pain are imitated and deceptively suggested, so that painful empathy with the *played* pain arises in the spectators. Postdramatic theatre, however, is above all familiar with 'mimesis *to* pain' ('Mimesis *an* den Schmerz' – Adorno): when the stage is becoming like life, when people really fall or really get hit on stage, the spectators start to fear for the players. The novelty resides in the fact that there is a transition from *represented pain* to *pain experienced in representation*. In its moral and aesthetic ambiguity it has become the indicator for the question of representation: exhausting and risky physical actions on stage (La La La Human Steps); exercises that often appear paramilitary (some dance theatre; Einar Schleef); masochism (La Fura dels Baus); the ethically provocative play with the fiction or reality of cruelty (Jan Fabre); the exhibition of diseased or disfigured bodies. A theatre of *bodies in pain* causes a schism for the perception: here the represented pain, there the playful, joyful act of its representation that is itself attesting to pain.

It is hardly a coincidence that we find in contemporary theatre a persistent return to the metaphor of the world as a hospital or delusional world, a world to which there is no alternative but the equally catastrophic withdrawal into solipsistic isolation. As in the work of Beckett and Heiner Müller, we find people in wheelchairs in the productions of *Dionysus* (1990) and *Elektra* (1995) by the Japanese director Tadashi Suzuki who stages strictly formalized, procession-like images of hell. The Catalonian group La Fura dels Baus places the audience into claustrophobically enclosed, demonic scenarios of agony that seem to be inspired by Dante's *Inferno*: naked bodies submerged in what looks like boiling water and oil, hanged, fallen and maltreated; fire flaring up everywhere, tied up people being flayed and whipped, torturers shouting out orders within a pandemonium of drumming, howling and screaming. While the dramatic theatre conceals the process of the body in the role, postdramatic theatre aims at the public exhibition of the body, its deterioration in an act that does not allow for a clear separation of art and reality. It does not conceal the fact that the body is moribund but rather emphasizes it. When the actor Ron Vawter shortly before his death (he died of AIDS) played two homosexuals in a double portrait, it was impossible to determine whether the sudden pauses in his performance were due to moments of 'acted' or real exhaustion. In the works of Reza Abdoh, who died of AIDS at a young age, the historical, theatrical and mediated ghosts entered into a symbiosis between show and provocation, bloody Grand Guignol and abysmal mourning. His theatre was baroque: displaying a brutal direct sensuality and the search for transcendence, a lust for life and the confrontation with death. Sarajevo, a hospital, and the frightening spectacle of a petty bourgeois interior became the 'writing on the wall' of a world emptied of meaning in which coldness, pain, disease, torture, death and depravity reign.

Media

In the theory of avant-garde theatre it has become commonplace to say that it analyses, reflects and deconstructs the conditions of seeing and hearing in the society of the media. Regardless of the cogency of this statement, it is to be doubted that the self-referentiality of the theatre works in question is really primarily driven by such a pathos of analysis which is more at home in theoretical efforts. Rather it seems realistic that an aesthetic is manifesting itself here that seeks proximity to an artificially changed perception. The often falsely 'dramatized' problem, that the seemingly limitless possibilities of reproduction, presentation and simulation of realities through media information technologies (supported by the universal medium of the computer) were leaving the representational possibilities of the theatre far behind, does *not* constitute the real explosive force of the question of the relationship between theatre and media. Theatre *per se* is already an art form of *signifying*, not of mimetic copying. (A tree on stage, even if it looks very real, remains a *sign* for a tree, not the reproduction of a tree, while a tree in film may mean all sorts of things as a sign but is above all a photographic reproduction of a tree.) Theatre does not simulate but obviously remains a concrete reality of the place, the time, the people who produce signs in the theatre – and these are always signs of signs.[17] What is a real cause of concern for the theatre, however, is the emerging transition to an *interaction* of distant partners by means of technology (at present still in the primitive stages of development). Will such an increasingly perfected inter-action in the end compete with the domain of the theatrical live arts whose main principle is *participation*? The point of theatre, however, is a communication structure at whose heart is not the process of a feedback of information but a different 'way of meaning what is meant' (Benjamin's 'Art des Meinens') which ultimately includes death. Information is outside of death, beyond the experience of time. Theatre, by contrast, in as much as within it sender and receiver age together, is a kind of 'intimation of mortality' – in the sense implied by Heiner Müller's remark that 'the potentially dying person' is what is special about theatre. In media communication technology the hiatus of mathematization separates the subjects from each other, so that their proximity and distance become irrelevant. The theatre, however, consisting of a shared time–space of mortality, articulates as a performative act the necessity of engaging with death, i.e. with the (a)liveness of life. Its themes are, to use Müller's words, the terrors and joys of transformation, while film is watching death at work. It is basically this aspect of the shared time–space of mortality with all its ethical and communication theoretical implications that ultimately marks a categorical difference between theatre and technological media.

Media in postdramatic theatre

We can roughly distinguish between different modes of media use in theatre. Either media are *occasionally* used without this use fundamentally defining the theatrical conception (mere media employment); or they serve as a source of *inspiration* for the theatre, its aesthetic or form without the media technology playing a major role in the productions themselves; or they are *constitutive* for certain forms of theatre (Corsetti, Wooster, Jesurun). And finally theatre and media art can meet in the form of *video installations*. Many directors use media on a case-by-case basis – as for example Peter Sellars in his London staging of Shakespeare's *Merchant of Venice* – without this defining their style. Particularly for a director who counts as 'postmodern', it is par for the course. Other theatre forms are primarily characterized not by the employment of media technology but by an *inspiration* through media aesthetic that is recognizable in the aesthetic of the staging. Among these are the rapid succession of images, the speed of conversation in shorthand, the gag consciousness of TV comedies, allusions to the popular entertainment of television, to film and television stars, to the day-to-day business of the entertainment industries and their movers and shakers, quotes from pop culture, entertainment films and controversial topics in the public sphere of the media. In these forms a parodic and ironic refraction of the media is predominant, but sometimes only the themes of the media are adopted. What is postdramatic about these attempts is that the quoted motifs, gags or names are not placed inside the frame of a coherent narrative dramaturgy but rather serve as musical phrases in a rhythm, as elements of a scenic image collage. René Pollesch showed in *Harakiri einer Bauchrednertagung* (*Harakiri of a Ventriloquist Convention*) and *Splatterboulevard* (1992) how entirely without drama the continually churned out dialogue punch lines form a text for which screwball comedy and sitcom serve as models. Accomplished taste-lessness, perpetual circling in a state of desolate listlessness and parodic media appropriations here produce their own *pop-theatre* atmosphere. In 1996 Stefan Pucher collaborated with the English company Gob Squad to produce the performance *Ganz nah dran* (*Close up*) at the Frankfurt TAT. Here the media repertoire, which influences the speech, gestures and emotional patterns of everyday life, was theatrically exhibited. A large part of the performance consisted in the self-presentations of the performers, which made it difficult to discern the 'real' biographical elements.

The work of The Wooster Group can serve as an example of the use of media as *constitutive* for certain forms of theatre. As a means of problematizing self-reflection, the electronic images in their 'post-epic' theatre refer directly to the everyday reality and/or the theatre process of the *players*. At most, they quote visual material – in *Hairy Ape*, for instance, a boxing match in which a white guy is fighting a black guy – as a *mental* extension of the stage, not as a document. It is therefore logical that video technology tends to be used for the co-presence of video image and live actor, functioning in general as the technically mediated *self-referentiality* of the theatre. It is a central element in the work of The Wooster Group, a company that originally emerged from Schechner's Performance Group and was named after the group's home in the Performance Garage located in Manhattan's Wooster Street. Theatre here demonstrates its technical possibilities dissected into individual components. The theatre machinery is clearly visible. The technical workings of the performance are openly exhibited: cables, apparatus, instruments are not shame-fully hidden or masked by lighting but integrated like props or almost like actors in their own right. The performers often imitate the affectations of television moderators. In *Brace Up!* based on Chekhov's *Three Sisters* a narrator (Kate Valk) guides us through the performance but also speaks text by figures who are not at that moment represented by other performers, introduces actors (for example the very old performer Beatrice Roth playing the youngest of the three sisters), and gives stage directions. During the performance debates may develop over whether a certain passage should be skipped or not – in short: what is shown is somewhere between a rehearsal and a performance, making the *production* of theatre visible and repeatedly addressing itself to the audience as in television. Particularly characteristic is the use of video in order to integrate absent performers, according to the motto: Michael Kirby can't be here tonight but we show him as a video image; one performer is too old to take part in the tour, we show her in the video. Very casually the illusions of the theatre and the familiar but actually quite amazing equal weighting of video presence and live presence are thus highlighted.

Theatre can also create 'virtual spaces' with its own means, as for example in the works of Helena Waldmann who in the 1990s attracted attention through a series of inventive theatrical 'viewing arrangements'. In the performance of *Wodka konkav*, the audience is seated opposite a wall and below several large, concave mirrors. When the performance starts, dancing bodies, who are not directly physically visible, appear in the mirrors, multiplied by them and partially distorted. In the multiple indirect reflection they look so similar that the spectators are long in doubt – some until the very end – about whether they are dealing with one body somehow doubled through the mirrors, two bodies, or more. Moreover, one can only see the images of the bodies – obviously dancing behind the wall – as they are mirrored at an angle from above, in addition to the multiple reflections there are also peculiar contractions, fragmentations, optical deformations that also unite with psychedelic bodiless figures of light. Added to this spectacle that removes the living body from view while simultaneously thematizing the gaze onto the body one hears from the loudspeakers a text by the Russian author Venedikt Jerofejev (spoken by the actor Thomas Thieme) which revolves exclusively around vodka and drunkenness. When at the end the two dancers – there really are two and they are twins! – step out in front of the wall for a 'curtain call' their presence seems the most natural thing – and yet they had been there, present in such a multiply fractured and refracted way that the question about representation becomes labyrinthine: what does presence consist of? What presents itself to the audience if not a presence that crosses itself out? This seems to be the case, but what can be experienced here is rather this: presence is the effect not simply of perception but of the *desire* to see. The withdrawal calls to mind what the perception of the 'present' body had actually also been: the hallucination of an absent other body, an imago equally invested with desire and rivalry and thus open to all variants of deadly conflicts and of Eros' promises of happiness. Moreover, it shows what the perception of the present body is also: not the perception of presence but the *consciousness* of presence, neither in need of sensuous confirmation, nor ultimately capable of it. It is obvious that this kind of theatre, even more so than traditional theatre productions, defies reproduction through film or television. Not because of the beauty of the live presence but because the (technically reproduced) image would level the layers and divisions between physical, imaginary and mental presence on which everything depends here.

Electronic images as a relief

One question media theatre poses for the spectator is this: why is it the image that fascinates us more? What constitutes the magic attraction that seduces the gaze to follow the image when given the choice between devouring something real or something imaginary? One possible answer is that the image is removed from real life, there is something liberating about the appearance of the image, which gives pleasure to the gaze. The gaze liberates desire from the bothersome 'other circumstance' of real, really producing bodies and transports it to a dream vision.

> Television, video cassettes, video tape recorders/players, video games, and personal computers all form an encompassing electronic representational system whose various forms 'interface' to constitute an alternative and absolute world that uniquely *incorporates* the spectator/user in a spatially decentered, weakly temporalized, and quasi-disembodied state ... Indeed, the electronic is phenomenologically experienced not as a discrete, intentional, and bodily centered *projection* in space but rather as a simultaneous, *dispersed*, and insubstantial *transmission* across a network ... Living in a schematized and intertextual meta-world far removed from all reference to a 'real' world liberates the spectator/user from what might be termed the latter's moral and physical gravity. The postmodern and electronic 'instant', in its break from the temporal structures of retension and pretension, constitutes a form of presence (one abstracted

from the continuity that gives meaning to the system past/present/future) and changes the nature of the space it occupies … In an important sense, electronic space *disembodies* … electronic 'presence' has neither a point of view nor a field of vision.[18]

In the face of such a seductive superiority of the virtual image world of cyborg, internet, virtual reality, etc., the question is: where can a practice that refuses such a 'relief' find a foothold? How can the scaled down model of the theatre situation turn the nature of seeing itself into the object of conscious perception? How can the disposition of the viewing subject as it experiences itself everywhere in media technology become visible itself? Paradoxically the answer is: in another version of the virtual itself.

Theatre-bodies cannot be captured by any video, because they are only 'there' in the 'between-the-bodies' of live performance. In this insecurity and forlornness, they store memory: they actualize (and appeal to) corporeal experience. And they store future, for what they remind us of is desire as something unfulfilled and unfulfillable. This is where the alternative to the electronic images resides: art as a theatrical process that actually preserves the virtual dimension, the dimension of desire and not knowing. Theatre is first of all anthropological, the name for a *behaviour* (playing, showing oneself, playing roles, gathering, spectating as a virtual or real form of participation), secondly it is a *situation*, and only then, last of all, is it *representation*. Media images are – in the first and in the last place – nothing but representation. The image as represention gives us a lot, to be sure: especially the feeling of being always on the track of something else. We are hunters in search of the lost treasure. Always 'in the picture', we are on the scent of a secret – but in doing so at any moment already 'content at the end' because we are satisfied by the image. The reason for this is that the electronic image lures through emptiness. Emptiness offers no resistance. Nothing can block us. Nothing stagnates. The electronic image is an idol (not simply an icon). The body or face in video is enough – for itself and for us. By contrast, an air of (productive) disappointment always surrounds the presence of real bodies. It is reminiscent of the air of mourning that, according to Hegel, surrounds the ancient Greek sculptures of gods: their all too complete and perfect presence allows for no transcendence of materiality to a more spiritual interiority. Similarly, one can say of the theatre: after the body there is nothing else. We have arrived. Nothing can be or become more present. Within any fascination with the live body there remains this invariably only desired 'rest' that we cannot get access to, a beyond the frame, a background. The gaze remains before the visibility of the real body like Kafka's man 'before the law'. There is nothing but this one gate and we cannot get through it because the object of desire is always elsewhere, (in the) background, never a presence as a form of being. In this way, the body in theatre is a signifier (not the object) of desire. The electronic image, by contrast, is pure foreground. It evokes a fulfilled, superficially fulfilled kind of seeing. Since no aim or desire enters consciousness as the background of the image, there can be no lack. The electronic image *lacks lack*, and is consequently leading only to – the next image, in which again nothing 'disturbs' or prevents us from enjoying the plenitude of the image.

'Representability', fate

A figure enters the stage. It interests us because the frame of the stage, of the staging, of the action, and of the visual constellation of the scene exhibits it. The peculiar suspense that accompanies its viewing is the curiosity about an impending explanation (that fails to occur). The restless suspense only lasts as long as there is still a remnant of this open question. The figure in its presence is nevertheless – absent. Shall we say: virtual? It remains *theatrical* only in the rhythm and to the degree of a certain not-knowing that keeps the perception in its searching motion. It is the dimension of not-knowing in theatrical perception (every figure is an oracle) that accounts for its constitutive virtuality. Theatre is real virtuality. For the theatrical gaze the body on stage turns into an 'image' in another sense of the word – not into an electronic image as it has been discussed here but into an 'image' in the sense of the term used by Max Imdahl. He postulates in a 'radical conjecture', as Bernhard Waldenfels stresses, the 'possibility of a withdrawal of reality in seeing itself' and calls image (in the emphatic sense) an occasion when a seeing takes place that leads to the invisible with seeing eyes:

> But perhaps the image is also a form of representation for something else, namely the illustrative model for a reality that withdraws forever from any immediate, as well as final, grasp – a reality to which it, as something visible, refers, and which itself has no appearance.[19]

Thus understood, the 'image' is about 'the experience of an insurmountable powerlessness to dispose' over reality. This insight helps us to analyse more precisely the *withdrawal of representation* in theatre that makes sure the spectator's seeing is not deceived by the illusion of the availability of the visible (an illusion inherent to the electronic image). Inherent to the curious gaze in theatre is the expectation that it will 'at one point' see the other. But this gaze does not reach for ever more distant unreal spaces but circles inside itself, pointing inwards, towards the clarification and visibility of the figure that nevertheless remains an enigma. Therefore this gaze is accompanied by a sense of lack instead of fulfilment. Naturally, this hope cannot be fulfilled because plenitude only persists in the question, in the curiosity, in the expectation, the non-appearance, the memory, not in the 'present' reality of the object. The figure of the other in theatre always has a reality only of *arrival*, not presence. In the light of the virtual objective – the 'representation' in its plenitude – we may call this essence of the theatrical figure its '*representability*' (*Darstellbarkeit*). Compared to this, the electronic images, which bridge the emptiness, fulfil the wish and deny the border, are realizations of *representation* (*Darstellung*). This requires some further explanation.

Walter Benjamin's essay on translation defines 'translatability' as the inherently necessary determination of certain texts. They imply translatability even if they were never actually going to be adequately translated. In the same text, Benjamin writes about the 'unforgettableness' of events, which can be called unforgettable even if all people had forgotten them but if it was in their essence not to be forgotten. According to Benjamin, they would still be the object of a memory, which he interprets as God's memory. In a similar sense, 'representability' can be thought of as an essential dimension of theatre. What ancient tragedy already articulated was the thought that there must be some coherence inhering in a human's life, a *Gestalt* that remains inaccessible to his/her own knowledge, however. This coherence is representable and visible only from a totally different perspective unattainable for the mortal human, namely that of the 'gods'. This inner logic is there, despite the fact that the discourse of ancient tragedy does not deny the accidental, chance nature that humans share with all other creatures and circumstances but rather highlights it in an extreme manner. Despite the human being's subjection to Chaos and Tyche, ancient tragedy insists that *representability* in this sense should be thought of as an inherent quality of its existence as a speaking creature. Namely in this sense: life never attains such representation but in being articulated theatrically its 'representability' appears. This truth about life is not 'given' at any moment, at any 'date', because it corresponds to its nature, to use Benjamin's words, to be represented in a *different* sphere. The mediated pictures, by contrast, are *nothing but data* (the given). In theatre, the actor is the interference (*Bildstörung*, literally 'picture trouble'). Electronic pictures, by contrast, evoke the image of fulfilment, the phantasm of 'immediate contact' with the desired. In theatre, what is perceived is not 'given' but only giving. It is arriving, an event that is an advent, and it depends upon the answer from chorus and audience in what Heiner Müller called an 'incandescent circuit'. In this circuit, the signifiers are only ever 'taken on' and all involved are called upon to pass them on: from the represented they come to the performer, from the performer to the visitors, and from these back to the performer. 'Representability' is inherent in this temporal process, remaining in irreconcilable tension with all fixed representations, which it traverses.

It may appear strange to introduce at this point the perhaps oldest theatre trick, namely what we are used to calling *fate*. Yet, it may actually be helpful to state for the theatre that *fate is another word for representability*. The electronic image, understood as the sphere of representation, is essentially a perpetual affirmation of 'fatelessness'. Representability as an experience that is simultaneously aesthetic and ethical is the manifestation of fate, the main theme of tragic theatre. However, while the dramatic theatre inspired by the ancient model relegated fate to the frame of a narration, the course of a fable, in postdramatic theatre it is articulated not through a plot but through the appearance of the body: fate here speaks through the gesture, not through myth. Aristotle (and in his wake almost the entire Western theory of the theatre) demands that tragedy has to be a whole with beginning, middle and end. Of course this was a paradoxical concept, since in reality – even in narrated reality – such a 'beginning', i.e. something that according to Aristotle has no presuppositions, simply does not exist; and neither does an 'end', i.e. something that has no consequences. What Aristotle articulates here, however, in his only seemingly self-evident formula, is nothing but the abstract formula for the *law of all representation*. The whole with beginning, middle, and end is the *frame*. It is to no avail, however, that each representation tries – and must try – to assert such framing. Fate (or representability) transcends the frame – in the same sense as human life transcends the biological life through the plethora and self-reflecting multiplication and intensification of images of it. Representability, the inner logic of theatrical reality, thus by no means contradicts the insight that human reality can only be dealt with under the premise that it remains unrepresentable.

The mediated image does know the possibility of representation in the sense of a mathematization that is in principle limitless. The question of a constitutive representability that always remains virtual does not come up here. The medium closes into a circuit of mathematical assumptions, existent givens, plain evidences. Representation is here a euphemism for information. Lyotard declared in 1979 in *The Postmodern Condition* that under the conditions of a generalized communication technology anything that cannot take the form of information would be excluded from the knowledge of society. This fate could hit theatre, for 'theatre' – in the emphatic and ideal sense that has been discussed here – actually works precisely the other way round, transferring all information into something else, namely into virtuality. It turns even representation into representability. What the spectators really see in front of them is already transformed into the mere sign, indication of an indeterminate possibility, thus at the same time leaving the sphere of beholding, transforming each perceived form into an index for one that is being missed. 'Theatre' transforms even the most simple representation of death into an unthinkable virtuality. Conversely, the electronic image allows and demands to see even the most impossible things. There is no void of another efficacy here, only evident reality. We are perhaps, quite possibly, already on the way to the images, our eyes meeting nothing but variations of the ideal of fatelessness, the Word Perfect of virtual communication. We do not know, for this fate, too, does not appear in any possible representation but will only have been. As Heiner Müller says: 'Nothing is the way it stays'.

Notes

1. B. Dort, *La représentation émancipée*, Arles: Actes Sud, 1988, p. 173.
2. D. Polaczek about Corsetti's *Beschreibung eines Kampfes* (*Description of a Struggle*), in *Frankfurter Allgemein Zeitung*, 3 February 1992.
3. Compare J.-J. Roubine, *Théâtre et mise en scène 1880-1980*, Paris: Presses Universitaires de France, 1980, p. 107.
4. For further details on this performance, see S. Seym, *Das Théâtre du Soleil: Ariane Mnouchkines Asthetik des Theaters*, Stuttgart: Metzler, 1992, esp. pp. 91-100.
5. Aston and Savona differentiate (1) 'Time present: the location of the spectator in the "here and now" of the fictional universe', (2) 'Chronological time: the linear time sequence of the story (fabula)', (3) 'Plot time: the structuring or ordering of events from the chronological time' (2) in order to shape the 'here and now' of (1), and (4) 'Performance time: the spectator in the theatre is aware there is a finite period of time for the events to take their course'. See A. Aston and G. Savona, *Theatre as Sign System: A Semiotics of Text and Performance*, London: Routledge, 1991, pp. 27–9. While the first three categories in this differentiation concern dramatic theatre, the fourth category of 'performance time' seems too narrowly conceived and would have to be subdivided into the time/rhythm of the actual staging and the time of the whole performance text as a theatre-going event.
6. H. Blumenberg, *Lebenszeit und Weltzeit*, Frankfurt am Main: Suhrkamp, 1986, p. 223.
7. See L. Althusser, ' "The Piccolo Teatro": Bertolazzi and Brecht', in L. Althusser, *For Marx*, trans. B. Brewster, London: Verso, 1986.
8. G. Deleuze, *Difference and Repetition*, trans. P. Patton, New York: Columbia University Press, 1994.
9. For a comprehensive discussion of the critical potential of repetition in art see ibid
10. B. Brecht, *Werke*, Vol. 22: 1 *Berliner and Frankfurter Ausgabe*, ed. W. Hecht and I. Gellert *et al.*, Frankfurt am Main: Suhrkamp, 1993, p. 2.
11. Aristotle, *Poetics*, London: Penguin, 1996, p. 14.
12. P. Corneille, 'Discours sur les trois unités', in *Œuvres complétès*, Paris: Editions du Seuil, 1963, p. 844. Compare this to the central importance of the concept of *dérégulation* in the poetics of modernism since Arthur Rimbaud who elevates the 'dérégulation de tous les sens' to a programmatic status for poetry.
13. Ibid, p. 845: 'moins on se charge d'actions passées, plus on a l'auditeur [not the 'spectacteur'] propice par le peu du gêne qu'on lui donne, en lui rendant toutes les choses présentes, sans demander aucune réflexion à sa mémoire que pour ce qu'il a vu'.
14. V. Novarina, *Le théâtre des Paroles*, Paris: Editions POL, 1988, pp. 22 and 24: 'L'acteur n'est pas un interpréte parce que le corps n'est pas un instrument.' And: 'L'acteur n'exécute pas … se fait sur la planche.'
15. G. Agamben, 'Noten zur geste', in J. G. Lauer (ed.), *Postmoderne und Politik*, Tübingen: Edition Diskord, 1992, pp. 97-107, 99.
16. Heiner Müller, *Heiner Müller Material*, ed. F. Hörnigk, Göttingen: Steidl Verlag, 1989, p. 50.
17. E. Fischer-Lichte, *The Semiotics of Theatre*, Bloomington: Indiana University Press, 1992, pp. 9ff.
18. V. Sobhchack, 'The Scene of the Screen: Envisioning Cinematic and Electronic "Presence"', in R. Stam and T. Miller (eds), *Film and Theory: An Anthology*, Oxford: Blackwell Publishers, 2000, pp. 67-84, here 78-80.
19. See the quotes from and discussion of Imdahl's theses in B. Waldenfels, *Sinnesschwellen*, Frankfurt am Main: Suhrkamp, 1999, p. 139.

5.9 Dramaturgy *and* Montage (1991)

Dramaturgy: Actions at work

EUGENIO BARBA

Translated by Richard Fowler

THE WORD 'TEXT', BEFORE referring to a written or spoken, printed or manuscripted text, meant 'a weaving together'. In this sense, there is no performance which does not have 'text'.

That which concerns the text (the weave) of the performance can be defined as 'dramaturgy', that is, *drama-ergon*, the 'work of the actions' in the performance. The way in which the actions work is the plot.

It is not always possible to differentiate between what, in the dramaturgy of a performance, may be 'direction' and what may be the author's 'writing'. This distinction is clear only in theatre which seeks to *interpret* a written text.

Differentiating between autonomous dramaturgy and the performance per se dates back to Aristotle's attitude towards the tradition of Greek tragedy, a tradition already well in the past even for him. He drew attention to two different fields of investigation: the written texts and the way they are performed. The idea that there exists a dramaturgy which is identifiable only in an autonomous, written text and which is the matrix of the performance is a consequence of those occasions in history when the memory of a theatre has been passed on by means of the words spoken by the characters in its performances. Such a distinction would not even be conceivable if it were the performances in their entirety that were being examined.

In a performance, actions (that is, all that which has to do with the dramaturgy) are not only what is said and done, but also the sounds, the lights and the changes in space. At higher level of organisation, actions are the episodes of the story or the different facets of a situation, the arches of time between two accents of the performance, between two changes in the space – or even the evolution of the musical score, the light changes, and the variations of rhythm and intensity which a performer develops following certain precise physical themes (ways of walking, of handling props, of using make-up or costume). The objects used in the performance are also *actions*. They are transformed, they acquire different meanings and different emotive colourations.

All the relationships, all the interactions between the characters or between the characters and the lights, the sounds and the space, are actions. Everything that works directly on the spectators' attention, on their understanding, their emotions, their kinaesthesia, is an action.

The list could become uselessly long. It is not so important to define what an action is, or to determine how many actions there may be in a performance. What is important is to observe that the actions come into play only when they are woven together, when they become texture: 'text'.

The plot can be of two types. The first type is accomplished through the development of actions in time by means of a *concatenation* of causes and effects or through an alternation of actions which represent two parallel developments. The second type occurs only by means of *simultaneity*: the simultaneous presence of several actions.

Concatenation and *simultaneity* are the two dimensions of the plot. They are not two aesthetic alternatives or two different choices of method. They are the two poles whose tension and dialectic determine the performance and its life: actions at work – dramaturgy.

Let us return to the important distinction – investigated especially by Richard Schechner – between theatre based on the mise-en-scène of a previously written text, and theatre based on a performance text. This distinction can be used to define two different approaches to the theatrical phenomenon and therefore two different performance results.

For example: while the written text is recognisable and transmissible before and independently of the performance, the performance text exists only at the end of the work process and cannot be passed on. It would in fact be tautological to say that the performance text (which is the performance) can be extracted from the performance. Even if one used a transcription technique similar to that used for music, in which various horizontal sequences can be arranged vertically, it would be impossible to pass on the information: the more faithful one tried to make it, the more illegible it would become. Even aural and visual mechanical recording of the performance captures only a part of the performance text, excluding (at least in the case of performances that do not use a proscenium stage) the complex montages of actor–spectator distance–proximity relationships, and favouring, in all those cases in which the actions are simultaneous, a single montage from among many. It reflects in fact only *one* observer's way of seeing.

The distinction between theatre based on a written text, or in any case on a text composed a priori and used as the matrix of the mise-en-scène, and theatre whose only meaningful text is the performance text, represents rather well the difference between 'traditional' and 'new' theatre. This distinction becomes even more useful if we wish to move from a classification of modern theatrical phenomena to a microscopic analysis or an anatomical investigation of scenic *bios*, of dramatic life: dramaturgy.

From this point of view, the relationship between a performance text and a text composed a priori no longer seems like a contradiction but like a complementary situation, a kind of dialectic opposition. The problem is not, therefore, the choice of one pole or another, the definition of one or another type of theatre. The problem is that of the balance between the *concatenation pole* and the *simultaneity pole*.

The only prejudicial thing that can occur is the loss of balance between these two poles.

When a performance is based on a text composed of words, there is a danger that the balance in the performance will be lost because of the prevalence of linear relationships (the plot as concatenation). This will damage the plot understood as the weaving together of simultaneously present actions.

If the fundamental meaning of the performance is carried by the interpretation of a written text, there will be a tendency to favour this dimension of the performance, which parallels the linear dimension of language. There will be a tendency to consider as ornamental elements all the interweavings that arise out of the conjunction of several actions at the same time, or simply to treat them as actions that are not woven together, as background actions.

The tendency to underestimate the importance of the simultaneity pole for the life of the play is reinforced, in the modern way of thinking, by the kind of performance which Eisenstein in his time was already calling the 'real level of theatre', that is, the cinema. In the cinema, the linear dimension is almost absolute and the dialectic life of the interwoven actions (the plot) depends basically on two poles: the concatenation of actions and the concatenation of an abstract observer's attention, the eye-filter which selects close-ups, long shots, etc.

The cinema's grip on our imagination increases the risk that the balance between the concatenation and simultaneity poles will be lost when we make theatre performances. The spectator tends not to attribute a significant value to the interweaving of simultaneous actions and behaves – as opposed to what happens in daily life – as if there was a favoured element in the performance particularly suited to establishing the meaning of the play (the words, the protagonist's adventures, etc.). This explains why a 'normal' spectator, in the West, often believes that he doesn't fully understand performances based on the simultaneous weaving together of actions, and why he finds himself in difficulty when faced with the logic of many Asian theatres, which seem to him to be complicated or suggestive because of their 'exoticness'.

If one impoverishes the simultaneity pole, one limits the possibility of making complex meanings arise out of the performance. These meanings do not derive from a complex concatenation of actions but from the interweaving of many dramatic actions, each one endowed with its own simple meaning, and from the assembling of these actions by means of a single unity of time. Thus the meaning of a fragment of a performance is not only determined by what precedes and follows it, but also by a multiplicity of facets whose three-dimensional presence makes it live in the present with a life of its own.

In many cases, this means that for a spectator, the more difficult it becomes for him to interpret or to judge immediately the meaning of what is happening in front of his eyes and in his head, the stronger is his sensation of living through an experience. Or, said in a way that is more obscure but perhaps closer to the reality: the stronger is the experience of an experience.

The simultaneous interweaving of several actions in the performance causes something similar to what Eisenstein describes in reference to El Greco's *View of Toledo*: that the painter does not reconstruct a real view but rather constructs a synthesis of several views, making a montage of the different sides of a building, including even those sides that are not visible, showing various elements – drawn from reality independently of each other – in a new and artificial relationship.

These dramaturgical possibilities apply to all the different levels and all the different elements of the performance taken one by one, as well as to the overall plot. The performer, for example, obtains simultaneous effects as soon as he breaks the abstract pattern of movements, just as the spectator is about to anticipate them. He composes his actions ('composes' used here in its original meaning, deriving from *cum-ponere*, 'to put together') into a synthesis that is far removed from a daily way of behaving. In this montage, he segments the actions, choosing and dilating certain fragments, composing the rhythms, achieving an equivalent to the real action by means of what Richard Schechner calls the 'restoration of behaviour'.

The use of the written text itself, when it is not interpreted only as a concatenation of actions, can guide elements and details, which are not themselves dramatic, into a simultaneous interweaving.

We can draw from *Hamlet*, for example, certain information: traces of the age-old strife between Norway and Denmark are to be found in the conflict between Hamlet's father and Fortinbras's father; England needing to pay taxes to Denmark echoes the days of the Vikings; the life of the Court recalls the Renaissance; the allusions to Wittenberg reflect Reformation issues. All these various historical facets (which we can really *use* as *different* historical facets) can be various choices by means of which the play can be interpreted: in this case, one chosen facet will eliminate the others.

They can also, however, be woven together into a synthesis with many simultaneously present historical elements, whose 'meaning' as it relates to the interpretation of *Hamlet* – that is, what the play will show to the spectators – is not foreseeable. The more the director has woven the different threads together, according to his own logic, the more the meaning of the performance will appear surprising, motivated and unexpected, even to the director himself.

Something similar can also be said for the play's protagonist, for Hamlet. The concatenation of Shakespeare's assembled actions (his montage) usually results in an image of Hamlet as a man in doubt, indecisive, consumed by melancholia, a philosopher ill-suited to action. But this image does not correspond to all the single elements of Shakespeare's total montage. Hamlet acts resolutely when he kills Polonius; he falsifies the message from Claudius to the King of England with cold decisiveness; he defeats the pirates; he challenges Laertes; he quickly notices and sees through the stratagems of his enemies; he kills the King. For an actor (and a director), all of these details, taken one by one, can be used as evidence with which to construct a coherent interpretation of Hamlet. But they can also be used as evidence of different and contradictory aspects of behaviour to be assembled into a synthesis which is not the result of a previous decision about what kind of character Hamlet is going to be.

As can be seen, this simple hypothesis brings us much closer to the creative process (that is, composition process) of many of the great actors in the Western tradition. In their daily work, they did not and do not begin with the interpretation of a character, but develop their work following a route not based on *what?* but on *how?*, assembling aspects that would at first seem incoherent from the point of view of habitual realism, and ending up with a formally coherent synthesis.

Actions at work (dramaturgy) come alive by means of the balance between the concatenation pole and the simultaneity pole. There is a risk of this life being lost with the loss of tension between the two poles.

While the alteration of balance for the sake of weaving through concatenation draws a performance into the somnolence of comfortable recognisability, the alteration of balance for the sake of weaving in the simultaneity dimension can result in arbitrariness, chaos. Or incoherent incoherence. It is easy to see that these risks are even greater for those who work without the guide of a previously composed text.

Written text, performance text, the concatenation or linear dimension, the simultaneity or three-dimensional dimension: these are elements without any value, positive or negative. Positive or negative value depends on the quality of the relationship between these elements.

The more the performance gives the spectator the experience of an experience, the more it must also guide his attention in the complexity of the actions which are taking place, so that he does not lose his sense of direction, his sense of the past and future – that is, the story, not as anecdote but as the 'historical time' of the performance.

All the principles that make it possible to direct the spectator's attention can be drawn from the life of the performance (from the actions that are at work): the interweaving means of concatenation and the interweaving by means of simultaneity.

To create the life of a performance does not mean only to interweave its actions and tensions, but also to direct the spectator's attention, his rhythms, to induce tensions in him without trying to impose an interpretation.

On the one hand, the spectator's attention is attracted by the action's complexity, its presence; on the other hand, the spectator is continuously required to evaluate this presence and this action in the light of his knowledge of what has occurred and in expectation of (or questioning about) what will happen next.

As with the performer's action, the spectator's attention must be able to live in a three-dimensional space, governed by a dialectic which is his own and which is the equivalent of the dialectic that governs life.

In the final analysis, one could relate the dialectic between the interweaving by means of concatenation and the interweaving by means of simultaneity to the complementary (and not the opposing) natures of the left and right hemispheres of the brain.

Each Odin Teatret production uses the scenic space in a different way. The actors do not adapt to given spatial dimensions (as happens on the proscenium stage) but model the architecture of the space according to the specific dramaturgical demands of each new production.

But it is not only the respective spaces occupied by the actors and spectators that change from production to production. During a given single production, the actors sometimes work on the sides of the performing area, at other times in the middle; thus certain spectators experience certain actions in close-up, as it were – when the actors are but a few centimetres from them – while other spectators see the whole picture from a much wider angle.

These same principles are used in outdoor performances, which take place in squares and streets, on balconies and on the rooftops of cities or villages. In this case the environment is given and apparently cannot change, but the actor can use his presence to make a dramatic character spring out of the architecture, which we are normally no longer able to see because of daily habits and usages and which we no longer experience with a fresh eye.

Montage: The Performer's Montage and the Director's Montage

'MONTAGE' IS A WORD which today replaces the former term 'composition'. 'To compose' (to put with) also means 'to mount', 'to put together', 'to weave actions together', 'to create the play'. Composition is a new synthesis of materials and fragments taken out of their original contexts. It is a synthesis that is equivalent to the phenomenon and to the real relationships which it suggests or represents.

It is also a dilation equivalent to the way in which a performer isolates and fixes certain physiological processes or certain behaviour patterns, as if putting them under a magnifying glass and making his body a dilated body. To dilate implies above all to isolate and to select:

'From afar, a city is a city and a landscape is a landscape, but little by little, as one approaches, there appear houses, trees, tiles, leaves, ants, ants' legs, *ad infinitum.*' The film director Robert Bresson quotes these words written by Pascal and deduces from them that in order to compose one must know how to see the reality that surrounds us and to subdivide it into its constituent parts. One must know how to isolate these parts, to make them independent, in order to give them a new dependence.

A performance is born out of a specific and dramatic relationship between elements and details which, considered in isolation, are neither dramatic nor appear to have anything in common. The concept of montage does not only imply a composition of words, images or relationships. Above all, it implies the montage of rhythm, but not in order to *represent* or *to reproduce* the movement. By means of the montage of rhythm, in fact, one aims at the very principle of motion, at tensions, at the dialectic process of nature or thought. Or better, at 'the thought which penetrates matter'.

Eisenstein's comments on El Greco are particularly important with respect to montage because they demonstrate how montage is actually the construction of meaning. Eisenstein shows how El Greco, assembling the individual parts of his paintings (Eisenstein calls them 'frames'), succeeds not in *representing* ecstatic characters but rather in creating an *ecstatic construction* of the paintings, forcing the observer's eye, even his body, to follow the route designed by the creator.

Making use of art critic J. E. Willumsen's accurate analyses, Eisenstein examines El Greco's *View and Map of Toledo*: the proportions of the huge Don Juan Tavera hospital on the slopes of the hill have been so reduced that the building appears only slightly larger than a house, 'otherwise it would have hidden the view of the city'. What El Greco paints, therefore, is not the landscape as it appears from a particular perspective but an *equivalent* of a *view* which does not allow the great bulk of the hospital to become an obstacle.

Moreover, the painter shows the hospital's principal and most beautiful façade, even though it is not actually visible from the angle from which the painting has been made.

Eisenstein writes: 'This view of Toledo is not possible from any real point of view. It is a mounted complex, a representation composed by means of a montage of objects, "photographed in isolation", which in nature mask each other or have their backs to the observer.' The painting, in short, is composed: 'of elements taken one by one and reunited in an arbitrary construction which is non-existent from a single point of view but which is fully consistent with respect to the internal logic of the composition.'

And again: 'El Greco did this painting at home, in his studio. That is to say, it is not based on a view, but on knowledge. Not on a single point of view, but on the assembling of isolated motifs collected while walking through the city and its surroundings.'

Montage is fundamental with regard to the effect the actions must have on the spectator. It guides the spectator's senses through the dramatic (*performance*) fabric (*text*), letting the spectator experience the *performance* text. The director guides, divides and reassembles the spectator's attention by means of the performer's actions, the words of the text, the relationships, the music, the sounds, the lights, the use of props.

The Performer's Montage

It is possible to differentiate two different spheres or directions of work: that of the performer who works inside a codified performance system and that of the performer who must invent and fix his way of being present every time he works in a new production, taking care not to repeat what he did in the previous production.

The performer who works in a codified performance system constructs the montage by altering his 'natural' and 'spontaneous' behaviour. Balance is modified and modelled, made precarious: new tensions are thus produced in the body, dilating it.

In the same way that particular physiological processes are dilated and codified, continuous eye

Figure 38 a–k Actor's first montage: Kosuke Nomura in Sequence A: how one picks and eats a fruit in a kyogen scene.

movements (*saccades*), which in daily life occur two or three times a second and which alternate with phases of stillness (*nystagmes*), are also codified. These formalisations recreate, by means of very precise rules which dictate how the eyes should move, an equivalent to the continuous life of the eyes in daily reality.

The same applies to the hands. In daily life the fingers are continuously animated by tensions that individualise each finger. These tensions are reconstructed in theatre by means of *mudras*, which can have either a semantic or a purely dynamic value. They recreate the equivalence of the fingers' life, which move continuously from one codified position to another equally precise position.

Analogously, in positions of non-movement, regulated as action in time by means of tensions in the postural muscles, the equivalent of the life which regulates daily balance is recreated. In daily life, immobility does not exist and apparent immobility is based on continuous, minuscule movements of adjustment (cf. *Eyes, Hands, Balance*).

The result of all these procedures, which amplify behavioural and physiological processes, is a series of very precise 'scores'. Richard Schechner speaks of a 'restoration of behaviour' which is used in all performance forms from shamanism to aesthetic theatre:

> A restored behaviour is a living behaviour treated the way a film director treats a strip of film. Each piece of film must be re-systemised, reconstructed. This is independent of the causal (social, psychological, technological) systems which have created it: it has its own behaviour. The original 'truth' or 'motivation' of that behaviour can be lost, ignored or covered, elaborated or distorted by myth. Originating a process – used in the course of rehearsals in order to obtain a new process, the performance – the strips of behaviour are themselves no longer processes but objects, *materials*.

What Schechner has written in order to explain how certain ritual dances (which today are considered classical) have been 'restored', applies perfectly well to the performer who works on the basis of a codification, or who fixes improvisations like 'strips of behaviour' on which montage work can be done. The restoration, that is, the work of selection and dilation, can only take place if there exists a process of fixing.

Thus, for example, when kabuki performers meet to perform, even if they have never before done the particular performance (or the variation of the performance) that they are about to present, they can make use of 'materials', already prepared for other scenic situations. These 'materials' are then re-edited in the new context. I have myself seen an *onnagata*, who had never performed a certain rôle, go on stage and perform it after only two rehearsals: he made a montage of materials available to him from rôles which he already knew.

The Director's Montage

If the performer's actions can be considered as analogous to strips of film which are already the result of a montage, it is possible to use this montage not as a final result but as material for a further montage. This is generally the task of the director, who can weave the actions of several performers into a succession in which one action seems to answer another, or into a simultaneous execution in which the meanings of both actions derive directly from the fact of their mutual presence.

Let us take an example, rough as all examples are, and even the more so here because we will use fixed images, photographs, to illustrate a process the meaning of which depends on the development of actions in space and in time and on their rhythm. But crude as it may be, this example can serve as a demonstration of the most elementary (grammatical) level of the director's montage.

Figure 39 a–n Actor's second montage: Etienne Decroux in Sequence B: how one picks a flower in mime

Let us imagine having the following text as a point of departure: 'Then the woman saw that the tree was good to eat, pleasing to the eye, desirable for the gaining of knowledge. She took its fruit and ate of it. She gave some to her husband, who was with her, and he also ate of it' (Genesis 3:6). We also have two performers' montages, two sequences of 'restored behaviour':

Sequence A: Kosuke Nomura, kyogen actor, shows how, in the tradition of his art, one picks a fruit (a plum) and eats it [Figure 38]. We see the principle of selection and dilation at work: [a] with one hand he grasps the branch, with the other, starting from the opposite side, he begins the movement to take the fruit; [b] he grasps the fruit and then, in order to pluck it, he does not pull it, but … [c] he turns it, showing its size; [d] the fruit is brought to the mouth, not in a direct line, but with a circular movement; the fingers squeeze the fruit and are composed in a way that shows the fruit's size, its softness, its weight; [e–h] with a movement that begins high up, the fruit is brought to the mouth; [i] it is not the mouth that squeezes the fruit but the hand, executing an action *equivalent* to that which, in reality, would be done by the mouth; [j] the fruit is swallowed (and again it is the hand which does the action): the performer does not show a man swallowing but his hand makes an otherwise invisible action – that of swallowing – visible; [k] having savoured the fruit, the man smiles with satisfaction.

Sequence B: Etienne Decroux, the great mime master, shows how one picks a flower according to the principles of his art. He also begins from a position that is opposite to that towards which he will direct the action, first with the eyes and then with the action itself [Figure 39].

The two sequences provided by the two performers, in spite of their different motivations and different original contexts, can be put together. We will thus obtain a new sequence whose meaning will depend on the new context into which it is inserted: the biblical text that we have chosen as the point of departure for our example. In this case, naturally, the sex of the two performers will not be taken into consideration: but there is no reason why the Japanese performer Kosuke Nomura cannot interpret the rôle of Eve.

Let's run through the two performers' sequences as if they now were a single sequence: Eve has just given in to the serpent's temptation, picks the fruit, tastes it. Her final reaction is a smile for the new world that has opened up in front of her eyes. Eve tempts Adam in her turn, puts the fruit of knowledge beside him on the ground, and now Adam glances sideways as if in fear of being watched by the angel of God. He begins the movement to take the fruit, starting in the extreme opposite direction: the principle of opposition now becomes legible as an initial reaction of refusal. Then Adam bends down, picks up the fruit and turns his back as if to leave, or as if to eat the fruit without being seen, or perhaps he is ashamed of what he has done or, having been left alone, he goes in search of Eve.

A montage of this type would be possible because the two performers are able to repeat each single action, each detail of each action, perfectly. And this is why the director can create a new relationship from the two sequences, can extrapolate them from their original contexts and create between them a new dependence, putting them in relationship with a text which is then faithfully followed. The biblical text does not in fact say *how* Eve gave Adam the fruit. At this point the director can fill the visual void in the text with the help of the sequences that have already been fixed by the performers. Some details of the actions can be amplified further, minimalised, accelerated.

Figure 40 a–j Director's montage: the new sequence obtained through the elaboration of the two actors' sequences, A and B, and the possible content variations: Genesis 3:6 and Strindberg's *The Father*, I, ix

Let us return to our example, to the 'material' furnished by the two performers, without adding anything new.

Since the two performers' sequences are already the result of a 'restoration of behaviour', since they are perfectly fixed and thus can be treated like two strips of film, the director can extract a few fragments from one performer's sequence and remount them, interweaving them with fragments from the other performer's sequence, taking care to ensure that, after the cuts and with the new montage, enough physical coherence remains so that the performers can go from one movement to another in an organic way.

Further montage by the director

Here is an example of a new montage which weaves together fragments from the original, autonomous and independent sequences furnished by the two performers [Figure 40].

If we apply this montage to our theme, Adam and Eve, we have the meaning of the new situation: [a] Adam looks incredulously ... [b] Eve has picked the forbidden fruit and is about to eat it. [c] Adam: 'We have promised not to eat the fruit of this tree!' [d] Eve persists, and brings the forbidden fruit up to her mouth. [e] Adam: 'God's sword will punish us.' [f] Eve is about to eat the fruit. [g] Adam: 'Don't do it!' [h] Eve eats the forbidden fruit. [i] Adam collapses on the floor. [j] Eve is intoxicated with knowledge.

The same montage that we have applied to the biblical story can also be applied to Strindberg's *The Father*: the wife Laura (once again, Kosuke Nomura is cast as the female) makes the Captain (her husband) suspect that he is not the father of their daughter. The man is ridiculed and crushed. The director has used Kosuke Nomura's actions (originally a sequence based on picking a plum and eating it) to create a sign of adultery and especially the image of the *vagina dentata* which emasculates and crushes the male. At the end, Laura says, 'It's strange, but I've never been able to look at a man without feeling superior to him' (*The Father*, Act I, scene x).

Seen in the light of their new Strindberg context, the performers' interwoven actions would have to change, small details would have to be modified in order to make these actions consistent with the meaning they have now acquired. Above all, the rhythm and intensity with which the actions are interwoven will allow unexpected meanings to emerge from the materials furnished by the performers.

The level of this montage of photographs, which we have used as a rough example, is the elementary, grammatical level: the essential work, that is the process of elaboration and refinement, is yet to come. We are face to face with a body that has been coldly constructed, an 'artificial body' in which there is no life. But this artificial body already has within it all the circuits in which *scenic bios*, that is, life recreated as art, will flow. In order for this to occur, there must be something burning, no longer analysable or anatomisable, which fuses the performer's and the director's work into a single whole in which it is no longer possible to distinguish the actions of the former and the montage of the latter. In this phase of work no rules exist. The rules serve only to make the event possible, to provide the conditions in which the real artistic creation can occur without further respect for limits or principles.

In the director's montage, the actions, in order to become dramatic, must take on a new value, must transcend the meaning and the motivations for which they were originally composed by the performers.

It is this new value which causes the actions to go beyond the literal act that they represent on their own. If I walk, I walk and nothing more. If I sit, I sit and nothing more. If I eat, I do nothing more than eat. If I smoke, I do nothing more than smoke. These are self-referential acts that do nothing more than illustrate themselves.

The actions transcend their illustrative meaning because of the relationships created in the new context in which they are placed. Put in relationship with something else, they become dramatic. To dramatise an action means to introduce a leap of tensions that obliges the action to develop meanings which are different from its original ones.

Montage, in short, is the art of putting actions in a context that causes them to deviate from their implicit meaning.

Note

Originally published in Eugenio Barba and Nicola Savarese, *A Dictionary of Theatre Anthropology: The Secret Art of the Performer*, 2nd edn, London: Routledge, 2006 [1991], pp. 66–9 and 178–84. Some of the photos from the original publication have not been reproduced in this version.

5.10 Laurie Anderson in Interview (1991)

NICHOLAS ZURBRUGG

LISTENING TO EARLY LP anthologies of avant-garde performance – such as One Ten Records' *Airwaves: Two Record Anthology of Artists' Aural Work and Music* (1977) and 1750 Arch Records' *New Music for Electronic and Recorded Media* (1977) – it seemed obvious that Laurie Anderson's multimedia performances offered remarkable syntheses of the experimental and the popular, the simulacral and the profound.

And later, watching Anderson from both stage-side and back-row seats in the Sydney Opera House in 1986, I was intrigued by her ability to project her persona across this vast auditorium, juggling with enough gadgets to keep two or three lesser mortals busy, while usually conveying 'something that's very intimate'.

I'd arranged to interview Anderson in New York in December 1990, but on arriving at her door heard her explain that she had to rush off that day to Europe, and so ... she hoped I'd understand. My mind whirled – I mentioned I was spending Christmas in England myself – and we finally met up at her London hotel, in January 1991.

Asked to what extent she felt her work with new media was 'avant-garde', Anderson disarmingly replied that she didn't really consider herself avant-garde and that she doubted whether there really could now be a New York avant-garde in a city where 'downtown art images are comped-up into ads' in a mere weekend, and where the life span of an artist could be 'eighteen months'.

Nevertheless, acknowledging 'a few exceptions', and arguing that 'until we're all dead, creativity isn't dead' (a point Rachel Rosenthal also makes, when observing, 'Art is the only thing that will remain as long as there's one person alive'), Anderson memorably warns, 'For anyone to say that creativity is dead just says that this particular person is creatively dead.'

Anderson's concluding remarks equally movingly discredit the myth that postmodern multimedia culture courts incomprehension: 'I always just wanted to make things that other people could understand. That's my only reason to be here. My only reason.'

London – January 30, 1991

Would you describe yourself as a multimedia artist?
I don't think of that first. I mean, I've used a lot of tools, and I think it's kind of strange to describe yourself by tools, although I suppose painters do – they use a paintbrush. But that hardly says anything about them. Although it might say more than 'multimedia' says about someone, because who doesn't work with multimedia? Often it gets a little bit blurry, especially in watching the Gulf War develop. A lot of artists talk about multimedia the way generals talk about F-16 bombers – you know, how efficient they are – it could be the same description as an artist describing tools. So I describe myself as a storyteller. That seems to work well enough.

Don't other storytellers tell stories in a more conventional way?
Yes, but it doesn't matter to me. People have told stories in a million kinds of ways. First it was sitting around a fire, with no tape recorders. But fire's magic, and so is technology. You just hover around something that has to do with light or circuitry, and that brings out stories, I think.

Does new circuitry inspire new kinds of storytelling?
It helps. It's an atmosphere. But it's not ever the point of the story. And I've been realizing that more and more, the last few things that I've done have really just been talking. I've been using maybe one slide, and some electronics, but not very much. Maybe it's a reaction to doing a lot of very big projects that involved two huge truckloads of stuff. And I thought, Well, this is an awful lot of equipment, just to tell these stories – why don't I just tell the stories instead? So, I started to do that.

This seems like a return to the register of your early performances at places like the Ear Inn, before relatively intimate audiences.
Well, it's just for a change. I'm not good at predicting what I'll do next year. I'm not saying that one thing's better than the other. It's just what I happen to be doing at the moment as a reaction to another thing. Which is often the way a lot of artists work. They work on a big monument, and then they decide, How about a nice little pencil sketch? And they can both be extremely beautiful.

Can you remember your first performance as a storyteller?
I can remember my first performance as a liar.

As a child?
Yes, sure. I'd just make up things for other kids. And these sort of had to do with the Bible. I'm from the Bible Belt, where everyone believed in the most amazing miracles. There were people who were just mowing their lawns and doing the most mundane things that you can imagine, and they believed that the oceans parted, and that snakes suddenly appeared on the earth. And they would talk about this quite matter-of-factly.

Was that a sort of local surrealism?
No, no, that was local truth. Surrealism is an art term. We were not artists.

How did you move from Bible Belt storytelling? When did you go through the art barrier?
I haven't. I try to tell the truth as I see it. I'm just telling the same mixture of midwestern Bible stories that I always have. They're a mixture of the most mundane things with a fabulous twist on them. It's only what I learned in Bible school. How Bible school related to public school is what I'm interested in. Always have been.

Didn't New York offer other opportunities for presenting things?
Yes, but they were still the same stories. In an art context they may have seemed a little odd. But some of the first performances I did were really about things that had happened to me as a

child, and what I thought about them. And I kind of branched out and included politics. And in including politics you have to include media, because media is politics, and vice versa. Just invert the 'M' of 'Music Television' and you get 'War Television'. It's still entertainment of the same order, complete with logos, soundtracks. '*War* in the Gulf – War *in* the Gulf – *da da da da da, da da da da da*' – and it immediately turns into a song.

The Gulf War has become a media war. People watch television and have the illusion that they're watching history. And for a day or so that was actually true. When the war first started, I was in Zurich, and I was transfixed by the way this story was being told. Firsthand, first person – you knew it was the beginning of the story, but you had no idea what the end would be. It was riveting. I watched them put their microphones out of the window and go, 'What do you hear? What's that sound?' And it was the first bomb that fell on Baghdad. You turn the dial, and for the first time in history you see someone putting on a mask because they think there's going to be a nerve gas attack.

After two days there was a blackout on that kind of reporting. Absolutely nothing after that. And you saw these huge objects moving into place – you saw the ways things functioned. You saw who wanted you to see what, who wanted you to hear what about this story, watching that network organizing itself. In other words – particularly in the United States – you can see quite easily how a story becomes propaganda, and becomes what people want to hear. On the other hand, I'm interested in what people want to hear, because so many people base their lives on what they want to hear, or on some future where everything will be perfect.

So telling stories is for me a futuristic experience. Not in the sense of Marinetti, who said war is the highest form of modern art. And his colleague in amateur art, Mussolini, happened to agree, as did the would-be painter Hitler, as do the would-be media stars George Bush and Hussein. You'd be hard pressed to say on a basic level how these groups differ from artists in what they want. They want their name in lights, they want to be in history.

I mean, I know that art is a supremely egotistical act, at one level. But another – the one I hope to get to – is one where my own sense of 'I', which is telling the story, becomes very unimportant. And the listener can identify enough with this to recognize that I'm not just talking about myself. Even if I don't use 'you', it becomes an experience in which the listener kind of goes, 'Did that happen to me or did that happen to you? Who did that happen to? It happened to someone – I can relate to it.'

What I'm really trying to do is find ordinary situations which people can understand in an immediate way. I have an ax, and there are huge frozen oceans inside everybody, and I just chip away at this, and look at it slightly differently from another angle. But it's not surrealistic. It's an incredibly ordinary old chunk of ice. And I know it works when people say, 'I know what you're talking about.'

All the same, you're orchestrating many contemporary technologies that other people don't bother to use.
I consider that unimportant. I use technology as just a way of amplifying or changing things. I use technology to change my voice. Storytellers have always assumed other voices. It's just a slightly different way of doing it. No better and no worse – it's really just a tool. And a lot of people focus on it as if it were something important. It's the least important thing about what I do, by far.

Why do you think people focus upon technology?

Maybe it resonates a little bit with their life, because so many parts of our lives come through speakers and circuitry, and we deal with that all the time. And so is this something everyday, like I hear in the subway? Or is this art? I thought art was supposed to be mute, and was supposed to be hanging somewhere in a museum – I thought art was supposed to have an aura. I think art has an aura, too – an aura that means that things resonate in the mind and the heart of the person who's receiving them. Real contact is very mysterious.

Do you think that your high-tech performances work as well as some of the earlier ones? I found your early pieces – like Time to Go *– very moving. Later, when I saw you in 1986, from the back of the Sydney Opera House, it seemed quite a job to project yourself to an enormous audience. I wondered if this involved any loss of immediacy and intimacy. Was this something you thought about very much?*

Well, I do. And that was the nature of that piece – it was not very intimate. The latest thing I did was extremely intimate, and at the same time had this huge amount of high-tech stuff. It was a solo thing. Seventeen people came along on tour for this so-called solo thing.

But I felt myself that it was by far the most intimate thing I've ever done. So it's not a question of size at all. It's a question of how you address people and what you say. Two people can sit at a table, and one can lecture the other in the most formal, remote kind of way you can imagine. And on the other hand, before an audience of ten thousand one can say something very intimate, in a way that's very intimate, and it will be received that way. There's a whole lot of things that are just not that simple.

You've remarked how the direct reporting of war becomes a certain sort of fiction. Does it worry you that use of the mass media might modify your work in that way?

Of course it modifies it. It does a lot of things to it. That's why I try to use several different ways of speaking. It's ventriloquism, what I'm doing. And so I can switch from something that is more authoritative to something that's very personal, to something that's conversational, to something that's anecdotal. And I'm very, very conscious of those voices and how I try to use them.

Do you find that certain voices become autonomous, so that their impact wanes a little bit?

It depends on a lot of things. I think you can use a confessional form of address for three hours, depending on what you're saying.

What kind of things do you find yourself wanting to say?

The last thing that I did, called *Empty Places*, was very, very political. It became almost poster-like in parts, because what I wanted to say, at times, didn't mean sixteen different things – it only meant one thing. This for me was the riskiest kind of talking, because I was vulnerable.

In what ways was it political?

Well, there's a long section about the relationship of songs to political tirades. That starts out with Hitler as a drummer – with the persuasive way that he spoke to get people excited by his drumming and marching to his drumming. Mussolini as an opera singer was another example.

He sang to people, operatically. And then an American example was Reagan, who was basically a crooner singing pretty corny 'When You Wish upon a Star' kinds of Disney numbers. This is the kind of singing that pushes American buttons. So you find, stylistically, there are many, many ways of saying words. I'm interested in the way they relate to music.

Another sense in which this was political – at least for me – was that it became a lot about women as well. I'd been taking singing lessons, and I suddenly realized I was a soprano, and that I had some different things to say with the soprano singing voice, than I had with a more neutral 'art voice'. So I used that voice to say things I probably would have said in my own voice. But the voice that we have – what is it? For me, it's a kind of mixture of my father's and my mother's voices. My father's voice – he learned English from Jimmy Cagney and Bob Hope and – way back – Abe Lincoln. And my mother's more of an academic voice, a Church of England voice. And I've mixed those up and found my own voice.

Of course, that's not to say I've *one*. Everyone has at least twenty – at the bottom line, at least twenty. They have their hail-a-cab voice, they have their interview voice, they have their confessional voice, their telephone voice, and their most intimate voice talking to their dearest loved ones, to name just a few.

What about our other faculties?
Well, our other faculties seem severely limited. The ears don't perk. They hang there. The eyes can't zoom, pan, or dolly very well. For example, you walk into a restaurant and you see a very jerky pan as you look for a place to sit and things go in and out of focus. If you looked at the rushes at the end of this day, you'd fire the cameraman. It's terrible stuff. The point is, you think back on it, and it looks pretty good. You see a bird's-eye view of the restaurant. You see a two-shot of you and the person sitting next to you. It's pretty well lit, it's fairly well cut. Your mind has fixed it up for you. What we see is actually very chaotic. This is the important point about memory and projections – our memories make things smooth, very smooth.

Would you say that all artistic memories become coherent?
I don't think art is necessarily coherent. Some writers and some painters try to duplicate this chaotic experience that we have with our vision, and some avant-garde films become almost unviewable – we see this stuff all day, so why see it at the movies? But art fixes it up, too. And when art fixes it up, it goes even another step past memory. It idealizes it. It gives it a certain meaning and a purpose.

How useful do you find the term avant-garde? Do you see yourself as an avant-garde artist?
I'd be pretty hard-pressed to find the avant-garde now. The existence of the avant-garde depends upon its ability to hide. In many places it's quite hard to hide – and the reason, in my view, is speed. The media is voracious for something – it's running out of topics – and has to go to downtown New York to find something new-new-new. If it's not new-new-new, it's nothing.

And so, for example, the lag time between up- and downtown New York is two days now. Your young painter, let's say, may have delusions about the life of an artist. Green plants, big lofts, parties, a little work, a little suffering, followed by your picture in a Gap ad, followed by media stardom. But, times are hard, so you can't afford this loft. To get a job in an ad agency, every

Saturday, you go to the galleries to see what's way cool. On Monday morning these downtown art images are comped-up into ads, for shoes, for cars, whatever. Two days' lag time.

It's hard for an artist who's so-called avant-garde to develop and nurture art. Because the avant-garde is eighteen, and he's selling his new hot stuff for five hundred thousand dollars a painting, because he's media star. And his career is eighteen months long, because our attention span is twelve minutes long. So by the time the media finally picks up on it, he's dead of a drug overdose. Jean-Michel Basquiat. The lifetime of an artist is getting more like a lifetime of a pop star – a year, eighteen months.

What about somebody like John Cage, who seems to go on forever, experimenting with new possibilities, which might not immediately prove user-friendly or commercially adaptable?
Well, Cage is one of the few artists who actually appeals to the senses, and not to the idea of what should be important this year, and what idea you're going to process and then discard, like any other commodity. He's not at all an intellectual artist – he's somebody who uses his ears, and that's such a shock to people when they're reminded of it, they can't believe it. Change is built into his work. He says, 'Listen to the way things constantly change.' So he's a definite exception to what I'm talking about. And fortunately, there are a few exceptions. But a general rule is that the art world, like any other consumer subculture, is interested in consuming and buying. I mean, salesmanship is not exclusively an American skill, although Americans are extremely good at it.

Do you feel very pressurized by this?
My father was a salesman – I know a lot about salesmanship. And of course, much of art is so specialized that you carve out your little territory and defend it. And when the army moves on, you're left defending your little patch of corn, and nobody cares, except that you fit into somebody's preconceived ideas of what history and the avant-garde are.

Or maybe nobody fits in? According to critics like Fredric Jameson, significant avant-garde art can no longer emerge in the 'postmodern' era, insofar as the media have allegedly neutralized creativity. According to this hypothesis, contemporary creativity can't possibly compete with that of the early twentieth century.
Well, you can imagine why he'd say some of those things because of the appropriation aspect of art of the last ten years. Sherrie Levine copies things. Rap artists appropriate phrases from music. But I think he's missing the point in a big way, because it's a very object-oriented way of thinking of things – you know, that they ought to present a new product, rather than a new way of seeing the product or seeing the thing. And Sherrie Levine, for example, asks some very interesting questions about that, and makes people think about it in a certain way. And it's an act of bravery and grace, to do that. And a very astute comment on the consumer aspect of art.

For anyone to say that creativity is dead just says that this particular person is creatively dead. Until we're all dead, creativity isn't dead. It changes, and I think a lot of people can't identify what it means, because they're looking for it in the wrong place.

Yes. Shakespeare appropriated left, right, and center, and nobody complains. All the same, I've always been a little confused by the appropriation of William Burrough's phrase 'language is a virus' in your film Home of

the Brave. *I felt this phrase had sort of walked out of Burrough's domain – and even beyond your domain – into a general anthem, rather than offering your particular version of it. How did you feel about this?*
I was glad that 'virus' didn't *rhyme* with anything, at least! I appreciate slogans like that because they can be repeated – they're not clichés, and each time you hear it, it sings itself a little bit differently. And sloganeering is something that not just one person does – it's contagious, like a virus. But the real reason I presented it like this was because I liked it as song, and I liked the harmony. And many things that I try to do on a very basic level of – I like the way they look, or I like the way they sound, I don't know what they mean. And I have to wait to see what they mean. I have to trust that they mean something, because I like them. That's why I'm not a pamphleteer – I'm an artist. I like color and sound. It makes me respond to something in a particular way.

If I was just interested in what things meant, if I was just some kind of French philosopher, I would really just write it down and Xerox it and hand it out. I would not bother to go to all this trouble of turning these words into colors, and colors back into words and notes, and finding the right tone of voice to say things in. You can say the same sentence in a hundred different tones of voice and it will mean a hundred different things. So I don't trust words enough to just read something on a piece of paper and expect to know what it means. If I can see and hear the person saying it, or if they have a really large context to put it in, then maybe I can guess at what they mean. But generally it's a cipher to me. It could mean anything.

Is that where the slides and the other things come in – as a way of establishing a more immediate set of contexts?
Yes, as a sensual field for these things, and as a way to become less judgmental and to make associations that you wouldn't necessarily make – like we're trying to make over this table. And to appreciate the craziness of life – that a lot of it doesn't make a lot of sense, and that you're always being pushed by the way things feel, and not just what they mean.

Do you find it frustrating to select a final version of a piece on record or video?
It depends on the piece. Some things go onto records very well, and some things just keep jumping off them and don't want to stick. When I try to force them to stick, sometimes they lose their life, and sometimes they have another, different life that I hadn't expected. So I always try and experiment with how things can stick, and see what the best way to do it is. Sometimes it's just the spoken word, and that's enough.

How important do you find collaborative experimentation?
A real collaboration to me is two people sit down and go, 'What shall we do?' I've only done that with one person – Peter Gabriel – and it was hard for me to do that. I'm a control freak, you know. I have to try to follow an idea through, and see if it works. In terms of my work, I don't feel control is a problem, because I don't collaborate. I feel very privileged in that way, but it's also a privilege that I took. It's a privilege that anyone can have.

Anyone could do their own work and sign their name to it, and that's that. And most people don't realize they are free to do this. They think they have to work their whole life to get to a point where they can do what they want, when they're sixty-five, instead of thinking, Well, maybe I don't need three cars, a dishwasher, four cats, and three kids. You know, it depends on your priorities. I always just wanted to make things that other people could understand. That's my only reason to be here. My only reason. Do you see what I mean?

Notes

Originally published in Nicholas Zurbrugg, ed., *Art, Performance, Media: 31 Interviews*, Minneapolis: University of Minnesota Press, 2004, pp. 25–34.

5.11 **Away From the Surveillance Cameras of the Art World** (2000)

Strategies for Collaboration and Community Activism

A CONVERSATION BETWEEN GUILLERMO GÓMEZ-PEÑA, ROBERTO SIFUENTES, AND LISA WOLFORD

(The text published below is part of the fourth in an ongoing series of conversations with members of Pocha Nostra [Guillermo Gómez-Peña, Roberto Sifuentes, Sara Shelton-Mann, and a fluctuating group of additional collaborators that includes Juan Ybarra and Rona Michele] that I recorded beginning in October 1998. This particular meeting took place over a long meal at a 'pan-Caribbean' restaurant in Ann Arbor, Michigan, decorated with murals of exotic birds and jungle foliage – true midwestern tropicalia. L.W.)

Lisa Wolford: During one of the rehearsals for *BORDERscape 2000*, you talked about being 'hunters of images'. I'm wondering if both of you could talk about that process.

Guillermo Gómez-Peña: In this oversaturated culture, it has become increasingly difficult to find original images that speak for the times. Most metaphors and symbols seem overused, hollow, or broken. I think that one of the many jobs of an artist is to look for new, fresh metaphors and symbols to help us understand our everchanging realities and fragmented cultures. We go about doing this in many ways. Sometimes we find images in everyday life, in the streets, and we capture them with our photographic eye and then re-enact them in more complex ways on stage. At other times, we create composite images by departing from a highly charged, traditional icon such as the crucifixion, the captured primitive, the political monster, the mariachi performing for outsiders and tourists, the witch doctor … Then we begin to do nasty things to these images. We begin to layer them as a kind of palimpsest. We add layers of contradiction or complexity, or we begin inserting details and features from other sources until these 'traditional' images implode. The result is like genetically engineered Mexicabilia. The ultimate goal is to look for images that will create a disturbing sediment in the consciousness of the spectator, images that the audience cannot easily escape from, that will haunt them in dreams, in conversations, in memories.

Roberto Sifuentes: It's very important for us that the complex images we use in performance be open to multiple interpretations that we may never have imagined ourselves. It's always interesting for us to hear the varied readings of our diverse audiences. For example, the image of the hanging chickens in our performances: on one level, there's our intention behind using this charged metaphor, which is that it recalls the fact that Mexican migrant workers were hung by the Texas Rangers.

Gómez-Peña: Even nowadays, migrant workers are derogatorily referred to as *pollos*. But we don't necessarily expect our audiences to know this. We welcome other readings of the hanging chickens. Every image we use is a polysemantic image. It changes meaning with the context …

Sifuentes: Bringing this image out of its culturally specific context and presenting the work in the deep South brought out a completely different reading, which had to do with the fact that African-American slaves were hung for stealing chickens. In the Caribbean, after hearing about the image, people thought we might be into some kind of Santeria or 'Mexican Voodoo' rituals …

Wolford: Are there ever moments when this process of interpretation becomes too elliptical, too open-ended? When audience members read something into an image that you didn't intend to communicate at all, or when a very specific message isn't recognized by the spectator? Like this idea that you're practicing Santeria …

Sifuentes: Yes, sometimes the interpretations of our images are really surprising. We were performing at a small college outside Kansas City, where the audience was described to us as right-wing Christian extremists who had, just a couple of weeks before, attacked a queer performance artist colleague of ours. So imagine how surprised we were to find out that these fundamentalists took an image on the publicity posters, that showed Guillermo in his mariachi suit, completely at face value. So these five hundred Republicans showed up to our performance with drums and maracas, ready to party, because they thought they were coming to 'Mariachi Karaoke' night. And imagine how surprised they were when they saw our particular brand of Mariachi night!

Gómez-Peña: I used to fear being misunderstood, five or six years ago. Since intercultural misunderstanding is often the source of racism, I used to think that for the performance to be understood was very important. Now I think that whether the audience feels they understand us or not is completely irrelevant. In fact, I now distrust people who come up to me right after a show and tell me 'I understood everything and I am with you.' I answer: 'Are you sure you are with me?' If you see a narrative film or a theater play, you immediately assume an ethical or emotional positionality. Whether you like it or not, you align yourself with certain characters, with certain notions of good, justice, freedom, rebellion, etc. You walk out of the theater and you say I got it, I liked it or I didn't.

Wolford: With some kinds of theater, not all.

Gómez-Peña: But with performance art, it's different. You walk out of a performance feeling troubled and perplexed. The performance triggers a process of reflexivity that continues through days and sometimes weeks, creating sediments in the consciousness of people. People slowly begin to come to terms with the images and make up their minds about what they saw, but it takes them weeks, even months. Sometimes people think they are offended because they don't want to face certain realities or certain scary feelings they harbor, and it's very easy to say 'I'm offended', as opposed to trying to understand what wound was opened.

Wolford: Guillermo, I think that really interesting, important theater can have that effect as well. But that's another conversation. In terms of the images, why do you think some people get offended? I don't mean something like the use of the chickens *per se* – I know that animal rights groups have been very vocal about objecting to that, but their reasons are fairly straightforward. I'm thinking about people who manifest strong reactions to some of the more poetical images, such as the crucifixion imagery, or the gang member's stigmata ...

Sifuentes: Most of the time, the audience is completely comfortable with images like a Chicano 'gang member' being beaten by the police, or dragged out of his home in front of his family by the LAPD. They see it on syndicated TV every night, on shows like 'COPS' and 'LAPD: Life in the Streets'. What our spectators find disturbing is witnessing these images of violence recontextualized in high art institutions by two Mexicans who talk back to them. I remember that during one performance we did, the melancholic image of Guillermo as a mariachi in a straightjacket confessing his intercultural desires so disturbed one upper-class Latina that she came onstage and whipped Guillermo so hard across the face and genitals that he crumbled to the ground and was unable to continue the piece for a few minutes. She ran out of the theater and was stopped by our agent and asked why. She only responded that this was offensive, and didn't represent her as a Latina. And this happened in the first five minutes of the piece.

Figure 41 Performance jamming session at Theater Arnaud (Gómez-Peña, Margaret Leonard, Roberto Sifuentes, Sara Shelton-Mann and Nao Bustamente). (Photographer: Eugenio Castro.)

Gómez-Peña: There's a very disturbing tendency in America to take things literally. Since our work is highly symbolic and metaphorical, it appears to be very much out of context in the current culture. We're living in a time in which confessional narrative is the primary means of communication, and we don't engage in confessional narratives of authenticity. Neither do we engage in psychological or social realism. The work is really not about 'us' . . .

Sifuentes: It's not autobiographical. We're not performing our authenticity as Chicanos; what we're doing is performing the multiplicity of mythologies and perceptions of Mexicans and Chicanos in the US. Unfortunately, some audiences don't think of Chicanos as 'cultural thinkers' or 'conceptual arists', so when I first began to portray the 'Vato' (street hipster) covered in tattoos, wearing baggie clothes, and manipulating weapons, many audience members and even some journalists thought I was a Latino gang member brought to town and put on display by Gómez-Peña.

Wolford: So the fact that you're both coming out of an experimental performance tradition already contradicts the ways in which people may tend to want to label your work. Also the incorporation of different media, the extent to which your performances reference theory and critical discourse, etc.

Gómez-Peña: Roberto and I are first and foremost conceptual artists. We always depart from a theoretical proposal, an idea which first becomes a blueprint for action, and eventually becomes a performance piece, a video, or a radio piece. But some of our collaborators come from very different traditions, especially when we work with actors, singers and dancers. Sara [Shelton-Mann] comes from the apocalypse dance theater movement that uses a lot of contact improvisation and physical movement to create original imagery and visceral rituals, and then the collaborating artists conceptualize around the imagery they have developed in the rehearsal room – that's basically the opposite of the way we work. Roberto and I don't spend that much time in the rehearsal room. What we do instead is write, brainstorm, debate with other artists and activists, and every now and then we rehearse. We usually only rehearse physically the month before launching a new project. But we are learning tremendously from Sara. We are beginning to shyly incorporate some of her methodologies into our work.

Sifuentes: And Sara is beginning to incorporate our methodologies. She now thinks of Doc's Clock (our local bar in the Mission) and La Boheme Cafe as viable rehearsal spaces.

Gómez-Peña: Imagine Roberto and I doing contact dance and Ch'i Kung. It sounds ridiculous, que no?

Wolford: Hey, I've seen it – it works. I really don't think you could have gotten to what you're doing now in terms of the physical images on stage without it.

Gómez-Peña: We are hoping to develop a kind of dialectic in which these two processes, the conceptual and the visceral, go together. When we brainstorm with our collaborators about how to incorporate a new vignette, we inevitably talk about politics, about other issues. Our discussions during the creative process are not just about the work itself. We talk about what we saw on TV the night before, about a new book we are reading, about cinema, computers, sex, anthropology, you name it … We share an experience we had the week before. We describe a rare prop we just found in a roadside museum on our last trip somewhere. And then, out of these eclectic discussions, where language and ideas are like personas in a conceptual mini-proscenium, the stage of the dinner table or the bar table, a new image or a new text begins to emerge. Then we try it out informally in front of friends. When we are in San Francisco, we have performance salons at least once a month. There we try out all the new material and invite other performers to try out fresh material.

Sifuentes: A text can begin in a salon, evolve into a radio commentary and then become the basis for a major section in a proscenium piece, or else the radio piece gets worked into the soundtrack for a diorama performance. But really, the performance personas, their actions, the texts, and juxtapositions of images, never get finalized. They are always in process of development. We test them in front of an audience and that's the moment when they begin to blossom, to really take form.

Wolford: When you stage a new piece, I know you often have a very short rehearsal period. Obviously, before you begin mounting a performance, you work conceptually, or you work with the text if it's a scripted piece. You work in your apartment, or in transit, but when you come into a venue with a script to mount a performance, normally you've got about a week to get it up on stage –

Gómez-Peña: At best.

Wolford: Often even less if it's an installation piece. And during the short time you're actually working in a performance space, you end up putting a lot of attention to the technical aspects of the piece, which can be very elaborate.

Sifuentes: Not to mention the shortness of the run. We've never performed more than three weekends in one city. Most of the time it's one show, two shows, a weekend at most … When we produce ourselves, we manage to squeeze out three weeks in a venue, but we don't normally have the luxury of presenting the work for the time that it really needs to evolve. As artists of color in the US, we aren't given the space, time, and funding to be able to sit and create a piece of work. Yes, we create on the road, in airplanes and hotel rooms, in cafes. No matter how visible we are, Chicanos don't have the infrastructure or financial support that would allow us to sit and create in peace, to spend half of the year in artist retreats.

Gómez-Peña: Let's face it, rehearsing all the time is a privilege that most Chicanos don't have. Besides, we have community responsibilities, and our community reminds us all the time of our civic duties, which include benefits for grassroots organizations, workshops in community centers, fundraisers for particular social causes, impromptu appearances at civic events or on Public Access

TV – you name it. And you cannot say no. You have to give back. It's a basic ethical issue. Besides, the work we do in the civic realm feeds the other work. It gives strength and weight to our work in and around the art world. We constantly cross the border back and forth between the civic realm and the art realm, and this is much more important to us than rehearsing all the time. In a sense, our grassroots activities are part of our rehearsal time.

Sifuentes: Traveling and performing is our sole means of economic survival. But at the same time, that's also our means of production. We have turned the necessity of working all the time into our creative process. We travel to the most unlikely places where our audience has never encountered Chicanos – which means that often our performance begins the moment we step off the plane. We become, in a sense, field workers conducting "reverse anthropological" research. I am also not about to begin complaining about the amount of touring we have, because that's something we've fought tooth and nail to achieve. It never gets any easier, even though because of our visibility, some people might get a false sense that we have the corner on the Latino performance art market. The fact of the matter is that we are constantly pushing, struggling, trying to find our niche, in order to make the work happen in the places where it needs to happen. We travel all the time, working in many different contexts from community centers to high art museums, from major urban centers to rural communities, from the US–Mexico border to New York and beyond . . .

Wolford: Could I ask you to talk a little bit about the structure of Pocha Nostra, your performance company? In the past, Guillermo, I know that you've collaborated with people whose primary professional identity wasn't as performers – theorists, cultural critics, visual artists. But in your more recent work, the two of you have been integrating a number of dancers and experimental theater artists.

Gómez-Peña: The way we work is that we have a core group of performance collaborators; for a long time, it was basically Roberto and myself, and more recently Sara. We also have another group of collaborators who are specialists in other areas. People like Mexican filmmaker Gustavo Vazquez, soundscape composer Rona Michele, or digital media advisor Suzanne Stefanac. Incredible performance artists from Mexico city like Juan Ybarra, Violet Luna and Yoshigiro Maeshiro. Chicana performance artists like Norma Medina and Isis Rodriguez. And all of these wonderful *locos y locas* bring something very special to the performances. Their individual creative output finds a new context and a new syntax within the frame of our installations and proscenium performances. Then we have a much bigger, outside circle of collaborators. Some of them are performance artists based in other countries or other cities, and we collaborate with them for specific projects, usually when we're doing a residency or presenting a performance in the areas where they live.

Sifuentes: Suomi violinists in 'traditional' costume sitting on stuffed reindeer in Helsinki, English singers interpreting traditional Welsh songs while doing erotic things with opera singers, gringo rasta tattoo artists tattooing performers onstage, neo-primitives naked on a platform displaying their bodies as art . . .

Gómez-Peña: Given what has happened to arts funding in the 90s, it's financially impossible for artists like us – politicized, experimental performance artists – to maintain any kind of big group. But we still have the desire to bring other people into the work, so the strategy we've developed is to create ephemeral communities that come together around a specific project, and once the project is over, they go back to their homes, to their own practice. Very often, we develop ongoing relationships with artists during our travels. For example, we've done several projects with our Crow friends from Montana, Susan and Tyler Medicine Horse, and we have plans to work with them again in the future. We are a tribe of nomads and misfits.

In some of our projects, we also like to collaborate with people who don't have specialized performance training. Along these lines, we have been working with all kinds of wonderful people: politicized strippers, activists with very theatrical personalities, hip hop poets, extremely articulate transsexuals who are willing to deconstruct their performance personas on stage, mariachis and other civic artists who have chosen to transgress their own tradition … We love to work with eccentrics who have performative personalities and important things to say. Whenever we collaborate with people who don't have formal performance experience, our work has been to contribute to shaping their material so that it gets presented in the best possible way.

Sifuentes: Then it can be incorporated into the larger context of the work that we are doing.

Gómez-Peña: Exactly. And they always get to have the last word about their own material and their representation. Our role is to coordinate, design, and stage the larger event, not necessarily to direct it. Our goal is to attempt a model that is not colonial, in which we don't manipulate these wonderful 'involuntary performance artists', and in which they get to have editorial say. We help them shape the material (I don't even want to use the word help, because it's condescending), but we work with them to structure their material because we have certain skills and experience that we have developed throughout the years.

Wolford: I want to shift back to the discussion of audience reception of the work, if that's okay. In the diorama performances, there is no spoken text – the text that exists is part of the soundscape. Because you work with multivalent, polysemantic images, and because irony is such a central aspect of your performance strategy, some of the journalistic responses to the diorama perform-ances suggest that without spoken text it's impossible for the work to deliver a clear political critique.

Gómez-Peña: Who can deliver a clear political critique nowadays? When all the philosophical and political systems are bankrupt, who can possibly claim that they have found a political positionality that is not susceptible to being challenged? I cannot assume a clear positionality vis-à-vis any progressive movement, even those closest to my heart. All the ideological systems that used to be sanctuaries of progressive thought are undergoing a permanent process of renego-tiation. We now know that obvious ethical or ideological borders are mere illusions, that the enemy is everywhere, even inside of us – especially inside of us. I think that in these senses, we cannot possibly assume one clear political position in the performance.

Sifuentes: Also, part of the point is that we want to see where people position themselves. The responses of our live audience in performance and the written intercultural fantasies, fears, and desires we've collected through the *Temple* and the website become a barometer for America's intolerance towards other cultures. In the 90s, handing the microphone to our audience, so to speak, has been a very effective performance strategy for dealing with sensitive issues.

Gómez-Peña: I think that what we are trying to do is to open up spaces of ambiguity where there are contradictory voices and contradictory ideas clashing in front of the audience – spaces of ambiguity in which audience members can undergo multiple emotional and intellectual journeys that lead to different responses and different political positionalities within the performance, especially if the performance lasts, say, five to six hours over a three-day period. Also, our own positionality is contextual.

Wolford: In what sense?

Gómez-Peña: When we're in Mexico we end up behaving a bit like Chicano nationalists, because Mexicans can be quite insensitive and ethnocentric toward Chicanos. But when we perform for primarily Chicano audiences, we question this type of nationalism. When we perform solely for Anglos, we tend to assume a pan-Latino or pan-subaltern space, but when we are performing for traditional or essentialist Latino audiences, we often defend cultural kleptomania, transvestism, and hybridity as a response to neo-essentialism in our own communities. Performance art allows us to shift these positionalities. We are constantly crossing invisible borders, reframing our voices, reinventing our identities.

Sifuentes: We tailor-make our performances to be specific to the context, regardless of where we are. When we go further away from the US/Mexican border, we adapt the work a little bit so as to ground the piece in different experience, say, to find the connections between the Chicano experience and the local subaltern or immigrant group. Performance art is all about contextualization, about doing site-specific pieces that speak to the moment and the context for which they are created.

Wolford: What are some of the aspects of your performance strategies that remain consistent even when you move among extremely different contexts?

Gómez-Peña: What we're attempting to do is to articulate unspoken complexities of race and gender relations in such a way that people don't close down. Discussions around sensitive issues of race and gender have reached a stalemate in contemporary America, and in order to get out of this stasis, we need to become almost like flashers. If people don't want to see something, we show it to them when they least expect it, and in a way that they actually accept it, even enjoy it. If they don't want to talk about a certain issue, we scream at them, but we make them laugh. If they just want us to whisper it, we say it louder and force them to confront the issues they don't want to talk about, but in such a way that they don't realize right away that we are forcing them to confront these issues. Performance art utilizes a very complex set of communication strategies.

Humor is a good way to deal with heavy issues so we don't get shot, because it takes people by surprise and disarms them for a little while. They bring their guard down a little, and that's exactly when we hit them with the tough question or with the bold image. It's a subversive strategy in our work. We often get criticized for being too humorous.

Wolford: What do you mean?

Gómez-Peña: In a Eurocentric tradition of conceptual art, humor is often equated with lack of seriousness and sophistication. There's an unwillingness in the US and European art world to understand that highly sophisticated conceptual constructions can coexist with very bald humor, so often when people from certain artistic milieus see our work, they just don't know what to think. These apparently sophisticated post-posty post-colonial Mexicans who travel all over are also capable of being crass, direct, sexually outrageous, and making people laugh. It just doesn't jive. There is also a kind of sacred irreverence in our work, a spirituality paired with satire, and that also takes people by surprise, because spirituality in the US is supposed to be a serious and solemn matter, and so are hardcore political subject matters, like racism, sexism, police brutality, etc.

Sifuentes: So when people see Sara crucified as an androgynous mariachi with a strap-on dildo, or when Guillermo as a 'holistic techno shaman' in a mechanical wheelchair baptizes the audience by spitting bad tequila on them, or when Tyler Medicine Horse sells audience members 'real' Indian names in the Crow language that translate to absurd things like 'itchy butt', reactions vary from utter repulsion to raucous laughter.

Gómez-Peña: Irreverent humor, merciless, uncompromising humor, has been at the core of Mexican and Chicano art, and it has always been one of our most effective political strategies. This humor has always taken many shapes, from social parody to self-parody to exaggerating a racist stereotype until it explodes or implodes. I would go so far as to say that humor is a quintessential feature of Mexican and Chicano art and activism. From the Royal Chicano Airforce to Superbarrio and Marcos, we've used humor to help fight our battles. But people forget this. Paradoxically, certain nationalist and essentialist sectors, mainly humorless activists and academicians, have become guardians of solemnity. They have forgotten that humor is profoundly political. They seem not to notice that Chicano and indigenous communities are actively engaged in humor as a mechanism of survival, as a means to generate attention to sensitive issues, as a way to elicit public dialogue. If you are funny, you can get away with murder, and you can appeal to a much larger audience. I'm not saying that all irreverence is subversive by any means – there is insensitive humor, and there are racist forms of irreverence – but our communities let us know how far we can go.

Sifuentes: Mexicano/Chicano audiences never let us take ourselves too seriously because they themselves are irreverent. They get it, they get a kick out of the humor, they laugh a lot. Maybe what makes some intellectuals uptight about our work is that they're afraid we're making fun of them, or that they'll do or say 'the wrong thing' in one of our interactive performances and end up getting laughed at by our 'less informed' Chicano audiences.

Gómez-Peña: These self-proclaimed guardians of our communities promote the idea that when you perform in a grassroots context, you've got to be extremely solemn and 'respectful', because the elders and the families won't be able to take our eccentricity, our transgressive behavior, our three-alarm spicy salsa. Reality tells us exactly the opposite. Every time we perform in a grassroots context, we find incredible tolerance for irreverence and extreme behavior, often a lot more tolerance than in artsy milieus.

Wolford: This brings up another important subject, Guillermo, because the extent to which you identify yourself in relation to the Chicano community is criticized as problematic.

Gómez-Peña: It used to be an ongoing source of pain for me, but not anymore. Now I don't have time to get entangled in that rhetoric. The fact is that my colleagues and I have chosen to speak from the epicentre of the earthquake, and because of that we become the easy targets of many conservative sectors on both the right and the left. When you open a wound and then rub chile into that wound, you are asking to be reprimanded. It's inevitable, especially nowadays when so many people are retrenching to essentialist positions. Neo-essentialism in the late 90s has reached ridiculous extremes. Essentialists nowadays are almost like eugenic intellectuals; if you don't show your birth certificate to prove that you were born in the barrio, if you were not present during the civil rights struggle, you can get conceptually deported back to Mexico. If your Spanglish is not 'street language', if you don't use each and every pc term, they disregard you. But I can deal with Chicano essentialists. I can put up a good fight. It's an internal family affair. What drives me crazy are the Anglo guardians of the Chicano community.

Wolford: What do you mean?

Gómez-Peña: Recently some Anglo scholar argued in her book that since I left the Tijuana/San Diego border region nine years ago, my work stopped being relevant – that I was no longer a true 'grassroots' artist, a real 'border' artist. Give me a million pinche breaks! How many times do we have to show our stinking badges to the Anglo cultural borderpatrol, so we can get their permission to travel across Mexamerica and out of our conceptual barrios? These people want us to remain in the margins forever, so that they can comfortably occupy the center, and from there pontificate about us.

Wolford: That reminds me of something bell hooks has said, about the fact that even well-intentioned white critics speaking about marginality sometimes reinforce the silencing of other voices and end up ventriloquizing for people of color, pointing out the absences, the spaces where they would be if they were allowed to speak for themselves ... But we're on the verge of opening a really huge Pandora's Box here if we're going to get into the issue of Anglo critics speaking about the work of artists of color. I know this isn't where you meant to go with that comment, but hey ... I'm sitting here with you guys and I still haven't really gotten over the interrogation I got last week at the conference about how 'unfortunate' it was that you had chosen Josh [Kun] and me to respond to your performance, and what that allegedly implied about your relationship to audiences of color. I mean, Josh is an amazing scholar, and his knowledge of rock en español gives him a very particular insight into your work, which is an important aspect of the perform-ances that I've never known another scholar to deal with as a central topic. But his presumed 'whiteness' became an issue at that conference, as did mine. I'm certainly not Chicana, but as an Appalachian woman from a mixed-race background, I don't exactly think of myself as 'white' in any simple way. Identity and affinity are so much more complicated than that, you can't judge those things by phenotype.

Gómez-Peña: No, you're totally right. But I hope you didn't really think that I was making an essentialist comment?

Wolford: Come on, I know you better than that.

Gómez-Peña: Anyone, regardless of their race, class, or gender, who is truly committed to social change and to the transformation of consciousness, has the moral authority to discuss these issues. The binary models that say only intellectuals and artists of color can talk about their own communities are totally ridiculous. The idea that only Chicanos can talk about Chicano art implies that all Chicanos are on the same side of a border and the same side of an issue, which is just not true. As a Mexicano, for example, I must say that I have more in common with an Asian-American intellectual or an Afro-American artist than I do with the Chief of Police of Mexico City, even if he's Mexican. Or as a Chicano, Roberto probably has more in common with a Jewish performance artist than he has with a Chicano borderpatrol officer. Our political coalitions and our artistic work have to do with more than just our ethnic and cultural backgrounds. But what I was talking about before was really specifically about the 'guardians', the self-proclaimed Anglo gatekeepers who believe they have the right to decide, from the outside, whose work gets canonized, included or excluded, who does or doesn't count as a member of a particular community.

Wolford: You're right, that's a very different issue, and an incredibly complicated one, with all sorts of problematic implications in terms of ways that white institutions, curators, or theorists try to maintain a position of privilege over artists of color.

Gómez-Peña: With all humility, I think that Roberto and I have paid our dues, and I'm getting a little pissed about theoreticians who say that we aren't involved in grassroots activism, that we've become mere darlings and pets of the 'liberal' art world.

Wolford: So there's more of a wound there than you were admitting before about your relationship with certain sectors of the Latino community?

Gómez-Peña: What can I say, the wound does open every now and then. We've been involved in political struggles for many years, and these struggles take place in the outside world, not in university department meetings. We've been working on the front lines, so to speak. We've been touring the Southwest and the Chicano communities of the US for many, many years, and we have very good relations with them.

Wolford: That's certainly true here in Ohio. You have very strong ties with Baldemar Velasquez and the Farm Labor Organizing Committee [FLOC], which is based here in Toledo.

Sifuentes: It makes perfect sense that a visionary like Baldemar has asked us to present our spoken word pieces and experimental work at the forefront of an ongoing farmworkers' movement. And Baldemar and all the campesinos have been responding very positively to the work. They see its value in the community centers, that it can speak very directly to the farmworker experience. That for me is a very encouraging affirmation of the work, because so often people want to believe that only muralism can speak to these communities, only campesino theater can speak to the campesinos, and that has not been our experience at all.

Gómez-Peña: Next weekend, it's possible that FLOC is going to bring a couple of vans with migrant workers to see the *Mexterminator* performance at the Detroit Institute of the Arts, just like they did last year when we did a public lecture in Bowling Green [Ohio]. That's not atypical of our work; it happens all the time. When we were in Kansas City a couple of years ago, there was a bus completely full of migrant workers who drove three hours in order to see the performance. This idea that we are speaking only to white 'liberal' audiences is really a misperception. It's completely misinformed. I don't want to suggest that there's anything heroic about what we're doing, because many of our Chicano/Latino performance colleagues have similar experiences. But it's paternalistic to pretend that the farm workers or the young homeboys in the barrio won't understand our work because it's too heavy, too dark, or too theoretically sophisticated.

For the last year and a half, we have been engaging in a dialogue with FLOC, and we have just formalized our association with them by having been declared honorary members, with very serious ethical responsibilities that go along with accepting this position. After our performances, when we engage in public discussions with the audience, we've committed to promote their boycott of corporations that are oppressing and mistreating migrant workers in North Carolina, and to teach audiences how they can effectively participate in this national boycott. I think that this is a very important part of our performance work, and we really don't care if this is lauded or not; whether it is visible to the art world or to academia is absolutely meaningless to us. We are simply trying to figure out ways to be useful to Latino communities in despair and in need, and we feel that we cannot shy away from direct activism. Perhaps one of the reasons why I was more careful about entering into direct activism in the past was because of my condition as a 'resident alien', because I'm not supposed to be affiliated with political organizations. That's part of the condition of receiving the resident card. If you are directly affiliated with a political organization considered to be a troublemaker, you risk being deported. But I'm hoping to acquire dual citizenship very soon, so that would no longer be a problem.

Sifuentes: You can begin to finally exercise your civic rights.

Gómez-Peña: Half of the work we do is in the civic realm rather than in the art world, but it goes unnoticed by the surveillance cameras of the art world. Wherever we go we have a double agenda. We work with a mainstream cultural institution that pays the bill and helps us to present a piece of work in the best possible way, and we also engage in a number of 'parallel' activities.

Those are often the most significant part of our work, but they go unnoticed. We're now on our way to Florida to do a residency at the Atlantic Center for the Arts, and also to do a number of presentations for farm worker communities; it's very likely that those presentations will never be documented, and that the piece at the Atlantic Center for the Arts will be covered in some way. There is no way out of this predicament. The art world is simply not interested in these other activities. And it's good that the art world is not interested, because that grants us special freedoms. They can see what we're doing with the right hand, but they never see what we're doing with the left hand.

Wolford: You're right that a spoken word performance at the Sofia Quintero Cultural Arts Center in Toledo probably isn't going to get written up in *Artforum*, but I certainly understand why it's important to do that work. Could I ask you to talk a bit more about some of the other facets of your work in the civic realm?

Gómez-Peña: We have been designing what we term 'experimental town meetings' in different cities across the US. The biggest up to now took place in Washington, DC. The premise was as follows: the performance artists designed the stage and structured the event carefully, as if a performance art piece was to take place, with lights, video projections, sound, etc. Inside this performance space, we placed a table with activists and radical scholars from the Latino, Indigenous and African-American communities. The performance artists, in character and in costume, with our voices processed by an SPX machine, would get to ask these panelists questions about lack of leadership, about the state of affairs in our communities, about intra-Latino conflicts, about inter-ethnic conflicts, and so on. There was a mediator, radical psychiatrist Leticia Nieto, who would broker between the panelists and the audience. So there were many things taking place simultaneously on different levels and fronts, and any time the conversation would drag or become uninteresting, the performance artists were allowed to 'intervene' with a skit or a spoken word text. At the main table where the panelists were seated, food was being served by performance artists dressed as waiters, and every now and then the waiters would go into performance mode. It was a very complicated script to write and put together, a sort of hypertextual script with lots of open ends. Initially there was some anxiety, especially from the activists. Of course they didn't want to make fools out of themselves. We had very prominent people working with us. Susan Harjo was there, and Baldemar Velasquez, among other people. Abel Lopez, the national director of NALAC at the time, he was there. One of the top immigration lawyers in Washington was there. Of course, some of these people were apprehensive in the beginning about what it meant for them as political activists, as lawyers and union organizers, to put themselves into this situation, which was framed in a very performative way. Susan was not, because she herself is a performance artist extraordinaire; she's one of the co-founders of Spiderwoman Theater and also a poet, along with being one of the most important Native American politicians we have in the country. She was also very familiar with our work, as was Baldemar. He was absolutely not apprehensive, as he himself is an involuntary performance artist, one of the most charismatic and compelling speakers I have ever met. But the others were. So it took a lot of talking to persuade them that we were not going to make fun of them. The event took place and it was a huge success, a strange hybrid of a hardcore political town meeting and an epic performance art piece. I wish all the performance art curators had been there, *esa*. A few days ago, for the closing ceremony of the Latino MacArthur Fellows visit to Toledo, we tried another version, smaller scale. The Latino MacArturos confronted the local political elite, and Roberto and I were asked by Baldemar to design the town meeting and to be the performance animateurs. We are very interested in continuing these experiments and fine-tuning this model, this new genre, utilizing performance art as a means to design, animate, layer, and reframe very tough political debates.

Sifuentes: It's important that we find a new forum to discuss these issues, because so often political panels or discussions around Latino issues and intra-community conflicts get stuck. People have gotten locked into particular ways of discussing identity and race relations. The discussion gets glazed over and audiences become completely uninterested, or else the debates wander into incredibly petty or inflammatory discourse, which is absolutely unproductive. In the context of these experimental town meetings, the performative interventions help us to break through these dynamics. Because the panelists have agreed to be part of this performance context where they can sense the energy of what's going on in the performance space, they tend to be much more concise, energetic and dynamic themselves in what they have to say. But if there are moments when the conversation starts to lag or go in an unproductive direction, the performative interventions are a good way to bring the discussion back around to the main issues we're trying to talk about, and also to diffuse the heaviness and the solemnity that often accompany political discussions. As performers, part of what we're trying to do in this context is to bring back the irreverence to these discussions, so that we don't take ourselves so seriously. That's the model that we're going for – looking for ways to keep the discussions dynamic so that people can encounter these issues in new ways.

Note

Originally published in Guillermo Gómez-Peña, *Dangerous Border Crossers: The Artist Talks Back*, London: Routledge, 2000, pp. 167-87.

Index